BATTLES AND LEADERS OF THE CIVIL WAR

VOLUME THREE

BETWEEN THE LINES DURING A TRUCE.

BATTLES AND LEADERS OF THE CIVIL WAR

VOLUME III

BEING FOR THE MOST PART CONTRIBUTIONS
BY UNION AND CONFEDERATE OFFICERS.
BASED UPON "THE CENTURY WAR SERIES."
EDITED BY ROBERT UNDERWOOD JOHNSON
AND CLARENCE CLOUGH BUEL, OF THE EDI-
TORIAL STAFF OF "THE CENTURY MAGAZINE."

CASTLE

CONTENTS OF VOLUME THREE.[J]

THE PERRYVILLE CAMPAIGN.

    [J] In order to save much repetition, particular credit is here given to the Massachusetts Commandery of the Loyal Legion, to Colonel Arnold A. Rand, General Albert Ordway, and Charles B. Hall for the use of photographs and drawings. War-time photographers whose work is of the greatest historical value, and has been freely drawn upon in the preparation of the illustrations, are M. B. Brady, Alexander Gardner, and Captain A. J. Russell in the North; and D. H. Anderson of Richmond, Va., and George S. Cook of Charleston, S. C.— the latter, since the war, having succeeded to the ownership of the Anderson negatives.

BURNSIDE AT FREDERICKSBURG.

CHANCELLORSVILLE.

GETTYSBURG.

THE VICKSBURG YEAR.

PORT HUDSON.

MURFREESBORO'.

MAPS.

ARTISTS.

BROWN, H. E.	GRIBAYEDOFF, V.	REDWOOD, ALLEN C.	TAYLOR, JAMES E.
DAVIDSON, J. O.	HALM, GEORGE R.	REED, C. W.	THULSTRUP, T. DE
DAVIS, THEO. R.	HOGAN, THOMAS	SCHELL, FRANK H.	VANDERHOOF, C. A.
FENN, HARRY	HOMER, WINSLOW	SCHELL, FRED. B.	WAUD, ALFRED R.
FORBES, EDWIN	MEEKER, EDWIN J	SHELTON, W. H	WOODWARD, J. D.
GAUL, GILBERT	OGDEN, HENRY A.	SHEPPARD, W. L.	ZOGBAUM, RUFUS F.
GIBSON, GEORGE	PENNELL, JOSEPH	TABER, WALTON	

DRAUGHTSMEN.

SITTS, FRED. E.	VAN GLÜMER, J.	WELLS, JACOB

ENGRAVERS.

AITKEN, PETER	DAVIS, SAMUEL	JONES, M.	POWELL, C. A.
ANDREWS, JOHN	DE LORME, E. H.	JUNGLING, J. F.	REED, C. H.
ATWOOD, K. C.	ENGBERG, J.	KING, F. S.	SCHOONMAKER, E.
BABCOCK, H. E.	ERTZ, EDWARD	KINGSLEY, ELBRIDGE	SCHUSSLER, T.
BARTLE, G. P.	EVANS, J. W.	KLASEN, W.	SPIEGLE, CHARLES
BERTRAM, W. A.	FAY, GASTON	KRUELL, G.	TIETZE, R. G.
BODENSTAB, W. R.	GAMM, ANTHONY	LE BLANC, FELIX	TYNAN, JAMES
BUTLER, T. A.	HEARD, T. H.	MILLER, WILLIAM	UNDERHILL, F.
CLEMENT, E.	HEINEMANN, E.	MULLER, R. A.	VELTEN, H.
CLOSSON, W. B.	HELD, E. C.	NICHOLS, DAVID	WHALEY, M. J.
COLLINS, R. C.	HELLAWELL, THOS.	NORTHCOTE, S.	WHITNEY, J. H. E.
DANA, W. J.	JOHNSON, THOMAS	OWENS, MARY L.	WILLIAMS, G. P.

CORRECTIONS IN VOLUME III.

Page 8, title to portrait. For " Major-General Preston Smith," read " Brigadier-General Preston Smith."

Page 19, title to portrait. For " Lieutenant-General B. F. Cheatham," read " Major-General B. F. Cheatham."

Page 25, note to picture. General Duke writes that his forces were not engaged in the attack on Cage's Ford. The note should read: " According to a note on the lithograph, a detachment of Morgan's cavalry, and of infantry," etc.

Page 60, title. For " John M. Wright," read " J. Montgomery Wright."

Page 62, 13th line. Omit the words " who joined me here."

Page 63, 15th line. For " Cumberland Gap," read " Cumberland Ford."

Page 122, first column, last line. For " 1877," read " 1878."

Page 136, title to picture. For " From a photograph," read " From an engraving by H. B. Hall."

Page 202, date in title to picture. For " May 2d," read " May 3d."

Page 260, note under portrait. For " The uniform is that of a field-officer in the regular infantry. Early in the war General Reynolds was Lieutenant-Colonel of the 14th United States Infantry," etc., read " The uniform is that of a field-officer in the regular army. Early in the war General Reynolds was promoted from Captain in the 3d Artillery to Lieutenant-Colonel of the 14th United States Infantry," etc.

Page 317, second column, 10th line from bottom. For " Stewart's and Nicholl's," read " Steuart's and Nicholls's."

Page 374. For " The batteries were found and brought up and Fitzhugh's, Weir's, and Parsons's," etc., read " The batteries were brought up and Fitzhugh's, Weir's, Wheeler's, and Parsons's," etc.

Page 388, second column, 4th line. For " Until Colonel Devereux repeated it," read " Until Colonel Devereux repeated it to Colonel Mallon."

Page 394 (including map) and page 395. Whenever the " Third Battalion of the 1st Vermont Cavalry " is mentioned, read " Second Battalion"; and whenever the latter is mentioned, read " Third Battalion."

Page 415, second column, 22d line. Omit the statement " nevertheless neither Howard nor Slocum was welcome in Meade's army, and they both sought service in the West under Sherman." General Slocum, on July 9th, 1888, wrote : " My relations with General Meade were always pleasant. I never sought service at the West, and regretted leaving the East."

Page 457. For " Colonel Lewis Merrall," read " Colonel Lewis Merrill."

Page 524, title to picture. For " Quinby's division of McClernand's Corps," read " Quinby's division of McPherson's Corps."

Page 580, first column, 7th line from bottom. For " In this way a belligerent vessel was 'neutralized,'" read " Thus a belligerent vessel was *first* 'neutralized.'"

Page 636, second column, 5th line. For " Colonel J. G. Wilder," read " Colonel J. T. Wilder." Fourteenth line. For " Garrison Fork of Elk River, which is about four miles south of Tullahoma," read " Garrison Fork, and pushed on to Elk River in rear of Tullahoma."

ADDITIONAL CORRECTIONS IN VOLUME II.

Page 200, first column, artillery of Kearny's division. For " 2d N. J., Captain John E. Beam," read " B, 1st N. J., Captain John E. Beam."

Page 309, title to picture. For " September, 1885," read " From a photograph taken in 1885."

Page 469, 9th line. General Pope says : " That this division [King's] was not reënforced by Reynolds and Sigel seems unaccountable." On this point General Doubleday informs the editors that upon hearing the noise of the firing, Reynolds rode through the woods about dusk and asked if he was needed. General Doubleday replied that he was hard pressed ; whereupon Reynolds started back through the woods for his division, but owing to the darkness of the night lost his way and did not reach his command till morning. Before the engagement was over, one of Sigel's batteries appeared on the right and opened fire.

Page 499, Kanawha Division. It should be noted that this division, under General J. D. Cox, was *en route*

from West Virginia to join Pope's Army of Virginia. Only the troops mentioned arrived in time to take part in the second Bull Run.

Page 612, title to article, and table of contents, p. xvi. For " The Surrender of Harper's Ferry," read " The Capitulation of Harper's Ferry."

Page 615, first column, 11th line. For " After our assault," read " After an assault."

Page 645. For " batteries of both corps were concentrated," read " cannon of both corps," etc.

Page 672, title to picture. For " Field Hospitals at Captain Smith's Barns near Sharpsburg," read " Field Hospitals of French's Division at Antietam "; and in the note, for " Captain Smith's barns," read " two or three barns."

Page 738, 17th line. For " and in the district of West Tennessee, commanded by General Grant," read " we were in the district of West Tennessee," etc.

ADDITIONAL CORRECTIONS IN VOLUME I.

Page 174. For " toward Vienna, June 9th," read " toward Vienna, June 7th."

Page 179. " Uniform of the 11th New York (Fire Zouaves), at Bull Run." According to William Murray, Superintendent in 1888 of the Police Department, New York City, this regiment, to which he belonged, wore a "red fez" at the first Bull Run.

Page 184. For " one or two miles east of Centreville," read " one or two miles east of Stone Bridge."

Page 332, foot-note. For " Colonel B. W. Share, 3d Texas Cavalry," read " Colonel B. W. Stone, 6th Texas Cavalry."

Page 337, second column, McCulloch's Division. For " Colonel J. T. Churchill," read " Colonel T. J. Churchill."

Page 429, first column, 6th line. Capt. Dresser's battery was " D, 2d Ill. Lt. Artillery," instead of " A, Ill. Lt. Artillery."

IN THE VAN.

BRAGG'S INVASION OF KENTUCKY.

BY JOSEPH WHEELER, LIEUTENANT-GENERAL, C. S. A.

GENERAL BRAGG succeeded General Beauregard in command of the Confederate troops at Tupelo, Miss., about fifty miles south of Corinth, on June 27th, 1862. The field returns of June 9th, a week after our army reached Tupelo, reported it at 45,080. ⌡ This return included the Army of Mississippi, reënforced by the troops brought from Arkansas by Generals Price and Van Dorn, together with detachments gathered from various localities. About two thousand cavalry not included in this return also belonged to the army. This was the maximum force General Bragg could expect to concentrate at that point. General Halleck, immediately confronting Bragg with the armies of Grant, Pope, and Buell, had in and about Corinth a force of 128,315 men, of which the field return of June 1st showed 108,538 present for duty. A division reporting 8682 for duty, under the Federal General George W. Morgan, was at Cumberland Gap; a division with 6411 for duty, under General Ormsby M. Mitchel, was in north Alabama, and three brigades were located at Nashville, Murfreesboro', and other points in middle Tennessee. Buell soon started *en route* to north Alabama, General Halleck remaining at or near Corinth with seventy thousand men for duty, a force strong enough to hold Corinth and west Tennessee, while Buell could menace or even invade Alabama or north Georgia.

The changed condition of the opposing armies during four months should now be considered. In January, 1862, the Confederates had held all of

⌡ To prevent misconception, and to avoid frequent repetitions, I will here state that throughout this paper when I mention the figures of field returns of Confederate troops I shall always include all officers, all non-commissioned officers, and all privates who are reported present for duty. — J. W.

Tennessee and most of Kentucky, and the Mississippi River from Columbus to the delta. Now, after a series of Confederate reverses, both States were virtually under the control of the armies under General Halleck, and the Federal flotilla sailed unmolested from St. Louis to Vicksburg. The Federal right was thrown forward into Mississippi. Its center occupied north Alabama, and its left was pressing the Confederates to the southern border of east Tennessee.

The Confederate problem was to devise some plan to turn the tide of disaster and recover at least a portion of our lost territory. Our soldiers had expected a battle at Corinth, in which they felt confident of as decisive a victory as was won by them on the first day of Shiloh; and the withdrawal to Tupelo had at last forced upon them a conviction that the numerical preponderance of the enemy was such that they could not expect to cope successfully with the combined armies then commanded by General Halleck.

Already the army had suffered much from sickness, and we could hardly expect any improvement while it remained idle in the locality where it had halted after its retreat from Corinth. An advance into west Tennessee would not afford protection to Alabama or Georgia. An advance into middle Tennessee by crossing the river at Florence, Decatur, or any neighboring point, would have the disadvantage of placing the Confederates between the armies of Grant and Buell under circumstances enabling these two commanders to throw their forces simultaneously upon General Bragg, who could not, in this event, depend upon any material coöperation from the army in east Tennessee under General Kirby Smith. There was another line for an aggressive movement. A rapid march through Alabama to Chattanooga would save that city, protect Georgia from invasion, and open the way into Tennessee and Kentucky, without the disadvantage of an intervening force between the column commanded by Bragg and that under the orders of General Kirby Smith. This movement was determined upon and resulted in what is called the Kentucky Campaign of 1862.

Major-General E. Kirby Smith had reached Knoxville March 8th, 1862, and assumed command of the Confederate troops in east Tennessee. The returns for June reported his entire force at 11,768 infantry, 1055 cavalry, ⚓ and 635 artillery. The occupation of Cumberland Gap, June 18th, by a Federal division, and the approach of Buell's forces toward Chattanooga seriously threatened his department.

MAP OF NORTH MISSISSIPPI AND WEST TENNESSEE.

⚓ Not including Allston's brigade.—EDITORS.

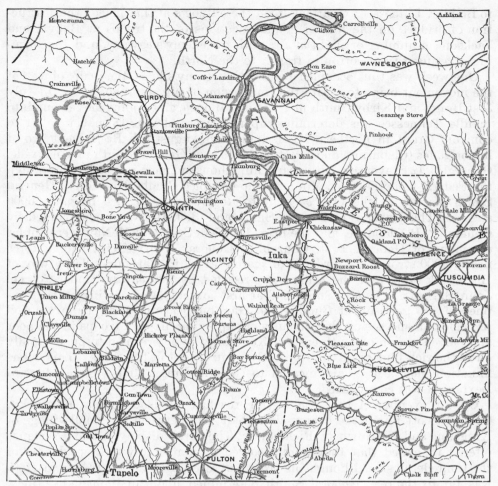

MAP OF THE CORINTH AND IUKA REGION.

General Bragg recognized the inadequacy of General Smith's force, and on June 27th he transferred the division commanded by Major-General John P. McCown from Tupelo to Chattanooga.‡ Forrest and John H. Morgan had already been sent into middle Tennessee and Kentucky, and the operations of these enterprising officers materially lessened the pressure upon General Smith. Correspondence between Generals Bragg and Smith resulted in an order, dated July 21st, transferring the entire Army of Mississippi to Chattanooga. To mislead the enemy and to prevent an advance upon Tupelo, Bragg had, on the 19th, sent Colonel Joseph Wheeler with a brigade of cavalry into west Tennessee, and Brigadier-General Frank C. Armstrong with a like force into north Alabama. Wheeler's operations in west Tennessee may be briefly summarized as a rapid march from Holly Springs, Mississippi,

‡ General Kirby Smith, in a letter dated July 14th, 1862, estimated Stevenson's division at 10,000, Heth's and McCown's at 10,000, Morgan's cavalry 1300. "Official Records," Vol. XVI., Pt. II., p. 727.— EDITORS.

to Bolivar, Tennessee; an attack upon the outposts at that place; the destruction of bridges on the line of communications of the troops at Bolivar and Jackson; a number of slight affairs with the enemy's cavalry, and the burning of a quantity of cotton in transit to the North.

One week was thus occupied behind the enemy's lines, the main object of the movement being to create the impression of a general advance. On July 31st Bragg and Kirby Smith met at Chattanooga, and a joint movement into middle Tennessee was determined upon, Price and Van Dorn being left to confront Grant in northern Mississippi. On August 5th Bragg sent two of his brigades (Cleburne's and Preston Smith's) to General Smith at Knoxville. General C. L. Stevenson, with nearly nine thousand men, was ordered to watch the Federal General G. W. Morgan, who occupied Cumberland Gap. General Smith started on the 14th *en route* to Rogers's Gap, with 4 brigades, 6000 strong. The brigades of Preston Smith and B. J. Hill were commanded by General P. R. Cleburne, and the brigades of McCray and McNair were under command of General T. J. Churchill. General Henry Heth, with a force nearly 4000 strong, was ordered to march direct to Barboursville by way of Big Creek Gap, and the army was preceded by 900 cavalry under Colonel John S. Scott. General Smith had at first contemplated cutting off the supplies of the garrison at Cumberland Gap, but learning that they were well provisioned, and seeing the difficulty of supplying his own troops in the poor and barren region of south-eastern Kentucky, he determined to push rapidly on to the rich blue-grass country in the central part of the State. This determination had been communicated to General Bragg, and a march toward Lexington was commenced.

On the evening of the 29th, having reached Madison County, Kentucky, Colonel Scott found the enemy about half way between the small village of Kingston and the town of Richmond. The force displayed and resistance offered indicated that they were resolved to contest any farther advance of the Confederates. Although his troops were quite weary and General Heth was far to the rear, General Smith determined upon an immediate attack. He was in the heart of Kentucky, and the Confederate commander rightly judged that boldness was the surest road to victory.

Early on the 30th, General Cleburne, being in advance with his two brigades, found that the Federal force had moved forward and was in line of battle about a mile north of Kingston and probably five miles south of Richmond. The extreme advance-guard of the enemy, about six hundred yards in front of their main line, became engaged with Cleburne's leading brigade, commanded by Colonel Hill, but after a light brush retired upon the main body of the Federal army. Hill's brigade was soon formed in line behind the crest of a low ridge which was nearly parallel with and about five hundred yards south of the position occupied by the enemy. Cleburne also brought up Douglas's battery, which he placed in a favorable position near the center of his line. A fire of artillery and infantry commenced, and Captain Martin, with a second battery, having arrived, it was also brought into action, and for two hours both infantry and artillery were engaged from their respective positions.

General Mahlon D. Manson, who was in command of the Federal army before General Nelson arrived, and who commenced the battle, now pushed his left forward to turn our right. Cleburne met this with one regiment of Preston Smith's brigade, which had been formed behind a crest in his rear, but the persistence of the enemy in that quarter made it necessary to reënforce the right with all of the reserve brigade under Preston Smith.

In the meantime General Kirby Smith had reached the field with the two brigades (McCray's and McNair's) forming General Churchill's division. He promptly dispatched that officer with one brigade to turn the enemy's right. The Federal commander, apparently disregarding this movement, still boldly advanced his own left to carry out his plan of turning the Confederate flank. This well-conceived manœuvre at first seemed to endanger the Confederate army, but Colonel Preston Smith with his brigade stood firm, and after a severe struggle checked and finally drove back the advancing enemy. General Cleburne, who up to this time had displayed both skill and gallantry, was severely wounded and left the field. General Churchill had now gained the enemy's right, and by a bold and determined charge threw the enemy into disorder.

Two miles farther north the Federal force made a stand, and McCray's gallant brigade, by a rapid march, struck their right, while Cleburne's division, now commanded by Colonel Preston Smith, moved to the attack in front. The celerity of McCray's movements brought him into action before the other troops reached the field, and he suffered from the concentration of a galling and destructive fire; but the approach of Preston Smith, with troops cheering as they advanced again, caused a rout of the Federal army, closely followed by our victorious soldiers. When in sight of the town of Richmond the enemy were seen forming for a final struggle upon a commanding ridge, which had been judiciously selected by the Federal commander, Major-General William Nelson, both of the enemy's flanks being protected by skirts of woods. General Smith promptly sent McNair's brigade again to turn the Federal flank, and with the remaining force attacked directly in front. A warm fusillade lasted a few moments, when the Federal army again retreated. Early in the morning Colonel Scott had been sent to gain the rear of the town. His arrival at this moment increased the dismay of the enemy, and assisted materially in securing prisoners. The reports of the division and brigade commanders show that General Smith's entire force was about five thousand. The enemy supposed it much greater, their estimate including General Heth, but his division did not join General Smith until the day after the battle. ♭ Kirby Smith's loss was 78 killed, 372 wounded, and 1 missing.

Nelson in his report speaks of his own command on the Kentucky River as 16,000 strong,♮ and the official report of casualties is given as 206 killed, 844 wounded, and 4303 captured. The Federal official reports admit that nine pieces of artillery and all their wagon trains were captured by the Confederates.

♭ In a letter to General Bragg dated August 24th, 1862, General Kirby Smith says he will have with him, in his advance to Lexington, "about 12,000 effective men."—EDITORS.
♮ This is the total force spoken of by Nelson as being on the Confederate flank.— EDITORS.

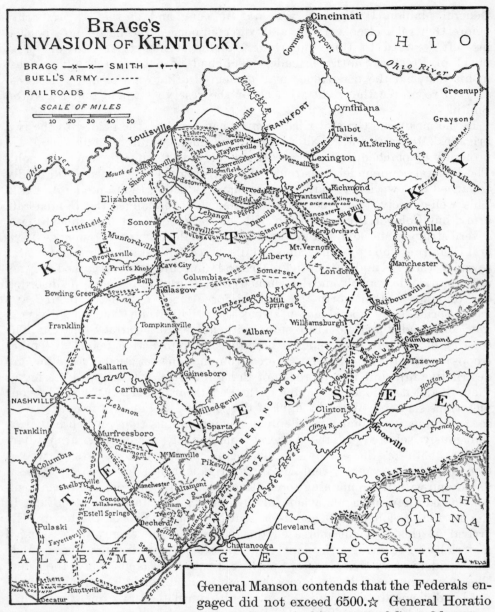

General Manson contends that the Federals engaged did not exceed 6500.☆ General Horatio G. Wright, who commanded the department, in his report of Sept. 2d, says:

"The force engaged in the battle in front of Richmond was utterly broken up, and after all the exertions that could be made to collect the stragglers, only some 800 or 900 could be found. The remainder of the force were killed, captured, or scattered over the country."

☆ According to the official reports the Union force engaged consisted of Manson's and Cruft's brigades, eight regiments and two detachments of infantry, one regiment and a battalion of cavalry and two batteries of artillery, *all new troops who had* *only been mustered into service a few days.* General Nelson says in his report that he had ordered General Manson not to fight, but to fall back, so as to concentrate on the Confederate flank. See the previous note.— EDITORS.

Elated with success, and reënforced by about four thousand troops just arrived under Heth, the victorious army moved forward to Lexington, and was designated by its commander as "The Army of Kentucky." During the month of September the greater portion of the army remained in that vicinity.

On September 4th Colonel Scott, with a brigade of cavalry, was ordered to push on as near as practicable to Louisville, and to destroy the Louisville and Nashville Railroad. Heth, with a division of infantry and a brigade of cavalry, marched north; some of his troops, on September 6th, reached the suburbs of Covington, but his instructions were not to make an attack upon the city. Smith used vigorous efforts to gather and concentrate supplies, arouse the people, and raise and organize troops for the Confederacy.

General George W. Morgan (Federal), who was left at Cumberland Gap with 8682 men, seeing these active movements in his rear, evacuated that position on September 17th and made his way through eastern Kentucky to the Ohio River at Greenupsburg, arriving there October 3d.

While these events were happening, Bragg had organized his army at Chattanooga into two wings. The right, commanded by General Polk, consisted of Cheatham's and Withers's divisions of infantry and Colonel Lay's brigade of cavalry. The left wing, commanded by General Hardee, consisted of Buckner's and Anderson's divisions of infantry and Wheeler's brigade of cavalry. This entire force, on August 27th, reported 27,816 officers and men for duty.⌡ On the 28th the army was fairly in motion, but up to this time General Bragg had not positively determined upon his plan of campaign, and much depended upon the course pursued by the Federal army.

As early as the 22d General Buell had established his headquarters at Decherd, on the Nashville Railroad, thirty miles north-west of Stevenson, and had all the supplies at Stevenson transferred to that place.⚓ Two parallel mountain ranges, running north-east and south-west, separated him from Chattanooga. A railroad, connecting McMinnville and Tullahoma, ran nearly parallel to the north-west slope of these mountain ranges. Already he had located General Thomas at McMinnville with Wood's and Ammen's divisions, while the divisions of Schoepf, McCook, and Thomas L. Crittenden were near the Nashville and Stevenson Railroad within easy call of headquarters at Decherd. Buell seemed impressed with the belief that Bragg's objective point was Nashville, and that he would take the short route over the mountain by way of Altamont, which movement, if made, would have placed Bragg between the force under Thomas and the rest of Buell's army. To prevent this Buell, on the 23d, ordered these five divisions to concentrate at Altamont. General Thomas reached his destination on the 25th, but, finding no enemy to confront him and learning that there was no enemy on the mountains, the nearest Confederates being at Dunlap's in the Sequatchie Valley, he reported

⌡ This return reports a total of 431 officers and men in the cavalry. September 10th (O. R., XVI., 893) Colonel Joseph Wheeler reported his command on the march (apparently a part of it) as 700 strong, and (p. 890) part of Colonel Lay's brigade is mentioned as 550 strong, August 27th.— EDITORS.

⚓ On August 6th, during this advance from Stevenson to Decherd, Brig.-Gen. Robert L. McCook (of Thomas's division; brother to Alex. McD. McCook), who, being ill, was riding in an ambulance, was mortally wounded by the enemy's scouts near New Market.— EDITORS.

MAJOR-GENERAL PRESTON SMITH, C. S. A.
FROM A PHOTOGRAPH.

these facts to Buell and returned to McMinnville. Crittenden's division halted near Pelham, and Schoepf at Hillsboro'. McCook pressed on and reached Altamont on the 29th, where, on the 30th, Wheeler attacked his outposts, and McCook retired down the mountain. The same day General Buell ordered his entire army to concentrate at Murfreesboro'.

By September 5th, the five divisions just mentioned had reached that place, together with all detachments from along the lines of railroad except Rousseau's division, which, being on the Nashville and Decatur Railroad, marched directly to Nashville. The strength of Buell's forces during the months of July, August, and September was estimated by witnesses before the Buell Commission, in 1863, at from 45,000 to 59,309. His own returns for June, deducting the force at Cumberland Gap, showed 56,706 present for duty, and his October returns, with the same deduction, 66,595.↓ General Buell presented a paper to the Commission which does not question any of these statements regarding strength, but states that he could not have concentrated more than 31,000 men at McMinnville to strike the Confederate forces as they debouched from the mountains; and the same paper estimated Bragg's army at 60,000, while his returns on August 27th showed but 27,816 officers and men for duty.♭ These facts prove the large preponderance of the Federals.

At Murfreesboro' Buell heard of Nelson's defeat at Richmond, and without halting he marched to Nashville. On September 7th he intrusted General Thomas with the defense of that city with the divisions of Palmer, Negley, and Schoepf, while with the infantry divisions of McCook, Crittenden, Ammen, Wood, Rousseau, and R. B. Mitchell, and a cavalry division under Kennett, General Buell determined to race with Bragg for Louisville.

↓ The October returns include the heavy reënforcements, placed by General Buell at 22,000, that were added to Buell's army on its arrival at Louisville, at the end of September.— EDITORS.

♭ In his official report, dated November 4th, 1862, General Buell estimated his whole effective force on the 7th and 8th of October, at 58,000, including 22,500 raw troops, with little or no instruction. He also estimated the total Confederate force engaged in the invasion at from 55,000 to 65,000. In "The Army under Buell" (N. Y.: D. Van Nostrand), General James B. Fry, Assistant Adjutant-General, Chief of Staff of the Army of the Ohio, after a careful study of all the data, estimates the force with which Buell moved against Bardstown (exclusive of Sill's division that moved against Frankfort) at 58,000; and Bragg's, including Kirby Smith's, at 68,000. By this estimate, when Sill joined the main body of Buell's army after the battle of Perryville, the armies were about equal in number.

EDITORS.

It, was a fair race, as on that day most of Bragg's army was south of the Cumberland River, at Carthage and Greensboro'. Bragg was nearest to Louisville by some twenty-five miles, but Buell had the advantage of a bridge at Nashville and the assistance of the railroad to aid in his march. With seven hundred cavalry, I hastened to strike and break the railroad at points between Bowling Green and Nashville, and otherwise sought to retard the northern march of the Federal army. By the 12th it was evident to Buell that no attack would be made on Nashville, and he ordered General Thomas to join him with his own division, which had been commanded by General

UNION FORT AT MUNFORDVILLE, CAPTURED BY BRAGG, SEPTEMBER 17, 1862—THE GREEN RIVER BRIDGE
ON THE LEFT. FROM A PHOTOGRAPH TAKEN IN 1886.

Schoepf. Buell reached Bowling Green with his cavalry and two divisions of infantry on the 14th, and turned his column in the direction of Munfordville. I interposed my cavalry on the Munfordville road, and also on the roads leading to Glasgow, and reported Buell's movements to Bragg. General Chalmers, with Bragg's advance, reached Munfordville at daylight on the 14th and learned that Colonel Scott, with a cavalry brigade, had demanded the surrender on the night previous.\ Chalmers was misinformed regarding the strength of the garrison and the character of the defensive works. He attacked with vigor, but was repulsed. He reported his force at 1913 men, and his loss at 35 killed and 253 wounded. On the 14th all of Buell's six divisions had reached Bowling Green, and on the 16th he advanced vigorously to succor the garrison at Munfordville, the head of his column being opposed by cavalry. Bragg, hearing of Chalmers's attack and of Buell's movements, ordered his entire army, which had rested two days at Glasgow, to start early on the 15th *en route* for Munfordville. On the next day he reached that place, boldly displayed his army, and on the 17th at 2 P. M. the

\ The post was commanded by Colonel J. T. Wilder (17th Indiana), whose force consisted of four regiments of infantry, a battery, and several detachments, aggregating about 4000 men.— EDITORS.

fort and garrison surrendered. The Federals reported their loss at 15 killed, 57 wounded, and 4076 prisoners. We also captured their armament, 10 pieces of artillery, and 5000 stand of small-arms. As might be expected, the Confederate army was much elated, and were eager to grapple with the dispirited army under General Buell.

Bragg placed his troops in a strong position south of the river, using the fort as a part of his line of defense. My command was thrown forward to meet and skirmish with the enemy, who, on the 19th, commenced preparations for an attack. On the 20th General Thomas joined the Federal army with his division. General Bragg, in referring to the situation of September 20th, wrote:

" With my effective force present reduced by sickness, exhaustion, and the recent affair before the intrenchments at Munfordville to half that of the enemy, I could not prudently afford to attack him there in his selected position."

If Kirby Smith's command had been ordered from Lexington to Munfordville even as late as the 12th, a battle with Buell could not have been other than a decided Confederate victory. Bragg at first had determined to fight with his four divisions, and no doubt would have done so had Buell advanced on the 17th, or 18th, or 19th. Early on the morning of the 18th, General Bragg sent for me and explained his plans. I never saw him more determined or more confident. The entire army was in the best of spirits. I met and talked with Generals Hardee, Polk, Cheatham, and Buckner; all were enthusiastic over our success, and our good luck in getting Buell where he would be compelled to fight us to such a disadvantage. It is true our back was to a river, but it was fordable at several places, and we felt that the objection to having it in our rear was fully compensated by the topographical features, which, with the aid of the fort, made our position a strong one for defense. So anxious was Bragg for a fight that he sent Buckner's division to the front in the hope that an engagement could thus be provoked; but after the arrival of General Thomas, Bragg did not deem it advisable to risk a battle with the force then under his command, believing that another opportunity would offer after being joined by Kirby Smith. He therefore withdrew to Bardstown, sending to me, who still confronted Buell, the following order, dated September 20th, through General Hardee:

"General Bragg directs that, if possible, the enemy be prevented from crossing Green River to-morrow, and General Hardee instructs me to say that he expects you will contest the passage of that river at Munfordville to that end."

Buell heard of Bragg's movements and pressed forward with determination. My small brigade of cavalry contested his advance on the 20th and 21st, in efforts to comply with the instructions from General Bragg. On the afternoon of the 21st, Buell's right approached the river above the town, and at the same time he pressed forward his line of battle so rapidly as almost to command the only ford by which I could cross Green River with both artillery and cavalry. Allen's 1st Alabama Regiment, being directly in front, was thrown into column and, charging gallantly, defeated the opposing cavalry and broke through their infantry. Among our killed was the noble

Lieutenant-Colonel T. B. Brown, but the charge sufficiently checked the advance to enable the command to cross the ford in good order. The following note, referring to this engagement, explains itself:

"HEADQUARTERS, SIXTH DIVISION, ARMY OF THE OHIO, September 22d, 1862. GENERAL WHEELER, Commanding Cavalry Brigade. GENERAL: I am directed by General Buell to say, in answer to your request to admit the brother of Lieutenant-Colonel Brown, killed in the affair of yesterday within our lines, he regrets he cannot, on account of the present state of the service, accede to your wishes. General Buell has referred your note to me to give you the desired information in regard to the fate of Colonel Brown. He was killed outright in the handsome cavalry charge executed by your troops yesterday afternoon. His body was taken to a neighboring house and cared for. He will be interred to-day, and doubtless in the vicinity. His watch was taken charge of by an officer of rank in our service, and I will make it a point to have it forwarded to you. I am not now informed whether there were any other valuables on the person of Colonel Brown. I am, General, very respectfully, your obedient servant, TH. J. WOOD, Brigadier-General of Volunteers, Commanding."

The watch was subsequently sent to Colonel Brown's daughter.

On the 22d, with a clear road to Louisville, Buell moved with celerity in that direction. My cavalry contested his advance, but the country was too open to allow of effective opposition with so small a force. On the 25th the leading Federal column reached the city, and the seven divisions were all up on the 27th. Bragg, Polk, and Hardee had been kept thoroughly informed of Buell's march and of the exposure of his flank, which presented an inviting opportunity for attack, but so worn and wearied was the condition of our army that these officers did not feel justified in attempting an aggressive movement. On the 28th Bragg left Bardstown with his staff to confer with Kirby Smith at Lexington, and then proceeded to Frankfort, where, on the 4th of October, a day was occupied in the installation of the Hon. Richard Hawes as Confederate Provisional Governor of the Commonwealth.

While these events were happening Buell was making active preparations for an aggressive campaign. On the 26th Major-General Wright, commanding the Department of the Ohio, went from Cincinnati to Louisville to confer with him, and on the 27th General Halleck issued an order placing Buell in command of the troops of both departments, then in Louisville. There has been much controversy as to the "strength of the opposing armies." After the most careful study of Federal and Confederate official statements, I have reached the following conclusions:

FEDERAL FORCES AVAILABLE TO MEET BRAGG. ☆

Collected at Cincinnati	45,000
Collected at Louisville	30,000
Carried to Louisville by Buell, September 25th to 29th	54,198
Morgan's Seventh Division	8,084
Total under Buell's and Wright's command	137,282 ǀ

☆ It will be contended, with some force, that a portion of these troops was necessary to guard Cincinnati and Louisville. But on the other hand it may be insisted, just as strenuously, that the most meager guard would have sufficed to protect those cities had the main body moved vigorously against the Confederates.—J. W.

ǀBut see other estimates, p. 31.—EDITORS.

To these we might with propriety add the 26,351 men which General Wright could have drawn from his command in West Virginia.

These stupendous armies did not include the 12,397 troops left at Nashville, which would make the entire force subject to Buell's and Wright's orders 176,030.

MAXIMUM CONFEDERATE FORCES.

General E. Kirby Smith's column taken to Kentucky	10,000
Humphrey Marshall, from West Virginia	2,160
Stevenson, joining after Perryville	7.500
John H. Morgan	1,300
Bragg's largest force before crossing Tennessee River — officers and men, for duty	27,816
Bragg, Smith, and Marshall	48,776 ⚓

The above was the reported strength of the Confederate troops when the campaign began, but to make sure and to compensate for any omitted cavalry let us add 1000, making the entire force 49,776. The losses at Richmond and Munfordville were very slight, compared to the daily depletion caused by dropping out along the route. Some were allowed to organize in squads and make their way back to east Tennessee; some sought shelter among the kind and hospitable people; some struggled along with the ambulance trains, and some were left at temporarily established hospitals, one of which, containing two hundred inmates, was captured by the enemy at Glasgow.

This character of loss always attends a rapidly moving army, and its extent can be realized when we see that Hardee's wing left Chattanooga 12,825 strong, was reënforced by Cleburne's brigade early in October; yet, even with Cleburne included, Hardee, in stating officially the force with which he fought at Perryville, says: "Thinned by battle and long and arduous service, my effective force did not exceed 10,000 men." It will be seen, therefore, that these causes reduced the Confederate ranks in much greater proportion than they were increased by enlistments and other accretions, and General Bragg in his official report of the campaign asserts that we were able "at no time to put more than forty thousand men of all arms and at all places in battle." This included Bragg's, Smith's, and Marshall's columns, and although it is probably true that their aggregate strength in August was 48,776, it would have been as difficult for Bragg and Smith to have concentrated that number as it would have been for Buell and Wright to have concentrated the 163,633 which they commanded. Even with such a force available to drive 40,000 men out of Kentucky, General Wright on the 16th appealed to the governors of Indiana, Illinois, Wisconsin, and Michigan for additional troops. What troops came in answer to these calls I would not venture to say; but leaving these and the troops in West Virginia under General Wright out of the calculation, our strength, even after Stevenson joined us, was less than half, and but little more than one-third that of the enemy, and that powerful enemy was directly on its base of supplies, with unlimited commissary and

⚓ But see other estimates, p. 31.— EDITORS.

ordnance stores, while the Confederate army had no base, was living off the country, and had no possibility of replenishing ammunition. Bragg felt very keenly the misfortune caused by his inability to concentrate and gain a victory over Buell before he should reach the reënforcements which awaited him at Louisville.

In writing to the Government, September 25th, Bragg says:

"I regret to say we are sadly disappointed in the want of action by our friends in Kentucky. We have so far received no accession to this army. General Smith has secured about a brigade — not half our losses by casualties of different kinds. Unless a change occurs soon we must abandon the garden spot of Kentucky. . . ."

On September 18th, Kirby Smith writes to General Bragg:

"The Kentuckians are slow and backward in rallying to our standard. Their hearts are evidently with us, but their blue-grass and fat-grass are against us. Several regiments are in process of organization, and if we remain long enough recruits will be found for all the disposable arms in our possession."

LIEUTENANT-GENERAL E. KIRBY SMITH, C. S. A.
FROM A PHOTOGRAPH.

These letters illustrated why a victory over Buell was necessary.

Although Kentucky maintained her neutrality as long as it was possible, the chivalric spirit of her gallant sons was fully manifested at the earliest opportunity — each obeying only the dictates of his own convictions of duty. While thousands united their fortunes with the South, other and more thousands flocked to the standard of the North.

The proud old families — descendants of the pioneers of the Commonwealth — each sent sons to do battle in the opposing armies. Friends, neighbors, kinsmen, and even brothers bade each other adieu — one to the Northern army, the other to the Confederate.‡ Wherever daring courage, rare intelligence, extraordinary fertility of resource, or fortitude under privation and suffering were displayed, Kentuckians were conspicuous; and when the fight was over and the battle-rent banner of the vanquished Con-

‡ The remarkable division of sentiment, upon the issue presented by the secession of the South, that existed in Kentucky is clearly illustrated by the course of some of her leading families. The three most prominent families in the State were the Breckinridges, the Clays, and the Crittendens, and each of them had representatives in both armies. Major-General Thomas L. Crittenden and Colonel Eugene W. Crittenden served in the army of the North, while their brother, Major-General George B. Crittenden, served in the army of the South. Of Henry Clay's grandchildren, I recall three who espoused the Federal cause, and four who joined the Southern army. Vice-President Breckinridge and three sons adhered to the South, while his two distinguished cousins, the eminent Presbyterian divines, were uncompromising in their devotion to the Union. The elder, and perhaps more famous of these cousins, Dr. Robert J. Breckinridge, had two sons in the Confederate and two in the Federal army; one of whom (Colonel J. C. Breckinridge, now [1888] of the regular army), in the fierce battle at Atlanta, July 22d, 1864, became a prisoner to his brother, W. C. P. Breckinridge, the present member of Congress, who made as brilliant a record as a soldier as he has since made as a statesman. They passed the night following that sanguinary battle with as much warmth of fraternal affection as though visiting each other from neighboring armies engaged in the same cause.— J. W.

federacy furled about its shattered staff was buried in that grave from which a resurrection is no less unwished for than impossible, the survivors of the contest from that State returned to their homes with no feelings of animosity, no brooding hopes of vengeance to be wreaked upon their late opponents.

On October 1st Buell commenced his march from Louisville upon Bragg at Bardstown. On September 29th General Thomas had been assigned by President Lincoln to the command of the army, but at Thomas's request the order was revoked, and he was announced in orders as second in command.

Buell organized his infantry into three army corps, of three divisions each. The First Corps on the left, under Major-General McCook, marched through Taylorsville. The Second Corps, under Major-General Crittenden, marched through Mount Washington, and the Third Corps, under Major-General Gilbert, which formed the Federal right, took the route by way of Shepherdsville. General Sill, of McCook's corps, reënforced by Dumont's independent division, marched direct to Frankfort to threaten Kirby Smith.

Buell, in his official report, says:

"Skirmishing with the enemy's cavalry and artillery marked the movement of each column from within a few miles of Louisville. It was more stubborn and formidable near Bardstown, but the rear of the enemy's infantry retired from that place eight hours before our arrival, when his rear-guard of cavalry and artillery retreated after a sharp engagement with my cavalry. The pursuit and skirmishing with the enemy's rear-guard continued toward Springfield."

General Smith prepared to meet Sill and Dumont, and on October 2d Bragg ordered General Polk to move the entire army from Bardstown via Bloomfield toward Frankfort, and to strike Sill's column in flank while Smith met it in front. For reasons which were afterward explained that order was not complied with, but, on the approach of Buell, Polk marched via Perryville toward Harrodsburg, where he expected the entire army would be concentrated. ♭ General Smith, confronted by Sill and Dumont near Frankfort, had several times on the 6th and 7th called upon Bragg for reënforcements, and Withers's division of Polk's corps was ordered to him. Reports reached Bragg exaggerating the strength of the movement upon Frankfort. He was thus led to believe that the force behind Polk was not so heavy as represented, and on the evening of October 7th he directed him to form the cavalry and the divisions of Cheatham, Buckner, and Patton Anderson at Perryville, and vigorously attack the pursuing column. Since October 1st our cavalry had persistently engaged the two most advanced of Buell's columns.

The reader should now observe, by the map [p. 6], that McCook's corps approached Perryville by the road through Bloomfield, Chaplin, and Mackville, its general direction being nearly south-east. General Gilbert's corps approached by the road from Springfield, its general direction being east, but bearing north-east as it approached the town. Crittenden's corps, accompanied by General Thomas and preceded by cavalry, having crossed Gilbert's line of march, was on a road which runs due east from Lebanon to Danville.

♭ General Polk, finding his own front threatened, availed himself of previous instructions as to how he should handle his force in certain contingencies, and retired slowly.— EDITORS.

At a point about five miles south-west of Perryville this road has a branch which turns north-east to that place. Now remember that our stores and supplies were at Bryantsville and Camp Dick Robinson about eighteen miles east of Perryville, and that Kirby Smith was at McCown's Ferry, on the Kentucky River, *en route* for Versailles, menaced by two divisions under General Sill. Also observe the important feature that McCook was at Mackville during the night of the 7th, at which place a road forks, running east to Harrodsburg and thence to our depot at Bryantsville; and also consider that Mackville was as near Bryantsville as were our troops in front of Perryville.

On the 7th our cavalry fought with considerable tenacity, particularly in the evening, when the enemy sought to get possession of the only accessible supply of water. General Buell, in his report, says:

" The advanced guard, consisting of cavalry and artillery, supported toward evening by two regiments of infantry, pressed successfully upon the enemy's rear-guard to within two miles of the town, against a somewhat stubborn opposition."

After dark, at General Hardee's request, I went to his bivouac and discussed the plans for the following day. I explained to him the topography of the country and the location of Buell's columns. I understood from him that the attack would be made very early the next morning, and I endeavored to impress upon him the great advantage which must follow an early commencement of the action. An early attack on the 8th would have met only the advance of Gilbert's corps on the Springfield road, which was four or five miles nearer to Perryville than any other Federal troops, and their overthrow could have been accomplished with little loss, while every hour of delay was bringing the rear divisions of the enemy nearer to the front, besides bringing the corps of McCook and Crittenden upon the field. I explained, also, that Thomas and Crittenden on the Lebanon and Danville road could easily gain our rear, while all our forces were engaged with McCook and Gilbert. For instance, if Crittenden turned toward Perryville at the fork five miles from that place, he would march directly in the rear of our troops engaged with Gilbert's corps. If he kept on toward Danville and Camp Dick Robinson, our position would be turned, and a rapid retreat to our depot of supplies, closely followed by McCook and Gilbert, would be the inevitable result. With equal ease, McCook, by marching from Mackville to Harrodsburg, could reach our depot, thus turning our right flank.

The reader will plainly see that Perryville was not a proper place for sixteen thousand men to form and await the choice of time and manner of attack by Buell, with his tremendous army, and that every moment's delay after daylight was lessening the probabilities of advantage to the Confederates. The cavalry under my command was pressed forward at dawn on the 8th, and skirmished with the outposts of the enemy, until, on the approach of a Federal brigade of cavalry supported by a line of infantry, we charged, dispersing the cavalry, and, breaking through both infantry and artillery, drove the enemy from their guns and took 140 prisoners.

The Federal army was now being placed in line: McCook's corps on the left, Gilbert's in the center, and Crittenden's corps, which reached the field

LIEUTENANT-GENERAL JOSEPH WHEELER, C. S. A.
FROM A PHOTOGRAPH.

at 11 o'clock,\ on the right, its flank being covered by Edward M. McCook's brigade of cavalry. The management of the Federal right wing was under the supervision of General Thomas.

General Bragg reached Perryville about 10 o'clock. General Liddell's brigade, of Buckner's division, had been advanced with his left near the Springfield road, and his skirmish line became engaged. The cavalry on the Confederate left apparently being able to hold their own against the enemy upon that part of the field, Cheatham's division, composed of Donelson's, Stewart's, and Maney's brigades, was ordered to the right, where, between 1 and 2 o'clock, with its right supported by cavalry, it moved forward to the attack. Generals Hardee and Buckner, seeing Cheatham fairly in action, ordered General Bushrod Johnson's and Cleburne's brigades forward. There being considerable space between Cheatham's left and Buckner's right, General John C. Brown's and Colonel Jones's brigades, of Anderson's division, and General S. A. M. Wood's, of Buckner's division, had been placed in position to fill the vacancy. Adams's and Powell's brigades, of Anderson's division, were to the left of Buckner, and the line thus arranged with cavalry on both flanks gallantly advanced upon the enemy. Cheatham was first in action and was almost immediately exposed to a murderous fire of infantry and artillery, which soon spread to the left of our line.

Our artillery, handled with great skill, told fearfully on the enemy, who sought, when practicable, to take shelter behind stone walls and fences. Fortunately we were enabled to enfilade many of their temporary shelters with a well-directed fire from our batteries, and this, added to our musketry, was so effective that first one regiment, then another, and finally the entire Federal line, gave way before the determined onset of our troops.

\ Crittenden testified before the Buell Commission that his leading division "was in line of battle between 10 and 11." This line was formed on the Lebanon pike about three miles from the battle-field.— EDITORS.

At one time Cleburne and Johnson seemed checked for a moment, as they assailed a very strong position, the fire from which cut down our men and severely wounded General Cleburne. But encouraged by the steady advance on both right and left, these troops recovered from the shock, and with increased speed the entire line overran the enemy, capturing three batteries and a number of prisoners. Among the dead and wounded Federals lay one who, the prisoners told us, was General James S. Jackson, the commander of one of McCook's divisions. General Liddell, who had been placed in reserve, followed the movement, and when the contest became warmest was sent to reënforce Cheatham, where he did valiant service.

During this sanguinary struggle, our line had advanced nearly a mile. Prisoners, guns, colors, and the field of battle were ours; not a step which had been gained was yielded. The enemy, though strongly reënforced, was still broken and disordered. He held his ground mainly because our troops were too exhausted for further effort. At one point just at dusk we captured a disorganized body, including a number of brigade and division staff-officers. Soon darkness came on and we rested on the field thus bravely won.

Our entire force engaged, infantry, cavalry and artillery, was but 16,000 men. Our loss was 510 killed, 2635 wounded, and 251 missing. Generals S. A. M. Wood and Cleburne were disabled, and a large proportion of higher officers were killed or wounded. Three of General Wood's staff were among the killed.

General Buell lost 916 killed, 2943 wounded, and 489 captured by the Confederates. General Jackson, commanding a division, and General Terrill and Colonel Webster, commanding brigades, were among the Federal killed, and Colonel Lytle was among the wounded.

At every point of battle the Confederates had been victorious. We had engaged three corps of the Federal army; ☆ one of these, McCook's, to use Buell's language, was "very much crippled," one division, again to use his language, "having in fact almost entirely disappeared as a body."

After darkness had closed a battle, it was a custom to send messengers or notes to the nearest generals, detailing results, telling of this or that one who had fallen, and asking information from other portions of the field. Resting quietly on the ground, the army expected, and would gladly have welcomed, a renewal of the fight on the next day, but the accumulation of Buell's forces was such as not to justify further conflict in that locality. Kirby Smith was near Lawrenceburg with his own troops and Withers's division, and after full consultation it was determined to march to Harrodsburg, where it was hoped the entire Confederate force in Kentucky might be concentrated. I was directed with the cavalry to prevent an advance on the road leading to Danville. At midnight the troops withdrew to Perryville, and at sunrise continued the march. It was long after this when the Federal pickets began to reconnoiter, and it was fully 10 o'clock when, standing on the edge of the town, I saw the advance of the skirmish line of Buell's army. Bragg prepared

☆ Only a small part of Crittenden's corps was in action; see p. 31.—EDITORS.

for battle on the Harrodsburg road, only eight miles from Perryville, and
awaited Buell's advance.

Two days elapsed, and the Federal army evinced no disposition to attack.
A division of infantry and a brigade of cavalry fought me back to near
Danville, and at the same time Buell formed with his right within four
miles of that place, making a feint in Bragg's immediate front on the road
leading from Perryville to Harrodsburg. Buell, no doubt, hoped to cut him
off from the crossing of the Dick River near Camp Dick Robinson.

I sent General Bragg information of Buell's dispositions, whereupon he
issued orders to his army and wrote me as follows:

"HARRODSBURG, KY., October 10th, 1862. COLONEL WHEELER. DEAR COLONEL: I
opened your dispatch to General Polk regarding the enemy's movements. The information
you furnish is very important. It is just what I needed and I thank you for it. This information leaves no doubt as to the proper course for me to pursue. Hold the enemy firmly till
to-morrow. Yours, etc., BRAXTON BRAGG."

Bragg had now determined to retreat to Knoxville by the way of Cumberland Gap. It was evident that Buell's large army would enable him to select
his own time and position for battle unless Bragg chose to attack. Bragg
already had 1500 sick and over 3000 wounded. A severe battle would
certainly have increased the wounded to 4000 or 5000 more. The care of
such a number of wounded would have embarrassed, possibly controlled,
our movements.

Hardee states that he had but 10,000 men before the battle of Perryville,
and Bragg said that the three divisions which fought that battle had but
14,500. If that was correct they had now but 11,000.

It was too hazardous to guard our depot of supplies and contend with the
Federal forces within easy march. Our wagon trains were immense, and our
artillery large in proportion to other arms.

The enemy pushed up close to Danville on the night of the 10th, but we
easily held him in check until all our army had crossed Dick River. On the
11th we contended against a force of infantry, which finally pressed us so
warmly that we were compelled to retire east of Danville. Here the enemy
was again driven back, and we held our position near the town.

Before day on the 13th I received the following appointment and instructions in a special order from General Bragg, dated Bryantsville:

"Colonel Wheeler is hereby appointed chief of cavalry, and is authorized to give orders
in the name of the commanding general. He is charged under Major-General Smith with
covering the rear of the army and holding the enemy in check. All cavalry will report to him
and receive his orders."

Compliance with the above of course involved considerable fighting, but by
using the cavalry to the best advantage, and adopting available expedients,
the movement of our infantry and trains in retreat was unmolested. These
engagements were constant, and were often warmly and bitterly contested.

The large trains of captured stores made the progress of our infantry very
slow, and the corps commanders sent frequent admonitions to me urging the

importance of persistent resistance to Buell's advance. In crossing Big Hill, and at other points, the trains hardly averaged five miles a day, and General Kirby Smith at one time regarded it as impossible for the cavalry to save them. In his letter to Bragg, on the 14th, he says: "I have no hope of saving the whole of my train"; and in his letter on the 15th he says: "I have little hope of saving any of the trains, and fear much of the artillery will be lost." But fortunately nothing was lost. Our cavalry at times dismounted and fought behind stone fences and hastily erected rail breastworks, and when opportunity offered charged the advancing enemy. Each expedient was adopted several times each day, and when practicable the road was obstructed by felling timber. These devices were continually resorted to until the 22d, when the enemy ceased the pursuit, and early in November the cavalry force, which covered the retreat from Kentucky, reached middle Tennessee and was close to the enemy, less than ten miles south of Nashville.

The campaign was over. Buell was deprived of his command for not having defeated Bragg, who, in turn, was censured by the Southern people for his failure to destroy the Federal army commanded by Buell.

LIEUTENANT-GENERAL B. F. CHEATHAM, C. S. A.
FROM A PHOTOGRAPH.

This campaign was made at a time when the opposing Governments hoped for more from their generals and armies than could reasonably be accomplished. The people of the South were misinformed regarding the resources at the disposal of Generals Bragg and Kirby Smith, and our first successes aroused expectations and hopes that the Kentucky movement would result in the defeat, or at least the discomfiture, of Buell's army, the possible invasion of the North, and certainly the recovery of Confederate power in the central and eastern portions of Kentucky and Tennessee. They were sorely disappointed when they heard of General Bragg's withdrawal through Cumberland Gap, and could not easily be convinced of the necessity of such a movement immediately following the battle of Perryville, which they regarded as a decisive victory. The censure which fell upon Bragg was therefore severe and almost universal. It somewhat abated after the prompt advance of the army to Murfreesboro'; but to this day there are many who contend that Bragg should have defeated Buell and maintained himself in the rich and productive plains of Kentucky. On the other hand the Federal Government was, if possible, more severe in denunciation of General Buell, and held that, far from allowing General Bragg to cross the Tennessee River and the mountains into middle Tennessee, Buell should have anticipated these movements, occupied Chattanooga, and, as some even contended, marched his army toward Atlanta. The Government was convinced that he could easily have met and halted Bragg as he debouched from the mountains before entering middle Tennessee. It was emphatic in its assertion that ordinary celerity on the part of General Buell would have saved Munfordville and its garrison of 4200 men; that proper concentration would have destroyed the Confederate forces at Perryville, and that the plainest principles of strategy presented the opportunity of throwing forward a column to cut off Bragg's retreat via Camp Dick Robinson, or that at least after the commencement of the conflict at Perryville he should have pressed close to his antagonist and forced Bragg to continuous battle, contending, as they did, that superior numbers and proximity to his base gave the Federal commander advantages that, if properly improved, would have resulted in the destruction of the Confederate army.

Buell's strategy and tactics were the subject of Congressional investigation and inquiry by a military commission. With regard to the adverse criticisms on Bragg's campaign it must be admitted that there were opportunities, had they been improved, to cripple, if not to defeat, the Federal army.

The failure to "concentrate and attack" tells the story of the campaign. The first opportunity was on September 18th, when we caught Buell south of Munfordville. Bragg could not have attacked at Altamont, because it will be remembered that on August 30th, at the first appearance of our cavalry, the Federal force retreated from that place down the mountain. Neither could he have overtaken Buell's troops at McMinnville, because, fully three days before Bragg could have reached that place, Buell had ordered all his army to Murfreesboro'.

Those who contend that Bragg should have followed Buell to Nashville do not consider that he would have found him in a good position, strengthened by fortifications, and defended by 9 divisions of infantry and 1 of cavalry; his available force for duty then being 66,595.

After the surrender of the Federal fort at Munfordville, it became painfully apparent that a single mind should control the Confederate troops in Kentucky, and concentrate our entire force and attack the divided enemy; but a condition existed which has been repeated in military operations for four thousand years, and always with disastrous results. The troops in Kentucky had two commanders. The troops of two different departments were expected to coöperate.

Both Kirby Smith and Bragg were brave and skillful generals. The devotion of each to the cause in which they were enlisted was absolute, and their only ambition was to contribute to its success. In their characters the pettiness of personal rivalry could find no place, and either would willingly have relinquished to the other the honor of being the victor, if the victory could only have been won.

It will be remembered how promptly, in the preceding June, General Bragg had weakened his own army and strengthened Smith's by sending McCown's division from Tupelo to Chattanooga, and again in August by sending the brigades of Cleburne and Preston Smith from Chattanooga to Knoxville;

SPRING NEAR PERRYVILLE, WHICH HELPED
TO RELIEVE BRAGG'S PARCHED ARMY.
FROM A PHOTOGRAPH TAKEN IN 1885.

PEAR-TREE, ONE HUNDRED YEARS OLD, AT THE LEFT OF
ROUSSEAU'S POSITION, PERRYVILLE. FROM A
PHOTOGRAPH TAKEN IN 1885.

and again, when Smith was pressed at Frankfort, that Bragg reënforced him promptly with one of his best divisions. That Kirby Smith would, at any time, have been as ready and prompt to give Bragg any part or all of his army there can be no doubt, but when the decisive moment came, the two independent armies were more than one hundred miles apart, and neither commander could be informed of the other's necessities. Bragg and Smith conferred together, but neither commanded the other. If all the troops had belonged to one army, Bragg would have ordered, and not conferred or requested.

To aggravate the difficulties inherent in the system of independent commands and divided responsibility, Brigadier-General Marshall, who had commanded in West Virginia, appeared upon the field of active operations with 2150 men. He was an able and distinguished man and determined in his devotion to the Confederacy. He wished to do his full duty, but he appeared to feel that he could render more efficient service with a separate command than if trammeled by subordination to a superior commander; and his aversion to having any intervening power between himself and the President was apparent.

While General Smith was anxious to coöperate, he nevertheless, in reply to Bragg's request for coöperation, wrote indicating very forcibly that he thought other plans were more important; and, in fact, the only coöperative action during the campaign was Bragg's compliance with Smith's request to transfer to him two brigades on August 5th, and to transfer Withers's division to him on October 7th.

In reply to the question as to what one supreme commander could have done, I confidently assert he could have concentrated and attacked and beaten Buell on September 18th south of Munfordville. He could then have turned and marched to Louisville and taken that city. If it should be argued that this plan involved unnecessary marching on the part of Kirby Smith, who was then at Lexington, a supreme commander could have adopted the one which was contemplated by Bragg early in the campaign. ⸙

After the surrender of Munfordville he could by September 21st have reached Louisville with all the force in Kentucky, taken the city, and then risked its being held by a small garrison, while making another concentration and attack upon Buell.

As an evidence of how easily we could have taken Louisville, it must be observed that on September 22d Buell sent Major-General Nelson orders containing these words:

" If you have only the force you speak of it would not, I should say, be advisable for you to attempt a defense of Louisville unless you are strongly intrenched; under no circumstances should you make a fight with his whole or main force. The alternative would be to cross the river or march on this side to the mouth of Salt River and bridge it so as to form a junction with me. . . ."

Nelson seemed to concur with Buell, and it was not until that officer was but a day's march from Louisville that Nelson telegraphed the fact to General Wright, saying, " Louisville is now safe; ' God and Liberty.' "

In further corroboration of this, " Harper's History," p. 311, says:

" Just before the Federal army entered Louisville, on the 25th of September, the panic there had reached its height. In twenty-four hours more Nelson would have abandoned the city."

But suppose neither plan had been adopted, the next chance for a supreme commander of the Kentucky forces was to " concentrate and attack" Buell's flank while his army was strung out *en route* to Louisville. Elizabethtown would have been a good place, and had it been done with vigor about September 23d it certainly would have resulted in victory. But at this time General Smith's forces were all moving to Mount Sterling, 130 miles to the east of that place (Elizabethtown), and General Smith was asking, not ordering, General Marshall to coöperate with him. The next field upon which a supreme commander had an opportunity to concentrate and attack was at Perryville. Three hundred cavalry could have played with Generals Sill and Dumont around Frankfort, and every other soldier, except a few

⸙ On the 1st of August General Bragg wrote from Chattanooga to Richmond: "As some ten days or two weeks must elapse before my means of transportation will reach here to such extent as to enable me to take the field with my main force, it has been determined that General Smith shall move at once against General [G. W.] Morgan in front of Cumberland Gap. Should he be successful, and our well-grounded hopes fulfilled, our entire force will be thrown into middle Tennessee with the fairest prospect of cutting off General Buell." On the 12th Bragg wrote to Smith, at Knoxville, as follows: "On Friday I shall probably commence crossing the river [Tennessee], by which I shall draw their attention from you. . . . I shall not desire to hold you longer in check than will enable me to get in motion to support you, for it would be too great a risk to allow Buell, by rapid railroad movements, to get in your front. In the meantime I hope you will bring Morgan to terms."— EDITORS.

scouts, could then have struck Gilbert's corps as day dawned on the 8th of October.

Since, in the final result, we neither defeated Buell nor took Louisville, it is now evident that it was unfortunate Bragg did not foresee the end immediately after his victory at Munfordville. He could certainly have crippled Buell to some extent as he attempted his hazardous flank movement *en route* to Louisville, and then, by a rapid march, he could have reached and captured Nashville and returned and established himself at Bowling Green.

I have pointed out these lost opportunities as an additional proof of the adage, as old as war itself, " that one bad general is better than two good ones." The very fact that both the generals are good intensifies the evil ; each, full of confidence in himself and determined to attain what he has in view, is unwilling to yield to any one ; but if both are weak the natural indisposition of such men to exertion, their anxiety to avoid responsibility, and their desire in a great crisis to lean on some one, will frequently bring about the junction of two independent armies without any

CORNER OF THE CONFEDERATE CEMETERY AT PERRYVILLE. FROM A PHOTOGRAPH TAKEN IN 1886.

The cemetery is situated on a knoll a few rods south-east of the hill on which General J. S. Jackson was killed. After the battle Squire Henry P. Bottom offered the friends of the Confederates any plot of ground they might choose on his farm for a burial spot. They chose this knoll because their dead lay thickest near its eastern slope. In the autumn of 1886 a fragment of a lime-stone wall was visible above the weeds. At that time Squire Bottom said that 435 Confederates were buried here, of whom about 100 were identified. Only one headstone was to be found, and that bore the name of Samuel H. Ransom, of the 1st Tenn., and was placed there by his wife. Several officers were buried with the unidentified dead.— EDITORS.

deliberately planned concert of action between the commanders. Both Bragg and Kirby Smith were men who had, to an eminent degree, those qualities that make good generals, and, once together with their armies upon the same field, victory would have been certain. Both fully appreciated the fact that, when an adversary is not intrenched, a determined attack is the beginning of victory. By this means Smith had been victorious at Manassas and at Richmond, Ky., and by vigorous attack Albert Sidney Johnston and Bragg had won at every point of battle at Shiloh, on the 6th of April. Later, the Confederate points of attack were Bragg's scene of victory the first day at Murfreesboro', and the boldness of his onset gave Bragg his great triumph at Chickamauga. Nothing was therefore wanting in Kentucky but absolute authority in one responsible commander. Coöperation of the most cordial character is a poor substitute. The word coöperation should be stricken from military phraseology.

In writing to the Government on August 1st, after he had met General Smith, General Bragg says : " We have arranged measures for mutual sup-

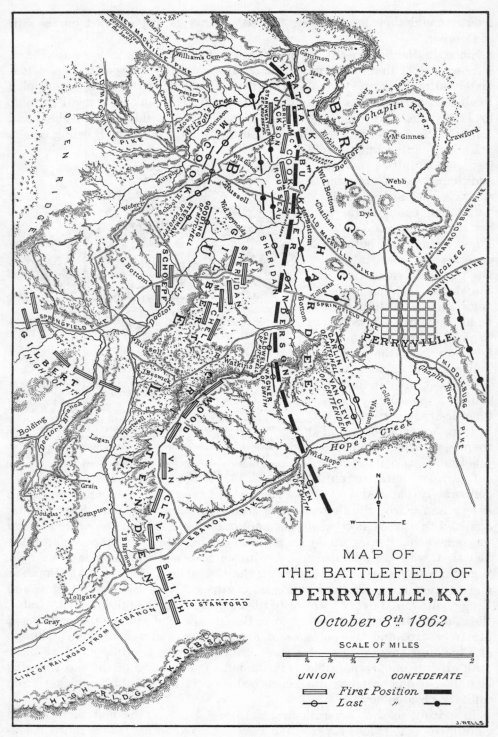

MAP OF
THE BATTLEFIELD OF
PERRYVILLE, KY.
October 8th 1862

SCALE OF MILES

UNION		CONFEDERATE
First Position		
Last	"	

J. WELLS

DEFENSE OF CAGE'S FORD, ON THE CUMBERLAND RIVER, NEAR GALLATIN, NOVEMBER 21, 1862.
FROM A LITHOGRAPH.

According to a note on the lithograph, a detachment of Morgan's cavalry, and of infantry, approached Cage's Ford at daybreak of November 21, 1862, hoping to surprise the 31st Ohio regiment, which had been encamped on the south side of the Cumberland. Finding that the Union troops had changed their camp to the north side, the Confederates threw shells from two 12-pounder howitzers until their cannoneers were driven from the pieces by the musketry fire of the Ohioans, under Lieutenant-Colonel Lister, three of whom were wounded. The Confederates made no serious attempt to cross, and soon withdrew.—EDITORS.

port and effective coöperation." On August 8th Bragg writes to Smith: "I find myself in your department; without explanation this might seem an unjustifiable intrusion." While it is no doubt true that General Smith was at all times willing to yield to the authority of General Bragg, yet the fact that Smith was the commander of an independent department, receiving orders from and reporting directly to the President, made him primarily responsible to the Executive, and this limited the authority of General Bragg. Nevertheless the Kentucky campaign was attended with great results to the Confederacy. Two months of marches and battle by the armies of Bragg and Smith had cost the Federals a loss in killed, wounded, and prisoners of 26,530. We had captured 35 cannon, 16,000 stand of arms, millions of rounds of ammunition, 1700 mules, 300 wagons loaded with military stores, and 2000 horses. We had recovered Cumberland Gap and redeemed middle Tennessee and north Alabama. Yet expectations had been excited that were not realized, and hopes had been cherished that were disappointed; and therefore this campaign of repeated triumphs, without a single reverse, has never received—save from the thoughtful, intelligent, and impartial minority—any proper recognition.

MORGAN'S CAVALRY DURING THE BRAGG INVASION.

BY BASIL W. DUKE, BRIGADIER-GENERAL, C. S. A.

WHILE Bragg was concentrating at Chattanooga, in August, 1862, preparatory to his march into Kentucky, Colonel John H. Morgan, with his cavalry command, numbering some nine hundred effectives, was actively engaged in middle Tennessee, operating chiefly against the Federal garrisons in the vicinity of Nashville, and the detachments employed immediately north and to the east of that city. All of these were successively captured or dispersed, and on the 21st of August Morgan defeated and completely routed a select body of cavalry, twelve hundred strong, sent under command of General R. W. Johnson to drive him out of Tennessee. Of this force 164 were killed and wounded, and a much larger number, including Johnson and his staff, were made prisoners.

Morgan had been notified of the intended invasion of Kentucky, and part of his duty was the destruction of the railroad track and bridges between Nashville and Bowling Green, for the purpose of retarding Buell's movements when the latter should begin his retreat to Louisville.

On the 28th of August Bragg crossed the Tennessee River at Chattanooga, and pushed northward. General Kirby Smith had previously entered Kentucky, and had ordered Morgan to report to him at Lexington, in the blue-grass region. Morgan marched from Hartsville, Tenn., on the 29th of August, and on the 4th of September reached Lexington, already occupied by General Smith. His command consisted of the 2d Kentucky Cavalry C. S. A., about 700 strong, and Gano's squadron, of 2 companies of Texan cavalry, about 150 strong. It was very largely recruited, however, during the occupation of Kentucky. A small detachment of the 2d Kentucky, leaving Lexington on the same day, made a rapid march of some 90 miles, and captured the garrison, 150 strong, of the stockade fort erected for the protection of the railroad bridge over Salt River, 17 miles south of Louisville. The bridge was burned in pursuance of the programme to destroy rail communication between Bowling Green and Louisville. By order of General Smith, the command was then divided for separate service. I was ordered to proceed with 600 men of the 2d Kentucky to the vicinity of Covington, whence General Heth, who had threatened Cincinnati, was then retiring. Colonel Morgan was ordered, with the remainder of the regiment, Gano's squadron, and all the cavalry recruits then organized, to march to the assistance of General Marshall in the mountains of eastern Kentucky. The Federal general, George W. Morgan, had evacuated Cumberland Gap, and followed by Stevenson, who had been instructed to observe and pursue him if he moved, was making his way to the Ohio. It was intended that Marshall and Morgan should intercept and arrest his march until Stevenson could overtake him and attack him in rear.

The detachment under my command became immediately very actively engaged with the enemy, who, in considerable numbers, had crossed the river and advanced to Walton, twenty-five miles south of Covington. For several days, skirmishing went on constantly, and I was steadily driven back, until I became convinced that it was an advance in force. Discovering, however, by careful reconnoissance that the entire Federal strength consisted of only 7000 or 8000 infantry, about 1000 cavalry, and 8 pieces of artillery, and that troops were being transported in large numbers by the river from Cincinnati, I became satisfied that the movement was intended to cover and divert attention from the real concentration at Louisville, and was not meant as a serious movement on Lexington, and I so reported to General Smith. Reports from my scouts and from citizens, to the effect that these troops were quite raw and inexperienced, and that, on account of the omission to scout or reconnoiter, the encampment at Walton, where the enemy had halted, could be easily approached, induced me to attack the camp. By a quick dash upon it, just after daybreak, I secured 90 or 100 prisoners, with very little loss on my part; but found that no effort by a force numerically so inferior could compel the enemy to retire.

It was important, however, that his column should be forced to fall back and not remain as a menace to Lexington, whence it was distant only two or three days' march. I learned that a regiment was organized for the Federal army out of some "home guard" companies at Augusta, a small town on the Ohio, about forty miles above Covington. I was also informed that at that season of year, when the river was at a very low stage of water, it was fordable immediately below this place. Leaving the greater part of my command in front of the enemy at Walton to observe and follow him if he retreated, I marched rapidly with 250 men to Augusta, believing that the recruits there could be captured or dispersed with ease, and without loss on my part, and that I could cross the river into Ohio, enter the suburbs of Cincinnati, and induce such consternation that the troops at Walton would be recalled. On the 27th of September I attacked, meeting, however, with fierce resistance. Two small river steamers were there, bulwarked with bales of hay, and each carrying a 12-pounder howitzer. On these boats were about one hundred infantry. The "Home Guards," 400 or 500 strong, were ensconced in the houses of the little town. I planted two small howitzers attached to my command on a hill overlooking the village, and within a half-mile range of the river. After the exchange of a few shots on each side, the boats, with the troops upon them, steamed off in disgraceful panic. I thought then that the affair was over, but when I entered the town I found nearly every house a fortress, and was met with severe volleys which did much damage. Before I could overcome the resistance of the inmates, I was forced to burn some of the houses, storm many others, and even double-shot the small field-pieces and fire them point-blank from the street into some whose defenders were unusually stubborn. The hand-to-hand fighting in this little skirmish was the fiercest I ever saw. In many instances when the firing from the windows was stopped by the volleys poured into them from the streets, the inmates still refused to surrender, and the details of my men who broke down the doors and entered were compelled to kill all they found inside. Captain S. D. Morgan killed seven men with his own hand, and was himself killed before the house he entered was taken. In some houses I saw blood dripping down the stairways.

My loss was 21 men killed and 18 wounded. A very much larger number of the "Home Guards" was killed, and I carried off between 300 and 400 prisoners. The combat lasted not more than fifteen minutes after I entered the town; but my loss, the number of prisoners, and especially the fact that I had nearly exhausted my ammunition, decided me not to cross the Ohio and carry out the movement on Cincinnati I had contemplated. I knew, also, that 500 or 600 Federal troops at Maysville, not far distant, would be ordered immediately to Augusta, and that my return by that point would be intercepted. On the next morning I was attacked at Brookville by these troops, under Lieutenant-Colonel H. B. Wilson, nine miles from Augusta; but the affair was trifling, the loss on either side slight, and I carried off my prisoners. Four or five days afterward I was ordered to return to Lexington.

Col. John H. Morgan had been sent to eastern Kentucky, as I have said, to intercept the retreat of the Federal general, George W. Morgan. He did not find Marshall in the vicinity where he was instructed to seek him, nor, indeed, at all. Learning that the Federal column was moving from Manchester via Booneville to Mount Sterling, doubtless to reach the Ohio at Maysville, Colonel Morgan expected to strike the enemy between Booneville and Mount Sterling. But General Morgan concentrated at Irvine on the 21st, and moved toward Proctor. The Confederate cavalry then moved as rapidly as the mountainous country permitted, and receiving further information that the enemy had turned to the right and was at Campton, in Wolfe County, succeeded in getting directly in his front near Hazel Green. From the 25th of September until the 1st of October every effort was made to arrest or delay the Federal retreat. The roads were barricaded, the column was attacked in front and flank, and the skirmishing was continuous. During that time the enemy progressed only thirty miles; nevertheless, John Morgan received no aid as promised him, nor did Stevenson overtake the Federal commander and force him to battle. At noon, October the 1st, Colonel Morgan received orders to withdraw from the enemy's front, and rejoin General Smith "at Lexington, *or wherever he might be.*" He reached Lexington on the 4th of October. I reported to him there the next day. The town was about to be evacuated, and General Smith's entire army, Stevenson having arrived, was marching to effect a junction with Bragg. We

left Lexington on the 6th, and until the 10th were employed in preventing the debouchment of Sill's and Dumont's divisions (Federal) from the rough country west of Frankfort, where they were demonstrating to induce Bragg to believe that Buell's attack would be delivered from that direction when the latter had in reality marched to Perryville.

After General Bragg had moved from Munfordville to Bardstown, the entire Confederate strategic line, including the disposition of the forces under General Smith, may be described as extending from Bardstown on the left flank, via Lexington, to Mount Sterling on the extreme right. It was one admirably adapted for defense. However threatened, the troops could be marched to the point menaced by excellent interior roads, and favorable ground for battle was available wherever attack was probable. The base at Bryantsville was secure, and was an exceedingly strong natural position. The aggregate strength of the Confederate armies was little, if any, less than 61,000 men.

On October 1st Buell moved out of Louisville with 58,000 effective men, of whom 22,000 were raw troops.

Under the impression that Buell was about to throw his entire army upon Smith at Frankfort, Bragg, on the 2d, ordered Polk to march with the Army of the Mississippi from Bardstown via Bloomfield toward Frankfort in order that he might strike the enemy in rear, while Kirby Smith should assail him in front. Until the 7th he remained apparently under the impression that Buell was advancing to attack Smith. But on the evening of the 7th, Gilbert, in command of Buell's center, came in contact with Hardee near Perryville, and compelled him to prepare for action. Hardee called for reënforcements, and Cheatham's division was sent him, while the remainder of Polk's corps continued its march toward Versailles with the view of joining the forces under General Smith.

It thus happened that General Bragg, completely misled by the mere demonstration upon Frankfort, kept more than two-thirds of the entire force under his control idly manœuvring in a quarter where nothing could possibly be accomplished, and permitted less than 20,000 men to become engaged upon a field where more than 45,000 of the enemy could have been hurled upon them. Buell's whole army (with the exception of the divisions of Sill and Dumont — together 10,000 or 12,000 strong) was concentrated at Perryville on the 8th, and but for the unaccountable circumstance that McCook had been fighting several hours before Buell was informed that a battle was in progress, the Confederate line would have been overwhelmed by an attack in force. If such had been the result at Perryville on the 8th, and Buell had then gotten between the scattered remnants of the troops that opposed him there, as he would almost surely have done, he would have been master of the situation, and nothing but disaster could have befallen the Confederates. For on the 9th Sill and Dumont were marching to rejoin the main body, and in another day Buell could have had his entire 58,000 — minus the loss sustained in the battle — well in hand.

After Perryville, Morgan was ordered to rejoin the army, when everything was concentrated at Harrodsburg, as if for a battle which General Bragg could have won but never meant to fight. When the army, leaving Harrodsburg, without battle, began its retreat to Tennessee, Morgan, assisted by Col. Henry Ashby with a small brigade of cavalry, was employed in covering its rear. This rear-guard was engaged very arduously, and almost constantly, in contact with Buell's advance regiments until the 17th. At that date Morgan received permission to retrace his march, capture Lexington, which was, of course, in the hands of the enemy, and then move southward, directly across Buell's rear, doing the latter all possible damage. Marching rapidly for twenty-four hours, he reached Lexington at dawn of the following morning, and immediately attacked the 4th Ohio Cavalry, which was encamped at Ashland — once the residence of Henry Clay — about two miles from the city. The enemy was defeated after a short combat, and nearly six hundred were made prisoners. The loss in killed and wounded on either side was slight. Resuming his march at noon that day, Morgan encamped on the following night at Shryock's ferry on the Kentucky River. At midnight he was attacked by Dumont, and fearing that he would be surrounded and entrapped in the rugged hills of that region, he marched with all speed for Lawrenceburg, four miles distant, reaching and passing through that little town just as a heavy Federal column, sent to intercept him there, was entering it upon the Frankfort turnpike. Passing around Bardstown on the next day, we encamped between that place and Elizabethtown. We were now directly in Buell's rear, and during the next twenty-four hours captured many laggards, and several wagon trains — one quite large and richly laden.

From the 20th to the 25th of October Morgan continued to march in a south-western direction, reaching Hopkinsville on the 25th. Here he had entirely passed beyond the zone of Federal garrisons in middle Kentucky, but still had arduous work before him in Tennessee and in front of Nashville, whither Buell, having turned aside from pursuit of Bragg through the mountains of south-eastern Kentucky, was now directing his course. After a short sojourn at Hopkinsville for much-needed rest, Colonel Morgan moved directly to Gallatin, Tennessee, with a view of completing the destruction of the Louisville and Nashville Railroad in that vicinity, and to that extent impeding the transportation of troops and supplies to Nashville. While engaged in this work he received orders from General John C. Breckinridge, who was stationed with a small infantry force at Murfreesboro', to coöperate with Forrest in a movement intended to effect the destruction of the rolling-stock of the Louisville and Nashville Railroad Company collected at Edgefield, on the bank of the Cumberland River, opposite Nashville. It was planned that Forrest should make such a demonstration south of Nash-

ville that the attention of the garrison would be attracted, while Morgan should dash into Edgefield and burn the cars, several hundred in number.

Leaving Gallatin on the night of November the 4th, Morgan entered Edgefield at daybreak the next morning, and immediately attacked the 16th Illinois and part of another regiment stationed there. After a sharp fight he drove this force back and obtained possession of the cars it was intended he should destroy. We heard Forrest's artillery at the same moment on the other side of the river. But Nashville was so strongly fortified on that side, and perhaps, also, the inadequacy of the small force under Forrest to make any serious attempt upon the place was so apparent, that although he advanced resolutely upon the works, the movement failed: a large portion of the garrison was dispatched to reënforce the detachment we had attacked; and before the work of demolition was fairly commenced, a column of infantry streamed at the double-quick over the pontoon-bridge, and reënforced the troops with which we were already engaged. The fight grew too hot to be maintained so near to yet stronger hostile forces, and under the heavy batteries which commanded the ground on which we stood. Morgan accordingly withdrew, followed a short distance by the enemy. Our loss in killed and wounded was not so heavy as the enemy's, and we carried off a few prisoners. Only a small number of the railroad cars were burned, and the expedition was a failure. Rosecrans's army ☆ was now close at hand, marching upon three or four roads leading into Nashville, and we were immediately in its path. Crittenden's corps was in advance, the major part of it marching on the Louisville and Nashville turnpike. Morgan sent strong detachments to harass these troops, and, if possible, delay their march. The leading division was ambuscaded near Tyree Springs, and a volley delivered at seventy-five yards' range inflicted some loss. Similar attacks were kept up all day on the 8th, but of course the efforts of so small a body against more than twenty thousand men were merely annoying. Early on the morning of the 9th Wood's and Van Cleve's divisions moved into and on either flank of Gallatin, nearly surrounding our people, who incautiously resisted the advance of the central column too long, thus necessitating brisk movement as well as sharp fighting to effect an escape. That afternoon Morgan crossed the Cumberland and encamped in a safe position between Lebanon and Murfreesboro'. Morgan's loss during the entire campaign, in killed and wounded, was not more than one hundred. He had inflicted a much greater loss on the enemy, and had captured nearly twelve hundred prisoners. He had entered Kentucky with less than 900 effectives; his command when he returned to Tennessee was nearly 2000 strong. It was admirably mounted, and well armed, and the recruits were fully the equals of the original "Morgan Men," in spirit, intelligence, and capacity to endure.

☆ General Buell was succeeded in the command of the troops of the Army of the Ohio by General W. S. Rosecrans on the 30th day of October. Under General Orders of October 24th the Department of the Cumberland was created, and the troops within it were designated the Fourteenth Army Corps.— EDITORS.

THE OPPOSING FORCES AT PERRYVILLE, KY.,

October 8th, 1862.

The composition, losses, and strength of each army as here stated give the gist of all the data obtainable in the Official Records. K stands for killed; w for wounded; m w for mortally wounded; m for captured or missing; c for captured.

THE UNION FORCES.

ARMY OF THE OHIO.— Maj.-Gen. Don Carlos Buell; Maj.-Gen. George H. Thomas, second in command.

Escort: Anderson (Pa.) Troop, Lieut. Thomas S. Maple; 4th U. S. Cav. (6 co's), Lieut.-Col. James Oakes. Escort loss: m, 1. *Unattached:* 7th Pa. Cav. (4 co's), Maj. John E. Wynkoop. Loss: w, 4; m, 3 = 7.

FIRST ARMY CORPS, Maj.-Gen. Alexander McD. McCook.

THIRD DIVISION, Brig.-Gen. Lovell H. Rousseau. Staff loss: m, 1.

Ninth Brigade, Col. Leonard A. Harris: 38th Ind., Col. Benjamin F. Scribner; 2d Ohio, Lieut.-Col. John Kell; 33d Ohio, Lieut.-Col. Oscar F. Moore (w and c), Maj. Frederick J. Lock; 94th Ohio, Col. Joseph W. Frizell; 10th Wis., Col. Alfred R. Chapin; 5th Ind. Battery, Capt. Peter Simonson. Brigade loss: k, 121; w, 419; m, 51 = 591.

Seventeenth Brigade, Col. William H. Lytle (w and c), Col. Curran Pope (m w): 42d Ind., Col. James G. Jones; 88th Ind., Col. George Humphrey; 15th Ky., Col. Curran Pope; 3d Ohio, Col. John Beatty; 10th Ohio, Lieut.-Col. Joseph W. Burke; 1st Mich. Battery, Capt. Cyrus O. Loomis. Brigade loss: k, 193; w, 606; m, 23 = 822.

Twenty-eighth Brigade, Col. John C. Starkweather: 24th Ill., Capt. August Mauff; 79th Pa., Col. Henry A. Hambright; 1st Wis., Lieut.-Col. George B. Bingham; 21st Wis., Col. Benjamin J. Sweet; 4th Ind. Battery, Capt. Asahel K. Bush; 1st Ky. Battery, Capt. David C. Stone. Brigade loss: k, 170; w, 477; m, 109 = 756. *Unattached:* 2d Ky. Cav. (6 co's), Col. Buckner Board; A, C, and H, 1st Mich., Eng'rs and Mech's, Maj. Enos Hopkins. Unattached loss: w, 18; m, 4 = 22.

TENTH DIVISION, Brig.-Gen. James S. Jackson (k). Staff loss: k, 1.

Thirty-third Brigade, Brig.-Gen. William R. Terrill (k); Col. Albert S. Hall: 80th Ill., Col. Thomas G. Allen; 123d Ill., Col. James Monroe; Detachments 7th and 32d Ky. and 3d Tenn., Col. Theophilus T. Garrard; 105th Ohio, Col. Albert S. Hall; Parsons's (improvised) Battery, Lieut. Charles C. Parsons. Brigade loss: k, 100; w, 336; m, 91 = 527. *Thirty-fourth Brigade,* Col. George Webster (k): 80th Ind., Lieut.-Col. Lewis Brooks; 50th Ohio, Col. Jonah R. Taylor, Lieut.-Col. Silas A. Strickland; 98th Ohio, Lieut.-Col. Christian L. Poorman; 121st Ohio, Col. William P. Reid; 19th Ind. Battery, Capt. Samuel J. Harris. Brigade loss: k, 87; w, 346; m, 146 = 579.

SECOND ARMY CORPS, } Maj.-Gen. Thomas L. Crittenden.

FOURTH DIVISION, Brig.-Gen. William S. Smith.

Tenth Brigade, Col. William Grose: 84th Ill., Col. Louis H. Waters; 36th Ind., Lieut.-Col. O. H. P. Carey; 23d Ky., Lieut.-Col. J. P. Jackson; 6th Ohio, Lieut.-Col. Nicholas L. Anderson; 24th Ohio, Lieut.-Col. Frederick C. Jones; H, 4th U. S. Art'y, Lieut. Samuel Canby; M, 4th U. S. Art'y, Capt. John Mendenhall. *Nineteenth Brigade,* Col. William B. Hazen: 110th Ill., Col. Thomas S. Casey; 9th Ind., Col. William H. Blake; 6th Ky., Col. Walter C. Whitaker; 27th Ky., Col. C. D. Pennebaker; 41st Ohio, Lieut.-Col. George S. Mygatt; F, 1st Ohio Art'y, Capt. Daniel T. Cockerill. *Twenty-second Brigade,* Brig.-Gen. Charles Cruft: 31st Ind., Lieut.-Col. John Osborn; 1st Ky., Lieut.-Col. David A. Enyart; 2d Ky., Col. Thomas D. Sedgwick; 20th Ky., Lieut.-Col. Charles S. Hanson; 90th Ohio, Col. Isaac N. Ross; B, 1st Ohio Art'y, Capt. William E. Standart. *Cavalry:* 2d Ky. (4 co's), Lieut.-Col. Thomas B. Cochran.

FIFTH DIVISION, Brig.-Gen. Horatio P. Van Cleve.

Eleventh Brigade, Col. Samuel Beatty: 79th Ind., Col.

Frederick Knefler; 9th Ky., Lieut.-Col. George H. Cram; 13th Ky., Lieut.-Col. J. B. Carlile; 19th Ohio, Lieut.-Col. E. W. Hollinsworth; 59th Ohio, Col. James P. Fyffe.

Fourteenth Brigade, Col. Pierce B. Hawkins: 44th Ind., Col. Hugh B. Reed; 86th Ind., Col. Orville S. Hamilton; 11th Ky., Lieut.-Col. S. P. Love; 26th Ky., Col. Cicero Maxwell; 13th Ohio, Col. Joseph G. Hawkins. *Twenty-third Brigade,* Col. Stanley Matthews: 35th Ind., Col. Bernard F. Mullen; 8th Ky., Col. Sidney M. Barnes; 21st Ky., Col. S. Woodson Price; 51st Ohio, Lieut.-Col. Richard W. McClain; 99th Ohio, Lieut.-Col. John E. Cummins. *Artillery:* 7th Ind., Capt. George R. Swallow; B, Pa., Lieut. Alanson J. Stevens; 3d Wis., Capt. Lucius H. Drury.

SIXTH DIVISION, Brig.-Gen. Thomas J. Wood.

Fifteenth Brigade, Brig.-Gen. Milo S. Hascall: 100th Ill., Col. Frederick A. Bartleson; 17th Ind., Lieut.-Col. George W. Gorman; 58th Ind., Col. George P. Buell; 3d Ky., Lieut.-Col. William T. Scott; 26th Ohio, Maj. Chris. M. Degenfield; 8th Ind. Battery, Lieut. George Estep. *Twentieth Brigade,* Col. Charles G. Harker: 51st Ind., Col. Abel D. Streight; 73d Ind., Col. Gilbert Hathaway; 13th Mich., Lieut.-Col. Frederick W. Worden; 64th Ohio, Col. John Ferguson; 65th Ohio, Lieut.-Col. William H. Young; 6th Ohio Battery, Capt. Cullen Bradley. *Twenty-first Brigade,* Col. George D. Wagner: 15th Ind., Lieut.-Col. Gustavus A. Wood; 40th Ind., Col. John W. Blake; 57th Ind., Col. Cyrus C. Hines; 24th Ky., Col. Louis B. Grigsby; 97th Ohio, Col. John Q. Lane; 10th Ind. Battery, Capt. Jerome B. Cox. Brigade loss (40th Ind.): w, 2. *Unattached:* B, E, I, and K, 1st Mich., Eng's and Mech's, Col. William P. Innes; 1st Ohio Cav. (detachment), Maj. James Laughlin.

THIRD ARMY CORPS, Maj.-Gen. Charles C. Gilbert.

FIRST DIVISION, Brig.-Gen. Albin Schoepf.

First Brigade, Col. Moses B. Walker: 82d Ind., Col. Morton C. Hunter; 12th Ky., Col. William A. Hoskins; 17th Ohio, Col. John M. Connell; 31st Ohio, Lieut.-Col. Frederick W. Lister; 38th Ohio, Lieut.-Col. William A. Choate. *Second Brigade,* Brig.-Gen. Speed S. Fry: 10th Ind., Col. William C. Kise; 74th Ind., Col. Charles W. Chapman; 4th Ky., Col. John T. Croxton; 10th Ky., Lieut.-Col. William H. Hays; 14th Ohio, Lieut.-Col. George P. Este. Brigade loss: k, 4; w, 7 = 11. *Third Brigade,* Brig.-Gen. James B. Steedman: 87th Ind., Col. Kline G. Shryock; 2d Minn., Col. James George; 9th Ohio, Lieut.-Col. Charles Joseph; 35th Ohio, Col. Ferdinand Van Derveer; 18th U. S., Maj. Frederick Townsend. Brigade loss: w, 6; m, 8 = 14. *Artillery:* 4th Mich., Capt. Josiah W. Church; C, 1st Ohio, Capt. Daniel K. Southwick; I, 4th U. S., Lieut. Frank G. Smith. Artillery loss: w, 1. *Cavalry:* 1st Ohio (detachment), Col. Minor Milliken.

NINTH DIVISION, Brig.-Gen. Robert B. Mitchell.

Thirtieth Brigade, Col. Michael Gooding: 59th Ill., Maj. Joshua C. Winters; 74th Ill., Lieut.-Col. James B. Kerr; 75th Ill., Lieut.-Col. John E. Bennett; 22d Ind., Lieut.-Col. Squire I. Keith (k); 5th Wis. Battery, Capt. Oscar F. Pinney. Brigade loss: k, 121; w, 314; m, 64 = 499. *Thirty-first Brigade,* Col. William P. Carlin: 21st Ill., Col. John W. S. Alexander; 38th Ill., Maj. Daniel H. Gilmer; 101st Ohio, Col. Leander Stem; 15th Wis., Col. Hans C. Heg; 2d Minn. Battery, Capt. William A. Hotchkiss. Brigade loss: w, 10. *Thirty-second Brigade,* Col. William W. Caldwell: 25th Ill., Lieut.-Col. James S. McClelland; 35th Ill., Lieut.-Col. William P. Chandler; 81st Ind.,

‖ Of the operations of this corps General Buell says, in his official report: "The corps of General Crittenden closed in, and Wagner's brigade, of Wood's division, became engaged and did good service on the right of Mitchell's division, but knowing nothing of the severity of the fight on the extreme left the rest of the corps did not get into action."— EDITORS.

Lieut.-Col. John Timberlake; 8th Kan. (battalion), Lieut.-Col. John A. Martin; 8th Wis. Battery, Capt. Stephen J. Carpenter. *Cavalry:* B, 36th Ill., Capt. Samuel B. Sherer.

ELEVENTH DIVISION, Brig.-Gen. Philip H. Sheridan.

Thirty-fifth Brigade, Lieut.-Col. Bernard Laiboldt: 44th Ill., Capt. Wallace W. Barrett; 73d Ill., Col. James F. Jaquess; 2d Mo., Capt. Walter Hoppe (k); 15th Mo., Maj. John Weber. Brigade loss: k, 22; w, 102; m, 1 = 125. *Thirty-sixth Brigade,* Col. Daniel McCook: 85th Ill., Col. Robert S. Moore: 86th Ill., Col. David D. Irons; 125th Ill., Col. Oscar F. Harmon; 52d Ohio, Lieut.-Col. D. D. T. Cowen. Brigade loss: k, 7; w, 63; m, 9 = 79. *Thirty-seventh Brigade,* Col. Nicholas Greusel: 36th Ill., Capt. Silas Miller; 88th Ill., Col. Francis T. Sherman; 21st Mich., Col. Ambrose A. Stevens; 24th Wis., Col. Charles H. Larrabee. Brigade loss: k, 15; w, 124; m, 4 = 143. *Artillery:* I, 2d Ill., Capt. Charles M. Barnett; G, 1st Mo., Capt. Henry Hescock. Artillery loss: w, 3.

CAVALRY: *Third Brigade,* Capt. Ebenezer Gay: 9th Ky. (detachment), Lieut.-Col. John Boyle; 2d Mich., Lieut.-Col. Archibald P. Campbell; 9th Pa., Lieut.-Col. Thomas C. James. Cavalry loss: k, 4; w, 13 = 17.

⚓ In March, 1888, General D. C. Buell wrote to the editors: "Adopting this estimate and adding Sill's Division, say 7000, which moved on the Frankfort road and did not join until after the battle *(i. e.,* on the 11th), will make the entire army 61,000 before the battle and 57,000 after. The corps

Total Union loss: killed, 845; wounded, 2851; captured or missing, 515 = 4211.

The most definite information afforded by the "Official Records" relative to the strength of the Union forces is contained in the testimony given before the Buell Commission by Major J. M. Wright, assistant adjutant-general at Buell's headquarters. On page 660, Vol. XVI., Part I., he says: "After the battle I do not think there were more than fifty thousand of the army which appeared in front of Perryville." Adding to this number the 4000 casualties sustained in the battle, would make the entire army at and about Perryville 54,000 strong. ⚓ Perhaps not over one-half of these were actually engaged. General McCook, commanding the First Corps (which bore the brunt of the fight), says that "Rousseau had present on the field 7000; Jackson, 5500; the brigade of Gooding [from Mitchell's division of Gilbert's corps] amounting to about 1500." The strength of Crittenden's (Second) and Gilbert's (Third) Corps is not anywhere officially, stated. Crittenden did not reach the field of action until the conflict was practically ended, and only parts of Wagner's and Hazen's brigades of his corps became slightly engaged.

were of about equal strength. Gilbert told me recently that he estimated his corps at about 18,000 before the battle. About one-third of the whole were raw troops. Jackson's division was composed almost entirely of raw regiments."— EDITORS.

THE CONFEDERATE FORCES.

General Braxton Bragg.

ARMY OF THE MISSISSIPPI: Maj.-Gen. Leonidas Polk. RIGHT WING, Maj.-Gen. Benjamin F. Cheatham.
CHEATHAM'S DIVISION, Brig.-Gen. Daniel S. Donelson.

First Brigade, Col. John H. Savage: 8th Tenn., Col. W. L. Moore; 15th Tenn., Col. R. C. Tyler; 16th Tenn., Lieut.-Col. D. M. Donnell; 38th Tenn., Col. John C. Carter; 51st Tenn., Col. John Chester; Tenn. Battery, Capt. W. W. Carnes. Brigade loss: k, 68; w, 272; m, 7 = 347. *Second Brigade,* Brig.-Gen. A. P. Stewart: 4th Tenn., Col. O. F. Strahl; 5th Tenn., Col. C. D. Venable; 24th Tenn., Lieut.-Col. H. L. W. Bratton; 31st Tenn., Col. E. E. Tansil; 33d Tenn., Col. W. P. Jones; Miss. Battery, Capt. T. J. Stanford. Brigade loss: k, 62; w, 340; m, 26 = 428. *Third Brigade,* Brig.-Gen. George Maney: 41st Ga., Col. Charles A. McDaniel (w), Maj. John Knight; 1st Tenn., Col. H. R. Field; 6th Tenn., Col. George C. Porter; 9th Tenn., Lieut.-Col. John W. Buford (w), Major George W. Kelsoe; 27th Tenn., Lieut.-Col. W. Frierson (w); Major A. C. Allen; Miss. Battery, Lieut. William B. Turner. Brigade loss: k, 136; w, 517; m, 34 = 687.

CAVALRY BRIGADE, Col. John A. Wharton: 1st Ky. (3 co's), ——; ↓ 4th Tenn., ——; 8th Tex., ——. Brigade loss (not separately reported).

LEFT WING, Maj.-Gen. William J. Hardee.

SECOND DIVISION, Brig.-Gen. J. Patton Anderson.

First Brigade, Brig.-Gen. John C. Brown (w), Col. William Miller: 1st Fla., Col. William Miller; 3d Fla., ——; 41st Miss., ——; Palmer's Battery, ——. Brigade loss (not separately reported). *Second Brigade,* Brig.-Gen. Daniel W. Adams: 13th La., Col. R. L. Gibson; 16th La., Col. D. C. Gober; 20th La., Col. Aug. Reichard, Lieut.-Col. Leon von Zinken; 25th La., Col. S. W. Fisk; 14th Battalion La. Sharp-shooters, Major J. E. Austin; 5th Co. Washington (La.) Art'y, Capt. C. H. Slocomb. Brigade loss: k, 6; w, 78; m, 68 = 152. *Third Brigade,* Col. Samuel Powell: 45th Ala., ——; 1st Ark., ——; 24th Miss., Col. William F. Dowd: 29th

↓ The dash indicates that the name of the commanding officer has not been found in the "Official Records."— EDITORS.

⚓ In March, 1888, General Buell wrote to the editors: "This probably did not include the cavalry. It is scarcely credible that the three divisions of infantry contained only 13,500.

Tenn., ——; Mo. Battery, Capt. Overton W. Barret. Brigade loss (not separately reported). *Fourth Brigade,* Col. Thomas M. Jones: 27th Miss., ——; 30th Miss., ——; 37th Miss., ——; Ala. Battery (Lumsden's). Brigade loss (not separately reported).

THIRD DIVISION, Maj.-Gen. Simon B. Buckner.

First Brigade, Brig.-Gen. St. John R. Liddell: 2d Ark., ——; 5th Ark., Col. L. Featherston; 6th Ark., ——; 7th Ark., Col. D. A. Gillespie; 8th Ark., Col. John H. Kelly; Miss. Battery (Swett's). Brigade loss: k, w, and m, 71. *Second Brigade,* Brig.-Gen. P. R. Cleburne (w): 13th Ark., ——; 15th Ark., ——; 2d Tenn., ——; Ark. Battery (Calvert's). Brigade loss (not separately reported). *Third Brigade,* Brig.-Gen. Bushrod R. Johnson: 5th Confederate, Col. J. A. Smith; 17th Tenn., Col. A. S. Marks; 23d Tenn., Lieut.-Col. R. H. Keeble; 25th Tenn., Col. John M. Hughs; 37th Tenn., Col. Moses White; 44th Tenn., Col. John S. Fulton; Miss. Battery (Jefferson Art'y), Capt. Put. Darden. Brigade loss: k, 30; w, 165; m, 9 = 204. *Fourth Brigade,* Brig.-Gen. S. A. M. Wood (w): 16th Ala., ——; 33d Ala., ——; 3d Confederate, ——; 45th Miss., ——; 15th Battalion Miss. Sharp-shooters, ——; Ala. Battery, Capt. Henry C. Semple. Brigade loss (not separately reported).

CAVALRY BRIGADE, Col. Joseph Wheeler: 1st Ala., Col. William W. Allen; 3d Ala., Col. James Hagan; 6th Confederate, Lieut.-Col. James A. Pell; 2d Ga. (battalion), Maj. C. A. Whaley; 3d Ga., Col. Martin J. Crawford; 1st Ky. (6 co's), Maj. J. W. Caldwell. Brigade loss (not separately reported).

Total Confederate loss: killed, 510; wounded, 2635; missing, 251 = 3396.

General Bragg reports ("Official Records," Vol. XVI., Pt. I., p. 1092) that "our forces . . . consisted of three divisions of infantry (about 14,500) and two small brigades of cavalry (about 1500)." General Polk reports (p. 1110): "The whole of our force, including all arms, did not exceed 15,000." ⚓

"However, the important question is as to the force that Bragg had in the field in Kentucky, for that was the force that was to be expected in a great battle. That question is not fully determined by official reports, but a careful study of the published records seems to place it at not less than 68,000 men."— EDITORS.

ON THE SKIRMISH LINE.

EAST TENNESSEE AND THE CAMPAIGN OF PERRYVILLE.

BY DON CARLOS BUELL, MAJOR-GENERAL, U. S. V.

THE invasion of Kentucky in the summer of 1862 by the Confederate forces under General Bragg was one of the most prominent incidents of the war; and both the officer who conducted it and the one who repelled it were the objects of much popular displeasure on their respective sides. On the one side there was severe condemnation of the withdrawal, and on the other unmeasured dissatisfaction that the invaders had not been captured in a body. Of course, there were in both cases numerous specifications to the general matter of complaint. With reference to the result, it must follow that the critics were wrong on one side or the other. It may even be that in the main, whatever may have been the incidental blunders, they were wrong on both sides: that is, that an invasion for a permanent occupation which lacked the support of the population, and was opposed by an army able and ready to contest the object, was wisely abandoned without further resistance; and that the contestant, in the presence of a skillful and not inferior adversary, wisely took his measures to make the result reasonably certain. The rashness of revolutionary ends might reject the former, but no rule of loyalty to the public welfare would condemn the latter.

In giving here a brief review of the subject—which properly includes the project for my advance into east Tennessee in the early summer—I shall undertake no more than a simple outline of the essential facts, and an exposition of the circumstances which controlled events.

The period immediately following the evacuation of Corinth, and lasting through the summer, found the Western armies in a less satisfactory state than at the first glance would be supposed. The early delusion of a ninety-days' campaign had not so completely passed away as not to give rise to disappointment in the ranks and among the people, at finding no signs in the

South of reconciliation or submission, after the signal successes which the Union cause had achieved; and it could hardly fail to happen that the disappointment would for a while act injuriously upon the temper and efficiency of unseasoned troops. It resulted, in fact, that the desire to get back to friends, or to find relief for a time from the hardships and restraints of service, caused large numbers to get away from the front on every possible pretext —on leave granted with or without proper authority, upon authority exercised too loosely, and even without any authority; and when once away their return was very difficult. Appeals were of little avail, and the recourse of sending officers to recall the absentees was attended with poor results.

But absence from the colors was not the worst form of the evil. Duty of every sort was performed with a sluggishness which greatly retarded every sort of work, of which there was much that had to be done, and the service of escorts and road guards was executed in very many cases with a fatal laxity. An idea grew up that a soldier on parole was virtually released from all restraint; and there was good reason to believe that large numbers of stragglers were quite willing to find themselves for a moment in the hands of the enemy, and that even the vigilance and resoluteness of escorts and guards were materially affected by the idea that captivity meant liberty and relaxation. ↓

Even in the routine of camp life, the weariness and impatience manifested themselves in some manner, actively or passively, in a protest against the interior demands and the exterior restraints of discipline. The thousands of letters which poured from the camps into the soldiers' homes and the public press were mediums for these manifestations, which put upon the general in

↓ To this rule there were of course honorable exceptions. The following orders concerning absentees and paroles were published in view of these evils, which were seriously impairing the strength and efficiency of the army:

"HEADQUARTERS, ARMY OF THE OHIO, "IN CAMP, NEAR FLORENCE, ALA., June 24th, 1862.

"GENERAL ORDERS, No. 26: There are 14,000 officers and soldiers absent from their duty with the various divisions of this army, i. e., the five divisions south of the Tennessee River. Some of them have gone off without any authority; others with the permission of officers not authorized to grant it. In general, sickness is given as the cause of absence, but in very many cases that cause has notoriously ceased to exist, and men remain away, drawing the same pay as their comrades who are faithfully performing their duty. To correct this abuse it is ordered ——

. . . .

"(4th.) All absent officers and soldiers who do not join their companies and regiments or are not satisfactorily accounted for as above by the 10th of July next, will be reported on their muster-roll as deserters, dating from the time that they may have been absent without authority. By act of Congress every deserter forfeits all claim on the Government for pay and allowances, besides being liable to arrest and trial by court-martial. Any person who apprehends and returns a deserter to the commanding officer of a military post is entitled to a reward of $5. By command of MAJOR-GENERAL BUELL. JAMES B. FRY, Assistant Adjutant-General, Chief-of-Staff."

"HEADQUARTERS, ARMY OF THE OHIO, "IN CAMP, HUNTSVILLE, ALA., August 8th, 1862.

"GENERAL ORDERS, No. 41: The system of paroles practiced in this army has run into an intolerable abuse. Hereafter no officer or soldier belonging to the forces in this district will give his parole not to take up arms, for the purpose of leaving the enemy's lines without the sanction of the general commanding this army, except when, by reason of wounds or disease, he could not be removed without endangering his life.

"Any parole given in violation of this order will not be recognized, and the person giving it will be required to perform military duty and take the risks prescribed by the laws of war.

"Any officer or soldier of this command, being in the hands of the enemy and desiring to be released on parole for the purpose of leaving the enemy's lines, will make application to the general commanding this army, inclosing in duplicate the parole which he proposes to give, and await its approval.

"The sanction of the officer commanding the forces by which he is held, being necessary to effect the arrangement, should be forwarded with the application. No such application will be approved when the capture has resulted from neglect or misbehavior on the part of the prisoner or of the command to which he belonged.

"The evidence of a lawful parole will be the parole itself, bearing the approval of the commanding general.

"The same rule will be observed by this army in paroling prisoners taken from the enemy. If they cannot be held until the sanction of such officer as the general commanding the enemy's forces may designate for that purpose is obtained, they will be released. By command of MAJOR-GENERAL BUELL. JAMES B. FRY, Colonel and Chief-of-Staff."

command the burthen of every complaint, and the responsibility of every miscarriage. If a command started upon a march, every soldier would be anxious to know how his haversack was to be replenished, but it never occurred to him that there was a question as to how the depots were to be supplied.

The Government, also, seemed to drop suddenly into a similar state of disappointment, discontent, and inaction. It had not apparently been imagined that the depletion which would unavoidably go on rapidly in the ranks must be replaced, and when at length the work of repair was taken up it was done by creating new regiments instead of replenishing the old ones. A vast waste of time, and material, and efficiency was caused by this plan of throwing large numbers of raw troops suddenly into service in distinct bodies. Moreover, party politics, which at first, under a spontaneous burst of patriotism, had put aside all party distinctions, began now to resume its old organization. That, of course, meant old ambitions and opposing policies with reference to means, however united men might be in motive upon the one great object of preserving the Union. No doubt all of these causes worked to the same end. At all events it resulted that during the summer of 1862, after the withdrawal of the Confederates from Corinth, the armies were weaker numerically than they

BREVET MAJOR-GENERAL JAMES B. FRY, CHIEF-OF-STAFF TO GENERAL BUELL; AFTERWARD PROVOST-MAR-SHAL-GENERAL. FROM A PHOTOGRAPH.

had been or ever were afterward, and that the tone of the troops, though always loyal, was in some respects seriously defective.

It was exactly the reverse on the other side. To the South the result of the battle of Shiloh was the disappointment of a great hope almost consummated, rather than a discouragement. The first depressing effect of the retreat from Corinth was more than compensated for by the splendid successes which were considered to have been gained in Virginia. Their Government acted vigorously. Their armies were speedily recruited, and never again entered the field in as great relative strength and as high spirit as in that summer. The army at Tupelo, no longer threatened, and under a new commander of established reputation for nerve and ability, paused for a moment to discover an opening for attack or a call for defense, and the disposition of the now unoccupied force under General Halleck soon pointed the way.

As soon as the expulsion of the Confederates from the line of the Memphis and Charleston Railroad was consummated by the definitive retreat of the Corinth army, the large Federal force that had been called together for the operations on that line was redistributed for ulterior objects. About 65,000 men were retained under General Halleck's immediate command to occupy the line from the Tennessee River to Memphis; the Army of the Ohio was restored to its original departmental territory, to advance into east Tennessee, perhaps even to penetrate Georgia; and the remainder of the force was sent to strengthen General Curtis in Arkansas. Thus the Army of the Ohio was the only army in the West that was assigned to an aggressive campaign.

The occupation of east Tennessee had from the first been a favorite measure with the President, apparently more from political than from military considerations. It had at one time been enjoined upon my predecessors in specific orders, and was urged upon my attention by General McClellan in the instructions with which I came to Kentucky. Some abortive steps had been taken in that direction by General Sherman before my arrival, but various causes, which need not here be enumerated, compelled its postponement then and afterward,—especially the inexpediency of the attempt upon military grounds under the circumstances, and finally the drift of events, which carried the bulk of the army to Shiloh and Corinth. A general view of the theater of war, and a consideration of the geography of east Tennessee, will show the importance of the lodgment that was now to be undertaken, and indicate the opposition it was sure to encounter, unless seconded by operations of a decisive character in other quarters.

East Tennessee is an elevated valley of great salubrity and considerable agricultural capacity, practically inclosed, though with some natural openings, by a mountainous and rugged belt of country in which rise the sources of the Tennessee River. The surplus of food products during the war was not large, but was not without value to the South at first, when so much of the country was absorbed in the growth of cotton. The railroad passing east and west through the valley afforded the most direct and convenient communication between Richmond and the Mississippi, while abreast of it, from Chattanooga, a branching railroad penetrated the Atlantic and Gulf States to the coast, affording a valuable system of internal communication for supply or defense, and an equally effective line for external invasion. On the northern side, the valley had a strong defensive line in the difficult, though not impracticable mountains, which, farther to the north, assume an expanse and ruggedness that present what might be considered practically a secure barrier between Kentucky and Virginia. East Tennessee might therefore be regarded as a doorway to the rear of Richmond, and a commanding rendezvous which looked down with a menacing adaptability upon the Gulf and Atlantic States. In the latter light, more than as a means of defense, its preservation was of vital moment to the Confederacy. The occupation of it by the Federal force would be like the last stage in a regular siege, when the glacis is crowned and batteries are established for breaching the walls and delivering the final assault. But the fact that it was the home of all that was loyal to the Union in the States in rebellion, seemed to blind the Government to the considerations which insured that it would be defended with all the energy of self-preservation. The powerful force and desperate battles that were finally found necessary to secure the object, afforded a vindication, to which nothing need be added, against the fatuity which demanded that the Army of the Ohio, without supplies and with severed communications, should accomplish it in the summer of 1862 with a movable force of 31,000 men against more than 60,000 that barred the way. [See maps, pp. 3 and 6.]

I was following the movements of the enemy retreating from Corinth, when, on the 9th of June, I received notice from General Halleck that my army was to resume its separate action, and advance into east Tennessee. My divisions started in the new direction the next day, and on the 11th I received my instructions verbally from General Halleck. I was to move as diligently as possible to the object specified, but I was to repair the Memphis and Charleston Railroad as I proceeded, guard it, and draw my supplies from it. The inexpediency of these conditions, as I had pointed out, was realized before the repairs were completed. The road, running along the enemy's front, was peculiarly exposed to attack — was in fact attacked while we were working on it and afterward; it was not supplied with rolling stock, and we derived no benefit from it, though the repairs detained us until the last of June. Foreseeing these embarrassments, I had given orders for the repair of the roads south from Nashville, and for the accumulation of supplies at that point. I desired also the option of making the advance through McMinnville and Kingston, which I imagined might be found to present decided advantages. It would avoid the heavy work on the railroads to the Tennessee River, the bridging of the river, and the extremely difficult ground that must at first be overcome by wagon transportation after crossing. It would establish a junction promptly with the force under G. W. Morgan operating against Cumberland Gap, and give actual possession of east Tennessee, which the mere occupation of Chattanooga would not. Halleck at first assented to my proposition, but a day or two afterward withdrew his consent, and enjoined that the movement should be made directly upon Chattanooga.

We crossed the Tennessee by extemporized ferries — three divisions at Florence, arriving at Athens on the Nashville and Decatur Railroad on the 28th of June, and one division between the 1st and 6th of July, by a very inefficient ferry prepared by General Mitchel at Decatur.

General Thomas with his division was still detained on the Corinth road under General Halleck's orders, and did not join at Huntsville until the last of July; so that the available effective force for an advance when I reached Huntsville on the 29th of June was between 24,000 and 25,000 men. The 16,000 already in middle Tennessee and north Alabama would still be required to guard Nashville and keep open the communications. But there was much to be done before an advance could be possible. We found ourselves already at the very limit of our means of transportation. Nothing had been accomplished in the way of repairing the railroads, and it required every wagon to haul supplies enough for the daily consumption. Much of the time thereafter the troops were on half rations. We could gather some forage from the country, but not enough for the animals.

Before my arrival General Mitchel had urgently reported demonstrations of the enemy from the direction of Chattanooga. To the Secretary of War he said, June 21st: "I am with difficulty maintaining my position in front of Chattanooga. I will endeavor to hold my position until reënforcements arrive." His nearest position was in fact at Battle Creek, twenty miles below Chattanooga, with the Tennessee River and a mountain range intervening. To me he telegraphed, June 21st: "I think everything depends on celerity of movement. If we should be driven from Stevenson (the junction of the Nashville and Chattanooga and the Memphis and Charleston railroads), or even from the position we now occupy (at Battle Creek, nine miles above Bridgeport), I should deem it a great misfortune." Partly therefore to oppose this supposed danger, and especially to place a strong working force on the Nashville and Chattanooga Railroad, McCook's and Crittenden's divisions were sent to Stevenson and Battle Creek. Nelson's and Wood's divisions were for the present kept on the Nashville and Decatur road; and the repairs by means of the troops and by experienced hired hands were urged energetically. At the same time mills were put to work to get out lumber, and the building of boats for a bridge was commenced. We had no pontoon train, and the Tennessee was a formidable river, requiring a bridge 1400 yards long.

The depredations of the small bands that had harassed Mitchel before my arrival were continued afterward, and soon demonstrated the necessity of defensive works for bridges and other vulnerable points. An inclosed earthwork of considerable strength, large enough for a regiment, was constructed at Stevenson for the protection of the depot to be established there for the advance; and a specific plan and instructions for small block-houses, or, more properly speaking, picket-houses, at the less important points were prescribed. An officer was specially assigned to the direction of these works, and the supervision of the guards. Iron-clad dummy cars were provided for such purposes and for express service. Much of the road-repairing and other engineering work was done and supervised by a splendid regiment of mechanics and engineers from Michigan, under Colonel William P. Innes.

These, from among the thousand other details, are mentioned, because they were infinitely important to our existence, and absolutely necessary for the first step in advance. Clearly the means of transportation, which were barely sufficient to provide us with a precarious subsistence where we were, would be insufficient to carry us at least thirty miles farther away, across a broad river and a mountainous country, into the presence of the enemy. The records show that laborious and unceasing efforts were used to bring about the necessary conditions for a forward movement, and that every officer employed in command or in staff positions was stimulated to the utmost by advice and instructions for the object before us. We had been engaged in this earnest manner just nine days from the time of my arrival at Huntsville [June 29th], when I received a dispatch from Halleck, saying that my progress was not satisfactory to the President. I was so astonished at the message that I made no reply until three days afterward, when I was called on for explanations.↓

The road from Nashville to Stevenson was completed on the 12th of July, and a train was started the next morning with supplies for the depot at Stevenson. My attention had been attracted to the importance of McMinnville as an outpost. It was at the foot of the mountain on the direct wagon road between Nashville and Chattanooga, and was the terminus of a branch railroad, twenty miles east of the Nashville and Chattanooga Railroad. I had just organized a new brigade at Murfreesboro' to occupy McMinnville. On the morning of the 13th Forrest, with a large body of cavalry, surprised the brigade, killed and wounded some and captured the rest, damaged the railroad seriously, and produced alarm in Nashville, where the force was not large. ♭

↓ "Official Records," Vol. XVI., Part II., pp. 104, 122.

♭ The following orders were published with reference to this and similar affairs. It is proper to add that a Court of Inquiry, instituted by General Rosecrans, at the request of General T. T. Crittenden, the commander of the brigade, after his exchange, acquitted the commander of blame, on the ground that he had only arrived the day before the attack, and had shown commendable energy in his new position. Colonel Duffield had also just arrived. He appeared to have behaved well in the attack, and was severely wounded:

"HEADQUARTERS, ARMY OF THE OHIO,
"IN CAMP, HUNTSVILLE, ALA., July 21st, 1862.

"GENERAL ORDERS, NO. 32: On the 13th instant the force at Murfreesborough, under command of Brigadier-General T. T. Crittenden, late colonel of the 6th Indiana Regiment, and consisting of 6 companies of the 9th Michigan, 9 companies of the 3d Minnesota, 2 sections of Hewett's (Kentucky) battery, 4 companies of the 4th Kentucky Cavalry, and three companies of the 7th Pennsylvania Cavalry, was captured at that place by a force of the enemy's cavalry variously estimated at from 1800 to 3500. It appears from the best information that can be obtained, that Brigadier-General Crittenden and Colonel Duffield of the 9th Michigan, with the 6 companies of that regiment and all of the cavalry, were surprised and captured early in the morning in the houses and streets of the town, or in their camp near by, with but slight resistance and without any timely warning of the presence of the enemy. The rest of the force, consisting of the 3d Minnesota and the artillery under Col. Lester, left its camp and took another position, which it maintained with but few casualties against the feeble attacks of the enemy until about 3 o'clock, when it was surrendered and marched into captivity.

"Take it in all its features, few more disgraceful examples of neglect of duty and lack of good conduct can be found in the history of wars. It fully merits the extreme penalty which the law provides for such misconduct. The force was more than sufficient to repel the attack effectually. The mortification which the army will feel at the result is poorly compensated by the exertion made by some — perhaps many — of the officers to retrieve the disgrace of the surprise. The action fit to be adopted with reference to those who are blamable, especially the officers highest in command, cannot be determined without further investigation.

"In contrast to this shameful affair, the general commanding takes pleasure in making honorable mention of the conduct of a detachment of twenty-two men of Companies I and H, 10th Wisconsin Regiment, under the command of Sergeants W. Nelson and A. H. Makinson.

The detachment was on duty guarding a bridge east of Huntsville, when it was attacked on April 28th by a force of some 200 or 300 cavalry, which it fought for two hours and repulsed in the most signal manner. Such is the conduct that duty and honor demand of every soldier; and this example is worthy of imitation by higher officers and larger commands. By command of MAJOR-GENERAL BUELL. JAMES B. FRY, Col. and Chief-of-Staff."

"HEADQUARTERS, ARMY OF THE OHIO,
"IN CAMP, HUNTSVILLE, ALA., August 1st, 1862.

"GENERAL ORDERS, No. 37: The major-general commanding has to announce other instances of disgraceful neglect and contrast them with another of gallantry:

"The guard at Courtland Bridge, consisting of companies A and H, 10th Kentucky, under the command of Captain Davidson, and a part of Captain Eggleston's company, 1st Ohio Cavalry, was completely surprised and captured with but trifling loss on the morning of the 25th ultimo, by a force of irregular cavalry. On the same day the companies of Captains Boyl and Goben, 10th Indiana, which were ordered to protect two bridges on the same road, respectively six and twelve miles east of Courtland, deemed it wiser to bring in an empty train which came up than to defend their posts, threatened with an attack from the same irregular cavalry; and so put themselves on the train and arrived safely at Decatur, a few miles distant, without the loss or injury of a man. On the same day, and on the same road, eight miles from Decatur, a guard, consisting of twenty-four men, of Company E, 31st Ohio, under the command of Lieutenant Harmon, were suddenly attacked by a greatly superior force of the same cavalry. They defended themselves gallantly, however, and repulsed the enemy, killing several of the number. Lieut. Harmon and eleven of his men were wounded, himself in two places, and two of his men were killed.

"The general submits these examples to the reflection of the troops. He reminds them that neglect and bad conduct on the part of guards brings dishonor upon them and may even jeopardize the safety of an army. If these appeals to their personal and professional pride should fail of their object, he warns them that the extreme penalty of the law must intervene to punish the guilty and save the army from the jeopardy in which they place it. The duty of guarding the communications of the army is among the most important with which an officer and his troops can be intrusted. Vigilance, determination, and the preparation of suitable defenses in the way of intrenchments or stockades will prevent such attacks, or enable a small force to repel a greatly superior one. Had the order for bridge-guards to fortify their posts been promptly executed and proper vigilance been observed, the attacks referred to, if made at all, would have had very different results. This order and General Orders, No. 32, will be read at the head of every company and detachment. By command of MAJOR-GENERAL BUELL. JAMES B. FRY, Colonel and Chief-of-Staff."

This was the first appearance of any large body of the enemy in our rear south of the Cumberland, though Morgan was at the same time engaged in a formidable raid in Kentucky. Nelson was immediately ordered to occupy Murfreesboro' and McMinnville with his division, himself and one brigade going by railroad. He had just reached Murfreesboro' with a portion of his troops when Forrest, on the 18th, appeared again on the railroad between him and Nashville, captured guards, and destroyed two more bridges. Work was immediately commenced to repair the damage. It was completed on the 28th of July, and the shipment of supplies for the depot at Stevenson was resumed.

As soon as my designs upon east Tennessee were known, the Confederate authorities took prompt measures to counteract them. The sudden appearance of large bodies of cavalry under Morgan and Forrest on my communications in Tennessee and Kentucky early in July, and the increased activity of small parties, were a part of these measures. It was at first in contemplation to move the Tupelo army upon my rear in middle Tennessee, but the wiser plan was adopted of concentrating in my front. One division of that army, and reënforcements from other quarters, reached Chattanooga in June. General Bragg arrived on the 30th of July, and by that time the transfer of his force from Tupelo was about completed. The nucleus of a force under Van Dorn and Price was left in Mississippi to neutralize the large Federal force on the Memphis and Charleston road, an object which was accomplished at first by inaction alone, and at last by bold though unsuccessful attacks with inferior numbers.

The foreshadowing of an aggressive campaign from east Tennessee soon began to be seen. By report, and actually, as the record now shows, the objective was at first middle Tennessee and Nashville. Rumor, as usual, placed the force that was ready for the work at very large numbers—80,000 or 100,000 men. I realized that the enemy in front of us was assuming formidable proportions, but I did not doubt that his strength was over-estimated, nor that, if necessary, my own force would be increased, and therefore my efforts for the accumulation of supplies for an advance were not relaxed.

On the 7th of August I informed General Halleck of the condition which the campaign was assuming, and told him that my force should be increased. I estimated the force opposed to me at sixty thousand men. The records now show that it was greater. He answered on the 8th that General Grant would turn over two divisions to my command " if I absolutely required them," but cautioned me not to ask for them if I could avoid it with safety. By the 12th the accumulating evidence showed that the call could not be dispensed with, and I requested General Grant to forward the divisions without delay. One of them joined on the 1st of September; the other did not arrive until the 12th, after the movement northward to follow Bragg had commenced. The strength of the two divisions was about 5000 men each.

Our communications south of the Cumberland had been made secure by the distribution of the troops, but to the north the depredations were prosecuted with increased vigor. Our cavalry was totally insufficient to cope with these incursions, which it must be said, also, were seldom resisted by the infantry guards with vigilance and resolution. On the 10th of August, Morgan again appeared on the railroad north of Nashville, captured the guard of about 150 men at Gallatin, effectually disabled the tunnel north of that place, and destroyed several bridges toward Nashville. Our communication with Louisville, on which we were dependent for supplies, was thus, for the present, effectually severed. Work was immediately commenced to repair the damage, but the constantly recurring presence of the enemy's cavalry interfered so effectually as to require a large increase of force from the front or the rear for the defense. I had already strengthened the guards at Bowling Green and Munfordville. To continue to draw from the front was not yet to be thought of. On the 16th, therefore, I gave General Nelson a couple of field-batteries and some experienced cavalry and infantry officers, and sent him to Kentucky to organize such troops as could be got together there to reëstablish our communications and operate against Morgan's incursions.

On the 18th a guard of a regiment belonging to Grant's command was captured without a show of resistance at Clarksville, ☆ where a considerable quantity of supplies had been deposited for transshipment in consequence of the suspension of navigation by low water in the Cumberland. Upon hearing of Morgan's appearance again on the Cumberland north of Nashville, General R. W. Johnson, a spirited cavalry officer, under whose command I had assembled all the cavalry that was available, moved promptly in pursuit, and with his inferior force attacked Morgan vigorously near Hartsville. Johnson was defeated with a loss of 80 killed and wounded and 75 prisoners, himself among the latter. The rest escaped and made their way as stragglers or in small bodies to Nashville.

These details, harassing and disappointing to the actors at the time, are now no less wearisome and uninteresting to the careless reader; but the consideration of them is essential to a correct appreciation of the campaign. It is a story familiar to history of the crippling of an invading army by a successful war upon its too long and inadequately protected communications, with an enemy in its front. The line in this case was a single railroad, 350 miles long, through a population either hostile to the invader, or at least in a considerable degree friendly to his opponent. Under the circumstances that were to ensue, it is not perhaps to be accounted a misfortune that the contemplated advance was checked at the start. A Union army of 31,000 men at Chattanooga in July, 1862, without supplies, with its communications broken for 400 miles, and the Government on the Potomac appealing for 25,000 men which could not be spared from Corinth, might well have been in a worse condition than the stronger army in November, 1863, which was reduced to horse and mule meat for its ration, with its communications complete to within 30 miles, and with an unoccupied army from Vicksburg and considerable reënforcements from the Potomac hastening to its succor.

☆ For an explanation of the surrender see Vol. XVI., Part I., pp. 862-869, "Official Records." Colonel Rodney Mason, 71st Ohio regiment, the commander, had less than 200 effective men. Soon after the surrender the colonel and all the line-officers present were cashiered by order of the President, but this action was subsequently revoked, and they were honorably discharged.— D. C. B.

The reports of the superior force assembled in east Tennessee were confirmed as the time passed, and there could be no doubt that our position in middle Tennessee was about to be assailed. Already there were rumors of crossing at Chattanooga, Harrison's Landing, and Kingston. These starting-points indicated no certain plan of attack. The enemy might descend the Sequatchie and Cumberland valleys and enter at north Alabama, in which case he would have a railroad for his supplies; or he might cross the mountains by direct roads toward middle Tennessee. In either case, Stevenson, on the south side of a declining spur of the Cumberland Mountains reaching to Huntsville, was unsuitable for our depot, and Decherd, on the north side, was adopted instead.

On the 19th of August I received information from General McCook, who was at Battle Creek with his own and Crittenden's divisions, that the enemy was crossing in force at Chattanooga. My plans were already matured and McCook had his orders for such a case, only waiting the signal to act, which was given on the 20th. He was to march with his division to the point at which the Anderson or Thurman road between Chattanooga and McMinnville crossed the Sequatchie valley, watching and opposing the enemy on that road, and gradually fall back toward McMinnville until he joined the remainder of the army. Crittenden was to follow him, and act similarly and in conjunction with him on the Higginbottom road, which crossed the valley a little lower down, and united with the Thurman road further north. They had previously been provided with rockets and a signal code for communicating with each other and with the rest of the army. The same day I went to Battle Creek and then to Decherd to superintend the further concentration, for which general instructions had already been given. Altamont, in advance of McMinnville, was designated as the point of junction, though that could have been modified, if desirable, after an examination of the locality. General McCook proceeded up the valley some distance until he received information on which he relied, that the enemy had already entered the valley in force, or would enter it before he could be intercepted. He therefore returned to Crittenden at the Higginbottom road, which he deemed to be impracticable for his artillery and train, and both divisions returned to Battle Creek, where, after hearing from them, I sent them further orders. The information was positive that the enemy was advancing on the Thurman road, where in fact his cavalry was encountered; and under the orders for the concentration Thomas went to Altamont from McMinnville with one division, but returned to McMinnville. McCook arrived there a little later and remained until the final concentration at Murfreesboro' under the orders of the 30th. A brigade under Colonel W. H. Lytle, of Rousseau's division, was still retained at Huntsville, and two regiments under Colonel L. A. Harris were at Battle Creek. The failure of McCook's movement up the Sequatchie was unfortunate. It gave a false impression of the enemy's progress, and of the route he was to pursue. But for the erroneous information under which it was abandoned, it ought to have led to important results. There would have been no advantage, however, in retiring on the Higginbottom road without meeting the enemy.

We were now reduced to ten days' provisions. Our railroad communication north of Nashville had been broken for twenty days, and no effort was being made at Louisville to reopen it. My orders to General Nelson had been of no avail. In fact, on his arrival there he found Kentucky organized into a separate department not under my command; and his report of my instructions and his representations of the necessity of opening the road to Nashville were answered with orders from Washington to first open communication with Cumberland Gap, where General G. W. Morgan was not in danger, and had abundant supplies for the present. The result of those orders, unnecessary for the relief of Morgan, and insufficient for stopping Kirby Smith, was the defeat of Nelson at Richmond on the 30th. Ten days had elapsed since the enemy's advance was positively reported, and there was no more evidence of his approach than at first. He was, of course, to be expected any day, but he might not come in two weeks.

Under the circumstances it was plainly necessary to concentrate nearer Nashville, where we could get to work on the railroad, and at the same time be ready for the enemy when he should come. Orders were accordingly given on the 30th of August for concentrating at Murfreesboro' on the 5th of September. Thomas, at McMinnville, was to march on the 2d, and other commands according to their position. To the last Thomas had no definite information of the approach of the enemy. It turned out that Bragg crossed at Chattanooga on the 28th of August, entered Sparta on the 3d of September, and made his way to Glasgow, where he arrived on the 14th, having crossed the Cumberland at Carthage and Gainsboro'. Something of these movements, though not of the entire force, was learned on the 6th, and that Bowling Green was threatened. Two divisions were, therefore, moved across the river at Nashville on the 7th,— one to go to the protection of Bowling Green, where there was a small garrison with some stores, and the other to Gallatin, to gain information of the movements of the enemy in the valley.

At the same time preparation was made to act with the remaining force as circumstances might require. Two and a half divisions, including Paine's division from Grant, which had not yet arrived, and a large number of convalescents, were designated to hold Nashville, under the command of General Thomas. It was ascertained on the 10th that the bulk of Bragg's army had marched north from the Cumberland, and my movable divisions were accordingly put in motion to follow. They were concentrated at Bowling Green on the evening of the 15th. I there learned that the garrison at Munfordville had been attacked, but the result was not certainly known. Bragg was reported at Glasgow, and on the 16th I marched to give battle to him at that place; but during the day it was ascertained that he had marched the day before for Munfordville, the garrison of which, it was also ascertained, had repelled the first attack, and my divisions were directed upon that point. The next day, at Prewett's Knob, thirteen miles from Munfordville, I learned that the garrison had that morning surrendered to Bragg's entire army, and that night Colonel Wilder reported to me with his command as prisoners of war.

The enemy was now concentrated in front of us, and had taken up a position of unusual strength upon and behind a rather low crest on the south side of Green River. My information of the aggregate force assembled in east Tennessee was sufficiently accurate, but at first there was no means of knowing what portion of it was with Bragg, and what portion had followed Kirby Smith. The proximity of the last three days had given a better knowledge of Bragg's strength. Colonel Wilder, who was competent, and had had some opportunity for observation, estimated it at from 35,000 to 40,000 men, and nobody estimated it at any less. I supposed it to be from 30,000 to 40,000. I

BRIGADIER-GENERAL JAMES S. JACKSON, KILLED AT PERRYVILLE. FROM A PHOTOGRAPH.

had with me 35,000 effective men, but on being satisfied at Bowling Green that no considerable force remained to threaten Nashville, I called up Thomas's division, and now determined, on its arrival, to attack Bragg's position if he should remain. Thomas arrived on the 20th. There was some skirmishing between the lines that evening, but the enemy withdrew during the night. His rear-guard was driven out of Munfordville the next day, and was pressed by our advanced guard until he turned off the main road toward Bardstown.☆

There was no reason to hesitate at this point as to the course which I should pursue. I did not know where Kirby Smith was, but the junction between himself and Bragg was to be considered as practically established. United for battle they would outnumber me very greatly. Louisville also, in the presence of this combined force, might be in danger. Besides, our provisions were nearly exhausted ; some of the troops were without rations after arriving at West Point, twenty-five miles from Louisville. I therefore pushed forward to Louisville, the leading division arriving there on the 25th, and the last on the 29th. The cavalry was kept as an outpost at Elizabethtown to guard the flank of the passing columns and watch any possible movements of the enemy toward Bowling Green. The large empty wagon train which the exhaustion of our supplies at Nashville had rendered useless and insupportable, had been pushed through from Bowling Green by the way of Brownsville, Litchfield, and West Point, under a cavalry escort.

The army was now to encounter grave danger from the influence of Oliver P. Morton, Governor of Indiana. He had from the beginning tried to retain a *quasi* authority over Indiana troops after they had been mustered into the

☆ In his official report General Bragg states that he "offered battle" at Munfordville. No doubt he was willing to fight on his own terms at more than one point. But the general who offers battle is he who stays to give or receive it.—D. C. B.

service of the United States and had joined my army. His interference was injurious to discipline; but he persisted in order to preserve his influence with the troops, the people, and the Government. The seeds of mischief, always present in his extra-official conduct toward the Indiana troops, were now being sown with a vigorous but crafty hand, in the counsels at Washington and among the executives of other States, to impair my authority and effect my removal from command. General Nelson, an officer of remarkable merit, was in command of the center corps of my army. He was assaulted and killed by General Davis, accompanied by Governor Morton, the very day before the army was to march against the invaders. Nelson, though often rough in command, was always solicitous about the well-being of his troops, and was held in high esteem for his conspicuous services, gallantry in battle, and great energy; and his death caused much indignation among the troops that knew him best. Davis, an Indianian, was unknown in my army except in his own division, which had just joined while he was absent; but Morton's relation to the affair brought to bear in Davis's behalf a State feeling inspired by Morton and strengthened by his habitual intervention in favor of Indiana troops against the rigidity of my control. The restraining influence of discipline was all that prevented an outbreak between the friends of Nelson and Davis, which might have added the most serious consequences to the criminal occurrence.

Nothing but the law of violence could, under any circumstances, justify the manner of the killing for the alleged provocation, and no mere merit of ordinary soldiership could ever atone for the sacrilege against discipline under the circumstances which existed. The dignity of a State was abused by the attitude of its governor in the affair, and the authority of the general government was even more degraded by its condonement of the act — a condonement made virtually, if not actually, at his dictation.☆

Davis was immediately placed in arrest, and the case reported to General Halleck, with the request that a court might be ordered from Washington for its trial, as the operations then in progress made it impracticable for me to spare the officers for the purpose at the moment. Instead of that, Davis

☆ Briefly stated, the particulars of the occurrence are as follows: Nelson was in command at Louisville, and was laboring to put the city in a state of defense against the expected attack. A few days before my arrival he rebuked Davis, no doubt harshly, for what he considered a neglectful or inefficient discharge of duty, and ordered him to report to General Wright at Cincinnati. Upon my arrival Davis was ordered by Wright to report to me for duty with his division. Instead of proceeding directly to Louisville, he went by Indianapolis and was joined by Morton. With him and with another friend Davis approached Nelson in the vestibule of the Galt House at Louisville at breakfast-time, in the presence of a considerable number of persons. The reception which Davis's demand for satisfaction received was no doubt such as he had expected. What the bystanders witnessed and what was reported at the time was a slap from the back of Nelson's hand in Davis's face. Nelson then turned to Morton, denounced him for appearing as an abettor of the insult forced upon him, and retired toward his room in the adjoining hall. Davis received a pistol from the hand of his other attendant, not Morton, and followed Nelson to the hall. Nelson, apparently changing his purpose, returned before reaching his room, and as he nearly reached the end of the hall where Davis was, the latter fired, inflicting a wound in the breast, of which Nelson died in about half an hour, after receiving the ministrations of the church and forgiving his slayer. It has recently been made known for the first time in a published statement of the affair by General James B. Fry, who at the moment placed Davis in arrest, and as a personal friend listened to his statement, that upon accosting Nelson Davis filliped into his face a paper-wad that he had been crumpling between his fingers. It was then that Nelson struck him. I was not aware of this circumstance until the appearance of the statement referred to. — D. C. B.

was released, ostensibly that the case might be turned over to the civil authority; and thus the military authority of the Government was abased over the grave of a high officer, whose slaughter by another officer under such circumstances, and as a purely military offense, it had not the character to bring to trial.|

In the midst of the excitement caused by the killing of Nelson, and the active preparation that was going on for an advance against the enemy the next day, an order was received from Washington relieving me from the command, and appointing General Thomas to succeed me. In a little while General Thomas came to my room and stated his intention to decline the command. I answered that I could not consent to his doing so on any ground that was personal to me, and that if his determination was fixed I must be allowed to see the message he proposed to send. He then prepared the following dispatch to General Halleck:

"Colonel McKibbin handed me your dispatch placing me in command of the Department of the Tennessee. General Buell's preparations have been completed to march against the enemy, and I therefore respectfully ask that he may be retained in command. My position is very embarrassing, not being as well informed as I should be as the commander of this army, and on the assumption of such a responsibility."

I could make no personal objection to his reasons, but I encouraged him to accept the duty assigned to him, saying that nothing remained to be done but to put the army in motion, and that I would cheerfully explain my plans to him and give him all the information I possessed. He persisted, however, and the message went off. I did not then know of the steps that were being taken for my retention by both of the senators and two representatives from Kentucky.⚓

Halleck replied to Thomas that the order had not been made by him or by his advice, and he had no power to revoke it, but that he would suspend it until the question could be submitted to the Government, and that Colonel McKibbin had been twice telegraphed to withhold the order. The order was accordingly suspended. I at once resumed the reins of command, which, indeed, had scarcely been laid aside, and proceeded with the preparations to advance.

On my arrival at Louisville I had found a considerable number of newly made regiments or fragments of regiments, which the crisis had hurried into

---

| The following order announced General Nelson's death to the army:

"HEADQUARTERS, ARMY OF THE OHIO, LOUISVILLE, September 29th, 1862. GENERAL ORDERS, NO. 47A. The general commanding announces with inexpressible regret the death of Major-General William Nelson, which occurred in this city at 8 : 30 o'clock this morning.

"The deceased was bred a sailor, and was an officer of the navy while holding a commission in the military service. History will honor him as one of the first to organize, by his individual exertion, a military force in Kentucky, his native State, to rescue her from the vortex of rebellion, toward which she was drifting.

"He was a man of extensive information, comprehensive views, and great energy and force of character. By his nature he was intolerant of disobedience, or neglect of public duty; but no man was more prompt to recognize and foster merit in his inferiors, and in his own conduct he set an example of that vigilance, industry, and prompt attention to duty which he exacted from others. In battle his example was equally marked. On more than one field — at Shiloh, Richmond, and Ivy Mountain — he was conspicuous for his gallant bearing.

"The funeral of the deceased will take place at 3 P. M. to-morrow, at Calvary Church, Third street. By command of MAJOR-GENERAL BUELL. JAMES B. FRY, Colonel and Chief-of-Staff."

⚓ Dispatch from Senators Crittenden and Davis, and Representatives Mallory and Dunlap, to the President ("Official Records," Vol. XVI., Part II., p. 557).

the State from Ohio, Indiana, and Illinois. After designating a portion as a guard for Louisville, mostly organized into a division under General Dumont, the remainder of the new regiments were assigned to places in the old divisions; the baggage, hospital, and supply trains were reorganized; the equipment of the soldier was repaired; each man was provided with individual cooking-utensils, so as almost to dispense with baggage-wagons; and on the arrival of the last division, on the 29th, the army was ready to march on the next day. One day was lost by the instructions from Washington, but orders were given for marching on the 1st of October. The army was divided into three corps: the First under General McCook, the Second under General T. L. Crittenden, and the Third under General Gilbert. This corps was to have been commanded by General Nelson. General Thomas was announced as second in command in the army. It is now proper to take a survey of the military situation which was before me.

BRIGADIER-GENERAL WILLIAM R. TERRILL, KILLED AT PERRYVILLE. FROM A PHOTOGRAPH.

My instructions of the 18th of March placed General G. W. Morgan in command of the Seventh division of the army, to operate in the Cumberland Gap road from Kentucky to east Tennessee, and required him to take the Gap if practicable, and if not, to hold the enemy in check on that route. The division was at first only partially formed, and some time elapsed before it was in a condition to advance. The Gap was naturally strong, and was occupied by a considerable force. Morgan turned the position on the 17th of June by marching through Big Creek and Rogers's Gaps. The Confederates thereupon evacuated the place without waiting for an attack, and Morgan took possession on the 18th. It was at once strongly intrenched under the supervision of an officer of engineers, but its importance in a general campaign was not in proportion to the force to which its maintenance gave occupation. It was chiefly as an encouragement to the loyal element in east Tennessee that the possession of it was desirable. The campaign inaugurated by the Confederates in east Tennessee employed the troops of two military departments, and labored under the inconvenience of coöperation between the two independent commanders, instead of subordination to a single authority. It was executed with a harmony and zeal unusual under such circumstances, but perhaps lacked the consistency which either of the two leaders would have been amply capable of imparting to it.

The original plan was for a combined movement into middle Tennessee for the recovery of Nashville. The invasion of Kentucky was at first probably not thought of at all, or at least only as a later possibility. But as Bragg could not be ready to cross the river from Chattanooga for about two weeks after his arrival, it was arranged that in the meantime Kirby Smith with his troops should attack and capture Morgan at Cumberland Gap. The strength of Morgan's fortified position, however, with 8000 good troops to defend it, was upon consideration deemed to preclude the attempt. The alternative was to invest him on the south side with 9000 men under Stevenson, while Smith with 12,000 should seize and hold his communications on the north; by which means, not being strong enough to break his way out on either side, Morgan, upon the exhaustion of his supplies, would be compelled to surrender. This plan being adopted, Smith commenced his movement through Rogers's and Big Creek Gaps on the 14th of August, and reached Morgan's rear at Barbourville on the 18th.

He now perceived that it would be impossible for him to gather supplies for his command from that poor and exhausted region, and later his embarrassment was increased by Morgan's occupation of Rogers's and Big Creek Gaps. Nothing therefore remained for him but to withdraw or advance boldly into the rich portion of Kentucky. Bragg was not at first in favor of the latter course, until he should be prepared to follow up the precipitate movement which it was not doubted I would make from middle Tennessee for the protection of Kentucky. However, his concurrence was readily yielded, for the proposition was alluring. The idea of invasion, which had now taken firm root, was coupled with the chimera of an uprising of the people and a transfer of the State to the Confederacy. I never had the slightest apprehension of such a result. Boys might join John Morgan's roving cavaliers, and some mature men might commit themselves with less romance to the cause of the Confederacy, and these phenomena would of course be multiplied by the backing of an army. But when Kentucky so far overcame her sympathy as to assume an attitude of neutrality, she listened to a call of reason and interest, not unmingled with genuine love of the Union, that was not to stop at half-measures; and as soon as it became apparent that neutrality was impracticable, it was the deliberate choice of the mass of the people — not any pressure of coercion — that arrayed her irrevocably on the side of the Union. To that choice she was thoroughly loyal, and no finer example of political and popular generosity can anywhere be found than that wherein, at the close of the conflict, she restored to all the rights of citizenship and the ties of fraternity her expatriated sons who for four years had made war upon her.

Smith advanced from Barbourville with 12,000 men on the 26th of August, encountered at Rogersville and Richmond the 5000 or 6000 raw troops assembled there, scattered them like chaff, making prisoners and capturing arms, proceeded to Lexington, where he established his headquarters on the 2d of September, occupied Frankfort and Cynthiana, and finally threw his pickets almost to the gates of Cincinnati and Louisville.

These events produced widespread effects. They were the signal for the movement of Humphrey Marshall with 3000 men into Kentucky through Pound Gap, and it would seem stimulated Bragg's advance from Chattanooga. They changed the concentration of my army from Murfreesboro' to Nashville, and would perhaps have caused the transfer of half of it into Kentucky, which seemed to be powerless, but for the sudden appearance of Bragg in the Valley of the Cumberland endangering Nashville. In Kentucky and other bordering States, they produced an excitement which was intense in some places, amounting almost to consternation. Business at Cincinnati was for a few days entirely suspended for the purpose of defense; intrenchments were vigorously prosecuted at Covington and Louisville by the labor of the citizens and the troops, and raw regiments in the process of formation were hurried into Cincinnati and Louisville from Ohio, Indiana, and Illinois. The Government of Kentucky sought refuge at Louisville, where on my arrival Nelson reported a force of 30,000 raw troops.

General Morgan at Cumberland Gap was promptly aware of Kirby Smith's movement, and informed me of it on the 16th of August. He had thirty days' provisions, and was instructed the same day to hold his position. The exhaustion of his supplies and the improbability of their being replenished in time made it necessary for him at last to withdraw, which he did on the night of the 17th of September. He was pursued by Stevenson and harassed by John Morgan's cavalry, but made his way successfully through Manchester, Boonesville, West Liberty, and Grayson to the Ohio River at Greenup, where he arrived about the 2d of October. Stevenson with his division joined Kirby Smith near Frankfort about the time of my arrival at Louisville, and was present in the operations around Perryville.

On his arrival in central Kentucky, Smith issued his proclamation inviting the people to join the cause of their deliverance, and Bragg did the same in pathetic terms at Glasgow. These appeals, like many of the orders promulgated to arouse the animosity and stimulate the valor of the Southern troops, would give a sad impression of the condition of the inhabitants, especially the innocent and helpless, and of the brutality of the oppressor; but they were not confirmed by the feebleness of the response. There was a sweet sympathy, so the Confederates thought, but that was all. The arms in abundance, which Kentuckians were advised to grasp, remained in the store-houses. Kentuckians suffered just as Ohioans would have suffered with armies in their midst, and they had as a body no more thought of changing their colors. During the whole occupation enough perhaps for a brigade joined the invaders.

The arrival of Bragg at Bardstown gave the Confederates virtual possession of the whole of Kentucky east of the Louisville and Nashville Railroad, excepting within the limits of Covington and Louisville, and Smith called his troops together near Frankfort to assist in the proposed attack upon Louisville. That project was postponed after my arrival; but Polk, Bragg having gone to Frankfort and Lexington, was ordered to occupy Shepherdsville, Taylorsville, and other near points around Louisville. Steps were being taken to that end when, on the 2d of October, the enemy's pickets announced to the leaders at Frankfort and Bardstown the advance of my army in force on four roads, threatening the whole of their front, which covered a distance of sixty miles.

The plan of my movement was to force the enemy's left back and compel him to concentrate as far as possible from any convenient line of retreat, while at the same time making a strong demonstration against his right, so as to mislead him as to the real point of attack, and prevent him from moving upon my left flank and rear. With that object General Sill, commanding a division in McCook's corps, was ordered to move boldly toward Frankfort through Shelbyville, followed temporarily by the division of raw troops under Dumont which had been organized as a guard for Louisville. McCook with his two remaining divisions moved upon Taylorsville, where he halted the second night in a position which pointed to either flank. The other two corps moved respectively through Shepherdsville and Mt. Washington, to converge upon Bardstown, and halted the second night at Salt River. The enemy's pickets were encountered on all of the roads within a few miles of the city, increasing in strength as the movement progressed, and opposing a sharp opposition at Bardstown and Shelbyville. Polk withdrew his army from Bardstown on the night of the 3d, going through Springfield, and Sill, against a considerable resistance, pushed back the force in front of him toward Frankfort. These measures brought to a hurried completion the inauguration of Provisional Governor Hawes at Frankfort on the 4th, under the supervision of General Bragg. Polk, on his part, was pressed so closely that Hardee, who was bringing up his rear, was compelled to make a stand at Perryville and call for assistance. Assuming that Smith was the object of my attack, and that my right and rear would thereby be exposed to Polk at Bardstown, Bragg ordered Polk on the 2d to attack in that manner, while Smith should attack my left, and that view of my design was persisted in; so that only one of the two divisions which were being pressed forward to reënforce Smith was returned to assist Hardee at Perryville on the night of the 7th.

The strength of the opposition to Sill and the continued presence of Kirby Smith about Frankfort pointed to a concentration in that direction, at least north of Perryville; but on the 6th the information was that Smith was moving upon Danville. McCook, who had been halted momentarily at Bloomfield until the question should be developed, was therefore directed on Harrodsburg, and Sill was ordered to join him by forced marches. During the night the information in regard to Smith was contradicted, and the expectation of a concentration

at or north of Perryville was confirmed. McCook was therefore promptly turned upon Perryville, and Sill was ordered to follow him. Under a stubborn resistance from Polk, during the 7th, the center corps halted in the evening about three and a half miles from Perryville without water, of which it had had but little since morning, and the corps was put in order of battle. It appeared now that the enemy was virtually concentrated in our front. Orders were therefore dispatched to McCook, who was supposed to be about seven miles back, on the left, and to Thomas, who had been ordered to halt the right corps (Crittenden's) for the night at Haysville, about four miles in rear, on the road from Lebanon to Perryville. They were to march precisely at 3 o'clock in the morning, prepared in every respect for battle, and on arriving at certain designated points were to be formed in order of battle on the left and right, respectively, of the center corps. They were then to be made as comfortable as possible, but not to leave ranks. A reconnoissance was to be made to ascertain the position of the enemy, and as soon as that was done Thomas and McCook were to report at headquarters for further orders.↓ I expected that these objects would be accomplished by 7 o'clock in the morning.

During the night it was ascertained that there were some pools of water in the bed of Doctor's Fork, which crossed the road in front of us, and of which the enemy's rear-guard held possession. Colonel Daniel McCook, commanding a brigade in Sheridan's division, was selected to attack the enemy and get possession of the water, which he did in a handsome manner at day dawn. Very soon the enemy attempted to recover the lost position, but Sheridan's and Mitchell's divisions were moved to the front and defeated the design. From that time a desultory cannonading was kept up between the two lines until it merged into the battle, which suddenly burst forth fiercely at 2 o'clock. The arrival of McCook's corps is dated from half-past 10 o'clock, but for the bulk of the corps it was later. He reported to me at about half-past 12, and I hastened his return to his command; for though the time had passed when I had somewhat apprehended an attack, while the center corps was alone, yet the occasion was critical, and he had not reconnoitered his front. Thomas had not reported, and no final instructions for attack could be given. When McCook reached his corps, it had materially changed its ground and was not in position. Artillery guns were exchanging distant shots, but evidently no one on our side was expecting an attack. It came at about 2 o'clock, while a line was moving forward to take possession of the water which could be discerned in the bed of Chaplin river, behind which the enemy were formed for the assault.

It turned out that Polk with three divisions, with cavalry on both flanks, had determined to fight a "defensive-offensive" battle; but as the morning wore away without the attack, which was awaited, Bragg came upon the ground and ordered an assault. It was delivered mainly upon McCook, but also fell heavily upon Sheridan, who repelled it handsomely on his side. McCook fought bravely, and by Gilbert's order was reënforced with Gooding's brigade from Mitchell's division; but he was steadily driven back for a mile, until the enemy's pursuing line came within the enfilading fire of Sheridan's artillery, which was delivered with great effect across the intervening valley of Doctor's Fork. At 4 o'clock Captain Fisher of McCook's staff arrived and reported to me that the left corps had been sustaining a severe conflict for a considerable time, and was being driven back. I was astonished. Not a sound of musketry had been heard, and my staff-officers had been at the front until dinner-time. I had noticed a sudden increase of cannonading at 2 o'clock, and General Gilbert, who had come in from his lines and was getting his dinner with me, immediately proceeded to his command; but as the firing as suddenly subsided, and no report came to me, I had ceased to think of the occurrence.

Reënforcements were immediately ordered to McCook from Schoepf's division, which was in reserve, and a staff-officer was dispatched to Thomas with orders to move the right corps forward vigorously and attack the enemy's left. Thomas could not be found until about 6 o'clock, and owing to the lateness of the hour the advance was not made; but McCook was relieved by the succor sent to him and the battle ceased about night-fall. Further orders were sent to Thomas at 6.30 P. M.:

OCTOBER 8TH, 1862, 6.30 P. M. GENERAL THOMAS, Second in Command: The First Corps (McCook's) on our left has been very heavily engaged. The left and center of this corps gained ground, but the right of it yielded a little. Press your lines forward as far as possible to-night, and get into position to make a vigorous attack in the morning at daylight. If you have got your troops into a position which you deem advantageous it will not be advisable to make a change for the purpose of complying with the general's instructions for you sent by Captain Mack. It may be as well to halt the division ordered to the center and let it wait where it is for further orders. The general desires to see you in person as soon to-night as your duties will permit you to come over. Respectfully, JAMES B. FRY, Colonel and Chief-of-Staff.

McCook had 12,500 men in the battle, and lost in killed and wounded about 3000 — nearly one-quarter; Gilbert lost in killed and wounded nearly 900, all of which belonged to Sheridan's division and one of Mitchell's brigades; and about 450 in all were taken prisoners; total loss, 4348. The force

actually engaged on the Union side numbered about 22,000, though more came into position for battle near the close. All of the force had a good number of new regiments. One of McCook's divisions was composed entirely of new regiments, with one exception. Its division commander, Jackson, and its two brigade commanders, Terrill and Webster, were killed. The enemy claim to have fought the battle, according to Bragg's report, with 16,000 men. His loss is reported at 3396, of which 251 were prisoners. He captured some artillery that he did not carry off, though he exchanged some of his pieces for better ones.

Not long before the commencement of this partial but fierce contest, a staff-officer arrived from General Thomas and reported two divisions of the right corps up — the last had not yet arrived. The enemy was in front, and Thomas thought it not advisable to leave to report in person. The want of definite information from both flanks, the failure of a meeting of the two commanders at my headquarters for explanations and final orders, and the lateness of the hour for effecting these preliminaries for the great battle which was to be fought, precluded the idea of bringing it on that evening. That conclusion had, indeed, been rendered probably unavoidable at the time of McCook's arrival at my headquarters, by two dispatches which had been received from Thomas during the morning: One dated the 7th, 6 o'clock P. M., at Haysville, ♭ saying that finding no water at that point he would march the right corps to the Rolling Fork for a camp; and the other, dated on the Rolling Fork, October 8th, 3 o'clock, A. M., ♮ reporting that my order to march at 3 o'clock had just been received, that the corps reached that place at 11 o'clock at night, and was then camping, the trains being not all yet up, and that he would be in front of Perryville as soon as possible. The staff-officer was, therefore, started back a few minutes before 2 o'clock with some minor instructions to General Thomas, and a desire that he should report in person after night-fall.

Thomas, McCook, and Gilbert met at my headquarters after dark, and after conversation upon the events of the day, orders were given for battle the following morning. Crittenden's corps on the right was to move forward at 6 o'clock and engage the enemy, and the center was to do likewise as soon as they were abreast. McCook was to close

♭ "HAYSVILLE, October 7th, 1862, 6 P. M.—MAJOR-GENERAL BUELL: About two and a half miles west of this place I can get a camp on the Rolling Fork, where there is said to be an abundance of water. As there is no water here, I propose to camp there. It will only throw us about one and a half miles farther from Perryville. It was reported to me on my arrival that the rebels had 200,000 pounds of pork at Lebanon. At first I ordered a regiment to go there and seize it. I afterward learned that it belonged to a company of pork-packers, who profess to be Union men. I therefore concluded not to send or seize it, as we can get it at any time by sending for it. Maxey's brigade is also reported as leaving Lebanon to-day for Danville, via Bradfordsville and Hustonville, with a train loaded with flour and pork from Lebanon. Shall I send and intercept him now, or capture him hereafter? Very respectfully, GEO. H. THOMAS."

♮ "HEADQUARTERS, UNITED STATES FORCES, ROLLING FORK, Ky., October 8th, 1862, 3 A. M.—GENERAL BUELL: Your letter of instruction came to hand at the time indicated for the Second Corps to march. Have given the necessary orders to General Crittenden, and will take position before Perryville as soon as possible. The roads over which we marched yesterday were exceedingly rough and tortuous, and, with one exception, without water. Reached this place at 11 o'clock last night, but all the trains are not up yet. I found, as night approached, that the troops must have water, which could not be obtained short of Rolling Fork, some two miles out of our way, to which place the command was ordered, and we are now camping. As soon as I decided to make Rolling Fork, I dispatched messengers to your headquarters, who must have reached you before this. Respectfully, etc., GEO. H. THOMAS, Major-General, U. S. Volunteers."

in and remain in reserve. In fact, only one of his divisions (Rousseau's) was in a condition to fight as a distinct body. At that hour not a man in the army who had any knowledge beyond the limit of his own vision doubted that the whole Confederate army was in our front, and that the battle was to be renewed in the morning.

The right corps did not commence the movement until 9 o'clock, owing, as was afterward explained, to Thomas's message to Crittenden by signal, from my camp, only specifying that he should be ready to advance at 6 o'clock; so that the orders to advance had to be repeated when it was discovered that the movement had not commenced. It was then ascertained that the enemy had withdrawn, and that only three of his divisions had been present. The battle had enabled him to perfect his junction with Kirby Smith at Harrodsburg, as originally intended, and I did not hesitate to await the arrival of Sill's division before precipitating the anticipated battle. In the meantime, the army was put in position for any emergency, and reconnoissances were actively employed to gain information of the movements of the enemy.

We had repelled the enemy's fierce attack when it was supposed his whole force was in front of us. My official report stated succinctly the causes which prevented us from winning a more fruitful success, namely, the difficulties which prevented the troops from getting on the ground simultaneously, and the fact that I was not apprised early enough of the condition of affairs on my left ("Official Records," Vol. XVI., Part I., p. 1031). When the orders in anticipation of battle were given on the evening of the 7th, McCook's exact position was not known. He was supposed to be about seven miles in rear. The orders did not reach him until 2:30 o'clock, and he marched at 5. It was 10:30 when the head of his column arrived. The road was hilly and rough, and the march was understood to be made in the vicinity of the enemy. It was therefore properly conducted with prudence, and was of course slow. The right corps had been ordered to halt for the night at Haysville, not more than four miles to the rear. But on arriving at that point, finding no water, General Thomas, who was conducting the corps, determined to go to the Rolling Fork to encamp. He was told the distance was two and one-half miles off to the right, but he did not arrive until 11 o'clock, after five hours of night marching. The courier did not find him until 3 o'clock in the morning, at which hour he was camping, his trains being not all yet up. It is evident from his dispatches that he did not realize the gravity of the occasion. It was impossible, under the circumstances, that marches should be regulated with reference to water. The center corps marched with no assurance of finding it, halted on the evening of the 7th without it, and only obtained it the next morning by wresting it from the hands of the enemy. Had the right corps been found at Haysville, it should have been in position for battle by 7 o'clock and, whatever else may have happened, would have been in such connection with

headquarters by signals, as the other corps were, that the orders of 4 o'clock for it to attack would have been delivered immediately, and would have given fully two hours of daylight for action.

On the other hand, had the battle on the left been reported at 2 o'clock, when it commenced, the succor which was ordered from the reserve at 4 would have come in the form of reënforcements two hours earlier; and the orders which were sent at the same time to the right corps would have had at least that much more time for execution. I make no prediction of all of the consequences that might have flowed from these conditions. It would have depended much upon the action of the right corps. They ought to have been of a very decisive character. For the rest, the reports show that the left corps was not fully prepared for the heavy blow that fell upon it, but the reverse which it sustained was largely due to the rawness of the troops. Fully one-half of the two divisions was made up of new regiments.

While the battle was in progress at Perryville, Kirby Smith, still thinking that my movement was upon his front, had prepared for a battle at or near Lawrenceburg. His cavalry attacked Sill at that point on that day, and the next day on the march, but Sill extricated himself skillfully, and continued his march, joining his corps at Perryville on the 11th. Smith now discovered his mistake, and dispatched Bragg on the 9th that he would join him immediately at Harrodsburg, which he accomplished partly on the 9th and fully on the 10th. On the latter day a strong reconnoissance found him in line of battle about four miles south of Harrodsburg. He withdrew entirely on the 11th, followed by my cavalry toward Camp Dick Robinson, where Bragg's whole force now took position, sheltered in front and on his right flank by the perpendicular cliffs of Dick's River and the Kentucky. I was moving on the 12th and 13th to turn his position and attack him on the left, when I learned that he was withdrawing. General Bragg states in his report that he was ready and desirous for battle at this point and previously after Perryville, and I have no doubt that was true, if he could have had his own terms. His order for withdrawal was announced on the 13th.

The pursuit was taken up that night, under the supervision of Thomas, with Crittenden's corps, followed by the other corps. The details afford no interesting or important fact, except that the retreating army was pressed into difficulties which involved it in great hardship and temporary disorganization. The pursuit was continued in that manner as far as London, and then, about the 20th, my several columns were turned by the most direct routes toward the ground in Tennessee and Alabama from which they had started six weeks before, and where it was foreseen the enemy would soon again be encountered. The repair of the railroad had been pushed forward with energy, and the army was arriving at Glasgow and Bowling Green on its route, when on the 30th of October I turned over the command to General Rosecrans, in obedience to orders from Washington. It would be useless to review the officio-personal part of the correspondence which immediately preceded that event between the Washington authorities and myself, or even the official part of it, relating chiefly to the plan of a movement into east Tennessee, to which my successor in a measure fell heir. Toward him, I may add, the transfer brought no heart-burning on my part, and the prayer expressed in my parting order was sincere, that the army might, under his command, be the means of speedily restoring the Union to its integrity.

In spite of my connection — I can scarcely speak of it as a personal interest — with the subject, I venture to make some observations that appear to me proper with reference to the campaign which I have outlined. It extended over a greater territory and involved greater hazard on the side of the Union than any other campaign of the war. In the early part, and up to the time of my arrival in Louisville, it was more neglected by the Government than any other. It was distinguished also from all others, except a part of Pope's operations in Virginia, in the relative strength of the contending forces.

The important results, favorable and adverse, were that the object for which I had started out, the occupation of east Tennessee, was not even in a condition to be attempted; and that on the other hand, a formidable political and strategical scheme which aimed at the conquest and absorption of Kentucky, was defeated with substantial disaster to the invader, and at the close the Federal arms returned with increased strength to the possessions from which they had been withdrawn to counteract the invasion. It has been said that territory was given up which was not recovered for a year; but that is not substantially true, except with reference to Cumberland Gap, and as to that, it is to be remarked that it had been held at a greater cost than it was worth, and that afterward it was no obstacle when the advance into east Tennessee was made with an adequate force. When the army on the way back changed commanders at Bowling Green, there was no new obstacle to its resumption of every position it had held in middle Tennessee and Alabama. The enemy, with broken fortune and relatively impaired strength, was only on the south side of the Tennessee from which he had started two months before. I do not comment upon what was afterward done, or raise the question whether it was desirable to resume the position which had been occupied as a point of departure; but if it was not desirable to resume it, certainly for stronger reasons it was not a position which it was advisable for me to hold.

If the campaign, with no more advantageous results, had been marked by one general and destructive, but not disastrous battle, it would no doubt have been received with more popular favor, and perhaps even have been more easy of professional praise. I shall not insist on that point, but I shall particularly make no apology for not having fought battles where the issue was reasonably doubtful, and where they in fact proved not to have been necessary for the success of my cause. Besides, in an open field, with capable commanders, it takes two parties to inaugurate a battle — one to begin the attack, and another to stand to receive it.

It was much talked of after the event, that Kentucky was known to be the immediate object for which Bragg moved from Chattanooga; that it was proposed to me to concentrate at Sparta to oppose him; and that that mountainous and comparatively barren region could have been relied upon to support my army, with exhausted magazines and in the presence of the enemy; but the facts were as erroneous as the theories were fallacious. There was never at the time an intelligent judgment or an accepted rumor that Bragg's first object, if he had any, was any other than the recovery of middle Tennessee and Nashville; and if, under the circumstances, a proposition had been made to me to concentrate the army at Sparta, I should have rejected it.

Various speculations and confident declarations have been indulged in by critics on both sides, as to the results that would have flowed from certain different action on the part of the two commanders. Such opinions with reference to extended operations are seldom of any value. They generally have no knowledge of the circumstances which would have prevented the prescribed action, and take no account of the modifying influence which it would have had on the conduct of the opposing commander. It is, therefore, idle to assert, as many have done, that Kirby Smith could and should have marched into Louisville after the battle of Richmond, or what would have been the substantial fruit of that proceeding if it had been accomplished; or that Bragg and Smith united would have overwhelmed me at Munfordville. The disappointment of calculations pending the events, affords no stronger marks of fallibility than do assumptions afterward. Of the former this campaign, like all campaigns, presents many examples. Thus, the military problem, as it appeared to my mind, was to be solved by a combined descent of the Confederates upon the inferior Union force in middle Tennessee. But instead of that, an army, embarrassed in its situation, to be sure, but intact and powerful, was left in the rear, and a distant invasion which had no well-founded prospect of success was undertaken. The boldness and formidable character of this alternative appeared to give assurance that it would not be abandoned without at least one vigorous blow in attack or defense; but when prudential measures were taken on the opposing side with reference to such a contingency, the invader, with a prudence, not to be expected from the audacity of his advance, withdrew from the contest. On the other side, to General Bragg's mind, as early as the 24th of August, the army opposed to him was demoralized and in full flight, with doubtful prospect of stopping short of the Ohio; later it was racing to get the lead of him at Munfordville; and at that point, astonished to find himself not attacked at sight, he imagined that his opponent must be in retreat by some secret route to the Ohio River. But all of these impressions were delusive. When to his mind the opposing army was in retreat, it was awaiting his approach from behind the

Tennessee River and the mountains. When he imagined it trying to get ahead of him, it was moving especially to keep him in front and away from Nashville, deeming the retention of that point of more consequence than his transient intrusion upon Kentucky; always pursuing him, always aiming to get nearer to him, always willing to avail itself of advantages, and confident in the end of triumphing over him.

A philosophical study of our civil conflict must recognize that influences of some sort operated fundamentally for the side of the Confederacy in every prominent event of the war, and nowhere with less effect than in the Tennessee and Kentucky campaign. They are involved in the fact that it required enormous sacrifices from 24,000,000 of people to defeat the political scheme of 8,000,000; 2,000,000 of soldiers to subdue 800,000 soldiers: and, descending to details, a naval fleet and 15,-000 troops to advance against a weak fort, manned by less than 100 men, at Fort Henry; 35,000 with naval coöperation to overcome 12,000 at Donelson; 60,000 to secure a victory over 40,000 at Pittsburg Landing; 120,000 to enforce the retreat of 65,000 intrenched, after a month of fighting and manœuvring, at Corinth; 100,000 repelled by 80,000 in the first Peninsular campaign against Richmond; 70,000, with a powerful naval force to inspire the campaign, which lasted nine months, against 40,000 at Vicksburg; 90,000 to barely withstand the assault of 70,000 at Gettysburg; 115,000 sustaining a frightful repulse from 60,000 at Fredericksburg. 100,000 attacked and defeated by 50,000 at Chancellorsville; 85,000 held in check two days by 40,000 at Antietam; 43,000 retaining the field uncertainly against 38,000 at Stone River; 70,000 defeated at Chickamauga, and beleaguered by 70,000 at Chattanooga; 80,000 merely to break the investing line of 45,000 at Chattanooga; 100,000 to press back 50,000, increased at last to 70,000, from Chattanooga to Atlanta, a distance of 120 miles, and then let go — an operation which is commemorated at festive reunions by the standing toast of "one hundred days under fire"; 50,000 to defeat the investing line of 30,000 at Nashville; and finally 120,000 to overcome 60,000 with exhaustion after a struggle of a year in Virginia. The rule which this summary establishes will not determine absolutely the relative merit of the different achievements, but is not to be ignored in a judgment upon particular events.

Individually, the Northern soldier was in no sense the inferior of the Southern. What, then, is the explanation of this rule which is so nearly invariable as to show that superior numbers were generally essential to Union victories, and the success of Union operations? Much was due to the character of the contest. Revolution is calculated to inspire bold and desperate action, and wars of sentiment, of the nature of which this partook more in the South than in the North, are always marked by unusual energy. In the North there was much

animosity, but it was more collective, and operated more in shaping public policy than upon the temper of the armies. The style of the orders and proclamations issued by many of the Southern generals shows how much they relied on the passionate enthusiasm of their soldiers, and how they tried to stimulate it. They recognized that the odds must generally be against them, and that they must find some means of overcoming the effect of the fact upon the spirits of their troops, and themselves set an example of audacity.

Of course the necessity of invasion against a hostile population placed the Federal cause at a disadvantage which had to be overcome by greater numbers. The simpler mode of life to which the bulk of the Southern troops were accustomed made them more contented with meager supplies; the lack of resources of every sort precluded the luxurious outfit to which the Northern troops were accustomed; and thus the impedimenta of military operations were more restricted without impairing their efficiency than in the Northern armies. It took some time to eradicate this inequality. Another sectional distinction produced a marked effect in the beginning of the war. The habits of the Southern people facilitated the formation of cavalry corps which were comparatively efficient even without instruction; and accordingly we see Stuart, and John Morgan, and Forrest riding with impunity around the Union armies, and destroying or harassing their communications. Late in the war that agency was reversed. The South was exhausted of horses, while the Northern cavalry increased in numbers and efficiency, and acquired the audacity which had characterized the Southern.

But still another influence must be found in the personal differences between the two sections,— differences due chiefly to the more rural condition of the South and the institution of slavery. In all popular movements the Southern leader was then, and is now in a less degree, followed with an implicit confidence which did not mean humility by any means, but produced subordination. This difference is illustrated by two historical incidents. At Cold Harbor, the Northern troops, who had proven their indomitable qualities by losses nearly equal to the whole force of their opponent, when ordered to another sacrifice, even under such a soldier as Hancock, answered the demand as one man, with a silent and stolid inertia : ☆ at Gettysburg, Pickett, when waiting for the signal which Longstreet dreaded to repeat, for the hopeless but immortal charge against Cemetery Hill, saluted and said, as he turned to his ready column : "I shall move forward, sir!"

Nor must we give slight importance to the influence of the Southern women, who in agony of heart girded the sword upon their loved ones and bade them go. It was to be expected that these various influences would give a confidence to leadership that would tend to bold adventure, and leave its mark upon the contest.

☆ General Francis A. Walker, in his "History of the Second Army Corps," says, p. 516, that Hancock declined the responsibility of renewing the attack as ordered by Meade; and that the statement that the troops refused to advance is erroneous.— EDITORS.

PERRYVILLE, KENTUCKY, LOOKING SOUTH-EAST FROM THE MACKVILLE PIKE. FROM A PHOTOGRAPH TAKEN IN 1885.

ON THE FIELD OF PERRYVILLE.⸗

BY CHARLES C. GILBERT, MAJOR-GENERAL, U. S. V.

AS the Army of the Ohio, moving from Bardstown, approached Perryville on the 7th of October, 1862, McCook's corps formed the left, Crittenden's the right, and mine—which was moving on the direct road by the way of Springfield, and was ahead of the others—the center. [See maps, pp. 6 and 24.] In my column, R. B. Mitchell's division had the lead; Schoepf followed, and Sheridan brought up the rear. Our advance was vigorously resisted by Wheeler's cavalry, forming the rear-guard of Hardee's corps, which was retiring before us. About 2 o'clock in the afternoon, when the head of the column was nearing the line of Doctor's Creek, a tributary of the Chaplin River, or more properly the Chaplin Fork of Salt River, the enemy, in force, was observed lining the crest of the ridge on the farther bank, obviously with the intention of disputing the possession of a few pools of water that remained in the water-course, which was otherwise nearly dry. An excessive drought had prevailed for months in this part of Kentucky. At sight of the enemy, orders were given to form Mitchell's division in order of battle across the Springfield road and along some high ground on the right. When Schoepf came up his division was massed in reserve in Mitchell's rear, on the left of the road, and Sheridan, arriving after Wheeler had been dislodged and was being pressed back toward Perryville, was posted in front and to the right of Mitchell. Before daybreak on the 8th, a position was gained that covered the pools in Doctor's Creek, and these formed our only water-supply for the next two days, or as long as the enemy held the Chaplin River.

⸗ Condensed from General Gilbert's articles in the "Southern Bivouac," and revised by him.— EDITORS.

During the night General Buell ordered McCook's and Crittenden's corps to march at 3 o'clock in the morning of the 8th, and to form in order of battle on the center corps—my own. The movements of these columns were delayed, and General Buell, apprehensive of an attack while the center corps was isolated, directed me to select a strong position, and my troops were soon moving out of their camps and taking positions for the main attack, which it was supposed would come on about 10 o'clock. As that hour drew near, I observed, in visiting General Sheridan's ground, that a part of it was vacant, and that one of his brigades was in march on the road to Perryville, and the remainder were preparing to follow. On inquiry it was discovered that this movement was in consequence of some misunderstanding of orders. General Sheridan was directed to recall the brigade, resume his position, and limit himself to its defense until a general advance to attack in force should be ordered. To this order was added the explanation that General Buell was particularly solicitous that nothing be done to bring on a general engagement until after the junction of the flank corps.

General Sheridan lost no time in reëstablishing his division on the ground to which he had been originally assigned. He had barely accomplished it when he was attacked in force and a fight ensued, in which the loss was severe on both sides. In the meantime the head of General McCook's corps, coming over the Mackville pike, appeared on the high ground marked

RIDGE ON THE UNION LEFT OCCUPIED BY STONE'S AND BUSH'S BAT-
TERIES—THE SCENE OF STARKWEATHER'S CONTEST [SEE P. 58].
FROM A PHOTOGRAPH FROM THE DIRECTION OF ROUS-
SEAU'S LINE, TAKEN IN 1885.

by Russell's house, due north of Sheridan's position about one mile. This was about 10:30 A. M. Marking out his line of battle, General McCook ordered General Rousseau to form it. Loomis's battery was established on a commanding piece of ground near Russell's house, and to the left of it. General Rousseau had been previously ordered to send a line of skirmishers to the left

TREE NEAR WHERE GENERAL
JAMES S. JACKSON FELL.

VIEW LOOKING NORTH-EAST FROM THE POSITION OF LOOMIS'S BATTERY, THE CENTER OF ROUSSEAU'S
LINE [SEE MAP, P. 24, AND NOTE ON P. 55]. FROM A PHOTOGRAPH TAKEN IN 1885.

and front to examine some wood on that quarter, and Captain Wickliffe,
with his company of cavalry, was sent to reconnoiter the ground to the left
of this line of skirmishers. At this time there was some light skirmishing
going on with Sheridan's division, at the head of the center corps, which was
still in column, as previously described; but this soon ceased, and General
McCook was satisfied that the enemy he found engaging my corps when
he arrived had retired from the field.

McCook's corps, as previously related, had been ordered to march at 3 A. M.,
but it was 2 : 30 A. M. before the order reached General McCook, and his
march began at 5 A. M. McCook had with him then two divisions, Rousseau's
and Jackson's.   Rousseau's division took the lead on the march, but when it
arrived at Perryville only two of the brigades were present — the remaining
one, Starkweather's, having been thrown to the rear by the interposition of
Jackson's division, which cut it off at Mackville. Without waiting for the
arrival of this brigade, General McCook, after giving his assistant adjutant-
general particular instructions to post Jackson's two brigades on a commanding piece of ground immediately to the right of the Mackville and Perryville
road, and to hold them in column so that they could be moved in any direction as occasion required, turned over the command to General Rousseau,
and galloped off to report to General Buell at headquarters. Buell was in
my camp, on the Springfield pike about two and a half miles distant from
McCook's position on the Mackville pike. At half-past 12 the Confederates
advanced, and in a few moments the skirmishers and artillery were engaged.
The attack fell upon Sheridan's division at the head of my corps and upon

POSITION OF LOOMIS'S BATTERY ON ROUSSEAU'S LINE, LOOKING ACROSS DOCTOR'S CREEK.
FROM A PHOTOGRAPH TAKEN IN 1885.

Loomis's battery occupied the highest part of the ridge above H. P. Bottom's house, at about the center of Rousseau's line (see map, p. 24). Lytle's brigade extended from the battery across the old Mackville pike to the "burnt barn." Lytle's brigade was assailed from the direction of Bottom's house, and from the right flank. The attack upon the position held by Loomis's battery was made chiefly from the ridge in the middle distance of the picture on page 54. The Confederates gained the north-east side of that ridge by following down the dry bed of Doctor's Creek under the shelter of its west bank.— EDITORS.

the head of McCook's corps, now advancing from its first position at Russell's house down the slope toward Chaplin River.

When General McCook returned to his troops after having reported at headquarters, he found that General Rousseau had advanced the right of the line about eight hundred or a thousand yards, and was occupying a commanding ridge which was to the left of the Mackville and Perryville pike. The enemy was firing on this line from three batteries, and Loomis's and Simonson's batteries were replying. As there was no Confederate infantry in sight McCook ordered the firing to cease, so as to economize ammunition, and then prepared to make a reconnoissance toward Chaplin River for water, as he had just been ordered to do by General Buell. Riding off to the left, General McCook found a commanding ridge about six hundred yards from the stream and overlooking it. Sending for Generals Jackson and Terrill, he showed them the water, marked his line of battle, and placed a battery on it with strong supports. General Terrill was then ordered to advance a body of skirmishers down the slope to the water as soon as the line was formed. Not being apprehensive of an attack, General McCook then went back to his right. It was now nearly 2 o'clock. At this time the line of the left corps stood with its right on the Mackville and Perryville pike near the crossing of Doctor's Creek and its left near Chaplin River, its direction being about due north and south. It was formed of two brigades of Rousseau's division

FARM-HOUSE OF H. P. BOTTOM. FROM A PHOTOGRAPH TAKEN IN 1885.

The farm-house stands near Doctor's Creek, under the ridge occupied by Rousseau; and the view
is from the old Mackville pike. [See map, p. 24.]

(Lytle's and Harris's) and Terrill's brigade of Jackson's division. Webster's
brigade of Jackson's division had not yet come into position, and Starkweather's brigade of Rousseau's division had not yet reached the field.

Just previously to this the enemy, in pursuance of his plan of attack, had
begun to engage Sheridan's division, the head of the center corps. Mitchell's
division was at that time closing up to take position within supporting distance of Sheridan. Caldwell's and Carlin's brigades of this division were to
the right and rear, under cover, and Gooding's brigade was north of Doctor's
Creek, near the stream. In this position the latter covered Sheridan's left,
and watched the interval between the two corps so long as the left corps
remained in its place in line of battle, and before it advanced to the front.
As Mitchell came into his position on the second line, the enemy appeared on
his right in force and engaged Carlin's brigade, but were repulsed. It was
now nearing half-past 2, and the enemy's entire line, from his left, where the
attack began on Sheridan, to his right, where it fell in heaviest force on
Rousseau, was in full progress, carrying everything before it. When Sheridan's assailants reached his main line he gave them a reception, cool, effective, and disastrous, and when their repulse was complete a brigade from the
second line (Carlin's), which had been called up to assist in the defense, pursued the enemy to Perryville, thus turning his left and establishing itself on
his rear. General Sheridan's action was according to the sound principles
of the profession, and, as he was amply and promptly supported, the operations on this part of the field, in which he had the lead, were fully successful,

and his conduct here foreshadowed the exceptionally successful career that lay before him.

General McCook was assailed by greatly superior numbers. His brigades, which General Rousseau had put in motion to the front in his absence, were surprised on the march by General Bragg's attack, and were taken in the act of forming, and on ground favorable to the attacking party. Rousseau's right brigade, the extreme right of the left corps, was attacked with great severity and pertinacity. Terrill's brigade on the left, and Starkweather's, which had now arrived, were in turn heavily assailed. Being composed of entirely raw troops, Terrill's brigade in a few moments gave way in confusion, losing Parsons's battery of eight Napoleon guns. General Jackson, who was with this brigade, was killed at the first fire. General Terrill did all in his power to steady his men, but in vain. An hour and a half later, while still striving to rally his broken troops, he was mortally wounded. ⚓ Starkweather's brigade and Stone's and Bush's batteries were on the extreme left and rear of Terrill's brigade, and checked the attack.

General McCook, perceiving that he was assailed by at least three times his number, sent an aide-de-camp, Lieutenant L. M. Hosea, to General Sheridan, requesting him to look to the right of his line and see that it was not turned. Just at this time Sheridan had his attention fully occupied with his own right, where two opposing batteries were in position, and troops were massing behind them to attack him front and flank. About half an hour later McCook sent Captain H. N. Fisher, of his staff, to General Schoepf, commanding the reserve of my corps, with an urgent request for reënforcement, reporting that his reserves were all exhausted and his corps upon the point of being compromised. General Schoepf was at the time on the march to the front with two of his brigades (Walker's and Steedman's), and although desirous of rendering assistance, he declined to take the responsibility of changing his line of march. He referred the officer to me, but I was at the time at General Buell's headquarters, where I had been since noon.

Owing to the conformation of the ground and to the limited use of artillery on both sides, no sound of the battle had been heard at General Buell's headquarters until the attack reached General Sheridan's position, which was about half-past 3 o'clock. Then the cannon firing became so continuous and was so well sustained and so different from the irregular shots, at wide intervals, which had characterized the "shelling of the woods" earlier in the day, that it was readily recognized as a battle. It was near 4 o'clock when there came up the valley of Doctor's Creek the sound of rapid artillery firing. It was too heavy and too well sustained to come from merely "shelling the woods." Listening attentively for a moment, General Buell said to me, "That is something more than shelling the woods; it sounds like a fight." I at once mounted and set off at a rapid pace down the

⚓ Colonel Charles Denby, of the 42d Indiana regiment, says:

"It is curious that the night before the battle [of Perryville] Generals Jackson and Terrill and Colonel Webster were discussing the chances of being hit in an engagement. Their opinion was that men would never be frightened if they considered the doctrine of probabilities and how slight the chance was of any particular person being killed. Theory failed, as it has often done before; all three were killed in the next day's fight." EDITORS.

ENGAGEMENT OF STARKWEATHER'S BRIGADE ON THE EXTREME UNION LEFT. FROM A LITHOGRAPH.

General John C. Starkweather, in his official report, says that the brigade, consisting at the time of the 24th Illinois, 1st and 21st Wisconsin, and 79th Pennsylvania, "arrived on the field of battle at about 1:30 P. M., having marched twelve miles — about three miles thereof being through fields, woods, etc. Finding the troops already engaged well on the right, center, and left, and thinking the extreme left position most accessible, and, from appearances, one that should be held at all hazards, I placed my command at once in position facing the enemy's right." General McCook, in his report on the part taken by Starkweather's brigade, says that the 21st Wisconsin was stationed "in a corn-field, lying down, awaiting the approach of the enemy, and when he approached with his overwhelming force this new regiment poured into his ranks a most withering fire."

road in the direction of the firing. Within a mile I met Captain Fisher coming at full speed and bearing General McCook's message. Instead of sending Captain Fisher back to General McCook with my answer to his appeal for help, I advised him to continue on and bear to General Buell the astounding news, and at once sent orders to Schoepf to go to the interval between the two corps,—on the left of Sheridan,—and to Mitchell to close toward Sheridan's right and support him. Directing my course toward the left, I found Gooding's brigade of Mitchell's division still standing to the left of Doctor's Creek, and at once put it in motion to the right to join the main body of the division and be nearer Sheridan, who had just reported that he was hard pressed in front and that the enemy was driving our left wing. General Schoepf was now on the ground with his leading brigade (Walker's). This he was ordered to deploy, to replace Gooding. In the midst of these movements, another staff-officer, Captain W. T. Hoblitzell, came from the left corps for help, with the information that the troops, though fighting stubbornly, were falling back everywhere, and that if assistance was not speedily afforded they must soon be driven from the field.

Up to this moment the fighting with Sheridan had been growing in intensity, and judging from the sound that it must soon culminate, I detained Captain Hoblitzell to await the issue. It was soon perceived that the firing was diminishing, and as there were no signs of defeat on our side, I turned to Walker's brigade to send it over to the left wing, when I discovered it had not yet deployed, and, moreover, did not seem to be sufficiently familiar with the tactics to make the simplest movements with promptness and intelligence. Accordingly I sent my adjutant-general, Captain J. E. Stacy, to recall Gooding and order him to proceed under the guidance of Captain Hoblitzell to report to General McCook. Gooding took with him Pinney's Wisconsin battery. Within twenty minutes after receiving the order, Gooding made himself felt on the flank of the Confederates, who had thus far been steadily driving Rousseau's troops back toward the Russell House. Within a few minutes after this brigade had started, Sheridan, having repulsed his assailants, turned his guns and opened fire across the valley of Doctor's Creek on Rousseau's assailants, who, in their advance, had come to present their flank within easy range, and from his commanding position he delivered a fire so effective as to force back the enemy in this part of the field, to the great relief of the right of General McCook's line. Just after Sheridan's artillery opened, General Steedman came up with his brigade of Schoepf's division and kept on his course down Doctor's Creek. The enemy had now been so far driven from McCook's front that they were beyond the reach of Steedman's infantry; but, passing under the fire of Sheridan's guns, Steedman halted and opened to the left with Smith's battery of his brigade.

Viewed from the Confederate stand-point, the battle of Perryville appears to have consisted of an attempt to turn the left flank of the Union line, in which, for the distance of a thousand or twelve hundred yards, the assailants drove all before them. At this juncture, after a fierce fight, the attack came to a stand, having expended its force, and the left of the Confederate line was now itself driven and turned, and its line of retreat threatened. This last the Confederates supposed had been effected by a fresh corps arriving on the field from the direction of Lebanon. In abandoning the battle-ground the Confederates, although obliged to leave their wounded behind, moved without any sense of humiliation, for they had made a good fight, and appeared only to be withdrawing from the presence of a greatly superior force.

From the Union side, the battle takes this appearance: The center corps, arriving on the ground alone on the afternoon of the 7th, met with considerable opposition in establishing itself in position. This opposition continued with only a brief interval till about 11 o'clock on the 8th, when the flank corps began to arrive on the line abreast of the center. After the lapse of about an hour four brigades from the left wing started to the front in quest of water. This movement coincided with the advance of the Confederates in full force to turn the left of the Union army. Those brigades were accordingly met and overpowered and driven back to their places in line, and some of them beyond it. But they made a most obstinate resistance. In the center corps the detachments thrown out to watch the approaches to the position held by the leading division were driven in, and that division was attacked in strong force and with great determination. But the assailants were repulsed and driven from the field, and then the center corps contributed about one-third of its effective force to the relief of the left wing and saved it from destruction.

NOTES OF A STAFF-OFFICER AT PERRYVILLE. ⸸

BY J. MONTGOMERY WRIGHT, MAJOR, ASSISTANT ADJUTANT-GENERAL, U. S. V.

THE situation at Louisville in the latter part of September, 1862, was not unlike that at Washington after the first battle of Bull Run. The belief was entertained by many that Bragg would capture the city, and not a few had removed their money and valuables across the Ohio River, not over-assured that Bragg might not follow them to the lakes. Nelson had sworn that he would hold the city so long as a house remained standing or a soldier was alive, and he had issued an order that all the women, children, and non-combatants should leave the place and seek safety in Indiana. He had only raw troops and convalescent veterans, and few citizens believed that he could hold out against an attack. His tragic death occurred a few days later. ⚓

Buell's arrival changed the situation of affairs. The uncertain defensive suddenly gave way to an aggressive attitude, and speculation turned from whether Bragg would capture Louisville to whether Buell would capture Bragg.

The country through which Buell's army marched is almost destitute of water, but at Perryville a stream flowed between the contending armies, and access to that water was equally important to both armies. Buell accompanied the center corps (Gilbert's), and the advance reached this stream on the evening of October 7th. From that time until the stream was crossed there was constant fighting for access to it, and the only restriction on this fighting was that it should not bring on an engagement until the time for the general attack should arrive. An incident will illustrate the scarcity of water. I obtained a canteenful, and about dark on October 7th, after giving myself a good brushing and a couple of dry rubs without feeling much cleaner, my careless announcement that I was about to take a tin-dipper bath brought General Buell out of his tent with a rather mandatory suggestion that I pour the water back into my canteen and save it for an emergency. The emergency did not come to

me, but on the morning of October 9th that water helped to relieve the suffering of some wounded men who lay between the two armies.

At Buell's headquarters, on the 8th, preparations were going on for the intended attack, and the information was eagerly waited for that Crittenden had reached his position on the right. Fighting for water went on in our front, and it was understood that it extended all along the line, but no battle was expected that day. McCook was at Buell's headquarters in the morning, and received, I believe, some oral instructions regarding the contemplated attack. It was understood that care would be taken not to bring on a general engagement, and no importance was attached to the sounds that reached us of artillery-firing at the front of the center. Of course the young officers of the staff, of whom I was one, were not taken into conference by General Buell, but we all knew that the subject of attention that morning was the whereabouts of Crittenden's corps, and the placing it in position on the right for the general engagement that was to be brought on as soon as the army was in line. We all saw McCook going serenely away like a general carrying his orders with him.

In the afternoon we moved out for a position nearer Crittenden, as I inferred from the direction taken. A message came from the line on the left center to General Buell, and in a few moments Colonel James B. Fry, our chief of staff, called me up, and sent me with an order to General Gilbert, commanding the center corps, to send at once two brigades to reënforce General McCook, commanding the left corps. Thus I came to be a witness to some of the curious features of Perryville.

I did not know what was going on at the left, and Colonel Fry did not inform me. He told me what to say to General Gilbert, and to go fast, and taking one of the general's orderlies with me, I

⸸ Condensed from a paper in "The Southern Bivouac."
EDITORS.

⚓ The facts in relation to the killing of General William Nelson by General Jefferson C. Davis are recounted by General James B. Fry in his pamphlet, "Killed by a Brother Soldier," from which the following account is condensed: Davis, who had been on sick leave in Indiana, hearing that general officers were needed about Cincinnati and Louisville to assist in repelling the invasion of Kirby Smith and Bragg, volunteered his services, and was sent by General H. G. Wright at Cincinnati to report to Nelson at Louisville. The latter assigned to Davis the work of arming the citizens of Louisville. A day or two afterward Davis called at Nelson's headquarters in the Galt House. Nelson inquired, "Well, Davis, how are you getting along with your command?" Davis replied, "I don't know," and gave similar answers to two or three questions as to the number of regiments and companies he had organized. Nelson, who was angered by his seeming indifference, rose and said, "But you should know. I am disappointed in you, General Davis; I selected you for this duty because you were an officer of the regular army,

but I find I made a mistake." Davis replied, deliberately, "General Nelson, I am a regular soldier, and I demand the treatment due to me as a general officer." Dr. Irwin, Nelson's medical director, was called in by Davis to be a witness to the altercation. In his presence Nelson repeated the reprimand, and ordered Davis to report to General Wright at Cincinnati. Davis replied, "You have no authority to order me." Nelson turned to his adjutant-general and said, "Captain, if General Davis does not leave the city by 9 o'clock to-night, give instructions to the provost-marshal to see that he is put across the Ohio." Davis was highly incensed by the manner and bearing of Nelson. He withdrew, and that night reported to Wright in Cincinnati. When Buell reached Louisville on September 25th, Wright ordered Davis to return and report to Buell. He arrived at the Galt House on the morning of September 29th. Nelson, after breakfast, was standing in the hotel office, and was leaning against the counter when he was approached by Davis in company with Governor Oliver P. Morton, of Indiana. Davis accosted Nelson with the remark that Nelson had insulted him at the last meeting and that he must have satisfaction. Nelson told him

started on my errand. I found General Gilbert at the front, and as he had no staff-officer at hand at the moment, he asked me to go to General Schoepf, one of his division commanders, with the order. Schoepf promptly detached two brigades, and he told me I had better go on ahead and find out where they were to go. There was no sound to direct me, and as I tried to take an air line I passed outside the Union lines and was overtaken by a cavalry officer, who gave me the pleasing information that I was riding toward the enemy's pickets. Now up to this time I had heard no sound of battle; I had heard no artillery in front of me, and no heavy infantry-firing. I rode back, and passed behind the cavalry regiment which was deployed in the woods, and started in the direction indicated to me by the officer who called me back. At some distance I overtook an ambulance train, urged to its best speed, and then I knew that something serious was on hand. This was the first intimation I had that one of the fiercest struggles of the war was at that moment raging almost within my sight.

Directed by the officers in charge of the ambulances I made another detour, and pushing on at greater speed I suddenly turned into a road, and there before me, within a few hundred yards, the battle of Perryville burst into view, and the roar of the artillery and the continuous rattle of the musketry first broke upon my ear. It was the finest spectacle I ever saw. It was wholly unexpected, and it fixed me with astonishment. It was like tearing away a curtain from the front of a great picture, or the sudden bursting of a thunder-cloud when the sky in front seems serene and clear. I had seen an unlooked-for storm at sea, with hardly a moment's notice, hurl itself out of the clouds and lash the ocean into a foam of wild rage. But here there was not the warning of an instant. At one bound my horse carried me from stillness into the uproar of battle. One turn from a lonely bridle-path through the woods brought me face to face with the bloody struggle of thousands of men.

Waiting for news to carry back, I saw and heard some of the unhappy occurrences of Perryville. I saw young Forman, with the remnant of his company of the 15th Kentucky regiment, withdrawn to make way for the reënforcements, and as they silently passed me they seemed to stagger and reel like men who had been beating against a great storm. Forman had the colors in his hand, and he and several of his little group of men had their hands upon their chests and their lips apart as though they had difficulty in breathing. They filed into a field, and without thought of shot or shell they lay down on the ground apparently in a state of exhaustion. I joined a mounted group about a young officer, and heard Rumsey Wing, one of Jackson's volunteer aides, telling of that general's death and the scattering of the raw division he commanded. I remembered how I had gone up to Shiloh with Terrill's battery in a small steamer, and how, as the first streak of daylight came, Terrill, sitting on the deck near me, had recited a line about the beauty of the dawn, and had wondered how the day would close upon us all. I asked about Terrill, who now commanded a brigade, and was told that he had been carried to the rear to die. I thought of the accomplished, good, and brave Parsons,— whom I had seen knocked down seven times in a fight with a bigger man at West Point, without ever a thought of quitting so long as he could get up, and who lived to take orders in the church, and die at Memphis of the yellow fever, ministering to the last to the spiritual wants of his parishioners,— and I asked about Parsons's battery. His raw infantry support had broken, and stunned by the disaster that he thought had overtaken the whole army, he stood by his guns until every horse and every man had gone, and the enemy was almost touching him, and had been dragged away at last by one of his men who had come back to the rescue. His battery was a wreck and no one knew then where he was. And so the news came in of men I knew and men with friends about me.

to go away. Davis pressed his demand and Nelson said, "Go away, you —— puppy. I don't want anything to do with you." Davis, who had picked up a blank visiting card and had squeezed it into a ball as he was talking, responded to the insulting words by flipping the card into Nelson's face. Nelson then slapped Davis in the face and said to Governor Morton, "Did you come here, sir, to see me insulted?" "No," replied Morton, whereupon Nelson walked toward his room on the office floor. After the slap Davis asked for a pistol, and a friend borrowed one and handed it to Davis, who started toward Nelson's room and met him in the corridor near the foot of the staircase, apparently on his way to Buell's apartment upstairs. When a yard apart Davis fired. Nelson walked upstairs and fell in the hall near Buell's door. To the proprietor of the hotel Nelson said, "Send for a clergyman; I wish to be baptized. I have been basely murdered." General T. L. Crittenden, who was at the breakfast table, hurried to the corridor, and, taking Nelson's hand, said, "Nelson, are you seriously hurt?" Nelson replied. "Tom, I am murdered." When Surgeon Robert Murray arrived Nelson was lying on the floor of a room near where he had fallen, insensible. The small pistol-ball entered just over the heart.

In less than an hour Nelson was dead. General Fry was in the grand hall of the hotel at the time of the encounter. On hearing the sound of the pistol he made his way through the crowd that had surrounded Davis and arrested him in the name of General Buell. Fry took Davis's arm, and they went to Davis's room on an upper floor. When the door was closed Davis said he wanted to relate the facts while they were fresh in his mind, and among other details mentioned the flipping of the paper into Nelson's face. General Gilbert was appointed to succeed Nelson, and two days afterward the army marched for Perryville. Buell could not then spare officers for a court-martial, and suggested to Halleck that a trial by commission appointed from Washington should take place immediately. As no charges were preferred against Davis within the period fixed by military rules, he was released by order of General Wright.

On October 27th, 1862, General Davis was indicted by a grand jury for manslaughter, and was admitted to bail in 'the sum of five thousand dollars. The case was continued from time to time until May 24th, 1864, when "it was stricken from the docket, with leave to reinstate."— EDITORS.

CUMBERLAND GAP.

BY GEORGE W. MORGAN, BRIGADIER-GENERAL, U. S. V.

O N the 11th of April, 1862, with the Seventh Division of the Army of the Ohio under my command, I arrived at Cumberland Ford with orders from General Buell to take Cumberland Gap, fourteen miles to the southward, and occupy east Tennessee, if possible; if not, then to prevent the Confederates from advancing from that direction. [See map, p. 6.] This movement and Mitchel's advance into northern Alabama formed detached parts of the general plan of operations arranged between General Buell and General Halleck.

The division under my command consisted of four brigades, commanded by Brigadier-Generals Samuel P. Carter and James G. Spears, Colonel John F. De Courcy, 16th Ohio regiment, and Colonel John Coburn, 33d Indiana regiment. (Coburn's brigade was afterward commanded by Brigadier-General Absalom Baird.) During the preceding winter, Carter, who joined me here, had occupied a position near the ford and threatening the Gap.

The condition of Carter's brigade was deplorable. The winter's storms, converting the narrow roads into torrents, had practically cut him off from his base of supplies, and, in spite of all he could do, his troops were half-famished and were suffering from scurvy. Of the 900 men of the 49th Indiana regiment, only 200 were fit for duty.

Reconnoissances at once satisfied me that the fastness could not be taken by a direct attack, nor without immense loss. I determined to try to force the enemy to abandon his stronghold by strategy.

The position of the Confederate commander in east Tennessee, Major-General E. Kirby Smith, was a difficult one. A large majority of the people of east Tennessee were devoted to the Union, and the war there had become a vendetta. The Union men regarded the Confederates as criminals, and were in turn denounced by the Confederates as insurgents. Kirby Smith recommended the arrest and incarceration in Southern prisons of leading citizens, not in arms, as a means of converting the majority to the Southern cause. ↓

For a distance of eighteen miles north of Big Creek Gap, a pass southwest of Cumberland Gap, the Confederates had heavily blockaded the narrow and abrupt defiles along that route. The work of clearing the blockades was thoroughly done. But while Spears was thus engaged Kirby Smith advanced with a large force of infantry through a bridle-path called Woodson's Gap, to cut him off. The attempt might well have succeeded but for the

---

↓ On our side acts not less vigorous were resorted to. A few days after our occupation of Cumberland Gap, June 18th, General Spears, without authority, sent out in the night, captured and wanted to hang a number of Confederate citizens, whose offense was that they had arrested T. A. R. Nelson, while on his way to take his seat in the United States Congress, and had sent him to Richmond. Their lives were saved by my interposition, and they were sent as prisoners to Indianapolis.—G. W. M.

heroic act of Mrs. Edwards, a noble woman, whose heart was wholly in the Union cause, although she had a son in each of the opposing armies. Well mounted, she passed the mountains by another path, and, by incredible efforts, reached my headquarters in time to enable me to send couriers at full speed with orders for Spears to fall back toward Barboursville, until his scouts should report that Smith had recrossed the mountains.

In order to succeed in the task committed to me it was necessary to compel Kirby Smith, who was at this time concentrating his whole army in my immediate front, to divide his forces. To this end I urged General Buell to direct General O. M. Mitchel to threaten Chattanooga, and thus draw the main force of the Confederates in that direction.

About four miles south of Cumberland Gap is a narrow defile formed by an abrupt mountain on one side, and the Cumberland River on the other, through which passes the State Road to Cumberland Gap, and on the edge of the defile was an abandoned cabin, known as "The Moss House," situated at the junction of the State Road and a pathway leading to Lambdin's on the main road to Big Creek Gap. On the morning of May 22d I sent forward the brigade of De Courcy, with a battery, with orders to oc-

BRIGADIER-GENERAL GEORGE W. MORGAN.
FROM A PHOTOGRAPH.

cupy the defile, and, as a stratagem intended to puzzle Smith, to construct a fort at the junction of the pathway and road.

I threw forward a strong party of pioneers to widen the path leading to Lambdin's, so as to enable my artillery and train to move forward. The mountain was steep and rugged, and skill and toil were necessary to the accomplishment of the work. Twenty-two guns, 2 of them 30-pounder and 2 20-pounder Parrott's, had to be dragged over the Pine and Cumberland mountains, at times by means of block and tackle, at others by putting in as many horses as could be used, and again by men—200 at a single piece — hauling with drag-ropes. The pathway leading from the Moss House had been made the width of a wagon, but two teams could not pass each other there.

On the 6th and 7th of June Buell caused diversions to be made by an advance of part of Mitchel's command to the river opposite Chattanooga, and Smith, with two brigades, hastened to its rescue. The brigade of De Courcy had gone forward; Baird occupied the defile at the Moss House, and Carter was assigned to hold the defile till the last moment, and then

bring up the rear of the column.   On the 9th of June General Buell telegraphed me from Booneville, Mississippi:

"The force now in Tennessee is so small that no offensive operation against east Tennessee
can be attempted, and you must therefore depend mainly on your own resources."

And on the 10th:

"Considering your force and that opposed to you, it will probably not be safe for you to
undertake any offensive operations.   Other operations will soon have an influence on your
designs, and it is better for you to run no risk at present."

It was, however, next to impossible to change my plans at this moment,
and move back on a road such as described.   We therefore continued to toil
forward over the almost impassable mountains.

Thinking that the series of feints against Chattanooga that were being
made at my request indicated an advance in force, Kirby Smith now concentrated for defense at that point, after evacuating Cumberland Gap and
removing the stores.   This was just what I wanted.   On the evening of the
17th of June, General Carter L. Stevenson of the Confederate forces sent
Colonel J. E. Rains to cover the evacuation of Cumberland Gap,⚓ which had
been commenced on the afternoon of that day; Rains withdrew in the night
and marched toward Morristown.   Unaware of that fact, at 1 o'clock on the
morning of June 18th we advanced in two parallel columns, of two brigades
each, to attack the enemy; but while the troops were at breakfast I learned
from a Union man who had come along the valley road that Rains had withdrawn and that the gap was being evacuated.   The advance was at once
sounded, the Seventh Division pressed forward, and four hours after the
evacuation by the Confederates the flag of the Union floated from the loftiest
pinnacle of the Cumberland Range.   The enemy had carried away his
field-guns, but had left seven of his heavy cannon in position, dismantling
the rest.

At the request of Carter, his brigade was sent forward in pursuit of the
enemy as far as Tazewell, but the enemy had fallen back south-eastward to
the Clinch Mountains.   Cumberland Gap was ours without the loss of a
single life.   Secretary Stanton telegraphed the thanks of the President, and
General Buell published a general order in honor of this achievement of the
Seventh Division.

Lieutenant (now Colonel) William P. Craighill, of the Corps of Engineers,
a soldier of distinguished merit and ability, was sent by Secretary Stanton
to strengthen the fortifications at the Gap, and he soon rendered them
impregnable against attack.

My hope and ambition now was to advance against Knoxville and arouse
the Union men of east Tennessee to arms.   I urgently asked for two additional
brigades of infantry, a battery, and two regiments of cavalry, and, thus reënforced, pledged myself to sweep east Tennessee of the Confederates.   My
guns were increased from 22 to 28, and a battery of east Tennessee artillery
was raised, commanded by Lieutenant Daniel Webster, of Foster's 1st Wis-

⚓ The Confederate forces covering the mountain and river passes north of Knoxville at this time
were under General C. L. Stevenson, First Division, Department of East Tennessee.—EDITORS.

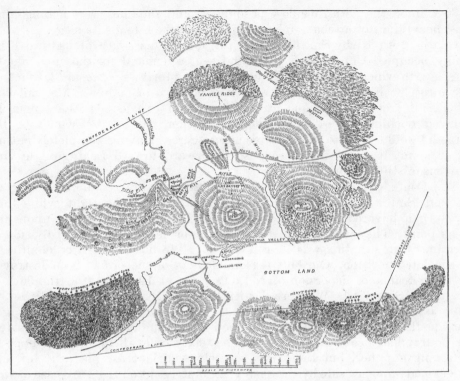

PLAN OF THE CONFEDERATE WORKS AT CUMBERLAND GAP, JUNE 14, 1862.
FROM A DRAWING BY CAPTAIN W. F. PATTERSON.

consin battery. Four thousand stand of arms, destined for east Tennessee, but left at Nicholasville and Crab Orchard during the winter on account of the impassable state of the roads, were now sent forward to Cumberland Gap with a large supply of ammunition, and magazines and an arsenal were got ready for them. A vast store-house, capable of containing supplies for 20,000 men for 6 months, was also built by Captain W. F. Patterson. The nerves and muscles of every man were stretched to the utmost tension, and the Gap became a vast workshop. Captain S. B. Brown, assistant quarter-master and acting commissary of subsistence, a man of fine intelligence and great energy, put on the road in small trains over four hundred wagons, and by this means the various munitions of war were dragged from the blue-grass region through the wilderness to Cumberland Gap.

Colonel De Courcy and Captain Joseph Edgar (afterward killed in action under De Courcy at Tazewell) were detailed as instructors of tactics for the officers of the new regiments of east Tennessee troops, who were brave, ambitious men and anxious to learn. Forage was collected with difficulty by armed parties.

About the middle of August Stevenson went into position in my immediate front. On the morning of the 17th I received intelligence, probable in its character, that Stevenson would attempt to carry the Gap that night. At

2:30 A. M. on the 18th reveille was sounded, and the lines were manned, but the enemy did not attack. It was evident that he intended a siege.

On the 16th Kirby Smith crossed the mountains south of us, into Kentucky, occupied Cumberland Ford, and sent a demand for the surrender of the Gap, to which I replied: "If you want this fortress, *come and take it*."

Smith's position was critical. He had no base of supplies; the valley in which his troops were concentrated was soon exhausted; the longer he delayed pushing toward the blue-grass region, the greater would be the force he would have to meet on reaching there. Having completely cut me off from my base, he therefore pushed forward toward Lexington, leaving Stevenson still in front of me.

The Confederates were invading Kentucky in three columns: Bragg on the left, Smith in the center, Humphrey Marshall on the right, while John H. Morgan hovered like an eagle on the wing, ready to pounce upon any weak point. They now regarded the capture or destruction of my division as certain. Our situation was indeed critical. We had been three months in this isolated position. Our only reasonable hope of succor had been destroyed by the defeat and dispersion of Nelson's force at Richmond on the 30th of August. [See p. 4.] We were destitute of forage. The horses of the 9th Ohio Battery literally starved to death, and their skeletons were dragged outside the lines. Our supplies of food were rapidly becoming exhausted. De Courcy had been sent to Manchester, sixty miles distant, in the hope of obtaining supplies, but there was scarcely sufficient for his own brigade. Enveloped on every side by the enemy, absolutely cut off from my base of supplies, and with starvation staring us in the face, I assembled a council of war, and, stating the situation in a few words, asked for the opinions of the members. Spears, Carter, and Baird (De Courcy being absent) gave it as their opinion, in which I concurred, that retreat was inevitable. In fact, I had already marked out in red chalk on the map of Kentucky my line of retreat, just as it was afterward carried out. Holding out the idea that we were seeking to obtain supplies by way of the barren wilderness through which I purposed to reach the Ohio, I had previously caused Lieutenant-Colonel George W. Gallup, of the 14th Kentucky, a soldier of rare merit, to send me at intervals men of his command familiar with the country through which each day's march would have to be made. The information given me by those brave mountaineers was discouraging. The want of water, the rugged character of the defiles, the almost absolute want of supplies, were stated by every one, but the opinion was expressed that a few wagons, laden with half a ton each, might get through. My topographical engineer, Captain Sidney S. Lyon, a man of fine intelligence and skill, had been the geologist of Kentucky, and was familiar with every foot of the State. Pointing out to him the region I had marked across the map I said, "Can I take my division by that route to the Ohio River?" "Yes, possibly, by abandoning the artillery and wagons." However, there was practically no choice. To retreat on Lexington would have placed my division, with its reduced numbers, between Stevenson in our immediate rear, Smith in our front, Bragg on our left, and Humphrey

VIEW OF CUMBERLAND GAP FROM THE SOUTH, SEPT. 14, 1862. FROM A LITHOGRAPH.

A, Battery No. 1; B, Battery No. 2; C, Fort McClellan; D, Battery No. 3; E, Fort Halleck; 1, 1st Tennessee Regt.;
2, 2d Tennessee; 5, 49th Indiana; 6, 14th Kentucky; 8, Headquarters Provost Guard; 9, 3d Kentucky;
10, 33d Indiana; 11, General Baird's Headquarters; 12, General Carter's Headquarters;
13, House used as General Morgan's Headquarters.

Marshall on our right, with the passes of the Wild Cat or of the Big Hill to overcome. I therefore determined to retreat by the red-chalk line, and at all hazards to take my artillery and wagons with me.↓

Stevenson, who knew as well as I did that I must attempt a retreat, was vigilant and energetic. From a knob on the east flank of Baptist Gap, with the aid of a good telescope, he could see all that was going on in Cumberland Gap. His line was nearly a semicircle, the opposite points of the diameter resting on the mountain's base to the right and left of the Gap. His policy was to starve us out.

During the night of the 16th of September, a long train of wagons was sent toward Manchester under the convoy of Colonel Coburn's 33d Indiana, two companies of Garrard's 3d Kentucky regiment, and the 9th Ohio Battery. This entire night and the following day, every preparation was made for the retreat. Mines had been constructed to blow up the magazines and arsenal and fire the vast store-houses constructed and under construction. Everything moved with the precision of a well-constructed and well-oiled piece of machinery, until late in the afternoon of the 17th, when a report came from our signal station on the crest of the mountain that a flag of truce from the enemy was approaching. This was in reality a party of observation. I therefore sent Lieutenant-Colonel Gallup, with a small escort and a few shrewd officers, to meet the enemy's flag outside our picket lines. The officers on

↓ The retreat was made across Kentucky by the way of Manchester, Booneville, and West Liberty to Greenup on the Ohio River. [See map, p. 6.] — EDITORS.

either side were laughing and joking together, when suddenly a glare of fire shone from the valley at the foot of the Gap and a volume of smoke curled over Poor Valley Ridge. One of the Confederates exclaimed, "Why, Colonel, what does that mean? It looks like an evacuation." With admirable coolness and address Gallup replied, "Not much. Morgan has cut away the timber obstructing the range of his guns, and they are now burning the brush on the mountain-side." This off-hand explanation was apparently satisfactory, but the fact was that some reckless person had fired a quartermaster's building,—a criminal blunder that might have cost us dear.

On the night of the 17th, Gallup, with a body of picked men, was left to guard the three roads leading from the camps of Stevenson, and to fire the vast quartermaster buildings, as well as the enormous store-house, nearly completed, on the crest of the mountain, and near the gap. The arsenal, containing four thousand stand of small-arms, and a large amount of shells and grenades, had been mined, and trains had been laid to the magazines.

At 8 o'clock that night my command wheeled into column with the coolness and precision of troops on review; and without hurry, without confusion, with no loud commands, but with resolute confidence, the little army, surrounded by peril on every side, set out on its march of more than two hundred miles through the wilderness. Toward morning Gallup fired the vast buildings and the trains leading to the mines. The shock of the explosion was felt fourteen miles away; the flaming buildings lighted up the sky as though the Gap and mountain crests were a volcano on fire, and from time to time till after dawn we heard the explosion of mines, shells, or grenades. At Manchester we halted for a day and a half, to concentrate the command, and to organize for the march before us. A day or two before a soldier had murdered a comrade in cold blood, under circumstances of great aggravation. I had ordered a court to try him. The sentence, of course, was death, and at the very moment of the execution the firing of our troops could be heard repelling the dash of Stevenson's cavalry on the wagon train of Spears.

I fully expected to be met by the enemy in force at Proctor, where the deep and abrupt banks would have rendered the passage of the Kentucky River perilous and difficult if disputed. We accordingly moved by two nearly parallel roads, and the two columns reached Proctor almost simultaneously. I at once threw a brigade, with a battery, across the river, and gave the command half a day's rest. The previous day and night the ever-vigilant John H. Morgan, with his daring followers, had been at Proctor, had burned the steam flouring-mill and its valuable contents, and had then withdrawn to Irvine, thirteen miles away.

In order to deceive the enemy as to my intended line of march, I directed Captain George M. Adams, Commissary of Subsistence, to send an officer toward Mount Sterling with written authority to purchase supplies. He set out, wearing his uniform, and attended only by two or three soldiers, knowing with certainty that he would be taken prisoner, and his papers seized. He was, of course, captured, since the Confederates were concentrating at Mount Sterling, believing my objective point to be Maysville.

Two roads run from Proctor to Hazel Green: the Ridge road, then destitute of water, and the North Fork road, which had water, but which the torrents of the previous rainy season had greatly damaged and in parts destroyed. De Courcy and Spears marched by the former, while Baird and Carter, with the wagon train, took the latter. It was largely through the energy of Baird that the wagon train was saved. After a day's halt at Hazel Green to rest and refresh the half-famished men and animals, the march was resumed toward West Liberty, supposed to be occupied by Humphrey Marshall. However, he was not there. During this march, John H. Morgan attacked the rear of De Courcy's brigade and scattered a lot of cattle intended for the use of the retreating column. Morgan then passed around us and commenced blockading the defiles between West Liberty and Grayson and destroying everything that could feed man or beast. He did his work gallantly and well. Frequent skirmishes took place, and it several times happened that while the one Morgan was clearing out the obstructions at the entrance to a defile, the other Morgan was blocking the exit from the same defile with enormous rocks and felled trees. In the work of clearing away these obstructions, one thousand men, wielding axes, saws, picks, spades, and block and tackle, under the general direction of Captain William F. Patterson, commanding his company of engineer-mechanics, and of Captain Sidney S. Lyon, labored with skill and courage. In one instance they were forced to cut a new road through the forest for a distance of four miles in order to turn a blockade of one mile. At Grayson, however, on the 1st of October, John Morgan abandoned the contest, to seek a new field for the exercise of his superior partisan skill and high courage; and on the 3d we reached the Ohio River at Greenup [see map, p. 6], without the loss of a gun or a wagon, and with the loss of but eighty men. Not only that, but, as General Bragg states in his report, we had detained General Kirby Smith, and thus prevented the junction of the Confederate armies in Kentucky, long enough to save Louisville.

THE OPPOSING FORCES AT CUMBERLAND GAP, JUNE 17TH—18TH, 1862.

UNION FORCES.—SEVENTH DIVISION, ARMY OF THE OHIO. Brig.-Gen. George W. Morgan.

Twenty-fourth Brigade, Brig.-Gen. Samuel P. Carter: 49th Ind., Lieut.-Col. James Keigwin; 3d Ky., Col. T. T. Garrard; 1st Tenn., Col. Robert K. Byrd; 2d Tenn., Col. James P. T. Carter. *Twenty-fifth Brigade*, Brig.-Gen. James G. Spears: 3d Tenn., Col. Leonidas C. Houk; 4th Tenn., Col. Robert Johnson; 5th Tenn., Col. James T. Shelley; 6th Tenn., Col. Joseph A. Cooper. *Twenty-sixth Brigade*, Col. John F. De Courcy: 22d Ky., Col. Daniel W. Lindsey; 16th Ohio, Lieut.-Col. George W. Bailey; 42d Ohio, Col. Lionel A. Sheldon. *Twenty-seventh Brigade*, Brig.-Gen. Absalom Baird: 33d Ind., Col. John Coburn; 14th Ky., Col. John C. Cochran; 19th Ky., Col. William J. Landram. *Artillery*, Capt. Jacob T. Foster: 7th Mich., Capt. Charles H. Lanphere; 9th Ohio, Lieut. Leonard P. Barrows; 1st Wis., Lieut. John D. Anderson; Siege Battery, Lieut. Daniel Webster. *Cavalry:* Ky. Battalion, Lieut.-Col. Reuben Munday. *Ky. Engineers,* Capt. William F. Patterson.

CONFEDERATE FORCES.—Their composition is not stated in the "Official Records." During the month of July Brig.-Gen. Carter L. Stevenson, First Division, Department of East Tennessee, was in position confronting Morgan at Cumberland Gap. The strength of this division was stated by General Kirby Smith on the 24th of the month to be 9000 effectives, "well organized and mobilized, and in good condition for active service." The organization on the 3d of July was as follows:

Second Brigade, Col. James E. Rains: 4th Tenn., Col. J. A. McMurry; 11th Tenn., Col. J. E. Rains; 42d Ga., Col. R. J. Henderson; 3d Ga. Battalion, Lieut.-Col. M. A. Stovall; 29th N. C., Col. R. B. Vance; Ga. Battery, Capt. J. G. Yeiser. *Third Brigade,* Brig.-Gen. S. M. Barton: 30th Ala., Col. C. M. Shelley; 31st Ala., Col. D. R. Hundley; 40th Ga., Col. A. Johnson; 52d Ga., Col. W. Boyd; 9th Ga. Battalion, Maj. J. T. Smith; Va. Battery, Capt. Joseph W. Anderson. *Fourth Brigade,* Col. A. W. Reynolds: 20th Ala., Col. I. W. Garrott; 36th Ga., Col. J. A. Glenn; 39th Ga., Col. J. T. McConnell; 43d Ga., Col. S. Harris; 39th N. C., Col. D. Coleman; 3d Md. Battery, Capt. H. B. Latrobe. *Fifth Brigade,* Col. T. H. Taylor: 23d Ala., Col. F. K. Beck; 46th Ala., Col. M. L. Woods; 3d Tenn., Col. J. C. Vaughn; 31st Tenn., Col. W. M. Bradford; 59th Tenn., Col. J. B. Cooke; Tenn. (Rhett) Battery, Capt. W. H. Burroughs.

THE BATTLE OF FREDERICKSBURG.

BY JAMES LONGSTREET, LIEUTENANT-GENERAL, C. S. A.

CONFEDERATE PICKET WITH BLANKET-CAPOTE
AND RAW-HIDE MOCCASINS.

IN the early fall of 1862, a distance of not more than thirty miles lay between the Army of the Potomac and the Army of Northern Virginia. A state of uncertainty had existed for several weeks succeeding the battle of Sharpsburg, but the movements that resulted in the battle of Fredericksburg began to take shape when on the 5th of November the order was issued removing General McClellan from command of the Federal forces. The order assigning General Burnside to command was received at General Lee's headquarters, then at Culpeper Court House, about twenty-four hours after it reached Warrenton, though not through official courtesy. General Lee, on receiving the news, said he regretted to part with McClellan, "for," he added, "we always understood each other so well. I fear they may continue to make these changes till they find some one whom I don't understand."

The Federal army was encamped around Warrenton, Virginia, and was soon divided into three grand divisions, whose commanders were Generals Sumner, Hooker, and Franklin.

Lee's army was on the opposite side of the Rappahannock River, divided into two corps, the First commanded by myself and the Second commanded by General T. J. (Stonewall) Jackson. At that time the Confederate army extended from Culpeper Court House (where the First Corps was stationed) on its right across the Blue Ridge down the Valley of Virginia to Winchester. There Jackson was encamped with the Second Corps, except one division which was stationed at Chester Gap on the Blue Ridge Mountains.

About the 18th or 19th of November, we received information through our scouts that Sumner, with his grand division of more than thirty thousand men, was moving toward Fredericksburg. Evidently he intended to surprise us and cross the Rappahannock before we could offer resistance. On receipt of the information, two of my divisions were ordered down to meet him. We made a forced march and arrived on the hills around Fredericksburg about 3 o'clock on the afternoon of the 21st. Sumner had already arrived, and his army was encamped on Stafford Heights, overlooking the town from the Federal side. Before I reached Fredericksburg, General Patrick, provost-marshal-general, crossed the river under a flag of truce and put the people in a state of great excitement by delivering the following letter:

"HEADQUARTERS OF THE ARMY OF THE POTOMAC, November 21st, 1862.

"TO THE MAYOR AND COMMON COUNCIL OF FREDERICKSBURG. GENTLEMEN: Under cover of the houses of your city, shots have been fired upon the troops of my command. Your mills and manufactories are furnishing provisions and the material for clothing for armed bodies in rebellion against the Government of the United States. Your railroads and other means of transportation are removing supplies to the depots of such troops. This condition of things must terminate, and by direction of General Burnside I accordingly demand the surrender of your city into my hands, as the representative of the Government of the United States, at or before 5 o'clock this afternoon. Failing in an affirmative reply to this demand by the hour indicated, sixteen hours will be permitted to elapse for the removal from the city of women and children, the sick and wounded and aged, etc., which period having expired I shall proceed to shell the town. Upon obtaining possession of the city every necessary means will be taken to preserve order and secure the protective operation of the laws and policy of the United States Government. I am, very respectfully, your obedient servant,

" E. V. SUMNER,
" Brevet Major-General, U. S. Army, Commanding Right Grand Division."

While the people were in a state of excitement over the receipt of this demand for the surrender of their town, my troops appeared upon the heights opposite those occupied by the Federals. The alarmed non-combatants heard of my arrival and immediately sent to me the demand of the Federal general. I stated to the town authorities that I did not care to occupy the place for military purposes and that there was no reason why it should be shelled by the Federal army. We were there to protect ourselves against the advance of the enemy, and could not allow the town to be occupied by the Federals. The mayor sent to General Sumner a satisfactory statement of the situation and was notified that the threatened shelling would not take place, since the Confederates did not purpose to make the town a base of military operations.

Before my troops reached the little city, and before the people of Fredericksburg knew that any part of the Confederate army was near, there was great excitement over the demand for surrender. No people were in the place except aged and infirm men, and women and children. That they should become alarmed when the surrender of the town was demanded by the Federals was quite natural, and a number proceeded with great haste to board a train then ready to leave. As the train drew out, Sumner's batteries on Stafford Heights opened fire on it, adding to the general terror, but fortunately doing no serious damage. The spectacle was nothing, however, to what we witnessed a short time after. About the 26th or 27th it became evident that Fredericksburg would be the scene of a battle, and we advised the people who were still in the town to prepare to leave, as they would soon be in danger if they remained. The evacuation of the place by the distressed women and helpless men was a painful sight. Many were almost destitute and had nowhere to go, but, yielding to the cruel necessities of war, they collected their portable effects and turned their backs on the town. Many were forced to seek shelter in the woods and brave the icy November nights to escape the approaching assault from the Federal army.

Very soon after I reached Fredericksburg the remainder of my corps arrived from Culpeper Court House, and as soon as it was known that all the Army of the Potomac was in motion for the prospective scene of battle Jackson was drawn down from the Blue Ridge. In a very short time the Army of Northern Virginia was face to face with the Army of the Potomac.

When Jackson arrived he objected to the position, not that he feared the result of the battle, but because he thought that behind the North Anna was a point from which the most fruitful results would follow. He held that we would win a victory at Fredericksburg, but it would be a fruitless one to us, whereas at North Anna, when we drove the Federals back, we could give pursuit to advantage, which we could not do at Fredericksburg. General Lee did not entertain the proposition, however, and we continued our preparations to meet the enemy at the latter place. ☆

At a point just above the town, a range of hills begins, extending from the river edge out a short distance and bearing around the valley somewhat in the form of a crescent. On the opposite side are the noted Stafford Heights, then occupied by the Federals. At the foot of these hills flows the Rappahannock River. On the Confederate side nestled Fredericksburg, and around it stretched the fertile bottoms from which fine crops had been gathered and upon which the Federal troops were to mass and give battle to the Confederates. On the Confederate side nearest the river was Taylor's Hill, and south of it the now famous Marye's Hill; next, Telegraph Hill, the highest of the elevations on the Confederate side (later known as Lee's Hill, because during the battle General Lee was there most of the time), where I had my headquarters in the field; next was a declination through which Deep Run Creek passed on its way to the Rappahannock River; and next was the gentle elevation at Hamilton's Crossing, not dignified with a

BRIGADIER-GENERAL MAXCY GREGG, C. S. A.,
KILLED AT FREDERICKSBURG.
FROM A PHOTOGRAPH.

name, upon which Stonewall Jackson massed thirty thousand men. It was upon these hills that the Confederates made their preparations to receive Burnside whenever he might choose to cross the Rappahannock. The Confederates were stationed as follows: On Taylor's Hill next the river and forming my left, R. H. Anderson's division; on Marye's Hill, Ransom's and McLaws's divisions; on Telegraph Hill, Pickett's division; to the right and about Deep Run Creek, Hood's division, the latter stretching across Deep Run Bottom.

☆ That General Lee was not quite satisfied with the place of battle is shown by a dispatch to the Richmond authorities on the second day after the battle, when it was uncertain what Burnside's next move would be. In that dispatch he says: "Should the enemy cross at Port Royal in force, before I can get this army in position to meet him, I think it more advantageous to retire to the Annas and give battle, than on the banks of the Rappahannock. My design was to have done so in the first instance. My purpose was changed not from any advantage in this position, but from an unwillingness to open more of our country to depredation than possible, and also with a view of collecting such forage and provisions as could be obtained in the Rappahannock Valley. With the numerous army opposed to me, and the bridges and transportation at its command, the crossing of the Rappahannock, where it is narrow and winding as in the vicinity of Fredericksburg, can be made at almost any point without molestation. It will, therefore, be more advantageous to us to draw him farther away from his base of operations."
EDITORS.

On the hill occupied by Jackson's corps were the divisions of A. P. Hill, Early, and Taliaferro, that of D. H. Hill being in reserve on the extreme right. To the Washington Artillery, on Marye's Hill, was assigned the service of advising the army at the earliest possible moment of the Federal advance. General Barksdale, with his Mississippi brigade, was on picket duty in front of Fredericksburg on the night of the advance.

The hills occupied by the Confederate forces, although over-crowned by the heights of Stafford, were so distant as to be outside the range of effective fire by the Federal guns, and, with the lower receding grounds between them, formed a defensive series that may be likened to natural bastions. Taylor's Hill, on our left, was unassailable; Marye's Hill was more advanced toward the town, was of a gradual ascent and of less height than the others, and we considered it the point most assailable, and guarded it accordingly. The events that followed proved the correctness of our opinion on that point. Lee's Hill, near our center, with its rugged sides retired from Marye's and rising higher than its companions, was comparatively safe.

This was the situation of the 65,000 Confederates massed around Fredericksburg, and they had twenty-odd days in which to prepare for the approaching battle.

The Federals on Stafford Heights carefully matured their plans of advance and attack. General Hunt, chief of artillery, skillfully posted 147 guns to cover the bottoms upon which the infantry was to form for the attack, and at the same time play upon the Confederate batteries as circumstances would allow. Franklin and Hooker had joined Sumner, and Stafford Heights held the Federal army, 116,000 strong, watching the plain where the bloody conflict was soon to be. In the meantime the Federals had been seen along the banks of the river, looking for the most available points for crossing. President Lincoln had been down with General Halleck, and it had been suggested by the latter to cross at Hoop-pole Ferry, about 28 or 30 miles below Fredericksburg. We discovered the movement, however, and prepared to meet it, and Burnside abandoned the idea and turned his attention to Fredericksburg, under the impression that many of our troops were down at Hoop-pole, too far away to return in time for this battle.⧧

The soldiers of both armies were in good fighting condition, and there was every indication that we would have a desperate battle. We were confident that Burnside could not dislodge us, and patiently awaited the attack.

On the morning of the 11th of December, 1862, an hour or so before daylight, the slumbering Confederates were awakened by a solitary cannon thundering on the heights of Marye's Hill. Again it boomed, and instantly the aroused Confederates recognized the signal of the Washington Artillery and knew that the Federal troops were preparing to cross the Rappahannock to give us the expected battle. The Federals came down to the river's edge and began the construction of their bridges, when Barksdale opened fire with such effect that they were forced to retire. Again and again they made an

---

⧧ It is more than probable that Burnside accepted the proposition to move by Hoop-pole Ferry for the purpose of drawing some of our troops from the points he had really selected for his crossing.—J. L.

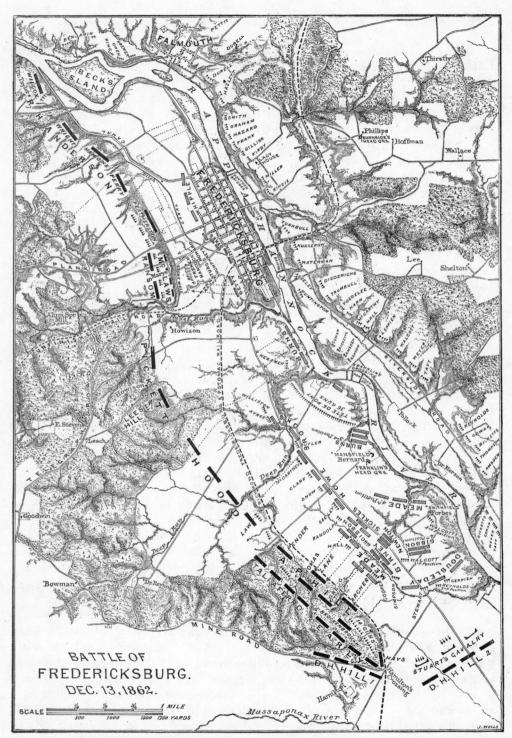

BATTLE OF
FREDERICKSBURG.
DEC. 13, 1862.

SCALE
500   1000   1500 1750 YARDS
¼   ½   ¾   1 MILE

J. WELLS

NOTE.—The batteries which had position on the outskirts of the town in rear of Sumner's attack were Waterman's, Kusserow's, Kirby's, Hazard's, Frank's, Arnold's, Phillips's, and Dickenson's. In placing the Union artillery, we have followed an official map made under direction of General Henry J. Hunt, chief of artillery.—EDITORS.

74

effort to cross, but each time they were met and repulsed by the well-directed bullets of the Mississippians. This contest lasted until 1 o'clock, when the Federals, with angry desperation, turned their whole available force of artillery on the little city, and sent down from the heights a perfect storm of shot and shell, crushing the houses with a cyclone of fiery metal. From our position on the heights we saw the batteries hurling an avalanche upon the town whose only offense was that near its edge in a snug retreat nestled three thousand Confederate hornets that were stinging the Army of the Potomac into a frenzy. It was terrific, the pandemonium which that little squad of Confederates had provoked. The town caught fire in several places, shells crashed and burst, and solid shot rained like hail. In the midst of the successive crashes could be heard the shouts and yells of those engaged in the struggle, while the smoke rose from the burning city and the flames leaped about, making a scene which can never be effaced from the memory of those who saw it. But, in the midst of all this fury, the little brigade of Mississippians clung to their work. At last, when I had everything in readiness, I sent a peremptory order to Barksdale to withdraw, which he did, fighting as he retired before the Federals, who had by that time succeeded in landing a number of their troops. The Federals then constructed their pontoons without molestation, and during the night and the following day the grand division of Sumner passed over into Fredericksburg.

About a mile and a half below the town, where the Deep Run empties into the Rappahannock, General Franklin had been allowed without serious opposition to throw two pontoon-bridges on the 11th, and his grand division passed over and massed on the level bottoms opposite Hamilton's Crossing, thus placing himself in front of Stonewall Jackson's corps. The 11th and 12th were thus spent by the Federals in crossing the river and preparing for battle.

Opposite Fredericksburg, the formation along the river-bank was such that the Federals were concealed in their approaches, and, availing themselves of this advantage, they succeeded in crossing and concealing the grand division of Sumner and, later, a part of Hooker's grand division in the city of Fredericksburg, and so disposing of Franklin in the open plain below as to give out the impression that the great force was with the latter and about to oppose Jackson.

Before daylight on the morning of the eventful 13th I rode to the right of my line held by Hood's division. General Hood was at his post in plain hearing of the Federals south of Deep Run, who were marching their troops into position for the attack. The morning was cold and misty, and everything was obscured from view, but so distinctly did the mist bear to us the sounds of the moving Federals that Hood thought the advance was against him. He was relieved, however, when I assured him that the enemy, to reach him, would have to put himself in a pocket and be subjected to attack from Jackson on one side, Pickett and McLaws on the other, and Hood's own men in front. The position of Franklin's men on the 12th, with the configuration of the ground, had left no doubt in my mind as to Franklin's intentions. I explained all this to Hood, assuring him that the attack would be

FRONT OF THE MARYE MANSION.   FROM A
WAR-TIME PHOTOGRAPH.

on Jackson. At the same time I ordered Hood, in case Jackson's line should be broken, to wheel around to his right and strike in on the attacking bodies, telling him that Pickett, with his division, would be ordered to join in the flank movement. These orders were given to both division generals, and at the same time they were advised that I would be attacked near my left center, and that I must be at that point to meet my part of the battle. They were also advised that my position was so well defended I could have no other need of their troops. I then returned to Lee's Hill, reaching there soon after sunrise.

Thus we stood at the eve of the great battle. Along the Stafford Heights 147 guns were turned upon us, and on the level plain below, in the town, and hidden on the opposite bank ready to cross, were assembled nearly 100,000 men, eager to begin the combat. Secure on our hills, we grimly awaited the onslaught. The valley, the mountain-tops, everything was enveloped in the thickest fog, and the preparations for the fight were made as if under cover of night. The mist brought to us the sounds of the preparation for battle, but we were blind to the movements of the Federals. Suddenly, at 10 o'clock, as if the elements were taking a hand in the drama about to be enacted, the warmth of the sun brushed the mist away and revealed the mighty panorama in the valley below.

Franklin's 40,000 men, reënforced by two divisions of Hooker's grand division, were in front of Jackson's 30,000. The flags of the Federals fluttered gayly, the polished arms shone brightly in the sunlight, and the beautiful uniforms of the buoyant troops gave to the scene the air of a holiday occasion rather than the spectacle of a great army about to be thrown into the tumult of battle. From my place on Lee's Hill I could see almost every soldier Franklin had, and a splendid array it was. But off in the distance was Jackson's ragged infantry, and beyond was Stuart's battered cavalry, with their soiled hats and yellow butternut suits, a striking contrast to the handsomely equipped troops of the Federals.

About the city, here and there, a few soldiers could be seen, but there was no indication of the heavy masses that were concealed by the houses. Those of Franklin's men who were in front of Jackson stretched well up toward Lee's Hill, and were almost within reach of our best guns, and at the other end they stretched out to the east until they came well under the fire of Stuart's

THE SUNKEN ROAD UNDER MARYE'S HILL. FROM A PHOTOGRAPH TAKEN IN 1884.

In the background is seen the continuation of Hanover street, which on the left ascends the hill to the Marye Mansion. The little square field lies in the fork made by the former road and the Telegraph road (see map, p. 74). Nearly all that remained in 1884 of the famous stone-wall is seen in the right of the picture. The horses are in the road, which is a continuation of the street south of Hanover street, and on which is the brick house mentioned in General Couch's article. The house in which General Cobb died would be the next object in the right of the picture if the foreground were extended. And beyond that house, following the Telegraph road south, there was, at the time of the battle, a long stretch of stone-wall (see map, p. 74), little if any of which was to be seen in 1884, the stone having been used for the gate-house of the National Cemetery.

In his official report General Kershaw, who succeeded General Cobb, thus describes the situation during the battle in that part of the road seen in the picture: "The road is about 25 feet wide, and is faced by a stone-wall about 4 feet high on the city side. The road having been cut out of the side of the hill, in many places this last wall is not visible above the surface of the ground. The ground falls off rapidly to almost a level surface, which extends about 150 yards, then, with another abrupt fall of a few feet, to another plain which extends some 200 yards, and then falls off abruptly into a wide ravine, which extends along the whole front of the city and discharges into Hazel Run. I found, on my arrival, that Cobb's brigade, Colonel McMillan commanding occupied our entire front, and my troops could only get into position by doubling on them. This was accordingly done, and the formation along most of the line during the engagement was consequently four deep. As

an evidence of the coolness of the command, I may mention here that, notwithstanding that their fire was the most rapid and continuous I have ever witnessed, not a man was injured by the fire of his comrades. . . . In the meantime line after line of the enemy deployed in the ravine, and advanced to the attack at intervals of not more than fifteen minutes until about 4:30 o'clock, when there was a lull of about a half hour, during which a mass of artillery was placed in position in front of the town and opened upon our position. At this time I brought up Colonel De Saussure's regiment. Our batteries on the hill were silent, having exhausted their ammunition, and the Washington Artillery were relieved by a part of Colonel Alexander's battalion. Under cover of this artillery fire, the most formidable column of attack was formed, which, about 5 o'clock, emerged from the ravine and, no longer impeded by our artillery, impetuously assailed our whole front. From this time until after 6 o'clock the attack was continuous, and the fire on both sides terrific. Some few, chiefly officers, got within 30 yards of our lines, but in every instance their columns were shattered by the time they got within 100 paces. The firing gradually subsided, and by 7 o'clock our pickets were established within thirty yards of those of the enemy.

"Our chief loss after getting into position in the road was from the fire of sharp-shooters, who occupied some buildings on my left flank in the early part of the engagement, and were only silenced by Captain [W.] Wallace, of the 2d Regiment, directing the continuous fire of one company upon the buildings. General Cobb, I learn, was killed by a shot from that quarter. The regiments on the hill suffered most, as they were less perfectly covered."—EDITORS.

horse artillery under Major John Pelham, a brave and gallant officer, almost a boy in years. As the mist rose, the Confederates saw the movement against their right near Hamilton's Crossing. Major Pelham opened fire upon Franklin's command and gave him lively work, which was kept up until Jackson ordered Pelham to retire. Franklin then advanced rapidly to the hill where Jackson's troops had been stationed, feeling the woods with shot as he progressed. Silently Jackson awaited the approach of the Federals until they were within good range, and then he opened a terrific fire which threw the Federals into some confusion. The enemy again massed and advanced, pressing through a gap between Archer and Lane. This broke Jackson's line and threatened very serious trouble. The Federals who had wedged themselves in through that gap came upon Gregg's brigade, and then the severe encounter ensued in which the latter general was mortally wounded. Archer and Lane very soon received reënforcements and, rallying, joined in the counter-attack and recovered their lost ground. The concentration of Taliaferro's and Early's divisions against this attack was too much for it, and the counter-attack drove the Federals back to the railroad and beyond the reach of our guns on the left. Some of our troops following up this repulse got

too far out, and were in turn much discomfited when left to the enemy's superior numbers, and were obliged to retire in poor condition. A Federal brigade advancing under cover of Deep Run was discovered at this time and attacked by regiments of Pender's and Law's brigades, the former of A. P. Hill's and the latter of Hood's division; and, Jackson's second line advancing, the Federals were forced to retire. This series of demonstrations and attacks, the partial success and final discomfiture of the Federals, constitute the hostile movements between the Confederate right and the Federal left.

HOUSE BY THE STONE-WALL, IN WHICH GENERAL
COBB DIED. FROM A WAR-TIME PHOTOGRAPH.

I have described, in the opening of this article, the situation of the Confederate left. In front of Marye's Hill is a plateau, and immediately at the base of the hill there is a sunken road known as the Telegraph road. On the side of the road next to the town was a stone-wall, shoulder-high, against which the earth was banked, forming an almost unapproachable defense. It was impossible for the troops occupying it to expose more than a small portion of their bodies. Behind this stone-wall I had placed about twenty-five hundred men, being all of General T. R. R. Cobb's brigade, and a portion of the brigade of General Kershaw, both of McLaws's division. It must now be understood that the Federals, to reach what appeared to be my weakest point, would have to pass directly over this wall held by Cobb's infantry.

An idea of how well Marye's Hill was protected may be obtained from the following incident: General E. P. Alexander, my engineer and superintendent of artillery, had been placing the guns, and in going over the field with him before the battle, I noticed an idle cannon. I suggested that he place it so as to aid in covering the plain in front of Marye's Hill. He answered: "General, we cover that ground now so well that we will comb it as with a fine-tooth comb. A chicken could not live on that field when we open on it."

A little before noon I sent orders to all my batteries to open fire through the streets or at any points where the troops were seen about the city, as a diversion in favor of Jackson. This fire began at once to develop the work in hand for myself. The Federal troops swarmed out of the city like bees out of a hive, coming in double-quick march and filling the edge of the field in front of Cobb. This was just where we had expected attack, and I was prepared to meet it. As the troops massed before us, they were much annoyed by the fire of our batteries. The field was literally packed with Federals from the vast number of troops that had been massed in the town. From the moment of their appearance began the most fearful carnage. With our artillery from the front, right, and left tearing through their ranks, the Federals pressed forward with almost invincible determination, maintaining their steady step and closing up their broken ranks. Thus resolutely they marched upon the stone fence behind which quietly waited the Confederate brigade of General Cobb. As they came within reach of this brigade, a storm of lead was poured into their advancing ranks and they were swept from the field like chaff before the wind. A cloud of smoke shut out the scene for a moment, and, rising, revealed the shattered fragments recoiling from their gallant but hopeless charge. The artillery still plowed through their retreating ranks and searched the places of concealment into which the troops had plunged. A vast number went pell-mell into an old railroad cut to escape fire from the right and front. A battery on Lee's Hill saw this and turned its fire into the entire length of the cut, and the shells began to pour down upon the Federals with the most frightful destruction. They found their position of refuge more uncomfortable than the field of the assault.

Thus the right grand division of the Army of the Potomac found itself repulsed and shattered on its first attempt to drive us from Marye's Hill. Hardly was this attack off the field before we saw the determined Federals again filing out of Fredericksburg and preparing for another charge. The Confederates under Cobb reserved their fire and quietly awaited the approach of the enemy. The Federals came nearer than before, but were forced to retire before the well-directed guns of Cobb's brigade and the fire of the artillery on the heights. By that time the field in front of Cobb was thickly strewn with the dead and dying Federals, but again they formed with desperate courage and renewed the attack and again were driven off. At each attack the slaughter was so great that by the time the third attack was

COBB'S AND KERSHAW'S TROOPS BEHIND THE STONE-WALL.

repulsed, the ground was so thickly strewn with dead that the bodies seriously impeded the approach of the Federals.   General Lee, who was with me on Lee's Hill, became uneasy when he saw the attacks so promptly renewed and pushed forward with such persistence, and feared the Federals might break through our line.   After the third charge he said to me: "General, they are massing very heavily and will break your line, I am afraid."   "General," I replied, "if you put every man now on the other side of the Potomac on that field to approach me over the same line, and give me plenty of ammunition, I will kill them all before they reach my line.   Look to your right; you are in some danger there, but not on my line."

I think the fourth time the Federals charged, a gallant fellow came within one hundred feet of Cobb's position before he fell.   Close behind him came some few scattering ones, but they were either killed or they fled from certain death. ♭ This charge was the only effort that looked like actual danger to Cobb, and after it was repulsed I felt no apprehension, assuring myself that there were enough of the dead Federals on the field to give me half the battle.   The anxiety shown by General Lee, however, induced me to bring up two or three brigades, to be on hand, and General Kershaw, with the remainder

BRIGADIER-GENERAL THOMAS R. R. COBB.
FROM A PHOTOGRAPH.

Before the war, General Cobb was a lawyer.   He was born in Georgia in 1820.   In 1851 he published a "Digest of the Laws of Georgia."

of his brigade, was ordered down to the stone-wall, rather, however, to carry ammunition than as a reënforcement for Cobb.   Kershaw dashed down the declivity and arrived just in time to succeed Cobb, who, at this juncture, fell from a wound in the thigh and died in a few minutes from loss of blood. [See also p. 94.]

A fifth time the Federals formed and charged and were repulsed.   A sixth time they charged and were driven back, when night came to end the dreadful carnage, and the Federals withdrew, leaving the battle-field literally heaped with the bodies of their dead.   Before the well-directed fire of Cobb's brigade, the Federals had fallen like the steady dripping of rain from the eaves of a house.   Our musketry alone killed and wounded at least 5000; and these,

♭ In his official report General Lafayette McLaws says: "The body of one man, believed to be an officer, was found within about thirty yards of the stone-wall, and other single bodies were scattered at increased distances until the main mass of the dead lay thickly strewn over the ground at something over one hundred yards off, and extending to the ravine, commencing at the point where our men would allow the enemy's column to approach before opening fire, and beyond which no organized body of men was able to pass."—EDITORS.

with the slaughter by the artillery, left over 7000 killed and wounded before the foot of Marye's Hill.   The dead were piled sometimes three deep, and when morning broke, the spectacle that we saw upon the battle-field was one of the most distressing I ever witnessed.   The charges had been desperate and bloody, but utterly hopeless.   I thought, as I saw the Federals come again and again to their death, that they deserved success if courage and daring could entitle soldiers to victory.

During the night a Federal strayed beyond his lines and was taken up by some of my troops.   On searching him, we found on his person a memorandum of General Burnside's arrangements, and an order for the renewal of the battle the next day.   This information was sent to General Lee, and immediately orders were given for a line of rifle-pits on the top of Marye's Hill for Ransom, who had been held somewhat in reserve, and for other guns to be placed on Taylor's Hill.

We were on our lines before daylight, anxious to receive General Burnside again.   As the gray of the morning came without the battle, we became more anxious; yet, as the Federal forces retained position during the 14th and 15th, we were not without hope.   There was some little skirmishing, but it did not amount to anything.   But when the full light of the next morning revealed an abandoned field, General Lee turned to me, referring in his mind to the dispatch I had captured and which he had just re-read, and said: "General, I am losing confidence in your friend General Burnside."   We then put it down as a *ruse de guerre*.   Afterward, however, we learned that the order had been made in good faith but had been changed in consequence of the demoralized condition of the grand divisions in front of Marye's Hill.   During the night of the 15th the Federal troops withdrew, and on the 16th our lines were reëstablished along the river. ☆

I have heard that, referring to the attack at Marye's Hill while it was in progress, General Hooker said: "There has been enough blood shed to satisfy any reasonable man, and it is time to quit."   I think myself it was fortunate for Burnside that he had no greater success, for the meeting with such discomfiture gave him an opportunity to get back safe.   If he had made any progress, his loss would probably have been greater.

Such was the battle of Fredericksburg as I saw it.   It has been asked why we did not follow up the victory.   The answer is plain.   It goes without saying that the battle of the First Corps, concluded after nightfall, could not have been changed into offensive operations.   Our line was about three miles long, extending through woodland over hill and dale.   An attempt at concentration to throw the troops against the walls of the city at that hour of the night would have been little better than madness.   The Confederate field was

☆ General Lee explained officially, as follows, why he expected the attack would be resumed:

"The attack on the 13th had been so easily repulsed, and by so small a part of our army, that it was not supposed the enemy would limit his efforts to an attempt which, in view of the magnitude of his preparations and the extent of his force, seemed to be comparatively insignificant.

"Believing, therefore, that he would attack us, it was not deemed expedient to lose the advantages of our position and expose the troops to the fire of his inaccessible batteries beyond the river by advancing against him; but we were necessarily ignorant of the extent to which he had suffered, and only became aware of it when, on the morning of the 16th, it was discovered that he had availed himself of the darkness of night, and the prevalence of a violent storm of wind and rain, to recross the river.   The town was immediately reoccupied and our position on the river-bank resumed."   EDITORS.

CONFEDERATE WORKS ON WILLIS'S HILL, NOW THE SITE OF THE NATIONAL CEMETERY.
FROM A WAR-TIME PHOTOGRAPH.

arranged for defensive battle. Its abrupt termination could not have been anticipated, nor could any skill have marshaled our troops for offensive operations in time to meet the emergency. My line was long and over broken country,—so much so that the troops could not be promptly handled in offensive operations. Jackson's corps was in mass, and could he have anticipated the result of my battle, he would have been justified in pressing Franklin to the river when the battle of the latter was lost. Otherwise, pursuit would have been as unwise as the attack he had just driven off. The Federal batteries on Stafford Heights were effectively posted to protect their troops against our advance, and Franklin would have been in good defensive position against attack on the next day. It is well known that after driving off attacking forces, if immediate pursuit can be made so that the victors can go along with the retreating forces pell-mell, it is well enough to do so; but the attack should be immediate. To follow a success by counter-attack against the enemy in position is problematical. In the case of the armies at Fredericksburg it would have been, to say the least, very hazardous to give counter-attack, the Federal position being about as strong as ours from which we had driven them back. Attempts to break up an army by following on its line of retreat are hazardous and rarely successful, while movements against the flanks and rear increase the demoralization and offer better opportunities for great results. The condition of a retreating army may be illustrated by a little incident witnessed thirty years ago on the western plains of Texas. A soldier of my regiment essayed to capture a rattlesnake. Being pursued, the reptile took refuge in a prairie-dog's hole, turning his head as he entered it, to defend the sally-port. The soldier, coming up in time, seized the tail as it was in the act of passing under cover, and at the same instant the serpent seized the index finger of the soldier's hand. The result was the soldier lost the use of his finger. The wise serpent made a successful retreat. The rear of a retreating army is always its best guarded point.

During the attack upon General Jackson, and immediately after his line was broken, General Pickett rode up to General Hood and suggested that

WELFORD'S MILL ON HAZEL RUN AND THE TELEGRAPH ROAD.
FROM A WAR-TIME PHOTOGRAPH.

The southern slope of Willis's Hill is seen in the background.

the moment was at hand for the movement anticipated by my orders, and requested that it be executed. Hood did not agree, so the opportunity was allowed to pass. Had Hood sprung to the occasion we would have enveloped Franklin's command, and might possibly have marched it into the Confederate camp. Hood commanded splendid troops, quite fresh and eager for occasion to give renewed assurances of their mettle.

It has been reported that the troops attacking Marye's Hill were intoxicated, having been plied with whisky to nerve them to the desperate attack. That can hardly be true. I know nothing of the facts, but no sensible commander will allow his troops strong drink upon going into battle. After a battle is over, the soldier's gill is usually allowed if it is at hand. No troops could have displayed greater courage and resolution than was shown by those brought against Marye's Hill. But they miscalculated the wonderful strength of the line behind the stone fence. The position held by Cobb surpassed courage and resolution, and was occupied by those who knew well how to hold a comfortable defense.

After the retreat, General Lee went to Richmond to suggest other operations, but was assured that the war was virtually over, and that we need not harass our troops by marches and other hardships. Gold had advanced in New York to two hundred, and we were assured by those at the Confederate capital that in thirty or forty days we would be recognized and peace proclaimed. General Lee did not share in this belief.

I have been asked if Burnside could have been victorious at Fredericksburg. Such a thing was hardly possible. Perhaps no general could have accomplished more than Burnside did, and it was possible for him to have suffered greater loss. The battle of Fredericksburg was a great and unprofitable sacrifice of human life made, through the pressure from the rear, upon a general who should have known better and who doubtless acted against his judgment. [See p. 99.] If I had been in General Burnside's place, I would have asked the President to allow me to resign rather than execute his order to force the passage of the river and march the army against Lee in his stronghold.

Viewing the battle after the lapse of more than twenty years, I may say, however, that Burnside's move might have been made stronger by throwing two of his grand divisions across at the mouth of Deep Run, where Franklin crossed with his grand division and six brigades of Hooker's. Had he thus placed Hooker and Sumner, his sturdiest fighters, and made resolute assault with them in his attack on our right, he would in all probability have given us trouble. The partial success he had at that point might have been pushed vigorously by such a force and might have thrown our right entirely from position, in which event the result would have depended on the skillful handling of the forces. Franklin's grand division could have made sufficient sacrifice at Marye's Hill and come as near success as did Sumner's and two-thirds of Hooker's combined. I think, however, that the success would have been on our side, and it might have been followed by greater disaster on the side of the Federals; still they would have had the chance of success in their favor, while in the battle as it was fought it can hardly be claimed that there was even a chance.

Burnside made a mistake from the first. He should have gone from Warrenton to Chester Gap. He might then have held Jackson and fought me, or have held me and fought Jackson, thus taking us in detail. The doubt about the matter was whether or not he could have caught me in that trap before we could concentrate. At any rate, that was the only move on the board that could have benefited him at the time he was assigned to the command of the Army of the Potomac. By interposing between the corps of Lee's army he would have secured strong ground and advantage of position. With skill equal to the occasion, he should have had success. This was the move about which we felt serious apprehension, and we were occupying our minds with plans to meet it when the move toward Fredericksburg was reported. General McClellan, in his report of August 4th, 1863, speaks of this move as that upon which he was studying when the order for Burnside's assignment to command reached him.

When Burnside determined to move by Fredericksburg, he should have moved rapidly and occupied the city at once, but this would only have forced us back to the plan preferred by General Jackson.

THE CONFEDERATE LEFT AT FREDERICKSBURG.

BY LAFAYETTE McLAWS, MAJOR-GENERAL, C. S. A.

ON the 25th of November, 1862, my division marched into Fredericksburg, and shortly after, by direction of General Longstreet, I occupied the city with one of my brigades and picketed the river with strong detachments from the dam at Falmouth to a quarter of a mile below Deep Run creek, the enemy's pickets being just across the river, within a stone's-throw of mine. Detachments were immediately set at work digging rifle-pits close to the edge of the bank, so close that our men, when in them, could command the river and the shores on each side. The cellars of the houses near the river were made available for the use of riflemen, and zigzags were constructed to enable the men to get in and out of the rifle-pits under cover. All this was done at night, and so secretly and quietly that I do not believe the enemy had any conception of the minute and careful preparations that had been made to defeat any attempt to cross the river in my front. No provision was made for the use of artillery, as the enemy had an enormous array of their batteries on the heights above the town, and could have demolished ours in five minutes.

Two or three evenings previous to the Federal attempt to cross, I was with General Barksdale, and we were attracted by one or more of the enemy's bands playing at their end of the railroad bridge. A number of their officers and a crowd of their men were about the band cheering their national airs, the "Star Spangled Banner," "Hail Columbia," and others, once so dear to us all. It seemed as if they expected some response from us, but none was given until, finally, they struck up "Dixie," and then both sides cheered, with much laughter. Surmising that this serenade meant mischief, I closely inspected our bank of the river, and at night caused additional rifle-pits to be constructed to guard more securely the approaches to the bridge.

Early in the night of the 10th General Barksdale reported that his pickets had heard noises, as if the enemy were hauling pontoon-boats to the brink of the river; a dense fog had prevented a clear view. About 2 A. M., of the 11th, General Barksdale notified me that the movements on the other side indicated that the enemy were preparing to lay down the pontoon-bridges. I told him to let the bridge building go on until the enemy were committed to it and the construction parties were within easy range. At 4:30 he reported that the bridge was being rapidly constructed and was nearly half done, and he was about to open fire. I then ordered the signal to be given by firing two guns of J. P. W. Read's battery, posted on the highest point along my front, on the edge of the hills alongside the main road running to the city.

Previous notice had been sent to General Lee and to corps headquarters that the bridge was being constructed. With the sound of the cannon was mingled the rattle of the rifles of the Mississippi men, who opened a concentrated fire from the rifle-pits and swept the bridge, now crowded with the construction parties. Nine distinct and desperate attempts were made to complete the bridge, but every one was attended with such heavy loss from our fire that the efforts were abandoned until about 10 A. M., when suddenly the tremendous array of the Federal artillery opened fire from the heights above the city.

It is impossible fitly to describe the effects of this iron hail hurled against the small band of defenders and into the devoted city. The roar of the cannon, the bursting shells, the falling of walls and chimneys, and the flying bricks and other material dislodged from the houses by the iron balls and shells, added to the fire of the infantry from both sides and

BARKSDALE'S MISSISSIPPIANS OPPOSING THE LAYING OF THE PONTOON-BRIDGES.

the smoke from the guns and from the burning houses, made a scene of indescribable confusion, enough to appall the stoutest hearts! Under cover of this bombardment the Federals renewed their efforts to construct the bridge, but the little band of Mississippians in the rifle-pits under Lieutenant-Colonel John C. Fiser, 17th Mississippi, composed of his own regiment, 10 sharp-shooters from the 13th Mississippi, and 3 companies from the 18th Mississippi (Lieutenant-Colonel Luse), held their posts, and successfully repelled every attempt. The enemy had been committed to that point, by having used half their pontoons.

About 4:30 P. M. the enemy began crossing in boats, and the concentrated fire from all arms, directed against Barksdale's men in the rifle-pits, became so severe that it was impossible for them to use their rifles with effect.↓

As the main purpose of a determined defense, which was to gain time for the other troops to take position, had been accomplished, Colonel Fiser was

↓Colonel Fiser himself had been knocked down and stunned by a portion of a falling wall, but, recovering consciousness, held to his post, and cheered on his men.— L. McL.

directed to draw his command back from the river and join the brigade in the city; and just in time, for the enemy, no longer impeded by our fire, crossed the river rapidly in boats, and, forming on the flanks, rushed down to capture the men in the rifle-pits, taking them in the rear. Some of the men in the cellars, who did not get the order to retire, were thus captured,↓ but the main body of them rejoined the brigade on Princess-Anne street, where it had been assembled, and all attempts made by the enemy, now crossing in large numbers, to gain possession of the city were defeated. The firing ceased by 7 o'clock, and as the grand division of Franklin had effected a crossing below the mouth of Deep Run, and thus controlled ground which was higher than the city, and other troops had crossed above the city, where, also, the ground was higher, so that our position would become untenable in the morning, I directed General Barksdale to retire to a strong position I had noticed along a sunken road cut through the foot of Marye's Hill and running perpendicular to the line of the enemy's advance.

We read in the accounts given by Federal officers of rank that although General Franklin's command had constructed a bridge or two across the Rappahannock, below the mouth of Deep Run, and had crossed the greater portion of his division on the 11th, yet, because of the failure of General Sumner's grand division to force a crossing in front of Fredericksburg, all but one brigade of Franklin's grand division had been recrossed to the left bank to await the result of Sumner's efforts, and that Franklin's grand division was not again crossed to our side until the 12th. The Federal accounts show that this determined defense offered by a small fraction of Barksdale's brigade not only prevented Sumner's crossing, but by this delay caused the whole of Franklin's Left Grand Division, except one brigade, to recross the Rappahannock, and thus gave General Lee twenty-four hours' time to prepare for the assault, with full notice of the points of attack.

Early on the night of the 11th General Thomas R. R. Cobb was directed to relieve the brigade of General Barksdale, and accordingly three Georgia regiments and the Phillips Legion of Cobb's brigade took position in the sunken road at foot of Marye's Hill, on the lower side of which there was a stone-wall something over four feet high, most of which was protected by the earth thrown from the road, and was invisible from the front. Barksdale's brigade retired to their originally assigned position as my rear line of defense, in Bernard's woods, where they constructed abatis and rifle-pits during the 12th.

Meanwhile the 18th Mississippi Regiment, of Barksdale's brigade, under Colonel Luse, which had been detached to defend the river-bank below the town on the night of the 10th, had offered such vigorous resistance from behind some old huts and thickets that the enemy had delayed the construction of their pontoon-bridges there until after daylight on the 11th, and therefore, instead of crossing the grand division by daylight of the 11th, did not cross until late on that day. The enemy on the 11th brought grape and canister against Colonel Luse, who was not fortified, not having rifle-pits

↓ Perhaps thirty or forty, not more.— L. McL.

FREDERICKSBURG FROM THE FOOT OF WILLIS'S HILL. FROM A WAR-TIME PHOTOGRAPH.

In the middle-ground is seen the south end of the stone-wall, and it may be seen that the front line of defense formed by the wall was continued still farther to the right by the sunken Telegraph road. At the base of the hill, this side of the stone-wall, is seen an earth-work which was a part of the second line. A third line [see p. 83] was on the brow of this hill, now the National Cemetery. Between the steeples on the outskirts of Fredericksburg is seen the end of Hanover street, by which, and by the street in the right of the picture, the Union forces filed out to form for the assault.— EDITORS.

even, and his regiment was withdrawn to the river road. The 16th Georgia, Colonel Bryan, and the 15th South Carolina, Colonel De Saussure, which had been ordered to the assistance of Colonel Luse, retired with his column. Early on the 11th a battalion of the 8th Florida, under Captain Lang, numbering 150 men, had been posted to the left of Colonel Fiser's command, above Fredericksburg, and while under Captain Lang did good service. But unfortunately the captain was badly wounded about 11 A. M., and the battalion was withdrawn. I think the defense of the river-crossing in front of Fredericksburg was a notable and wonderful feat of arms, challenging comparison with anything that happened during the war.

On the 12th close and heavy skirmishing was kept up between my advanced parties and the enemy, and whole divisions were employed in fortifying their positions and preparing for the coming assaults. The grounds in my front had been well studied by myself, in company with my brigade commanders and colonels of regiments, and all the details for the supply of ammunition, provisions, water, care for the wounded, and other necessary arrangements had been attended to, so that we waited for the enemy with perfect calmness and with confidence in our ability to repel them.

A heavy fog hung over the valley, concealing the town from our view, and until late in the day the banks below were not visible. As I was anxiously inquiring for some news from the pickets, since the point of attack had not yet been developed, my aide-de-camp, Captain H. L. P. King, volunteered to go to

the river and collect information by personal observation, and I consented to
his going, but did not send him. He rode off, and in about two hours returned,
reporting that he had ridden down Deep Run as far as he could go in safety
on horseback, and, dismounting and concealing his horse, had gone on foot
down the run to its mouth, and from there he had watched the enemy crossing the river on two bridges. One or two hundred yards below the mouth of
the run large bodies of infantry, artillery, and some cavalry had crossed,
while heavy forces on the opposite side were waiting their turn to cross. On
his return he had gone into a two-story wooden dwelling on the banks of the
river, and had taken a leisurely view of the whole surroundings, confirming
his observations taken from the mouth of Deep Run. This was a daring
reconnoissance, as, at the time, none of our troops were within a mile of him.
Up to this time the enemy had not shown us any very large body of troops,
either in Fredericksburg, on the opposite side, or below.

On the 13th, during the early morning, a thick fog enveloped the town in
my front and the valley of the river, but between 9 and 10 o'clock it lifted,
and we could see on our right, below Deep Run, long lines of the enemy
stretching down the river, and near it, but not in motion. Reconnoitering
parties on horseback were examining the grounds in front of our army, coming
within range without being fired on. After they retired a strong body of
infantry advanced from a point on the river somewhat below my extreme
right, as if to gain possession of the Bernard woods, but I had seven rifle-
guns on the hill above those woods to meet this very contingency, and these
opening on this advancing body, it fell back to the river before coming
within reach of Barksdale.

As the fog lifted higher an immense column of infantry could be seen
halted on the other side of the river, along the road leading from the hills
beyond to the pontoon-bridges in front of the town, and extending back for
miles, as it looked to us, and still we could not see the end. In Jackson's front
the enemy had advanced, and their forming lines were plainly visible, while in
Longstreet's front we could see no body of troops on the Fredericksburg side
of the river. The indications were that Jackson was to receive the first blow,
and General Longstreet came to me and said he was going over to that flank.
I called his attention to the immense column of troops opposite us, on the
other side of the river, with its head at the pontoon-bridges, crossing to
Fredericksburg in our immediate front, and told him that in my judgment
the most desperate assault was to be made on his front, and it would be
developed close to us, without our knowing that it was forming, nor would we
know when it commenced to move against us; that the assault would be
sudden and we should be ready to meet it, and that there were certainly as
many of the enemy in that column threatening us as appeared in the lines
opposite General Jackson. General Longstreet agreed with me, and remained.

Not long after, the grand division of General Franklin, in plain view from
where we stood, was seen advancing in two lines against Jackson's front,
marching in most magnificent order. No perceptible check could I observe
in the advance, and the first line in good order entered the woods and was

lost to our view. But the immediate crash of musketry and the thunder of artillery told of a desperate conflict, and we waited anxiously for some sign of the result. Soon masses of the enemy were seen emerging from the woods in retreat, and the whole body of the enemy marched back in the direction they came from, in excellent order, and very deliberately. Now began the trial against Longstreet's lines; but our confidence in our ability to resist all assaults against us had been wonderfully increased by seeing the repulse of Franklin.

My line of defense was a broken one, running from the left along the sunken road, near the foot of Marye's Hill, where General Cobb's brigade (less the 16th Georgia) was stationed. During the 12th the defenses of this line had been extended beyond the hill by an embankment thrown up to protect the right from sharp-shooters, as also to resist assaults that might be made from that direction, and then the line was retired a hundred or more yards to the foot of the hills in the rear, along which was extended Kershaw's brigade of South Carolina troops, and General Barksdale's Mississippians, from left to right, the brigade of General Semmes being held in reserve. The Washington Artillery, under Colonel Walton, were in position on the crest of Marye's Hill over the heads of Cobb's men [see p. 97], and two brigades under General Ransom were held here in reserve. The heights above Kershaw and Barksdale were crowned with 18 rifle-guns and 8 smooth-bores belonging to batteries, and a number of smooth-bores from the reserve artillery. The troops could not be well seen by the enemy, and the artillery on my rear line was mostly concealed, some covered with brush. The enemy, from their position, could not see the sunken road, near the foot of Marye's Hill, nor do I think they were aware, until it was made known to them by our fire, that there was an infantry force anywhere except on top of the hill, as Ransom's troops could be seen there, in reserve, and the men in the sunken road were visible at a short distance only.

Soon after 11 A. M. the enemy approached the left of my line by the Telegraph road, and, deploying to my right, came forward and planted guidons or standards (whether to mark their advance or to aid in the alignment I do not know), and commenced firing; but the fire from our artillery, and especially the infantry fire from Cobb's brigade, so thinned their ranks that the line retreated without advancing, leaving their guidons planted. Soon another force, heavier than the first, advanced, and were driven back with great slaughter. They were met on retiring by reënforcements, and advanced again, but were again repulsed, with great loss. This continued until about 1 P. M., when General Cobb reported to me that he was short of ammunition. I sent his own very intelligent and brave courier, little Johnny Clark, from Augusta, Georgia, to bring up his ordnance supplies, and directed General Kershaw to reënforce General Cobb with two of his South Carolina regiments, and I also sent the 16th Georgia, which had been detached, to report to General Cobb. A few minutes after these orders had been given I received a note from General Cobb, informing me that General R. H. Anderson, whose division was posted on the left and rear of Cobb's, had just told him that if the attack was turned on him he would retire his troops to the hills in their rear. As this would leave my troops in the sunken road with their left flank unprotected, and at the mercy of the enemy, should they come up on my left, I went over to General Longstreet and represented to him that if this were done I would have to provide in some other way for the protection of the troops in the sunken road, or move them out, so soon as there was a

lull in the attack, which would be virtually giving up the defense of Marye's Hill. General Longstreet at once ordered General Pickett to reënforce Anderson, and directed Anderson to hold his position until forced back. I then went over and examined the ground where Anderson's force was on my left, and finding that the preparations for defense made to resist an assault were incomplete and inconsiderable, I thought it best to take measures to protect my own flank with my own troops, and therefore directed General Kershaw to take his brigade, and, sending two of his regiments to strengthen General Cobb's line be-

BRIGADIER-GENERAL ROBERT RANSOM, C. S. A.
FROM A PHOTOGRAPH.

neath the hill, to hold the rest of his command on top of the hill, to the left of Cobb's line, to meet emergencies, and especially to hold in check, or aid in repelling, any force coming on Cobb's flank, until the force in the sunken road could be withdrawn by the right flank — the only chance it would have of retiring without very heavy loss. I then tore a leaf from my memorandum-book and wrote to General Cobb, "General: Hold your position, with no fear of your flank, it will be protected," and handing it to Captain King, my aide-de-camp, told him to carry it to General Cobb, and to inform him that both ammunition and reënforcements were on the way.↓ General Kershaw at once moved his brigade as ordered, but while it was in motion a courier came from General Cobb and informed me that the general was desperately wounded. General Kershaw was directed to go at once and take command of the force at the foot of Marye's Hill.

Kershaw doubled his 2d and 8th regiments on Phillips's Legion and 24th Georgia, commanded by Colonel McMillan, who succeeded General Cobb in command of the brigade, leaving the 3d and 7th South Carolina on the hill, and holding the 15th, Colonel De Saussure, in reserve. His 3d Battalion was posted on the right at Howison's mill to repulse any attack up Hazel Run, and the 16th Georgia was doubled on the right of Cobb's brigade in the road. The 3d and 7th South Carolina suffered severely while getting into position, Colonel Nance, Lieutenant-Colonel Rutherford, Major Maffett, Captains P. Todd and

↓ This was the last I saw of Captain King until we found this gallant officer's body, after the battle.—L. McL.

John C. Summer being shot down. Summer was killed. The 2d and 8th arrived just in time to resist a heavy assault made on the left about 2:45 P. M., and all of these reënforcements were opportune. The enemy, then deploying in a ravine about three hundred yards from the stone-wall, advanced with fresh lines of attack at short intervals, but were always driven back with great loss. This was kept up until about 4:30 P. M., when the assaults ceased for a time; but the enemy, posting artillery on the left of the Telegraph road, opened on our position; however, they did no damage worth particularizing.

The batteries on Marye's Hill were at this time silent, having exhausted their ammunition, and were being relieved by guns from Colonel E. P. Alexander's battalion. Taking advantage of this lull in the conflict, the 15th South Carolina was brought forward from the cemetery, where it had been in reserve, and was posted behind the stone-wall, supporting the 2d South Carolina regiment.

The enemy in the meanwhile formed a strong column of lines of attack, and advancing under cover of their own artillery, and no longer impeded by ours, came forward along our whole front in the most determined manner; but by this time, as just explained, I had lines four deep throughout the whole sunken road, and beyond the right flank. The front rank, firing, stepped back, and the next in rear took its place and, after firing, was replaced by the next, and so on in rotation. In this way the volley firing was made nearly continuous, and the file firing very destructive. The enemy were repulsed at all points.

The last charge was made after sundown—in fact, it was already dark in the valley. A Federal officer who was in that assault told me that the first discharge at them was a volley, and the bullets went over their heads " in sheets," and that his command was ordered to lie down, and did lie down for a full half-hour and then retired, leaving a large number of killed and wounded. The firing ceased as darkness increased, and about 7 P. M. the pickets of the opposing forces were posted within a short distance of each other, my pickets reporting noises as of movements of large bodies of troops in the city.

Thus ended the battle. The enemy remained in possession of the city until the night of the 15th, and then retired across the Rappahannock, resuming their former positions, and Kershaw's brigade of my division re-occupied the city. My loss in killed, wounded, and missing was 853; of which number 67 were missing, 62 being from Barksdale's brigade, 100 of the 853 being killed. Over 200 of the number were killed or disabled in Kershaw's command while taking positions to defend my left flank.

There was a ravine in my front, distant between 200 or 300 yards, where large masses of the enemy were constantly deployed, and they controlled the slope of Marye's Hill, so that it would have been a hazardous feat, even for a dog, to have attempted to run down it; and yet a Georgia boy named Crumley, an orderly of General Kershaw's, finding that the general had no use for his horse in the sunken road, or thinking that it was no place for a fine animal, deliberately rode him up that slope without injury either to the horse or to himself,—and going back to his camp, returned with an inferior horse, rode down the slope unscathed, and joined his chief, who, until his return, was ignorant of Crumley's daring feat.

General Cobb, who was wounded by a musket-ball in the calf of the leg, ⚓ died shortly after he was removed to the field-hospital in rear of the division. He and I were on intimate terms, and I had learned to esteem him warmly, as I believe every one did who came to know his great intellect and his good heart. Like Stonewall Jackson, he was a religious enthusiast, and, being firmly convinced that the South was right, believed that God would give us visible sign that Providence was with us, and daily prayed for His interposition in our behalf.

⚓ The statement in the text is made on the authority of Surgeon Todd, of Cobb's brigade, who says he saw the wound, and I am assured that General Cobb received all possible attention, and that everything that skill could do was done to save his life.— L. McL.

RANSOM'S DIVISION AT FREDERICKSBURG.

BY ROBERT RANSOM, BRIGADIER-GENERAL, C. S. A.

IN "The Century" magazine for August, 1886, General James Longstreet published what he "saw of the battle of Fredericksburg, Va., December 13th, 1862." [See p. 70.]

The omissions in that article were so glaring, and did such injustice, that I wrote to him and requested him to correct what would produce false impressions. His answer was unsatisfactory, but promised that, "I [Longstreet] expect in the near future to make accounts of all battles and put them in shape, in a form not limited by words, but with full details, when there will be opportunity to elaborate upon all points of interest."

General Lee, in his report of the battle of Fredericksburg, December 13th, 1862, writes as follows:

. . . "Longstreet's corps constituted our left, with Anderson's division resting upon the river, and those of McLaws, Pickett, and Hood extending to the right in the order named. Ransom's division supported the batteries on Marye's and Willis's hills, at the foot of which Cobb's brigade of McLaws's division and the 24th North Carolina of Ransom's brigade were stationed, protected by a stone-wall. *The immediate care of this point was committed to General Ransom.*"

The italics in this paper are all mine. The positions are stated by General Lee exactly as the troops were posted. Lee's report continues farther on:

. . . "About 11 A. M., having massed his [the enemy's] troops under cover of the houses of Fredericksburg, he moved forward in strong columns to seize Marye's and Willis's hills. General Ransom advanced Cooke's brigade to the top of the hill, and placed his own, with the exception of the 24th North Carolina, ♀ short distance in rear." . . . "In the *third* assault," his report continues, "the brave and lamented Brigadier-General Thomas R. R. Cobb fell at the head of his gallant troops, and almost at the same moment Brigadier-General Cooke was borne from the field severely wounded. Fearing that Cobb's brigade might exhaust its ammunition, General Longstreet had directed General Kershaw to take two regiments to its support. Arriving after the fall of Cobb, he assumed command, his troops taking position on the crest and at the foot of the hill, *to which point General Ransom also advanced three other regiments.*"

General Kershaw took command of Cobb's brigade, which I had had supplied with ammunition from my wagons, and I repeated the supply during the day.

General Longstreet, in his official report, says:

. . . "*General Ransom on Marye's Hill was charged with the immediate care of the point attacked*, with orders to send forward additional reënforcements if it should become necessary, and to use Featherston's brigade of Anderson's division if he should require it." And continuing, "I directed Major-General Pickett to send me two of his brigades: one, Kemper's, *was sent to General Ransom* to be placed in some secure position to be ready in case it should be wanted." And again, "I would also mention, as particularly distinguished in the engagement of the 13th, Brigadier-Generals Ransom, Kershaw, and Cooke (severely wounded)."

General McLaws was not upon the part of the field in the vicinity of Marye's and Willis's hills during the battle, but his aide, Captain King, was killed on the front slope of the hill near Marye's house.

My own permanent command was a small division of two brigades of infantry,—my own, containing the 24th, 25th, 35th, and 49th; and Cooke's, the 15th, 27th, 46th, and 48th regiments,—*all from North Carolina ;* and attached to my brigade was Branch's battery, and to Cooke's brigade the battery of Cooper.

At the time the fog began to lift from the field, I was with Generals Lee and Longstreet on what has since been known as Lee's Hill. Starting to join my command as the Federals began to emerge from the town, General Longstreet said to me: "Remember, General, I place that salient in your keeping. Do what is needed; and call on Anderson if you want help."

I brought up Cooke before the first assault to the crest of the hill, and before that assault ended Cooke took the 27th and the 46th and part of the 15th North Carolina into the sunken road in front. The 48th North Carolina fought on top of the hill all day.

At the third assault I brought up the 25th North Carolina just in time to deliver a few deadly volleys, and then it "took position shoulder to shoulder with Cobb's and Cooke's men in the road."

During this third attack General Cobb was mortally hit, and almost at the same instant, and within two paces of him, General Cooke was severely wounded and borne from the field, Colonel E. D. Hall, 46th North Carolina, assuming command of Cooke's brigade.

At this juncture I sent my adjutant-general, Captain Thomas Rowland, to the sunken road to learn the condition of affairs. "His report was most gratifying, representing the troops in fine spirits and an abundance of ammunition. I had ordered Cobb's brigade supplied from my wagons."

After this third attack I was bringing up the 35th and 49th North Carolina of my brigade, when General Kershaw, by a new road leading from the mill below, came up on horseback with his staff at the head of *one regiment*, which he took in just at Marye's house. He was followed by a second regiment, which halted behind a brick-walled graveyard upon Willis's Hill. [See below.]

About sundown Brigadier-General Kemper was brought up, and relieved the 24th North Carolina with two of his regiments and held the others in closer supporting distance. On the 20th of December, 1862, he sent me a list of his casualties, with this note:

"HEADQUARTERS, KEMPER'S BRIGADE,
"December 20th, 1862.

"GENERAL: I inclose herewith the statement of the losses of my brigade on the 13th and 14th inst. while acting as part of your command. While a report of my losses has been called for by my permanent division commander, and rendered to him, it has occurred to me that a similar one rendered to yourself would be proper and acceptable. Permit me to add, General, that our

brief service with you was deeply gratifying to myself and to my entire command. I have the honor to be, General, very respectfully, your obedient servant,

"J. L. KEMPER, Brigadier-General.
"BRIG.-GEN. RANSOM, Commanding Division."

As stated in my letter to General Longstreet dated August 14th, 1886, when I brought to his attention his extraordinary omissions, it gave me unfeigned pleasure to mention properly in my official report the meritorious conduct of those who were a part of my permanent command and those others who that day fell under my direction by reason of my "*immediate care of the point attacked.*" My official report exhibits no self-seeking nor partial discriminations.

Upon a letter from me (of the 17th of December, 1862) to General R. H. Chilton, assistant adjutant-general Army of Northern Virginia, wherein I protest against the ignoring of my command in some telegraphic dispatches to the War Department at Richmond relative to the battle of the 13th, General Longstreet indorses these words: "*General Ransom's division was engaged throughout the battle and was quite as distinguished as any troops upon the field*"; and the same day, the 19th of December, I received from both him and General Chilton notes expressing the regret felt by General Lee at the injustice of which I complained. Those original letters are now among the "Official Records" in Washington.

I may be pardoned for remembering with pride that among the Confederate troops engaged on the *whole* battle-field of Fredericksburg, Va., December 13th, 1862, none were more honorably distinguished than the sons of North Carolina, and those of them who, with brother soldiers from other States, held the lines at Marye's Hill against almost ten times their number of as brave and determined foes as ever did battle, can well trust their fame to history when written from truthful official records. ⬇

⬇ Where credit is not given for quotations, they are from my official report of the battle.— R. R.

KERSHAW'S BRIGADE AT FREDERICKSBURG.

GENERAL J. B. KERSHAW writes to the editors as follows, December 6th, 1887:

"General Ransom's letter, in 'The Century' for December, 1887, in regard to his services at Fredericksburg, contains an error in relation to the operations of my brigade. In the morning of that day, my troops were stationed at the foot of Lee's Hill. After the assaults on General Cobb's position had commenced, I was directed to send two of my regiments to reënforce Cobb, and did so. Before they had reached him, tidings arrived of the fall of General Cobb, and I was immediately ordered to take the rest of my brigade to the position held by his forces, and assume command of the troops of McLaws's division there. I preceded my troops, and as soon as possible arrived at the Stevens House at the foot of Marye's Hill. As my brigade arrived they were placed — two regiments, the 3d and the 7th South Caro-

lina, at Marye's House on the hill, and the rest of them in the sunken road, with the left resting about the Stevens House. The last regiment that arrived was the 15th South Carolina (Colonel De Saussure's). He sheltered his command behind the cemetery on the hill until his proper position was made known, when he moved deliberately and in perfect order down the road to the Stevens House, and proceeded to the right of my line. Instead of having two regiments engaged at that point, as General Ransom supposes, I had five regiments and a battalion (my entire brigade), each of which suffered more or less severely. During these operations I received no orders or directions from any officer but my division commander, General McLaws. I requested not to be relieved that night, and remained in that position until the evacuation of Fredericksburg by the Union forces. These facts were officially reported at the time, and were then too well known to be the subject of mistake."

THE WASHINGTON ARTILLERY ON MARYE'S HILL FIRING UPON THE UNION COLUMNS FORMING FOR THE ASSAULT.

A HOT DAY ON MARYE'S HEIGHTS.

BY WILLIAM MILLER OWEN, FIRST LIEUTENANT, C. S. A.

ON the night of the 10th of December we, of the New Orleans Washington Artillery, sat up late in our camp on Marye's Heights, entertaining some visitors in an improvised theater, smoking our pipes, and talking of home. A final punch having been brewed and disposed of, everybody crept under the blankets and was soon in the land of Nod. In an hour or two we were aroused by the report of a heavy gun. I was up in an instant, for if there should be another it would be the signal that the enemy was preparing to cross the river. Mr. Florence, a civilian in the bivouac, bounced as if he had a concealed spring under his blanket, and cried out, "Wake up! wake up! what's that?" The deep roar of the second gun was heard, and we knew what we had to do. It was 4 o'clock. Our orders were that upon the firing of these signal guns we should at once take our places in the redoubts prepared for us on Marye's Hill, and await developments. "Boots and saddles" was sounded, and the camp was instantly astir, and in the gray of the morning we were on the Plank road leading to the hill. The position reached, our nine guns were placed as follows: Two 12-pounder howitzers and two 12-pounder light Napoleon guns of the 4th Company, under Captain Eshleman and Lieutenants Norcom and Battles, were put in the work on the extreme right of the line next to the Telegraph road; two 12-pounder Napoleon guns of the 3d Company, under Captain Miller and Lieutenant McElroy, in the center; two 3-inch rifle-guns of the 1st Company, under Captain Squires and Lieutenant Brown, on the left, next to the brick-house and in front of the Welford graveyard, and one 10-pounder Parrott rifle, under Lieutenant Galbraith, of the 1st Company, next to the Plank road leading into Fredericksburg.

The 2d Company, under Captain Richardson, with four Napoleon guns, moved on across the Telegraph road to the right, and reported as ordered to General Pickett for service with his troops. Without delay the men made the redoubts as snug as possible, and finding the epaulements not to their liking, went to work with pick and shovel throwing the dirt a little higher, and fashioning embrasures to fire through. The engineers objected, and said they were "ruining the works," but the cannoneers said, "We have to fight here, not you; we will arrange them to suit ourselves." And General Longstreet approvingly said, "If you save the finger of a man's hand, that does some good." A dense fog covered the country, and we could not discern what was going on in the town.

The morning of the 12th was also foggy, and it was not until 2 P. M. that it cleared off, and then we could see the Stafford Heights, across the river, densely packed with troops. At 3 P. M. a heavy column moved down toward one of the bridges near the gas-works, and we opened upon it, making some splendid practice and apparently stirring them up prodigiously, for they soon sought cooler localities. While our guns were firing, the enemy's long range batteries on the Stafford Heights opened upon us, as much as to say, "What are you about over there?" We paid no attention to their inquiry, as our guns could not reach them.

At dawn the next morning, December 13th, in the fresh and nipping air, I stepped upon the gallery overlooking the heights back of the little old-fashioned town of Fredericksburg. Heavy fog and mist hid the whole plain between the heights and the Rappahannock, but under cover of that fog and within easy cannon-shot lay Burnside's army. Along the heights, to the right and left of where I was standing, extending a length of nearly five miles, lay Lee's army. The bugles and the drum corps of the respective armies were now sounding reveille, and the troops were preparing for their early meal. All knew we should have a battle to-day and a great one, for the enemy had crossed the river in immense force, upon his pontoons during the night. On the Confederate side all was ready, and the shock was awaited with stubborn resolution. Last night we had spread our blankets upon the bare floor in the parlor of Marye's house, and now our breakfast was being prepared in its fire-place, and we were impatient to have it over. After hastily dispatching this light meal of bacon and corn-bread, the colonel, chief bugler, and I (the adjutant of the battalion) mounted our horses and rode out to inspect our lines. Visiting first the position of the 10-pounder Parrott rifle on the Plank road, we found Galbraith and his boys wide-awake and ready for business. Across the Plank road, in an earthwork, was the battery of Donaldsonville Cannoneers, of Louisiana, all Creoles and gallant soldiers. Riding to the rear of Marye's house, we visited in turn the redoubts of Squires, Miller, and Eshleman, and found everything ready for instant action. The ammunition chests had been taken off the limbers and placed upon the ground behind the traverses close to the guns. The horses and limbers had been sent to the rear out of danger. We drew rein and spoke a few words to each in passing, and at the 3d Company's redoubt we were invited by Sergeant "Billy" Ellis to partake of some "café noir" which his mess had prepared in a horse bucket. Nothing loath, we drank a tin-cupful, and found, not exactly "Mocha," or "Java," but the best of parched corn. However, it was hot, the morning was raw, and it did very well.

At 12 o'clock the fog had cleared, and while we were sitting in Marye's yard smoking our pipes, after a lunch of hard crackers, a courier came to Colonel Walton, bearing a dispatch from General Longstreet for General Cobb, but, for our information as well, to be read and then given to him. It was as follows: "Should General Anderson, on your left, be compelled to fall back to the second line of heights, you must conform to his movements." Descending the hill into the sunken road, I made my way through the troops, to a little house where General Cobb had his headquarters, and handed him the dispatch. He read it carefully, and said,

JAMES A. SEDDON, SECRETARY OF WAR TO THE SOUTHERN
CONFEDERACY, FROM NOVEMBER 20, 1862, TO JAN-
UARY 28, 1865. FROM A PHOTOGRAPH.

"Well! if they wait for me to fall back, they will
wait a long time." Hardly had he spoken, when
a brisk skirmish fire was heard in front, toward
the town, and looking over the stone-wall we saw
our skirmishers falling back, firing as they came;
at the same time the head of a Federal column
was seen emerging from one of the streets of the
town. They came on at the double-quick, with
loud cries of "Hi! Hi! Hi!" which we could distinctly hear. Their arms were carried at "right
shoulder shift," and their colors were aslant the
shoulders of the color-sergeants. They crossed the
canal at the bridge, and getting behind the bank to
the low ground to deploy, were almost concealed
from our sight. It was 12:30 P. M., and it was
evident that we were now going to have it hot and
heavy.

The enemy, having deployed, now showed himself above the crest of the ridge and advanced in
columns of brigades, and at once our guns began
their deadly work with shell and solid shot. How
beautifully they came on! Their bright bayonets
glistening in the sunlight made the line look like
a huge serpent of blue and steel. The very force
of their onset leveled the broad fences bounding
the small fields and gardens that interspersed the
plain. We could see our shells bursting in their
ranks, making great gaps; but on they came, as
though they would go straight through and over
us. Now we gave them canister, and that staggered

them. A few more paces onward and the
Georgians in the road below us rose up,
and, glancing an instant along their rifle
barrels, let loose a storm of lead into the
faces of the advance brigade. This was
too much; the column hesitated, and then,
turning, took refuge behind the bank.
But another line appeared from behind
the crest and advanced gallantly, and
again we opened our guns upon them,
and through the smoke we could discern
the red breeches of the "Zouaves," and
hammered away at them especially. But
this advance, like the preceding one, although passing the point reached by the
first column, and doing and daring all
that brave men could do, recoiled under
our canister and the bullets of the infantry in the road, and fell back in great confusion. Spotting the fields in our front,
we could detect little patches of blue —
the dead and wounded of the Federal
infantry who had fallen facing the very
muzzles of our guns. Cooke's brigade
of Ransom's division was now placed in
the sunken road with Cobb's men. At
2 P. M. other columns of the enemy left
the crest and advanced to the attack; it
appeared to us that there was no end of
them. On they came in beautiful array
and seemingly more 'determined to hold
the plain than before; but our fire was
murderous, and no troops on earth could
stand the *feu d'enfer* we were giving
them. In the foremost line we distinguished the green flag with the golden
harp of old Ireland, and we knew it to be Meagher's Irish brigade. The gunners of the two rifle-
pieces, Corporals Payne and Hardie, were directed
to turn their guns against this column; but
the gallant enemy pushed on beyond all former
charges, and fought and left their dead within five
and twenty paces of the sunken road. Our position
on the hill was now a hot one, and three regiments
of Ransom's brigade were ordered up to reënforce
the infantry in the road. We watched them as
they came marching in line of battle from the rear,
where they had been lying in reserve. They
passed through our works and rushed down the hill
with loud yells, and then stood shoulder to shoulder
with the Georgians. The 25th North Carolina
regiment, crossing Miller's guns, halted upon the
crest of the hill, dressed its line, and fired a deadly
volley at the enemy at close range, and then at the
command "Forward!" dashed down the hill. It
left dead men on Miller's redoubt, and he had to
drag them away from the muzzles of his guns. At
this time General Cobb fell mortally wounded, and
General Cooke was borne from the field; also
wounded. Among other missiles a 3-inch rifle-ball
came crashing through the works and fell at our
feet. Kursheedt picked it up and said, "Boys,
let's send this back to them again"; and into the
gun it went, and was sped back into the dense
ranks of the enemy.

General Kershaw now advanced from the rear

with two regiments of his infantry, to reënforce the men in the sunken road, who were running short of ammunition, and to take command.

The sharp-shooters having got range of our embrasures, we began to suffer. Corporal Ruggles fell mortally wounded, and Perry, who seized the rammer as it fell from Ruggles's hand, received a bullet in the arm. Rodd was holding "vent," and away went his "crazy bone." In quick succession Everett, Rossiter, and Kursheedt were wounded. Falconer in passing in rear of the guns was struck behind the ear and fell dead. We were now so short-handed that every one was in the work, officers and men putting their shoulders to the wheels and running up the guns after each recoil. The frozen ground had given way and was all slush and mud. We were compelled to call upon the infantry to help us at the guns. Eshleman crossed over from the right to report his guns nearly out of ammunition; the other officers reported the same. They were reduced to a few solid shot only. It was now 5 o'clock, P. M., and there was a lull in the storm. The enemy did not seem inclined to renew his efforts, so our guns were withdrawn one by one, and the batteries of Woolfolk and Moody were substituted.

The little whitewashed brick-house to the right of the redoubt we were in was so battered with bullets during the four hours and a half engagement that at the close it was transformed to a bright brick-dust red. An old cast-iron stove lay against the

house, and as the bullets would strike it it would give forth the sound of "bing! bing!" with different tones and variations. During the hottest of the firing old Mr. Florence, our non-combatant friend, was peering around the end of the house (in which, by the way, our wounded took refuge), looking out to see if his son, who was at the gun, was all right. A cannon-ball struck the top of the work, scattering dirt all over us and profusely down our necks, and, striking the end of the house, carried away a cart-load of bricks, just where Mr. Florence had been looking an instant before. We thought surely he had met his fate, but in a moment we were pleased to see his gray head "bob up serenely," determined to see "what was the gage of the battle."

After withdrawing from the hill the command was placed in bivouac, and the men threw themselves upon the ground to take a much-needed rest. We had been under the hottest fire men ever experienced for four hours and a half, and our loss had been three killed and twenty-four wounded. Among them was Sergeant John Wood, our leading spirit in camp theatricals, who was severely injured and never returned to duty. One gun was slightly disabled, and we had exhausted all of our canister, shell and case shot, and nearly every solid shot in our chests. At 5:30 another attack was made by the enemy, but it was easily repulsed, and the battle of Fredericksburg was over, and Burnside was baffled and defeated.

WINTER SPORT IN A CONFEDERATE CAMP.

CONFEDERATE THEATRICALS.

NOTES OF A CONFEDERATE STAFF-OFFICER.

BY W. ROY MASON, MAJOR, C. S. A.

FREDERICKSBURG was the first great battle that I saw in its entire scope. Here the situation of the country — a champaign tract inclosed in hills — offered the opportunity of seeing the troops on both sides, and the movements down the entire lines. I witnessed the magnificent charges made on our left by Meagher's Irish Brigade, and was also a sorrowful witness of the death of our noble T. R. R. Cobb of Georgia, who fell mortally wounded at the foot of the stone-wall just at the door of Mrs. Martha Stevens. This woman, the Molly Pitcher of the war, attended the wounded and the dying fearless of consequences, and refused to leave her house, although, standing just between the advancing line of the enemy and the stone-wall, the position was one of danger. It is said that after using all the materials for bandages at her command, she tore from her person most of her garments, even on that bitter cold day, in her anxiety to administer to necessities greater than her own.

Mrs. Stevens still lives in her old home at the foot of Marye's Heights, honored by every Confederate soldier. Not long ago, hearing that she was very sick, I went out with a party of gentlemen friends who were visitors in Fredericksburg to inquire for her. Being told of our visit, she requested her son-in-law to ask me in. When jocularly asked by him if she was going to invite a gentleman into her sick-room, the old lady replied: "Yes, ask Major Mason in, — we were old soldiers together."

After Burnside had withdrawn his forces across the Rappahannock, General Lee rode over to Marye's Heights, where I then was, and said to me: "Captain, those people [meaning the enemy] have sent over a flag of truce, asking permission to send

a detachment to bury their dead. They have landed near your house, 'The Sentry Box.' Have you any objection to taking this reply down?" As he spoke, he handed me a sealed envelope directed to General Burnside. I accordingly rode into town and made my way down to the river-front of my residence, from which Burnside had only that morning removed his pontoons. There I found a Federal lieutenant-colonel with two soldiers in a boat, holding a flag of truce. I handed him the dispatch and at the same time asked where Burnside was. He answered, "Just up the hill across the river, under an old persimmon-tree, awaiting the dispatch." Telling him my name, I said: "Give my regards to General Burnside, and say to him that I thought he was too familiar with the surroundings of Fredericksburg to butt his brains out deliberately against our stone-walls."

"Do you know General Burnside?" inquired the officer.

"Oh, yes!" I replied, "he is an old acquaintance of mine."

"Then will you wait till I deliver your message and return? He may have something to say."

"I will wait then," was my answer.

In a very short time the flag of truce returned with a request from Burnside that I would come over in the boat to see him. I thoroughly appreciated the fact that I was running the risk of a court-martial from my own side in thus going into the enemy's lines without permission; but being that rather privileged person, a staff-officer, from whom no pass was required and of whom no questions were asked, I determined to accept this invitation and go over.

After passing the river and walking leisurely up the hill, the idle Federal soldiers, seeing a Confederate officer on their side and feeling curious about it, ran down in numbers toward the road. For the first time I was frightened by this result of my act, as I feared that our generals on the hills with their strong glasses, seeing the commotion, might inquire into it. As soon as I approached Burnside, who met me with the greatest cordiality, I expressed to him this fear. He at once sent out couriers to order the soldiers back to camp, and we then sat down on an old log, and being provided with crackers, cheese, sardines, and a bottle of brandy (all luxuries to a Confederate), we discussed this lunch as well as the situation. General Burnside seemed terribly mortified and distressed at his failure, but said that he wanted me to tell his old army friends on the other side that he was not responsible for the attack on Fredericksburg in the manner in which it was made, as he was himself under orders, and was not much more than a figure-head, or words to that effect.

We talked pleasantly for an hour about old times, Burnside asking me many questions about former friends and comrades, now on our side of the fratricidal struggle. When I expressed my wish to return, he wrapped up a bottle of brandy to give me at parting, and sent me under escort to the river. Having recrossed, I mounted my horse and rode back to Marye's Heights, but, enjoyable as this escapade had been, I said nothing, of course, about it to my army friends till long afterward.

That day I witnessed with pain the burial of many thousands of Federal dead that had fallen at Fredericksburg. The night before, the thermometer must have fallen to zero, and the bodies of the slain had frozen to the ground. The ground was frozen nearly a foot deep, and it was necessary to use pick-axes. Trenches were dug on the battle-field and the dead collected and laid in line for burial. It was a sad sight to see these brave soldiers thrown into the trenches, without even a blanket or a word of prayer, and the heavy clods thrown upon them; but the most sickening sight of all was when they threw the dead, some four or five hundred in number, into Wallace's empty ice-house, where they were found — a hecatomb of skeletons — after the war. In 1865–66 some shrewd

Yankee contractors obtained government sanction to disinter all the Federal dead on the battle-fields of Fredericksburg, Chancellorsville, the Wilderness, and Spotsylvania Court House. They were to be paid *per capita*. When I went out to see the skeletons taken from the ice-house, I found the contractor provided with unpainted boxes of common pine about six feet long and twelve inches wide; but I soon saw that this scoundrel was dividing the remains so as to make as much by his contract as possible. I at once reported what I had seen to Colonel E. V. Sumner, Jr., then in command of the Sub-district of the Rappahannock. He was utterly shocked at this vandalism. I afterward heard that the contract was taken away from the fellow and given to more reliable parties.

One morning about this time I was at breakfast, when the servant, terribly frightened, announced a sergeant and file of soldiers in my porch asking for me. The ladies immediately imagined that this squad had been sent to arrest me, as they had heard more than once that charges would be preferred against me by the United States Government for extreme partisanship. Going to the door, I was told by the sergeant that Colonel Sumner had sent him to me to inquire as to the burial places of the Federal soldiers whom I had found dead upon my lot and in my house after the battle of Fredericksburg. I told him that I had found one Federal soldier stretched on one of my beds. In my parlor, lying on the floor, was another whose entire form left its imprint in blood on the floor,— as may be seen to this day. In my own chamber, sitting up in an old-fashioned easy-chair, I had found a Federal lieutenant-colonel. When I entered, I supposed him to be alive, as the back of his head was toward me. Much startled, I approached him, to find that he had been shot through the neck, and, probably, placed in that upright position that he might better breathe. He was quite dead. I had all these bodies, and five or six others found in my yard, buried in one grave on the wharf. They had been killed, no doubt, by Barksdale's Mississippi brigade, in their retreat from my lot. I made my report at Sumner's headquarters, after which I took the burial squad to the grave, and then returned home to quiet the apprehensions of my family.

NEWSPAPERS IN CAMP. FROM A WAR-TIME SKETCH.

THE REMOVAL OF McCLELLAN.

BY RICHARD B. IRWIN, LIEUTENANT-COLONEL, ASSISTANT ADJUTANT-GENERAL, U. S. V.

IN some former notes↓ I tried to trace with an impartial hand, and without intruding any prejudice or opinion of my own, the course of the unfortunate differences that had arisen between the Government and the commander of the Army of the Potomac. The acute stage was reached on the Peninsula; Pope's campaign marked the first crisis. On the 1st of September McClellan found himself a general without an army. On the 2d the Government gave him what was left of two armies, and only asked him to defend the capital. On the 5th the troops were in motion; on the 7th, without another word, and thus, as appears probable, overstepping the intentions of the Government, ⚓ he set out to meet Lee in Maryland; and, moving deliberately under repeated cautions, ten days later he once more grappled fiercely with his antagonist, who stood waiting on the banks of the Antietam. Antietam strained the back of the Confederacy.

Hardly had the echo of the guns died away than again the angry ink began to flow. To follow its track would here be as tedious and unnecessary as it must always be painful. The sullen stage of the disorder had been reached; collapse was soon to follow. As one turns the pages of the history of the seven weeks after Antietam, or the scattered leaves that are some time to be gathered into history, it is impossible not to realize that we are reading of the last days of the first and best-loved commander of the Army of the Potomac; that the last hour is not far off.

Without going into the details, and without attempting to pass judgment, it must be said that no candid person, knowing anything of war and armies, can doubt that the Army of the Potomac, in the last days of September and early October, 1862, needed nearly *everything* before beginning a fresh campaign of its own choice. For some things, such as shoes, the troops were really suffering. It is

↓ "The Administration in the Peninsular Campaign," Vol. II. of this work, p. 435; "Washington under Banks," Vol. II. of this work, p. 541.

⚓ See Vol. II., p. 542, and note. This is strongly confirmed by Chase's diary, September 2 (Warden's "Life of Chase," p. 549): "The President repeated that the whole scope of the order was simply to direct McClellan to put the troops into the fortifications and command them for the defense of Washington." September 3d (*Ibid.*, p. 460), the diary says: " . . . the President . . . assured him [Pope] . . . that McClellan's command was only temporary, and gave him reason to expect that another army of active operations would be organized at once which he [Pope] would lead." The same evening (September 3d) the President gave General Halleck an order,

which never became known to General McClellan, "to organize an army for active operations . . . independent of the forces he may deem necessary for the defense of Washington, when such active army shall take the field." ("Official Records," Vol. XIX., Part II., p. 169.)

The published extracts from Chase's diary, though voluminous in the earlier stages, are silent on the subject of McClellan's final removal. In Warden's "Life of Chase" (p. 506) we read: "Another chapter[2] offers a few words relating to our hero's responsibility for that fall," and the foot-note refers us to "[2] Post Chapter LVII.," but not another word is said, and "Chapter LVI., Conclusion," ends the book. This is at least curious, if not significant.— R. B. I.

equally evident that the duty of providing these essential supplies rested with the administrative services in Washington; that some of the supplies did not reach the troops for a long time,⟂ and that certain subordinate chiefs were at least indulged in expending an amount of energy in combating the earnest representations that came pouring in from the army on the field; that they, or some one, might well have been required to devote to the task of seeing that the supplies reached the troops who needed them, instead of resting content with perfunctory declarations that the stores had "been sent." Nor can any commander of an army be blamed for not liking this. The wonder is, that a railway journey of a few hours should have stood in the way of a complete understanding and swift remedy, on one side or the other.

President Lincoln visited General McClellan on the 1st of October, and went over the battle-fields of South Mountain, Crampton's Gap, and Antietam in his company. When the President left him on the 4th, General McClellan appears to have been under the impression that his military acts and plans were satisfactory. ♭ What these plans were at this time, beyond the reorganization and refitting of his army, in the absence of direct evidence, one can but conjecture from a passage that occurs in a private letter dated October 2d, printed in "McClellan's Own Story" (p. 654). "His [the President's] ostensible purpose is to see the troops and the battle-field; I incline to think that the real purpose of his visit is to push on into a premature advance into Virginia. . . . The real truth is that my army is not fit to advance."⟨ However, on the 6th, two days after Mr. Lincoln's departure, General Halleck telegraphed to General McClellan:

"The President directs that you cross the Potomac and give battle to the enemy or drive him south. Your army must move now, while the roads are good. If you cross the river between the enemy and Washington and cover the latter by your operation, you can be reënforced with 30,000 men. If you move up the valley of the Shenandoah, not more than 12,000 or 15,000 can be sent to you. The President advises the interior line between Washington and the enemy, but does not order it. He is very desirous that your army move as soon as possible."

General McClellan at first selected the valley route, but the tardy delivery of supplies delayed his movement, and when he crossed the Potomac on the 25th and began the advance the circum-

stances had somewhat changed.☆ Then, leaving the Twelfth Corps to hold Harper's Ferry, he marched down the eastern side of the Blue Ridge, as the President had originally desired, picked up the Third and Eleventh Corps and Bayard's division of cavalry on striking the railway opposite Thoroughfare Gap, and on the 5th of November made his headquarters at Rectortown, with all his arrangements in progress for concentrating the army near Warrenton.

This movement in effect placed the Army of the Potomac, with a force double that of the Army of Northern Virginia,⟂ between the two halves of that army, farther separated by the Blue Ridge; for Lee, with Longstreet's corps, had kept pace with McClellan's movement and advanced to Culpeper, and Jackson was still in the Valley of Virginia, distant several days' march behind Thornton's Gap, with D. H. Hill holding the western entrance to the gap against Pleasonton, who was on the east, observing its debouch.

On that very day, the 5th of November, 1862, President Lincoln, with his own hand, wrote the following order : ⚓

"EXECUTIVE MANSION,
WASHINGTON,   , 186 .
"By direction of the President it is ordered that Major-General McClellan be relieved from the command of the Army of the Potomac, and that Major-General Burnside take command of that army. Also that Major-General Hunter take command of the corps in said army now commanded by General Burnside.

"That Major-General Fitz John Porter be relieved from the command of the corps he now commands in said army, and that Major-General Hooker take command of said corps.

"The general-in-chief is authorized, in [his] discretion, to issue an order substantially as the above, forthwith or as soon as he may deem proper.   "A. LINCOLN.
"November 5th, 1862."

Forthwith the following orders were issued:

"HEADQUARTERS OF THE ARMY,
WASHINGTON, November 5th, 1862.
"MAJOR-GENERAL McCLELLAN, Commanding, etc.—
GENERAL: On receipt of the order of the President, sent herewith, you will immediately turn over your command to Major-General Burnside, and repair to Trenton, N. J., reporting, on your arrival at that place, by telegraph, for further orders.

"Very respectfully, your obedient servant,
"H. W. HALLECK,
"General-in-Chief."

⟂ In particular the statement of General Rufus Ingalls ("Official Records," Vol. XIX., Part I., p. 95) seems to me conclusive, although the contrary view is strongly held by high authority.— R. B. I.

♭ "We spent some time on the battle-field and conversed fully on the state of affairs. He told me that he was entirely satisfied with me and with all that I had done; that he would stand by me against 'all comers'; that he wished me to continue my preparations for a new campaign, not to stir an inch until fully ready, and when ready to do what I thought best. He repeated that he was entirely satisfied with me; that I should be let alone; that he would stand by me. I have no doubt he meant exactly what he said. He parted from me with the utmost cordiality. We never met again on this earth." ["McClellan's Own Story," pp. 627, 628.]

⟨ President Lincoln's views as to the comparative readiness to move of the Federal and Confederate armies may be found tersely expressed in his letter to General McClellan, dated October 13th, 1862, printed on p. 105.

☆ Among other things, Stuart crossed the Potomac at Williamsport on the 10th of October, on his famous raid into Maryland and Pennsylvania, rode completely around the rear of the Army of the Potomac, and, eluding Pleasonton's vigorous but ineffectual pursuit, safely recrossed the river near the mouth of the Monocacy. One effect of this raid on the mind of the President is indicated in an anecdote related in "Washington under Banks," Vol. II. of this work, p. 544.— R. B. I.

⟂ The "Official Records" show that at this time McClellan's effective force was about 145,000, Lee's about 72,000. Longstreet and Jackson each had about 32,000.— R. B. I.

⚓ It is virtually certain that General McClellan never saw this order, which, in the form as written by the President, was never promulgated. General Hunter was not placed in command of Burnside's corps. Hooker was ordered to relieve Porter by Special Orders from the War Department, Adjutant-General's Office, dated November 10th, 1862.

This order was inclosed:

"WAR DEPARTMENT, ADJUTANT-GENERAL'S OFFICE, WASHINGTON, November 5th, 1862.

"GENERAL ORDERS, NO. 182: By direction of the President of the United States, it is ordered that Major-General McClellan be relieved from the command of the Army of the Potomac, and that Major-General Burnside take the command of that army.

"By order of the Secretary of War:
"E. D. TOWNSEND,
"Assistant Adjutant-General."

If we except Halleck's report of October 28th, obviously called for and furnished as a record, and containing nothing new, no cause or reason has ever been made public, either officially or in any one of the many informal modes in which official action so often finds it convenient to let itself be known. It is hard to credit that the Government did not know, or that knowing they did not appreciate, the military situation on the 5th of November; still harder to believe that, knowing and appreciating it, they threw away such an opportunity for any cause that appears in Halleck's letter.

General C. P. Buckingham, the confidential assistant adjutant-general of the Secretary of War, bore these orders from Washington by a special train. He arrived at Rectortown in a blinding snow-storm. First calling upon Burnside to deliver to him a counterpart of the order, late on the night of November 7th these two officers proceeded together to General McClellan's tent. McClellan says: ✰

"I at once [when he heard of Buckingham's arrival] suspected that he brought the order relieving me from command, but kept my own counsel. Late at night I was sitting alone in my tent, writing to my wife. All the staff were asleep. Suddenly some one knocked upon the tent-pole, and upon my invitation to enter there appeared Burnside and Buckingham, both looking very solemn. I received them kindly and commenced conversation upon general subjects in the most unconcerned manner possible. After a few moments Buckingham said to Burnside: 'Well, General, I think

we had better tell General McClellan the object of our visit.' I very pleasantly said that I should be glad to learn it. Whereupon Buckingham handed me the two orders of which he was the bearer. . . .

"I saw that both—especially Buckingham—were watching me most intently while I opened and read the orders. I read the papers with a smile, immediately turned to Burnside, and said: 'Well, Burnside, I turn the command over to you.' " ⎦

The movements of troops that had already been begun were completed on the 8th and 9th, at General Burnside's request; but there the execution of General McClellan's plans stopped. Burnside turned to the left and massed his army on the Rappahannock, opposite Fredericksburg; Lee conformed to this movement, called in Jackson, and concentrated on the opposite heights. The disaster of Fredericksburg followed.

On the 10th McClellan bade farewell to the Army of the Potomac. As he rode between the lines, formed almost of their own accord to do honor for the last time to their beloved commander, grief and disappointment were on every face, and manly tears stood in many an eye that had learned to look on war without a tremor. In the simple, touching words of the gallant and accomplished Walker: "Every heart was filled with love and grief; every voice was raised in shouts expressive of devotion and indignation; and when the chief had passed out of sight, the romance of war was over for the Army of the Potomac." ⚓

In all that these brave men did, in all that they suffered, and great were their deeds, unspeakable their sufferings, never, perhaps, were their devotion and loyalty more nobly proved than by their instant obedience to this order, unwisely wrung from the President as many of them believed it to have been, yet still for them, as American soldiers, as American citizens, an implicit mandate. The men who could talk so glibly of "prætorian guards" knew little of the Army of the Potomac.

✰ "McClellan's Own Story," pp. 652, 653.

⎦ General Buckingham, in a letter printed in the "Chicago Tribune," of September 4th, 1875 (quoted in the "History of the Civil War in America," by the Comte de Paris, Vol. II., p. 555), writes substantially to the same effect. He also states that General Burnside at first declined the command (as there is good reason for believing he had done twice before, namely, in August, and again early in September). He adds: "General McClellan has himself borne testimony to the kind manner in which I communicated the order, and I can bear testimony to his prompt and cheerful obedience to it."—R. B. I.

⚓ "History of the Second Army Corps," by General Francis A. Walker, p. 137.

From "McClellan's Last Service to the Republic," by George Ticknor Curtis (N. Y.: D. Appleton & Co.), pp. 81-83, we take the following description of McClellan's farewell to the Army of the Potomac:

"After he had reached Warrenton, a day was spent in viewing the position of the troops and in conferences with General Burnside respecting future operations. In the course of that day the order was published, and General McClellan issued a farewell address to the army. On the evening of Sunday, the 9th, there was an assembly of officers who came to take leave of him. On the 10th he visited some of the various camps, and amid the impassioned cries and demonstrations of the men he took a last look of the troops who had followed him with such unfaltering devotion. 'His-

tory,' he said to the officers who crowded around him—'history will do justice to the Army of the Potomac, even if the present generation does not. I feel as if I had been intimately connected with each and all of you. Nothing is more binding than the friendship of companions in arms. May you all in future preserve the high reputation of our army, and serve all as well and faithfully as you have served me.' On the 11th, at Warrenton Junction, he entered with his staff a railroad train that was about to start toward Washington. Here there was stationed a detachment of 2000 troops. They were drawn up in line, and a salute was fired. The men then broke their ranks, surrounded the car in which he was seated, uncoupled it from the train and ran it back, insisting wildly that he should not leave them, and uttering the bitterest imprecations against those who had deprived them of their beloved commander. The scene has been described to us by an officer who was present as one of fearful excitement. The moment was critical. One word, one look of encouragement, the lifting of a finger, would have been the signal for a revolt against lawful authority, the consequences of which no man can measure. McClellan stepped upon the front platform of the car, and there was instant silence. His address was short. It ended in the memorable words, 'Stand by General Burnside as you have stood by me, and all will be well.' The soldiers were calmed. They rolled the car onward, recoupled it to the train, and with one long and mournful huzza bade farewell to their late commander, whom many of them were destined never to behold again. General McClellan reached Washington on the following day, and without tarrying for an hour proceeded at once to Trenton, where he arrived at 4 o'clock in the morning of the 12th. From that time he never again saw Lincoln, or Stanton, or Halleck."—EDITORS.

HOT WORK FOR HAZARD'S BATTERY.   SEE P. 115.

SUMNER'S "RIGHT GRAND DIVISION."†

BY DARIUS N. COUCH, MAJOR-GENERAL, U. S. V.

ON the evening of October 15th, 1862, a few days after McClellan had placed me in command of the Second Corps, then at Harper's Ferry, the commanding general sent an order for Hancock to take his division the next morning on a reconnoissance toward Charlestown, about ten miles distant. The division started in good season, as directed. About 10 in the morning General McClellan reined up at my headquarters and asked me to go out with him to see what the troops were doing. Our people had met the enemy's outpost five miles from the Ferry, and while artillery shots were being exchanged, both of us dismounted, walked away by ourselves, and took seats on a ledge of rocks. After a little while McClellan sent to an aide for a map of Virginia. Spreading it before us, he pointed to the strategic features of the valley of the Shenandoah, and indicated the movements he intended to make, which would have the effect of compelling Lee to concentrate in the vicinity, I think, of Gordonsville or Charlottesville, where a great battle would be fought. Continuing the conversation, he said, "But I may not have command of the army much longer. Lincoln is down on me," and, taking a paper from his pocket, he gave me my first intimation of the President's famous letter. ⚓

---

†It is due to General Couch to state that, with limited time in which to prepare this paper, he dictated it to a stenographer in answer to questions by the editors bearing chiefly on his personal recollections.— EDITORS.

⚓ Lincoln's letter is dated October 13th, 1862, and begins: "MY DEAR SIR,—You remember my speaking to you of what I called your over-cautiousness. Are you not over-cautious when you assume that you cannot do what the enemy is constantly doing? Should you not claim to be at least his equal in prowess, and act upon the claim?" Further on the President says: "Change positions with the enemy, and think you not he would break your communication with Richmond within the next twenty-four hours? You dread his going into Pennsylvania; but if he does so in full force, he gives up his communication to you absolutely, and you have nothing to do but to follow and ruin him. . . . Exclusive of the water-line, you are

He read it aloud very carefully, and when it was finished I told him I thought there was no ill-feeling in the tone of it. He thought there was, and quickly added, "Yes, Couch, I expect to be relieved from the Army of the Potomac, and to have a command in the West; and I am going to take three or four with me," calling off by their names four prominent officers. I queried if "so and so" would be taken along, naming one who was generally thought to be a great favorite with McClellan. His curt reply was, "No, I sha'n't have him."

This brief conversation opened a new world for me. I had never before been to any extent his confidant, and I pondered whether on a change of the commanders of the Army of the Potomac the War Department would allow him to choose the generals whose names had been mentioned. I wondered what would be the future of himself and those who followed his fortunes in that untried field. These and a crowd of other kindred thoughts quite oppressed me for several days. But as the time wore on, and preparations for the invasion of Virginia were allowed to go on without let or hindrance from Washington, I naturally and gladly inferred that McClellan's fears of hostile working against him were groundless. However, the blow came, and soon enough.

On the 8th of November, just at dark, I had dismounted, and, standing in the snow, was superintending the camp arrangements of my troops, when McClellan came up with his staff, accompanied by General Burnside. McClellan drew in his horse, and the first thing he said was:

"Couch, I am relieved from the command of the army, and Burnside is my successor."

I stepped up to him and took hold of his hand, and said, "General McClellan, I am sorry for it." Then, going around the head of his horse to Burnside, I said, "General Burnside, I congratulate you."

Burnside heard what I said to General McClellan; he turned away his head, and made a broad gesture as he exclaimed:

"Couch, don't say a word about it."

His manner indicated that he did not wish to talk about the change; that he thought it was not good policy to do so, nor the place to do it. He told me afterward that he did not like to take the command, but that he did so to keep it from going to somebody manifestly unfit for it. I assumed that he meant Hooker. Those of us who were well acquainted with Burnside knew that he was a brave, loyal man, but we did not think that he had the military ability to command the Army of the Potomac.

McClellan took leave on the 10th. Fitz John Porter sent notes to the corps commanders, informing them that McClellan was going away, and suggesting that we ride about with him. Such a scene as that leave-taking

now nearer Richmond than the enemy is, by the route that you *can* and he *must* take." And in conclusion: "It is all easy if our troops march as well as the enemy, and it is unmanly to say they cannot do it. This letter is in no sense an order."

In his "Life of Abraham Lincoln" (Chicago: Jan-sen, McClurg & Company) Isaac N. Arnold makes President Lincoln say: "With all his failings as a soldier, McClellan is a pleasant and scholarly gentleman. He is an admirable engineer, but he seems to have a special talent for a *stationary engine*."— EDITORS.

CHATHAM, OPPOSITE FREDERICKSBURG, ALSO KNOWN AS THE "LACY HOUSE." FROM A WAR-TIME PHOTOGRAPH.

had never been known in our army. Men shed tears and there was great excitement among the troops. [See p. 104.]

I think the soldiers had an idea that McClellan would take care of them,— would not put them in places where they would be unnecessarily cut up; and if a general has the confidence of his men he is pretty strong. But officers and men were determined to serve Burnside loyally.

A day or two afterward Burnside called the corps commanders together, mapped out a course that he intended to pursue; and, among other things, he said that he intended to double the army corps, and he proposed to call the three new commands — or doubles — "grand divisions." Under this arrangement my corps, the Second, and Willcox's, the Ninth, which had been Burnside's, formed the Right Grand Division under General Sumner. When Sumner and I arrived near Falmouth, opposite Fredericksburg, November 17th, we found the enemy in small force in readiness to oppose our crossing the Rappahannock. Everybody knew that Lee would rush right in; we could see it. If the pontoons had been there, we might have crossed at once. [See p. 121.] Yet we lay there nearly a month, while they were fortifying before our eyes; besides, the weather was against us. Under date of December 7th, my diary contains this entry: "Very cold; plenty of snow. Men suffering; cold outdoors, ice indoors in my room."

Sumner's headquarters were at the Lacy House, while the Second Corps lay back of the brow of the hill behind Falmouth.

On the night of the 9th, two nights before the crossing, Sumner called a council to discuss what we were to do, the corps, division, and brigade commanders being present. The result was a plain, free talk all around, in which words were not minced, for the conversation soon drifted into a marked disapprobation of the manner in which Burnside contemplated meeting the enemy.

Sumner seemed to feel badly that the officers did not agree to Burnside's mode of advance. That noble old hero was so faithful and loyal that he wanted, even against impossibilities, to carry out everything Burnside suggested. I should doubt if his judgment concurred. It was only chivalrous attacnment to Burnside, or to any commander. But there were not two opinions among the subordinate officers as to the rashness of the undertaking.

Somebody told Burnside of our views, and he was irritated. He asked us to meet him the next night at the Lacy House. He said he understood, in a general way, that we were opposed to his plans. He seemed to be rather severe on Hancock,—to my surprise, for I did not think that officer had said as much as myself in opposition to the plan of attack. Burnside stated that he had formed his plans, and all he wanted was the devotion of his men. Hancock made a reply in which he disclaimed any personal discourtesy, and said he knew there was a line of fortified heights on the opposite side, and that it

THE PHILLIPS HOUSE, BURNSIDE'S HEADQUARTERS.
FROM A PHOTOGRAPH TAKEN WHILE THE HOUSE WAS BURNING.

would be pretty difficult for us to go over there and take them. I rose after him, knowing that I was the more guilty, and expressed a desire to serve Burnside, saying, among other things, that if I had ever done anything in any battle, in this one I intended to do twice as much. French came in while I was talking. He was rather late, and in his bluff way exclaimed: "Is this a Methodist camp-meeting?"

The heights on the morning of the 11th, before the bridges were thrown across, did not offer a very animated scene, because the troops were mostly hidden. The bombardment for the purpose of dislodging the sharp-shooters who under cover of the houses were delaying the bridge-making, was terrific, while the smoke settled down and veiled the scene. After the bombardment had failed to dislodge the enemy, the 7th Michigan and the 19th and the 20th Massachusetts of Howard's division sprang into the pontoons, and rowing themselves over drove away Barksdale's sharp-shooters. This gallant action enabled the engineers to complete the bridges. Howard's division was the first to cross by the upper bridge [see map, p. 74], his advance having a lively fight in the streets of Fredericksburg. Hawkins's brigade of Willcox's corps occupied the lower part of the town on the same evening, and the town was not secured without desperate fighting. I went over the next morning, Friday, the 12th, with Hancock's and French's divisions. The remainder of Willcox's corps crossed and occupied the lower part of the town. There was considerable looting. I placed a provost-guard at the bridges, with orders that nobody should go back with plunder. An enormous pile of booty was collected there by evening. But there came a time when we were too busy to guard it, and I suppose it was finally carried off by another set of spoilers. The troops of the two corps bivouacked that night in the streets and were not per-

mitted to make fires. Late on that day we had orders to be ready to cross Hazel Run, which meant that we were to join Franklin. That was the only proper move to make, since we had done just what the enemy wanted us to do,—had divided our army. The conditions were favorable for a change of position unknown to the enemy, since the night was dark and the next morning was foggy. But it would have been very difficult to make the movement. I was much worried in regard to building the necessary bridges over Hazel Run and the dangers attending a flank movement at night in the presence of the enemy. But the order to march never came. The orders that were given by Burnside showed that he had no fixed plan of battle. After getting in the face of the enemy, his intentions seemed to be continually changing.

Early the next morning, Saturday, the 13th, I received orders to make an assault in front. My instructions came from General Sumner, who did not

cross the river during the fight, owing to a special understanding with which
I had nothing to do, and which related to his supposed rashness. At Fair
Oaks, Antietam, and on other battle-fields he had shown that he was a hard
fighter. He was a grand soldier, full of honor and gallantry, and a man of
great determination.

FREDERICKSBURG FROM THE EAST BANK OF THE RAPPAHANNOCK — I.

As I have said, on that Saturday morning we were enveloped in a heavy
fog. At 8:15, when we were still holding ourselves in readiness to move
to the left, I received the following order:

"HEADQUARTERS, RIGHT GRAND DIVISION, NEAR FALMOUTH, VA., December 12th, 1862.
"MAJOR-GENERAL COUCH, Commanding Second Corps d'Armée.
"GENERAL: The major-general commanding directs me to say to you that General Willcox has
been ordered to extend to the left, so as to connect with Franklin's right. You will extend your
right so far as to prevent the possibility of the enemy occupying the upper part of the town.
You will then form a column of a division for the purpose of pushing in the direction of the
Plank and Telegraph roads, for the purpose of seizing the heights in rear of the town. This
column will advance in three lines, with such intervals as you may judge proper, this movement
to be covered by a heavy line of skirmishers in front and on both flanks. You will hold another
division in readiness to advance in support of this movement, to be formed in the same manner
as the leading division. Particular care and precaution must be taken to prevent collision with
our own troops in the fog. The movement will not commence until you receive orders. The
watchword will be, 'Scott!' Very respectfully, your most obedient servant,

"J. H. TAYLOR, Chief of Staff and Assistant Adjutant-General.

"P. S. The major-general thinks that, as Howard's division led into the town, it is proper
that one of the others take the advance."

French was at once directed to prepare his division in three brigade lines for the advance, and Hancock was to follow with his division in the same order. The distance between the brigade lines was to be about 200 yards.

Toward 10 o'clock the fog began to lift; French reported that he was ready, I signaled to Sumner, and about 11 o'clock the movement was ordered to begin. French threw out a strong body of skirmishers, and his brigades filed out of town as rapidly as possible by two parallel streets, the one on the right, which

FREDERICKSBURG FROM THE EAST BANK OF THE RAPPAHANNOCK — II.

was Hanover street, running into the Telegraph road, and both leading direct to Marye's Hill, the stronghold of the enemy. On the outskirts of the town the troops encountered a ditch, or canal, so deep as to be almost impassable except at the street bridges, and, one of the latter being partly torn up, the troops had to cross single file on the stringers. Once across the canal, the attacking forces deployed under the bank bordering the plain over which they were to charge. This plain was obstructed here and there by houses and fences, notably at a fork of the Telegraph road, in the narrow angles of which was a cluster of houses and gardens; and also on the parallel road just south of it, where stood a large square brick house. This cluster of houses and the brick house were the rallying-points for parts of our disordered lines of attack. The fork in the road and the brick house were less than 150 yards from the stone-wall, which covered also as much more of the plain to the left of the brick house. A little in advance of the brick house a slight rise in the ground afforded protection to men lying down, against the musketry behind the stone-wall, but not against the converging fire of the artillery on the heights. My headquarters were in the field on the edge of the town, overlooking the plain.

A few minutes after noon French's division charged in the order of Kimball's, Andrews's, and Palmer's brigades, a part of Kimball's men getting into the cluster of houses in the fork of the road. Hancock followed them in the order of Zook's, Meagher's, and Caldwell's brigades, the two former getting

THE BOMBARDMENT OF FREDERICKSBURG, DECEMBER 11, 1862.

nearer to the stone-wall than any who had gone before, except a few of Kimball's men, and nearer than any brigade which followed them.

Without a clear idea of the state of affairs at the front, since the smoke and light fog veiled everything, I sent word to French and Hancock to carry the enemy's works by storm. Then I climbed the steeple of the court-house, and from above the haze and smoke got a clear view of the field. Howard, who was with me, says I exclaimed, " Oh, great God ! see how our men, our poor fellows, are falling ! " I remember that the whole plain was covered with men, prostrate and dropping, the live men running here and there, and in front closing upon each other, and the wounded coming back. The commands seemed to be mixed up. I had never before seen fighting like that, nothing approaching it in terrible uproar and destruction. There was no cheering on the part of the men, but a stubborn determination to obey orders and do their duty. I don't think there was much feeling of success. As they charged the artillery fire would break their formation and they would get mixed; then they would close up, go forward, receive the withering infantry fire, and those who were able would run to the houses and fight as best they could; and then the next brigade coming up in succession would do its duty and melt like snow coming down on warm ground.

I was in the steeple hardly ten seconds, for I saw at a glance how they were being cut down, and was convinced that we could not be successful in front, and that our only chance lay by the right. I immediately ordered Howard to work in on the right with the brigades of Owen and Hall, and attack the enemy behind the stone-wall in flank, which was done. Before he could begin this movement both Hancock and French had notified me that they must have support or they would not be responsible for the maintenance of their position. Sturgis, of Willcox's corps, who had been supporting my left, sent the brigades of Ferrero and Nagle to the fruitless charge.

About 2 o'clock General Hooker, who was in command of the Center Grand Division (Stoneman's and Butterfield's corps), came upon the field. At an earlier hour Whipple's division of Stoneman's corps had crossed the river and relieved Howard on the right, so that the latter might join in the attack in the center, and Griffin's division of Butterfield's corps had come over to the support of Sturgis. Humphreys and Sykes, of the latter corps, came to my support. Toward 3 o'clock I received the following dispatch:

" HEADQUARTERS, RIGHT GRAND DIVISION, ARMY OF THE POTOMAC, Dec. 13th, 1862.—2:40 P. M. GENERAL COUCH : Hooker has been ordered to put in everything. You must hold on until he comes in. By command of Brevet Major-General SUMNER. W. G. JONES, Lieut., Aide-de-camp, etc."

NOTE TO ILLUSTRATION.— The Artillery Reserve posted on the eastern bank of the river comprised four commands, as follows : the Right Division, under Lieutenant-Colonel William Hays, extending from Falmouth down to the ravine, about 500 yards below Falmouth (see map, p. 74), and consisting of 40 rifled guns ; the Right Center Division, under Colonel C. H. Tompkins, consisted of 38 guns ; the Left Center Division, under Colonel R. O. Tyler, occupying the crest of the ridge from the middle bridge southward to the wooded ravine near the center of the ridge, and consisting of 27 guns ; the Left Division, under Captain G. A. De Russy, numbering 42 guns. When the order was given to fire upon the town, only the guns of the Right Center and Left Center could be brought to bear effectually. Hays's batteries delivered a few shots. Tyler's guns opened fire, doing but little execution. Colonel Tompkins reported that his batteries opened at 12 : 30 P. M. under orders to burn the town, and ceased firing at 2 : 30 P. M., at which time several buildings were burning.—EDITORS.

CROSSING THE RIVER IN PONTOONS TO
DISLODGE THE CONFEDERATE
SHARP-SHOOTERS.

Hooker was the ranking general, and as I understood that he was to take command of the whole fighting line, the putting in of his fresh men beside mine might make a success. His very coming was to me, therefore, like the breaking out of the sun in a storm. I rode back to meet him, told him what had been done, and said, "I can't carry that hill by a front assault; the only chance we have is to try to get in on the right." Hooker replied, "I will talk with Hancock." He talked with Hancock, and after a few minutes said, "Well, Couch, things are in such a state I must go over and tell Burnside it is no use trying to carry this line here,"— or words to that effect,— and then he went off. His going away left me again in command. Burnside was nearly two miles distant. It was not much after 2 o'clock when he went away, and it was about 4 when he returned. This was after Humphreys had made his charge and the fighting for the day was substantially finished. We were holding our lines. Hooker left word that Humphreys, whose division was ready to advance, should take his cue from me. Butterfield also gave Humphreys orders to that effect. After a lull in the battle General Caldwell, a brigade commander under Hancock, sent word to the latter that the enemy were retreating from Marye's house. It was probably only a shifting of the enemy's troops for the relief of the front line. But, assuming that the report was true, I said, "General Humphreys, Hancock reports the enemy is falling back; now is the time for you to go in!" He was ready, and his troops around him were ready. The order had evidently been expected, and after an interval of more than twenty-five years I well recollect the grim determination which settled on the face of that gallant hero when he received the words, "Now is the time for you to go in!" Spurring to his work he led his two brigades, who charged over precisely the same ground, but who did not get quite so near to the stone-wall as some of French's and Hancock's men.↓

The musketry fire was very heavy, and the artillery fire was simply terrible. I sent word several times to our artillery on the right of Falmouth that they were firing into us, and were tearing our own men to pieces. I thought they had made a mistake in the range. But I learned later that the fire came from the guns of the enemy on their extreme left.

Soon after 4 o'clock, or about sunset, while Humphreys was at work, Getty's division of Willcox's corps was ordered to the charge on our left by the unfinished railroad. I could see them being dreadfully cut up, although they had not advanced as far as our men. I determined to send a battery upon the plain to shell the line that was doing them so much harm; so I ordered an aide to tell Colonel Morgan to send a battery across the canal and plant it near the brick house. Morgan came to me and said: "General, a battery can't live there." I replied, "Then it must die there!"

Hazard took his battery out in gallant style and opened fire on the enemy's lines to the left of the Marye House. Men never fought more gallantly, and he lost a great many men and horses. When Hooker came he ordered Frank's battery to join Hazard. But this last effort did not last long. In the midst of it I rode to the brick house, accompanied by Colonel Francis A. Walker, Lieutenant Cushing, and my orderly, Long. The smoke lay so thick that we could not see the enemy, and I think they could not see us, but we were aware

↓ Lieutenant-Colonel Carswell McClellan, Assistant Adjutant-General, serving on General Humphreys's staff at Fredericksburg, writes to the editors to correct a statement made in Walker's "History of the Second Army Corps" [p. 181], as well as by other writers, implying that the charge of Humphreys's division was supported by Sykes. Colonel McClellan says:

"Sykes's division *had not crossed the Rappahannock* when General Humphreys's first assault was made, and the head of his column reached the bridge crossing the mill-race on the Telegraph road, only after the last charge made by General Humphreys had been repulsed. General Sykes's First and Second Brigades *afterward* relieved the troops upon the advanced line on the Telegraph road, and experienced one of the most trying tours of duty exacted from troops

during the war. His Third Brigade remained massed in Fredericksburg during the night of December 13th–14th."

Noticing, also, the denials of General Walker and others that General Humphreys's men approached "nearer to the wall than any other troops had reached," Colonel McClellan cites the fact that General Humphreys, who made this statement, was an eye-witness of the scene from his position in front of his division, while on the other hand the officers of the burial-parties sent out a week later (whose evidence has been relied on to support the opposite view) could hardly have identified the men of the different commands, because nearly all the bodies had in the meantime been stripped of their clothing.— EDITORS.

THE NINTH CORPS CROSSING BY THE PONTOON-BRIDGE TO THE STEAM-
BOAT LANDING AT THE LOWER END OF THE TOWN.

of the fact that some-body in our front was doing a great deal of shooting. I found the brick house packed with men ; and behind it the dead and the living were as thick as they could be crowded to-gether. The dead were rolled out for shelter, and the dead horses were used for breastworks. I know I tried to shelter myself behind the brick house, but found I could not, on account of the men already there. The plain thereabouts was dotted with our fallen. I started to cross to the fork of the road where our men, under Colonel John R. Brooke, were holding the cluster of houses.

When it became dark the wounded were being brought off the plain, and Hooker was talking about relieving my men in front by putting in Sykes's division, and I said, "No! No men shall take the place of the Second Corps unless General Sumner gives the orders. It has fought and gained that ground and it shall hold it." Later the order came for Sykes to relieve the Second Corps, which was done about 11 o'clock.

That night was bitter cold and a fearful one for the front line hugging the hollows in the ground, and for the wounded who could not be reached. It was a night of dreadful suffering. Many died of wounds and exposure, and as fast as men died they stiffened in the wintry air, and on the front line were rolled forward for protection to the living. Frozen men were placed for dumb sentries.

My corps again bivouacked in the town, and they were not allowed fires lest they should draw the fire of the enemy's artillery.

At 2 o'clock in the morning Burnside came to my headquarters near the center of the town. I was lying down at the time. He asked me to tell him about the battle, and we talked for about an hour. I told him everything that had occurred. "And now," I said, "General Burnside, you must know that everything that could be done by troops was done by the Second Corps." He said, "Couch, I know that; I am perfectly satisfied that you did your best." He gave no intimation of his plans for the next day. He was cheerful in his tone and did not seem greatly oppressed, but it was plain that he felt he had led us to a great disaster, and one knowing him so long and well as myself could see that he wished his body was also lying in front of Marye's Heights. I never felt so badly for a man in my life.

The next day, Sunday, the 14th, our men began digging trenches along the edge of the town. We were on the alert, for there was some fear of an assault. Of course there is no need of denying that after the battle the men became strained. The pressure of a fight carries you through, but after it is all over and you have been whipped you do not feel very pugnacious.

WAREHOUSE IN FREDERICKSBURG USED AS A HOSPITAL.

The men, knowing that they had been unsuccessful, were in a nervous state, and officers suffered also from the reaction, the worst of it being that the mass of the army had lost confidence in its commander.

About midday of the 14th Burnside called a council of war, in which it was decided to fall back, but to hold Fredericksburg. No attack was made by us that day, though Burnside had said that he should renew the assault on Marye's Hill, with his old Ninth Corps, and that he would place himself at its head. General Getty of that corps, a very gallant officer, touched me as I passed him and said: "I understand that Burnside has given out that he intends to lead seventeen regiments to the attack." He urged me strongly to dissuade him if possible, as it would be a perfect slaughter of men.

At the council Hooker expressed himself as against the movement of retreat, saying, "We must fight those people. We are over there and we must fight them." But, as I remember, he did not advocate the plan of holding Fredericksburg if we were not to renew the fight. I urged that the army was not in a condition, after our repulse, to renew the assault, but that we ought to hold Fredericksburg at all hazards. I had an argument with General Burnside upon that point, telling him that I was willing to have him throw all the responsibility upon me; that if we held the town we should

THE GROUND BETWEEN FREDERICKSBURG AND MARYE'S HEIGHTS. FROM A WAR-TIME PHOTOGRAPH.

The portico of the Marye mansion is faintly marked among the trees of the hill in the middle-background. The road on the right is the end of Hanover street and the beginning of the Telegraph road, by which most of the attacking troops crossed the canal, or ditch, and, filing to the left, formed line under the low bank. In the middle-ground, to the left of the road, is seen the square brick house mentioned by General Couch. Part of the troops crossed the canal by a street on the left parallel with Hanover street, and a few waded. Most of the dead lay a short distance beyond the brick house.

Colonel John R. Brooke, of Hancock's division, was sent on the fourth day after the battle with a large detail to bury the dead. In his official report he says: "Those bodies nearest the enemy's works were recognized as belonging to Kimball's brigade of French's division and to the different regiments of Hancock's division." In the two days occupied by the burial he says he "found and buried 913 of our soldiers, and brought to this side of the river the bodies of five officers, making a total of 918. Nearly all the dead were stripped entirely naked by the enemy." A woman who lived in one of the houses near the stone-wall has related that "the morning after the battle the field was blue; but the morning after the Federals withdrew the field was white."— EDITORS.

have a little something to show for the sacrifice of the day before; that the people would feel we had not failed utterly. It was agreed that Fredericksburg should be held. Then Burnside dismissed us and sent Hooker and myself to Fredericksburg to arrange for the defense. We held a council at the corner of Hanover street.

It was decided that Hooker's troops should hold the town. The question was how many men would he leave for that purpose, opinions varying from ten to eighteen thousand. My limit was ten thousand men. General Tyler turned to me and said: "Make it higher, General." We compromised on twelve thousand. We remained in the town on the 15th, and that evening my corps and the Ninth Corps recrossed the river. Next morning we found that Fredericksburg had been evacuated. When Willcox and I left, we thought, of course, it would be held. The talk was that during the night Hooker prevailed upon Burnside to evacuate the town.

Our wing of the army thought the failure of the campaign was due in part to the fact that we were put in where we ought not to have been. We were asked to achieve an impossibility. We had something to do that was not possible for us to do.

After the battle Burnside tried to regain the confidence of the army, and there is no doubt that Sumner did a good deal to help him. Burnside conceived the plan of crossing the Rappahannock a few miles above Fredericksburg, where the enemy were unprepared to receive us. The result was the "mud march" of January 20th–21st. It was Burnside's effort to redeem himself. To start off in the mud as we did with the army in its discouraged state was perfect folly. There did not seem to be anything in the move to recommend itself. If the weather had happened to turn cold, possibly he might have surprised Lee and gotten across the river, above Fredericksburg, but it was a hazardous move, with the army out of confidence with its commander and the enemy elated with brilliant success. The general demoralization that had come upon us made two or three months of rest a necessity. ♭

When Hooker, on January 25th, was placed in command of the army, many of us were very much surprised; I think the superior officers did not regard him competent for the task. He had fine qualities as an officer, but not the weight of character to take charge of that army. Nevertheless, under his administration the army assumed wonderful vigor. I have never known men to change from a condition of the lowest depression to that of a healthy fighting state in so short a time. President Lincoln with his wife came down to spend a few days with General Hooker, and to see the different officers and talk with them. To further that, General Hooker gave a dinner party at

♭ In the course of a correspondence, relating to their several controversies with General Burnside, Franklin wrote to Halleck, under date of June 1st, 1863: "I was of your opinion with regard to the honesty and integrity of purpose of General Burnside, until after his relief from the command of the Army of the Potomac. I lost all confidence in his ability at the first Fredericksburg battle. There was not a man in my command who did not believe that everything he would undertake would fail, and General Hooker informed me that that was the general feeling in his command. General Sumner's feelings were not so decided, but they were nearly so. You can imagine that the beds of the grand division commanders were not of roses, and I came to the conclusion that Burnside was fast losing his mind. So I looked upon the rain which stopped his second attempt to cross the river [the 'mud march'] as almost a providential interference in our behalf."—EDITORS.

STUCK IN THE MUD—A FLANK MARCH ACROSS COUNTRY. FROM A WAR-TIME SKETCH.

THE GRAND REVIEW AT FALMOUTH DURING PRESIDENT LINCOLN'S VISIT.
FROM A WAR-TIME SKETCH.

which all the corps commanders were present, and also Mrs. Lincoln. Mr.
Lincoln would talk to the officers on the subject that was uppermost in our
minds—how we were to get the better of the enemy on the opposite hills.
Before he went away he sent for Hooker and for me, I being second in
command, and almost his last injunction was: "Gentlemen, in your next
battle *put in all your men*." Yet that is exactly what we did not do at Chancellorsville.

We had a grand review of the army in honor of the President. The Second
Corps paraded with Howard's Eleventh Corps, I think, for after I had saluted
at the head of my corps I rode to the side of the President, who was on horseback, and while near him General Schurz approached at the head of his division. I said: "Mr. Lincoln, that is General Schurz," pronouncing it *Shurs*,
after the American fashion. Mr. Lincoln turned to me and said: "Not *Shurs*,
General Couch, but *Shoortz*." But he did it very pleasantly, and I was just
a little surprised that our Western President should have the advantage of
me. It was a beautiful day, and the review was a stirring sight. Mr. Lincoln, sitting there with his hat off, head bent, and seemingly meditating, suddenly turned to me and said: "General Couch, what do you suppose will
become of all these men when the war is over?" And it struck me as very
pleasant that somebody had an idea that the war would sometime end.

THE CROSSING OF THE RAPPAHANNOCK BY THE 19TH MASSACHUSETTS.

BY H. G. O. WEYMOUTH, CAPTAIN, 19TH MASSACHUSETTS REGIMENT.

ON the morning of the 11th of December, 1862, about two hours before daylight, the regimental commanders of Colonel Norman J. Hall's Third Brigade, of Howard's Second Division, Second Army Corps, were assembled at brigade headquarters to receive preliminary orders for the approaching battle. Our brigade commander informed us that our regiment was to be the first to cross the upper pontoon-bridge, which was to be laid by the engineer corps by daylight, and that we were to hold and occupy the right of the town until the whole army should have crossed, when the Right Grand Division, comprising the Second and Ninth Corps, would charge the heights, supported by artillery in front and on the right flank. On our arrival at the river at daylight we found but a very small section of the bridge laid, in consequence of the commanding position which the enemy held on the right bank of the river, secreted as they were behind fences made musket-proof by piling cord-wood and other materials against them. After a fruitless attempt of eight hours' duration to lay the bridge where the enemy had absolute control of the river front, the idea was abandoned, and notice was sent down to us at the river that the enemy would be shelled from the heights, with orders to take to the pontoon-boats and cross and dislodge the enemy in order to enable the engineer corps to complete the bridge. The instant the artillery ceased firing, the 7th Michigan and 19th Massachusetts took to the boats and poled across the river under a heavy musketry fire from the enemy. The 7th Michigan was the first to make a landing, and marched up Farquhar street in a direct line from the bridge. They immediately became severely engaged, and the first two companies of the 19th Massachusetts that had crossed went forward and joined them. A few minutes later the remainder of the 19th crossed, formed in line on the bank of the river, left resting on Farquhar street, and advanced, deploying as skirmishers in order to drive back the enemy from the western part of the city. We were met with such resistance by Barksdale's brigade, very aptly styled by General Longstreet "Confederate hornets," that it was nearly dusk before we gained the north side of Caroline street. It was now apparent that our thin line could not make any farther advance against the formidable barricades the enemy had erected on the south side of the street, consisting of barrels and boxes, filled with earth and stones, placed between the houses, so as to form a continuous line of defense, and the left of our line was forced to fall back down Farquhar street, fully one-half the distance from Caroline street. On reporting our position to a staff-officer our brigade commander ordered the 20th Massachusetts to clear the streets. They marched up Farquhar street in company or division front, and on reaching Caroline street wheeled to the right; but before the full regiment had entered the street the enemy, from their snug retreats, poured such a deadly fire on them as to force them to retire with great loss.

This action of the 20th enabled our left to regain our position on Caroline street, which was maintained until Barksdale withdrew his command to the heights, about an hour after dark. At about 11 o'clock General Howard crossed over to learn our position. Informing him that the enemy had retired in our front, I asked him if we should move forward. After making some inquiries concerning our right, he thought nothing would be gained by doing so. We remained in this position until about noon of the 13th.

THE PONTONIERS AT FREDERICKSBURG.

BY WESLEY BRAINERD, MAJOR 50TH, AND COLONEL 15TH, NEW YORK ENGINEERS.

FROM certain remarks made by various writers [see pp. 107 and 126] on the battle of Fredericksburg, it might be inferred that there was some foundation for the general impression that had the pontoons arrived in time, the crossing could have been made before the enemy concentrated, and the disastrous defeat which followed might thus have been avoided.

The fact is that the engineers (15th and 50th New York), with two full trains and material for two pontoon-bridges, each 420 feet in length, arrived opposite Fredericksburg and bivouacked in rear of the Lacy house on the afternoon of November 27th, and could have thrown two bridges across the stream without opposition that night had they been allowed to do so. There was no force of the enemy in the city, and General Longstreet, with the advance of the Confederate army, had by a forced march occupied a portion of the heights in rear of the city on the 21st.

I distinctly remember that General Sumner rode up to our position soon after our arrival on the 27th and asked Major Ira Spaulding, of the 50th New York, and myself if we could throw a bridge across the river that night, to which we replied that we could throw two bridges across in three hours if he would give us the order to do so. After a little hesitation, he replied that he would like to give us the order, as there was certainly nothing to oppose its execution, but that he did not care to assume the responsibility, fearing that it might conflict with General Burnside's plans. He also remarked that he could have forded the stream with a part of his command at Falmouth several days before had he been allowed to do so; he then rode away. We were ordered back into camp, and the "golden opportunity" passed — a blunder for which we were in no way responsible, but for which we were destined to suffer.

We did not receive the order to leave Berlin, six miles below Harper's Ferry, until late on the *seventh day* after it was issued.┃ We took up two bridges, each 1100 feet long, loaded and moved them by canal and land transportation to Washington, where we received 500 unbroken mules. We then fitted up two trains, moved through the mud to Occoquan, where we divided the trains, part going by water and part by land to Aquia Creek, where we again reloaded the entire equipment, and arrived at the Lacy house but six days behind Longstreet's advance, which had made a forced march from the vicinity of Culpeper to reach the heights in rear of Fredericksburg. These being the facts, it can hardly be said, with justice, that the engineers were slow in their movements.

The idea of crossing immediately in front of the town seemed to have passed, temporarily at least, from General Burnside's mind, and "demonstrations" on an extensive scale were made to the right and left.

Twice I crossed the river below the town and examined the country for some distance inland, it being rather difficult to find ground suitable for the passage of artillery on both sides of the stream at all stages of the tide. The second time I crossed at "Skinker's Neck," and made a thorough examination of the country for several miles around, pacing off the distances, and furnished General Burnside, in person, with my sketches. These expeditions were, of course, made in the night.

"Skinker's Neck" seemed to me to be the proper place for a crossing. At the time of my visit it was not occupied by the enemy, except by a cavalry patrol, which I easily avoided.

Six or eight miles above, where I made my first crossing, it was somewhat difficult to make my way through the picket lines. General Burnside appeared to be greatly pleased and relieved when I reported favorably on the "Skinker's Neck" crossing. He gave me to understand that we should throw our bridges there, and we made our arrangements accordingly.

What was my surprise when, a few days after, the orders came that mine was to be one of two bridges that were to be thrown across directly in front of the city, near the Lacy house.

┃The "Official Records" show that this order, issued by Captain J. C. Duane, Chief-Engineer of the Army of the Potomac at Rectortown, on the 6th of November, did not reach Major Spaulding, at Berlin, until the afternoon of November 12th. General Halleck's report exonerates the engineers from all blame.— EDITORS.

IN FRONT OF THE STONE WALL AT FREDERICKSBURG. ⚓

BY JOHN W. AMES, BREVET BRIGADIER-GENERAL, U. S. V.

O
N Saturday, December 13th, our brigade ┃ had been held in reserve, but late in the day we were hurried to the battle only to see a field full of flying men and the sun low in the west shining red through columns of smoke,— six deserted field-pieces on a slight rise of ground in front of us, and a cheering column of troops in regular march disappearing on our left. But the day was then over and the battle lost, and our line felt hardly bullets enough to draw blood before darkness put an end to the uproar of all hostile sounds, save desultory shell-firing. For an hour or two afterward shells from Marye's Heights traced bright lines across the black sky with their burning fuses. Then, by command, we sank down in our lines, to get what sleep the soggy ground and the danger might allow us. Experience had taught us that when the silent line of fire from the shells had flashed across the sky and disappeared behind us the scream and explosion that followed were harmless, but still it required some effort to overcome the discomfort of the damp ground, and the flash and report of bursting shells, and to drop quietly asleep at an order. We finally slept, but we were roused before midnight, and formed into line with whispered commands, and then filed to the right, and, reaching the highway, marched away from the town. There were many dead horses at exposed points of our turning and many more dead men. Here stood a low brick house, with an open door in its gable end, from which shone a light, and into which we peered when passing. Inside sat a woman, gaunt and hard-featured, with crazy hair and a Meg Merrilies face, still sitting by a smoking candle, though it was nearly two hours past midnight. But what woman could sleep, though never so masculine and tough of fiber, alone in a house between two hostile armies,— two corpses lying across her door-steps, and within, almost at her feet, four more! So, with wild eyes and face lighted by her smoky candle, she stared across the dead barrier into the darkness outside with the look of one who heard and saw not, and to whom all sounds were a terror.

We formed in two lines,— the right of each resting near and in front of this small brick house, and the left extending into the field at right angles with the highway. Here we again bivouacked, finding room for our beds with no little difficulty, because of the shattered forms of those who were here taking their last long sleep. We rose early. The heavy fog was penetrating and chilly, and the damp turf was no warm mattress to tempt us to

⚓ Condensed from the "Overland Monthly," 1869, Vol. III., p. 432, by permission of Fisher Ames. General John W. Ames, U. S. Surveyor-General of California, died in San Rafael, in that State, in 1877.

┃The 2d Brigade of regulars (Sykes's division, Fifth Army Corps), commanded by Major George L. Andrews, 17th U. S. Infantry. General Ames was then a captain in the 11th U. S. Infantry.— EDITORS.

a morning nap. So we shook off sloth from our moistened bodies willingly, and rolling up the gray blankets set about breakfast. The bivouac breakfast is a nearer approach to its civilized congener than the bivouac bed. Coffee can be made hot and good in blackened tins; pork can be properly frizzled only on a stick over an open fire; hard-tack is a better, sweeter morsel than the average American housewife has yet achieved with her saleratus, sour-milk, "empt'ins," and what-not; and a pipe! — who can estimate what that little implement has done for mankind? Certainly none better than those who have sought its solace after the bivouac breakfast that succeeds a bivouac bed, in December.

We now began to take note, through the misty veil, of the wreck of men and horses cumbering the ground about us, and a slight lifting of the gray fog showed us the story of yesterday's repeated assaults and repeated failures. When our pipes were exhausted we got up to inspect and criticise the situation. Just here was the wreck of a fence, which seemed to have been the high-tide mark of our advance-wave of battle. The fence was a barrier which, slight as it was, had turned back the already wavering and mutilated lines of assault. Almost an army lay about us and scattered back over the plain toward the town. Not only corpses, but many of the badly wounded, hardly distinguishable from the dead, were here too. To die, groveling on the ground or fallen in the mire, is dreadful indeed. The pallid faces, and the clammy hands clenching their muskets, looked ghastly by the fog-light. The new, bright, blue overcoats only made the sight the ghastlier.

About eighty yards in front the plowed field was bounded by a stone-wall, and behind the wall were men in gray uniforms moving carelessly about. This picture is one of my most distinct memories of the war — the men in gray behind this wall, talking, laughing, cooking, cleaning muskets, clicking locks,— there they were! — Lee's soldiers! — the Army of Northern Virginia! We were so absurdly near this host of yesterday's victors that we seemed wholly in their hands and a part of their great mass; cut off and remote from the Federal army ♭ and almost within the lines of the enemy — prisoners, of course. That was the immediate impression, as we stupidly gazed in the first moment of the awkward discovery.

But the sharp whistle of a bullet sounded in our ears, and a rebel's face peered through the puff of smoke, as he removed the rifle from his shoulder; then rapidly half-a-dozen more bullets whistled by us, and the warning sent us all to earth. The order to lie down is theoretically infrequent, but practically it is often given in modern warfare. Napoleon's maxim that "an army travels on its belly" was metaphorical, but long-range and repeating rifles have gone far to make it true in a literal sense. Our double lines of battle sought the shelter of the ground as soon as blood was drawn. This had the effect of hiding us from

the enemy, or partially so, for the fusillade slackened.

It was irksome to keep one position, even at full length, but the watch over us was very vigilant; hardly a movement was made at any part of our line that did not draw fire from the wall. Necessity compelled us, however, to keep up something of a lookout upon the enemy at any risk. A cautious inspection showed great carelessness in their lines, the men still strolling and lounging — a group at cards, even, evidently ignorant or careless of our proximity.

What to do about it was to us a topic second only in interest to the probable action of the enemy. Could we long lie thus without waking up the big guns, whose black muzzles looked down at us from the hill-tops on our right? And if not, what then? From these guns there would be no possible shelter. Retreat alone was more dangerous than to remain as we were, or even to advance. The field behind us stretched away toward the town, level and exposed — the focus of an arc of battery-crowned hills, with no inequality of ground to protect us from a convergence of fire that would be singularly effective.

The situation had already forced upon us a policy of masterly inactivity, which alone seemed to meet our immediate difficulties. So we drifted into a common understanding that no doubt an abler council of war would have approved. Shots might rouse the enemy from his carelessness or ignorance; certainly a volley from our line would not go unanswered, and the odds were great. Let them stick to their cards and forget us if they would! But we arrived at this policy only as the least of many evils.

The enemy riddled every moving thing in sight: horses tied to the wheels of a broken gun-carriage behind us; pigs that incautiously came grunting from across the road; even chickens were brought down with an accuracy of aim that told of a fatally short range, and of a better practice than it would have been wise for our numbers to face. They applauded their own success with a hilarity we could hardly share in, as their chicken-shooting was across our backs, leaving us no extra room for turning. But this was mere wantonness of slaughter, not indulged in when the higher game in blue uniform was in sight. The men who had left our ranks for water, or from any cause, before we were pinned to the earth, came back at great peril. Indeed, I believe not one of them reached our line again unhurt. Some were killed outright; others were mortally wounded, and died within a few steps of us; and several who tried to drag themselves away flat upon their faces were put out of their misery. This, too, showed us plainly what we might expect, and fixed our bounds to such segments of the field as were hidden from the enemy. This was not alike throughout the line. At one point the exposure was absolute, and stillness as absolute was the only safety. A slight barrier was afterward formed at this point by a

---

♭ The force here consisted of Buchanan's and Andrews's brigades of regulars, of Sykes's division, and Stockton's brigade of volunteers, of Griffin's division, Fifth Army Corps.— EDITORS.

disposal of the dead bodies in front, so that the dead actually sheltered the living.

After two or three hours of this experience we became somewhat accustomed to the situation,— for man becomes accustomed to almost anything that savors of routine,—and learned with considerable exactness the limit inside which we might move with safety, and the limit also of endurable constraint. It was somewhat curious to see how strong the tobacco hunger was with many,— perhaps with most. Men would jump to their feet and run the length of a regiment to borrow tobacco, and in so doing run the gauntlet of a hundred shots. This was so rarely accomplished in entire safety that it won the applause of our line and hearty congratulations to any one fortunate enough to save his life and sweeten it with the savory morsel.

All this would have been ludicrous but for the actual suffering inflicted upon so many. Men were mortally hit, and there was no chance to bind up their wounds; they were almost as far beyond our help as if they had been miles away. A little was accomplished for their relief by passing canteens from hand to hand, keeping them close to the ground out of sight, and some of the wounded were where a little manipulation could be done in safety. It was sad to hear the cries fade away to low moans, and then to silence, without a chance to help. The laugh over a successful chase for tobacco would die away only to change into a murmur of indignation at the next cruel slaughter. A young officer, boyish and ruddy, fresh from a visit home, with brighter sword and shoulderstraps than most of us, raised his head to look at the enemy, and a bullet at once pierced his brain. Without a word or groan his head sank again, his rosy cheek grew livid, and his blood crimsoned his folded hands. Next a leg or arm was shattered as it became exposed in shifting from the wearisomeness of our position. Presently a system of reporting the casualties became established; the names of the injured were passed from mouth to mouth;—"Captain M——, 17th, just killed"; "Private ——, Co. C, 11th ——, knocked over." Those who were fortunate enough to have paper and pencil, and elbow-room enough to get them from pocket-depths, kept a list of the names of the killed and wounded; the occupation this gave proved a blessing, for the hours were very long and weary.

I suppose *ennui* is hardly the word where nerves are on the rack, and danger pinions one to a single spot of earth, yet something like *ennui* came over us. By chance I found a fragment of newspaper which proved a charm that for a time banished the irksome present with its ghastly field of dead men and its ceaseless danger. Through this ragged patch of advertisements I sailed away from Fredericksburg with the good bark *Neptune*, which had had quick dispatch a month before,—for the paper was of ancient date,—and was well on her way to summer seas, when I obeyed the printed injunction and applied on board for passage. And oh, pleasant summer meadows of the peaceful North! who would have suspected you to lurk in

extracts of sarsaparilla and ointment for eruptive skins? But I found you there, and forgot the sunshine and the chill earth, the grim war, the rifle's crack and the bullet's whistle,—forgot even the dead hand that had stretched itself toward me all the morning with its clutch of grass.

I was called back to the dull wet earth and the crouching line at Fredericksburg by a request from Sergeant Read, who "guessed he could hit that cuss with a spy-glass,"— pointing, as he spoke, to the batteries that threatened our right flank. Then I saw that there was commotion at that part of the Confederate works, and an officer on the parapet, with a glass, was taking note of us. Had they discovered us at last, after letting us lie here till high noon, and were we now to receive the plunging fire we had looked for all the morning? Desirable in itself as it might be to have "that cuss with a spy-glass" removed, it seemed wiser to repress Read's ambition. The shooting of an officer would dispel any doubts they might have of our presence, and we needed the benefit of all their doubts. Happily, they seemed to think us not worth their powder and iron.

Were we really destined to see the friendly shades of night come on and bring us release from our imprisonment? For the first time we began to feel it probable when the groups left the guns without a shot. I grew easy enough in mind to find that sleep was possible, and I was glad to welcome it as a surer refuge from the surroundings than the scrap of newspaper. It was a little discouraging to see a sleeping officer near me wakened by a bullet, but as his only misfortune, besides a disturbed nap, seemed to be a torn cap and scratched face, he soon wooed back the startled goddess. I had enjoyed sleep for its quiet and rest, but never before for *mere* oblivion.

When I returned to consciousness I found the situation unchanged, except that the list of casualties had been swelled by the constant rifle practice, which was still as pitiless and as continuous as before. It was almost startling to see, on looking at the brick house, the Meg Merrilies of the night before standing at her threshold. With the same lost look of helpless horror that her face had worn by candle-light, she gazed up and down our prostrate lines, and the disenchantment of day and sunshine failed to make her situation seem in any way prosaic and commonplace. The desolate part she had to play suited well her gaunt and witch-like features. Shading her eyes with her hand at last, as if to banish a vision and call her senses back to earth, she searched our lines once more; then, with a hopeless shake of the head, she moved slowly back into the dismal little tomb she was forced to occupy. In which army was her husband serving? Did she search our lines and the dead ranks for any friend of hers? Was maternal anxiety added to the physical terrors of her forced isolation?

Slowly the sun declined. He had been our friend all day, shining through the December air with an autumn glow that almost warmed the chill earth; but at his last half-hour he seemed to hang motionless in the western sky. His going down would set us free; free from the fire that was galling and decimating us; free from the fear of guns on the right, and advance from the front; free from numbness, and constraint, and irksomeness, and free from the cold, wet earth. Also it would bring us messengers from the town to call us back from the exposed position and the field of dead bodies. But he lingered and stood upon the order of his going, until it seemed as if a Joshua of the Confederates had caused him to stand still.

When at last the great disc stood, large and red, upon the horizon, every face was turned toward it, forgetting constraint, thirst, tobacco, and rebel fire, in the eagerness to see the end of a day that had brought us a new experience of a soldier's life, and had combined the dangers of a battle-field and the discomfort of a winter's bivouac with many new horrors of its own.

At last the lingering sun went down. December twilights are short; the Federal line sprang to its feet with almost a shout of relief. The repel fire grew brisker as they saw such a swarm of blue-coats rising from the ground, but it was too late to see the fore-sights on the rifles, and shots unaimed were not so terrible as the hated ground. So we contemptuously emptied our rifles at them, and before the smoke rolled away the coming darkness had blotted out the wall and the hostile line.

With our line rose also a few men from the ghastly pile of yesterday's dead, who hobbled up on muskets used as crutches. These poor fellows had bound up their own wounds, and the coffee we had given them had cheered them into life and hope. Their cheerfulness grew into hilarity and merriment as they found themselves clear, at last, from the dead, and facing toward home, with a hope not by any means so impossible of realization as it had seemed not long before. Poor fellows! their joy was more touching than their sufferings,—which, indeed, they seemed to have forgotten.

In our own brigade we found we had lost nearly 150, ⸮ out of a present-for-duty strength of about 1000 men. This would have been a fair average loss in any ordinary battle, but we had suffered it as we lay on the ground inactive, without the excitement and dash of battle and without the chance to reply: a strain upon nerves and physical endurance which we afterward remembered as severer than many more fatal fields. In the midst of our buzz of relief and mutual congratulation, the expected summons came for us to fall back to the town. Once more we formed an upright line of battle, then faced by the rear rank and marched

in retreat, with muffled canteens and many halts and facings about toward a possible pursuit. Reaching a slight bank, we descended to the meadow through which the Fredericksburg raceway was dug, and here we changed to a flank march and filed into the highway. The highway soon became a street, and we were once more in Fredericksburg.

We marched past the court-house,—past churches, schools, bank-buildings, private houses, —all lighted for hospital purposes, and all in use, though a part of the wounded had been transferred across the river. Even the door-yards had their litter-beds, and were well filled with wounded men, and the dead were laid in rows for burial. The hospital lights and camp-fires in the streets, and the smoldering ruins of burned buildings, with the mixture of the lawless rioting of the demoralized stragglers, and the suffering and death in the hospitals, gave the sacked and gutted town the look of pandemonium.

In our new freedom we wandered about for the first half of the night, loath to lie on the earth again after our day's experience. At last we spread our blankets on a sidewalk and slept in the lurid firelight with a sense of safety not warranted by our position. The next morning we made our toilets in wanton plenty. Water from a pump! and we bathed in the falling splash. Our "contraband" brought us a box of soap and an uncut, unhemmed bolt of toweling from the despised plunder of a store. The same source gave us a table-cloth for our breakfast. This we spread upon the sidewalk and furnished with variously assorted crockery from an ownerless pantry. Cabbage fresh from a kitchen garden, with vinegar from the deserted kitchen, added a welcome and unusual luxury to the meal. And at the end we rolled dishes and débris together into the paved gutter by a comprehensive pull at the table-cloth. Then we smoked the emblem of peace, tilted back against the buildings in borrowed chairs, and were very comfortable and happy. This was the holiday of war,—vastly better than yesterday! But we were hardly safer here, though more comfortable. Lee might open his guns at any moment. The drum-beat made us tip down our chairs and fall into line. We had roll-call and something like a dress parade without music, then stacked arms along the curb-stone and mounted sentinels over them. A bright, beautiful day and the freedom of an uninhabited and plundered city were before us.

⸮ The "Official Records" (Vol. XXI., Pt. I., p. 136) give the loss as 12 killed, 114 wounded, 14 missing; total, 140.— EDITORS.

WHY BURNSIDE DID NOT RENEW THE ATTACK AT FREDERICKSBURG.

BY RUSH C. HAWKINS, BREVET BRIGADIER-GENERAL, U. S. V.

NOVEMBER 22d, 1862, the whole Union army had reached Falmouth, opposite Fredericksburg, and General Lee, who had proved upon more than one occasion his watchfulness and enterprise, took means to insure the arrival, about the same time, of the Army of Northern Virginia on the heights in the immediate rear of Fredericksburg.

Without the slightest delay the enemy's line of defense was marked out, nor did their labors cease until their defensive lines were made formidable and complete by the mounting of a large number of guns. In the meantime the Army of the Potomac had drawn its abundant supply of daily rations, subjected itself to some drilling and several reviews, while its commander had been carrying on an animated correspondence with the powers at Washington, chiefly in relation to pontoons which had been promised but had failed to reach Falmouth until long after the arrival of both armies at the points they then occupied. [See p. 121.] Some time during the first week in December the much-looked-for pontoon train appeared, and then came the oft-repeated camp rumor of a "movement over the river," which in a few days assumed a more definite form, the actual plan of attack becoming the topic of many a camp-fire. It was freely stated that the whole army was to cross the river about such a time, and that the chief attack was to be made by General Sumner's Right Grand Division upon the enemy's center immediately back of Fredericksburg, where the hills were steepest and the fortifications strongest.

There were a few officers in the Army of the Potomac who had watched the gradual growth of the enemy's lines, and knew something of the natural formations in that direction,— a succession of steep hills which, in themselves, were almost as potent for defensive purposes as the average artificial fortifications. I, for one, had been over that ground several times the August before while engaged in ascertaining the best line for a grand guard for the protection of the roads leading from the back country into Fredericksburg. The three or four officers who were possessed of this knowledge expressed themselves very strongly in opposition to the plan of attack as foreshadowed by the gossips of the camp, and the news of these adverse opinions having come to General Burnside, he sent a circular to the general officers of the Right Grand Division and colonels commanding brigades to meet him at the Phillips house on the evening of December 9th. At the time appointed the large room of that mansion was filled with general officers, with here and there a colonel and a few grand division staff-officers. General Burnside made a speech in which he partly disclosed and explained his plan for the coming battle. It was received without any particular criticism or comment, but General French, who was very enthusiastic, said the battle would be won in forty-eight hours, and called for three cheers for the commander, which were given.

The meeting ended, Colonel J. H. Taylor, assistant adjutant-general of the Right Grand Division, and myself were standing together in the hall of the house, when General Burnside came along and said to me, "What do you think of it?" I answered, "If you make the attack as contemplated it will be the greatest slaughter of the war; there isn't infantry enough in our whole army to carry those heights if they are well defended." He then turned to Colonel Taylor and said, "Colonel, what do you say about it?" The response came quickly and was sufficiently definite, "I quite agree with Colonel Hawkins. The carrying out of your plan will be murder, not warfare." The commanding general was very much surprised and irritated at these answers, and made a remark about my readiness to throw cold water upon his "plans"; he repeated the assertion of French about victory within forty-eight hours, and passed on.

The meeting dispersed, the officers who had composed it going to their respective commands and giving their final orders for the movement of the following day. Besides attending to the details of moving my command on the morrow, I found time to write three letters — one to my mother, another to my wife, and a third to Charles P. Kirkland, of the city of New York. In each of these defeat was distinctly and without qualification predicted. The first letter in the order mentioned has been preserved, and from it the following quotations are given:

"CAMP, NEAR FALMOUTH, VA., December 10th, 1862.

"DEAR MOTHER—. . . . To-morrow, if our present plans are carried out, the great battle of the war will commence. . . . I have little hope of the plans succeeding. I do not think them good,— there will be a great loss of life and nothing accomplished. I am sure we are to fight against all chances of success. There is a rumor and a hope that Banks may have landed on the James River; if so, a large part of the enemy's force will be diverted from this point, but if they have a force anywhere near our own in number we are pretty certain to get whipped."

The letter to Judge Kirkland was much stronger and more explicit, and evoked an answer from which one paragraph is quoted:

"NEW YORK, December 18th, 1862.

"How wonderfully *prophetic* is your letter, written on the 10th of December. It *foretells* exactly the awful disaster and reverse that our cause has met with. How is it possible, if you thus knew all this, that those *having control* were ignorant of it? This whole transaction seems now almost incredible. To think of the thousands of splendid, brave, patriotic fellows absolutely butchered without the least beneficial result : on the contrary, with a result disgraceful and disheartening to us, but I fervently trust a result from which we can recover."

This matter of the letters is here referred to, not in a spirit of pride, but simply to show a want of knowledge, judgment, and foresight on the part of those high in command.

We now pass over the bombardment of December 11th, the many disastrous attempts to lay the pontoons in front of Fredericksburg, and come to 3 o'clock of that day, when volunteers were called for to cross the river in open boats for the purpose of dislodging the enemy from the opposite bank. For this service the 7th Michigan, 19th and 20th Massachusetts of General Howard's division, and the 89th New York of my brigade answered the call. The first three regiments crossed under fire where the first bridge was afterward laid, and the fourth under sharper fire where the second was completed. By 9 o'clock that night the division of General Howard and my brigade had obtained possession of the town, the former taking the right of the line and the latter the left. The whole of the 12th of December into the night was occupied in crossing the army, and on the morning of the 13th the battle began and continued at intervals until darkness set in. During a considerable portion of that day, while the attacks upon the enemy's center, known as "Marye's Heights," were being made, General George W. Getty, my division commander, and myself were on the roof of the Slaughter house, a high residence at the lower end of the city, named after its owner. From this prominent position our repeated repulses and the terrible destruction of the Union troops had been witnessed. At about half-past 3 o'clock the order came for General Getty's Third Division of the Ninth Corps to make an attack upon that part of the enemy's line to the left of where the principal attacks had been made. The order was obeyed, but not until I had tried to induce General Getty to protest against its obedience and the further useless waste of life. The attack of our division closed a battle which was one of the most disastrous defeats to the Union forces during the war. The sadness which prevailed throughout the whole army on that night can neither be described nor imagined. The surgeons were the happiest of all, for they were so busy that they had no time to think of our terrible defeat.

About 9 o'clock that evening I found myself near a building situated upon the main street of the town, where several of the generals of the Right Grand Division had assembled for the purpose of discussing the attack to be made the next morning. When I entered the room these officers were looking at a map upon a table, showing the position of the enemy. There were present Generals Willcox, Humphreys, Getty, Butterfield, Meade, and three or four others. They were seriously discussing the proposed renewal of the attack the next day as though it had been decided upon. I listened until I was thoroughly irritated because of the ignorance displayed in regard to our situation, and then uttered a solemn, earnest, and emphatic protest against even the consideration of another attack. With a pencil I made a rough drawing of the first line then occupied by the enemy, and also showed a second position a little to the rear, to which they could fall back and make a strong stand in the event of their being driven out of their first line. It did not take long to convince these officers that a second attack would probably end more disastrously than the first, and they united in a request that I should go at once to try to persuade Burnside that the attack ought not to be renewed.

It was a cheerless ride in the wet and cold, and through the deep mud of an army-traveled road that dark night, for I was already weary from much care, watching, and loss of sleep, and besides I was fully aware of the unpleasant fact that an officer of very inferior rank was bent upon an ungrateful errand to a general commanding one of the largest armies of modern times. But a solemn sense of duty, and a humane desire to save further useless slaughter, convinced me that any sacrifice of self ought to be made in the interest of the men who were fighting our battles.

I arrived at the Phillips house about 11 o'clock to learn that I had probably passed General Burnside on the road, who had gone to perfect the details for a second attack. Those present at the Phillips house were Generals Sumner, Hooker, Franklin, Hardie, and Colonel Taylor. I made a brief statement and explanation of the object of my mission, which deeply interested all present. They united in a desire that I should wait until the arrival of General Burnside, which occurred about 1 o'clock. As he came through the door he said: "Well, it's all arranged; we attack at early dawn, the Ninth Corps in the center, which I shall lead in person"; and then seeing me he said: "Hawkins, your brigade shall lead with the 9th New York on the right of the line, and we'll make up for the bad work of to-day."

When he had ceased there was perfect silence, and he was evidently astonished that no one approved. With hesitation and great delicacy General Sumner then stated the object of my visit, and suggested that General Burnside should examine the rough drawing then upon the table, and listen to some reasons why the attack contemplated ought not to be made. After I had explained the enemy's positions, called attention to several pertinent circumstances, and made something of an argument, General Burnside asked General Sumner what he thought, and he replied that the troops had undergone such great fatigue and privation, and met with such a disaster, that it would not be prudent to make another attack so soon. General Hooker, who was lying full length upon a bed in one corner of the room, upon being appealed to by General Burnside, sat up and said in the most frank and decided manner that the attack ought not to be renewed that morning. Then a general consultation took place, in which all who were present joined, the result of which was a verbal order, transmitted through me, countermanding the arrangements for a second attack.

Of those present at the first interview, on the Fredericksburg side, Generals Getty, Willcox, Butterfield, and probably several others whom I do not now remember, are living. The only survivors of the Phillips house interview are General Franklin and myself. In one of his letters to me, dated Hartford, Conn., December 17th, 1866, he says:

". . . I distinctly recollect your talk to Burnside, to which you refer, and had he been so talked to before he crossed the river, many lives would have been saved, as well as much credit to himself and reputation to the gallant Army of the Potomac."

FRANKLIN'S MEN CHARGING ACROSS THE RAILROAD.

FRANKLIN'S "LEFT GRAND DIVISION."

BY WILLIAM FARRAR SMITH, BREVET MAJOR-GENERAL, U. S. A.

WHEN General Burnside assumed the command of the Army of the Potomac on the 9th of November, 1862, he gave up the immense strategic advantage which McClellan had gained, and led the army to Falmouth on the Rappahannock River, opposite the city of Fredericksburg. A few days after his arrival on the Rappahannock he called a council of war. It was a conference rather than a council, for he stated that he called the generals together to make known something of his plans, and not to put any question before them for decision. The grand division commanders, Sumner, Franklin, and Hooker, were present, and also, I think, the corps commanders. I was present as commander of the Sixth Army Corps. The entire army was massed within a few miles of Falmouth, and the first object was to cross the river in our front, and gain a fair field for a battle. From the same ground Hooker afterward marched north-west, and by a series of fine movements placed himself in a position to offer battle at Chancellorsville on at least equal terms. The outcome of Hooker's campaign belied its beginning, but it led to the battle of Gettysburg, which more than compensated in results for the previous failure. ↓

General Burnside opened the conference by stating that within a few days he proposed to cross the river to offer battle to General Lee, and that after a close study of the reports of his engineers he had chosen Skinker's Neck as

↓ When General Burnside determined to occupy Fredericksburg it was not held by a large force of the enemy. A body of cavalry, sent from Warrenton, could have seized the place without serious opposition, and could have held it until the advance of the infantry came up. In the preliminary discussion of the move from Warrenton to Fredericks- burg, the notion that a serious battle was necessary to enable the army to get into Fredericksburg was not entertained by any one. Sumner, who had the advance, reported that when he arrived at Falmouth he could even then have occupied Fredericksburg without opposition, had his orders justified him in crossing the river.— W. B. FRANKLIN.

the point of crossing. Skinker's Neck is a shoe-shaped bend in the Rappahannock River, about twelve miles below Fredericksburg. It offered all the necessary military features for forcing a crossing, but, like Butler's famous "bottle" at Bermuda Hundred, also presented great facilities for preventing the egress of an army which had effected an entrance on its peninsula. After developing to a limited extent his plans, the general said that any one present was at liberty to express his views on the subject. General Sumner, if I recollect aright, remarked only that he would do his utmost to carry out the plans of the commanding general. General Franklin said that we could doubtless effect a crossing at the designated place; he assumed that the movements, after crossing, had been carefully studied, and he stood ready to execute any orders he might receive. General Hooker then said, in substance, that it was preposterous to talk about our crossing the river in the face of Lee's army; that he would like to be in command of fifty thousand men on the other side of the river, and have an enemy make the attempt. I then stated that I would guarantee the crossing of the river if my command had the advance. General Burnside closed the conference by stating that his mind was made up; that we must prepare our commands for the work before them; and that we should receive the proper orders in due time.

Three or four days after that I was at Burnside's headquarters, and he invited me to take a ride with him. Riding along on the hills near the river,

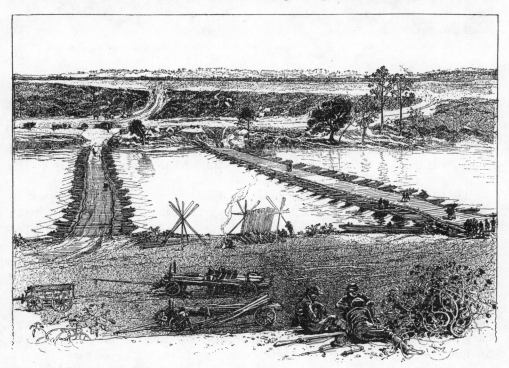

THE PONTOON-BRIDGES AT FRANKLIN'S CROSSING. FROM A WAR-TIME PHOTOGRAPH.
The hills occupied by Stonewall Jackson's command are seen in the distance.

FRANKLIN'S BATTLE-FIELD AS SEEN FROM HAMILTON'S CROSSING — FREDERICKSBURG STEEPLES
IN THE DISTANCE. FROM A SKETCH MADE IN 1884.

he pointed out some fine positions for artillery, and said: "My reserve artillery has as yet had no chance to show its value, and I am going to make the crossing here and below, under cover of the guns of the reserve artillery."

To this I replied, "You can cross here without great difficulty, for this bank dominates the other, but when your army is across your troubles will begin," calling his attention at the same time to the range of hills on the other side, a mile or more back from the river.

"Oh!" said Burnside, "I know where Lee's forces are, and I expect to surprise him. I expect to cross and occupy the hills before Lee can bring anything serious to meet me."

I then said, "If you are sure of that, there is no more to be said on the subject."

On parting General Burnside said, "I wish you to say nothing to any one about my change of plan. I will make it known at the proper time."

Though General Franklin and myself were on the most intimate terms, and occupied the same tent, I gave him no hint of the change. Two or three days before the movement General Franklin was notified of the point selected for his crossing, and I then told him the story of the change of plan.

He merely said, "Your command is the strongest, and you must take the advance."

As I remember, it was on the afternoon of the 10th of December that General Franklin received an order to have the head of his command at a designated point on the river, about one and a half miles below Fredericksburg, and since known as Franklin's Crossing, at daylight on the morning of the 11th, where he would at once begin crossing by bridges which would be found ready.

On the morning of the 11th of December, at 5 o'clock, the First Corps, under Major-General John F. Reynolds, marched to take position at the bridges, and cover the crossing of the Sixth Corps over the Rappahannock. A brigade of the corps had moved at 2 o'clock A. M., to protect the engineer troops while throwing the bridges, which were expected to be finished by daylight. The work was for a while suspended on account of the fire of sharpshooters, covered by some fishing-huts and a thicket on the opposite shore. Two batteries placed on the bank opened with canister and shell, and caused the enemy to disappear, and work was resumed. When the head of the Sixth Corps reached the bank at 7:30 A. M., only three or four pontoons of each bridge had been placed in position, and the bridges were not completed till about 1 P. M. It was not until about 4 P. M. that I received orders to begin the crossing.

General Devens's brigade held the post of honor and began the movement, using both bridges. One of the commanders of the leading regiments, more patriotic than wise, had placed his band at the head of the column, and it was ordered to begin playing as it reached the bridge. This threw the men on the bridges into "step," and for some minutes it looked as though both bridges must go down. Fortunately, through the reckless riding of a "Wild Irishman" on the staff, an order reached the colonel, and the music was stopped before any harm was done.

The troops were rapidly thrown across, when an order came to recross all but one brigade. This was done and General Devens's brigade was left to keep the bridge-head. The cause of this was that the upper bridges opposite the town, intended for the use of the right wing, had not yet been finished. Sharp-shooters in the brick houses near the river had interfered with the work, and the heavy guns of the reserve artillery could not make the same impression on masonry walls that our field-batteries had produced on thicket and hut. Some volunteers finally crossed the river to Fredericksburg in boats and cleared the other bank, and the bridge was rapidly laid.

Of course all chance of effecting a surprise was now over, and if we persisted in crossing we must fight for the hills south of the river. There was, however, a very fine opportunity for turning what had been done into a feint, and crossing the main army elsewhere. But this was not done, and early on the morning of the 12th the Sixth Corps recommenced the passage of the river, marched to the front about a mile, and formed line of battle. Its right was thrown across Deep Run, which, between the Sixth Corps and the river, was an impassable stream, separating us, until bridged, from the right wing of the army. In the right front was an open field, traversed by Deep Run from left to right, bounded by the hills and narrowing as it

FROM A PHOTOGRAPH TAKEN ABOUT 1884.

W B Franklin

approached a gorge a mile or more away. In front of the left and right at a
distance of perhaps half a mile was the ridge of hills occupied by the enemy.

The First Corps, under Major-General John F. Reynolds, followed the
Sixth, and, forming on its left, curved back across the Richmond road and
rested its left on the Rappahannock River. In its right front was the range of
hills at a short distance, which broke away, leaving an open space on the
left between it and the river. Here were two corps with an impassable stream
on their right, a formidable range of hills occupied by the enemy covering
almost their entire front, and at their back a river with two frail bridges connecting its shores. It takes soldiers who do not believe that war is an art to
be perfectly at their ease under such circumstances.

General Franklin, General Reynolds, and myself were on the most intimate
social and official terms. We always discussed questions of general interest
to the command, and after General Reynolds had placed his corps in position

we met and looked over the situation as it then appeared to us. We unanimously agreed that there was but one thing to do, and that was to put the forty thousand men of the Left Grand Division into columns of assault on the right and left of the Richmond road, carry the ridge, and turn Lee's right flank at any cost. To do this the Sixth Corps must be relieved from its position in line, where it was covering the bridge. This could only be done after dark, but as it would take some time to get the columns formed, and as it was necessary that the men should get some rest before morning, the work of preparation must begin directly after dusk. In coming to this conclusion we had considered the fact that Lee being on the exterior had longer lines than those of our army, and that therefore he could not have force enough on his right to resist an assault by forty thousand men, and that the demonstration made on his left would prevent the withdrawal of any of his force from that flank. Besides this we had in front of Reynolds open country of sufficient width to turn the hills which terminated to the right of the Richmond road.

About 5 P. M. General Burnside came to the left wing, and after he had taken a hurried gallop along the lines General Franklin asked him to go to his tent, and there gave him the above-described plan as the only one that in our judgment offered a fair hope of success. When General Burnside left us we were all of the opinion that he agreed with us, and the last request, urgently pressed upon him, was that he should at once give the order for Birney's and Sickles's divisions of the Third Corps (Hooker's Center Grand Division) to cross the bridge and be ready to begin to relieve the Sixth Corps in the lines at dusk. Under the supposition that the orders asked for would soon be received, General Franklin gave General Reynolds and myself orders to do all the preliminary work possible; which being done, we returned to General Franklin's headquarters to await the arrival of the messenger from General Burnside. As the precious time passed by we fell to discussing the condition of affairs. Burnside had proposed to effect a surprise, and now before Lee could be attacked he would have had forty-eight hours for concentration against us and for fortifying his positions on the hills. Burnside had persisted in crossing the river after all hope of a surprise had faded away, and now we must fight our way out under great disadvantages. Had Burnside been forced into a move by the Administration? Under the circumstances would he make a desperate fight or only go far enough to keep up appearances? Whatever was in store for us the Left Grand Division was a unit in sentiment; the men were brave and well disciplined, and we felt sure that with our forty thousand men we could force back Lee's right flank and get a better position for a general battle, if one were then necessary. Would Burnside adopt our plan, and if so, why this delay which was costing us so much valuable time? We had all known Burnside socially, long and intimately, but in his new position of grave responsibility he was to us entirely unknown.

The weary hours of that long winter night wore away in this profitless manner until about 3 o'clock, when General Reynolds said: "I know I have hard work ahead of me and I must get some sleep. Send for me if I am

RUINS OF "MANSFIELD," ALSO KNOWN AS THE "BERNARD HOUSE." FROM A WAR-TIME PHOTOGRAPH.

wanted." General Franklin then sent an aide to headquarters, who returned with the answer that the orders would "come presently."

The order came, I think, at 7:45 A. M.: "Keep your whole command in position for a rapid movement down the old Richmond road." Two-thirds of the command (the Sixth Corps) was so placed that it could not move, without danger of losing the bridges, until relieved by other troops or until Lee's right wing should be in full retreat. "And you will send out at once a division, at least, to pass below Smithfield,"—a hamlet occupied by Reynolds on the previous evening,—"to seize if possible the heights near Captain Hamilton's, on this side of the Massaponax, taking care to keep it well supported and its *line of retreat open*."

The peculiar wording of the order is positive evidence that when it was penned Burnside's mind was still filled with the fallacy of effecting a surprise. The order recites that the division to be sent out by Franklin—and also one to be pushed forward by Sumner on the right—was to *seize*, or attempt to seize, certain heights. The military man is habituated to use the word seize when an unguarded position is to be occupied, or a point in the lines of the enemy left weak through ignorance or neglect is to be taken by a sudden rush. Both of these operations are in the nature of a military surprise. When an advantage is to be gained by hard fighting or the weight of a mass of troops, the word *carry* is instinctively used. In corroboration of this proposition, I will state that in the third interview I had with Burnside, after the battle, he said, "I should have ordered Franklin to carry the heights at Captain Hamilton's at all hazards." ⸹

⸹ Just as General Burnside was leaving, shortly after nightfall, I asked to be permitted to order General Stoneman's corps (the Third) to cross at once. He declined to give the permission, but as- sured me I would have the orders before midnight. Had the permission been granted, the First and Sixth Corps would have been in position for the at- tack by daylight, the Third Corps taking the place of

The Sixth Corps had two divisions in line and one in reserve. It remained in an exposed position during the day, and suffered severely from artillery fire, while the enemy in its front were well covered by woods and rifle-pits.

In obedience to his orders Reynolds moved to the attack at 8:30 A. M., with his center division under Meade, which was to be supported by the division of Gibbon on the right and next to the Sixth Corps. The third division, under Doubleday, was in reserve and guarding Meade's left. ☆ Meade crossed the ravine in his front, and directed his course toward a point of woods coming down from the heights. The artillery on the crest was silenced by three batteries, and Meade pushed on, supported on his right by Gibbon, and, after severe fighting, carried the crest, capturing flags and prisoners. In the dense woods on the height, the connection with Gibbon

A JACK-KNIFE RECORD ON THE STONE WALL
OF THE BERNARD HOUSE.

was lost, and Meade, after a stubborn contest, was finally driven back, Gibbon yet holding his ground. Two regiments from the Third Corps arriving were sent to Gibbon's left, but were soon overpowered, and they were forced back with Gibbon. The enemy made a strong show of following up their success, but the arrival of two fresh brigades from the Third Corps checked them and drove them back to their sheltered positions. Gibbon's division, after its retreat, was relieved by Sickles's division of the Third Corps. Newton's division, the reserves of the Sixth Corps, arrived late in the afternoon and took position on the left, but was not engaged. The enemy's batteries on their extreme right, having a reverse fire upon Meade, when he advanced up the crest, maintained their position throughout the battle. Owing to the foggy character of the day our artillery on the left bank of the Rappahannock was obliged to fire somewhat at random, and for the same reason the fire from the enemy's batteries was not very well directed. The contest ended at nightfall, our troops having made no material permanent advance.

The military reader will see that had Meade and Gibbon had behind them, when they carried the enemy's lines, the 25,000 men of the Sixth Corps instead of 2 regiments, simply, of the Third Corps, the probabilities would all

the Sixth, which would have attacked with the First Corps. Had the necessary orders been received, even by midnight, the movements would have been made under cover of the darkness, and the whole night after midnight would have been required to make them. It seems that General Burnside went to bed as soon as he arrived at his headquarters, and did not write the orders until the next morning. None of my urgent messages sent to him during the night were delivered to him, although their receipt at headquarters was acknowledged.

It will be seen that the order sent by General Burnside under which the attack was made is entirely different from that for an attack by forty thousand men, which I had a right to expect from what took place at our interview of the previous evening. And its receipt at 7:45 in the morning [it was dated 5:55 A. M.], instead of midnight, was unaccountable, except under the supposition that Burnside, for some reason that was unknown to us on the left, disapproved of the plan to which we thought he had assented, or that no serious attack was to be made from the left.—W. B. FRANKLIN.

☆ It came into action shortly after Meade's advance, to repel a threatened attack from a large force of cavalry which developed between our left and the Massaponax Creek.—W. B. FRANKLIN.

BRIGADIER-GENERAL GEORGE D. BAYARD, KILLED AT FREDERICKSBURG.
FROM A PHOTOGRAPH.

have been in favor of a success. When night fell there were no longer forty thousand men in the Left Grand Division, and we had gained no important advance.

After Meade's division had been withdrawn from the front he came to General Franklin's headquarters, and on being asked some question about the fight said, " I found it quite hot enough for me," taking off his slouched hat and showing two bullet-holes between which and the top of his head there must have been little space. During one of the feeble, skirmishing attacks made on the lines of the Sixth Corps later in the day, Meade, who was still at headquarters, was expressing great uneasiness lest the enemy should break through and capture the bridges. General Franklin quieted him by saying that the Sixth Corps could not be driven from its position.

"Mansfield," as the Bernard house was called, was a large, stone mansion, that looked down on the Rappahannock River close beneath it, and was approached by an imposing drive, while behind was an open grove of magnificent trees; in this grove was the headquarters of General Franklin. The house was evidently one of Virginia's ancestral homes, and had been in former days the center of generous hospitality. Though under artillery fire, it was used as a temporary hospital, and in it the brave Bayard died. The grove was filled with saddled horses, not for the use of fair ladies and gay cavaliers, as in the olden time, but for staff-officers and orderlies to carry orders into the fight and bring back reports from the field. The testy owner, who remained about the house during the early part of the day, and whose word had been law for so many years to all the country side, did not realize, when he demanded the immediate evacuation of his premises, that he spoke to a man who commanded 40,000 men, and one who on that day had little regard for proprietary rights, and did not stand much in awe of a Virginia magnate or constable.∤

∤ When I first arrived at the Bernard house I found Mr. Bernard holding a lively interview with Reynolds. It seemed that Mr. Bernard protested against the use of his house and grounds by the troops because they would spoil them, and insisted upon staying at the house to protect it. Reynolds on such occasions was a man of few words, and I presently saw Mr. Bernard hurrying toward the pontoon-bridges between two soldiers, and he was not seen again in that vicinity.— W. B. FRANKLIN.

During this day, as in all days of battle, many sad and many humorous incidents occurred. Some of the shots that were fired too high for the line of battle went hurtling through the headquarters of General Franklin into the open grove of large trees. General George D. Bayard, much endeared to us by his social qualities and his rare merits as a cavalry leader, was mortally wounded by a round shot through the thigh. Bayard and his friend, Captain H. G. Gibson, commanding a battery of flying artillery, were within ten feet of Franklin, and were just rising from the ground to go to luncheon when the shot came. It severed Gibson's sword-belt without injury to him, and struck Bayard. Many generals could have better been spared from the service.

A few days before the battle there had come to the Sixth Corps the first importation of bounty men. They had been placed in the front to save the veterans for heavy work, and as their wounded men were carried back through the ranks of the old soldiers, the latter would cry out, "Take good care of those men; they have cost the Government a great deal of money." The bounty men were at first a by-word and a cause of irritation to the real volunteers. During the afternoon, hearing some heavy musketry firing in my front, I went to ascertain the cause, and while riding along behind a regiment lying with their faces to the ground, a round shot struck the knapsack of a soldier, and, cutting it open, sent a cloud of underclothes into the air, and high above them floated a scattered pack of cards. The soldier, hearing the shouts of laughter, turned over to see what was the matter, and when he saw the mishap which had befallen him made a feeble effort to join in the laugh.

Between 1 and 2 A. M. of December 14th a council of war of the

FROM A PHOTOGRAPH.

C. F. Jackson

Killed at Fredericksburg, December 13, 1862.
See p. 141.

grand division commanders was ordered, and General Burnside announced his intention of leading the Ninth Corps (his old command) in an assault against the works which the Second Corps, led by such men as Couch and Hancock, had failed to carry. For some reason the project was abandoned. [See p. 127.] During the next two days the Left Grand Division remained in position, with no disturbance except that produced by an angry skirmish line with an occasional artillery engagement.

On Monday afternoon (the 15th) I received an order from General Franklin, then detained at headquarters, to withdraw the Left Grand Division after dark to the left bank of the river, and what remained of the forty thousand men of that command recrossed during the night without loss and without molestation from the enemy.

After the battle I had four interviews with Burnside. The first was on Sunday, the 14th of December. I found him alone in his tent walking up and down, apparently in great distress of mind, and turning to me he said, "Oh! those men! oh! those men!" I asked what he meant, and he said, "Those men over there!" pointing across the river where so many thousands lay dead and wounded, "I am thinking of them all the time."

I made some remark about the fate of soldiers and changed the subject. Burnside also said that he did not lead the Ninth Corps to the charge as he had said he would, because the generals on the right made such statements with reference to the demoralization of their commands that he feared to make the attempt. After we had recrossed the river I saw him again, when he told me that he had it in his mind to relieve Sumner from command, place Hooker in arrest, and Franklin in command of the army.

In the third interview General Reynolds was with me. Burnside said that the men on the left did not fight well enough. To this we replied that the list of killed and wounded proved the contrary. He then said, "I did not mean that; I meant there were not muskets enough fired," adding, "I made a mistake in my order to Franklin; I should have directed him to carry the hill at Hamilton's at all hazards." ☆

At the fourth interview he stated that the mistake was that Franklin did not get the order early enough; that he had started it at 4 o'clock in the morning, but that General Hardie, to whom the order was committed, had stopped an hour and a half in camp to get breakfast. I then told him that we should have had the order before midnight in order to form such a column of attack as we had proposed.

For a few days General Burnside was dazed by the defeat and grief-stricken at the loss of life; but he soon recovered, and planned and attempted to carry out his harmless "Mud Campaign," his last at the head of the Army of the Potomac.

☆ The Committee on the Conduct of the War received from General Burnside responses to questions as follows:

Q. "Do I understand you to say that you expected General Franklin to carry the point at the extreme left of the ridge in the rear of the town, and thereby enable our troops to storm and carry their fortifications?"

A. "I did expect him to carry that point; which being done would have placed our forces in rear of their extreme right, and which I thought at the time would shake their forces to such an extent that the position in front could be easily stormed and carried."

Q. "To what do you attribute his failure to accomplish that?"

A. "To the great strength of the position, and the accumulation of the enemy's forces there."

General Burnside then explained that the delay in building the bridges gave the enemy time to accumulate his forces before he was able to order the attack.—W. B. FRANKLIN.

TRAFFIC BETWEEN THE LINES DURING A TRUCE.

WITH JACKSON AT HAMILTON'S CROSSING. †

BY J. H. MOORE, C. S. A.

THE morning of the 13th [of December] dawned with a dense fog enveloping the plain and city of Fredericksburg, through which the brilliant rays of the sun struggled about 10 in the morning. In front of the right of the Confederate army was displayed the vast force of Franklin, marching and countermarching, hastily seeking the places assigned for the coming conflict. Here was a vast plain, now peopled with an army worthy of its grand dimensions. A slight but dazzling snow beneath, and a brilliant sun above, intensified the leaping reflections from thousands of gleaming bayonets. Officers, on restless horses, rushed from point to point in gay uniforms. Field-artillery was whisked into position as so many fragile toys. Rank and file, foot and horse, small-arms and field-ordnance presented so magnificent a pageant as to call forth the unbounded admiration of their adversaries. In a word, this was the grandest martial scene of the war. The contrast between Stonewall Jackson's corps and Franklin's grand division was very marked, and so far as appearances went the former was hardly better than a caricature of the latter.

When all was in readiness, adjutants stepped to the front and, plainly in our view, read the orders of the day. This done, the fatal advance across the plain commenced. With gay pennants, State, regimental, and brigade standards flying, this magnifi-

cent army advanced in three closely compacted lines of battle. At intervals, in front, preceded by horse-artillery and flanked on either side by numerous field-pieces, hundreds of heavy field-pieces from the north bank of the Rappahannock belched forth their missiles of destruction and swept the plain in advance of Franklin's columns, while at the same moment his smaller field-pieces in front and on the flanks joined in to sweep the open space on all sides. This mighty cannonading was answered by the Confederate ordnance. Onward, steady and unwavering, these three lines advanced, preceded by a heavy skirmish line, till they neared the railroad, when Jackson's right and right center poured into these sturdy ranks a deadly volley from small-arms. Spaces, gaps, and wide chasms instantly told the tale of a most fatal encounter. Volley after volley of small-arms continued the work of destruction, while Jackson's artillery posted on the Federal left and at right angles to their line of advance kept up a withering fire on the lessening ranks. The enemy advanced far in front of the River road [and crossing the railroad charged the slopes upon which our troops were posted], but at length wavered, halted, and suddenly retreated to the protection of the railroad embankments. The struggle was kept up by sharp-shooters for some time, when another general advance was made against a furious cannonade of

† Condensed from an article in the "Southern Bivouac" for August, 1886.

HAYS'S BRIGADE OF STONEWALL JACKSON'S CORPS, AT HAMILTON'S CROSSING.   SEE MAP, P. 74.

small-arms and artillery. Again the scene of destruction was repeated; still the Federals crossed the railroad, when a gap in Jackson's line between Archer's and Thomas's brigades was discovered by some of the assailants. [See map, p. 74.] This interval was rushed for by a part of Franklin's troops as a haven of safety, while the rest of his command were repulsed in the utmost confusion.

The extreme left of Archer's brigade, and the extreme right of Thomas's brigade, that is, the 14th Tennessee and 19th Georgia, commanded by Colonel Forbes, and a part of the 7th Tennessee, commanded by Colonel Goodner, of the former brigade, believing they were about to be surrounded, gave way. Their comrades on the right, unaware of the condition of affairs on the left, and seeing the enemy routed in their front, were amazed at this confusion. Officers and men on the right were enraged at what seemed to be cowardice, and, rushing toward the broken lines, officers leveled their pistols and, with many privates, fired into these fleeing comrades.

Presently the true condition of affairs appeared when the victorious brigades of Franklin emerged from the woods. Line and field officers rushed to and fro, wildly shouting, "Into line, into line!" and, even in the face of a flanking foe, the gallant Colonel Turney, who temporarily commanded Archer's brigade, succeeded in re-forming his regiments at right angles to the former line of attack. This gave a brief check to the victors. Still the infantry

and artillery fire scourged the line. The rout or capture of the Confederates seemed inevitable. Turney was struck by a minie-ball, which entered his mouth and came out at his neck, and his apparently lifeless body was hurriedly placed on a blanket, and four of his devoted followers attempted to carry him to the rear. They had not proceeded far when a shell burst among them, and they in turn lay helpless by the side of their bleeding commander. ⚓ Colonel Goodner also did gallant service in preventing a rout, for, with the part of the 7th that still held its ground, he formed a line at right angles to their former position, and aided in checking this dangerous reverse.

Up to the time of the break in our line no one in the ranks apprehended any danger. Those in front and near this scene of defeat and confusion made desperate efforts to rally the men and prevent a stampede, for we looked for nothing but defeat or capture. We were unaware of the fact that we had any reserves. Presently Early's division, in the very mood and spirit that had characterized Archer's brigade before the breaking of the lines, came at double-quick to our relief, jesting and yelling at us: "Here comes old Jubal! Let old Jubal straighten that fence! Jubal's boys are always getting Hill out o' trouble!"

A desperate encounter followed. The Federals fought manfully, but the artillery on our right, together with the small-arms, literally mowed them down. Officers and men lost courage at the sight of their lessening ranks, and in the utmost confusion

⚓ Colonel Turney, thus painfully and dangerously wounded, has, for the last fifteen years, served the State of Tennessee as one of its supreme judges.— J. H. M.

they again sought the shelter of the railroad. Archer's brigade, of Jackson's corps, was on the extreme right of A. P. Hill's front line, composed of the following regiments, posted in the order named: 19th Georgia, 14th Tennessee, 7th Tennessee, 1st Tennessee, and extended from the interval or space left unoccupied by Gregg's brigade to the railroad curve near Hamilton's Crossing. We occupied ground slightly higher than the level of the plain over which the Federals had to pass. In our immediate rear and left was an irregular growth of timber of varied size, which obstructed the view in the direction of the Gregg interval.

As the battle opened in the morning, the enemy was plainly in our view, and we could distinctly see their approach to the railroad in our front and to the left, where in every attempt to advance they halted. Now and then they would make an effort to advance from the railroad to our lines. We who were on the right had no trouble to repulse those in our front, and, in fact, we successfully met every assault made on the right, and that, too, with little or no loss. We regarded the efforts of the Federals, so far as the right was concerned, as futile in the extreme. In fact, their assaults on this part of the line appeared like the marching of men to certain defeat and slaughter. Our infantry fire, aided by fifteen pieces of artillery placed at our right, did terrible execution as the poor fellows emerged from a slight railroad cut in front of a part of our line. ↓

On the morning of the 13th General Jackson rode down his lines dressed in a new suit, presented to him, as we understood, by General Stuart. Some of our men facetiously remarked that they preferred seeing him with his rusty old cap on, as they feared he wouldn't get down to work. He inspected all of his positions, riding alone. After halting near the extreme right, the artillery fire was begun, and here I had an excellent opportunity to see him under fire. I watched him closely, and was unable to detect the slightest change in his demeanor. In a few minutes he rode off in the direction of Lee's headquarters.

A very general impression prevails, and it is in a great measure confirmed by writers on Fredericksburg, that Jackson's lines were strongly fortified. This is not correct: we had no time to construct anything like fortifications. D. H. Hill's division had been at Port Royal, eighteen miles below Fredericksburg, to prevent the Federals from crossing at that point; he left Port Royal after the enemy had abandoned the project of crossing there, and did not reach the position assigned him until about daylight of the morning of the battle.

The next morning the scenes of carnage were heart-sickening. To intensify the horrible picture, the dead and the mortally wounded were in many instances burned in the sedge-grass, which was set on fire by bursting shells.

↓ The report of General John F. Reynolds, commanding the First Corps, contains the following account of the engagement of his troops at Hamilton's Crossing: "About 8:30 A. M. Meade's division advanced across the Smithfield ravine, formed in column of two brigades, with the artillery between them, the Third Brigade marching by the flank on the left and rear. It moved down the river some 500 or 600 yards, when it turned sharp to the right and crossed the Bowling Green road. The enemy's artillery opened fire from the crest and the angle of the Bowling Green road. I directed General Meade to put his column directly for the nearest point of wood, and, having gained the crest, to extend his attack along it to the extreme point of the heights, where most of the enemy's artillery was posted. As the column crossed the Bowling Green road the artillery of his division was ordered into position on the rise of the ground between this road and the railroad; Cooper's and Ransom's batteries, to the front, soon joined by Amsden's, to oppose those of the enemy on the crest, while Simpson's had to be thrown to the left, to oppose that on the Bowling Green road, which was taking the column in flank. Hall's battery was at the same time thrown to the front, on the left of Gibbon's division, which was advancing in line on Meade's right. The artillery combat here raged furiously for some time, until that of the enemy was silenced, when all of our batteries were directed to shell the wood, where his infantry was supposed to be posted. This was continued some half-hour, when the column of Meade, advancing in fine order and with gallant determination, was directed into the point of wood which extended this side of the railroad, with instructions, when they carried the crest and road which ran along it in their front, to move the First Brigade along the road, the Second Brigade to advance and hold the road, while the Third moved across the open field, to support the First in carrying the extreme point of the ridge. At this time I sent orders to General Gibbon to advance, in connection with General Meade, and carry the wood in his front. The advance was made under the fire of the enemy's batteries on his right and front, to which Gib-

bon's batteries replied, while those of Smith joined in on the right.

"Meade's division successfully carried the wood in front, crossed the railroad, charged up the slope of the hill, and gained the road and edge of the wood, driving the enemy from his strong positions in the ditches and railroad cut, capturing the flags of 2 regiments and sending about 200 prisoners to the rear. At the same time Gibbon's division had crossed the railroad and entered the wood, driving back the first line of the enemy and capturing a number of prisoners; but, from the dense character of the wood, the connection between his division and Meade's was broken. The infantry combat was here kept up with great spirit for a short time, when Meade's column was vigorously assailed by the enemy's masked force, and, after a severe contest, forced back. Two regiments of Berry's brigade, Birney's division, arrived about this time, and were immediately thrown into the wood on Gibbon's left, to the support of the line; but they, too, were soon overpowered, and the whole line retired from the wood, Meade's in some confusion, and, after an ineffectual effort by General Meade and myself to rally them under the enemy's fire, that of the artillery having resumed almost its original intensity, I directed General Meade to re-form his division across the Bowling Green road, and ordered the remainder of Berry's brigade, which had come up, to the support of the batteries.

"The enemy, showing himself in strong force in the wood, seemed disposed to follow our retiring troops, but the arrival of the other brigades of Birney's division on the ground at this critical moment, to occupy our line of battle, materially aided in saving Hall's battery, which was now seriously threatened by the enemy, and, together with our artillery fire, soon drove him to his sheltered positions and cover, from which his infantry did not again appear.

"General Gibbon's division was assailed in turn in the same manner, and compelled to retire from the wood soon after Meade's." General C. Feger Jackson commanding the Third Brigade of Meade's division, was killed within the enemy's lines.— EDITORS.

IN THE RANKS AT FREDERICKSBURG.

I. BY GEORGE E. SMITH, PRIVATE, CO. E, 2D WISCONSIN VOLUNTEERS.

GENERAL W. F. SMITH, in his article on "Franklin's Left Grand Division" [p. 137], makes mention of a round shot that ripped open a soldier's knapsack and distributed his clothing and cards. It was not a round shot, but the second "bolt" that came from the Whitworth gun that the "Johnnies" had run in on our flank. And although we were surprised and dumfounded at this attack from a new arm that appeared to take in about five miles of our line, the boys could not forego their little joke; so when that column of cards was thrown some twenty feet in the air, on all sides could be heard the cry, "Oh, deal me a hand!"

Three other shots in that battle did queer work. Ours was the last brigade (the "Iron Brigade" under Meredith) to cross on the pontoons, and we came to a halt upon the river-bank, for a few moments, before going into position among the big cotton-wood trees at the Bernard House. We had been paid off that day, and the gamblers began to play at cards the moment we halted. A man who was about to "straddle" a "fifty-cent blind" had his knapsack knocked from under him by a solid shot, and he "straddled" half a dozen soldiers, who were covered with a cart-load of dirt. This was the first shot from the "Johnnies" on our left. Their second passed over the river and struck a paymaster's tent. The struggle between the paymaster and the stragglers for possession of the flying greenbacks was both exciting and ridiculous.

The next day, December 13th, our officers and the enemy's batteries kept us on the jump. During a moment's halt, behind a slight rise of ground, we lay down. A soldier facing to the rear was in earnest conversation with a comrade. Suddenly he made a terrific leap in air, and from the spot of ground on which he had been sitting a solid shot scooped a wheelbarrow-load of dirt. It was a clear case of premonition, for the man could give no reason for having jumped.

General Smith also speaks of the veterans' ridicule of the bounty men. The 24th Michigan became part of our brigade shortly after Antietam, and we were told they were mostly bounty men. [See below.] We made unmerciful sport of them, but never a joke or word of abuse did I hear after the 24th had shown its mettle in the battle of Fredericksburg.

On the evening of December 14th, General Doubleday wanted our regiment (the 2d Wisconsin) to go on picket and make an effort to stop the firing upon the picket-line, for the shots of the Confederates covered the whole field, and no one could get any rest. We had not been in the picket-line more than twenty minutes before we made a bargain with the "Rebs," and the firing ceased, and neither they nor ourselves pretended to keep under cover. But at daylight the 24th Michigan came to relieve us. Before they were fairly in line they opened fire upon the Confederates without the warning we had agreed to give. We yelled lustily, but the rattle of musketry drowned the sound, and many a confiding enemy was hit. This irritated the Confederates, who opened a savage fire, and the 24th Michigan were put upon their good behavior; it was with difficulty a general engagement was prevented. All that day, until about 4 o'clock, the picket-firing was intense; it was abruptly ended by a Confederate challenging a 6th Wisconsin man to a fist-fight in the middle of the turnpike. The combatants got the attention of both picket-lines, who declared the fight a "draw." They ended the matter with a coffee and tobacco trade and an agreement to do no more firing at picket-lines, unless an advance should be ordered. It was this agreement that enabled Lieutenant Rogers to save a long picket-line that was to have been sacrificed when we fell back.

RACINE, WIS., October 3d, 1886.

II. BY ORSON B. CURTIS, CORPORAL, CO. D, 24TH MICHIGAN.

SINCE Private Smith, above, mentions the 24th Michigan as "bounty men," let me state that in July, 1862, a war meeting held in Detroit to promote enlistments under Lincoln's call for 300,000 men was broken up by the disturbance created by a large number of Confederate refugees from Windsor, Canada, with the aid of some anti-war men here. To wipe out the unexpected insult, a second war meeting was held, which resolved to raise immediately an entire regiment,—the 24th Michigan,—in Wayne County alone, *in addition to its regular quota;* and within 20 days said regiment was recruited and mustered, 1027 strong. Not a man of us received a cent of State or county bounty. Each man, however, did receive, in advance, one month's pay and $25 of the regular $100 government bounty promised to all soldiers enlisting for two years; 673 of the men who were credited to Detroit received sums varying from $25 to $50 apiece as a gratuity from patriotic friends, while the remaining 354 of us never received a cent.

Assigned to the "Iron Brigade," our regiment shared its hardships till the spring of 1865, when its remnant was sent to guard conscripts at Springfield, Ill., and formed the escort at President Lincoln's funeral. At Gettysburg it suffered probably as great a loss as any regiment of its size. One of the first infantry regiments to engage the enemy in the first day's fight, it went into that battle with 28 officers and 468 men; total, 496. It lost that day 24 officers and 339 men; total, 363, of which number 272, *or about 55 per cent. of the command, were killed and wounded;* 91 were taken prisoners, over a third of whom died in Southern prisons; twice that day was its entire color-guard shot down, and only 3 officers and 95 men were left to respond at roll-call. General Wadsworth thus commended its conduct on that day: "Colonel Morrow, the only fault I find with you is that you fought the 24th Michigan too long, *but God only knows what would have become of us had you not held the ground as long as you did.*"

THE OPPOSING FORCES AT FREDERICKSBURG, VA.

The composition, losses, and strength of each army as here stated give the gist of all the data obtainable in the Official Records. K stands for killed; w for wounded; m w for mortally wounded; m for captured or missing; c for captured.

THE UNION ARMY.

ARMY OF THE POTOMAC.— Major-General Ambrose E. Burnside.

Escort, etc.: Oneida (N. Y.) Cav., Capt. Daniel P. Mann; 1st U. S. Cav. (detachment), Capt. Marcus A. Reno; A and E, 4th U. S. Cav., Capt. James B. McIntyre. *Provost Guard,* Brig.-Gen. Marsena R. Patrick: A and B, McClellan (Ill.) Dragoons, Capts. George W. Shears and David C. Brown; G, 9th N. Y., Capt. Charles Child; 93d N. Y., Col. John S. Crocker; 2d U. S. Cav., Maj. Charles J. Whiting; 8th U. S., Capt. Royal T. Frank. *Volunteer Engineer Brigade,* Brig.-Gen. Daniel P. Woodbury: 15th N. Y., Maj. James A. Magruder; 50th N. Y., Maj. Ira Spaulding. Brigade loss: k, 8; w, 48 = 56. *Battalion U. S. Engineers,* Lieut. Charles E. Cross. Loss: w, 1; m, 2 = 3.

ARTILLERY, Brig.-Gen. Henry J. Hunt. *Artillery Reserve,* Lieut.-Col. William Hays: 5th N. Y., Capt. Elijah D. Taft; A, 1st Batt. N. Y., Capt. Otto Diederichs; B, 1st Batt. N. Y., Capt. Adolph Voegelee; C, 1st Batt. N. Y., Lieut. Bernhard Wever; D, 1st Batt. N. Y., Capt. Charles Kusserow; K, 1st U. S., Capt. William M. Graham; A, 2d U. S., Capt. John C. Tidball; G, 4th U. S., Lieut. Marcus P. Miller; K, 5th U. S., Lieut. David H. Kinzie; C, 32d Mass. (train guard), Capt. Josiah C. Fuller. *Unattached Artillery,* Maj. Thomas S. Trumbull: B, 1st Conn. Heavy, Capt. Albert F. Brooker; M, 1st Conn. Heavy, Capt. Franklin A. Pratt. Artillery reserve loss: w, 8.

RIGHT GRAND DIVISION, Major-Gen. Edwin V. Sumner.

SECOND ARMY CORPS, Maj.-Gen. Darius N. Couch. Staff loss: w, 1.

FIRST DIVISION, Brig.-Gen. Winfield S. Hancock. Staff loss: w, 3.

First Brigade, Brig.-Gen. John C. Caldwell (w), Col. George W. von Schack: 5th N. H., Col. Edward E. Cross (w), Maj. E. E. Sturtevant (k), Capt. James E. Larkin, Capt. Horace T. H. Pierce; 7th N. Y., Col. George W. von Schack, Capt. G. A. von Bransen; 61st N. Y., Col. Nelson A. Miles ⌡ (w); 64th N. Y., Lieut.-Col. Enos C. Brooks; ⌡ 81st Pa., Col. H. Boyd McKeen (w), Capt. William Wilson (w), Col. Hiram L. Brown (w), Lieut.-Col. David B. McCreary. Brigade loss: k, 108; w, 729; m, 115 = 952. *Second Brigade,* Brig.-Gen. Thomas F. Meagher: 28th Mass., Col. Richard Byrnes; 63d N. Y., Maj. Joseph O'Neill (w), Capt. Patrick J. Condon; 69th N. Y., Col. Robert Nugent (w), Capt. James Saunders; 88th N. Y., Col. Patrick Kelly; 116th Pa., Col. Dennis Heenan (w), Lieut.-Col. St. Clair A. Mulholland (w), Lieut. Francis T. Quinlan. Brigade loss: k, 50; w, 421; m, 74 = 545. *Third Brigade,* Col. Samuel K. Zook: 27th Conn., Col. Richard S. Bostwick; 2d Del., Col. William P. Baily (w); 52d N. Y., Col. Paul Frank; 57th N. Y., Lieut.-Col. Alford B. Chapman (w), Maj. N. Garrow Throop (w), Capt. James W. Britt; 66th N. Y., Lieut.-Col. James H. Bull (k), Capt. Julius Wehle (k), Capt. John S. Hammell (w), Lieut. James G. Derrickson; 53d Pa., Col. John R. Brooke. Brigade loss: k, 60; w, 427; m, 40 = 527. *Artillery:* B, 1st N. Y., Capt. Rufus D. Pettit; C, 4th U. S., Lieut. Evan Thomas. Artillery loss: k, 1; w, 4 = 5.

SECOND DIVISION, Brig.-Gen. Oliver O. Howard. Staff loss: w, 1.

First Brigade, Brig.-Gen. Alfred Sully: 19th Me., Col. Frederick D. Sewall, Lieut.-Col. Francis E. Heath; 15th Mass., Maj. Chase Philbrick (w), Capt. John Murkland, Capt. Charles H. Watson; 1st Co. Mass. Sharp-shooters, Capt. William Plumer; 1st Minn., Col. George N. Morgan; 2d Co. Minn. Sharp-shooters, Capt. William F.

Russell; 34th N. Y., Col. James A. Suiter; 82d N. Y. (2d Militia), Lieut.-Col. James Huston. Brigade loss: k, 14; w, 77; m, 31 = 122. *Second Brigade,* Col. Joshua T. Owen: 69th Pa., Lieut.-Col. Dennis O'Kane; 71st Pa., Lieut.-Col. John Markoe; 72d Pa., Col. De Witt C. Baxter; 106th Pa., Col. Turner G. Morehead. Brigade loss: k, 27: w, 203; m, 28 = 258. *Third Brigade,* Col. Norman J. Hall: 19th Mass., Capt. H. G. O. Weymouth; 20th Mass. Capt. George N. Macy; 7th Mich., Lieut.-Col. Henry Baxter (w), Maj. Thomas H. Hunt: 42d N. Y., Lieut.-Col. George N. Bomford; 59th N. Y., Lieut.-Col. William Northedge; 127th Pa., Col. William W. Jennings. Brigade loss: k, 63; w, 419; m, 33 = 515. *Artillery:* A, 1st R. I., Capt. William A. Arnold; B, 1st R. I., Capt. John G. Hazard. Artillery loss: w, 18.

THIRD DIVISION, Brig.-Gen. William H. French.

First Brigade, Brig.-Gen. Nathan Kimball (w), Col. John S. Mason: 14th Ind., Maj. Elijah H. C. Cavins; 24th N. J., Col. Wm. B. Robertson; 28th N. J., Col. Moses N. Wisewell (w), Lieut -Col. E. A. L. Roberts; 4th Ohio, Col. John S. Mason, Lieut.-Col. James H. Godman (w), Capt. Gordon A. Stewart; 8th Ohio, Lieut.-Col. Franklin Sawyer; 7th W. Va., Col. Joseph Snider (w), Lieut.-Col. Jonathan H. Lockwood. Brigade loss: k, 36; w, 420; m, 64 = 520. *Second Brigade,* Col. Oliver H. Palmer: 14th Conn., Lieut.-Col. Sanford H. Perkins (w), Capt. Samuel H. Davis; 108th N. Y., Lieut.-Col. Charles J. Powers; 130th Pa., Col. Henry I. Zinn (k), Capt. William M. Porter. Brigade loss: k, 20; w, 207; m, 64 = 291. *Third Brigade,* Col. John W. Andrews, Lieut.-Col. William Jameson, Lieut.-Col. John W. Marshall: 1st Del., Maj. Thomas A. Smyth; 4th N. Y., Col. John D. MacGregor (w), Lieut.-Col. William Jameson, Maj. Charles W. Kruger; 10th N. Y., Col. John E. Bendix (w), Capt. Salmon Winchester (m w), Capt. George F. Hopper; 132d Pa., Lieut.-Col. Charles Albright. Brigade loss: k, 32; w, 271; m, 39 = 342. *Artillery:* G, 1st N. Y., Capt. John D. Frank; G, 1st R. I., Capt. Charles D. Owen. Artillery loss: k, 1; w, 6 = 7.

ARTILLERY RESERVE, Capt. Charles H. Morgan: I, 1st U. S., Lieut. Edmund Kirby; A, 4th U. S., Lieut. Rufus King, Jr. Artillery Reserve loss: w, 7.

NINTH ARMY CORPS, Brig.-Gen. Orlando B. Willcox. *Escort:* B, 6th N. Y. Cav., Capt. Hillman A. Hall; C, 6th N. Y. Cav., Capt. William L. Heermance.

FIRST DIVISION, Brig.-Gen. William W. Burns.

First Brigade, Col. Orlando M. Poe: 2d Mich., Lieut.-Col. Louis Dillman; 17th Mich., Col. William H. Withington; 20th Mich., Col. Adolphus W. Williams; 79th N. Y., Lieut.-Col. David Morrison. Brigade loss: k, 1; w, 12 = 13. *Second Brigade,* Col. Benjamin C. Christ: 29th Mass., Lieut.-Col. Joseph H. Barnes; 8th Mich., Maj. Ralph Ely; 27th N. J., Col. George W. Mindil; 46th N. Y., Lieut.-Col. Joseph Gerhardt; 50th Pa., Lieut.-Col. Thomas S. Brenholtz. Brigade loss: w, 7; m, 1 = 8. *Third Brigade,* Col. Daniel Leasure: 36th Mass., Col. Henry Bowman; 45th Pa., Col. Thomas Welsh; 100th Pa., Lieut.-Col. David A. Leckey. Brigade loss: w, 3. *Artillery:* D, 1st N. Y., Capt. Thomas W. Osborn; L and M, 3d U. S., Lieut. Horace J. Hayden. Artillery loss: w, 2; m, 1 = 3.

SECOND DIVISION, Brig.-Gen. Samuel D. Sturgis. Staff loss: w, 1.

First Brigade, Brig.-Gen. James Nagle: 2d Md., Col. Thomas B. Allard; 6th N. H., Col. Simon G. Griffin; 9th N. H., Lieut.-Col. John W. Babbitt; 48th Pa., Col. Joshua K. Sigfried; 7th R. I., Col. Zenas R. Bliss; 12th R. I., Col.

⌡ Commanded 61st and 64th N. Y., consolidated.

George H. Browne. Brigade loss: k, 31; w, 421; m, 48 =500. *Second Brigade*, Brig.-Gen. Edward Ferrero: 21st Mass., Col. William S. Clark; 35th Mass., Maj. Sidney Willard (k), Capt. Stephen H. Andrews; 11th N. H., Col. Walter Harriman; 51st N. Y., Col. Robert B. Potter; 51st Pa., Col. John F. Hartranft. Brigade loss: k, 60; w, 393; m, 38 = 491. *Artillery:* L, 2d N. Y., Capt. Jacob Roemer; D, Pa., Capt. George W. Durell; D, 1st R. I., Capt. William W. Buckley; E, 4th U. S., Lieut. George Dickenson (k), Lieut. John Egan. Artillery loss: k, 3; w, 12 = 15.

THIRD DIVISION, Brig.-Gen. George W. Getty.

First Brigade, Col. Rush C. Hawkins: 10th N. H., Col. Michael T. Donohoe; 13th N. H., Col. Aaron F. Stevens; 25th N. J., Col. Andrew Derrom; 9th N. Y., Lieut.-Col. Edgar A. Kimball; 89th N. Y., Col. Harrison S. Fairchild; 103d N. Y., Col. Benjamin Ringold. Brigade loss: k, 14; w, 187; m, 54 = 255. *Second Brigade*, Col. Edward Harland: 8th Conn., Maj. John E. Ward, Capt. Henry M. Hoyt; 11th Conn., Col. Griffin A. Stedman, Jr.; 15th Conn., Lieut.-Col. Samuel Tolles; 16th Conn., Capt. Charles L. Upham; 21st Conn., Col. Arthur H. Dutton; 4th R. I., Lieut.-Col. Joseph B. Curtis (k), Maj. Martin P. Buffum. Brigade loss: k, 2; w, 29; m, 10 = 41. *Artillery:* E, 2d U. S., Lieut. Samuel N. Benjamin; A, 5th U. S., Lieut. James Gilliss.

CAVALRY DIVISION, Brig.-Gen. Alfred Pleasonton.

First Brigade, Brig.-Gen. John F. Farnsworth: 8th Ill., Col. William Gamble; 3d Ind., Maj. George H. Chapman; 8th N. Y., Col. Benjamin F. Davis. *Second Brigade*, Col. David McM. Gregg, Col. Thomas C. Devin: 6th N. Y., Col. Thomas C. Devin, Lieut.-Col. Duncan McVicar; 8th Pa., Lieut.-Col. Amos E. Griffiths; 6th U. S., Capt. George C. Cram. *Artillery:* M, 2d U. S., Lieut. Alexander C. M. Pennington, Jr.

CENTER GRAND DIVISION, Maj.-Gen. Jos. Hooker.

THIRD ARMY CORPS, Brig.-Gen. George Stoneman.

FIRST DIVISION, Brig.-Gen. David B. Birney.

First Brigade, Brig.-Gen. John C. Robinson: 20th Ind., Col. John Van Valkenburg; 63d Pa., Maj. John A. Danks; 68th Pa., Col. Andrew H. Tippin; 105th Pa., Col. Amor A. McKnight; 114th Pa., Col. Charles H. T. Collis; 141st Pa., Col. Henry J. Madill. Brigade loss: k, 14; w, 106; m, 26 = 146. *Second Brigade*, Brig.-Gen. J. H. Hobart Ward: 3d Me., Col. Moses B. Lakeman; 4th Me., Col. Elijah Walker; 38th N. Y., Lieut.-Col. William Birney (w); 40th N. Y., Lieut.-Col. Nelson A. Gesner (w); 55th N. Y., Col. P. Regis de Trobriand; 57th Pa., Col. Charles T. Campbell (w), Lieut.-Col. Peter Sides; 99th Pa., Col. Asher S. Leidy (w), Lieut.-Col. Edwin R. Biles. Brigade loss: k, 79; w, 397; m, 153 = 629. *Third Brigade*, Brig.-Gen. Hiram G. Berry: 17th Me., Col. Thomas A. Roberts; 3d Mich., Maj. Moses B. Houghton; 5th Mich., Lieut.-Col. John Gilluly (k), Maj. Edward T. Sherlock; 1st N. Y., Col. J. Frederick Pierson; 37th N. Y., Col. Samuel B. Hayman; 101st N. Y., Col. George F. Chester. Brigade loss: k, 19; w, 144; m, 2 = 165. *Artillery*, Capt. George E. Randolph: E, 1st R. I., Lieut. Pardon S. Jastram; F and K, 3d U. S., Lieut. John G. Turnbull. Artillery loss: k, 2; w, 8 = 10.

SECOND DIVISION, Brig.-Gen. Daniel E. Sickles.

First Brigade, Brig.-Gen. Joseph B. Carr: 1st Mass., Lieut.-Col. Clark B. Baldwin, Col. Napoleon B. McLaughlen; 11th Mass., Col. William Blaisdell; 16th Mass., Col Thomas R. Tannatt; 2d N. H., Col. Gilman Marston; 11th N. J., Col. Robert McAllister; 26th Pa., Lieut.-Col. Benjamin C. Tilghman. Brigade loss: k, 11; w, 68; m, 2 = 81. *Second Brigade*, Col. George B. Hall: 70th N. Y., Col. J. Egbert Farnum; 71st N. Y., Maj. Thomas Rafferty; 72d N. Y., Col. William O. Stevens; 73d N. Y., Col. William R. Brewster; 74th N. Y., Lieut.-Col. William H. Lounsbury; 120th N. Y., Col. George H. Sharpe. Brigade loss: w, 16. *Third Brigade*, Brig.-Gen. Joseph W. Revere: 5th N. J., Col. William J. Sewell; 6th N. J., Col. George C. Burling; 7th N. J., Col. Louis R. Francine; 8th N. J., Col. Adolphus J. Johnson; 2d N. Y., Col. Sidney W. Park; 115th Pa., Lieut.-Col. William A. Olmsted. Brigade loss: k, 1; w, 1 = 2. *Artillery*, Capt. James E. Smith: 2d N. J., Capt. A. Judson Clark; 4th N. Y., Lieut. Joseph E. Nairn; H, 1st U. S., Lieut. Justin E. Dimick; K, 4th U. S., Lieut. Francis W. Seeley. Artillery loss: m, 1.

THIRD DIVISION, Brig.-Gen. Amiel W. Whipple. Staff loss: m, 1.

First Brigade, Brig.-Gen. A. Sanders Piatt, Col. Emlen Franklin: 86th N. Y., Lieut.-Col. Barna J. Chapin; 124th N. Y., Col. A. Van Horne Ellis; 122d Pa., Col. Emlen Franklin. Brigade loss: w, 3; m, 6 = 9. *Second Brigade*, Col. Samuel S. Carroll: 12th N. H., Col. Joseph H. Potter; 163d N. Y., Maj. James J. Byrne; 84th Pa., Col. Samuel M. Bowman; 110th Pa., Lieut.-Col. James Crowther. Brigade loss: k, 19; w, 88; m, 11 = 118. *Artillery:* 10th N. Y., Capt. John T. Bruen; 11th N. Y., Capt. Albert A. von Puttkammer; H, 1st Ohio, Lieut. George W. Norton. Artillery loss: w, 1.

FIFTH ARMY CORPS, Brig.-Gen. Daniel Butterfield. Staff loss: k, 1; w, 1 = 2.

FIRST DIVISION, Brig.-Gen. Charles Griffin.

First Brigade, Col. James Barnes: 2d Me., Lieut.-Col. George Varney (w), Maj. Daniel F. Sargent; 2d Co. Mass. Sharp-shooters, Capt. Lewis E. Wentworth; 18th Mass., Lieut.-Col. Joseph Hayes; 22d Mass., Lieut.-Col. William S. Tilton; 1st Mich., Lieut.-Col. Ira C. Abbott (w); 13th N. Y., Col. Elisha G. Marshall (w), Lieut.-Col. Francis A. Schoeffel; 25th N. Y., Capt. Patrick Connelly; 118th Pa., Lieut.-Col. James Gwyn. Brigade loss: k, 30; w, 381; m, 89 = 500. *Second Brigade*, Col. Jacob B. Sweitzer: 9th Mass., Col. Patrick R. Guiney; 32d Mass., Col. Francis J. Parker; 4th Mich., Lieut.-Col. George W. Lumbard; 14th N. Y., Lieut.-Col. Thomas M. Davies; 62d Pa., Lieut.-Col. James C. Hull. Brigade loss, k, 23; w, 193; m, 6 = 222. *Third Brigade*, Col. T. B. W. Stockton: 20th Me., Col. Adelbert Ames; Brady's Co. Mich. Sharp-shooters, Lieut. Jonas H. Titus, Jr.; 16th Mich., Lieut.-Col. Norval E. Welch; 12th N. Y., Lieut.-Col. Robert M. Richardson; 17th N. Y., Capt. John Vickers; 44th N. Y., Lieut.-Col. Freeman Conner (w), Maj. Edward B. Knox; 83d Pa., Col. Strong Vincent. Brigade loss: k, 18; w, 158; m, 25 = 201. *Artillery:* 3d Mass., Capt. Augustus P. Martin; 5th Mass., Capt. Charles A. Phillips; C, 1st R. I., Capt. Richard Waterman; D, 5th U. S., Lieut. Charles E. Hazlett. Artillery loss: k, 2; w, 1 = 3. *Sharp-shooters:* 1st U. S., Lieut.-Col. Casper Trepp.

SECOND DIVISION, Brig.-Gen. George Sykes.

First Brigade, Lieut.-Col. Robert C. Buchanan: 3d U. S., Capt. John D. Wilkins; 4th U. S., Capt. Hiram Dryer; 1st Battalion, 12th U. S., Capt. Matthew M. Blunt; 2d Battalion, 12th U. S., Capt. Thomas M. Anderson; 1st Battalion, 14th U. S., Capt. John D. O'Connell; 2d Battalion, 14th U. S., Capt. Giles B. Overton. Brigade loss: k, 5; w, 42; m, 4 = 51. *Second Brigade*, Maj. George L. Andrews, Maj. Charles S. Lovell: 1st and 2d U. S. (battalion), Capt. Salem S. Marsh; 6th U. S., Capt. Levi C. Bootes; 7th U. S. (battalion), Capt. David P. Hancock; 10th U. S., Capt. Henry E. Maynadier; 11th U. S., Capt. Charles S. Russell; 17th and 19th U. S. (battalion), Capt. John P. Wales. Brigade loss: k, 12; w, 114; m, 14 = 140. *Third Brigade*, Brig.-Gen. Gouverneur K. Warren: 5th N. Y., Col. Cleveland Winslow; 140th N. Y., Col. Patrick H. O'Rorke; 146th N. Y., Col. Kenner Garrard. Brigade loss: w, 6; m, 30 = 36. *Artillery:* I, 1st Ohio, Lieut. Frederick Dorries; I, 5th U. S., Lieut. Malbone F. Watson. Artillery loss: w, 1.

THIRD DIVISION, Brig.-Gen. Andrew A. Humphreys. Staff loss: w, 3.

First Brigade, Brig.-Gen. Erastus B. Tyler: 91st Pa., Col. Edgar M. Gregory (w); 126th Pa., Col. James G. Elder (w), Lieut.-Col. David W. Rowe; 129th Pa., Col. Jacob G. Frick; 134th Pa., Lieut.-Col. Edward O'Brien. Brigade loss: k, 52; w, 321; m, 81 = 454. *Second Brigade*, Col. Peter H. Allabach: 123d Pa., Col. John B. Clark; 131st Pa., Lieut.-Col. William B. Shaut; 133d Pa., Col. Franklin B. Speakman; 155th Pa., Col. Edward J. Allen. Brigade loss: k, 63; w, 448; m, 51 = 562. *Artillery:* C, 1st N. Y., Lieut. William H. Phillips; E and G, 1st U. S., Capt. Alanson M. Randol.

CAVALRY BRIGADE, Brig.-Gen. William W. Averell: 1st Mass., Col. Horace B. Sargent; 3d Pa., Lieut.-Col. Edward S. Jones; 4th Pa., Col. James K. Kerr; 5th U. S., Capt. James E. Harrison. Brigade loss: k, 1. *Artillery:* B and L, 2d U. S., Capt. James M. Robertson.

LEFT GRAND DIVISION, Maj.-Gen. William B. Franklin.

Escort: 6th Pa. Cav., Col. Richard H. Rush.

FIRST ARMY CORPS, Maj.-Gen. John F. Reynolds.

Escort: L, 1st Me. Cav., Capt. Constantine Taylor. Escort loss: w, 3.

FIRST DIVISION, Brig.-Gen. Abner Doubleday.

First Brigade, Col. Walter Phelps, Jr.: 22d N. Y., Lieut.-Col. John McKie, Jr.; 24th N. Y., Lieut.-Col. Samuel R. Beardsley; 30th N. Y., Lieut.-Col. Morgan H. Chrysler; 84th N. Y. (14th Militia), Lieut.-Col. William H. de Bevoise; 2d U. S. Sharp-shooters, Maj. Homer R. Stoughton. Brigade loss: k, 3; w, 24; m, 3 = 30. *Second Brigade*, Col. James Gavin: 7th Ind., Lieut.-Col. John F. Cheek; 76th N. Y., Col. William P. Wainwright; 95th N. Y., Col. George H. Biddle; 56th Pa., Lieut.-Col. J. William Hofmann. Brigade loss: k, 5; w, 21 = 26. *Third Brigade*, Col. William F. Rogers: 21st N. Y., Capt. George N. Layton; 23d N. Y., Col. Henry C. Hoffman; 35th N. Y., Col. Newton B. Lord; 80th N. Y. (20th Militia), Lieut.-Col. Jacob B. Hardenbergh. Brigade loss: k, 10; w, 54; m, 3 = 67. *Fourth Brigade*, Brig.-Gen. Solomon Meredith, Col. Lysander Cutler: 19th Ind., Lieut.-Col. Samuel J. Williams; 24th Mich., Col. Henry A. Morrow; 2d Wis., Col. Lucius Fairchild; 6th Wis., Col. Lysander Cutler, Lieut.-Col. Edward S. Bragg; 7th Wis., Col. William W. Robinson. Brigade loss: k, 9; w, 40; m, 16 = 65. *Artillery*, Capt. George A. Gerrish (w), Capt. John A. Reynolds: 1st N. H., Lieut. Frederick M. Edgell; L, 1st N. Y., Capt. John A. Reynolds; B, 4th U. S., Lieut. James Stewart. Artillery loss: k, 4; w, 22 = 26.

SECOND DIVISION, Brig.-Gen. John Gibbon (w), Brig.-Gen. Nelson Taylor. Staff loss: w, 1.

First Brigade, Col. Adrian R. Root: 16th Me., Lieut.-Col. Charles W. Tilden; 94th N. Y., Maj. John A. Kress; 104th N. Y., Maj. Gilbert G. Prey; 105th N. Y., Maj. Daniel A. Sharp (w), Capt. Abraham Moore; 107th Pa., Col. Thomas F. McCoy. Brigade loss: k, 47; w, 373; m, 55 = 475. *Second Brigade*, Col. Peter Lyle: 12th Mass., Col. James L. Bates; 26th N. Y., Lieut.-Col. Gilbert S. Jennings, Maj. Ezra F. Wetmore; 90th Pa., Lieut.-Col. William A. Leech; 136th Pa., Col. Thomas M. Bayne. Brigade loss: k, 51; w, 377; m, 32 = 460. *Third Brigade*, Brig.-Gen. Nelson Taylor, Col. Samuel H. Leonard: 13th Mass., Col. Samuel H. Leonard, Lieut.-Col. N. Walter Batchelder; 83d N. Y. (9th Militia), Capt. John Hendrickson (w), Capt. Joseph A. Moesch (w), Lieut. Isaac E. Hoagland; 97th N. Y., Col. Charles Wheelock; 11th Pa., Col. Richard Coulter (w), Capt. Christian Kuhn; 88th Pa., Maj. David A. Griffith. Brigade loss: k, 41; w, 258; m, 15 = 314. *Artillery*, Capt. George F. Leppien: 2d Me., Capt. James A. Hall; 5th Me., Capt. George F. Leppien; C, Pa., Capt. James Thompson; F, 1st Pa., Lieut. R. Bruce Ricketts. Artillery loss: k, 2; w, 15 = 17.

THIRD DIVISION, Maj.-Gen. George G. Meade.

First Brigade, Col. William Sinclair (w), Col. William McCandless: 1st Pa. Reserves, Capt. William C. Talley; 2d Pa. Reserves, Col. William McCandless, Capt. Timothy Mealey; 6th Pa. Reserves, Maj. Wellington H. Ent; 13th Pa. Reserves (1st Rifles), Capt. Charles F. Taylor; 121st Pa., Col. Chapman Biddle. Brigade loss: k, 47; w, 386; m, 77 = 510. *Second Brigade*, Col. Albert L. Magilton: 3d Pa. Reserves, Col. Horatio G. Sickel; 4th Pa. Reserves, Lieut.-Col. Richard H. Woolworth; 7th Pa. Reserves, Col. Henry C. Bolinger; 8th Pa. Reserves, Maj. Silas M. Baily; 142d Pa., Col. Robert P. Cummins. Brigade loss: k, 65; w, 426; m, 141 = 632. *Third Brigade*, Brig.-Gen. C. Feger Jackson (k), Col. Joseph W. Fisher, Lieut.-Col. Robert Anderson: 5th Pa. Reserves, Col. Joseph W. Fisher, Lieut.-Col. George Dare; 9th Pa. Reserves, Lieut.-Col. Robert Anderson, Maj. James McK. Snodgrass; 10th Pa. Reserves, Maj. James B. Knox; 11th Pa. Reserves, Lieut.-Col. Samuel M. Jackson; 12th Pa. Reserves, Capt. Richard Gustin. Brigade loss: k, 56; w, 410; m, 215 = 681. *Artillery*: A, 1st Pa., Lieut. John G. Simpson; B, 1st Pa., Capt. James H. Cooper; G, 1st Pa., Capt. Frank P. Amsden; C, 5th U. S., Capt. Dunbar R. Ransom. Artillery loss: k, 7; w, 19; m, 4 = 30.

SIXTH ARMY CORPS, Maj.-Gen. William F. Smith.

Escort: L, 10th N. Y. Cav., Lieut. George Vanderbilt; I, 6th Pa. Cav., Capt. James Starr; K, 6th Pa. Cav., Capt. Frederick C. Newhall.

FIRST DIVISION, Brig.-Gen. William T. H. Brooks.

First Brigade, Col. Alfred T. A. Torbert: 1st N. J., Lieut.-Col. Mark W. Collet; 2d N. J., Col. Samuel L. Buck; 3d N. J., Col. Henry W. Brown; 4th N. J., Col. William B. Hatch (w), Lieut.-Col. James N. Duffy; 15th N. J., Lieut.-Col. Edward L. Campbell; 23d N. J., Col. Henry O. Ryerson. Brigade loss: k, 18; w, 94; m, 50 = 162. *Second Brigade*, Col. Henry L. Cake: 5th Me., Col. Edward A. Scammon; 16th N. Y., Col. Joel J. Seaver; 27th N. Y., Col. Alexander D. Adams; 121st N. Y., Col. Emory Upton; 96th Pa., Lieut.-Col. Peter A. Filbert. Brigade loss: k, 4; w, 13 = 17. *Third Brigade*, Brig.-Gen. David A. Russell: 18th N. Y., Col. George R. Myers; 31st N. Y., Lieut.-Col. Leopold C. Newman; 32d N. Y., Capt. Charles Hubbs; 95th Pa., Lieut.-Col. Elisha Hall. Brigade loss: w, 10. *Artillery:* A, Md., Capt. John W. Wolcott; 1st Mass., Capt. William H. McCartney; 1st N. J., Capt. William Hexamer; D, 2d U. S., Lieut. Edward B. Williston. Artillery loss: k, 2; w, 6 = 8.

SECOND DIVISION, Brig.-Gen. Albion P. Howe.

First Brigade, Brig.-Gen. Calvin E. Pratt: 6th Me., Col. Hiram Burnham; 43d N. Y., Col. Benjamin F. Baker; 49th Pa., Col. William H. Irwin; 119th Pa., Col. Peter C. Ellmaker; 5th Wis., Col. Amasa Cobb. Brigade loss: w, 23; m, 3 = 26. *Second Brigade*, Col. Henry Whiting: 26th N. J., Col. Andrew J. Morrison; 2d Vt., Lieut.-Col. Charles H. Joyce; 3d Vt., Col. Breed N. Hyde; 4th Vt., Col. Charles B. Stoughton; 5th Vt., Col. Lewis A. Grant; 6th Vt., Col. Nathan Lord, Jr. Brigade loss: k, 21; w, 121; m, 2 = 144. *Third Brigade*, Brig.-Gen. Francis L. Vinton (w), Col. Robert F. Taylor, Brig.-Gen. Thomas H. Neill: 21st N. J., Col. Gilliam Van Houten; 20th N. Y., Col. Ernst von Vegesack; 33d N. Y., Col. Robert F. Taylor; 49th N. Y., Col. Daniel D. Bidwell; 77th N. Y., Lieut.-Col. Winsor B. French. Brigade loss: k, 1; w, 14 = 15. *Artillery:* B, Md., Capt. Alonzo Snow; 1st N. Y., Capt. Andrew Cowan; 3d N. Y., Lieut. William A. Harn; F, 5th U. S., Lieut. Leonard Martin. Artillery loss; w, 1.

THIRD DIVISION, Brig.-Gen. John Newton.

First Brigade, Brig.-Gen. John Cochrane: 65th N. Y., Col. Alexander Shaler; 67th N. Y., Col. Nelson Cross; 122d N. Y., Col. Silas Titus; 23d Pa., Maj. John F. Glenn; 61st Pa., Col. George C. Spear; 82d Pa., Col. David H. Williams. Brigade loss: k, 2; w, 19; m, 3 = 24. *Second Brigade*, Brig.-Gen. Charles Devens, Jr.: 7th Mass., Lieut.-Col. Franklin P. Harlow; 10th Mass., Col. Henry L. Eustis; 37th Mass., Colonel Oliver Edwards; 36th N. Y., Col. William H. Browne; 2d R. I., Col. Frank Wheaton, Lieut.-Col. Nelson Viall. Brigade loss: k, 3; w, 14 = 17. *Third Brigade*, Col. Thomas A. Rowley, Brig.-Gen. Frank Wheaton: 62d N. Y., Maj. Wilson Hubbell; 93d Pa., Maj. John M. Mark; 98th Pa., Lieut.-Col. Adolph Mehler; 102d Pa., Lieut.-Col. Joseph M. Kinkead; 139th Pa., Lieut.-Col. James D. Owens. Brigade loss: w, 6; m, 6 = 12. *Artillery:* C, 1st Pa., Capt. Jeremiah McCarthy; D, 1st Pa., Capt. Michael Hall; G, 2d U. S., Lieut. John H. Butler. Artillery loss: k, 2; w, 8 = 10.

CAVALRY BRIGADE, Brig.-Gen. George D. Bayard (k), Col. David McM. Gregg: Indep't Co., D. C., Lieut. Williams H. Orton; 1st Me., Lieut.-Col. Calvin S. Douty; 1st N. J., Lieut.-Col. Joseph Kargé; 2d N. Y., Maj. Henry E. Davies; 10th N. Y., Lieut.-Col. William Irvine; 1st Pa., Col. Owen Jones. Brigade loss: k, 1; w, 3 = 4. *Artillery:* C, 3d U. S., Capt. Horatio G. Gibson.

Total Union loss: killed, 1284; wounded, 9600; captured or missing, 1769 = 12,653.

Regarding the strength of his army on the morning of December 13th, General Burnside says ("Official Records," Vol. XXI., p. 90): "The forces now under command of General Franklin consisted of about 60,000 men, as shown by the morning reports, and was composed as follows: Sixth Corps, 24,000; First Corps, 18,500; Third Corps (two divisions), 10,000; Ninth Corps (Burns's division), 4000; Bayard's cavalry, 3500. General Sumner had about 27,000 men, comprising his own grand division, except Burns's division of the Ninth Corps. General Hooker's command was about 26,000 strong, two of General Stoneman's divisions having reported to General Franklin." These numbers aggregate 113,000.

According to Burnside's return for December 10th ("Official Records," Vol. XXI., p. 1121), the "present for duty equipped," or available for line of battle, was 104,903 infantry, 5884 cavalry, and 5896 artillery = 116,683.

THE CONFEDERATE ARMY.

ARMY OF NORTHERN VIRGINIA.— General Robert E. Lee.

FIRST ARMY CORPS, Lieut.-Gen. James Longstreet.
McLAWS'S DIVISION, Maj.-Gen. Lafayette McLaws. Staff loss : k, 1 ; w, 1 = 2.
Kershaw's Brigade, Brig.-Gen. Joseph B. Kershaw : 2d S. C., Col. John D. Kennedy ; 3d S. C., Col. James D. Nance (w), Lieut.-Col. William D. Rutherford (w), Maj. Robert C. Maffett (w), Capt. William W. Hance (w), Capt. John C. Summer (k), Capt. John K. G. Nance ; 7th S. C., Lieut.-Col. Elbert Bland ; 8th S. C., Capt. E. T. Stackhouse ; 15th S. C., Col. W. D. De Saussure ; 3d S. C. Battalion, Lieut.-Col. W. G. Rice. Brigade loss : k, 38 ; w, 341 = 379. *Barksdale's Brigade*, Brig.-Gen. William Barksdale : 13th Miss., Col. J. W. Carter ; 17th Miss., Lieut.-Col. John C. Fiser ; 18th Miss., Lieut.-Col. William H. Luse ; 21st Miss., Col. Benjamin G. Humphreys. Brigade loss : k, 29 ; w, 151 ; m, 62 = 242. *Cobb's Brigade*, Brig.-Gen. Thomas R. R. Cobb (m w), Col. Robert McMillan : 16th Ga., Col. Goode Bryan ; 18th Ga., Lieut.-Col. S. Z. Ruff; 24th Ga., Col. Robert McMillan ; Cobb (Ga.) Legion, —— ; Phillips (Ga.) Legion, Col. B. F. Cook. Brigade loss : k, 33 ; w, 198 ; m, 4 = 235. *Semmes's Brigade*, Brig.-Gen. Paul J. Semmes : 10th Ga., —— ; 50th Ga., —— ; 51st Ga., —— ; 53d Ga., ——. Brigade loss : w, 4. *Artillery*, Col. Henry C. Cabell : N. C. Battery, Capt. Basil C. Manly ; Ga. Battery, Capt. J. P. W. Read ; 1st Richmond (Va.) Howitzers, Capt. E. S. McCarthy ; Ga. Battery (Troup Art'y), Capt. Henry H. Carlton. Artillery loss : w, 2. (Colonel Cabell also commanded Nelson's battalion, and Branch's, Cooper's, Dearing's, Ells's, Eubank's, Lane's, Macon's, and Ross's batteries.)
ANDERSON'S DIVISION, Maj.-Gen. Richard H. Anderson.
Wilcox's Brigade, Brig.-Gen. Cadmus M. Wilcox : 8th Ala., —— ; 9th Ala., —— ; 10th Ala., —— ; 11th Ala., —— ; 14th Ala., ——. Brigade loss : k, 3 ; w, 15 = 18. *Mahone's Brigade*, Brig.-Gen. William Mahone : 6th Va., —— ; 12th Va., —— ; 16th Va., —— ; 41st Va., —— ; 61st Va., ——. Brigade loss : k, 2 ; w, 6 = 8. *Featherston's Brigade*, Brig.-Gen. W. S. Featherston : 12th Miss., —— ; 16th Miss., —— ; 19th Miss., —— ; 48th Miss. (5 co's) ——. Brigade loss : k, 5 ; w, 38 = 43. *Wright's Brigade*, Brig.-Gen. A. R. Wright : 3d Ga., Col. Edward J. Walker ; 22d Ga., —— ; 48th Ga., Capt. M. R. Hall ; 2d Ga. Battalion, Capt. C. J. Moffett. Brigade loss : k, 2 ; w, 1 = 3. *Perry's Brigade*, Brig.-Gen. E. A. Perry : 2d Fla., —— ; 5th Fla., —— ; 8th Fla., Capt. David Lang (w), Capt. Thomas R. Love. Brigade loss : k, 7 ; w, 38 ; m, 44 = 89. *Artillery* : La. Battery (Donaldsonville Art'y), Capt. Victor Maurin ; Va. Battery, Capt. Frank Huger ; Va. Battery, Capt. John W. Lewis ; Va. Battery (Norfolk Light Art'y Blues), Lieut. William T. Peet. Artillery loss : k, 1 ; w, 8 = 9.
PICKETT'S DIVISION, Maj.-Gen. George E. Pickett.
Garnett's Brigade, Brig.-Gen. Richard B. Garnett : 8th Va., —— ; 18th Va., —— ; 19th Va., —— ; 28th Va., —— ; 56th Va., ——. *Armistead's Brigade*, Brig.-Gen. Lewis A. Armistead : 9th Va., —— ; 14th Va., —— ; 38th Va., —— ; 53d Va., —— ; 57th Va., ——. *Kemper's Brigade*, Brig.-Gen. James L. Kemper : 1st Va., —— ; 3d Va., —— ; 7th Va., —— ; 11th Va., —— ; 24th Va., ——. *Jenkins's Brigade*, Brig.-Gen. Micah Jenkins : 1st S. C. (Hagood's) ; 2d S. C. Rifles, —— ; 5th S. C., —— ; 6th S. C., —— ; Hampton (S. C.) Legion, —— ; Palmetto (S. C.) Sharp-shooters, ——. *Corse's Brigade*, Brig.-Gen. Montgomery D. Corse : 15th Va., —— ; 17th Va., —— ; 30th Va., —— ; 32d Va., ——. *Artillery* (composition incomplete) : Va. Battery, Capt.

James Dearing ; Va. Battery (Fauquier Art'y), Capt. R. M. Stribling ; Va. Battery (Richmond Fayette Art'y), Capt. Miles C. Macon. Division loss : k, 3 ; w, 50 ; m, 1 = 54.
HOOD'S DIVISION, Maj.-Gen. John B. Hood.
Law's Brigade, Brig.-Gen. E. McIver Law : 4th Ala., —— ; 44th Ala., —— ; 6th N. C., —— ; 54th N. C., Col. J. C. S. McDowell ; 57th N. C., Col. A. C. Godwin. Brigade loss : k, 50 ; w, 164 ; m, 5 = 219. *Robertson's Brigade*, Brig.-Gen. J. B. Robertson : 3d Ark., —— ; 1st Tex., —— ; 4th Tex., —— ; 5th Tex., ——. Brigade loss : k, 1 ; w, 4 = 5. *Anderson's Brigade*, Brig.-Gen. George T. Anderson : 1st Ga. (Regulars), —— ; 7th Ga., —— ; 8th Ga., —— ; 9th Ga., —— ; 11th Ga., ——. Brigade loss : k, 2 ; w, 8 ; m, 4 = 14. *Toombs's Brigade*, Col. H. L. Benning : 2d Ga., —— ; 15th Ga., —— ; 17th Ga., —— ; 20th Ga., ——. Brigade loss : k, 1 ; w, 12 ; m, 2 = 15. *Artillery* : S. C. Battery (German Art'y), Capt. W. K. Bachman ; S. C. Battery (Palmetto Light Art'y), Capt. Hugh R. Garden ; N. C. Battery (Rowan Art'y), Capt. James Reilly.
RANSOM'S DIVISION, Brig.-Gen. Robert Ransom, Jr.
Ransom's Brigade, Brig.-Gen. Robert Ransom, Jr. : 24th N. C., —— ; 25th N. C., Lieut.-Col. Samuel C. Bryson ; 35th N. C., —— ; 49th N. C., —— ; Va. Battery, Capt. J. R. Branch. Brigade loss : k, 27 ; w, 127 = 154. *Cooke's Brigade*, Brig.-Gen. John R. Cooke (w), Col. E. D. Hall : 15th N. C., —— ; 27th N. C., Col. John A. Gilmer, Jr. ; 46th N. C., Col. E. D. Hall ; 48th N. C., Lieut.-Col. Samuel H. Walkup ; Va. Battery (Cooper's). Brigade loss : k, 52 ; w, 328 = 380.
CORPS ARTILLERY (not assigned to divisions).
Washington (La.) Artillery, Col. J. B. Walton : 1st Co., Capt. C. W. Squires ; 2d Co., Capt. J. B. Richardson ; 3d Co., Capt. M. B. Miller ; 4th Co., Capt. B. F. Eshleman. Battalion loss : k, 3 ; w, 24 = 27. *Alexander's Battalion*, Lieut.-Col. E. Porter Alexander : Va. Battery (Bedford Art'y), Capt. Tyler C. Jordan ; Va. Battery, Capt. J. L. Eubank ; La. Battery (Madison Light Art'y), Capt. George V. Moody ; Va. Battery, Capt. William W. Parker ; S. C. Battery, Capt. A. B. Rhett ; Va. Battery, Capt. P. Woolfolk, Jr. Battalion loss : k, 1 : w, 10 = 11.
SECOND ARMY CORPS, Lieut.-General Thomas J. Jackson.
HILL'S DIVISION, Maj.-Gen. Daniel H. Hill.
First Brigade, Brig.-Gen. R. E. Rodes : 3d Ala., —— ; 5th Ala., —— ; 6th Ala., —— ; 12th Ala., —— ; 26th Ala., ——. Brigade loss : k, 2 ; w, 14 = 16. *Second Brigade*, Brig.-Gen. George Doles : 4th Ga., —— ; 44th Ga., Col. John B. Estes : 1st N. C., —— ; 3d N. C., ——. Brigade loss : k, 2 ; w, 25 = 27. *Third Brigade*, Brig.-Gen. A. H. Colquitt : 13th Ala., —— ; 6th Ga., —— ; 23d Ga., —— ; 27th Ga., —— ; 28th Ga., ——. Brigade loss : w, 15. *Fourth Brigade*, Brig.-Gen. Alfred Iverson : 5th N. C., —— ; 12th N. C., —— ; 20th N. C., —— ; 23d N. C., ——. Brigade loss : k, 1 ; w, 12 = 13. *Fifth Brigade*, Col. Bryan Grimes : 2d N. C., —— ; 4th N. C., —— ; 14th N. C., —— ; 30th N. C., ——. Brigade loss : k, 8 ; w, 51 = 59. *Artillery*, Major H. P. Jones : Ala. Battery, Capt. R. A. Hardaway ; Ala. Battery (Jeff Davis Art'y), Capt. J. W. Bondurant ; Va. Battery, (King William Art'y), Capt. Thomas H. Carter ; Va. Battery (Morris Art'y), Capt. R. C. M. Page ; Va. Battery (Orange Art'y), Capt. C. W. Fry. Artillery loss : k, 4 ; w, 8 = 12.
LIGHT DIVISION, Maj.-Gen. Ambrose P. Hill.
First Brigade, Col. J. M. Brockenbrough : 40th Va., —— ; 47th Va., Col. Robert M. Mayo ; 55th Va., —— ; 22d Va. Battalion, Lieut.-Col. E. P. Tayloe. Brigade

The dash indicates that the name of the commanding officer has not been found in the "Official Records."—EDITORS.

loss: k, 10; w, 73 = 83. *Second Brigade*, Brig.-Gen. Maxcy Gregg (m w), Col. D. H. Hamilton: 1st S. C. (Prov. Army), Col. D. H. Hamilton; 1st S. C. Rifles, ——; 12th S. C., ——; 13th S. C., ——; 14th S. C., Col. Samuel McGowan. Brigade loss: k and w, 363. *Third Brigade*, Brig.-Gen. Edward L. Thomas: 14th Ga., ——; 35th Ga., ——; 45th Ga., ——; 49th Ga., ——. Brigade loss: k, 42; w, 288 = 330. *Fourth Brigade*, Brig.-Gen. James H. Lane: 7th N. C., Lieut.-Col. J. L. Hill; 18th N. C., Col. Thomas J. Purdie (w); 28th N. C., Col. S. D. Lowe; 33d N. C., Col. Clark M. Avery; 37th N. C., Col. W. M. Barbour (w). Brigade loss: k, 62; w, 257; m, 216 = 535. *Fifth Brigade*, Brig.-Gen. James J. Archer: 5th Ala., Battalion, Major A. S. Van de Graaff (w), Capt. S. D. Stewart; 19th Ga., Lieut.-Col. Andrew J. Hutchins; 1st Tenn. (Prov. Army), Col. Peter Turney (w), Lieut.-Col. N. J. George (w), Capt. M. Turney (w), Capt. H. J. Hawkins; 7th Tenn., Col. John F. Goodner; 14th Tenn., Lieut.-Col. James W. Lockert. Brigade loss: k, 40; w, 211; m, 166 = 417. *Sixth Brigade*, Brig.-Gen. William D. Pender (w), Col. Alfred M. Scales: 13th N. C., Col. Alfred M. Scales; 16th N. C., Col. John S. McElroy; 22d N. C., Maj. Christopher C. Cole; 34th N. C., ——; 38th N. C., ——. Brigade loss: k, 16; w, 153 = 169. *Artillery*, Lieut.-Col. R. L. Walker: N. C. Battery (Branch Art'y — section), Lieut. J. R. Potts; Va. Battery (Crenshaw's — section), Lieut. James Ellett (k); Va. Battery (Fredericksburg Art'y), Lieut. E. A. Marye; Va. Battery (Johnson's — section), Lieut. V. J. Clutter (w); Va. Battery (Letcher Art'y), Capt. G. Davidson; S. C. Battery (Pee Dee Art'y), Capt. D. G. McIntosh; Va. Battery (Purcell Art'y), Capt. W. J. Pegram. Artillery loss: k, 11; w, 88 = 99. Division loss: k, 231; w, 1474; m, 417 = 2122.
EWELL'S DIVISION, Brig.-Gen. Jubal A. Early.

Lawton's Brigade, Col. E. N. Atkinson (w and c), Col. Clement A. Evans: 13th Ga., Col. J. M. Smith; 26th Ga., Capt. B. F. Grace; 31st Ga., Col. Clement A. Evans; 38th Ga., Capt. William L. McLeod; 60th Ga., Col. W. H. Stiles; 61st Ga., Col. J. H. Lamar (w), Maj. C. W. McArthur. Brigade loss: k, 86; w, 633 = 719. *Trimble's Brigade*, Col. Robert F. Hoke: 15th Ala., ——; 12th Ga., ——; 21st Ga., Lieut.-Col. Thomas W. Hooper; 21st N. C., ——; 1st N. C. Battalion ——. Brigade loss: k, 8; w, 98 = 106. *Early's Brigade*, Col. James A. Walker: 13th Va., Lieut.-Col. James B. Terrill; 25th Va., ——; 31st Va., ——; 44th Va., ——; 49th Va., ——; 52d Va., ——; 58th Va., ——. Brigade loss: k, 17; w, 140 = 157. *Hays's Brigade*, Brig.-Gen. Harry T. Hays: 5th La., ——; 6th La., ——; 7th La., ——; 8th La., ——; 9th La., ——. Brigade loss: k, 9; w, 44; m, 1 = 54. *Artillery*, Capt. J. W. Latimer: Va. Battery (Charlottesville Art'y), Capt. J. McD. Carrington; Md. Battery (Chesapeake Art'y), Lieut. John E. Plater; 1st Md. Battery, Capt. William F. Dement; Va. Battery (Courtney Art'y), Lieut. W. A. Tanner; La. Battery (Guard Art'y), Capt. Louis D'Aquin (k); Va. Battery (Staunton Art'y), Lieut. Asher W. Garber. Artillery loss: k, 4; w, 21 = 25.
JACKSON'S DIVISION, Brig.-Gen. William B. Taliaferro.

First Brigade, Brig.-Gen. E. F. Paxton: 2d Va., Capt. J. Q. A. Nadenbousch; 4th Va., Lieut.-Col. R. D. Gardner (w), Maj. William Terry; 5th Va., Lieut.-Col. H. J. Williams; 27th Va., Lieut.-Col. James K. Edmondson; 33d Va., Col. Edwin G. Lee. Brigade loss: k, 3; w, 44; m, 1 = 48. *Second Brigade*, Brig.-Gen. John R. Jones; 21st Va., ——; 42d Va., ——; 48th Va., ——; 1st Va.

Battalion, ——. Brigade loss: k, 3; w, 34 = 37. *Third Brigade*, Col. E. T. H. Warren: 47th Ala., Capt. James M. Campbell; 48th Ala., Capt. C. B. St. John; 10th Va., Capt. W. B. Yancey; 23d Va., Capt. A. J. Richardson; 37th Va., Col. T. V. Williams. Brigade loss: w, 9. *Fourth Brigade*, Col. Edmund Pendleton: 1st La., Lieut.-Col. M. Nolan; 2d La., Maj. M. A. Grogan; 10th La., Maj. John M. Legett; 14th La., Capt. H. M. Verlander; 15th La., Lieut.-Col. McG. Goodwyn. Brigade loss: k, 2; w, 35 = 37. *Artillery*, Capt. J. B. Brockenbrough: Va. Battery (Carpenter's), Lieut. George McKendree; Va. Battery (Danville Art'y), Capt. George W. Wooding (w); Va. Battery (Hampden Art'y), Capt. William H. Caskie; Va. Battery (Lee Art'y), Lieut. C. W. Statham; Va. Battery (Lusk's). Artillery loss: k, 2; w, 48; m, 1 = 51.
RESERVE ARTILLERY, ☆ Brig.-Gen. W. N. Pendleton.

Brown's Battalion, Col. J. Thompson Brown: Va. Battery, Capt. James V. Brooke; Va. Battery (Powhatan Art'y), Capt. Willis J. Dance; Va. Battery (Salem Art'y, Hupp's), ——; Va. Battery (Rockbridge Art'y), Capt. William T. Poague; Va. Battery (3d Howitzers), Lieut. James Utz (k); Va. Battery, Capt. David Watson. Battalion loss: k, 10; w, 26 = 36. *Sumter (Ga.) Battalion*, Lieut.-Col. Allen S. Cutts: Co. A, Capt. H. M. Ross; Co. B, Capt. George M. Patterson; Co. C, Capt. John Lane. *Nelson's Battalion*, Maj. William Nelson: Va. Battery (Amherst Art'y), Capt. Thomas J. Kirkpatrick; Va. Battery (Fluvanna Art'y), Capt. John L. Massie; Ga. Battery, Capt. John Milledge, Jr. *Miscellaneous Batteries* (assignments not indicated): Ga. Battery (Ells's), Lieut. W. F. Anderson; Va. Battery (Hanover Art'y), Capt. George W. Nelson.
CAVALRY, Maj.-Gen. James E. B. Stuart.

First Brigade (a detachment was on a raid to the rear of the Union army), Brig.-Gen. Wade Hampton: 1st N. C., Col. L. S. Baker; 1st S. C., Col. J. L. Beach; 2d S. C., Col. M. C. Butler; Cobb (Ga.) Legion, Lieut.-Col. P. M. B. Young; Phillips's (Ga.) Legion, Lieut.-Col. William W. Rich. *Second Brigade*, Brig.-Gen. Fitzhugh Lee: 1st Va., Col. James H. Drake; 2d Va., Col. Thomas T. Munford; 3d Va., Col. T. H. Owen; 4th Va., Col. Williams C. Wickham; 5th Va., ——. *Third Brigade*, Brig.-Gen. W. H. F. Lee: 2d N. C., Col. S. Williams; 9th Va., Col. R. L. T. Beale; 10th Va., Col. J. Lucius Davis; 13th Va., Col. J. R. Chambliss, Jr.; 15th Va., Col. William B. Ball. Brigade loss: w, 7. *Artillery*, Maj. John Pelham: Va. Battery, Capt. James Breathed; Va. Battery, Capt. R. P. Chew; S. C. Battery, Capt. J. F. Hart; Va. Battery, Capt. M. W. Henry; Va. Battery, Capt. M. N. Moorman. Artillery loss: k, 3; w, 22 = 25.

Total Confederate loss: killed, 608; wounded, 4116; captured or missing, 653 = 5377.

The "present for duty" in Lee's army (including all of Stuart's cavalry), as shown by his return for December 10th, was 78,513. To arrive at Lee's effective strength in the battle (not officially stated) there should be deducted the usual proportion of non-combatants, the detachment of Hampton's cavalry brigade, on a raid to the north of the Rappahannock, and the cavalry brigade of W. E. Jones serving in the Shenandoah Valley. According to the estimate of Mr. Thomas White, as given in Taylor's "Four Years with General Lee" (p. 158), this was 58,500 of all arms. Colonel Taylor (p. 81) says: "Less than 20,000 Confederate troops (about one-fourth of the army under General Lee) were actively engaged."— EDITORS.

☆ Majors Garnett, Hamilton, and T. J. Page, Jr., are mentioned in the reports as commanding artillery battalions, but the composition of their commands is not given.— EDITORS.

UNION CAMP SCENE.— A QUIET GAME. FROM A WAR-TIME SKETCH.

A BIT OF PARTISAN SERVICE.

BY JOHN S. MOSBY, COLONEL, C. S. A.

BEFORE the first battle of Bull Run I had enlisted as a private in a company of Confederate cavalry of which William E. Jones, a West Point officer, was the captain, and that had been assigned to the 1st Virginia regiment of cavalry, commanded by Colonel J. E. B. Stuart. We joined Stuart at Bunker Hill, a small village on the pike leading from Winchester, where General Johnston had his headquarters, to Martinsburg, where Patterson with his army was lying. Stuart was watching Patterson. In a few days Patterson advanced and took possession of our camp, and our regiment retired toward Winchester. Here I took my first lessons in war. Patterson had no cavalry except a battalion of regulars, and we had no artillery; so he contented himself with throwing an occasional shell at us, and we got out of the way of them as fast as we could. One day we were lying down in a large open field holding our horses when a battery suddenly appeared upon a hill about a mile off and opened on us. I saw a shell burst within a few yards of Captain Jones, who coolly ordered us to mount and fall into line. I do not think I was so much frightened at any time after that. Stuart sent one company of cavalry down toward Charlestown to observe Patterson, and with the remainder of his regiment started for Manassas and took part in that battle. I served also with Stuart on the Peninsula and in the Antietam campaign.

When the year 1863 arrived Fredericksburg had been fought, and the two armies, in winter quarters, were confronting each other on the Rappahannock. Both sides sought rest; the pickets on the opposite banks of the river had ceased firing and gone to swapping coffee and tobacco. The cavalry had been sent to the rear to forage. But "quiet to quick

bosoms is a hell." I did not want to rust away my life in camp, so I asked Stuart to give me a detail of men to go over to Loudoun County, where I thought I could make things lively during the winter months. Always full of enterprise, Stuart readily assented, and I started off on my career as a partisan. At the time I had no idea of organizing an independent command, but expected to return to Stuart when the campaign opened in the spring. I was indifferent to rank, and would have been as contented to be a lieutenant as a colonel.

I was somewhat familiar with the country where I began operations, having picketed there the year before. The lines of the troops attached to the defenses of Washington extended from about Occoquan, on the lower Potomac, through Centreville, in Fairfax County, to the Falls of the upper Potomac, and thence as far west as Harper's Ferry. This was a long line to defend, and before I went there had not been closely guarded. I began on the picket-lines; my attacks were generally in the night-time, and usually the surprise compensated for the disparity in numbers. They would be repeated the next, and often during the same night at a different point, and this created a vastly exaggerated idea of my force. Some conception may be formed of the alarm it produced from a fact stated by General Hooker, that in the spring of 1863 the planks on Chain Bridge were taken up every night to keep me out of Washington. At that time I could not muster over twenty men. A small force moving with celerity and threatening many points on a line can neutralize a hundred times its own number. The line must be stronger at every point than the attacking force, else it is broken. At that time Hooker asked that the cavalry division belonging to the defenses of Washington be sent to the front to reënforce Pleasonton when he crossed the Rappahannock to engage Stuart in the great cavalry combat of June 9th. [It was refused on the ground that it was necessary to keep it where it was, in order to protect the communication between the army and Washington. A few days before that fight we struck the railroad within two miles of this cavalry camp, and captured and burned a train of supplies going up to Pleasonton. The 3000 men who came after me could not run any faster than the twenty with me. We vanished like the children of the mist, and the major-general who pursued reported that we had been annihilated. But within less than a week I pulled myself together again, crossed the Potomac about twelve miles above Washington, and captured the cavalry camp near Seneca.

I recur now to the time when I first arrived in the country which became the theater of the partisan war which I carried on until the surrender at Appomattox. As I have said, the line of outposts belonging to the defenses of Washington formed the arc of a circle extending from the upper to the lower Potomac. The troops had been having an easy, lazy life, which was described in the stereotyped message sent every night to the Northern press, "All quiet along the Potomac." I saw that here was a bountiful harvest to be gathered, and that the reapers were few. I gave constant employment to the Union troops, and they no longer led a life of drowsy indolence. I procured some guides who knew every path of the country, and with the aid of friendly citizens found out where every picket was posted. A certain major-general came after me with a division of cavalry and a battery of artillery. After shelling the woods in every direction so as to be sure of my extermination, and destroying many bats and owls, he took off as prisoners all the old men he could find. He had the idea that I was a myth and that these old farmers were the raiders. One old man appealed to his crutch to show the physical impossibility of his being a guerrilla. But the major-general was inexorable. He returned with his prizes to camp, but I was there almost as soon as he was.

In the month of February, 1863, Brigadier-General E. H. Stoughton was in command of the troops in front of Washington, with his headquarters at Fairfax Court House. There was a considerable body also at Centreville, and a cavalry brigade was encamped on the pike leading from that place to Fairfax Court House, under command of Colonel Percy Wyndham. Stoughton was a West Point officer, and had served with distinction under McClellan on the Peninsula. Wyndham was an Englishman serving as Colonel of the 1st New Jersey Cavalry. The year before he had started up the Shenandoah Valley to bag Ashby, but the performance did not come up to the manifesto; in their first encounter Ashby bagged him. He was now given a chance to redeem his reputation. My attacks on his lines had been incessant and very annoying. He struck blindly around like the Cyclops in his cave, but nobody was hurt. The methodical

tactics he had learned in European wars were of no more use to him than a suit of armor of the Middle Ages. My men would dart down on his outposts like a hawk on its prey; but when Wyndham came up in solid column the partisans had gone. In his vexation he sent me word that I was a horse-thief; to which I replied that all the horses I had stolen had had riders, and the riders had had sabers and pistols.

While operating against the outposts it had been my custom to examine my prisoners separately, and in this way I learned all the interior arrangements of their camps. I was then meditating a bolder enterprise than I had ever undertaken, but had communicated it to no one. This was to penetrate the outer lines, and go right up to their headquarters and carry off the general commanding and Colonel Wyndham. It looked extremely hazardous to attempt it; but as nothing of the sort ever had been done, I calculated there would be no precaution to prevent it. I was right. While I was maturing my plan I received aid from an unexpected source. One day a deserter, named Ames, wearing the stripes of a sergeant, came to me from a New York cavalry regiment of Wyndham's brigade. The Emancipation Proclamation which had been put in operation was the reason he gave for deserting the cause of the Union, but I always suspected that it was some personal wrong he had suffered. He seemed to be animated by the most vindictive hatred for his former comrades. I felt an instinctive confidence in his sincerity which he never betrayed. After I had thoroughly tested his fidelity I made him a lieutenant. He served with me until he was killed in October, 1864.

I questioned Ames closely about the location of the camps and outposts, and he confirmed the knowledge I had previously obtained. I determined first to take him on a trial-trip down into Fairfax County. There was a cavalry post at a certain school-house, and I started with Ames one afternoon to attack it. A deep snow was on the ground, and it was raining and sleeting. About two weeks before, I had captured the same post, but I thought they would not expect me back so soon. To satisfy my men I did not let Ames carry any arms, for they all were certain that he had been sent to decoy me into a trap. The soldiers in the Union camps slept soundly that night, for they felt sure that nothing but a wild animal would be abroad in such weather. I stopped when I got near the place I intended to attack, to make an inquiry of a farmer who lived near there as to the number of men on the post. I called him out of bed. He came to the door in his night-dress, and the first thing he asked was, "How many men have you?" I said, "Seventeen." "How many," I asked, "are at the picket-post?" "One hundred," he answered. "I have been down there this evening. You are certainly not going to attack them with so few men?" "Yes," I replied; "it is so dark they can't see us, and will think I have got a hundred too." Contrary to my usual practice, I went straight along the road. We got close on the vedette, who challenged us, fired, and started into camp at full speed. We dashed on as close to his heels as the witches were on Tam O'Shanter's. The men were asleep in the school-house and their horses were tied with halters to the trees. If they had staid inside they could easily have driven us

COLONEL JOHN S. MOSBY, C. S. A.
FROM A PHOTOGRAPH.

off with their carbines. But every man ran for his horse, and we were just in time to scatter them. We got all the horses, but most of the men escaped in the darkness. In the charge, Ames rode by my side. We got off safe with our booty and prisoners. After daybreak, Colonel Wyndham followed at full speed for twenty miles on our

track. All that he did was to go back to camp with a lot of broken down horses. Ames, like the saints, had been tried by fire; he was never doubted afterward. The time had now come for me to take a bolder flight and execute my plan of making a raid on headquarters.

It was on the afternoon of March 7th, 1863, that I started from Aldie with 29 men on this expedition. Ames was the only one who knew its object. It was pitch-dark before we got near the cavalry pickets at Chantilly. We passed in between them and Centreville. Here a good point in the game was won, for once inside the Union lines we would be mistaken for their own men. By an accident one-half of my command got separated in the dark from the other, and it was nearly an hour before I could find them. We passed along close by the camp-fires, but the sentinels took us for a scouting party of their cavalry. I had felt very cold in the early part of the night, but my blood grew warmer as I got farther in the lines, and the chill passed away. I had no reputation to lose by failure but much to gain by success. I remembered, too, the motto that Ixion in heaven wrote in Minerva's album —" Adventures are to the adventurous." We struck the road leading from Fairfax Court House to the railroad station and then went on to the village. There were a few guards about, but they did not suspect us until they saw a pistol pointed at them. Of course they surrendered. Some refused to believe we were Confederates after we told them who we were. A few sentinels hailed us with the formula, " Who comes there?" and were answered, "5th New York Cavalry." It was past midnight, and it was necessary to do our work quickly if it was to be done at all. The first thing I did was to detail squads of men to gather prisoners and horses. I was more anxious to catch Wyndham than any one else; so I sent Ames, with a detachment, after him. But for once fortune had been propitious to him. He had gone down to Washington that evening. Ames got two of his staff and his uniform, and brought them to me. One of these officers was Captain Barker, of the 5th New York Cavalry, who had been Ames's captain. Ames brought him to me as a trophy, and seemed to feel a malicious pride in introducing him. I had sent another party to the house where Lieut.-Col. Robert Johnstone, commanding the cavalry brigade, was sleeping. In some manner he had heard the alarm and had slipped out through the back way into the garden in his night-clothes. His wife met my men like a lioness at the door. I was greatly disappointed in not getting Wyndham. The capture of his staff-officers and fine horses was not an equivalent for the loss of the chief. The other details did their work rapidly, and soon collected at our rendezvous in the court-yard a large number of prisoners and fine steeds. The prisoners seemed to be utterly dumfounded. About this time Joe Nelson rode up to me with a prisoner who said he belonged to the guard at General Stoughton's headquarters, and with a party of five or six I immediately went there. We dismounted, and with a loud rap on the front door awoke the inmates. An upper window was raised and some one called out, "Who is there?"

The answer was, "We have a dispatch for General Stoughton." An officer (Lieutenant Prentiss) came to the front door to get it. I caught hold of his shirt and whispered my name in his ear, and told him to lead me to the general's room. Resistance was useless, and he did so. A light was struck, and before us lay the sleeping general. He quickly raised up in bed and asked what this meant. I said, "General, get up—dress quick—you are a prisoner." "What!" exclaimed the indignant general. "My name is Mosby; Stuart's cavalry are in possession of this place, and General Jackson holds Centreville." "Is Fitz Lee here?" "Yes." "Then take me to him; we were classmates." "Very well; but dress quick." Two of my men assisted him to put on his clothes. My motive in deceiving him in regard to the amount of my force was to deprive him of all hope of rescue. I was in a most critical situation, for in addition to several thousand troops in the surrounding camps, a considerable number were quartered in the houses in the village. If there had been the least concert among them they could easily have driven us out; but, although we remained there an hour, not a shot was fired; as soon as our presence became known each man tried to save himself. Stoughton did not delay a moment, for he had no idea how few of us there were. A couple of men had been left to hold our horses while we were in the house. One of these, George Whitescarver, surrounded and captured a guard of six men sleeping in a tent. Stoughton's horses all stood at the door as we came out, with saddles and bridles on. Lieutenant Prentiss started, but soon parted company with us. We could not see where he went. When I got to the court-yard I found all my different squads collected there with their prisoners and spoils. No sign of resistance had been shown. The prisoners outnumbered us three or four to one, and each was mounted and leading a horse. The cavalcade started in an opposite direction from where we intended to go, in order to deceive our pursuers. After going a few hundred yards we turned and flanked the cavalry camp, and struck the pike to Centreville.

Stoughton soon discovered how few of us there were. I did not allow him to hold his bridle-reins, but gave them to one of my men (Hunter), who rode beside him. Stoughton remarked, "This is a bold thing you have done; but you will certainly be caught; our cavalry will soon be after you." "Perhaps so," I said. It was so dark that the blue could not be distinguished from the gray. Hence the prisoners all thought there were at least one hundred of us. We lost many of them before we got beyond the lines. They were all formed in a column of fours, and after we got on the pike I rode some distance in the rear while Hunter, with Stoughton, was leading in front. We went at a trot and the chances of our escape were improving. No one seemed to be on our track, as our winding

about had baffled pursuit. It never entered the head of any one that I would march up the pike in the face of two or three thousand troops at Centreville. When within a mile of that place, and just about the break of day, we came upon a camp-fire which had evidently just been deserted. A picket had been posted there on the evening before to stay during the night. The officer, thinking it unnecessary to remain longer, had gone into camp. As we had taken the precaution to cut the telegraph wires, no news had yet reached Centreville of our work at the Court House. When I saw the picket-fire on the pike I halted the column and galloped forward to reconnoiter. Seeing that no one was there, I called to Hunter to come on. It was necessary to make a circuit around Centreville, and to pass between encampments of Union troops on both sides of it. I was certain to be lost if I went either too far to the left or the right. Just as we turned off from the pike Captain Barker made a desperate attempt to escape. He darted from the line, but my Hungarian Jake was at his heels, and sent a harmless shot after him just as his horse fell in a ditch. I rode up to him and inquired if he was hurt. He said "No," and Jake assisted him to mount. No one else cared to repeat the experiment. We passed within a few hundred yards of the forts, and could see the guns pointing through the embrasures and hear the challenge of the sentinels as they walked on the parapets. My heart began to beat with joy. The odds were now rapidly getting in my favor. We were soon on the other side of Centreville. Although we could be plainly seen from there, it was probably supposed that we were a scouting party of Federal cavalry. When we got to Cub Run, it was so swollen by the melting snows that it could not be forded. We were still within easy cannon-shot of the guns on the heights, and there was no time to be lost. I acted on the maxim of plucking the flower safety from the nettle danger, and plunging into the brimming stream swam over. The rest followed, Stoughton being next to me. The first thing he said as he shivered with cold was, "This is the first rough treatment I have received." I knew that no cavalry would ever swim after me. Leaving Hunter to come on with my men and prisoners, I galloped on ahead with George Slater and once more got on the pike at Groveton. This was the very spot where, the year before, Fitz John Porter had made his disastrous assault on Jackson. From this hill I had a view of the pike seven miles back to Centreville. No enemy was in pursuit. I was safe. Just then Hunter appeared and the sun rose. It seemed to me that it never shone with such splendor before. I turned over my prisoners to Stuart at Culpeper Court House. He was as much delighted by what I had done as I was, and published a general order announcing it to the cavalry, in which he said that it was "a feat unparalleled in the war."

THE original instructions to General George Stoneman for the coöperation of the cavalry in the Chancellorsville campaign directed him to cross the Rappahannock on the 13th of April, at some point west of the Orange and Alexandria railroad, and throw his whole force, excepting one brigade, between Lee's position on the Rappahannock and his base at Richmond. The object was the isolation of the enemy "from his supplies, checking his retreat, and inflicting on him every possible injury which will tend to his discomfiture and defeat." This movement was delayed by heavy rains, and on the 28th of April the instructions were modified. The new plan was to cross the Rappahannock at the fords immediately north-west of Fredericksburg on the evening of the 28th, or the morning of the 29th, and move in two columns, operating on the lines of the Orange and Alexandria and the Richmond and Fredericksburg railroads toward Richmond. The movements of the corps are given in detail in the report of General Stoneman:

"On April 27th, I, then being at Warrenton Junction, with the corps encamped along the Orange and Alexandria railroad, received a telegram directing me with my commanders to meet some persons from headquarters Army of the Potomac at Morrisville on the following day [the 28th] at 2 P. M. Arriving there with my commanders, I found the commanding general and his staff, and learned that a portion of the army was about to cross the Rappahannock at Kelly's Ford that day. . . . From Morrisville to where the cavalry corps lay was thirteen miles; from there to where some of the extreme pickets were was thirteen more, so that it was quite late at night before the command was all assembled and ready to start, and owing to the state of the roads, the result of the recent heavy rains, and the darkness of the night, rendered doubly obscure by a dense fog, the corps did not reach the river until nearly 8 A. M. of the 29th. Arriving at the river, we found but one ford within the limits prescribed in our instructions which could be passed over, and that not by packed mules or artillery. By dint of great exertion we succeeded in getting all over the river by 5 P. M. I assembled the division and brigade commanders, spread our maps, and had a thorough understanding of what we were to do. . . . Instructions were given to have all the packed mules and led horses sent in the direction of Germanna Mills, and to follow in the rear of the army and remain with it until we formed a junction therewith, which we expected would be in the vicinity of Richmond, and for each officer and man to take with him no more than he could carry on his horse, myself and staff setting the example."

Averell, with three brigades, was to advance on Culpeper Court House, while Stoneman, with three brigades numbering about 3500, under D. McM. Gregg, was to take the shorter route via Stevensburg, a hamlet 7 miles east of Culpeper Court House. The operations the first day, the 29th, after crossing, consisted in driving in the outposts which were encountered on both roads. The report continues:

"About 9 A. M., April 30th, a staff-officer of General Averell overtook me. . . . He also handed me a note picked up by some one, and sent me by General Averell, and to the following effect :

"'[Important.] HEADQUARTERS, CAVALRY DIVISION, near Brandy Station, Va., April 29th, 1863. COLONEL CHAMBLISS,

13th Virginia Cavalry. COLONEL: The major-general commanding directs me to say that he wishes you to get a man posted so as to have a view of the road leading down on the other side to Kelly's Ford, and find out what kind of troops marched down behind the wagons. The enemy have made a demonstration toward Stevensburg, but so far it amounts to nothing. The general is very anxious to know where to look for Stoneman, as we have heard nothing from him. Most respectfully, your obedient servant, R. CHANNING PRICE, Assistant Adjutant-General.'

"Feeling satisfied that we should find Raccoon Ford guarded, and that its passage would be disputed, I struck the Rapidan River about six miles below ; crossed over the portion of the command under General Buford, who sent a party under Captain Peter Penn Gaskell, of his staff, who, at a dash, cleared the ford above, capturing an officer, Lieutenant Bourier [James Boulware] of the 9th Virginia Cavalry, and six privates of the 9th and 10th

MAJOR-GENERAL GEORGE STONEMAN.
FROM A PHOTOGRAPH.

Virginia Cavalry. The rest of the cavalry and the artillery made their escape. The main body immediately crossed at the Raccoon Ford, the rear getting over about 10 P.M. No fires built to-night, as we were in plain view from Clark's Mountain, a few miles to the south of the ford, and on the top of which the enemy have a signal station. We learned here that Stuart, with Fitzhugh Lee's brigade, had that morning crossed at Somerville Ford, five miles above Raccoon Ford, and had gone toward Fredericksburg, and we thought it more than probable that we should find him on the Plank road at Verdierville, where we had to strike it on our way south. Orders were issued to be in the saddle at 2 o'clock in the morning, and we lay down on the wet ground to get a couple of hours' sleep. Two o'clock came, but the fog was so thick that it was impossible to move, more particularly as we had no guide to show us the road. Daylight came, and we pushed on ; struck the turnpike ; found no enemy, but saw by his trail that he had gone toward Fredericksburg. From here I pushed Gregg's division on to Louisa Court House, on the Virginia Central Railroad, where it arrived about 2 A. M., May 2d, and immediately commenced tearing up the track of the railroad, destroying the telegraph, etc. Buford's brigade encamped that night on the south bank of the North Anna. About 10 A. M., May 2d, I had the whole force united at Louisa Court House. From here I pushed a squadron

‡ See map, p. 155 of this volume, and also p. 164 of Volume II.—EDITORS.

152

of the 1st Maine, under Captain Tucker of that regiment, toward Gordonsville to find out the whereabouts of the enemy in that direction, as we knew that six or seven trains had passed up the evening previous loaded with troops. The captain drove in their pickets upon the main body, the 9th Virginia Cavalry, which in turn attacked him, killing 1 man, wounding 1, and capturing 1 lieutenant and 23 men. Captain Lord, with the 1st U. S. Cavalry, was sent to Tolersville Station, and from there to Frederickshall Station, twelve miles from Louisa Court House. From here a party under Lieutenant —— went to the North Anna and destroyed Carr's Bridge, which is on the main road leading from Spotsylvania to Goochland, on the James River, and is one of the principal highways. After having destroyed the Virginia Central railroad and telegraph, burned the depots, water-tanks, etc., for eighteen miles, and accomplished all that time would permit, we pushed on to Yanceyville, on the South Anna, and from there to Thompson's Cross-roads, ten miles lower down the river, where we arrived about 10 P. M., May 2d.

"At this point the James and South Anna rivers are less than 12 miles apart, and here I determined to make the most of my 3500 men in carrying out my previously conceived plan of operations. . . . One party, the 1st New Jersey, under Colonel [Percy] Wyndham, was to strike the James River at Columbia, at the junction of the James and Rivanna rivers, to destroy, if possible, the large canal aqueduct over the Rivanna, and from thence proceed along the canal in the direction of Richmond, doing all the harm possible. . . . Another party, the 2d New York, Colonel [Judson] Kilpatrick, was to push on to the railroad bridges over the Chickahominy, destroy them and the telegraph, and operate in the direction of Richmond, four miles distant from the bridges. Another force, the 12th Illinois Cavalry, Colonel Hasbrouck Davis, was to strike the two railroads at or in the vicinity of Ashland, on the Fredericksburg, and Atlee's, on the Virginia Central, and do all the harm it could. Another party, the 1st Maine and 1st Maryland, with a section of artillery, all under General Gregg, was to follow down the South Anna River, destroy all the road bridges thereon, and, if possible, the two railroad bridges across that river. Another party, the 5th U. S. Cavalry, under Captain Drummond, was to follow this last and see that the destruction was complete. Captain Merritt, with a flying party of the 1st Maryland, was sent out to do what he thought he could accomplish in the way of destroying bridges, etc. These different parties all got off by 3 A. M. on the 3d.

" . . . Colonels Wyndham, Kilpatrick, and Davis were directed either to return or to push on and bring up at either Yorktown or Gloucester Point. The rest were ordered to return to the reserve with myself. Colonel Wyndham and Captain Lord returned the same day. General Gregg and Captains Merritt and Drummond the next day. Colonels Kilpatrick and Davis pushed on through to Gloucester Point. . . . We remained at Shannon's Cross-roads during the 4th, and on the morning of the 5th moved to Yanceyville, on the South Anna, where we were joined by General Gregg, Colonel Wyndham, and Captains Merritt and Drummond, each with his command."

The operations of the column under General Averell are thus described by him in a communication to the editors dated May 11th, 1888:

"We encountered the enemy's cavalry, two thousand strong, under General W. H. F. Lee on the morning of the 30th, and drove it through Culpeper Court House in the direction of Rapidan Station.

"On the 1st we pressed the enemy's cavalry and pushed our right to within three miles of Orange Court House in an effort to dislodge the enemy from a strong position occupied by him on the south bank of the Rapidan, after he had crossed and destroyed the bridge.

"While thus engaged on the morning of the 2d we were recalled to the Army of the Potomac at U. S. Ford by orders from General Hooker. We reached Ely's Ford of the Rapidan after dark on the evening of the 2d, and were fired upon by the enemy's infantry from the opposite bank. A part of McIntosh's brigade forded the river, dismounted, drove away the enemy, some of the 13th North Carolina, and captured some prisoners. Early on the morning of the 3d we crossed the Rapidan and entered the right of our lines.

"It was found necessary to issue immediate orders sending cavalry to protect the right and rear of the army, which had become exposed to danger from the enemy's cavalry set free by our recall."

The column with Stoneman now prepared to return to the army. His report continues:

"The six days having now expired, during which we were assured by the commanding general he would certainly communicate with us, and no communication having been received, no retreating enemy having been seen or heard of, and no information as to the condition of things in the vicinity of Fredericksburg, except vague rumors of our defeat and capture, having been obtained, supplies for man and beast becoming scarce, having accomplished all that we were sent to perform, and having come to the conclusion that Colonels Kilpatrick and Davis, with their commands, had gone in the direction of Yorktown, I determined to make the best of our way back to the Army of the Potomac.

"To take the enemy by surprise and penetrate his country was easy enough; to withdraw from it was a more difficult matter. We knew that Lee and Hampton were to the west of us. . . . We knew also that there was a strong force at and in the vicinity of Gordonsville, and heard that another force was at Louisa Court House, and a small force of infantry at Tolersville.

"After thinking the matter over, I determined to send General Buford, with 650 picked horses of his brigade, to threaten any force in the vicinity of Gordonsville, and induce Lee and Hampton to believe that we were going to get out by that way; and another force, under Captain Rodenbough, was sent in the direction of Bowling Green, with the view of threatening the enemy's communication in that direction, and, under cover of night, with the main body, to take the middle road leading through Tolersville, and crossing the North Anna near the Victoria Iron Works; from thence to Orange Springs, where all were to rendezvous the next day.

"All our plans and calculations worked admirably, and though we had no little difficulty in finding and following the almost impassable roads, owing to the inky darkness of the night and the incessant pouring of the rain, the whole command was assembled at Orange Springs at 12 M. on the 6th. Here we first began to hear rumors, through negroes, of the repulse and withdrawal of our army to the north side of the Rappahannock.

"After watering and feeding our animals, we pushed on to the Plank road leading from Fredericksburg to Orange Court House, and from thence to Raccoon Ford, which, to our great joy, we found fordable, and were all over safe by daylight on the morning of the 7th."

EDITORS.

CORPS BADGES OF THE ARMY OF THE POTOMAC UNDER HOOKER.

THE CHANCELLORSVILLE CAMPAIGN.⌡

BY DARIUS N. COUCH, MAJOR-GENERAL, U. S. V.

IN the latter part of January, 1863, the Army of the Potomac under Burnside was still occupying its old camps on the left bank of the Rappahannock, opposite Fredericksburg. After the failures under Burnside it was evident that the army must have a new commander. For some days there had been a rumor that Hooker had been fixed upon for the place, and on the 26th of January it was confirmed. This appointment, undoubtedly, gave very general satisfaction to the army, except perhaps to a few, mostly superior officers, who had grown up with it, and had had abundant opportunities to study Hooker's military character; these believed that Mr. Lincoln had committed a grave error in his selection. The army, from its former reverses, had become quite disheartened and almost sulky; but the quick, vigorous measures now adopted and carried out with a firm hand had a magical effect in toning up where there had been demoralization and inspiring confidence where there had been mistrust. Few changes were made in the heads of the general staff departments, but for his chief-of-staff Hooker applied for Brigadier-General Charles P. Stone, who, through some untoward influence at Washington, was not given to him. This was a mistake of the war dignitaries, although the officer finally appointed to the office, Major-General Daniel Butterfield, proved himself very efficient. Burnside's system of dividing the army into three grand divisions was set aside, and the novelty was introduced of giving to each army corps a distinct badge, an idea which was very popular with officers and men. ⚓

⌡ Reprinted with permission from the "Philadelphia Times."— EDITORS.

⚓ This idea originated with General Butterfield, who not only instituted the badges, but devised them in detail. As organized by Hooker the First Corps was commanded by Reynolds; the Second by Couch; the Third by Sickles; the Fifth by Meade; the Sixth by Sedgwick; the Eleventh by Howard; the Twelfth by Slocum, and the cavalry corps by Stoneman. In each corps the badge of the First Division was red; of the Second Division, white; of the Third Division, blue. After the battle of Chickamauga (Sept. 19th and 20th, 1863), the Eleventh and Twelfth corps were sent west, and on April 4th, 1864, they were consolidated to form the new Twentieth Corps, which retained the star of the Twelfth for a badge. The old Twentieth lost its designation Sept. 28th, 1863.—EDITORS.

Some few days after Mr. Lincoln's visit to the army in April [see p. 119] I was again thrown with the President, and it happened in this wise. My pickets along the river were not only on speaking terms with those of the enemy on the other side of the river, but covertly carried on quite a trade in exchanging coffee for tobacco, etc. This morning it was hallooed over to our side: "You have taken Charleston," which news was sent to head-quarters. Mr. Lincoln hearing of it wished me to come up and talk the matter over. I went and was ushered into a side tent, occupied only by himself and Hooker. My entrance apparently interrupted a weighty conversation, for both were looking grave. The President's manner was kindly, while the general, usually so courteous, forgot to be conventionally polite. The Charleston rumor having been briefly discussed, Mr. Lincoln remarked that it was time for him to leave. As he stepped toward the general, who had risen from his seat, as well as myself, he said: "I want to impress upon you two gentlemen in your next fight,"—and turning to me he completed the sentence,—"put in all of your men"—in the long run a good military maxim.

The weather growing favorable for military operations, on April 12th were commenced those suggestive preliminaries to all great battles, clearing out the hospitals, inspecting arms, looking after ammunition, shoeing animals, issuing provisions, and making every preparation necessary to an advance. The next day, the 13th, Stoneman was put in motion at the head of ten thousand finely equipped and well organized cavalry to ascend the Rappahannock and, swinging around, to attack the Confederate cavalry wherever it might be found, and "Fight! fight! fight!" At the end of two days' march Stoneman found

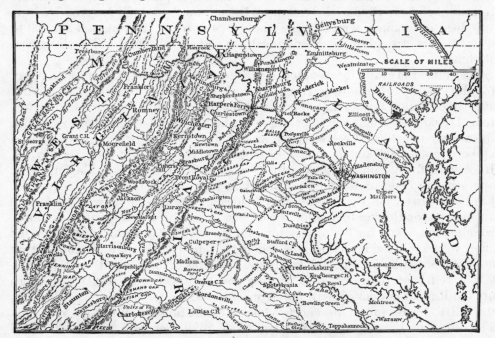

OUTLINE MAP OF THE CHANCELLORSVILLE CAMPAIGN.

THE RIGHT WING OF HOOKER'S ARMY CROSSING THE RAPPAHANNOCK AT KELLY'S FORD.
FROM A WAR-TIME SKETCH.

the river so swollen by heavy rains that he was constrained to hold up, upon which Hooker suspended his advance until the 27th. This unexpected delay of the cavalry seemingly deranged Hooker's original plan of campaign. He had hoped that Stoneman would have been able to place his horsemen on the railroad between Fredericksburg and Richmond, by which Lee received his supplies, and make a wreck of the whole structure, compelling that general to evacuate his stronghold at Fredericksburg and vicinity and fall back toward Richmond.

I estimate the grand total of Hooker's seven corps at about 113,000 men ready for duty, although the data from which the conclusion is arrived at are not strictly official. This estimate does not include the cavalry corps of not less than 11,000 duty men, nor the reserve artillery, the whole number of guns in the army being 400. Lee's strength in and around Fredericksburg was placed at between 55,000 and 60,000, not including cavalry. It is not known if Hooker's information concerning the Confederate force was reliable, but Peck, operating in front of Norfolk, notified him that two of Lee's divisions under Longstreet were on the south side of the James. The hour was, therefore, auspicious for Hooker to assume the offensive, and he seized it with a boldness which argued well for his fitness to command. The aim was to transfer his army to the south side of the river, where it would have a manœuvring footing not confronted by intrenched positions. On the 27th of April the Eleventh and Twelfth corps were set in motion for Kelly's Ford, twenty-five miles up the Rappahannock, where they concentrated on the evening of the 28th, the Fifth, by reason of its shorter marching distance, moving on the 28th. The object of the expedition was unknown to the corps commanders until communicated to them after their arrival at the ford by the commanding general in person.‡ The Eleventh Corps crossed the Rappahannock, followed in the morning by the Twelfth and Fifth corps—the two former striking for Germanna Ford, a crossing of the Rapidan, the latter for Ely's Ford, lower down the same stream. Both columns, successfully effecting crossings with little opposition from the enemy's pickets, arrived that evening, April 30th, at the point of concentration, Chancellorsville. It had been a brilliantly conceived and executed movement.

In order to confound Lee, orders were issued to assemble the Sixth, Third, and First corps under Sedgwick at Franklin's Crossing and Pollock's Mill, some three miles below Fredericksburg, on the left, before daylight of the morning of the 29th, and throw two bridges across and hold them. This was done under a severe fire of sharp-shooters. The Second Corps, two divisions, marched on the 28th for Banks's Ford, four miles to the right; the other division, Gibbon's, occupying Falmouth, near the river-bank, was directed to remain in its tents, as they were in full view of the enemy, who would readily observe their withdrawal. On the 29th the two divisions of the Second Corps reached United States Ford, held by the enemy; but the advance of the right wing down the river uncovered it, whereupon a bridge of pontoons was thrown across and the corps reached Chancellorsville the same night as the Fifth, Eleventh, and Twelfth. The same day, the 30th, Sedgwick was instructed to place a corps across the river and make a demonstration upon the enemy's right, below Fredericksburg, and the Third Corps received orders to join the right wing at Chancellorsville, where the commanding general arrived the same evening, establishing his headquarters at the Chancellor House, which, with the adjacent grounds, is Chancellorsville. All of the army lying there that night were in exuberant spirits at the success of their general in getting "on the other side" without fighting for a position. As I rode into Chancellorsville that night the general hilarity pervading the camps was particularly noticeable; the soldiers, while chopping wood and lighting fires, were singing merry songs and indulging in peppery camp jokes.

The position at Chancellorsville not only took in reverse the entire system of the enemy's river defenses, but there were roads leading from it directly to his line of communication. [See maps, pp. 155, 158.] But in order to gain the advantages now in the commanding general's grasp he had divided his army into two wings, and the enemy, no ordinary enemy, lay between them. The line of communication connecting the wings was by way of United States Ford and twenty miles long. It was of vital importance that the line be shortened in order to place the wings within easy support of each other. The possession of Banks's Ford, foreshadowed in the instructions given to Slocum, would accomplish all that at present could be wished.

There were three roads over which the right wing could move upon Fredericksburg: the Orange turnpike, from the west, passed through Chancellors-

‡ General Hooker sent for me on the night of the 27th to ride over to his headquarters, where he explained to me, as next in rank, his plan of campaign. He informed me that, under certain contingencies, the right wing would be placed at my command. Although anticipating the narrative, I may say I think it was a signal misfortune to our arms that he did not delay joining that wing until the morning of May 1st, when he would have found Banks's Ford in our possession.—D. N. C.

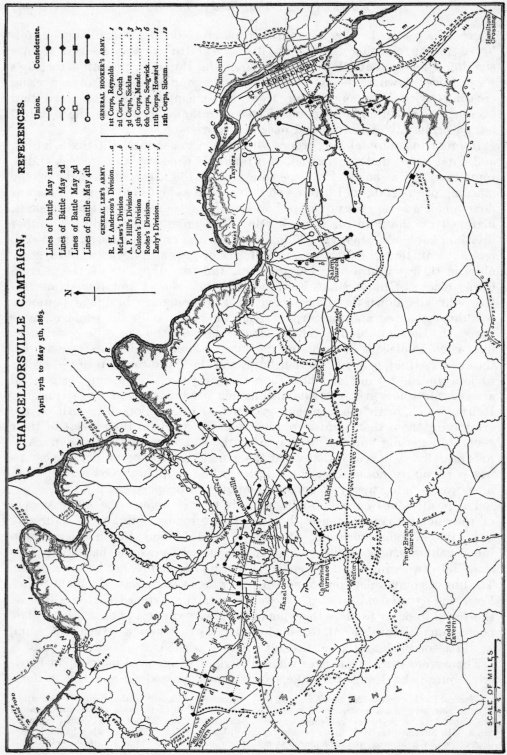

CHANCELLORSVILLE CAMPAIGN,

April 27th to May 5th, 1863.

REFERENCES.

Lines of battle May 1st .... a
Lines of Battle May 2d .... b
Lines of Battle May 3d c
Lines of Battle May 4th .... d

GENERAL LEE'S ARMY.

R. H. Anderson's Division .... a
McLaw's Division .... b
A. P. Hill's Division c
Colston's Division .... d
Rodes's Division .... e
Early's Division .... f

GENERAL HOOKER'S ARMY.

1st Corps, Reynolds 1
2d Corps, Couch 2
3d Corps, Sickles 3
5th Corps, Meade 5
6th Corps, Sedgwick 6
11th Corps, Howard 11
12th Corps, Slocum 12

Union.   Confederate.

SCALE OF MILES

ville, and was the most direct; the United States Ford road, crossing the former at Chancellorsville, became the Plank road, bent to the left and united with the turnpike five miles or so from Chancellorsville; the third road fell back from Chancellorsville toward the Rappahannock, passed along by Banks's Ford, six miles distant, and continued to Fredericksburg. That wing was ready for the advance at an early hour in the morning of May 1st, but somehow things dragged; the order defining the movement, instead of being issued the previous night, was not received by the corps commanders, at least by me, until hours after light. Meade was finally pushed out on the left over the Banks's Ford and turnpike roads, Slocum and Howard on the right along the Plank road, the left to be near Banks's Ford by 2 P. M., the right at the junction of its line of movement with the turnpike at 12 M. No opposition was met, excepting that the division marching over the turnpike came upon the enemy two or three miles out, when the sound of their guns was heard at Chancellorsville, and General Hooker ordered me to take Hancock's division and proceed to the support of those engaged. After marching a mile and a half or so I came upon Sykes, who commanded, engaged at the time in drawing back his advance to the position he then occupied. Shortly after Hancock's troops had got into a line in front, an order was received from the commanding general " to withdraw both divisions to Chancellorsville." Turning to the officers around me, Hancock, Sykes, Warren, and others, I told them what the order was, upon which they all agreed with me that the ground should not be abandoned, because of the open country in front and the commanding position. An aide, Major J. B. Burt, dispatched to General Hooker to this effect, came back in half an hour with positive orders to return. Nothing was to be done but carry out the command, though Warren suggested that I should disobey, and then he rode back to see the general. In the meantime Slocum, on the Plank road to my right, had been ordered in, and the enemy's advance was between that road and my right flank. Sykes was first to move back, then followed by Hancock's regiments over the same road. When all but two of the latter had withdrawn, a third order came to me, brought by one of the general's staff: " Hold on until 5 o'clock." It was then perhaps 2 P. M. Disgusted at the general's vacillation and vexed at receiving an order of such tenor, I replied with warmth unbecoming in a subordinate : " Tell General Hooker he is too late, the enemy are already on my right and rear. I am in full retreat."

The position thus abandoned was high ground, more or less open in front, over which an army might move and artillery be used advantageously; moreover, were it left in the hands of an enemy, his batteries, established on its crest and slopes, would command the position at Chancellorsville. Everything on the whole front was ordered in. General Hooker knew that Lee was apprised of his presence on the south side of the river, and must have expected that his enemy would be at least on the lookout for an advance upon Fredericksburg. But it was of the utmost importance that Banks's Ford should fall into our hands, therefore the enemy ought to have been pressed until their strength or weakness was developed; it would then have been time enough to run away.

FROM A PHOTOGRAPH

J. Hooker

Mott's Run, with a considerable brushy ravine, cuts the turnpike three-fourths of a mile east of Chancellorsville. Two of Hancock's regiments, under Colonel Nelson A. Miles, subsequently the Indian fighter, were directed to occupy the ravine. Continuing my way through the woods toward Chancellorsville, I came upon some of the Fifth Corps under arms. Inquiring for their commanding officer, I told him that in fifteen minutes he would be attacked. Before finishing the sentence a volley of musketry was fired into us from the direction of the Plank road. This was the beginning of the battle of Chancellorsville. Troops were hurried into position, but the observer required no wizard to tell him, as they marched past, that the high expectations which had animated them only a few hours ago had given place to disappointment. Proceeding to the Chancellor House, I narrated my operations in front to Hooker, which were seemingly satisfactory, as he said: "It is all right, Couch, I have got Lee just where I want him; he must fight me on my own ground." The retrograde movement had prepared me for something of the kind, but to hear from his own lips that the advantages gained by the successful marches of his lieutenants were to culminate in fighting a defensive battle in that nest of thickets was too much, and I retired from his presence with the belief that my commanding general was a whipped man. The army was directed to intrench itself. At 2 A. M. the corps commanders reported to General Hooker that their positions could be held; at least so said Couch, Slocum, and Howard.

Until after dark on May 1st the enemy confined his demonstrations to finding out the position of our left with his skirmishers. Then he got some guns upon the high ground which we had abandoned as before mentioned, and cannonaded the left of our line. There were not many casualties, but that day a shell severely wounded the adjutant-general of the Second Corps, now General F. A. Walker. Chancellorsville was a strategic point to an offensive or retreating army, as roads diverged from it into every part of Virginia; but for a defensive position it was bad, particularly for such an army as Hooker had under him, which prided itself upon its artillery, which was perhaps equal to any in the world. There were no commanding positions for artillery, and but little open country to operate over; in fact, the advantages of ground for this arm were mainly with the attacking party.

During the 29th and 30th the enemy lay at Fredericksburg observing Sedgwick's demonstrations on the left, entirely unconscious of Hooker's successful crossing of the right wing, until midday of the latter date, but that night Lee formed his plan of operations for checking the farther advance of the force which had not only turned the left flank of his river defenses but was threatening his line of communication with Richmond as well as the rear of his center at Fredericksburg. Stonewall Jackson, who was watching Sedgwick, received instructions to withdraw his corps, march to the left, across the front of Hooker's intrenched position, until its right flank was attained, and assault with his column of 22,000 men, while his commanding general would, with what force he could spare, guard the approaches to Fredericksburg.

HOOKER'S HEADQUARTERS AT CHANCELLORSVILLE, SATURDAY MORNING, MAY 2 — THE PICTURE
FACES SOUTH. FROM A WAR-TIME SKETCH.

On the morning of May 2d our line had become strong enough to resist a
front attack unless made in great force; the enemy had also been hard at
work on his front, particularly that section of it between the Plank road and
turnpike. Sedgwick, the previous night, had been ordered to send the First
Corps (Reynolds's) to Chancellorsville. At 7 A. M. a sharp cannonade was
opened on our left, followed by infantry demonstrations of no particular
earnestness. Two hours later the enemy were observed moving a mile or
so to the south and front of the center, and later the same column was
reported to the commander of the Eleventh Corps by General Devens, whose
division was on the extreme right flank. At 9:30 A. M. a circular directed to
Generals Slocum and Howard called attention to this movement and to the
weakness of their flanks. ⟩

At 11 A. M. our left was furiously cannonaded by their artillery, established
on the heights in front of Mott's Run, followed by sharp infantry firing on the
fronts of the Second and Twelfth corps. As time flew along and no attack
came from the enemy seen moving in front, Hooker conceived that Lee was
retreating toward Gordonsville. There was color for this view, as the main
road from Fredericksburg to that point diverged from the Plank road two
miles to the left of Chancellorsville, and passed along his front at about the
same distance. Hooker therefore jumped at the conclusion that the enemy's
army was moving into the center of Virginia. But instead of the hostile
column being on the Gordonsville road in retreat, it was Stonewall's corps moving on an interior neighborhood road, about one mile distant, and in search

⟩ See p. 219 for a copy of this circular order. Maps showing the positions of the Eleventh and
Twelfth corps appear on pages 191–201.—EDITORS.

of our right flank and rear. At 2 P. M. I went into the Chancellor House, when
General Hooker greeted me with the exclamation: "Lee is in full retreat
toward Gordonsville, and I have sent out Sickles to capture his artillery."
I thought, without speaking it: "If your conception is correct, it is very
strange that only the Third Corps should be sent in pursuit." Sickles
received orders at 1 P. M. to take two divisions, move to his front and attack,
which he did, capturing some hundreds of prisoners. The country on the
front being mostly wooded enabled the enemy to conceal his movements and
at the same time hold Sickles in check with a rear-guard, which made such
a show of strength that reënforcements were called for and furnished. In
the meantime Jackson did not for a moment swerve from his purpose, but
steadily moved forward to accomplish what he had undertaken.

It was about 5:30 in the evening when the head of Jackson's column
found itself on the right and rear of the army, which on that flank consisted
of the Eleventh Corps, the extreme right brigade receiving its first intimation
of danger from a volley of musketry fired into their rear, followed up so
impetuously that no efficient stand could be made by the brigades of the
corps that successively attempted to resist the enemy's charge. When
General Hooker found out what that terrific roar on his right flank meant
he quickly mounted and flew across the open space to meet the onset, passing
on his way stampeded pack-mules, officers' horses, caissons, with men and
horses running for their lives. Gathering up such troops as were nearest to
the scene of action, Berry's division from the Third Corps, some from the
Twelfth, Hays's brigade of the Second, and a portion of the Eleventh, an
effectual stand was made. Pleasonton, who was returning from the front,
where he had been operating with Sickles (at the time Jackson attacked),
taking in the state of things, rapidly moved his two regiments of cavalry
and a battery to the head and right flank of the enemy's advance columns,
when, making a charge and bringing up his own guns, with others of the
Eleventh and Third Corps, he was enabled to punish them severely.

Pickets had been thrown out on Howard's flank, but not well to the right
and rear. I suspect that the prime reason for the surprise was that the
superior officers of the right corps had been put off their guard by adopting
the conjecture of Hooker, "Lee's army is in full retreat to Gordonsville," as
well as by expecting the enemy to attack precisely where ample preparations
had been made to receive him. It can be emphatically stated that no corps
in the army, surprised as the Eleventh was at this time, could have held its
ground under similar circumstances.

At half-past two that afternoon the Second Corps' lines were assaulted by
artillery and infantry. Just previous to Jackson's attack on the right a
desperate effort was made by Lee's people to carry the left at Mott's Run, but
the men who held it were there to stay. Hooker, desiring to know the enemy's
strength in front of the Twelfth Corps, advanced Slocum into the thicket,
but that officer found the hostile line too well defended for him to penetrate
it and was forced to recall the attacking party. When night put an end to
the fighting of both combatants, Hooker was obliged to form a new line for

STAMPEDE OF THE ELEVENTH CORPS ON THE PLANK ROAD.

his right flank perpendicular to the old one and barely half a mile to the right of Chancellorsville. Sickles was retired, with the two columns, from his advanced position in the afternoon to near where Pleasonton had had his encounter, before mentioned, some distance to the left of the new line of our right flank and close up to the enemy. The situation was thought to be a very critical one by General Hooker, who had simply a strong body in front of the enemy, but without supports, at least near enough to be used for that purpose. At the same time it was a menace to Jackson's right wing or flank. Before midnight some of the latter's enterprising men pushed forward and actually cut off Sickles's line of communication. When this news was carried to Hooker it caused him great alarm, and preparations were at once made to withdraw the whole front, leaving General Sickles to his fate; but that officer showed himself able to take care of his rear, for he ordered after a little while a column of attack, and communication was restored at the point of the bayonet.

The situation of Jackson's corps on the morning of May 3d was a desperate one, its front and right flank being in the presence of not far from 25,000 men, with the left flank subject to an assault of 30,000, the corps of Meade and Reynolds, by advancing them to the right, where the thicket did not present an insurmountable obstacle. It only required that Hooker should brace himself up to take a reasonable, common-sense view of the state of things, when the success gained by Jackson would have been turned into an overwhelming defeat. But Hooker became very despondent. I think that his being outgeneraled by Lee had a good deal to do with his depression. After the right flank had been established on the morning of the 3d by Sickles getting back into position our line was more compact, with favorable positions for artillery, and the reserves were well in hand. Meade had been drawn in from the left and Reynolds had arrived with the First Corps. The engineers had been directed on the previous night to lay out a new line, its front a half mile in rear of Chancellorsville, with the flanks thrown back,— the right to the Rapidan, a little above its junction with the Rappahannock, the left resting on the latter river. The Eleventh Corps, or at least that portion which formed line of battle, was withdrawn from the front and sent to the rear to reorganize and get its scattered parts together, leaving the following troops in front: one division of the Second Corps on the left from Mott's Run to Chancellorsville, the Twelfth Corps holding the center and right flank, aided by the Third Corps and one division of the Second Corps (French's), on the same flank; the whole number in front, according to my estimate, being 37,000 men. The First and Fifth corps in reserve numbered 30,000, and, placing the number of reliable men in the Eleventh Corps at 5000, it will be seen that the reserves nearly equaled those in line of battle in front.

After the day's mishaps Hooker judged that the enemy could not have spared so large a force to move around his front without depleting the defenses of Fredericksburg. Accordingly, at 9 P. M., an imperative order was sent to the commander of the left wing to cross the river at Fredericksburg, march upon Chancellorsville, and be in the vicinity of the commanding general at daylight. But Sedgwick was already across the river and three miles below Fredericksburg. It was 11 P. M., May 2d, when he got the order, and twelve or fourteen miles had to be marched over by daylight. The night was moonlight, but any officer who has had experience in making night marches with infantry will understand the vexatious delays occurring even when the road is clear; but when, in addition, there is an enemy in front, with a line of fortified heights to assault, the problem which Sedgwick had to solve will be pronounced impossible of solution. However, that officer set his column in motion by flank, leaving one division that lay opposite the enemy, who were in force to his left. The marching column, being continually harassed by skirmishers, did not arrive at Fredericksburg until daylight. The first assault upon the heights behind the town failed. Attempts to carry them by flank movements met with no success. Finally a second storming party was organized, and the series of works were taken literally at the point of the bayonet, though at heavy loss. It was then 11 A. M. The column immediately started for Chancellorsville, being more or less obstructed by the enemy until its arrival near Salem Heights, 5 or 6 miles out, where seven brigades under Early, six of which had been driven from the defenses of Fredericksburg, made a stand in conjunction with supports sent from Lee's army before Chancellorsville. This was about the middle of the afternoon, when Sedgwick in force attacked the enemy. Though at first successful, he was subsequently compelled to withdraw those in advance and look to his own safety by throwing his own flanks so as to cover Banks's Ford, the friendly proximity of which eventually saved this wing from utter annihilation.

STAYING JACKSON'S ADVANCE, SATURDAY EVENING, MAY 2, WITH ARTILLERY PLACED ACROSS
THE PLANK ROAD. FROM A WAR-TIME SKETCH.

At about 5 A. M., May 3d, fighting was begun at Chancellorsville, when
the Third (Sickles's) Corps began to retire to the left of our proper right
flank, and all of that flank soon became fiercely engaged, while the battle ran
along the whole line. The enemy's guns on the heights to our left, as well as
at every point on the line where they could be established, were vigorously
used, while a full division threw itself on Miles at Mott's Run. On the right
flank our guns were well handled, those of the Twelfth Corps being conspicuous, and the opposing lines of infantry operating in the thicket had almost
hand-to-hand conflicts, capturing and recapturing prisoners. The enemy
appeared to know what he was about, for pressing the Third Corps vigorously
he forced it back, when he joined or rather touched the left of Lee's main
body, making their line continuous from left to right. Another advantage
gained by this success was the possession of an open field, from which guns
covered the ground up to the Chancellor House. Upon the south porch of
that mansion General Hooker stood leaning against one of its pillars, observing the fighting, looking anxious and much careworn. After the fighting had
commenced I doubt if any orders were given by him to the commanders on
the field, unless, perhaps, "to retire when out of ammunition." None were
received by me, nor were there any inquiries as to how the battle was going
along my front. On the right flank, where the fighting was desperate, the
engaged troops were governed by the corps and division leaders. If the ear
of the commanding general was, as he afterward stated, strained to catch
the sound of Sedgwick's guns, it could not have heard them in the continuous
uproar that filled the air around him ; but as Sedgwick, who was known as a
fighting officer, had not appeared at the time set—daylight—nor for some
hours after, it was conclusive evidence that he had met with strong opposition, showing that all of Lee's army was not at Chancellorsville, so that the

moment was favorable for Hooker to try his opponent's strength with every available man. Moreover, the left wing might at that very time be in jeopardy, therefore he was bound by every patriotic motive to strike hard for its relief. If he had remembered Mr. Lincoln's injunction (" Gentlemen, in your next fight put in all of your men "), the face of the day would have been changed and the field won for the Union arms.

Not far from 8:30 A. M. the headquarters pennants of the Third and Twelfth corps suddenly appeared from the right in the open field of Chancellorsville; then the Third began to fall back, it was reported, for want of ammunition, followed by that portion of the Twelfth fighting on the same flank, and the division of the Second Corps on its right. It is not known whether any efforts were made to supply the much-needed ammunition to the Third as well as the Twelfth Corps, whose ammunition was nearly used up when it retired. My impression is that the heads of the ordnance, as well as of other important departments, were not taken into the field during this campaign, which was most unfortunate, as the commanding general had enough on his mind without charging it with details.

The open field seized by Jackson's old corps after the Third Corps drew off was shortly dotted with guns that made splendid practice through an opening in the wood upon the Chancellor House, and everything else, for that matter, in that neighborhood. Hooker was still at his place on the porch, with nothing between him and Lee's army but Geary's division of the Twelfth and Hancock's division and a battery of the Second Corps. But Geary's right was now turned, and that flank was steadily being pressed back along his intrenched line to the junction of the Plank road and the turnpike, when a cannon-shot struck the pillar against which Hooker was leaning and knocked him down. A report flew around that he was killed. I was at the time but a few yards to his left, and, dismounting, ran to the porch. The shattered pillar was there, but I could not find him or any one else. Hurrying through the house, finding no one, my search was continued through the back yard. All the time I was thinking, " If he is killed, what shall I do with this disjointed army?" Passing through the yard I came upon him, to my great joy, mounted, and with his staff also in their saddles. Briefly congratulating him on his escape — it was no time to blubber or use soft expressions — I went about my own business. This was the last I saw of my commanding general in front. The time, I reckon, was from 9:15 to 9:30 A. M., I think nearer the former than the latter. He probably left the field soon after his hurt, but he neither notified me of his going nor did he give any orders to me whatever. Having some little time before this seen that the last stand would be about the Chancellor House, I had sent to the rear for some of the Second Corps batteries, which had been ordered there by the commanding general, but word came back that they were so jammed in with other carriages that it was impossible to extricate them. General Meade, hearing of my wants, kindly sent forward the 5th Maine battery belonging to his corps. It was posted in rear of the Chancellor House, where the United States Ford road enters the thicket. With such precision did the artillery of Jackson's old corps play upon this battery that

THE 29TH PENNSYLVANIA (OF KANE'S BRIGADE, GEARY'S DIVISION, TWELFTH CORPS) IN THE TRENCHES
UNDER ARTILLERY FIRE, MAY 3.

all of the officers and most of the non-commissioned officers and men were killed or wounded. The gallant Kirby, whose guns could not be brought up, was mortally wounded in the same battery ⸜ of which I had for the time placed him in command, and my horse was killed under me while I was trying to get some men to train a gun on the flank of the force then pushing Geary's division. The enemy, having 30 pieces in position on our right, now advanced some of his guns to within 500 or 600 yards of the Chancellor House, where there were only four of Pettit's Second Corps guns to oppose them, making a target of that building and taking the right of Hancock's division in reverse, a portion of which had been withdrawn from its intrenchments and thrown back to the left to meet the enemy should he succeed in forcing Mott's Run. This flank was stoutly held by Colonel Miles, who, by the bye, had been carried off the field, shot through the body. Lee by this time knew well enough, if he had not known before, that the game was sure to fall into his hands, and accordingly plied every gun and rifle that could be brought to bear on us. Still everything was firmly held excepting Geary's right, which was slowly falling to pieces, for the enemy had his flank and there was no help for it. Riding to Geary's left, I found him there dismounted, with sword swinging over his head, walking up and down, exposed to a severe infantry fire, when he said: "My division can't hold its place; what shall I do?" To which I replied: "I don't know, but do as we are doing; fight it out."

⸜ The 5th Maine battery, Capt. G. F. Leppien, belonged to the First Corps. Captain Leppien and Lieutenants G. T. Stevens and A. B. Twitchell were wounded, Capt. Leppien mortally. Lieut. E. Kirby was the proper commander of Battery I, 1st U. S. Artillery, Second Corps. The 5th Maine lost 6 men killed and 19 wounded; 43 horses were disabled, and the guns were hauled off by hand.— EDITORS.

It was not then too late to save the day. Fifty pieces of artillery, or even forty, brought up and run in front and to the right of the Chancellor House, would have driven the enemy out of the thicket, then forcing back Geary's right, and would have neutralized the thirty guns to the right which were pounding us so hard. But it is a waste of words to write what might have been done. Hooker had made up his mind to abandon the field, otherwise he would not have allowed the Third and part of the Twelfth Corps to leave their ground for want of ammunition. A few minutes after my interview with Geary a staff-officer from General Hooker rode up and requested my presence with that general. Turning to General Hancock, near by, I told him to take care of things and rode to the rear. The Chancellor House was then burning, having been fired in several places by the enemy's shells.

At the farther side of an open field, half a mile in the rear of Chancellorsville, I came upon a few tents (three or four) pitched, around which, mostly dismounted, were a large number of staff-officers. General Meade was also present, and perhaps other generals. General Hooker was lying down I think in a soldier's tent by himself. Raising himself a little as I entered, he said: "Couch, I turn the command of the army over to you. You will withdraw it and place it in the position designated on this map," as he pointed to a line traced on a field-sketch. This was perhaps three-quarters of an hour after his hurt. He seemed rather dull, but possessed of his mental faculties. I do not think that one of those officers outside of the tent knew what orders I was to receive, for on stepping out, which I did immediately on getting my instructions, I met Meade close by, looking inquiringly as if he expected that

SECOND LINE OF UNION DEFENSE AT THE JUNCTION OF THE ROADS TO ELY'S AND UNITED STATES
FORDS. FROM A WAR-TIME SKETCH.

finally he would receive the order for which he had waited all that long morning, " to go in." Colonel N. H. Davis broke out: "We shall have some fighting now." These incidents are mentioned to show the temper of that knot of officers. No time was to be lost, as only Hancock's division now held Lee's army. Dispatching Major John B. Burt with orders for the front to retire, I rode back to the thicket, accompanied by Meade, and was soon joined by Sickles, and after a little while by Hooker, but he did not interfere with my dispositions. Hancock had a close shave to withdraw in safety, his line being three-fourths of a mile long, with an exultant enemy as close in as they dared, or wished, or chose to be, firing and watching. But everything was brought off, except five hundred men of the Second Corps who, through the negligence of a lieutenant charged by Hancock with the responsibility of retiring the force at Mott's Run, were taken prisoners. However, under the circumstances, the division was retired in better shape than one could have anticipated. General Sickles assisted in getting men to draw off the guns of the Maine battery before spoken of. General Meade wished me to hold the strip of thicket in rear of Chancellorsville, some six hundred yards in front of our new line of defense. My reply was: "I shall not leave men in this thicket to be shelled out by Lee's artillery. Its possession won't give us any strength. Yonder [pointing to the rear] is the line where the fighting is to be done." Hooker heard the conversation, but made no remarks. Considerable bodies of troops of different corps that lay in the brush to the right were brought within the lines, and the battle of Chancellorsville was ended. My pocket diary, May 3d, has the following: " Sickles opened at about 5 A. M. Orders sent by me at 10 for the front to retire; at 12 M. in my new position"; the latter sentence meaning that at that hour my corps was in position on the new or second line of defense.

As to the charge that the battle was lost because the general was intoxicated, I have always stated that he probably abstained from the use of ardent spirits when it would have been far better for him to have continued in his usual habit in that respect. The shock from being violently thrown to the ground, together with the physical exhaustion resulting from loss of sleep and the anxiety of mind incident to the last six days of the campaign, would tell on any man. The enemy did not press us on the second line, Lee simply varying the monotony of watching us by an occasional cannonade from the left, a part of his army having been sent to Salem Church to resist Sedgwick. Sedgwick had difficulty in maintaining his ground, but held his own by hard fighting until after midnight, May 4th–5th, when he recrossed at Banks's Ford.

Some of the most anomalous occurrences of the war took place in this campaign. On the night of May 2d the commanding general, with 80,000 men in his wing of the army, directed Sedgwick, with 22,000, to march to his relief. While that officer was doing this on the 3d, and when it would be expected that every effort would be made by the right wing to do its part, only one-half of it was fought (or rather half-fought, for its ammunition was not replenished), and then the whole wing was withdrawn to a place where it could not be hurt, leaving Sedgwick to take care of himself.

At 12 o'clock on the night of the 4th-5th General Hooker assembled his corps commanders in council. Meade, Sickles, Howard, Reynolds, and myself were present; General Slocum, on account of the long distance from his post, did not arrive until after the meeting was broken up. Hooker stated that his instructions compelled him to cover Washington, not to jeopardize the army, etc. It was seen by the most casual observer that he had made up his mind to retreat. We were left by ourselves to consult, upon which Sickles made an elaborate argument, sustaining the views of the commanding general. Meade was in favor of fighting, stating that he doubted if we could get off our guns. Howard was in favor of fighting, qualifying his views by the remark that our present situation was due to the bad conduct of his corps, or words to that effect. Reynolds, who was lying on the ground very much fatigued, was in favor of an advance. I had similar views to those of Meade as to getting off the guns, but said I " would favor an advance if I could designate the point of attack." Upon collecting the suffrages, Meade, Reynolds, and Howard voted squarely for an advance, Sickles and myself squarely no; upon which Hooker informed the council that he should take upon himself the responsibility of retiring the army to the other side of the river. As I stepped out of the tent Reynolds, just behind me, broke out, " What was the use of calling us together at this time of night when he intended to retreat anyhow?"

On the morning of May 5th, corps commanders were ordered to cut roads, where it was necessary, leading from their positions to the United States Ford. During the afternoon there was a very heavy rainfall. In the meantime Hooker had in person crossed the river, but, as he gave orders for the various corps to march at such and such times during the night, I am not aware that any of his corps generals knew of his departure. Near midnight I got a note from Meade informing me that General Hooker was on the other side of the river, which had risen over the bridges, and that communication was cut off from him. I immediately rode over to Hooker's headquarters and found that I was in command of the army, if it had any commander. General Hunt, of the artillery, had brought the information as to the condition of the bridges, and from the reports there seemed to be danger of losing them entirely. After a short conference with Meade I told him that the recrossing would be suspended, and that "we would stay where we were and fight it out," returning to my tent with the intention of enjoying what I had not had since the night of the 30th ultimo — a good sleep; but at 2 A. M., communication having been reëstablished, I received a sharp message from Hooker, to order the recrossing of the army as he had directed, and everything was safely transferred to the north bank of the Rappahannock.

In looking for the causes of the loss of Chancellorsville, the primary ones were that Hooker expected Lee to fall back without risking battle. Finding himself mistaken he assumed the defensive, and was outgeneraled and became demoralized by the superior tactical boldness of the enemy.

THE SUCCESSES AND FAILURES OF CHANCELLORSVILLE.

BY ALFRED PLEASONTON, BREVET MAJOR-GENERAL, U. S. A.

UNION CAVALRY-MAN'S HAT.

IN the latter part of April, 1863, General Hooker decided to undertake an offensive campaign with the Army of the Potomac against the Army of Northern Virginia, under General Lee. At this time the two armies faced each other: Lee's, numbering about 60,000 men, being at Fredericksburg, and the Army of the Potomac, numbering about 130,000 men, at Falmouth, on the north side of the Rappahannock River opposite Fredericksburg. Hooker directed three corps of the army, the First, the Third, and the Sixth, comprising 59,000 men, under the command of General Sedgwick, to cross the Rappahannock River below Fredericksburg and hold Lee's army in that position, while he himself moved secretly and with celerity three corps, the Fifth, the Eleventh, and the Twelfth, numbering 42,000 men, up the river, crossing it and concentrating them at Chancellorsville, ten miles west of Fredericksburg, with the purpose of moving down upon General Lee's army to take it in rear and flank—two divisions of the Second Corps being placed to cover Banks's Ford, the third division being left at Falmouth, while a brigade and battery were stationed at United States Ford to facilitate the crossing. The Cavalry Corps, with the exception of one small brigade of three regiments and a battery of horse artillery, which was left under my command with the army, was ordered under the command of General Stoneman to make a raid in rear of Lee's army, and destroy his railroads and his communications with Richmond. ⌡

PARADE AT FALMOUTH OF THE 110TH PENNSYLVANIA VOLUNTEERS. FROM A PHOTOGRAPH.

This regiment (of Whipple's division, Third Corps) with the 84th Pennsylvania performed desperate service near Fairview on Sunday morning, May 3d, the 84th losing 215 men and the 110th losing 45 men.— EDITORS.

⌡ This corps did great service by drawing off General Lee's cavalry, under General J. E. B. Stuart, to Brandy Station and Culpeper, thus depriving General Lee of their services; for General Hooker moved the three corps with him with such celerity that they passed between Stuart and Lee's army, and Stuart could not get through to communicate to Lee what was going on. It will be seen later on what a loss this was to Lee, and what a great advantage it was to the Army of the Potomac.— A. P.

ABANDONING THE WINTER CAMP AT FALMOUTH.   FROM A WAR-TIME SKETCH.

On the 26th of April General Hooker gave his orders for the right wing of the army to move, the Eleventh and Twelfth corps to be followed by the Fifth; the Eleventh and Twelfth to cross the Rappahannock at Kelly's Ford, and the Rapidan River at Germanna Ford; the Fifth Corps marching from Kelly's Ford to Ely's Ford, nearer to the mouth of the Rapidan and to Chancellorsville. The left wing of the army, under General Sedgwick, was ordered to cross the Rappahannock below Fredericksburg on the morning of the 29th; its duty was to keep the enemy as long as possible before Fredericksburg, to pursue him if he attempted to fall back on Richmond, and to take possession of his works and his line of retreat if he marched upon Chancellorsville; in other words, Sedgwick was told to hold Lee at Fredericksburg until Hooker could come down upon him from Chancellorsville and crush him.

The right wing of the army crossed Kelly's Ford on the morning of the 29th, and the Eleventh and Twelfth corps reached Germanna Ford that evening. I had the advance of this column with two regiments of cavalry and a battery of horse artillery; the third regiment of the cavalry brigade I sent with the Fifth Corps to Ely's Ford. In the afternoon, at Germanna Ford, I surprised and captured a picket of some fifty of Stuart's cavalry soldiers. With them was an engineer officer belonging to Stuart's staff. On searching the party, as is done with all prisoners, I found on this engineer officer a very bulky volume, which proved to be a diary that he had been keeping throughout the war. I spent the greater part of the night in reading it, in hopes of finding something that would be of advantage to us; nor was I disappointed. This diary stated that in the first week in March a council of war had been held at General Stuart's headquarters, which had been attended by Generals Jackson, A. P. Hill, Ewell, and Stuart. They were in conference over five hours, and came to the decision that the next battle would be at or near Chancellorsville, and that that position must be prepared.

The next day, the 30th of April, I moved on toward Chancellorsville, and at 1 o'clock in the day I captured a courier or orderly from General Lee, who had a dispatch from Lee, dated at Fredericksburg, noon of that day, and addressed to Major-General McLaws, stating that he had just been informed that the enemy had concentrated in force near Chancellorsville, inquiring why he had not been kept advised, and saying that he wished to see McLaws as soon as possible at headquarters. At 2 o'clock P. M., one hour later, I reported to General Hooker at Chancellorsville, and submitted to him the diary and General Lee's dispatch, both of which he retained, and I suggested that we had evidently surprised General Lee by our rapid movements across the river, and, as Lee had prepared for a battle at Chancellorsville, we had better anticipate him by moving on toward Fredericksburg. A march of three or four miles would take us out of the woods into a more open country, where we could form our line of battle, and where our artillery could be used to advantage; we would then be prepared to move on Fredericksburg in the morning. Besides, such a movement would enable us to uncover Banks's Ford, which would shorten our communication with General Sedgwick over 5 miles, and bring us within 3½ miles of Falmouth by that Ford.

I was much surprised to find that General Hooker, who up to that time had been all vigor, energy, and activity, received the suggestion as a matter of secondary importance, and that he considered the next morning sufficiently early to move on Fredericksburg. Up to that time General Hooker's strategy had been all that could have been desired. He had outflanked the enemy and had surprised him by the rapidity of his movements. At 2 o'clock P. M., on the 30th of April, General Hooker had ninety chances in his favor to ten

UNION TROOPS CROSSING THE RAPIDAN AT ELY'S FORD.   FROM A WAR-TIME SKETCH.

against him. The very cavalry under Stuart that Lee depended on to keep him advised had been cut off by the prompt action of the army, and we had it over the signature of General Lee himself that his army had been surprised. General Hooker had it in his power at that time to have crushed Lee's army and wound up the war. The Army of the Potomac never had a better opportunity, for more than half its work had been done before a blow had been struck, by the brilliancy of its strategy in moving upon Chancellorsville.

I camped my command about a mile from General Hooker's headquarters, which were at the Chancellor House, and such were my misgivings as regarded the situation of the army that about dusk I called upon the general again and stated to him our perilous position.

To the east, toward Fredericksburg, the woods were thick for three or four miles; to the south, toward Spotsylvania Court House, the woods extended about the same distance; to the west, from Hazel Grove, the same condition of things existed; while the country between Chancellorsville and the Rappahannock River, in our rear, was rough, broken, and not at all suitable for the operations required of an army. The position of the army at Chancellorsville extended about three miles from east to west in the narrow clearings, which did not afford sufficient ground to manœuvre an army of the size of the Army of the Potomac. Besides this, we were ignorant of what might be going on outside of this cordon of woods, and were giving the enemy every opportunity to take us at a disadvantage. Every instinct induced me to suggest to General Hooker, to relieve ourselves from our embarrassments, to send the Eleventh Corps, which was in a miserable position in the woods, down to Spotsylvania Court House by the Jack Shop road, and make the line of battle from Chancellorsville to Spotsylvania. This proposition was not approved, and I then asked permission to send some cavalry to Spotsylvania, to find out what was going on in the open country beyond the woods. General Hooker assented to this, and I ordered the 6th New York Cavalry, under Lieutenant-Colonel Duncan McVicar, to proceed down the road from Chancellorsville to Spotsylvania, ascertain if the enemy were anywhere in that vicinity, and, having done so, return before daybreak. This could easily be done, as the distance was not more than eight miles. Colonel McVicar executed his orders in splendid style; he went to Spotsylvania, saw no enemy, but on his return, it being moonlight, he found a body of cavalry in his front, barring his passage to Chancellorsville. He immediately deployed his regiment, some three or four hundred strong, and after a murderous fire from the saddle he charged the enemy with sabers and completely routed them. This force was the 5th Virginia Cavalry, and with it were General Stuart and staff. They scattered in every direction and were pursued by the 6th New York Cavalry until the 2d Virginia Regiment, coming to their assistance, stopped the pursuit. The 6th New York Cavalry then, unmolested, returned to Chancellorsville, but without their brave commander, who was killed in the thickest of the fray.

This action made a strong impression on the Confederates, and Stuart, in order to avoid another such encounter, started his cavalry in the direction

MAJOR-GENERAL HIRAM G. BERRY, COMMANDING
SECOND DIVISION, THIRD CORPS, KILLED MAY
3, 1863. FROM A PHOTOGRAPH.

of Spotsylvania Court House, but his rear-guard threw the whole column into confusion by the cry, "The enemy is upon us." Major von Borcke, a distinguished officer, who was on General Stuart's staff, and was present on this occasion, in describing it, says: "Shots were fired at hazard in every direction. The 1st and 3d Virginia Regiments, no longer recognizing each other, charge upon each other mutually; Stuart's mounted men, generally so brave and so steadfast, no longer obey the orders of their officers, and gallop off in great disorder. At last quiet is restored, and the brigade finally reaches Spotsylvania Court House, while the small band which has caused so much alarm to Stuart was quietly returning to Chancellorsville."

The next morning at daylight (Friday, May 1st) I reported to General Hooker the result of this reconnoissance, and he began to realize the importance of the information that had been conveyed the day before in the diary of Stuart's engineer officer. The 6th New York Cavalry were only able to report that they had cut their way through a heavy body of cavalry, and this by moonlight; they were unable to say whether any infantry or artillery were in that direction.

To move the army down on Fredericksburg with an unknown force on its rear and flank was a hazardous experiment. What could have been done with safety the day before now became doubtful, and it was this uncertainty that paralyzed the vigor and action of General Hooker throughout the 1st of May. Although he started the Second, Fifth, Twelfth, and Third corps in the direction of Tabernacle Church on the way to Fredericksburg, the movement was not of such a character as to bring success. Upon meeting a stubborn resistance from General Jackson's forces, and fearing that if he should become deeply engaged a force from Spotsylvania would take him in the rear and flank, he withdrew the army and placed it in position at Chancellorsville.

From that time the whole situation was changed. Without striking a blow, the army was placed on the defensive. The golden moment had been lost, and it never appeared again to the same extent afterward—an illustration that soldiers' legs have as much to do with winning victories as their arms.

General Lee knew that General Hooker had taken his army back to its position at Chancellorsville. The Third Corps had already been taken from

General Sedgwick at Fredericksburg, and at 2 o'clock on the morning of May 2d the First Corps was also ordered up to Chancellorsville, leaving Sedgwick with the Sixth Corps. These movements did not escape the attention of General Lee, so he decided to assume the offensive and put in operation the plan which had been suggested by Generals Jackson, A. P. Hill, Ewell, and Stuart at their council of war in the first week in March. He left a sufficient force at Fredericksburg to watch Sedgwick, while with the bulk of his army he moved on Chancellorsville, sending a force under Generals Jackson, A. P. Hill, and Stuart, to make a turning movement and to attack the Union forces in the rear and right flank, and roll them up. Lee himself, in the meantime, with the remainder of his forces, occupied the attention of the left and center of Hooker's army, to prevent any interference with the flank movement. General Lee's strategy was the same that Hooker had carried out so successfully until he stopped at Chancellorsville. Lee was equally successful in his movements, and we will now investigate the causes of his failure to give the Army of the Potomac a crushing blow.

On the 2d day of May the right of the Army of the Potomac was the Eleventh Corps, in the woods near Dowdall's Tavern (Melzi Chancellor's); the Third Corps connected it with the Twelfth Corps at Fairview and Chancellorsville, facing south toward the woods; while the Second and the Fifth corps were posted to prevent any attack taking the position in the rear and flank from the east. Throughout the morning of the 2d of May, attacks were made on different portions of our line from the east to the west. These attacks occurred at intervals of an hour or more, but always farther to the west. I was satisfied this was done to withdraw our attention from the real point of attack, and I mentioned this to Hooker, who had become more and more impressed with the belief that the information contained in the diary of Stuart's engineer officer was correct, and that Lee had adopted a plan to carry it out.

In the afternoon of May 2d General Sickles, commanding the Third Corps, sent in word that the enemy were retreating toward Gordonsville, and that their wagons and artillery could be seen passing by the Furnace road some three miles to the south. General Hooker sent for me on receiving this report, and stated that he was not sure the enemy were retreating; that he wanted an officer of experience in that part of the field, and that he wished me to take my command there and keep him promptly informed of everything that was going on. I asked him if he considered me to be under the orders of any one. He replied quickly, " You are under my orders only ; use your best judgment in doing whatever you think ought to be done."

On arriving at Hazel Grove, about one mile from Chancellorsville, I found that General Sickles was moving two of the divisions of the Third Corps in the direction of Catherine Furnace, and shortly after he became engaged there with a strong rear-guard. Hazel Grove was the highest ground in the neighborhood and was the key of our position, and I saw that if Lee's forces gained it the Army of the Potomac would be worsted.

General Sickles wanted some cavalry to protect his flanks, and I gave him the 6th New York. This left me with only the 8th and 17th Pennsylvania

REPULSE OF JACKSON'S MEN AT HAZEL GROVE, BY ARTILLERY UNDER GENERAL PLEASONTON.

regiments and Martin's New York battery of horse artillery. I posted this command at the extreme west of the clearing, about two hundred yards from the woods in which the Eleventh Corps was encamped. This position at Hazel Grove was about a quarter of a mile in extent, running nearly north-east and south-west, but was in no place farther than two hundred yards from the woods, and on the south and east it sloped off into a marsh and a creek. It commanded the position of the army at Fairview and Chancellorsville and enfiladed our line. The moving out to the Furnace of the two divisions of the Third Corps left a gap of about a mile from Hazel Grove to the right of the Twelfth Corps. Shortly after General Sickles had been engaged at the Furnace, he sent me word that the enemy were giving way and cavalry could be used to advantage in pursuit. Before moving my command I rode out to the Furnace to comprehend the situation. It was no place for cavalry to operate, and as I could hear spattering shots going more and more toward the north-west, I was satisfied that the enemy were not retreating. I hastened back to my command at Hazel Grove; when I reached it, the Eleventh Corps to our rear and our right was in full flight, panic-stricken beyond description. We faced about, having then the marsh behind us. It was an ugly marsh, about fifty yards wide, and in the stampede of the Eleventh Corps, beef cattle, ambulances, mules, artillery, wagons, and horses became stuck in the mud, and others coming on crushed them down, so that when the fight was over the pile of débris in the marsh was many feet high. I saw that something had to be done, and that very quickly, or the Army of the Potomac would receive a crushing defeat. The two cavalry regiments were in the saddle, and as I rode forward Major Keenan of the 8th Pennsylvania came out to meet me, when I ordered him to take the regiment, charge into the woods, which, as we had previously stood, were to our rear, and hold the enemy in check until I could get some guns into position.⚓ He replied, with a smile at the size of the task, that he would do it, and started off immediately. Thirty men, including Major Keenan, Captain Arrowsmith, and Adjutant Haddock, never came back. I then directed Captain Martin to bring his guns into battery, load with double charges of canister, and aim them so that the shot would hit the ground half-way between the guns and the woods. I also stated that I would give the order to fire. Just then a handsome young lieutenant of the 4th U. S. Artillery, Frank B. Crosby (son of a distinguished lawyer of New York City), who was killed the next day, galloped up and said, "General, I have a battery of six guns; where shall I go? what shall I do?" I told him to place his battery in line on the right of Martin's battery, and gave him the same instructions I had given Martin as to how I wanted him to serve his guns. These 2 batteries gave me 12 guns, and to obtain more I then charged 3 squadrons of the 17th Pennsylvania Cavalry on the stragglers of the Eleventh Corps to clear the ground, and with the assistance of the rest of the regiment succeeded in placing 10 more pieces of artillery in line. The line was then ready for Stonewall Jackson's onset. It was dusk when his men swarmed out of the woods for a quarter of a mile in our front

⚓ See also statements of Major Edward J. Carpenter and others on p. 187.— EDITORS.

(our rear ten minutes before). They came on in line five and six deep, with but one flag—a Union flag dropped by the Eleventh Corps.

I suspected deception and was ready for it. They called out not to shoot, they were friends; at the same time they gave us a volley from at least five thousand muskets. As soon as I saw the flash I gave the command to fire, and the whole line of artillery was discharged at once. ↓ It fairly swept them from the earth; before they could recover themselves the line of artillery had been loaded and was ready for a second attack. After the second discharge, suspecting that they might play the trick of having their men lie down, draw the fire of the artillery, then jump up and charge before the pieces could be reloaded, I poured in the canister for about twenty minutes, and the affair was over. ♭

When the Eleventh Corps was routed, the situation was this: The nearest infantry to me was the right of the Twelfth Corps, over a mile off, and engaged by the forces under General Lee, who was trying to prevent them from impeding the movements of General Jackson. The two divisions of the Third Corps were nearly a mile to the west, at the Furnace. Had Jackson

↓ Major Clifford Thomson, aide-de-camp on General Pleasonton's staff, in a letter written in 1866 gives the following account of the fight at Hazel Grove:

"General Pleasonton rode from gun to gun, directing the gunners to aim low, not to get excited, to make every shot tell; the staff-officers, catching their cue from him, did the same, and while at first there had been considerable excitement and apprehension among us, it soon quieted down, and every thought and action was directed to getting the best service out of those guns that they were capable of rendering. Recovering from the disorder into which Keenan's charge had thrown them, the enemy could be seen forming line of battle in the edge of woods now in our front. They were scarcely two hundred yards distant; yet such was the gloom that they could not be clearly distinguished. General Pleasonton was about to give the order to fire, when a sergeant at one of the guns said:

"'General, aren't those our troops? I see our colors in the line!' This was true, for where he pointed our colors could be seen—trophies picked up on the field. General Pleasonton turned to me and said:

"'Mr. Thomson, ride out there and see who those people are.'

"For myself, I was not at all curious about 'those people,' being perfectly willing to wait till they introduced themselves. Riding out between our guns, I galloped to within thirty or forty yards of them; all along the line they cried out to me, 'Come on; we're friends!' It was quite dark and I could not make out their uniforms, but I could see three of our flags, and these caused me to hesitate; I came to a halt, peering into the darkness to make sure, when a bullet whistled by me, and then came 'the rebel yell.' The line charged up the hill toward our guns, and I led it! Lying down upon my horse's neck, I gave him the spur, and the yells of the 'Johnnies' behind further stimulated him, so that we got over the ground in a lively manner. But with the report of the first shot fired at me General Pleasonton had opened fire, and those twenty-two guns belched forth destruction at a fearfully rapid rate. Although lying down on my horse I kept an eye on the guns and guided my horse between the flashes, and in less time than it takes to tell it I was on the safe side of them. It was load and fire at will for some minutes; the enemy was mowed down in heaps; they could make no headway against such a cyclone, and ran back down the slope to

the cover of the woods. But still the canister was poured into them, and a second attempt to charge the guns failed. Soon Sickles's corps moved from its advanced position and interposed between us and the woods; parties sent out over the field which had been swept by our guns found the dead and dying lying in heaps. Old artillery officers have informed me that they never before heard such rapid firing as occurred at that engagement; the roar was a continuous one, and the execution terrific. After it had ceased I rode up to General Pleasonton and said:

"'General, those people out there are rebels!'

"There was a grave twinkle in his eye as he held out his hand and replied:

"'Thomson, I never expected to see you again; I thought if they didn't kill you I should, but that was no time to stop for one man.'

"I should have agreed with him more cordially if that one man had been somebody else. After Sickles had made his dispositions in our front, we were withdrawn to get forage for our horses, and our part in the battle of Chancellorsville was done. Word had gone out through the army that Pleasonton and his staff had been killed; so, when tired, sleepy, very dirty, and extremely hungry, we next morning rode quietly into our headquarters camp, at the rear, we were looked upon as persons risen from the dead. One thing I have forgotten to mention, and that is that we had virtually no support for those twenty-two guns during the action. There was a portion of the 17th Pennsylvania Cavalry under the hill, but the men were new recruits and had not, I believe, been under fire previous to that occasion. Had the enemy succeeded in gaining the crest of the knoll, the support would not have made a mouthful for a single company of Jackson's men. When President Lincoln visited the army a day or two after this fight, General Pleasonton chanced to call at Hooker's headquarters, when that officer said:

"'Mr. President, this is General Pleasonton, who saved the Army of the Potomac the other night.'

"The President acknowledged the service in his usual grateful manner. Only inspiration, or the instinct of a natural soldier, could have enabled Pleasonton to accomplish so much in so short a time with so small a force. The fight at Hazel Grove was one of those sharp and decisive actions pregnant with great results."

♭ See also statements of Captain James F. Huntington on p. 188.—EDITORS.

captured the position at Hazel Grove, these two divisions would have been cut off from the army. He would have seen General Hooker and his staff getting what troops he could to prevent the routed Eleventh Corps from demoralizing the rest of the army, and the fatal position which that portion of the army occupied rendered it an easy task to have crushed it. Neither the Second Corps nor the Twelfth Corps was in position to have defended itself against an attack by Jackson from Hazel Grove.

For half an hour General Jackson had the Army of the Potomac at his mercy. That he halted to re-form his troops in the woods, instead of forging ahead into the clearing, where he could re-form his troops more rapidly, and where he could have seen that he was master of the situation, turned out to be one of those fatalities by which the most brilliant prospects are sacrificed. When he advanced upon the artillery at Hazel Grove Jackson had another opportunity to win, if his infantry had been properly handled. The fire of his infantry was so high it did no harm; they should have been ordered to fire so low as to disable the cannoneers at the guns. Had his infantry fire been as effective as that of our artillery, Jackson would have carried the position. The artillery fire was effective because I applied to it that principle of dynamics in which the angle of incidence is equal to the angle of reflection,—that is to say, if the muzzle of a gun is three feet from the ground and it is discharged so that the shot will strike the ground at a distance of one hundred yards, it will glance from the earth at the same angle at which it struck it, and in another one hundred yards will be three feet from the ground. I knew my first volley must be a crushing one, or Jackson, with his superior numbers, would charge across the short distance which separated us and capture the artillery before the guns could be reloaded.

MAJOR-GENERAL AMIEL W. WHIPPLE, COM-MANDER OF THE THIRD DIVISION OF THE THIRD CORPS, MORTALLY WOUNDED BY A SHARP-SHOOTER ON THE MORNING OF MAY 4, 1863. FROM A PHOTOGRAPH.

After the fight at Hazel Grove I sent into the woods and captured a number of Jackson's men. I asked them to what command they belonged. One of them said to General A. P. Hill's corps, and added, "That was a pretty trick you played us this evening." I asked to what he referred. He replied, "By withdrawing your infantry, and catching us on your guns,"—thus showing that the flight of the Eleventh Corps was looked upon as a ruse. To my question, if they had suffered much, he said that they had been badly cut up; that General Jackson had been badly wounded; also General A. P. Hill, and their chief of artillery. I asked how he knew General Jackson had been wounded. He stated that he saw him when he was carried off the field in a litter. This information I immediately reported to General Hooker, when he directed me to withdraw my command from that position and go into camp on the north side of the Rappahannock River. It was 4 A. M. of the 3d of

May when I moved from Hazel Grove. Sickles, with the two divisions of the Third Corps, reached Hazel Grove from the Furnace between half-past nine and ten on the night of the 2d of May. Some of his troops had fighting in the woods before I left, but I am unable to say what was its character.

On the morning of the 3d of May (Sunday) General Stuart was in command of Jackson's forces, Jackson and A. P. Hill having been wounded, as reported by the prisoner taken the night before. Stuart prepared, with his usual impetuosity, to renew the attack early that morning, and by one of those unfortunate occurrences so prevalent during the war, he caught the Third Corps in motion to take up a new position, connecting with the Twelfth Corps at Fairview, and facing to the west. This withdrawal enabled Stuart to take the position at Hazel Grove from which Jackson had been repulsed the evening before. He saw its advantages at once, and, placing some thirty pieces of artillery there, he enfiladed the Twelfth Corps at Fairview and Chancellorsville, and punished the Third Corps severely. The Third Corps was fighting throughout the day under great disadvantages. To add to the embarrassments of the army, General Hooker that morning was disabled by a concussion, and the army was virtually without a head, the different corps commanders fighting their commands on the defensive. Such extraordinary conditions forced the Army of the Potomac to fall back from Chancellorsville and Fairview, and form a new line of battle to the north and some distance from Chancellorsville. This line presented a front to the enemy that could not be enfiladed or turned. Desultory fighting, especially with artillery, was kept up on the 4th of May; but Hooker's battle ended on the 3d, after the army had gained its new position.

It is useless to speculate what General Hooker would have done if he had not been disabled. Up to the evening of the 2d of May the enemy had suffered severely, while the Army of the Potomac had comparatively but few killed and wounded; but the unfortunate circumstances that contracted the lines of our army enabled the enemy to inflict the severest punishment upon all the troops that were engaged. In fact, the greatest injury was inflicted on the 3d of May, while the army had no commander. Had the First Corps, which had not been engaged, and the Fifth Corps, still fresh, been thrown into the action in the afternoon of Sunday, the 3d of May, when Lee's troops were exhausted from the struggle, they would certainly have made Chancellorsville what it should have been,— a complete success. These two corps mustered from 25,000 to 30,000 men. There was no one to order them into the fight, and a second golden opportunity was lost. The army recrossed the Rappahannock River on the night of May 5th, and took up again the position at Falmouth which they had occupied before the campaign.

WHEN STONEWALL JACKSON TURNED OUR RIGHT.

BY JOHN L. COLLINS, 8TH PENNSYLVANIA CAVALRY.

ON the afternoon of May 2d, 1863, the 8th Pennsylvania Cavalry were ordered to dismount, slack saddle-girths, and rest in the vicinity of General Hooker's headquarters at Chancellorsville. Some of the men fell asleep holding their horses, some began talking of the battle, while a knot of officers, who always improved such occasions in this way, sat down to their favorite game of poker. Suddenly an order from headquarters made a complete change in the scene. At the word "Mount!" the sleepers as well as the talkers sprang to their saddles, the gamblers snatched up their stakes and their cards, and a regiment of cavalry took the place of a lounging crowd.

Passing to the left of the Chancellorsville House, we crossed our line of battle at the edge of a wood and came up with a reconnoitering party that had captured the 23d Georgia. We had heard that Lee was retreating, and supposed that this unfortunate regiment had been sacrificed to give the main body a chance to escape; but while we were commiserating the poor fellows, one of them defiantly said, "You may think you have done a big thing just now, but wait till Jackson gets round on your right."

We laughed at his harmless bravado, for we did not think he would betray Jackson's move had he known anything about it; but while we were yet trying to get through the thick wood the roar of musketry and artillery on our right confirmed his speech. We now came back at a gallop toward a point between the place where we were resting and the place where the battle was raging. As we rode into an elevated clearing, called Hazel Grove, the regiment (the 8th Pennsylvania) was brought into line. We surmised a disaster and nervously braced ourselves for the ordeal, not knowing whether we were to make an attack or wait there to receive one.

The roar of musketry was now heavier and nearer; the vast woods between us and Dowdall's tavern seemed to shake with it. There was no time to ask or to wonder what had happened, for the regiment was ordered off at a gallop. After riding about three hundred yards we turned into a narrow road that promised to take us into the midst of the enemy. Half a dozen horsemen in cadet gray — most likely a general's staff reconnoitering, as they did not ride in ranks — were in the road ahead of us, and turned and fled back to their lines.

The word "Charge!" was now passed from the leading squadron, and sabers flew into the air along our line; but none too soon, for we were already in the midst of the foe, and they were ready for us. The unfortunate squadron that led caught all the fire as we dashed along the narrow lane, and we who rode next it got only the smoke from the enemy's guns. We could reach nothing as yet, and could see nothing but fire and smoke, for their line of battle was safely posted behind a thicket that lined

the left of the road, while their rifles were aimed through it.

It was a long lane and a hot lane to go through; but the lane had a turn, and we got to it at last when we reached the Plank road and struck Rodes's division right in the front. We struck it as a wave strikes a stately ship: the ship is staggered, maybe thrown on her beam ends, but the wave is dashed into spray, and the ship sails on as before.

Major Keenan, who led his battalion in the charge, the captain in command of the leading squadron, the adjutant, and a few score of their followers went down at this shock together. The detail sent over to recover their bodies after the battle said that the major had thirteen bullets in his body, the adjutant nine, and others fewer. It was reported by some who rode close upon the major that in falling he shouted, "To the right!" seeing that the impenetrable masses on his left could not be forced, and that there was no way out but over the thinner lines on the right. When turning at full speed, my horse was killed and I was pitched over his neck on the roadside. Here I parted company with the regiment. When I jumped to my feet I had time to take only one glance at my surroundings. My sole thought was to escape capture or death. On one side were the heavy lines of Confederate infantry doubled and bent by the charge, their officers trying to recover their alignment; on the other side the survivors of the leading squadrons were galloping in the Plank road, the others breaking over the Confederate skirmish lines as far back as I could see into the woods.

By instinct I turned toward the woods on the right of the Plank road as the best way out, and made a dash at the lines, which had just recovered from their surprise that a cavalry regiment should have ridden over them, and were firing after it. They were loading when I ran out between them, and when they began to fire I dropped down behind some trees that had been cut to make an abatis, or had been shot down by the cannon; when the volley was over I jumped up and ran as fast as before.

The Plank road, and the woods that bordered it, presented a scene of terror and confusion such as I had never seen before. Men and animals were dashing against one another in wild dismay before the line of fire that came crackling and crashing after them. The constantly approaching rattle of musketry, the crash of the shells through the trees, seemed to come from three sides upon the broken fragments of the Eleventh Corps that crowded each other on the road. The horses of the men of my regiment who had been shot, mingled with the pack-mules that carried the ammunition of the Eleventh Corps, tore like wild beasts through the woods. I tried in vain to catch one.

This employment of the mules for ammunition

MAJOR PETER KEENAN, KILLED IN THE CHARGE OF
THE 8TH PENNSYLVANIA CAVALRY.

service was a device of General Hooker's, and this was the only field where they played their part. Each mule carried four or five boxes of spare ammunition, and being tied in couples, they seemed easier to catch than a horse. As a pair of them made for opposite sides of a tree, I ran toward them to get one, but before I could succeed a shell from the direction of the Plank road struck the tree, exploded the ammunition, and slaughtered the mules.

I now gave up hope of a mount, and seeing the Confederate lines coming near me, tried to save myself on foot. Once, when throwing myself down to escape the fury of the fire, I saw a member of my own regiment, whose horse also had been shot, hiding in a pine top that had been cut down by a shell. He had thrown his arms away that he might run the faster, and he begged me to do the same. This I refused to do, and I got in safely with my arms, while he was never seen again. I turned into the Plank road to join the very bad company that came pouring in by that route. More than half of the runaways had thrown their arms away, and all of them were talking a language that I did not understand, but, by their tones, evidently blaming some one for the disgrace and disaster that had befallen their corps. They appeared to share the prevailing confusion on that part of the field, where the front and the rear seemed reversed. Yet, as misery loves company, I cast my lot with them and continued my flight.

I doubt if any of us knew where we were going, further than that we were fleeing before the pursuing lines of the enemy. One of my own company, who was captured in the charge, afterward told me that in leaping an abatis, he was lifted from his saddle by a vine and remained suspended till made a prisoner.

In the very height of the flight, we came upon General Howard, who seemed to be the only man in his own command that was not running at that moment. He was in the middle of the road and mounted, his maimed arm embracing a stand of colors that some regiment had deserted, while with his sound arm he was gesticulating to the men to make a stand by their flag. ⌡ With bared head he was pleading with his soldiers, literally weeping as he entreated the unheeding horde. Under different circumstances I should have considered it my duty to follow and find my command, and report for duty with it. But I could not go past the general. Maimed in his person and sublime in his patriotism, he seemed worthy to stand by, and out of pure compliment to his appearance I hooked up my saber and fell into the little line that gathered about him. As the front became clear, we fired a few shots at the advance line of the Confederates, but a fresh mass of fugitives in blue soon filled the road, and we had to stop firing. The general now ordered us to cover the whole line of retreat so as to let none pass, and the officers, inspired by his devotion, ran in front of their men, drew their swords, and attempted to stop them. As the number constantly increased, the pressure became greater upon the line that blocked the way; but this line was constantly reënforced by officers and others, and offered some resistance to the pressure. At last the seething, surging sea of humanity broke over the feeble barrier, and General Howard and his officers were carried away by main force with the tide. Pharaoh and his chariots could have held back the walls of the Red Sea as easily as those officers could resist this retreat. I started again on my race for life, this time alone, and toward the slopes of the Chancellorsville plateau, where it seemed to me probable that my regiment would re-form after the charge.

My course was right-oblique from the road, and I had not gone far before I saw lines that I knew were not retreating. Their flags were flying, and my heart took a bound as I beheld battery after battery galloping into position, and regiment after regiment wheeling into line behind them. A line of battle showed itself at last; the Third Corps had come up to stop the successful charge, and Jackson's men would find a difference between attacking the Third Corps in front and the Eleventh in the rear. Seeing the guns unlimber and load, I made my greatest effort at speed, but not caring for a few fugitives, the guns belched forth their fire before I could get in. However, I came safely through, and at last paused for a long breath. While congratulating myself upon my escape, I looked behind the line of battle, and there saw my own regiment drawn up for a charge, the line not so long as half an hour before by one-third, but still as shapely and resolute as ever. The horses were blown and nervous, and the men were, no doubt, a little depressed by the rough usage they had met with. A horse, that had followed the company riderless from the charge, was given to me,

⌡ See General Howard's description on p. 200.—EDITORS.

and my confidence and self-respect came back as I mounted him, for I was no longer a fugitive, but a soldier.

The fighting now began in earnest. The splendid divisions of Birney, Berry, and Whipple had to be met and vanquished before a farther advance could be made, and before Jackson could attain the great object of his march to our rear. The gathering darkness was favorable to the Confederates, for they could get near the guns before being seen; but it also added to the terror of the batteries, which were discharged double-shotted at the assailants, and lit up the heavens with fire that seemed supernat-

The slope was so steep that a line of battle could be formed in front of the guns and a double skirmish line in front of that.

Our regiment now moved up to the guns, enabling us to see better the slopes and the woods when lit up by the flashes. Sometimes darkness and stillness would reign for a few minutes, and we would

GENERAL HOWARD STRIVING TO RALLY HIS TROOPS.

ural. The dusky lines fell back into the woods in disorganized masses as often as they advanced, and the cheers of our troops rang out at each retreat. From the boldness and the frequency of the Confederate charges it was found necessary to move the infantry in front of the guns, lest the enemy should seize them before being discovered.

think the long day's fighting was over, but it would presently break out again. The stealthy rush from the woods could be heard first, then the sharp crack of the skirmisher's rifle, then a yell and a louder rushing of their lines met by the loud roll of the line of battle's fire. As the cheer of our men announced that the enemy's line was again in retreat, the blaze of forty or fifty cannons from the right to the left would light up the scene and carry death over the heads of our men into the woods beyond.

At last Jackson's men paused, for they had been marching and fighting since morning, and human nature could endure no more. But they were not allowed to hold the ground they had won; an advance was now ordered on our side, and it was made with a vigor that avenged the discomfiture of our comrades. Though it was now midnight the woods were lit up with the flame of the musketry as the combatants came face to face among the trees, and the battle began anew. The artillerists pushed on their guns by hand a hundred yards behind the infantry line, and shook the woods in their depths, as they had the hills to their foundations. At last, at 2 o'clock in the morning, we were told to sleep on our arms. But who could sleep while counting the dead of our commands? Comrades were gone; file-leaders and file-closers were gone; officers of every grade had perished. Stonewall Jackson himself had gone down in his greatest charge; and his men never again fought as on that day, nor came down on our flank with such fury.

THE CHARGE OF THE EIGHTH PENNSYLVANIA CAVALRY. ⚓

I. BY PENNOCK HUEY, BREVET BRIGADIER-GENERAL, U. S. V.

JUST as we reached Hazel Grove, at Scott's Run Crossing, at half-past 6 o'clock P. M., May 2d, a staff-officer rode up in a state of great excitement and reported to General Sickles that the enemy had flanked General Howard's corps, and that he had been sent for a regiment of General Pleasonton's cavalry. General Sickles immediately ordered General Pleasonton to send a regiment. General Pleasonton then ordered me to report with my regiment as quickly as possible to General Howard, whom I would probably find near the old Wilderness church. There were no other orders given to me or to any officer of my regiment. ↓

I found the regiment, standing to horse, on the opposite or north side of Hazel Grove, near the road. The wood in front was so thick with underbrush that a bird could scarcely fly through it; much less could a cavalry charge have been made. On inquiring for the adjutant of the regiment, and on being informed by some of the men where he was, I rode to the point designated and found Major Peter Keenan, Captain William A. Dailey, Adjutant J. Haseltine Haddock, and Lieutenant Andrew B. Wells playing cards under a tree. When I ordered them to mount their commands they were all in high spirits about the game, Keenan remarking: "Major, you have spoiled a good game!"

After mounting the regiment I rode off at its head in my proper place, followed by four other officers, all of whom belonged in front except Lieutenant Carpenter, who commanded the second company of the first squadron, and might properly have been in the rear of the first company, where he undoubtedly would have been had I supposed there was danger ahead. The officers in front were: Major Pennock Huey, commander of the regiment; Major Peter Keenan, commander of the first battalion; Captain Charles Arrowsmith, commander of the first squadron; Lieutenant J. Edward Carpenter, commander of the second company; and Adjutant J. Haseltine Haddock, whose place was with me unless otherwise ordered. We rode through the wood toward the Plank road; there was no unusual stir or excitement among the men or officers of the regiment, the impression being that the enemy were retreating, and all who had not heard of General Howard's disaster felt happy with the thought that the battle was almost over. No one in the regiment, with the exception of myself, knew where we were going or for what purpose.

From the information I had received from General Pleasonton, and from hearing the aide make his report before I started, I had no idea that we would meet the enemy till after I had reported to General Howard. Therefore the surprise was as great to us as to the enemy, as we were entirely unprepared, our sabers being in their scabbards. When we arrived almost at the Plank road, we discovered that we had ridden right into the enemy, the Plank road in our front being occupied by them in great force, and that we were completely surrounded, the woods at that point being filled with flankers of Jackson's column, who were thoroughly hidden from our view by the thick undergrowth. It was here that I gave the command to "draw sabers and charge," which order was repeated by Major Keenan and other officers. The charge was led by the five officers already named, who were riding at the head of the regiment when we left Hazel Grove. On reaching the Plank road it appeared to be packed about as closely with the enemy as it possibly could be.

We turned to the left, facing the Confederate column, the regiment crowding on, both men and horses in a perfect frenzy of excitement, which nothing but death could stop. We cut our way through, trampling down all who could not escape us, and using our sabers on all within reach, for a distance of about 100 yards, when we received a volley from the enemy, which killed Major Keenan, Captain Arrowsmith, and Adjutant Haddock, three of the noblest and most gallant officers of the war, besides a large number of men. All three of the above-named officers fell at the same time and from the same volley, Major Keenan falling against me and lighting on the ground under my horse. A few days afterward his body was found near the spot where he had fallen.

⚓ Extracted by permission and condensed from "A True History of the Charge of the 8th Pennsylvania Cavalry at Chancellorsville," by Pennock Huey, Philadelphia, 1885.— EDITORS.

↓ General Huey was at this time Major (afterward Colonel) of the 8th Pennsylvania cavalry, and was the senior officer present with it. [See also p. 187.]— EDITORS.

II. BY J. EDWARD CARPENTER, MAJOR, 8TH PENNSYLVANIA CAVALRY. ♭

THERE was no confusion at Hazel Grove when the regiment received its orders and left that place. No enemy was in sight. Indeed, until after the 8th Pennsylvania had left the place there was not the slightest evidence that the enemy was in the immediate neighborhood, excepting, perhaps, that the musketry-firing seemed to be drawing nearer. The charge of the regiment was made on the Plank road, about three-quarters of a mile from where Pleasonton was at Hazel Grove, and was first ordered by the commanding officer of the regiment at the moment when the emergency arose.

The writer of this, although himself a participator in the charge, was unable to recognize General Pleasonton's description of it and the surrounding scenes attending it. [See p. 179.] A letter from the writer to a member of his family, written three days after the charge, is now before him. From this letter the following is extracted:

" We lost, however, I regret to say, three gallant officers, Major Keenan, Captain Arrowsmith and Adjutant Haddock. Major Huey and . . . were the only ones who came out from the head of the column. All the rest were killed, wounded, or prisoners."

When this letter was written on the 5th of May, 1863, there was no thought of controversy. It was intended only for the eye of the person to whom it was written, with no idea that it would be preserved.

General Pleasonton's report of the operations of his command at Chancellorsville, dated May 18th, 1863, makes no mention of Keenan, but commends Huey as the commander of the regiment and indorses his report. In Major Huey's report of the operations of the 8th Pennsylvania cavalry, dated May 9th, 1863, he states that he was ordered to report, with his command, to General Howard, and no mention is made of any order from General Pleasonton to charge. This report was before Pleasonton when his own report was made, and no exception was ever taken to it. In Colonel Thomas C. Devin's report of the 2d brigade, dated May 12th, 1863, he states that the 8th Pennsylvania cavalry was sent to the support of General Howard, and Major Huey is complimented as the commander of the regiment. No mention is made of an order to Keenan to charge, and Keenan is only referred to as having gallantly fallen.

III. BY ANDREW B. WELLS, CAPTAIN, CO. F, 8TH PENNSYLVANIA CAVALRY. ♭

OUR regiment, on the second day of May, 1863, was awaiting orders in a clearing of wooded country called Hazel Grove. We had been there some little time. Everything was quiet on the front. The men were gathered in groups, chatting and smoking, and the officers were occupied in much the same manner, wondering what would turn up next.

About 4 o'clock I suggested a game of draw poker. An empty cracker-box, with a blanket thrown over it, served as a card-table. The party playing, if I mistake not, was composed of Major Keenan, Adjutant Haddock, Captain Goddard, Lieutenant W. A. Daily, and myself. We had been playing about two hours — the game was a big one and we were all absorbed in it — when, about 6 P. M., it was brought to an abrupt end by the appearance of a mounted officer. Riding up to where we were playing, he asked in an excited manner: " Who is in command of this regiment?" Major Keenan, who was seated beside me, turned his head and said, in a joking way: "I am; what's the trouble?" Our visitor replied: " General Howard wants a cavalry regiment." And before we had time to ask further questions he was off, and the next moment we were all on our feet, and our game was ended. I remember it perfectly well, for I was out of pocket on the play. ♎ The regiment was mounted, I mounting at the same time and alongside of Major Keenan. We then moved out of Hazel Grove by twos. Keenan, Haddock, Arrowsmith, Huey, and Carpenter moved

out with the first squadron. I remember distinctly seeing that group of officers, and did not see General Pleasonton at the time.

I was under the impression, and believe that the other officers also were, that we were on our road to report to General Howard. Anyhow, I fell in with the second squadron, Captain William A. Corrie being in command, and he and I rode together at the head of it. When we passed out of the clearing there were no officers or men on our flank, all was in order ahead, and the command was moving at a walk. The command entered the woods and was still moving on a walk, when, at the distance of about one mile from where we had mounted, Captain Corrie and myself saw the first squadron take the trot, leaving a space between us of about twenty-five yards. At the same time we heard the command, " Draw sabers," and saw the first squadron draw them. We then heard the musketry-firing. In was given in continuous but distant volleys.

We of the second squadron knew that our time was at hand, and Captain Corrie gave the order to draw sabers and charge. Taking a trot, we found that the road took a bend as we proceeded. When we turned the corner of the wood-road a sight met our eyes that it is impossible for me to describe. After charging over the dead men and horses of the first squadron we charged into Jackson's column, and, as luck would have it, found them with empty guns — thanks to our poor comrades ahead.

♭ Taken by permission from the "Philadelphia Weekly Press," October 13th, 1886, and condensed.— EDITORS.
♎ Captain Wells has elsewhere said that at 6:20 by his watch, Major Huey rode up and gave the order to mount.— EDITORS.

The enemy were as thick as bees, and we appeared to be among thousands of them in an instant.

After we reached the Plank road we were in columns of fours and on the dead run, and when we struck the enemy there occurred a "jam" of living and dead men, friends and enemies, and horses, and the weight of the rear of our squadron broke us into utter confusion, so that at the moment every man was for himself.

The third squadron, which Captain P. L. Goddard commanded, was in our rear, and came thundering along after us, but as to the balance of the regiment I do not know how they came in or got out.

The enemy were as much surprised as we were, and thought, no doubt, as they now say, that the whole cavalry corps of the Army of the Potomac was charging them. I distinctly remember hearing a number of them call out, "I surrender, I surrender." We did not stop to take any prisoners for fear of being captured ourselves,— I had been

caught once and was just out of Libby prison and did not want to be captured again,— but made for our lines as best we could.

The whole affair was accidental. We were on our way to report to General Howard, some three miles from where we were encamped, and the country that General Howard's staff-officer had just passed over in quest of the cavalry had in the meantime been crossed by Stonewall Jackson's troops, and in following the same track we naturally ran into them. The officers who were at the head of our column, seeing the situation, had only an instant to determine what was to be done. We could not turn around and get out in the face of the enemy, and the only thing left for us was to go through them, "sink or swim."

Can any man who was a soldier for one moment imagine an officer deliberately planning a charge by a regiment of cavalry, strung out by twos in a column half a mile long in a thick wood?

THE ARTILLERY AT HAZEL GROVE. ☆

BY JAMES F. HUNTINGTON, CAPTAIN, BATTERY H, 1ST OHIO ARTILLERY.

WHEN Jackson's advance struck the Eleventh Corps, four batteries had been for some time waiting orders in the extensive clearing known as Hazel Grove. Of these, "H," 1st Ohio Light Artillery, and the 10th and 11th New York Independent Batteries belonged to Whipple's division of the Third Corps. They were left there when that division passed through *en route* to join the force operating under General Sickles near the Furnace. Later, Martin's horse battery, with Devin's cavalry brigade, arrived and took ground on the opposite or south side of the field. When the sound of battle indicated that the enemy were driving in the right of the army, and were approaching Hazel Grove, the batteries of Whipple's division were brought into position under my direction, as acting chief of artillery. Although the movement was delayed by causes beyond my control until its execution had become exceedingly difficult, our eighteen guns were established in battery, ready to open before the enemy fired a shot or were in a position to do so. General Pleasonton seems to be unaware of that fact, or he would hardly have failed to allude to it. It is,

therefore, fair to presume that his attention was engrossed by the supervision of Martin's battery, as detailed in his paper. General Sickles, on his arrival, soon after the firing ceased, sent for me and warmly expressed his approbation of the manner in which my command had held the ground. ‖

Nothing on wheels from the Eleventh Corps passed through Hazel Grove. The vehicles that stampeded through my lines while in process of formation were forges, battery-wagons, ambulances, etc., belonging to the Third Corps, left in the cross-road leading to the Plank road, when that corps went out to the Furnace to attack Jackson's column. So whatever else may have formed the components of the remarkable *tumulus* described by General Pleasonton, it certainly did not contain the débris of the Eleventh Corps. As for the *tumulus* itself, it escaped my observation when I crossed the bog he refers to on Sunday morning with my battery, or what there was left of it, at the pressing solicitation of Archer's Confederate brigade.

BOSTON, October 14th, 1886.

☆ In reply to statements contained in General Pleasonton's paper, p. 179.— EDITORS.

‖ General Sickles says in his official report: "I confided to Pleasonton the direction of the artillery — three batteries of my reserve — Clark's, Lewis's [10th New York, of Huntington's command] and Turnbull's, and his own horse-battery. . . . The fugitives of the Eleventh Corps swarmed from the woods and swept frantically over the cleared fields in which my artillery was parked. . . . The enemy showing himself on the plain, Pleasonton met the attack at short range with the well-directed fire of twenty-two pieces double-shotted with canister." According to this one of Huntington's three

batteries (Lewis's 10th New York) was placed under Pleasonton's control. Probably this battery, with Turnbull's, Clark's, and Martin's, made up the twenty-two guns mentioned by both Sickles and Pleasonton. General Hunt, the chief of artillery of the army, says: "When the Eleventh Corps was broken up and routed on the 2d, . . . General Pleasonton collected some batteries belonging to different corps (Martin's Horse Artillery, 6th New York, six 3-inch guns, Clark's B, 1st New Jersey, six 10-pounders; Lewis's 10th New York, six light 12-pounders; Turnbull's F and K, 3d U. S., six 12-pounders), and with them formed a large battery of twenty-four guns."— EDITORS.

RACE ON THE PLANK ROAD FOR RIGHT OF WAY, BETWEEN THE NINTH MASSACHUSETTS BATTERY AND A BAGGAGE TRAIN.

THE ELEVENTH CORPS AT CHANCELLORSVILLE.

BY OLIVER O. HOWARD, MAJOR-GENERAL, U. S. A.

THE country around Chancellorsville for the most part is a wilderness, with but here and there an opening. If we consult the recent maps (no good ones existed before the battle), we notice that the two famous rivers, the Rapidan and the Rappahannock, join at a point due north of Chancellorsville; thence the Rappahannock runs easterly for two miles, till suddenly at the United States Ford it turns and flows south for a mile and a half, and then, turning again, completes a horse-shoe bend. Here, on the south shore, was General Hooker's battle-line on the morning of the 2d of May, 1863. Here his five army corps, those of Meade, Slocum, Couch, Sickles, and Howard, were deployed. The face was toward the south, and the ranks mainly occupied a ridge nearly parallel with the Rapidan. The left touched the high ground just west of the horse-shoe bend, while the bristling front, fringed with skirmishers, ran along the Mineral Spring road, bent forward to take in the cross-roads of Chancellorsville, and then, stretching on westerly through lower levels, retired to Dowdall's Tavern. Just beyond Dowdall's was a slight backward hook in the line, partially encircling Talley's Hill, a sunny spot in the forest between the Orange Plank road and the pike. This pike is an old roadway which skirts the northern edge of Talley's farm, and makes an angle of some forty degrees with the Orange Plank road.

At dawn of that eventful day General Hooker was at Chancellorsville. Slocum and Hancock were just in his front, infantry and artillery deployed to the right and left. French's division was in his rear. Meade occupied the extreme left, and my corps, the Eleventh, the right. Sickles connected me with Slocum. Our lines covered between five and six miles of frontage, and Hooker was near the middle point. The main body of our cavalry, under Stoneman, had gone off on a raid upon Lee's communications, and the remainder of the Army of the Potomac was under the sturdy Sedgwick, beyond Fredericksburg.

Our opponents, under General Robert E. Lee, the evening before, were about two miles distant toward Fredericksburg, and thus between us and Sedgwick. Lee had immediately with him the divisions of McLaws, Anderson, Rodes, Colston, and A. P. Hill, besides some cavalry under Stuart. He

THE OLD CHANCELLOR HOUSE, BURNED DURING THE BATTLE. FROM A PHOTOGRAPH.

held, for his line of battle, a comparatively short front between the Rappahannock and the Catherine Furnace, not exceeding two miles and a half in extent. His right wing, not far from the river, was behind Mott's Run, which flows due east, and his left was deployed along the Catherine Furnace road.

Could Hooker, on the first day of May, have known Lee's exact location, he never could have had a better opportunity for taking the offensive. But he did not know, and after the few troops advancing toward Fredericksburg had met the approaching enemy he ordered all back to the "old position," the Chancellorsville line, which I have just described.

On the preceding Thursday, the last of April, the three corps that constituted the right wing of the army, Meade's, Slocum's, and mine, had crossed from the north to the south side of the Rapidan, and by 4 o'clock in the afternoon had reached the vicinity of Chancellorsville, where Slocum, who was the senior commander present, established his headquarters. I, approaching from Germanna Ford, halted my divisions at Dowdall's Tavern and encamped them there. Then I rode along the Plank road through the almost continuous forest to the Chancellorsville House. There I reported to Slocum. He said that the orders were for me to cover the right of the general line, posting my command near Dowdall's Tavern. He pointed to a place on the map marked "Mill" near there, on a branch of Hunting Run [see map, p. 193], and said, "Establish your right there." General Slocum promised, with the Twelfth Corps, to occupy the space between his headquarters and Dowdall's clearing; but, finding the distance too great, one of his division commanders sent me word that I must cover the last three-quarters of a mile of the Plank road.

This was done by a brigade of General Steinwehr, the commander of my left division, though with regret on our part, because it required all the corps reserves to fill up that gap.

The so-called Dowdall's Tavern was at that time the home of Melzi Chancellor. He had a large family, including several grown people. I placed my headquarters at his house. In front of me, facing south along a curving ridge, the right of Steinwehr's division was located. He had but two brigades, Barlow on the Plank road and Buschbeck on his right. With them Steinwehr covered a mile, leaving but two regiments for reserve. These he put some two hundred yards to his rear, near the little "Wilderness Church."

Next to Steinwehr, toward our right, came General Carl Schurz's division. First was Captain Dilger's battery. Dilger was one of those handsome, hearty, active young men that everybody liked to have near. His guns pointed to the south-west and west, along the Orange Plank road. Next was Krzyzanowski's brigade, about half on the front and half in reserve. Schurz's right brigade was that of Schimmelfennig, disposed in the same manner, a part deployed and the remainder kept a few hundred yards back for a reserve. Schurz's front line of infantry extended along the old turnpike and faced to the south-west. The right division of the corps was commanded by General Charles Devens,

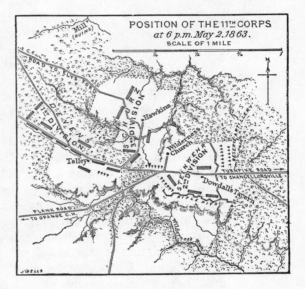

afterward attorney-general in the cabinet of President Hayes. Devens and I together had carefully reconnoitered both the Orange Plank road and the old turnpike for at least three miles toward the west. After this reconnoissance he established his division,— the Second Brigade, under McLean, next to Schurz's first, and then pushing out on the pike for half a mile he deployed the other, Gilsa's, at right angles facing west, connecting his two parts by a thin skirmish-line. Colonel Gilsa's brigade was afterward drawn back, still facing west at right angles to the line, so as to make a more solid connection, and so that, constituting, as it did, the main right flank, the reserves of the corps could be brought more promptly to its support, by extending its right to the north, should an enemy by any possible contingency get so far around. A section of Dieckmann's battery which looked to the west along the old pike was located at the angle.

The reserve batteries, twelve guns, were put upon a ridge abreast of the little church and pointed toward the north-west, with a view to sweep all approaches to the north of Gilsa, firing up a gradually ascending slope. This ridge, where I stood during the battle, was central, and, besides, enabled the artillerymen to enfilade either roadway, or meet an attack from south, west, or north. Here epaulments for the batteries were constructed, and cross-intrenchments for the battery supports were dug, extending from the little church across all the open ground that stretched away from the tavern to the right of Devens's line.

DOWDALL'S TAVERN, HOWARD'S HEADQUARTERS.
FROM A WAR-TIME PHOTOGRAPH.

To my great comfort, General Sickles's corps came up on Friday, May 1st, and took from our left Steinwehr's three-quarters of a mile of the Plank road. Thus he relieved from the front line Barlow's large brigade, giving me, besides the several division reserves, General Barlow with 1500 men as a general reserve for the corps. These were massed near the cross-intrench-ments, and held avowedly to support the batteries and protect General Devens's exposed right flank.

As to pickets, each division had a good line of them. My aide, Major Charles H. Howard, assisted in connecting them between divisions, and during the 2d of May that fearless and faithful staff-officer, Major E. Whittlesey, rode the entire circuit of their front to stimulate them to special activity. Those of Devens were "thrown out at a distance from a half-mile to a mile and stretching well around covering our right flank"; ⫾ and the picket-posts in front on the pike were over two miles beyond the main line.

The nature of the country in the neighborhood of the three adjoining farms, Dowdall's, Talley's, and Hawkins's, became well known to the Army of the Potomac in subsequent experiences, never to be forgotten. It is the terrible "Wilderness" where, later in the war, so many brave men fell. Here were stunted trees, such as scraggy oaks, bushy firs, cedars, and junipers, all entangled with a thick, almost impenetrable undergrowth, and criss-crossed with an abundance of wild vines. In places all along the south-west and west front the forest appeared impassable, and the skirmishers could only work their way through with extreme difficulty.

To the officers of the Eleventh Corps the position was never a desirable one. It presented *a flank in the air.* We were more than four miles south from Ely's ford, where were Hooker's nearest cavalry flankers. In his report after the battle, General Schurz says:

DOWDALL'S TAVERN IN 1884.

⫾ See General Devens's report of Chancellorsville ("Official Records," Vol. XXV., Part I., p. 632).—O. O. H.

THE WILDERNESS CHURCH (IN THE LEFT MIDDLE-GROUND) AND HAWKINS'S FARM (ON THE RIGHT)
AS SEEN FROM THE PLANK ROAD IN FRONT OF DOWDALL'S TAVERN.

"Our right ought to have been drawn back toward the Rapidan, to rest on that river at or near the mouth of Hunting Run, the corps abandoning so much of the Plank road as to enable it to establish a solid line." Yes; but we were ordered to Dowdall's Tavern, and not to the Rapidan, three or four miles in our rear! And our right was fixed for us at the "Mill." It is true the mill no longer existed, but the point required was not doubted. Again, this position, which Schurz recommended in his report subsequent to our battle, was the very one into which Hooker's whole army was forced two days afterward. He was so cramped by it that he did not dare to take the offensive. In that position, "solid" and fortified as it was, our army, out-numbering Lee's, was so badly handled by the enemy that Hooker at last deemed it safer to return to the north side of the Rappahannock.

The strength of Hooker's five corps, and Reynolds's, which was not far behind, was, on the morning of the 2d of May, about 90,000 effectives. The right corps, the Eleventh, had in all, artillery and infantry, twelve thousand men. Lee faced us with five large divisions, having on the spot about 40,000 rifles, with considerable artillery.

In my youth my brother and I had a favorite spot in an upper field of my father's farm from which we were accustomed, after the first symptoms of a coming storm, to watch the operations of the contending winds; the sudden gusts and whirlwinds; the sideling swallows excitedly seeking shelter; the swift and swifter, black and blacker clouds, ever rising higher and pushing their angry fronts toward us. As we listened we heard the low rumbling from afar; as the storm came nearer the woods bent forward and shook fiercely their thick branches; the lightning zigzagged in flashes, and the deep-bassed thunder echoed more loudly, till there was scarcely an interval between its ominous crashing discharges. In some such manner came on that battle of May 2d to the watchers at Dowdall's Tavern and Talley's farm-house.

The first distant symptom occurred on the evening of May 1st. Then was heard the sudden crack of rifle-shooting. It began with Steinwehr's skirmishers, and then passed on to Schurz. Schimmelfennig pushed out a brigade straightforward toward the south-west and received a sudden fire of artillery from the intruders. They left him and pushed on.

It was "a rolling reconnoissance," evidently to determine, for Lee's and Jackson's information, the position of our flank. They probably had, however, some more certain knowledge, gained from one or two of the enterprising residents let loose during that Friday by our general forward movement. We forgot these friends to Lee as we excitedly marched to Friday's battle. When we unexpectedly came back, some of these residents, with little baskets of provisions in hand, were gone beyond recall. I suspect that the commander of the "rolling reconnoissance" and the said residents formed part of the famous night conference of Lee and Jackson, where cracker-boxes served as seats and tables. General Lee says: "It was therefore resolved to endeavor to turn his right flank and gain his rear, leaving a force in front to hold him in check and conceal the movement. The execution of this plan was intrusted to Lieutenant-General Jackson with his three divisions."

Jackson's movement, with a stronger indication of battle, began at sunrise, Rodes, Colston, and A. P. Hill, in the order named, following the old road by the Catherine Furnace, there shoving off farther south to get beyond the sight of our men; then sweeping around by a private road, well known to them, up to the Orange Plank road; and thence on, perhaps a mile farther, through the wild forest till the old turnpike was found and crossed. The Catherine Furnace, nearly opposite Sickles's right and two and a half miles distant, gave an open reach and fully exposed the moving column to view. Except at that point the Confederates were covered by woods and by Stuart's busy and noisy cavalry.

THE WILDERNESS CHURCH. FROM A WAR-TIME PHOTOGRAPH. SEE PREVIOUS PAGE.

THE CONFEDERATES CARRYING HOWARD'S BREASTWORKS.

About sunrise at Dowdall's I heard cheering. It was a hearty sound, with too much bass in it for that of the enemy's charge. It was occasioned by General Hooker, with Colonel Comstock and a few staff-officers, riding along slowly and inspecting the lines. General Sickles says of this: "It is impossible to pass over without mention the irrepressible enthusiasm of the troops for Major-General Hooker, which was evinced in hearty and prolonged cheers as he rode along the lines of the Third, Eleventh, and Twelfth corps."

I was ready, mounted, and with my officers joined the ever-increasing cavalcade. Hooker observed the troops in position; Barlow, who filled the cross-trenches an hour later, had not yet come out of the front line, so that my reserves just at that time were small. Hooker noticed the breastworks, unusually well built by Schurz and Devens. He passed to the extreme right, and then returned by the shortest route. As he looked over the barricades, while receiving the salutes and cheers of the men, he said to me, "How strong! How strong!"

I still had much extension, so that there were gaps along Schurz's and Devens's fronts. Colonel Comstock spoke to me in his quiet way: "General, do close in those spaces!"

I said, "The woods are thick and entangled; will anybody come through there?"

"Oh, they may!"

His suggestion was heeded. During the forenoon General Sickles discovered Jackson's moving column. It was passing toward Orange Court House, so everybody said. Sickles forwarded all reports to General Hooker, who now returned to Chancellorsville. He tried to divine Jackson's purpose.

About midday Sickles received General Hooker's orders to advance south cautiously. Soon after, perhaps by 2 P. M., there was a stronger apprehension

of a conflict, for there was a sharp skirmish in the direction of Catherine
Furnace. The rattle of musketry followed; then in a little time was heard
the booming of cannon. I sent the news to every division and said, " Be
ready."‡ Slocum went forward to the aid of Sickles, and Hancock was behind
him with support. Next, the enemy was reported to be in full retreat.
General Hooker so telegraphed to Sedgwick; Captain Moore, of his staff,
who had gone out with Birney to see the attack upon Jackson, came hurriedly
to me with an order from General Hooker for my reserve brigade, Barlow's.
Major Howard rode rapidly to Sickles, that he might point out exactly
where to locate the brigade. The major was also to ascertain the nearest
route, so as to save time and not weary the men by a circuitous march.

It was already past 4. There was much excitement among the groups of
officers at the different points of observation. We who were at Dowdall's had
been watching the enemy's cavalry, which kept pushing through the woods
just far enough to receive a fire, and then withdrawing. Devens and his brigade and regimental commanders gathered, in various ways, all the information possible, while from a high point they obtained glimpses of a moving
column crossing the Plank road and apparently making off. I sent out scouts,
who returned with reports that the enemy was not more than three or four
miles off, and in motion. Schurz was anxious and, with my approval, moved
a part of his reserves to the north of Hawkins's farm into good position to
cover Devens's flank. Devens held at least two regiments well in hand, for the
same purpose, and Steinwehr's whole division I knew could just face about
and defend the same point. A few companies of cavalry came from Pleasonton. I sent them out. " Go out beyond my right; go far, and let me know
if an assault is coming." All my staff, Asmussen, Meysenberg, Whittlesey,
C. H. Howard, Schofield, Dessauer, Stinson, Schirmer, and Hoffmann, were
keenly on the alert. We had not a very good position, it is true, but we did
expect to make a good strong fight should the enemy come.

General Hooker's circular order to " Slocum and Howard " neither reached
me, nor, to my knowledge, Colonel Meysenberg, my adjutant-general.↓ From
some confused notion it was issued to " Slocum and Howard," when Slocum
was no longer within two miles of me, and had not been in command of my
corps after Hooker's arrival at Chancellorsville. Slocum, naturally supposing
that I had a copy, would not think of forwarding a joint order to me after
that, and certainly no such order came to me. But Generals Devens, Schurz,
and Steinwehr, my division commanders, and myself did precisely what we
should have done had that order come. The three reserve batteries were
put in position, and the infantry reserves were held well in hand for the possible emergency. My aide had now returned from Sickles, near the Furnace,

‡ Devens states in his official report that at intervals between 11 A. M. and 6:30 P. M. he reported to
corps headquarters that the enemy in force was
threatening his front and his right flank.—EDITORS.

↓ See pp. 219 and 220. The original dispatch
is not on file in the War Records Office, but a copy
of it exists in Hooker's " Letters Sent " book and

in one of the two " Letters Received " books of
Howard's headquarters. The entry in Howard's
book appears to have been made in the latter part
of June. In Hooker's book a notation in red ink
reads, " Copy furnished General Howard "; and
the inference is that it was this " copy " that was
entered in Howard's book in June.—EDITORS.

and reported in substance that he (Sickles) was glad to receive the help ; that he was about to make a grand attack, having been for some time driving the enemy, and expected soon a brilliant result; that he desired to place my reënforcement upon his right flank in the forward movement.

Such was the state of things when, through Captain Moore, General Hooker directed to Sickles's attack, at the Furnace, all of my general infantry reserves, consisting of Barlow's stanch brigade. Steinwehr and I, with Major Howard as guide, went far enough southward to see what was to be done with our men, and to see if Steinwehr's di-

vision, as was probable, must swing in to the left in support of Sickles's promised attack. There was no real battle there, so we returned rapidly to our post at the tavern and dismounted.

Meanwhile the Confederate General Rodes had been reaching his place in the Wilderness. At 4 P. M. his men were in position; the line of battle of his own brigade touched the pike west of us with its right and stretched away to the north ; beyond his brigade came Iverson's in the same line. On the right of the pike was Doles's brigade, and to his right Colquitt's. One hundred yards to the rear was Trimble's division (Col-

MAJOR-GENERAL CARL SCHURZ. FROM A PHOTOGRAPH.

ston commanding), with Ramseur on the right following Colquitt. After another interval followed the division of A. P. Hill. The advance Confederate division had more men in it than there were in the Eleventh Corps, now in position. Counting the ranks of this formidable column, beginning with the enveloping skirmish line, we find 7, besides the 3 ranks of file-closers. Many of them were brought into a solid mass by the entanglements of the forest, and gave our men the idea that battalions were formed in close columns doubled on the center. With as little noise as possible, a little after 5 P. M., the steady advance of the enemy began. Its first lively effects, like a cloud of dust driven before a coming shower, appeared in the startled rabbits, squirrels, quail, and other game flying wildly hither and thither in evident terror, and escaping, where possible, into adjacent clearings.

The foremost men of Doles's brigade took about half an hour to strike our advance picket on the pike. This picket, of course, created no delay. Fifteen minutes later he reached our skirmishers, who seem to have resisted effectively for a few minutes, for it required a main line to dislodge them. Doles says, concerning the next check he received, " After a resistance of about ten minutes we drove him [Devens] from his position on the left and carried his battery of two guns, caissons, and horses."

This was the fire that Steinwehr and I heard shortly after our return from Barlow. Somebody's guns thundered away for a few short minutes, and then came the fitful rattle of musketry; and before I could again get into the saddle there arose the ceaseless roar of the terrible storm.

I sent out my chief-of-staff, Colonel Asmussen, who was the first officer to mount,—"The firing is in front of Devens, go and see if all is in order on the extreme right." He instantly turned and galloped away. I mounted and set off for a prominent place in rear of Schurz's line, so as to change front to the north-west of every brigade south-east of the point of attack, if the attack should extend beyond Devens's right flank; for it was divined at once that the enemy was now west of him. I could see numbers of our men—not the few stragglers that always fly like chaff at the first breeze, but scores of them—rushing into the opening, some with arms and some without, running or falling before they got behind the cover of Devens's reserves, and before General Schurz's waiting masses could deploy or charge. The noise and the smoke filled the air with excitement, and to add to it Dieckmann's guns and caissons, with battery men scattered, rolled and tumbled like runaway wagons and carts in a thronged city. The guns and the masses of the right brigade struck the second line of Devens before McLean's front had given way; and, more quickly than it could be told, with all the fury of the wildest hailstorm, everything, every sort of organization that lay in the path of the mad current of panic-stricken men,⟩ had to give way and be broken into fragments.

My own horse seemed to catch the fury; he sprang—he rose high on his hind legs and fell over, throwing me to the ground. My aide-de-camp, Dessauer, was struck by a shot and killed, and for a few moments I was as helpless as any of the men who were speeding without arms to the rear. But faithful orderlies helped me to remount. Schurz was still doing all he could to face regiments about and send them to Devens's northern flank to help the few who still held firm. Devens, already badly wounded, and several officers were doing similar work. I rode quickly to the reserve batteries. A staff-officer of General Hooker, Lieutenant-Colonel Joseph Dickinson, Assistant Adjutant-General, joined me there; my own staff gathered around me. I was eager to fill the trenches that Barlow would have held. Buschbeck's second line was ordered to change front there. His men kept their ranks, but at first they appeared slow. Would they never get there!

Dickinson said, "Oh, General, see those men coming from that hill way off to the right, and there's the enemy after them. Fire, oh, fire at them; you may stop the flight!"

"No, Colonel," I said, "I will never fire on my own men!"

⟩ Colonel von Gilsa's report of the crisis is as follows:

" . . . A patrol of the 45th New York regiment reported masses of the enemy in an open field opposite my line. I reported this fact at once to the division commander, and at the same moment my skirmishers were driven in by overwhelming forces of the enemy. The whole line at once became engaged furiously, and my brigade stood bravely, fired three times, and stood still until after they had outflanked me on my right.

"The enemy attacked now from the front and rear, and then of course my brave boys were obliged to fall back, the 54th New York and the right wing of the 153d Pennsylvania forcing their way back through the enemy's skirmishers in their rear. . . . Retreating I expected surely to rally my brigade behind our second line, formed by the Third Division, but I did not find the second line; it was abandoned before we reached it."

Von Gilsa's brigade lost 133 killed and wounded out of an effective of 1400 men.— EDITORS.

As soon as our men were near enough the batteries opened, firing at first shells and then canister over their heads. As the attacking force emerged from the forest and rushed on, the men in front would halt and fire, and, while these were reloading, another set would run before them, halt and fire, in no regular line, but in such multitudes that our men went down before them like trees in a hurricane.

By extraordinary effort we had filled all our long line of cross-intrenchments, mainly with fragments of organizations and individual soldiers. Many officers running away stopped there and did what they could, but others shouted, "We've done all we can," and ran on. Schirmer managed

1. UNION BREASTWORKS IN THE WOODS BETWEEN DOWDALL'S TAVERN AND CHANCELLORSVILLE.

2. RELICS OF THE DEAD IN THE WOODS NEAR THE PLANK ROAD.

3. THE PLANK ROAD NEAR WHERE JACKSON FELL.

FROM PHOTOGRAPHS TAKEN IN 1864.

the reserve artillery fairly. Dilger, the battery commander on Schurz's left, rolled the balls along the Plank road and shelled the wood. General Steinwehr was on hand, cool, collected, and judicious. Like Blair at Atlanta, he had made his men (who were south of Dowdall's) spring to the reverse side of their intrenchments and be ready to fire the instant it was possible.

Let us pause here a moment and follow Doles, who led the enemy's attack. He states that, after his first success-

⌐ General Schurz states in his report that the masses which were rallied here were reorganized and led forward two or three times, but were dispersed by the enemy's flank fire.—EDITORS.

ful charge, "the command moved forward at the double-quick to assault the enemy, who had taken up a strong position on the crest of a hill in the open field." This position was the one on Hawkins's farm where Devens's and Schurz's reserves began their fight. But wave after wave of Confederate infantry came upon them, and even their left flank was unprotected the instant the runaways had passed it. To our sorrow, we, who had eagerly observed their bravery, saw these reserves also give way, and the hill and crest on Hawkins's farm were quickly in the hands of the men in gray. ☆

Doles, who must have been a cool man to see so clearly amid the screeching shells and all the hot excitement of battle, says again: "He" (meaning our forces from Schimmelfennig's and Buschbeck's brigades, and perhaps part of McLean's, who had faced about and had not yet given way) "made a stubborn resistance from behind a wattling fence on a hill covered thickly with pines."

Among the stubborn fighters at this place was Major Jeremiah Williams. The enemy was drawing near him. His men fired with coolness and deliberation. His right rested among scrubby bushes and saplings, while his left was in comparatively open ground. The fire of the approaching enemy was murderous, and almost whole platoons of our men were falling; yet they held their ground. Williams waited, rapidly firing, till not more than thirty paces intervened, and then ordered the retreat. Out of 333 men and 16 commissioned officers in the regiment (the 25th Ohio), 130, including 5 officers, were killed or wounded. Major Williams brought a part of the living to the breastworks near me; the remainder, he says, were carried off to the rear by another regimental commander.

During the delays we had thus far caused to the first division of our enemy, all his rear lines had closed up, and the broad mass began to appear even below me on my left front to the south of Steinwehr's knoll. Then it was, after we had been fighting an hour, that Sickles's and Pleasonton's guns began to be heard, for they had faced about at Hazel Grove obliquely toward the north-west, and were hurrying artillery, cavalry, and infantry into position to do what they could against the attack now reaching them.

I had come to my last practicable stand. The Confederates were slowly advancing, firing as they came. The twelve guns of Schirmer, the corps chief of artillery, increased by a part of Dilger's battery, fired, at first with rapidity; but the battery men kept falling from death and wounds. Suddenly, as if by an order, when a sheet of the enemy's fire reached them, a large number of the men in the supporting trenches vacated their positions and went off.

No officers ever made more strenuous exertions than those that my staff and myself put forth to stem the tide of retreat and refill those trenches,

☆ In justice to the men of Devens's division who first resisted Doles it should be stated that the official report of the latter shows that his column was engaged at the outset by Union skirmishers, and "subjected to a heavy musketry fire, with grape, canister, and shell."—EDITORS.

but the panic was too great. Then our artillery fire became weaker and weaker.

I next ordered a retreat to the edge of the forest toward Chancellorsville, so as to uncover Steinwehr's knoll, the only spot yet firmly held. The batteries, except four pieces, were drawn off and hurried to the rear. The stand at the edge of the forest was necessarily a short one.

General Steinwehr, being now exposed from flank and rear, having held his place for over an hour, drew off his small remnants and all moved rapidly through openings and woods, through low ground and swamps, the two miles to the first high land south of Hooker's headquarters.

Captain Hubert Dilger with his battery sturdily kept along the Plank road, firing constantly as he retired. The Confederate masses rushed after us in the forest and along all paths and roads with triumphant shouts and redoubled firing, and so secured much plunder and many prisoners.

It was after sundown and growing dark when I met General Hiram G.

POSITIONS OF THE 12TH CORPS AND PART OF THE 3D CORPS, COVERING THE CHANCELLORSVILLE PLATEAU, MAY 2 AND 3.

Berry, commanding a division of the Third Corps, as I was ascending the high ground above named. "Well, General, where now?" he asked. "You take the right of this road and I will take the left and try to defend it," I replied.

Our batteries, with many others, were on the crest facing to the rear, and as soon as Steinwehr's troops had cleared the way these guns began a terrible cannonade and continued it into the night. They fired into the forest, now full of Confederates, all disorganized by their exciting chase, and every effort of the enemy to advance in that direction in the face of the fire was effectually barred by the artillery and supporting troops.

Stonewall Jackson fell that evening from bullet-wounds, in the forest in front of Berry's position. And here, on the forenoon of the next day, May 3d, the gallant General Berry met his death. It was here, too, that officers of the Eleventh Corps, though mortified by defeat, successfully rallied the scattered brigades and divisions, and, after shielding the batteries, went during the night to replace the men of the Fifth Corps and thereafter defend the left of the general line.

Twenty-three years ago, in my report to General Hooker, I wrote the following:

"Now, as to the causes of this disaster to my corps: 1st. Though constantly threatened and apprised of the moving of the enemy, yet the woods were so dense that he was able to mass a large force, whose exact whereabouts ⅃ neither patrols, reconnoissances, nor scouts ascertained. He succeeded in forming a column opposite to and outflanking my right.

"2d. By the panic produced by the enemy's reverse fire, regiments and artillery were thrown suddenly upon those in position.

"3d. The absence of General Barlow's brigade, which I had previously located in reserve and *en échelon* with Colonel von Gilsa's, so as to cover his right flank. This was the only general reserve I had."

Stonewall Jackson was victorious. Even his enemies praise him; but, providentially for us, it was the last battle that he waged against the American Union. For, in bold planning, in energy of execution, which he had the power to diffuse, in indefatigable activity and moral ascendency, Jackson stood head and shoulders above his confrères, and after his death General Lee could not replace him.

⅃ General Devens's report is very explicit upon this point, and states as follows:

"Colonel von Gilsa's skirmishers were, between 3 and 4 o'clock in the afternoon, attacked by the skirmishers of the enemy with the evident intention of feeling our position. After this Colonel von Gilsa's skirmishers were pushed farther to the front, and the major-general commanding the corps again rode down the line. After his return a company of cavalry was sent me for the purpose of making further examination of the woods, which examination, though not thoroughly made, was still sufficient to show that the enemy's cavalry were deployed along the front of my First Brigade, accompanied by some pieces of horse artillery. I directed the captain commanding the cavalry to return and report at corps headquarters."

See also note on p. 198.—EDITORS.

RESCUING THE WOUNDED ON SUNDAY, MAY 3D, FROM THE BURNING WOODS.
FROM A WAR-TIME SKETCH.

STONEWALL JACKSON'S LAST BATTLE.

BY THE REV. JAMES POWER SMITH, CAPTAIN AND ASSISTANT ADJUTANT-GENERAL, C. S. A.

STONEWALL JACKSON'S
CAP.

Major Jed. Hotchkiss, who owns the "old gray cap," writes that Jackson wore it through the Valley, Seven Days, and Second Manassas campaigns. At Frederick City, in the Antietam campaign, he bought a soft hat for his general, who, at Fredericksburg, gave him the cap as a souvenir.— EDITORS.

AT daybreak on the morning of the 29th of April, 1863, sleeping in our tents at corps headquarters, near Hamilton's Crossing, we were aroused by Major Samuel Hale, of Early's staff, with the stirring news that Federal troops were crossing the Rappahannock on pontoons under cover of a heavy fog. General Jackson had spent the night at Mr. Yerby's hospitable mansion near by, where Mrs. Jackson [his second wife] had brought her infant child for the father to see. He was at once informed of the news, and promptly issued to his division commanders orders to prepare for action. At his direction I rode a mile across the fields to army headquarters, and finding General Robert E. Lee still slumbering quietly, at the suggestion of Colonel Venable, whom I found stirring, I entered the general's tent and awoke him. Turning his feet out of his cot he sat upon its side as I gave him the tidings from the front. Expressing no surprise, he playfully said: "Well, I thought I heard firing, and was beginning to think it was time some of you young fellows were coming to tell me what it was all about. Tell your good general that I am sure he knows what to do. I will meet him at the front very soon."

It was Sedgwick who had crossed, and, marching along the river front to impress us with his numbers, was now intrenching his line on the river road, under cover of Federal batteries on the north bank.

All day long we lay in the old lines of the action of December preceding, watching the operation of the enemy. Nor did we move through the next day, the 30th of April. During the forenoon of the 29th General Lee had been informed by General J. E. B. Stuart of the movement in force by General Hooker across the Rappahannock upon Chancellorsville; and during the night of Thursday, April 30th, General Jackson withdrew his corps, leaving Early and his division with Barksdale's brigade to hold the old lines from Hamilton's Crossing along the rear of Fredericksburg.

By the light of a brilliant moon, at midnight, that passed into an early dawn of dense mist, the troops were moved, by the Old Mine road, out of sight of the enemy, and about 11 A. M. of Friday, May 1st, they reached Anderson's position, confronting Hooker's advance from Chancellorsville, near the Tabernacle Church on the Plank road. To meet the whole Army of the Potomac, under Hooker, General Lee had of all arms about 60,000 men. General Longstreet, with part of his corps, was absent below Petersburg. General Lee had two divisions of Longstreet's corps, Anderson's, and McLaws's, and Jackson's corps, consisting of four divisions, A. P. Hill's, D. H. Hill's, commanded by Rodes, Trimble's, commanded by Colston, and Early's;

LEE AND JACKSON IN COUNCIL ON THE NIGHT OF MAY 1.

and about 170 pieces of field-artillery. The divisions of Anderson and McLaws had been sent from Fredericksburg to meet Hooker's advance from Chancellorsville; Anderson on Wednesday, and McLaws (except Barksdale's brigade, left with Early) on Thursday. At the Tabernacle Church, about four miles east of Chancellorsville, the opposing forces met and brisk skirmishing began. On Friday, Jackson, reaching Anderson's position, took command of the Confederate advance, and urged on his skirmish line under Brigadier-General Ramseur with great vigor. How the muskets rattled along a front of a mile or two, across the unfenced fields, and through the woodlands! What spirit was imparted to the line, and what cheers rolled along its length, when Jackson, and then Lee himself, appeared riding abreast of the line along the Plank road! Slowly but steadily the line advanced, until at night-fall all Federal pickets and skirmishers were driven back upon the body of Hooker's force at Chancellorsville.

Here we reached a point, a mile and a half from Hooker's lines, where a road turns down to the left toward the old Catherine Furnace [see map, p. 158]; and here at the fork of the roads General Lee and General Jackson spent the night, resting on the pine straw, curtained only by the close shadow of the pine forest. A little after night-fall I was sent by General Lee upon an errand to General A. P. Hill, on the old stone turnpike a mile or two north; and returning some time later with information of matters on our right, I found General Jackson retired to rest, and General Lee sleeping at the foot of a tree, covered with his army cloak. As I aroused the sleeper, he slowly sat up on the ground and said, "Ah, Captain, you have returned, have you? Come here and tell me what you have learned on the right." Laying his hand on me he drew me down by his side, and, passing his arm around my shoulder, drew me near to him in a fatherly way that told of his warm and kindly heart. When I had related such information as I had secured for him, he thanked me for accomplishing his commission, and then said he regretted that the young men about General Jackson had not relieved him of annoyance, by finding a battery of the enemy which had harassed our advance, adding that the young men of that day were not equal to what they were when he was a young man. Seeing immediately that he was jesting and disposed to rally me, as he often did young officers, I broke away from the hold on me which he tried to retain, and, as he laughed heartily through the stillness of the night, I went off to make a bed of my saddle-blanket, and, with my head in my saddle, near my horse's feet, was soon wrapped in the heavy slumber of a wearied soldier.

Some time after midnight I was awakened by the chill of the early morning hours, and, turning over, caught a glimpse of a little flame on the slope above me, and sitting up to see what it meant, I saw, bending over a scant fire of twigs, two men seated on old cracker boxes and warming their hands over the little fire. I had but to rub my eyes and collect my wits to recognize the figures of Robert E. Lee and Stonewall Jackson. Who can tell the story of that quiet council of war between two sleeping armies? Nothing remains on record to tell of plans discussed, and dangers weighed, and a great purpose formed, but the story of the great day so soon to follow.

It was broad daylight, and the thick beams of yellow sunlight came through the pine branches, when some one touched me rudely with his foot, saying: "Get up, Smith, the general wants you!" As I leaped to my feet the rhythmic click of the canteens of marching infantry caught my ear. Already in motion! What could it mean? In a moment I was mounted and at the side of the general, who sat on his horse by the roadside, as the long line of our troops cheerily, but in silence as directed, poured down the Furnace road. His cap was pulled low over his eyes, and, looking up from under the visor, with lips compressed, indicating the firm purpose within, he nodded to me, and in brief and rapid utterance, without a superfluous word, as though all were distinctly formed in his mind and beyond question, he gave me orders for our wagon and ambulance trains. From the open fields in our rear, at the head of the Catharpin road, all trains were to be moved upon that road to Todd's Tavern, and thence west by interior roads, so that our troops would be between them and the enemy at Chancellorsville. My orders having been delivered and the trains set in motion, I returned to the site of our night's bivouac, to find that General Jackson and his staff had followed the marching column.

Slow and tedious is the advance of a mounted officer who has to pass, in narrow wood roads through dense thickets, the packed column of marching infantry, to be recognized all along the line and good-naturedly chaffed by many a gay-spirited fellow: "Say, here's one of Old Jack's little boys, let him by, boys!" in the most patronizing tone. "Have a good breakfast this morning, sonny?" "Better hurry up, or you'll catch it for getting behind." "Tell Old Jack we're all a-comin'." "Don't let him begin the fuss till we get thar!" And so on, until about 3 P. M., after a ride of ten miles of tortuous road, I found the general, seated on a stump by the Brock road, writing this dispatch, which, through the courtesy of the Virginia State Library, is here given in fac-simile:

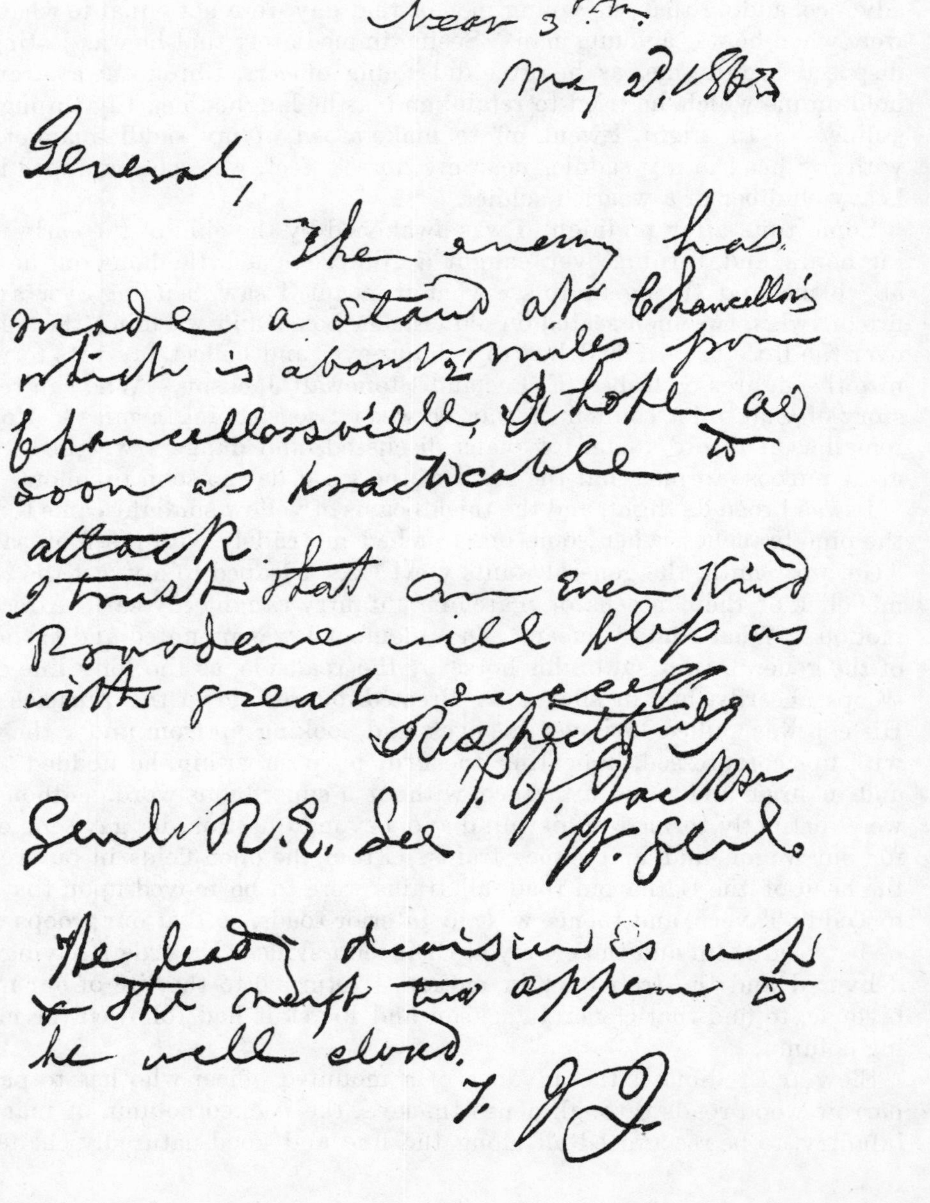

Near 3 P.M.
May 2, 1863

General,

The enemy has made a stand at Chancellor's which is about 2 miles from Chancellorsville, I hope as soon as practicable to attack.
I trust that an ever Kind Providence will bless us with great success.
Respectfully
T. J. Jackson
W. Genl.
Genl R. E. Lee

The leading division is up & the next two appear to be well closed.
T. J. J.

LIEUTENANT-GENERAL THOMAS JONATHAN JACKSON, C. S. A. FROM A PHOTOGRAPH
TAKEN IN WINCHESTER, VA., IN 1862.

The place here mentioned as Chancellor's was also known as Dowdall's Tavern. It was the farm of the Rev. Melzi Chancellor, two miles west of Chancellorsville, and the Federal force found here and at Talley's, a mile farther west, was the Eleventh Corps, under General Howard. General Fitz Lee, with cavalry scouts, had advanced until he had view of the position of Howard's corps, and found them unsuspicious of attack.

Reaching the Orange Plank road, General Jackson himself rode with Fitz Lee to reconnoiter the position of Howard, and then sent the Stonewall brigade of Virginia troops, under Brigadier-General Paxton, to hold the point where the Germanna Plank road obliquely enters the Orange road. Leading the main column of his force farther on the Brock road to the old turnpike, the head of the column turned sharply eastward toward Chancellorsville. [See maps, pp. 158, 191.] About a mile had been passed, when he halted and began the disposition of his forces to attack Howard. Rodes's division, at the head of the column, was thrown into line of battle, with Colston's forming the second line and A. P. Hill's the third, while the artillery under Colonel Stapleton Crutchfield moved in column on the road, or was parked in a field on the right. The well-trained skirmishers of Rodes's division, under Major Eugene Blackford, were thrown to the front. It must have been between 5 and 6 o'clock in the evening, Saturday, May 2d, when these dispositions were completed. Upon his stout-built, long-paced little sorrel, General Jackson sat, with visor low over his eyes and lips compressed, and with his watch in his hand. Upon his right sat General Robert E. Rodes, the very picture of a soldier, and every inch all that he appeared. Upon the right of Rodes sat Major Blackford.

"Are you ready, General Rodes?" said Jackson.

"Yes, sir!" said Rodes, impatient for the advance.

"You can go forward then," said Jackson.

A nod from Rodes was order enough for Blackford, and then suddenly the woods rang with the bugle call, and back came the responses from bugles on the right and left, and the long line of skirmishers, through the wild thicket of undergrowth, sprang eagerly to their work, followed promptly by the quick steps of the line of battle. For a moment all the troops seemed buried in the depths of the gloomy forest, and then suddenly the echoes waked and swept the country for miles, never failing until heard at the headquarters of Hooker at Chancellorsville — the wild "rebel yell" of the long Confederate lines.

STONEWALL JACKSON'S "OLD SORREL."

This picture is from a photograph taken at the Maryland State Fair at Hagerstown, in 1884. At that time "Old Sorrel" was thought to be about thirty-four years old. At the fair, relic-hunters plucked away much of his mane and tail.—EDITORS.

Never was assault delivered with grander enthusiasm. Fresh from the long winter's waiting, and confident from the preparation of the spring, the troops were in fine condition and in high spirits. The boys were all back from home or sick leave. "Old Jack" was there upon the road in their midst; there could be no mistake and no failure. And there were Rodes and A. P. Hill. Had they not seen and cheered, as long and as loud as they were permitted, the gay-hearted Stuart and the long-bearded Fitz Lee on his fiery charger? Was not Crutchfield's array of brass and iron "dogs of war" at hand, with Poague and Palmer, and all the rest, ready to bark loud and deep with half a chance?

Alas! for Howard and his unformed lines, and his brigades with guns stacked, and officers at dinner or asleep under the trees, and butchers deep in the blood of beeves! Scattered through field and forest, his men were preparing their evening meal.⸗ A little show of earth-work facing the south was quickly taken by us in reverse from the west. Flying battalions are not

⸗ But see notes, pp. 198 and 202.— EDITORS.

flying buttresses for an army's stability. Across Talley's fields the rout begins. Over at Hawkins's hill, on the north of the road, Carl Schurz makes a stand, soon to be driven into the same hopeless panic. By the quiet Wilderness Church in the vale, leaving wounded and dead everywhere, by Melzi Chancellor's, on into the deep thicket again, the Confederate lines pressed forward,—now broken and all disaligned by the density of bush that tears the clothes away; now halting to load and deliver a volley upon some regiment or fragment of the enemy that will not move as fast as others. Thus the attack upon Hooker's flank was a grand success, beyond the most sanguine expectation.

The writer of this narrative, an aide-de-camp of Jackson's, was ordered to remain at the point where the advance began, to be a center of communication be-

BRIGADIER-GENERAL E. F. PAXTON, COMMANDING THE "STONEWALL" BRIGADE OF COLSTON'S DIVISION, KILLED MAY 3. FROM A TINTYPE.

tween the general and the cavalry on the flanks, and to deliver orders to detachments of artillery still moving up from the rear. A fine black charger, with elegant trappings, deserted by his owner and found tied to a tree, became mine only for that short and eventful night-fall; and about 8 P. M., in the twilight, thus comfortably mounted, I gathered my couriers about me and went forward to find General Jackson. The storm of battle had swept far on to the east and become more and more faint to the ear, until silence came with night over the fields and woods. As I rode along that old turnpike, passing scattered fragments of Confederates looking for their regiments, parties of prisoners concentrating under guards, wounded men by the roadside and under the trees at Talley's and Chancellor's, I had reached an open field on the right, a mile west of Chancellorsville, when, in the dusky twilight, I saw horsemen near an old cabin in the field. Turning toward them, I found Rodes and his staff engaged in gathering the broken and scattered troops that had swept the two miles of battle-field. " General Jackson is just ahead on the road, Captain," said Rodes; " tell him I will be here at this cabin if I am wanted." I had not gone a hundred yards before I heard firing, a shot or two, and then a company volley upon the right of the road, and another upon the left. A few moments farther on I met Captain

STONEWALL JACKSON GOING FORWARD ON THE PLANK ROAD IN ADVANCE OF HIS LINE OF BATTLE.

Murray Taylor, an aide of A. P. Hill's, with tidings that Jackson and Hill were wounded, and some around them killed, by the fire of their own men. Spurring my horse into a sweeping gallop, I soon passed the Confederate line of battle, and, some three or four rods on its front, found the general's horse beside a pine sapling on the left, and a rod beyond a little party of men caring for a wounded officer. The story of the sad event is briefly told, and, in essentials, very much as it came to me from the lips of the wounded general himself, and in everything confirmed and completed by those who were eye-witnesses and near companions.

When Jackson had reached the point where his line now crossed the turnpike, scarcely a mile west of Chancellorsville, and not half a mile from a line of Federal troops, he had found his front line unfit for the farther and vigorous advance he desired, by reason of the irregular character of the fighting, now right, now left, and because of the dense thickets, through which it was impossible to preserve alignment. Division commanders found it more and more difficult as the twilight deepened to hold their broken brigades in hand. Regretting the necessity of relieving the troops in front, General Jackson had ordered A. P. Hill's division, his third and reserve line, to be placed in front. While this change was being effected, impatient and anxious, the general rode forward on the turnpike, followed by two or three of his staff and a number of couriers and signal sergeants. He passed the swampy depression and began the ascent of the hill toward Chancellorsville, when he came upon a line of the Federal infantry lying on their arms. Fired at by one or two muskets (two musket-balls from the enemy whistled over my head as I came to the front), he turned and came back toward his line, upon the side of the road to his left. As he rode near to the Confederate troops, just placed in position and ignorant that he was in the front, the

MAJOR-GENERAL R. E. COLSTON, C. S. A.
FROM A PHOTOGRAPH.

left company began firing to the front, and two of his party fell from their saddles dead—Captain Boswell, of the Engineers, and Sergeant Cunliffe, of the Signal Corps. Spurring his horse across the road to his right, he was met by a second volley from the right company of Pender's North Carolina brigade. Under this volley, when not two rods from the troops, the general received three balls at the same instant. One penetrated the palm of his right hand and was cut out that night from the back of his hand. A second passed around the wrist of the left arm and out through the left hand. A third ball passed through the left arm half-way from shoulder to elbow. The large bone of the upper arm was splintered to the elbow-joint, and the wound bled freely. His horse turned quickly from the fire, through the thick bushes which swept the cap from the general's head, and scratched his forehead, leaving drops of blood to stain his face. As he lost his hold upon the bridle-rein, he reeled from the saddle, and was caught by the arms of Captain Wilbourn, of the Signal Corps. Laid upon the ground, there came at once to his succor General A. P. Hill and members of his staff. The writer reached his side a minute after, to find General Hill holding the head and shoulders of the wounded chief. Cutting open the coat-sleeve from wrist to shoulder, I found the wound in the upper arm, and with my handkerchief I bound the arm above the wound to stem the flow of blood. Couriers were sent for Dr. Hunter McGuire, the surgeon of the corps and the general's trusted friend, and for an ambulance. Being outside of our lines, it was urgent that he should be moved at once. With difficulty litter-bearers were brought from the line near by, and the general was placed upon the litter and carefully raised

BRIGADIER-GENERAL F. T. NICHOLLS, C. S. A.
FROM A PHOTOGRAPH.

to the shoulder, I myself bearing one corner. A moment after, artillery from the Federal side was opened upon us; great broadsides thundered over the woods; hissing shells searched the dark thickets through, and shrapnels swept the road along which we moved. Two or three steps farther, and the litter-bearer at my side was struck and fell, but, as the litter turned, Major Watkins Leigh, of Hill's staff, happily caught it. But the fright of the men was so great that we were obliged to lay the litter and its burden down upon the road. As the litter-bearers ran to the cover of the trees, I threw myself by the general's side and held him firmly to the ground as he attempted to rise. Over us swept the rapid fire of shot and shell — grape-shot striking fire upon the flinty rock of the road all around us, and sweeping from their feet horses and men of the artillery just moved to the front. Soon the firing veered to the other side of the road, and I sprang to my feet, assisted the general to rise, passed my arm around him, and with the wounded man's weight thrown heavily upon me, we forsook the road. Entering the woods, he sank to the ground from exhaustion, but the litter was soon brought, and again rallying a few men, we essayed to carry him farther, when a second bearer fell at my side. This time, with none to assist, the litter careened, and the general fell to the ground, with a groan of deep pain. Greatly alarmed, I sprang to his head, and, lifting his head as a stray beam of moonlight came through clouds and leaves, he opened his eyes and wearily said: "Never mind me, Captain, never mind me." Raising him again to his feet, he was accosted by Brigadier-General Pender: "Oh, General, I hope you are not seriously wounded. I will have to retire my troops to re-form them, they are so much broken by this fire." But Jackson, rallying his strength, with firm voice said: "You must hold your ground, General Pender; you must hold your ground, sir!" and so uttered his last command on the field.

THE NEW CHANCELLOR HOUSE.

This picture is from a photograph taken at a reunion of Union and Confederate officers and soldiers in May, 1884. The original house (see p. 190) was set on fire by Confederate shells on Sunday, May 3d, shortly after Hooker was injured while standing on the porch. The picture faces south; Jackson attacked the Eleventh Corps from the left (west) by the Plank road, which passes in front of the Chancellor House. The cross-road in the foreground leads northward to Ely's Ford and United States Ford. See map, p. 158.— EDITORS.

Again we resorted to the litter, and with difficulty bore it through the bush, and then under a hot fire along the road. Soon an ambulance was reached, and stopping to seek some stimulant at Chancellor's (Dowdall's Tavern), we were found by Dr. McGuire, who at once took charge of the wounded man. Passing back over the battle-field of the afternoon, we reached the Wilderness store, and then, in a field on the north, the field-hospital of our corps under Dr. Harvey Black. Here we found a tent prepared, and after midnight the left arm was amputated near the shoulder, and a ball taken from the right hand.

All night long it was mine to watch by the sufferer, and keep him warmly wrapped and undisturbed in his sleep. At 9 A. M., on the next day, when he aroused, cannon firing again filled the air, and all the Sunday through the fierce battle raged, General J. E. B. Stuart commanding the Confederates in Jackson's place. A dispatch was sent to the commanding general to announce formally his disability,— tidings General Lee had received during the night with profound grief. There came back the following note:

"GENERAL: I have just received your note, informing me that you were wounded. I cannot express my regret at the occurrence. Could I have directed events, I should have chosen, for the good of the country, to have been disabled in your stead. I congratulate you upon the victory which is due to your skill and energy. Most truly yours, R. E. LEE, GENERAL."

When this dispatch was handed to me at the tent, and I read it aloud, General Jackson turned his face away and said, "General Lee is very kind, but he should give the praise to God."

The long day was passed with bright hopes for the wounded general, with tidings of success on the battle-field, with sad news of losses, and messages to and from other wounded officers brought to the same infirmary.

On Monday the general was carried in an ambulance, by way of Spotsylvania Court House, to most comfortable lodging at Chandler's, near Guinea's Station, on the Richmond, Fredericksburg and Potomac railroad. And here, against our hopes, notwithstanding the skill and care of wise and watchful surgeons, attended day and night by wife and friends, amid the prayers and tears of all the Southern land, thinking not of himself, but of the cause he loved, and for the troops who had followed him so well and given him so great a name, our chief sank, day by day, with symptoms of pneumonia and some pains of pleurisy, until, at 3:15 P. M. on the quiet of the Sabbath afternoon, May 10th, 1863, he raised himself from his bed, saying, "No, no, let us pass over the river, and rest under the shade of the trees"; and, falling again to his pillow, he passed away, "over the river, where, in a land where warfare is not known or feared, he rests forever 'under the trees.'"

His shattered arm was buried in the family burying-ground of the Ellwood place—Major J. H. Lacy's—near his last battle-field.

His body rests, as he himself asked, "in Lexington, in the Valley of Virginia." The spot where he was so fatally wounded in the shades of the Wilderness is marked by a large quartz rock, placed there by the care of his chaplain and friend, the Rev. Dr. B. T. Lacy, and the latter's brother, Major Lacy.

Others must tell the story of Confederate victory at Chancellorsville. It has been mine only, as in the movement of that time, so with my pen now, to follow my general himself. Great, the world believes him to have been in many elements of generalship; he was greatest and noblest in that he was good, and, without a selfish thought, gave his talent and his life to a cause that, as before the God he so devoutly served, he deemed right and just.

STONEWALL JACKSON'S GRAVE, LEXINGTON, VA.   FROM A PHOTOGRAPH.

HOOKER'S COMMENTS ON CHANCELLORSVILLE.

BY SAMUEL P. BATES, HIS LITERARY EXECUTOR.

LANCE USED BY THE 6TH PENNSYLVANIA
CAVALRY. (RUSH'S LANCERS).

IN October, 1876, I accompanied General Hooker to the battle-fields of Fredericksburg, Chancellorsville, and Antietam,— fields on which he had borne conspicuous parts. It was the only occasion on which he visited them after the battles. He had previously placed in my hands his official papers and memoranda for the preparation of a history of the Battle of Chancellorsville, at the same time requesting me to make this journey with him, that I might have the advantage of a thorough knowledge of the field, and of his interpretation of the manner in which the battle was fought. At this period he was partly paralyzed from the injury received in the Chancellorsville battle, and he could move only with great difficulty by the aid of his valet.

After our arrival at Fredericksburg, General Hooker was the recipient of many courteous attentions from the leading citizens, and at night he was serenaded, when a great crowd assembled in front of the hotel, to whose repeated cheers he made a brief response, in which he said that he had visited their city but once before, and although his reception now was not nearly so warm as on that former day, yet it was far more agreeable to him,—a conceit which greatly pleased his hearers.

Our drive over the Fredericksburg field, which we visited on the way, was on one of the most perfect of autumnal days, and at every turn fresh reminiscences of that battle were suggested. As we approached the flag-staff of the National Cemetery, on the hill adjoining Marye's Heights, where more than fifteen thousand of the Union dead of Fredericksburg, Chancellorsville, the Wilderness, and Spotsylvania are buried, General Hooker said:

"I never think of this ground but with a shudder. The whole scene is indelibly fixed in my mind, as it appeared on that fatal day. Here on this ground were ranged the enemy's cannon, and the heights farther to his left were thickly planted with pieces; all the infantry he could use was disposed behind earthworks and stone walls. How this could have been selected as the point, above all others, for attack, and followed up until four whole divisions had been sacrificed, I cannot comprehend. As I stand here to-day, the impossibility of carrying this ground by direct assault is no more apparent than it was when I made my observation preparatory to ordering Humphreys's division forward. But it is evident that General Burnside never forgave me for counseling him on that occasion as I did, for on January 23d he drew up an order, known as General Orders, No. 8, of his series, dishonorably dismissing me from the service, together with three other prominent general officers, at the same time relieving five other officers from duty. I was grossly maligned by the press of that day, and it was generally believed by the people at the North that I had not faithfully supported General Burnside in this battle, and that I was aiming thereby to supplant him. If these brave men who are sleeping here beneath our feet could speak, they would bear testimony to my sincerity and fidelity to the cause we were battling for; and though I have suffered in silence, and my reputation has been grossly aspersed, I have rested in the firm belief that my conduct on that day would be justified by the American people."

These Orders, No. 8, ⸴ were prepared on the 23d of January, 1863, and would have been immediately promulgated had not General Burnside been counseled first to lay them before President Lincoln, of whom he asked that they be approved, as drawn, or that his own resignation be accepted. The President refused to accept his resignation, but relieved him of the command of the Army of the Potomac; and so little effect had the order upon the mind of Mr. Lincoln that he decided to place Hooker, at whom the shaft was chiefly aimed, at the head of the army. And yet so strong a hold had this unjust opinion on the public mind that even the President was tinctured with it, and in his remarkable letter of January 26th to General Hooker, informing him of his appointment, he said:

"I have placed you at the head of the Army of the Potomac. Of course I have done this upon what appears to me to be sufficient reasons, and yet I think it best for you to know that there are some things in regard to which I am not quite satisfied with you. I believe you to be a brave and skillful soldier, which, of course, I like. I also believe you do not mix politics with

⸴ Following is the text of the orders: "HEAD-QUARTERS, ARMY OF THE POTOMAC, January 23d, 1863. GENERAL ORDERS, No. 8. (1.) General Joseph Hooker, major-general of volunteers and brigadier-general, U. S. Army, having been guilty of unjust and unnecessary criticisms of the actions of his superior officers, and of the authorities, and having, by the general tone of his conversation, endeavored to create distrust in the minds of officers who have associated with him, and having, by omissions and otherwise, made reports and statements which were calculated to create incorrect impressions, and for habitually speaking in disparaging terms of other officers, is hereby dismissed the service of the United States as a man unfit to hold an important commission during a crisis like the present, when so much patience, charity, confidence, consideration, and patriotism are due from every soldier in the field. This order is issued subject to the approval of the President of the United States. (2.) Brigadier-General W. T. H. Brooks, commanding First Division, Sixth Army Corps, for complaining of the policy of the Government, and for using language tending to demoralize his command, is, subject to the approval of the President, dismissed from the mili-

tary service of the United States. (3.) Brigadier-General John Newton, commanding Third Division, Sixth Army Corps, and Brigadier-General John Cochrane, commanding First Brigade, Third Division, Sixth Army Corps, for going to the President of the United States with criticisms upon the plans of their commanding officer, are, subject to the approval of the President, dismissed from the military service of the United States. (4.) It being evident that the following-named officers can be of no further service to this army, they are hereby relieved from duty, and will report in person, without delay, to the Adjutant-General, U. S. Army: Major-General W. B. Franklin, commanding Left Grand Division; Major-General W. F. Smith, commanding Sixth Corps; Brigadier-General Samuel D. Sturgis, commanding Second Division, Ninth Corps; Brigadier-General Edward Ferrero, commanding Second Brigade, Second Division, Ninth Army Corps; Brigadier-General John Cochrane, commanding First Brigade, Third Division, Sixth Corps; Lieutenant-Colonel J. H. Taylor, Assistant Adjutant-General, Right Grand Division. By command of MAJOR-GENERAL A. E. BURNSIDE. LEWIS RICHMOND, Assistant Adjutant-General." ⚓

⚓ In the "Official Records" the above order is accompanied by the following note of explanation: "This order was not approved by the President, and was, therefore, never issued. It appeared in the public

prints, is referred to in the correspondence between Halleck and Franklin, and in Burnside's testimony before the Committee on the Conduct of the War."
EDITORS.

your profession, in which you are right. You have confidence in yourself, which is a valuable, if not an indispensable, quality. You are ambitious, which, within reasonable bounds, does good rather than harm; but I think that during General Burnside's command of the army you have taken counsel of your ambition, and thwarted him as much as you could, in which you did a great wrong to the country and to a most meritorious and honorable brother officer. I have heard, in such way as to believe it, of your recently saying that both the army and the Government needed a Dictator. Of course it was not for this, but in spite of it, that I have given you the command. Only those generals who gain successes can set up dictators. What I now ask of you is military success, and I will risk the dictatorship. The Government will support you to the utmost of its ability, which is neither more nor less than it has done and will do for all commanders. I much fear that the spirit which you have aided to infuse into the army, of criticising their commander and withholding confidence from him, will now turn upon you. I shall assist you as far as I can to put it down. Neither you nor Napoleon, if he were alive again, could get any good out of an army while such a spirit prevails in it. And now beware of rashness. Beware of rashness, but with energy and sleepless vigilance go forward, and give us victories."

The caution against rashness may have been suggested to the mind of Mr. Lincoln by the epithet of "Fighting Joe Hooker," which the general never heard without expressing his deep regret that it was ever applied to him. "People will think I am a highwayman or a bandit," he said; when in fact he was one of the most kindly and tender-hearted of men.

We were accompanied on our ride to the Chancellorsville field, some ten or twelve miles above Fredericksburg, by Major George E. Chancellor, a son of Melzi Chancellor, whose home at the time of the battle was at Dowdall's Tavern, where General Howard had his headquarters. On setting out, General Hooker suggested that we should take some lunch along with us, as, when he was there last there was very little to eat in all that region. Major Chancellor thought it unnecessary, and, in fact, we were feasted most sumptuously at his father's house.

Upon our arrival at the broad, open, rolling fields opposite Banks's Ford, some three or four miles up the stream, General Hooker exclaimed, waving his hand significantly: "Here, on this open ground, I intended to fight my battle. But the trouble was to get my army on it, as the banks of the stream are, as you see, rugged and precipitous, and the few fords were strongly fortified and guarded by the enemy. By making a powerful demonstration in front of and below the town of Fredericksburg with a part of my army, I was able, unobserved, to withdraw the remainder, and, marching nearly thirty miles up the stream, to cross the Rappahannock and the Rapidan unopposed, and in four days' time to arrive at Chancellorsville, within five miles of this coveted ground,⚓—and all this without General Lee having discovered that I had left my position in his front. So far, I regarded my movement as a

⚓ The demonstrations began on April 21st, and were made at intervals at Kelly's Ford, Rappahannock Bridge, and Port Royal. The movement of Sedgwick below the town was disclosed to Lee on the 29th, when the pontoons were laid and the crossing took place at the point where Franklin's Left Grand Division crossed in December, 1862. Hooker's flanking column, consisting of the Fifth, Eleventh, and Twelfth corps and two divisions of the Second Corps, crossed the Rappahannock at Kelly's Ford on the 28th and 29th by pontoon-bridges, and passed the Rapidan by fording and by means of pontoons, arriving at Chancellorsville on the 30th. The Third Corps, after taking part in the demonstrations before Fredericksburg, crossed the Rappahannock at United States Ford and reached Chancellorsville on May 1st, and was followed by the First Corps on the 2d.—EDITORS.

great success.   On the morning of the fifth day my army was astir, and was put in motion on three lines through the tangled forest (the Wilderness) which covers the whole country around Chancellorsville, and in three hours' time I would have been in position on these crests, and in possession of Banks's Ford, in short and easy communication with the other wing of my army.   But at midnight General Lee had moved out with his whole army, and by sunrise was in firm possession of Banks's Ford, had thrown up this line of breastworks which you can still follow with the eye, and it was bristling with cannon from one end to the other.   Before I had proceeded two miles the heads of my columns, while still upon the narrow roads in these interminable forests, where it was impossible to manœuvre my forces, were met by Jackson with a full two-thirds of the entire Confederate army.   I had no alternative but to turn back, as I had only a fragment of my command in hand, and take up the position about Chancellorsville which I had occupied during the night, as I was being rapidly outflanked upon my right, the enemy having open ground on which to operate.

" And here again my reputation has been attacked because I did not undertake to accomplish an impossibility, but turned back at this point; and every history of the war that has been written has soundly berated me because I did not fight here in the forest with my hands tied behind me, and allow my army to be sacrificed.   I have always believed that impartial history would vindicate my conduct in this emergency."

Soon after leaving the open ground opposite Banks's Ford we entered the dense forest, or " Wilderness," which covers the entire Chancellorsville battle-ground,—" a dense forest," says General Warren, " of not very large trees, but very difficult to get through; mainly of scrubby oak, what they call black-jack there, so that a man could hardly ride through it, and a man could not march through it very well with musket in hand, unless he trailed it."

Every important position was observed and commented upon by the man who on those fierce battle-days had wielded, on this very ground, an army of a hundred thousand men.   On approaching the pine-tree under which Generals Lee and Jackson had planned the mode of attack, General Hooker observed: " It was under that tree that the mischief was devised which came near ruining my army.   My position at Chancellorsville was a good one for this monotonous country.   I felt confident when I reached it that I had eighty chances in a hundred to win.   To make sure that everything was firm and strong, very early on the 2d of May, the first day of the battle, I rode along the whole line, and personally examined every part, suggesting some changes and counseling extreme vigilance.   Upon my return to headquarters I was informed that a continuous column of the enemy had been marching past my front since early in the morning, as of a corps with all its *impedimenta*.   This put an entirely new phase upon the problem, and filled me with apprehension for the safety of my right wing, which was posted to meet a front attack from the south, but was in no condition for a flank attack from the west; for this marching of the enemy's corps, to my mind, meant a flank movement upon my right. I immediately dictated a dispatch ‡ to 'Generals Slocum and Howard,' the latter commanding the Eleventh Corps, which stood upon the extreme right, saying that I had good reason to believe that the enemy was moving to our right, and that they must be ready to meet an attack from the west. This was at 9:30 in the morning. In the course of two hours I got a dispatch from General Howard, saying that he could see a column of the enemy moving westward, and that he was taking the precautions necessary 'to resist an attack from the west.' ♭ I had previously put Williams's division of the Twelfth Corps on an interior line looking westward, and had it fortified, so that if Howard should give way, this interior line would be for safety, as it afterward proved my salvation.

"I sent Sickles to pierce this moving column of the enemy, and made preparations to flank the portion of Lee's army that was still upon my front, in the direction of Fredericksburg, and, sweeping down in reverse, to destroy it if possible. But a swamp intervened which had to be corduroyed, and a small stream had to be bridged, which consumed time; and though Sickles was successful in breaking in upon the enemy's column and making some captures, yet, before he was in position to make his decisive attack, Jackson, who had led his column by a long circuit, out of sight and hearing, through the dense forest, came in upon my right flank, and by one concentrated blow of his whole corps, some 25,000 men, had crushed and put to flight almost the entire corps of Howard; and it was with the utmost difficulty that I could lead up my reserves to the interior line of Williams, and bring Jackson's victorious forces to a halt. This failure of Howard to hold his ground cost us our position, and I was forced, in the presence of the enemy, to take up a new one. Upon investigation I found that Howard had failed properly to obey my instructions to prepare to meet the enemy from the west." In this connection the following extracts from a letter to Hooker from Schurz (who subsequently gave General Hooker leave to print it) will be read with interest:

"40 W. 32D ST., NEW YORK, April 22d, 1876.

"MY DEAR GENERAL: Your letter of the 8th inst. was forwarded to me from St. Louis, and reached me here early this morning, and I hasten to reply. I regret very much that, my papers being boxed up, I have no access to a memorandum of the circumstances connected with the

‡ "H'DQ'RS, ARMY OF THE POTOMAC, CHANCELLORSVILLE, VA., May 2d, 1863, 9:30 A. M. *Circular*. MAJOR-GENERALS SLOCUM AND HOWARD: I am directed by the Major-General commanding to say that the disposition you have made of your corps has been with a view to a front attack by the enemy. If he should throw himself upon your flank, he wishes you to examine the ground and determine upon the position you will take in that event, in order that you may be prepared for him in whatever direction he advances. He suggests that you have heavy reserves well in hand to meet this contingency. The right of your line does not appear to be strong enough. No artificial defenses worth naming have been thrown up, and there appears to be a scarcity of troops at that point, and not, in the general's opinion, as favorably posted as might be. We have good reason to suppose that the enemy is moving to our right. Please advance your pickets for purposes of observation as far as may be safe, in order to obtain timely information of their approach. J. H. VAN ALEN, Brigadier-General and Aide-de-camp." [This is the dispatch which General Howard states he did not receive at the time. See p. 196. In the "Official Records" the word circular does not appear, and the address is "Major-Generals Howard and Slocum."— EDITORS.]

♭ "HEADQUARTERS, 11TH CORPS, May 2d, 10 m. to 11 o'k [10:50 A. M.] MAJ.-GENL. HOOKER, Comd'g Army. GENERAL: From Gen. Devens's headquarters we can observe a column of infantry moving westward on a road parallel with this on a ridge about 1½ to 2 miles south of this. I am taking measures to resist an attack from the west. Respectfully, O. O. HOWARD, Maj.-Gen."

battle of Chancellorsville, as they came under my observation, which memorandum I put on paper shortly after that event. So I have to depend upon my memory in answering your questions. According to my recollection, you are mistaken in your impression that General Howard put your dispatches and orders into his pocket without communicating them to his division commanders. About noon or a little after on the day of the attack on the Eleventh Corps I was at General Howard's headquarters, a house on the Chancellorsville road near the center of our position. General Howard, being very tired, wanted to rest a little, and asked me as next in rank to open dispatches that might arrive and to wake him in case they were of immediate importance. Shortly after a courier arrived with a dispatch from you calling General Howard's attention to the movement of the enemy toward our right flank, and instructing him to take precautionary measures against an attack from that quarter. I went into General Howard at once and read it to him, and, if I remember rightly, while we were speaking about it another courier, or one of your young staff-officers, arrived with a second dispatch of virtually the same purport. We went out and discussed the matter on the porch of the house. I am not sure whether General Steinwehr was present or not. . . .

"I have seen it stated that my troops were already gone when General Devens's division in its hurried retreat reached my position. This is utterly untrue. Some of my regiments, which had remained in their old position, succeeded in wheeling round under the fire of the enemy; others were swept away, but those whose front I had changed during the afternoon in anticipation of the attack held their ground a considerable time after the débris of General Devens's division had swept through our line. I saw General Devens, wounded, carried by, and he had long been . . . in the rear when we were overpowered and fell back upon Colonel Buschbeck's position, where General Howard in the meantime had been trying to rally the routed troops. This also you will find in my report. My loss in killed and wounded was quite heavy : if I remember rightly, about twenty per cent.

"I ought to add that he [General Howard] thought he could not carry out as well as he desired your instruction to hold a strong reserve in hand, for the reason that General Barlow's brigade of Steinwehr's division had been ordered to the support of Sickles. All the precaution that was taken against a flank attack, aside from what I did without orders, was the construction of a small rifle-pit across the Chancellorsville road in the rear of my division, near the house [Dowdall's Tavern] occupied by General Howard as headquarters. . . . Of course this hasty note is not written with any expectation on my part to see it printed as part of an historical narrative. It is simply to give *you* the information you wish for, and which it gives me pleasure to furnish.   Very truly yours,   C. SCHURZ.
"MAJOR-GENERAL HOOKER.

"P. S.—Whether General Howard received on that day any dispatches or instructions from you subsequent to those mentioned, I do not know." ⸱

When we arrived at the Chancellor House (which is all there is of Chancellorsville), where General Hooker had his headquarters, and where he received the hurt that came near proving mortal, General Hooker said, " I was standing on this step of the portico on the Sunday morning of the 3d of May, and

⸱ The following are extracts from the official report of General Schurz, who shows, besides, that his division made strenuous efforts to stem the assaults of Jackson's men :

"In the course of the forenoon I was informed that large columns of the enemy could be seen from General Devens's headquarters, moving from east to west. . . . I observed them plainly as they moved on. I rode back to your [General Howard's] headquarters, and on the way ordered Captain Dilger to look for good artillery positions on the field fronting west, as the troops would in all probability have to execute a change of front. The matter was largely discussed at your headquarters, and I entertained and expressed in our informal conversations the opinion that we should form upon the open ground we then occupied, with our front at right angles with the Plank road, lining the church grove and the border of the woods east of the open plain with infantry, placing strong échelons behind both wings, and distributing the artillery along the front on ground most favorable for its action, especially on the eminence on the right and left of Dowdall's Tavern. . . . In the absence of orders, but becoming more and more convinced that the enemy's attack would come from the west and fall upon our right and rear, I took it upon my own responsibility to detach two regiments from the second line of my Second Brigade and to place them in a good position on the right and left of Ely's Ford road, west of Hawkins's farm, so as to check the enemy if he should attack our extreme right and penetrate through the woods at that point. This was subsequently approved by you. . . .

was giving direction to the battle, which was now raging with great fury, the cannon-balls reaching me from both the east and the west, when a solid shot struck the pillar near me, splitting it in two, and throwing one-half longitudinally against me, striking my whole right side, which soon turned livid. For a few moments I was senseless, and the report spread that I had been killed. But I soon revived, and, to correct the misapprehension, I insisted on being lifted upon my horse, and rode back toward the white house, which subsequently became the center of my new position. Just before reaching it, the pain from my hurt became so intense that I was likely to fall, when I was assisted to dismount, and was laid upon a blanket spread out upon the ground, and was given some brandy. This revived me, and I was assisted to remount. Scarcely was I off the blanket when a solid shot, fired by the enemy at Hazel Grove, struck in the very center of that blanket, where I had a moment before been lying, and tore up the earth in a savage way." As he ended this recital General Hooker turned to Major Chancellor, who was standing by, and said, "Ah, Major! Your people were after me with a sharp stick on that day."

A short distance from the Chancellor House, in the direction of Dowdall's Tavern, our carriage was halted, and, dismounting, Major Chancellor led us a few paces out of the road, along a faint cart-path, when he said, " This is the place where Stonewall Jackson received the wounds that proved mortal." " I have always been struck," observed General Hooker, " with the last words of General Jackson, evincing how completely he was absorbed in the progress of the battle. In his delirium he was still upon the field, and he cried out, ' Order A. P. Hill to prepare for action — pass the infantry to the front rapidly — tell Major Hawks —' when he stopped with the sentence unfinished. After a little his brow relaxed, as if from relief, and he said, ' Let us cross over the river, and rest under the shade of the trees,'— and these were his last words."

Arriving at Dowdall's Tavern, General Hooker pointed out the excellent position here afforded for Howard's corps to have made a stout defense. "Buschbeck's brigade of that corps," said he, " did wonders here, and held the whole impetuous onset of the enemy in check for an hour or more, which gave me opportunity to bring my reserves into position. The loss of this ground brought me into so cramped a condition that I was obliged to take up a new position, which I successfully accomplished. I now ordered Sedgwick, who commanded the Sixth Corps, the largest in my army, some 22,000 men,

With these exceptions, no change was made in the position occupied by the corps. The losses suffered by my division in the action of May 2d were very severe in proportion to my whole effective force. I had 15 officers killed, 23 wounded, and 15 missing, and 102 men killed, 365 wounded, and 441 missing,— total, 953. ☆ . . . My whole loss amounted to about 23 per cent. . . . In closing this report I beg leave to make one additional remark. The Eleventh Corps, and, by error or malice, especially the Third Division, has been held up to the whole country as a band of cowards. My division has been made responsible for the defeat of the Eleventh Corps, and the Eleventh Corps for the failure of the campaign. Preposterous as this is, yet we have been overwhelmed by the army and the press with abuse and insult beyond measure. We have borne as much as human nature can endure. I am far from saying that on May 2d everybody did his duty to the best of his power.

"But one thing I will say, because I know it: these men are no cowards. . . . I have seen, with my own eyes, troops who now affect to look down upon the Eleventh Corps with sovereign contempt behave much worse under circumstances far less trying. . . ."

EDITORS.

☆ This was the loss reported by General Schurz, but a recently revised table of the War Department shows 9 officers and 120 men killed, 32 officers and 461 men wounded, and 8 officers and 290 men captured or missing,— a total of 920.— EDITORS.

RETREAT OF THE UNION ARMY ACROSS THE RAPPAHANNOCK AT UNITED STATES FORD.
FROM A WAR-TIME SKETCH.

which had been left to demonstrate in front of Fredericksburg, to cross the
river and move rapidly up to my left. The effect of so heavy a body of fresh
troops coming in upon the enemy's flank I calculated would be decisive. But
Sedgwick was dilatory in moving, ↓ which gave the enemy time to concentrate and stop him before he had moved over half the distance, and I
consequently got no help from him."

I ventured to ask why he did not attack when he found that the enemy had
weakened his forces in the immediate front and sent them away to meet Sedgwick. "That," said he, "would seem to have been the reasonable thing to do.
But we were in this impenetrable thicket. All the roads and openings leading through it the enemy immediately fortified strongly, and planted thickly
his artillery commanding all the avenues, so that with reduced numbers he
could easily hold his lines, shutting me in, and it became utterly impossible
to manœuvre my forces. My army was not beaten. Only a part of it had been
engaged. The First Corps, commanded by Reynolds, whom I regarded as the
ablest officer under me, was fresh and ready and eager to be brought into
action, as was my whole army. But I had been fully convinced of the futil-
ity of attacking fortified positions, and I was determined not to sacrifice my
men needlessly, though it should be at the expense of my reputation as a fighting officer. We had already had enough grievous experience in that line.
I made frequent demonstrations to induce the enemy to attack me, but he
would not accept my challenge. Accordingly, when the eight days' rations
with which my army started out were exhausted, I retired across the river.
Before doing so I sent orders to General Sedgwick to hold his position near

↓ See statements in "Sedgwick at Fredericksburg and Salem Heights," p. 224.—EDITORS.

Banks's Ford, on the south side of the stream, and I would bring my whole army to his support; but the order failed to reach him until he had already recrossed the river.⚓ Could I have had my army on the open grounds at that point where I could have manœuvred it properly, I felt assured that I could have gained a decisive victory. But this, my last chance, was frustrated." |

⚓ The "Official Records" (Vol. XXV., Part II., p. 418) show that Sedgwick recrossed the Rappahannock in obedience to an order from General Hooker, dated May 5th, 1 A. M., and received by Sedgwick at 2 A. M. At 1:20 A. M. Hooker sent the following order to Sedgwick (*Ibid.*, p. 419): "Yours received, saying you should hold position [as ordered]. Order to withdraw countermanded." This countermand was received by Sedgwick at 3:20 A. M., but meanwhile almost his entire command had recrossed under the order of 1 A. M.— EDITORS.

| The subjoined letter has been kindly furnished to us for publication by Lieutenant Worth G. Ross, son of the late Colonel Samuel Ross, to whom it is addressed. It is believed that it had not been printed before its appearance in "The Century" for April, 1888.— EDITORS.

"LOOKOUT VALLEY, TENN., February 28th, 1864.

"MY DEAR COLONEL: For some reason your letter was a long time in reaching me. When the Eleventh Corps gave way on Saturday, Berry's division and Hays's brigade were dispatched to seize and hold the ground occupied by the left of that corps. Berry double-quicked his men to the point, but was too late. The enemy were already in possession. When this was reported to me I directed my engineers to establish a new line, which was pointed out to them on the map, and at the same time stated to them that we would probably have to move on it as soon as the enemy opened on us in the morning, as his batteries would sweep the plain in front of the Chancellorsville House, and, besides, enfilade the line held by the Second and Twelfth corps nearly its entire length. Soon after these instructions were given to the engineers, peremptory orders were sent to General Sedgwick to advance over the Plank road from Fredericksburg and attack the enemy in front of the Second and Twelfth corps at daylight. My single object in holding on to the position as long as I did was to hear Sedgwick's guns, which I momentarily expected,

of course. General Warren had been sent to guide him. The orders reached him between 10 and 11 o'clock, [he] had but eight miles to march, a bright moonlight night, with only a small force to oppose. Probably had he marched as directed, not a gun would have been fired. With Lee in my front and Jackson on my flank I was unwilling to attempt to force my way through Lee, especially as the roads through the forests would only enable me to present my columns with narrow fronts, which the enemy could cut down as fast as they were exposed. I knew that I could do this, and I gave the enemy credit for being able to do as much as I could, but no more. Had Sedgwick come up on Lee's rear, the latter would have found himself between two armies, and would doubtless have followed Jackson's flank movement, which I desired, as that would throw the enemy off the short road to Richmond and our troops on it. I do not know that you ever heard that I had one and a half millions of rations afloat in the Potomac to throw up the Pamunkey River in view of this contingency.

"I recrossed the Rappahannock, expecting to return at or near Franklin's Crossing, where I had elbow-room [see p. 74], and at least an even chance for being victorious, and so stated to the President at the time. No general battle was fought at Chancellorsville, for I was unwilling to give battle with such great odds against me. I rejoice that what was not gained was not lost.

"We lost no honors at Chancellorsville. With all of our misfortunes the enemy's loss exceeded our own by one-third. Of this I have abundant evidence in the official returns of the enemy's casualties, as they have from time to time been published. [But see p. 238.] If I did not cross the river again it will appear that it was for reasons over which I had no control. The rains had nothing to do with our returning from Chancellorsville, for it had been determined on in my mind long before the rain commenced falling. I do not like to be quoted as authority on this subject until after the official report is published, and for the flattering terms in which you speak of me—*not ever.* I hope that you and yours are well. My kindest regards to Mrs. Ross and my best wishes for yourself. Your friend,

"JOSEPH HOOKER.

"COLONEL SAMUEL ROSS,
    Commanding Brigade, Twelfth Corps."

FORAGING IN THE WILDERNESS.

FEELING THE ENEMY. FROM A WAR-TIME SKETCH.

SEDGWICK AT FREDERICKSBURG AND SALEM HEIGHTS.

BY HUNTINGTON W. JACKSON, BREVET LIEUTENANT-COLONEL, U. S. V.

FROM our encampment on the Stafford Heights, the bright camp-fires of the enemy and the scenes of the terrible encounters under Burnside were daily presented to our sight from December, 1862, until the following April. During this period, with the exception of a futile movement on the right known as the "Mud March," the army remained quiet. The pickets stationed on either bank of the Rappahannock were within hailing distance of each other, and dress and faces could be easily distinguished. By the comity that prevailed, there was no firing from either side. One could ride or walk down to the banks of the river with perfect security. Sometimes "Johnny Reb," as he was called, would rig up a little raft, and, loading it with tobacco, start it with sails and rudder set for the other shore. When the precious freight was unloaded, the craft, generously burdened with coffee and salt, would be headed by "Yank" in an opposite direction, where it would be received with loud expressions of thanks. In this and other ways the asperities of the war were mollified. As time rolled on and the weather improved, arrangements were made for an advance. The men were well clothed, rested, and eager to move again to test the fortunes of war.

Of the several plans of attack, Hooker determined to march around the enemy's left flank to Chancellorsville, leaving a portion of the army at Fredericksburg to conceal the real movement. The army struck camp on the 27th of April, and on the 30th Hooker established his headquarters at Chancellorsville. The same evening, in general orders, he said, "It is with heartfelt satisfaction the commanding general announces to the army that the operations of the last three days have determined that our enemy must either ingloriously fly, or come out from behind his defenses and give us battle on our own ground, where certain destruction awaits him." Hooker forgot the injunction of Ahab to Benhadad: "Tell him," he said, "Let not him that girdeth on his harness boast himself as he that putteth it off."

While the right wing was concentrating at Chancellorsville, the corps of Sedgwick and Reynolds, after considerable opposition, crossed the Rappahannock on pontoon-bridges below Fredericksburg, and by the evening of the 30th were deployed on the wide plain where Franklin's Left Grand Division had fought in the previous battle. Sickles's corps was in supporting distance. The position of Lee's army remained unchanged until the 29th, when Lee was informed that large bodies of Federals were moving toward Chancellorsville. It was the first information he had received of Hooker's movement on his left, and it is said he was incensed at the delay of the communication. [See p. 233.] At midnight Anderson's division of Lee's army hurriedly moved from Fredericksburg and intrenched about four or five miles from Hooker's headquarters.

In an address of Fitzhugh Lee delivered to the Association of the Army of Northern Virginia he stated: "General Robert E. Lee said that Jackson had first preferred to attack Sedgwick's corps in the plain at Fredericksburg; Lee told him he felt it was as impracticable as at the first battle of Fredericksburg; it was hard to get at the enemy and harder to get away, on account of the artillery on the north bank, if we drove them into the river; but, said he to Jackson, 'If you think it can be done, I will give you orders for it.' Jackson then asked to be allowed to examine the grounds, and did so during the afternoon, and at night came to Lee and said he thought he (Lee) was right; it would be inexpedient to attack them. 'Move then,' said Lee, 'at dawn to-morrow, up to Anderson.'"

Sickles's and Reynolds's corps having subsequently been ordered to Chancellorsville by Hooker, Sedgwick was left alone below Fredericksburg with about 24,000 men, the Sixth Corps being by several thousand the largest in the army.

During the evening of the 2d of May Hooker sent word to Sedgwick "to take up his line on the Chancellorsville road and attack and destroy any forces he might meet." He also added that "he (Sedgwick) would probably fall upon the rear of Lee's forces, and between them they would use Lee up." If Hooker thought an insignificant force was in Sedgwick's front, the engagement soon to take place showed how mistaken he was. Sedgwick received the order about 11 o'clock at night. He at once advanced his command to the Bowling Green road and then marched by the right flank toward Fredericksburg. Newton's division was in the advance. The night was dark and the road made darker by the foliage of the trees on either side. The progress was necessarily slow. Frequent short halts were made while the skirmishers were feeling their way. Once, when the halt was prolonged and nothing broke the deep silence of the night except an occasional shot followed by the never-to-be-forgotten *ping* of the minie-ball, General Newton, who was riding with the third or fourth regiment from the advance, called out: "Is any one of my staff here?" Those present promptly responded, and I was directed to "ride ahead and tell Colonel Shaler to brush away the enemy's

THE STONE WALL UNDER MARYE'S HEIGHTS. FROM A PHOTOGRAPH TAKEN IMMEDIATELY AFTER SEDGWICK CARRIED THE POSITION BY ASSAULT.

pickets." The road was filled with soldiers, some lying down, others resting on their guns, but a passage was quickly cleared. At Hazel Run Colonel Shaler and Colonel Hamblin were found standing together. Here the enemy made a determined resistance. Their pickets were but a few yards distant. On the other side of the creek the road made a sharp ascent and curved to the right. In a subdued tone Colonel Shaler said: "Colonel Hamblin, you have heard the order from General Newton?" At once Colonel Hamblin left. In a moment there was the noise of hurrying feet, the troops quickly disappeared in the dark; a shout, a bright, sudden flash, a roll of musketry followed, and the road was open.

It was the gray of morning when the advance reached the rear and left of Fredericksburg. A negro who came into the lines reported the heights occupied and that the enemy were cutting the canal to flood the roads. To ascertain whether this was true, another delay was caused. No one in the command was acquainted with the topography of the country, and the advance was compelled to move with great caution through the streets and in the outskirts of the town. As the morning dawned, Marye's Heights, the scene of the fierce attacks under Burnside in the previous December, were presented to our view. Several regiments were speedily moved along the open ground in the rear of the town toward the heights, and this movement discovered the enemy in force behind the famous stone wall at the base of the hill. Lee had left Early with his division and Barksdale's brigade, a force of about ten thousand men, to hold Fredericksburg Heights. They were protected by strong works and supported by well-served artillery. It was at once felt that a desperate encounter was to follow, and the recollections of the previous disaster were by no means inspiriting.

It was Sunday morning, the 3d of May, and the weather was beautiful. The town was perfectly quiet, many of the inhabitants had fled, not a person was to be seen on the streets, and the windows and blinds of the houses were closed. The marks of the fierce cannonade to which the place had previously been exposed were everywhere visible.

As soon as practicable and as secretly as possible, Sedgwick prepared to attack the heights. Gibbon, of the Second Corps, who had been left on the north bank, crossed shortly after Sedgwick had captured the town and moved to the right, but his advance was stopped by the canal in front, over which it was impossible to lay bridges in face of the fire from the artillery and infantry on the hill. Sedgwick says, "Nothing remained but to carry the works by direct assault." The attack on Marye's Heights was made under direction of Newton. Two columns, each marching by fours, were formed on the Plank and Telegraph roads, and were supported by a line of infantry from the Light Brigade on the left, commanded by Colonel Burnham. The right column, under Colonel George C. Spear, was composed of the 61st Pennsylvania and the 43d New York. These two regiments belonged to the Light Brigade. This column was supported by the 67th New York and 82d Pennsylvania, under Colonel Alexander Shaler. The left column consisted of the 7th Massachusetts and the 36th New York, under Colonel Thomas D. Johns.

The line of battle, commanded by Colonel Hiram Burnham, was composed of the 5th Wisconsin (acting as skirmishers), the 6th Maine, 31st New York (these three regiments also belonging to the Light Brigade), and the 23d Pennsylvania. Howe's division was posted south of Hazel Run, and coöperated handsomely, capturing five guns.

The order to advance was given at 11 o'clock. Sedgwick and Newton with the deepest interest watched the attack from the garden of a brick residence situated on the outskirts of the town and to the left of the Telegraph road, which commanded a full view of the assault. The movements of the enemy showed that they were actively preparing to receive the attack, but the men behind the stone wall were concealed from view. As the left column emerged from the town and was passing near Sedgwick

THE CAPTURE OF A GUN OF THE WASHINGTON ARTILLERY, ON MARYE'S HEIGHTS.

and Newton, the enemy's battery opened, and a portion of a bursting shell struck and killed Major Elihu J. Faxon, of the 36th New York, while mounted and riding with his command, and wounded several others. There was an exclamation of horror and a momentary scattering of the rear of the column, but the men quickly closed up and pressed on. Colonel Spear, commanding the right column, was killed at about the same time. Both columns and line, in light marching order, advanced at double-quick without firing a shot. The enemy kept up an incessant artillery fire, and the noise was deafening. Their musketry fire was reserved until our men were within easy range. Then a murderous storm of shot from the stone wall, and grape and canister from the hill, burst upon the columns and line. For a moment the head of the left column was checked and broken. The column on the right was also broken. Colonel Burnham's line of blue on the green field paused as if to recover breath, and

Brooks's division was posted along Deep Run as far as Bernard's house. Bartlett's brigade of this division held the railroad crossing at Deep Run to guard against an attack on the flank of the storming column, and was sharply engaged during the forenoon.—EDITORS.

slightly wavered. Sedgwick and Newton looked on with unconcealed anxiety, and turned to each other, but remained silent. The suspense was intense. Was it to be a victory or a defeat? Was the place a second time to be a "slaughter-pen?" Was the Sixth Corps to be driven into the river? Staff-officers, waving their swords and hurrahing to the men, dashed down the Telegraph road. A blinding rain of shot pierced the air. It was more than human nature could face. The head of the column as it reached the lowest part of the decline near a fork in the road seemed to melt away. Many fell; others bending low to the earth hurriedly sought shelter from the undulations of ground and the fences and the two or three wooden structures along the road. Out of 400 comprising the 7th Massachusetts, 150 were killed and wounded. Colonel Johns, commanding, was severely wounded. Then, as if moved by a sudden impulse and nerved for a supreme effort, both columns and the line in the field simultaneously sprang forward. The stone wall was gained and the men were quickly over it.✝ Just as my horse was jumping through a break in the wall one of the enemy, standing slightly to the left and about a horse's length from me, raised his gun and fired. The excitement of the hour must have unnerved his hand, for the ball *zipped* harmlessly by to my right. In a second a bayonet was thrust into his breast by one of our men on my left. Along the wall a hand-to-hand fight took place, and the bayonet and the butt of the musket were freely used. The brilliant and successful charge occupied perhaps ten or fifteen minutes, and immediately after the wall was carried the enemy became panic-stricken. In the flight they threw away guns, knapsacks, pistols, swords, and everything that might retard their speed. One thousand prisoners were taken, besides several battle-flags and pieces of artillery. The commander of a Louisiana battery handed his saber to Colonel Thomas S. Allen, of the 5th Wisconsin. This regiment out of 500 men lost 123, and the 6th Maine out of about the same number lost 167 in killed and wounded. Over 600 were killed and wounded in the direct assault upon the heights, and the loss to the corps on the entire front was about 1000.

General G. K. Warren, who had arrived that morning with instructions from headquarters, said in his telegram to Hooker: "The heights were carried splendidly at 11 A. M. by Newton." Upon reaching the summit of the sharp hill, after passing through the extensive and well-wooded grounds of

---

✝ A private of Company F, 7th Massachusetts, writes to the editors:

"The assault took place Sunday, May 3d, at about 11 o'clock A. M., the 7th Massachusetts leading the left column, the 36th New York Volunteers in support. Both marched by the flank. Our company (F), leading the 7th, consequently caught the whole body of the first fire of the 'Johnnies,' which they withheld until we were certainly within twenty-five yards. As some of the officers sang out 'Retreat, Retreat,' the men began to yell 'Forward! don't go back! we sha'n't get so close up again.' Lieutenant-Colonel Franklin P. Harlow was the man above all others who held the men up to their work, and I have never yet seen his name even worthily mentioned. Just before and in front of the wall facing down the street is a house standing in a small plat, V-shaped, and inclosed by a high board fence. This wall in our front along the base of the hill was a rough stone wall forming the rear bank of the sunken road, while on

our side in front of the sunken road was a good stone wall even with the level of the field. In this sunken road were two Confederate lines of battle, the front line firing on our charging lines on the left of the road and the rear line sitting on their heels, with their backs against the terrace wall at the base of the hill and rear of the road. About opposite the right of our regiment was a depression on the hill made some time, I should think, by water from the land above, but now grassed over; at the head of this depression was a battery placed, I suppose, to rake the ravine or depression. Some one looked through the board fence, and saw the enemy's flank. In a moment the men rushed to the fence, and we went through pell-mell right upon the flank of the Confederates, at the same time giving them the contents of the muskets point-blank without aiming. The whole thing was a surprise; they were not prepared for anything from this quarter, as we were hidden from them, and they from us, by the house and fence."   EDITORS.

the Marye House, an exciting scene met the eye. A single glance exhibited to view the broad plateau alive with fleeing soldiers, riderless horses, and artillery and wagon trains on a gallop. The writer hurried back to Sedgwick, who was giving directions for Brooks and Howe to come up, and suggested that it was a rare opportunity for the use of cavalry. With evident regret Sedgwick replied that he did not have a cavalryman. The carrying of the heights had completely divided the enemy's forces, throwing either flank with much confusion on opposite roads, and it seemed as though a regiment of cavalry might not only have captured many prisoners, guns, ammunition, and wagons, but also have cleared the way for the corps almost as far as the immediate rear of Lee's army at Chancellorsville.

SALEM CHURCH. FROM A RECENT PHOTOGRAPH.

The view is from the Plank road. On the left is what remains of the Confederate trenches. The bricks on the four sides of the church are spotted with bullet-marks, and especially on the line of the upper windows toward the road, showing that many Union soldiers aimed high. This church was a refuge for many Fredericksburg families during Burnside's battle.—EDITORS.

Newton's division, exhausted by the night march, the weight of several days' rations and sixty rounds of ammunition, and by the heat, fatigue, and excitement of battle, were allowed to halt for a short time. Many were soon asleep, while others made coffee and partook of their first meal that day.

Brooks's division soon came up from below Hazel Run, and took the advance. Newton and Howe followed. The enemy in the meantime had united their forces, and delayed the rapid advance by frequent stands, retiring successively from hill to hill, and opening with artillery. Ravines running at right angles to the main road and the rolling character of the country were favorable for impeding the pursuit, which was continued for three or four miles until we reached Salem Church, an unpretentious red-brick structure situated on a ridge covered with dense woods and undergrowth. To-day it bears many scars of the contest waged around it.

At this point the enemy were in position with four fresh brigades withdrawn from Hooker's front, and prepared to contest any farther advance. Lee had met with such complete success in his attack upon Hooker that he felt he could well spare these troops and not suffer. Brooks on the left of the road and Newton on the right quickly formed their commands and made several gallant assaults. The fight was very severe in the thick woods, and for a time was waged with varying success. The crest of the woods and a little school-house near the church were gained, and once it was thought they could be held, but the enemy, in superior numbers, pressed on, and the ground and the church were left in their possession. The contest did not last long, but nearly 1500 were killed and wounded. Bartlett's brigade, numbering less than 1500, lost 580 officers and men. That night the soldiers slept on their arms.

It was understood throughout the Sixth Corps that as soon as it should become engaged with the enemy Hooker would immediately attack in his front, and prevent any reënforcements from being sent against Sedgwick. All during that Sabbath day and the next the sound of Hooker's guns were eagerly listened for. No sound would have been more welcome. But after 10 o'clock Sunday morning axes and spades were used at Chancellorsville more than the guns. The feeling became widely prevalent that the Sixth Corps would be compelled to take care of itself. At first it was cautiously whispered that Hooker had failed, and soon the worst was surmised, and it was concluded that no help could be expected from him. His dash, promptness, and confidence as a division and corps commander were gone.

Lee that night withdrew his troops, flushed with their brilliant success, from the front of Hooker, with the exception of Jackson's corps, and marched against Sedgwick. Still Hooker remained inactive; with a force greatly in excess of the enemy in his front, he made no effort to relieve Sedgwick from his perilous position. Works were thrown up by the enemy along the Salem Church ridge, and they extended their right until on Monday morning Marye's Heights and Fredericksburg, won at so great a sacrifice, were again theirs.

Sedgwick's position, as finally established, was in the shape of a horseshoe, both flanks resting on the river, the line covering Banks's Ford. His line of battle was between five and six miles in length. Frequent attempts had been made, during Sunday morning, to communicate with Banks's Ford and to direct the laying of pontoon-bridges, but for some time roving bodies of cavalry frustrated this. The late Colonel Henry W. Farrar, then on the staff of Sedgwick, while carrying a message for this purpose, was captured and taken to Richmond. The 4th of May dragged wearily, skirmishing continued all day, the weather was hot, Sedgwick's position was most critical, and the keenest anxiety was felt. Lee was in our front with a force much larger than Sedgwick's then available command of about eighteen thousand men, and an attack was momentarily expected, but fortunately Lee consumed the whole day in establishing his lines. The greatest vigilance and activity were exercised by our men in throwing up rifle-pits. Hooker sent word to Sedgwick to look well to the safety of his corps, and either to fall back upon Fredericksburg or recross at Banks's Ford; he also added that he could do nothing to relieve him.⸸ Sedgwick accordingly intrusted Newton with the arrange-

---

⸸ These instructions to Sedgwick were sent through General G. K. Warren, Hooker's chief of engineers, who had been sent to Sedgwick to render what assistance he might, and who had returned to Hooker on Sunday evening. Warren says:

"As soon as General Sedgwick's advance had caused the retreat of the troops at Banks's Ford [about 1 P. M., May 3d], General Benham had thrown a bridge across and communicated with him. By this route and the United States Mine Ford, I returned to headquarters, near Chancellorsville, which I reached at 11 P. M. I found, as the result of the battle at that point, that our line had fallen back from the Chancellorsville house about a mile. After reporting to the general, and getting his ideas, I telegraphed the following to General Sedgwick at midnight:

"'I find everything snug here. We contracted the line a little, and repulsed the last assault with ease. General

THE ATTACK ON SEDGWICK AT BANKS'S FORD, MONDAY EVENING, MAY 4, AS SEEN FROM
THE SAND-BAG BATTERY NEAR FALMOUTH. FROM A WAR-TIME SKETCH.

ments for the withdrawal. Newton quickly made himself acquainted with
the roads leading to Banks's Ford and succeeded in establishing communication with General Henry W. Benham, who was in charge of the pontoons at
that place.

At 6 o'clock in the evening the enemy attacked Brooks and Howe on the
center and left, with the design of cutting off the corps from Banks's Ford.
Howe not only maintained his position until night-fall, but also made several
counter-charges, capturing several hundred prisoners. Brooks also held on
until dark, but in retiring was closely pursued by the enemy. The whole corps
then successfully fell back to Banks's Ford, and the long and painful suspense
of the day was over. The picket line in front and on the left of Salem ridge
was withdrawn by General David A. Russell in person. I had been directed
to assist him. That sterling soldier dismounted, moved along the line saying,
"Quietly, men, quietly; don't make any noise"; but the jingle of the canteens
and other unavoidable sounds on the evening air revealed the movement to
the vigilant enemy, and they followed closely, yelling and firing until the
double-quick step brought us to our main column on the march, about a mile
distant. Several of the enemy's scouts penetrated almost to the ford and
threw up rockets to mark our position. The enemy's artillery responded to
the signal, shelling both troops and bridges, but with little injury. During
the night we recrossed the river and took position to meet the enemy should
they, as expected at the time, cross to the north side to renew their attack,
or attempt to destroy our depots for supplies near Fredericksburg. We
captured 5 battle-flags and 15 pieces of artillery, 9 of which were brought off.
Fourteen hundred prisoners were taken, including many officers of rank.

Hooker wishes them to attack him to-morrow, if they will.
He does not desire you to attack again in force unless he
attacks him at the same time. He says you are too far away
from him to direct. Look well to the safety of your corps,
and keep up communication with General Benham at Banks's
Ford and Fredericksburg. You can go to either place, if you
think best. To cross at Banks's Ford would bring you in
supporting distance of the main body, and would be better
than falling back to Fredericksburg.'

"This dispatch was written at a time when I was exceedingly exhausted. It did not reach Genera Sedgwick till late in the forenoon of the 4th, so I have been
told, and was the only instruction he received. The
enemy attacked him in strong force the next day, and,
having resisted them till the evening, he withdrew
across the river at Banks's Ford."

EDITORS.

LEE'S KNOWLEDGE OF HOOKER'S MOVEMENTS.

BY R. E. COLSTON, MAJOR-GENERAL, C. S. A.

THE assertion that Hooker's move upon Chancellorsville was a surprise to General Lee is a great mistake. Every day Lee had information of Hooker's movements. The following letter, sent by Lee to Jackson, and by the latter to me, has never been out of my possession since. It shows the remarkable intuition that enabled General Lee on so many occasions to foresee and penetrate the intentions of his antagonist. In this case a demonstration had been made on our extreme right at Port Royal, and without waiting for orders I had gone with a brigade and battery to meet it. I reported the facts to General Jackson, and it is my letter to him to which Lee refers:

"HEADQUARTERS, A. N. VA., April 23, 1863. LIEUT.-GEN'L T. J. JACKSON, Com'g Corps. GEN'L: 1 have received General Colston's letter of 8½ o'clock to-day which you forwarded to me. I think from the account given me by L't-Col. Smith of the Engineers, who was at Port Royal yesterday, of the enemy's operations there, the day and night previous, that his present purpose is to draw our troops in that direction while he attempts a passage elsewhere. I would not, then, send down more troops than are actually necessary. I will notify Gen'ls McLaws and Anderson to be on the alert, for I think that if a real attempt is made to cross the river it will be above Fredericksburg. Very respectfully, R. E. LEE, Gen'l."

The letter was indorsed by Jackson, "Respectfully referred to General Colston for his guidance." It was also marked "confidential," and both the front and the back of the envelope were marked "private," so that not even my adjutant-general should open it in case of my absence.

The Federal writers have wondered why Jackson's corps did not complete its work on the evening of May 2d. They do not realize the condition of our troops after their successful charge on Howard. We had forced our way through brush so dense that the troops were nearly stripped of their uniforms. Brigades, regiments, and companies had become so mixed that they could not be handled; besides which the darkness of evening was so intensified by the shade of the dense woods that nothing could be seen a few yards off. The halt at that time was not a mistake, but a necessity. So far from intending to stop, Jackson, when he was wounded, was hurrying A. P. Hill's division to the front to take the place of Rodes's

and mine and to continue the attack; A. P. Hill was also wounded soon afterward, and the advance of his troops in the narrow road on which alone they could move was checked by the shell and canister of twelve Napoleon guns, from an elevation within five hundred yards. The slaughter and confusion were greatly increased by this terrible fire in the night, so that the pause in the attack was one of those fatalities of war that no foresight can prevent.

It was about 1 o'clock on Sunday, May 3d, that Lee received information that Early had been driven from Marye's Heights and was falling back before Sedgwick. Jackson's corps, which had been fighting since 6 o'clock the previous evening, with very little rest during the night, renewing the conflict at daylight, and capturing the positions at Chancellorsville, was much diminished by casualties and much exhausted by fatigue, hunger, and thirst; but it was preparing to move upon Hooker's last line of intrenchments, erected during the night on very strong positions. My division was in the lead in line of battle. It was then that I received an order to report at once in person to General Lee. I found him standing in a small tent pitched by the roadside. His plain gray sack-coat, with only three stars on the rolling collar, was, like his face, well sprinkled with the dust of the battle-field. In low, quiet tones he said to me: "General, I wish you to advance with your division on the United States Ford road. I expect you will meet with resistance before you come to the bend of the road. I do not want you to attack the enemy's positions, but only to feel them. Send your engineer officer with skirmishers to the front to reconnoiter and report. Don't engage seriously, but keep the enemy in check and prevent him from advancing."

I am confident that these were almost the exact words of General Lee, to which he added, "Move at once," which I did. I was not a little puzzled at the time (not knowing the situation at Fredericksburg), and I wondered why we were not to continue our advance and hurl Hooker into the river. Lee left the field at Chancellorsville immediately after giving me the above orders, and hastened to Early's support with McLaws's division, Mahone's brigade, and other troops, and compelled Sedgwick to retreat across the Rappahannock.

THE OPPOSING FORCES IN THE CHANCELLORSVILLE CAMPAIGN.

The composition, losses, and strength of each army as here stated give the gist of all the data obtainable in the Official Records. K stands for killed; w for wounded; m w for mortally wounded; m for captured or missing; c for captured.

THE UNION ARMY.

ARMY OF THE POTOMAC.— Major-General Joseph Hooker. Staff loss: w, 1.

Provost Guard, Brig.-Gen. Marsena R. Patrick: 93d N. Y., Col. John S. Crocker; E and I, 6th Pa. Cav., Capt. James Starr; 8th U. S. (6 co's), Capt. E. W. H. Read; Detachment Regular Cav., Lieut. Tattnall Paulding. *Patrick's Brigade*, Col. William F. Rogers: B, Md. Art'y,

Capt. Alonzo Snow; 21st N. Y., Lieut.-Col. Chester W. Sternberg; 23d N. Y., Col. Henry C. Hoffman; 35th N. Y., Col. John G. Todd; 80th N. Y. (20th Militia), Col. Theodore B. Gates; 12th Ohio Battery, Capt. Aaron C. Johnson. *Engineer Brigade*, Brig.-Gen. Henry W. Benham: 15th N. Y., Col. Clinton G. Colgate; 50th N. Y., Col. Charles B. Stuart; Battalion U. S. Engineers, Capt. Chauncey B. Reese. Brigade loss: k, 1; w, 6; m, 1 = 8. *Guards and Orderlies*, Oneida (N. Y.) Cav., Capt. Daniel P. Mann.

ARTILLERY, Brig.-Gen. Henry J. Hunt. *Artillery Reserve*, Capt. William M. Graham, Brig.-Gen. Robert O. Tyler: B, 1st Conn., Lieut. Albert F. Brooker; M, 1st Conn., Capt. Franklin A. Pratt; 5th N. Y., Capt. Elijah D. Taft; 15th N. Y., Capt. Patrick Hart; 29th N. Y., Lieut. Gustav von Blucher; 30th N. Y., Capt. Adolph Voegelee; 32d N. Y., Lieut. George Gaston; K, 1st U. S., Lieut. Lorenzo Thomas, Jr.; C, 3d U. S., Lieut. Henry Meinell; G, 4th U. S., Lieut. Marcus P. Miller; K, 5th U. S., Lieut. David H. Kinzie; C, 32d Mass., Capt. Josiah C. Fuller. *Train Guard*, 1st N. J. (7 co's), Col. William Birney, Capt. Robert S. Johnston.

FIRST ARMY CORPS, Maj.-Gen. John F. Reynolds. *Escort*: L, 1st Me. Cav., Capt. Constantine Taylor.

FIRST DIVISION, Brig.-Gen. James S. Wadsworth.

First Brigade, Col. Walter Phelps, Jr.: 22d N. Y., Maj. Thomas J. Strong; 24th N. Y., Col. Samuel R. Beardsley; 30th N. Y., Col. Wm. M. Searing; 84th N. Y. (14th Militia), Col. Edward B. Fowler. Brigade loss: w, 37. *Second Brigade*, Brig.-Gen. Lysander Cutler: 7th Ind., Lieut.-Col. Ira G. Grover; 76th N. Y., Col. William P. Wainwright; 95th N. Y., Col. George H. Biddle; 147th N. Y., Col. John G. Butler; 56th Pa., Col. J. William Hofmann. Brigade loss: k, 3; w, 25; m, 5 = 33. *Third Brigade*, Brig.-Gen. Gabriel R. Paul: 22d N. J., Col. Abraham G. Demarest; 29th N. J., Col. William R. Taylor; 30th N. J., Col. John J. Cladek; 31st N. J., Lieut.-Col. Robert R. Honeyman; 137th Pa., Col. Joseph B. Kiddoo. Brigade loss: k, 1; w, 15 = 16. *Fourth Brigade*, Brig.-Gen. Solomon Meredith: 19th Ind., Col. Samuel J. Williams; 24th Mich., Col. Henry A. Morrow; 2d Wis., Col. Lucius Fairchild; 6th Wis., Col. Edward S. Bragg; 7th Wis., Col. William W. Robinson. Brigade loss: k, 11; w, 46; m, 3 = 60. *Artillery*, Capt. John A. Reynolds: 1st N. H., Capt. Frederick M. Edgell; L, 1st N. Y., Capt. John A. Reynolds; B, 4th U. S., Lieut. James Stewart. Artillery loss: w, 9; m, 2 = 11.

SECOND DIVISION, Brig.-Gen. John C. Robinson.

First Brigade, Col. Adrian R. Root: 16th Me., Col. Charles W. Tilden; 94th N. Y., Capt. Samuel A. Moffett; 104th N. Y., Col. Gilbert G. Prey; 107th Pa., Col. Thomas F. McCoy. Brigade loss: w, 5. *Second Brigade*, Brig.-Gen. Henry Baxter: 12th Mass., Col. James L. Bates; 26th N. Y., Lieut.-Col. Gilbert S. Jennings; 90th Pa., Col. Peter Lyle; 136th Pa., Col. Thomas M. Bayne. Brigade loss: k, 1; w, 16; m, 5 = 22. *Third Brigade*, Col. Samuel H. Leonard: 13th Mass., Lieut.-Col. N. Walter Batchelder; 83d N. Y. (9th Militia), Lieut.-Col. Joseph A. Moesch; 97th N. Y., Col. Charles Wheelock; 11th Pa., Col. Richard Coulter; 88th Pa., Col. Louis Wagner. Brigade loss: k, 2; w, 13; m, 1 = 16. *Artillery*, Capt. Dunbar R. Ransom: 2d Me., Capt. James A. Hall; 5th Me., Capt. George F. Leppien (w), Lieut. Edmund Kirby (m w), Lieut. Greenleaf T. Stevens; C, Pa., Capt. James Thompson; C, 5th U. S., Capt. Dunbar R. Ransom. Artillery loss: k, 7; w, 25 = 32.

THIRD DIVISION, Maj.-Gen. Abner Doubleday.

First Brigade, Brig.-Gen. Thomas A. Rowley: 121st Pa., Col. Chapman Biddle; 135th Pa., Col. James R. Porter; 142d Pa., Col. Robert P. Cummins; 151st Pa., Col. Harrison Allen. Brigade loss: k, 1; w, 12; m, 36 = 49. *Second Brigade*, Col. Roy Stone: 143d Pa., Col. Edmund L. Dana; 149th Pa., Lieut.-Col. Walton Dwight; 150th Pa., Col. Langhorne Wister. Brigade loss: w, 3. *Artillery*, Maj. Ezra W. Matthews: B, 1st Pa., Capt. James H. Cooper; F, 1st Pa., Lieut. R. Bruce Ricketts; G, 1st Pa., Capt. Frank P. Amsden. Artillery loss: w, 9; m, 2 = 11.

SECOND ARMY CORPS, Maj.-Gen. Darius N. Couch. Staff loss: w, 1.

Escort, D and K, 6th N. Y. Cav., Capt. Riley Johnson. Loss: w, 2.

FIRST DIVISION, Maj.-Gen. Winfield S. Hancock.

First Brigade, Brig.-Gen. John C. Caldwell: 5th N. H., Col. Edward E. Cross,‡ Lieut.-Col. Charles E. Hapgood; 61st N. Y., Col. Nelson A. Miles (w), Lieut.-Col. K. Oscar Broady; 81st Pa., Col. H. Boyd McKeen (w); 148th Pa., Col. James A. Beaver (w), Maj. George A. Fairlamb. Brigade loss: k, 36; w, 196; m, 46 = 278. *Second Brigade*, Brig.-Gen. Thomas F. Meagher: 28th Mass., Col. Richard Byrnes; 63d N. Y., Lieut.-Col. Richard C. Bentley; 69th N. Y., Capt. James E. McGee; 88th N. Y., Col. Patrick Kelly; 116th Pa. (battalion), Maj. St. Clair A. Mulholland. Brigade loss: k, 8; w, 63; m, 31 = 102. *Third Brigade*, Brig.-Gen. Samuel K. Zook: 52d N. Y., Col. Paul Frank, Lieut.-Col. Charles G. Freudenberg; 57th N. Y., Lieut.-Col. Alford B. Chapman; 66th N. Y.,⚓ Col. Orlando H. Morris; 140th Pa., Col. Richards P. Roberts. Brigade loss: k, 13; w, 97; m, 78 = 188. *Fourth Brigade*, Col. John R. Brooke: 27th Conn., Col. Richard S. Bostwick; 2d Del., Lieut.-Col. David L. Stricker; 64th N. Y., Col. Daniel G. Bingham; 53d Pa., Lieut.-Col. Richards McMichael; 145th Pa., Col. Hiram L. Brown. Brigade loss: k, 19; w, 64; m, 446 = 529. *Artillery*, Capt. Rufus D. Pettit: B, 1st N. Y., Capt. Rufus D. Pettit; C, 4th U. S., Lieut. Evan Thomas. Artillery loss: k, 2; w, 25 = 27.

SECOND DIVISION, Brig.-Gen. John Gibbon.

First Brigade, Brig.-Gen. Alfred Sully, Col. Henry W. Hudson, Col. Byron Laflin: 19th Me., Col. Francis E. Heath; 15th Mass., Maj. George C. Joslin; 1st Minn., Lieut.-Col. William Colvill, Jr.; 34th N. Y., Col. Byron Laflin, Lieut.-Col. John Beverly; 82d N. Y. (2d Militia), Col. Henry W. Hudson, Lieut.-Col. James Huston. Brigade loss: w, 16; m, 4 = 20. *Second Brigade*, Brig.-Gen. Joshua T. Owen: 69th Pa., Col. Dennis O'Kane; 71st Pa., Col. Richard P. Smith; 72d Pa., Col. De Witt C. Baxter; 106th Pa., Col. Turner G. Morehead. *Third Brigade*, Col. Norman J. Hall: 19th Mass., Lieut.-Col. Arthur F. Devereux; 20th Mass., Lieut.-Col. George N. Macy; 7th Mich., Capt. Amos E. Steele, Jr.; 42d N. Y., Col. James E. Mallon; 59th N. Y., Lieut.-Col. Max A. Thoman; 127th Pa., Col. William W. Jennings. Brigade loss: k, 3; w, 56; m, 8 = 67. *Artillery*: A, 1st R. I., Capt. William A. Arnold; B, 1st R. I., Lieut. T. Fred. Brown. *Sharp-shooters*: 1st Co. Mass., Capt. William Plumer.

THIRD DIVISION, Maj.-Gen. William H. French.

First Brigade, Col. Samuel S. Carroll: 14th Ind., Col. John Coons; 24th N. J., Col. William B. Robertson; 28th N. J., Lieut.-Col. John A. Wildrick (c), Maj. Samuel K. Wilson; 4th Ohio, Lieut.-Col. Leonard W. Carpenter; 8th Ohio, Lieut.-Col. Franklin Sawyer; 7th W. Va., Col. Joseph Snider, Lieut.-Col. Jonathan H. Lockwood. Brigade loss: k, 29; w, 182; m, 57 = 268. *Second Brigade*, Brig.-Gen. William Hays (c), Col. Charles J. Powers: 14th Conn., Maj. Theodore G. Ellis; 12th N. J., Col. J. Howard Willets (w), Maj. John T. Hill; 108th N. Y., Col. Charles J. Powers, Lieut.-Col. Francis E. Pierce; 130th Pa., Col. Levi Maish (w), Maj. Joseph S. Jenkins. Brigade loss: k, 26; w, 242; m, 61 = 319. *Third Brigade*, Col. John D. MacGregor, Col. Charles Albright: 1st Del., Col. Thomas A. Smyth; 4th N. Y., Lieut.-Col. William Jameson; 132d Pa., Col. Charles Albright, Lieut.-Col. Joseph E. Shreve. Brigade loss: k, 8; w, 80; m, 11 = 99. *Artillery*: G, 1st N. Y., Lieut. Nelson Ames; G, 1st R. I., Capt. George W. Adams. Artillery loss: k, 5; w, 18 = 23.

ARTILLERY RESERVE: I, 1st U. S., Lieut. Edmund Kirby (m w while commanding 5th Maine Battery); A, 4th U. S., Lieut. Alonzo H. Cushing. Artillery loss: w, 2.

THIRD ARMY CORPS, Maj.-Gen. Daniel E. Sickles. Staff loss: w, 1.

FIRST DIVISION, Brig.-Gen. David B. Birney. Staff loss: w, 2.

First Brigade, Brig.-Gen. Charles K. Graham, Col. Thomas W. Egan: 57th Pa., Col. Peter Sides; 63d Pa., Lieut.-Col. William S. Kirkwood (m w), Capt. James F. Ryan; 68th Pa., Col. Andrew H. Tippin; 105th Pa., Col.

‡ In temporary command of a force consisting of the 5th N. H., 88th N. Y., and 81st Pa.
⚓ Served temporarily with the First Brigade.

Amor A. McKnight (k), Lieut.-Col. Calvin A. Craig; 114th Pa., Col. Charles H. T. Collis, Lieut.-Col. Frederick F. Cavada; 141st Pa., Col. Henry J. Madill. Brigade loss: k, 72; w, 490; m, 194 = 756. *Second Brigade*, Brig.-Gen. J. H. Hobart Ward: 20th Ind., Col. John Wheeler; 3d Me., Col. Moses B. Lakeman; 4th Me., Col. Elijah Walker; 38th N. Y., Col. P. Regis de Trobriand; 40th N. Y., Col. Thomas W. Egan; 99th Pa., Col. Asher S. Leidy. Brigade loss: k, 11; w, 124; m, 113 = 248. *Third Brigade*, Col. Samuel B. Hayman: 17th Me., Lieut.-Col. Charles B. Merrill, Col. Thomas A. Roberts; 3d Mich., Col. Byron R. Pierce (w), Lieut.-Col. Edwin S. Pierce; 5th Mich., Lieut.-Col. Edward T. Sherlock (k), Maj. John Pulford; 1st N. Y., Lieut.-Col. Francis L. Leland; 37th N. Y., Lieut.-Col. Gilbert Riordan. Brigade loss: k, 30; w, 283; m, 253 = 566. *Artillery*, Capt. A. Judson Clark: 2d N. J., Lieut. Robert Sims; E, 1st R. I., Lieut. Pardon S. Jastram; F and K, 3d U. S., Lieut. John G. Turnbull. Artillery loss: k, 6; w, 26; m, 3 = 35.

SECOND DIVISION, Maj.-Gen. Hiram G. Berry (k), Brig.-Gen. Joseph B. Carr. Staff loss: k, 1.

First Brigade, Brig.-Gen. Joseph B. Carr, Col. William Blaisdell: 1st Mass., Col. Napoleon B. McLaughlen; 11th Mass., Col. William Blaisdell, Lieut.-Col. Porter D. Tripp; 16th Mass., Lieut.-Col. Waldo Merriam; 11th N. J., Col. Robert McAllister; 26th Pa., Col. Benjamin C. Tilghman (w), Maj. Robert L. Bodine. Brigade loss: k, 52; w, 387; m, 65 = 504. *Second Brigade*, Brig.-Gen. Joseph W. Revere, Col. J. Egbert Farnum: 70th N. Y., Col. J. Egbert Farnum, Lieut.-Col. Thomas Holt; 71st N. Y., Col. Henry L. Potter; 72d N. Y., Col. William O. Stevens (k), Maj. John Leonard; 73d N. Y., Maj. Michael W. Burns; 74th N. Y., Lieut.-Col. William H. Lounsbury (w), Capt. Henry M. Alles (w), Capt. Francis E. Tyler; 120th N. Y., Lieut.-Col. Cornelius D. Westbrook. Brigade loss: k, 26; w, 160; m, 131 = 317. *Third Brigade*, Brig.-Gen. Gershom Mott (w), Col. William J. Sewell: 5th N. J., Col. William J. Sewell, Maj. Ashabel W. Angel (w), Capt. Virgil M. Healy; 6th N. J., Col. George C. Burling (w), Lieut.-Col. Stephen R. Gilkyson; 7th N. J., Col. Louis R. Francine, Lieut.-Col. Francis Price; 8th N. J., Col. John Ramsey (w), Capt. John G. Langston; 2d N. Y., Col. Sidney W. Park (w), Lieut.-Col. William A. Olmsted; 115th Pa., Col. Francis A. Lancaster (k), Maj. John P. Dunne. Brigade loss: k, 57; w, 422; m, 48 = 527. *Artillery*, Capt. Thomas W. Osborn: D, 1st N. Y., Lieut. George B. Winslow; 4th N. Y., Lieut. George F. Barstow, Lieut. William T. McLean; H, 1st U. S., Lieut. Justin E. Dimick (m w), Lieut. James A. Sanderson; K, 4th U. S., Lieut. Francis W. Seeley. Artillery loss: k, 12; w, 68 = 80.

THIRD DIVISION, Maj.-Gen. Amiel W. Whipple (m w), Brig.-Gen. Charles K. Graham. Staff loss: w, 1.

First Brigade, Col. Emlen Franklin: 86th N. Y., Lieut.-Col. Barna J. Chapin (k), Capt. Jacob H. Lansing; 124th N. Y., Col. A. Van Horne Ellis; 122d Pa., Lieut.-Col. Edward McGovern. Brigade loss: k, 47; w, 304; m, 32 = 383. *Second Brigade*, Col. Samuel M. Bowman: 12th N. H., Col. Joseph H. Potter (w); 84th Pa., Lieut.-Col. Milton Opp; 110th Pa., Col. James Crowther (k), Maj. David M. Jones (w and c). Brigade loss: k, 51; w, 290; m, 236 = 577. *Third Brigade*, Col. Hiram Berdan: 1st U. S. Sharpshooters, Lieut.-Col. Caspar Trepp; 2d U. S. Sharpshooters, Maj. Homer R. Stoughton. Brigade loss: k, 11; w, 61; m, 12 = 84. *Artillery*, Capt. Albert A. von Puttkammer, Capt. James F. Huntington: 10th N. Y., Lieut. Samuel Lewis; 11th N. Y., Lieut. John E. Burton; H, 1st Ohio, Capt. James F. Huntington. Artillery loss: k, 2; w, 26; m, 9 = 37.

FIFTH ARMY CORPS, Maj.-Gen. George G. Meade.

FIRST DIVISION, Brig.-Gen. Charles Griffin.

First Brigade, Brig.-Gen. James Barnes: 2d Me., Col. George Varney; 18th Mass., Col. Joseph Hayes; 22d Mass., Col. William S. Tilton; 2d Co. Mass. Sharp-shooters, Lieut. Robert Smith; 1st Mich., Col. Ira C. Abbott; 13th N. Y. (battalion), Capt. William Downey; 25th N. Y., Col. Charles A. Johnson; 118th Pa., Col. Charles M. Prevost. Brigade loss: k, 4; w, 40; m, 4 = 48. *Second Brigade*, Col. James McQuade, Col. Jacob B. Sweitzer: 9th Mass., Col. Patrick R. Guiney; 32d Mass., Lieut.-Col. Luther Stephenson; 4th Mich., Col. Harrison H. Jeffords;

14th N. Y., Lieut.-Col. Thomas M. Davies; 62d Pa., Col. Jacob B. Sweitzer, Lieut.-Col. James C. Hull. Brigade loss: k, 9; w, 46; m, 7 = 62. *Third Brigade*, Col. Thomas B. W. Stockton: 20th Me., Lieut.-Col. Joshua L. Chamberlain; Brady's Co. Mich. Sharp-shooters; 16th Mich., Lieut.-Col. Norval E. Welch; 12th N. Y., Capt. William Huson; 17th N. Y., Lieut.-Col. Nelson B. Bartram; 44th N. Y., Col. James C. Rice; 83d Pa., Col. Strong Vincent. Brigade loss: k, 2; w, 18 = 20. *Artillery*, Capt. Augustus P. Martin: 3d Mass., Capt. Augustus P. Martin; 5th Mass., Capt. Charles A. Phillips; C, 1st R. I., Capt Richard Waterman; D. 5th U. S., Lieut. Charles E. Hazlett. Artillery loss: k, 2; w, 4; m, 2 = 8.

SECOND DIVISION, Maj.-Gen. George Sykes.

First Brigade, Brig.-Gen. Romeyn B. Ayres: 3d U. S. (6 co's), Capt. John D. Wilkins; 4th U. S. (4 co's), Capt. Hiram Dryer; 12th U. S. (5 co's 1st Battalion and 3 co's 2d Battalion), Maj. Richard S. Smith; 14th U. S. (6 co's 1st Battalion and 2 co's 2d Battalion), Capt. Jonathan B. Hagar. Brigade loss: k, 4; w, 17; m, 30 = 51. *Second Brigade*, Col. Sidney Burbank: 2d U. S. (5 co's), Capt. Salem S. Marsh (k), Capt. Samuel A. McKee; 6th U. S. (5 co's), Capt. Levi C. Bootes; 7th U. S. (4 co's), Capt. David P. Hancock; 10th U. S. (3 co's), Lieut. Edward G. Bush; 11th U. S. (6 co's 1st Battalion and 2 co's 2d Battalion), Maj. De L. Floyd-Jones; 17th U. S. (5 co's 1st Battalion and 2 co's 2d Battalion), Maj. George L. Andrews. Brigade loss: k, 17; w, 108; m, 22 = 147. *Third Brigade*, Col. Patrick H. O'Rorke: 5th N. Y., Col. Cleveland Winslow; 140th N. Y., Lieut.-Col. Louis Ernst; 146th N. Y., Col. Kenner Garrard. Brigade loss: k, 4; w, 29; m, 38 = 71. *Artillery*, Capt. Stephen H. Weed: L, 1st Ohio, Capt. Frank C. Gibbs; I, 5th U. S., Lieut. Malbone F. Watson. Artillery loss: k, 2; w, 13; m, 1 = 16.

THIRD DIVISION, Brig.-Gen. Andrew A. Humphreys.

First Brigade, Brig.-Gen. Erastus B. Tyler: 91st Pa., Col. Edgar M. Gregory (w), Lieut.-Col. Joseph H. Sinex; 126th Pa., Lieut.-Col. David W. Rowe (w); 129th Pa., Col. Jacob G. Frick; 134th Pa., Col. Edward O'Brien. Brigade loss: k, 21; w, 166; m, 53 = 240. *Second Brigade*, Col. Peter H. Allabach: 123d Pa., Col. John B. Clark; 131st Pa., Maj. Robert W. Patton; 133d Pa., Col. Franklin B. Speakman; 155th Pa., Lieut.-Col. John H. Cain. Brigade loss: k, 4; w, 31; m, 2 = 37. *Artillery*, Capt. Alanson M. Randol: C, 1st N. Y., Capt. Almont Barnes; E and G, 1st U. S., Capt. Alanson M. Randol.

SIXTH ARMY CORPS, Maj.-Gen. John Sedgwick. Staff loss, w, 1; m, 1 = 2.

Escort: Maj. Hugh M. Janeway: L, 1st N. J. Cav., Lieut. Voorhees Dye; H, 1st Pa. Cav., Capt. William S. Craft.

FIRST DIVISION, Brig.-Gen. William T. H. Brooks. Staff loss: w, 1.

Provost Guard: A, C, and H, 4th N. J., Capt. Charles Ewing. Loss: w, 1. *First Brigade*, Col. Henry W. Brown (w), Col. William H. Penrose, Col. Samuel L. Buck (w), Col. William H. Penrose: 1st N. J., Col. Mark W. Collet (k), Lieut.-Col. William Henry, Jr.; 2d N. J., Col. Samuel L. Buck, Lieut.-Col. Charles Weibecke; 3d N. J., Maj. J. W. H. Stickney; 15th N. J., Col. William H. Penrose, Lieut.-Col. Edward L. Campbell; 23d N. J., Col. E. Burd Grubb. Brigade loss: k, 66; w, 359; m, 86 = 511. *Second Brigade*, Brig.-Gen. Joseph J. Bartlett: 5th Me., Col. Clark S. Edwards; 16th N. Y., Col. Joel J. Seaver; 27th N. Y., Col. Alexander D. Adams; 121st N. Y., Col. Emory Upton; 96th Pa., Maj. William H. Lessig. Brigade loss: k, 101; w, 368; m, 143 = 612. *Third Brigade*, Brig.-Gen. David A. Russell: 18th N. Y., Col. George R. Myers; 32d N. Y., Col. Francis E. Pinto; 49th Pa., Lieut.-Col. Thomas M. Hulings; 95th Pa., Col. Gustavus W. Town (k), Lieut.-Col. Elisha Hall (k), Capt. Theodore H. McCalla; 119th Pa., Col. Peter C. Ellmaker. Brigade loss: k, 35; w, 197; m, 136 = 368. *Artillery*, Maj. John A. Tompkins: 1st Mass., Capt. William H. McCartney; 1st N. J., Lieut. Augustin N. Parsons; A, Md., Capt. James H. Rigby; D, 2d U. S., Lieut. Edward B. Williston. Artillery loss: k, 2; w, 5 = 7.

SECOND DIVISION, Brig.-Gen. Albion P. Howe.

Second Brigade, Col. Lewis A. Grant: 26th N. J., Col. Andrew J. Morrison, Lieut.-Col. Edward Martindale; 2d

Vt., Col. James H. Walbridge; 3d Vt., Col. Thomas O. Seaver, Lieut.-Col. Samuel E. Pingree; 4th Vt., Col. Charles B. Stoughton; 5th Vt., Lieut.-Col. John R. Lewis; 6th Vt., Col. Elisha L. Barney. Brigade loss: k, 39; w, 295; m, 97 = 431. *Third Brigade,* Brig.-Gen. Thomas H. Neill; 7th Me., Lieut.-Col. Selden Connor; 21st N. J., Col. Gilliam Van Houten (m w), Lieut.-Col. Isaac S. Mettler; 20th N. Y., Col. Ernst von Vegesack; 33d N. Y., Col. Robert F. Taylor; 49th N. Y., Col. Daniel B. Bidwell; 77th N. Y., Lieut.-Col. Winsor B. French. Brigade loss: k, 52; w, 394; m, 404 = 850. *Artillery,* Maj. J. Watts de Peyster: 1st N. Y., Capt. Andrew Cowan; F, 5th U. S., Lieut. Leonard Martin. Artillery loss: w, 8; m, 1 = 9.

THIRD DIVISION, Maj.-Gen. John Newton.

First Brigade, Col. Alexander Shaler: 65th N. Y., Lieut.-Col. Joseph E. Hamblin; 67th N. Y., Col. Nelson Cross; 122d N. Y., Col. Silas Titus; 23d Pa., Col. John Ely; 82d Pa., Maj. Isaac C. Bassett. Brigade loss: k, 7; w, 86; m, 67 = 160. *Second Brigade,* Col. William H. Browne (w), Col. Henry L. Eustis: 7th Mass., Col. Thomas D. Johns (w), Lieut.-Col. Franklin P. Harlow; 10th Mass., Lieut.-Col. Joseph B. Parsons; 37th Mass., Col. Oliver Edwards; 36th N. Y., Lieut.-Col. James J. Walsh; 2d R. I., Col. Horatio Rogers, Jr. Brigade loss: k, 42; w, 278; m, 22 = 342. *Third Brigade,* Brig.-Gen. Frank Wheaton: 62d N. Y., Lieut.-Col. Theodore B. Hamilton; 93d Pa., Capt. John S. Long; 98th Pa., Col. John F. Ballier (w), Lieut.-Col. George Wynkoop; 102d Pa., Col. Joseph M. Kinkead; 139th Pa., Col. Frederick H. Collier. Brigade loss: k, 48; w, 237; m, 200 = 485. *Artillery,* Capt. Jeremiah McCarthy: C and D, 1st Pa., Capt. Jeremiah McCarthy; G, 2d U. S., Lieut. John H. Butler. Artillery loss: k, 1; w, 4; m, 4 = 9.

LIGHT DIVISION, Col. Hiram Burnham: 6th Me., Lieut.-Col. Benjamin F. Harris; 31st N. Y., Col. Frank Jones; 43d N. Y., Col. Benjamin F. Baker; 61st Pa., Col. George C. Spear (k), Maj. George W. Dawson; 5th Wis., Col. Thomas S. Allen; 3d N. Y. Battery, Lieut. William A. Harn. Division loss: k, 94; w, 404; m, 310 = 808.

ELEVENTH ARMY CORPS, Maj.-Gen. Oliver O. Howard.

Escort: I and K, 1st Ind. Cav., Capt. Abram Sharra.

FIRST DIVISION, Brig.-Gen. Charles Devens, Jr. (w), Brig.-Gen. Nathaniel C. McLean. Staff loss: w, 1.

First Brigade, Col. Leopold von Gilsa: 41st N. Y., Maj. Detleo von Einsiedel; 45th N. Y., Col. George von Amsberg; 54th N. Y., Lieut.-Col. Charles Ashby, Maj. Stephen Kovacs; 153d Pa., Col. Charles Glanz, Lieut.-Col. Jacob Dachrodt. Brigade loss: k, 16; w, 117; m, 131 = 264. *Second Brigade,* Brig.-Gen. Nathaniel C. McLean, Col. John C. Lee: 17th Conn., Col. William H. Noble (w), Maj. Allen G. Brady; 25th Ohio, Col. William P. Richardson (w), Maj. Jeremiah Williams; 55th Ohio, Col. John C. Lee, Lieut.-Col. Charles B. Gambee; 75th Ohio, Col. Robert Reily (k), Capt. Benjamin Morgan; 107th Ohio, Col. Seraphim Meyer (w), Lieut.-Col. Charles Mueller. Brigade loss: k, 45; w, 348; m, 299 = 692. *Unattached,* 8th N. Y. (1 co.), Lieut. Herman Rosenkranz. *Artillery:* 13th N. Y., Capt. Julius Dieckmann. Artillery loss: w, 11; m, 2 = 13.

SECOND DIVISION, Brig.-Gen. Adolph von Steinwehr.

First Brigade, Col. Adolphus Buschbeck: 29th N. Y., Lieut.-Col. Louis Hartmann (w), Maj. Alex. von Schluembach; 154th N. Y., Col. Patrick H. Jones (w), Lieut.-Col. Henry C. Loomis; 27th Pa., Lieut.-Col. Lorenz Cantador; 73d Pa., Lieut.-Col. William Moore (w). Brigade loss: k, 26; w, 229; m, 228 = 483. *Second Brigade,* Brig.-Gen. Francis C. Barlow: 33d Mass., Col. Adin B. Underwood; 134th N. Y., Col. Charles R. Coster; 136th N. Y., Col. James Wood, Jr.; 73d Ohio, Col. Orland Smith. Brigade loss: w, 9; m, 14 = 23. *Artillery:* I, 1st N. Y., Capt. Michael Wiedrich. Artillery loss: k, 1; w, 10; m, 2 = 13.

THIRD DIVISION, Maj.-Gen. Carl Schurz. Staff loss: w, 1.

First Brigade, Brig.-Gen. Alexander Schimmelfennig: 82d Ill., Col. Frederick Hecker (w), Maj. Ferdinand H. Rolshausen (w), Capt. Jacob Lasalle; 68th N. Y., Col.

Gotthilf Bourry; 157th N. Y., Col. Philip P. Brown, Jr.; 61st Ohio, Col. Stephen J. McGroarty; 74th Pa., Lieut.-Col. Adolph von Hartung. Brigade loss: k, 84; w, 215; m, 120 = 419. *Second Brigade,* Col. W. Krzyzanowski: 58th N. Y., Capt. Frederick Braun (k), Capt. Emil Koenig; 119th N. Y., Col. Elias Peissner (k), Lieut.-Col. John T. Lockman; 75th Pa., Col. Francis Mahler; 26th Wis., Col. William H. Jacobs. Brigade loss: k, 36; w, 219; m, 153 = 408. *Unattached,* 82d Ohio, Col. James S. Robinson. Loss: k, 8; w, 48; m, 25 = 81. *Artillery:* I, 1st Ohio, Capt. Hubert Dilger. Artillery loss: k, 1; w, 10 = 11.

RESERVE ARTILLERY, Lieut.-Col. Louis Schirmer: 2d N. Y., Capt. Hermann Jahn; K, 1st Ohio, Capt. William L. De Beck; C, 1st W. Va., Capt. Wallace Hill. Reserve artillery loss: w, 3.

TWELFTH ARMY CORPS, Maj.-Gen. Henry W. Slocum. Staff loss: w, 1.

Provost Guard: 10th Me. (battalion), Capt. John D. Beardsley. Loss: w, 2; m, 1 = 3.

FIRST DIVISION, Brig.-Gen. Alpheus S. Williams. Staff loss: m, 1.

First Brigade, Brig.-Gen. Joseph F. Knipe: 5th Conn., Col. Warren W. Packer (c), Lieut.-Col. James A. Betts, Maj. David F. Lane; 28th N. Y., Lieut.-Col. Elliott W. Cook (c), Maj. Theophilo Fitzgerald; 46th Pa., Maj. Cyrus Strous (k), Capt. Ed. L. Witman; 128th Pa., Col. Joseph A. Matthews (c), Maj. Cephas W. Dyer. Brigade loss: k, 5; w, 53; m, 394 = 452. *Second Brigade,* Col. Samuel Ross: 20th Conn., Lieut.-Col. William B. Wooster (c), Maj. Philo B. Buckingham; 3d Md., Lieut.-Col. Gilbert P. Robinson; 123d N. Y., Col. Archibald L. McDougall; 145th N. Y., Col. E. Livingston Price (w), Capt. George W. Reid. Brigade loss: k, 42; w, 253; m, 204 = 499. *Third Brigade,* Brig.-Gen. Thomas H. Ruger: 27th Ind., Col. Silas Colgrove (w); 2d Mass., Col. Samuel M. Quincy; 13th, N. J., Col. Ezra A. Carman, Maj. John Grimes (w), Capt. George A. Beardsley; 107th N. Y., Col. Alexander S. Diven; 3d Wis., Col. William Hawley. Brigade loss: k, 81; w, 465; m, 68 = 614. *Artillery,* Capt. Robert H. Fitzhugh: K, 1st N. Y., Lieut. Edward L. Bailey; M, 1st N. Y., Lieut. Charles E. Winegar (c), Lieut. John D. Woodbury; F, 4th U. S., Lieut. Franklin B. Crosby (k), Lieut. Edward D. Muhlenberg. Artillery loss: k, 7; w, 30; m, 9 = 46.

SECOND DIVISION, Brig.-Gen. John W. Geary.

First Brigade, Col. Charles Candy: 5th Ohio, Lieut.-Col. Robert L. Kilpatrick (w), Maj. Henry E. Symmes; 7th Ohio, Col. William R. Creighton; 29th Ohio, Lieut.-Col. Thomas Clark; 66th Ohio, Lieut.-Col. Eugene Powell; 28th Pa., Maj. Lansford F. Chapman (k); Capt. Conrad U. Meyer; 147th Pa., Lieut.-Col. Ario Pardee, Jr. Brigade loss: k, 58; w, 314; m, 151 = 523. *Second Brigade,* Brig.-Gen. Thomas L. Kane: 29th Pa., Lieut.-Col. William Rickards, Jr.; 109th Pa., Col. Henry J. Stainrook (k), Capt. John Young, Jr.; 111th Pa., Col. George A. Cobham, Jr.; 124th Pa., Lieut.-Col. Simon Litzenberg; 125th Pa., Col. Jacob Higgins. Brigade loss: k, 16; w, 90, m, 33 = 139. *Third Brigade,* Brig.-Gen. George S. Greene: 60th N. Y., Lieut.-Col. John C. O. Redington; 78th N. Y., Maj. Henry R. Stagg, Capt. William H. Randall; 102d N. Y., Col. James C. Lane; 137th N. Y., Col. David Ireland; 149th N. Y., Maj. Abel G. Cook (w), Capt. Oliver T. May, Lieut.-Col. Koert S. Van Voorhis. Brigade loss: k, 49; w, 219; m, 260 = 528. *Artillery,* Capt. Joseph M. Knap: E, Pa., Lieut. Charles Atwell (w), Lieut. James D. McGill; F, Pa., Capt. Robert B. Hampton (k), Lieut. James P. Fleming. Artillery loss: k, 3; w, 15 = 18.

CAVALRY CORPS,↓ Brig.-Gen. George Stoneman.

FIRST DIVISION, Brig.-Gen. Alfred Pleasonton.

First Brigade, Col. Benjamin F. Davis: 8th Ill., Lieut.-Col. David R. Clendenin; 3d Ind., Col. George H. Chapman; 8th N. Y., —— (w), Col. William Sackett. Brigade loss: k, 1; w, 8; m, 22 = 31. *Second Brigade,* Col. Thomas C. Devin: L, 1st Mich., Lieut. John K. Truax; 6th N. Y., Lieut.-Col. Duncan McVicar (k), Capt. William E. Beardsley; 8th Pa., Maj. Pennock Huey; 17th Pa., Col. Josiah H. Kellogg; 6th N. Y. Battery,

↓ The Second and Third Divisions, First Brigade, First Division, and the Regular Reserve Brigade, with Robertson's and Tidball's batteries, on the "Stoneman Raid."

Lieut. Joseph W. Martin. Brigade loss: k, 12; w, 54; m, 134 = 200.

SECOND DIVISION, Brig.-Gen. William W. Averell.

First Brigade, Col. Horace B. Sargent: 1st Mass., Lieut.-Col. Greely S. Curtis; 4th N. Y., Col. Louis P. Di Cesnola; 6th Ohio, Maj. Benjamin C. Stanhope; 1st R. I., Lieut.-Col. John L. Thompson. Brigade loss: w, 6; m, 2 = 8. *Second Brigade*, Col. John B. McIntosh: 3d Pa., Lieut.-Col. Edward S. Jones; 4th Pa., Lieut.-Col. William E. Doster: 16th Pa., Lieut.-Col. Lorenzo D. Rogers. *Artillery :* A, 2d U. S., Capt. John C. Tidball.

THIRD DIVISION, Brig.-Gen. David McM. Gregg.

First Brigade, Col. Judson Kilpatrick: 1st Me., Col. Calvin S. Douty; 2d N. Y., Lieut.-Col. Henry E. Davies, Jr.; 10th N. Y., Lieut.-Col. William Irvine. Brigade loss: k, 1; w, 1; m, 24 = 26. *Second Brigade*, Col. Percy Wyndham: 12th Ill., Lieut.-Col. Hasbrouck Davis; 1st Md., Lieut.-Col. James M. Deems; 1st N. J., Lieut.-Col. Virgil Brodrick; 1st Pa., Col. John P. Taylor. Brigade loss: k, 2; w, 3; m, 40 = 45. *Reserve Cavalry Brigade*, Brig.-Gen. John Buford: 6th Pa., Maj. Robert Morris, Jr.; 1st U. S., Capt. R. S. C. Lord; 2d U. S., Maj. Charles J. Whiting; 5th U. S., Capt. James E. Harrison; 6th U. S., Capt. George C. Cram. Brigade loss: k, 1; w, 3; m, 75 = 79. *Artillery*, Capt. James M. Robertson: B and L, 2d U. S., Lieut. Albert O. Vincent; M, 2d U. S., Lieut. Robert Clarke; E, 4th U. S., Lieut. Samuel S. Elder.

The casualties in the Union forces during the campaign were as follows:

	Killed.	Wounded.	Captured or Missing.	Total.
Germanna Ford, April 29	1	4	......	5
Franklin's Crossing, April 29 — May 2	2	18	......	20
Fitzhugh's Crossing, April 29 — May 2	19	144	9	172
Stoneman's Raid, Apl. 29 — May 11	4	7	139	150
Old Wilderness Tavern, April 30	1	1	......	2
Chancellorsville, April 30	......	3	......	3
Spotsylvania C. H., April 30	3	12	36	51
Rapidan Station, May 1	1	14	24	39
Chancellorsville, May 1 — 6	1082	6849	4214	12,145
Fredericksburg, or Marye's and Salem Heights, May 3, 4	493	2710	1497	4,700
Grand total	1606	9762	5919	17,287

According to the returns for April 30, 1863 ("Official Records," Vol. XXV., Pt. II., p. 320), the effective strength of Hooker's army was, in round numbers, about 130,000, distributed as follows: Infantry, 111,000; cavalry, 11,000; and artillery, 8000, with 404 pieces of the latter arm.

THE CONFEDERATE ARMY.

ARMY OF NORTHERN VIRGINIA.— General Robert E. Lee.

FIRST ARMY CORPS. ♪

MCLAWS'S DIVISION, Maj.-Gen. Lafayette McLaws.

Wofford's Brigade, Brig.-Gen. W. T. Wofford: 16th Ga., —— ; ♩ 18th Ga., —— ; 24th Ga., —— ; Cobb's (Ga.) Legion, —— ; Phillips's (Ga.) Legion, —— . Brigade loss: k, 74; w, 479; m, 9 = 562. *Semmes's Brigade*, Brig.-Gen. Paul J. Semmes: 10th Ga., Lieut.-Col. W. C. Holt; 50th Ga., Lieut.-Col. F. Kearse; 51st Ga., Col. W. M. Slaughter (k), Lieut.-Col. Edward Ball (w); 53d Ga., Col. James P. Simms. Brigade loss: k, 85; w, 492; m, 26 = 603. *Kershaw's Brigade*, Brig.-Gen. Joseph B. Kershaw: 2d S. C., Col. John D. Kennedy; 3d S. C., Maj. R. C. Maffett; 7th S. C., Col. Elbert Bland; 8th S. C., Col. John W. Henagan; 15th S. C., Lieut.-Col. Joseph F. Gist; 3d S. C. Battalion, Lieut.-Col. W. G. Rice. Brigade loss: k, 12; w, 90; m, 2 = 104. *Barksdale's Brigade*, Brig.-Gen. William Barksdale : 13th Miss., Col. J. W. Carter; 17th Miss., Col. W. D. Holder; 18th Miss., Col. Thomas M. Griffin; 21st Miss., Col. B. G. Humphreys. Brigade loss: k, 43; w, 208; m, 341 = 592. *Artillery*, Col. Henry C. Cabell: Ga. Battery (Troup Art'y), Capt. H. H. Carlton; Ga. Battery, Capt. John C. Fraser; Va. Battery (1st Howitzers), Capt. E. S. McCarthy; N. C. Battery, Capt. B. C. Manly. Artillery loss: k, 5; w, 21; m, 2 = 28.

ANDERSON'S DIVISION, Maj.-Gen. Richard H. Anderson.

Wilcox's Brigade, Brig.-Gen. Cadmus M. Wilcox: 8th Ala., Col. Y. L. Royston (w), Lieut.-Col. H. A. Herbert; 9th Ala., Maj. J. H. J. Williams; 10th Ala., Col. William H. Forney; 11th Ala., Col. J. C. C. Sanders; 14th Ala., Col. L. Pinckard (w). Brigade loss: k, 72; w, 372; m, 91 = 535. *Wright's Brigade*, Brig.-Gen. A. R. Wright: 3d Ga., Maj. J. F. Jones (w), Capt. C. H. Andrews; 22d Ga., Lieut.-Col. J. Wasden; 48th Ga., Lieut.-Col. R. W. Carswell; 2d Ga. Battalion, Maj. George W. Ross. Brigade loss: k, 25; w, 271 = 296. *Mahone's Brigade*, Brig.-Gen. William Mahone: 6th Va., Col. George T. Rogers; 12th Va., Lieut.-Col. E. M. Feild; 16th Va., Lieut.-Col. R. O. Whitehead; 41st Va., Col. William A. Parham; 61st Va., Col. V. D. Groner. Brigade loss: k, 24; w, 134; m, 97 = 255. *Posey's Brigade*, Brig.-Gen. Carnot Posey: 12th Miss., Lieut.-Col. M. B. Harris (w), Maj. S. B. Thomas;

16th Miss., Col. Samuel E. Baker; 19th Miss., Col. N. H. Harris; 48th Miss., Col. Joseph M. Jayne (w). Brigade loss: k, 41; w, 184; m, 65 = 290. *Perry's Brigade*, Brig.-Gen. E. A. Perry: 2d Fla., —— ; 5th Fla., —— ; 8th Fla., —— . Brigade loss: k, 21; w, 88 = 109. *Artillery*, Lieut.-Col. J. J. Garnett: Va. Battery, Capt. C. R. Grandy; Va. Battery (Lewis's), Lieut. Nathan Penick; La. Battery, Capt. Victor Maurin; Va. Battery, Capt. Joseph D. Moore. Artillery loss: k, 1; w, 13 = 14.

ARTILLERY RESERVE.

Alexander's Battalion, Col. E. P. Alexander: Va. Battery (Eubank's); Va. Battery (Jordan's); La. Battery (Moody's); Va. Battery (Parker's); S. C. Battery (Rhett's); Va. Battery (Woolfolk's). Battalion loss: k, 6; w, 35; m, 21 = 62. *Washington (La.) Artillery*, Col. J. B. Walton: 1st Co. (Squires's); 2d Co. (Richardson's); 3d Co. (Miller's); 4th Co. (Eshleman's). Battalion loss: k, 4; w, 8; m, 33 = 45.

SECOND ARMY CORPS, Lieut.-Gen. Thomas J. Jackson (m w), Maj.-Gen. Ambrose P. Hill (w), Brig.-Gen. R. E. Rodes, Maj.-Gen. James E. B. Stuart. Staff loss: k, 2; w, 3 = 5.

LIGHT DIVISION, Maj.-Gen. Ambrose P. Hill, Brig.-Gen. Henry Heth (w), Brig.-Gen. William D. Pender (w), Brig.-Gen. James J. Archer. Staff loss: k, 2; w, 2 = 4.

Heth's Brigade, Brig.-Gen. Henry Heth, Col. J. M. Brockenbrough: 40th Va., Col. J. M. Brockenbrough, Lieut.-Col. F. W. Cox (w), Capt. T. E. Betts; 47th Va., Col. Robert M. Mayo; 55th Va., Col. Francis Mallory (k), Lieut.-Col. William S. Christian (w), Maj. A. D. Saunders (k), Lieut. R. L. Williams, Maj. Evan Rice; 22d Va. Battalion, Lieut.-Col. E. P. Tayloe. Brigade loss: k, 33; w, 270 = 303. *Thomas's Brigade*, Brig.-Gen. E. L. Thomas: 14th Ga., Col. R. W. Folsom; 35th Ga., Capt. John Duke; 45th Ga., Lieut.-Col. W. L. Grice; 49th Ga., Maj. S. T. Player. Brigade loss: k, 21; w, 156 = 177. *Lane's Brigade*, Brig.-Gen. James H. Lane: 7th N. C., Col. E. G. Haywood (w), Lieut.-Col. J. L. Hill (k), Maj. William L. Davidson (w), Capt. N. A. Pool; 18th N. C., Col. Thomas J. Purdie (k), Lieut.-Col. Forney George (w), Maj. John D. Barry; 28th N. C., Col. S. D. Lowe, Capt. Edward F.

♪ Lieut.-Gen. James Longstreet, with Hood's and Pickett's divisions and Dearing's and Henry's artillery battalions, absent in South-eastern Virginia.

♩ The dash indicates that the name of the commanding officer has not been found in the "Official Records."—EDITORS.

Lovill; 33d N. C., Col. Clark M. Avery (w), Capt. Joseph H. Saunders; 37th N. C., Col. W. M. Barbour (w). Brigade loss: k, 161; w, 626; m, 122 = 909. *McGowan's Brigade*, Brig.-Gen. Samuel McGowan (w), Col. O. E. Edwards (w), Col. Abner Perrin, Col. D. H. Hamilton: 1st S. C. (Prov. Army), Col. D. H. Hamilton, Capt. W. P. Shooter; 1st S. C. Rifles, Col. James M. Perrin (m w), Lieut.-Col. F. E. Harrison; 12th S. C., ———; 13th S. C., Col. O. E. Edwards, Lieut.-Col. B. T. Brockman; 14th S. C., Col. Abner Perrin. Brigade loss: k, 46; w, 402; m, 7 = 455. *Archer's Brigade*, Brig.-Gen. James J. Archer, Col. B. D. Fry: 13th Ala., Col. B. D. Fry; 5th Ala. Battalion, Capt. S. D. Stewart (k), Capt. A. N. Porter; 1st Tenn. (Prov. Army), Lieut.-Col. N. J. George; 7th Tenn., Lieut.-Col. John A. Fite; 14th Tenn., Col. William McComb (w), Capt. R. C. Wilson. Brigade loss: k, 44; w, 305; m, 16 = 365. *Pender's Brigade*, Brig.-Gen. W. D. Pender: 13th N. C., Col. Alfred M. Scales (w), Lieut.-Col. J. H. Hyman; 16th N. C., Col. John S. McElroy (w), Lieut.-Col. William A. Stowe (w); 22d N. C., Lieut.-Col. Chris. C. Cole (k); 34th N. C., ———; 38th N. C., Lieut.-Col. John Ashford. Brigade loss: k, 116; w, 567; m, 68 = 751. *Artillery*, Col. R. L. Walker, Maj. William J. Pegram: S. C, Battery, Capt. E. B. Brunson; Va. Battery (Crenshaw's), Lieut. John H. Chamberlayne; Va. Battery, Capt. Greenlee Davidson (m w); Va. Battery, Lieut. Joseph McGraw; Va. Battery, Capt. E. A. Marye. Artillery loss: k, 5; w, 28 = 33.

D. H. HILL'S DIVISION, Brig.-Gen. R. E. Rodes, Brig.-Gen. S. D. Ramseur.

Rodes's Brigade, Brig.-Gen. R. E. Rodes, Col. E. A. O'Neal (w), Col. J. M. Hall: 3d Ala., Capt. M. F. Bonham; 5th Ala., Col. J. M. Hall, Lieut.-Col. E. L. Hobson (w), Capt. W. T. Rufus (m w), Capt. T. M. Riley; 6th Ala., Col. James N. Lightfoot; 12th Ala., Col. Samuel B. Pickens; 26th Ala., Col. E. A. O'Neal, Lieut.-Col. John S. Garvin (w), Lieut. M. J. Taylor. Brigade loss: k, 90; w, 538; m, 188 = 816. *Colquitt's Brigade*, Brig.-Gen. A. H. Colquitt: 6th Ga., Col. John T. Lofton; 19th Ga., Col. A. J. Hutchins; 23d Ga., Col. Emory F. Best; 27th Ga., Col. C. T. Zachry; 28th Ga., Col. Tully Graybill. Brigade loss: k, 9; w, 128; m, 312 = 449. *Ramseur's Brigade*, Brig.-Gen. S. D. Ramseur (w), Col. F. M. Parker: 2d N. C., Col. W. R. Cox (w); 4th N. C., Col. Bryan Grimes; 14th N. C., Col. R. T. Bennett; 30th N. C., Col. F. M. Parker. Brigade loss: k, 151; w, 529; m, 108 = 788. *Doles's Brigade*, Brig.-Gen. George Doles: 4th Ga., Col. Philip Cook (w), Lieut.-Col. D. R. E. Winn; 12th Ga., Col. Edward Willis; 21st Ga., Col. J. T. Mercer; 44th Ga., Col. J. B. Estes. Brigade loss: k, 66; w, 343; m, 28 = 437. *Iverson's Brigade*, Brig.-Gen. Alfred Iverson: 5th N. C., Col. Thomas M. Garrett (w), Lieut.-Col. J. W. Lea (w), Maj. William J. Hill (w), Capt. S. B. West; 12th N. C., Maj. D. P. Rowe (k), Lieut.-Col. R. D. Johnston; 20th N. C., Col. T. F. Toon (w), Lieut.-Col. Nelson Slough; 23d N. C., Col. D. H. Christie. Brigade loss: k, 67; w, 330; m, 73 = 470. *Artillery*, Lieut.-Col. T. H. Carter: Ala. Battery, Capt. William J. Reese; Va. Battery, Capt. W. P. Carter; Va. Battery, Capt. C. W. Fry; Va. Battery, Capt. R. C. M. Page. Artillery loss: k, 9; m, 37 = 46.

EARLY'S DIVISION, Maj.-Gen. Jubal A. Early.

Gordon's Brigade, Brig.-Gen. John B. Gordon: 13th Ga., ———; 26th Ga., ———; 31st Ga., ———; 38th Ga., ———; 60th Ga., ———; 61st Ga., ———. Brigade loss: k, 16; w, 145 = 161. *Hoke's Brigade*, Brig.-Gen. Robert F. Hoke (w): 6th N. C., ———; 21st N. C., ———; 54th N. C., ———; 57th N. C., ———; 1st N. C. Battalion, ———. Brigade loss: k, 35; w, 195 = 230. *Smith's Brigade*, Brig.-Gen. William Smith: 13th Va., ———; 49th Va., ———; 52d Va., ———; 58th Va., Col. F. H. Board. Brigade loss: k, 11; w, 75 = 86. *Hays's Brigade*, Brig.-Gen. Harry T. Hays: 5th La., ———; 6th La., ———; 7th La., ———; 8th La., ———; 9th La., ———. Brigade loss: k, 63; w, 306 = 369. *Artillery*, Lieut.-Col. R. S. Andrews: Md. Battery (Brown's); Va. Battery (Carpenter's); Md. Battery (Dement's); Va. Battery (Raine's). Artillery loss (not reported).

TRIMBLE'S DIVISION, Brig.-Gen. R. E. Colston.

First Brigade, Brig.-Gen. E. F. Paxton (k), Col. J. H. S. Funk: 2d Va., Col. J. Q. A. Nadenbousch; 4th Va., Maj. William Terry; 5th Va., Col. J. H. S. Funk, Lieut.-Col. H. J. Williams; 27th Va., Col. J. K. Edmondson (w), Lieut.-Col. D. M. Shriver; 33d Va., Col. A. Spengler. Brigade loss: k, 54; w, 430; m, 9 = 493 *Second Brigade*, Brig.-Gen. J. R. Jones, Col. T. S. Garnett (k), Col. A. S. Vandeventer: 21st Va., Capt. John B. Moseley; 42d Va., Lieut.-Col. R. W. Withers; 44th Va., Maj. N. Cobb, Capt. Thomas R. Buckner; 48th Va., Col. T. S. Garnett, Maj. Oscar White; 50th Va., Col. A. S. Vandeventer, Maj. L. J. Perkins, Capt. Frank W. Kelly. Brigade loss: k, 52; w, 420 = 472. *Third Brigade* (Colston's), Col. E. T. H. Warren (w), Col. T. V. Williams (w), Lieut.-Col. S. D. Thruston (w), Lieut.-Col. H. A. Brown: 1st N. C., Col. J. A. McDowell (w); 3d N. C., Lieut.-Col. S. D. Thruston; 10th Va., Col. E. T. H. Warren, Lieut.-Col. S. T. Walker (k), Maj. Joshua Stover (k), Capt. A. H. Smals; 23d Va., Lieut.-Col. Simeon T. Walton; 37th Va., Col. T. V. Williams. Brigade loss: k, 128; w, 594; m, 80 = 802. *Fourth Brigade*, Brig.-Gen. F. T. Nicholls (w), Col. J. M. Williams: 1st La., Capt. E. D. Willett; 2d La., Col. J. M. Williams, Lieut.-Col. R. E. Burke; 10th La., Lieut.-Col. John M. Legett (k); 14th La., Lieut.-Col. D. Zable; 15th La., Capt. William C. Michie. Brigade loss: k, 47; w, 266; m, 10 = 323. *Artillery*, Lieut.-Col. H. P. Jones: Va. Battery, Capt. J. McD. Carrington; Va. Battery (Garber's), Lieut. Alexander H. Fultz; Va. Battery, Capt. W. A. Tanner; La. Battery, Capt. C. Thompson. Artillery loss (not reported).

ARTILLERY RESERVE, Col. S. Crutchfield.

Brown's Battalion, Col. J. Thompson Brown: Va. Battery (Brooke's); Va. Battery (Dance's); Va. Battery (Graham's); Va. Battery (Hupp's); Va. Battery (Smith's); Va. Battery (Watson's). Battalion loss (not reported). *McIntosh's Battalion*, Maj. D. G. McIntosh: Ala. Battery (Hurt's), Va. Battery (Johnson's); Va. Battery (Lusk's); Va. Battery (Wooding's). Battalion loss (not reported).

RESERVE ARTILLERY, Brig.-Gen. William N. Pendleton. *Sumter (Ga.) Battalion*, Lieut.-Col. A. S. Cutts: Battery A (Ross's); Battery B (Patterson's); Battery C (Wingfield's). Battalion loss: w, 3. *Nelson's Battalion*, Lieut.-Col. William Nelson: Va. Battery (Kirkpatrick's); Va. Battery (Massie's); Ga. Battery (Milledge's). Battalion loss (not reported).

CAVALRY, Maj.-Gen. James E. B. Stuart.

Second Brigade, Brig.-Gen. Fitzhugh Lee: 1st Va., ———; 2d Va., ———; 3d Va., Col. Thomas H. Owen; 4th Va., Col. Williams C. Wickham. Brigade loss: k, 4; w, 7 = 11. *Third Brigade* (engaged in resisting "the Stoneman raid"), Brig.-Gen. W. H. F. Lee: 2d N. C., Lieut.-Col. William H. Payne; 5th Va., Col. Thomas L. Rosser; 9th Va., Col. R. L. T. Beale; 10th Va., ———; 13th Va., Col. John R. Chambliss, Jr.; 15th Va., ———. Brigade loss (not reported). *Horse Artillery*, Maj. R. F. Beckham: Va. Battery, Capt. M. N. Moorman; Va. Battery, Capt. James Breathed; Va. Battery, Capt. William M. McGregor. Horse Artillery loss: k, 4; w, 6 = 10.

The total loss of the Confederate Army, based mainly upon the reports of brigade and division commanders, aggregated 1649 killed, 9106 wounded, and 1708 captured or missing = 12,463.

The return of the Army of Northern Virginia for March 31st, 1863 ("Official Records," Vol. XXV., Pt. II., p. 696), shows an "effective total" of all arms of 57,112. To this number there should be added the net increase during the month of April, a period of "rest and recruiting," of perhaps 3000, and say 1500 for the reserve artillery of Jackson's corps, not reported on the return for March. This addition gives a total of 61,612. Then, deducting Hampton's brigade of cavalry, recruiting south of the James River, and numbering, perhaps, 1600, the effective force of Lee's Army on the Rappahannock may be estimated at not less than 60,000, with probably 170 pieces of artillery.

BREAKING UP THE UNION CAMP AT FALMOUTH. FROM A PHOTOGRAPH.

HOOKER'S APPOINTMENT AND REMOVAL.

BY CHARLES F. BENJAMIN. ⌡

WHEN, after the Mud March ⚓ that succeeded the disaster of Fredericksburg, General Burnside, in a fit of humiliation, telegraphed to Washington requesting, for the second time, to be relieved, the question of his successor was already being considered as a probability. Though stung by the loud call that went up for McClellan from the army that had twice met disaster after parting with him, the cabinet were not shaken in the conclusion that McClellan must not be restored, for the jocund Seward, equally with the patient Lincoln, drew the line at a military dictatorship, such as would be virtually implied by a second restoration, under such pressure. But while firm, the authorities were circumspect, and concluded that it would not be prudent to increase the tension between themselves and a possible prætorian camp by sending an outsider to take the command from Burnside. Subject to this conclusion, General Halleck and Secretary Stanton favored the transfer of Rosecrans, for whom McClellan might

be expected to say a good word to supplement his inherent strength as a repeatedly victorious commander; but it was then thought injudicious to put another Western man in command.

The choice being narrowed to the Army of the Potomac, a process of exclusion began. Franklin was under a cloud [see note, p. 216] and was considered out of the question; Sumner had many qualifications, but his age and growing feebleness were beyond remedy; Couch was a possible second, and still more likely third choice; and, briefly, the selection was found to lie among Hooker, Reynolds, and Meade. ⌡ The first-named had a strong popular lead, but General Halleck, backed by the Secretary of War, contended that there were reasons of an imperative character why he should not be intrusted with an independent command of so high a degree of responsibility. Stress was laid upon the fact that in the dispositions for the attack on Marye's Heights, General Burnside, who at that time could have had no valid motive for jealousy

⌡ The writer of this paper occupied responsible and confidential positions at the headquarters of the Army of the Potomac and in the War Department.— EDITORS.

⚓ In his official report of the Rappahannock campaign, General Burnside says: "I made four distinct attempts, between November 9th, 1862, and January 25th, 1863. The first failed for want of pontoons; the second was the battle of Fredericksburg; the third was stopped by the President; and the fourth was defeated by the elements or other causes. After the last attempt to move I was, on January 25th, 1863, relieved of the command of the Army of the Potomac." The fourth attempt mentioned by General Burnside has passed into history as the "Mud March." The plan was to move Franklin's two corps, or the Left Grand Division, to Banks's Ford, where Franklin was to cross and seize the heights on the river road north of the Orange Turnpike. Franklin was to be supported by Hooker and Sumner, with the Center and Right Grand Divisions. Franklin and Hooker marched from their camps and bivouacked near Banks's Ford on January 20th; but a rain storm set

in that evening making the roads impassable for pontoon wagons, and after several attempts to haul the boats to the river by hand the movement was abandoned. The artillery and wagons became mired, and the army, with all of its necessary material, was in fact foot-fast in the soft, clayey soil that abounds in that region. In a dejected mood the army splashed back to its old camps around Falmouth. See also p. 118.— EDITORS.

↓ I have been told recently, on hearsay testimony, that Sedgwick was sounded and said he ought not to be appointed because he was a McClellan man. I never heard that Sedgwick was ever proposed as successor to Burnside, and I cannot believe it, knowing the *limited* though warm regard of Secretary Stanton for him. Stanton always spoke of Sedgwick as a brave, thoroughgoing soldier, who staid in camp, gave Washington a wide berth, and did not intrigue against his superiors; but I never heard him attribute to Sedgwick such high qualities for a great command as he imputed to some other officers of that army.— C. F. B.

of Hooker, had intrusted him with no important part, although he was present on the field and of equal rank with Sumner and Franklin, to whom the active duties of the battle were assigned. President Lincoln apparently yielded to the views of those in charge of the military department of affairs, and thereupon Halleck confidentially inquired of Reynolds if he was prepared to accept the command. Reynolds replied that he expected to obey all lawful orders coming to his hands, but as the communication seemed to imply the possession of an option in himself, he deemed it his duty to say frankly that he could not accept the command in a voluntary sense, unless a liberty of action should be guaranteed to him considerably beyond any which he had reason to expect. He was thereupon dropped, and the choice further and finally restricted to Hooker and Meade, with the chances a hundred to one in favor of the latter by reason of the fixed conviction of the Secretary of War that the former ought not to be chosen in any contingency. Stanton knew that there were two Hookers in the same man. He knew one as an excellent officer, mentally strong, clever and tireless, and charming (almost magnetic) in address. It was the other Hooker on whom he wished to take no chances.

Hooker and Meade were in camp, attending to such military duties as the lull of action gave occasion for, neither having taste nor talent for intrigue, each aware that "something" was afoot, but both supposing that the ferment concerned Hooker and Reynolds, and, possibly, some third man beyond the lines of the army. But there were men about Hooker who believed in, and hoped to rise with him, and who, at all events, could afford to take the chances of success or failure with him; and these men were rich in personal and external resources of the kinds needed for the combination of political, financial, and social forces to a common end. By their exertions, such influences had been busy for Hooker ever since the recent battle, greatly aided by the unselfish labor of earnest men who believed that Hooker's military reputation (the pugnacious disposition implied in his popular cognomen of "Fighting Joe") and his freedom from suspicion of undue attachment to the fortunes of General McClellan, pointed him out as the man for the occasion by the unerring processes of natural selection. The attitude and character of the Secretary of War, however, justified nothing but despair until connection was made with a powerful faction which had for its object the elevation of Mr. Chase to the Presidency at the end of Mr. Lincoln's term. Making every allowance for the strength and availability of Mr. Chase, as against Mr. Lincoln or any other civilian candidate, his friends did not conceal from themselves that the general who should conquer the rebellion would have the disposal of the next Presidency, and they were on the lookout for the right military alliance when they came into communication with Hooker's friends and received their assurances that, if it should be his good fortune to bring the war to a successful close, nothing could possibly induce him to accept other than military honors in recognition of his services. General

Hooker thereupon became the candidate of Mr. Chase's friends. Hooker probably knew of these dickerings. Certainly Stanton did, through a friend in Chase's own circle.

As soon as Burnside's tenure of the command had become a question rather of hours than of days, new efforts were made to win over the Secretary of War, but necessarily without avail, because, apart from any personal considerations that may have had place in his mind, he had certain convictions on the subject of a kind that strong men never abandon when once formed. At this critical moment the needed impulse in the direction of Hooker was supplied by a person of commanding influence in the councils of the Administration, and Mr. Lincoln directed the appointment to be made. [See Lincoln's letter to Hooker, p. 216.]

Mr. Stanton's first conclusion was that he should resign; his second, that duty to his chief and the public forbade his doing so; his third, that Hooker must be loyally supported so long as there was the least chance of his doing anything with the army placed in his keeping. This latter resolution he faithfully kept, and General Hooker, who soon had occasion to know the facts connected with his appointment, was both surprised and touched by the generous conduct of his lately implacable opponent.

Mr. Chase found his situation as sponsor for the new commander embarrassing. As a member of the cabinet he could freely express his views with reference to any military question coming up for cabinet discussion, and upon any matter introduced to him by the President he had fair opportunity of making a desired impression; but further than this he could not directly go without disclosing a personal interest inconsistent with his place and duty. Yet the circumstances connected with the appointment of Hooker made it imperatively necessary that the influence of Mr. Chase should be exerted in respect of matters that could not formally come to him for consideration, although, on the other hand, they could not safely be intrusted wholly to the keeping of a suspicious and probably hostile War Department. Fortunately for the perplexed statesman, the influence that had proved sovereign when the balance had hung in suspense between Hooker and Meade was safely and wholly at his service, and, being again resorted to, provided a *modus vivendi* so long as one was needed. Out of all these anomalies a correspondence resulted between Mr. Chase and General Hooker, the publication of which is historically indispensable to the saying of the final word on the leading events of Mr. Lincoln's administration.

When General Hooker telegraphed to Washington that he had brought his army back to the north side of the river, because he could not find room for it to fight at Chancellorsville, President Lincoln grasped General Halleck and started for the front post-haste. He would likewise have taken the Secretary of War, in his anxiety, but for the obvious indelicacy of the latter's appearance before Hooker at such a moment. Mr. Lincoln went back to Washington that night, enjoining upon Halleck to remain till he knew "everything." Halleck was a keen lawyer, and the reluctant generals and staff-officers had but poor success in stopping anywhere short of the whole truth. When he got back to his post, a conference of the President and Secretary of War with himself was held at the War Department, whereat it was concluded that both the check at Chancellorsville and the retreat were inexcusable, and that Hooker must not be intrusted with the conduct of another battle. Halleck had brought a message from Hooker to the effect that as he had never sought the command, he could resign it without embarrassment, and would be only too happy if, in the new arrangement, he could have the command of his old division and so keep in active service.

The friends of Mr. Chase considered that the fortunes of their leader were too much bound up with Hooker to permit of the latter's ignominious removal and, although the President had learned much that he did not dream of at the time he parted company with the War Department in the matter of appointing a successor to Burnside, the Treasury faction had grown so powerful that he could not consent to a rupture with it, and a temporizing policy was adopted all around, which General Couch, commander of the Second Corps, all unconsciously, nearly spoiled by contemptuously refusing to serve any longer under Hooker, despite an abject appeal to him by Hooker not to leave the army. ◗

General Lee's invasion of Pennsylvania broke up the nearly intolerable situation, and Hooker's diligent and skillful management of his army rapidly brought matters back to the hopeful state

◗ General F. A. Walker says in his "History of the Second Army Corps" (pp. 253–255) :

"One of the results of the Chancellorsville campaign was a change in the command of the Second Corps. General Couch had felt outraged in every nerve and fiber of his being by the conduct of General Hooker from the 1st to the 5th of May. . . .

"Not that General Couch was alone in this feeling, which was shared by nearly all the commanders of the army ; but at once his nature as a man and his position as the senior corps commander made him peculiarly the spokesman in the representations and remonstrances addressed to General Hooker, . . . and when consulted by President Lincoln on the 22d of May he advised that General Meade should be placed in command, stating that he himself would have great pleasure in serving under that officer, though senior to him. To the suggestion of his own succession to the command General Couch returned a firm and sincere negative. . . .

"In this spirit [having lost confidence in Hooker], with pain inexpressible, General Couch asked to be relieved from further service with the Army of the Potomac."—EDITORS.

◖ On the 5th of June General Hooker sent to the President a long dispatch, which Mr. Lincoln replied on the same day. These communications throw an interesting light on Hooker's relations with the Administration. After stating his suspicion that Lee was about to undertake an aggressive movement, Hooker says:

"As I am liable to be called on to make a movement with the utmost promptitude, I desire that I may be informed as early as practicable of the views of the Government concerning this army. Under instructions from the major-general commanding the army, dated January 31st, I am instructed to 'keep in view always the importance of covering Washington and Harper's Ferry, either directly or by so operating as to be able to punish any force of the enemy sent against them.' In the event the enemy should move, as I almost anticipate he will, the head of his column will probably be headed toward the Potomac, *via* Gordonsville or Culpeper, while

they were in before the late battle. ◗ But Mr. Stanton was determined that the deliberate decision of the council of war, held after Halleck's return from the front, should not be set aside, and he was now the master of the situation. Hooker was so full of hope and energy that severe measures had to be resorted to in order to wring from him that tender of resignation deemed to be necessary to enable his supporters at Washington to keep on outward terms with the Administration. When it did come, the impending battle was evidently so close at hand that the Secretary of War was seized with the fear that, either by accident or design, the change of command to General Meade would not be effected in time to avoid the very contingency aimed at by the change. At the last moment, the President too became alarmed, and there was another conference at the Department to settle the means of insuring the transfer.

Duplicate copies of the President's order, changing the command, were made, authenticated by the signature of the adjutant-general and addressed, severally, to Generals Hooker and Meade. General James A. Hardie, chief of the staff of the Secretary of War, and a personal friend of both the officers concerned, was then called into the conference room and directed to start at once for Frederick City and, without disclosing his presence or business, make his way to General Meade and give him to understand that the order for him to assume the command of the army immediately was intended to be as unquestionable and peremptory as any that a soldier could receive. He was then, as the representative of the President, to

the rear will rest on Fredericksburg. After giving the subject my best reflection, I am of opinion that it is my duty to pitch into his rear, although in so doing the head of his column may reach Warrenton before I can return. Will it be within the spirit of my instructions to do so? In view of these contemplated movements of the enemy, I cannot too forcibly impress upon the mind of His Excellency, the President, the necessity of having one commander for all of the troops whose operations can have an influence on those of Lee's army. Under the present system, all independent commanders are in ignorance of the movements of the others ; at least such is my situation. I trust that I may not be considered in the way to this arrangement, as it is a position I do not desire, and only suggest it, as I feel the necessity for concert as well as vigorous action. It is necessary for me to say this much that my motives may not be misunderstood. JOSEPH HOOKER, Major-General."

President Lincoln's reply is as follows :

"WASHINGTON, June 5th, 1863, 4 P. M.— MAJOR-GENERAL HOOKER : Yours of to-day was received an hour ago. So much of professional military skill is requisite to answer it that I have turned the task over to General Halleck. He promises to perform it with his utmost care. I have but one idea which I think worth suggesting to you, and that is, in case you find Lee coming to the north of the Rappahannock, I would by no means cross to the south of it. If he should leave a rear force at Fredericksburg, tempting you to fall upon it, it would fight in intrenchments and have you at disadvantage, and so, man for man, worst you at that point, while his main force would in some way be getting an advantage of you northward. In one word, I would not take any risk of being entangled upon the river, like an ox jumped half over a fence, and liable to be torn by dogs front and rear without a fair chance to gore one way or kick the other. If Lee would come to my side of the river, I would keep on the same side and fight him or act on the defense, according as might be my estimate of his strength relatively to my own. But these are mere suggestions, which I desire to be controlled by the judgment of yourself and General Halleck. A. LINCOLN."—EDITORS.

MAJOR-GENERAL GEORGE G. MEADE.　FROM A PHOTOGRAPH.

take General Meade to the headquarters of General Hooker and transfer the command from the latter to the former. General Hardie manifested some reluctance to doing his appointed task in the prescribed manner, but Mr. Stanton sententiously remarked that in this case the manner was of the substance of the matter, to which Mr. Lincoln added that he would take the responsibility upon himself for any wound to the feelings of the two generals, or of the bearer of the order. General Hardie was supplied with passes and orders to facilitate his progress, and with money to buy his way through to his destination if delayed or obstructed on the road. If compelled by the imminency of capture by Stuart's raiders to destroy his papers, and he could still make his way through, he was to deliver verbally the order for the changing of the command and supervise its execution.

General Hardie, in civilian's dress, reached Frederick in safety, and by diligent inquiry ascertained the whereabouts of General Meade's headquarters, several miles from town. By some oversight at headquarters, no governor or provost-marshal had been appointed for the town, and the streets and all the roads leading to the camps were thronged with boisterous soldiers, more or less filled with Maryland whisky, and many of them ripe for rudeness or mischief. By liberal use of money he at last obtained a buggy and a driver who knew the roads; but his progress through straggling parties of soldiers and trains of wagons was so slow, and he was so often obliged to appeal to officers to secure passage and safety from one stage to another, that the night was far spent when he reached General Meade's headquarters and, after some wrangling, penetrated to his tent.

Meade was asleep, and when awakened was confounded by the sight of an officer from the War Department standing over him. He afterward said that, in his semi-stupor, his first thought was that he was to be taken to Washington in arrest, though no reason occurred to him why he should be. When he realized the state of affairs he became much agitated, protesting against being placed in command of an army that was looking toward Reynolds as the successor, if Hooker should be displaced; referring to the personal friendship between Reynolds and himself, which would make the President's order an instrument of injustice to both; urging the heaviness of the responsibility so suddenly placed upon him in presence of the enemy and when he was totally ignorant of the positions and dispositions of the army he was to take in charge; and strenuously objecting to the requirement that he should go to Hooker's headquarters to take over the command without being sent for by the commanding general, as McClellan had sent for Burnside ☆ and Burnside for Hooker. Meade proposed to Hardie that he should telegraph to Stanton to be relieved from taking the command, but Hardie told him that in the council it had been assumed that he would wish to be excused, that he would prefer Reynolds first and anybody else but himself afterward, and that he might even deem it too late to displace Hooker; but that, notwithstanding, it had been determined that Hooker should be relieved, and by Meade alone, and that it should be done immediately upon Hardie's arrival. It was a mental relief to the stern Secretary of War, when General Meade's spontaneous utterances were reported to him, to note that he had uttered no protest against Hooker's being relieved of the command, even in what might almost be called the presence of the enemy. This silence on the part of a man so regardless of himself, so regardful of others, Mr. Stanton accepted as being, in itself, his complete vindication.

After taking General Hardie's opinion, as a professional soldier, that he had no lawful discretion to vary from the orders given, horses and an escort were ordered out and the party proceeded to general headquarters, some miles distant.⎰ Hardie undertook to break the news to Hooker, who did not need to be told anything after seeing who his visitors were. It was a bitter moment to all, for Hooker had construed favorably the delay in responding to his tender of resignation, and could not wholly mask the revulsion of feeling. General Butterfield, the chief of staff, between whom and General Meade much coldness existed, was called in, and the four officers set themselves earnestly to work to do the state some service by honestly transferring the command and all that could help

to make it available for good. During the interview Meade unguardedly expressed himself as shocked at the scattered condition of the army, and Hooker retorted with feeling. Tension was somewhat eased by Meade's insisting upon being regarded as a guest at headquarters while General Hooker was present, and by his requesting General Butterfield, upon public grounds, not to exercise his privilege of withdrawing with his chief; but Hooker's chagrin and Meade's overstrung nerves made the lengthy but indispensable conference rather trying to the whole party.

When Reynolds heard the news, he dressed himself with scrupulous care and, handsomely attended, rode to headquarters to pay his respects to the new commander. Meade, who looked like a wagonmaster in the marching clothes he had hurriedly slipped on when awakened in his tent, understood the motive of the act, and after the exchange of salutations all around, he took Reynolds by the arm, and, leading him aside, told him how surprising, imperative, and unwelcome were the orders he had received; how much he would have preferred the choice to have fallen on Reynolds; how anxious he had been to see Reynolds and tell him these things, and how helpless he should hold himself to be did he not feel that Reynolds would give him the earnest support that he would have given to Reynolds in a like situation. Reynolds answered that, in his opinion, the command had fallen where it belonged, that he was glad that such a weight of responsibility had not come upon him, and that Meade might count upon the best support he could give him. Meade then communicated to Reynolds all that he had learned from Hooker and Butterfield concerning the movements and positions of the two armies, and hastily concerted with him a plan of coöperation which resulted in the fighting of the battle of Gettysburg upon ground selected by Reynolds.

During the afternoon the consultations were ended, and, with the aid of the representative of the War Department, the two generals drew up the orders that were to announce formally the change of command. In the evening, standing in front of the commanding general's tent, General Hooker took leave of the officers, soldiers, and civilians attached to headquarters, and, amid many a "God bless you, General!" got into the spring wagon that was to convey him and General Hardie to the railroad station, the former *en route* to Baltimore, the latter to Washington. When all was ready for the start, the throng about the vehicle respectfully drew back as Meade approached with uncovered head; the two men took each other by the hand, some words passed between them in a low tone, the wagon moved off, and Meade walked silently into the tent just vacated by his predecessor.

☆ Meade was mistaken in thinking that McClellan had sent for Burnside when the command was turned over to him. —C. F. B.

⎰ Hardie told me that Meade at last said, half playfully, "Well, I've been tried and condemned without a hearing, and I suppose I shall have to go to execution."—C. F. B.

UNION CAVALRY SCOUTING IN FRONT OF THE CONFEDERATE ADVANCE.

LEE'S INVASION OF PENNSYLVANIA.

BY JAMES LONGSTREET, LIEUTENANT-GENERAL, C. S. A.

ONE night in the spring of 1863 I was sitting in my tent opposite Suffolk, Virginia, when there came in a slender, wiry fellow about five feet eight, with hazel eyes, dark hair and complexion, and brown beard. He wore a citizen's suit of dark material, and except for his stooping shoulders was well formed and evidently a man of great activity. He handed me a note from Mr. Seddon, Secretary of War. That was my first meeting with the famous scout, Harrison, who in his unpretending citizen's dress passed unmolested from right to left through the Federal army, visited Washington City, ate and drank with the Federal officers, and joined me at Chambersburg with information more accurate than a force of cavalry could have secured.

While my command was at Suffolk, engaged in collecting supplies from the eastern coasts of Virginia and North Carolina, General Burnside was relieved and General Hooker put in command of the Federal Army of the Potomac. General Lee was not expecting Hooker to move so early, and gave me no warning until the Federals moved out to turn his left by Chancellorsville. He then sent urgent demand for me, but it so happened that all my trains were down on the eastern coasts, and I could not move my troops without leaving the trains to the enemy. I made haste to get them back as quickly as possible, and the moment we got them within our lines I pulled up from around Suffolk, and, recrossing the Blackwater, started back on my march to join General Lee at Fredericksburg. Before we got to Richmond, however, we received dispatches announcing the Confederate success. But with these tidings of victory came the sad intelligence that General Stonewall Jackson was seriously wounded, a piece of news that cast a deep gloom over the army.

On the 9th of May I joined General Lee at his headquarters at Fredericksburg. At our first meeting we had very little conversation; General Lee merely stated that he had had a severe battle, and the army had been very much broken up. He regarded the wound accidently inflicted on Jackson as a terrible calamity. Although we felt the immediate loss of Jackson's services, it was supposed he would rally and get well. He lingered for several days, one day reported better and the next worse, until at last he was taken from us to the shades of Paradise. The shock was a very severe one to men and officers, but the full extent of our loss was not felt until the remains of the beloved general had been sent home. The dark clouds of the future then began to lower above the Confederates.

General Lee at that time was confronted by two problems: one, the finding a successor for Jackson, another, the future movements of the Army of Northern Virginia. After considering the matter fully he decided to reorganize his army, making three corps instead of two. I was in command of the First Corps, and he seemed anxious to have a second and third corps under the command of Virginians. To do so was to overlook the claims of other generals who had been active and very efficient in the service. He selected General Ewell to command the Second, and General A. P. Hill for the Third Corps. General Ewell was entitled to command by reason of his rank, services, and ability. Next in rank was a North Carolinian, General D. H. Hill, and next a Georgian, General Lafayette McLaws, against whom was the objection that they were not Virginians. ⌡

In reorganizing his army, General Lee impaired to some extent the *morale* of his troops, but the First Corps, dismembered as it was, still considered itself, with fair opportunities, invincible, and was ready for any move warranted by good judgment.

While General Lee was reorganizing his army he was also arranging the new campaign. Grant had laid siege to Vicksburg, and Johnston was concentrating at Jackson to drive him away. Rosecrans was in Tennessee and Bragg was in front of him. The force Johnston was concentrating at Jackson gave us no hope that he would have sufficient strength to make any impression upon Grant, and even if he could, Grant was in position to reënforce rapidly and could supply his army with greater facility. Vicksburg was doomed unless we could offer relief by strategic move. I proposed to send a force through east Tennessee to join Bragg and also to have Johnston sent to join him, thus concentrating a large force to move against Rosecrans, crush out his

⌡General D. H. Hill was the superior of General A. P. Hill in rank, skill, judgment, and distinguished services. He had served with the army in Virginia, on the Peninsula in the battles of Williamsburg, Seven Pines, and the Seven Days' battles around Richmond. In the Maryland campaign he made the battle of South Mountain alone from morning till late in the afternoon, with five thousand against a large part of McClellan's army. [See foot-note, Vol. II., p. 578.] He also bore the brunt of the battle of Sharpsburg. He came, however, not from Virginia but from North Carolina, and had just been detailed for service in that State.

Next in rank after General D. H. Hill was General Lafayette McLaws, who had served with us continuously from the Peninsular campaign. His attack on Maryland Heights in the campaign of 1862 was the crowning point in the capture of Harper's Ferry with its garrison and supplies. With Maryland Heights in our hands Harper's Ferry was untenable. Without Maryland Heights in our possession Jackson's forces on the south side of the Potomac could not have taken the post. At Fredericksburg McLaws held the ground at Marye's Hill with 5000 men (his own and Ransom's division) against 40,000, and put more than double his defending forces *hors de combat*, thus making, for his numbers, the best battle of the war. General McLaws was not in vigorous health, however, and was left to command his division in the campaign. He called on General Lee to know why his claims had been overlooked, but I do not know that Lee gave him satisfactory reasons.— J. L.

See Colonel William Allan's comments, to follow.— EDITORS.

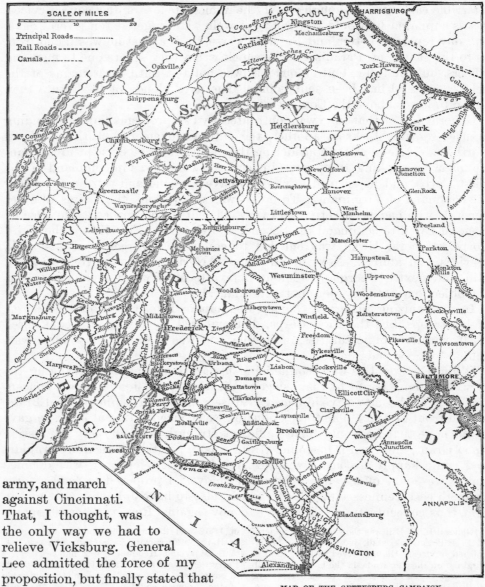

MAP OF THE GETTYSBURG CAMPAIGN.

army, and march against Cincinnati. That, I thought, was the only way we had to relieve Vicksburg. General Lee admitted the force of my proposition, but finally stated that he preferred to organize a campaign into Maryland and Pennsylvania, hoping thereby to draw the Federal troops from the southern points they occupied. After discussing the matter with him for several days, I found his mind made up not to allow any of his troops to go west. I then accepted his proposition to make a campaign into Pennsylvania, provided it should be offensive in strategy but defensive in tactics, forcing the Federal army to give us battle when we were in strong position and ready to receive them. One mistake of the Confederacy was in pitting force against force. The only hope we had was to outgeneral the Federals. We

RELIEF MAP OF THE GETTYSBURG CAMPAIGN.

FROM A PHOTOGRAPH OF THE ORIGINAL CAST MADE BY A. E. LEHMAN FOR THE CUMBERLAND VALLEY RAILROAD COMPANY.

were all hopeful and the army was in good condition, but the war had advanced far enough for us to see that a mere victory without decided fruits was a luxury we could not afford. Our numbers were less than the Federal forces, and our resources were limited while theirs were not. The time had come when it was imperative that the skill of generals and the strategy and tactics of war should take the place of muscle against muscle. Our purpose should have been to impair the *morale* of the Federal army and shake Northern confidence in the Federal leaders. We talked on that line from day to day, and General Lee, accepting it as a good military view, adopted it as the key-note of the campaign. I suggested that we should have all the details and purposes so well arranged and so impressed upon our minds that when the critical moment should come, we could refer to our calmer moments and know we were carrying out our original plans. I stated to General Lee that if he would allow me to handle my corps so as to receive the attack of the Federal army, I would beat it off without calling on him for help except to guard my right and left, and called his attention to the battle of Fredericksburg as an instance of defensive warfare, where we had thrown not more than five thousand troops into the fight and had beaten off two-thirds of the Federal army with great loss to them and slight loss to my own troops. I also called his attention to Napoleon's instructions to Marmont at the head of an invading army.

A few days before we were ready to move General Lee sent for General Ewell to receive his orders. I was present at the time and remarked that if we were ever going to make an offensive battle it should be done south of the

FROM A PHOTOGRAPH TAKEN AFTER THE WAR.

GENERAL ROBERT E. LEE.

Potomac — adding that we might have an opportunity to cross the Rappahannock near Culpeper Court House and make a battle there. I made this suggestion in order to bring about a discussion which I thought would give Ewell a better idea of the plan of operations. My remark had the desired effect and we talked over the possibilities of a battle south of the Potomac. The enemy would be on our right flank while we were moving north. Ewell's corps was to move in advance to Culpeper Court House, mine to follow, and the cavalry was to move along on our right flank to the east of us. Thus, by threatening his rear we could draw Hooker from his position on Stafford Heights opposite Fredericksburg. Our movements at the beginning of the campaign were necessarily slow in order that we might be sure of having the proper effect on Hooker.

Ewell was started off to the valley of Virginia to cross the mountains and move in the direction of Winchester, which was occupied by considerable forces under Milroy. I was moving at the same time east of the Blue Ridge with Stuart's cavalry on my right so as to occupy the gaps from Ashby on to Harper's Ferry. Ewell, moving on through the valley, captured troops and supplies at Winchester, and passed through Martinsburg and Williamsport into Maryland. As I moved along the eastern slope of the Blue Ridge we heard from day to day of the movements of Hooker's army, and that he had finally abandoned his position on Stafford Heights, and was moving up the Potomac in the direction of Washington. Upon receipt of that information, A. P. Hill was ordered to draw off from Fredericksburg and follow the movements of General Ewell, but to cross the Potomac at Shepherdstown. When Hill with his troops and well-supplied trains had passed my rear, I was ordered to withdraw from the Blue Ridge, pass over to the west of the Shenandoah and follow the movements of the other troops, only to cross the Potomac at Williamsport. I ordered General Stuart, whom I considered under my command, to occupy the gaps with a part of his cavalry and to follow with his main force on my right, to cross the Potomac at Shepherdstown, and move on my right flank. Upon giving him this order, he informed me that he had authority from General Lee to occupy the gaps with a part of his cavalry, and to follow the Federal army with the remainder. At the same time he expressed his purpose of crossing the river east of the Blue Ridge and trying to make way around the right of the Federal army; so I moved my troops independent of the cavalry, and, following my orders, crossed at Williamsport, came up with A. P. Hill in Maryland, and moved on thence to Chambersburg.

Before we left Fredericksburg for the campaign into Maryland and Pennsylvania, I called up my scout, Harrison, and, giving him all the gold he thought he would need, told him to go to Washington City and remain there until he was in possession of information which he knew would be of value to us, and directed that he should then make his way back to me and report. As he was leaving, he asked where he would find me. That was information I did not care to impart to a man who was going directly to the Federal capital. I answered that my command was large enough to be found without

CONFEDERATES AT A FORD.

difficulty.   We had reached Chambersburg on the 27th of June and were remaining there to give the troops rest, when my scout straggled into the lines on the night of June 28th.   He told me he had been to Washington and had spent his gold freely, drinking in the saloons and getting upon confidential terms with army officers.   In that way he had formed a pretty good idea of the general movements of the Federal army and the preparation to give us battle.   The moment he heard Hooker had started across the Potomac he set out to find me.   He fell in with the Federal army before reaching Frederick—his plan being to walk at night and stop during the day in the neighborhood of the troops.   He said there were three corps near Frederick when he passed there, one to the right and one to the left, but he did not succeed in getting the position of the other.   This information proved more accurate than we could have expected if we had been relying upon our cavalry.   I sent the scout to report to General Lee, who was near, and suggested in my note that it might be well for us to begin to look to the east of the Blue Ridge.   Meade was then in command of the Federal army, Hooker having been relieved.

The two armies were then near each other, the Confederates being north and west of Gettysburg, and the Federals south and south-east of that memorable field.   On the 30th of June we turned our faces toward our enemy and marched upon Gettysburg.   The Third Corps, under Hill, moved out first and my command followed. We then found ourselves in a very unusual condition: we were almost in the immediate presence of the enemy with our cavalry gone. Stuart was undertaking another wild ride around the Federal army. We knew nothing of Meade's movements further then the report my scout had made. We did not know, except by surmise, when or where to expect to find Meade, nor whether he was lying in wait or advancing. The Confederates moved down the Gettysburg road on June 30th, encountered the Federals on July 1st, and a severe engagement followed. The Federals were driven entirely from the field and forced back through the streets of Gettysburg to Cemetery Hill, which had been previously selected as a Federal rallying-point and was occupied by a reserve force of the Eleventh Corps.

THE CONFEDERATE CAVALRY IN THE GETTYSBURG CAMPAIGN.

I. BY JOHN S. MOSBY, COLONEL, C. S. A.

IT is generally agreed by Southern writers that the battle of Gettysburg was the result of an accidental collision of armies. General Lee in effect says in his report of the campaign that his failure was due to his ignorance of the movements of the enemy; and the absence of a portion of the cavalry under Stuart, or rather its separation from the army, is assigned as the primary cause of its failure by General Long, the biographer of Lee, and by General Longstreet. Both ignore the fact that Stuart left with General Lee, under command of General Beverly H. Robertson, a larger body of cavalry than he took with him. General Long charges that Stuart's expedition around Hooker was made either from "a misapprehension of orders or love of the *éclat* of a bold raid" (which, of course, implies disobedience); and General Longstreet, while admitting that Stuart may have acted by authority of Lee, says that it was undertaken against his own orders, which were to cross the Potomac at Shepherdstown, west of the Blue Ridge.

That General Lee was greatly embarrassed by want of intelligence of the movements of the enemy was not due to the lack of cavalry; and Stuart is not responsible for the inefficient manner in which Lee was served.

When it was determined that Stuart should take three brigades of cavalry to join Ewell on the Susquehanna and leave his other two to perform outpost duty for the army in Virginia, General Lee

was in the Shenandoah Valley with the corps of Hill and Longstreet. The latter was holding the gaps and Stuart was guarding the approaches to them east of the ridge. Hence Stuart came under Longstreet's orders. Hooker's headquarters were in Fairfax, with his army spread out like a fan—his left being at Thoroughfare Gap and his right on the Potomac at Leesburg. On returning from a scout, I reported to Stuart the scattered condition of Hooker's corps, and he determined, with the approval of General Lee, to pass around, or rather through, them, as the shortest route to Ewell. There was an opportunity besides to inflict much damage and to cut off communication between Washington and the North.

I have lately discovered documents in the archives of the War Department that set at rest the question of Stuart's alleged disobedience of orders, and show that General Longstreet then approved a plan which he now condemns as "a wild ride around the Federal army." He directed Stuart to pass around *the rear of the enemy* in preference to crossing west of the ridge, in order to prevent disclosing our designs.☆

Under date of June 22d, 7:30 P. M., he writes to General Lee: "I have forwarded your letter to General Stuart, with the suggestion that he *pass by the enemy's rear* if he thinks he may get through."

Up to the morning of June 25th it was perfectly practicable for Stuart to have done so. In accordance with Lee's and Longstreet's instruc-

☆ "HEADQUARTERS, MILLWOOD, June 22d, 1863, 7 P. M. MAJOR-GENERAL J. E. B. STUART, Commanding Cavalry. GENERAL: General Lee has inclosed to me this letter for you to be forwarded to you provided you can be spared from my front, and provided I think you can move across the Potomac without disclosing our plans. He speaks of your leaving *via* Hopewell Gap and passing by the rear of the enemy. If you can get through by that route, I think that you will be less likely to indicate what our plans are than if you should cross by passing to our rear. I forward the letter of instructions with these suggestions. Please advise me of the condition of affairs before you leave, and order General Hampton—whom I suppose you will leave here in command—to report to me at Millwood either by letter or in person, as may be

most agreeable to him. Most respectfully, J. LONGSTREET, Lieutenant-General.—N. B. I think that your passage of the Potomac by our rear at the present moment will in a measure disclose our plans. You had better not leave us, therefore, unless you can take the proposed route in rear of the enemy. J. LONGSTREET, Lieutenant-General."

"HEADQUARTERS, 22d June, 1863. MAJOR-GENERAL J. E. B. STUART, Commanding Cavalry. GENERAL: I have just received your note of 7:45 this morning to General Longstreet. I judge the efforts of the enemy yesterday were to arrest our progress and ascertain our whereabouts. Perhaps he is satisfied. Do you know where he is and what he is doing? I fear he will steal a march on us and get across the Potomac before we are aware.

tions Stuart withdrew from the front on the evening of the 24th to pass around Hooker, leaving Robertson about Middleburg with 3000 cavalry and 2 batteries of artillery to observe the enemy. Stuart's success depended upon preserving the *status quo* of the Federal army until he could get through it. *Hooker was on the defensive waiting for his adversary to move.* It did not seem to occur to General Longstreet that the march of the infantry down the Shenandoah Valley would disclose all to the enemy that the cavalry would have done. It was no fault of Stuart's that he was foiled by events which he could not control. When on the morning of the 25th he reached Hooker's rear, he found his whole army moving to the Potomac and all the roads occupied by his troops. This compelled a wide *détour*, and instead of crossing the river in advance of the enemy, as he had expected, he was two days behind him. Thus all communication was broken with Generals Lee and Ewell. The march of Hill's and Longstreet's corps on the day before had been in full view of the signal stations on Maryland Heights and was telegraphed to Hooker, who made a corresponding movement.

On the morning of June 26th the enemy disappeared from Robertson's front and crossed the Potomac. In that event his instructions from Stuart were, "to watch the enemy and harass his rear — to cross the Potomac and follow the army, keeping on its right and rear," and to "report anything of importance to Lieutenant-General Longstreet, with whose position you will communicate by relays through Charlestown."

Robertson retired to the mountain gaps and remained until the afternoon of the 29th, when he was recalled to the army by a courier from General Lee. At night on the 28th General Lee heard, through a scout at Chambersburg, of Hooker's advance. As no information of it had come from the cavalry he had left in Hooker's front in Virginia, he thought that Hooker was still there. He

immediately issued an order for the concentration at Gettysburg, and sent for Robertson's command, that had been left, he says, to hold the mountain passes, "*as long as the enemy remained south of the Potomac.*" It had staid there three days after they had gone. As Stuart had been ordered to Ewell on the Susquehanna, it could not have been expected that he should also watch Hooker on the Potomac. Stuart's instructions to divide the cavalry and take three brigades with him to Ewell, on the Susquehanna, were peremptory; he was only given discretion as to *the point of crossing the Potomac.* It was therefore immaterial, so far as giving information to Lee was concerned, whether he crossed east or west of the ridge. In either event they would have been separated and out of communication with each other. Lee must then have relied on Robertson or nobody to watch Hooker.

Instead of keeping on the right of the army and in close contact with the enemy, as Stuart had ordered, Robertson's command marched *on the left* by Martinsburg and did not reach the battle-field. The rear-guard of the Federal army moving into Pennsylvania crossed the Potomac on June 26th, east of the Blue Ridge; Robertson crossed at Williamsport, about twenty-five miles to the *west* of it, on July 1st, the day the fighting began at Gettysburg. When General Lee crossed the Potomac, he left General Robertson between him and the enemy. By July 3d Robertson had so manœuvred that Lee was between him and the enemy. Stuart had ridden around General Hooker while Robertson was riding around General Lee. If, in accordance with Stuart's instructions, Robertson had promptly followed on the right of the army when the enemy left, Lee's forces would have been concentrated and ready for attack; a defensive battle would have been fought, and Gettysburg might have been to Southern hearts something more than a

" Glorious field of grief."

WASHINGTON, Feb. 9th, 1887.

If you find that he is moving northward, and that two brigades can guard the Blue Ridge and take care of your rear, you can move with the other three into Maryland and take position on General Ewell's right, place yourself in communication with him, guard his flank and keep him informed of the enemy's movements, and collect all the supplies you can for the use of the army. One column of General Ewell's army will probably move toward the Susquehanna by the Emmitsburg route, another by Chambersburg. Accounts from him last night state that there was no enemy west of Fredericktown. A cavalry force (about one hundred) guarded the Monocacy bridge, which was barricaded. You will, of course, take charge of Jenkins's brigade and give him necessary instructions. All supplies taken in Maryland must be by authorized staff-officers for their respective departments, by no one else. They will be paid for or receipts for the same given to the owners. I will send you a general order on this subject, which I wish you to see is strictly complied with. I am, very respectfully, your obedient servant, R. E. LEE, General."

On the following day General Lee wrote as follows:

"HEADQUARTERS, ARMY OF NORTHERN VIRGINIA, June 23d, 1863, 5 P. M. MAJOR-GENERAL J. E. B. STUART, Commanding Cavalry. GENERAL: Your notes of 9 and 10:30 A. M. to-day have just been received. . . . If General

Hooker's army remains inactive you can leave two brigades to watch him and withdraw with the three others, but should he not appear to be moving northward, I think you had better withdraw this side of the mountain to-morrow night, cross at Shepherdstown next day, and move over to Fredericktown. You will, however, be able to judge whether you can pass around their army without hindrance, doing them all the damage you can, and cross the river east of the mountains. In either case, after crossing the river, you must move on and feel the right of Ewell's troops, collecting information, provisions, etc. Give instructions to the commander of the brigades left behind to watch the flank and rear of the army and (in event of the enemy leaving their front) retire from the mountains west of the Shenandoah, leaving sufficient pickets to guard the passes, and bringing everything clean along the valley, closing upon the rear of the army. As regards the movements of the two brigades of the enemy moving toward Warrenton, the commander of the brigades to be left in the mountains must do what he can to counteract them; but I think the sooner you cross into Maryland, after to-morrow, the better. The movements of Ewell's corps are as stated in my former letter. Hill's first division will reach the Potomac to-day, and Longstreet will follow to-morrow. Be watchful and circumspect in all your movements. I am very respectfully and truly yours, R. E. LEE, General."—J. S. M.

II. BY BEVERLY H. ROBERTSON, BRIGADIER-GENERAL, C. S. A.

COLONEL JOHN S. MOSBY has seen proper to make mention of my command in the cavalry of the Army of Northern Virginia during the Gettysburg campaign, and as a means of defending General J. E. B. Stuart from an imaginary attack, has misrepresented a portion of General Stuart's cavalry. Colonel Mosby knows very little of Stuart's character if he supposes that so true a soldier would have silently passed over such disobedience of orders as Colonel Mosby imputes to me. The fact that Colonel Mosby has "lately discovered documents in the archives" at Washington, which are to "set at rest" something that has not been set in motion, will not excuse him for attempting in 1887 to prove by argument that in 1863 Stuart did not know whether I had obeyed his orders in the Gettysburg campaign.

The orders left with me by General Stuart, dated June 24th, were exactly obeyed by me, to his entire satisfaction as well as to that of General R. E. Lee. These orders embraced the duty of holding Ashby's and Snicker's gaps, to prevent Hooker from interrupting the march of Lee's army; and "in case of a move by the enemy on Warrenton," to counteract it if possible. I was also ordered when I withdrew from the gaps to "withdraw to the west side of the Shenandoah," to cross the Potomac where Lee crossed, and to "follow the army, keeping on its right and rear." The full text of my orders was as follows:

"HEADQUARTERS, CAVALRY DIVISION, ARMY NORTHERN VIRGINIA, June 24th, 1863. BRIGADIER-GENERAL B. H. ROBERTSON, Commanding Cavalry. GENERAL: Your own and General Jones's brigades will cover the front of Ashby's and Snicker's Gaps, yourself, as senior officer, being in command.

"Your object will be to watch the enemy, deceive him as to our designs, and harass his rear if you find he is retiring. Be always on the alert; let nothing escape your observation, and miss no opportunity which offers to damage the enemy.

"After the enemy has moved beyond your reach, leave sufficient pickets in the mountains and withdraw to the west side of the Shenandoah and place a strong and reliable picket to watch the enemy at Harper's Ferry, cross the Potomac and follow the army, keeping on its right and rear.

"As long as the enemy remains in your front, in force, unless otherwise ordered by General R. E. Lee, Lieutenant-General Longstreet, or myself, hold the gaps with a line of pickets reaching across the Shenandoah by Charlestown to the Potomac.

"If, in the contingency mentioned, you withdraw, sweep the valley clear of what pertains to the army and cross the Potomac at the different points crossed by it.

"You will instruct General Jones from time to time as the movements progress, or events may require, and report anything of importance to Lieutenant-General Longstreet, with whose position you will communicate by relays through Charlestown.

"I send instructions for General Jones, which please read. Avail yourself of every means in your power to increase the efficiency of your command and keep it up to the highest number possible. Particular attention will be paid to shoeing horses, and to marching off of the turnpikes.

"In case of an advance of the enemy you will offer such resistance as will be justifiable to check him and discover his intentions, and if possible you will prevent him from gaining possession of the gaps. In case of a move by the enemy upon Warrenton, you will counteract it as much as you can, compatible with previous instructions.

"You will have with the two brigades two batteries of horse-artillery. Very respectfully, your obedient servant, J. E. B. STUART, Major-General Commanding.

"Do not change your present line of pickets until daylight to-morrow morning unless compelled to do so."

The only road by which the orders (which particularly specified the avoidance of "turnpikes" on account of the difficulty and delay of shoeing horses) could be complied with, carried my command to Martinsburg; at which place, *and not in the gaps of the mountains,* as Colonel Mosby insinuates, a courier from General Lee met me. My command was hurried from there to Chambersburg, and thence by forced march, on the night of July 2d, to Cashtown, where it arrived at about 10 A. M. on July 3d. Ascertaining at Cashtown that General Pleasonton was moving from Emmitsburg directly on the baggage and ammunition trains of General Lee's army, which were exposed to his attack without defense of any kind, I pressed forward with my command and intercepted the advance of General Pleasonton, under the command of Major Samuel H. Starr. A severe and gallant fight was made at Fairfield, in which Major Starr of the 6th United States Regular Cavalry was wounded and captured with a large portion of his staff, while his regiment was severely damaged. Adjutant John Allan and three others of the 6th Virginia Cavalry were killed, 19 were wounded, and 5 were reported missing.

That fight at Fairfield, on the last day of the fighting at Gettysburg, refutes the imputation intended by Colonel Mosby to be conveyed in his remark that my command "did not reach the battle-field."

From that fight at Fairfield I was ordered by General R. E. Lee to cover his wagon trains, and in obeying the same my command was engaged in repeated skirmishes, particularly at Funkstown and Hagerstown, after which it returned to Virginia — the last command that recrossed the Potomac.

If there existed the least ground for Colonel Mosby's statements, there would be found among the reports of general officers some reference to the imputed dereliction of duty on my part. As no such reference is made, and no imputation of disobedience of orders is there intimated, it may be assumed that neither Stuart nor Lee had any reason to complain of my command.

FROM A PHOTOGRAPH.

James Longstreet

BUFORD'S CAVALRY OPPOSING THE
CONFEDERATE ADVANCE UPON GETTYSBURG.

THE FIRST DAY AT GETTYSBURG.

BY HENRY J. HUNT, BREVET MAJOR-GENERAL, U. S. A., CHIEF OF ARTILLERY OF THE
ARMY OF THE POTOMAC.

THE battles of Fredericksburg and Chancellorsville raised the confidence
of the Confederate Army of Northern Virginia to such a height as to
cause its subordinate officers and soldiers to believe that, as opposed to the
Army of the Potomac, they were equal to any demand that could be made
upon them. Their belief in the superiority of the Southerner to the Northerner
as a fighter was no longer, as at the beginning of the war, a mere provincial
conceit, for it was now supported by signal successes in the field. On each
of these two occasions the Army of the Potomac had been recently reorganized
under a new general, presumably abler than his predecessor and possessing
the confidence of the War Department, and the results were crowning victories
for the Confederates. Yet at Fredericksburg defeat was not owing to any
lack of fighting qualities on the part of the Federal soldiers, but rather to
defective leadership.

At Chancellorsville both qualities were called in question. In none of the
previous battles between these armies had the disparity of numbers been so
great. The Federal general had taken the initiative, his plan of operations
was excellent, and his troops were eager for battle. The Confederates could
at first oppose but a portion of their inferior force to the attack of greatly
superior numbers, and the boast of the Federal commander, that "the Army
of Northern Virginia was the legitimate property of the Army of the Potomac," seemed in a fair way to be justified, when at first contact the advantages already gained were thrown away by the assumption of a timid,
defensive attitude. Lee's bold offensive, which followed immediately on this
exhibition of weakness, the consequent rout of a Federal army-corps, and the
subsequent retreat of the whole army, a large portion of which had not been
engaged, confirmed the exultant Confederates in their conviction—which
now became an article of faith—that both in combat and in generalship the
superiority of the Southerner was fully established. The Federal soldiers

returned from Chancellorsville to their camps on the northern bank of the
Rappahannock, mortified and incensed at finding themselves, through no
fault of their own, in the condition of having in an offensive campaign lost
the battle without fighting, except when the enemy forced it upon them.

Yet in this battle the Northern soldier fought well. Under the circumstances no men could have withstood such a sudden attack as that made by
"Stonewall" Jackson on the flank and rear of the Eleventh Corps; but as
soon as Jackson encountered troops in condition for action, his pursuit was
checked and he was brought to a stand. The panic did not extend beyond
the routed corps, nor to all of that, for its artillery and so much of its infantry
as could form a proper line did their duty, and the army, far from being
"demoralized" by this mishap, simply ridiculed the corps which, from its
supposed want of vigilance, had allowed itself to be surprised in a position in
which it could not fight. The surprise itself was not the fault of the troops,
and in subsequent battles the corps redeemed its reputation. Both armies
were composed in the main of Americans, and there was little more difference
between their men than might be found between those of either army at
different periods, or under varying circumstances; for although high bounties
had already brought into the Federal ranks an inferior element which swelled
the muster-rolls and the number of stragglers, "bounty jumping"⌡ had not
as yet become a regular business.

The morale of the Confederate army was, however, much higher at this
time than that of its adversary. It was composed of men not less patriotic,
many of whom had gone into the war with reluctance, but who now felt that
they were defending their homes. They were by this time nearly all veterans,
led by officers having the confidence of their Government, which took pains
to inspire its soldiers with the same feeling. Their successes were extolled and
magnified, their reverses palliated or ignored. Exaggerations as to the relative numbers of the troops had been common enough on both sides, but those
indulged in at the South had been echoed, sometimes suggested, in the North
by a portion of the press and people, so that friends and enemies united in
inspiring in the Confederate soldier a belief in himself and a contempt for his
enemy. In the Army of the Potomac it was different; the proportion of veterans was much smaller; a cessation of recruiting at the very beginning of
active operations, when men were easily obtainable to supply losses in existing regiments, had been followed, as emergencies arose, by new levies, for short
periods of service, and in new organizations which could not readily be assim-
ilated by older troops. Moreover, there were special difficulties. The Army
of the Potomac was not in favor at the War Department. Rarely, if ever, had
it heard a word of official commendation after a success, or of sympathy or
encouragement after a defeat. From the very beginning its camps had been
filled with imputations and charges against its leaders, who were accused on
the streets, by the press, in Congress, and even in the War Department itself,
and after victories as well as after defeats, not only of incapacity or miscon-

⌡ This term was applied to the practice of enlisting and securing bounty money, and then, either
deserting outright, or shirking the serious work of the field.— EDITORS.

GENERAL MEADE IN THE FIELD.
FROM A PHOTOGRAPH.

duct, but sometimes of "disloyalty" to their superiors, civil and military, and even to the cause for which they fought. These accusations were followed or accompanied by frequent changes of commanders of the army, of army-corps, and even of divisions. Under such circumstances, but little confidence could be felt by the troops, either in the wisdom of a war office which seemed to change its favorites with the caprice of a coquette, or in the capacity of new generals who followed each other in such rapid succession. But it is due to that patient and sorely tried army, to say that the spirit of both officers and men was of the best, and their devotion to duty unconquerable. The army itself had originally been so admirably disciplined and tempered, that there always remained to it a firm self-reliance and a stern sense of duty and of honor that was proof against its many discouragements. In battle it always acquitted itself well and displayed the highest soldierly qualities, no matter who commanded it or whence he came. Chancellorsville furnishes no exception to this assertion, nor evidence of inferiority of the Northern to the Southern soldier, but it does furnish striking illustrations of Napoleon's well-known saying, "In war *men* are nothing, *a man* is everything."

General Lee, who felt great confidence in his own troops, and overrated the effects of successive reverses on the Federal soldiers, now resolved to assume the offensive, for he knew that to remain on the defensive would in the end force him back on Richmond. He determined, therefore, in case the Army of the Potomac could not be brought to action under favorable circumstances in Virginia, to transfer, if permitted, the field of operations to Northern soil, where a victory promptly followed up might give him possession of Baltimore or Washington, and perhaps lead to the recognition of the Confederacy by foreign powers. The valley of the Shenandoah offered a safe line of operations; the Federal troops occupying it were rather a bait than an obstacle, and to capture or destroy them seemed quite practicable to one who controlled absolutely all Confederate troops within the sphere of his operations. The sharp lesson he had administered the previous year had not been heeded by the Federal War Office; an opportunity now offered to repeat it, and he took his measures accordingly. In case his Government would not consent to a bolder offensive, he could at least clear the valley of Virginia of the enemy,—a distinct operation, yet a necessary preliminary to an invasion of the North. This work was assigned to Lieutenant-General Ewell, an able officer, in every way qualified for such an enterprise.

In anticipation of the new campaign, Lee's army was strengthened and reorganized into three army-corps of three divisions each. Each division consisted of four brigades, except Rodes's and Anderson's, which had five each, and Pickett's, which had three at Gettysburg,—in all, thirty-seven infantry brigades. The cavalry were the select troops of the Confederacy. Officers and men had been accustomed all their lives to the use of horses and arms, "and to the very end the best blood in the land rode after Stuart, Hampton, and the Lees." They were now organized as a division, under Major-General J. E. B. Stuart, consisting of the six brigades of Hampton, Robertson, Fitzhugh Lee, Jenkins, W. E. Jones, and W. H. F. Lee, and six batteries of horse-artillery under Major R. F. Beckham. To these should be added Imboden's command, a strong brigade of over 2000 effective horsemen and a battery of horse-artillery, which had been operating in the mountain country and was now near Staunton, awaiting orders. The artillery had recently received an excellent organization under its commandant-in-chief, General Pendleton. It consisted, besides the horse-artillery, of fifteen so-called " battalions," each of four batteries, with one lieutenant-colonel and a major. To each army-corps were attached five battalions, one for each division and two as a reserve, the whole under a colonel as chief of artillery. The total number of batteries was 69, of guns 287, of which 30 were with the cavalry. With few exceptions the batteries were of four guns each. The army was commanded by a full general, each army-corps, except the artillery, by a lieutenant-general, each division by a major-general, each brigade, except two, by brigadier-generals. Nearly all these officers were veterans of proved ability and many had served in the Mexican war.

In the Army of the Potomac the discharge of 58 regiments had reduced its strength since Chancellorsville by 25,000 effectives, partly replaced by 5 brigades numbering less than 12,000 men. At the battle of Gettysburg the 7 army-corps consisted of 19 infantry divisions, 7 of which had 2 brigades, 11 had 3, and 1 had 4; in all 51 brigades. [See lists of organizations and commanders in "The Opposing Forces in the Gettysburg Campaign," to follow.] The army and army-corps were commanded by major-generals, the divisions by 3 major-generals and 16 brigadier-generals, the infantry brigades by 22 brigadier-generals and 29 colonels. The average strength of army-corps and divisions was about half that of the Confederates, a fact that should be kept in mind, or the terms will be misleading. The cavalry had been raised under disadvantages. Men accustomed to the use of both horses and arms were comparatively few in the North and required training in everything that was necessary to make a trooper. The theater of war was not considered favorable for cavalry, and it was distributed to the various headquarters for escort duty, guards, and orderlies. It was not until 1863 that it was united under General Pleasonton in a corps consisting of three weak divisions, Buford's, D. McM. Gregg's, and Duffié's, afterward consolidated into two, Stahel's cavalry, which joined at Frederick, June 28th, becoming the third division. The corps was then organized as follows: First Division, Buford: brigades, Gamble, Devin, Merritt; Second Division, Gregg: brigades, McIntosh, Huey, J. Irvin Gregg; Third Division, Kilpatrick: brigades, Farnsworth, Custer. The divisions and three of the brigades were commanded by brigadier-generals, the other five brigades by colonels. To the cavalry were attached Robertson's and Tidball's brigades of horse-artillery. Under excellent chiefs and the spirit created by its new organization, the Federal cavalry soon rivaled that of the Confederates.

The field-artillery was in an unsatisfactory condition. The high reputation it had gained in Mexico was followed by the active and persistent hostility of the War Department, which almost immediately dismounted three-fourths of its authorized batteries. Congress in 1853 made special provision for remounting them as schools of instruction for the whole arm, a duty which the War Department on shallow pretexts evaded. Again in 1861 Congress amply provided for the proper organization and command of the artillery in the field, but as there was no chief nor special administration for the arm, and no regulations for its government, its organization, control, and direction were left to the fancies of the various army commanders. General officers were practically denied it, and in 1862 the War Department announced in orders that field-officers of artillery were an unnecessary expense and their muster into service forbidden. Promotion necessarily ceased, and such able artillerists as Hays, DeRussy, Getty, Gibbon, Griffin, and Ayres could only receive promotion by transfer to the infantry or cavalry. No adequate measures were taken for the supply of recruits, and the batteries were frequently dependent on the troops to which they were attached for men enough to work their guns in battle. For battery-draft they were often glad to get the refuse horses after the ambulance and quartermasters' trains were supplied. Still, many of the batteries attained a high degree of excellence, due mainly to the self-sacrifice, courage, and intelligence of their own officers and men.

On taking command of the army, General Hooker had transferred the military command of the artillery to his own headquarters, to be resumed by the chief of artillery only under specific orders and for special occasions, which resulted in such mismanagement and confusion at Chancellorsville that he consented to organize the artillery into brigades. This was a decided improvement, which would have been greater if the brigade commanders had held adequate rank. As it was, there was no artillery commandant-in-chief for months before the battle of Gettysburg, and of the 14 brigades 4 were commanded by field-officers, 9 by captains, and 1 by a lieutenant, taken from their batteries for the purpose. The number of field-batteries at Gettysburg was 65, of guns 370, of which 212 were with the infantry, 50 with the cavalry, 108 in the reserve. The disadvantages under which the artillery labored all through the war, from want of proper regulations, supervision, and command

MAJOR-GENERAL JOHN F. REYNOLDS.

The uniform is that of a field-officer in the regular infantry. Early in the war General Reynolds was Lieutenant-Colonel of the 14th United States Infantry, and was made Brigadier-General of Volunteers in September, 1861.— EDITORS.

were simply disgraceful to our army administration from the close of the Mexican to that of the Civil war, and caused an unnecessary expenditure of both blood and treasure.

It will be perceived by comparison that the organization of the Army of the Potomac was at this period in every way inferior to that of its adversary. The army-corps and divisions were too numerous and too weak. They required too many commanders and staffs, and this imposed unnecessary burdens on the general-in-chief, who was often compelled to place several army-corps under the commander of one of them, thus reproducing the much-abused " grand divisions " of Burnside, under every possible disadvantage. Had the number of infantry corps been reduced to four at most, and the divisions to twelve, the army would have been more manageable and better commanded, and the artillery, without any loss, but rather a gain of efficiency, would have been reduced by a dozen or fifteen batteries.

EARLY in June Lee's army began to move, and by the 8th Longstreet's and Ewell's corps had joined Stuart's cavalry at Culpeper. A. P. Hill's corps was left in observation at Fredericksburg; and so skillfully were the changes concealed that Hooker, believing that all the enemy's infantry were still near that town, ordered Pleasonton to beat up Stuart's camps at Culpeper, and get information as to the enemy's position and proposed movements. For these purposes he gave Pleasonton two small brigades of infantry, 3000 men under Generals Ames and Russell, which carried his total force to 10,981. They were echeloned along the railroad, which crosses the river at Rappahannock Station, and runs thence ten miles to Culpeper. [See map, p. 55.] About midway is Brandy Station a few hundred yards north of which is Fleetwood Hill. Dividing his force equally, Pleasonton ordered Buford and Ames to cross at Beverly Ford, and Gregg, Duffié, and Russell at Kelly's Ford. All were to march to Brandy Station, Duffié being thrown out to Stevensburg, seven miles east of Culpeper, to watch the Fredericksburg road. Then the whole force was to move on Culpeper. On the 8th, General Lee, having sent Jenkins's brigade as Ewell's advance into the valley, reviewed the other 5 brigades of Stuart, 10,292 combatants, on the plains near Brandy Station. After the review they were distributed in the neighborhood with a view to crossing the Rappahannock on the 9th, Stuart establishing his headquarters at Fleetwood. Accident had thus disposed his forces in the most favorable manner to meet Pleasonton's converging movements.

At daybreak Buford crossed and drove the enemy's pickets from the ford back to the main body, near St. James's church. Stuart, on the first report of the crossing, sent Robertson's brigade toward Kelly's to watch that ford, and Colonel M. C. Butler's 2d South Carolina to Brandy Station. He himself took the command at the church, where he was attacked by Buford. At Brandy Station W. H. F. Lee was wounded, and Colonel Chambliss took command of his brigade. Meantime Gregg had crossed at Kelly's Ford, and Duffié, leading, took a southerly road, by which he missed Robertson's brigade. Learning that Duffié's advance had reached Stevensburg and that Buford

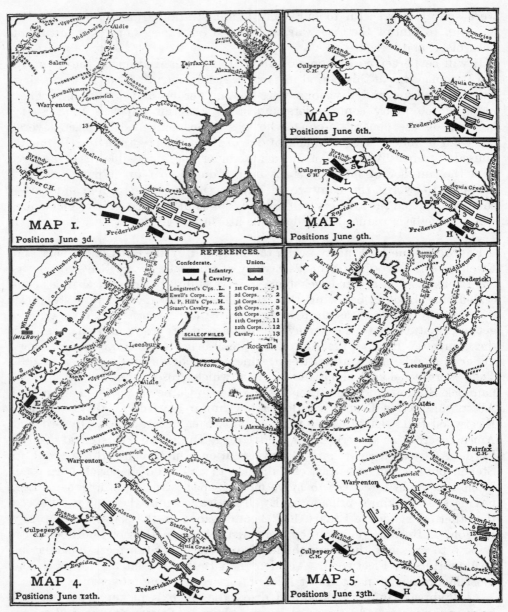

MAP 1.
Positions June 3d.

MAP 2.
Positions June 6th.

MAP 3.
Positions June 9th.

REFERENCES.
Confederate.   Union.
                 Infantry.
                 Cavalry.
Longstreet's C'ps .L.   1st Corps 1
Ewell's Corps .... E.   2d Corps 2
A. P. Hill's C'ps ..H.   3d Corps 3
Stuart's Cavalry .. S.   5th Corps 5
                          6th Corps 6
                          11th Corps 11
                          12th Corps 12
                          Cavalry 13
SCALE OF MILES

MAP 4.
Positions June 12th.

MAP 5.
Positions June 13th.

These maps and the others relating to the campaign and battle of Gettysburg are compilations by Abner Doubleday,
Brevet Major-General, U. S. A., from the official reports of the commanders on both sides, and from the maps
of Colonel John B. Bachelder, which were purchased by Congress for the War Department.—EDITORS.

was heavily engaged, Gregg pushed direct for Brandy Station, sending orders
to Duffié to follow his movement. Stuart, notified of his approach, had sent
in haste some artillery and two of Jones's regiments to Fleetwood, and
Colonel Butler started at once for Stevensburg, followed soon after by Wickham's 4th Virginia. On their approach two squadrons of the 6th Ohio, in

occupation of the place, fell back skirmishing. Duffié sent two regiments to their aid, and after a severe action, mainly with the 2d South Carolina, reoccupied the village. In this action Colonel Butler lost a leg, and his lieutenant-colonel, Hampton, was killed.

On Gregg's arrival near Brandy Station the enemy appeared to be in large force, with artillery, on and about Fleetwood Hill. He promptly ordered an attack; the hill was carried, and the two regiments sent by Stuart were driven back. Buford now attacked vigorously and gained ground steadily, for Stuart had to reënforce his troops at Fleetwood from the church. In the struggles that followed, the hill several times changed masters; but as Duffié did not make his appearance, Gregg was finally overmatched and withdrew, leaving three of his guns, two of them disabled, in the enemy's hands, nearly all of their horses being killed and most of their cannoneers *hors de combat*. There were some demonstrations of pursuit, but the approach of Buford's reserve brigade stopped them. Duffié finally came up and Gregg reported to Pleasonton, informing him of the approach of Confederate infantry from Culpeper. Pleasonton, who had captured some important dispatches and orders, now considered his mission accomplished, and ordered a withdrawal of his whole command. This was effected leisurely and without molestation. Gregg recrossed at Rappahannock Station, Buford at Beverly Ford, and at sunset the river again flowed between the opposing forces. Stuart reports his losses at 485, of whom 301 were killed or wounded. Pleasonton reports an aggregate loss (exclusive of Duffié's, which would not exceed 25) of 907, of whom 421 were killed or wounded. In nearly all the previous so-called "cavalry" actions, the troops had fought as dismounted dragoons. This was in the main a true cavalry battle, and enabled the Federals to dispute the superiority hitherto claimed by, and conceded to, the Confederate cavalry. In this respect the affair was an important one. It did not, however, delay Lee's designs on the valley; he had already sent Imboden toward Cumberland to destroy the railroad and canal from that place to Martinsburg.

Milroy's Federal division, about 9000 strong, occupied Winchester, with McReynolds's brigade in observation at Berryville. Kelley's division of about 10,000 men was at Harper's Ferry, with a detachment of 1200 infantry and a battery under Colonel B. F. Smith at Martinsburg. On the night of June 11th, Milroy received instructions to join Kelley, but, reporting that he could hold Winchester, was authorized to remain there. Ewell, leaving Brandy Station June 10th, reached Cedarville *via* Chester Gap on the evening of the 12th, whence he detached Jenkins and Rodes to capture McReynolds, who, discovering their approach, withdrew to Winchester. They then pushed on to Martinsburg, and on the 14th drove out the garrison. Smith's infantry crossed the Potomac at Shepherdstown, and made its way to Maryland Heights; his artillery retreated by the Williamsport road, was pursued, and lost five guns.

Meanwhile Ewell, with Early's and Edward Johnson's divisions, marched direct on Winchester. Arriving in the neighborhood on the evening of the 13th, he ordered Early on the 14th to leave a brigade in observation on the south of the town, move his main force under cover of the hills to the north-

MAP 6.
Positions June 17th.

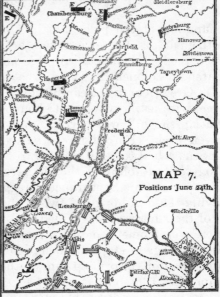

MAP 7.
Positions June 24th.

MAP 8.
Positions June 28th.

western side, and seize the outworks which commanded the main fort. He also ordered Johnson to deploy his division on the east of the town, so as to divert attention from Early. This was so successfully done that the latter placed, unperceived, twenty guns and an assaulting column in position, and at 6 P. M., by a sudden attack, carried the outworks, driving the garrisons into the body of the place. This capture was a complete surprise, and Milroy called a council of war, which decided on an immediate retreat, abandoning the artillery and wagons. Ewell had anticipated this, and ordered Johnson to occupy with a brigade a position on the Martinsburg pike, north of Winchester. The retreat commenced at

2 A. M. of the 15th, and after proceeding three or four miles, the advance encountered Johnson's troops, attacked vigorously, and at first successfully, but, the enemy receiving reënforcements, a hard fight ensued in which the Federals lost heavily. The retreat was then continued; the troops separated in the darkness, one portion reaching Harper's Ferry, another crossing the Potomac at Hancock. On the 15th Ewell crossed the river, occupied Hagerstown and Sharpsburg, and sent Jenkins's cavalry to Chambersburg to collect supplies. On the 17th the garrison of Harper's Ferry was removed to Maryland Heights, and the valley of the Shenandoah was cleared of Federal troops. In these brilliant operations General Lee claims for Ewell the capture of 4000 prisoners and small-arms, 28 pieces of artillery, 11 colors, 300 loaded wagons, as many horses, and a considerable quantity of stores of all descriptions, the entire Confederate loss, killed, wounded, and missing, being 269.

These operations indicate on the part of General Lee either contempt for his opponent, or a belief that the chronic terror of the War Department for the safety of Washington could be safely relied upon to paralyze his movements,— or both. On no other reasonable hypothesis can we account for his stretching his army from Fredericksburg to Williamsport, with his enemy concentrated on one flank, and on the shortest road to Richmond.

General Hooker's instructions were to keep always in view the safety of Washington and Harper's Ferry, and this necessarily subordinated his operations to those of the enemy. On June 5th he reported that in case Lee moved via Culpeper toward the Potomac with his main body, leaving a corps at Fredericksburg, he should consider it his duty to attack the latter, and asked if that would be within the spirit of his instructions. In reply he was warned against such a course, and its dangers to Washington and Harper's Ferry were pointed out. On June 10th, learning that Lee was in motion, and that there were but few troops in Richmond, he proposed an immediate march on that place, from which, after capturing it, he could send the disposable part of his force to any threatened point north of the Potomac, and was informed that Lee's army, and not Richmond, was his true objective. Had he taken Richmond, Peck's large force at Suffolk and Keyes's 10,000 men ♭ in the Peninsula might have been utilized, and Hooker's whole army set free for operations against Lee.

As yet an invasion of the North had not been definitely fixed upon. On June 8th, the day before the engagement at Brandy Station, Lee, in a confidential letter to Mr. Seddon, Confederate Secretary of War, stated that he was aware of the hazard of taking the aggressive, yet nothing was to be gained by remaining on the defensive; still, if the department thought it better to do so, he would adopt that course. Mr. Seddon replied, June 10th, the date of Hooker's proposal to march on Richmond, concurring in General Lee's views.

♭ The forces referred to consisted (January 1st, 1863) of three brigades and some unassigned commands at Suffolk, under General John J. Peck, and two brigades, and three cavalry commands — also unassigned, stationed at Yorktown, Gloucester Point, and Williamsburg, under General E. D. Keyes. The troops under Peck belonged to the Seventh Corps. Keyes's command was known as the Fourth Corps. Both were included in the Department of Virginia, commanded by General John A. Dix, with headquarters at Fort Monroe.

While Lee was invading the North an expedition was sent by General Dix from White House to the South Anna River and Bottom's Bridge to destroy Lee's communications and threaten Richmond. — EDITORS.

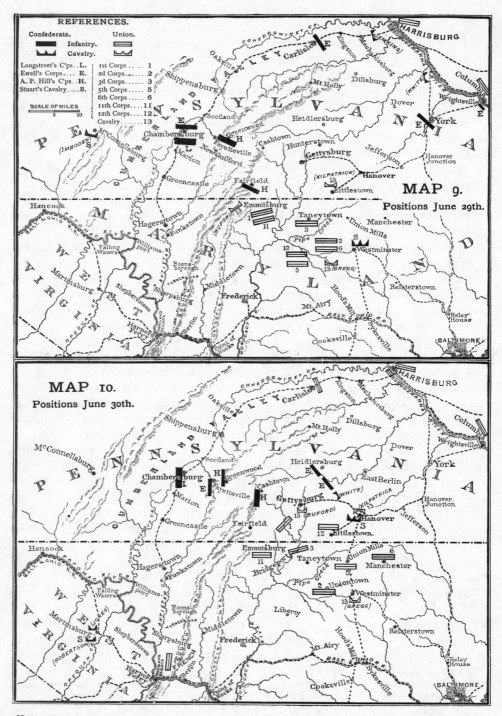

REFERENCES.

Confederate.   Union.

Infantry.   Infantry.

Cavalry.   Cavalry.

Longstreet's C'ps ..L.   1st Corps 1
Ewell's Corps.... E.   2d Corps.... 2
A. P. Hill's C'ps . H.   3d Corps 3
Stuart's Cavalry . S.   5th Corps 5
    6th Corps 6
    11th Corps....11
    12th Corps....12
    Cavalry 13

SCALE OF MILES

MAP 9.

Positions June 29th.

MAP 10.

Positions June 30th.

NOTE.—In considering the comparative value of Gettysburg and Westminster (behind Pipe Creek) to Lee and Meade, the maps, above, should make more of the mountain ridge, west of the Monocacy, and defined in general by Point of Rocks, Fairfield, and Cashtown; and there should be represented on the maps the lesser range called Parr's Ridge, east of Pipe Creek, at the foot of which lie Westminster and Manchester.—EDITORS.

He considered aggressive action indispensable, that "all attendant risks and sacrifices must be incurred," and adds, "I have not hesitated, in coöperating with your plans, to leave this city almost defenseless." General Lee now had full liberty of action, with the assured support of his Government,—an immense advantage over an opponent who had neither.

As soon as Hooker learned from Pleasonton that a large infantry force was at Culpeper, he extended his right up the Rappahannock, and when informed of Ewell's move toward the valley, being forbidden to attack A. P. Hill at Fredericksburg or to spoil Lee's plans by marching to Richmond, he moved his army, on the night of June 13th, toward the line of the Orange and Alexandria Railroad, and occupied Thoroughfare Gap in advance of it. On the 15th Longstreet left Culpeper, keeping east of the Blue Ridge and so covering its gaps. Hill left Fredericksburg on the 14th, and reached Shepherdstown via Chester Gap on the 23d. Stuart's cavalry had been thrown out on Longstreet's right to occupy the passes of the Bull Run mountains and watch Hooker's army. On the 17th he encountered, near Aldie, a portion of Pleasonton's command; a fierce fight ensued, which left the Federals in possession of the field. During the four following days there was a succession of cavalry combats; those of the 19th near Middleburg, and of the 21st near Upperville, were especially well contested, and resulted in the retreat of Stuart through Ashby's Gap. Longstreet had already withdrawn through the gaps and followed Hill

PENNSYLVANIA COLLEGE, GETTYSBURG. FROM A PHOTOGRAPH.

The cupola was first used by Union officers, and then by Confederate, as a station for observation and signals. During the withdrawal of the First and Eleventh corps through the town to Cemetery Hill, there was hard fighting in the college grounds.— EDITORS.

to the Potomac. Imboden, his work of destruction completed, had taken post at Hancock. Longstreet and Hill crossed the Potomac on the 24th and 25th and directed their march on Chambersburg and Fayetteville, arriving on the 27th. Stuart had been directed to guard the mountain passes until the Federal army crossed the river, and, according to General Lee's report, "to lose no time in placing his command on the right of our [Confederate] column as soon as he should perceive the enemy moving northward," in order to watch and report his movements. According to Stuart's report, he was authorized to cross between the Federal army and Washington, and directed after crossing to proceed with all dispatch to join Early in Pennsylvania.

General Lee so far had been completely successful; his army was exultant, and he lost no time in availing himself of his advantages. On the 21st he ordered Ewell to take possession of Harrisburg; and on the 22d Ewell's whole corps was on the march, Rodes's and Johnson's divisions via Chambersburg to Carlisle, which they reached on the 27th, and Early via Greenwood and Gettysburg to York, with orders from Ewell to break up the Northern Central Railroad, destroy the bridge across the Susquehanna at Wrightsville, and then rejoin the main body at Carlisle. Early entered York on the 28th, and sent Gordon's brigade, not to destroy but to secure possession of the bridge, which would enable him to operate upon Harrisburg from the rear; but a small militia force under Colonel Frick, retreating from Wrightsville across the bridge, after an unsuccessful attempt to destroy one of its spans, set fire to and entirely destroyed that fine structure, Gordon's troops giving their aid to the citizens to save the town from the flames. On the 29th Ewell received orders from General Lee to rejoin the army at Cashtown; the next evening,

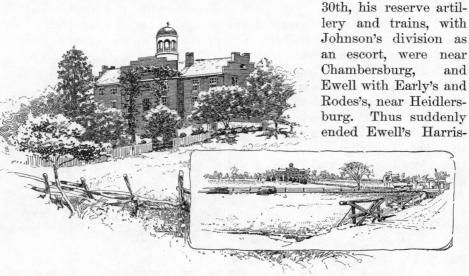

30th, his reserve artillery and trains, with Johnson's division as an escort, were near Chambersburg, and Ewell with Early's and Rodes's, near Heidlersburg. Thus suddenly ended Ewell's Harris-

THE LUTHERAN SEMINARY. THE UPPER PICTURE FROM A WAR-TIME PHOTOGRAPH.

Both pictures show the face of the seminary toward the town, and in the right-hand view is seen the Chambersburg Pike. On the first day, Buford and Reynolds used the cupola for observations; thereafter it was the chief signal-station and observatory for the Confederates — EDITORS.

burg expedition. One object was to collect supplies, and contributions were accordingly levied. Much damage was done to roads and bridges, but the prompt advance of the Army of the Potomac made this useless to the Confederates.

Before committing his army to an invasion of the North, General Lee recommended the proper steps to cover and support it. In a letter of June 23d, addressed to President Davis, he states that the season was so far advanced as to stop further Federal operations on the Southern coast, and that Confederate troops in that country and elsewhere were now disposable. He proposed, therefore, that an army should as soon as possible be organized at Culpeper, as " the well-known anxiety of the Northern Government for the safety of its capital would induce it to retain a large force for its defense, and thus relieve the opposition to our advance"; and suggested that General Beauregard be placed in command, " as his presence would give magnitude

Oak Hill is a mile north-west of Gettysburg, and the view here is south-east, showing Stevens Hall (named after Thaddeus Stevens), the preparatory department of the Pennsylvania College on the left; then Culp's Hill; then Pennsylvania College, and, to the right of its cupola, the observatory on Cemetery Hill.

even to a small demonstration." On the 25th he wrote twice to Mr. Davis urging the same views. The proposition embarrassed Mr. Davis, who could not see how, with the few troops under his hand, it could be carried out. In fact, although General Lee had pointed out the means, the proposition came too late, as the decisive battle took place much earlier than was expected. This correspondence, however, with that between Lee and Mr. Seddon, shows that Hooker's project to capture Richmond by a *coup-de-main* was feasible. It was not now a question of "swapping queens." Washington was safe, being well fortified and sufficiently garrisoned, or with available troops within reach, without drawing on Hooker; and to take Richmond and scatter the Confederate Government was the surest way to ruin Lee's army — "his true objective."

On the first appearance of danger of invasion, Pennsylvania's vigilant governor, Curtin, warned the people of the State and called out the militia. General Couch was sent to Harrisburg to organize and command them, but disbelief in the danger — due to previous false alarms — caused delays until the fugitives from Milroy's command, followed by Jenkins's cavalry, roused the country. Defensive works were then thrown up at Harrisburg and elsewhere, and local forces were raised and moved toward the enemy.

Early in June Hooker represented in strong terms the necessity of having one commander for all the troops whose operations would have an influence on those of Lee's army, and in reply was informed by Halleck that any movements he might suggest for other commands than his own would be ordered *if practicable*. Misunderstandings and confusion naturally resulted, and authority was given Hooker from time to time to exercise control over the troops of Heintzelman, commanding the Department of Washington, and of Schenck, commanding the Middle Department, followed, June 24th, by orders specifically placing the troops in Harper's Ferry and its vicinity at his disposal.

Disregarding Ewell's movements, Hooker conformed his own to those of the enemy's main body, and crossed the Potomac at Edwards's Ferry on the 25th and 26th of June. On the 27th three army-corps under Reynolds occupied Middletown and the South Mountain passes. The Twelfth Corps was near Harper's Ferry, and the three other corps at or near Frederick. Hooker now ordered the Twelfth Corps to march early on the 28th to Harper's Ferry,

GENERAL LEE'S HEADQUARTERS ON THE CHAMBERSBURG PIKE.
FROM A WAR-TIME PHOTOGRAPH.

there to be joined by its garrison from Maryland Heights, in order to cut Lee's communications with Virginia, and in conjunction with Reynolds to operate on his rear. General Halleck, however, objected to the abandonment of the Heights, notwithstanding Hooker's representations that the position was utterly useless for any purpose; whereupon Hooker abandoned his project, and finding now that he was "not allowed to manœuvre his own army in the presence of the enemy," asked to be relieved from his command. He had encountered some of the difficulties which had beset a predecessor whom he had himself mercilessly criticised, and promptly succumbed to them. His request was complied with, and Major-General George G. Meade was appointed his successor, this being the fifth change of commanders of the army in front of Washington in ten months. Meade was an excellent officer of long service, who had always proved equal to his position, whether as a specialist or a commander of troops. Many welcomed his advent—some regretted Hooker's departure. All thought the time for the change unfortunate, but accepted loyally, as that army ever did, the leader designated by the President, and gave Meade their hearty support. He was succeeded in the command of the Fifth Corps by Major-General George Sykes, a veteran of the Mexican war and a distinguished soldier.

When General Meade assumed command, June 28th, the best information placed Longstreet at Chambersburg, A. P. Hill between that place and Cashtown, and Ewell in occupation of Carlisle, York, and the country between them, threatening Harrisburg. Unacquainted with Hooker's plans and views [see p. 243], he determined at once to move on the main line from Frederick to Harrisburg, extending his wings as far as compatible with a ready concentration, in order to force Lee to battle before he could cross the Susquehanna. With this view he spent the day in ascertaining the position of his army, and brought up his cavalry, Buford to his left, Gregg to his right, and Kilpatrick to the front. Directing French to occupy Frederick with seven thousand men of the garrison of Harper's Ferry, he put his army in motion early on the morning of the 29th. Kilpatrick reached Littlestown that night; and on the morning of the 30th the rear of his division, while passing through Hanover, was attacked by a portion of Stuart's cavalry. Stuart, availing himself of the discretion allowed him, had left Robertson's and Jones's brigades to guard the passes of the Blue Ridge, and on the night of the 24th, with those of Hampton, Fitzhugh Lee, and Chambliss, had started to move round the Army of the Potomac, pass between it and Centreville into Maryland, and so rejoin Lee; but the movements of that army forced him so far east that he was compelled to ford the Potomac near Seneca [20 miles above Washington], on the night of the 27th. Next morning, learning that Hooker had already crossed the river, he marched north by Rockville, where he captured a wagon train. Paroling his prisoners and taking the train with him, he pushed on—through Westminster, where he had a sharp action with a squadron of Delaware horse—to Union Mills, and encamped there on the 29th. During the night, he learned that the Federal army was still be-

tween him and Lee on its march north, and his scouts reported its cavalry in strong force at Littlestown, barring his direct road to Gettysburg; wherefore, on the morning of the 30th he moved across country to Hanover, Chambliss in front and Hampton in rear of his long train of two hundred wagons, with Fitzhugh Lee well out on his left flank. About 10 A. M. Chambliss, reaching Hanover, found Kilpatrick passing through the town and attacked him, but was driven out before Hampton or Lee could come to his support. Stuart's men and horses were now nearly worn out; he was encumbered with a large captured train; a junction with some part of Lee's army was a necessity, and he made a night march for York, only to learn that Early

NORTH-EAST CORNER OF THE McPHERSON WOODS, WHERE GENERAL REYNOLDS WAS KILLED. FROM A PHOTOGRAPH.

had left the day before. Pushing on to Carlisle, he found that Ewell was gone, and the place occupied by a militia force under General W. F. Smith.↓ His demand of a surrender was refused; he threw a few shells into the town and burned the Government barracks. That night he learned that Lee's army was concentrating at Gettysburg, and left for that place next day. Thus ended a raid which greatly embarrassed Lee, and by which the services of three cavalry brigades were, in the critical period of the campaign, exchanged for a few hundred prisoners and a wagon train.

Hearing nothing from Stuart, and therefore believing that Hooker was still south of the Potomac, Lee, on the afternoon of the 28th, ordered Longstreet and A. P. Hill to join Ewell at Harrisburg; but late that night one of Longstreet's scouts came in and reported that the Federal army had crossed the river, that Meade had relieved Hooker and was at Frederick. Lee thereupon changed the rendezvous of his army to Cashtown, which place Heth reached on the 29th. Next day Heth sent Pettigrew's brigade on to Gettysburg, nine miles, to procure a supply of shoes. Nearing this place, Pettigrew

↓ General Smith commanded the First Division, Department of the Susquehanna, and was charged with the protection of Harrisburg.— EDITORS.

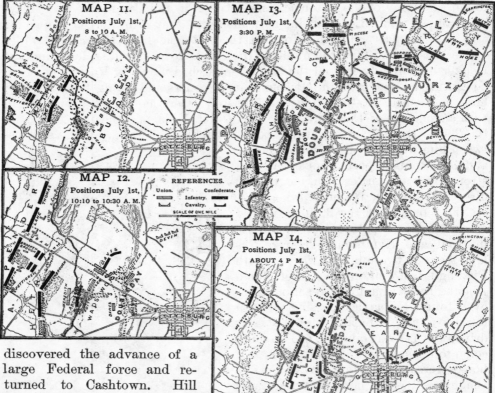

discovered the advance of a
large Federal force and returned to Cashtown. Hill
immediately notified Generals
Lee and Ewell, informing the
latter that he would advance
next morning on Gettysburg.
Buford, sending Merritt's brigade to Mechanicstown as guard to his trains,
had early on the morning of the 29th crossed into and moved up the Cumberland valley via Boonsboro' and Fairfield with those of Gamble and Devin,
and on the afternoon of Tuesday, June 30th, under instructions from Pleasonton, entered Gettysburg, Pettigrew's brigade withdrawing on his approach.

From Gettysburg, near the eastern base of the Green Ridge, and covering
all the upper passes into the Cumberland valley, good roads lead to all important points between the Susquehanna and the Potomac. It is therefore
an important strategic position. On the west of the town, distant nearly half
a mile, there is a somewhat elevated ridge running north and south, on which
stands the "Lutheran Seminary." This ridge is covered with open woods
through its whole length, and is terminated nearly a mile and a half north of
the seminary by a commanding knoll, bare on its southern side, called Oak
Hill. From this ridge the ground slopes gradually to the west, and again
rising forms another ridge about 500 yards from the first, upon which, nearly
opposite the seminary, stand McPherson's farm buildings. The second ridge
is wider, smoother, and lower than the first, and Oak Hill, their intersection,

has a clear view of the slopes of both ridges and of the valley between them. West of McPherson's ridge Willoughby Run flows south into Marsh Creek. South of the farm buildings and directly opposite the seminary, a wood borders the run for about 300 yards, and stretches back to the summit of McPherson's ridge. From the town two roads run: one south-west to Hagerstown via Fairfield, the other north-westerly to Chambersburg via Cashtown. The seminary is midway between them, about 300 yards from each. Parallel to and 150 yards north of the Chambersburg pike, is the bed of an unfinished railroad, with deep cuttings through the two ridges. Directly north of the town the country is comparatively flat and open; on the east of it, Rock Creek flows south.

On the south, and overlooking it, is a ridge of bold, high ground, terminated on the west by Cemetery Hill and on the east by Culp's Hill, which, bending to the south, extends half a mile or more and terminates in low grounds near Spangler's Spring. Culp's Hill is steep toward the east, is well wooded, and its eastern base is washed by Rock Creek.

CONFEDERATE DEAD ON THE FIELD OF THE FIRST DAY.
FROM A PHOTOGRAPH.

Impressed by the importance of the position, Buford, expecting the early return of the enemy in force, assigned to Devin's brigade the country north, and to Gamble's that west of the town; sent out scouting parties on all the roads to collect information, and reported the condition of affairs to Reynolds. His pickets extended from below the Fairfield road, along the eastern bank of Willoughby Run, to the railroad cut, then easterly some 1500 yards north of the town, to a wooded hillock near Rock Creek.

On the night of June 30th Meade's headquarters and the Artillery Reserve were at Taneytown; the First Corps at Marsh Run, the Eleventh at Emmitsburg, Third at Bridgeport, Twelfth at Littlestown, Second at Uniontown, Fifth at Union Mills, Sixth and Gregg's cavalry at Manchester, Kilpatrick's at Hanover. A glance at the map [p. 266] will show at what disadvantage Meade's army was now placed. Lee's whole army was nearing Gettysburg, while Meade's was scattered over a wide region to the east and south of that town.

Meade was now convinced that all designs on the Susquehanna had been abandoned; but as Lee's corps were reported as occupying the country from

UNION DEAD WEST OF THE SEMINARY. FROM A PHOTOGRAPH.

Chambersburg to Carlisle, he ordered, for the next day's moves, the First and Eleventh corps to Gettysburg, under Reynolds, the Third to Emmitsburg, the Second to Taneytown, the Fifth to Hanover, and the Twelfth to Two Taverns, directing Slocum to take command of the Fifth in addition to his own. The Sixth Corps was left at Manchester, thirty-four miles from Gettysburg, to await orders. But Meade, while conforming to the current of Lee's movement, was not merely drifting. The same afternoon he directed the chiefs of engineers and artillery to select a field of battle on which his army might be concentrated, whatever Lee's lines of approach, whether by Harrisburg or Gettysburg,—indicating the general line of Pipe Creek as a suitable locality. Carefully drawn instructions were sent to the corps commanders as to the occupation of this line, should it be ordered; but it was added that developments might cause the offensive to be assumed from present positions. These orders were afterward cited as indicating General Meade's intention not to fight at Gettysburg. They were, under any circumstances, wise and proper orders, and it would probably have been better had he concentrated his army behind Pipe Creek rather than at Gettysburg; but events finally controlled the actions of both leaders.

At 8 A. M., July 1st, Buford's scouts reported Heth's advance on the Cashtown road, ⚓ when Gamble's brigade formed on McPherson's Ridge, from the

⚓ The opening of the battle on the Chambersburg road, on July 1st, is thus described by Captain Newel Cheney, of the 9th N. Y. Cavalry, in a paper prepared for the Gettysburg Monument Commission of New York:

"Colonel William Sackett, commanding the 9th N. Y. Cavalry, was brigade officer of the day and in charge of

the brigade picket-line made up of details from each regiment of Devin's brigade (9th N. Y., 6th N. Y., 4th N. Y., and 17th Pa.) the night of June 30th, and extending from the south side of the Chambersburg road, on the east side of Willoughby Run, northerly and eastwardly across the Mummasburg, Carlisle, and Harrisburg roads. He had his headquarters on the Chambersburg road, near the Lutheran Seminary. The advanced picket put on the Chambersburg road near Willoughby

Fairfield road to the railroad cut; one section of Calef's battery A, 2d United States, near the left of his line, the other two across the Chambersburg or Cashtown pike. Devin formed his disposable squadrons from Gamble's right toward Oak Hill, from which he had afterward to transfer them to the north of the town to meet Ewell. As Heth advanced, he threw Archer's brigade to the right, Davis's to the left of the Cashtown pike, with Pettigrew's and Brockenbrough's brigades in support. The Confederates advanced skirmish-

UNION DEAD NEAR McPHERSON'S WOODS. FROM A PHOTOGRAPH.

Run consisted of a corporal and three men, relieved every two hours, with orders not to fire on any one approaching from the front, but to notify the pickets in each direction and the reserve. No one approached from the front until daylight next morning, July 1st, when Corporal Alphonse Hodges, of Company F, 9th N. Y. Cavalry, was on this post with three men. At daylight he saw men approaching along the road, nearly a mile away, across Willoughby Run. Acting on his orders, he immediately sent his men to notify the line and the reserve, while he advanced across the Run till near enough to see that those approaching were the enemy, when he turned back, and as he did so the enemy fired at him. He retired to the Run, and from behind the abutments of the bridge fired several shots back at the enemy. These are supposed to be the first shots fired from our side on the morning of July 1st at Gettysburg, and occurred about 5:30 A. M., as near as Hodges can remember. When he fell back from the bridge to the higher ground, he found Colonel Sackett had formed a skirmish-line of the whole of his picket force, which, as I have said, consisted of detachments from the different regiments of the (Devin's) brigade. Here the advance of the enemy was first seriously disputed by this skirmish-line, which he held till after Hall's battery (2d Maine) came up and took position on the right of the Chambersburg road in rear of this skirmish-line and fired. . . . The First Brigade of Buford's division (Colonel Gamble's) coming up on the left of the road, the line of the Second Brigade, still under command of Colonel Sackett, moved farther to the right and occupied the line from the Chambersburg road to the Mummasburg road. That portion of the 9th Cavalry which

had remained in camp received orders to water their horses by squadrons in Rock Creek about 7 A. M. As soon as they had watered, they saddled up and proceeded out on the Mummasburg road to the skirmish-line on Oak Ridge. The first squadron, under Captain Hanley (afterward Lieutenant-Colonel), was the first to reach the line, and he immediately ordered Lieutenant A. C. Robertson (afterward Captain) with twenty men to advance down the road into the woods, where he found the enemy's line near the residence of N. Hoffman. Finding the enemy had a strong line, he retired to a position a little back of the residence of J. Forney, from behind which some of the enemy were firing at him. He dismounted his men and drove the enemy from behind Forney's buildings, then fell back to the stone wall on the ridge, where the balance of the regiment were formed dismounted. Here the regiment held their ground for some time while the enemy approached on their hands and knees through the wheat-field in front. Daniel Cornish, of Company F, getting sight of a rebel not far away in the field, fired and killed him. The regiment cheered, and the enemy, evidently thinking our men would charge on them, hastily withdrew out of the wheat-field. As they fell back one man stopped behind a tree in the field near the road, and Perry Nichols, of Company F, advanced and captured him. This is said to be the first prisoner captured. He was immediately taken to Buford's headquarters, and gave the first information we received from the enemy's side. It was during this skirmish that Cyrus W. James, Company G, 9th N. Y. Cavalry, was killed by a rebel bullet, and he is said to have been the first man killed that morning on our side."—EDITORS.

JOHN L. BURNS, "THE OLD HERO OF GETTYSBURG." }
FROM A PHOTOGRAPH TAKEN SOON AFTER
THE BATTLE.

ing heavily with Buford's dismounted troopers. Calef's battery, engaging double the number of its own guns, was served with an efficiency worthy of its former reputation as "Duncan's battery" in the Mexican war, and so enabled the cavalry to hold their long line for two hours. When Buford's report of the enemy's advance reached Reynolds, the latter, ordering Doubleday and Howard to follow, hastened toward Gettysburg with Wadsworth's small division (two brigades, Meredith's and Cutler's) and Hall's 2d Maine battery. As he approached he heard the sound of battle, and directing the troops to cross the fields toward the firing, galloped himself to the seminary, met Buford there, and both rode to the front, where the cavalry, dismounted, were gallantly holding their ground against heavy odds. After viewing the field, he sent back to hasten up Howard, and as the enemy's main line was now advancing to the attack, directed Doubleday, who had arrived in advance of his division, to look to the Fairfield road, sent Cutler with three of his five regiments north of the railroad cut, posted the other two under Colonel Fowler, of the 14th New York, south of the pike, and replaced Calef's battery by Hall's, thus relieving the cavalry. Cutler's line

⎰ I have seen it stated in an account of Burns, that he was an old regular soldier who had served in the Florida war.— H. J. H.

Sergeant George Eustice, of Company F, 7th Wisconsin Volunteers, in a letter from Gilroy, Santa Clara County, California, gives this account of John Burns's action in the ranks of that regiment:

"It must have been about noon when I saw a little old man coming up in the rear of Company F. In regard to the peculiarities of his dress, I remember he wore a swallow-tailed coat with smooth brass buttons. He had a rifle on his shoulder. We boys began to poke fun at him as soon as he came amongst us, as we thought no civilian in his senses would show himself in such a place. Finding that he had really come to fight I wanted to put a cartridge-box on him to make him look like a soldier, telling him he could not fight without one. Slapping his pantaloons-pocket, he replied, 'I can get my hands in here quicker than in a box. I'm not used to them new-fangled things.' In answer to the question what possessed him to come out there at such a time, he replied that the rebels had either driven away or milked his cows, and that he was going to be even with them. About this time the enemy began to advance. Bul-

lets were flying thicker and faster, and we hugged the ground about as close as we could. Burns got behind a tree and surprised us all by not taking a double-quick to the rear. He was as calm and collected as any veteran on the ground. We soon had orders to get up and move about a hundred yards to the right, when we were engaged in one of the most stubborn contests I ever experienced. Foot by foot we were driven back to a point near the seminary, where we made a stand, but were finally driven through the town to Cemetery Ridge. I never saw John Burns after our movement to the right, when we left him behind his tree, and only know that he was true blue and grit to the backbone, and fought until he was three times wounded."

In his official report, General Doubleday says:

"My thanks are specially due to a citizen of Gettysburg named John Burns, who, although over seventy years of age, shouldered his musket and offered his services to Colonel Wister, 150th Pennsylvania Volunteers. Colonel Wister advised him to fight in the woods, as there was more shelter there; but he preferred to join our line of skirmishers in the open fields. When the troops retired, he fought with the Iron Brigade [Meredith's]. He was wounded in three places."—EDITORS.

was hardly formed when it was struck by Davis's Confederate brigade on its front and right flank, whereupon Wadsworth, to save it, ordered it to fall back to Seminary Ridge. This order not reaching the 147th New York, its gallant major, Harney, held that regiment to its position until, having lost half its numbers, the order to retire was repeated. Hall's battery was now imperiled, and it withdrew by sections, fighting at close canister range and suffering severely. Fowler thereupon changed his front to face Davis's brigade, which held the cut, and with Dawes's 6th Wisconsin — sent by Doubleday to aid

the 147th New York — charged and drove Davis from the field. The Confederate brigade suffered severely, losing all its field-officers but two, and a large proportion of its men killed and captured, being disabled for further effective service that day. In the meantime Archer's Confederate brigade had occupied McPherson's wood, and as the regiments of Meredith's "Iron Brigade" came up, they were sent forward by Doubleday, who fully recognized the importance of the position, to dislodge Archer. At the entrance of the wood they found Reynolds in person, and, animated by his presence, rushed to the charge, struck successive heavy blows, outflanked and turned the enemy's right, captured General Archer and a large portion of his brigade, and pursued the remainder across Willoughby Run. Wadsworth's small division had thus won decided successes against superior numbers, but it was at grievous cost

MAJOR-GENERAL ABNER DOUBLEDAY.
FROM A PHOTOGRAPH.

to the army and the country, for Reynolds, while directing the operations, was killed in the wood by a sharp-shooter. It was not, however, until by his promptitude and gallantry he had determined the decisive field of the war, and had opened brilliantly a battle which required three days of hard fighting to close with a victory. To him may be applied in a wider sense than in its original one, Napier's happy eulogium on Ridge: "No man died on that field with more glory than he, yet many died, and there was much glory."

After the repulse of Davis and Archer, Heth's division was formed in line mostly south of the Cashtown pike, with Pender's in second line, Pegram's and McIntosh's artillery (nine batteries) occupying all the commanding positions west of Willoughby Run. Doubleday reëstablished his former lines, Meredith holding McPherson's wood. Soon after, Rowley's and Robinson's divisions (two brigades each) and the four remaining batteries of the corps

ASSAULT OF BROCKENBROUGH'S CONFEDERATE BRIGADE (HETH'S DIVISION) UPON THE STONE
BARN OF THE McPHERSON FARM.

The line of the stone barn was held by Stone's bri-gade, Pennsylvania Bucktails (Doubleday's division), its right resting on the Chambersburg pike (the left of the picture) and its left on the McPherson woods, where a part of Archer's Confederate brigade of Heth's division was captured by Meredith's brigade.— EDITORS.

arrived. Rowley's division was thrown forward, Stone's brigade to the inter-val between Meredith and Cutler, and Biddle's with Cooper's battery to occupy the ridge between the wood and the Fairfield road. Reynolds's bat-tery replaced Hall's, and Calef's rejoined Gamble's cavalry, now in reserve. Robinson's division was halted near the base of Seminary Ridge. By this time, near noon, General Howard arrived, assumed command, and directed General Schurz, commanding the Eleventh Corps, to prolong Doubleday's line toward Oak Hill with Schimmelfennig's and Barlow's divisions and three batteries, and to post Steinwehr's division and two batteries on Cemetery Hill, as a rallying-point. By 1 o'clock, when this corps was arriving, Buford had reported Ewell's approach by the Heidlersburg road, and Howard called on Sickles at Emmitsburg and Slocum at Two Taverns for aid, to which both these officers promptly responded. It was now no longer a question of prolonging Doubleday's line, but of protecting it against Ewell whilst engaged in front with Hill. Schurz's two divisions, hardly 6000 effectives, accordingly formed line on the open plain half a mile north of the town. They were too weak to cover the ground, and a wide interval was left between the two corps, covered only by the fire of Dilger's and Wheeler's batteries (ten guns) posted behind it.

That morning, whilst on the march to Cashtown, Ewell received Hill's notice that his corps was advancing to Gettysburg, upon which he turned the heads of his own columns to that point. Reporting the change by a staff-officer to General Lee, Ewell was instructed that if the Federals were in force at Gettysburg a general battle was not to be brought on until the rest of the army was up. Approaching Gettysburg, Rodes, guided by the sounds of battle, followed the prolongation of Seminary Ridge; Iverson's, Daniel's, and Ramseur's brigades on the western, O'Neal's and Doles's on the eastern slope. Ewell, recognizing the importance of Oak Hill, ordered it to be occupied by Carter's artillery battalion, which immediately opened on both the Federal corps, enfilading Doubleday's line. This caused Wadsworth again to

withdraw Cutler to Seminary Ridge, and Reynolds's battery was posted near McPherson's house, under partial cover. Stone therefore placed two of his three regiments on the Cashtown pike, so as to face Oak Hill. This left an interval between Stone and Cutler, through which Cooper and Reynolds could fire with effect, and gave to these lines a cross-fire on troops entering

CONFEDERATE DEAD GATHERED FOR BURIAL NEAR THE McPHERSON WOODS. FROM PHOTOGRAPHS.

the angle between them. Robinson now sent his two brigades to strengthen Cutler's right. They took post behind the stone walls of a field, Paul's brigade facing west, Baxter's north. Rodes, regarding this advance as a menace, gave orders at 2:30 P. M. to attack. Iverson, sweeping round to his left, engaged Paul, who prolonged Cutler's line, and O'Neal attacked Baxter. The repulse of O'Neal soon enabled Baxter to turn upon Iverson. Cutler also attacked him in flank, and after losing 500 men killed and wounded, 3 of Iverson's regiments surrendered. General Robinson reports the capture of 1000 prisoners and 3 colors; General Paul was severely wounded, losing both eyes. Meanwhile Daniel's brigade advanced directly on Stone, who maintained his lines against this attack and also Brockenbrough's, of Hill's corps,

LIEUTENANT BAYARD WILKESON HOLDING HIS BATTERY (G, 4TH UNITED STATES ARTILLERY) TO ITS WORK IN AN EXPOSED POSITION.

but was soon severely wounded. Colonel Wister, who succeeded him, met the same fate, and Colonel Dana took command of the brigade. Ramseur, who followed Daniel, by a conversion to the left, now faced Robinson and Cutler with his own brigade, the remnant of Iverson's, and one regiment of O'Neal's, his right connecting with Daniel's left, and the fighting became hot. East of the ridge, Doles's brigade had been held in observation, but about 3:30 P. M., on the advance of Early, he sent his skirmishers forward and drove those of Devin—who had gallantly held the enemy's advance in check with his dismounted troopers—from their line and its hillock on Rock Creek. Barlow, considering this an eligible position for his own right, advanced his division, supported by Wilkeson's battery, and seized it. This made it necessary for Schurz to advance a brigade of Schimmelfennig's division to connect with Barlow, thus lengthening his already too extended line.

The arrival of Early's division had by this time brought an overwhelming force on the flank and rear of the Eleventh Corps. On the east of Rock Creek, Jones's artillery battalion, within easy range, enfiladed its whole line and took it in reverse, while the brigades of Gordon, Hays, and Avery in line, with Smith's in reserve, advanced about 4 P. M. upon Barlow's position, Doles, of Rodes's division, connecting with Gordon. An obstinate and bloody contest ensued, in which Barlow was desperately wounded, Wilkeson killed, and the whole corps forced back to its original line, on which, with the aid of Coster's brigade and Heckman's battery, drawn from Cemetery Hill, Schurz endeavored to rally it and cover the town. The fighting here was well sustained, but the Confederate force was overpowering in numbers, and the troops retreated to Cemetery Hill, Ewell entering the town about 4:30 P. M. These retrograde movements had uncovered the flank of the First Corps and made its right untenable.

Meanwhile, that corps had been heavily engaged along its whole line; for, on the approach of Rodes, Hill attacked with both his divisions. There were thus opposed to the single disconnected Federal line south of the Cashtown pike two solid Confederate ones which outflanked their left a quarter of a mile or more. Biddle's small command, less than a thousand men, after a severe contest, was gradually forced back. In McPherson's wood and beyond, Meredith's and Dana's brigades repeatedly repulsed their assailants, but as Biddle's retirement uncovered their left, they too fell back to successive positions from which they inflicted heavy losses, until finally all three reached the

NOTE TO CUT, P. 280.— The death of Lieutenant Bayard Wilkeson, who commanded Battery G, Fourth U. S. Artillery, was one of the most heroic episodes of the fight. He was but nineteen years old and was the son of Samuel Wilkeson, who, as correspondent of the "New-York Times," was at Meade's headquarters during the fight. Young Wilkeson, by his fearless demeanor, held his battery in an exposed position on the Union right. General John B. Gordon, finding it impossible to advance his Confederate division in the face of Wilkeson's fire, and realizing that if the officer on the horse could be disposed of the battery would not remain, directed two batteries of his command to train every gun upon him. Wilkeson was brought to the ground, desperately wounded, and his horse was killed. He was carried by the Confederates to the Alms House (or dragged himself there — the accounts differ), where he died that night. Just before he expired, it is said, he asked for water; a canteen was brought to him; as he took it a wounded soldier lying next to him begged, "For God's sake give me some!" He passed the canteen untouched to the man, who drank every drop it contained. Wilkeson smiled on the man, turned slightly, and expired.— EDITORS.

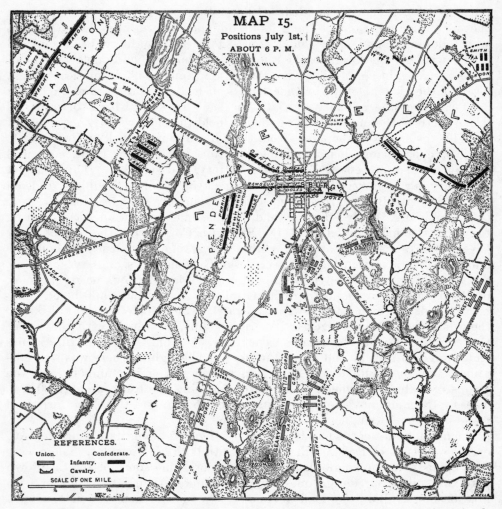

MAP 15.
Positions July 1st,
ABOUT 6 P. M.

REFERENCES.
Union.   Confederate.
Infantry.
Cavalry.
SCALE OF ONE MILE

NOTE.—Edward Johnson's Confederate division (upper right-hand corner) did not reach the position assigned
them on this map until after sunset or about dusk of July 1st. See p. 284.— EDITORS.

foot of Seminary Ridge, where Colonel Wainwright, commanding the corps
artillery, had planted twelve guns south of the Cashtown pike, with Stewart's
battery, manned in part by men of the Iron Brigade, north of it. Buford had
already thrown half of Gamble's dismounted men south of the Fairfield road.
Heth's division had suffered so severely that Pender's had passed to its front,
thus bringing fresh troops to bear on the exhausted Federal line.

It was about 4 P. M. when the whole Confederate line advanced to the final
attack. On their right Gamble held Lane's brigade for some time in check,
Perrin's and Scales's suffered severely, and Scales's was broken up, for Stewart,
swinging half his guns, under Lieutenant Davison, upon the Cashtown pike,
raked it. The whole corps being now heavily pressed and its right uncovered,
Doubleday gave the order to fall back to Cemetery Hill, which was effected in

THE LINE OF DEFENSE AT THE CEMETERY GATE-HOUSE. FROM A PHOTOGRAPH.

comparatively good order, the rear, covered by the 7th Wisconsin, turning when necessary to check pursuit. Colonel Wainwright, mistaking the order, had clung with his artillery to Seminary Hill, until, seeing the infantry retreating to the town, he moved his batteries down the Cashtown pike until lapped on both sides by the enemy's skirmishers, at close range, when they were compelled to abandon one gun on the road, all its horses being killed. The Eleventh Corps also left a disabled gun on the field. Of the troops who passed through the town, many, principally men of the Eleventh Corps, got entangled in the streets, lost their way, and were captured.

On ascending Cemetery Hill, the retreating troops found Steinwehr's division in position covered by stone fences on the slopes, and occupying by their skirmishers the houses in front of their line. As they arrived they were formed, the Eleventh Corps on the right, the First Corps on the left of Steinwehr. As the batteries came up, they were well posted by Colonels Wainwright and Osborn, and soon a formidable array of artillery was ready to cover with its fire all the approaches. Buford assembled his command on the plain west of Cemetery Hill, covering the left flank and presenting a firm front to any attempt at pursuit. The First Corps found a small reënforcement awaiting it, in the 7th Indiana, part of the train escort, which brought up nearly five hundred fresh men. Wadsworth met them and led them to Culp's Hill, where, under direction of Captain Pattison of that regiment, a defensive line was marked out. Their brigade (Cutler's) soon joined them; wood and stone were plentiful, and soon the right of the line was solidly established.

Nor was there wanting other assurance to the men who had fought so long that their sacrifices had not been in vain. As they reached the hill they were received by General Hancock, who arrived just as they were coming up from the town, under orders from General Meade to assume the command. His person was well known; his presence inspired confidence, and it implied also the near approach of his army-corps. He ordered Wadsworth at once to

Culp's Hill to secure that important position, and aided by Howard, by Warren who had also just arrived from headquarters, and by others, a strong line, well flanked, was soon formed.

General Lee, who from Seminary Hill had witnessed the final attack, sent Colonel Long, of his staff, a competent officer of sound judgment, to examine the position, and directed Ewell to carry it if practicable, renewing, however, his previous warning to avoid bringing on a general engagement until the army was all up. Both Ewell, who was making some preparations with a view to attack, and Long found the position a formidable one, strongly occupied and not accessible to artillery fire. Ewell's men were indeed in no condition for an immediate assault. Of Rodes's eight thousand, nearly three thousand were *hors de combat.* Early had lost over five hundred, and had but two brigades disposable, the other two having been sent on the report of the advance of Federal troops, probably the Twelfth Corps, then near by, to watch the York road. Hill's two divisions had been very roughly handled, and had lost heavily, and he withdrew them to Seminary Hill as Ewell entered the town, leaving the latter with not more than eight thousand men to secure the town and the prisoners. Ewell's absent division (Edward Johnson's) was expected soon, but it did not arrive until near sunset, when the Twelfth Corps and Stannard's Vermont brigade were also up, and the Third Corps was arriving. In fact an assault by the Confederates was not practicable before 5:30 P. M., and after that the position was perfectly secure. For the first time that day the Federals had the advantage of position, and sufficient troops and artillery to occupy it, and Ewell would not have been justified in attacking without the positive orders of Lee, who was present, and wisely abstained from giving them. [Continuation on page 290.]

INCIDENTS OF THE FIRST DAY AT GETTYSBURG. ⎰

BY E. P. HALSTEAD, BREVET-MAJOR AND ASSISTANT ADJUTANT-GENERAL, U. S. V.

COUNTING THE SCARS IN THE COLORS.

Soon after daylight on July 1st, General Reynolds, then at Marsh Run, gave orders to move with all possible dispatch to Gettysburg, where General Buford, with a small division of cavalry, was contending against Heth's division of infantry and vastly superior numbers.

The First Corps moved promptly, covered a distance of nearly eight miles, and the First Division, commanded by General Wadsworth, reached the field about 10 o'clock in the forenoon.

In returning for the Second and Third divisions I met John Burns in the field east of the Seminary, with an old musket on his shoulder and a powder-horn in his pocket, hurrying to the front, looking terribly earnest. When near me he inquired, "Which way are the rebels? Where are our troops?" I informed him that they were just in front, that he would soon overtake them. He then said, with much enthusiasm, "I know how to fight, I have fit before!"

Wadsworth's division was immediately engaged, except the Sixth Wisconsin, held in reserve by General Doubleday's orders. General Robinson and General Rowley were soon up with their divi-

⎰ From a paper read before the District of Columbia Commandery of the Loyal Legion, March 2d, 1887.—EDITORS.

sions and hotly engaged, the former on the right of the line, extending to near the Mummasburg road, and the latter in the center between Meredith's and Cutler's brigades of Wadsworth's division.

The advantages of position were, perhaps, favorable to us, but in numbers the enemy was vastly superior. We had 6 brigades, numbering, with the artillery assigned to duty with us, 8200 men, and we maintained our position for six hours and a half against General A. P. Hill's corps of 13 brigades. General Archer and most of his brigade were captured early in the day by Meredith's "Iron Brigade." He evidently had expected an easy "walk over," judging from his disappointed manner after he was captured. A guard brought him back to General Doubleday, who, in a very cordial manner,— they having been cadets at West Point together,— said: "Good-morning, Archer! How are you? I am glad to see you!" General Archer replied: "Well, I am *not* glad to see *you*, by a —— sight!" Very soon after this episode the 6th Wisconsin, under Lieutenant-Colonel Dawes, made a successful charge, resulting in the capture of a force of the enemy in the railroad cut north of the Cashtown road, and a little later General Baxter captured nearly all of Iverson's [Confederate] brigade.

About 2 o'clock in the afternoon the Eleventh Corps reached the field and formed in line of battle at about a right angle to the general line of the First Corps, but did not connect with its right by several hundred yards, so that both flanks were in the air. When Ewell's troops approached from Carlisle and York they struck the Eleventh Corps in front and on both flanks almost simultaneously. The result was an easy victory to the enemy, giving them possession of Gettysburg before the First Corps had ceased fighting or had left its position west of the Seminary. Thus the First Corps was enveloped on its right and rear and was contending against vastly superior numbers in its front.

About 4 o'clock in the afternoon General Doubleday sent me to General Howard for reënforcements and orders. I found the latter in the cemetery near the gate. He looked the picture of despair. On receipt of the message he replied: "Tell General Doubleday that I have no reënforcements to send him. I have only one regiment in reserve." I then asked if he had any orders to give, and called his attention to the enemy then advancing in line of battle overlapping our left by nearly half a mile. He looked in that direction and replied rather sharply: "Those are nothing but rail fences, sir!" I said: "I beg your pardon, General; if you will take my glass you will see something besides rail fences." Turning to a staff-officer, he bade him take the glass and see what it was. The officer looked, and in an instant lowered the glass, saying: "General, those are long lines of the enemy!" General Howard then turned to me and said: "Go to General Buford, give him my compliments, and tell him to go to General Doubleday's support." When asked where General Bu-

ford could be found, he replied: "I don't know! I think he is over this way," pointing toward the east.

After riding in that direction as far as I deemed it wise or prudent, I returned to where General Howard sat, just as General Hancock approached at a swinging gallop. When near General Howard, who was then alone, he saluted, and with great animation, as if there was no time for ceremony, said General Meade had sent him forward to take command of the three corps. General Howard replied that he was the senior. General Hancock said: "I am aware of that, General, but I have written orders in my pocket from General Meade, which I will show you if you wish to see them." General Howard said: "No; I do not doubt your word, General Hancock, but you can give no orders here while I am here." Hancock replied: "Very well, General Howard, I will second any order that you have to give, but General Meade has also directed me to select a field on which to fight this battle in rear of Pipe Creek." Then, casting one glance from Culp's Hill to Round Top, he continued: "But I think this the strongest position by nature upon which to fight a battle that I ever saw, and if it meets your approbation I will select this as the battle-field." General Howard responded: "I think it a very strong position, General Hancock; a very strong position!" "Very well, sir, I select this as the battle-field." General Hancock immediately turned away to rectify our lines.

There was no person present besides myself when the conversation took place between Howard and Hancock. A number of years since I reminded General Hancock of that fact and what I had heard pass between them. He said that what I have repeated here was true, and requested a written statement, which I subsequently furnished him.

When I left General Howard to return to the front, I discovered General Buford's cavalry only a little to the west of the cemetery and delivered the order I had received from General Howard. Buford rose in his stirrups upon his tiptoes and exclaimed: "What does he think I can do against those long lines of the enemy out there?" "I don't know anything about that, General; those are General Howard's orders." "Very well," said he, "I will see what I can do," and, like the true soldier that he was, he moved his command out in plain view of the enemy and formed for the charge. The enemy, seeing the movement, formed squares in echelon, which delayed them and materially aided in the escape of the First Corps, if it did not save a large portion of the remnant from capture. The formation of squares by the enemy that day has been doubted by nearly every one with whom I have conversed upon the subject, and not until the meeting of the survivors of the First Corps at Gettysburg, in May, 1885, was I able to satisfy Colonel Bachelder, who has made a study of that battle, of the correctness of my statement, and only then after it had been corroborated by two of Buford's officers who were in the engagement.

FROM A PHOTOGRAPH TAKEN DURING THE WAR OR SOON AFTER.

HANCOCK AND HOWARD IN THE FIRST DAY'S FIGHT.

I. FROM GENERAL HANCOCK'S OFFICIAL REPORT.

GENERAL HANCOCK'S report bears no date except 1863, but a supplemental report, by way of correction, dated October 24th, shows that the paper was written prior to that time, and during his convalescence from the wound received near the end of the battle. There are passages in the report which show a determination on the part of Meade to fight at Pipe Creek. General Hancock says:

"On the morning of July 1st the command marched to Taneytown, going into bivouac about 11 A. M. I then proceeded in person to General Meade's headquarters, and, on reporting to him, was informed as to his intention with reference to giving battle to the enemy, the orders for preparatory movements being then ready for issue. A few minutes before 1 P. M. I received orders to proceed in person to the front and assume command of the First, Third, and Eleventh corps, in consequence of the death of Major-General Reynolds. Having been fully informed by the major-general commanding as to his intentions, I was instructed by him to give the necessary directions upon my arrival at the front for the movement of troops and trains to the rear toward the line of battle he had selected, should I deem it expedient to do so. If the ground was suitable, and circumstances made it wise, I was directed to establish the line of battle at Gettysburg. . . . At 3 P. M. I arrived at Gettysburg and assumed the command. At this time the First and Eleventh corps were retiring through the town, closely pursued by the enemy. The cavalry of General Buford was occupying a firm position on the plain to the left of Gettysburg, covering the rear of the retreating corps. The Third Corps had not yet arrived from Emmitsburg. Orders were at once given to establish a line of battle on Cemetery Hill, with skirmishers occupying that part of the town immediately in our front. The position just on the southern edge of Gettysburg, overlooking the town and commanding the Emmitsburg and Taneytown roads and the Baltimore turnpike, was already partially occupied on my arrival by direction of Major-General Howard. Some difficulty was experienced in forming the troops of the Eleventh Corps, but by vigorous efforts a sufficiently formidable line was established to deter the enemy from any serious assault on the position. They pushed forward a line of battle for a short distance east of the Baltimore turnpike, but it was easily checked by the fire of our artillery. In forming the lines, I received material assistance from Major-General Howard, Brigadier-Generals Warren and Buford, and officers of General Howard's command. . . . The trains of all the troops under my command were ordered to the rear, that they might not interfere with any movement of troops that might be directed by the major-general commanding. My aide, Major Mitchell, was then sent to General Meade to inform him of the state of affairs, and to say that I would hold the position until night. Shortly after, I addressed a communication to the major-general commanding, sending it by Captain Parker, of my staff, giving in detail the information in my possession, and informing him that the position at Gettysburg was a very strong one, having for its disadvantage that it might be easily turned, and leaving to him the responsibility whether the battle should be fought at Gettysburg or at a place first selected by him. Between 5 and 6 o'clock, my dispositions having been completed, Major-General Slocum arrived on the field, and, considering that my functions had ceased, I transferred the command to him. The head of the Third Corps appeared in sight shortly afterward, on the Emmitsburg road.

"About dark I started for the headquarters of the army, still at Taneytown, thirteen miles distant, and reported in person to General Meade. I then ascertained that he had already given orders for the corps in the rear to advance at once to Gettysburg, and was about proceeding there in person."

II. FROM GENERAL HOWARD'S OFFICIAL REPORT.

GENERAL HOWARD'S detailed report is dated August 31st, 1863, and speaks specifically of the course of events after he took command on the morning of the First Day's battle. He says:

"Just at sunset [June 30th] I received a request from General Reynolds, commanding First Corps, to meet him at his headquarters [at Marsh Run, midway between Emmitsburg and Gettysburg]. He then showed me the orders from your headquarters placing him in command of the First, Eleventh, and Third corps; also the circulars of the commanding general dated June 30th, together with a confidential communication. The purport of these papers was that a general engagement was imminent, the issues involved immense, and all commanders urged to extraordinary exertions. General Reynolds and I consulted together, comparing notes and information until a late hour. I then returned to Emmitsburg. A circular from your headquarters, of June 30th, required corps commanders to hold their commands in readiness to move at a moment's notice. . . . At 8 A. M. [July 1st] orders were received from him [Reynolds] directing the corps to march to Gettysburg. . . . As soon as the corps was set in motion, I pushed on with my staff by the direct road, and when within two miles of Gettysburg received word from General Reynolds, pointing out the place where I was to encamp; but, on approaching the town, heavy artillery firing was heard. For some little time I endeavored, by sending in different directions, to find General Reynolds, in order to report to him in person. In the meantime I went to the top of a high building in Gettysburg facing westward. I saw firing beyond Seminary Ridge and not far from the seminary. Toward the right masses of cavalry were drawn up in order, to the east of the ridge and to the north-east of the town. A portion of the First Corps, of General Wadsworth's command, was between me and the seminary, taking position near the railroad. Another division of this corps was moving by the flank with considerable rapidity, along the ridge and in a north-easterly direction. I had studied the position a few moments, when a report reached me that General Reynolds was wounded. At first I hoped his wound might be slight, and that he would continue to command; but in a short time I was undeceived. His aide-de-camp, Major [William] Riddle, brought the sad tiding of his death. This was about 11:30 A. M. Prior to this the general had sent me orders to move up at double-quick, for he was severely engaged. On hearing of the death of General Reynolds, I assumed command of the left wing, instructing General Schurz to take command of the Eleventh Corps. After an examination of the general features of the country, I came to the conclusion that the only tenable position for my limited force was the ridge to the south-east of Gettysburg, now so well known as Cemetery Ridge. The highest point at the cemetery commanded every eminence within easy range. The slopes toward the west and south were gradual, and could be completely swept by artillery. To the north, the ridge was broken by a ravine running transversely. I at once established my headquarters near the cemetery and on the highest point north of the Baltimore pike. Here General Schurz joined me before 12 M., when I instructed him to make the following dispositions of the Eleventh Corps. Learning from General Doubleday, commanding the First Corps, that his right was hard pressed, and receiving continued assurance that his left was safe and pushing the enemy back, I ordered the First and Third divisions of the Eleventh Corps to seize and hold a prominent height [Oak Hill, which they did not reach — the Confederates getting there first. — EDITORS] on the right of the Cashtown road and on the prolongation of Seminary Ridge, each division to have a battery of artillery, the other three batteries, supported by General Steinwehr's division (Second), to be put in position near me on Cemetery Hill.

"About 12:30 [P. M.] General Buford sent me word that the enemy was massing between the York and Harrisburg roads, to the north of Gettysburg, some three or four miles from the town. Quite a large number of prisoners had already been taken by the First Corps. They reported that we were engaging Hill's corps, or a portion of it, and that an aide of General Longstreet had arrived, stating that he would be up with one division in a short time. About this time the head of column of the Eleventh Corps entered and passed through the town, moving forward rapidly toward the position ordered. The news of Ewell's advance from the direction of York was confirmed by reports from General Schurz, General Buford, and Major Charles H. Howard, my aide-de-camp, who had been sent in that direction to reconnoiter. I therefore ordered General Schurz to halt his command, to prevent his right flank being turned, but to push forward a thick line of skirmishers to seize the point first indicated [Oak Hill], as a relief and support to the First Corps. Meanwhile word was sent to General Sickles, commanding Third Corps, and General Slocum, commanding Twelfth, informing them of the situation of affairs, with a request that General Sickles forward my dispatch to General Meade. General Sickles was at that time, about 1 P. M., near Emmitsburg, and General Slocum reported to be near Two Taverns, distant between four and five miles from Gettysburg. At 2 P. M. a report of the state of things as then existing was sent to General Meade directly. About this time I left my chief-of-staff to execute orders, and went to the First Corps. I found General Doubleday about a quarter of a mile beyond the seminary. His Third Division was drawn up to his front and left, facing toward the north-west, making a large angle with the ridge. The artillery of this division was engaging the enemy at this time. His First Division (Wadsworth's) was located a little to the right of the railroad, and his Second Division (Robinson's) on Wadsworth's right. The First Corps, in this position, made a right angle with the Eleventh Corps, the vertex being near the Mummasburg road. The cavalry of General Buford was located mainly upon the flanks. After inspecting the position of the First Corps, and examining the topography of that part of the field, I returned to my former position at the cemetery. About this time (2:45 P. M.) the enemy showed himself in force in front of the Eleventh Corps. His batteries could be distinctly seen on a prominent slope between the Mummasburg and the Harrisburg roads. From this point he opened fire upon the Eleventh Corps, and also more or less enfilading Robinson's division of the First Corps. The batteries attached to the First and Third divisions, Eleventh Corps, immediately replied, and with evident effect. One battery of the enemy, a little more than a mile north from the cemetery, near the Harrisburg road, could be distinctly seen, and as I had a battery of 3-inch rifled guns, under Wiedrich, near my position, I directed him to fire, provided he could reach the enemy. He did so, but his shells for the most part fell short. Soon after complaint came that they reached no farther than our own cavalry; however, I never heard that any of our own men were killed or wounded by this fire. The reason of this irregularity was the poor quality of the ammunition there used. Subsequently these guns did most excellent service.

"I now sent again to General Slocum, stating that my right flank was attacked and asking him if he was moving up, and stating that I was in danger of being turned and driven back. Before this my aide-de-camp, Captain [Edward P.] Pearson, had been sent to General Sickles,

requesting him to move up to Gettysburg as rapidly as possible. Owing to difficulty in finding General Sickles's headquarters, this message was not delivered until 3:30 P. M.

At 3:20 P. M. the enemy renewed his attack upon the First Corps, hotly pressing the First and Second divisions. Earnest requests were made upon me for reënforcements, and General Schurz, who was engaged with a force of the enemy much larger than his own, asked for a brigade to be placed en échelon on his right. I had then only two small brigades in reserve, and had already located three regiments from these in the edge of the town and to the north, and I felt sure that I must hold the point where I was as an ultimate resort. Therefore I at first replied that I could not spare any troops, but did afterward permit General Steinwehr to push out Colonel Coster's brigade beyond the town, to cover the retreat. General Buford was requested to support the center, near the right of the First Corps, as well as he could with his cavalry. A third battery was sent to the front, and put in position near the Third Division, Eleventh Corps. At 3:45 P. M. Generals Doubleday and Wadsworth besought me for reënforcements. I directed General Schurz, if he could spare one regiment or more, to send it to reënforce General Wadsworth, and several times sent urgent requests to General Slocum to come to my assistance. To every application for reënforcements, I replied, " Hold out, if possible, a while longer, for I am expecting General Slocum every moment." At this time General Doubleday's left was turned, and troops of the enemy appeared far outflanking him, and the enemy were also extending beyond my right flank. About 4 P. M. I sent word to General Doubleday that, if he could not hold out longer, he must fall back, fighting, near to Cemetery Hill and on the left of the Baltimore pike; also a request to General Buford to make a show of force opposite the enemy's right, which he immediately did. I now dispatched Major Howard, my aide-de-camp, to General Slocum, to inform him of the state of affairs, requesting him to send one of his divisions to the left, the other to the right of Gettysburg, and that he would come in person to Cemetery Hill. He met the general on the Baltimore pike, about a mile from Gettysburg, who replied that he had already ordered a division to the right, and that he would send another to cover the left, as requested, but that he did not wish to come up in person to the front and take the responsibility of that fight. In justice to General Slocum, I desire to say that he afterward expressed the opinion that it was against the wish of the commanding general to bring on a general engagement at that point.

"At 4:10 P. M., finding that I could hold out no longer, and that the troops were already giving way, I sent a positive order to the commanders of the First and Eleventh corps to fall back gradually, disputing every inch of ground, and to form near my position, the Eleventh Corps on the right and the First Corps on the left of the Baltimore pike. General Steinwehr's division of the Eleventh Corps and the batteries which he was supporting were so disposed as to check the enemy attempting to come through the town, or to approach upon the right or left of Gettysburg. The movement ordered was executed, though with considerable confusion, on account of the First and Eleventh corps coming together in the town.

"At 4:30 P. M. the columns reached Cemetery Hill, the enemy pressing hard. He made a single attempt to turn our right, ascending the slope north-east of Gettysburg, but his line was instantly broken by Wiedrich's battery, in position on the heights. General Hancock came to me about this time and said General Meade had sent him on hearing the state of affairs; that he had given him his instructions while under the impression that he was my senior. We agreed at once that that was no time for talking, and that General Hancock should further arrange the troops and place the batteries upon the left of the Baltimore pike, while I should take the right of the same. In a very short time we put the troops in position, as I had previously directed, excepting that

General Wadsworth's division was sent to occupy a height to the right and rear of our position. In passing through the town we lost many prisoners, but the enemy, perceiving the strength of our position on the heights, made no further attempts to renew the engagement that evening.

"About 7 P. M. Generals Slocum and Sickles arrived at the cemetery. A formal order was at the same time put into my hands placing General Hancock in command of the left wing. But General Slocum being present, and senior, I turned the command over to him, and resumed the direct command of the Eleventh Corps, whereupon General Hancock repaired to the headquarters of General Meade. The eventful day was over. The First and Eleventh corps, numbering less than eighteen thousand men, nobly aided by Buford's division of cavalry, had engaged and held in check nearly double their numbers from 10 in the morning until 7 in the evening. They gave way, it is true, after hard fighting, yet they secured and held the remarkable position which, under the able generalship of the commander of this army, contributed to the grand results of July 2d and 3d."

In a letter to President Lincoln, dated Near Berlin, July 18th, 1863 ("Official Records," Vol. XXVII., p. 700), General Howard says:

"The successful issue of the battle of Gettysburg was due mainly to the energetic operations of our present commanding general prior to the engagement, and to the manner in which he handled his troops on the field. The reserves have never before during this war been thrown in at just the right moment. In many cases when points were just being carried by the enemy, a regiment or brigade appeared to stop his progress and hurl him back. Moreover, I have never seen a more hearty coöperation on the part of general officers as since General Meade took command."

In a resolution dated January 28th, 1864, the thanks of Congress were tendered to General Joseph Hooker and his army for the movement covering Washington and Baltimore; "and to Major-General George G. Meade, Major-General Oliver O. Howard, and the officers and soldiers of that army, for the skill and heroic valor which, at Gettysburg, repulsed, defeated, and drove back, broken and dispirited, beyond the Rappahannock, the veteran army of the Rebellion." On May 30th, 1866, the thanks of Congress were given to Major-General W. S. Hancock, "for his gallant, meritorious, and conspicuous share in that great and decisive victory"— meaning Gettysburg. EDITORS.

CITIZENS OF GETTYSBURG IN THE UNION ARMY.

BY H. M. M. RICHARDS, COMPANY A, 26TH PENNSYLVANIA MILITIA.

FOR twenty-three years we have heard it asserted that the people of Gettysburg were lacking in patriotism because they did not spring to arms *en masse*, and assist in repelling the invaders. I am glad to see young Weakley cited, in addition to old John Burns, as one who volunteered in the defense of his home during the battle ; but these are not all.

Upon the first indication of an invasion of Pennsylvania, the 26th Regiment, P. V. M., was organized and mustered into the United States service at Harrisburg, under the command of Colonel W. W. Jennings of that city. Company A of this regiment, to which I belonged, was composed of students from the Lutheran Theological Seminary and the Pennsylvania College of Gettysburg, and of citizens of the town ; one other company came from Hanover, but a few miles distant.

On June 23d we left Harrisburg for Gettysburg, to be used, I believe, as riflemen among the hills near Cashtown. A railroad accident prevented this plan from being carried into effect, and kept us from reaching Gettysburg until the 26th, by which time General Early had reached Cashtown. In accordance with orders received from Major Granville O. Haller,‡ in command of the post, we were marched out on the Chambersburg pike at 10 A. M., June 26th, for a distance of about three and a half miles, accompanied by Major Robert Bell, who commanded a troop of horse, also raised, I understand, in Gettysburg. Having halted, our colonel, accompanied by Major Bell, rode to the brow of an elevation distant several hundred yards,

and there saw General Early's troops a few miles distant. Early says in his report: "I sent General Gordon with his brigade and White's battalion of cavalry on the pike through Cashtown toward Gettysburg, and moved with the rest of the command to the left through Hilltown to Mummasburg. The object of this movement was for Gordon to amuse and skirmish with the enemy while I should get on his flank and rear so as to capture his whole force." We, a few hundred men at the most, were in the toils ; what should be done ? We would gladly have marched to join the Army of the Potomac, under Meade, but where was it ? Our colonel, left to his own resources, wisely decided to make an effort to return to Harrisburg, and immediately struck off from the pike, the Confederates capturing many of our rear-guard after a sharp skirmish, and sending their cavalry in pursuit of us. These latter overtook us in the afternoon at Witmer's house, about four and a half miles from Gettysburg on the Carlisle road, where after an engagement they were repulsed with some loss. After many vicissitudes, we finally reached Harrisburg, having marched 54 out of 60 consecutive hours, with a loss of some 200 men.

It should be added that Gettysburg, small town as it was, had already furnished its quota to the army. Moreover, on the first day of the battle hundreds of the unfortunate men of Reynolds's gallant corps were secreted, sheltered, fed, and aided in every way by the men and women of the town.

READING, PA., November 2d, 1886.

‡ Acting aide-de-camp to General Couch, commanding the Department of the Susquehanna.— EDITORS.

HALL'S BATTERY ON THE FIRST DAY RESISTING THE CONFEDERATE ADVANCE ON THE CHAMBERSBURG ROAD.

THE SECOND DAY AT GETTYSBURG.

BY HENRY J. HUNT, BREVET MAJOR-GENERAL, U. S. A., CHIEF OF ARTILLERY A. P.

ON June 30th, at Taneytown, General Meade received information that the enemy was advancing on Gettysburg, and corps commanders were at once instructed to hold their commands in readiness to march against him. The next day, July 1st, Meade wrote to Reynolds that telegraphic intelligence from Couch, and the movements reported by Buford, indicated a concentration of the enemy's army either at Chambersburg or at some point on a line drawn from that place through Heidlersburg to York. Under these circumstances, Meade informed Reynolds that he had not yet decided whether it was his best policy to move to attack before he knew more definitely Lee's point of concentration. He seems, however, soon to have determined not to advance until the movements or position of the enemy gave strong assurance of success, and if the enemy took the offensive, to withdraw his own army from its actual positions and form line of battle behind Pipe Creek, between Middleburg and Manchester. The considerations probably moving him to this are not difficult to divine. Examination of the maps [see page 266] will show that such a line would cover Baltimore and Washington in all directions from which Lee could advance, and that Westminster, his base, would be immediately behind him, with short railroad communication to Baltimore. It would, moreover, save much hard marching, and restore to the ranks the thousands of stragglers who did not reach Gettysburg in time for the battle.

From Westminster—which is in Parr's Ridge, the eastern boundary of the valley of the Monocacy—good roads led in all directions, and gave the place the same strategic value for Meade that Gettysburg had for Lee. The new line could not be turned by Lee without imminent danger to his own army, nor could he afford to advance upon Baltimore or Washington, leaving the Army of the Potomac intact behind and so near him;—that would be to invite the fate of Burgoyne. Meade, then, could safely select a good "offensive-defensive line" behind Pipe Creek and establish himself there, with perfect liberty of action in all directions. Without magazines or assured

↓ Continued from page 284.

communications, Lee would have to scatter his army more or less in order to subsist it, and so expose it to Meade; or else keep it united, and so starve it, a course which Meade could compel by simple demonstrations. There would then be but two courses for Lee,—either to attack Meade in his chosen position or to retreat without a battle. The latter, neither the temper of his army nor that of his Government would probably permit. In case of a defeat Meade's line of retreat would be comparatively short, and easily covered, whilst Lee's would be for two marches through an open country before he could gain the mountain passes. As Meade believed Lee's army to be at least equal to his own, all the elements of the problem were in favor of the Pipe Creek line. But Meade's orders for July 1st, drawing his corps toward the threatened flank, carried Reynolds to Gettysburg, and Buford's report hastened this movement. Reynolds, who probably never received the Pipe Creek circular, was eager for the conflict, and his collision with Heth assuming the dimensions of a battle, caused an immediate concentration of both armies at Gettysburg. Prior to this, the assembling of Meade's army behind Pipe Creek would have been easy, and all fears of injuring thereby the *morale* of his troops were idle; the Army of the Potomac was of " sterner stuff" than that implies. The battle of July 1st changed the situation. Overpowered by numbers, the First and Eleventh corps had, after hard fighting and inflicting as well as incurring heavy losses, been forced back to their reserve, on Cemetery Hill, which they still held. To have withdrawn them now would have been a retreat, and might have discouraged the Federal, as it certainly would have elated the Confederate troops; especially as injurious reports unjust to both the corps named had been circulated. It would have been to acknowledge a defeat when there was no defeat. Meade therefore resolved to fight at Gettysburg. An ominous dispatch from General Halleck to Meade, that afternoon, suggesting that whilst his tactical arrangements were good, his strategy was at fault, that he was too far east, that Lee might attempt to turn his left, and that Frederick was preferable as a base to Westminster, may have confirmed Meade in this decision.

In pursuance of his instructions, I had that morning (July 1st) reconnoitered the country behind Pipe Creek for a battle-ground. On my return I found General Hancock at General Meade's tent. He informed me that Reynolds was killed, that a battle was going on at Gettysburg, and that he was under orders to proceed to that place. His instructions were to examine it and the intermediate country for a suitable field, and if his report was favorable the troops would be ordered forward. Before the receipt that evening of Hancock's written report from Cemetery Hill, which was not very encouraging, General Meade received from others information as to the state of affairs at the front, set his troops in motion toward Gettysburg, afterward urged them to forced marches, and under his orders I gave the necessary instructions to the Artillery Reserve and Park for a battle there. The move was, under the circumstances, a bold one, and Meade, as we shall see, took great risks. We left Taneytown toward 11 P. M., and reached Gettysburg after midnight. Soon after, General Meade, accompanied by General Howard and myself, inspected

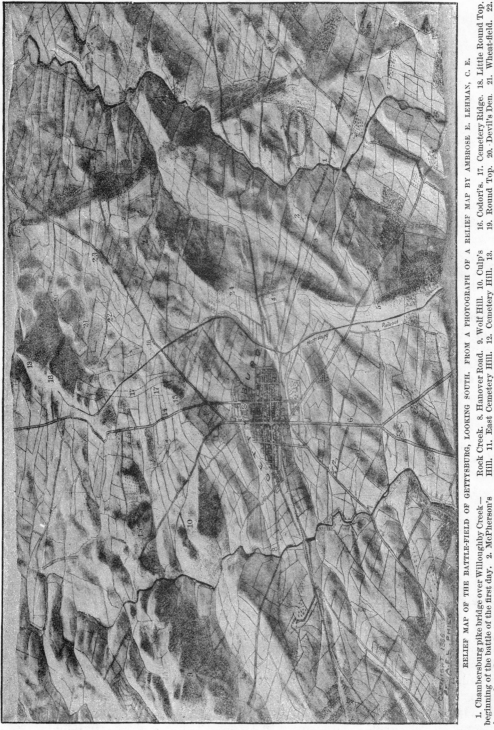

RELIEF MAP OF THE BATTLE-FIELD OF GETTYSBURG, LOOKING SOUTH, FROM A PHOTOGRAPH OF A RELIEF MAP BY AMBROSE E. LEHMAN, C. E.

1. Chambersburg pike bridge over Willoughby Creek — beginning of the battle of the first day. 2. McPherson's farm and woods. 3. Railway cuts. 4. Seminary. 5. Oak Hill. 6. Carlisle Road. 7. Harrisburg Road bridge over Rock Creek. 8. Hanover Road. 9. Wolf Hill. 10. Culp's Hill. 11. East Cemetery Hill. 12. Cemetery Hill. 13. Ziegler's Grove. 14. Meade's headquarters on the Taney-town Road. 15. Slocum's headquarters on Power's Hill. 16. Codori's. 17. Cemetery Ridge. 18. Little Round Top. 19. Round Top. 20. Devil's Den. 21. Wheat-field. 22. Trostle's farm. 23. Peach Orchard. 24. Seminary Ridge. 19 to 25. About extreme right of Longstreet's line.

our lines so far as then occupied, after which he directed me to examine them again in the morning, and to see that the artillery was properly posted. He had thus recognized my "command" of the artillery; indeed, he did not know it had been suspended. I resumed it, therefore, and continued it to the end of the battle.

At the close of July 1st Johnson's and Anderson's divisions of the Confederate army were up. Ewell's corps now covered our front from Benner's Hill to the Seminary, his line passing through the town—Johnson on the left, Early in the center, Rodes on the right. Hill's corps occupied Seminary Ridge, and during the next morning extended its line from the Seminary south nearly to the Peach Orchard on the Emmitsburg road; Trimble—*vice* Pender, wounded—on the left; Anderson on the right; Pettigrew—*vice* Heth, wounded—in reserve. Of Longstreet's corps, McLaws's division and Hood's—except Law's brigade not yet up—camped that night on Marsh Creek, four miles from Gettysburg. His Reserve Artillery did not reach Gettysburg until 9 A. M. of the 2d. Pickett's division had been left at Chambersburg as rear-guard, and joined the corps on the night of the 2d.

It had not been General Lee's intention to deliver a general battle whilst so far from his base, unless attacked, but he now found himself by the mere force of circumstances committed to one. If it must take place, the sooner the better. His army was now nearly all on the ground, and delay, whilst it could not improve his own position, would certainly better that of his antagonist. Longstreet, indeed, urged General Lee instead of attacking to turn Meade's left, and by interposing between him and Washington and threatening his communications, to force him to attack the Confederate army in position; but General Lee probably saw that Meade would be under no such necessity; would have no great difficulty in obtaining supplies, and—disregarding the clamor from Washington—could play a waiting game, which it would be impossible for Lee to maintain in the open country. He could not advance on Baltimore or Washington with Meade in his rear, nor could his army subsist itself in a hostile region which would soon swarm with additional enemies. His communications could be cut off, for his recommendation to assemble even a small army at Culpeper to cover them and aid him had not been complied with.

A battle was a necessity to Lee, and a defeat would be more disastrous to Meade, and less so to himself, at Gettysburg than at any point east of it. With the defiles of the South Mountain range close in his rear, which could be easily held by a small force, a safe retreat through the Cumberland Valley was assured, so that his army, once through these passes, would be practically on the banks of the Potomac, at a point already prepared for crossing. Any position east of Gettysburg would deprive him of these advantages. It is more probable that General Lee was influenced by cool calculation of this nature than by hot blood, or that the opening success of a chance battle had thrown him off his balance. Whatever his reasons, he decided to accept the gage of battle offered by Meade, and to attack as soon as practicable. Ewell had made arrangements to take possession of Culp's Hill in the early morn-

GENERAL MEADE'S HEADQUARTERS ON THE TANEYTOWN ROAD. FROM A WAR-TIME PHOTOGRAPH.

General Meade arrived at Cemetery Hill at one o'clock in the morning of July 2d, and after daylight established his headquarters in a small farm-house on the Taneytown road, little more than an eighth of a mile east of Hancock's line of battle, which was the Union center. In the afternoon of July 2d, headquarters became the target of a heavy artillery fire which caused a scattering of officers and staffs and the headquarters signal corps. During the terrific cannonade which preceded Pickett's charge on July 3d, Meade's headquarters received a still greater storm of shot and shell, with the same result.— EDITORS.

ing, and his troops were under arms for the purpose by the time General Meade had finished the moonlight inspection of his lines, when it was ascertained by a reconnoitering party sent out by Johnson, that the hill was occupied, and its defenders on the alert; and further, from a captured dispatch from General Sykes to General Slocum, that the Fifth Corps was on the Hanover road only four miles off, and would march at 4 A. M. for Culp's Hill. Johnson thereupon deferred his attack and awaited Ewell's instructions.

General Lee had, however, during the night determined to attack the Federal left with Longstreet's corps, and now instructed Ewell, as soon as he heard Longstreet's guns, to make a diversion in his favor, to be converted, if opportunity offered, into a real attack.

Early on the morning of July 2d, when nearly all the Confederate army had reached Gettysburg or its immediate vicinity, a large portion of the Army of the Potomac was still on the road. The Second Corps and Sykes, with two divisions of the Fifth, arrived about 7 A. M., Crawford's division not joining until noon; Lockwood's brigade—two regiments from Baltimore—at 8; De Trobriand's and Burling's brigades of the Third Corps, from Emmitsburg, at 9, and the Artillery Reserve and its large ammunition trains from Taneytown at 10:30 A. M. Sedgwick's Sixth Corps, the largest in the army, after a long night march from Manchester, thirty-four miles distant, reached Rock Creek at 4 P. M. The rapidity with which the army was assembled was creditable to it and to its commander. The heat was oppressive, the long marches, especially the night marches, were trying and had caused much straggling.

All this morning Meade was busily engaged personally or by his staff in rectifying his lines, assigning positions to the commands as they came up, watching the enemy, and studying the field, parts of which we have described in general terms. We now refer the reader to the map [p. 299] to aid our further description of some necessary even if tedious details. Near the western base of Cemetery Hill is Ziegler's Grove. From this grove the distance nearly due south to the base of Little Round Top is a mile and a half. A well-defined ridge known as Cemetery Ridge follows this line from Ziegler's for 900 yards to another small grove, or clump of trees, where it turns sharply to the east for 200 yards, then turns south again, and continues in a direct line toward Round Top, for 700 yards, to George Weikert's. So far the ridge is smooth and open, in full view of Seminary Ridge opposite, and distant from 1400 to 1600 yards. At Weikert's, this ridge is lost in a large body of rocks, hills, and woods, lying athwart the direct line to Round Top, and forcing a bend to the east in the Taneytown road. This rough space also stretches for a quarter of a mile or more *west* of this direct line, toward Plum Run. Toward the south it sinks into low marshy ground which reaches to the base of Little Round Top, half a mile or more from George Weikert's. The west side of this broken ground was wooded through its whole extent from north to south. Between this wood and Plum Run is an open cleared space 300 yards wide—a continuation of the open country in front of Cemetery Ridge; Plum Run flows south-easterly toward Little Round Top, then makes a bend to the south-west, where it receives a small stream or "branch" from Seminary Ridge. In the angle between these streams is Devil's Den, a bold, rocky height, steep on its eastern face, and prolonged as a ridge to the west. It is 500 yards due west of Little Round Top, and 100 feet lower. The northern extremity is composed of huge rocks and bowlders, forming innumerable crevices and holes, from the largest of which the hill derives its name. Plum Run valley is here marshy but strewn with similar bowlders, and the slopes of the Round Tops are covered with them. These afforded lurking-places for a multitude of Confederate sharp-shooters whom, from the difficulties of the ground, it was impossible to dislodge, and who were opposed by similar methods on our part; so that at the close of the battle these hiding-places, and especially the "Den" itself, were filled with dead and wounded men. This kind of warfare was specially destructive to Hazlett's battery on Round Top, as the cannoneers had to expose themselves in firing, and in one case three were shot in quick succession, before the fourth succeeded in discharging the piece. A cross-road connecting the Taneytown and Emmitsburg roads runs along the northern base of Devil's Den. From its Plum Run crossing to the Peach Orchard is 1100 yards. For the first 400 yards of this distance, there is a wood on the north and a wheat-field on the south of the road, beyond which the road continues for 700 yards to the Emmitsburg road along Devil's Den ridge, which slopes on the north to Plum Run, on the south to Plum Branch. From Ziegler's Grove the Emmitsburg road runs diago-

MAJOR-GENERAL DANIEL E. SICKLES. FROM A WAR-TIME PHOTOGRAPH.

nally across the interval between Cemetery and Seminary ridges, crossing the latter two miles from Ziegler's Grove. From Peach Orchard to Ziegler's is nearly a mile and a half. For half a mile the road runs along a ridge at right angles to that of Devil's Den, which slopes back to Plum Run. The angle at the Peach Orchard is thus formed by the intersection of two bold ridges, one from Devil's Den, the other along the Emmitsburg road. It is distant about 600 yards from the wood which skirts the whole length of Seminary Ridge and covers the movement of troops between it and Willoughby Run, half a mile beyond. South of the Round Top and Devil's Den ridge the country is open, and the principal obstacles to free movement are the fences — generally of stone — which surround the numerous fields.

As our troops came up they were assigned to places on the line: the Twelfth Corps, General A. S. Williams,— *vice* Slocum, commanding the right wing,— to Culp's Hill, on Wadsworth's right; Second Corps to Cemetery Ridge — Hays's and Gibbon's divisions, from Ziegler's to the clump of trees, Caldwell's to the short ridge to its left and rear. This ridge had been occupied by the Third Corps, which was now directed to prolong Caldwell's line to Round Top, relieving Geary's division, which had been stationed during the night on the extreme left, with two regiments at the base of Little Round Top. The Fifth Corps was placed in reserve near the Rock Creek crossing of the Baltimore pike; the Artillery Reserve and its large trains were parked in a central position on a cross-road from the Baltimore pike to the Taneytown road; Buford's cavalry, except Merritt's brigade (then at Emmitsburg), was near Round Top, from which point it was ordered that morning to Westminster, thus uncovering our left flank; Kilpatrick's and Gregg's divisions were well out on the right flank, from which, after a brush with Stuart on the evening of the 2d, Kilpatrick was sent next morning to replace Buford, Merritt being also ordered up to our left.

The morning was a busy and in some respects an anxious one; it was believed that the whole Confederate army was assembled, that it was equal if not superior to our own in numbers, and that the battle would commence before our troops were up. There was a gap in Slocum's line awaiting a division of infantry, and as some demonstrations of Ewell about daylight indicated an immediate attack at that point, I had to draw batteries from other parts of the line — for the Artillery Reserve was just then starting from Taneytown — to cover it until it could be properly filled. Still there was no hostile movement of the enemy, and General Meade directed Slocum to hold himself in readiness to attack Ewell with the Fifth and Twelfth, so soon as the Sixth Corps should arrive. After an examination Slocum reported the ground as unfavorable, in which Warren concurred and advised against an attack there. The project was then abandoned, and Meade postponed all offensive operations until the enemy's intentions should be more clearly developed. In the meantime he took precautionary measures. It was clearly now to his advantage to fight the battle where he was, and he had some apprehension that Lee would attempt to turn his flank and threaten his communications,—just what Longstreet had been advising. In this case it might be necessary to fall back to the Pipe Creek line, if possible, or else to follow Lee's movement into the open country. In either case, or in that of a forced withdrawal, prudence dictated that arrangements should be made in advance, and General Meade gave instructions for examining the roads and communications, and to draw up an order of movement, which General Butterfield, the chief-of-staff, seems to have considered an order absolute for the withdrawal of the army without a battle.

These instructions must have been given early in the morning, for General Butterfield states that it was on his arrival from Taneytown, which place he left at daylight. An order was drawn up accordingly, given to the adjutant-general, and perhaps prepared for issue in case of necessity to corps commanders; but it was not recorded nor issued, nor even a copy of it preserved. General Meade declared that he never contemplated the issue of such an order unless contingencies made it necessary; and his acts and dispatches during the day were in accordance with his statement. There is one circumstance pertaining to my own duties which to my mind is conclusive, and I relate it because it may have contributed to the idea that General Meade intended to withdraw from Gettysburg. He came to me that morning before the Artillery Reserve had arrived, and, therefore, about the time that the order was in course of preparation, and informed me that one of the army corps had left its whole artillery ammunition train behind it, and that others were also deficient, notwithstanding his orders on that subject. He was very much disturbed, and feared that, taking into account the large expenditure of the preceding day by the First and Eleventh corps, there would not be sufficient to carry us through the battle. This was not the first nor the last

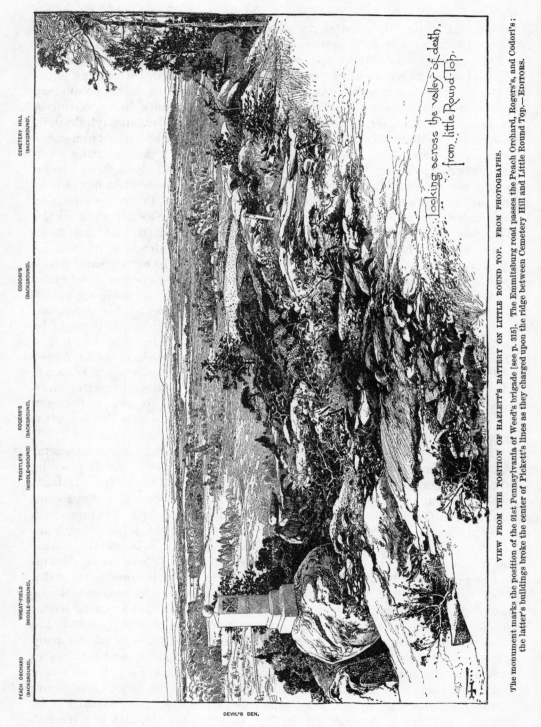

PEACH ORCHARD (BACKGROUND). WHEAT-FIELD (MIDDLE-GROUND). TROSTLE'S (MIDDLE-GROUND). ROGERS'S (BACKGROUND). CODORI'S (BACKGROUND). CEMETERY HILL (BACKGROUND).

DEVIL'S DEN.

Looking across the valley of death, from Little Round-Top.

VIEW FROM THE POSITION OF HAZLETT'S BATTERY ON LITTLE ROUND TOP. FROM PHOTOGRAPHS.

The monument marks the position of the 91st Pennsylvania of Weed's brigade [see p. 315]. The Emmitsburg road passes the Peach Orchard, Rogers's, and Codori's; the latter's buildings broke the center of Pickett's lines as they charged upon the ridge between Cemetery Hill and Little Round Top.— EDITORS.

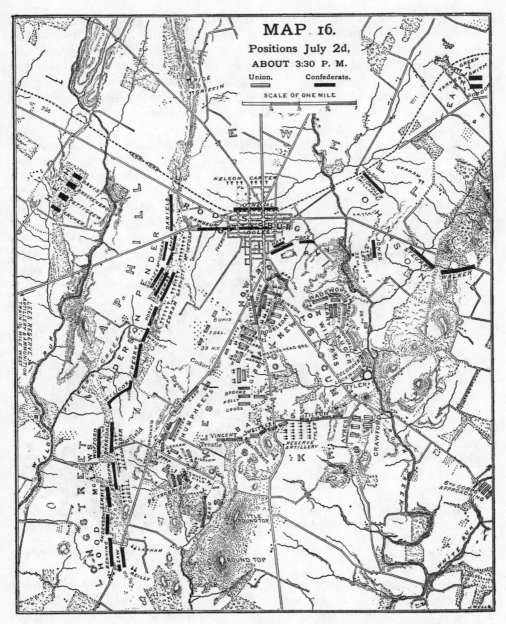

MAP 16.

Positions July 2d,
ABOUT 3:30 P. M.
Union.   Confederate.

SCALE OF ONE MILE

time that I was called upon to meet deficiencies under such circumstances, and I was, therefore, prepared for this, having directed General Tyler, commanding the Artillery Reserve, whatever else he might leave behind, to bring up every round of ammunition in his trains, and I knew he would not fail me. Moreover, I had previously, on my own responsibility, and unknown to General Hooker, formed a special ammunition column attached to the Artillery Reserve, carrying twenty rounds per gun, over and above the authorized amount, for every gun in the army, in order to meet such emergencies. I was, therefore, able to assure General Meade that there would be enough ammunition for the battle, but none for idle cannonades, the besetting sin of some of our commanders. He was much relieved, and expressed his satisfaction. Now, had he had at this time any intention of withdrawing the army, the first thing to get rid of would have been this Artillery Reserve and its large trains, which were then blocking the roads in our rear; and he would surely have told me of it.

Still, with the exception of occasional cannonading, and some skirmishing near the Peach Orchard, the quiet remained unbroken, although Lee had

determined upon an early attack on our left. He says in his detailed report that our line extended " upon the high ground along the Emmitsburg road, with a steep ridge

[Cemetery] in rear, which was also occupied "; and in a previous "outline" report he says: "In front of General Longstreet the enemy held a position [the salient angle at the Peach Orchard] from which, if he could be driven, it was thought our artillery could be used to advantage in

UNION BREASTWORKS ON LITTLE ROUND TOP — BIG ROUND TOP IN THE DISTANCE. FROM WAR-TIME PHOTOGRAPHS.

assailing the more elevated ground beyond, and thus enable us to gain the crest of the ridge." It would appear from this that General Lee mistook the few troops on the Peach Orchard ridge in the morning for our main line, and that by taking it and sweeping up the Emmitsburg road under cover of his batteries, he expected to " roll up " our lines to Cemetery Hill. That would be an " oblique order of battle," in which the attacking line, formed obliquely to its opponent, marches directly forward, constantly breaking in the *end* of his enemy's line and gaining his rear. General Longstreet was ordered to form the divisions of Hood and McLaws on Anderson's right, so as to envelop our left and drive it in. These divisions were only three miles off at daylight, and moved early, but there was great delay in forming them for battle, owing principally to the absence of Law's brigade, for which it would have been well to substitute Anderson's fresh division, which could have been replaced by Pettigrew's, then in reserve. There seems to have been no good reason why the attack should not have been made by 8 or 9 A. M. at the latest (but see p. 351), when the Federal Third Corps was not yet all up, nor Crawford's division, nor the Artillery Reserve, nor the Sixth Corps, and our lines were still very incomplete. This is one of the cheap criticisms after all the facts on both sides are known; but it is apt for its purpose, as it shows how great a risk Meade took in abandoning his Pipe Creek line for Gettysburg on the chances of Lee's army not yet being assembled; and also, that there was no lack of boldness and decision on Meade's part. Indeed, his course, from the hour that he took command, had been marked by these qualities.

A suggestive incident is worth recording here. In the course of my inspection of the lines that morning, while passing along Culp's Hill, I found the men hard at work intrenching, and in such fine spirits as at once to attract attention. One of them finally dropped his work, and, approaching me, inquired if the reports just received were true. On asking what he referred to, he replied that twice word had been passed along the line that General McClellan had been assigned to the command of the army, and the second time it was added that he was on the way to the field and might soon be expected. He continued, "The boys are all jubilant over it, for they know that if *he* takes command everything will go right." I have been told recently by the commander of a Fifth Corps battery that during the forced march of the preceding night the same report ran through that corps, excited great enthusiasm amongst the men, and renewed their vigor. It was probably from this corps—just arrived—that the report had spread along the line. ↓

On my return to headquarters from this inspection General Meade told me that General Sickles, then with him, wished me to examine a new line, as he thought that assigned to him was not a good one, especially that he could not use his artillery there. I had been as far as Round Top that morning, and had noticed the unfavorable character of the ground, and, therefore, I accompanied Sickles direct to the Peach Orchard, where he pointed out the ridges, already described, as his proposed line. They commanded all the ground behind, as well as in front of them, and together constituted a favorable position for *the enemy* to hold. This was one good reason for our taking possession of it. It would, it is true, in our hands present a salient angle, which generally exposes both its sides to enfilade fires; but here the ridges were so high that each would serve as a " traverse " for the other, and reduce that evil to a minimum. On the other hand it would so greatly lengthen

↓ Lieutenant O. S. Barrett, in a pamphlet sketch of the "Old Fourth Michigan Infantry" [Detroit, 1888], relates a similar occurrence in the Second Corps. He says:

"We arrived at Hanover, Pennsylvania, on the afternoon of July 1st. . . . An aide-de-camp came riding along, saying, 'Boys, keep up good courage, McClellan is in command of the army again.' Instantly the space above was filled with the hats and caps of the gratified soldiers. . . . I knew this was untrue myself, but it served its purpose, as intended."—EDITORS.

our line—which in any case must rest on Round Top, and connect with the left of the Second Corps—as to require a larger force than the Third Corps alone to hold it, and it would be difficult to occupy and strengthen the angle if the enemy already held the wood in its front. At my instance General Sickles ordered a reconnoissance to ascertain if the wood was occupied.

About this time a cannonade was opened on Cemetery Hill, which indicated an attack there, and as I had examined the Emmitsburg Ridge, I said I

would not await the result of the reconnoissance but return to headquarters by way of Round Top, and examine that part of the proposed line. As I was leaving, General Sickles asked me if he should move forward his corps. I answered, "Not on my authority; I will report to General Meade for his instructions." I had not reached the wheat-field when a sharp rattle of musketry showed that the enemy held the wood in front of the Peach Orchard angle.

As I rode back a view from that direction showed how much farther Peach Orchard was to the front of the direct line than it appeared from the orchard itself. In fact there was a

COLONEL EDWARD E. CROSS, COMMANDING THE FIRST
BRIGADE OF CALDWELL'S DIVISION, KILLED NEAR
DEVIL'S DEN, JULY 2. FROM A PHOTOGRAPH.

third line between them, which appeared, as seen from the orchard, to be continuous with Cemetery Ridge, but was nearly six hundred yards in front of it. This is the open ground east of Plum Run already described, and which may be called the Plum Run line. Its left where it crosses the run abuts rather on Devil's Den than Round Top; it was commanded by the much higher Peach Orchard crests, and was therefore not an eligible line to occupy, although it became of importance during the battle.

As to the other two lines, the choice between them would depend on circumstances. The direct short line through the woods, and including the Round Tops, could be occupied, intrenched, and made impregnable to a front attack. But, like that of Culp's Hill, it would be a purely defensive one, from which, owing to the nature of the ground and the enemy's commanding position on the ridges at the angle, an advance in force would be impracticable. The salient line proposed by General Sickles, although much longer, afforded excellent positions for our artillery; its occupation would cramp the movements of the enemy, bring us nearer his lines, and afford us facilities for taking the offensive. It was in my judgment tactically the better line of the two, provided it were strongly occupied, for it was the only one on the field from which we could have passed from the defensive to the offensive with a prospect of decisive results. But General Meade had not, until the arrival of the Sixth Corps, a sufficient number of troops at his disposal to risk such an extension of his lines; it would have required both the Third and the Fifth corps, and left him without any reserve. Had he known that Lee's attack would be postponed until 4 P. M., he might have occupied this line in the morning; but he did not know this, expected an attack at any moment, and, in view of the vast interests involved, adopted a defensive policy, and ordered the occupation of the *safe* line. In taking risks, it would not be for his army alone, but also for Philadelphia, Baltimore, and Washington. Gettysburg was not a good strategical position for us, and the circumstances under which our army was assembled limited us tactically to a strictly defensive battle. But even a strictly defensive battle gained here would be, in its results, almost as valuable as an offensive one with a brilliant victory, since it would necessarily be decisive as to both the campaign and the invasion, and its moral effect abroad and at home, North and South, would be of vast importance in a political as well as a military sense. The additional risks of an offensive battle were out of all proportion to the prospective gains. The

decision then to fight a defensive rather than an offensive battle, to look rather to solid than to brilliant results, was wise.

After finishing my examination I returned to headquarters and briefly reported to General Meade that the proposed line was a good one in itself, that it offered favorable positions for artillery, but that its

WEED'S POSITION ON LITTLE ROUND TOP, LOOKING IN THE DIRECTION OF THE PEACH ORCHARD. FROM A WAR-TIME SKETCH.

relations to other lines were such that I could not advise it, and suggested that he examine it himself before ordering its occupation. He nodded assent, and I proceeded to Cemetery Hill.

The cannonade there still continued; it had been commenced by the enemy, and was accompanied by some movements of troops toward our right. As soon as I saw that it would lead to nothing serious, I returned direct to the Peach Orchard, knowing that its occupation would require large reënforcements of artillery. I was here met by Captain Randolph, the corps chief of artillery, who informed me that he had been ordered to place his batteries on the new line. Seeing Generals Meade and Sickles, not far off, in conversation, and supposing that General Meade had consented to the occupation, I sent at once to the reserve for more artillery, and authorized other general officers to draw on the same source. Here, perhaps, I may be allowed to say *en passant* that this large reserve, organized by the wise forethought of General McClellan, sometimes threatened with destruction, and once actually broken up, was often,

GENERAL G. K. WARREN AT THE SIGNAL STATION ON LITTLE ROUND TOP.
FROM A SKETCH MADE AT THE TIME.

as at Malvern Hill, and now at Gettysburg, an invaluable resource in the time of greatest need. When in 1864, in the Rapidan campaign, it was "got rid of," it reconstituted itself, without orders, and in a few weeks, through the necessities of the army, showing that "principles vindicate themselves."

When I arrived Birney's division was already posted on the crest, from Devil's Den to the Peach Orchard, and along the Emmitsburg road, Ward's brigade on the left, Graham's at the angle, De Trobriand's connecting them by a thin line. Humphreys's division was on Graham's right, near the Emmitsburg road, Carr's brigade in the front line, about the Smith house, Brewster's in second line. Burling's, with the exception of Sewell's 5th New Jersey Regiment, then in skirmish order at the front, was sent to reënforce Birney. Seeley's battery, at first posted on the right, was soon after sent to the left of the Smith house, and replaced on the right by Turnbull's from the Artillery Reserve. Randolph had ordered Smith's battery, 4th New York, to the rocky hill at the Devil's Den; Winslow's to the wheatfield. He had placed Clark on the crest looking south, and his own ("E," 1st Rhode Island) near the angle, facing west. The whole corps was, however, too weak to cover the ground, and it was too late for Meade to withdraw it. Sykes's Fifth Corps had already been ordered up and was momentarily expected. As soon as fire opened, which was just as he arrived on the ground, General Meade also sent for Caldwell's division from Cemetery Ridge, and a division of the Twelfth Corps from Culp's, and soon after for troops from the Sixth Corps. McGilvery's artillery brigade soon arrived from the reserve, and Bigelow's, Phillips's, Hart's, Ames's, and Thompson's batteries had been ordered into position on the crests, when the enemy opened from a long line of guns, stretching down to the crossing of the Emmitsburg pike. Smith's position at Devil's Den gave him a favorable oblique fire on a part of this line, and as he did not reply I proceeded to the Den. Finding the acclivity steep and rocky, I dismounted and tied my horse to a tree before crossing the valley. My rank, brigadier-general, the command being that of a lieutenant-general, gave me a very small and insufficient staff, and even this had been recently cut down. The inspector of artillery, Lieutenant-Colonel Warner, adjutant-general, Captain Craig, my only aide, Lieutenant Bissell, my one orderly, and even the flag-bearer necessary to indicate my presence to those seeking me, were busy conveying orders or messages, and I was alone; a not infrequent and an awkward thing for a general who had to keep up communications with every part of a battle-field and with the general-in-chief. On climbing to the summit, I found that Smith had just got his guns, one by

BRIGADIER-GENERAL STRONG VINCENT, MORTALLY WOUNDED, JULY 2, IN THE STRUGGLE FOR THE ROUND TOPS. FROM A PHOTOGRAPH.

one, over the rocks and chasms, into an excellent position. After pointing out to me the advancing lines of the enemy, he opened, and very effectively. Many guns were immediately turned on him, relieving so far the rest of the line. Telling him that he would probably lose his battery, I left to seek infan-

BRIGADIER-GENERAL STEPHEN H. WEED, COMMANDING THE THIRD BRIGADE OF AYRES'S DIVISION, KILLED JULY 2. FROM A PHOTOGRAPH.

General Weed was picked off by sharp-shooters at Devil's Den soon after getting his brigade in position on Little Round Top.—EDITORS.

try supports, very doubtful if I would find my horse, for the storm of shell bursting over the place was enough to drive any animal wild. On reaching the foot of the cliff, I found myself in a plight at once ludicrous, painful, and dangerous. A herd of horned cattle had been driven into the valley between Devil's Den and Round Top, from which they could not escape. A shell had exploded in the body of one of them, tearing it to pieces; others were torn and wounded. All were *stampeded*, and were bellowing and rushing in their terror, first to one side and then to the other, to escape the shells that were bursting over them and among them. Cross I must, and in doing so I had my most trying experience of that battle-field. Luckily the poor beasts were as much frightened as I was, but their rage was subdued by

TROSTLE'S FARM, THE SCENE OF THE FIGHTING BY BIGELOW'S NINTH MASSACHUSETTS BATTERY.
FROM A WAR-TIME PHOTOGRAPH.

terror, and they were good enough to let me pass through scot-free, but "badly demoralized." However, my horse was safe, I mounted, and in the busy excitement that followed almost forgot my scare.

It was not until about 4 P. M. that Longstreet got his two divisions into position in two lines, McLaws's on the right of Anderson's division of Hill's corps, and opposite the Peach Orchard; Hood's on the extreme Confederate right and crossing the Emmitsburg road. Hood had been ordered, keeping his left on that road, to break in the end of our line, supposed to be at the orchard; but perceiving that our left was "refused" (bent back toward Devil's Den), and noticing the importance of Round Top, he suggested to Longstreet that the

TROSTLE'S HOUSE, SCENE OF THE FIGHTING OF BIGELOW'S BATTERY.   FROM A WAR-TIME PHOTOGRAPH.

latter be turned and attacked [see p. 322]. The reply was that General Lee's orders were to attack along the Emmitsburg road. Again Hood sent his message and received the same reply, notwithstanding which he directed Law's brigade upon Round Top, in which movement a portion of Robertson's brigade joined; the rest of the division was thrown upon Devil's Den and the ridge between it and the Peach Orchard. The first assaults were repulsed, but after hard fighting, McLaws's division being also advanced, toward 6 o'clock the angle was broken in, after a resolute defense and with great loss on both sides. In the meantime three of Anderson's brigades were advancing on Humphreys, and the latter received orders from Birney, now in command of the corps (Sickles having been severely wounded soon after 6 o'clock near the Trostle house), to throw back his left, form an oblique line in his rear, and connect with the right of Birney's division, then retiring. The junction was not effected, and Humphreys, greatly outnumbered, slowly and skillfully fell back to Cemetery Ridge, Gibbon sending two regiments and Brown's Rhode Island battery to his support. But the enemy was strong and covered the whole Second Corps front, now greatly weakened by detach-

ments. Wilcox's, Perry's, and Wright's Confederate brigades pressed up to the ridge, outflanking Humphreys's right and left, and Wright broke through our line and seized the guns in his front, but was soon driven out, and not being supported they all fell back, about dusk, under a heavy artillery fire.

MONUMENT OF BIGELOW'S NINTH MASSACHUSETTS BATTERY. FROM A PHOTOGRAPH TAKEN IN 1886.

As soon as Longstreet's attack commenced, General Warren was sent by General Meade to see to the condition of the extreme left. The duty could not have been intrusted to better hands. Passing along the lines he found Little Round Top, the key of the position, unoccupied except by a signal station. The enemy at the time lay concealed, awaiting the signal for assault, when a shot fired in their direction caused a sudden movement on their part which, by the gleam of reflected sunlight from their bayonets, revealed their long lines outflanking the position. Fully comprehending the imminent danger, Warren sent to General Meade for a division.♭ The enemy was already

♭ Before the Committee on the Conduct of the War General Warren testified that he went to Little Round Top "by General Meade's direction." In a letter dated July 13th, 1872, General Warren says:

"Just before the action began in earnest, on July 2d, I was with General Meade, near General Sickles, whose troops seemed very badly disposed on that part of the field. At my suggestion, General Meade sent me to the left to examine the condition of affairs, and I continued on till I reached Little Round Top. There were no troops on it, and it was used as a signal station. I saw that this was the key of the whole position, and that our troops in the woods in front of it could not see the ground in front of them, so that the enemy would come upon them before they would be aware of it. The

long line of woods on the west side of the Emmitsburg road (which road was along a ridge) furnished an excellent place for the enemy to form out of sight, so I requested the captain of a rifle battery just in front of Little Round Top to fire a shot into these woods. He did so, and as the shot went whistling through the air the sound of it reached the enemy's troops and caused every one to look in the direction of it. This motion revealed to me the glistening of gun-barrels and bayonets of the enemy's line of battle, already formed and far outflanking the position of any of our troops; so that the line of his advance from his right to Little Round Top was unopposed. I have been particular in telling this, as the discovery was intensely thrilling to my feelings, and almost appalling. I immediately sent a hastily written dispatch to General Meade to send a division at

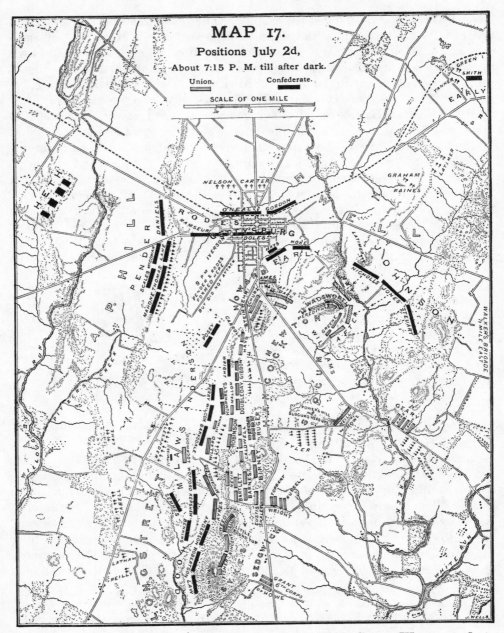

advancing when, noticing the approach of the Fifth Corps, Warren rode to
meet it, caused Weed's and Vincent's brigades and Hazlett's battery to be

least to me, and General Meade directed the Fifth Army
Corps to take position there. The battle was already
beginning to rage at the Peach Orchard, and before a
single man reached Round Top the whole line of the
enemy moved on us in splendid array, shouting in the
most confident tones. While I was still all alone with
the signal officer, the musket-balls began to fly around

us, and he was about to fold up his flags and withdraw,
but remained, at my request, and kept waving them in
defiance. Seeing troops going out on the Peach Orchard
road, I rode down the hill, and fortunately met my old
brigade. General Weed, commanding it, had already
passed the point, and I took the responsibility to detach Colonel O'Rorke, the head of whose regiment I

detached from the latter and hurried them to the summit [see p. 298]. The passage of the six guns through the roadless woods and amongst the rocks was marvelous. Under ordinary circumstances it would have been considered an impossible feat, but the eagerness of the men to get into action with their comrades of the infantry, and the skillful driving, brought them without delay to the very summit, where they went immediately into battle. They were barely in time, for the enemy were also climbing the hill. A close and bloody hand-to-hand struggle ensued, which left both Round Tops in our possession. Weed and Hazlett were killed, and Vincent was mortally wounded — all young men of great promise. Weed had served with much distinction as an artillerist in the Peninsular, Second Bull Run, and Antietam campaigns, had become chief of artillery of his army corps, and at Chancellorsville showed such special aptitude and fitness for large artillery commands that he was immediately promoted from captain to brigadier-general and transferred to the infantry. Hazlett was killed whilst bending over his former chief, to receive his last message. Lieutenant Rittenhouse efficiently commanded the battery during the remainder of the battle.

COLONEL GEORGE L. WILLARD, COMMANDING THE THIRD BRIGADE OF HAYS'S DIVISION, KILLED ON JULY 2. FROM A PHOTOGRAPH.

The enemy, however, clung to the woods and rocks at the base of Round Top, carried Devil's Den and its woods, and captured three of Smith's guns, who, however, effectively deprived the enemy of their use by carrying off all the implements.

The breaking in of the Peach Orchard angle exposed the flanks of the batteries on its crests, which retired firing, in order to cover the retreat of the infantry. Many guns of different batteries had to be abandoned because of the destruction of their

BRIGADIER-GENERAL SAMUEL K. ZOOK, COMMANDING THE THIRD BRIGADE OF CALDWELL'S DIVISION, KILLED IN THE "WHEAT-FIELD" JULY 2. FROM A PHOTOGRAPH.

struck, who, on hearing my few words of explanation about the position, moved at once to the hill-top. About this time First Lieutenant Charles E. Hazlett of the Fifth Artillery, with his battery of rifled cannon, arrived. He comprehended the situation instantly and planted a gun on the summit of the hill. He spoke to the effect that though he could do little execution on the enemy with his guns, he could aid in giving confidence to the infantry, and that his battery was of no consequence whatever compared with holding the position. He staid there till he was killed. I was wounded with a musket-ball while talking with Lieutenant Hazlett on the hill, but not seriously ; and, seeing the position saved while the whole line to the right and front of us was yielding and melting away under the enemy's fire and advance, I left the hill to rejoin General Meade near the center of the field, where a new crisis was at hand."

EDITORS.

CULP'S HILL.

VIEW OF CULP'S HILL FROM THE POSITION OF THE BATTERIES NEAR THE CEMETERY GATE. FROM PHOTOGRAPHS.

1. Position of Stevens's 5th Maine Battery which enfiladed Early's division in the charge upon East Cemetery Hill.   2. Left of the line of field-works on Culp's Hill.   3. Position of the 33d Massachusetts behind the fence of a lane where the left of the Confederate charge was repulsed.—EDITORS.

horses and men; many were hauled off by hand; all the batteries lost heavily. Bigelow's 9th Massachusetts made a stand close by the Trostle house in the corner of the field through which he had retired fighting with prolonges fixed. Although already much cut up, he was directed by McGilvery to hold that point at all hazards until a line of artillery could be formed in front of the wood beyond Plum Run; that is, on what we have called the "Plum Run line." This line was formed by collecting the serviceable batteries, and fragments of batteries, that were brought off, with which, and Dow's Maine battery fresh from the reserve, the pursuit was checked. Finally some twenty-five guns formed a solid mass, which unsupported by infantry held this part of the line, aided General Humphreys's movements, and covered by its fire the abandoned guns until they could be brought off, as all were, except perhaps one. When, after accomplishing its purpose, all that was left of Bigelow's battery was withdrawn, it was closely pressed by Colonel Humphreys's 21st Mississippi, the only Confederate regiment which succeeded in crossing the run. His men had entered the battery and fought hand-to-hand with the cannoneers; one was killed whilst trying to spike a gun, and another knocked down with a handspike whilst endeavoring to drag off a prisoner. The battery went into action with 104 officers and men. Of the four battery officers one was killed, another mortally, and a third, Captain Bigelow, severely wounded. Of 7 sergeants, 2 were killed and 4 wounded; or a total of 28 men, including 2 missing; and 65 out of 88 horses were killed or wounded. As the battery had sacrificed itself for the safety of the line, its work is specially noticed as typical of the service that artillery is not infrequently called upon to render, and did render in other instances at Gettysburg besides this one.

When Sickles was wounded General Meade directed Hancock to take command of the Third as well as his own corps, which he again turned over to Gibbon. About 7:15 P. M. the field was in a critical condition. Birney's division was now broken up; Humphreys's was slowly falling back, under cover of McGilvery's guns; Anderson's line was advancing. On its right, Barksdale's brigade, except the 21st Mississippi, was held in check only by McGilvery's artillery, to whose support Hancock now brought up Willard's brigade of the Second Corps. Placing the 39th New York in reserve, Willard with his other three regiments charged Barksdale's brigade and drove it back nearly to the Emmitsburg road, when he was himself repulsed by a heavy artillery and infantry fire, and fell back to his former position near the sources of Plum Run. In this affair Willard was killed and Barks-

EARLY'S CHARGE ON THE EVENING OF JULY 2 UPON EAST CEMETERY HILL.

dale mortally wounded. Meanwhile the 21st Mississippi crossed the run from the neighborhood of the Trostle house, and drove out the men of Watson's battery ("I," 5th United States), on the extreme left of McGilvery's line, but was in turn driven off by the 39th New York, led by Lieutenant Peeples of the battery, musket in hand, who thus recovered his guns, Watson being severely wounded.

Birney's division once broken, it was difficult to stem the tide of defeat. Hood's and McLaws's divisions—excepting Barksdale's brigade—compassed the Devil's Den and its woods, and as the Federal reënforcements from other corps came piecemeal, they were beaten in detail until by successive accretions they greatly outnumbered their opponents, who had all the advantages of position, when the latter in turn retired, but were not pursued. This fighting was confined almost wholly to the woods and wheat-field between the Peach Orchard and Little Round Top, and the great number of brigade and regimental commanders, as well as of inferior officers and soldiers, killed and wounded on both sides, bears testimony to its close and desperate character. General Meade was on the ground active in bringing up and putting in reënforcements, and in doing so had his horse shot under him. At the close of the day the Confederates held the base of the Round Tops, Devil's Den, its woods, and the Emmitsburg road, with skirmishers thrown out as

CONFEDERATE SKIRMISHERS AT THE FOOT OF CULP'S HILL.

far as the Trostle house; the Federals had the two Round Tops, the Plum Run line, and Cemetery Ridge. During the night the Plum Run line, except the wood on its left front (occupied by McCandless's brigade, Crawford's division, his other brigade being on Big Round Top), was abandoned; the Third Corps was massed to the left and rear of Caldwell's division, which had reoccupied its short ridge, with McGilvery's artillery on its crest. The Fifth Corps remained on and about Round Top, and a division [Ruger's] which had been detached from the Twelfth Corps returned to Culp's Hill.

When Longstreet's guns were heard, Ewell opened a cannonade, which after an hour's firing was overpowered by the Federal artillery on Cemetery Hill. Johnson's division then advanced, and found only one brigade— Greene's—of the Twelfth Corps in position, the others having been sent to the aid of Sickles at the Peach Orchard. Greene fought with skill and determination for two or three hours, and, reënforced by seven or eight hundred men of the First and Eleventh corps, succeeded in holding his own intrenchments, the enemy taking possession of the abandoned works of Geary and Ruger. This brought Johnson's troops near the Baltimore pike, but the darkness prevented their seeing or profiting by the advantage then within their reach. When Ruger's division returned from Round Top, and Geary's from Rock Creek, they found Johnson in possession of their intrenchments, and immediately prepared to drive him out at daylight.

It had been ordered that when Johnson engaged Culp's Hill, Early and Rodes should assault Cemetery Hill. Early's attack was made with great spirit, by Hoke's and Avery's brigades, Gordon's being in reserve; the hill was ascended through the wide ravine between Cemetery and Culp's hills, a line of infantry on the slopes was broken, and Wiedrich's Eleventh Corps and Ricketts's reserve batteries near the brow of the hill were overrun; but the excellent position of Stevens's 12-pounders at the head of the ravine, which enabled him to sweep it, the arrival of Carroll's brigade sent unasked by Hancock,—a happy inspiration, as this line had been weakened to send supports both to Greene and Sickles,—and the failure of Rodes to coöperate with Early, caused the attack to miscarry. The cannoneers of the two batteries, so summarily ousted, rallied and recovered their guns by a vigorous attack — with pistols by those who had them, by others with handspikes, rammers, stones, and even fence-rails — the "Dutchmen" showing that they were in no way inferior to their "Yankee" comrades, who had been taunting them ever since Chancellorsville. After an hour's desperate fighting the enemy was driven out with heavy loss, Avery being among the killed. At the close of this second day a consultation of corps commanders was held at Meade's headquarters. I was not present, although summoned, but was informed that the vote was unanimous to hold our lines and to await an attack for at least one day before taking the offensive, and Meade so decided. [Continuation on p. 369.]

THE COUNCIL OF WAR ON THE SECOND DAY.

BY JOHN GIBBON, MAJOR-GENERAL, U. S. V.

SOON after all firing had ceased a staff-officer from army headquarters met General Hancock and myself and summoned us both to General Meade's headquarters, where a council was to be held. We at once proceeded there, and soon after our arrival all the corps commanders were assembled in the little front room of the Liester House — Newton, who had been assigned to the command of the First Corps over Doubleday, his senior; Hancock, Second; Birney, Third; Sykes, Fifth; Sedgwick, who had arrived during the day with the Sixth, after a long march from Manchester; Howard, Eleventh; and Slocum, Twelfth, besides General Meade, General Butterfield, chief of staff; Warren, chief of engineers; A. S. Williams, Twelfth Corps, and myself, Second. It will be seen that two corps were doubly represented, the Second by Hancock and myself, and the Twelfth by Slocum and Williams. These twelve were all assembled in a little room not more than ten or twelve feet square, with a bed in one corner, a small table on one side, and a chair or two. Of course all could not sit down; some did, some lounged on the bed, and some stood up, while Warren, tired out and suffering from a wound in the neck, where a piece of shell had struck him, lay down in the corner of the room and went sound asleep, and I don't think heard any of the proceedings.

The discussion was at first very informal and in the shape of conversation, during which each one made comments on the fight and told what he knew of the condition of affairs. In the course of this discussion Newton expressed the opinion that "this was no place to fight a battle in." General Newton was an officer of engineers (since chief-engineer of the army), and was rated by me, and I suppose most others, very highly as a soldier. The assertion, therefore, coming from such a source, rather

startled me, and I eagerly asked what his objections to the position were. The objections he stated, as I recollect them, related to some minor details of the line, of which I knew nothing except so far as my own front was concerned, and with those I was satisfied; but the prevailing impression seemed to be that the place for the battle had been in a measure selected for us. Here we are; now what is the best thing to do? It soon became evident that everybody was in favor of remaining where we were and giving battle there. General Meade himself said very little, except now and then to make some comment, but I cannot recall that he expressed any decided opinion upon any point, preferring apparently to listen to the conversation. After the discussion had lasted some time, Butterfield suggested that it would, perhaps, be well to formulate the question to be asked, and General Meade assenting he took a piece of paper, on which he had been making some memoranda, and wrote down a question; when he had done he read it off and formally proposed it to the council.

I had never been a member of a council of war before (nor have I been since) and did not feel very confident I was properly a member of this one; but I had engaged in the discussion, and found myself (Warren being asleep) the junior member in it. By the custom of war the junior member votes first, as on courts-martial; and when Butterfield read off his question, the substance of which was, "Should the army remain in its present position or take up some other?" he addressed himself first to me for an answer. To say "Stay and fight" was to ignore the objections made by General Newton, and I therefore answered somewhat in this way: "Remain here, and make such correction in our position as may be deemed necessary, but take no step which even looks like retreat." The question was put to

Taken by permission from the "Philadelphia Weekly Press" of July 6th, 1887, and condensed.— EDITORS.

each member and his answer taken down, and when it came to Newton, who was the first in rank, he voted in pretty much the same way as I did, and we had some playful sparring as to whether he agreed with me or I with him; the rest voted to remain.

The next question written by Butterfield was, "Should the army attack or wait the attack of the enemy?" I voted not to attack, and all the others voted substantially the same way; and on the third question, "How long shall we wait?" I voted, "Until Lee moved." The answers to this last question showed the only material variation in the opinion of the members.

When the voting was over General Meade said quietly, but decidedly, "Such then is the decision"; and certainly he said nothing which produced a doubt in my mind as to his being perfectly in accord with the members of the council.

In 1881 (eighteen years after the battle) I was shown in Philadelphia, by General Meade's son [Colonel George Meade], a paper found amongst General Meade's effects after his death. It was folded, and on the outside of one end was written, in his well-known handwriting, in ink, "Minutes of Council, July 2d, '63." On opening it, the following was found written in pencil in a handwriting [General Daniel Butterfield's] unknown to me:

Minutes of Council, July 2d, 1863.

Page 1, Questions asked:

1. Under existing circumstances is it advisable for this army to remain in its present position, or to retire to another nearer its base of supplies?
2. It being determined to remain in present position, shall the army attack or wait the attack of the enemy?
3. If we wait attack, how long?

Page 2, Replies.

Gibbon: 1. Correct position of the army, but would not retreat. 2. In no condition to attack, in his opinion. 3. Until he moves.
Williams: 1. Stay. 2. Wait attack. 3. One day.
Birney: Same as General Williams.
Sykes: "   "   "
Newton: 1. Correct position of the army, but would not retreat. 2. By all means not attack. 3. If we wait it will give them a chance to cut our line.

Page 3.

Howard: 1. Remain. 2. Wait attack until 4 P. M. to-morrow. 3. If don't attack, attack them.

⚓ The words in *italics*, noted as illegible in the "Official Records," have been deciphered on a careful examination of the original document deposited by Colonel George Meade with the Penn. Hist. Society.— EDITORS.

Hancock: 1. Rectify position without moving so as to give up field. 2. Not attack unless our communications are cut. 3. Can't wait long; can't be idle.
Sedgwick: 1. Remain. [2.] and wait attack. [3.] At least one day.
Slocum: Stay and fight it out.

[On the back, or *first* page of the sheet]:

Slocum stay and fight it out. Newton thinks it a bad position; Hancock puzzled about practicability of retiring; thinks by holding on *inviting* ⚓ to mass forces and attack. Howard favor of not retiring. Birney don't know. Third Corps used up and not in good condition to fight. Sedgwick *doubtful whether we ought to attack.* ⚓ Effective strength about 9000, 12,500, 9000, 6000, 8500, 6000, 7000. Total, 58,000.

[*Endorsement:*]

Minutes of Council, held Thursday, P. M., July 2d, 1863. D. B., M. G., C. of S. [Daniel Butterfield, Major-General, Chief of Staff].

The memoranda at the bottom of the paper were doubtless made while the discussion was going on, and the numbers at the foot refer probably to the effective strength of each corps. ↓

Several times during the sitting of the council reports were brought to General Meade, and now and then we could hear heavy firing going on over on the right of our line. I took occasion before leaving to say to General Meade that his staff-officer had regularly summoned me as a corps commander to the council, although I had some doubts about being present. He answered, pleasantly, "That is all right. I wanted you here."

Before I left the house Meade made a remark to me which surprised me a good deal, especially when I look back upon the occurrence of the next day. By a reference to the votes in council it will be seen that the majority of the members were in favor of acting on the defensive and awaiting the action of Lee. In referring to the matter, just as the council broke up, Meade said to me, "If Lee attacks to-morrow, it will be in *your front*." I asked him why he thought so, and he replied, "Because he has made attacks on both our flanks and failed, and if he concludes to try it again it will be on our center." I expressed the hope that he would, and told General Meade, with confidence, that if he did we would defeat him.

↓A careful study of the original suggests that these notes "at the bottom" (on the back) were made *before* the questions were formulated. See p. 313.
EDITORS.

THE 20TH MAINE AT LITTLE ROUND TOP. ♪

BY H. S. MELCHER, 20TH MAINE REGIMENT.

THE Confederate force designated to take possession of Little Round Top appears to have been Robertson's brigade, consisting of the 1st, 4th, and 5th Texas and the 3d Arkansas; and Law's brigade, consisting of the 4th, 44th, 48th, 47th, and 15th Alabama, both of Hood's division. The former was to assault in front, while Law's brigade was to attack in the rear of the hill [see p. 318]; but Robertson, finding he could not cover the entire front with his brigade, detached the

44th, 48th, and 4th Alabama from Law's brigade about the time they arrived at the foot of Round Top in their advance and connected them with Robertson's line, then well in front of Little Round Top. This left the 47th and 15th Alabama to carry out the flanking movement alone, which they did, passing up the southern side of Round Top, and halting some ten minutes on the crest for rest. This halt proved fatal to the success of their undertaking, as it enabled our brigade (Vincent's)

♪ Condensed from the "Lincoln County News," Waldoboro, Maine, March 13th, 1885.— EDITORS.

to reach Little Round Top in time to resist their advance. ⸮

Resuming their march, these two regiments passed down the north-easterly side of Round Top and advanced across the wooded depression between the hills to charge up the rear of Little Round Top and sweep off Vincent's brigade, then fiercely engaged with Robertson's Texans and the three regiments of Law's brigade that had been assigned to his command, who were trying to get possession from the front. But just here these two Alabama regiments met the 20th Maine, which was the left regiment of Vincent's brigade, and also the left of the whole Army of the Potomac, and, to conform to the crest of the hill, was bent back at about right angles with the line of the rest of the brigade. This was fortunate, for in their advance the 47th Alabama, commanded by Lieutenant-Colonel Bulger, struck our regiment squarely in front and opened a murderous fire on our unprotected line, as we had just got into position, and had no time to throw up breastworks. At the same time the 15th Alabama, commanded by Colonel William C. Oates, numbering 644 men and 42 officers, moved around to attack us in flank and rear. Our colonel, Chamberlain, met this movement by putting the right wing of the regiment into single rank to resist the 47th, and bent back the five left companies of the regiment at a right angle.

Our regiment numbered 358 men, but as Company B, numbering 50 men, had been sent out to "protect our flank," we had 308 men in line to resist the furious assault of these two strong regiments, outnumbering us more than 3 to 1. The conflict was fierce, but necessarily brief, as it was a question of only a short time when every man must fall before the superior fire of our enemy.

When 130 of our brave officers and men had been shot down where they stood, and only 178 remained,—hardly more than a strong skirmish line,—and each man had fired the 60 rounds of cartridges he carried into the fight, and the survivors were using from the cartridge-boxes of their fallen comrades, the time had come when it must be decided whether we should fall back and give up this key to the whole field of Gettysburg, or charge and try and throw off this foe. Colonel Chamberlain gave the order to "fix bayonets," and almost before he could say "charge!" the regiment leaped down the hill and closed in with the foe, whom we found behind every rock and tree. Surprised and overwhelmed, most of them threw down their arms and surrendered.

Some fought till they were slain; the others ran "like a herd of wild cattle," as Colonel Oates himself expressed it. In their flight they were met by Company B, Captain Morrill, which we supposed had been captured, but now attacked so vigorously that over one hundred of the fugitives were compelled to surrender.

Lieutenant-Colonel Bulger, commanding the 47th, was wounded, and fell into our hands, with over three hundred prisoners and all the wounded.

The 20th Maine returned with its prisoners to the original position, and staid there until ordered forward in the early evening to Round Top.

⸮ Vincent's brigade appears to have been sent by General Sykes to occupy the position to the left, or southward, of Little Round Top, between it and Round Top, about the same time that Colonel O'Rorke with the 140th New York and Hazlett's battery, the advance of Weed's brigade, at the call of Warren was hastening up the northern slope of Little Round Top to seize the crest.— EDITORS.

THE 146TH NEW YORK AT LITTLE ROUND TOP.

BY JAMES G. GRINDLAY, BREVET BRIGADIER-GENERAL, U. S. V.

UNIFORM OF THE 146TH NEW YORK REGIMENT.

IN "The Century" for December, 1886 [see p. 298 of this volume], in the illustration, "View from the position of Hazlett's battery on Little Round Top," it is stated, "the monument marks the position of the 91st Pennsylvania of Weed's brigade." I beg to say that the location of the monument is exactly where the headquarters of the 146th New York Volunteers were established and maintained during the battle of Gettysburg. Weed's brigade comprised the 140th and 146th New York and the 91st and 155th Pennsylvania Volunteers, and they formed the line of battle on Little Round Top in the order as named from left to right.

The Big Rock stands upon the summit of Little Round Top, and was the headquarters of the 146th New York, Colonel Kenner Garrard, and also brigade headquarters, when Colonel Garrard succeeded General Weed in command when the latter was killed. The 146th New York occupied the ground immediately in front of the Big Rock, and the center and colors of our regiment were opposite the rock—the 91st being on our right, as before stated; and the extreme left of the 91st Pennsylvania was at least one hundred yards to the right of the rock. I am confirmed in this statement by correspondence with brother officers, among others Major C. K. Dutton, of New York City, who writes me: "Your statement of the position of 146th is correct. One thing I do know, viz., that my company (H) was to the right of the rock, and several companies of the regiment on the right of my company before the 91st Pennsylvania came in line. Jenkins, Armstrong, and myself had our position a hundred feet to the right of the rock." The writer commanded the color company, and his memory is refreshed from the fact that at the reunion of the regiment at Rome, N. Y., August 6th last, the subject was fully discussed and steps taken to erect a monument to mark the position, also by a recent examination of the maps and photographs of the field of battle at the residence of General Sickles by a committee of our regiment.

UTICA, N. Y., Dec. 26th, 1886.

THE BREASTWORKS AT CULP'S HILL.

I. BY JESSE H. JONES, CAPTAIN, 60TH N. Y. V.

THE Second Division of the Twelfth Corps camped on the night of the first day under the shadow of Little Round Top. About 6 o'clock the next morning it was marched over from that point, which was then the extreme left of our line, and posted on Culp's Hill, its left forming a right angle with the right of General Wadsworth's division of the First Corps. Our brigade, commanded by Brigadier-General George S. Greene and comprising five New York regiments, the 60th, 78th, 102d, 137th, and 149th, was on the left of the division, and our regiment, the 60th, was on the left of the brigade. This regiment was largely composed of men accustomed to woodcraft, and they fell to work to construct log breastworks with unaccustomed heartiness. All instinctively felt that a life-and-death struggle was impending, and that every help should be used. Culp's Hill was covered with woods; so all the materials needful were at our disposal. Right and left the men felled the trees, and blocked them up into a close log fence. Piles of cordwood which lay near by were quickly appropriated. The sticks, set slanting on end against the outer face of the logs, made excellent battening. All along the rest of the line of the corps a similar defense was constructed. Fortunate regiments, which had spades and picks, strengthened their work with earth. By 10 o'clock it was finished.

At 6 o'clock in the evening General Meade, finding himself hard pressed on the left, and deeming an attack on the right wing improbable at so late an hour, called for the Twelfth Corps. Our brigade was detailed to remain and hold the lines of the corps. Word was brought from the officer in charge of our pickets that the enemy was advancing in heavy force in line of battle, and, with all possible celerity, such dispositions as the case admitted of were made. The brigade was strung out into a thin line of separate men as far along the breastworks as it would reach. The intention was to place the men an arm's-length apart, but, by the time the left of the brigade had fairly undoubled files, the enemy was too near to allow of further arrangements being made.

In a short time the woods were all flecked with the flashes from the muskets of our skirmishers. Down in the hollow there, at the foot of the slope, you could catch a glimpse now and then, by the blaze of the powder, of our brave boys as they sprang from tree to tree, and sent back defiance to the advancing foe. With desperation they clung to each covering. For half an hour they obstructed the enemy's approach.

The men restrained their nervous fingers; the hostile guns flamed out against us not fifteen yards in front. Our men from the front were tumbling over the breastwork, and for a breathless moment those behind the breastwork waited. Then out into the night like chain-lightning leaped the zigzag line of fire. Now was the value of breastworks apparent, for, protected by these, few of our men were hit, and feeling a sense of security, we worked with corresponding energy. Without breastworks our line would have been swept away in an instant by the hailstorm of bullets and the flood of men. The enemy worked still farther around to our right, entered the breastwork beyond our line, and crumpled up and drove back, a short distance, our extreme right regiment. They advanced a little way, but were checked by the fire of a couple of small regiments borrowed for the emergency from General Wadsworth, and placed in echelon.

General Meade hardly mentioned this affair at the breastworks in his original report of the battle, and those who were there think justice has never been done in the case, ☆ and that what was there achieved has never been adequately apprehended and stated by any writer.

The left of our brigade was only about eighty rods from the Baltimore turnpike, while the right was somewhat nearer. There were no supports. All the force that there was to stay the onset was that one thin line. Had the breastworks not been built, and had there been only the thin line of our unprotected brigade, that line must have been swept away like leaves before the wind, by the oncoming of so heavy a mass of troops, and the pike would have been reached by the enemy. Once on the pike, the Confederate commander would have been full in the rear of one-third of our army, firmly planted on the middle of the chord of the arc upon which that portion was posted. What the effect must have been it is not needful to describe. The least disaster would have sufficed to force us from the field.

During the night our commanders brought back the remainder of the corps, and, stumbling upon the enemy's pickets, found out what had taken place, something of which until that moment they had been entirely unaware.

☆ On the 25th of February, 1864, General Meade made the following substitution in his official report:

"The detachment of so large a portion of the Twelfth Corps, with its temporary commander, Brigadier-General A. S. Williams, left the defense of the line previously held to the remaining brigade of the Second Division, commanded by Brigadier-General Greene, who held the left of the Twelfth Corps, now become the extreme right of the army. The enemy, perceiving the withdrawal of our troops, advanced and attacked General Greene with great vigor, who, making a gallant defense, and being soon reënforced by portions of the First and Eleventh corps, contiguous to him, succeeded in repulsing all the efforts of the enemy to dislodge him."

Also, on the same day, in reply to a letter from General Slocum on the subject, General Meade wrote in part:

"I am willing to admit that, if my attention had been called to the services of Greene's Brigade in the pointed manner it now is, I would have given it credit for this special service." EDITORS.

II. BY GEORGE S. GREENE, BREVET-MAJOR-GENERAL, U. S. V.

THE breastworks on Culp's Hill referred to in the foregoing article were constructed under my immediate direction. Orders were given to throw up breastworks as soon as the troops came on the line. The approximate shape of the line at first held by the entire corps and afterward by my single brigade was this:

Wadsworth.

Greene's Brigade.

Kane's Brigade (Ireland's regiment).

First Division.

When Meade ordered the whole of the Twelfth Corps from Culp's Hill to reënforce his left, Slocum ordered my brigade to remain and "occupy the breastworks thrown up by the corps." The rest of the corps moved off just before dusk (about 7 P. M.) I immediately extended my men to the right to comply with the order as far as possible. Ireland's regiment (the 149th N. Y.), which was on my right, occupied the intrenchments vacated by Kane's brigade, his left at *b*, and a regiment from Howard's corps was placed on Ireland's right. This regiment, without being specially attacked, was marched to the rear by its colonel, when an attack upon it was imminently probable, much to the disgust of his men, as reported. As soon as I received orders to occupy the intrenchments, I applied to Wadsworth and received two regiments, which were placed in rear of my right, behind the points *b* and *d*, but sufficiently in the rear to support any part of the line.

The movement of the 149th Regiment had hardly been made when the regiment on picket was driven in by a vigorous attack by Johnson's division of Ewell's corps, which was continued with great perseverance. The enemy finally extended their left to cover Ireland's right, which had been left in the air by the desertion of the Pennsylvania regiment from Howard's corps. Ireland was forced back and rallied his regiment behind the traverse, *b d*, which had been built to protect my right, and which now served its purpose. As soon as Ireland's movement was seen — or, rather heard, for it was dark — I brought up the reserve, which checked any further advance of the enemy on the right. Very soon after this movement, Kane, with his brigade, arrived and took post on the right of my reserve, and the enemy ceased their attacks, after about three hours' continuous fighting.

As the troops marched out, General Kane followed the First Brigade of the Second Division toward the left. When the column arrived at the Baltimore pike the First Division followed the staff-officer sent to conduct it toward the left. The Second Division marched down the pike to the rear. Kane, hearing the firing on my posi-

tion, inquired as to their destination, and, not being satisfied, took the responsibility of returning to the fight, and immediately countermarched; as he came near the position which had been occupied by the First Division, the enemy's pickets fired on him, and this being heard by me, I sent an officer to conduct Kane in by the safer route of the turnpike. He arrived about 10 o'clock P. M., just after the enemy had been repulsed on my right. His presence tended to render the enemy cautious, and they rested on their arms till morning. The First Brigade (Candy's) of the Second Division arrived at Culp's Hill about 1 A. M., long after the fighting had ceased. General Williams, who commanded the Twelfth Corps, and General Slocum, who commanded the right wing, having been advised of the enemy's position, the artillery was placed in position before daylight, and after a heavy bombardment, the infantry, by a gallant and successful charge, drove the enemy from the position they had occupied in the night in the lines of the First Division.

The attack on my front, on the morning of the 3d of July, was renewed by Johnson's division simultaneously with our attack on the enemy in our lines on our right, and was conducted with the utmost vigor. The greater part of their heavy losses were sustained within a few yards of our breastworks. His adjutant, Major Watkins Leigh persisted in riding up to the very front of our lines, pushing his men to an assault on my works, where both horse and rider were killed, pierced simultaneously with several bullets. About fifty of the men got too near to our lines to retreat, and threw down their arms, ran up close to our works, threw up their handkerchiefs or white rags, and were allowed to come unarmed into our lines. Shaler's and Canda's brigades were sent to our support and took part in the defense of our lines on the morning of July 3d. By 10 A. M. the fighting ceased, and at 1 P. M. the enemy had disappeared from our front, and our men went to Rock Creek for water.

Of the disastrous consequences to the Union army, had Lee succeeded in penetrating our lines and placing himself square across the Baltimore pike in rear of the center and right wing of the entire army, there can be no question. Fortunately it was averted by the steady and determined courage of the five New York regiments above named. The assailants were Johnson's division of Ewell's (Second) Corps, consisting of twenty-two regiments, organized into four brigades — Steuart's, Nicholls's, Jones's, and Walker's — the latter being the famous "Stonewall Brigade," first commanded by Stonewall Jackson.

To the discernment of General Slocum, who saw the danger to which the army would be exposed by the movement ordered, and who took the responsibility of modifying the orders which he had received, is due the honor of having saved the army from a great and perhaps fatal disaster.

AT CLOSE QUARTERS ON THE FIRST DAY AT GETTYSBURG.

THE STRUGGLE FOR "ROUND TOP."

BY E. M. LAW, MAJOR-GENERAL, C. S. A.

MORE has been written concerning the battle of Gettysburg than any other "passage of arms" between the Federal and Confederate troops during the civil war. The engagement of the 1st of July, brought on by accident, on the part of the Confederates at least, in which two corps of the Federal army under General Reynolds were defeated and driven through Gettysburg by portions of Hill's and Ewell's corps, has been often and fully described by the officers on both sides. Ewell's attack on the Federal right in the vicinity of Culp's Hill on the 2d of July, and Longstreet's advance upon the Federal left on the same day, so far as relates to one division of the latter's command (McLaws's), have been detailed with equal minuteness by those engaged. The magnificent charge of Pickett's division on the Federal center on the third day has been the theme of a host of writers who deemed it an honor to have stood in the lines of blue by which that charge was repelled, and those who, on the other hand, thought it no less an honor to have shared the fortunes of the torn and shattered columns of gray which only failed to accomplish impossibilities.

But concerning the operations of Lee's extreme right wing, extending to the foot of Round Top, little or nothing has been written on the Confederate side.   This part of the line was held by Hood's division of Longstreet's corps, and was really the key to the whole position of Gettysburg.   Here some of the most stubborn fighting of that desperate battle was done, and here a determined effort of the Federal cavalry to reach the right rear of the Confederate army on the 3d of July was frustrated — an attempt which, if successful, must have resulted disastrously to that army.

The meagerness of the details of the operations referred to may be accounted for by the fact that General Longstreet personally superintended the left of his line, consisting of McLaws's division of his own corps, supported by R. H. Anderson's division of Hill's corps, and hence knew comparatively little from personal observation of the movements of Hood's division; and, also, that General Hood was wounded early in the engagement on the 2d of July, and, relinquishing the command of the division, could not report its subsequent operations.   As senior brigadier, I succeeded to the command of Hood's division, and directed its movements during the engagements of the 2d and 3d of July.   But owing to the active and constant movements of our army for some weeks after the battle, I was only able to obtain the reports of brigade commanders a very short time previous to being ordered to the army of General Bragg at Chickamauga.   This prevented me from making a report at the time, and it was afterward neglected.

The facts stated in this paper are therefore many of them published for the first time.   It remains for the impartial reader to decide whether they do not constitute an important part of the history of the most memorable battle of the war; for Gettysburg was the turning-point in the great struggle.   Together with the fall of Vicksburg, which occurred simultaneously with the retreat of Lee's army toward the Potomac, it inspired the armies and people of the North with fresh courage and stimulated anew the hopes of ultimate success which were visibly flagging under an almost uninterrupted series of reverses to the Federal arms in Virginia, extending over a period of nearly two years.   On the other hand, it was at Gettysburg that the right arm of the South was broken, and it must always stand out in Confederate annals as in the history of a brave and kindred people stands

" Flodden's fatal field,
Where shivered was fair Scotland's spear,
And broken was her shield."

When the fight began at Gettysburg on the 1st of July, three brigades of Hood's division were at Greenwood on the Chambersburg road and on the west side of South Mountain.   My own brigade, with Bachman's battery, was at New Guilford, some miles south of Greenwood, watching our right flank. At 3 o'clock on the morning of the 2d, under orders from General Longstreet, I moved as rapidly as possible toward Gettysburg, and arrived there shortly before noon, having marched the intervening distance of twenty-four miles in that time.   On my arrival I found the other brigades of Hood's division resting about a mile from the town, on the Chambersburg road.   In a short time after my brigade came up, the division was moved to our right (south), traversing the angle between the Chambersburg and Emmitsburg roads, following McLaws, who was in advance. Pickett's division had not yet come up. We moved very slowly, with frequent halts and deflections from the direct course — the latter being necessary to conceal our movements from the Federal signal station on Little Round Top.

At length, after many vexatious delays, Hood's division was pushed forward until it uncovered McLaws, and soon reached the Emmitsburg road in front of Round Top. Here our line of battle was formed at an acute angle

BREVET MAJOR-GENERAL HENRY J. HUNT, CHIEF OF
ARTILLERY OF THE ARMY OF THE POTOMAC.
FROM A PHOTOGRAPH.

with the road, the right being in advance of it, between the road and the mountain, and the left extending across and in rear of the road. The formation was in two lines, Law's Alabama and Robertson's Texas brigades in front, supported, at a distance of about 200 yards, by the Georgia brigades of Benning and G. T. Anderson. McLaws's division extended the line to our left, with a similar formation. The Artillery Battalion, composed of Reilly's, Latham's, Garden's, and Bachman's batteries, twenty guns in all, were disposed at advantageous points upon the ridge occupied by the line of infantry. There were no signs of Federal cavalry or troops of any kind on our right. As a precautionary measure, however, a regiment was detached from Anderson's brigade and stationed at Kern's house, half a mile down the road toward Emmitsburg.

It was now past 4 o'clock in the afternoon and our troops were in position for the attack. The flank movement by which they came into position is referred to in the following dispatch from the Federal signal station on Little Round Top: "To General Meade—4 o'clock P. M. The only infantry of the enemy visible is on the extreme [Federal] left; it has been moving toward Emmitsburg." It will thus be seen that the movement, in spite of our precautions, was not unobserved.

The Confederate line of battle occupied a ridge, partly wooded, with a valley intervening between it and the heights held by the Federal troops in front. The position occupied by the Federal left wing in front of us was now fully disclosed to view, and it was certainly one of the most formidable it had ever been the fortune of any troops to confront. Round Top rose like a huge sentinel guarding the Federal left flank, while the spurs and ridges trending off to the north of it afforded unrivaled positions for the use of artillery. The puffs of smoke rising at intervals along the line of hills, as the Federal batteries fired upon such portions of our line as became exposed to view, clearly showed that these advantages had not been neglected. The thick woods which in great part covered the sides of Round Top and the adjacent hills concealed from view the rugged nature of the ground, which increased fourfold the difficulties of the attack.

How far up the slope of Round Top the Federal left extended we could not tell, as the woods effectually concealed from view everything in that quarter.

In order to gain information upon this important point, I sent out a detail of six picked men as scouts, with instructions to move as rapidly as possible to the summit of Round Top, making a détour to their right, and "feeling" down from that point, to locate the left of the Federal line. The entire absence of Federal cavalry on our right, as well as other indications leading to the same conclusion, convinced me that the Federals, relying upon the protection of the mountain, considered their flank secure; that it was therefore their most vulnerable point. Impressed with this view, I further instructed the scouts when they reached the summit to observe carefully the state of affairs on the other side, and to send a "runner" back to me with such intelligence as they might be able to gain. They moved off at a trot. A few moments after they had started, I saw in the valley, some distance to our right, several dark figures moving across the fields from the rear of Round Top in the direction of the Emmitsburg road. These on being captured proved to be Federal soldiers, who seemed surprised at our sudden appearance in that quarter, and who, on being questioned, stated that they had surgeons' certificates and were "going to the rear." They indicated "the rear" by pointing toward Emmitsburg, and in reply to the question where they came from, they said from the "medical train behind the mountain"—referring to Round Top. They also stated that the medical and ordnance trains "around the mountain" were insecurely guarded, no attack being expected at that point; and that the other side of the mountain could be easily reached by a good farm road, along which they had just traveled, the distance being a little more than a mile. On my way to convey this information to General Hood, I met a messenger from my scouts, who had reached the crest of Round Top. He reported that there was no Federal force on the summit, and confirmed in every particular the statements of the prisoners I had just captured. If there had previously been any question in regard to the policy of a front attack, there now remained not a shadow of doubt that our true *point d'appui* was Round Top, from which the Confederate right wing could be extended toward the Taneytown and Baltimore roads, on the Federal left and rear.

I found General Hood on the ridge where his line had been formed, communicated to him the information I had obtained, and pointed out the ease with which a movement by the right flank might be made. He coincided fully in my views, but said that his orders were positive to attack in front, as soon as the left of the corps should get into position. I therefore entered a formal protest against a direct attack, on the grounds: 1. That the great natural strength of the enemy's position in our front rendered the result of a direct assault extremely uncertain. 2. That, even if successful, the victory would be purchased at too great a sacrifice of life, and our troops would be in no condition to improve it. 3. That a front attack was unnecessary,—the occupation of Round Top during the night by moving upon it from the south, and the extension of our right wing from that point across the enemy's left and rear, being not only practicable, but easy. 4. That such a movement would compel a change of front on the part of the enemy, the abandonment of his strong position on the heights, and force him to attack us in position.

General Hood called up Captain Hamilton, of his staff, and requested me to repeat the protest to him, and the grounds on which it was made. He then directed Captain Hamilton to find General Longstreet as quickly as possible and deliver the protest, and to say to him that he (Hood) indorsed it fully. Hamilton rode off at once, but in about ten minutes returned, accompanied by a staff-officer of General Longstreet, who said to General Hood, in my hearing, " General Longstreet orders that you begin the attack at once." Hood turned to me and merely said, " You hear the order ? " I at once moved my brigade to the assault. I do not know whether the protest ever reached General Lee. From the brief interval that elapsed between the time it was sent to General Longstreet and the receipt of the order to begin the attack, I am inclined to think it did not. General Longstreet has since said that he repeatedly advised against a front attack and suggested a movement by our right flank. He may have thought, after the rejection of this advice by General Lee, that it was useless to press the matter further.

Just here the battle of Gettysburg was lost to the Confederate arms. It is useless to speculate upon the turn affairs might have taken if the Confederate cavalry had been in communication with the rest of the army, and if General Stuart had kept General Lee informed, as he should have done, of the movements of the Federal army. In considering the causes of the Confederate failure on that particular field, we must take the situation just as we find it. And the situation was as follows: The advance of the two armies encountered each other on the 1st of July. An engagement ensued in which the Confederates were victorious. The Federal troops retired through Gettysburg and took position along the height east of the town—a position which, if properly defended, was practicably impregnable to a direct attack.

The whole matter then resolves itself into this: General Lee failed at Gettysburg on the 2d and 3d of July because he made his attack precisely where his enemy wanted him to make it and was most fully prepared to receive it. Even had he succeeded in driving the Federal army from its strong position by a general and simultaneous assault along the whole front (which was the only possible chance of success in that direction), he would have found his army in very much the same condition in which Pyrrhus found his, when, after driving the Romans from the field of Asculum, he exclaimed, " Another such victory, and I am undone ! "

The failure of General Ewell to seize Cemetery Hill and adjacent positions, on the evening of July 1st, has been frequently assigned as one of the causes of our loss of the battle. It is very doubtful whether General Ewell could have occupied those heights had he made the attempt, for General Pleasonton has asserted very positively that, on the night of the 1st of July, " we [the Federals] had more troops in position than Lee." And General Lee qualified his instructions to General Ewell to seize the heights by the words "if practicable." Under the circumstances, the fact that General Ewell did not seize them is very strong presumptive evidence that it was not practicable.

The two armies being face to face on the 2d of July, and setting aside all question of a retreat by either, General Lee's alternative of a direct attack was a movement by his right flank to the Federal left and rear. The first promised nothing but desperate fighting, heavy loss, and probable failure. The second certainly promised nothing worse, with the probabilities all in favor of a "fair field and a free fight," and that was all his army asked. Referring to this suggested movement upon the Federal left flank, General Pleasonton, who commanded the Federal cavalry at that time, has expressed the opinion that it was impracticable, and has stated further that he "had two divisions of cavalry, one in rear of the Federal position and one on Lee's right flank," to prevent it. If the cavalry had been there, as he states, they

THE STRUGGLE FOR DEVIL'S DEN, (LOOKING TOWARD THE CONFEDERATE LINES). FROM A WAR-TIME SKETCH.

would not have amounted to even a single "ounce of prevention," as far as the movements of our infantry were concerned. But if there *was* a division, or even a single picket-post of cavalry, either Federal or Confederate, on our right flank, at any time on the 2d of July, it was kept most persistently out of sight, as my scouts, who were sent out in all directions, failed to find it.

Our order of attack—issued as soon as the two divisions of Longstreet's corps came into position on the line already described—was, that the movement should begin on the right, my brigade on that flank leading, the other commands taking it up successively toward the left. It was near 5 o'clock P. M. when we advanced to the attack. The artillery on both sides had been warmly engaged for about fifteen minutes, and continued to fire heavily until we became engaged with the Federal infantry, when the Confederate batteries ceased firing to avoid injury to our own troops, who were then, for the most part, concealed by the woods about the base of Round Top and the spurs to the north of it. General Hood was severely wounded in the arm by a shot from the Federal artillery as we moved into action.

Advancing rapidly across the valley which separated the opposing lines,— all the time under a heavy fire from the batteries,— our front line struck the enemy's skirmishers posted along the farther edge of the valley. Brushing these quickly away, we soon came upon their first line of battle, running along the lower slopes of the hills known as Devil's Den, to our left of Round Top, and separated from the latter by Plum Run valley. The fighting soon became close and severe. Exposed to the artillery fire from the heights in front and on our left, as well as to the musketry of the infantry, it required all the courage and steadiness of the veterans who composed the Army of Northern Virginia — whose spirit was never higher than then — to face the storm. Not one moment was lost. With rapidly thinning ranks the gray line swept on, until the blue line in front wavered, broke, and seemed to dissolve in the woods and rocks on the mountain-side. The advance continued steadily, the center of the division moving directly upon the guns on the hill adjoining Devil's Den on the north, from which we had been suffering so severely. In order to secure my right flank, I extended it well up on the side of Round Top, and my brigade, in closing to the right, left a considerable interval between its left and the right of the Texas brigade of Robertson. Into this interval I threw Benning's Georgia brigade, which had up to that time occupied the second line. At the same time seeing a heavy Federal force on Robertson's left, and no Confederate troops having come up to extend our line in that direction, Anderson's Georgia brigade, till then also in the second line, was thrown out on that flank.

Thus disposed, the division continued to move forward, encountering, as it ascended the heights around the battery on the spur and to the right and left of it, a most determined resistance from the Federal troops, who seemed to be continually reënforced. The ground was rough and difficult, broken by rocks and bowlders, which rendered an orderly advance impossible. Sometimes the Federals would hold one side of the huge bowlders on the slope until the Confederates occupied the other. In some cases my men, with reckless daring, mounted to the top of the large rocks in order to get a better view and to deliver their fire with greater effect. One of these, Sergeant Barbee of the Texas brigade, having reached a rock a little in advance of the line, stood erect on the top of it, loading and firing as coolly as if unconscious of danger, while the air around him was fairly swarming with bullets. He soon fell helpless from several wounds; but he held his rock, lying upon the top of it until the litter-bearers carried him off.

In less than an hour from the time we advanced to the attack, the hill by Devil's Den opposite our center was taken, with three pieces of the artillery that had occupied it. The remaining piece was run down the opposite slope by the gunners, and escaped capture.

In the meantime my brigade, on the right, had swept over the northern slope of Round Top, cleared it of the enemy, and then, making a partial change of front to the left, advanced upon Little Round Top, which lay in rear of the spur on which the battery had been taken. This change of direction soon exposed it to a flank attack on the right by fresh troops (Vincent's brigade), rendering it necessary to retire it to the general line.

While our center and right wing were engaged as I have described, Anderson's brigade, on the left, was subjected to great annoyance and loss by movements of the enemy upon its left flank, being frequently compelled to change the front of the regiments on that flank to repel attacks from that direction.

Up to this time I had seen nothing of McLaws's division, which was to have extended our left and to have moved to the attack at the same time. I therefore halted my line, which had become broken and disorganized by the roughness of the ground over which it had been fighting, and placing it in as advantageous a position as possible for receiving any attack that the Federals

THE "SLAUGHTER PEN" AT THE BASE AND ON THE LEFT SLOPE OF LITTLE ROUND TOP. FROM PHOTOGRAPHS.

might be disposed to make, I hurried back to the ridge from which we had originally advanced. I found McLaws still in position there, his troops suffering considerably from a severe fire of artillery from the opposite hills. I was informed by General Kershaw, who held the right of this division, that although he understood the general instructions that the forward movement was to be taken up from the right, he had not yet received the order to move, from his division commander. I pointed out the position of Hood's division, and urged the necessity of immediate support on its left. General Kershaw requested me to designate the point on which his right flank should be directed, and promptly moved to the attack, the movement being taken up by the whole division.

When Hood's division first attacked, General Meade, alarmed for the safety of his left wing, and doubtless fully alive to the importance of holding so vital a point as Round Top and its adjacent spurs, commenced sending reën-forcements to the threatened points. We encountered some of these in our first advance, and others were arriving as McLaws came up on our left. In its advance this division extended from the "Peach Orchard" near the Emmitsburg road, on its left, to the "Wheat-field" north of the hill on which we had captured the Federal battery, where its right wing connected with my left. As McLaws advanced, we again moved forward on his right, and the fighting continued in "see-saw" style—first one side and then the other gaining ground or losing it, with small advantage to either, until dark.

At the close of the engagement Hood's division held the hill where the battery had been taken and the ridge to its left—our right extending across Devil's Den and well up on the north-western slope of Round Top. During the night this line was strengthened by the construction of a breastwork of the loose stones that abounded all along the positions occupied by the troops, and the light of the next morning disclosed the fact that the Federal troops in front of us had improved their time in the same way. In fact, all through the night we could hear them at work as the rocks were dropped in place on the works, and no doubt they heard us just as distinctly, while we were engaged in the same life-preserving operation.

Though the losses had been severe on both sides, comparatively few prisoners had been taken. But early in the night, in the confusion resulting from the fight over such rugged ground, and the darkness of the wooded mountain-side, men of both armies, in search of their commands, occasionally wandered into the opposing picket-lines and were captured. Many of the Federal wounded were left in our lines on the ground from which their troops had been forced back, and some of ours remained in their hands in the most advanced positions which we had reached and had been compelled to abandon. Among these latter was Colonel Powell of the 5th Texas regiment, who was shot through the body and afterward died. Powell was a stout, portly man, with a full beard, resembling, in many respects, General Longstreet, and the first impression of his captors was that they had taken that officer. Indeed, it was asserted positively by some of the prisoners we picked up during the night that Longstreet was badly wounded and a prisoner in their hands, and they obstinately refused to credit our statements to the contrary.

Early in the morning of the 3d two of my batteries, Latham's and Garden's, were sent to Colonel (afterward General) E. P. Alexander, who commanded our artillery in the center, to assist in the cannonade of the Federal position south of Cemetery Hill, preparatory to the assault of General Pickett's division at that point; and about 9 o'clock A. M. General Longstreet came over to my position on the right, and instructed me to be ready to renew the attack on our front. Under the circumstances that then existed, such an attack would have been simply madness. I have already described the difficult nature of the ground in our front. These difficulties were greatly increased by extemporized breastworks of rock all along the Federal line, which afforded good protection for their infantry, and were fully manned by a force much superior to our own. On the other hand, we had been weakened in the desperate attack of the preceding evening by losses amounting to one-fourth of the whole force carried into action. More than two thousand officers and men of our division had been killed and wounded, among them Generals J. B. Anderson and G. T. Robertson, and about one-half of the field-officers of the various regiments. McLaws's division, on our left, had suffered nearly as severely, General Barksdale of that division being killed and General Semmes mortally wounded.

The cannonade in the center soon began, and presented one of the most magnificent battle-scenes witnessed during the war. Looking up the valley toward Gettysburg, the hills on either side were capped with crowns of flame and smoke, as 300 guns, about equally divided between the two ridges, vomited their iron hail upon each other. Dense clouds of smoke settled over the valley, through which the shells went hissing and screaming on their errand of death. Numbers of these from opposite directions exploded midway over the valley, apparently with venomous impatience, as they met each other in mid-air, lighting up the clouds with their snake-like flashes.

While this grand artillery duel was progressing, and before our infantry had moved to the attack, a new danger threatened us on the right. This was the appearance of Kilpatrick's division of cavalry, which moved up on that flank and commenced massing in the body of timber which extended from the base of Round Top westward toward Kern's house, on the Emmitsburg road. Reilly's and Bachman's batteries were ordered to change front to the right so as to bear upon this position, and at once opened fire upon the cavalry, which retired beyond the wood and out of sight. In order to protect my flank more fully, I withdrew the 1st Texas regiment of Robertson's brigade from the main line, and placed it in position midway between Round Top and the Emmitsburg road, with skirmishers extending from its left and connecting at right angles with the extreme right of the main line on the slope of the mountain. I also detached the 7th and 8th Georgia regiments of Anderson's brigade, and sent them to the support of the 9th, which had been stationed at Kern's house. About the time these dispositions were completed, Colonel Black, of the 1st South Carolina Cavalry, reported to me with about 100 men who had been gathered up from the medical trains, most of them partly disabled and only a part mounted, and with three guns of Hart's battery of horse artillery. Hart's guns were stationed on the Emmitsburg road, and the cavalry extended the right flank beyond that road. This new flanking line was formed at right angles to the main line, and crossed the Emmitsburg road near Kern's house.

One brigade of the Federal cavalry (Merritt's) moved across the road and deployed a strong line of dismounted skirmishers in front of Colonel Black's command, which was too weak to offer any effectual resistance. Hart's guns, however, were well handled, and did good service as long as the enemy remained in reach of them. To meet this flanking movement, I had to extend the 7th and 8th Georgia regiments to the right, and heavy skirmishing continued as the lines developed, with occasional efforts of the Federals to break through, until about half-past three o'clock P. M., when my two regiments were stretched out to a bare line of skirmishers.

It is not an easy task to operate against cavalry with infantry alone, on an extended line, and in an open country where the former, capable of moving much more rapidly, can choose its own points of attack and can elude the blows of its necessarily more tardy adversary. But Merritt's brigade was now dismounted and deployed as skirmishers, and I lost no time in taking advantage of this temporary equality as to the means of locomotion. Detaching the two remaining regiments of Anderson's brigade (11th and 59th Georgia) from the main line, I moved them rapidly to our extreme right, now about a mile from Kern's house, attacked Merritt's reserve, and then, changing front to the left, struck his skirmish-line " on its end " and " doubled it up " as far as the Emmitsburg road. This re-

DEAD CONFEDERATE SHARP-SHOOTER IN THE DEVIL'S DEN.
FROM A PHOTOGRAPH.

duced my front to manageable dimensions and left some force at my disposal to meet any concentrated attack that the cavalry might make.

I had just returned to the position occupied by our artillery, which was in the angle formed by the main and flanking lines, when Farnsworth's cavalry brigade charged the line held by the 1st Texas regiment. It was impossible to use our artillery to any advantage owing to the " close quarters " of the attacking cavalry with our own men — the leading squadrons forcing their horses up to the very muzzles of the rifles of our infantry. That portion of the cavalry which covered the front of the 1st Texas regiment was handsomely repulsed; but the 1st Vermont regiment, forming the Federal right wing, overlapped the 1st Texas on its left, and, striking the skirmish-line only, rode through it into the open valley in rear of our main line on the spurs of Round Top. When I first became satisfied, through information from the Texas skirmishers, that Farnsworth's brigade was massing in their front, the 9th Georgia regiment was ordered from Kern's house to the support of the batteries, the former position being now safe, as the other four regiments of Anderson's brigade were concentrated near that point. Hearing the firing and knowing its cause, the 9th Georgia came up at a run, just as the 1st Vermont Cavalry rode through our skirmish-line, led by General Farnsworth in person. Instead of moving directly upon our batteries, the cavalry directed its course up the valley toward Gettysburg, passing between the position of our artillery and our main line. Watching the direction they had taken, I sent Lieutenant Wade, of my staff, rapidly across the valley in advance of them, with orders to detach the first regiment he should come to on the main line and send it down on a run to "head them off" in that direction. He was also ordered to follow the line to the extreme right and direct Colonel Oates (15th Alabama) to strengthen his flanking skirmish-line and to close up the gap on the left of the 1st Texas where the cavalry had broken in.

Farnsworth and his cavalry in the meantime were riding in gallant style, with drawn sabers and unopposed, up the valley. As they approached Sly-der's house, and as I stood intently watch-ing them, I saw a ragged Confederate battle-flag fluttering among the trees at the foot of the opposite ridge, and the men with it soon after appeared, running out into the open ground on the farther side of the valley. It was the 4th Alabama regiment, Law's brigade, which had been taken from the main line and sent down by Lieutenant Wade. The men opened fire as they ran. The course of the cav-alry was abruptly checked and saddles were rapidly emptied. Recoiling from this fire, they turned to their left and rear, and directed their course up the hill toward the position occupied by our batteries. Bachman's battery promptly changed front to its left, so as to face the ap-

BRIGADIER-GENERAL WILLIAM N. PENDLETON, C. S. A., LEE'S CHIEF OF ARTILLERY. FROM A PHOTOGRAPH.

proaching cavalry, and, together with its infantry supports, opened a wither-ing fire at close range. Turning again to their left, Farnsworth and the few of his men who remained in their saddles directed their course toward the point where they had originally broken in, having described by this time almost a complete circle. But the gap where they had entered was now closed, and receiving another fire from that point, they again turned to the left and took refuge in the woods near the base of Round Top. When the last turn to the left was made, about half a dozen of their number separated from the main body and escaped by "running the gauntlet" to the right of the 1st Texas regiment. Farnsworth, with his little handful of gallant followers, rode upon the skirmish-line of the 15th Alabama regiment, and, pistol in hand, called upon Lieutenant Adrian, who commanded the line, to surrender. The skirmishers in return fired upon him, killing his horse and wounding Farnsworth in several places. [See p. 391.]

General Longstreet, aware of the danger that threatened our right from the attack of Kilpatrick's division, came over to my position late in the afternoon and expressed his satisfaction at the result and the promptness and good conduct of the troops engaged. We had all day held our front line, gained the evening before, and with troops drawn from that line had repulsed General Kilpatrick on our right flank. It seemed to us on the Confederate right that there was at least one little spot of "silver lining" in the cloud that hung so darkly over the field of Gettysburg after the disastrous charge of Pickett.

Late in the afternoon of July 3d I was ordered to withdraw the division from the lines it had held since the evening of the 2d to the ridge near the Emmitsburg road, from which it had advanced to the attack on that day.   McLaws's division, which had held the line to our left during the

MAJOR-GENERAL J. B. KERSHAW, C. S. A.
FROM A PHOTOGRAPH.

day, retired first, and I ordered my brigade commanders to take up the movement from left to right.   The courier who delivered the order to General Benning holding the left of the division, in designating the position to which he was to retire, pointed to the line McLaws had just abandoned. Benning, supposing that McLaws had been moved for the purpose of reënforcing our line on some other part of the field, dispatched Colonel DuBose with the 15th Georgia regiment in that direction.   McCandless's Federal brigade had, in the meantime, advanced to the ground previously held by McLaws, and attacked the 15th Georgia when it attempted to take up that position.   Colonel DuBose made a gallant but fruitless attempt to hold his ground, expecting support from the other regiments of his brigade. Being attacked in front and on both flanks by McCandless's brigade, reënforced by Nevin's, he was driven back with considerable loss.   He retired from one position to another, fighting as he retreated, and finally succeeded in extricating his regiment and rejoining his brigade.   The loss of the 15th Georgia in this affair was very heavy, including 101 prisoners, besides the killed and wounded.   In the meantime General Benning, having received a second order to retire, withdrew the remainder of his brigade without loss. The other brigades were quietly withdrawn, the Federals making no advance. We remained in our new position across the Emmitsburg road until near daylight on the 5th, when we took up our march with the rest of the army toward Fairfield Gap and the Potomac.

DEVIL'S DEN, FACING LITTLE ROUND TOP.

KERSHAW'S BRIGADE AT GETTYSBURG.

BY J. B. KERSHAW, MAJOR-GENERAL, C. S. A.

MY brigade, composed of South Carolinians,[1] constituted, with Semmes's, Wofford's, and Barksdale's brigades, the division of Major-General Lafayette McLaws, and that, with the divisions of Pickett and Hood, formed the First Corps of the Army of Northern Virginia, known as Longstreet's.

About sunset on the 1st of July we reached the top of the range of hills overlooking Gettysburg, from which could be seen and heard the smoke and din of battle, then raging in the distance. We encamped about midnight two miles from Gettysburg, on the left of the Chambersburg pike. On the 2d we were up and ready to move at 4 A. M., in obedience to orders, but, owing, as we understood at the time, to the occupancy of the road by trains of the Second Corps, Ewell's, did not march until about sunrise. With only a slight detention from trains in the way, we reached the high grounds near Gettysburg, and moved to the right of the Third Corps, Kershaw's brigade being at the head of the column, which was halted at the end of the lane leading to the Black Horse Tavern, situated some five hundred yards to our right. We lay there awaiting orders until noon, or an hour after. This position commanded a view of the Emmitsburg road about Kern's house, and during the morning a large body of troops, with flankers out in our direction, passed over that point and joined the Federal army. At length, General McLaws ordered me to move by a flank to the rear, get under the cover of the hill, and move along the bank of Marsh Creek toward the enemy, taking care to keep out of their view. In executing this order, we passed the Black Horse Tavern and followed the road leading from that point toward the Emmitsburg pike, until the head of column reached a point where the road passed over the top of a hill, from which our movement would have been plainly visible from the Federal signal station on Little Round Top. Here we were halted by General McLaws in person, while he and General Longstreet rode forward to reconnoiter. Very soon those gentlemen returned, both manifesting considerable irritation, as I thought. General McLaws ordered me

[1] The 2d, 3d, 7th, 8th and 15th South Carolina regiments, and the 3d South Carolina Battalion.—EDITORS.

to countermarch, and in doing so we passed Hood's division, which had been following us. We moved back to the place where we had rested during the morning, and thence by a country road to Willoughby Run, then dry, and down that to the school-house beyond Pitzer's. There we turned to the left through the lane, moving directly toward Little Round Top. General Longstreet here commanded me to advance with my brigade and attack the enemy at the Peach Orchard, which lay a little to the left of my line of march, some six hundred yards from us. I was directed to turn the flank of that position, extend my line along the road we were then in beyond the Emmitsburg pike, with my left resting on that road. At the same time a

battery of artillery was moved alongside of the column, parallel to my line of march. At 3 P. M. the head of my column emerged from the woods, and came into the open field in front of the stone wall which extends along by Flaherty's farm, and to the east past Snyder's. Here we were in full view of the Federal position. Their main line appeared to extend from Little Round Top, where their signal flags were flying, until it was lost to sight far away to the left. An advanced line occupied the Peach Orchard, heavily supported by artillery, and extended from that point toward our left along the Emmitsburg road. The intervening ground was occupied by open fields, interspersed

MAJOR-GENERAL E. M. LAW, C. S. A.
FROM A PHOTOGRAPH.

and divided by stone walls. The position just here seemed almost impregnable. I immediately formed line of battle along the stone wall just mentioned, my left resting about Flaherty's house, and my right near Snyder's. This was done under cover of my skirmishers, who engaged those of the enemy near the Emmitsburg road. In the meantime I examined the position of the Federals with some care. I found them in superior force, strongly posted in the Peach Orchard, which bristled with artillery, with a main line of battle in their rear, apparently intrenched, and extending to, if not upon, Little Round Top, far beyond the point at which their left had been supposed to rest. To carry out my instructions would have been, if successful in driving the enemy from the Peach Orchard, to present my own right flank and rear to a large portion of the enemy's main line of battle. I therefore placed my command in position under the cover of the stone wall, and communicated the condition of matters to Major-General McLaws. The division was then formed on this line, Semmes's brigade two hundred yards in rear and supporting Kershaw's; Barksdale's on the left of Kershaw's, with Wofford's in Barksdale's rear supporting him. Cabell's battalion of artillery was placed along the wall to Kershaw's right, and the 15th South Carolina regiment, Colonel de Saussure, was thrown to their right to support them on that flank.

In the meantime General Hood's division was moving in our rear to the right, to gain the enemy's left flank, and I was directed to commence the attack as soon as General Hood became engaged, swinging around toward the Peach Orchard, and at the same time establishing connection with Hood on my right, and coöperating with him. It was understood that he was to sweep down the Federal lines in a direction perpendicular to our line of battle. I was informed that Barksdale would move

MAJOR-GENERAL LAFAYETTE McLAWS, C. S. A. FROM A PHOTOGRAPH.

with me and conform to my movement; that Semmes would follow me, and Wofford follow Barksdale. These instructions I received in sundry messages from General Longstreet and General McLaws, and in part by personal communication with them. In my center-front was a stone farm-house [supposed to be Rose's], with a barn also of stone. These buildings were about five hundred yards from our position, and on a line with the crest of the Peach Orchard hill.

The Federal infantry was posted along the front of the orchard, and also on the face looking toward Rose's. Six of their batteries were in position, three at the orchard near the crest of the hill, and the others about two hundred yards in rear, extending in the direction of Little Round Top. Behind Rose's was a morass, and, on the right of that, a stone wall running parallel with our line, some two hundred yards from Rose's. Beyond the morass was a stony hill, covered with heavy timber and thick undergrowth, interspersed with bowlders and large fragments of rock, extending some distance toward the Federal main line, and in the direction of Round Top, and to our left and in rear of the orchard and the batteries posted there. Beyond the stone wall last mentioned, and to the right of the stony hill, was a dense forest extending far to the right. From the morass a small stream ran into this wood and along the base of the mountain. Between the stony hill and

SICKLES'S POSITION AT THE PEACH ORCHARD, VIEWED FROM THE EMMITSBURG ROAD, LOOKING SOUTH.

This and the other outline sketches were made in 1885 by C. W. Reed, of Bigelow's 9th Mass. Battery.

the forest was an interval of about one hundred yards, only sparsely covered with a scrubby undergrowth, through which a narrow road led in the direction of the mountain. Looking down this road from Rose's a large wheat-field was seen. In rear of the wheat-field, and between that and the mountain, there was a heavy force of Federals, posted in line behind a stone wall. Under my instructions I determined to move upon the stony hill, so as to strike it with my center, and thus attack the orchard on its left rear. About 4 o'clock I received the order to move, at a signal from Cabell's artillery. They were to fire for some minutes, then pause, and then fire three guns in rapid succession. At this I was to move without further orders. I communicated these instructions to the commanders of each of the regiments in my command, directing them to convey them to the company officers. They were told, at the signal, to order the men to leap the wall without further orders, and to align the troops in front of it. Accordingly, at the signal, the men leaped over the wall and were promptly aligned; the word was given, and the brigade moved off at the word, with great steadiness and precision, followed by Semmes with equal promptness. General Longstreet accompanied me in this advance on foot, as far as the Emmitsburg road. All the field and staff officers were dismounted on account of the many obstacles in the way. When we were about the Emmitsburg road, I heard Barksdale's drums beat the assembly, and knew *then* that I should have no immediate support on my left, about to be squarely presented to the heavy force of infantry and artillery at and

THE "WHEAT-FIELD," LOOKING TOWARD KERSHAW'S POSITION IN FRONT OF ROSE'S HOUSE.

PEACH ORCHARD.

THE PEACH ORCHARD, VIEWED FROM LONGSTREET'S EXTREME RIGHT ON THE EMMITSBURG ROAD.

in rear of the Peach Orchard. The 2d and 8th South Carolina regiments and James's (Third) battalion constituted the left wing of the brigade, and were then moving majestically across the fields to the left of the lane leading to Rose's, with the steadiness of troops on parade. They were ordered to change direction to the left, and attack the batteries in rear of the Peach Orchard, and accordingly moved rapidly on that point. In order to aid this attack, the direction of the 3d and 7th regiments was changed to the left, so as to occupy the stony hill and wood. After passing the buildings at Rose's, the charge of the left wing was no longer visible from my position; but the movement was reported to have been magnificently conducted until the cannoneers had left their guns and the caissons were moving off, when the order was given to "move *by the right flank*," by some unauthorized person, and was immediately obeyed by the men. The Federals returned to their guns and opened on these doomed regiments a raking fire of grape and canister, at short distance, which proved most disastrous, and for a time destroyed their usefulness. Hundreds of the bravest and best men of Carolina fell, victims of this fatal blunder. While this tragedy was being enacted, the 3d and 7th regiments were conducted rapidly to the stony hill. In consequence of the obstructions in the way, the 7th Regiment had lapped the 3d a few paces, and when they reached the cover of the stony hill I halted the line at the edge of the wood for a moment, and ordered the 7th to move by the right flank to uncover the 3d Regiment, which was promptly done. It was, no

CONFEDERATES MOVING ABOUT DEVIL'S DEN.   PEACH ORCHARD.   POSITION OF CLARK'S, PHILLIPS'S AND BIGELOW'S BATTERIES.

SICKLES'S ANGLE AT THE PEACH ORCHARD, AS SEEN FROM THE ROAD LEADING FROM THE WHEAT-FIELD TO THE PEACH ORCHARD.

doubt, this movement, observed by some one from the left, that led to the terrible mistake which cost so dearly.

The moment the line was rectified the 7th and 3d regiments advanced into the wood and occupied the stony hill, the left of the 3d Regiment swinging around and attacking the batteries to the left of that position, which, for the reasons already stated, had resumed their fire. Very soon a heavy column moved in two lines of battle across the wheat-field to attack my position in such manner as to take the 7th Regiment in flank on the right. The right wing of this regiment was then thrown back to meet this attack, under the command of Lieutenant-Colonel Bland. I then hurried in person to General Semmes, then 150 yards in my right rear, to bring him up to meet the attack on my right, and also to bring forward my right regiment, the 15th, commanded by Colonel W. G. de Saussure, which, separated from the brigade by the artillery at the time of the advance, was cut off by Semmes's brigade. In the act of leading his regiment, this gallant and accomplished commander of the 15th had just fallen when I reached it. He fell some paces in front of the line, with sword drawn, leading the advance.

General Semmes promptly responded to my call, and put his brigade in motion toward the right, preparatory to moving to the front. While his troops were moving he fell, mortally wounded. Returning to the 7th Regiment, I reached it just as the advancing column of Federals had arrived at a point some two hundred yards off, whence they poured into us a volley from their whole line, and advanced to the charge. They were handsomely received and entertained by this veteran regiment, which long kept them at bay in its front. One regiment of Semmes's brigade came at a double-quick as far as the ravine in our rear, and checked the advance of the Federals in their front. There was still an interval of a hundred yards, or thereabout, between this regiment and the right of the 7th, and into this the enemy was forcing his way, causing my right to swing back more and more; still fighting, at a distance not exceeding thirty paces, until the two wings of the regiment were nearly doubled on each other.⚓

About this time, the fire of the battery on my left having ceased, I sent for the 2d South Carolina regiment to come to the right. Before I could hear anything of them the enemy had swung around and lapped my whole line at close quarters, and the fighting was general and desperate all along the line, and so continued for some time. These men were brave veterans who had fought from Bull Run to Gettysburg, and knew the strength of their position, and so held it as long as it was tenable. The 7th Regiment finally gave way, and I directed Colonel Aiken to re-form it at the stone wall about Rose's. I passed to the 3d Regiment, then hotly engaged on the crest of the hill, and gradually swung back its right as the enemy made progress around that flank. Semmes's advanced regiment had given way. One of his regiments had mingled with the 3d, and amid rocks and trees, within a few feet of each other, these brave men, Confederates and Federals, maintained a desperate

⚓ The Union force engaged in this movement consisted of De Trobriand's brigade (Birney's division) of the Third Corps.— EDITORS.

conflict. The enemy could make no progress in front, but slowly extended around my right. Separated from view of my left, of which I could hear nothing, all my staff being with that wing, the position of the 15th Regiment being wholly unknown, the 7th having retreated, and nothing being heard of the other troops of the division, I feared the brave men around me would be surrounded by the large force of the enemy constantly increasing in numbers and all the while gradually enveloping us. In order to avoid such a catastrophe, I ordered a retreat to the buildings at Rose's. On emerging from the wood as I followed the retreat, I saw Wofford riding at the head of his fine brigade, then coming in, his left being in the Peach Orchard, which was then clear of the enemy. His movement was such as to strike the stony hill on the left, and thus turn the flank of the troops that had driven us from that position. On his approach the enemy retreated across the wheatfield, where, with the regiments of my left wing, Wofford attacked with great effect, driving the Federals upon and near to Little Round Top. I now ascertained that Barksdale had advanced upon the Peach Orchard after I had become engaged; that he had cleared that position with the assistance of my 8th South Carolina regiment, driving all before him, and, having advanced far beyond that point, until enveloped by superior forces, had fallen mortally wounded, and been left in the Federals' hands. He had passed too far to my left to afford me any relief except in silencing the batteries that had so cruelly punished my left. When Barksdale passed to the left, the regiments of my left wing moved up into the wood on the left of the stony hill, and maintained that position against heavy odds, until the advance of Wofford's brigade.

When the enemy fell back from the stony hill on General Wofford's advance, the 15th South Carolina and a portion of Semmes's brigade followed them and joined Wofford in his attack upon the retreating column. I rallied the remainder of my brigade and Semmes's at Rose's, with the assistance of Colonel Sorrel of Longstreet's staff, and advanced with them to the support of Wofford, taking position at the stone wall overlooking the forest to the right of Rose's house, some two hundred yards in front. Finding that Wofford's men were coming out, I retained them at that point to check any attempt of the enemy to follow. It was now near nightfall, and the operations of the day were over. That night we occupied the ground over which we had fought, with my left at the Peach Orchard, on the hill, and gathered the dead and wounded—a long list of brave and efficient officers and men. Captain Cunningham's company of the 2d Regiment was reported to have gone into action with forty men, of whom but four remained unhurt to bury their fallen comrades. My losses exceeded 600 men killed and wounded,—about one-half the force engaged.

A glance at the map [see pp. 299, 308] showing the positions occupied by the troops on the 2d of July, will reveal the remarkable fact that the stony hill and wood occupied by this brigade and part of Semmes's was assailed or defended by the Federal brigades of De Trobriand, Sweitzer, Tilton, and Zook, of the divisions of Birney, Barnes, and Caldwell, and of the Second, Third, and Fifth corps. Nowhere have I found any more forcible evidence

of the nature and magnitude of this struggle by McLaws's and Hood's
divisions than is contained in General Meade's report. He says:

"About 3 P. M. I rode out to the extreme left. . . . Having found Major-General Sickles, I
was explaining to him that he was too far in the advance, and discussing with him the propriety
of withdrawing, when the enemy opened upon him with several batteries, in his front and
flank, and immediately brought forward columns of infantry and made a vigorous assault. The
Third Corps sustained the shock most heroically. Troops from the Second Corps were immediately sent by Major-General Hancock to cover the right flank of the Third Corps, and soon
after the assault commenced the Fifth Corps most fortunately arrived and took position on
the left of the Third, Major-General Sykes, commanding, immediately sending a force to occupy
Round Top Ridge, where a most furious contest was maintained, the enemy making desperate
but unsuccessful efforts to secure it. Notwithstanding the stubborn resistance of the Third
Corps under Major-General Birney (Major-General Sickles having been wounded early in the
action), superiority in numbers of corps of the enemy enabling him to outflank its advance
position, General Birney was compelled to fall back and re-form behind the line originally
designed to be held.

"In the meantime, perceiving the great exertions of the enemy, the Sixth Corps, Major-
General Sedgwick, and part of the First Corps to the command of which I had assigned Major-
General Newton, particularly Lockwood's Maryland Brigade, with detachments from the Second
Corps, were all brought up at different periods, and succeeded, together with a gallant resist-
ance of the Fifth Corps, in checking and finally repulsing the assault of the enemy, who retired
in confusion and disorder about sunset, and ceased any further efforts on our extreme left." ‡

These mighty shocks of contending armies were sustained, on our part, by
two divisions of infantry numbering, with the artillery, not more than 10,000,
or at the highest estimate 13,000 men.

Kershaw's brigade remained unemployed during the 3d of July, in the position it held the evening before, along the stony hill and wood. It will be
evident to the reader that the causes of the failure of the operations here
described to achieve greater results, may be reduced to one, to wit: the want
of simultaneous movement and coöperation between the troops employed. A
careful examination of all that has been written of that eventful series of battles will show that this was the cause of all the failures. Every attack was
magnificent and successful, but failed in the end for the want of coöperation
between corps, divisions, brigades, and, in some instances, regiments of the
same brigade. The want of coöperation, or, as the Comte de Paris terms
it, the want of "coördination," caused the loss of Gettysburg to the Confederates. It will be seen, too, that there was no loss of time on the part
of McLaws's division, from the day it left Culpeper to that of its arrival at
Gettysburg. If any ensued after that, it was due to circumstances wholly
unknown to the writer. Certainly, the loss of time, if any, would not have lost
the fight, if there had been perfect coöperation of all the troops. But, except
to vindicate the truth, it is vain to inquire into the causes of our failure.

‡ In a supplementary report, General Meade amended this paragraph so as to include the First Division
of the Twelfth Corps. Lockwood's brigade belonged to the Twelfth Corps, unattached.—EDITORS.

THE LAST CONFEDERATE GUN AT GETTYSBURG—ON LONGSTREET'S RIGHT, OPPOSITE ROUND TOP.

LEE'S RIGHT WING AT GETTYSBURG.

BY JAMES LONGSTREET, LIEUTENANT-GENERAL, C. S. A.

GETTYSBURG lies partly between Seminary Ridge on the west and Cemetery Ridge on the south-east, a distance of about fourteen hundred yards dividing the crests of the two ridges. As General Lee rode to the summit of Seminary Ridge and looked down upon the town he saw the Federals in full retreat and concentrating on the rock-ribbed hill that served as a burying-ground for the city. He sent orders to Ewell to follow up the success if he found it practicable and to occupy the hill on which the enemy was concentrating. As the order was not positive, but left discretion with General Ewell, the latter thought it better to give his troops a little rest and wait for more definite instructions. I was following Hill's Corps as fast as possible, and as soon as I got possession of the road went rapidly forward to join General Lee. I found him on the summit of Seminary Ridge watching the enemy concentrate on the opposite hill. He pointed out their position to me. I took my glasses and made as careful a survey as I could from that point. After five or ten minutes I turned to General Lee and said:

"If we could have chosen a point to meet our plans of operation, I do not think we could have found a better one than that upon which they are now concentrating. All we have to do is to throw our army around by their left, and we shall interpose between the Federal army and Washington. We can get a strong position and wait, and if they fail to attack us we shall have everything in condition to move back to-morrow night in the direction of Washington, selecting beforehand a good position into which we can place our troops to receive battle next day. Finding our object is Washington or that army, the Federals will be sure to attack us. When they attack, we shall beat them, as we proposed to do before we left Fredericksburg, and the probabilities are that the fruits of our success will be great."

"No," said General Lee; "the enemy is there, and I am going to attack him there."

I suggested that such a move as I proposed would give us control of the roads leading to Washington and Baltimore, and reminded General Lee of

LUTHERAN CHURCH ON CHAMBERSBURG STREET,
GETTYSBURG, USED AS A HOSPITAL.
FROM A PHOTOGRAPH.

our original plans. If we had fallen behind Meade and had insisted on staying between him and Washington, he would have been compelled to attack and would have been badly beaten. General Lee answered, "No; they are there in position, and I am going to whip them or they are going to whip me." I saw he was in no frame of mind to listen to further argument at that time, so I did not push the matter, but determined to renew the subject the next morning. It was then about 5 o'clock in the afternoon.

On the morning of the 2d I joined General Lee and again proposed the move to Meade's left and rear. He was still unwilling to consider the proposition, but soon left me and rode off to see General Ewell and to examine the ground on our left with a view to making the attack at that point. After making the examination and talking to General Ewell, he determined to make the attack by the right, and, returning to where I was, announced his intention of so doing. His engineer officers had been along the line far enough to find a road by which the troops could move and be concealed from the Federal signal stations.

About 11 o'clock on the morning of the 2d he ordered the march, and put it under the conduct of his engineer officers, so as to be assured that the troops would move by the best route and encounter the least delay in reaching the position designated by him for the attack on the Federal left, at the same time concealing the movements then under orders from view of the Federals.

McLaws's division was in advance, with Hood following. After marching some distance there was a delay in front, and I rode forward to ascertain the cause, when it was reported to me that part of the road just in advance of us was in plain view of the Federal signal station on Round Top. To avoid that point the direction of the troops was changed. Again I found there was some delay, and ordering Hood's division, then in the rear, to move on and double with the division in front, so as to save as much time as possible, I went forward again to see the cause of the delay. It seemed there was doubt again about the men being concealed, when I stated that I could see the signal station, and there was no reason why they could not see us. It seemed to me useless, therefore, to delay the troops any longer with the idea of concealing the movement, and the two divisions advanced. As the line was deployed I rode along from left to right, examining the Federal position and putting my troops in the best position we could find. General Lee at the same time gave orders for the attack to be made by my right — following up the direction of the Emmitsburg road toward the Cemetery Ridge, holding Hood's left as well as could be toward the Emmitsburg road, McLaws to follow the movements of Hood, attacking at the Peach Orchard the Federal Third Corps, with a part of R. H. Anderson's division following the movements of McLaws to guard his left flank. As soon as the troops were in position, and we could find the points against which we should march and give the guiding points, the advance was ordered — at half-past 3 o'clock in the afternoon. The attack was made in splendid style by both divisions, and the Federal line was broken by the first impact. They retired, many of them, in the direction of Round Top behind bowlders and fences, which gave them shelter, and where they received reën-forcements.

BRIGADIER-GENERAL PAUL SEMMES, C. S. A.,
MORTALLY WOUNDED, JULY 2.
FROM A PHOTOGRAPH.

This was an unequal battle. General Lee's orders had been that when my advance was made, the Second Corps (Ewell), on his left, should move and make a simultaneous attack; that the Third Corps (Hill) should watch closely and engage so as to prevent heavy massing in front of me. Ewell made no move

BRIGADIER-GENERAL WILLIAM BARKSDALE, C. S. A.,
WOUNDED JULY 2, DIED JULY 3.
FROM A PHOTOGRAPH.

at all until about 8 o'clock at night, after the heat of the battle was over, his line having been broken by a call for one of his brigades to go elsewhere. Hill made no move whatever, save of the brigades of his right division that were covering our left.

When the battle of the 2d was over, General Lee pronounced it a success, as we were in possession of ground from which we had driven the Federals and had taken several field-pieces. The conflict had been fierce and bloody, and my troops had driven back heavy columns and had encountered a force three or four times their number, ⸗ but we had accomplished little toward victorious results. Our success of the first day had led us into

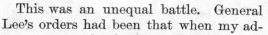

⸗ General Meade's report shows that all of the Third and parts of the Second, Fifth, Sixth, and Twelfth corps were engaged in the second day's fight. — EDITORS.

battle on the 2d, and the battle on the 2d was to lead us into the terrible and hopeless slaughter on the 3d.

On the night of the 2d I sent to our extreme right to make a little reconnoissance in that direction, thinking General Lee might yet conclude to move around the Federal left. The morning of the 3d broke clear and indicated a day on which operations would not be interrupted by the elements. The Confederate forces still occupied Seminary Ridge, while the Federals occupied the range stretching from Round Top to Cemetery Hill and around Culp's Hill. The position of the Federals was quite strong, and the battle of the 2d had concentrated them so that I considered an attack from the front more hazardous than the battle on the 2d had been. The Federals were concentrated, while our troops were stretched out in a long, broken—

DEAD IN THE "WHEAT-FIELD" GATHERED FOR BURIAL. FROM PHOTOGRAPHS.

and thus a weak—line. However, General Lee hoped to break through the Federal line and drive them off. I was disappointed when he came to me on the morning of the 3d and directed that I should renew the attack against Cemetery Hill, probably the strongest point of the Federal line. For that purpose he had already ordered up Pickett's division, which had been left at Chambersburg to guard our supply trains. In the meantime the Federals had placed batteries on Round Top, in position to make a raking fire against troops attacking the Federal front. Meade knew that if the battle was renewed it would be virtually over the same ground as my battle of the 2d. I stated to General Lee that I had been examining the ground over to the right, and was much inclined to think the best thing was to move to the Federal left.

"No," he said; "I am going to take them where they are on Cemetery Hill. I want you to take Pickett's division and make the attack. I will reënforce you by two divisions [Heth's under Pettigrew and Pender's under Trimble] of the Third Corps."

"That will give me fifteen thousand men," I replied. "I have been a soldier, I may say, from the ranks up to the position I now hold. I have been in pretty much all kinds of skirmishes, from those of two or three soldiers up to those of an army corps, and I think I can safely say there never was a body of fifteen thousand men who could make that attack successfully."

The general seemed a little impatient at my remarks, so I said nothing more. As he showed no indication of changing his plan, I went to work at once to arrange my troops for the attack. Pickett was put in position and received directions for the line of his advance as indicated by General Lee. The divisions of the Third Corps were arranged along his left with orders to take up the line of march, as Pickett passed before them, in short echelon. We were to open with our batteries, and Pickett was to move out as soon as we silenced the Federal batteries. The artillery combat was to begin with the rapid discharge of two field-pieces as our signal. As soon as the orders were communicated along the line, I sent Colonel E. P. Alexander (who was commanding a battalion of artillery and who had been an engineer officer) to select carefully a point from which he could observe the effect of our batteries. When he could discover the enemy's batteries silenced or crippled, he should give notice to General Pickett, who was ordered, upon receipt of that notice, to move forward to the attack. When I took Pickett to the crest of Seminary Ridge and explained where his troops should be sheltered, and pointed out the direction General Lee wished him to take and the point of the Federal line where the assault was to be made, he seemed to appreciate the severity of the contest upon which he was about to enter, but was quite hopeful of success. Upon receipt of notice, he was to march over the crest of the hill down the gentle slope and up the rise opposite the Federal stronghold. The distance was about fourteen hundred yards, and for most of the way the Federal batteries would have a raking fire from Round Top, while the sharp-shooters, artillery, and infantry would subject the assaulting column to a terrible and destructive fire. With my knowledge of the situation, I could see the desperate and hopeless nature of the charge and the cruel slaughter it would cause. My heart was heavy when I left Pickett. I rode once or twice along the ground between Pickett and the Federals, examining the positions and studying the matter over in all its phases so far as we could anticipate.

About 1 o'clock everything was in readiness. The signal guns broke the prevailing stillness, and immediately 150 Confederate cannon burst into a deafening roar, which was answered by a thunder almost as great from the Federal side. The great artillery combat proceeded. The destruction was, of course, not great; but the thunder on Seminary Ridge, and the echo from the Federal side, showed that both commanders were ready. The armies seemed like mighty wild beasts growling at each other and preparing for a death struggle. For an hour or two the fire was continued, and met such steady response on the part of the Federals, that it seemed less effective than

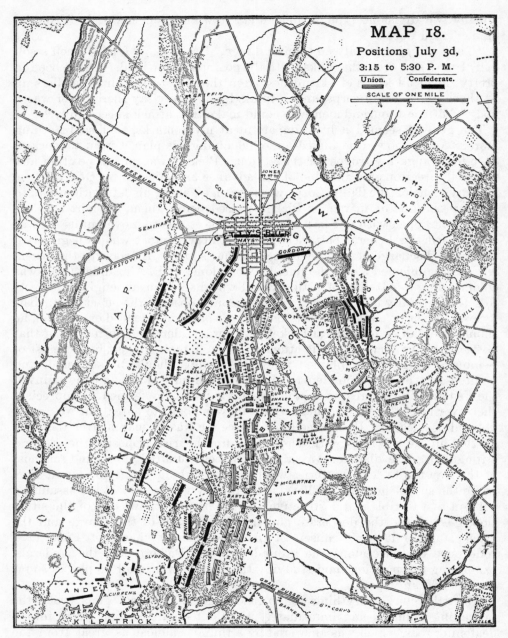

MAP 18.

Positions July 3d,
3:15 to 5:30 P. M.
Union.   Confederate.
SCALE OF ONE MILE

we had anticipated.   I sent word to Alexander that unless he could do something more, I would not feel warranted in ordering the troops forward.   After
a little, some of the Federal batteries ceased firing, possibly to save ammunition, and Alexander thought the most suitable time for the advance had
come.   He sent word to Pickett, and Pickett rode to my headquarters.   As
he came up he asked if the time for his advance had come.   I was convinced

that he would be leading his troops to needless slaughter, and did not speak. He repeated the question, and without opening my lips I bowed in answer. In a determined voice Pickett said : " Sir, I shall lead my division forward." He then remounted his horse and rode back to his command. I mounted my horse and rode to a point where I could observe the troops as they marched forward. Colonel Alexander had set aside a battery of seven guns to advance with Pickett, but General Pendleton, from whom they were borrowed, recalled them just before the charge was ordered. Colonel Alexander told me of the seven guns which had been removed, and that his ammunition was so low he could not properly support the charge. I ordered him to stop Pickett until the ammunition could be replenished, and he answered, " There is no ammunition with which to replenish." In the hurry he got together such guns as he could to move with Pickett.

MAJOR-GENERAL WILLIAM D. PENDER, WOUNDED JULY 2, DIED JULY 18. FROM A PHOTOGRAPH.

It has been said that I should have exercised discretion and should not have sent Pickett on his charge. It has been urged that I had exercised discretion on previous occasions. It is true that at times when I saw a certainty of success in another direction, I did not follow the orders of my general, but that was when he was not near and could not see the situation as it existed. When your chief is away, you have a right to exercise discretion; but if he sees everything that you see, you have no right to disregard his positive and repeated orders. I never exercised discretion after discussing with General Lee the points of his orders, *and* when, after discussion, he had ordered the execution of his policy. I had offered my objections to Pickett's battle and had been overruled, and I was in the immediate presence of the commanding general when the order was given for Pickett to advance. [See p. 355.]

That day at Gettysburg was one of the saddest of my life. I foresaw what my men would meet and would gladly have given up my position rather than share in the responsibilities of that day. It was thus I felt when Pickett at the head of 4900 brave men marched over the crest of Seminary Ridge and began his descent of the slope. As he passed me he rode gracefully, with his jaunty cap raked well over on his right ear and his long auburn locks, nicely dressed, hanging almost to his shoulders. He seemed rather a holiday soldier than a general at the head of a column which was about to make one of the grandest, most desperate assaults recorded in the annals of wars. Armistead and Garnett, two of his brigadiers, were veterans of nearly a quarter of a century's service. Their minds seemed absorbed in the men behind, and in the bloody work before them. Kemper, the other brigadier, was younger but had experienced many severe battles. He was leading my old brigade that I had drilled on Manassas plains before the first battle on that noted field. The troops advanced in well-closed ranks and with elastic step, their faces lighted

ROUND TOPS.

CLUMP OF TREES.

PROFILE OF CEMETERY RIDGE AS SEEN FROM PICKETT'S POSITION BEFORE THE CHARGE.

CEMETERY HILL.

with hope. Before them lay the ground over which they were to pass to the point of attack. Intervening were several fences, a field of corn, a little swale running through it and then a rise from that point to the Federal stronghold. As soon as Pickett passed the crest of the hill, the Federals had a clear view and opened their batteries, and as he descended the eastern slope of the ridge his troops received a fearful fire from the batteries in front and from Round Top. The troops marched steadily, taking the fire with great coolness. As soon as they passed my batteries I ordered my artillery to turn their fire against the batteries on our right then raking my lines. They did so, but did not force the Federals to change the direction of their fire and relieve our infantry. As the troops were about to cross the swale I noticed a considerable force of Federal infantry moving down as though to flank the left of our line. I sent an officer to caution the division commanders to guard against that move, at the same time sending another staff-officer with similar orders so as to feel assured the order would be delivered. Both officers came back bringing their saddles, their horses having been shot under them. After crossing the swale, the troops kept the same steady step, but met a dreadful fire at the hands of the Federal sharpshooters; and as soon as the field was open the Federal infantry poured down a terrific fire which was kept up during the entire assault. The slaughter was terrible, the enfilade fire of the batteries on Round Top being very destructive. At times one shell would knock down five or six men. I dismounted to relieve my horse and was sitting on a rail fence watching very closely the movements of the troops. Colonel Freemantle, who had taken a position behind the Third Corps where he would be out of reach of fire and at the same time have a clear view of the field, became so interested that he left his position and came with speed to join me. Just as he came up behind me, Pickett had reached a point near the Federal lines. A pause was made to close ranks and mass for the final plunge. The troops on Pickett's left, although advancing, were evidently a little shaky. Colonel Freemantle, only observing the troops of Pickett's command, said to me, " General, I would not have missed this for anything in the world." He believed it to be a complete success. I was watching the troops supporting Pickett and saw plainly they could not hold together ten minutes longer. I called his attention to the wavering condition of the two divisions of the Third Corps, and said they would not hold, that Pickett would strike and be crushed and the attack would be a failure. As Pickett's division concentrated in making the final assault, Kemper fell severely wounded. As the division threw itself against the Federal line Garnett fell and expired. The Confederate flag was planted in the Federal line, and immediately Armistead fell mortally wounded at the feet of the Federal soldiers. The wavering divisions then seemed appalled, broke their ranks, and retired. Immediately the Federals swarmed around Pickett, attacking on all sides, enveloped and broke up his command, having killed and wounded more than two thousand men in about thirty minutes. They then drove the fragments back upon our lines. As they came back I fully expected to see Meade ride to the front and lead

BRIGADIER-GENERAL LEWIS A. ARMISTEAD, C. S. A., KILLED JULY 3. FROM A PHOTOGRAPH.

his forces to a tremendous counter-charge. Sending my staff-officers to assist in collecting the fragments of my command, I rode to my line of batteries, knowing they were all I had in front of the impending attack, resolved to drive it back or sacrifice my last gun and man. The Federals were advancing a line of skirmishers which I thought was the advance of their charge. As soon as the line of skirmishers came within reach of our guns, the batteries opened again and their fire seemed to check at once the threatened advance. After keeping it up a few minutes the line of skirmishers disappeared, and my mind was relieved of the apprehension that Meade was going to follow us.

General Lee came up as our troops were falling back and encouraged them as well as he could; begged them to re-form their ranks and reorganize their forces, and assisted the staff-officers in bringing them all together again. It was then he used the expression that has been mentioned so often:

"It was all my fault; get together, and let us do the best we can toward saving that which is left us."

As our troops were driven back from the general assault an attack was made on my extreme right by several squadrons of cavalry, which succeeded in breaking through our line of pickets. They were met by a counter-move of the 9th Georgia and the well-directed fire of Captain Bachman's battery and driven back, the 11th and 59th Georgia joining in the counter-move.

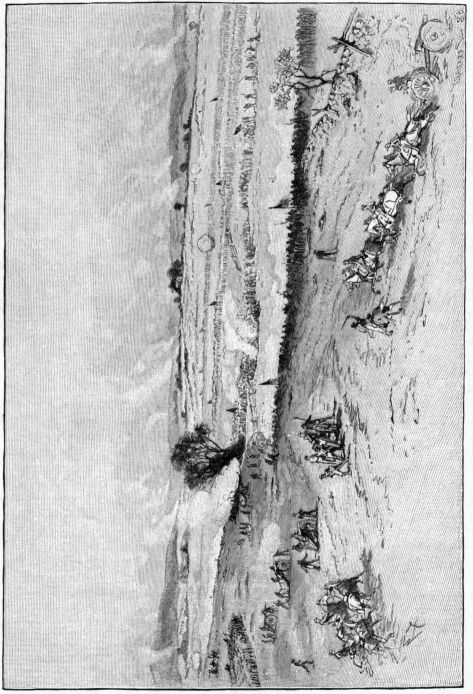

THE CHARGE OF PICKETT, PETTIGREW, AND TRIMBLE. FROM A WAR-TIME SKETCH FROM THE UNION POSITION.

Finding that Meade was not going to follow us, I prepared to withdraw my line to a better defensive position. The batteries were withdrawn well over Seminary Ridge, and orders were sent to the right for McLaws's and Hood's divisions to be withdrawn to corresponding positions. The armies remained in position, the Confederates on Seminary Ridge extending around Gettysburg, the left also drawn back, the Federals on Cemetery Ridge, until the night of the 4th, when we took up the march in retreat for Virginia.

That night, while we were standing round a little fire by the roadside, General Lee said again the defeat was all his fault. He said to me at another time, "You ought not to have made that last attack." I replied, "I had my orders, and they were of such a nature there was no escape from them." During that winter, while I was in east Tennessee, in a letter I received from him he said, "If I only had taken your counsel even on the 3d, and had moved around the Federal left, how different all might have been."

The only thing Pickett said of his charge was that he was distressed at the loss of his command. He thought he should have had two of his brigades that had been left in Virginia; with them he felt that he would have broken the line.

While I was trying to persuade General Lee to turn the Federal left on the 1st of July, Halleck telegraphed Meade as follows:

"WASHINGTON, D. C., July 1st, 1863.

"The movements of the enemy yesterday indicate his intention to either turn your left, or to cover himself by the South Mountain and occupy Cumberland Valley. Do not let him draw you too far to the east."

Again on the same day:

". . . Your tactical arrangements for battle seem good, so far as I can judge from my knowledge of the character of the country; but in a strategic view, are you not too far east, and may not Lee attempt to turn your left and cut you off from Frederick? Please give your full attention to this suggestion. . . . "

The next day, just thirty minutes before my assault, General Meade telegraphed General Halleck at 3 P. M.:

". . . If I find it hazardous to do so [meaning to attack], or am satisfied that the enemy is endeavoring to move to my rear and interpose between me and Washington, I shall fall back to my supplies at Westminster. . . . "

From this we know that the ground of the Gettysburg cemetery could have been occupied without the loss of a man, yet even at this late day, some of the Virginians, not satisfied with the sacrifice already made, wish that I, who would and could have saved every man lost at Gettysburg, should now be shot to death.

If we had made the move around the Federal left, and taken a strong position, we should have dislodged Meade without a single blow; but even if we had been successful at Gettysburg, and had driven the Federals out of their stronghold, we should have won a fruitless victory, and returned to Virginia conquered victors. The ground they occupied would have been worth no more to us than the ground we were on. What we needed was a battle that would give us decided fruits, not ground that was of no value. I do not think there was any necessity for giving battle at Gettysburg. All of our cavalry was absent, and while that has been urged by some as a reason why the battle should have been made at once, to my mind it was one of the strongest reasons for delaying the battle until everything was well in hand. The cause of the battle was simply General Lee's determination to fight it out from the position in which he was at that time. He did not feel that he was beaten on the second day, but that he was the victor, and still hoped he would be able to dislodge Meade; but he made a mistake in sending such a small number of men to attack a formidable force in a position of great natural strength, reënforced by such temporary shelter as could be collected and placed in position to cover the troops. Lee's hope in entering the campaign was that he would be in time to make a successful battle north of the Potomac, with such advantages as to draw off the army at Vicksburg as well as the Federal troops at other points.

MAJOR-GENERAL GEORGE E. PICKETT, C. S. A.   FROM A PHOTOGRAPH.

I do not think the general effect of the battle was demoralizing, but by a singular coincidence our army at Vicksburg surrendered to Grant on the 4th, while the armies of Lee and Meade were lying in front of each other, each waiting a movement on the part of the other, neither victor, neither vanquished. This surrender, taken in connection with the Gettysburg defeat, was, of course, very discouraging to our superior officers, though I do not know that it was felt as keenly by the rank and file. For myself, I felt that our last hope was gone, and that it was now only a question of time with us. When, however, I found that Rosecrans was moving down toward Georgia against General Bragg, I thought it possible we might recover some of our lost prospects by concentrating against Rosecrans, destroying his army, and advancing through Kentucky.

General Lee evidently felt severely mortified and hurt at the failure, so much so that at times he was inclined to listen to some of those who claimed to be his friends, and to accept their proposition to find a scapegoat. He resisted them, however, and seemed determined to leave the responsibility on his own hands.

For several reasons I will take occasion here to answer some serious charges that have been made against me by men who claim to have been the friends of General Lee.

Mr. Jefferson Davis, in his "Rise and Fall of the Confederate Government" (p. 441, Vol. II.), quotes from a memorial address the old story of the Rev. W. N. Pendleton:

"The ground south-west of the town was carefully examined by me after the engagement on July 1st. Being found much less difficult than the steep ascent fronting the troops already up, its practicable character was reported to our commanding general. He informed me that he had ordered Longstreet to attack on that front at sunrise the next morning. And he added to myself, 'I want you to be out long before sunrise, so as to reëxamine and save time.'

"He also desired me to communicate with General Longstreet as well as with himself. The reconnoissance was accordingly made as soon as it was light enough on the 2d, and made through a long distance — in fact, very close to what there was of the enemy's line. No insuperable difficulty appearing, and the marching up — far off, the enemy's reënforcing columns being seen, the extreme desirableness of immediate attack there was at once reported to the commanding general; and, according to his wish, message was also sent to the intrepid but deliberate corps commander, whose sunrise attack there had been ordered. There was, however, unaccountable delay. My own messages went repeatedly to General Lee, and his I know was urgently pressed on General Longstreet until, as I afterward learned from officers who saw General Lee — as I could not at the time — he manifested extreme displeasure with the tardy corps commander. That hard-fighting soldier, to whom it had been committed there to attack early in the day, did not in person reach the commanding general and with him ride to a position whence to view the ground and see the enemy's arriving masses, until 12 o'clock, and his column was not up and ready for the assault until 4 P. M. All this, as it occurred under my personal observation, it is nothing short of imperative duty that I should thus fairly state."

Mr. Davis indorses the statement thus:

"For the reasons set forth by General Pendleton, whose statement in regard to a fact coming under his personal observation none who knew him will question, preparations for a general engagement were unfortunately delayed until the afternoon instead of being made at sunrise; then troops had been concentrated, and Round Top, the commanding position unoccupied in the morning, had received the force which inflicted such disaster on our assaulting columns. The question as to the responsibility for this delay has been so fully discussed in the 'Southern Historical Society Papers' as to relieve me from the necessity of entering into it."

As General Pendleton's lecture was the capital upon which it was proposed to draw funds for a memorial church, it was natural, perhaps, that Mr. Davis should, *as a sentiment*, claim the statements made as beyond question. Most Virginia writers on this subject have taken up and followed the false scent announced by General Pendleton. Outside that State, I believe Mr. Davis and General Wilcox are the only persons who do not spurn it as false. Facts connected with this battle have been so distorted and misrepresented that a volume of distinct maps must be written in order to make a demonstration, to the letter, of all its features.

General C. M. Wilcox, in an article in the number of the "Southern Historical Society Papers" for September, 1877, refers to the order for early attack, viz.:

"It has been asserted that General Longstreet was ordered to attack at daylight or early the next morning. Of this I have no knowledge personally, but am inclined to believe that he was so ordered."

But from the *official accounts* of Generals Pendleton and Wilcox ♭ we see that the right of General Lee's army was not deployed as far as the Fairfield road on the 1st of July, that General Pendleton did not pass beyond this road, and only noted the location of the ridge on the right from his position on the Fairfield road especially as likely to be important "toward a flank movement." With this idea in his mind he leaves us to infer that he left our right and moved over to our left to supervise the posting of artillery battalions just then coming up. Soon after General Pendleton passed from about the Fairfield road to our left, the division of General R. H. Anderson,—of the Third Corps,—led by the brigade of General C. M. Wilcox, filed off to the right from the Chambersburg road, marched in an oblique direction toward the Fairfield road, where it was halted for the night, lying in bivouac till the next day, the brigade of Wilcox being on picket or guard service during the night about a mile farther to the right. In the absence of other evidence, one might be at a loss to know which of these accounts was intended in a Pickwickian sense, but the account of General R. H. Anderson, who was guileless and truthful, supports the official reports. General A. A. Humphreys (of the other side), late chief of the United States Corps of Engineers, a man whose entire life and service were devoted to official accuracy, gives similar evidence in his official report. ↓

All the subordinate reports on the Confederate side confirm the account by General Anderson, while the reports of subordinate officers on the Federal side conform to that of General Humphreys. It is conclusive therefore that the Confederates occupied no ground east of the Fairfield road till R. H. Anderson's division advanced on the morning of the 2d at 10 to find its position on the right of Hill's corps, after a clever fight between the 3d Maine and 1st U. S. Sharp-shooters against the 10th and 11th Alabama regiments.

When it is remembered that my command was at the close of the first day's fight fifteen to twenty miles west of the field, that its attack as ordered was to be made along the east side of the Emmitsburg road, that no part of General Lee's army touched that road till 9 A. M of the 2d, that up to that hour it was in possession of the Federals, and that their troops had been marching in by that road from early on the 1st till 8 A. M. on the 2d, it will be seen that General Pendleton's reconnoissance on the 1st was made, if made at all, by his passing through the Federal lines on the afternoon of the 1st and again on the morning of the 2d.

General Wilcox confesses want of personal information of the order for daylight or early attack, but expresses his confidence that the order was given. That is, he, occupying our extreme right on the 1st, on picket at a point considerably west of the Emmitsburg road, believes that General Lee ordered troops some fifteen or twenty miles off, and yet on the march, to pass his picket guard in the night to the point of attack, east of the Emmitsburg road, through the Federal lines, in order to make a daylight attack east of the road. While I am prepared to admit that General Lee ordered, at times,

♭ "Official Records," Vol. XXVII., Part II., pp. 346, 616.
↓ "Official Records," Vol. XXVII., Part I., p. 529.

desperate battles, I cannot admit that he, blindfold, ever led or ordered his next in rank, also blindfold, into night marches through the enemy's lines to gain position and make a battle at daylight next morning.

In articles formerly published on this charge of General Pendleton, masses of evidence were adduced showing that my column when ordered to the right, east of the Emmitsburg road, was conducted by General Lee's engineer officer; that when halted under the conduct of that officer I doubled the rear division on the leading one so as to save time; that my arrangements were promptly made, and that my attack was made many hours before any of our other troops were ready to obey their orders to coöperate. As I was the only one prepared for battle, I contended against the Federal army throughout the contest with two divisions and some misguided brigades sent to cover my left.

Colonel Taylor, of General Lee's staff, takes exception to the delay in the attack of Pickett on the last day under the impression that, had I attacked earlier and before Edward Johnson was driven from the Federal right, the latter might have held his ground longer and to some advantage to the Confederates. He seems to lose sight of the fact that General Lee, not I, was commanding our left under Johnson, and that he alone could order concert of action. On the 2d, notwithstanding his orders to move in concert with my attack at 4 P. M., Johnson did not go in till 8 at night, long after my battle was ended. Colonel Taylor thinks the forlorn-hope should have gone in sooner. The universal opinion now is that it should not have gone in at all; and, as already stated, that was the opinion General Lee expressed soon after the battle.

Some of our North Carolina troops seem to consider the less conspicuous part given them a reflection upon them as soldiers of true mettle and dash. This sensitiveness is not well founded. Every officer of experience knows that the best of veteran soldiers, with bloody noses from a fresh battle, are never equal to those going in fresh in their first stroke of the battle. Had Pickett's men gone through the same experience as the other troops on the 1st, they could not have felt the same zest for fighting that they did coming up fresh and feeling disparaged that the army had won new laurels in their absence. There is no doubt that the North Carolinians did as well as any soldiers could have done under the circumstances. I can truthfully attest that the old North State furnished as fine and gallant troops as any that fought in the Confederate ranks — and that is saying as much as can be said for soldiers. They certainly made sufficient sacrifice, and that was all we had left to do on that day.

During the Franco-Prussian war I kept a map of the field of operations with colored pegs, that were moved from day to day to indicate the movements of the two armies. Bazaine had been driven to shelter at Metz, McMahon had been driven back to the route leading from Paris to Metz and seemed in doubt whether he would go to Paris or to Bazaine's relief. He suffered himself to be forced north of the route between these points. On the morning that the wires brought us that information, two or three of the French Creoles of New Orleans visited my office to ask my views of the movements then proceeding. I replied, "McMahon's army will be prisoners of war in ten days." They were very indignant and stated that I was a Republican and in sympathy with the Prussians. My reply was that I had only given them my solution of a military problem. The Prussians were on the shorter route to Paris or to Metz, so that if McMahon should attempt to move in either direction the Prussians, availing themselves of the shorter lines, would interpose and force McMahon to attack; but as he had already been so beaten and demoralized, that he could not be expected to make a successful attack and would therefore be obliged to surrender. If he had gone direct to Paris before giving up his shorter route, it is possible that he could have organized a succoring army for the relief of Metz.

Had we interposed between Meade and Washington our army in almost as successful prestige as was that of the Prussians, Meade would have been obliged to attack us wherever we might be pleased to have him. He would have been badly beaten like the French, and the result would have been similar. I do not mean to say that two governments would have been permanently established; for I thought before the war, and during its continuance, that the people would eventually get together again in stronger bonds of friendship than those of their first love.

THE CHARGE OF PICKETT, PETTIGREW, AND TRIMBLE.⌡

BY J. B. SMITH.

In an address delivered by Colonel Andrew Cowan to his comrades at Gettysburg on the 3d of July, 1886, he, like nearly every other speaker and writer, ascribes all the praise of the Confederate charge of the third day to Pickett's division. He says: "Beyond the wall nothing but the gray-clad Virginians." He speaks of no other troops except Pickett's. Some writers have gone so far as to say Pickett made the immortal charge with five thousand Virginians, etc. Pickett's division was fresh, not having engaged the enemy on the first or second day, while the other troops of the assaulting body fought on the previous days with unsurpassed bravery, and some of the brigades were almost annihilated.

The grand assaulting column was formed in three divisions, and the divisions were commanded and led to the slaughter by Pickett, Pettigrew, and Trimble.

General George E. Pickett's division, composed of three brigades commanded by Generals Richard B. Garnett, Lewis A. Armistead, and James L. Kemper, was 4900 strong. Garnett fell during the progress of the charge while at the head of his column urging his men on. Armistead led his men through the terrific storm of battle to the base of the Federal works, and there he placed his cap on his sword and scaled the wall, appealing to his troops to follow him. A few of his disorganized men imitated his heroic example, and died at his feet. General Kemper was wounded in the charge.

General J. Johnston Pettigrew's command embraced the following brigades: Archer's Tennessee brigade, commanded by Colonel Fry, of the 13th Alabama; Pettigrew's North Carolina brigade, Jo Davis's Mississippi brigade, and Brockenbrough's brigade of Virginians, aggregating five thousand troops. All were of Heth's division of A. P. Hill's corps. General Pettigrew was wounded in the charge, but he did not quit the field, and remained in command until he fell at Falling Waters.

I will now notice the conduct of Archer's Tennessee brigade. It opened the battle on the first day and lost its brave and gallant commander. While leading his men he was captured by a flank movement made by the enemy. The brigade suffered heavy losses in other ways on that day. When the grand assault was made on the 3d, the 1st and 7th Tennessee regiments made the first breach in the Federal works on Cemetery Hill, and they were the only organized regiments that entered into and beyond the enemy's walls.

The 14th Tennessee, after losing heavily on the first day, went into the grand charge with 375 men, and planted its colors on the stone wall and left them there. The heroic conduct of the 13th Alabama in that awful and trying scene has been carefully written up, and the record is in the archives of the Southern Historical Society, in its native State, and will be loved and admired as long as heroism is admired. It was Archer's worn, tattered, and bleeding brigade that fought the last

⌡ From the "Bivouac" of March, 1887, and editorially revised.— Editors.

battle north of the Potomac — the battle of Falling Waters — where the lamented Pettigrew fell.

Davis's Mississippi brigade, that fought so gallantly on the first day, and crossed bayonets with the Iron Brigade, had a prominent part in the grand charge. The 2d Mississippi of that brigade lost half of its men on that day, but was still intact, ready and willing to fight, and its courage in the great charge has become a matter of history. Its battle-flag is in the possession of the old color-bearer, who lives at Blossom Prairie, Texas, and has the names of more than a score of battles stamped on it.

Scales's and Lane's North Carolina brigades, commanded by General Isaac R. Trimble, belonged to General W. D. Pender's division of A. P. Hill's corps, and were 2500 strong. General Pender was mortally wounded on the second day. When General Lee saw the men of Scales's brigade, bleeding from wounds received on the first day, he said, "Many of these poor fellows should go to the rear." When a brigade would fight under such circumstances as Scales's did, it ought not to be robbed of its military fame. General Trimble was wounded in the charge.

PRAIRIE GROVE, TEX.

A REPLY TO GENERAL LONGSTREET.

BY WILLIAM ALLAN, COLONEL, C. S. A.

GENERAL LONGSTREET'S account of Gettysburg [see pp. 244, 339] is notable for its mistakes as well as for its attitude toward General Lee and others.

First. The statement that General Lee passed over more deserving officers from other States in order to give the command of his corps to Virginians is an unworthy attack upon a man who was as singularly free from such prejudices as he was from self-seeking, either during the war or after it. Lee said in a letter to President Davis, October 2d, 1862, at the close of the Antietam campaign:

"In reference to commanders of corps with the rank of lieutenant-general, of which you request my opinion, I can confidently recommend Generals Longstreet and Jackson, in this army. My opinion of the merits of General Jackson has been greatly enhanced during this expedition. He is true, honest, and brave; has a single eye to the good of the service, and spares no exertion to accomplish his object. Next to these two officers I consider General A. P. Hill the best commander with me. He fights his troops well and takes good care of them. At present I do not think that more than two commanders of corps are necessary for this army."

This was Lee's judgment after a campaign in which both the Hills and McLaws had served, and long before there was any question of making either of them a lieutenant-general. It would be about as just to accuse Lee of undue partiality to Georgia in making Longstreet his senior lieutenant, as it is to accuse him of partiality to Virginia in selecting A. P. Hill rather than D. H. Hill or McLaws for the command of his Third Corps.

Second. In regard to the battle of Gettysburg: The first day's fight was brought on unexpectedly to Lee. In the absence of Stuart he was not aware of the proximity of the Federal army. The first day's operations were very successful. Two of the seven infantry corps of the Federal army were virtually demolished, having been defeated and driven in disorder completely from the field, leaving many killed and wounded and several thousand prisoners to the victors.

Third. It was at the close of this day's work that General Lee, in view of its results, and of the indications it gave of the position of the Federal army, decided to follow up the fight. General Longstreet advised a movement across Meade's front

to threaten his left and rear. Such a movement would have been difficult in the absence of Stuart; it could not have been executed in the position then occupied by the army with sufficient promptness to surprise Meade; and if successful it simply would have forced the Federal army back to some position nearer Baltimore and Washington where the issue of battle was still to be tried. General Longstreet begs the question when he assumes that Meade would then have been obliged to attack at a disadvantage. General Lee decided that this plan did not promise as good results as to follow up the partial victory already gained. More than one-fourth of the Federal army was beaten. (Of the First and Eleventh corps that had numbered 20,931 on June 30th, not 5700 were in line on July 2d.) That army was not concentrated, and hours must elapse before its full strength could be marshaled for battle. The absent portions would reach the field jaded by forced marches, to meet the depressing news of the defeat of their comrades. Doubt and uncertainty would prevail, increased perhaps by the fact that the present Federal commander was so new in his place. Lee's troops were much more nearly up, only Pickett's division and Law's brigade being out of reach. Not to press the Union army was to lose the greater part of the advantage of the first day's victory. The Federals would soon recover from their depression if not pressed, and his own troops would be disappointed. Lee believed if he could attack early on the second day he would have but part of the Federal army to deal with, and that if he could repeat his success of the first day the gain would be great. He therefore determined upon attack. On the night of the 1st (not on the forenoon of the 2d, as General Longstreet has it) he decided, after a conference with Ewell and his division commanders, to make the attack early next day from his right with Longstreet's two divisions that were within reach, this attack to be supported by Hill and Ewell. (See Ewell's and Early's reports: Early's paper in "Southern Historical Society Papers," Vol. IV., p. 214; and Long's "Memoirs of Lee.")

Fourth. General Longstreet would have us infer that he was not ordered by General Lee to attack early on the second day; but that his memory is at fault on this point has been abundantly shown by Generals Fitz Lee, Pendleton, Early, Wilcox, and many others. No testimony on this point is more direct and conclusive than that of General A. L. Long, then military secretary to General Lee. He says in his recently published "Memoirs of R. E. Lee" (page 277), that on the evening of the 1st, when General Lee had decided not to renew the attack on Cemetery Hill that day, he said (in Long's presence) to Longstreet and Hill: "Gentlemen, we will attack the enemy in the morning as early as practicable." Long continues: "In the conversation that succeeded he [Lee] directed them to make the necessary preparations and be ready for prompt action the next day." Long shows plainly that General Lee's design was to attack the troops in front before the whole Federal army could get up, and he described graphically the impatience Lee showed next morning, as early as 9 A. M., at Longstreet's delay. General Longstreet is wrong, too, in giving the impression that his divisions were fifteen or twenty miles away on the night of the 1st, for in his official report he says that "McLaws's division . . . reached Marsh Creek, four miles from Gettysburg, a little after dark, and Hood's division [except Law's brigade] got within nearly the same distance of the town about 12 o'clock at night." Hood says he was with his staff "in front of the heights of Gettysburg shortly after daybreak" on the 2d, and his troops were close behind. Kershaw (of McLaws's division) says in his official report that on the 1st of July they "marched to a point on the Gettysburg road some two miles from that place, going into camp at 12 P. M."

General Longstreet, to explain his delay, besides the above reasons scrapes together a number of others,— such as the presence of some Federal scouts and pickets west of the Emmitsburg road, the movement of Sickles's rear-guard along that road, the presence of one of General Lee's engineers (who had been sent to give information, not to command his corps). No time need be wasted on these. The fact is that General Longstreet, though knowing fully the condition of things on the night of the 1st, knowing that Lee had decided to attack that part of the Federal army in his front, knowing that every hour strengthened Meade and diminished the chances of Confederate success, and knowing that his corps was to open the battle and deliver the main assault, consumed the time from daylight to nearly 4 P. M., on July 2d, in moving his troops about four miles, over no serious obstacle, and in getting them into battle. Meantime on the Federal side Hancock's corps, which had camped three miles from Gettysburg, reached the field by 6 or 7 A. M.; Sickles's two brigades that had been left at Emmitsburg came up by 9 A. M.; the rear of the Fifth Corps by midday, and the Sixth Corps, after a march of thirty-two miles in thirty hours, by 2 P. M. Had Longstreet attacked not later than 9 or 10 A. M., as Lee certainly expected, Sickles's and Hancock's corps would have been defeated before part of the Fifth and the Sixth corps arrived. Little Round Top (which, as it was, the Fifth Corps barely managed to seize in time) would have fallen into Confederate possession; and even if nothing more had been done this would have given the field to the Confederates, since the Federal line all the way to Cemetery Hill was untenable with Round Top in hostile hands.

Fifth. That Longstreet's attack when made was poorly seconded by the other corps may be true, and thus another chance of winning a complete victory on July 2d was lost, but this does not change the fact that the first and great opportunity of that day for the Confederates was lost by Longstreet's delay.

Sixth. Victory on the third day was for the Confederates a far more difficult problem than on the second, but it was still within their reach. But one need not be surprised at the failure of Pickett's attack after reading of the hesitation, the want of confidence and hearty coöperation, with which General Longstreet directed it. Lee never intended that Pickett, Pettigrew, and Trimble should fight unsupported by the remainder of the army. He expected "that with proper concert of action . . . we should ultimately succeed." (Lee's report.) Longstreet was directed to use his whole corps, and when he felt embarrassed by the Federal forces on or near the Round Tops he was given a division and a half from A. P. Hill's corps, with power to call for more. General Long says: "The original intention of General Lee was that Pickett's attack should be supported by the divisions of McLaws and Hood, and General Longstreet was so ordered." ("Memoirs of Lee," p. 294. See also statements of Colonels Venable and Taylor, "Four Years with General Lee," p. 108.) Lee's efforts for a concerted attack were ineffectual. Pickett was overwhelmed not by troops in front but by those on his flanks, especially by those on his right flank, where Wilcox was sent forward too late to be of use, and where he was too weak to have effected much at best. Yet Longstreet did not use any part of Hood's and McLaws's divisions to support Pickett, or to make a diversion in his favor, or to occupy the troops on his flank which finally defeated him. These divisions were practically idle, except that one of Hood's brigades was occupied in driving off the Federal cavalry which made a dash on that flank. Longstreet, in a word, sent forward one-third of his corps to the attack, but the remainder of his troops did not coöperate. And yet he reproaches Lee for the result!

McDonogh, Md., February 16th, 1887.

CHARGE OF
ALEXANDER'S ARTILLERY.
SEE PAGE 360.

THE GREAT CHARGE AND ARTILLERY FIGHTING
AT GETTYSBURG.

BY E. PORTER ALEXANDER, BRIGADIER-GENERAL, C. S. A.

THE Reserve Artillery of Longstreet's corps, in the Gettysburg campaign, consisted of the Washington Artillery of New Orleans, then under Major Eshleman, nine guns, and my own battalion of twenty-six guns. Besides these, the artillery of the corps comprised Cabell's, Henry's, and Dearing's battalions of eighteen guns each. The latter battalions were usually attached, on the march, respectively to McLaws's, Hood's, and Pickett's divisions of infantry.

On the first of July, 1863, the Reserve Artillery was encamped near Greenwood, and we had no idea that the great battle of the campaign had already opened about eighteen miles away. Early in the night, however, rumors reached us that Hill's corps had been heavily engaged, and that Ewell's had come to his assistance; that the enemy had been driven some distance, but had finally made a stand in a very strong position. These rumors were soon followed by orders for the artillery to march at 1 o'clock for the front. There was little time for sleep before taking the road, and I think but few improved even that little. There was the usual lively interest, of course, to hear of the personal fortunes of friends in the two corps which had been engaged. Who was killed and who safe? Then there was no one so dull as not to appreciate the tremendous gravity to us of the results of the battle which the next day was to bring. We had penetrated farther into the enemy's country than ever before. Our only communication with our arsenals and depots was by an unguarded wagon-road to Staunton, Virginia, about two hundred miles, over mountains and across unbridged rivers; much of it through a hostile country, and all of it liable to cavalry raids by the enemy. But we felt that we were now, somehow, nearer the enemy's heart than we had ever been before,—within easy reach of some vital part,—and that a blow struck now must have many times the effect it would have if given in Virginia against only an invading army. Our confidence in Lee was, of course, supreme, and the opportune arrival of Ewell to Hill's aid gave fresh confirmation of the skill that would direct our efforts.   There seemed to be a prevalent feeling that fortune now favored us and that victory or defeat now depended solely on ourselves.

Except in equipment, I think a better army, better nerved up to its work, never marched upon a battle-field.   But many of our infantry still carried smooth-bore muskets, and our artillery ammunition was inferior, especially that of the rifles.   The Confederacy did not have the facilities for much nice work of that sort, and we had to take what we could get without rigid inspection.   How our rifled batteries always envied our friends in the opposition their abundant supply of splendid ammunition! For an unreliable fuse or a rifle-shell which "tumbles" sickens not only the gunner but the whole battery, more than "misfires" at large game dishearten a sportsman. There is no encouragement to careful aiming when the ammunition fails, and the men feel handicapped.   But for all our confidence that Providence had now at last consented to "come down and take a proper view of the situation," as one of our good chaplains used to pray, there was a very natural anxiety to know how the enemy had fought the day before at Gettysburg. As we met the wounded and staff-officers who had been in the action, I remember many questions asked on that subject.   There was no great comfort to be derived from the answers, which were generally in profane simile. Indeed, I have heard survivors of the war say since that some of the Federal fighting that day equaled or surpassed any they ever saw from first to last.

We marched quite steadily, with a good road and a bright moon, until about 7 A. M. on the 2d, when we halted in a grassy open grove about a mile west of Seminary Ridge, and fed and watered.   Here, soon afterward, I was sent for by General Longstreet, and, riding forward, found him with General Lee on Seminary Ridge.   Opposite, about a mile away, on Cemetery Ridge, overlooking the town, lay the enemy, their batteries making considerable display, but their infantry, behind stone walls and ridges, scarcely visible. In between us were only gentle rolling slopes of pasture and wheat-fields, with a considerable body of woods to the right and front.   The two Round Tops looked over everything, and a signal-flag was visible on the highest. Instinctively the idea arose, "If we could only take position here and have them attack us through this open ground!"   But I soon learned that we were in no such luck—the boot, in fact, being upon the other foot.

It was explained to me that our corps was to assault the enemy's left flank, and I was directed to reconnoiter it and then to take charge of all the artillery of the corps and direct it in the attack, leaving my own battalion to the command of Major Huger.   I was particularly cautioned, in moving the artillery, to keep it out of sight of the signal-station upon Round Top. ⫿

⫿ This suggests the remark that I have never understood why the enemy abandoned the use of military balloons early in 1863, after having used them extensively up to that time. Even if the observers never saw anything, they would have been worth all they cost for the annoyance and delays they caused us in trying to keep our movements out of their sight. That wretched little signal-station upon Round Top that day caused one of our divisions to lose over two hours, and probably delayed our assault nearly that long. During that time a Federal corps arrived near Round Top and became an important factor in the action which followed.—E. P. A.

CONFEDERATE ARTILLERY AT DINNER.

I immediately started on my reconnoissance, and in about three hours had a good idea of all the ground, and had Cabell's, Henry's, and my own battalions parked near where our infantry lines were to be formed and the attack begun. Dearing's battalion with Pickett's infantry was not yet up, and the Washington Artillery was left in reserve.

Through some blunder, part of our infantry had been marched on a road that brought them in sight of Round Top, and instead of taking to the fields and hollows, they had been halted for an hour, and then had been counter-marched and sent around by a circuitous road, via Black Horse Tavern, about five miles out of the way, thereby losing at least two hours.

We waited quite a time for the infantry, and I think it was about 4 o'clock when at last the word was given for Hood's division to move out and endeavor to turn the enemy's left, while McLaws awaited the development of Hood's attack, ready to assault the Peach Orchard. Henry's battalion moved out with Hood and was speedily and heavily engaged ; Cabell was ready to support him, and at once went into action near Snyder's house, about seven hundred yards from the Peach Orchard.

The Federal artillery was ready for us and in their usual full force and good practice. The ground at Cabell's position gave little protection, and he suffered rapidly in both men and horses. To help him I ran up Huger with 18 guns of my own 26, to Warfield's house, within 500 yards of the Peach Orchard, and opened upon it. This made fifty-four guns in action, and I hoped they would crush that part of the enemy's line in a very short time, but the fight was longer and hotter than I expected. So accurate was the enemy's fire, that two of my guns were fairly dismounted, and the loss of men was so great that I had to ask General Barksdale, whose brigade was lying down close behind in the wood, for help to handle the heavy 24-pounder howitzers of Moody's battery. He gave me permission to call for volunteers, and in a minute I had eight good fellows, of whom, alas! we buried two that night, and sent to the hospital three others mortally or severely wounded. At last I sent for my other two batteries, but before they arrived McLaws's division charged past our guns, and the enemy deserted their line in confusion. Then I believed that Providence was indeed " taking the proper view," and that the war was very nearly over. Every battery was limbered to the front, and the two batteries from the rear coming up, all six charged in line across the plain and went into action again at the position the enemy had deserted. I can recall no more splendid sight, on a small scale,— and certainly no more inspiriting moment during the war,— than that of the charge of these six batteries. An artillerist's heaven is to follow the routed enemy, after a tough resistance, and throw shells and canister into his disorganized and fleeing masses. Then the explosions of the guns sound louder and more powerful, and the very shouts of the gunners, ordering " Fire ! " in rapid succession, thrill one's very soul. There is no excitement on earth like it. It is far prettier shooting than at a compact, narrow line of battle, or at another battery. Now we saw our heaven just in front, and were already breathing the very air of victory. Now we would have our revenge, and make them sorry they had staid so long. Everything was in a rush. The ground was generally good, and pieces and caissons went at a gallop, some cannoneers mounted, and some running by the sides — not in regular line, but a general race and scramble to get there first.

But we only had a moderately good time with Sickles's retreating corps after all. They fell back upon fresh troops in what seemed a strong position extending along the ridge north of Round Top. Hood's troops under Law gained the slope of Little Round Top, but were driven back to its base. Our infantry lines had become disjointed in the advance, and the fighting became a number of isolated combats between brigades. The artillery took part wherever it could, firing at everything in sight, and a sort of pell-mell fighting lasted until darkness covered the field and the fuses of the flying shells looked like little meteors in the air. But then both musketry and artillery slackened off, and by 9 o'clock the field was silent. It was evident that we had not finished the job, and would have to make a fresh effort in the morning. The firing had hardly ceased when my faithful little darkey, Charlie, came up hunting for me, with a fresh horse, affectionate congratulations on my safety, and, what was equally acceptable, something to eat. Negro servants hunting for their masters were a feature of the landscape that night. I then found General Longstreet, learned what I could of the fortunes of the day on other parts of the field, and got orders for the morning. They were, in brief, that our present position was to be held and the attack renewed as soon as Pickett arrived, and he was expected early.

CONFEDERATES WAITING FOR THE END OF THE ARTILLERY DUEL.

There was a great deal to do meanwhile. Our sound horses were to be fed and watered, those killed and disabled were to be replaced from the wagon-teams, ammunition must be replenished, and the ground examined and positions of batteries rectified. But a splendid moon made all comparatively easy, and greatly assisted, too, in the care of the wounded, many of whom, both our own and the enemy's, lay about among our batteries nearly all night. About 1 o'clock I made a little bed of fence-rails, as preferable to the trampled ground in the Peach Orchard, and got two hours' sleep. At 3 I began to put the batteries in position again and was joined by the Washington Artillery, which had been in reserve the day before. As daylight came I found I had placed about twenty guns so that the enemy's batteries on Cemetery Hill enfiladed the line, and I had a panic, almost, for fear the enemy would discover my blunder and open before I could rectify it. They could not, perhaps, see down into the valley as early as I could see them, and all was right before they opened. They never could have resisted the temptation to such pot-shooting. Apparently to feel us, they fired a few shots, and hit one or two men and some horses; but we did not respond, wanting to save our ammunition for the real work, and we were grateful to them for their moderation, our ground being very unfavorable as regarded shelter.

Early in the morning General Lee came around, and I was then told that we were to assault Cemetery Hill, which lay rather to our left. This necessitated a good many changes of our positions, which the enemy did not altogether approve of, and they took occasional shots at us, though we shifted about, as inoffensively as possible, and carefully avoided getting into bunches. But we stood it all meekly, and by 10 o'clock, Dearing having come up, we had seventy-five guns in what was virtually one battery, so disposed as to fire on Cemetery Hill and the batteries south of it, which would have a fire on our advancing infantry. Pickett's division had arrived, and his men were resting and eating. Along Seminary Ridge, a short distance to our left, were sixty-three guns of A. P. Hill's corps, under Colonel R. L. Walker. As their distance was a little too great for effective howitzer fire, General Pendleton offered me the use of nine howitzers belonging to that corps. I accepted them, intending to take them into the charge with Pickett; so I put them in a hollow behind a bit of wood, with no orders but to wait there until I sent for them. About 11, some of Hill's skirmishers and the enemy's began fighting over a barn between the lines, and gradually his artillery and the enemy's took part, until over a hundred guns were engaged, and a tremendous roar was kept up for quite a time. But it gradually died out, and the whole field became as silent as a churchyard until 1 o'clock. The enemy, aware of the strength of his position, simply sat still and waited for us. It had been arranged that when the infantry column was ready, General Longstreet should order two guns fired by the Washington Artillery. ⚓ On that signal all our guns were to open on Cemetery Hill and the ridge extending toward Round Top, which was covered with batteries. I was to observe the fire and give Pickett the order to charge. I accordingly took position, about 12, at the most favorable point, just on the left of the line of guns and with one of Pickett's couriers with me. Soon after I received the following note from Longstreet:

"COLONEL: If the artillery fire does not have the effect to drive off the enemy or greatly demoralize him, so as to make our efforts pretty certain, I would prefer that you should not advise General Pickett to make the charge. I shall rely a great deal on your good judgment to determine the matter, and shall expect you to let General Pickett know when the moment offers."

This note rather startled me. If that assault was to be made on General Lee's judgment it was all right, but I did not want it made on mine. I wrote back to General Longstreet to the following effect:

"GENERAL: I will only be able to judge of the effect of our fire on the enemy by his return fire, for his infantry is but little exposed to view and the smoke will obscure the whole field. If, as I infer from your note, there is any alternative to this attack, it should be carefully considered before opening our fire, for it will take all the artillery ammunition we have left to test this one thoroughly, and, if the result is unfavorable, we will have none left for another effort. And even if this is entirely successful, it can only be so at a very bloody cost."

⚓ In the "United Service Magazine" for August, 1885, Lieutenant-Colonel William Miller Owen, of the Washington Artillery, says:

"Returning to the position of the Washington Artillery, we all quietly awaited the order to open the ball. At 1:30 P. M. a courier dashed up in great haste, holding a little slip of paper, torn evidently from a memorandum-book, on which, written in pencil and addressed to Colonel Walton, was the following:

'HEADQUARTERS, July 3d, 1863. Colonel: Let the batteries open. Order great care and precision in firing. If the batteries at the Peach Orchard cannot be used against the point we intend attacking, let them open on the enemy on the rocky hill. Most respectfully, J. LONGSTREET, Lieutenant-General Commanding.'

"The order to fire the signal-gun was immediately communicated to Major Eshleman, commanding the Washington Artillery, and the report of the first gun rang out upon the still summer air. There was a moment's delay with the second gun, a friction-primer having failed to explode. It was but a little space of time, but a hundred thousand men were listening. Finally a puff of smoke was seen at the Peach Orchard, then came a roar and a flash, and 138 pieces of Confederate artillery opened upon the enemy's position, and the deadly work began with the noise of the heaviest thunder." EDITORS.

To this presently came the following reply:

"COLONEL: The intention is to advance the infantry if the artillery has the desired effect of driving the enemy's off, or having other effect such as to warrant us in making the attack. When the moment arrives advise General Pickett, and of course advance such artillery as you can use in aiding the attack."

I hardly knew whether this left me discretion or not, but at any rate it seemed decided that the artillery must open. I felt that if we went that far we could not draw back, but the infantry must go too. General A. R. Wright, of Hill's corps, was with me looking at the position when these notes were received, and we discussed them together. Wright said, "It is not so hard to *go* there as it looks; I was nearly there with my brigade yesterday. The trouble is to *stay* there. The whole Yankee army is there in a bunch."

I was influenced by this, and somewhat by a sort of camp rumor which I had heard that morning, that General Lee had said that he was going to send every man he had upon that hill. At any rate, I assumed that the question of supports had been well considered, and that whatever was possible would be done. But before replying I rode to see Pickett, who was with his division a short distance in the rear. I did not tell him my object, but only tried to guess how he felt about the charge. He seemed very sanguine, and thought himself in luck to have the chance. Then I felt that I could not make any delay or let the attack suffer by any indecision on my part. And, that General Longstreet might know my intention, I wrote him only this: "GENERAL: When our artillery fire is at its best, I shall order Pickett to charge."

Then, getting a little more anxious, I decided to send for the nine howitzers and take them ahead of Pickett up nearly to musket range, instead of following close behind him as at first intended; so I sent a courier to bring them up in front of the infantry, but under cover of the wood. The courier could not find them. He was sent again, and only returned after our fire was opened, saying they were gone. I afterward learned that General Pendleton had sent for a part of them, and the others had moved to a neighboring hollow to get out of the line of the enemy's fire at one of Hill's batteries during the artillery duel they had had an hour before.

At exactly 1 o'clock by my watch the two signal-guns were heard in quick succession. In another minute every gun was at work. The enemy were not slow in coming back at us, and the grand roar of nearly the whole artillery of both armies burst in on the silence, almost as suddenly as the full notes of an organ would fill a church. [See p. 371.]

The artillery of Ewell's corps, however, took only a small part, I believe, in this, as they were too far away on the other side of the town. Some of them might have done good service from positions between Hill and Ewell, enfilading the batteries fighting us. The opportunity to do that was the single advantage in our having the exterior line, to compensate for all its disadvantages. But our line was so extended that all of it was not well studied, and the officers of the different corps had no opportunity to examine each other's ground for chances to coöperate.

The enemy's position seemed to have broken out with guns everywhere, and from Round Top to Cemetery Hill was blazing like a volcano. The air seemed full of missiles from every direction. The severity of the fire may be illustrated by the casualties in my own battalion under Major Huger.

Under my predecessor, General S. D. Lee, the battalion had made a reputation at the Second Manassas and also at Sharpsburg. At the latter battle it had a peculiarly hard time fighting infantry and superior metal nearly all day, and losing about eighty-five men and sixty horses. Sharpsburg they called "artillery hell." At Gettysburg the losses in the same command, including the infantry that volunteered to help serve the guns, were 144 men and 116 horses, nearly all by artillery fire. Some parts of the Federal artillery suffered in the same proportion under our fire. I heard of one battery losing 27 out of 36 horses in 10 minutes.

MAJOR-GENERAL CADMUS M. WILCOX, C. S. A.
FROM A PHOTOGRAPH.

Before the cannonade opened I had made up my mind to give Pickett the order to advance within fifteen or twenty minutes after it began. But when I looked at the full development of the enemy's batteries, and knew that his infantry was generally protected from our fire by stone walls and swells of the ground, I could not bring myself to give the word. It seemed madness to launch infantry into that fire, with nearly three-quarters of a mile to go at midday under a July sun. I let the 15 minutes pass, and 20, and 25, hoping vainly for something to turn up. Then I wrote to Pickett: "If you are coming at all you must come at once, or I cannot give you proper support; but the enemy's fire has not slackened at all; at least eighteen guns are still firing from the cemetery itself." Five minutes after sending that message, the enemy's fire suddenly began to slacken, and the guns in the cemetery limbered up and vacated the position.

We Confederates often did such things as that to save our ammunition for use against infantry, but I had never before seen the Federals withdraw their guns simply to save them up for the infantry fight. So I said, "If he does not run fresh batteries in there in five minutes, this is our fight." I looked anxiously with my glass, and the five minutes passed without a sign of life on the deserted position, still swept by our fire, and littered with dead men and horses and fragments of disabled carriages. Then I wrote Pickett, urgently: "For God's sake, come quick. The eighteen guns are gone; come quick, or my ammunition won't let me support you properly."

I afterward heard from others what took place with my first note to Pickett.

Pickett took it to Longstreet, Longstreet read it, and said nothing. Pickett said, "General, shall I advance?" Longstreet, knowing it had to be, but unwilling to give the word, turned his face away. Pickett saluted and said, "I am going to move forward, sir," galloped off to his division and immediately put it in motion. ↓

Longstreet, leaving his staff, came out alone to where I was. It was then about 1:40 P. M. I explained the situation, feeling then more hopeful, but afraid our artillery ammunition might not hold out for all we would want. Longstreet said, "Stop Pickett immediately and replenish your ammunition." I explained that it would take too long, and the enemy would recover from the effect our fire was then having, and we had, moreover, very little to replenish with. Longstreet said, "I don't want to make this attack. I would stop it now but that General Lee ordered it and expects it to go on. I don't see how it can succeed."

I listened, but did not dare offer a word. The battle was lost if we stopped. Ammunition was far too low to try anything else, for we had been fighting three days. There was a chance, and it was not my part to interfere. While Longstreet was still speaking, Pickett's division swept out of the wood and showed the full length of its gray ranks and shining bayonets, as grand a sight as ever a man looked on. Joining it on the left, Pettigrew stretched farther than I could see. General Dick Garnett, just out of the sick ambulance, and buttoned up in an old blue overcoat, riding at the head of his brigade passed us and saluted Longstreet. Garnett was a warm personal friend, and we had not met before for months. We had served on the plains together before the war. I rode with him a short distance, and then we wished each other luck and a good-bye, which was our last.

Then I rode down the line of guns, selecting such as had enough ammunition to follow Pickett's advance, and starting them after him as fast as possible. I got, I think, fifteen or eighteen in all, in a little while, and went with them. Meanwhile, the infantry had no sooner debouched on the plain than all the enemy's line, which had been nearly silent, broke out again with all its batteries. The eighteen guns were back in the cemetery, and a storm of shell began bursting over and among our infantry. All of our guns — silent as the infantry passed between them — reopened over their heads when the lines had got a couple of hundred yards away, but the enemy's artillery let us alone and fired only at the infantry. No one could have looked at that advance without feeling proud of it.

But, as our supporting guns advanced, we passed many poor, mangled victims left in its trampled wake. ⟩ A terrific infantry fire was now opened upon Pickett, and a considerable force of the enemy moved out to attack the right flank of his line. We halted, unlimbered, and opened fire upon it. Pickett's men never halted, but opened fire at close range, swarmed over the fences and among the enemy's guns — were swallowed up in smoke, and that

---

↓ See General Longstreet's statement on pp. 344, 345.—EDITORS.

⟩ I remember one with the most horrible wound that I ever saw. We were halted for a moment by a fence, and as the men threw it down for the guns to pass, I saw in one of the corners a man sitting down and looking up at me. A solid shot had carried away both jaws and his tongue. I noticed the powder smut from the shot on the white skin around the wound. He sat up and looked at me steadily, and I looked at him until the guns could pass, but nothing, of course, could be done for him.—E. P. A.

was the last of them. The conflict hardly seemed to last five minutes before they were melted away, and only disorganized stragglers pursued by a moderate fire were coming back. Just then, Wilcox's brigade passed by us, moving to Pickett's support. There was no longer anything to support, and with the keenest pity at the useless waste of life, I saw them advance. The men, as they passed us, looked bewildered, as if they wondered what they were expected to do, or why they were there. However, they were soon halted and moved back. They suffered some losses, and we had a few casualties from canister sent at them at rather long range.

From the position of our guns the sight of this conflict was grand and thrilling, and we watched it as men with a life-and-death interest in the result. If it should be favorable to us, the war was nearly over ; if against us, we each had the risks of many battles yet to go through. And the event culminated with fearful rapidity. Listening to the rolling crashes of musketry, it was hard to realize that they were made up of single reports, and that each musket-shot represented nearly a minute of a man's life in that storm of lead and iron. It seemed as if 100,000 men were engaged, and that human life was being poured out like water. As soon as it appeared that the assault had failed, we ceased firing in order to save ammunition in case the enemy should advance. But we held our ground as boldly as possible, though we were entirely without support, and very low in ammunition. The enemy gave us an occasional shot for a while and then, to our great relief, let us rest. About that time General Lee, entirely alone, rode up and remained with me for a long time. He then probably first appreciated the full extent of the disaster as the disorganized stragglers made their way back past us. The Comte de Paris, in his excellent account of this battle, remarks that Lee, as a soldier, must at this moment have foreseen Appomattox — that he must have realized that he could never again muster so powerful an army, and that for the future he could only delay, but not avert, the failure of his cause. However this may be, it was certainly a momentous thing to him to see that superb attack end in such a bloody repulse. But, whatever his emotions, there was no trace of them in his calm and self-possessed bearing. I thought at the time his coming there very imprudent, and the absence of all his staff-officers and couriers strange. It could only have happened by his express intention. I have since thought it possible that he came, thinking the enemy might follow in pursuit of Pickett, personally to rally stragglers about our guns and make a desperate defense. He had the instincts of a soldier within him as strongly as any man. Looking at Burnside's dense columns swarming through the fire of our guns toward Marye's Hill at Fredericksburg, he had said : " It is well war is so terrible or we would grow too fond of it." No soldier could have looked on at Pickett's charge and not burned to be in it. To have a personal part in a close and desperate fight at that moment would, I believe, have been at heart a great pleasure to General Lee, and possibly he was looking for one. We were here joined by Colonel Fremantle of Her Majesty's Coldstream Guards, who was visiting our army. He afterward published an excellent account of the battle in " Blackwood," and described many little incidents that took place here, such as General Lee's encouraging the retreating stragglers to rally as soon as they got back to cover, and saying that the failure was his fault, not theirs.   Colonel Fremantle especially noticed that General Lee reproved an officer for spurring a foolish horse, and advised him to use only gentle measures.   The officer was Lieutenant F. M. Colston of my staff, whom General Lee had requested to ride off to the right and try to discover the cause of a great cheering we heard in the enemy's lines.   We thought it might mean an advance upon us, but it proved to be only a greeting to some general officer riding along the line.

That was the end of the battle.   Little by little we got some guns to the rear to replenish and refit, and get in condition to fight again, and some we held boldly in advanced positions all along the line.   Sharp-shooters came out and worried some of the men, and single guns would fire on these, sometimes very rapidly, and manage to keep them back; some parts of the line had not even a picket in front.   But the enemy's artillery generally let us alone, and I certainly saw no reason to disturb the *entente cordiale*.   Night came very slowly, but came at last; and about 10 the last gun was withdrawn to Willoughby Run, whence we had moved to the attack the afternoon before.

Of Pickett's three brigadiers, Garnett and Armistead were killed and Kemper dangerously wounded.   Fry, who commanded Pettigrew's brigade, which adjoined Garnett on the left, and in the charge was the brigade of direction for the whole force, was also left on the field desperately wounded. Of all Pickett's field-officers in the three brigades only one major came out unhurt.   The men who made the attack were good enough : the only trouble was, there were not enough of them.

Next day, July 4th, we took a pretty fair position, except that it had no right flank, and awaited the enemy, who we thought would be inspired by the day to attack us.   Meanwhile the wounded and the trains were started back to the Potomac, and at night, in a pouring rain and over roads that were almost gulfs of mud, the army followed.   Providence had evidently not yet taken a " proper view of the situation."   We had not finished the war, but had to go back to Virginia and start afresh.   Yet the *morale* of the army seemed not at all affected. The defeat was attributed entirely to the position, and, if anything, it rather gave to the men confidence in what position could do for them if they had it on their side.   Had Meade attacked us at Downsville, where we were stopped for several days by high water in the Potomac, I believe we should have repulsed him easily, barring exhaustion of ammunition.

The retreat was a terrible march for the artillery, crippled as we were by the loss of so many horses in battle, and the giving out of many more on the stony roads for the lack of horseshoes.   We were compelled to trespass on the reluctant hospitality of the neighboring farmers, and send squads in every direction to get horses.   Wherever found they were to be bought, whether the owner desired to sell or not.   Of course our only money was Confederate bills, but we explained to the farmers that these would be as good as greenbacks if only they would make their own Government stop fighting us. Such transactions we called "pressing" for short; and, by the way, we often practiced it both at home and abroad, but our own people took it more complacently than did the "Dutch" farmers of Pennsylvania.

Near Hagerstown I had an experience with an old Dunkard which gave me a high and lasting respect for the people of that faith. My scouts had had a horse transaction with this old gentleman, and he came to see me about it. He made no complaint, but said it was his only horse, and as the scouts had told him we had some hoof-sore horses we should have to leave behind, he came to ask if I would trade him one of those for his horse, as without one his crop would be lost.

I recognized the old man at once as a born gentleman in his delicate characterization of the transaction as a trade. I was anxious to make the trade as square as circumstances would permit. So I assented to his taking a foot-sore horse, and offered him besides payment in Confederate money. This he respectfully but firmly declined. Considering how the recent battle had gone, I waived argument on the point of its value, but tried another suggestion. I told him that we were in Maryland as the guests of the United States; that after our departure the Government would pay all bills that we left behind, and that I would give him an order on the United States for the value of his horse and have it approved by General Longstreet. To my surprise he declined this also. I supposed then that he was simply ignorant of the bonanza in a claim against the Government, and I explained that; and, telling him that money was no object to us under the circumstances, I offered to include the value of his whole farm. He again said he wanted nothing but the foot-sore horse. Still anxious that the war should not grind this poor old fellow in his poverty, I suggested that he take two or three foot-sore horses which we would have to leave anyhow, when we marched. Then he said, "Well, sir, I am a Dunkard, and the rule of our church is an eye for an eye, and a tooth for a tooth, and a horse for a horse, and I can't break the rule."

I replied that the Lord, who made all horses, knew that a good horse was worth a dozen old battery scrubs; and after some time prevailed on him to take two, by calling one of them a gift. But that night, about midnight, we were awakened by approaching hoofs and turned out expecting to receive some order. It was my old Dunkard leading one of his foot-sores. "Well, sir," he said, "you made it look all right to me to-day when you were talking; but after I went to bed to-night I got to thinking it all over, and I don't think I can explain it to the church, and I would rather not try." With that he tied old foot-sore to a fence, and rode off abruptly. Even at this late day it is a relief to my conscience to tender to his sect this recognition of their integrity and honesty, in lieu of the extra horse which I vainly endeavored to throw into the trade. Their virtues should commend them to all financial institutions in search of incorruptible employees.

HAND-TO-HAND FOR RICKETTS'S GUNS ON
THE EVENING OF THE SECOND DAY.
SEE P. 313.

THE THIRD DAY AT GETTYSBURG.↓

BY HENRY J. HUNT, BREVET MAJOR-GENERAL, U. S. A., CHIEF OF ARTILLERY, A. P.

IN view of the successes gained on the second day, General Lee resolved to renew his efforts. These successes were:

1st. *On the right*, the lodgment at the bases of the Round Tops, the possession of Devil's Den and its woods, and the ridges on the Emmitsburg road, which gave him the coveted positions for his artillery.

2d. *On the left*, the occupation of part of the intrenchments of the Twelfth Corps, with an outlet to the Baltimore pike, by which all our lines could be taken in reverse.

3d. *At the center*, the partial success of three of Anderson's brigades in penetrating our lines, from which they were expelled only because they lacked proper support. It was thought that better concert of action might have made good a lodgment here also.

Both armies had indeed lost heavily, but the account in that respect seemed in favor of the Confederates, or at worst balanced. Pickett's and Edward Johnson's divisions were fresh, as were Posey's and Mahone's brigades of R. H. Anderson's, and William Smith's brigade of Early's division. These could be depended upon for an assault; the others could be used as supports, and to follow up a success. The artillery was almost intact. Stuart had arrived with his cavalry, excepting the brigades of Jones and Robertson, guarding the communications; and Imboden had also come up. General Lee, therefore, directed the renewal of operations both on the right and left. Ewell had been ordered to attack at daylight on July 3d, and during the night reënforced Johnson with Smith's, Daniel's, and O'Neal's brigades. Johnson had made his preparations, and was about moving, when at dawn Williams's artillery opened upon him, preparatory to an assault by Geary and Ruger for the recovery of their works. The suspension of this fire was followed by an immediate advance by both sides. A conflict ensued which lasted with varying success until near 11 o'clock, during which the Confederates were driven

↓ Continued from p. 313.— EDITORS.

out of the Union i trenchments by Geary and Ruger, aided by Shaler's brigade of the Sixth Corps. They made one or two attempts to regain possession, but were unsuccessful, and a demonstration to turn Johnson's left caused him to withdraw his command to Rock Creek. At the close of the war the scene of this conflict was covered by a forest of dead trees, leaden bullets proving as fatal to them as to the soldiers whose bodies were thickly strewn beneath them.

Longstreet's arrangements had been made to attack Round Top, and his orders issued with a view to turning it, when General Lee decided that the assault should be made on Cemetery Ridge by Pickett's and Pettigrew's divisions, with part of Trimble's. Longstreet formed these in two lines—Pickett on the right, supported by Wilcox; Pettigrew on the left, with Lane's and Scales's brigades under Trimble in the second line. Hill was ordered to hold his line with the remainder of his corps,—six brigades,—give Longstreet assistance if required, and avail himself of any success that might be gained. Finally a powerful artillery force, about one hundred and fifty guns, was ordered to prepare the way for the assault by cannonade. The necessary arrangements caused delay, and before notice of this could be received by Ewell, Johnson, as we have seen, was attacked, so that the contest was over on the left before that at the center was begun. The hoped-for concert of action in the Confederate attacks was lost from the beginning.

On the Federal side Hancock's corps held Cemetery Ridge with Robinson's division, First Corps, on Hays's right in support, and Doubleday's at the

STEUART'S BRIGADE RENEWING THE CONFEDERATE ATTACK ON CULP'S HILL, MORNING OF THE THIRD DAY.

THE 29TH PENNSYLVANIA FORMING LINE OF BATTLE ON CULP'S HILL AT 10 A. M., JULY 3.

angle between Gibbon and Caldwell. General Newton, having been assigned to the command of the First Corps, *vice* Reynolds, was now in charge of the ridge held by Caldwell. Compactly arranged on its crest was McGilvery's artillery, forty-one guns, consisting of his own batteries, reënforced by others from the Artillery Reserve. Well to the right, in front of Hays and Gibbon, was the artillery of the Second Corps under its chief, Captain Hazard. Woodruff's battery was in front of Ziegler's Grove; on his left, in succession, Arnold's Rhode Island, Cushing's United States, Brown's Rhode Island, and Rorty's New York. In the fight of the preceding day the two last-named batteries had been to the front and suffered severely. Lieutenant T. Fred Brown was severely wounded, and his command devolved on Lieutenant Perrin. So great had been the loss in men and horses that they were now of four guns each, reducing the total number in the corps to twenty-six. Daniels's battery of horse artillery, four guns, was at the angle. Cowan's 1st New York battery, six rifles, was placed on the left of Rorty's soon after the cannonade commenced. In addition, some of the guns on Cemetery Hill, and Rittenhouse's on Little Round Top, could be brought to bear, but these were offset by batteries similarly placed on the flanks of the enemy, so that on the Second Corps line, within the space of a mile, were 77 guns to oppose nearly 150. They were on an open crest plainly visible from all parts of the opposite line. Between 10 and 11 A. M., everything looking favorable at Culp's Hill, I crossed over to Cemetery Ridge, to see what might be going on at other points. Here a magnificent display greeted my eyes. Our whole front for two miles was covered by batteries already in line or going into position. They stretched — apparently in one unbroken mass — from opposite the town to the Peach Orchard, which bounded the view to the left, the ridges of which were planted thick with cannon. Never before had such a sight been witnessed on this continent, and rarely, if ever, abroad. What did it mean? It might possibly be to hold that line while its infantry was sent to aid Ewell, or to guard against a counter-stroke from us, but it most probably meant an assault on our center, to be preceded by a cannonade in order to crush our batteries and shake our infantry; at least to cause us to exhaust our ammunition in reply, so that the assaulting troops might pass in good condition over the half mile of open ground which was beyond our effective musketry fire. With such an object the cannonade would be long and followed immediately by the assault, their whole army being held in readiness to follow up a success. From the great extent of ground occupied by the enemy's batteries, it was evident that all the artillery on our west front, whether of the army corps or the reserve, must concur as a *unit*, under the chief of artillery, in the defense. This is provided for in all well-organized armies by special

BREVET MAJOR-GENERAL GEORGE S. GREENE.
FROM A PHOTOGRAPH.

rules, which formerly were contained in our own army regulations, but they had been condensed in successive editions into a few short lines, so obscure as to be virtually worthless, because, like the rudimentary toe of the dog's paw, they had become, from lack of use, mere survivals — unintelligible except to the specialist. It was of the first importance to subject the enemy's infantry, from the first moment of their advance, to such a cross-fire of our artillery as would break their formation, check their impulse, and drive them back, or at least bring them to our lines in such condition as to make them an easy prey. There was neither time nor necessity for reporting this to General Meade, and beginning on the right, I instructed the chiefs of artillery and battery commanders to withhold their fire for fifteen or twenty minutes after the cannonade commenced, then to concentrate their fire with all possible accuracy on those batteries which were most destructive to us — but slowly, so that when the enemy's ammunition was exhausted, we should have sufficient left to meet the assault. I had just given these orders to the last battery on Little Round Top, when the signal-gun was fired, and the enemy opened with all his guns. From that point the scene was indescribably grand. All their batteries were soon covered with smoke, through which the flashes were incessant, whilst the air seemed filled with shells, whose sharp explosions, with the hurtling of their fragments, formed a running accom-

GETTYSBURG FROM CULP'S HILL. FROM A PHOTOGRAPH TAKEN ABOUT 1886.

paniment to the deep roar of the guns. Thence I rode to the Artillery Reserve to order fresh batteries and ammunition to be sent up to the ridge as soon as the cannonade ceased; but both the reserve and the train had gone to a safer place. Messengers, however, had been left to receive and convey orders, which I sent by them; then I returned to the ridge. Turning into the Taneytown pike, I saw evidence of the necessity under which the reserve had "decamped," in the remains of a dozen exploded caissons, which had been placed under cover of a hill, but which the shells had managed to search out. In fact, the fire was more dangerous behind the ridge than on its crest, which I soon reached at the position occupied by General Newton behind McGilvery's batteries, from which we had a fine view as all our own guns were now in action.

Most of the enemy's projectiles passed overhead, the effect being to sweep all the open ground in our rear, which was of little benefit to the Confederates—a mere waste of ammunition, for everything here could seek shelter. And just here an incident already published may be repeated, as it illustrates a peculiar feature of civil war. Colonel Long, who was at the time on General Lee's staff, had a few years before served in my mounted battery expressly to receive a course of instruction in the use of field-artillery. At Appomattox we spent several hours together, and in the course of conversation I told him I was not satisfied with the conduct of this cannonade which I had heard was under his direction inasmuch as he had not done justice to his instruction; that his fire, instead of being concentrated on the point of attack, as it ought to have been, and as I expected it would be, was scattered over

MONUMENT OF THE 2D MASSACHUSETTS INFAN-
TRY, FACING THE EAST BASE OF CULP'S HILL.

the whole field. He was amused at the criticism and said: "I remembered my lessons at the time, and when the fire became so scattered, wondered what you would think about it!"

I now rode along the ridge to inspect the batteries. The infantry were lying down on its reverse slope, near the crest, in open ranks, waiting events. As I passed along, a bolt from a rifle-gun struck the ground just in front of a man of the front rank, penetrated the surface and passed under him, throwing him "over and over." He fell behind the rear rank, apparently dead, and a ridge of earth where he had been lying reminded me of the backwoods practice of "barking" squirrels. Our fire was deliberate, but on inspecting the chests I found that the ammunition was running low, and hastened to General Meade to advise its immediate cessation and preparation for the assault which would certainly follow. The headquarters building, immediately behind the ridge, had been abandoned, and many of the horses of the staff lay dead. Being told that the general had gone to the cemetery, I proceeded thither. He was not there, and on telling General Howard my object, he concurred in its propriety, and I rode back along the ridge, ordering the fire to cease. This was followed by a cessation of that of the enemy, under the mistaken impression that he had silenced our guns, and almost immediately his infantry came out of the woods and formed for the assault. On my way to the Taneytown road to meet the fresh batteries which I had ordered up, I met Major Bingham, of Hancock's staff, who informed me that General Meade's aides were seeking me with orders to "cease firing"; so I had only anticipated his wishes. The batteries were found and brought up, and Fitzhugh's, Weir's, and Parsons's were put in near the clump of trees. Brown's and Arnold's batteries had been so crippled that they were now withdrawn, and Brown's was replaced by Cowan's. Meantime the enemy advanced, and McGilvery opened a destructive oblique fire, reënforced by that of Rittenhouse's six rifle-guns from Round Top, which were served with remarkable accuracy, enfilading Pickett's lines. The Confederate approach was magnificent, and excited our admiration; but the story of that charge is so well

SLOCUM'S HEADQUARTERS, POWER'S HILL.

known that I need not dwell upon it further than as it concerns my own command. The steady fire from McGilvery and Rittenhouse, on their right, caused Pickett's men to "drift" in the opposite direction, so that the weight of the assault fell upon the positions occupied by Hazard's batteries. I had counted on an artillery cross-fire that would stop it before it reached our lines, but, except a few shots here and there, Hazard's batteries were silent until the enemy came within canister range. They had unfortunately exhausted their long range projectiles during the cannonade, under the orders of their corps commander, and it was too late to replace them. Had my

MENCHEY'S SPRING, BETWEEN CULP'S HILL AND THE CEMETERY GATE.

instructions been followed here, as they were by McGilvery, I do not believe that Pickett's division would have reached our line. We lost not only the fire of one-third of our guns, but the resulting cross-fire, which would have doubled its value. The prime fault was in the obscurity of our army regulations as to the artillery, and the absence of all regulations as to the proper relations of the different arms of service to one

SPANGLER'S SPRING, EAST OF CULP'S HILL.

another. On this occasion it cost us much blood, many lives, and for a moment endangered the integrity of our line if not the success of the battle. Soon after Pickett's repulse, Wilcox's, Wright's, and Perry's brigades were moved forward, but under the fire of the fresh batteries in Gibbon's front, of McGilvery's and Rittenhouse's guns and the advance of two regiments of Stannard's Vermont brigade, they soon fell back. The losses in the batteries of the Second Corps were very heavy. Of the five battery commanders and their successors on the field, Rorty, Cushing, and Woodruff were killed, and Milne was mortally and Sheldon severely wounded at their guns. So great was the destruction of men and horses, that Cushing's and Woodruff's United States, and Brown's and Arnold's Rhode Island batteries were consolidated to form two serviceable ones.

The advance of the Confederate brigades to cover Pickett's retreat showed that the enemy's line opposite Cemetery Ridge was occupied by infantry.

Our own line on the ridge was in more or less disorder, as the result of the conflict, and in no condition to advance a sufficient force for a counter-assault. The largest bodies of organized troops available were on the left, and General Meade now proceeded to Round Top and pushed out skirmishers to feel the enemy in its front. An advance to the Plum Run line, of the troops behind it, would have brought them directly in front of the numerous batteries which crowned the Emmitsburg Ridge, commanding that line and all the intervening ground; a farther advance, to the attack, would have brought them under additional heavy flank fires. McCandless's brigade,

COLONEL ELIAKIM SHERRILL, COMMANDING THE THIRD BRIGADE OF HAYS'S DIVISION, SECOND CORPS. KILLED JULY 3, 1863. FROM A PHOTOGRAPH.

supported by Nevin's, was, however, pushed forward, under cover of the woods, which protected them from the fire of all these batteries; it crossed the Wheat-field, cleared the woods, and had an encounter with a portion of Benning's brigade, which was retiring. Hood's and McLaws's divisions were falling back under Longstreet's orders to their strong position, resting on Peach Orchard and covering Hill's line. It needs but a moment's examination of the official map to see that our troops on the left were locked up. As to the center, Pickett's and Pettigrew's assaulting divisions had formed no part of A. P. Hill's line, which was virtually intact. The idea that there must have been "a gap of at least a mile" in that line, made by throwing forward these divisions, and that a prompt advance

from Cemetery Ridge would have given us the line, or the artillery in front of it, was a delusion. A prompt counter-charge after a combat between two small bodies of men is one thing; the change from the defensive to the offensive of an army, after an engagement at a single *point*, is quite another. *This* was not a "Waterloo defeat" with a fresh army to follow it up, and to have made such a change to the offensive, on the assumption that Lee had made no provision against a reverse, would have been rash in the extreme. An advance of 20,000 men from Cemetery Ridge in the face of the 140 guns then in position would have been stark madness; an immediate advance from any point, in force, was simply impracticable, and before due preparation could have been made for a change to the offensive, the favorable moment — had any resulted from the repulse — would have passed away.

Whilst the main battle was raging, sharp cavalry combats took place on both flanks of the army. On the left the principal incident was an attack made by order of General Kilpatrick on infantry and artillery in woods and behind stone fences, which resulted in considerable losses, and especially in the death of General Farnsworth, a gallant and promising officer who had but a few days before been appointed brigadier-general and had not yet received his commission. On the right an affair of some magnitude took

PICKETT'S CHARGE, I.—LOOKING DOWN THE UNION LINES FROM THE "CLUMP OF TREES."

General Hancock and staff are seen in the left center of the picture.—This and the two pictures that follow are from the Cyclorama of Gettysburg, by permission of the National Panorama Company.

place between Stuart's command of four and Gregg's of three brigades; but Jenkins's Confederate brigade was soon thrown out of action from lack of ammunition, and two only of Gregg's were engaged. Stuart had been ordered to cover Ewell's left and was proceeding toward the Baltimore pike, where he hoped to create a diversion in aid of the Confederate infantry, and in case of Pickett's success to fall upon the retreating Federal troops. From near Cress's Ridge, two and a half miles east of Gettysburg, Stuart commanded a view of the roads in rear of the Federal lines. On its northern wooded end he posted Jackson's battery, and took possession of the Rummel

PICKETT'S CHARGE, II.—THE MAIN COLLISION TO THE RIGHT OF THE "CLUMP OF TREES."
FROM THE CYCLORAMA OF GETTYSBURG.

In this hand-to-hand conflict General Armistead, of Pickett's Division, was killed, and General Webb,
of Gibbon's Division, was wounded.

farm-buildings, a few hundred yards distant. Hampton and Fitzhugh Lee
were on his left, covered by the wood, Jenkins and Chambliss on the
right, along the ridge. Half a mile east on a low parallel ridge, the
southern part of which bending west toward Cress's Ridge furnished excellent positions for artillery, was the Federal cavalry brigade of McIntosh, who
now sent a force toward Rummel's, from which a strong body of skirmishers
was thrown to meet them, and the battery opened. McIntosh now demanded
reënforcements, and Gregg, then near the Baltimore pike, brought him
Custer's brigade and Pennington's and Randol's batteries. The artillery soon
drove the Confederates out of Rummel's, and compelled Jackson's Virginia
battery to leave the ridge. Both sides brought up reënforcements and the
battle swayed from side to side of the interval. Finally the Federals were
pressed back, and Lee and Hampton, emerging from the wood, charged,
sword in hand, facing a destructive artillery fire — for the falling back of the
cavalry had uncovered our batteries. The assailants were met by Custer's
and such other mounted squadrons as could be thrown in; a *mêlée* ensued, in
which Hampton was severely wounded and the charge repulsed. Breathed's
and McGregor's Confederate batteries had replaced Jackson's, a sharp
artillery duel took place, and at nightfall each side held substantially its
original ground. Both sides claim to have held the Rummel house. The
advantage was decidedly with the Federals, who had foiled Stuart's plans.

PICKETT'S CHARGE, III.—(CONTINUATION OF THE PICTURE ON P. 378.)
FROM THE GETTYSBURG CYCLORAMA.

Thus the battle of Gettysburg closed as it had opened, with a very creditable cavalry battle.

General Lee now abandoned the attempt to dislodge Meade, intrenched a line from Oak Hill to Peach Orchard, started all his *impedimenta* to the Potomac in advance, and followed with his army on the night of July 4th, via Fairfield. This compelled Meade to take the circuitous routes through the lower passes; and the strategic advantage to Lee and disadvantage to Meade of Gettysburg were made manifest.

General Meade has been accused of slowness in the pursuit. The charge is not well founded; he lost no time in commencing, or vigor in pushing, it. As early as the morning of the 4th he ordered French at Frederick to seize and hold the lower passes, and he put all the cavalry except Gregg's and Mc-Intosh's brigades in motion to harass the enemy's anticipated retreat, and to destroy his trains and bridges at Williamsport. It stormed heavily that day, and the care of the wounded and burial of the dead proceeded whilst the enemy's line was being reconnoitered. As soon, on the 5th, as it was certain that Lee was retreating, Gregg was started in pursuit on the Chambersburg pike, and the infantry—now reduced to a little over 47,000 effectives, short of ammunition and supplies—by the lower passes. The Sixth Corps taking the Hagerstown road, Sedgwick reported the Fairfield pass fortified, a large force present, and that a fight could be had; upon which, on the 6th, Meade halted the rest of the infantry and ordered two corps to his support, but soon learning that although the pass could be carried it would cause too much delay, he resumed the march, leaving McIntosh and a brigade of the Sixth

INSIDE EVERGREEN CEMETERY, CEMETERY HILL. FROM A WAR-TIME SKETCH.

Corps to follow the enemy through the Fairfield pass. On the evening of the 4th — both armies being still in position at Gettysburg — Kilpatrick had a sharp encounter with the enemy in Monterey pass, and this was followed by daily cavalry combats on the different routes, in which much damage was done to trains and many captures of wagons, caissons, and prisoners effected. On the 5th, whilst Lee was moving through the passes, French destroyed the pontoon-bridge at Falling Waters. On the 6th — as Meade was leaving Gettysburg — Buford attacked at Williamsport and Kilpatrick toward Hagerstown, on his right, but as Imboden's train guard was strong, Stuart was up, and Longstreet close by, they had to withdraw. [See p. 427.] The enemy proceeded to construct a new bridge and intrench a strong line covering Williamsport and Falling Waters. There were heavy rains on the 7th and 8th, but the infantry corps reached Middleton on the morning of the 9th, received supplies, crossed the mountains that day, and at its close the right was at Boonsboro', and the left at Rohrersville, on the roads to Hagerstown and Williamsport. By this time the Potomac was swollen and impassable. On the 10th Meade continued his advance, and received information that the enemy had occupied a line extending from near Falling Waters, through Downsville to Funkstown, which he was intrenching. This at 1 P. M. he reported to Halleck, informing him at the same time that his cavalry had driven that of Lee to within a mile of Funkstown, and that he would next day move cautiously until he had developed the enemy's force and position. Halleck, at 9 P. M., sent him a cipher dispatch as follows:

"I think it will be best for you to postpone a general battle till you can concentrate all your forces and get up your reserves and reënforcements; I will push on the troops as fast as they arrive. It would be well to have staff-officers at the Monocacy, to direct the troops arriving where to go, and to see that they are properly fitted out. They should join you by forced marches. Beware of partial combats. Bring up and hurl upon the enemy all your forces, good and bad."

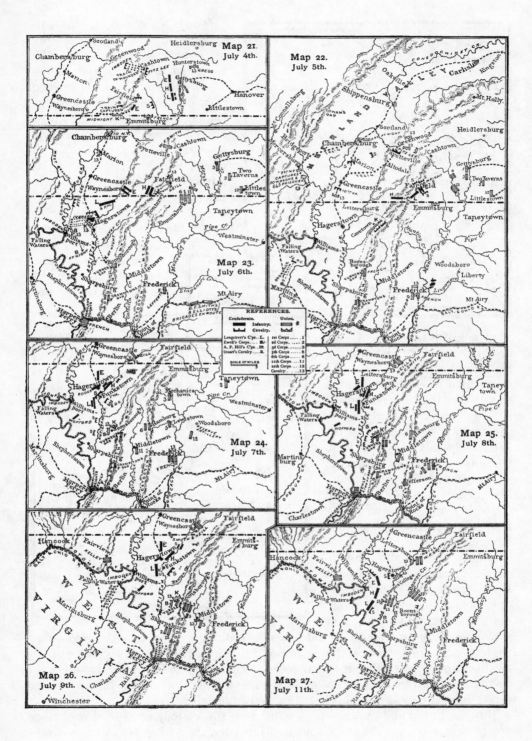

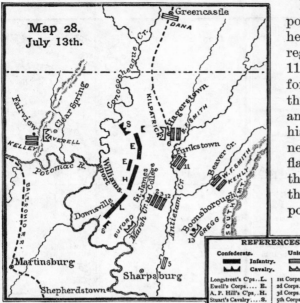

Meade, fully alive to the importance of striking Lee before he could cross the Potomac, disregarded this, advanced on the 11th, and on the 12th pushed forward reconnoissances to feel the enemy. After a partial examination made by himself and his chiefs of staff and of engineers, which showed that its flanks could not be turned, and that the line, so far as seen by them, presented no vulnerable points, he determined to make a demonstration in force on the next morning, the 13th, supported by the whole army, and to attack if a prospect of success offered. On assembling his corps commanders, however, he found their opinion so adverse that he postponed it for further examination, after which he issued the order for the next day, the 14th. On advancing that morning, it was found that the enemy had abandoned his line and crossed the river, partly by fording, partly by a new bridge.

A careful survey of the enemy's intrenched line after it was abandoned justified the opinion of the corps commanders against an attack, as it showed that an assault would have been disastrous to us. It proved also that Meade in overriding that opinion did not shrink from a great responsibility, notwithstanding his own recent experience at Gettysburg, where all the enemy's attacks on even partially intrenched lines had failed. If he erred on this occasion it was on the side of temerity.

But the hopes and expectations excited by the victory of Gettysburg were as unreasonable as the fears that had preceded it; and great was the disap-

pointment that followed the " escape " of Lee's army. It was promptly manifested, too, and in a manner which indicates how harshly and unjustly the
Army of the Potomac and its commanders were usually judged and treated;
and what trials the latter had to undergo whilst subjected to the meddling
and hectoring of a distant superior, from which they were not freed until
the general-in-chief accompanied them in the field. On the day following
Lee's withdrawal, before it was possible that all the circumstances could be
known, three dispatches passed between the respective headquarters.

First. Halleck to Meade July 14th (in part):

" I need hardly say to you that the escape of Lee's army without another battle has created
great dissatisfaction in the mind of the President, and it will require an active and energetic pursuit on your part to remove the impression that it has not been sufficiently active heretofore."

Second. Meade to Halleck July 14th:

" Having performed my duty conscientiously and to the best of my ability, the censure of the
President conveyed in your dispatch of 1 P. M. this day, is, in my judgment, so undeserved that I
feel compelled most respectfully to ask to be immediately relieved from the command of this army."

Third. Halleck to Meade July 14th:

" My telegram stating the disappointment of the President at the escape of Lee's army was
not intended as a censure, but as a stimulus to an active pursuit. It is not deemed a sufficient
cause for your application to be relieved." ☆

Whatever the object of these dispatches of General Halleck, they are perfectly consistent with a determination on the part of the War Department to

☆ At the end of July the following letters passed
between Halleck and Meade:

" [UNOFFICIAL.] HEADQUARTERS OF THE ARMY, WASH-
INGTON, July 28th, 1863. MAJOR-GENERAL MEADE, ARMY
OF THE POTOMAC, WARRENTON, VA. GENERAL: I take
this method of writing you a few words which I could not
well communicate in any other way. Your fight at Gettysburg met with universal approbation of all military
men here. You handled your troops in that battle as well,
if not better, than any general has handled his army
during the war. You brought all your forces into action
at the right time and place, which no commander of the
Army of the Potomac has done before. You may well
be proud of that battle. The President's order or proclamation of July 4th showed how much he appreciated
your success. And now a few words in regard to subsequent events. You should not have been surprised or
vexed at the President's disappointment at the escape
of Lee's army. He had examined into all the details of
sending you reënforcements to satisfy himself that
every man who could possibly be spared from other
places had been sent to your army. He thought that
Lee's defeat was so certain that he felt no little impatience at his unexpected escape. I have no doubt, General, that you felt the disappointment as keenly as any
one else. Such things sometimes occur to us without any
fault of our own. Take it all together, your short campaign has proved your superior generalship, and you
merit, as you will receive, the confidence of the Government and the gratitude of the country. I need not assure you, General, that I have lost none of the confidence
which I felt in you when I recommended you for the
command. Very respectfully, your obedient servant,
H. W. HALLECK."

" [UNOFFICIAL.] HEADQUARTERS, A. P., July 31, 1863.
MAJOR-GENERAL HALLECK, General-in-Chief. MY DEAR

GENERAL: I thank you most sincerely and heartily
for your kind and generous letter of the 28th inst., received last evening. It would be wrong in me to deny
that I feared there existed in the minds both of the
President and yourself an idea that I had failed to do
what another would and could have done in the withdrawal of Lee's army. The expression you have been
pleased to use in a letter, *to wit*, a feeling of disappointment, is one that I cheerfully accept and readily admit
was as keenly felt by myself as any one. But permit
me, dear General, to call your attention to the distinction
between disappointment and dissatisfaction. The one
was a natural feeling in view of the momentous consequences that would have resulted from a *successful* attack, but does not necessarily convey with it any censure.
I could not view the use of the latter expression in any
other light than as intending to convey an expression
of opinion on the part of the President, that I had failed
to do what I might and should have done. Now let me
say in the frankness which characterizes your letter,
that perhaps the President was right. If such was the
case, it was my duty to give him an opportunity to replace me by one better fitted for the command of the
army. It was, I assure you, with such feelings that I
applied to be relieved. It was not from any personal
considerations, for I have tried in this whole war to
forget all personal considerations, and I have always
maintained they should not for an instant influence any
one's action. Of course you will understand that I do
not agree that the President was right—and I feel sure
when the true state of the case comes to be known,
however natural and great may be the feeling of disappointment, that no blame will be attached to any one.
Had I attacked Lee the day I proposed to do so, and
in the ignorance that then existed of his position, I
have every reason to believe the attack would have
been unsuccessful and would have resulted disastrously.
This opinion is founded on the judgment of numerous

CONFEDERATE PRISONERS ON THE BALTIMORE PIKE. FROM A WAR-TIME SKETCH.

discredit under all circumstances the Army of the Potomac and any commander identified with it,—and that was the effect in this case.

The losses of both armies were very large. The revised returns show for
the Army of the Potomac: killed, 3072; wounded, 14,497; missing, 5434,—
total, 23,003 ; and for the Army of Northern Virginia: killed, 2592; wounded,
12,709; missing, 5150,—total, 20,451. But the returns for the latter army
are not complete; some commands are not reported, and in others the regimental show larger losses than do the brigade returns from which the foregoing numbers are compiled.

As to the comparative strength of the two armies on the field of battle, we
have no satisfactory data. The last Confederate return was for May 31st,
showing "Present for duty, under arms," 59,484, infantry. The morning
report of the Army of the Potomac for June 30th shows "Present for duty,
equipped," 77,208, infantry. Neither return is worth much except as a basis

distinguished officers, after inspecting Lee's vacated
works and position. Among these officers I could name
Generals Sedgwick, Wright, Slocum, Hays, Sykes, and
others.

"The idea that Lee had abandoned his lines early in
the day that he withdrew, I have positive intelligence
is not correct, and that not a man was withdrawn until
after dark. I mention these facts to remove the impression which newspaper correspondents have given
the public: that it was only necessary to advance to
secure an easy victory. I had great responsibility
thrown on me: on one side were the known and important fruits of victory, and on the other, the equally
important and terrible consequences of a defeat. I
considered my position at Williamsport very different
from that at Gettysburg. When I left Frederick it was
with the firm determination to attack and fight Lee
without regard to time or place as soon as I could come
in contact with him. But, after defeating him and requiring him to abandon his schemes of invasion, I did

not think myself justified in making a blind attack,
simply to prevent his escape, and running all the risks
attending such a venture. Now, as I said before, in
this perhaps I erred in judgment, for I take this occasion
to say to you, and through you to the President—that
I have no pretensions to any superior capacity for the
post he has assigned me to—that all I can do is to ex-
ert my utmost efforts and do the best I can; but that
the moment those who have a right to judge my actions
think or feel satisfied either that I am wanting, or
that another would do better, that moment I earnestly
desire to be relieved, not on my own account, but on
account of the country and the cause. You must excuse
so much egotism, but your kind letter in a measure
renders it necessary. I feel, General, very proud of
your good opinion, and assure you I shall endeavor in
the future to continue to merit it. Reciprocating the
kind feeling you have expressed, I remain, General,
most truly and respectfully yours, GEORGE G. MEADE,
Major-General."   EDITORS.

for guessing; the long marches, followed by the forced ones of July 1–2, of the Army of the Potomac left thousands of stragglers on the roads. These totals are of little importance; they would have been of some significance had the larger army been defeated; but it was not. At the "points of contact" the Confederates were almost always the stronger. On July 1st 18,000 Federal combatants contended against at least 25,000 Confederates, and got the worst of it. On July 2d Longstreet's 15,000 overcame Sickles's 10,000, and had to halt when a larger force was opposed to them. Williams's Twelfth Corps retook its works from a larger body of Ewell's troops, for at the contested point they were opposed by an inferior number; and then held them, for Johnson's superior force was as much hampered here by the nature of the ground as was Meade's on the left, the evening before. In many respects the Confederates had the advantage: they had much better ground for their artillery; they were fresher; they were all veterans; they were better organized; they were commanded by officers who had been selected for their experience and abilities, and in whom they had implicit confidence. These were enormous advantages, sufficient to counterbalance the difference of numbers, which, if any existed, was small; and whilst all the Confederate army, except here and there a brigade, were fought to the utmost, the strongest Federal corps (the Sixth) was hardly in action, the total loss of its eight brigades being but two hundred and forty-two killed, wounded, and missing. But the Southerners were subjected here to the disadvantages that the Northerners had to contend with in Virginia: they were surrounded by enemies, not friends who supplied them with aid and information; and they were not by choice, but by necessity, the assailants on the chosen ground of their opponents.

Right gallantly did they act their part, and their failure carried no discredit with it. Their military honor was not tarnished by their defeat, nor their spirit lowered, but their respect for their opponents was restored to what it had been before Fredericksburg and Chancellorsville.

GENERAL HANCOCK AND THE ARTILLERY AT GETTYSBURG.

I. BY FRANCIS A. WALKER, BREVET BRIGADIER-GENERAL, U. S. V.

GENERAL HUNT, in his article on "The Third Day at Gettysburg" [see p. 375], criticises General Hancock's conduct of his artillery, on the ground that his directing the Second Corps batteries to continue firing throughout the Confederate cannonade was both an encroachment upon his own (General Hunt's) proper authority, as chief of artillery of the Army of the Potomac, and an act of bad policy. On the latter point he says:

"Had my instructions been followed here, as they were by McGilvery, I do not believe that Pickett's division would have reached our line. We lost not only the fire of one-third of our guns, but the resulting cross-fire, which would have doubled its value."

This, it will be seen, constitutes a very severe impeachment. I have had much correspondence and conversation with General Hancock on the subject; and, as the heroic leader of the Second

Corps can no longer reply for himself, I beg leave to speak on his behalf.

In the first place, two antagonistic theories of authority are advanced. General Hancock claimed that he commanded *the line of battle* along Cemetery Ridge. General Hunt, in substance, alleges that General Hancock commanded the infantry of that line, and that he himself commanded the artillery. Winfield S. Hancock did not read his commission as constituting him a major-general of infantry, nor did he believe that a line of battle was to be ordered by military specialists. He knew that by both law and reason the defense of Cemetery Ridge was intrusted to him, subject to the actual, authentic orders of the commander of the Army of the Potomac, but not subject to the discretion of one of General Meade's staff-officers. General Meade could, under the President's order, have placed a junior at the head of the Second Corps, but whomsoever he did place over the corps became thereby invested with the whole undiminished substance, and with all the proper and ordinary incidents of command.

So much for the question of authority. On the question of policy there is only to be said that a difference of opinion appears between two highly meritorious officers — one, the best artillerist of the army, the other, one of the best, if not the best, commander of troops in the army — as to what was most expedient in a given emergency. Unquestionably it would have been a strong point for us if, other things being equal, the limber chests of the artillery had been full when Pickett's and Pettigrew's divisions began their great charge. But would other things have been equal? Would the advantage so obtained have compensated for the loss of *morale* in the infantry which might have resulted from allowing them to be scourged, at will, by the hostile artillery? Every soldier knows how trying and often how demoralizing it is to endure artillery fire without reply.

Now, on the question thus raised, who was the better judge, General Hunt or General Hancock? Had Henry J. Hunt taken command of a brigade

of infantry in 1861, had he for nearly two years lived with the infantry, marching with them, camping among them, commanding them in numerous actions, keeping close watch of their temper and spirit, observing their behavior under varying conditions and trials, I believe that by the 3d of July, 1863, he would have become one of the most capable and judicious corps commanders of the army. But in so doing he would necessarily have forfeited nearly all of that special experience which combined with his high intelligence and great spirit to make him one of the best artillerists whom the history of war has known. Certainly a service almost wholly in the artillery could not yield that intimate knowledge of the temper of troops which should qualify him, equally with Hancock, to judge what was required to keep them in heart and courage under the Confederate cannonade at Gettysburg, and to bring them up to the final struggle, prepared in spirit to meet the fearful ordeal of Longstreet's charge. Hancock had full authority over that line of battle; he used that authority according to his own best judgment, and he beat off the enemy. That is the substance of it.

BOSTON, January 12th, 1887.

II. REJOINDER BY HENRY J. HUNT, BREVET MAJOR-GENERAL, U. S. A.

GENERAL F. A. WALKER, of General Hancock's staff, comments on my expressed belief that, had my instructions for the cannonade of July 3d been carried out by Captain Hazard, commander of the artillery of the Second Corps, the Confederate assault would not have reached our lines, and considers this "a very severe impeachment" of General Hancock's conduct of his artillery. I fully appreciate and honor the motive of General Walker's courteous criticism, and his very kind references to myself, but he writes under misapprehensions which are widespread and misleading, and which, as they place me in a false position, I beg leave to explain.

General Hancock's claim that he commanded all the troops of every description posted on his part of Cemetery Ridge is perfectly valid. It cannot be disputed, and I never questioned it; but all commands must be exercised subject to the established principles for the government of armies. Under these, commanders of special arms issue their own orders direct to their subordinates serving with army corps, who must submit them to the corps commanders with whom they serve. The latter, being supreme on their own lines, can modify or countermand these orders, but by doing so they make themselves responsible for the result. Thus all conflicts or theories as to authority are avoided. Our "Regulations" (Scott's), adopted in 1821, read:

"The superior officer of the corps of engineers, or of the artillery, serving with one of the army corps . . . will receive the orders of the commandant thereof, to whom the said superior officer of engineers or of artillery will communicate any orders he may receive from his own particular commandant-in-chief, attached to general headquarters."

Separate paragraphs provided rules for the military "staff" and administration,—the latter including the supply departments. "Staff-officers" are forbidden to give orders except in the names of their generals. From this rule administrative officers are specially exempted, their chiefs directing their respective departments in their own names, but subject to the control of the generals under whom they serve.

All these regulations are essential to the management of a large army, but are only partly applicable to a two-company post, the school in which most of our officers, both of the war office and of the regiments, were trained. So in the "Regulations" of 1861–3, they were all condensed into one short paragraph:

"Staff-officers and commanders of artillery, engineers, and ordnance, report to their immediate commanders the state of the supplies and whatever concerns the service under their direction, and receive their orders, and communicate to them the orders they receive from their superiors in their own corps."

Closely examined, this is correct, but it is obscure and misleading. It lumps together officers of the staff and of administration as "staff-officers," and so connects them with those of the special arms as seemingly to confirm the erroneous idea that engineer officers are staff-officers, and of course that artillery officers must be the same. It is an odd notion, which could not find a lodgment in any other army than our own, that an artillery commandant-in-chief, himself a "corps commander," and provided with a staff of his own, is "one of the staff-officers" who runs about a battle-field carrying "the actual and authentic orders" of the general-in-chief to *other* corps commanders. A "staff-officer" is an officer attached to the person or headquarters of a general as his aide or assistant.

To illustrate the general principle as to the service of the special arms, I quote from the "Instructions of Frederick the Great" to his artillery. He was himself, by the way, an "artillery specialist" of the highest order, yet I have never heard it suggested that this unfitted him for "ordering a line of battle." He was also a disciplinarian of the sternest school, yet he "almost preached insubordination" in order to reduce to a minimum the mischief that meddling with the artillery by any general, even the general-in-chief, might occasion. He says:

" It sometimes happens that the general in command, or some other general, is himself forgetful, and orders the fire to be opened too soon, without considering what injurious consequences may result from it. In such case the artillery officer must certainly obey, but he should fire as slowly as possible, and point the pieces with the utmost accuracy, in order that his shots may not be thrown away."

As to the other question, that of policy, each general must decide it for himself, and General Hancock presumably acted according to his best judgment in the emergency suddenly presented to him when the cannonade opened. I do not know his reasons for countermanding my orders, and therefore cannot discuss them, even were I disposed to do so. As to the hypothetical case presented by General Walker, the possible effect of the enemy's cannonade on the *morale* of our troops, and his question, "Who was the better judge, General Hunt or General Hancock?" I may be permitted to reply, that a corps commander ought to be, so far as his own corps is concerned. It is, however, one of the necessary duties of an artillery commander to study the qualities of the other arms, for these must be considered in organizing and distributing the artillery, and are, as we see in this very case, important elements in determining its service. I had studied the Army of the Potomac, believed in its high qualities, and when, for special reasons, I instructed our batteries to withhold their fire for a given period, I knew the severity of the trial to which I was subjecting all the troops. I knew, also, that while the batteries would be the direct object of the enemy's fire, their men must stand idle at the guns and bear its full fury, while the infantry, lying on the reverse slope of the ridge and out of the enemy's sight, would be partly sheltered from it. Yet I felt no misgiving as to the fortitude of my cannoneers, and no doubt as to that of the infantry. I think I was justified by the event, for the troops on General Hancock's line, where my instructions were not followed, and those on General Newton's line (on Hancock's immediate left), where they *were* followed, were equal in "heart and courage" for the "fearful ordeal of Longstreet's charge." The object of my orders, however, was to spare them this ordeal altogether by breaking up the charge before it reached our lines. Had my orders been fully carried out, I think their whole line would have been — as half of it was — driven back before reaching our position, and this would have given us our only chance for a successful counter-attack. As it was, the splendid valor of Pickett's division alone enabled the Confederates, although defeated, to preserve their *morale* intact. Had they been repulsed without coming into immediate contact with our infantry, their *morale* would have been seriously impaired, their sense of superiority humbled.

REPELLING LEE'S LAST BLOW AT GETTYSBURG.

I. BY EDMUND RICE, BREVET LIEUTENANT-COLONEL, U. S. A.

THE brigades of Harrow, Webb, and Hall, of Gibbon's division, Hancock's corps, occupied the crest on Cemetery Ridge on July 3d. The right of Hall's and the left of Webb's brigades were in a clump of trees, called by the enemy the salient of our position, and this grove was the focus of the most fearful cannonade that preceded Pickett's charge. One regiment, the 72d Pennsylvania, in Webb's command, was a little in rear of the left of its brigade; two regiments, the 19th Massachusetts and 42d New York, Colonel A. F. Devereux commanding, of Hall's brigade, were in rear of the right of their brigade.

From the opposite ridge, three-fourths of a mile away, a line of skirmishers sprang lightly forward out of the woods, and with intervals well kept moved rapidly down into the open fields, closely followed by a line of battle, then by another, and by yet a third. Both sides watched this never-to-be-forgotten scene,— the grandeur of attack of so many thousand men. Gibbon's division, which was to stand the brunt of the assault, looked with admiration on the different lines of Confederates, marching forward with easy, swinging step, and the men were heard to exclaim: "Here they come!" "Here they come!" "Here comes the infantry!"

Soon little puffs of smoke issued from the skirmish line, as it came dashing forward, firing in reply to our own skirmishers in the plain below, and with this faint rattle of musketry the stillness was broken; never hesitating for an instant, but driving our men before it, or knocking them over by a biting fire as they rose up to run in, their skirmish line reached the fences of the Emmitsburg road. This was Pickett's advance, which carried a front of five hundred yards or more. I was just in rear of the right of the brigade, standing upon a large bowlder, in front of my regiment, the 19th Massachusetts, where, from the configuration of the ground, I had an excellent view of the advancing lines, and could see the entire formation of the attacking column. Pickett's separate brigade lines lost their formation as they swept across the Emmitsburg road, carrying with them their chain of skirmishers. They pushed on toward the crest, and merged into one crowding, rushing line,

GROUND OVER WHICH PICKETT, PETTIGREW, AND TRIMBLE CHARGED.   FROM A PHOTOGRAPH
TAKEN SINCE THE WAR.

On the left of the picture (which shows the view from the Union lines) is seen the clump of trees which was the point of direction for Pickett's men; also the monument of Webb's brigade of Gibbon's division (Second Corps), near which General Alexander S. Webb was wounded. General Armistead, of Pickett's division, was killed in the middle foreground of the picture; Codori's house is seen on the right [see also map, p. 344].—EDITORS.

many ranks deep. As they crossed the road, Webb's infantry, on the right of the trees, commenced an irregular, hesitating fire, gradually increasing to a rapid file firing, while the shrapnel and canister from the batteries tore gaps through those splendid Virginia battalions.

The men of our brigade, with their muskets at the ready, lay in waiting. One could plainly hear the orders of the officers as they commanded, "Steady, men, steady ! Don't fire !" and not a shot was fired at the advancing hostile line, now getting closer every moment. The heavy file firing on the right in Webb's brigade continued.

By an undulation of the surface of the ground to the left of the trees, the rapid advance of the dense line of Confederates was for a moment lost to view; an instant after they seemed to rise out of the earth, and so near that the expression on their faces was distinctly seen. Now our men knew that the time had come, and could wait no longer. Aiming low, they opened a deadly concentrated discharge upon the moving mass in their front. Nothing human could stand it. Staggered by the storm of lead, the charging line hesitated, answered with some wild firing which soon increased to a crashing roll of musketry, running down the whole length of their front, and then all that portion of Pickett's division which came within the zone of this terrible close musketry fire appeared to melt and drift away in the powder-smoke of both sides. At this juncture some one behind me gave the quick, impatient order : "Forward, men ! Forward ! Now is your chance !"

I turned and saw that it was General Hancock, who was passing the left of the regiment. He checked his horse and pointed toward the clump of trees to our right and front. I construed this into an order for both regiments — the 19th Massachusetts and the 42d New York — to run for the trees, to prevent the enemy from breaking

through. The men on the left of our regiment heard the command, and were up and on the run forward before the 42d New York, which did not hear Hancock's order until Colonel Devereux repeated it, had a chance to rise. The line formation of the two regiments was partially broken, and the left of the 19th Massachusetts was brought forward, as though it had executed a right half-wheel. All the men who were now on their feet could see, to the right and front, Webb's wounded men with a few stragglers and several limbers leaving the line, as the battle-flags of Pickett's division were carried over it. With a cheer the two regiments left their position in rear of Hall's right, and made an impetuous dash, racing diagonally forward for the clump of trees. Many of Webb's men were still lying down in their places in ranks, and firing at those who followed Pickett's advance, which, in the meantime, had passed over them. This could be determined by the puffs of smoke issuing from their muskets, as the first few men in gray sprang past them toward the cannon, only a few yards away. But for a few moments only could such a fire continue, for Pickett's disorganized mass rolled over, beat down, and smothered it.

One battle-flag after another, supported by Pickett's infantry, appeared along the edge of the trees, until the whole copse seemed literally crammed with men. As the 19th and 42d passed along the brigade line, on our left, we could see the men prone in their places, unshaken, and firing steadily to their front, beating back the enemy. I saw one leader try several times to jump his horse over our line. He was shot by some of the men near me.

The two regiments, in a disorganized state, were now almost at right angles with the remainder of the brigade, — the left of the 19th Massachusetts being but a few yards distant, — and the officers and men were falling fast from the enfilading fire of the hostile line in front, and from the direct fire of those who were crowded in among the trees. The advance of the two regiments became so thinned that for a moment there was a pause. Captain Farrell, of the 1st Minnesota, with his company, came in on my left. As we greeted each other he received his death-wound, and fell in front of his men, who now began firing. As I looked back I could see our men, intermixed with those who were driven out of the clump of trees a few moments before, coming rapidly forward, firing, some trying to shoot through the intervals and past those who were in front.

The gap in the line seemed to widen, for the enemy in front, being once more driven by a terrible musketry in their very faces, left to join those who had effected an entrance through Webb's line.

The men now suffered from the enfilading fire of the enemy who were in the copse. Seeing no longer an enemy in front, and annoyed by this galling fire from the flank, the 7th Michigan and 59th New York, followed directly by the 20th Massachusetts and the regiments of Harrow's brigade, left their line, faced to the right, and in groups, without regimental or other organization, joined in the rush with those already at the edge of the clump of trees, all cheering and yelling, "Hurrah! for the white trefoil!" "Clubs are trumps!" "Forward the white trefoil!" [The badge of Gibbon's division — the Second, of the Second Corps — was a white trefoil. — EDITORS.]

This was one of those periods in action which are measurable by seconds. The men near seemed to fire very slowly. Those in rear, though coming up at a run, seemed to drag their feet. Many were firing through the intervals of those in front, in their eagerness to injure the enemy. This manner of firing, although efficacious, sometimes tells on

friend instead of foe. A sergeant at my side received a ball in the back of his neck by this fire. All the time the crush toward the enemy in the copse was becoming greater. The men in gray were doing all that was possible to keep off the mixed bodies of men who were moving upon them swiftly and without hesitation, keeping up so close and continuous a fire that at last its effects became terrible. I could feel the touch of the men to my right and left, as we neared the edge of the copse. The grove was fairly jammed with Pickett's men, in all positions, lying and kneeling. Back from the edge were many standing and firing over those in front. By the side of several who were firing, lying down or kneeling, were others with their hands up, in token of surrender. In particular I noticed two men, not a musket-length away, one aiming so that I could look into his musket-barrel; the other, lying on his back, coolly ramming home a cartridge. A little farther on was one on his knees waving something white in both hands. Every foot of ground was occupied by men engaged in mortal combat, who were in every possible position which can be taken while under arms, or lying wounded or dead.

A Confederate battery, near the Peach Orchard, commenced firing, probably at the sight of Harrow's men leaving their line and closing to the right upon Pickett's column. A cannon-shot tore a horrible passage through the dense crowd of men in blue, who were gathering outside the trees; instantly another shot followed, and fairly cut a road through the mass. My thoughts were now to bring the men forward; it was but a few steps to the front, where they could at once extinguish that destructive musketry and be out of the line of the deadly artillery fire. Voices were lost in the uproar; so I turned partly toward them, raised my sword to attract their attention, and motioned to advance. They surged forward, and just

CEMETERY RIDGE AFTER PICKETT'S CHARGE. FROM A WAR-TIME SKETCH.

then, as I was stepping backward with my face to the men, urging them on, I felt a sharp blow as a shot struck me, then another; I whirled round, my sword torn from my hand by a bullet or shell splinter. My visor saved my face, but the shock stunned me. As I went down our men rushed forward past me, capturing battle-flags and making prisoners.

Pickett's division lost nearly six-sevenths of its officers and men. Gibbon's division, with its leader wounded, and with a loss of half its strength, still held the crest.

II. FROM THE OFFICIAL REPORT OF NORMAN J. HALL, COLONEL, U. S. V.

"THE object [of the heavy cannonading] was evidently to destroy our batteries and drive the infantry from the slight crest which marked the line of battle, while the concentration of fire upon the hill occupied by the Second [Webb's] and the right of the Third [Hall's] brigades indicated where the real attack was to be made. The experience of the terrible grandeur of that rain of missiles and that chaos of strange and terror-spreading sounds, unexampled, perhaps, in history, must ever remain undescribed, but can never be forgotten by those who survived it. I cannot suffer this opportunity to pass without paying just tribute to the noble service of the officers and men of the batteries that were served within my sight. Never before during this war were so many batteries subjected to so terrible a test. Horses, men, and carriages were piled together, but the fire scarcely slackened for an instant so long as the guns were standing. Lieutenant [A. H.] Cushing, of Battery A, 4th U. S. Artillery, challenged the admiration of all who saw him.☆ Three of his limbers were blown up and changed with the caisson limbers under fire. Several wheels were shot off his guns and replaced, till at last, severely wounded himself, his officers all killed or wounded, and with but cannoneers enough to man a section, he pushed his gun to the fence in front, and was killed while serving his last canister into the ranks of the advancing enemy. Knowing that the enemy's infantry would attack soon, I sent Lieutenant [William R.] Driver, acting assistant adjutant-general, to the Artillery Reserve for batteries, with orders to conduct them to the crest, if they were granted, with all possible speed. He arrived with one, which, though too late for service in arresting the advance of the enemy, yet had the opportunity to do him much damage.

"At 3 o'clock exactly the fire of the enemy slackened, and his first line of battle advanced from the woods in front in beautiful order. About one hundred yards in rear came a second line, and opposite the main point of attack was what appeared to be a column of battalions. . . . The perfect order and steady but rapid advance of the enemy called forth praise from our troops, but gave their line an appearance of being fearfully irresistible. My line was single, the only support (the 72d Pennsylvania Volunteers) having been called away by General Webb before the action had fairly commenced. There was a disposition in the men to reserve their fire for close quarters, but when I observed the movement the enemy was endeavoring to execute, I caused the 7th Michigan and 20th Massachusetts Volunteers to open fire at about two hundred yards. The deadly aim of the former regiment was attested by the line of slain within its range. This had a great effect upon the result, for it caused the enemy to move rapidly at one point, and consequently to crowd in front. Being occasioned at the point where his column was forming, he did not recover from this disorder. The remainder of our line reserved its fire until one hundred yards, some regiments waiting even until but fifty paces intervened between them and the enemy.

"There was but a moment of doubtful contest in front of the position of this brigade. The enemy halted to deliver his fire, wavered, and fled, while the line of the fallen perfectly marked the limit of his advance. The troops were pouring into the ranks of the fleeing enemy that rapid and accurate fire, the delivery of which victorious lines always so much enjoy, when I saw that a portion of the line of General Webb on my right had given way, and many men were making to the rear as fast as possible, while the enemy was pouring over the rails [surmounting a low stone wall.—EDITORS] that had been a slight cover for the troops.

"Having gained this apparent advantage, the enemy seemed to turn again and reëngage my whole line. Going to the left, I found two regiments that could be spared from some command there, and endeavored to move them by the right flank to the break; but, coming under a warm fire, they crowded to the slight cover of the rail fence, mixing with the troops already there. Finding it impossible to draw them out and re-form, and seeing no unengaged troops within reach, I was forced to order my own brigade back from the line, and move it by the flank under a heavy fire. The enemy was rapidly gaining a foothold; organization was mostly lost; in the confusion commands were useless, while a disposition on the part of the men to fall back a pace or two each time to load gave the line a retiring direction. With the officers of my staff and a few others, who seemed to comprehend what was required, the head of the line, still slowly moving by the flank, was crowded closer to the enemy, and the men obliged to load in their places. I did not see any man of my command who appeared disposed to run away, but the confusion first caused by the two regiments above spoken of so destroyed the formation in two ranks that in some places the line was several files deep. . . . During this time the 15th Massachusetts Volunteers, 1st Minnesota, and 19th Maine Volunteers from the

☆ Cushing was a brother of Lieutenant W. B. Cushing, famous for his destruction of the Confederate ram *Albemarle*.—EDITORS.

First Brigade [Harrow's] of this division had joined the line, and are entitled to a full share in the credit of the final repulse.

"The line remained in this way for about ten minutes, rather giving way than advancing, when, by a simultaneous effort on the part of all the officers I could instruct, aided by the general advance of many of the colors, the line closed with the enemy, and after a few minutes of desperate, often hand-to-hand fighting, the crowd—for such

had become that part of the enemy's column that had passed the fence—threw down their arms and were taken prisoners of war, while the remainder broke and fled in great disorder. The Second Brigade had again joined the right of my line, which now occupied the position originally held by that command. Generals Garnett and Armistead [of Pickett's Division] were picked up near this point, together with many colonels and officers of other grades."

III. FROM THE REPORT OF ALEXANDER S. WEBB, BREVET MAJOR-GENERAL, U. S. A.

"ABOUT 1 P. M. the enemy opened with more than twenty batteries upon our line; by 2:45 o'clock had silenced the Rhode Island battery and all the guns but one of Cushing's battery, and had plainly shown by his concentration of fire on this and the Third Brigade that an important assault was to be expected. I had sent, at 2 P. M., Captain Banes, assistant adjutant-general of the brigade, for two batteries to replace Cushing's and Brown's. Just before the assault, Captain Wheeler's [Cowan's] battery, First New York Artillery [First New York Independent Battery], had gotten in position on the left, in the place occupied by the Rhode Island battery, which had retired with a loss of all its officers but one.

"At 3 o'clock the enemy's line of battle left the woods in our front, moved in perfect order across the Emmitsburg road, formed in the hollow in our immediate front several lines of battle, under a fire of spherical case from Wheeler's [Cowan's] battery and Cushing's gun, and advanced for the assault. The 71st Pennsylvania Volunteers were advanced to the wall on the right of the 69th Pennsylvania Volunteers. Three of Cushing's guns were run down to the fence, carrying with them their canister. The 72d Pennsylvania Volunteers were held in reserve under the crest of the hill. The enemy advanced steadily to the fence, driving out a portion of the 71st Pennsylvania Volunteers. General Armistead passed over the fence with probably over one hundred of his command, and with several battle-flags. The 72d Pennsylvania Volunteers were ordered up to hold the crest, and advanced to within forty paces of the enemy's line. Colonel R. P. Smith, commanding the 71st Pennsylvania Volunteers, threw two

companies of his command behind the stone wall on the right of Cushing's battery, fifty paces retired from the point of attack. This disposition of his troops was most important. Colonel Smith showed true military intelligence on the field. The 69th Pennsylvania Volunteers and most of the 71st Pennsylvania Volunteers, even after the enemy were in their rear, held their position. The 72d Pennsylvania Volunteers fought steadily and persistently, but the enemy would probably have succeeded in piercing our lines had not Colonel Hall advanced with several of his regiments to my support. Defeated, routed, the enemy fled in disorder. General Armistead was left, mortally wounded, within my lines, and forty-two of the enemy who crossed the fence lay dead.

"This [Webb's] brigade captured nearly 1000 prisoners, 6 battle-flags (4 have been turned in), and picked up 1400 stand of arms and 903 sets of accouterments. . . . The conduct of this brigade was most satisfactory; officers and men did their whole duty. The 69th Pennsylvania Volunteers lost all its field-officers, but held its ground; the cover in its front was not well built, and it lost many men lying on the ground; still, I saw none retire from the fence. A portion of the 106th Pennsylvania Volunteers, left behind the previous evening under Captain Ford, took part in repelling the assault. I lost gallant officers and men; they need no tribute from me; a nominal list has been sent in. . . . Lieutenant A. H. Cushing, 4th United States Artillery, fell, mortally wounded, at the fence by the side of his guns. Cool, brave, competent, he fought for an hour and a half after he had reported to me that he was wounded in both thighs."

IV. BY L. E. BICKNELL, LIEUTENANT, 1ST MASS. SHARP-SHOOTERS.

UPON the excursion of Massachusetts veterans to Gettysburg, I found a monument in Ziegler's Grove to the 88th Pennsylvania Volunteers. It marks the spot where our infantry were being rapidly cut down by the enemy's sharp-shooters in their front on the morning of the 3d of July, the third day's fight. In fact, when, with twenty of the 1st Company of Massachusetts sharp-shooters, I entered the grove, our infantry were virtually driven from it. We held the grove, to the right and left of the monument, until the heavy cannonading checked the sharp-shooting. A shattered remnant of some regiment, perhaps the one which had suf-

fered so in front of and in the grove, lay along the remnants of a stone wall in our rear, and during the heavy cannonading which preceded the many others sought the seeming shelter of the grove.

Just before the grand charge, at the request of General Alexander Hays, who commanded the Third Division, Second Corps, I gathered up all these men who lay in the grove, and General Hays formed them in line to the right of the Bryan House, which is the first house to the left of the monument on the line of battle as you go toward Round Top. At the time of the battle the grove extended to this house. I took position, with the remnant of my squad of sharp-shooters, on the right of this line.

While the enemy were advancing to the Emmitsburg road, General Hays drilled the line in the manual of arms, allowed them to fire left oblique while the enemy were closing with our line to the left of the Bryan House, and then swung them down by a left wheel to the lane which then ran from the Bryan House to the Emmitsburg road, across which lane they then fired. The moment chosen for the left wheel or flanking movement was just as the last division of the charging column was crossing the Emmitsburg road, moving direct for Ziegler's Grove. As the entire front of the Second Corps to the left of the Bryan House was already covered, and in many places penetrated, this fresh division would probably have forced our line back and gained the shelter of Ziegler's Grove had it not been subjected to our flank fire, which destroyed its formation and sent its shattered and disordered masses along the other side of the lane and in front of the Third Division of the Second Corps.

I finally drew back our line a little from the fence to prevent our rear being gained by the enemy moving north on the Emmitsburg road, and also to uncover a gun (or two guns, I forget which) that had, during the melee, been got in position at the head of the lane near the Bryan House. As the enemy crowded forward into the lane, the fire of these guns ended the contest.

The "clump of trees" upon Bachelder's chart is near the point where Stannard struck the right flank. Ziegler's Grove, farther north, is the clump of trees where I was, and to which I refer, and to which General Longstreet refers in his letter to me mentioned further on. It is the blow upon the left flank, and not upon the right flank, to which we all refer.

That there might not be any mistake I sent General Longstreet a chart of the battle-field furnished me by the Gettysburg Battle-Field Memorial Association, on which I marked the lane running down from Ziegler's Grove to the Emmitsburg road.

I have not yet learned what regiments, or frag-

ments of regiments, composed the line swung down, but they were strangers to me and I have just learned that the 39th, 111th, 125th, and 126th New-York were added to the Third Division, Second Corps, *on the march to Gettysburg*. I left the army after the battle, and so had no opportunity to learn afterward.

With regard to the blow struck on Pettigrew's left by the 8th Ohio Regiment, the Ohio men say that they lay *west* of the *Emmitsburg road*. If so, they must have been north and in front of the right of Ziegler's Grove, as we faced. |

After we had swung down on the left flank to the lane we were struck by A. P. Hill's men, who faced Ziegler's Grove upon our right and rear so forcibly that I had given the order to "Left wheel backwards, firing," and the order was being executed when Hill's men abandoned our rear. It is my strong impression that the Ohio regiment pitched into Hill's men, who were pitching into our flank and rear. I remember distinctly that our artillerists at our right, seeing our imminent danger, poured in the grape and canister upon our rear assailants in a lively manner.

General Longstreet writes to me from Atlanta, Georgia, January 4th, 1884:

"The move of which you speak I remember quite well, and my impression is that it was made against Pickett's men.

"At its first appearance I sent orders for a counter-move. I think the order was sent by Colonel Osman Latrobe, now of Baltimore. Colonel Latrobe can probably give you more definite information of the troops you may have struck.

"At the first appearance of the troops in this move I recognized it as one that would break up my assault, but I looked on the movements of the Third Corps — A. P. Hill's — as certain to break the intended flank move.

"Soon after the flank movement was disclosed, a severe fire from artillery, etc., coming in across our line from the right as we advanced, hurt our supporting columns badly.

"If you struck their left you may claim to have put in very heavy blows at the critical moment, for the breaking up of the supporting force broke up the attack or hope of success from it. We could not look for anything from Pickett except to break your line. The supports were to secure the fruits of that break."

| General Franklin Sawyer, Lieutenant-Colonel of the 8th Ohio Volunteers, in the history of the regiment, gives the following description of Pettigrew's column in the assault:

"They moved up splendidly, deploying into column as they crossed the long, sloping interval between the Second Corps and their base. At first it looked as if their line of march would sweep our position, but as they advanced their direction lay considerably to our left; but soon a strong line, with flags, directed its march immediately upon us. . . . We changed our front, and, taking position by a fence, facing the left flank of the advancing column of rebels, the men were ordered to fire into their flank at will. Hardly a musket had been fired at this time. The front of the column was nearly up the slope, and within a few yards of the line of the Second Corps' front and its batteries, when suddenly a terrific fire from every available gun from the Cemetery to Round Top Mountain burst upon them. The distinct, graceful lines of the rebels underwent an instantaneous transformation. They were at once enveloped in a dense cloud of smoke and dust. Arms, heads, blankets, guns and knapsacks were thrown and tossed into the clear air. Their track, as they

advanced, was strewn with dead and wounded. A moan went up from the field, distinctly to be heard amid the storm of battle; but, on they went, too much enveloped in smoke and dust now to permit us to distinguish their lines or movements, for the mass appeared more like a cloud of moving smoke and dust than a column of troops. Still it advanced amid the now deafening roar of artillery and storm of battle. Suddenly the column gave way, the sloping landscape appeared covered all at once with the scattered and retreating foe. A withering sheet of missiles swept after them, and they were torn and tossed and prostrated as they ran. It seemed as if not one would escape. Of the mounted officers who rode so grandly in the advance, not one was to be seen on the field; all had gone down. The 8th [Ohio] advanced and cut off three regiments, or remnants of regiments, as they passed us, taking their colors, and capturing many prisoners. The colors captured were those of the 34th North Carolina, 38th Virginia, and one that was taken from the captor, Sergeant Miller, Company G, by a staff-officer, the number of the regiment not being remembered. The battle was now over. The field was covered with the slain and wounded, and everywhere were to be seen white handkerchiefs held up asking for quarter."   EDITORS.

FARNSWORTH'S CHARGE.

FARNSWORTH'S CHARGE AND DEATH.

BY H. C. PARSONS, CAPTAIN, 1ST VERMONT CAVALRY.

ON the eve of the battle of Gettysburg Captain Elon J. Farnsworth, of the 8th Illinois Cavalry, an aide on General Pleasonton's staff, was promoted for gallantry to be brigadier-general and given command oɟ a brigade in Kilpatrick's division, consisting of the 5th New York, 18th Pennsylvania, 1st Vermont, and 1st West Virginia regiments.

On the evening of the 2d of July we were on Meade's right wing, and by noon of the third day of the battle we went into position on his left wing, near the enemy's artillery line, on the south end of Seminary Ridge. When the cannonading which preceded Pickett's charge opened, General Farnsworth rode to the position marked "A" upon the map [p. 394], and I think Kilpatrick joined him. A long skirmish line of the enemy was at that moment moving toward us. I was commanded to take one squadron, charge as foragers, ride to cover of the stone house (Bushman's), and wait for orders. At our approach the enemy's skirmish line fell back. We rode to the house with the loss of two men. Captain Stone was sent with a squadron to my support. We remained some time at the Bushman house, near the enemy's batteries, and returned under fire without loss.

At 5 o'clock that afternoon we went into position, and were resting behind a battery on the low, wooded hill at the left of Round Top, and separated from it by a narrow valley. The enemy's picket line confronted our own near the base of the hill, but there was no firing. There was an oppressive stillness after the day's excitement. I rode out to the brow of the hill and had an excellent view of the field. Directly in front of us opened the valley toward Gettysburg, with its wheat-fields; at the right, and less than half a mile distant, rose Round Top; in the intervening valley lay the Slyder farm, with low, cross fences. Projecting from Round Top was a hill, perhaps one hundred feet high, on the top of which was a field surrounded by high stone walls. The slopes of this hill were covered with immense granite bowlders; a road or lane extended from the Emmitsburg pike to its base, and then turned to the left toward Devil's Den. Beyond this road ran a high rail fence the only openings being at the right and left of the walled field on the hill. Above this, and along the rocky and wooded slopes of Round Top, Law's brigade was firmly intrenched, and pressing him in front and on the right was the Union army. Toward the openings described, the charge that was afterward made was directed. While I was looking out upon the field General Kilpatrick rode near, showing great impatience and eagerness for orders, and an orderly dashed by shouting, "We turned the charge; nine acres of prisoners!"

From this point the position of the troops on the Confederate right appeared to be full of peril. Law's brigade had held an almost untenable but essential position through two hard-fought days, while their batteries and support, nearly a mile in the rear, were at that moment turned upon Merritt's advancing squadrons. The gates to the valley behind Round Top, toward which Longstreet's eye turned so eagerly, were held by them, and the valley in the rear was protected by a single Texas regiment and a weak skirmish line. Kilpatrick had been given large discretion by General Pleasonton when he had been sent in the morning against Lee's right, with Merritt's and Farnsworth's brigades. (Custer had been detached and sent to General Gregg.) Kilpatrick's orders were to press the enemy, to threaten him at every point, and to strike at the first opportunity, with an emphatic intimation that the best battle news could be brought by the wind. His opportunity had now come. If he could bring on a battle, drive back the Texas regiment, and break the lines on the mountain, Meade's infantry on Round Top would surely drive them into the valley, and then the five thousand cavalry in reserve could strike the decisive blow.

The 1st West Virginia was selected to attack the Texas regiment. The Second Battalion of the 1st Vermont was thrown out as skirmishers; the First and Third battalions were held for the charge on the mountain. The 1st West Virginia charged at our left and front down the open valley, nearly in the direction but toward the right of the Bushman house, upon the 1st Texas regiment, which was in line behind a rail fence that had been staked and bound with withes. A thin line shot forward and attempted to throw the rails, tugging at the stakes, cutting with their sabers, and falling in the vain effort. The regiment came on in magnificent style, received a deadly volley, before which it recoiled, rallied, charged the second time, and fell back with great loss.

I was near Kilpatrick when he impetuously gave the order to Farnsworth to make the last charge. Farnsworth spoke with emotion: "General, do you mean it? Shall I throw my handful of men over rough ground, through timber, against a brigade of infantry? The 1st Vermont has already been fought half to pieces; these are too good men to kill." Kilpatrick said: "Do you refuse to obey my orders? If you are afraid to lead this charge, I will lead it." Farnsworth rose in his stirrups — he looked magnificent in his passion — and cried, "Take that back!" Kilpatrick returned his defiance, but, soon repenting, said, "I did not mean it; forget it." For a moment there was silence, when Farnsworth spoke calmly, "General,

if you order the charge, I will lead it, but you must take the responsibility." I did not hear the low conversation that followed, but as Farnsworth turned away he said, "I will obey your order." Kilpatrick said earnestly, "I take the responsibility."

I recall the two young generals at that moment in the shadow of the oaks and against the sunlight — Kilpatrick with his fine features, his blonde beard, his soft hat turned up jauntily, and his face lighted with the joy that always came into it when the charge was sounded; Farnsworth, tall, slight, stern, and pale, but rising with conscious strength and consecration. Kilpatrick was eager for the fray. He believed that cavalry could "fight anywhere except at sea." He was justified by his orders and by results, and he was brave enough to withdraw the hot imputation, even in the presence of a regiment. Farnsworth was courage incarnate, but full of tender regard for his men, and his protest was manly and soldierly.

The direction of our guns was changed; new guns were brought into position. A shell shrieked down the line of my front company a few feet above their heads, covering them with leaves and branches. We rode out in columns of fours with drawn sabers. General Farnsworth, after giving the order to me, took his place at the head of the Third Battalion. In this action I commanded the First Battalion and Major Wells commanded the Third. Captain Cushman and Lieutenant

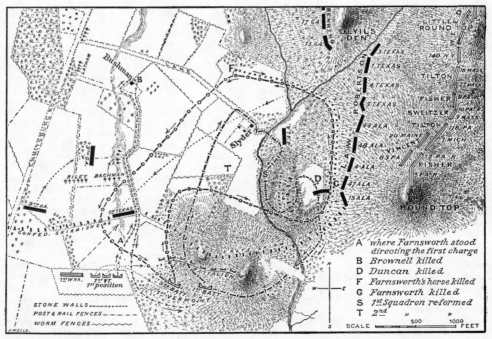

MAP OF FARNSWORTH'S CHARGE. FROM A SKETCH MAP BY CAPTAIN H. C. PARSONS.

NOTE.—The reader is referred to the map on page 344 for the full position of Kilpatrick's Cavalry division, and Merritt's brigade of Buford's division.— EDITORS.

Watson rode with me; General Farnsworth and Adjutant-General Estes rode with Major Wells.

As the First Battalion rode through the line of our dismounted skirmishers, who were falling back, they cried to us to halt. As we passed out from the cover of the woods the 1st West Virginia was retiring in disorder on our left. A frantic horse with one leg torn off by a cannonball rushed toward us as if for protection. We rode through the enemy's skirmish line across the fields, over the low fences, past the Slyder house, and down the road. The sun was blinding; Captain Cushman shaded his eyes with his hand and cried, "An ambuscade!" We were immediately upon the enemy, within thirty paces, and the deadly volley, which is referred to in the Confederate reports, was fired, but it passed over our heads; although they report that half our saddles were emptied, not a man was shot, yet the fire was the close and concentrated volley of a regiment. Captain (afterward Colonel) Jones, who commanded on the right of the 4th Alabama, says: "I was ordered to face about to resist cavalry; we marched rapidly to the rear over the rocks, and the Vermonters were upon us before we could form. They were within a few paces when we gave the order to fire. . . . The whole regiment fired, but when the smoke cleared I only saw one horse fall. A private at my left said, 'Captain, I shot that black.' I said, 'Why didn't you shoot his rider?' He replied, 'Oh, we'll get him anyhow; but I'm a hunter, and for three years I haven't looked at a deer's eye — I couldn't stand it.'"

Taken by surprise, they had shot over us; the next, a random volley, was effective. With the head of the column we cleared the wall at the right and formed under cover of the hill. The rear companies fell back and formed behind a cross fence and in the edge of timber. In the meantime the most important movement of the day was being made. The Third Battalion, under Major Wells,—a young officer who bore a charmed life and was destined to pass through many daring encounters to the rank of brigadier-general,— moved out in splendid form to the left of the First Battalion and swept in a great circle to the right, around the front of the hill and across our track; then, guiding to the left across the valley and up the side of the low hill at the base of Round Top, they charged along the wall, and between it and the mountain, directly in the rear of several Confederate regiments in position and between them and the 4th Alabama. It was a swift, resistless charge over rocks, through timber, under close enfilading fire. Colonel A. W. Preston had taken my Second Squadron and rode with part of the Second Battalion in support.] The direction was toward Devil's Den. At the foot of the declivity the column turned left and passed a battery, receiving the fire of its support, then divided into three parties. One swept across the open field and upon the rear of the Texas skirmish line, carrying

in a part of this line as prisoners, and one rode through into the Union lines. Farnsworth's horse had fallen; a trooper sprang from the saddle, gave the general his horse, and escaped on foot. Captain Cushman and a few others, with Farnsworth, turned back and rode at full gallop toward the point of entering. My First Squadron was again ordered forward. The enemy's sharp-shooters appeared in the rocks above us and opened fire.

BRIGADIER-GENERAL ELON J. FARNSWORTH.
FROM A PHOTOGRAPH.

We rode obliquely up the hill in the direction of Wells, then wheeling to the left, between the picket line and the wall. As we turned, Corporal Sperry fell at my side. Part of my men turned back with prisoners. The head of the column leapt the wall into the open field. Farnsworth, seeing our horsemen, raised his saber and charged as if with an army; at almost the same moment his followers, and what remained of the First Battalion, cut their way through the 15th Alabama, which was wheeling into position at a run and offered little resistance. We charged in the same general direction, but on opposite sides of the wall that runs parallel with the Round Top range, and within two hundred paces of each other. Sergeant Duncan, a black-eyed, red-cheeked boy, splendidly mounted, standing in his stirrups, flew past me with his saber raised, shouted, "I'm with you!" threw up his left arm, and fell. My horse recoiled over his dead body, my men swept past, and I was for a moment alone on the field. The enemy ran up crying "Surrender!" as if they did not want to shoot me, but as I raised my saber a gun was planted against my breast and fired; my horse was struck at the same moment and broke frantically through the men, over the wall, and down the hill. Corporal Waller overtook me from the left, and, riding close, supported me on my horse.

] Colonel Preston, in his report, does not refer to the repulse by the 4th Alabama; he refers to Major Wells as leading the Second Battalion, but the latter says he was with the Third.— EDITORS.

As we rode on, he told me how Farnsworth and Cushman had fallen together.

I have spoken of the battalions as distinct. They were not, nor were the companies. At the sharp turn at the top of the hill, Captain Cushman and Sergeant Stranahan, who commanded Company L after Watson's horse was shot, kept straight on with part of his company, and rode in the main charge. A number of my men had turned back with prisoners, so that not over fifty men, ✠ including those with Farnsworth, cut their way through in the outward charge.

The whole number who rode with Farnsworth was about three hundred. Their casualties were sixty-five. They brought in over one hundred prisoners; they rode within the Confederate lines nearly two miles; they received at short range the direct or enfilading fire of three regiments of infantry and of a battery of artillery; they drew two regiments out of line and held them permanently in new positions, breaking the Confederate front and exposing it to an infantry charge if one had been immediately ordered. Their assault was so bold that the Confederates received it as the advance of a grand attack, and, finding themselves exposed to infantry in front and cavalry in the rear, they were uncertain of their position. Why no advantage was taken of this it is not for us to explain. Why the infantry, when they heard fighting in Law's rear, or when, afterward, we delivered to their skirmish line our prisoners, did not advance and drive his brigade into the valley where it would have been exposed to a general flank attack, has never been explained; but it was not "a charge of madmen with a mad leader." We believed, and yet believe, that Farnsworth's charge was wisely ordered, well timed, well executed, and effective. ↓

The behavior of the horses in this action was admirable. Running low and swift, as in a race; in their terror surrendering to their masters, and guiding at the slightest touch on the neck; never

refusing a fence or breaking from the column; crowding together and to the front, yet taking or avoiding the obstacles with intelligence, they carried their riders over rocks and fallen timber and fences that the boldest hunter would hardly attempt to-day; and I doubt if there was a single fall of man or horse, except from the shot of the enemy. I may be permitted a remorseful tribute. My powerful bay had been disabled in the action at Hanover, and I was riding my bugler's horse, a gentle sorrel, scarred and stiff with long service. When I saw the work before us I condemned him, and would have ordered some trooper to change if it had not seemed like exposing another's life,—and yet, how he sprang into the charge! How he leaped the four walls! How he cleared Farrington's horse as it rolled over in the rocks! And how gently he carried me from the field, although blood spurted from his side at every step. Four better horses passed him in the race, but only to fall or carry their riders to death! And when I was lifted down into unconsciousness, my last recollection was of his great eyes turned upon me as in sympathy and reproof.

There was no charging of cannon, no sabering of men. Farnsworth and his troopers understood that they were to draw the enemy's fire, to create a diversion, preparatory to the main movement. They were to ride as deep into the enemy's lines as possible, to disclose his plan and force his positions. The taking of the prisoners on the return was the accident, not the order, of the charge. There was no encouragement of on-looking armies, no cheer, no bravado; and each man felt, as he tightened his saber belt, that he was summoned to a ride to death.

Farnsworth fell in the enemy's lines with his saber raised, dead with five mortal wounds, and without fame. So fell this typical volunteer soldier of America—a man without military training or ambition, yet born with a genius for war which carried him to high command and to the threshold of a great career.

✠ The officers of the 15th Alabama say there were not over ten men with Farnsworth when he fell. His horse dashed through their lines riderless. Colonel Oates kept for a long time the star cut from Farnsworth's coat, hoping some time to return it to his family, but it was accidentally lost or destroyed.—H. C. P.

↓ A strange story which appears in all the Confederate reports shows how a mistake may make history. It is stated that Farnsworth wore a linen coat and a havelock; that he fought desperately with his revolver after he was down, and that he blew out his brains rather than surrender.

When Farnsworth was notified of his promotion ⸶ on the field it was impossible to secure a new uniform, but Pleasonton, as a token of esteem, divided his own wardrobe with him. Farnsworth wore in the action Pleasonton's blue coat, with a single star, and a soft black hat; he fell with his saber raised, and as if dead; and when his remains were taken from the field

by Doctors Edson and Wood there were five mortal wounds in his body and no wound in his head. Captain Cushman wore a white duck "fighting jacket," trimmed with yellow braid. To my objection, he answered, "A lady sent this to me, and said it was made with her own hands, and no rebel bullet could pierce it. It may be a good day to try magic mail." While we sat behind the guns in the heat he threw a silk handkerchief over his cap, pinning it to the visor. This he forgot to remove; he, and not Farnsworth, rode in the charge on the 4th Alabama; he rode with Farnsworth in the charge on the 15th Alabama; he fell at Farnsworth's side, terribly wounded in the face, and fought with his revolver until he fainted. He was a notably handsome officer, and it was clear that he was mistaken throughout the fight for General Farnsworth. Captain Cushman lay insensible and apparently dead until the next day, but finally revived, only to die in his next battle.—H. C. P.

⸶ Major Clifford Thomson, of General Pleasonton's staff, writes to the editors: "Farnsworth's commission was dated June 29th, four days before his death. As he had been on

detached service, it had not reached him, being carried among Pleasonton's headquarters papers until after the battle."—EDITORS.

THE CAVALRY BATTLE NEAR GETTYSBURG.

BY WILLIAM E. MILLER, CAPTAIN, 3D PENNSYLVANIA CAVALRY.

MONUMENT ON THE FIELD OF THE CAVALRY
FIGHT BETWEEN THE FORCES OF GREGG
AND STUART. FROM A PHOTOGRAPH.

THE 3d Pennsylvania Cavalry, after participating in the different cavalry engagements from Brandy Station to Upperville, was the last regiment to cross the Potomac into Maryland by the pontoon-bridge at Edwards's Ferry, except McCandless's brigade of the Pennsylvania Reserves. Well do the men of Gregg's cavalry command remember the evening of the 27th of June, 1863, while they were drawn up on the slope of the northern bank of the Potomac awaiting the crossing of McCandless's infantry, which was somewhat delayed on the opposite side. As soon as the band of McCandless's brigade placed foot on the bridge it began to play "Maryland, My Maryland." The men took up the refrain, and it was echoed back by the cavalrymen on the northern hillside. The scene was beautiful and touching beyond description, and formed one of the happy incidents that broke the monotony of the long and weary march from Falmouth to Gettysburg.

About dusk "to horse" was sounded, and the division again put in motion. A tedious night's march along a road blockaded with wagons and other impediments brought us to Monocacy Junction, on the Baltimore and Ohio Railroad, between which place and Frederick we halted on Sunday morning, the 28th. A reorganization of the cavalry there took place. General Kilpatrick, who had commanded the Second Brigade of Gregg's division, was promoted to the command of Stahel's division, which was then added to the Cavalry Corps of the Army of the Potomac as the Third Division, and Colonel Pennock Huey, with the 8th Pennsylvania Cavalry, was transferred from Buford's division to the Second Brigade of the Second Division, Huey succeeding Kilpatrick in command of the brigade. [For organization, see p. 437.]

Before leaving Frederick the 1st Pennsylvania Cavalry was ordered to report to General Meade's headquarters, where it remained until after the battle of Gettysburg; it did not rejoin its brigade before the 12th of July, at Boonsboro'. The 1st Massachusetts was also sent on detached service.

While we were halted near Frederick it was discovered that Stuart was making a detour around our army and had crossed the Potomac below Edwards's Ferry. Our cavalry was sent out on all the roads leading from Frederick to the north and east to prevent his gaining information, and to push him as far away as possible, so that he might be delayed in communicating with his chief. On the evening of the 28th McIntosh's brigade was sent eastward on the Baltimore pike, and passing New Market it halted at Ridgeville, and from there scouting parties were sent in every direction. On the morning of the 29th a portion of the 3d Pennsylvania was sent to Lisbon, and from there one squadron went northward to Woodbine, on the Baltimore and Ohio Railroad. It was ascertained that Stuart was tearing up the tracks near Hood's Mill, the next station east of Woodbine, and that he was moving northward. Information was sent to headquarters, and by 4 o'clock P. M. Gregg's division was concentrated at Mount Airy, north of Ridgeville, where it was supplied with a scanty allowance of rations and forage. Five o'clock found it on the march for Westminster, with the 3d Pennsylvania of McIntosh's brigade in advance. Having been on almost continuous duty, night and day, since the battle of Brandy Station, on the 9th, the prospect of another night march was, to say the least, discouraging.|

BREVET MAJOR-GENERAL D. McM. GREGG.
FROM A PHOTOGRAPH.

Our march to Westminster was one of unusual severity, for the night was very dark and both men and horses were worn out. The men fell asleep in their saddles, and whenever the column halted the horses would fall asleep too. As the officers were responsible for keeping the column closed up, they had to resort to all sorts of expedients to keep awake, such as pinching themselves, pounding their heads, and pricking themselves with pins. When within about five miles of Westminster it was discovered that the left of the line was not up. A halt was ordered, and, on sending back, the fact was disclosed that the artillerymen and battery horses were sound asleep, and that, whilst the portion of the column in front of them had been moving on, that in the rear was standing still. As soon as the latter was brought up the whole command moved forward, and at daylight on the 30th the advance, under Captain Charles Treichel, of the 3d Pennsylvania, charged into Westminster and captured a lot of Stuart's stragglers. Here we met with a cordial reception. The majority of the houses were thrown open, and the women, standing on their door-steps and at the windows, waved their handkerchiefs and cheered the old flag. It was noticed, however, that some of the houses remained closed, and upon inquiry it was

|To one not familiar with a cavalry night march in the face of the enemy it may be difficult to comprehend why it should differ materially from an advance by daylight, but to those who have had some experience this is easily understood. On a night march, in order to guard against surprise, flankers are thrown out on either side, who are supposed to keep abreast of the advance-guard. These flankers are under the supervision of the officer in charge of the advance, and no matter how dark the night is he must keep them sufficiently deployed to protect the column, and yet always have them well in hand. These flankers encounter all sorts of obstacles, such as ditches, ravines, fences, underbrush, woods, etc., and necessarily make slow progress. The time thus occupied compels the main body in the rear to make innumerable stops and starts, which are not only tedious and wearying, but annoying and irksome, and hard upon the horses, often causing the men to grow impatient and the officers to become irritable.—W. E. M.

ascertained that these had in a similar manner been open the day before for the reception of Stuart and his men.

At Manchester a halt of a few hours was made, during which the men consumed what was left of the rations procured at Mount Airy, gave their horses the last grain of feed they had with them, and obtained a little sleep. Mounting again we moved north along the Carlisle pike for half a mile, and then by the Grove Mill road to Hanover Junction, Pennsylvania, on the Northern Central Railroad, where we arrived during the forenoon of July 1st. Our movements at this place illustrate to some extent the uncertainties of the campaign After a short delay General Gregg received an order to proceed south toward Baltimore. Scarcely was the division drawn out on the road when a second order came directing him to turn about and move north as rapidly as possible toward York. Just as we were starting in the latter direction the final order came to send Huey's brigade back to Manchester, Maryland, and to march with McIntosh's and Irvin Gregg's brigades westward to Gettysburg. After losing some valuable time in consequence of these conflicting orders, we (McIntosh's and Gregg's brigades) advanced over a crooked road to Hanover, where we went into bivouac.

At Hanover we found the streets barricaded with boxes, old carriages and wagons, hay, ladders, barbers' poles, etc., the marks of Kilpatrick's encounter with Stuart on the previous day, for the Third Division, while we were making the detour on the right flank, had taken the direct road from Frederick, and at Hanover had intercepted the line of march of the Confederate cavalry while we had been following it up.

By this time we had become a sorry-looking body of men, having been in the saddle day and night almost continuously for over three weeks, without a change of clothing or an opportunity for a general wash; moreover we were much reduced by short rations and exhaustion, and mounted on horses whose bones were plainly visible to the naked eye. ⚓

Leaving Hanover at 3 o'clock on the morning of July 2d we had proceeded along the Littlestown road for two miles when Dr. T. T. Tate, one of the assistant surgeons of the 3d Pennsylvania Cavalry, who was a citizen of Gettysburg and familiar with the country, advised General Gregg that the shortest route to Gettysburg was by way of the Bonaughtown or Hanover road. The doctor piloted the column across the fields and we reached the Bonaughtown road at McSherrystown. On reaching Geiselman's Woods, Colonel McIntosh, who had been suffering from exhaustion, became very sick. The column was halted, and Dr. Tate took him to Mr. Geiselman's house, where with careful medical attention he was in a short time restored and again

⚓ As an evidence of how the division was reduced by hard marching and hard fighting it may be stated that the morning report of the 3d Pennsylvania on the 30th of June — one of the strongest regiments in the division — showed present for duty 29 officers, including field and staff, 365 enlisted men, and 322 serviceable horses. It will thus be manifest that we had seventy-two men whose horses had dropped from the ranks. Many of these men were traveling along on foot and carrying their saddles in the hope of procuring remounts. The above report was made out at Westminster. Our march from there through the broiling sun and clouds of dust entailed a still larger loss of men and horses from exhaustion, so that by the time we reached Gettysburg the 3d Pennsylvania did not number three hundred officers and men all told. — W. E. M.

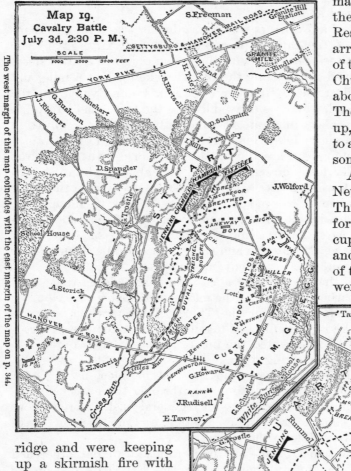

Map 19.
Cavalry Battle
July 3d, 2:30 P. M.

SCALE
1000   2000   3000 FEET

The west margin of this map coincides with the east margin of the map on p. 344.

made his appearance at the head of his command. Resuming the march we arrived at the intersection of the Low Dutch (or Salem Church) and Hanover roads about noon on July 2d. The regiments were closed up, and we halted in a field to allow the men and horses some much-needed rest.

About 3 o'clock the 10th New York cavalry of the Third Brigade was ordered forward and directed to occupy Brinkerhoff's Ridge and relieve some infantry of the Eleventh Corps, who were in possession of the

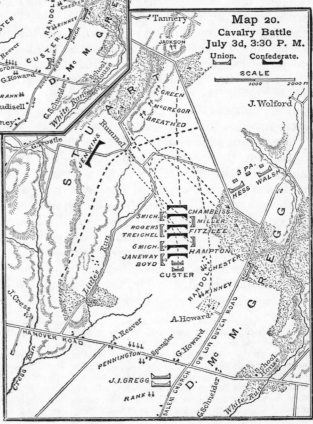

Map 20.
Cavalry Battle
July 3d, 3:30 P. M.
Union.   Confederate.

SCALE
1000   2000 ft

ridge and were keeping up a skirmish fire with the enemy in their front. General Gregg took two guns, a section of Battery H, 3d Pennsylvania Heavy Artillery, Captain W. D. Rank (serving as Light Artillery), and placed them on the Hanover road opposite the Reever house, about three miles east of Gettysburg. Near 6 o'clock some mounted men, who seemed to be making observations, appeared in the road on the top of Brinkerhoff's Ridge, about three-fourths of a mile distant, whereupon Gregg ordered Rank to send them a "feeler," which he did in the most approved style — the two shells bursting in their midst and scattering the party like chaff in a wind storm. The First Brigade was now ordered forward, and on passing beyond Rank's guns the 3d Pennsylvania, being in the advance, was ordered into Cress's Woods, on the right of the road. The squadron of Captain Hess and my own were directed to dismount and advance across Cress's Run to the top of Brinkerhoff's Ridge — Hess on the left, with his left resting on the road and deployed to the right, and Miller [the writer] deployed to the right of Hess. On the left side of the road, connecting with Hess, two battalions of the 1st New Jersey, under Major Janeway and Captain Boyd, and Duvall's Maryland troop were deployed — the whole supported by the Third Battalion of the 1st New Jersey, under Major Beaumont. After crossing Cress's Run and gaining the elevated ground beyond, it was discovered that a stone fence ran along the crest of the ridge, and that some Confederate infantry were advancing from the opposite direction. "Double quick" was ordered, and a race for the fence ensued. The men seeing the importance of the position quickened their steps and arrived at the wall about twenty paces in advance of the enemy. As soon as our men reached the wall they opened fire with their carbines, and drove back their opponents. They punched holes through the wall with their carbines, and behind this formidable breastwork they were enabled, though repeatedly charged, to hold their position until daylight disappeared. Rank's guns in the meantime kept up a lively fire and did effective work. After dark a charge was made against our right which was driven in, but the men, not being discouraged, made a counter-charge and regained their position. Our opponents proved to be Walker's brigade, of Johnson's division, of Ewell's corps, and it was our good fortune to hold them in check long enough to prevent them from participating in the assault on Culp's Hill.

About 10 o'clock the whole division was withdrawn and moved over a country cross-road to the Baltimore pike, where it bivouacked for the night along White Run.

Between 9 and 10 o'clock on the morning of the 3d "to horse" was sounded, and we were again in the saddle. Retracing our steps, we resumed our position on the right, but with a more extended line. Irvin Gregg connected with the right of the infantry line near Wolf's Hill and stretched his line to the Hanover road, while McIntosh moved to and halted at the crossing of the Low Dutch and Hanover roads. Custer's brigade occupied the ground to the right and front of McIntosh. After some delay McIntosh moved forward to relieve Custer, who had been ordered to report to his division commander (Kilpatrick) in the vicinity of Round Top. The 3d Pennsylvania and 1st Maryland were drawn up in column of squadrons in a clover-field in front of and across the road from Lott's house, while the 1st New Jersey was sent to relieve Custer's men on outpost.

General J. E. B. Stuart, who was in command of the Confederate cavalry, now occupied what is known as Cress's Ridge, about three-fourths of a mile north of Lott's house.   On the south-eastern slope of the ridge there were cultivated fields, while its summit was covered with heavy timber.   North of this ridge there were open fields, almost surrounded by woods, through which ran a country cross-road leading from the York pike to the Low Dutch road. The place was most admirably adapted to the massing and screening of troops. Behind the woods Stuart, who had come out from the direction of Gettysburg along the York pike, concentrated his forces on what was known as the Stall- smith farm.   Gregg's troops were not so favorably situated.   Occupying a line about three miles long from Wolf's Hill to Lott's house, through an open country, they were in full view of the enemy.   [See maps, pp. 344, 400.]

A party of Confederate skirmishers thrown out in front of Stuart's center occupied the Rummel farm buildings, which were situated in the plain about three-fourths of a mile north-west of the Lott house, and near the base of Cress's Ridge.   About 2 o'clock McIntosh, who well understood Stuart's tac- tics, and had correctly discerned his position, dismounted the 1st New Jersey and moved it forward under Major Beaumont in the direction of Rummel's. To meet this advance the Confederates pushed out a line of skirmishers and occupied a fence south of Rummel's.   The 1st New Jersey soon adjusted their line to correspond with that of their antagonists, and firing began.   At the same time a Confederate battery appeared on the top of the ridge and com- menced shelling.   Lieutenant A. C. M. Pennington's battery (M, 2d U. S. Artillery), in position in front of Spangler's house on the Hanover road, instantly replied.   The 3d Pennsylvania was ordered forward, and two squad- rons under Captains Treichel and Rodgers were moved across to Little's Run (which flowed southward from Rummel's spring-house) and placed to the left of the 1st New Jersey, while Duvall's troop was extended to their left.   Captains Walsh and Hess were ordered out the Low Dutch road beyond Lott's woods, with instructions to hold the position and protect the right. My squadron was deployed along the edge of the woods north of Lott's house (near where the cavalry shaft now stands) and extended to the cross-roads running toward Stallsmith's, facing north-west.   It will thus be seen that the 3d Pennsylvania was divided — one-half being on the left of the line, whilst the other occupied the right.   The 1st Maryland was posted near the Lott house and held in reserve.   Captain A. M. Randol's battery (E, 1st U. S. Artillery), stationed across the road from the Howard house, was also ordered forward, and a section under Lieutenant Chester placed in position a little south-west of Lott's house.   Pennington and Chester soon silenced the Confederate battery, and finding Rummel's barn filled with sharp-shooters, who were picking off our men, they turned their guns on it and drove them out.   In the meantime our front line was advanced and we drove back that of the Confederates, occupying their position.   A lull in the firing now ensued, during which Custer's brigade returned.   After the engagement had opened McIntosh had discovered that the force in his front was too strong for his command, and consequently he had sent word to General Gregg to that effect, requesting that Irvin Gregg's brigade be forwarded to his support.   As this brigade was some distance to the rear, and therefore not immediately avail-

BATTLE BETWEEN THE UNION CAVALRY UNDER GREGG AND THE CONFEDERATE CAVALRY UNDER STUART.
FROM A SKETCH MADE AT THE TIME.

able, Gregg, meeting Custer, who was about to begin his march in the opposite direction, had ordered him to return, and at the same time had sent
word to Irvin Gregg to concentrate as much of his command as possible in
the vicinity of Spangler's house. Custer, eager for the fray, had wheeled
about and was soon on the field.

Gregg at this juncture appeared and took command in person. Custer, as
soon as he arrived, extended the left of the line along Little's Run with a portion of the 6th Michigan, dismounted, and at the same time Randol placed in
position to the left and rear of Chester the second section of his battery under
Lieutenant Kinney.

At this stage the ammunition of that portion of the 3d Pennsylvania which
was on the left, and of the 1st New Jersey, began to run short, and the 5th
Michigan was ordered to relieve them. The latter was dismounted, and whilst
it was moving to the front a dismounted regiment from W. H. F. Lee's brigade came to the support of the Confederate skirmishers. A heated contest
followed, in which the 1st New Jersey and the 3d Pennsylvania remained to
take part. After the firing abated these regiments attempted to withdraw,
but they were followed up so closely that they were obliged to face about
and resume the conflict. However, they soon drove the enemy back, inflicting severe punishment. The short supply of ammunition of the 5th Michigan
having by this time given out, and Major Noah H. Ferry, who was in command of the line, having been killed, the whole line was driven in. Improving this opportunity, Fitz. Lee sent forward the 1st Virginia, which charged
our right and center. The 7th Michigan at once moved forward from the
direction of the Reever house in close column of squadrons and advanced to
the attack. The right of the 5th Michigan swung back, and the 7th pressed
forward to a stone-and-rail fence and opened fire with their carbines. The

1st Virginia advanced with steadiness, and soon the two regiments were face to face, the fence alone separating them. My squadron, which occupied the right center and which up to this time had not been engaged, opened a flank fire on the Virginians, which aided materially in holding them in check. The 1st North Carolina Cavalry and the Jeff Davis Legion coming up to their support, they crowded the 7th Michigan back, and it was obliged to give way, the Confederates following in close pursuit. A more determined and vigorous charge than that made by the 1st Virginia it was never my fortune to witness. But they became scattered by the flank fire they received, together with the shells from our artillery, and were in the end obliged to fall back on their main body.

About half a mile distant from the last-mentioned fence, where the cross-road passes through the woods on the Stallsmith farm, there appeared moving toward us a large mass of cavalry, which proved to be the remaining portions of Hampton's and Fitzhugh Lee's brigades. They were formed in close column of squadrons and directed their course toward the Spangler house. A grander spectacle than their advance has rarely been beheld. They marched with well-aligned fronts and steady reins. Their polished saber-blades dazzled in the sun. All eyes turned upon them. Chester on the right, Kinney in the center, and Pennington on the left opened fire with well-directed aim. Shell and shrapnel met the advancing Confederates and tore through their ranks. Closing the gaps as though nothing had happened, on they came. As they drew nearer, canister was substituted by our artillerymen for shell, and horse after horse staggered and fell. Still they came on. Our mounted skirmishers rallied and fell into line; the dismounted men fell back, and a few of them reached their horses. The 1st Michigan, drawn up in close column of squadrons near Pennington's battery, was ordered by Gregg to charge. Custer, who was near, placed himself at its head, and off they dashed. As the two columns approached each other the pace of each increased, when suddenly a crash, like the falling of timber, betokened the crisis. So sudden and violent was the collision that many of the horses were turned end over end and crushed their riders beneath them. The clashing of sabers, the firing of pistols, the demands for surrender and cries of the combatants now filled the air. As the columns were drawing nearer to each other McIntosh sent his adjutant-general, Captain Walter S. Newhall, to the left with orders to Treichel and Rogers to mount and charge, and also sent Captain S. C. Wagner, of his staff, to rally the headquarters staff, buglers, and orderlies, whilst he himself rode to the Lott house for the 1st Maryland. But Gregg, when he first arrived and looked over the field, had moved the 1st Maryland over to the Low Dutch road, just north of the Hanover road, in order to strengthen his right, and so failing to find this regiment where he had expected, McIntosh gathered up what loose men he could, joined them to his headquarters party and charged. My squadron was still deployed along the edge of Lott's woods. Standing in company with Lieutenant William Brooke-Rawle on a little rise of ground in front of his command, and seeing that the situation was becoming critical, I turned to him and said: "I have been ordered to hold this position, but, if you will back me up in case I am court-martialed for disobedience, I will order a charge." The lieutenant, always ready to "pitch in," as he expressed it, with an energetic reply convinced me that I would not be deserted. I accordingly directed him to close in the left and Sergeant Heagy the right, while the former should select the proper place for the attack. As soon as his line had rallied, the men fired a volley from their carbines, drew their sabers, sent up a shout, and "sailed in," striking the enemy's left flank about two-thirds down the column. Hart, of the 1st New Jersey, whose squadron was in the woods on my left, soon followed, but directed his charge to the head of the enemy's column. Newhall, when he reached Treichel and Rogers, joined them in their charge, which struck the right flank of the enemy's column, near the color-guard. The standard-bearer, seeing that Newhall was about to seize the colors, lowered his spear, which caught his opponent on the chin, tearing and shattering his lower jaw, and sending him senseless to the earth. Every officer of the party was wounded. My command pressed through the Confederate column, cut off the rear portion and drove it back. In the charge my men became somewhat scattered. A portion of them, however, got into Rummel's lane, in front of the farm-buildings, and there encountered some of Jenkins's men, who seemed stubborn about leaving. ‡ Breathed's battery, unsupported, was only one hundred yards away, but my men were so disabled and scattered that they were unable to take it back.

These flank attacks demoralized the Confederate column. Custer and McIntosh, whose tenacity had kept the head of the column at bay, now got the advantage. Many of the enemy had fallen, Wade Hampton was wounded, and at length the enemy turned. Their column was swept back to its starting-point, and the field was ours.

After the repulse of the enemy's grand charge, McIntosh took the 1st New Jersey and part of the 3d Pennsylvania and Duvall's troop, and established a skirmish line along Little's Run, by Rummel's spring-house and along his lane toward the cross-road, the field of the hand-to-hand contest thus remaining in our possession. The Confederates established their line along the edge of the woods on the summit of Cress's Ridge. Some artillery firing and light skirmishing was kept up until after dark. In the meantime Custer's brigade was relieved and sent to its division. ♭

‡ Since the war, while going over the field in company with Mr. Rummel, he told me that he had dragged thirty dead horses out of this lane.— W. E. M.

♭ The following incidents will illustrate in some degree with what desperation the men of both sides fought, as well as the character of the struggle. The first two incidents were related by Mr. Rummel, who aided in removing the dead. The last came under my personal notice. On going over the field, Mr. Rummel found two men — one a private in the 3d Pennsylvania, the other a Confederate — who had cut each other down with their sabers, and were lying with their feet together, their heads in opposite directions, and the blood-stained saber of each still tightly in his grip. At another point he found two men — one a Virginian, the other a 3d Pennsylvania man — who fought on horseback with their sabers until they finally clinched and their horses ran from under them. Their heads and shoulders were severely cut, and when found, their fingers, though stiff in death, were so firmly imbedded in each other's flesh that they could not be removed without the aid of force.

In the midst of the engagement, and immediately in front of Rummel's house, E. G. Eyster of H Company, 3d Pennsylvania Cavalry, captured a

With the exception of the Rummel farm buildings, the Confederates held virtually the same line at dark that they held in the morning, but this did not include the field of the main engagement. This was no mere reconnoissance to develop the position or movements of the enemy. Stuart had with him the main strength and the flower of the Confederate cavalry, led by their most distinguished commanders. His force comprised 4 brigades with 20 regiments and battalions and 4 batteries. His avowed object was to strike the rear of the Federal army in coöperation with Pickett's grand attack upon its center. For this movement he succeeded in attaining a most commanding position, and, according to the surmise of Major H. B. McClellan, Stuart's adjutant-general, gave to Lee the preconcerted signal for the attack. The field of this cavalry fight was south of the Rummel buildings. To this field Stuart advanced his whole force, engaged in an obstinate and desperate struggle with the Federal cavalry, was driven back out of the field and forced to retire to his original position. At the opening of the engagement Gregg's outposts were on the southern side of the battle-field; at its close they were advanced to its northern side. The losses on both sides show the importance and determined character of the fight. ↖

dismounted Confederate and covered him with his carbine. Eyster's attention becoming drawn off by the firing around him, the Confederate drew his revolver, shot Eyster's horse, and held the rider a prisoner. Just then Sergeant Gregg of A Company came upon the scene, and with his saber cut the Confederate to the ground. Before Gregg had time to turn another Confederate came up, and, with a right cut, sliced off the top of Gregg's scalp. Gregg, who subsequently rose to a captaincy in his regiment, and who died in 1886, had only to remove his hat to show a head as neatly tonsured as a priest's.

A singular coincidence occurred in connection with the above circumstance. Eyster and Gregg were both taken prisoners in the fight. Gregg, being wounded, was removed in an ambulance, and Eyster, with other prisoners, was compelled to walk. They were separated on the field. Eyster was sent to prison, Sergeant Gregg was taken to the hospital and was soon afterward exchanged. It so happened that when one came back to the regiment the other was absent, and *vice versa*, so that they never met again until sixteen years afterward at Gettysburg, where the regiment was holding a reunion. In going over the field Eyster was relating the story to Colonel John B. Bachelder, on the very spot where the above scene had occurred, when Gregg came up and they met for the first time since their separation on the ground.—W. E. M.

↖ The Union loss, July 3d, was 30, k; 149, w; 75, m,—total, 254. Confederate: 41, k; 50, w; 90 m,—total, 181. The loss in Jenkins's (Confederate) brigade is not included in this computation.—EDITORS.

MEADE AT GETTYSBURG.

BY FRANCIS A. WALKER, BREVET BRIGADIER-GENERAL, U. S. V.

THERE is probably no other battle of which men are so prone to think and speak without a conscious reference to the commanding general of the victorious party, as they are regarding Gettysburg. For this there are several reasons.

First, General Meade had been in command of the army but three days when the action began.

Second, the collision of the two armies on the 1st of July took place while headquarters were at a distance.

Third, the battle, on the Union side, was a defensive one. The sword is ever of higher honor than the shield.

Fourth, the fact that the Union army occupied a convex line, broke up the battles of the 2d and 3d of July into a series of actions, regarding which it was inevitable that attention should be fixed especially upon those who commanded at the points successively assaulted.

Fifth, the fact that so many eminent officers were killed or severely wounded during the action, had a tendency to concentrate interest upon them. Reynolds, the commander of the left wing, was killed at the first onset. Hancock, the commander of the left center; Sickles, the commander of the Third Corps, and Gibbon, commanding, in Hancock's absence, the Second, were desperately wounded. Such an unusual succession of casualties could not fail to have an effect in distracting attention from the commander-in-chief.

Sixth, the people of the North have ever loved to think of Gettysburg as a soldier's battle. In a great measure the wish has been father to the thought. But, indeed, there was something in the change of tone in the Army of the Potomac, as it turned from the gloomy region of Fredericksburg and Chancellorsville to throw itself in the path of the invading army, which justifies that view.

Seventh, much of the effect we are considering was due to General Meade's disinclination to assert himself against hostile criticism. He did, indeed, show a proper resentment of the blame thrown upon him for allowing the retreat of Lee; but during the years of life which remained he took little pains to vindicate himself against aspersion and disparagement, or even to put upon record the orders and dispositions of the battle.

It is my purpose to show that at Gettysburg the Army of the Potomac had a commander in every sense; that, in spite of misadventures and miscarriages, the action was fought according to his plans and under his direction as nearly as usually happens in war; and that his presence and watchful care, his moral courage and tenacity of purpose, contributed largely to the result.

When, on the 28th of June, 1863, General Meade relieved General Hooker, who, since the 13th, had been moving northward, interposing the Army of the Potomac continually between the Confederate forces and Washington, the right wing of that army lay at Frederick, Maryland, while the left occupied Boonsboro' and Middletown, and held the passes of the South Mountain. One corps, however, had been detached, but was returning to Frederick. It is in the disposition General Meade made of this corps that we find the chief difference between his conception of the strategy suitable to the campaign then approaching its culmination and that which had been entertained by his predecessor. The absent corps was the Twelfth, under Slocum, which had been pushed toward Harper's Ferry, with a view to advancing thence upon Lee's line of supply, and even following up the rear of the Confederate army. This corps Hooker had desired to reënforce by the large garrison of Harper's Ferry, abandoning that post as useless for strategic purposes. This General Halleck, at Washington, positively refused to permit. Thereupon Hooker ordered the Twelfth Corps back, and requested to be relieved.

When, however, Meade had been placed in command, Halleck conceded to him the power of diminishing the garrison at Harper's Ferry to any extent consistent with holding that post. The new commander was thus in a position to prosecute the contemplated enterprise in Lee's rear. Instead of doing so, he included the Twelfth Corps in his plan for a forward movement of the whole army directly northward, to be undertaken on the 29th and pushed with the utmost vigor till the encounter should take place.

This abandonment of the projected movement

against Lee's line of communication has been severely criticised by General Doubleday. That writer assumes that it was intelligence of Slocum's enterprise which caused Lee to loose his hold upon the Susquehanna and concentrate his forces at Gettysburg. ☆ He adds the opinion that "if he (Lee) had known that Meade was about to withdraw all the troops acting against his line of retreat, he would probably have gone on and taken Harrisburg."

Whatever General Lee might have thought of the projected enterprise under Slocum, had he known of it, he, in fact, knew nothing whatever concerning it. The only intelligence that reached him was that the Union army had crossed the Potomac on the 25th, at Edwards's Ferry, moving toward Frederick and Boonsboro', It was this, and only this, which determined his march upon Gettysburg. ⌡

More remains to be said. Meade's movement northward from Frederick, with his whole army, was a severer threat to Lee than a persistence in Hooker's plan. The movement against the Confederate communications through Harper's Ferry was correct enough, provided the bulk of the army was to remain at Frederick; but had the army moved northward while Slocum followed up Lee's rear, on the other side of the river and the mountains, there would have been every reason to anticipate essentially the same result as that which followed Hooker's division of his forces at Chancellorsville. On the other hand, Meade, by marching northward, did not relinquish the opportunity of moving to the west against Lee's communications, which could at any time have been done through Mechanicstown (to Hagerstown) just as effectively as from Harper's Ferry. [See map, p. 246.]

How far Meade's better choice was a mere matter of military judgment; how far it was due to the accident that the new commander was himself a Pennsylvanian it is difficult to say. There can, I think, be no doubt that the special instincts of local patriotism had much to do with bringing on and fighting through to a successful conclusion the battle of Gettysburg. It is remarkable that, in the one Pennsylvania battle of the war, the men of that State should have borne so prominent a part. It was a Pennsylvanian who directed the movement on Gettysburg and commanded there in chief. It was a Pennsylvanian who hurried the left wing into action and lost his life in determining that the battle should be fought at Gettysburg, and not on any line more remote. It was a Pennsylvanian who came up to check the rout and hold Cemetery Hill for the Union arms, who commanded the left center in the great battle of the second day, and on the third received and repelled the attack of Pettigrew and Pickett.

For one, I entertain no doubt that the military

☆ "The wisdom of Hooker's policy in desiring to assail the rebel communications is demonstrated by the fact that Lee immediately turned back. The head of the serpent faced about as soon as its tail was trodden upon." (Doubleday's "Chancellorsville and Gettysburg.")

⌡ General Lee's official report says: "The advance against Harrisburg was arrested by intelligence received from a scout, on the night of the 28th, to the effect that the army of General Hooker had crossed the Potomac and was approaching the South Mountain."

judgment of General Meade, which dictated his decision on the 28th of June to adopt the direct and more effective plan of moving straight northward from Frederick, instead of persisting in the division of the army which Hooker had initiated, was largely influenced by that intensity of feeling which actuated him as a Pennsylvanian. At such a crisis, stress of feeling drives the intellect to its highest work. So long as moral forces enter into the conduct of war, can we doubt that it was fortunate for the Union arms that they so largely were Pennsylvanians who hurried forward the troops in their long and painful marches northward, and who threw the veteran corps of the Potomac upon the invading army?

Widely spread as the Confederate army was when General Meade took command of the Union forces,— Longstreet at Chambersburg, Ewell at Carlisle and York,— it was a matter of course that the serious collision should be a surprise to one or the other party, and that accident should determine which should encounter its antagonist with the advantage in concentration. It turned out that the collision was a surprise to both commanders, and chance gave the advantage of greater concentration to the Confederates. Meade, leaving Frederick on the 29th, moved rapidly northward, extending his wings sufficiently to cover alike the road by which Lee might attempt to move to Washington and that by which he might march to Baltimore. He could not conjecture where, amid the fiery cloud of Southern raiders extending from the Cumberland Valley to the Susquehanna, was to be found the real nucleus of that formidable army; nor had the Confederate commander furnished any indication of his purpose. But on the same day, General Lee, having the evening before learned of the crossing of the Potomac by Hooker, recalled his advanced divisions from Carlisle and York, and threw forward Hill and Longstreet, with a view to a concentration at Gettysburg. During the 30th the two armies continued rapidly to approach each other, until, on the morning of the 1st of July, a stunning collision took place between the heads of Lee's columns and our left wing under Reynolds. In the two days that had passed, the Union forces had made nearly twice as long marches as the Confederates. The risk that one of Meade's columns would somewhere encounter the enemy in greater force, was an inevitable incident of so impetuous a forward movement.

But while Meade intended, by his rapid advance, to compel Lee to loose his hold upon the Susquehanna, he had wisely determined to fight a de-

fensive battle, and had selected the line of Pipe Creek as that most suitable for covering Washington and Baltimore.

It was the noble impetuosity of Reynolds, pushing forward to support Buford's hard-pressed but stubborn cavalry, which transformed the movement of the left wing from a reconnoissance into an attack upon Lee's advancing columns, and committed the Union army to battle at Gettysburg. The reports which, at noon of the 1st of July, reached the new commander at Taneytown, brought news that Reynolds had fallen, together with intimations of disaster to his adventurous column. The first act of General Meade, as commander-in-chief in the immediate presence of the enemy, was one which exhibited moral courage, insight into character, and rapidity of decision. This was to dispatch Hancock to the front, ⚓ with full powers to take command and do whatever might be necessary to save the day, and with instructions to report upon the nature of the position. It is difficult for us, now, to appreciate what this decision meant, on the part of Meade. Himself but three days at the head of the army, he was sending an officer, who had but three weeks before left his division, to assume command of three corps, over two officers who were his seniors. When one remembers how strong is the respect for rank among the higher officers, and how greatly the oldest commander is subject to the public sentiment of his army,— when one recalls that even Grant recognized Burnside's claim to command at the Mine,— this act of General Meade becomes one of the boldest in the history of our war. That it was also one of the most judicious, is abundantly established. No other man except, perhaps, Sheridan, arriving on that field of disaster, could have done what Hancock did in checking the rout, in establishing order, in restoring confidence, and in making the dispositions which caused Lee to postpone his contemplated assault on Cemetery Hill.

The further news of the opening battle brought upon General Meade the necessity for a choice which might well have caused deep anxiety and protracted doubt to a veteran commander. The Fifth and Sixth corps were still far distant from the field; the former about twenty, the latter more than thirty miles away. The fighting of the day had shown the superior concentration of Lee's forces; and all night long his fast-marching divisions would, doubtless, be pressing down the roads leading to Gettysburg, and wheeling into their places in the Confederate line. Two of the

---

⚓ The Comte de Paris says that Meade "should have gone in person to reconnoiter the localities around which the conflict was carried on, being only separated from it by about thirteen miles." He says that Meade was "unwilling to go," and "declined assuming the responsibility" of deciding whether it was expedient to deliver battle at Gettysburg or fall back to Pipe Creek; that, had he gone forward himself, "the concentration of the army would have been effected with more speed."

The last-indicated advantage certainly is fictitious. Why should the transmission of orders to the more distant points have been more rapid from Gettysburg than

from Taneytown? The manner in which the Fifth and Sixth corps were actually brought up showed no loss of time in effecting "the concentration of the army."

The charge that Meade, in remaining at Taneytown, declined to assume the proper responsibilities of his position, is unfounded and unjust. How could the Union commander know that he might not the very next hour hear of a collision at some other point? His true place, *until he had made up his mind where to concentrate*, was the most central point. To go to Gettysburg was to leave a position which was midway between his two wings, and was also between Gettysburg and the proposed line on Pipe Creek.— F. A. W.

Union corps, the First and Eleventh, had been put nearly *hors de combat*. With only three corps in fair fighting condition which could be upon the ground at daybreak, should the risks of an early morning battle be taken? General Meade's decision was here as brave as it proved fortunate; and his inspired rashness, like that of Reynolds in the morning, was of the kind which wins battles and saves states.

In his dispositions to meet the enemy's attack, on the 2d of July, it seems probable that General Meade, who had come upon the ground after midnight, and, in the cemetery, had met and conferred with Howard, anticipated that the weight of the Confederate force would be thrown upon Cemetery Hill, or else that the enemy would work around our right in order to get possession of the Baltimore pike. The fighting of the previous day had given undue emphasis to the importance of this end of the line. I am disposed to believe that General Meade's somewhat vague orders to Sickles, and his failure personally to inspect the left of the line after daybreak in the morning, ↓ were the result of a conviction that the battle was to be fought upon the center and right.

I have spoken of the orders to Sickles as somewhat vague. It would be more correct to speak of them as lacking emphasis rather than distinctness. Those orders were explicit enough to have been obeyed without difficulty, had proper care been taken to observe them. They were, that Sickles should take up the position from which Geary's division was to withdraw, in order to rejoin its own corps, the Twelfth, on the extreme right. Little Round Top, which forms a natural bastion, enfilading the low "curtain" known as Cemetery Ridge, strongly attracted the attention of Hancock on the afternoon of the 1st, and he dispatched that division, the first of the Twelfth Corps to arrive, with instructions to take position on the left of the First Corps and extend its own left to the hill. These instructions Geary had intelligently carried out, some of his regiments passing the night on Little Round Top. The slow development of Sickles's corps ♭ had allowed Geary, in pursuance of his own orders, to withdraw from his position of the night without being actually relieved therein; but a very little of good staff work would have sufficed to show where the line had been. Troops do not occupy ground without leaving palpable evidence of their presence. Meanwhile, the Second Corps had come up and taken position on Cemetery Ridge; the First Corps had been concentrated on the right; and Sickles's orders were repeated to him, by General Meade in person, to extend his command from the left of the Second Corps over the ground previously held

by Geary. Those instructions should have sufficed; and yet the presence of General Meade for but a few moments, at that time, upon that part of the line, would have added an assurance that his plans were being carried out. As it proved, it was left to Meade to ascertain, in the crisis of the battle, that Little Round Top was unoccupied and uncovered. The promptitude and energy of that brilliant young officer, General G. K. Warren, and his instantaneous acceptance of grave responsibility in detaching troops of the Fifth Corps on a hurried march to reënforce Sickles, finally secured that vitally important position.

It does not come within the scope of this paper, nor is it necessary, to comment on the action of General Sickles in advancing his troops to the Emmitsburg road, breaking connection with Hancock on the right, and leaving Little Round Top undefended on his left and rear. There can be no question that he both made a mistake in point of judgment and failed properly to subordinate his views and acts to the instructions of his commander. That he defended the position he had taken with courage and address, and that his splendid troops exhibited unsurpassed gallantry and resolution, must be admitted by even the severest critic. General Meade, who had sought to withdraw the Third Corps from its false position, was compelled to desist when the roar of musketry told that the conflict had begun, and had to content himself with reënforcing the widely extended lines and hastily stopping the gaps through which the Confederates streamed in continually swelling numbers. Few commanders ever showed more resolution in fighting a seemingly lost battle, advanced their reserves more promptly, or stripped other parts of their lines with less hesitation. The Fifth Corps was instantly sent forward; Caldwell's division and Willard's brigade, of the Second Corps, were thrown into the furious fight; General Meade himself brought up the reënforcements from the First and Twelfth corps, which finally completed the new line behind Plum Run, from which the exhausted Confederates fell back at nightfall. If one will compare the energy in which this action was conducted by General Meade with previous experiences of the Army of the Potomac, especially remembering the manner in which Porter was left to be overwhelmed at Gaines's Mill, the disconnected and desultory fighting at Antietam, and the conduct of affairs at Chancellorsville, one cannot fail to acknowledge that never before had the divisions of that army so closely supported each other or been so unreservedly thrown into the fight when and where most needed. ⌐

The fall of night found the Potomac army in a situation that demanded the most grave and seri-

---

↓ General Meade did, indeed, ride over the line on the left, about 1 o'clock; but it was then too dark to see the whole field, or to get a very clear view of anything.—F. A. W.

♭ In his letter to Colonel Benedict, March 16th, 1870, General Meade states that Geary informed him that, "after waiting for some time to be relieved, he sent to General Sickles a staff-officer with instructions to explain the position and its importance, and to ask, if troops could not be sent to relieve him, that General

Sickles would send one of his staff to see the ground and to place troops there on their arrival. He received, for reply, that General Sickles would attend to it in due time. No officer or troops came."—F. A. W.

⌐ "You handled your troops in that battle as well, if not better, than any general has handled his army during the war. You brought all your forces into action at the right time and place, which no commander of the Army of the Potomac has done before."—HALLECK to MEADE, July 28th, 1863.—F. A. W.

MONUMENT TO THE 1ST MASSACHUSETTS CAVALRY, ON THE SITE OF SEDGWICK'S HEADQUARTERS.
FROM A PHOTOGRAPH.

ous consideration. We had repulsed the last assaults; but nearly twelve thousand men had fallen in the desperate battle of the afternoon; our whole left had been beaten back to the position assigned it in the morning; the two corps chiefly engaged, the Third and Fifth, had been shockingly depleted; the enemy had taken advantage of the absence of the greater portion of the Twelfth Corps to push around our right and seize a part of our line, holding, thus, an open gateway through which their troops could be advanced to seize the Baltimore pike. It was, indeed, a gloomy hour when General Meade assembled his corps commanders to consult upon the situation and to frame plans for the morrow. Fortunately, the spirit of the army was high and stern; the corps commanders were unanimous in the opinion that the battle should be fought out on existing lines; and the commander-in-chief remained resolute in the face of the terrible responsibilities confronting him.

It has been alleged, with much of circumstance, that General Meade sought to retreat from Gettysburg, and he carried to his grave this arrow rankling in his breast. Had that charge been substantiated it would have answered the double

purpose of diminishing the fame of the commander-in-chief, and of giving to the advance upon the left the high credit of a movement which held the army at Gettysburg and brought about the conflict from which its commander was disposed to slink away.

The day of the 2d of July divides itself, for the present purpose, into three periods : before, during, and after the battle of the afternoon. Regarding the first period, General Butterfield declares that General Meade directed him, as chief-of-staff, to prepare plans for the withdrawal of the army. Were this admitted, it would prove nothing, since every general is bound to consider the contingency of defeat. Moreover, at Gettysburg there was an especial reason for being prepared for a sudden movement to the rear, inasmuch as the position which the army occupied was liable to be turned on the left. There was another weakness of the position calling for special precautions, viz. : the roads by which the Union army would have had to retreat, if beaten, ran back from the line of battle at an acute angle. But Butterfield's statement was directly contradicted by General Meade, ☆ than whom no man was more truthful. It is, moreover, inconsistent with the dispatch sent to Halleck

☆ Before the Committee on the Conduct of the War General Meade testified as follows:

"I have understood that an idea has prevailed that I intended an order should be issued on the morning of the 2d of July, requiring the withdrawal of the army or the

retreat of the army from Gettysburg, which order was not issued owing simply to the attack of the enemy having prevented it. In reply to that, I have only to say that I have no recollection of ever having directed such an order to be issued, or ever having contemplated the issuing of such an order, and that it does seem to me that to any intelligent mind who

at 3 o'clock in the afternoon: "I have delayed attacking, to allow the Sixth Corps and parts of other corps to reach this place and rest the men. Expecting a battle, I ordered all my trains to the rear. If not attacked, and I can get any positive information of the position of the enemy which will justify me in so doing, I shall attack."

The charge that General Meade, *during* the battle of the afternoon, actually undertook to retreat from the presence of the enemy, is founded upon a statement of General Pleasonton, dated October 16th, 1865, that at 5 o'clock, which was be-

is made acquainted with the great exertions I made to mass my army at Gettysburg on the night of July 1st, it must appear entirely incomprehensible that I should order it to retreat, after collecting all my army there, before the enemy had done anything to require me to make a movement of that kind."

At another time General Meade testified as follows:

"I deny under the full solemnity and sanctity of my oath, and in the firm conviction that the day will come when the secrets of all men shall be known — I utterly deny ever having intended or thought, for one instant, to withdraw that army, unless the military contingencies, which the future should develop during the course of the day, might render it a matter of necessity that the army should be withdrawn."

Of the witnesses referred to by General Meade, General Henry J. Hunt denied any knowledge of such an order or of such intention to retreat. See also p. 297.

That part of General Daniel Butterfield's testimony relating to the matter reads as follows:

"General Meade then directed me to prepare an order to withdraw the army from that position. I stated to him that it would be necessary that I should know the exact position of the troops."

Question: "What day of the fight was this?"

Answer: "This was in the morning of the 2d of July, before the battle of that day had commenced. I stated to General Meade that I could not prepare the order properly without first going over the field and ascertaining the positions of each division and corps of the army with relation to the roads. General Meade replied that he could not wait for that — that he could show me where the troops were. He then took a pencil and a piece of paper and made a rough sketch, showing the position of the different corps. I stated to him that the order was one requiring a great deal of care in its preparation; that it involved something more than logistics, as we were in the presence of the enemy, and that while preparing it I must not be interrupted by anybody coming to me with dispatches or orders. He said, 'Very well, you shall not be interrupted.' I told him I thought I could not prepare the order without a more accurate sketch, and I would have to send out to the corps commanders to give me a report of the position of their troops in regard to the various roads; that in the meanwhile I could be studying the maps. He said, 'Very well, do so.' I went upstairs, and, after carefully studying the maps, I prepared the order for the withdrawal of the army from the field of Gettysburg. After finishing it I presented it to General Meade, and it met his approval. I then stated to him that it would be a great deal better if that order was to be executed, as it might involve grave consequences if not properly executed, to submit it for careful examination to such general officers as were then present, with a view of giving them an opportunity of finding any fault with it then, so that no misunderstanding should arise from the manner in which it was worded or expressed. He said there was no objection to having it done. I called General Gibbon, who was present, and, I think, General Williams and General Ingalls, and stated to them that I had been directed to prepare this order, and that I would be very much obliged to any of them if they would look it over and point out any faults in it then, rather than after it was put into execution; that I desired it scrutinized carefully with a view of discovering anything in it which might be misunderstood. Some of these officers — I do not remember which; I am very sure General Gibbon was one — I think General Hancock was there, but whether he read it over or not I am not sure — some of

the officers read it over and said that they thought it was correctly prepared. The corps commanders were then sent for by General Meade to report to headquarters. The order which I had prepared was given to General Williams, and was copied by the clerks, or was in process of being copied by them. As General Sickles rode up to headquarters, in pursuance of the request of General Meade, the battle broke out in front of General Sickles's corps, and there was no council held. General Sickles returned immediately, and every corps commander then rode immediately to his command. Without my memoranda I cannot fix the hour of this occurrence, but it was during the 2d day of July. . . ."

Question: "Did this collision of General Sickles's corps with the enemy prevent the order being executed which you had prepared?"

Answer: "It is impossible for me to state that, because General Meade had not communicated to me his intention to execute the order regardless of the opinion of the corps commanders, or whether he intended to have the order submitted to them. He merely directed me to prepare such an order, which I did. It is for him to say whether he intended to execute it or not. He may have desired it prepared for an emergency without any view of executing it then, or he may have had it prepared with a full view of its execution."

Question: "The collision of Sickles's troops with the enemy broke up the council?"

Answer: "It prevented any consultation of corps commanders at that time. . . ."

General Seth Williams, assistant adjutant-general on Meade's staff, testified:

"In regard to the order of the 2d of July, to the best of my recollection and belief, the chief-of-staff either handed to me or to my clerk an order looking to a contingency which possibly might happen, of the army being compelled to assume a new position. To the best of my belief such an order was prepared, and I presume it may have been signed by me and possibly copies may have been prepared for the corps and other commanders. Orders of such character are usually made out in manifold in order to save time. The particular order in question, however, was never distributed; no vestige of it is to be found among any of the records of my office, and it must have been destroyed within a day or two after it was prepared. I have no reason to suppose other than the fact that the order was given to me or my chief clerk by the chief-of-staff, that General Meade had any knowledge of it. It was not for me to look beyond the orders of the chief-of-staff. Whether or not a copy of that order was given to Major-General Butterfield, who was then acting as chief-of-staff, I am unable to say, and I cannot certainly state whether the rough draft was ever handed back to him. I only know that there is nothing in relation to that order to be found among the records in my charge. The order was never recorded, or issued in any sense. I do not now remember the exact tenor of the order, but to the best of my belief it was an order which, if carried out, would have involved a retrograde movement of the army."

General John Gibbon testified that General Butterfield asked him to read the order for retreat and to compare it with a map. He added:

"General Butterfield did not say General Meade did intend to leave; he merely said something to the effect that it was necessary to be prepared in case it should be necessary to leave, or some remark of that kind. He then showed me the order, and either he read it over and I pointed out the places on the map, or I read it over and he pointed out the places to which each corps was to go. When he got through, I remarked that it was all correctly drawn up."

EDITORS.

remember." What is the degree of probability that a chief of cavalry, who had, on so important an occasion as this, been engaged from 5 until 12 o'clock in bringing up and disposing his troops to cover the retreat of his army, should, first, have omitted to mention it in his official report, and, secondly, have failed to remember it nine months later, in reply to a specific and highly suggestive inquiry?

That on the evening of the 2d, after the battle, General Meade was disinclined to await further attacks in his position, is an imputation which rests upon much higher authority, for it has the word of General Slocum, an officer of honor, dignity of character, and firmness of purpose. Referring to the council of war, General Slocum, in a letter dated February 19th, 1883, makes the following statement: "When each officer had expressed his views General Meade said: 'Well, gentlemen, the question is settled; we will remain here, but I wish to say I consider this no place to fight a battle.'"

I would not speak lightly of any word of General Slocum, but it is far more probable that, at such a distance of time, he was mistaken, than that General Sedgwick had forgotten the incidents of the council when he wrote, on March 10th, 1864, "At no time, in my presence, did the general commanding insist upon or advise a withdrawal of the army."

On the same point, General Gibbon wrote: "I never heard General Meade say one word in favor of a retreat, nor do I believe that he did so." General A. S. Williams testified: "I heard no expression from him which led me to think he was in favor of withdrawing the army from before Gettysburg." At a later date, General Howard wrote to Colonel George Meade, "I did not hear your father utter a word which made me think that he then favored a withdrawal of his troops."

Certainly, if General Meade had such a momentary feeling as General Slocum understood him to express, it was in direct contradiction to his acts and words and bearing throughout those three memorable days. At all other times his spirit was bold and martial. From first to last he bore himself as one who came to fight, who wanted to fight, and who could not have too much fighting on equal terms. Whatever opinion men may hold as to the grade of Meade's generalship, those do him a gross injustice who represent him as ever, in any case, timid, vacillating, or reluctant to encounter the enemy. On the contrary, he was a man in whom high military scholarship and a serious sense of responsibility were often in conflict with "creature pugnacity" and stubbornness of temper.

Of the battle of the third day, the purpose of this paper requires us to say but little. When the lines had been rectified upon the left, and the Round Tops had been made secure, when the positions of the troops had been readjusted to secure due strength in every part, when all the points from which effective artillery fire could be obtained had been occupied, and when the intruding enemy upon the right had been driven out in the early morning by the energetic attack of the Twelfth Corps, reënforced from the Sixth,—when all this had been done, little remained but to await the assault which it was known General Lee must needs deliver, whether to prosecute his enterprise or to excuse his retreat. All that long morning, amid the dread silence, no man in the Potomac army could conjecture where that assault would be delivered; but no man in all that army doubted that it was to come.

At last the blow fell. As the spear of Menelaus pierced the shield of his antagonist, cut through the shining breastplate, but spared the life, so the division of Pickett, launched from Seminary Ridge, broke through the Union defense, and for the moment thrust its head of column within our lines, threatening destruction to the Army of the Potomac; then the broken brigades fled, with the loss of more than half their numbers, across the plain, which was shrieking with the fire of a hundred guns, and Gettysburg had been fought and won for the Union arms.

Into the questions, whether Meade should not have followed up the repulse of Pickett with a general advance of his own line, or, failing this, have attacked Lee at Falling Waters, on the 13th of July, we have no call to enter. General Meade was here entirely within his competence as the commander of an army. Any officer who is fit to be intrusted with such a charge is entitled to the presumption that, for decisions such as these, he had good and sufficient reasons, whatever may, at the time, have been the opinion of subordinates on whom did not rest the final responsibility of success or failure; yet in fact, in both these decisions General Meade was supported by a preponderance of authoritative opinion among his corps commanders and the staff-officers of greatest reputation.

I believe that, as time goes on and the events of the last days of June and the first days of July, 1863, are more and more carefully studied, in the light of all the facts, and with an impartial and dispassionate spirit, the weighty judgment of the illustrious chief of the Union artillery, General Henry J. Hunt, ♭ will be more and more fully approved. "He was right in his orders as to Pipe Creek; right, in his determination under certain circumstances to fall back to it; right, in pushing up to Gettysburg after the battle commenced; right, in remaining there; right, in making his battle a purely defensive one; right, therefore, in taking the line he did; right, in not attempting a counter-attack at any stage of the battle; right, as to his pursuit of Lee."

♭ In his letter to General A. S. Webb, January 19th, 1888, quoted by permission.—F. A. W.

I. A LETTER FROM GENERAL MEADE.

HEADQUARTERS, MILITARY DIVISION OF THE AT-
LANTIC, PHILADELPHIA, March 16th, 1870.

[Private.]

[COLONEL] G. G. BENEDICT, Burlington, Vt.

DEAR SIR: I am in receipt of your letter of the
13th inst., as also the copies of the "Free Press,"
with editorials and comments on the address of
Colonel [W. W.] Grout before the Officers' Society
and Legislature of the State.

I have carefully read your articles and feel
personally under great obligations to you for the
clear and conclusive manner in which you have
vindicated the truth of history. I find nothing to
correct in your statements except a fact you mention, which is a misapprehension.

I did not invite General Humphreys to be my
chief-of-staff till after the battle, because I did not
see him after assuming command till I met him on
the field, and besides I relied on him as a mainstay
in handling the Third Corps, and did not wish to
withdraw him from that position.

I did ask General [Seth] Williams to assume the
duties in addition to those of adjutant-general, but
he declined. I also asked General Warren, then
my chief-of-engineers, to act temporarily as chief-
of-staff, but he also declined taking on himself
additional duties. Under these circumstances I
asked General Butterfield to remain till I had time
to make permanent arrangements [see p. 243].
On the third day General Butterfield, having been
disabled by being struck with a fragment of a
spent shell, left the army, and a few days afterward General Humphreys accepted my invitation.

My defense against the charges and insinuations
of Generals Sickles and Butterfield is to be found
in my testimony before the Committee on the Conduct of the War. I have avoided any controversy
with either of these officers — though both have
allowed no opportunity to pass unimproved which
permitted them to circulate their ex-parte statements, and, as you justly say, to *distort* history for
their purposes. Both perfectly understand what
I meant by my ante-battle order, referring to Pipe
Creek, also my instructions to Butterfield on the
morning of the 2d, which he persists in calling an
order for retreat, in the face of all my other acts,
and of the fact that I did not retreat when I could
have done so with perfect ease *at any moment.*
Longstreet's advice to Lee [to move from his right
upon General Meade's communications] was sound
military sense; it was the step I feared Lee would
take, and to meet which and be prepared for
which was the object of my instructions to Butterfield, which he has so misrepresented. Now, let

me tell you another historical fact. Lieutenant-
General Ewell, in a conversation held with me
shortly after the war, asked what would have been
the effect if at 4 P. M. on the 1st he had occupied
Culp's Hill and established batteries on it. I told
him that in my judgment, in the condition of
the Eleventh and First corps, with their *morale*
affected by their withdrawal to Cemetery Ridge
with the loss of over half their numbers in killed,
wounded, and missing (of the 6000 prisoners we
lost in the field nearly all came from these corps

MONUMENT IN THE GETTYSBURG CEMETERY.

in the first day), his occupation of Culp's Hill, with
batteries commanding the whole of Cemetery Ridge,
would have produced the evacuation of that ridge
and the withdrawal of the troops there by the
Baltimore Pike and Taneytown and Emmitsburg
roads. He then informed me that at 4 P. M. on
the 1st he had his corps, 20,000 strong, in column
of attack, and on the point of moving on Culp's
Hill, which he saw was unoccupied and commanded
Cemetery Ridge, when he received an order from
General Lee directing him to assume the defensive
and not to advance; that he sent to General Lee
urging to be permitted to advance with his reserves, but the reply was a reiteration of the

See also the preceding article.— EDITORS.

The substance of these editorials in the Burlington
"Free Press" will be found in the appendix to the second
edition of Colonel Benedict's work, "Vermont at Gettysburg."— EDITORS.

According to General A. A. Humphreys's statement

to the Committee on the Conduct of the War, General
Meade, on assuming command of the army at Frederick,
expressed his desire to appoint General Humphreys his
chief-of-staff, but that officer wishing to retain command
of his division in the Third Corps during the impending
battle, the decision was postponed.— EDITORS.

previous order. To my inquiry why Lee had restrained him, he said our troops coming up (Slocum's) were visible, and Lee was under the impression that the greater part of my army was on the ground and deemed it prudential to await the rest of his — as you quote from his report.

But suppose Ewell with 20,000 men had occupied Culp's Hill, and our brave soldiers had been compelled to evacuate Cemetery Ridge and withdraw on the roads above referred to, would the Pipe Creek order have been so very much out of place?

That order was to meet the very contingency here in question, to wit: A part of my army, overwhelmed by superior numbers, compelled to fall back, and a line of battle, formed to the rear of my most advanced position, thus necessitated.

As to General Sickles having by his advance brought on an attack, and thus compelled the battle which decided the war, you have completely answered — and it is a very favorite theory with the partisans of this officer. But these gentlemen ignore the fact that of the 18,000 men killed and wounded on the field during the whole battle more than two-thirds were lost on the second day, and but for the timely advance of the Fifth Corps and the prompt sending a portion on Round Top, where they met the enemy almost on the crest and had a desperate fight to secure the position — I say but for these circumstances, over which Sickles had neither knowledge nor control, the enemy would have secured Round Top, planted his artillery there, commanding the whole battle-field, and what the result would have been I leave you to judge. Now, when I wrote my report of the battle I honestly believed General Sickles did not know where I wished him to go, and that his error arose from a misapprehension of my orders; but I have recently learned from General Geary, who had the day before been sent by Hancock to hold the left, and who in doing so had seen the great importance of Round Top, and *posted a brigade on it*, that on the morning of the 2d, when he received my order that he would be relieved by the Third Corps and on being relieved would rejoin his own corps (Twelfth) on the right, after waiting for some time to be relieved he sent to General Sickles a staff-officer with instructions to explain the position and its importance, and to ask, if troops could not be sent to relieve him, that General Sickles would send one of his staff to see the ground, and to place troops there on their arrival. He received for reply that General Sickles would attend to it in due time. No officer or troops came, and after waiting till his patience was exhausted General Geary withdrew and joined his corps. Now my first orders to General Sickles were to relieve the Twelfth Corps division (Geary's) and occupy their position. Here is evidence that he knew the position occupied by Geary's division, or could have known, and yet failed to occupy it. Furthermore, when he came to my headquarters at about noon and said he did not know where to go, I answered, "Why you were to relieve the Twelfth Corps." He said they had no position; they were massed, awaiting events. Then it was I told him his *right* was to be *Hancock's left*, his *left* on *Round Top, which I pointed out*. Now his right was three-quarters of a mile in front of Hancock's left and his left one-quarter of a mile in front of the base of Round Top, leaving that *key-point unoccupied*, which ought to have been occupied by Longstreet before we could get there with the Fifth Corps. Sickles's movement practically destroyed his own corps, the Third, caused a loss of 50 per cent. in the Fifth Corps, and very heavily damaged the Second Corps; as I said before, producing 66 per cent. of the loss of the whole battle; and with what result? — driving us back to the position he was ordered to hold originally. These losses of the first and second day affected greatly the efficiency and *morale* of the army and prevented my having the audacity in the offense that I might otherwise have had.

If this is an advantage — to be so crippled in battle without attaining an object — I must confess I cannot see it.

Pardon my writing with so much prolixity, but your generous defense and the clear view you have taken of the battle have led me to wander thus far.

Very truly yours,   GEO. G. MEADE.

II. REPLY BY DANIEL E. SICKLES, MAJOR-GENERAL, U. S. A.⟩

ONLY a cursory perusal of General Meade's letter suggests the reason why he wished it treated as confidential. It must have been written without deliberation, without revision, and without comparison with the official records. It contradicts his own official report of the battle made in October, 1863, and his testimony before the Committee on the Conduct of the War, in March, 1864.

General Meade is altogether mistaken in speaking of charges and insinuations and attacks upon him made by me. I have never spoken of his conduct at Gettysburg except in my testimony before the Committee on the Conduct of the War, in February, 1864. General Meade's testimony was given in the following month and with full knowledge of all my statements, none of which were contradicted by him when he testified. The report of the Committee on the Conduct of the War justified me and censured General Meade.

It must not be supposed that General Meade had a controversy with me only. Other corps commanders made protests when I was silent. I will only speak now of one or two as examples. Immediately after General Meade's report of the battle of Gettysburg, Major-General Slocum, commanding the right wing of the Army of the Potomac at Gettysburg, in an official communication to General Meade, arraigned him for a series of inaccuracies, to use the mildest phrase, in General Meade's official report of Gettysburg, by which

⟩ From the "New York Times" of August 14th, 1886. Revised by General Sickles for this work, June 26th, 1888.—EDITORS.

grave injustice was done to Major-General Slocum and the corps under his command. After reciting so much of General Meade's report as relates to the operations of his command, General Slocum says: "Yet the facts in the case are very nearly the reverse of the above in every particular, and directly in contradiction to the facts as set forth in the reports of General Geary and General Williams."

Brigadier-General Williams, commanding the Twelfth Corps, in an official communication to Major-General Slocum, dated December 26th, 1863, points out four serious misstatements in General Meade's official report relating to the operations of the Twelfth Corps on the 2d of July. The character of these complaints will be understood when I quote from General Williams that they consist "in wholly ignoring the operations of the First Division" and "in repudiating most of the material statements of my report as temporary commander of this army corps"; also "in ignoring the splendid conduct of Greene's brigade, which held our intrenched line on the right," and in giving credit for Greene's fight to Geary's division, which was not in the fight at all, but got lost on the road to Two Taverns. General Williams concludes his protest in these words, referring to General Meade's official report of Gettysburg: "I confess to have read that part of his official report relating to the Twelfth Corps with a mixed feeling of astonishment and regret." ⸸

I could amplify similar proofs, showing the characteristic inaccuracy of General Meade in his official reports of his military operations, but will not now trespass upon your space in that direction. General Meade knew nothing of Gettysburg. He so stated to the Committee on the Conduct of the War. He speaks of Gettysburg in these words: "A place I had never seen in my life and had no more knowledge of than you have now" (addressing the committee). This is not said censoriously, for General Meade had only been in command three days and had already chosen another battle-field, on the line of Pipe Clay Creek, twenty miles distant. General Meade was drawn to Gettysburg in spite of his plans, because Lee had chosen Gettysburg as his place of concentration, and because Buford and Reynolds had accepted battle there, forcing General Meade to give up his Pipe Creek line and come to Gettysburg. I assisted in this, first, by moving my corps twelve miles from Emmitsburg to Gettysburg, on the afternoon of July 1st, to help Howard after Reynolds fell; also by my letter to General Meade, written at Gettysburg at 9 o'clock on the night of July 1st, asking his approval of my march, made without orders, and urging him to come to Gettysburg with his army, describing it as "a good place to fight a battle," and pointing out to him that its weak place would be "on his left," as it proved to be the next day, when I was unsupported for two hours in resisting Longstreet's assault. After General Meade had brought his forces up to Gettysburg and had reconnoitered the position, he was dissatisfied, and frequently

spoke of it, during the 2d, as "no place to fight a battle." He so expressed himself in the council of war held on the night of the 2d. After this council had decided to stay and fight it out, General Slocum thus describes what took place: General Meade said, "Well, gentlemen, the question is settled; we will remain here; but I wish to say that I consider this no place to fight a battle." This was after the combats of the 1st and 2d of July, and after twenty thousand Union soldiers had fallen on that field.

General Meade seemed to manifest resentment against every corps commander who had been instrumental in the choice of Gettysburg as our battle-field. He owed his splendid position there to Buford, Reynolds, and Howard, and the divisions of Wadsworth, Doubleday, and Robinson. Yet all of these officers, except Reynolds, who was killed, suffered marks of his displeasure or were mentioned with the scantiest recognition of their heroic conduct. In Howard's case Congress interposed to do him justice, when he received its formal vote of thanks for his choice of our position on Cemetery Ridge, the Gibraltar of Gettysburg.

General Meade was surprised by the attack of Longstreet, on the Union left, on the afternoon of the 2d of July. No preparations whatever were made by the commanding general to meet Longstreet's assault. There was no order of battle. General Meade had not personally reconnoitered the position, though frequently solicited by General Hunt, General Meade's chief of artillery, General Warren, his chief of engineers, and myself, to do so. This appears in the testimony of General Hunt and in the report of General Tremain, my senior aide-de-camp. Not only was no preparation made by General Meade to meet the attack upon his left,— the position I held,— but he deprived me and himself of the most effective support he had on his left flank by the unaccountable withdrawal of Buford's division of cavalry, which held the Emmitsburg road and covered our left flank, including Round Top, until a late hour on the morning of the 2d. Geary's division of infantry had been withdrawn from the left very early in the morning of the 2d. These dispositions imposed upon me, thus weakened by the withdrawal of two divisions, the sole responsibility of resisting the formidable attack of General Lee upon our left flank. The first support that reached me was Barnes's division of the Fifth Corps; it got into position after 5 o'clock in the afternoon, two hours after the battle opened.

The Comte de Paris, in his critical history of the war, incomparably the ablest yet written, thus speaks of the withdrawal of General Buford's division:

"One of those blunders that frequently occur on the battle-field was the means of compromising the safety of the Federal line just in that part which will be the first to be menaced."

This was my front. The Count continues:

"Buford alone covered this flank. Meade only learned this fact at 1 o'clock. He immediately directed Pleasonton not to strip him entirely, but it is too late. Buford is gone; Merritt, who is coming from Emmitsburg, is still far away, and Sickles has therefore only the skirmishers of his infantry to watch the movements of the enemy, whose numerous indications reveal his presence in force on that side. . . . when, shortly after, Sickles, being apprised of the untimely departure of Buford, decided, in order to ward off all surprise, to replace him by causing his whole line of skirmishers to advance as far as the Emmitsburg road. This general, whose military instinct has fathomed the enemy's intentions, justly suspecting that Lee's main effort would shortly be directed against that portion of the Federal line which has been intrusted to him, . . . has charged Colonel Berdan to push forward a reconnoissance. . . . This . . . has revealed the presence of a numerous enemy, who is masking his movements and seems disposed to turn the Federal left. In the meanwhile Sickles, thinking only of the attack with which he believes himself menaced, has requested Meade to send him fresh instructions: . . . receiving no reply, he repairs to headquarters for the purpose of obtaining them. . . . he immediately requests his chief either to ascertain for himself the necessity for making this movement, or to send General Warren to settle the matter in his place. Meade, being under the impression, no doubt, that the attack of the enemy would not be aimed at his left, . . . declined either to leave his headquarters or to separate himself from General Warren."

Unfortunately, General Meade's whole attention, tactically, was fixed upon his right flank. He did not believe that the enemy would attack his left, although Hancock and myself had both of us pointed out that his left was his vulnerable point for attack. Apart from this tactical preoccupation on his right, General Meade, as I have already said, did not like Gettysburg as a battle-field and wanted to get away from it. Hence we can understand, and in another way, the withdrawal of Geary and Buford from the left and his failure to send timely reënforcements to the almost uncovered left flank. At 3 o'clock in the afternoon of July 2d, a few moments before Longstreet opened his assault, Meade telegraphed to Halleck: "If satisfied the enemy is endeavoring to move to my rear, I shall fall back to my supplies at Westminster." He had already sent Buford there, two hours before. General Meade's chief-of-cavalry, Major-General Alfred Pleasonton, states that in the afternoon of the 2d of July General Meade "gave me the order to get what cavalry and artillery I could as soon as possible, and take up a position in the rear to cover the retreat of the army from Gettysburg. I was thus occupied until 10 o'clock at night, when I was recalled by an order from General Meade."

Meanwhile, although General Meade had no order of battle, although his chief-of-artillery, General Hunt, as he states in his testimony, knew nothing of the intentions of his commanding general, whether to stay or to go, or whether his tactics were offensive or defensive if he staid; while his left flank was being stripped of cavalry and of infantry vital to its protection; while the commander of the Third Corps, General Sickles, was left unsupported and without definite instructions, all was different on the side of the enemy. From early dawn on the morning of the 2d General Lee, with his lieutenants and his staff, was in the saddle carefully reconnoitering our left and making elaborate preparations for the assault made at a later hour. General Lee promulgated his order of battle. He placed his infantry and his artillery in position. He designated the divisions of his center and left to support Longstreet's assault. These dispositions made by General Lee were disclosed by reconnoissances made by General Birney, one of the greatest soldiers produced by Pennsylvania. Birney commanded my left division. To his vigilance and unerring military intuition General Meade owed the timely warnings, again and again repeated by myself and General Tremain, my senior aide, of the enemy's movements imperiling the left flank of our army. All admonitions were unheeded, derided. General Meade declined to accept any suggestion that his left was in danger of attack.

It is a significant fact, never contradicted, that at the moment when the battle of the 2d began, General Meade was in consultation with his corps commanders, a consultation which I was called away from my front to attend. Finding myself in the presence of the enemy, I asked to be excused from attending the council of war. I was at once peremptorily ordered to repair to General Meade's headquarters. The report of my aide-de-camp that I was momentarily expecting to be engaged with the enemy was disregarded, and the order to leave my command and report to headquarters was made imperative. While I was on my way to headquarters the battle began on my front. General Meade met me at the door of his house, excused me from dismounting, authorized me to return to my command, and said he would follow immediately. This broke up the council, and the corps commanders repaired to their commands. This was at 3 in the afternoon. General Meade soon afterward met me at the front and witnessed the dispositions which I was making, and which he did not modify. And from that hour until 6 o'clock, when I was wounded, I did not receive any order or instruction whatever from General Meade as to the conduct of the battle.

The truth is that when I was summoned to headquarters at 3 o'clock in the afternoon to attend this council of war, I had become weary of so many visits to headquarters during the day. Besides my own repeated requests made in person to General Meade for instructions, General Tremain and Colonel Moore, my aides, had been sent again and again to General Meade with reports of the enemy's movements on his left and with urgent representations from me of the necessity of proper dispositions and of reënforcements.

General Meade states in his confidential letter to Colonel Benedict: "When Sickles came to my headquarters about noon and said he did not know where to go I answered, 'Why, you were to relieve the Twelfth Corps.' He said they had no position; they were massed awaiting events." To this I answer from the record: First, that the Twelfth Corps was never at any time, until the very close of the battle on the 2d of July, in position on the left. The position of the Twelfth Corps during all the day of the 2d was on the right flank, miles away from the left—as far away as Culp's Hill is from Round Top; second, that Geary's division of the Twelfth Corps was ordered by General Hancock, on the evening of July 1st, "to the high ground to the right of and near Round Top mountain, commanding the Gettysburg and Emmitsburg road, as well as the Gettysburg and Taneytown road, to our rear" (see Hancock's Official Report); third, that Birney, "under orders from Major-General Sickles, relieved Geary's division and formed a line resting its left on the Sugar Loaf Mountain (Round Top), and the right thrown in a direct line toward the Cemetery, connecting on the right with the Second Division of this corps. My picket line was in the Emmitsburg road with sharp-shooters some three hundred yards in advance." (See Official Report of Major-General Birney, commanding First Division, Third Corps.)

These citations from the official reports of Hancock and Birney prove that only one division (Geary's) of the Twelfth Corps was temporarily on the left; that this division was ordered there by Hancock; that, pursuant to my orders, Birney relieved Geary's division and occupied a position identical with that indicated by Hancock,—to wit, "to the right of and near Round Top mountain, commanding the Gettysburg and Emmitsburg road," etc.

General Meade is as unfortunate in dealing with the Twelfth Corps, in his letter to Benedict seven years after the battle, as he was in dealing with the Twelfth Corps' movements in his official report of Gettysburg. I have already quoted General Williams, commanding the Twelfth Corps, when he exclaimed: "I have read General Meade's report of the operations of the Twelfth Corps with astonishment and regret." I may be permitted to share General Williams's astonishment and regret when I read General Meade's report of the operations of the Third Corps, my own.

General Meade proceeds in his confidential statement to Colonel Benedict: "Then it was I told him his right was to be Hancock's left; his left on Round Top, which I pointed out." To this I answer: First, that this statement is contradicted by General Meade's official report of the battle, and by his testimony before the Committee on the Conduct of the War; second, it is contradicted by the report of his chief-of-artillery, General Hunt; third, it is absurd, topographically and tactically; fourth, my testimony before the Committee on the Conduct of the War, in February, 1864, presented the facts, which are wholly different from General Meade's statement in the Benedict letter, and which were not denied by him when he testified in the following month. My statement in regard to the operations of the Third Corps at Gettysburg from the beginning to the end was never publicly contradicted by General Meade, so far as I have been informed. Certainly it was never contradicted by him or any one else officially. The War Department records have been ransacked and searched in vain for testimony to uphold these assertions of General Meade in regard to the position of the Third Corps. Failing to find any testimony from the records contradicting my declarations at Gettysburg on the 2d of July last, this confidential letter of General Meade, written in 1870, is brought to light, most impru-

dently, I think, to uphold a contention absolutely unsupported by anything in the official records of the battle.

You have not the space to give me for citations from the testimony of Meade, Hunt, and Sickles before the Committee on the Conduct of the War, nor for extracts from the official reports of Generals Meade, Birney, and Humphreys. It is enough for me to state distinctly, and this can be verified by any one who chooses to consult the record, that General Meade nowhere pretends in his official report, or in his testimony before the Committee on the Conduct of the War, that I was to occupy Round Top. He states that he expected me to occupy Geary's position. Hancock's report proves that Geary was ordered to the right of Round Top, — precisely the ground I held, extending my left to the Devil's Den and my right toward the Emmitsburg road. General Tremain, my aide-de-camp, in compliance with my instructions, pointed out to General Meade, during the morning of the 2d, the importance of Round Top and the need of troops to occupy it; likewise the importance of the Emmitsburg road and the intersecting roads leading to our left, all of which positions, including Round Top, had been stripped of defense by the removal of Buford and his division of cavalry. Against this abandonment of Round Top and the Emmitsburg road I personally protested to General Meade at his headquarters, and so testified to the Committee on the Conduct of the War, uncontradicted by General Meade.

General Meade's statement, I repeat, is absurd, tactically and topographically, because it designates a line and positions for the Third Corps which it could not have occupied by reason of the great extension of the line and the number of troops required to hold Round Top. The distance from Hancock's left to Round Top is stated by the Comte de Paris to be a mile and a quarter, that is to say, 2200 yards. The front of the Second Corps, Hancock's, which was stronger than mine, was only twelve hundred yards, so that my line, if taken according to General Meade's confidential letter, from Hancock's left to and including Round Top, and the necessary force to hold that natural fortress, would have been a mere skirmish line utterly incapable of resisting assaulting columns. Moreover, the direct line from Hancock's left to Round Top was a line through swale, morass, swamp, bowlders, and forest and tangled undergrowth, impracticable for infantry, impracticable for artillery, and hopelessly dominated by the ridge in front, which I would have surrendered to Lee without a blow if I had attempted to execute the impossible order General Meade confidentially states to his correspondent that he gave me. Nay, more, if I had occupied the line General Meade represents in 1870 that he told me to take, I would have had no positions whatever for my artillery over one half of my line, and would have surrendered to Lee the positions for his artillery which he states in his official report it was the object of his movement to gain. In other words, the line indicated by General Meade in his confidential letter is one that would have abandoned to the enemy all the vantage-ground he sought and had to fight for all the afternoon. And this vantage-ground, by which I mean the Emmitsburg road ridge, the Devil's Den, the Emmitsburg road itself, and the intersecting roads leading to our left, once in possession of the enemy without loss, would have enabled him to deliver his assault upon me in the position indicated by General Meade, three hours before it was delivered, and with advantage of position and force that would have given Lee the victory.

General Meade proceeds: "Now, his right was three-quarters of a mile in front of Hancock's left and his left one-quarter of a mile in front of the base of Round Top, leaving that key-point unoccupied, which ought to have been occupied by Longstreet before we could get there with the Fifth Corps." To this I answer: First, that I was in the right place to defend Round Top when I put myself in front of it, and I staid there until after 5 o'clock, giving General Meade time to bring up the Fifth Corps from the right, where he had kept it all day; second, that if I had not put my troops in position in front of Round Top, Longstreet would have occupied it at any time during the two hours that elapsed before the Fifth Corps was brought over from the right to occupy it; third, my line was a good one, but there were not troops enough at hand early in the day to hold that line, or any other line, against the forces employed by Lee in the attack. If the reënforcements which came up from 5 o'clock to 6:30 had arrived three hours earlier, Longstreet's assault on the second would have been repulsed as promptly and decisively as on the third day; fourth, look at the ground occupied by my corps, and then compare its advantages over Meade's line, extending from Cemetery Ridge to Round Top,— and the discussion will not last long.

General Meade proceeds: "Sickles's movement practically destroyed his own corps, the Third; caused a loss of 50 per cent. in the Fifth Corps, and very heavily damaged the Second Corps, producing 66 per cent. of the loss of the whole battle." To this I answer: First, that the losses of the Fifth Corps in the entire Gettysburg campaign, killed, wounded, captured, and missing, were 2187, out of an aggregate of 12,000, by which it appears — I speak from the official record — that General Meade confidentially more than doubled the loss of the Fifth Corps, an inexcusable disregard of fact with the record before him; second, when General Meade says that the Third Corps was practically destroyed on the 2d of July he is contradicted by the two division commanders, Humphreys and Birney, and by Graham and Carr, and by De Trobriand, Ward, Burling, and Brewster. Not to weary the readers with extracts from the reports of all these distinguished Third Corps commanders, I will cite an example from the report of General Joseph B. Carr. General Carr, in his official report, states: "Notwithstanding my apparently critical position I could and would have maintained it but for an order received direct from Major-General Birney, commanding the corps, to fall back to the crest of the hill in my rear." This was between 6 and 7 o'clock in the evening, after I had been wounded. General Carr proceeds:

"At that time I have no doubt I could have charged on the rebels and driven them in confusion, for my line was still perfect and unbroken and my troops in the proper spirit for the performance of such a task. After I had reached the position designated by General Birney, the brigade was rallied by my assistant adjutant-general and aides and moved forward, driving the enemy and capturing many prisoners. I continued to advance until I again occupied the field I had a few moments before vacated. Here my command remained until morning." This was the right of my line.

General Meade declares that my movement produced "66 per cent. of the loss of the whole battle, and with what result? Driving us back to the position he [Sickles] was ordered to hold originally." To this I answer: First, that the position of the troops on our left at the close of the battle on the 2d of July, was not in any particular, in any part of the line on the left, as General Meade confidentially informs Colonel Benedict. On my extreme right, as I have just proved from Carr's report, the Third Corps held its advanced position. On my left, that is to say, on the left flank of the army, General Crawford's splendid division of Pennsylvania Reserves held my advanced position to the stone wall, south of the wheat-field, in advance of Round Top. The other divisions of the Fifth Corps occupied both Round Tops, Little and Big, with the Sixth Corps—the strongest corps in the army, under Sedgwick—in reserve to our left, and the Twelfth Corps, under Williams, brought over from the right, and the First Corps, under Newton, in support; making a total of over 40,000 infantry in position on the left to protect that flank against the assault which General Meade intimates he expected the Third Corps to repel alone. Second, General Meade, in his exaggerated estimate of his losses on July 2d, which he represents as 66 per cent. of the entire loss of his army during the three days of conflict, would seem to hold me not only responsible for the losses in my own corps and for the other corps moved up to save the left and rear of his army, but also for the losses on the right at Culp's Hill. In other words, General Meade's statement is difficult to reconcile with the respect due to his high position and the ample means of information always accessible to him.

The losses on the 2d of July, although large and serious, were inevitable. So far as my observation enabled me to judge, and I was on the line of battle until I was wounded, our losses are attributable only to the assaults, vigorous, persistent, and prolonged, from 3 o'clock until dark, of an ably led enemy, one who had staked everything upon the issue; and the official Confederate reports show that Lee's losses on the 2d of July, especially in the divisions of Hood, McLaws, and Anderson, and in their artillery, were quite as large as ours, and perhaps larger. As I have already shown, if I had received this assault in the position General Meade says he designed I should take, then indeed would my corps have been virtually destroyed and the enemy in possession of our left flank and rear before the troops I have enumerated could have been brought up.

In conclusion allow me to show that General Meade's letter, so far as it relates to the orders and instructions therein alleged to have been given to me, is flatly contradicted by his own official report of the battle and by his sworn testimony before the Committee on the Conduct of the War. In his official report General Meade says that "the Second and Third corps were directed to occupy the continuation of the Cemetery Ridge on the left of the Eleventh Corps." That is the only statement in General Meade's official report to indicate the position of the Third Corps. No mention is made of the occupation of Round Top, which is a mile and more from Cemetery Ridge and in advance of it. Now we will see how guardedly he speaks of it in his testimony: "About 3 or 3:30 o'clock in the afternoon I proceeded from my headquarters to the extreme left in order to see to the posting of the Fifth Corps, also to inspect the position of the Third Corps, about which I was in doubt. General Sickles had said to me earlier in the day that there was in the neighborhood of where his corps was some very good ground for artillery, and that he should like to have some staff-officer of mine go out there and see as to the posting of artillery. He also asked me whether he was not authorized to post his corps in such manner as in his judgment he should deem the most suitable. I answered General Sickles: 'Certainly, within the limits of the general instruction I have given you. Any ground within those limits you choose to occupy I leave to you,' and I directed Brigadier-General Hunt, my chief-of-artillery, to accompany Sickles and examine and inspect such positions as General Sickles thought good for artillery, and to give General Sickles the benefit of his judgment."

General Meade's "general instructions" to me were all verbal and extremely vague and indefinite. As I have said, he was wholly preoccupied with his right flank. None of his instructions contemplated the probability of an attack on his left. The only definite instruction that reached me from General Meade before the battle opened on July 2d was that I should relieve Geary's division, which he had ordered over to the right. I at once reported to him that I found no troops on the left, except Buford's cavalry; that Geary's division had not been in position at all; that it was massed to the right of Round Top during the night of the 1st of July, and had moved over to Culp's Hill before I had received his instructions to relieve it. In fact this was the only instruction, general or particular, the only order of any nature or kind, that I had received from General Meade on the 2d of July from daybreak in the morning until 6 o'clock in the evening, when I was wounded. I had no communication from General Geary whatever. He had left the field, and there was no staff-officer or representative of General Geary to indicate his position, and for obvious reasons, because he was not in position. He had bivouacked for the night

on the left, and when his corps, under Slocum, went into position on Culp's Hill on the right he followed it.

I am persuaded that Generals Slocum, Howard, Pleasonton, Doubleday, Robinson, Howe, and Williams, and other corps and division commanders of the Army of the Potomac would agree with me in the observation that General Meade was very imperfectly informed as to the movements and operations of his corps, divisions, and brigades of the army, during the first and second days of July, 1863. I am unwilling to attribute to General Meade an intention to do injustice to any of the troops under his command, yet much, very much, injustice was done. No adequate recognition was accorded to the First and Eleventh corps, by whose sacrifices and by the sagacity of whose leaders we seized from the enemy the impregnable position of Cemetery Ridge. The heroic stand made by John Buford on the Cashtown road on the morning of the 1st of July; the brilliant deployments of his cavalry, holding the enemy in check for hours until Reynolds came up with his leading division under Wadsworth, are barely mentioned. In truth the cavalry under Pleasonton and Buford and Gregg and Kilpatrick, to which General Meade owed so much of his success, and the artillery under General Hunt, equally brilliant in its service, received no adequate appreciation. I have already given examples in which whole corps and divisions of infantry are placed in positions by General Meade, in his report, other than those they occupied, so that it will be seen that it is by no means myself alone who complain of injustice at the hands of General Meade. In my belief the forced march I made of twelve miles over a difficult road in the heat of a July afternoon, with troops which had been without rest from the Rappahannock to the heart of Pennsylvania, a march made without orders, on my own responsibility, to help the overtasked troops of Howard — in my belief this was a soldierly act that deserved recognition at the hands of the commanding general. Yet it is not mentioned either in General Meade's official report or in his confidential letter. Why is it that General Meade is so unwilling to praise where praise might be bestowed, and is so lavish of censure where censure might be more gracefully suppressed, even if an error of judgment had been committed by an officer who paid dearly enough for the zeal which exposed himself and his command to the shock of the enemy's assaults? "I am of the opinion," says General Meade in his testimony before the Committee on the Conduct of the War, "that General Sickles did what he thought was for the best, but I differed from him in judgment." Here is no question of orders disobeyed or of instructions disregarded, and here I leave the issue where General Meade puts it. Military critics more competent than I will decide whether General Meade's judgment or my judgment was correct.

THE CONFEDERATE RETREAT FROM GETTYSBURG.

BY JOHN D. IMBODEN, BRIGADIER-GENERAL, C. S. A.

D URING the Gettysburg campaign, my command—an independent brigade of cavalry—was engaged, by General Lee's confidential orders, in raids on the left flank of his advancing army, destroying railroad bridges and cutting the canal below Cumberland wherever I could—so that I did not reach the field till noon of the last day's battle. I reported direct to General Lee for orders, and was assigned a position to aid in repelling any cavalry demonstration on his rear. None of a serious character being made, my little force took no part in the battle, but were merely spectators of the scene, which transcended in grandeur any that I beheld in any other battle of the war.

"CARRY ME BACK TO OLE VIRGINNY."

When night closed the struggle, Lee's army was repulsed. We all knew that the day had gone against us, but the full extent of the disaster was only known in high quarters. The carnage of the day was generally understood to have been frightful, yet our army was not in retreat, and it was surmised in camp that with to-morrow's dawn would come a renewal of the struggle. All felt and appreciated the momentous consequences to the cause of Southern independence of final defeat or victory on that great field.

It was a warm summer's night; there were few camp-fires, and the weary soldiers were lying in groups on the luxuriant grass of the beautiful meadows, discussing the events of the day, speculating on the morrow, or watching that our horses did not straggle off while browsing. About 11 o'clock a horseman came to summon me to General Lee. I promptly mounted and, accompanied by Lieutenant George W. McPhail, an aide on my staff, and guided by the courier who brought the message, rode about two miles toward Gettysburg to where half a dozen small tents were pointed out, a little way from the roadside to our left, as General Lee's headquarters for the night. On inquiry I found that he was not there, but had gone to the headquarters of General A. P. Hill, about half a mile nearer to Gettysburg. When we reached the place indicated, a single flickering candle, visible from the road through the open front of a common wall-tent, exposed to view Generals Lee and Hill seated on camp-stools with a map spread upon their knees. Dismounting, I approached on foot. After exchanging the ordinary salutations General Lee directed me to go back to his headquarters and wait for him. I did so, but he did not make his appearance until about 1 o'clock, when he came riding alone, at a slow walk, and evidently wrapped in profound thought.

When he arrived there was not even a sentinel on duty at his tent, and no one of his staff was awake. The moon was high in the clear sky and the silent scene was unusually vivid. As he approached and saw us lying on the grass under a tree, he spoke, reined in his jaded horse, and essayed to dismount.   The effort to do so betrayed so much physical exhaustion that I hurriedly rose and stepped forward to assist him, but before I reached his side he had succeeded in alighting, and threw his arm across the saddle to rest, and fixing his eyes upon the ground leaned in silence and almost motionless upon his equally weary horse,—the two forming a striking and never-to-be-forgotten group.   The moon shone full upon his massive features and revealed an expression of sadness that I had never before seen upon his face. Awed by his appearance I waited for him to speak until the silence became embarrassing, when, to break it and change the silent current of his thoughts, I ventured to remark, in a sympathetic tone, and in allusion to his great fatigue:

"General, this has been a hard day on you."

He looked up, and replied mournfully:

"Yes, it has been a sad, sad day to us," and immediately relapsed into his thoughtful mood and attitude.   Being unwilling again to intrude upon his reflections, I said no more.   After perhaps a minute or two, he suddenly straightened up to his full height, and turning to me with more animation and excitement of manner than I had ever seen in him before, for he was a man of wonderful equanimity, he said in a voice tremulous with emotion:

"I never saw troops behave more magnificently than Pickett's division of Virginians did to-day in that grand charge upon the enemy.   And if they had been supported as they were to have been,—but, for some reason not yet fully explained to me, were not,—we would have held the position and the day would have been ours."   After a moment's pause he added in a loud voice, in a tone almost of agony, "Too bad! *Too bad!* Oh! Too bad!" ⌡

I shall never forget his language, his manner, and his appearance of mental suffering.   In a few moments all emotion was suppressed, and he spoke feelingly of several of his fallen and trusted officers; among others of Brigadier-Generals Armistead, Garnett, and Kemper of Pickett's division.   He invited me into his tent, and as soon as we were seated he remarked:

⌡ Of interest in this connection is a letter written by General Lee to Mr. Davis from Camp Orange on the 8th of August, 1863, and first printed in "A Piece of Secret History," by Colonel C. C. Jones, Jr., in "The Century" (old series) for February, 1876.   In this letter General Lee speaks in the highest terms of his army, and says, in part:

" . . . We must expect reverses, even defeats.   They are sent to teach us wisdom and prudence, to call forth greater energies, and to prevent our falling into greater disasters.   Our people have only to be true and united, to bear manfully the misfortunes incident to war, and all will come right in the end.

"I know how prone we are to censure, and how ready to blame others for the nonfulfillment of our expectations.   This is unbecoming in a generous people, and I grieve to see its expression.   The general remedy for the want of success in a military commander is his removal.   This is natural, and in many instances proper. For, no matter what may be the ability of the officer, if he loses the confidence of his troops, disaster must sooner or later ensue.

"I have been prompted by these reflections more than once since my return from Penna. to propose to your Exc'y the propriety of selecting another commander for this army.   I have seen and heard of expressions of discontent in the public journals at the result of the expedition.   I do not know how far this feeling extends in the army.   My brother officers have been too kind to report it, and so far the troops have been too generous to exhibit it.   It is fair, however, to suppose that it does exist, and success is so necessary to us that nothing should be risked to secure it.   I therefore, in all sincerity, request your Exc'y to take measures to supply my place.   I do this with the more earnestness because no one is more aware than myself of my inability for the duties of my position.   I cannot even accomplish what I myself desire.   How can I fulfill the expectations of others? . . .

"I have no complaints to make of any one but myself. I have received nothing but kindness from those above me, and the most considerate attention from my comrades and companions in arms.   To your Excellency I am specially indebted for uniform kindness and consideration.   You have done everything in your power to aid me in the work committed to my charge, without omitting anything to promote the general welfare. . . ."

"We must now return to Virginia. As many of our poor wounded as possible must be taken home. I have sent for you, because your men and horses are fresh and in good condition, to guard and conduct our train back to Virginia. The duty will be arduous, responsible, and dangerous, for I am afraid you will be harassed by the enemy's cavalry. How many men have you?"

"About 2100 effective present, and all well mounted, including McClanahan's six-gun battery of horse artillery."

"I can spare you as much artillery as you require," he said, "but no other troops, as I shall need all I have to return safely by a different and shorter route than yours. The batteries are generally short of ammunition, but you will probably meet a supply I have ordered from Winchester to Williamsport. Nearly all the transportation and the care of all the wounded will be intrusted to you. You will recross the mountain by the Chambersburg road, and then proceed to Williamsport by any route you deem best, and without a halt till you reach the river. Rest there long enough to feed your animals; then ford the river, and do not halt again till you reach Winchester, where I will again communicate with you."

After a good deal of conversation about roads, and the best disposition of my forces to cover and protect the vast train, he directed that the chiefs of his staff departments should be waked up to receive, in my presence, his orders to collect as early next day as possible all the wagons and ambulances which I was to convoy, and have them in readiness for me to take command of them. His medical director [Dr. Lafayette Guild] was charged to see that all the wounded who could bear the rough journey should be placed in the empty wagons and ambulances. He then remarked to me that his general instructions would be sent to me in writing the following morning. As I was about leaving to return to my camp, as late, I think, as 2 A. M., he came out of his tent to where I was about to mount, and said in an undertone: "I will place in your hands by a staff-officer, to-morrow morning, a sealed package for President Davis, which you will retain in your possession till you are across the Potomac, when you will detail a reliable commissioned officer to take it to Richmond with all possible dispatch and deliver it into the President's own hands. And I impress it on you that, whatever happens, this package must not fall into the hands of the enemy. If unfortunately you should be captured, destroy it at the first opportunity."

On the morning of July 4th my written instructions, and a large official envelope addressed to President Davis, were handed to me by a staff-officer.

It was apparent by 9 o'clock that the wagons, ambulances, and wounded could not be collected and made ready to move till late in the afternoon. General Lee sent to me eight Napoleon guns of the famous Washington Artillery of New Orleans, under the immediate command of Major Eshleman, one of the best artillery officers in the army, a four-gun battery under Captain Tanner, and a Whitworth under Lieutenant Pegram. Hampton's cavalry brigade, then under command of Colonel P. M. B. Young, with Captain James F. Hart's four-gun battery of horse artillery, was ordered to cover the rear of all trains

GOOD-BYE!

moving under my convoy on the Chambersburg road. These 17 guns and McClanahan's 6 guns gave us 23 pieces in all for the defense of the trains.

Shortly after noon of the 4th the very windows of heaven seemed to have opened. The rain fell in blinding sheets; the meadows were soon overflowed, and fences gave way before the raging streams. During the storm, wagons, ambulances, and artillery carriages by hundreds—nay, by thousands—were assembling in the fields along the road from Gettysburg to Cashtown, in one confused and apparently inextricable mass. As the afternoon wore on there was no abatement in the storm. Canvas was no protection against its fury, and the wounded men lying upon the naked boards of the wagon-bodies were drenched. Horses and mules were blinded and maddened by the wind and water, and became almost unmanageable. The deafening roar of the mingled sounds of heaven and earth all around us made it almost impossible to communicate orders, and equally difficult to execute them.

About 4 P. M. the head of the column was put in motion near Cashtown, and began the ascent of the mountain in the direction of Chambersburg. I remained at Cashtown giving directions and putting in detachments of guns and troops at what I estimated to be intervals of a quarter or a third of a mile. It was found from the position of the head of the column west of the mountain at dawn of the 5th—the hour at which Young's cavalry and Hart's battery began the ascent of the mountain near Cashtown — that the entire column was seventeen miles long when drawn out on the road and put in motion. As an advance-guard I had placed the 18th Virginia Cavalry, Colonel George W. Imboden, in front with a section of McClanahan's battery.

Next to them, by request, was placed an ambulance carrying, stretched side by side, two of North Carolina's most distinguished soldiers, Generals Pender and Scales, both badly wounded, but resolved to bear the tortures of the journey rather than become prisoners. I shared a little bread and meat with them at noon, and they waited patiently for hours for the head of the column to move. The trip cost poor Pender his life. General Scales appeared to be worse hurt, but stopped at Winchester, recovered, and fought through the war.

After dark I set out from Cashtown to gain the head of the column during the night. My orders had been peremptory that there should be no halt for any cause whatever. If an accident should happen to any vehicle, it was immediately to be put out of the road and abandoned. The column moved rapidly, considering the rough roads and the darkness, and from almost every wagon for many miles issued heart-rending wails of agony. For four hours I hurried forward on my way to the front, and in all that time I was never out of hearing of the groans and cries of the wounded and dying. Scarcely one in a hundred had received adequate surgical aid, owing to the demands on the hard-working surgeons from still worse cases that had to be left behind. Many of the wounded in the wagons had been without food for thirty-six hours. Their torn and bloody clothing, matted and hardened, was rasping the tender, inflamed, and still oozing wounds. Very few of the wagons had even a layer of straw in them, and all were without springs. The road was rough and rocky from the heavy washings of the preceding day. The jolting was enough to have killed strong men, if long exposed to it. From nearly every wagon as the teams trotted on, urged by whip and shout, came such cries and shrieks as these:

" O God! why can't I die?"

" My God! will no one have mercy and kill me?"

" Stop! Oh! for God's sake, stop just for one minute; take me out and leave me to die on the roadside."

"I am dying! I am dying! My poor wife, my dear children, what will become of you?"

Some were simply moaning; some were praying, and others uttering the most fearful oaths and execrations that despair and agony could wring from them; while a majority, with a stoicism sustained by sublime devotion to the cause they fought for, endured without complaint unspeakable tortures, and even spoke words of cheer and comfort to their unhappy comrades of less will or more acute nerves. Occasionally a wagon would be passed from which only low, deep moans could be heard. No help could be rendered to any of the sufferers. No heed could be given to any of their appeals. Mercy and duty to the many forbade the loss of a moment in the vain effort then and there to comply with the prayers of the few. On! On! we *must* move on. The storm continued, and the darkness was appalling. There was no time even to fill a canteen with water for a dying man; for, except the drivers and the guards, all were wounded and utterly helpless in that vast procession of misery. During this one night I realized more of the horrors of war than I had in all the two preceding years.

And yet in the darkness was our safety, for no enemy would dare attack where he could not distinguish friend from foe. We knew that when day broke upon us we should be harassed by bands of cavalry hanging on our flanks. Therefore our aim was to go as far as possible under cover of the night. Instead of going through Chambersburg, I decided to leave the main road near Fairfield after crossing the mountains, and take "a near cut" across the country to Greencastle, where daybreak on the morning of the 5th of July found the head of our column. We were now twelve or fifteen miles from the Potomac at Williamsport, our point of crossing into Virginia.

Here our apprehended troubles began. After the advance — the 18th Virginia Cavalry — had passed perhaps a mile beyond the town, the citizens to the number of thirty or forty attacked the train with axes, cutting the spokes out of ten or a dozen wheels and dropping the wagons in the streets. The moment I heard of it I sent back a detachment of cavalry to capture every citizen who had been engaged in this work, and treat them as prisoners of war. This stopped the trouble there, but the Union cavalry began to swarm down upon us from the fields and cross-roads, making their attacks in small bodies, and striking the column where there were few or no guards, and thus creating great confusion. I had a narrow escape from capture by one of these parties — of perhaps fifty men that I tried to drive off with canister from two of McClanahan's guns that were close at hand. They would perhaps have been too much for me, had not Colonel Imboden, hearing the firing turned back with his regiment at a gallop, and by the suddenness of his movement surrounded and caught the entire party.

To add to our perplexities still further, a report reached me a little after sunrise, that the Federals in large force held Williamsport. I did not fully credit this, and decided to push on. Fortunately the report was untrue. After a great deal of desultory fighting and harassments along the road during the day, nearly the whole of the immense train reached Williamsport on the afternoon of the 5th. A part of it, with Hart's battery, came in next day, General Young having halted and turned his attention to guarding the road from the west with his cavalry. We took possession of the town to convert it into a great hospital for the thousands of wounded we had brought from Gettysburg. I required all the families in the place to go to cooking for the sick and wounded, on pain of having their kitchens occupied for that purpose by my men. They readily complied. A large number of surgeons had accompanied the train, and these at once pulled off their coats and went to work, and soon a vast amount of suffering was mitigated. The bodies of a few who had died on the march were buried. All this became necessary because the tremendous rains had raised the river more than ten feet above the fording stage of water, and we could not possibly cross then. There were two small ferry-boats or "flats" there, which I immediately put into requisition to carry across those of the wounded, who, after being fed and having their wounds dressed, thought they could walk to Winchester. Quite a large number were able to do this, so that the "flats" were kept running all the time.

THE RETREAT FROM GETTYSBURG.

Our situation was frightful. We had probably ten thousand animals and nearly all the wagons of General Lee's army under our charge, and all the wounded, to the number of several thousand, that could be brought from Gettysburg. Our supply of provisions consisted of a few wagon-loads of flour in my own brigade train, a small lot of fine fat cattle which I had collected in Pennsylvania on my way to Gettysburg, and some sugar and coffee procured in the same way at Mercersburg.

The town of Williamsport is located in the lower angle formed by the Potomac with Conococheague Creek. These streams inclose the town on two sides, and back of it about one mile there is a low range of hills that is crossed by four roads converging at the town. The first is the Greencastle road leading down the creek valley; next the Hagerstown road; then the Boonsboro' road; and lastly the River road. [See map, p. 246.]

Early on the morning of the 6th I received intelligence of the approach from Frederick of a large body of cavalry with three full batteries of six rifled guns. These were the divisions of Generals Buford and Kilpatrick, and Huey's brigade of Gregg's division, consisting, as I afterward learned, of 23 regiments of cavalry, and 18 guns, a total force of about 7000 men.

I immediately posted my guns on the hills that concealed the town, and dismounted my own command to support them—and ordered as many of the wagoners to be formed as could be armed with the guns of the wounded that we had brought from Gettysburg. In this I was greatly aided by Colonel J. L. Black of South Carolina, Captain J. F. Hart commanding a battery from the same State, Colonel William R. Aylett of Virginia, and other wounded officers. By noon about 700 wagoners were organized into companies of 100 each and officered by wounded line-officers and commissaries and quartermasters,—about 250 of these were given to Colonel Aylett on the right next the river,—about as many under Colonel Black on the left, and the residue were used as skirmishers. My own command proper was held well in hand in the center.

The enemy appeared in our front about half-past one o'clock on both the Hagerstown and Boonsboro' roads, and the fight began. Every man under my command understood that if we did not repulse the enemy we should all be captured and General Lee's army be ruined by the loss of its transportation, which at that period could not have been replaced in the Confederacy. The fight began with artillery on both sides. The firing from our side was very rapid, and seemed to make the enemy hesitate about advancing. In a half hour J. D. Moore's battery ran out of ammunition, but as an ordnance train had arrived from Winchester, two wagon-loads of ammunition were ferried across the river and run upon the field behind the guns, and the boxes tumbled out, to be broken open with axes. With this fresh supply our guns were all soon in full play again. As the enemy could not see the supports of our batteries from the hill-tops, I moved the whole line forward to his full view, in single ranks, to show a long front on the Hagerstown approach. My line passed our guns fifty or one hundred yards, where they were halted awhile, and then were withdrawn behind the hill-top again, slowly and steadily.

Leaving Black's wagoners and the Marylanders on the left to support Hart's and Moore's batteries, Captain Hart having been put in command by Colonel Black when he was obliged to be elsewhere, I moved the 18th Virginia Cavalry and 62d Virginia Mounted Infantry rapidly to the right, to meet and repel five advancing regiments (dismounted) of the enemy. My three regiments, with Captain John H. McNeill's Partisan Rangers and Aylett's wagoners, had to sustain a very severe contest. Hart, seeing how hard we were pressed on the right, charged the enemy's right with his little command, and at the same time Eshleman with his eight Napoleons advanced four hundred yards to the front, and got an enfilading position, from which, with the aid of McClanahan's battery, he poured a furious fire into the enemy's line. The 62d and Aylett, supported by the 18th Cavalry, and McNeill, charged the enemy who fell back sullenly to their horses.

Night was now rapidly approaching, when a messenger from Fitzhugh Lee arrived to urge me to "hold my own," as he would be up in a half hour with three thousand fresh men. The news was sent along our whole line, and was received with a wild and exultant yell. We knew then that the field was won, and slowly pressed forward. Almost at the same moment we heard distant guns on the enemy's rear and right on the Hagerstown road. They were Stuart's, who was approaching on that road, while Fitzhugh Lee was coming on the Greencastle road. That settled the contest. The enemy broke to the left and fled by the Boonsboro' road. It was too dark to follow. When General Fitzhugh Lee joined me with his staff on the field, one of the enemy's shells came near striking him. General Lee thought it came from Eshleman's battery, till, a moment later, he saw a blaze from its gun streaming away from us.

We captured about 125 of the enemy who failed to reach their horses. I could never ascertain the loss on either side. I estimated ours at about 125. The wagoners fought so well that this came to be known as "the wagoners' fight." Quite a number of them were killed in storming a farm from which sharp-shooters were rapidly picking off Eshleman's men and horses.

My whole force engaged, wagoners included, did not exceed three thousand men. The ruse practiced by showing a formidable line on the left, then withdrawing it to fight on the right, together with our numerous artillery, 23 guns, led to the belief that our force was much greater.

By extraordinary good fortune we had thus saved all of General Lee's trains. A bold charge at any time before sunset would have broken our feeble lines, and then we should all have fallen an easy prey to the Federals. The next day our army arrived from Gettysburg, and the country is familiar with the way it escaped across the Potomac on the night of the 13th of July.

It may be interesting to repeat one or two facts to show the peril in which the army was till the river could be bridged. Over four thousand prisoners taken at Gettysburg were ferried across the river by the morning of the 9th, and I was ordered with a single regiment, the 62d Virginia, to guard them to Staunton and send them on to Richmond. When the general assigned me to this duty he expressed an apprehension that before I could reach Winchester the Federal cavalry would cross at Harper's Ferry, intercept and capture my guard and release the prisoners. Before we had left the river I had an interview with him at his headquarters near Hagerstown, in which he expressed great impatience at the tardiness in building rude pontoons at the river, and calling in Colonel James L. Corley, his chief quartermaster, told him to put Major John A. Harman in charge of the work; remarking that without Harman's extraordinary energy to conduct the work, the pontoons would not be done for several days. Harman took charge that day, and by tearing down warehouses on the canal got joists to build boats with, and in twenty-four hours had enough of them ready to float down to Falling Waters and construct a bridge. As we were talking General Longstreet came into the tent, wet and muddy, and was cordially greeted by General Lee in this wise: "Well, my old warhorse, what news do you bring us from the front?" That cordial greeting between chief and lieutenant is a sufficient answer, in my mind, to the statements of alleged ill feeling between the two men growing out of affairs at Gettysburg. It has been said that if "Stonewall" Jackson had been in command at Gettysburg, Longstreet would have been shot. This is a monstrous imputation upon General Lee, no less than upon Longstreet, and utterly without foundation, in my opinion. They were surely cordial on the 9th of July, 1863.

Before I had gone two miles on my anxious march toward Winchester a courier overtook me with a note from General Lee directing me to return immediately to his headquarters. I halted my column, hurried back, was ferried over the river, and galloped out on the Hagerstown road to where I had parted from the general that morning. He had left with his staff to ride toward Hagerstown, where a heavy artillery fire indicated an attack by the enemy in considerable force. When I overtook him he said that he understood I was familiar with the fords of the Potomac from Williamsport to Cumberland, and with the roads to them. I replied that I was. He then called up one of his staff, either General Long or General Alexander, I think, and directed him to write down my answers to his questions, and required me to name and describe ford after ford all the way up to Cumberland, and to describe minutely their character, and the roads and surrounding country on both sides of the river, and directed me, after I had given him all the information I could, to send to him my brother and his regiment, the 18th Virginia Cavalry, to act as an advance and guide if he should require it. He did not say so, but I felt that his situation was precarious in the extreme. When about to dismiss me, referring to

BRIGADIER-GENERAL J. JOHNSTON PETTIGREW,
C. S. A., KILLED IN AN ACTION AT FALL-
ING WATERS, MD., JULY 14, 1863.
FROM A PHOTOGRAPH.

the freshet in the river he laughingly said: "You know this country well enough to tell me whether it ever quits raining about here? If so, I should like to see a clear day soon." I did not see him again till he left the Shenandoah Valley for the east side of the Blue Ridge.

A PRISONER'S MARCH FROM GETTYSBURG TO STAUNTON.

BY JOHN L. COLLINS, 8TH PENNSYLVANIA CAVALRY.

ON the 4th, when Lee's movement of withdrawal became known, the cavalry was ordered to throw itself between the Confederate army and the Potomac. To do this the different divisions were headed for the gaps and passes through which the trains sent under escort in advance were escaping over the mountains to Williamsport.

The regiment to which I belonged was in Gregg's division, but

CONFEDERATE VIDETTE.

having become detached with the rest of the brigade during the three days of the battle, it united with two other brigades under General Kilpatrick and made an attack upon a Confederate train near Monterey. The fight took place before midnight the first day of the march, the train was burned, the guard was made prisoners, and then our command pushed on after another train that was reported ahead of the one we destroyed. A few whose horses were killed or disabled were ordered back to the division for a remount, instead of being mounted upon the enemy's horses. I disobeyed the orders, and hoping to get one of the enemy's horses I led my own and followed on foot. I soon lost sight of the brigade, however, but toiled along the dark and rough road, until my horse, which at first could walk with only the weight of the saddle, refused to go any farther. As the day was breaking, I was examining and washing the poor creature's wounded shoulder, when I was surprised by about 150 Confederate cavalry, whose approach I had hailed as that of friends. At a motion from their colonel three men dismounted, the foremost of whom held out his hand to me and cheerfully said: "Good morning, sir! I am sorry to say you are a prisoner." The other two went toward my arms, which were piled on the saddle on the roadside, and, holding them up, exclaimed, "What splendid arms he has!" Surprise and the novelty of the first man's greeting kept me from realizing my position until I saw them take my carbine, saber, and pistol. Then my heart sank.

Those "splendid arms" had been my companions for two years, and two months previously I had been publicly commended for bringing them with me through the enemy's ranks when my horse was shot inside their lines as we charged upon Jackson's men at Chancellorsville. But such is war, and I bade them a sorrowful adieu, as I looked from them to the faces of my captors, some of which showed sympathy, some indifference, while all seemed manly and soldierly. The commander alone took no notice of me or my arms; he gazed up the road through the gray light of the morning as if bent on some bold manœuvre, and then said to one of his men in a loud voice: "Tell General Lee (Fitzhugh) that there is a regiment of Yankee cavalry half a mile up the road, and ask him if I shall charge them."

The man galloped back, and without waiting for General Lee's orders, the colonel wheeled his men and galloped after him,—such a piece of cheap braggadocio as I had seen displayed by some of our own colonels. I was left in the care of two men to put the saddle on my horse and follow at a walk. My guards were frank, and in answer to my question told me that they belonged to General William E. Jones's brigade, that they had been captured in the fight just mentioned, and had escaped during the night from Kilpatrick who was more intent in overtaking larger bodies than in watching the few hundred he had taken. Between midnight and daybreak the colonel and about 150 men came together in the woods and fell in with General Fitzhugh Lee, who was then slipping out between two divisions of our cavalry.

About noon I was introduced to about thirty of those who had been sent back for horses to the division, and had shared my fate. We were with General Stuart's headquarters, as he was moving in the center of his brigades — they being pushed out in every direction, trying to keep a road clear for their infantry and artillery.

A young Virginian about my own age, but with much more suavity and self-complacency than I could claim, introduced himself to me and told me that he belonged to the "King and Queen" cavalry (1st Virginia, I think), and said that they knew my regiment well, and considered it a "rough one to deal with." He asked me if I remembered all the skirmishes we had as we advanced from New Kent Court House to the Chickahominy, which I did well, and then when we had become quite well acquainted, asked me if I would have any objections to exchanging saddles with him. I had not the least, as I never expected to sit on mine again, and when we stopped on the roadside to make the exchange I walked back into the ranks without my horse, as I saw no reason why I should bother leading him along for my captors to ride, if he should

ever get well. Fresh prisoners were added all the time, mostly cavalry, and we marched along through the mountains the entire day. Stuart and his staff rode in our midst — rather an imprudent thing, I thought, for many of the men observed him closely with reference to a future meeting. I know it was in my mind every time I looked at him, though I had no malice and nothing to complain of in regard to my treatment. Within a year he fell by the carbine of a cavalryman whose regiment was at this time well represented among the prisoners.

The day was a hard one for me, used to fatigue and fasting though I was. The roads were the roughest and narrowest that could be found, and I had eaten nothing since the previous day, having lost my haversack during the night. I was at last compelled to tell one of the guards that I was very hungry, and he apologized for having nothing to give me, but promised to see that I got something before we went much farther. He left the ranks soon and shortly afterward returned with some bread and butter, which he divided with me. Later in the afternoon foragers brought us in rations collected from the farm-houses.

Just before sunset, as we were going through a gap, a rapid exchange of shots was heard ahead of us, and both prisoners and captors became excited. A few moments later we were near enough to look out into the plain beyond; we saw the Confederates in front of us dismounting and deploying as skirmishers, and my heart bounded as I saw my own regiment drawn up for a charge about five hundred yards away! I began to cry like a child; I thought that I would be free again in about ten minutes, with my friends; that I would be armed and mounted as twenty-four hours before. The question, How did I know my regiment? naturally comes, and is as easily answered. I could distinguish the companies by the color of their horses, and knew the order of the squadrons in the line. The black horses of troop C and the light bays of H formed the first squadron, the sorrel horses of E and the dark bays of G formed the next, and so on. The troops changed squadron often to suit the seniority of the captains, and the squadrons changed positions in the regiment for the same reason, but the combination of companies before me now had been that of the regiment for a week at least.

A call was made for sharp-shooters, and those who dismounted and presented themselves were supplied with cartridges and sent into the cornfield in front of us. But my regiment seemed disinclined to charge, and merely threw out skirmishers to meet them. Some of the Confederates enthusiastically cried, "My! won't the sharpshooters make it hot for that cavalry!"

Though the firing became brisk, it wearied me; I wanted the charge, because I was sure that a vigorous attack would send our guards fleeing without us in less than five minutes. One of them, a quiet, pleasant-faced man, as were many of the others, noticed my dejected look, came to me, and, swinging himself from his saddle to a fence-rail, took a Testament from his pocket, and asked me if I objected to his reading a chapter aloud. I thankfully asked him to do so, as I had not had heart enough to read my own that day. He read a chapter in one of Paul's epistles, and when he had concluded remarked that he would feel fifty per cent. better if the country were at peace and he at home that night. I must add that while he was reading I held Quaker principles myself, for I was pained to think I was an enemy of that fair-minded Christian young man who, like myself, thought he was right in engaging in a career of destruction to life and property. But we were both reminded that it was war and not peace by the call of "More ammunition" for the sharp-shooters, and our guards had to supply it from their boxes, it being apparently scarce.

Now is the time for a charge, I thought. General Stuart had not more than three hundred men, encumbered by as many prisoners, and the regiment in front had five hundred in line. But while their commander hesitated, General Stuart, whose genius and courage had gotten him out of many a difficulty, proved himself equal to the present emergency. While his skirmishers were firing their last cartridges he made us fall in by fours, and marched us two or three times across the opening. We were mistaken in the twilight for Confederate infantry coming up, and then his whole column was moved along the edge of the corn-field, keeping the skirmishers between us and my regiment, which moved parallel with us, until darkness shut them out from my view.

The next morning Stuart's men were gone, and we were guarded toward the Potomac by Pickett's division. I regretted the change, the rank and file of the cavalry were so different from what I had expected to find the Southern soldiers. They were quiet, courteous, and considerate; they all seemed young, of light build with fair or sandy complexions predominant; and, better than all, they had more by far than the average share of intelligence. The infantry that took their place were nearer my conception of the Southern soldier. But I must not blame the poor fellows if they had not the kindness and elasticity of the cavalry. They were out of heart — a large part of their division had been left on the field on the 3d of July, and besides the commander of the division there was only one officer above the rank of captain left in it.

We were halted by the roadside often during the day to let Confederate troops hurry past us. In one of these halts General Longstreet was pointed out to me with evident pride by a staff-officer who had turned aside to make some courteous remarks to me. I told the officer as politely as I could that I thought they were badly beaten, and would hardly get across the Potomac. He laughed and said that they were not trying to get across, — that Baltimore was their objective point just then; from there, he explained, it was but a forced march to Washington, and once there they could conquer a peace in thirty days. His hopes amused me; I remembered that when retreating from the Chickahominy and from Chancellorsville *I* did not know anything of defeat, but thought I was marching to victory by another road.

The next time we were halted I was not so pleasantly entertained. I sat on a high bank watching the various regiments and batteries go by, when a haughty young officer rode up, looking at the prisoners' feet, as if he wanted a pair of boots. Several of the men concealed theirs by drawing them up, but I did not; the soles of mine were coming off, for two days' march over rough roads was something the contractor for cavalry boots had not contemplated. The officer pulled up in front of me, however, and said in an overbearing manner, "I want those spurs." I merely looked at them and nodded. "Hand them to me," he said sternly. "They were given to me for the United States service, not for rebel service," I said, stung by his manner. "Oh!" he scornfully remarked, "I suppose you know you are a prisoner?" "Yes, I have been nearly two days without food; that convinces me." "And when a soldier is taken, his horse, his arms, and equipments are his captor's?" "Yes, mine are all gone." "And his spurs, too?" "Yes, and his boots sometimes." "Hand me your spurs, then." "Take them, if you want them, I won't hand them to you." He took out his pistol and raised it, but controlling himself lowered it and moved away. Then he turned his horse and demanded them again. The same answer, and the same arguments were repeated; the pistol was pointed at me, but his soldierly qualities triumphed over his temper as before. There seemed no way out of the difficulty; he was determined to have the spurs, but too proud to dismount and unbuckle them, and I was too stubborn to yield. At last one of Pickett's men came up and took them off, and the officer rode away with them.

Before I left the spot I kicked off my boots, for they seemed made only to carry spurs, and went barefoot the rest of the way to Richmond. The prisoners who on the first day had numbered only about 300, mostly cavalry, were now increased to nearly as many thousands, as the men taken at Gettysburg were added to us. Besides these, fresh cavalry prisoners were brought in every day. From them we heard of the extent of the victory, and the fighting that was still in progress, and we were assured by them that neither we nor our guards could ever reach the Potomac. This helped to restore the self-respect that a soldier partly loses when his arms are taken from him, and which continued captivity almost entirely destroys.

We were marched past a handsome house which had attracted our attention on our way to Gettysburg by the number of United States flags and the gayly dressed ladies waving handkerchiefs to us. They were waving them as boldly to the Confederates now, and the stars and stripes had been transformed into the stars and bars.

Some of the newly captured were badly wounded, but had no attention given them, except such crude service as their fellow-prisoners could do for them. None of our surgeons were captured, and I suppose those of the enemy had plenty to do among their own. One poor fellow of the 5th New York Cavalry had seventeen wounds which he got from the 11th Virginia. He was cut and slashed at every angle, and when we had gotten some bandages and patched him up he looked ludicrously odd.

Before we entered Williamsport a correspondent, whom the Confederates had decided to let go, took the names of those who chose to give them to him, that their friends might learn their fate from the papers. I gave him mine, and though it was printed in a leading Philadelphia paper, I was afterward mortified to learn that only one of all my friends in that city had seen it. A dozen others there with whom I had correspondence supposed I had been killed.

At Williamsport all was crowded and in confusion. The Confederates were throwing up weak defenses in expectation of an attack. Our cavalry had cut their way in and destroyed the only bridge that Lee had left in his rear. Some of the poor fellows that must always get left on such occasions cheered us by telling us how they did it. Three regiments charged in,—one fought to the right, another to the left, while the third, supplied with straw and turpentine, dashed at the bridge, set fire to it, then cut it loose from its moorings and let it float down the river, a burning wreck. "Score another for the cavalry," we cried.

My hopes rose with the river, which was a seething flood, boiling over its banks; it seemed impossible to get us across the Potomac now. Rigging up a rope ferry, and getting the prisoners across on flat-boats was the work of two or three days, and then they encamped us on a hill a few days more, waiting for their army to follow. I think they feared an advance by Harper's Ferry and Martinsburg. The cavalry and flying artillery came from that direction; Imboden's men told us so, and I never gave up hope until we had passed Winchester. A brigade composed of infantry, cavalry, and artillery under General Imboden guarded us from this point to Staunton, a distance of over 120 miles, I think. It seemed five hundred miles to me, for I was barefooted and the pike had been recently repaired.

The mode of marching us was now for the first time systematic. We numbered at least four thousand men, and were divided into divisions, marching by columns of fours. The cavalry and artillery marched *en masse* between the divisions, while the infantry marched in two files, one at each side of the column. Imboden's brigade did not seem to have seen much hard service, at least I thought so because their clothes were new, yet the general had a new suit of gray on, and certainly he had seen plenty of hard service. The men were as kind to us as could be expected; only one unpleasant affair came under my observation all the way. In the heat of a discussion a guard clubbed his musket and struck a wounded man on the head. I have no doubt that the latter had his tongue to blame for it; but he was a prisoner and a wounded man, and the guard was promptly placed under arrest.

I have said nothing so far of the commissary arrangements simply because there was nothing to be said. I do not now remember getting anything to eat until we crossed the Potomac, except from Stuart's cavalry the first day of my captivity.

But my memory must fail me, for I could not have lived unless I had gotten something occasionally. After we left Williamsport the arrangements were regular—in their meagerness, too regular. We got about a pint of flour every other day, and with it now and then a piece of rusty flitch. Some of the men tried to make bread of the flour as we camped, but the greater number stirred it up in water, and drank the paste, saying that "it stuck to their ribs longer" that way. We got an extra ration at Martinsburg, that, out of compliment to the ladies, I ought not to forget. As we marched through the town the whole populace turned out to greet us, not as enemies but as friends and sympathizers. They cried out to us, to cheer up—not to be downhearted—that we had won a great victory at Gettysburg, and though we were being marched to prison we were already avenged by the thousands of rebels that were left dead or prisoners in Pennsylvania. They appeared to be well posted by the Northern newspapers, and right in the teeth of the guards they upbraided the Confederates for theft and violence north of the Potomac. It must have been very galling to Imboden's command to be reviled that way by their countrywomen, but they bore it with cast-down heads, and made no reply. We could not have done it, I fear, had we been the guards, and in Pennsylvania. At last some of our men, in reply to questions on the subject, said they did not give us anything to eat. There was a sudden rush for the houses, and in a few seconds the street was lined with women with dishes of cake, bread, and everything they could lay hands on with so short a notice.

The sight of the food threw our column into disorder. Some men tried to break out of the ranks, and this being resisted, the women tried to break in. In the confusion that followed a few women were pushed back to the street-curb and fell down. The falls were, I think, accidental; but the prisoners became furious when they saw them fall, they struck at the guards right and left, and overpowered many of them, bearing them to the ground. It looked for the moment as if there would be a general fight, which must result in the death of many prisoners and the escape of others; but this was prevented by the prompt action of the cavalry and artillery, marching near the scene of the revolt. Then the general, or some one for him, promised the people and the prisoners that the latter would be halted outside the town to receive the contributions. In an open wood by the roadside we were halted, and the guards themselves soon brought us the coveted food. The sly rascals must have tossed the dainties up in the blankets as they brought them along so that every man of us at a single grab could get a sample of all they sent. I got one good handful only, but it was a mixture of ginger-bread, cookies, cake, corn-bread, and everything else that the people of Martinsburg ate. It was here that the Barbara Frietchies lived. After the battle of Antietam these women had laid planks on a torn up bridge for us, so that we could cross and drive Stuart's cavalry out of the town.

But notwithstanding this extra food at Martinsburg the low diet and the sharp stones soon told on my strength. My feet were sore, and my stomach was faint beyond endurance, and the climax was reached one day when my sight left me, and I threw myself down on the roadside to die. The rallying cry of "A cavalry charge" had no more effect on me; I knew they could not approach us now, and I gave up in despair as soon as I found I was blind. The guards tried to make me get up, but I listened with indifference to their threats to shoot me. The rear-guard of each division passed me with the same result for their efforts to rouse me, until at last the rear-guard of all came up; the officer in command assured me that it was his duty to kill me rather than leave me behind, and though I believed him I could not move, and merely told him so. At last he told a man to "run me through" with his bayonet, but I suppose there was a saving sign that I did not see, for after a pause I heard him tell the man to stay with me until a wagon came along and I could be taken and given something to eat. I never saw that officer, but I hope God saw his act of forbearance and humanity and rewarded him for it. There have been miserable cowards in either army who bullied and mistreated unfortunate prisoners when they had the power to do so, but the true soldier never did, and I never saw anything but kindness shown to the prisoners that my regiment took, and I never experienced anything but kindness from the men who guarded me from Gettysburg to Staunton.

After a long rest I was placed in a wagon and taken to a house where I got a big slice of bread and butter, and in a short time sight and strength returned, and I was able to march with the column. I ought to add for my own credit that I did not fall out again, though faint and hungry often enough. The towns through which we passed on our way up the Shenandoah Valley were apprised of our coming, and manifested a different spirit, of course, from that exhibited at Martinsburg. Many insulted and upbraided us, but some of our men who excelled in nothing else were mighty in vituperation and abusive eloquence, and these

paid back with interest all the taunts we received, often, I am sorry to say, surpassing the bounds of self-respect and decency.

We usually encamped in large meadows, through which streams of good water ran, and were here allowed to wash, eat, and sleep while our guards were posted around the fences. At one of those halts, as we approached Staunton, a farmer with his wife drove up close to the fence, and after taking a critical survey of the crowd he said indignantly: "Forty thousand Yankee prisoners! Why, I would bet the best farm in the valley that there isn't a quarter of them here!" The heralds everywhere had doubtless added a harmless cipher to our real number.

At length—about the 20th of July, I think—we arrived at Staunton, weary and sore. We had marched about fifteen miles a day since we left Williamsport. As we entered Staunton some showed their love to their enemies by supplying us with tracts, but I am not sure that their kindness was appreciated by the prisoners as generally as was the attention paid to our hungry stomachs by the people of Martinsburg. While waiting there for transportation to Richmond we were amused to note the esteem in which the people held the Confederate money. Those who brought wares into our camp for sale at first refused to sell at all except for Federal money. When the officers threatened to expel from the camp any who did that, they would ask to see the money before naming the price, and if it was Federal, the pie was a quarter, but if Confederate, it would cost a dollar. One young army sharper—not one of our guards and not a Virginian—must have made a small fortune by exchanging money with our men at the rate of about two for one. He told them that at Richmond the respective values were even, but when we were marched through that city we found it to be as ten to one.

Our marches ended here; we were placed in box, or gravel cars, and at a slightly increased rate of speed were taken to Richmond.

CONFEDERATES CAPTURED AT GETTYSBURG. FROM A PHOTOGRAPH.

THE OPPOSING FORCES AT GETTYSBURG, PA.

July 1st–3d, 1863.

The composition, losses, and strength of each army as here stated give the gist of all the data obtainable in the Official Records. K stands for killed; w for wounded; m w for mortally wounded; m for captured or missing; c for captured.

THE UNION ARMY.

ARMY OF THE POTOMAC— Major-General George G. Meade. Staff loss: w, 4.

Command of the Provost Marshal General, Brig.-Gen. Marsena R. Patrick: 93d N. Y.,⎰ Lieut.-Col. Benjamin C. Butler; 8th U. S.,⎰ Capt. Edwin W. H. Read: 2d Pa. Cav., Col. R. Butler Price; E and I, 6th Pa. Cav., Capt. James Starr; Detachments 1st, 2d, 5th and 6th, U. S. Cav. *Guards and Orderlies:* Oneida (N. Y.) Cav., Capt. Daniel P. Mann. *Artillery,*✠ Brig.-Gen. Henry J. Hunt. *U. S. Engineer Battalion,*⎰ Capt. George H. Mendell.

FIRST ARMY CORPS,↓ Maj.-Gen. Abner Doubleday, Maj.-Gen. John Newton. Staff loss: k, 1; w, 1 = 2.

General Headquarters: L, 1st Me. Cav., Capt. Constantine Taylor. Loss: k, 1; w, 2 = 3.

FIRST DIVISION, Brig.-Gen. James S. Wadsworth.

First Brigade, Brig.-Gen. Solomon Meredith, Col. William W. Robinson: 19th Ind., Col. Samuel J. Williams; 24th Mich., Col. Henry A. Morrow (w), Capt. Albert M. Edwards; 2d Wis., Col. Lucius Fairchild (w), Maj. John Mansfield (w), Capt. George H. Otis; 6th Wis., Lieut.-Col. Rufus R. Dawes; 7th Wis., Col. William W. Robinson, Maj. Mark Finnicum. Brigade loss: k, 162; w, 724; m, 267 = 1153. *Second Brigade*, Brig.-Gen. Lysander Cutler: 7th Ind., Col. Ira G. Grover; 76th N. Y., Maj. Andrew J. Grover (k), Capt. John E. Cook; 84th N. Y. (14th Militia), Col. Edward B. Fowler; 95th N. Y., Col. George H. Biddle (w), Maj. Edward Pye; 147th N. Y., Lieut.-Col. Francis C. Miller (w), Maj. George Harney; 56th Pa., Col. J. William Hofmann. Brigade loss: k, 111; w, 498; m, 366 = 975.

SECOND DIVISION, Brig.-Gen. John C. Robinson. Staff loss : w, 1.

First Brigade, Brig.-Gen. Gabriel R. Paul (w), Col. Samuel H. Leonard (w), Col. Adrian R. Root (w and c), Col. Richard Coulter (w), Col. Peter Lyle, Col. Richard Coulter: 16th Me., Col. Charles W. Tilden (c), Maj. Archibald D. Leavitt; 13th Mass., Col. Samuel H. Leonard, Lieut.-Col. N. Walter Batchelder; 94th N. Y., Col. Adrian R. Root, Maj. Samuel A. Moffett; 104th N. Y., Col. Gilbert G. Prey; 107th Pa., Lieut.-Col. James MacThomson (w), Capt. Emanuel D. Roath. Brigade loss : k, 51; w, 357; m, 633 = 1041. *Second Brigade*, Brig.-Gen. Henry Baxter: 12th Mass., Col. James L. Bates (w), Lieut.-Col. David Allen, Jr.; 83d N. Y. (9th Militia), Lieut.-Col. Joseph A. Moesch; 97th N. Y., Col. Charles Wheelock (c), Maj. Charles Northrup; 11th Pa.,⎰ Col. Richard Coulter, Capt. Benjamin F. Haines (w), Capt. John B. Overmyer; 88th Pa., Maj. Benezet F. Foust (w), Capt. Henry Whiteside; 90th Pa., Col. Peter Lyle, Maj. Alfred J. Sellers, Col. Peter Lyle. Brigade loss : k, 39; w, 255; m, 350 = 644.

THIRD DIVISION, Brig.-Gen. Thomas A. Rowley, Maj.-Gen. Abner Doubleday. Staff loss : w, 1.

First Brigade, Col. Chapman Biddle (w), Brig.-Gen. Thomas A. Rowley, Col. Chapman Biddle: 80th N. Y. (20th Militia), Col. Theodore B. Gates; 121st Pa., Maj. Alexander Biddle, Col. Chapman Biddle, Maj. Alexander Biddle; 142d Pa., Col. Robert P. Cummins (k), Lieut.-Col. Alfred B. McCalmont; 151st Pa., Lieut.-Col. George F. McFarland (w), Capt. Walter L. Owens, Col. Harrison Allen. Brigade loss : k, 91; w, 548; m, 257 = 896. *Second Brigade*, Col. Roy Stone (w), Col. Langhorne Wister (w),

Col. Edmund L. Dana: 143d Pa., Col. Edmund L. Dana, Lieut.-Col. John D. Musser; 149th Pa., Lieut.-Col. Walton Dwight (w), Capt. James Glenn; 150th Pa., Col. Langhorne Wister, Lieut.-Col. Henry S. Huidekoper (w), Capt. Cornelius C. Widdis. Brigade loss : k, 84; w, 462; m, 306 = 852. *Third Brigade*, Brig.-Gen. George J. Stannard (w), Col. Francis V. Randall : 12th Vt., ⎰ Col. Asa P. Blunt; 13th Vt., Col. Francis V. Randall, Maj. Joseph J. Boynton, Lieut.-Col. William D. Munson; 14th Vt., Col. William T. Nichols; 15th Vt., ⎰ Col. Redfield Proctor; 16th Vt., Col. Wheelock G. Veazey. Brigade loss : k, 45; w, 274; m, 32 = 351.

ARTILLERY BRIGADE, Col. Charles S. Wainwright: 2d Me., Capt. James A. Hall; 5th Me., Capt. Greenleaf T. Stevens (w), Lieut. Edward N. Whittier; L, 1st N. Y. (E, 1st N. Y. attached), Capt. Gilbert H. Reynolds (w), Lieut. George Breck; B, 1st Pa., Capt. James H. Cooper; B, 4th U. S., Lieut. James Stewart (w). Brigade loss : k, 9; w, 86; m, 11 = 106.

SECOND ARMY CORPS, ☆Maj.-Gen. Winfield S. Hancock (w), Brig.-Gen. John Gibbon (w). Staff loss: w, 3.

General Headquarters: D and K, 6th N. Y. Cav., Capt. Riley Johnson. Loss : k, 1; w, 3 = 4.

FIRST DIVISION, Brig.-Gen. John C. Caldwell.

First Brigade, Col. Edward E. Cross (k), Col. H. Boyd McKeen: 5th N. H., Lieut.-Col. Charles E. Hapgood; 61st N. Y., Lieut.-Col. K. Oscar Broady; 81st Pa., Col. H. Boyd McKeen, Lieut.-Col. Amos Stroh; 148th Pa., Lieut.-Col. Robert McFarlane. Brigade loss : k, 57; w, 260; m, 13 = 330. *Second Brigade*, Col. Patrick Kelly : 28th Mass., Col. Richard Byrnes; 63d N. Y. (2 co's), Lieut.-Col. Richard C. Bentley (w), Capt. Thomas Touhy; 69th N. Y. (2 co's), Capt. Richard Moroney (w), Lieut. James J. Smith; 88th N. Y. (2 co's), Capt. Denis F. Burke; 116th Pa. (4 co's), Maj. St. Clair A. Mulholland. Brigade loss : k, 27; w, 109; m, 62 = 198. *Third Brigade*, Brig.-Gen. Samuel K. Zook (k), Lieut.-Col. John Fraser: 52d N. Y., Lieut.-Col. C. G. Freudenberg (w), Capt. William Scherrer; 57th N. Y., Lieut.-Col. Alford B. Chapman; 66th N. Y., Col. Orlando H. Morris (w), Lieut.-Col. John S. Hammell (w), Maj. Peter Nelson ; 140th Pa., Col. Richard P. Roberts (k), Lieut.-Col. John Fraser. Brigade loss : k, 49; w, 227; m, 82 = 358. *Fourth Brigade*, Col. John R. Brooke (w) : 27th Conn. (2 co's), Lieut.-Col. Henry C. Merwin (k), Maj. James H. Coburn ; 2d Del., Col. William P. Baily, Capt. Charles H. Christman ; 64th N. Y., Col. Daniel G. Bingham (w), Maj. Leman W. Bradley; 53d Pa., Lieut.-Col. Richards McMichael; 145th Pa. (7 co's), Col. Hiram L. Brown (w), Capt. John W. Reynolds (w), Capt. Moses W. Oliver. Brigade loss : k, 53; w, 281 ; m, 49 = 383.

SECOND DIVISION, Brig.-Gen. John Gibbon, Brig.-Gen. William Harrow. Staff loss: w, 3.

First Brigade, Brig.-Gen. William Harrow, Col. Francis E. Heath : 19th Me., Col. Francis E. Heath, Lieut.-Col. Henry W. Cunningham ; 15th Mass., Col. George H. Ward (k), Lieut.-Col. George C. Joslin ; 1st Minn. (2d Co. Minn. S. S. attached), Col. William Colvill, Jr. (w), Capt. Nathan S. Messick (k), Capt. Henry C. Coates ; 82d N. Y. (2d Militia), Lieut.-Col. James Huston (k), Capt. John

---

↓ At Taneytown and not engaged in the battle.

✠ See artillery brigades attached to army corps and the reserve.

↓ Maj.-Gen. John F. Reynolds of this corps was killed July 1st, while in command of the left wing of the army.

⎰ Transferred on afternoon of July 1st to the First Brigade.

⎰ Guarding trains and not engaged in the battle.

☆ After the death of General Reynolds General Hancock was assigned to the command of all the troops on the field

of battle, relieving General Howard, who had succeeded General Reynolds. General Gibbon of the Second Division assumed command of the corps. These assignments terminated on the evening of July 1. Similar changes in commanders occurred during the battle of the 2d, when General Hancock was put in command of the Third Corps, in addition to his own. He and General Gibbon were wounded on the 3d, and Brig.-Gen. William Hays was assigned to the command of the corps.

Darrow. Brigade loss: k, 147; w, 569; m, 48 = 764. *Second Brigade,* Brig.-Gen. Alexander S. Webb (w): 69th Pa., Col. Dennis O'Kane (m w), Capt. William Davis; 71st Pa., Col. Richard Penn Smith; 72d Pa., Col. DeWitt C. Baxter (w), Lieut.-Col. Theodore Hesser; 106th Pa., Lieut.-Col. William L. Curry. Brigade loss: k, 114; w, 337; m, 39 = 490. *Third Brigade,* Col. Norman J. Hall: 19th Mass., Col. Arthur F. Devereux; 20th Mass., Col. Paul J. Revere (m w), Lieut.-Col. George N. Macy (w), Capt. Henry L. Abbott; 7th Mich., Lieut.-Col. Amos E. Steele, Jr. (k), Maj. Sylvanus W. Curtis; 42d N. Y., Col. James E. Mallon; 59th N. Y. (4 co's), Lieut.-Col. Max A. Thoman (m w), Capt. William McFadden. Brigade loss: k, 81; w, 282; m, 14 = 377. *Unattached:* 1st Co. Mass. Sharp-shooters, Capt. William Plumer, Lieut. Emerson L. Bicknell. Loss: k, 2; w, 6 = 8.

THIRD DIVISION, Brig.-Gen. Alexander Hays.

First Brigade, Col. Samuel S. Carroll: 14th Ind., Col. John Coons; 4th Ohio, Lieut.-Col. Leonard W. Carpenter; 8th Ohio, Lieut.-Col. Franklin Sawyer; 7th W. Va., Lieut.-Col. Jonathan H. Lockwood. Brigade loss: k, 38; w, 166; m, 7 = 211. *Second Brigade,* Col. Thomas A. Smyth (w), Lieut.-Col. Francis E. Pierce: 14th Conn., Maj. Theodore G. Ellis; 1st Del., Lieut.-Col. Edward P. Harris, Capt. Thomas B. Hizar (w), Lieut. William Smith (k), Lieut. John T. Dent; 12th N. J., Maj. John T. Hill; 10th N. Y. (battalion), Maj. George F. Hopper; 108th N. Y., Lieut.-Col. Francis E. Pierce. Brigade loss: k, 61; w, 279; m, 26 = 366. *Third Brigade,* Col. George L. Willard (k), Col. Eliakim Sherrill (k), Lieut.-Col. James M. Bull: 39th N. Y. (4 co's), Maj. Hugo Hildebrandt (w); 111th N. Y., Col. Clinton D. MacDougall (w), Lieut.-Col. Isaac M. Lusk, Capt. Aaron P. Seeley; 125th N. Y., Lieut.-Col. Levin Crandell; 126th N. Y., Col. Eliakim Sherrill, Lieut.-Col. James M. Bull. Brigade loss: k, 139; w, 542; m, 33 = 714.

ARTILLERY BRIGADE, Capt. John G. Hazard: B, 1st N. Y. (14th N. Y. Battery attached), Lieut. Albert S. Sheldon (w), Capt. James McKay Rorty (k), Lieut. Robert E. Rogers; A, 1st R. I., Capt. William A. Arnold; B, 1st R. I., Lieut. T. Fred. Brown (w), Lieut. Walter S. Perrin; I, 1st U. S., Lieut. George A. Woodruff (m w), Lieut. Tully McCrea; A, 4th U. S., Lieut. Alonzo H. Cushing (k), Sergt. Frederick Fuger. Brigade loss: k, 27; w, 119; m, 3 = 149.

THIRD ARMY CORPS, Maj.-Gen. Daniel E. Sickles (w), Maj.-Gen. David B. Birney. Staff loss: w, 2.

FIRST DIVISION, Maj.-Gen. David B. Birney, Brig.-Gen. J. H. Hobart Ward.

First Brigade, Brig.-Gen. Charles K. Graham (w and c), Col. Andrew H. Tippin: 57th Pa. (8 co's), Col. Peter Sides (w), Capt. Alanson H. Nelson; 63d Pa., Maj. John A. Danks; 68th Pa., Col. Andrew H. Tippin, Capt. Milton S. Davis; 105th Pa., Col. Calvin A. Craig; 114th Pa., Lieut.-Col. Frederick F. Cavada (c), Capt. Edward R. Bowen: 141st Pa., Col. Henry J. Madill. Brigade loss: k, 61; w, 508; m, 171 = 740. *Second Brigade,* Brig.-Gen. J. H. Hobart Ward, Col. Hiram Berdan: 20th Ind., Col. John Wheeler (k), Lieut.-Col. William C. L. Taylor; 3d Me., Col. Moses B. Lakeman; 4th Me., Col. Elijah Walker (w), Capt. Edwin Libby; 86th N. Y., Lieut.-Col. Benjamin L. Higgins (w); 124th N. Y., Col. A. Van Horne Ellis (k), Lieut.-Col. Francis M. Cummins (w); 99th Pa., Maj. John W. Moore; 1st U. S. Sharp-shooters., Col. Hiram Berdan, Lieut.-Col. Casper Trepp; 2d U. S. Sharp-shooters (8 co's), Maj. Homer R. Stoughton. Brigade loss: k, 129; w, 482; m, 170 = 781. *Third Brigade,* Col. P. Regis De Trobriand: 17th Me., Lieut.-Col. Charles B. Merrill; 3d Mich., Col. Byron R. Pierce (w), Lieut.-Col. Edwin S. Pierce; 5th Mich., Lieut.-Col. John Pulford (w); 40th N. Y., Col. Thomas W. Egan; 110th Pa. (6 co's), Lieut.-Col. David M. Jones (w), Maj. Isaac Rogers. Brigade loss: k, 75; w, 394; m, 21 = 490.

SECOND DIVISION, Brig.-Gen. Andrew A. Humphreys. Staff loss: k, 2; w, 9 = 11.

First Brigade, Brig.-Gen. Joseph B. Carr: 1st Mass., Lieut.-Col. Clark B. Baldwin; 11th Mass., Lieut.-Col.

Porter D. Tripp; 16th Mass., Lieut.-Col. Waldo Merriam (w), Capt. Matthew Donovan; 12th N. H., Capt. John F. Langley; 11th N. J., Col. Robert McAllister (w), Capt. Luther Martin (w), Lieut. John Schoonover (w), Capt. William H. Lloyd (w), Capt. Samuel T. Sleeper, Lieut. John Schoonover; 26th Pa., Maj. Robert L. Bodine; 84th Pa.,⫶ Lieut.-Col. Milton Opp. Brigade loss: k, 121; w, 604; m, 65 = 790. *Second Brigade,* Col. William R. Brewster: 70th N. Y., Col. J. Egbert Farnum; 71st N. Y., Col. Henry L. Potter; 72d N. Y., Col. John S. Austin (w), Lieut.-Col. John Leonard; 73d N. Y., Maj. Michael W. Burns; 74th N. Y., Lieut.-Col. Thomas Holt; 120th N. Y., Lieut.-Col. Cornelius D. Westbrook (w), Maj. John R. Tappen. Brigade loss: k, 130; w, 573; m, 75 = 778. *Third Brigade,* Col. George C. Burling: 2d N. H., Col. Edward L. Bailey (w); 5th N. J., Col. William J. Sewell (w), Capt. Thomas C. Godfrey, Capt. Henry H. Woolsey; 6th N. J., Lieut.-Col. Stephen R. Gilkyson; 7th N. J., Col. Louis R. Francine (m w), Maj. Frederick Cooper; 8th N. J., Col. John Ramsey (w), Capt. John G. Langston; 115th Pa., Maj. John P. Dunne. Brigade loss: k, 59; w, 376; m, 78 = 513.

ARTILLERY BRIGADE, Capt. George E. Randolph (w), Capt. A. Judson Clark: 2d N. J., Capt. A. Judson Clark, Lieut. Robert Sims; D, 1st N. Y., Capt. George B. Winslow; 4th N. Y., Capt., James E. Smith; E, 1st R. I., Lieut. John K. Bucklyn (w), Lieut. Benjamin Freeborn; K, 4th U. S., Lieut. Francis W. Seeley (w), Lieut. Robert James. Brigade loss: k, 8; w, 81; m, 17 = 106.

FIFTH ARMY CORPS, Maj.-Gen. George Sykes.

General Headquarters: D and E, 12th N. Y. Inf., Capt. Henry W. Rider; D and H, 17th Pa. Cav., Capt. William Thompson.

FIRST DIVISION, Brig.-Gen. James Barnes.

First Brigade, Col. William S. Tilton: 18th Mass., Col. Joseph Hayes; 22d Mass., Lieut.-Col. Thomas Sherwin, Jr.; 1st Mich., Col. Ira C. Abbott (w), Lieut.-Col. William A. Throop; 118th Pa., Lieut.-Col. James Gwyn. Brigade loss: k, 12; w, 102; m, 11 = 125. *Second Brigade,* Col. Jacob B. Sweitzer: 9th Mass., Col. Patrick R. Guiney; 32d Mass., Col. G. L. Prescott; 4th Mich., Col. Harrison H. Jeffords (k), Lieut.-Col. George W. Lumbard; 62d Pa., Lieut.-Col. James C. Hull. Brigade loss: k, 67; w, 239; m, 121 = 427. *Third Brigade,* Col. Strong Vincent (m w), Col. James C. Rice: 20th Me., Col. Joshua L. Chamberlain; 16th Mich., Lieut.-Col. Norval E. Welch; 44th N. Y., Col. James C. Rice, Lieut.-Col. Freeman Conner; 83d Pa., Capt. Orpheus S. Woodward. Brigade loss: k, 88; w, 253; m, 11 = 352.

SECOND DIVISION, Brig.-Gen. Romeyn B. Ayres.

First Brigade, Col. Hannibal Day: 3d U. S. (6 co's), Capt. Henry W. Freedley (w), Capt. Richard G. Lay; 4th U. S. (4 co's), Capt. Julius W. Adams; 6th U. S. (5 co's), Capt. Levi C. Bootes; 12th U. S. (8 co's), Capt. Thomas S. Dunn; 14th U. S. (8 co's), Maj. Grotius R. Giddings. Brigade loss: k, 46; w, 318; m, 18 = 382. *Second Brigade,* Col. Sidney Burbank: 2d U. S. (6 co's), Maj. Arthur T. Lee (w), Capt. Samuel A. McKee; 7th U. S. (4 co's), Capt. David P. Hancock; 10th U. S. (3 co's), Capt. William Clinton; 11th U. S. (6 co's), Maj. DeLancey Floyd-Jones; 17th U. S. (7 co's), Lieut.-Col. J. Durell Greene. Brigade loss: k, 78; w, 342; m, 27 = 447. *Third Brigade,* Brig.-Gen. Stephen H. Weed (k), Col. Kenner Garrard: 140th N. Y., Col. Patrick H. O'Rorke (k), Lieut.-Col. Louis Ernst; 146th N. Y., Col. Kenner Garrard, Lieut.-Col. David T. Jenkins; 91st Pa., Lieut.-Col. Joseph H. Sinex; 155th Pa., Lieut.-Col. John H. Cain. Brigade loss: k, 40; w, 142; m, 18 = 200.

THIRD DIVISION, Brig.-Gen. Samuel W. Crawford.

First Brigade, Col. William McCandless: 1st Pa. Reserves, Col. William C. Talley; 2d Pa. Reserves, Lieut.-Col. George A. Woodward; 6th Pa. Reserves, Lieut.-Col. Wellington H. Ent; 13th Pa. Reserves, Col. Charles F. Taylor (k), Maj. William R. Hartshorne. Brigade loss: k, 20; w, 132; m, 3 = 155. *Third Brigade,* Col. Joseph W. Fisher: 5th Pa. Reserves, Lieut.-Col. George Dare; 9th Pa. Reserves, Lieut.-Col. James McK. Snodgrass; 10th Pa. Reserves, Col. Adoniram J. Warner; 11th Pa. Re-

⫶ Guarding trains and not engaged in the battle.

serves, Col. Samuel M. Jackson; 12th Pa. Reserves, Col. Martin D. Hardin. Brigade loss: k, 6; w, 49 = 55.

ARTILLERY BRIGADE, Capt. Augustus P. Martin: 3d Mass., Lieut. Aaron F. Walcott; C, 1st N. Y., Col. Almont Barnes; L, 1st Ohio, Capt. Frank C. Gibbs; D, 5th U. S., Lieut. Charles E. Hazlett (k), Lieut. Benjamin F. Rittenhouse; I, 5th U. S., Lieut. Malbone F. Watson (w), Lieut. Charles C. MacConnell. Brigade loss: k, 8; w, 33; m, 2 = 43.

SIXTH ARMY CORPS, Maj.-Gen. John Sedgwick.

General Headquarters: L, 1st N. J., and H, 1st Pa. Cav., Capt. William S. Craft.

FIRST DIVISION, Brig.-Gen. Horatio G. Wright.

Provost Guard: 4th N. J. (3 co's), Capt. William R. Maxwell. *First Brigade,* Brig.-Gen. A. T. A. Torbert: 1st N. J., Lieut.-Col. William Henry, Jr.; 2d N. J., Lieut.-Col. Charles Wiebecke; 3d N. J., Lieut.-Col. Edward L. Campbell; 15th N. J., Col. William H. Penrose. Brigade loss: w, 11. *Second Brigade,* Brig.-Gen. Joseph J. Bartlett: ☆ 5th Me., Col. Clark S. Edwards; 121st N. Y., Col. Emory Upton; 95th Pa., Lieut.-Col. Edward Carroll; 96th Pa., Maj. William H. Lessig. Brigade loss: k, 1; w, 4 = 5. *Third Brigade,* Brig.-Gen. David A. Russell: 6th Me., Col. Hiram Burnham; 49th Pa. (4 co's), Lieut.-Col. Thomas M. Hulings; 119th Pa., Col. Peter C. Ellmaker; 5th Wis., Col. Thomas S. Allen. Brigade loss: w, 2.

SECOND DIVISION, Brig.-Gen. Albion P. Howe.

Second Brigade, Col. Lewis A. Grant: 2d Vt., Col. James H. Walbridge; 3d Vt., Col. Thomas O. Seaver; 4th Vt., Col. Charles B. Stoughton; 5th Vt., Lieut.-Col. John R. Lewis; 6th Vt., Col. Elisha L. Barney. Brigade loss: w, 1. *Third Brigade,* Brig.-Gen. Thomas H. Neill: 7th Me. (6 co's), Lieut.-Col. Selden Connor; 33d N. Y. (detachment), Capt. Henry J. Gifford; 43d N. Y., Lieut.-Col. John Wilson; 49th N. Y., Col. Daniel D. Bidwell; 77th N. Y., Lieut.-Col. Winsor B. French; 61st Pa., Lieut.-Col. George F. Smith. Brigade loss: k, 2; w, 11; m, 2 = 15.

THIRD DIVISION, Maj.-Gen. John Newton, Brig.-Gen. Frank Wheaton.

First Brigade, Brig.-Gen. Alexander Shaler: 65th N. Y., Col. Joseph E. Hamblin; 67th N. Y., Col. Nelson Cross; 122d N. Y., Col. Silas Titus; 23d Pa., Lieut.-Col. John F. Glenn; 82d Pa., Col. Isaac C. Bassett. Brigade loss: k, 15; w, 56; m, 3 = 74. *Second Brigade,* Col. Henry L. Eustis: 7th Mass., Lieut.-Col. Franklin P. Harlow; 10th Mass., Lieut.-Col. Joseph B. Parsons; 37th Mass., Col. Oliver Edwards; 2d R. I., Col. Horatio Rogers, Jr. Brigade loss: k, 3; w, 41; m, 25 = 69. *Third Brigade,* Brig.-Gen. Frank Wheaton, Col. David J. Nevin: 62d N. Y., Col. David J. Nevin, Lieut.-Col. Theodore B. Hamilton; 93d Pa., Maj. John I. Nevin; 98th Pa., Maj. John B. Kohler; 102d Pa., ⚓ Col. John W. Patterson; 139th Pa., Col. Frederick H. Collier, Lieut.-Col. William H. Moody. Brigade loss: k, 2; w, 51 = 53.

ARTILLERY BRIGADE, Col. Charles H. Tompkins: 1st Mass., Capt. William H. McCartney; 1st N. Y., Capt. Andrew Cowan; 3d N. Y., Capt. William A. Harn; C, 1st R. I., Capt. Richard Waterman; G, 1st R. I., Capt. George W. Adams; D, 2d U. S., Lieut. Edward B. Williston; G, 2d U. S., Lieut. John H. Butler; F, 5th U. S., Lieut. Leonard Martin. Brigade loss: k, 4; w, 8 = 12.

ELEVENTH ARMY CORPS, ⎰ Maj.-Gen. Oliver O. Howard. Staff loss: w, 1.

General Headquarters: I and K, 1st Ind. Cav., Capt. Abram Sharra; 8th N. Y. (1 co.), Lieut. Hermann Foerster. Loss: m, 3.

FIRST DIVISION, Brig.-Gen. Francis C. Barlow (w), Brig.-Gen. Adelbert Ames. Staff loss: w, 1.

First Brigade, Col. Leopold von Gilsa: 41st N. Y., Lieut.-Col. Detleo von Einsiedel; 54th N. Y., Maj. Stephen Kovacs (c), Lieut. Ernest Both; 68th N. Y., Col. Gotthilf Bourry; 153d Pa., Maj. John Frueauff. Brigade loss: k, 54; w, 310; m, 163 = 527. *Second Brigade,* Brig.-

Gen. Adelbert Ames, Col. Andrew L. Harris: 17th Conn., Lieut.-Col. Douglas Fowler (k), Maj. Allen G. Brady; 25th Ohio, Lieut.-Col. Jeremiah Williams (c), Capt. Nathaniel J. Manning, Lieut. William Maloney (w), Lieut. Israel White; 75th Ohio, Col. Andrew L. Harris, Capt. George B. Fox; 107th Ohio, Col. Seraphim Meyer, Capt. John M. Lutz. Brigade loss: k, 68; w, 366; m, 344 = 778.

SECOND DIVISION, Brig.-Gen. Adolph von Steinwehr. Staff loss: w, 1.

First Brigade, Col. Charles R. Coster: 134th N. Y., Lieut.-Col. Allan H. Jackson; 154th N. Y., Lieut.-Col. D. B. Allen; 27th Pa., Lieut.-Col. Lorenz Cantador; 73d Pa., Capt. D. F. Kelley. Brigade loss: k, 55; w, 228; m, 314 = 597. *Second Brigade,* Col. Orland Smith: 33d Mass., Col. Adin B. Underwood; 136th N. Y., Col. James Wood, Jr.; 55th Ohio, Col. Charles B. Gambee; 73d Ohio, Lieut.-Col. Richard Long. Brigade loss: k, 51; w, 278; m, 19 = 348.

THIRD DIVISION, Maj.-Gen. Carl Schurz.

First Brigade, Brig.-Gen. Alex. Schimmelfennig, Col. George von Amsberg: 82d Ill., Lieut.-Col. Edward S. Salomon; 45th N. Y., Col. George von Amsberg, Lieut.-Col. Adolphus Dobke; 157th N. Y., Col. Philip P. Brown, Jr.; 61st Ohio, Col. Stephen J. McGroarty; 74th Pa., Col. Adolph von Hartung (w), Lieut.-Col. Alexander von Mitzel (c), Capt. Gustav Schleiter, Capt. Henry Krauseneck. Brigade loss: k, 58; w, 296; m, 453 = 807. *Second Brigade,* Col. W. Krzyzanowski: 58th N. Y., Lieut.-Col. August Otto, Capt. Emil Koenig; 119th N. Y., Col. John T. Lockman (w), Lieut.-Col. Edward F. Lloyd; 82d Ohio, Col. James S. Robinson (w), Lieut.-Col. David Thomson; 75th Pa., Col. Francis Mahler (w), Maj. August Ledig; 26th Wis., Lieut.-Col. Hans Boebel (w), Capt. John W. Fuchs. Brigade loss: k, 75; w, 388; m, 206 = 669.

ARTILLERY BRIGADE, Maj. Thomas W. Osborn: I, 1st N. Y., Capt. Michael Wiedrich; 13th N. Y., Lieut. William Wheeler; I, 1st Ohio, Capt. Hubert Dilger; K, 1st Ohio, Capt. Lewis Heckman; G, 4th U. S., Lieut. Bayard Wilkeson (k), Lieut. Eugene A. Bancroft. Brigade loss: k, 7; w, 53; m, 9 = 69.

TWELFTH ARMY CORPS, Maj.-Gen. Henry W. Slocum, ⎰ Brig.-Gen. Alpheus S. Williams.

Provost Guard: 10th Me. (4 co's), Capt. John D. Beardsley.

FIRST DIVISION, Brig.-Gen. Alpheus S. Williams, Brig.-Gen. Thomas H. Ruger.

First Brigade, Col. Archibald L. McDougall: 5th Conn., Col. Warren W. Packer; 20th Conn., Lieut.-Col. William B. Wooster; 3d Md., Col. Joseph M. Sudsburg; 123d N. Y., Lieut.-Col. James C. Rogers, Capt. Adolphus H. Tanner; 145th N. Y., Col. E. Livingston Price; 46th Pa., Col. James L. Selfridge. Brigade loss: k, 12; w, 60; m, 8 = 80. *Second Brigade,* Brig.-Gen. Henry H. Lockwood: 1st Md. Potomac Home Brigade, Col. William P. Maulsby; 1st Md. Eastern Shore, Col. James Wallace; 150th N. Y., Col. John H. Ketcham. Brigade loss: k, 35; w, 121; m, 18 = 174. *Third Brigade,* Brig.-Gen. Thomas H. Ruger, Col. Silas Colgrove: 27th Ind., Col. Silas Colgrove, Lieut.-Col. John R. Fesler; 2d Mass., Lieut.-Col. Charles R. Mudge (k), Maj. Charles F. Morse; 13th N. J., Col. Ezra A. Carman; 107th N. Y., Col. Nirom M. Crane; 3d Wis., Col. William Hawley. Brigade loss: k, 49; w, 225; m, 5 = 279.

SECOND DIVISION, Brig.-Gen. John W. Geary.

First Brigade, Col. Charles Candy: 5th Ohio, Col. John H. Patrick; 7th Ohio, Col. William R. Creighton; 29th Ohio, Capt. Wilbur F. Stevens (w), Capt. Edward Hayes; 66th Ohio, Lieut.-Col. Eugene Powell; 28th Pa., Capt. John Flynn; 147th Pa. (8 co's), Lieut.-Col. Ario Pardee, Jr. Brigade loss: k, 18; w, 117; m, 3 = 138. *Second Brigade,* Col. George A. Cobham, Jr., Brig.-Gen. Thomas L. Kane, Col. George A. Cobham, Jr.: 29th Pa., Col. William Rick-

---

☆ Also commanded Third Brigade, Third Division, July 3d.
⚓ Guarding trains and not engaged in the battle.
⎰ During the interval between the death of General Reynolds and the arrival of General Hancock on the afternoon of July 1st, all the troops on the field of battle were

commanded by General Howard, General Schurz taking command of the Eleventh Corps, and General Schimmelfennig of the Third Division.
⎰ General Slocum exercised command of the right wing during a part of the battle.

ards, Jr.; 109th Pa., Capt. F. L. Gimber; 111th Pa., Lieut.-Col. Thomas M. Walker, Col. George A. Cobham, Jr., Lieut.-Col. Thomas M. Walker. Brigade loss: k, 23; w, 66; m, 9=98. *Third Brigade,* Brig.-Gen. George S. Greene: 60th N. Y., Col. Abel Godard; 78th N. Y., Lieut.-Col. Herbert von Hammerstein; 102d N. Y., Col. James C. Lane (w), Capt. Lewis R. Stegman; 137th N. Y., Col. David Ireland; 149th N. Y., Col. Henry A. Barnum, Lieut.-Col. Charles B. Randall (w). Brigade loss: k, 67; w, 212; m, 24=303.

ARTILLERY BRIGADE, Lieut. Edward D. Muhlenberg: M, 1st N. Y., Lieut. Charles E. Winegar; E, Pa., Lieut. Charles A. Atwell; F, 4th U. S., Lieut. Sylvanus T. Rugg; K, 5th U. S., Lieut. David H. Kinzie. Brigade loss: w, 9.

CAVALRY CORPS, Maj.-Gen. Alfred Pleasonton.
FIRST DIVISION, Brig.-Gen. John Buford.
First Brigade, Col. William Gamble: 8th Ill., Maj. John L. Beveridge; 12th Ill. (4 co's) and 3d Ind. (6 co's), Col. George H. Chapman; 8th N. Y., Lieut.-Col. William L. Markell. Brigade loss: k, 13; w, 58; m, 28=99. *Second Brigade,* Col. Thomas C. Devin: 6th N. Y., Maj. Wm. E. Beardsley; 9th N. Y., Col. William Sackett; 17th Pa., Col. J. H. Kellogg; 3d W. Va. (2 co's), Capt. Seymour B. Conger. Brigade loss: k, 2; w, 3; m, 23=28. *Reserve Brigade,* Brig.-Gen. Wesley Merritt: 6th Pa., Maj. James H. Haseltine; 1st U. S., Capt. Robert S. C. Lord; 2d U. S., Capt. T. F. Rodenbough; 5th U. S., Capt. Julius W. Mason; 6th U. S., Maj. Samuel H. Starr (w and c), Lieut. Louis H. Carpenter, Lieutenant Nicholas Nolan, Captain Ira W. Claflin. Brigade loss: k, 13; w, 55; m, 223=291.

SECOND DIVISION, Brig.-Gen. David McM. Gregg. *Head-quarters Guard:* A, 1st Ohio, Capt. Noah Jones.
First Brigade, Col. John B. McIntosh: 1st Md., Lieut.-Col. James M. Deems; A, Purnell (Md.) Legion, Capt. Robert E. Duvall; 1st Mass., Lieut.-Col. Greely S. Curtis; 1st N. J., Maj. M. H. Beaumont; 1st Pa., Col. John P. Taylor; 3d Pa., Lieut.-Col. E. S. Jones; Section Battery H, 3d Pa. Art'y, Captain William D. Rank. Brigade loss: w, 26; m, 9=35. *Second Brigade,* ⚓ Col. Pennock Huey: 2d N. Y., Lieut.-Col. Otto Harhaus; 4th N. Y., Lieut.-Col. Augustus Pruyn; 6th Ohio, Maj. William Stedman; 8th Pa., Capt. William A. Corrie. *Third Brigade,* Col. J. Irvin Gregg: 1st Me., Lieut.-Col. Charles H. Smith; 10th N. Y., Major M. Henry Avery; 4th Pa., Lieut.-Colonel William E. Doster; 16th Pa., Lieut.-Colonel John K. Robison. Brigade loss: k, 6; w, 12; m, 3=21.

THIRD DIVISION, Brig.-Gen. Judson Kilpatrick. *Head-quarters Guard:* C, 1st Ohio, Capt. Samuel N. Stanford.

⚓ At Westminster, etc., and not engaged in the battle.
ᕠ With Huey's cavalry brigade, and not in the battle.

First Brigade, Brig.-Gen. Elon J. Farnsworth (k), Col. Nathaniel P. Richmond: 5th N. Y., Maj. John Hammond; 18th Pa., Lieut.-Col. William P. Brinton; 1st Vt., Lieut.-Col. Addison W. Preston; 1st W. Va., Col. Nathaniel P. Richmond, Maj. Charles E. Capehart. Brigade loss: k, 21; w, 34; m, 43=98. *Second Brigade,* Brig.-Gen. George A. Custer (k): 1st Mich., Col. Charles H. Town; 5th Mich., Col. Russell A. Alger; 6th Mich., Col. George Gray; 7th Mich., Col. William D. Mann. Brigade loss: k, 32; w, 147; m, 78=257.

HORSE ARTILLERY. *First Brigade,* Capt. James M. Robertson: 9th Mich., Capt. Jabez J. Daniels; 6th N. Y., Capt. Joseph W. Martin; B and L, 2d U. S., Lieut. Edward Heaton; M, 2d U. S., Lieut. A. C. M. Pennington; E, 4th U. S., Lieut. Samuel S. Elder. Brigade loss: k, 2; w, 6=8. *Second Brigade,* Capt. John C. Tidball: E and G, 1st U. S., Capt. Alanson M. Randol; K, 1st U. S., Capt. William M. Graham; A, 2d U. S., Lieut. John H. Calef; C, 3d U. S., ᕠ Lieut. William D. Fuller. Brigade loss: k, 2; w, 13=15.

ARTILLERY RESERVE, Brig.-Gen. Robert O. Tyler, Capt. James M. Robertson.
Headquarters Guard: C, 32d Mass., Capt. Josiah C. Fuller.
First Regular Brigade, Capt. Dunbar R. Ransom (w): H, 1st U. S., Lieut. Chandler P. Eakin (w), Lieut. Philip D. Mason; F and K, 3d U. S., Lieut. John G. Turnbull; C, 4th U. S., Lieut. Evan Thomas; C, 5th U. S., Lieut. Gulian V. Weir. Brigade loss: k, 13; w, 53; m, 2=68. *First Volunteer Brigade,* Lieut.-Col. Freeman McGilvery: 5th Mass. (10th N. Y. attached), Capt. Charles A. Phillips; 9th Mass., Capt. John Bigelow (w), Lieut. Richard S. Milton; 15th N. Y., Capt. Patrick Hart (w); C and F, Pa., Capt. James Thompson (w). Brigade loss: k, 16; w, 71; m, 6=93. *Second Volunteer Brigade,* Capt. Elijah D. Taft: B, 1st Conn., ᕠ Capt. Albert F. Brooker; M, 1st Conn., ᕠ Capt. Franklin A. Pratt; 2d Conn., Capt. John W. Sterling; 5th N. Y., Capt. Elijah D. Taft. Brigade loss: k, 1; w, 5; m, 2=8. *Third Volunteer Brigade,* Capt. James F. Huntington: 1st N. H., Capt. Frederick M. Edgell; H, 1st Ohio, Lieut. George W. Norton; F and G, 1st Pa., Capt. R. Bruce Ricketts; C, W. Va., Capt. Wallace Hill. Brigade loss: k, 10; w, 24; m, 3=37. *Fourth Volunteer Brigade,* Capt. Robert H. Fitzhugh: 6th Me., Lieut. Edwin B. Dow; A, Md., Capt. James H. Rigby; 1st N. J., Lieut. Augustin N. Parsons; G, 1st N. Y., Capt Nelson Ames; K, 1st N. Y. (11th N. Y. attached), Capt. Robert H. Fitzhugh. Brigade loss: k, 2; w, 34=36.

Train Guard: 4th N. J. (7 co's), Maj. Charles Ewing.
The total loss of the Union army was 3072 killed, 14,497 wounded, and 5434 captured or missing =23,003.

ᕠ At Taneytown and Westminster, and not engaged in the battle.

THE CONFEDERATE ARMY.

ARMY OF NORTHERN VIRGINIA — General Robert E. Lee.

FIRST ARMY CORPS, Lieut.-Gen. James Longstreet.
McLAWS'S DIVISION, Maj.-Gen. Lafayette McLaws.
Kershaw's Brigade, Brig.-Gen. Joseph B. Kershaw: 2d S. C., Col. J. D. Kennedy (w), Lieut.-Col. F. Gaillard; 3d S. C., Maj. R. C. Maffett, Col. J. D. Nance; 7th S. C., Col. D. Wyatt Aiken; 8th S. C., Col. J. W. Henagan; 15th S. C., Col. W. G. De Saussure (k), Maj. William M. Gist; 3d S. C. Battalion, Lieut.-Col. W. G. Rice. Brigade loss: k, 115; w, 483; m, 32=630. *Semmes's Brigade,* Brig.-Gen. Paul J. Semmes (m w), Col. Goode Bryan: 10th Ga., Col. John B. Weems; 50th Ga., Col. W. R. Manning; 51st Ga., Col. E. Ball; 53d Ga., Col. James P. Simms. Brigade loss: k, 55; w, 284; m, 91=430. *Barksdale's Brigade,* Brig.-Gen. William Barksdale (m w), Col. Benjamin G. Humphreys: 13th Miss., Col. J. W. Carter; 17th Miss., Col. W. D. Holder, Lieut.-Col. John C. Fiser; 18th Miss., Col. T. M. Griffin, Lieut.-Col. W. H. Luse; 21st Miss., Col. B. G. Humphreys. Brigade loss: k, 105; w, 550; m, 92=747. *Wofford's Brigade,* Brig.-Gen. William T. Wofford: 16th Ga., Col. Goode Bryan; 18th Ga., Lieut.-

Col. S. Z. Ruff; 24th Ga., Col. Robert McMillan; Cobb's (Ga.) Legion, Lieut.-Col. Luther J. Glenn; Phillips's (Ga.) Legion, Lieut.-Col. E. S. Barclay. Brigade loss: k, 30; w, 192; m, 112=334. *Artillery Battalion,* Col. Henry C. Cabell: A, 1st N. C., Capt. B. C. Manly; Ga. Battery (Pulaski Art'y), Capt. J. C. Fraser (m w), Lieut. W. J. Furlong; Va. Battery (1st Richmond Howitzers), Capt. E. S. McCarthy; Ga. Battery (Troup Art'y), Capt. H. H. Carlton (w), Lieut. C. W. Motes. Battalion loss: k, 8; w, 29=37.

PICKETT'S DIVISION, Maj.-Gen. George E. Pickett.
Garnett's Brigade, Brig.-Gen. Richard B. Garnett (k), Maj. Charles S. Peyton: 8th Va., Col. Eppa Hunton (w); 18th Va., Lieut.-Col. H. A. Carrington (w); 19th Va., Col. Henry Gantt (w), Lieut.-Col. John T. Ellis (k); 28th Va., Col. R. C. Allen (k), Lieut.-Col. William Watts (w); 56th Va., Col. W. D. Stuart (m w), Lieut.-Col. P. P. Slaughter. Brigade loss: k, 78; w, 324; m, 539=941. *Armistead's Brigade,* Brig.-Gen. Lewis A. Armistead (k), Col. W. R. Aylett: 9th Va., Maj. John C. Owens (k); 14th Va., Col.

James G. Hodges (k), Lieut.-Col. William White; 38th Va., Col. E. C. Edmonds (k), Lieut.-Col. P. B. Whittle; 53d Va., Col. W. R. Aylett (w) ; 57th Va., Col. John Bowie Magruder (k). Brigade loss : k, 88 ; w, 460 ; m, 643 = 1191. *Kemper's Brigade*, Brig.-Gen. James L. Kemper (w and c), Col. Joseph Mayo, Jr. (w) : 1st Va., Col. Lewis B. Williams (w), Lieut.-Col. F. G. Skinner; 3d Va., Col. Joseph Mayo, Jr., Lieut.-Col. A. D. Callcote (k) ; 7th Va., Col. W. T. Patton (k), Lieut.-Col. C. C. Flowerree; 11th Va., Maj. Kirkwood Otey (w) ; 24th Va., Col. William R. Terry (w). Brigade loss : k, 58 ; w, 356 ; m, 317 = 731. *Artillery Battalion*, Maj. James Dearing : Va. Battery (Fauquier Art'y), Capt. R. M. Stribling ; Va. Battery (Hampden Art'y), Capt. W. H. Caskie ; Va. Battery (Richmond Fayette Art'y), Capt. M. C. Macon ; Va. Battery, Capt. Joseph G. Blount. Battalion loss : k, 8 ; w, 17 = 25.

HOOD'S DIVISION, Maj.-Gen. John B. Hood (w), Brig.-Gen. E. McIver Law.

Law's Brigade, Brig.-Gen. E. McIver Law, Col. James L. Sheffield : 4th Ala., Lieut.-Col. L. H. Scruggs ; 15th Ala., Col. William C. Oates, Capt. B. A. Hill ; 44th Ala., Col. William F. Perry ; 47th Ala., Col. James W. Jackson, Lieut.-Col. M. J. Bulger, (w and c), Maj. J. M. Campbell ; 48th Ala., Col. James L. Sheffield, Capt. T. J. Eubanks. Brigade loss : k, 74 ; w, 276 ; m, 146 = 496. *Anderson's Brigade*, Brig.-Gen. George T. Anderson (w), Lieut.-Col. William Luffman : 7th Ga., Col. W. W. White ; 8th Ga., Col. John R. Towers ; 9th Ga., Lieut.-Col. John C. Mounger (k), Maj. W. M. Jones (w), Capt. George Hillyer ; 11th Ga., Col. F. H. Little (w), Lieut.-Col. William Luffman, Maj. Henry D. McDaniel, Capt. William H. Mitchell ; 59th Ga., Col. Jack Brown (w), Capt. M. G. Bass. Brigade loss ; k,105 ; w, 512 ; m, 54 = 671. *Robertson's Brigade*, Brig.-Gen. Jerome B. Robertson (w) : 3d Ark., Col. Van H. Manning (w), Lieut.-Col. R. S. Taylor ; 1st Tex., Lieut.-Col. P. A. Work ; 4th Tex., Col. J. C. G. Key (w), Maj. J. P. Bane ; 5th Tex., Col. R. M. Powell (m w), Lieut.-Col. K. Bryan (w), Maj. J. C. Rogers. Brigade loss : k, 84 ; w, 393 ; m, 120 = 597. *Benning's*, Brig.-Gen. Henry L. Benning : 2d Ga., Lieut.-Col. William T. Harris (k), Maj. W. S. Shepherd ; 15th Ga., Col. D. M. Du Bose ; 17th Ga., Col. W. C. Hodges ; 20th Ga., Col. John A. Jones (k), Lieut.-Col. J. D. Waddell. Brigade loss : k, 76 ; w, 299 ; m, 122 = 497. *Artillery Battalion*, Maj. M. W. Henry : N. C. Battery (Branch Art'y), Capt. A. C. Latham ; S. C. Battery (German Art'y), Capt. William K. Bachman ; S. C. Battery (Palmetto Light Art'y), Capt. Hugh R. Garden ; N. C. Battery (Rowan Art'y), Capt. James Reilly. Battalion loss : k, 4 ; w, 23 = 27.

RESERVE ARTILLERY, Col. J. B. Walton.

Alexander's Battalion, Col. E. Porter Alexander : La. Battery (Madison Light Art'y), Capt. George V. Moody ; S. C. Battery (Brooks Art'y), Lieut. S. C. Gilbert ; Va. Battery (Ashland Art'y), Capt. P. Woolfolk, Jr. (w), Lieut. James Woolfolk ; Va. Battery (Bedford Art'y), Capt. T. C. Jordan ; Va. Battery, Capt. William W. Parker ; Va. Battery, Capt. O. B. Taylor. Battalion loss : k, 19 ; w, 114 ; m, 6 = 139. *Washington (La.) Artillery*, Maj. B. F. Eshleman : 1st Co., Capt. C. W. Squires ; 2d Co., Capt. J. B. Richardson ; 3d Co., Capt. M. B. Miller ; 4th Co., Capt. Joe Norcom (w), Lieut. H. A. Battles. Battalion loss : k, 3 ; w, 26 ; m, 16 = 45.

SECOND ARMY CORPS, Lieut.-Gen. Richard S. Ewell. Staff loss : w, 1.

EARLY'S DIVISION, Maj.-Gen. Jubal A. Early.

Hays's Brigade, Brig.-Gen. Harry T. Hays: 5th La., Maj. Alexander Hart (w), Capt. T. H. Biscoe; 6th La., Lieut.-Col. Joseph Hanlon ; 7th La., Col. D. B. Penn; 8th La., Col. T. D. Lewis (k), Lieut.-Col. A. de Blanc (w), Maj. G. A. Lester ; 9th La., Col. Leroy A. Stafford. Brigade loss : k, 36 ; w, 201 ; m, 76 = 313. *Hoke's Brigade*, Col. Isaac E. Avery (m w), Col. A. C. Godwin : 6th N. C., Maj. S. McD. Tate ; 21st N. C., Col. W. W. Kirkland ; 57th N. C., Col. A. C. Godwin. Brigade loss : k, 35 ; w, 216 ; m, 94 = 345. *Smith's Brigade*, Brig.-Gen. William Smith : 31st Va., Col. John S. Hoffman ; 49th Va., Lieut.-Col. J. Catlett Gibson ; 52d Va., Lieut.-Col. James H. Skinner. Brigade loss : k, 12 ; w, 113 ; m, 17 = 142. *Gordon's Bri-*

gade, Brig.-Gen. John B. Gordon : 13th Ga., Col. James M. Smith ; 26th Ga., Col. E. N. Atkinson ; 31st Ga., Col. Clement A. Evans ; 38th Ga., Capt. William L. McLeod ; 60th Ga., Capt. W. B. Jones ; 61st Ga., Col. John H. Lamar. Brigade loss : k, 71 ; w, 270 ; m, 39 = 380. *Artillery Battalion*, Lieut.-Col. H. P. Jones : Va. Battery (Charlottesville Art'y), Capt. James McD. Carrington ; Va. Battery (Courtney Art'y), Capt. W. A. Tanner ; La. Battery (Guard Art'y), Capt. C. A. Green ; Va. Battery (Staunton Art'y), Capt. A. W. Garber. Battalion loss : k, 2 ; w, 6 = 8.

JOHNSON'S DIVISION, Maj.-Gen. Edward Johnson. Staff loss : w, 1 ; m, 1 = 2.

Steuart's Brigade, Brig.-Gen. George H. Steuart: 1st Md. Battalion, Lieut.-Col. James R. Herbert (w), Maj. W. W. Goldsborough (w), Capt. J. P. Crane ; 1st N. C., Lieut.-Col. H. A. Brown ; 3d N. C., Maj. W. M. Parsley; 10th Va., Col. E. T. H. Warren ; 23d Va., Lieut.-Col. S. T. Walton ; 37th Va., Maj. H. C. Wood. Brigade loss : k, 83 ; w, 409 ; m, 190 = 682. *Nicholls's Brigade*, Col. J. M. Williams : 1st La., Capt. E. D. Willett ; 2d La., Lieut.-Col. R. E. Burke ; 10th La., Maj. T. N. Powell ; 14th La., Lieut.-Col. David Zable ; 15th La., Maj. Andrew Brady. Brigade loss : k, 43 ; w, 309 ; m, 36 = 388. *Stonewall Brigade*, Brig.-Gen. James A. Walker : 2d Va., Col. J. Q. A. Nadenbousch ; 4th Va., Maj. William Terry ; 5th Va., Col. J. H. S. Funk ; 27th Va., Lieut.-Col. D. M. Shriver ; 33d Va., Capt. J. B. Golladay. Brigade loss : k, 35 ; w, 208 ; m, 87 = 330. *Jones's Brigade*, Brig.-Gen. John M. Jones (w), Lieut.-Col. R. H. Dungan : 21st Va., Capt. W. P. Moseley ; 25th Va., Col. J. C. Higginbotham (w), Lieut.-Col. J. A. Robinson ; 42d Va., Lieut.-Col. R. W. Withers (w), Capt. S. H. Saunders ; 44th Va., Maj. N. Cobb (w), Capt. T. R. Buckner ; 48th Va., Lieut.-Col. R. H.Dungan ; Maj. Oscar White ; 50th Va., Lieut.-Col. L. H. N. Salyer. Brigade loss : k, 58 ; w, 302 ; m, 61 = 421. *Artillery Battalion*, Maj. J. W. Latimer (m w), Capt. Charles I. Raine : 1st Md. Battery, Capt. William F. Dement ; Va. Battery (Alleghany Art'y), Capt. J. C. Carpenter ; Md. Battery (Chesapeake Art'y), Capt. William D. Brown (w) ; Va. (Lee) Battery, Capt. Charles I. Raine, Lieut. William W. Hardwicke. Battalion loss : k, 10 ; w, 40 = 50.

RODES'S DIVISION, Maj.-Gen. Robert E. Rodes.

Daniel's Brigade, Brig.-Gen. Junius Daniel : 32d N. C., Col. E. C. Brabble ; 43d N. C., Col. T. S. Kenan (w and c), Lieut.-Col. W. G. Lewis ; 45th N. C., Lieut.-Col. S. H. Boyd (w and c), Maj. John R. Winston (w and c), Capt. A. H. Gallaway (w), Capt. J. A. Hopkins ; 53d N. C., Col. W. A. Owens ; 2d N. C. Battalion, Lieut.-Col. H. L. Andrews (k), Capt. Van Brown. Brigade loss : k, 165 ; w, 635 ; m, 116 = 916. *Iverson's Brigade*, Brig.-Gen. Alfred Iverson : 5th N. C., Capt. Speight B. West (w), Capt. Benjamin Robinson (w) ; 12th N. C., Lieut.-Col. W. S. Davis ; 20th N. C., Lieut.-Col. Nelson Slough (w), Capt. Lewis T. Hicks ; 23d N. C., Col. D. H. Christie (m w), Capt. William H. Johnston. Brigade loss : k, 130 ; w, 328 ; m, 308 = 820. *Doles's Brigade*, Brig.-Gen. George Doles : 4th Ga., Lieut.-Col. D. R. E. Winn (k), Maj. W. H. Willis ; 12th Ga., Col. Edward Willis ; 21st Ga., Col. John T. Mercer ; 44th Ga., Col. S. P. Lumpkin (w), Maj. W. H. Peebles. Brigade loss : k, 24 ; w, 124 ; m, 31 = 179. *Ramseur's Brigade*, Brig.-Gen. Stephen D. Ramseur : 2d N. C., Maj. D. W. Hurtt (w), Capt. James T. Scales ; 4th N. C., Col. Bryan Grimes ; 14th N. C., Col. R. Tyler Bennett (w), Maj. Joseph H. Lambeth ; 30th N. C., Col. Francis M. Parker (w), Maj. W. W. Sellers. Brigade loss : k, 23 ; w, 122 ; m, 32 = 177. *O'Neal's Brigade*, Col. Edward A. O'Neal : 3d Ala., Col. C. A. Battle ; 5th Ala., Col. J. M. Hall ; 6th Ala., Col. J. N. Lightfoot (w), Capt. M. L. Bowie ; 12th Ala., Col. S. B. Pickens ; 26th Ala., Lieut.-Col. John C. Goodgame. Brigade loss : k, 73 ; w, 430 ; m, 193 = 696. *Artillery Battalion*, Lieut.-Col. Thomas H. Carter : Ala. Battery (Jeff Davis Art'y), Capt. W. J. Reese ; Va. Battery (King William Art'y), Capt. W. P. Carter ; Va. Battery (Morris Art'y), Capt. R. C. M. Page (w) ; Va. Battery (Orange Art'y), Capt. C. W. Fry. Battalion loss : k, 6 ; w, 35 ; m, 24 = 65.

RESERVE ARTILLERY, Col. J. Thompson Brown.

Brown's Battalion, Capt. Willis J. Dance : Va. Battery

(2d Richmond Howitzers), Capt. David Watson; Va. Battery (3d Richmond Howitzers), Capt. B. H. Smith, Jr.; Va. Battery (Powhatan Art'y), Lieut. John M. Cuningham; Va. Battery (Rockbridge Art'y), Capt. A. Graham; Va. Battery (Salem Art'y), Lieut. C. B. Griffin. Battalion loss: k, 3; w, 19 = 22. *Nelson's Battalion,* Lieut.-Col. William Nelson: Va. Battery (Amherst Art'y), Capt. T. J. Kirkpatrick; Va. Battery (Fluvanna Art'y), Capt. J. L. Massie; Ga. Battery, Capt. John Milledge, Jr. Battalion loss (not reported).

THIRD ARMY CORPS, Lieut.-Gen. Ambrose P. Hill.

ANDERSON'S DIVISION, Maj.-Gen. Richard H. Anderson.

Wilcox's Brigade, Brig.-Gen. Cadmus M. Wilcox: 8th Ala., Lieut.-Col. Hilary A. Herbert; 9th Ala., Capt. J. H. King (w); 10th Ala., Col. William H. Forney (w and c), Lieut.-Col. James E. Shelley; 11th Ala., Col. J. C. C. Sanders (w), Lieut.-Col. George E. Tayloe; 14th Ala., Col. L. Pinckard (w), Lieut.-Col. James A. Broome. Brigade loss: k, 51; w, 469; m, 257 = 777. *Mahone's Brigade,* Brig.-Gen. William Mahone: 6th Va., Col. George T. Rogers; 12th Va., Col. D. A. Weisiger; 16th Va., Col. Joseph H. Ham; 41st Va., Col. William A. Parham; 61st Va., Col. V. D. Groner. Brigade loss: k, 8; w, 55; m, 39 = 102. *Wright's Brigade,* Brig.-Gen. Ambrose R. Wright, Col. William Gibson, Brig.-Gen. Ambrose R. Wright: 3d Ga., Col. E. J. Walker; 22d Ga., Col. Joseph Wasden (k), Capt. B. C. McCurry; 48th Ga., Col. William Gibson, Capt. M. R. Hall, Col. William Gibson (w and c); 2d Ga. Battalion, Maj. George W. Ross (m w), Capt. Charles J. Moffett. Brigade loss: k, 40; w, 295; m, 333 = 668. *Perry's Brigade,* Col. David Lang: 2d Fla., Maj. W. R. Moore (w and c); 5th Fla., Capt. R. N. Gardner (w); 8th Fla., Col. David Lang. Brigade loss: k, 33; w, 217; m, 205 = 455. *Posey's Brigade,* Brig.-Gen. Carnot Posey: 12th Miss., Col. W. H. Taylor; 16th Miss., Col. Samuel E. Baker; 19th Miss., Col. N. H. Harris; 48th Miss., Col. Joseph M. Jayne. Brigade loss: k, 12; w, 71 = 83. *Sumpter (Ga.) Artillery Battalion,* Maj. John Lane: Co. A, Capt. Hugh M. Ross; Co. B, Capt. George M. Patterson; Co. C, Capt. John T. Wingfield (w). Battalion loss: k, 3; w, 21; m, 6 = 30.

HETH'S DIVISION, Maj.-Gen. Henry Heth (w), Brig.-Gen. J. Johnston Pettigrew (w). Staff loss: w, 2.

First Brigade, Brig.-Gen. J. Johnston Pettigrew, Col. James K. Marshall (w and c): 11th N. C., Col. Collett Leventhorpe (w); 26th N. C., Col. Henry K. Burgwyn, Jr. (k), Capt. H. C. Albright; 47th N. C., Col. G. H. Faribault (w); 52d N. C., Col. James K. Marshall, Lieut.-Col. Marcus A. Parks (w). Brigade loss: k, 190; w, 915 = 1105. *Second Brigade,* Col. J. M. Brockenbrough: 40th Va., Capt. T. E. Betts, Capt. R. B. Davis; 47th Va., Col. Robert M. Mayo; 55th Va., Col. W. S. Christian; 22d Va. Battalion, Maj. John S. Bowles. Brigade loss: k, 25; w, 123 = 148. *Third Brigade,* Brig.-Gen. James J. Archer (c), Col. B. D. Fry (w and c), Lieut.-Col. S. G. Shepard: 13th Ala., Col. B. D. Fry; 5th Ala. Battalion, Maj. A. S. Van de Graaff; 1st Tenn. (Prov. Army), Maj. Felix G. Buchanan; 7th Tenn., Lieut.-Col. S. G. Shepard; 14th Tenn., Capt. B. L. Phillips. Brigade loss: k, 16; w, 144; m, 517 = 677. *Fourth Brigade,* Brig.-Gen. Joseph R. Davis: 2d Miss., Col. J. M. Stone (w); 11th Miss., Col. F. M. Greene; 42d Miss., Col. H. R. Miller; 55th N. C., Col. J. K. Connally (w). Brigade loss: k, 180; w, 717 = 897. *Artillery Battalion,* Lieut.-Col. John J. Garnett: La. Battery (Donaldsonville Art'y), Capt. Victor Maurin; Va. Battery (Huger Art'y), Capt. Joseph D. Moore; Va. Battery, Capt. John W. Lewis; Va. Battery (Norfolk Light Art'y Blues), Capt. C. R. Grandy. Battalion loss: w, 5; m, 17 = 22.

PENDER'S DIVISION, Maj.-Gen. William D. Pender (m w), Brig.-Gen. James H. Lane, Maj.-Gen. Isaac R. Trimble (w and c), Brig.-Gen. James H. Lane. Staff loss: k, 1; w, 4 = 5.

First Brigade, Col. Abner Perrin: 1st S. C. (Prov. Army), Maj. C. W. McCreary; 1st S. C. (Rifles), Capt. William M. Hadden; 12th S. C., Col. John L. Miller; 13th S. C., Lieut.-Col. B. T. Brockman; 14th S. C., Lieut.-Col. Joseph N. Brown (w). Brigade loss: k, 100; w, 477 = 577. *Second Brigade,* Brig.-Gen. James H. Lane,

Col. C. M. Avery, Brig.-Gen. James H. Lane (w), Col. C. M. Avery: 7th N. C., Capt. J. McLeod Turner (w and c), Capt. James G. Harris; 18th N. C., Col. John D. Barry; 28th N. C., Col. S. D. Lowe (w), Lieut.-Col. W. H. A. Speer; 33d N. C., Col. C. M. Avery; 37th N. C., Col. W. M. Barbour. Brigade loss: k, 41; w, 348; m, 271 = 660. *Third Brigade,* Brig.-Gen. Edward L. Thomas: 14th Ga., ——; 35th Ga., ——; 45th Ga., ——; 49th Ga., Col. S. T. Player. Brigade loss: k, 16; w, 136 = 152. *Fourth Brigade,* Brig.-Gen. Alfred M. Scales (w), Lieut.-Col. G. T. Gordon, Col. William Lee J. Lowrance: 13th N. C., Col. J. H. Hyman (w); 16th N. C., Capt. L. W. Stowe; 22d N. C., Col. James Conner; 34th N. C., Col. William Lee J. Lowrance (w), Lieut.-Col. G. T. Gordon; 38th N. C., Col. W. J. Hoke (w). Brigade loss: k, 102; w, 323; m, 110 = 535. *Artillery Battalion,* Maj. William T. Poague: Va. Battery (Albemarle Art'y), Capt. James W. Wyatt; N. C. Battery (Charlotte Art'y), Capt. Joseph Graham; Miss. Battery (Madison Light Art'y), Capt. George Ward; Va. Battery, Capt. J. V. Brooke. Battalion loss: k, 2; w, 24; m, 6 = 32.

RESERVE ARTILLERY, Col. R. Lindsay Walker.

McIntosh's Battalion, Maj. D. G. McIntosh: Ala. Battery (Hardaway Art'y), Capt. W. B. Hurt; Va. Battery (Danville Art'y), Capt. R. S. Rice; Va. Battery (2d Rockbridge Art'y), Lieut. Samuel Wallace; Va. Battery, Capt. M. Johnson. Battalion loss: k, 7; w, 25 = 32. *Pegram's Battalion,* Maj. W. J. Pegram, Capt. E. B. Brunson: S. C. Battery (Pee Dee Art'y), Lieut. William E. Zimmerman; Va. Battery (Crenshaw), ——; Va. Battery (Fredericksburg Art'y), Capt. E. A. Marye; Va. Battery, (Letcher Art'y), Capt. T. A. Brander; Va. Battery (Purcell Art'y), Capt. Joseph McGraw. Battalion loss: k, 10; w, 37; m, 1 = 48.

CAVALRY, Maj.-Gen. James E. B. Stuart.

Fitz Lee's Brigade, Brig.-Gen. Fitzhugh Lee: 1st Md. Battalion (serving with Ewell's corps), Maj. Harry Gilmor, Maj. Ridgely Brown; 1st Va., Col. James H. Drake; 2d Va., Col. T. T. Munford; 3d Va., Col. Thomas H. Owen; 4th Va., Col. Williams C. Wickham; 5th Va., Col. T. L. Rosser. Brigade loss: k, 5; w, 16; m, 29 = 50. *Hampton's Brigade,* Brig.-Gen. Wade Hampton (w), Col. Lawrence S. Baker: 1st N. C., Col. Lawrence S. Baker; 1st S. C., ——; 2d S. C., ——; Cobb's (Ga.) Legion, ——; Jeff Davis Legion, ——; Phillips's (Ga.) Legion, ——. Brigade loss: k, 17; w, 58; m, 16 = 91. *W. H. F. Lee's Brigade,* Col. John R. Chambliss, Jr.: 2d N. C., ——; 9th Va., Col. R. L. T. Beale; 10th Va., Col. J. Lucius Davis; 13th Va., ——. Brigade loss: k, 2; w, 26; m, 13 = 41. *Jenkins's Brigade,* Brig.-Gen. Albert G. Jenkins (w), Col. M. J. Ferguson: 14th Va., ——; 16th Va., ——; 17th Va., Col. W. H. French; 34th Va. Battalion, Lieut.-Col. V. A. Witcher; 36th Va. Battalion, ——; Va. Battery, Capt. Thomas E. Jackson. *Robertson's Brigade,* Brig.-Gen. Beverly H. Robertson (commanded his own and W. E. Jones's brigades): 4th N. C., Col. D. D. Ferebee; 5th N. C., ——. *Jones's Brigade,* Brig.-Gen. William E. Jones: 6th Va., Maj. C. E. Flournoy; 7th Va., Lieut.-Col. Thomas Marshall; 11th Va., Col. L. L. Lomax; 35th Va. Battalion, Lieut.-Col. E. V. White. Brigade loss: k, 12; w, 40; m, 6 = 58. *Stuart's Horse Artillery,* Maj. R. F. Beckham: Va. Battery, Capt. James Breathed; Va. Battery, Capt. R. P. Chew; Maryland Battery, Capt. W. H. Griffin; S. C. Battery, Capt. J. F. Hart; Va. Battery, Capt. W. M. McGregor; Va. Battery, Capt. M. N. Moorman. *Imboden's Command,* Brig.-Gen. John D. Imboden: 18th Va. Cav., Col. George W. Imboden; 62d Va. (mounted infantry), Col. George H. Smith; Va. Partisan Rangers, Capt. John H. McNeill; Va. Battery, Capt. J. H. McClanahan.

According to the reports of brigade and other subordinate commanders the total loss of the Confederate Army was 2592 killed, 12,709 wounded, and 5150 captured or missing = 20,451. Several of the reports indicate that many of the "missing" were killed or wounded. Rolls on file in the office of the Adjutant-General, U. S. Army, bear the names of 12,227 wounded and unwounded Confederates captured at and about Gettysburg from July 1st to 5th, inclusive. The number of wounded prisoners is reported by the medical director of Meade's army as 6802.

RELATIVE STRENGTH OF THE ARMIES.

The consolidated morning reports of the Union Army for June 30th, 1863, give the numbers "actually available for line of battle," or the effective force, including officers and men, as follows:

COMMAND.	Cavalry.	Artillery.	Infantry.	Total.
First Army Corps.......	67	619	9,403	10,089
Second Army Corps.....	82	551	12,363	12,996
Third Army Corps......	......	677	11,247	11,924
Fifth Army Corps......	......	555	11,954	12,509
Sixth Army Corps......	124	1,039	14,516	15,679
Eleventh Army Corps..	52	644	9,197	9,893
Twelfth Army Corps....	......	396	8,193	8,589
Cavalry Corps...........	12,653	491	......	13,144
Artillery Reserve......	......	2,211	335	2,546
Aggregate	12,978	7,183	77,208	97,369

Between June 30th and July 3d, the reënforcements that joined the army may be estimated as follows:

Stannard's brigade to First Corps........ 2,500
Lockwood's brigade to Twelfth Corps.... 1,700
Duvall's company Maryland cavalry to
    Gregg's cavalry division.............. 60
Rank's Pennsylvania artillery to Gregg's
    cavalry division........................ 50

      Total reënforcements............... 4,310

This number, added to the strength as per returns of June 30th, makes a maximum of 101,679 effectives of all arms.

The severe marches following the roll-call of June 30th considerably reduced by sickness and straggling the strength of the commands, but a satisfactory computation of the shrinkage from these causes does not seem possible. It may have ranged from five to ten per cent.

The field returns of the infantry and artillery of the army corps, for July 4th, give the following effective figures:

First Corps (except one regiment detailed
    as wagon guard)........................ 5,430
Second Corps 6,923
Third Corps.............................. 6,130
Fifth Corps 9,553
Sixth Corps 12,832
Eleventh Corps 5,513
Twelfth Corps (except one battery on re-
    connoissance)........ 9,757

      Total 56,138

Adding to this the loss of 21,905 sustained by the commands mentioned, gives an approximate calculation of the strength of the seven army corps, viz., 78,043.

There are no field returns of the Cavalry Corps or the Artillery Reserve for July 4th. But by assuming, in round numbers, 78,000 as the maximum fighting strength of the seven army corps, and adding 13,000 for the Cavalry Corps, and 2500 for the Artillery Reserve (as shown by the return for June 30th), *an aggregate of 93,500* is obtained.

The effective strength as reported by the seven army corps commanders at the council held on the evening of July 2d, was as follows: "About 9000, 12,500, 9000, 6000, 8500, 6000, 7000,—total 58,000.

Unfortunately the particular corps represented by these figures are not stated in the minutes of the council.

According to the returns of the Confederate Army for May 31st, 1863 (the latest immediately preceding the battle), the "effective total" of enlisted men was:

Infantry..................................... 54,356
Stuart's Cavalry............................. 9,536
Artillery................................... 4,460

Alexander's and Garnett's artillery battalions, consisting of ten batteries, are not included in the above figures. Their effective strength may, however, be put at 800 officers and men. There were also 6116 officers borne on the return as "present for duty," which, added to the foregoing, give an aggregate of 75,268 officers and men.

The accessions by organizations to the army between May 31st and July 3d, were as follows:

                             *Estimated at
                             not less than*
1st. Pettigrew's infantry brigade......... 2,000
2d.   Jenkins's cavalry brigade............. 1,600
3d.   Imboden's cavalry brigade........... 2,000

      Total gain......................... 5,600

The loss by organizations during the same period was:

1st. Corse's brigade and one regiment of
     Pettigrew's brigade left at Hanover
     Court House, Va................... 2,000
2d. Three regiments of Early's division
     left at Winchester, Va.............. 1,000
3d. One regiment of Stuart's cavalry left
     in Virginia........................ 350

      Total loss (estimated)......... 3,350

or a net gain of 2250, which, added to the strength on May 31st, of 75,268, makes a maximum in the campaign of 77,518. After making a liberal allowance for losses by sickness, straggling, guards to prisoners and casualties in the various encounters between June 1st and June 30th inclusive, it seems reasonable to conclude that *General Lee had at his command on the field of battle, from first to last, an army numbering at least* 70,000 *men of all arms.*

CONSECRATION OF THE GETTYSBURG CEMETERY, NOVEMBER 19, 1863—THE GATHERING THAT
PRESIDENT LINCOLN ADDRESSED. FROM A PHOTOGRAPH.

UNION CAVALRYMAN — THE WATER-CALL.

THE CONQUEST OF ARKANSAS.↓

BY COLONEL THOMAS L. SNEAD.

I HAVE already sketched in this work the chief events of the war west of the Mississippi, down to the defeat of Van Dorn and Price by Curtis, in the battle of Elkhorn [see Vol. I., p. 263], and the withdrawal of the Confederate forces to Des Arc, whither boats were to be sent by Beauregard to transport them to Memphis.

Van Dorn, after issuing orders for the transfer of the army from Des Arc to Memphis, to reënforce the army of Albert Sidney Johnston, in west Tennessee, went, on March 29th, 1862, to Corinth, accompanied by Colonel Dabney H. Maury, in order to confer personally with Johnston and Beauregard as to the movement of his command. He was directed to return forthwith to Arkansas and bring every man that he could to Corinth, in all haste, so as to take part in the projected attack upon Grant, who was then at Pittsburg Landing.

Until Van Dorn returned to Des Arc, on April 5th, it was not generally known that the Trans-Mississippi army was to be sent across the river, and that Missouri and Arkansas were to be abandoned to the enemy. The governors of both of these States protested earnestly against the movement, and the troops themselves manifested the greatest unwillingness to leave their homes in possession of the enemy, while they should go far away to fight for others. But Van Dorn assured them that they were to be brought back to Arkansas as soon as the impending battle on the Tennessee had been

↓Including the battles of Prairie Grove and the capture of Arkansas Post, Helena, and Little Rock. See also "Naval Operations in the Vicksburg Campaign," to follow.—EDITORS.

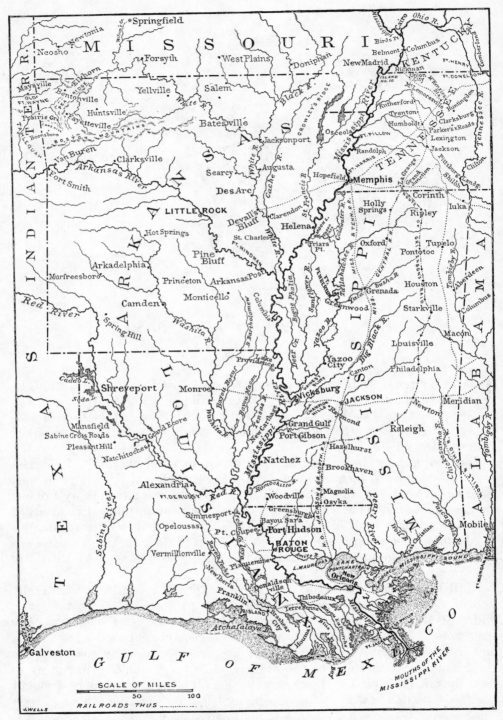

CAMPAIGNS OF THE MISSISSIPPI VALLEY.

fought, and Price, though he utterly disapproved of the movement, used his influence with the men to induce them to go willingly. They all consented to go, and the mounted men were even persuaded to leave their horses behind them. On the 8th of April, 1862, Little's Missouri brigade embarked for Memphis, quickly followed by the remainder of the Army of the West, twenty thousand men. Few of these ever got back to their Western homes, and Arkansas and Missouri were abandoned to their fate; moreover, Van Dorn was too late for the battle of Shiloh.

The transfer of Van Dorn's forces to Corinth resulted before the middle of May not only in the abandonment of Missouri and northern Arkansas to the enemy, but in the transfer by Halleck of more than thrice as many Union troops from the Trans-Mississippi to the Tennessee to meet them there. This policy of depleting the forces west of the Mississippi, persisted in by the Confederate authorities, thenceforth down to the fall of Vicksburg, was one of the gravest of those blunders whereby the downfall of the Confederacy was precipitated.

Curtis meanwhile moved without opposition from Elkhorn into north-eastern Arkansas, and on the 3d of May occupied Batesville, a small town on White River within ninety miles of Little Rock. His effective force, after sending two divisions, under Generals Asboth and Jeff. C. Davis, to the Tennessee, still amounted to 12,422 men.✠ Nothing now prevented him from moving against the capital and the valley of the Arkansas, but the difficulty of subsisting his army so far from its base of supply, which was St. Louis.

In spite of this difficulty he had begun to advance to Little Rock, and his outposts were within thirty-five miles of that city (where he was to assume the position of military governor), when the evacuation of Corinth and the consequent opening of the Mississippi to Vicksburg also opened the White River to the Federal fleet and furnished him, as he hoped, a safe and convenient water communication with his base. While waiting for the opening of this new line of communication, for which gun-boats and transports were being made ready, he lay inactive at Batesville.

Van Dorn, on leaving Arkansas, had assigned Brigadier-General Roane to the command of that State. There were no troops there except a few companies of State militia, and these were badly organized and poorly armed; and Roane, though he had been governor of the State and was a brave and estimable gentleman, amiable and popular, was wholly unfit for a military command. Besides these militia companies there were some 5000 or 6000 Indian and mixed (Indian and white) troops in the Indian Territory under Brigadier-General Albert Pike, but they could hardly be accounted a force, as they were of no value except on furlough, and had even then to be fed and clothed, and supplied with all sorts of things, and treated with great consideration and gentleness.

Arkansas was thus utterly undefended, and her people, feeling that they

---

✠ The Army of the South-west consisted, May 13th, 1862, of three divisions under Generals Frederick Steele, E. A. Carr, and P. J. Osterhaus. General Sigel was assigned to duty in the East by orders dated June 1st, 1862.— EDITORS.

had been abandoned by the Confederate Government, were fast becoming despondent or apathetic. Those living to the north of the Arkansas among the mountains which rise west of the White and Black rivers were fast submitting to the authority of the Union, and many of them were enlisting in the Union army. The slave-holders that lived in the valley of the Arkansas and on the rich alluvial lands south of that river and along the Mississippi were in despair. The governor and State officers were making ready to abandon the capital, and that part of the population which still remained loyal

LIEUTENANT-GENERAL T. H. HOLMES, C. S. A.
FROM A PHOTOGRAPH.

to the Confederacy was panic-stricken. In these straits a delegation was sent to Beauregard, to whose Department the Trans-Mississippi still belonged, to beg him to appoint Major-General Hindman to the command, from which Van Dorn had been taken, and to authorize him to raise an army for the defense of the State.

Hindman was consequently assigned, on the 26th of May, to the command of the Trans-Mississippi District, comprising the States of Missouri and Arkansas and that part of Louisiana north of the Red River and the Indian Territory. He had commanded a brigade at Shiloh, was wounded there, and had been promoted for good conduct.

Leaving Corinth at once Hindman went to Memphis, which the Confederates were preparing to evacuate as soon as Corinth should be abandoned. There he collected a few supplies for his army, and "impressed" a million dollars that was in the banks. Thus equipped, he hastened to Little Rock, where he assumed command of his district and established headquarters on the 31st of May, 1862. With great energy and with administrative ability of the highest order, he went to work to create an army and provide supplies for it. He declared martial law, and scattered his provost-marshals all over the State; enforced the Conscript Law‡ remorselessly; collected thousands of stragglers that were skulking in all directions; arrested deserters and shot scores of them; sent recruiting officers into north Arkansas and Missouri; stopped five Texas regiments that were on their way to Beauregard; established workshops for making powder, shot, arms, clothing, and other supplies

‡ The first Confederate Conscript Law, entitled "An act to provide for the public defense," was approved April 16th, 1862. This act annulled all previous contracts made by volunteers, and virtually constituted all men over eighteen years of age and under thirty-five, soldiers during the continuance of the war. The provisions withdrew from State control all male citizens within the ages prescribed and made them subject to the control of the President of the Confederacy during the war. The act further provided that all persons under the age of eighteen years or over the age of thirty-five years, who were in military service at the time of the passage of the act, should be held to duty in the organizations where they were then serving, for a period of ninety days, unless their places in the ranks should be filled by other recruits.—EDITORS.

for his forces; and worked in every way so intelligently and earnestly that early in July he had an army of about 20,000 armed men and 46 pieces of artillery.

Not only had Little Rock and the valley of the Arkansas been saved to the Confederacy, but Curtis's position at Batesville was fast becoming untenable. In front he was threatened by Hindman, who was growing stronger and bolder every day, while behind him the Missourians were organizing in all directions to break his long line of communication with St. Louis. The failure of a gun-boat expedition ♭ to relieve him from this precarious situation determined him to retreat across the swamps to Helena. Hindman resolved to attack him. Sending a considerable force under Brigadier-General Albert Rust to get between the retreating army and Helena, and to hold the crossing of the almost impassable Cache, he himself set off in pursuit. But Rust, though a very successful politician, was one of the most incompetent of all "political generals," and was easily brushed out of the way by Curtis, who, conquering the greater obstacles which Nature opposed to his march, got safely to Helena on the 13th of July.

Meanwhile the Confederate Government, yielding to the importunities of General Price and of the representatives of the States west of the Mississippi, and alarmed by the progress of the Union armies in that direction, determined to prosecute more vigorously the war in the West, and to make some effort to recover Missouri and that part of Louisiana which the Union armies had conquered.

Accordingly, just after McClellan's "change of base" to the James, General J. B. Magruder, who had won distinction in the Virginia campaign and was believed to be an officer of great ability and force, was assigned to the command of the Trans-Mississippi, which was now, for the first time, made a separate department. He was told that Hindman, Dick Taylor, and Price would be ordered to report to him — Taylor to command the forces in Louisiana, Hindman the District of Arkansas, and Price

MAJOR-GENERAL T. C. HINDMAN, C. S. A.
FROM A PHOTOGRAPH.

the army which was to be sent into Missouri. But hardly had this wise plan been agreed upon before it was set aside. Magruder, who was already on his way to the West, was recalled to Richmond, and subsequently ordered to Texas; Price was directed to remain in Mississippi; ⟨ and Major-General Theophilus H. Holmes was assigned to the command of the Trans-Mississippi.

♭ See "Naval Operations," to follow.— EDITORS.
⟨ See "With Price East of the Mississippi," Vol. II., p. 717. After the battle of Corinth and the retreat to Ripley, General Price and his forces continued to be attached to the Department of Mississippi and East Louisiana.— EDITORS.

General Holmes reached Vicksburg on the 30th of July, and on the 12th of August established the headquarters of his department at Little Rock. The force which Hindman turned over to him consisted of about 18,000 infantry "effectives," some 6000 mounted men, 54 pieces of artillery, and 7000 or 8000 unarmed men in camps of instruction.

Hindman was now ordered by Holmes to concentrate the greater part of this force near Fort Smith on the western border of the State, and to organize there an expedition into Missouri, which State was at that time in the utmost commotion.

When Halleck went to the Tennessee in April, 1862, to assume command of the armies which he was to lead against Corinth, he left Schofield in command of the Union troops in Missouri. This force consisted chiefly of the State militia which Schofield had himself organized. Before the end of the summer this militia had an effective strength of about fifty thousand men. Great as this force was, Schofield did not find it sufficient to hold the Missourians in subjection and to disperse the roving bands which kept up the fight for their State upon its own soil, and he had to call to his assistance several considerable bodies of Union troops. With the aid of these he was gradually driving the Confederate bands out of the State when he learned, toward the last of August, that Hindman was gathering an army for the invasion of Missouri. Rumor so magnified the greatness of this invasion that Schofield fancied that Hindman was at the head of from 40,000 to 70,000 men. He accordingly called eagerly for help. The Department of the Missouri was thereupon enlarged by the addition of Kansas; and on the 24th of September Curtis was assigned to the command of it. Curtis ordered Schofield, who was then at Springfield, to take command of all the troops in the south-west. At the same time he ordered General J. G. Blunt, who was commanding in Kansas, to reënforce Schofield with all his available men. This order was promptly obeyed, and Schofield found himself by the 1st of October at the head of about 11,000 effectives with 16 pieces of artillery. This force he called the "Army of the Frontier."

MAJOR-GENERAL JOHN S. MARMADUKE, C. S. A.
FROM A PHOTOGRAPH.

Hindman assumed personal command of the Confederate troops in northwestern Arkansas on the 24th of August. These consisted of between 9000 and 10,000 men, of whom about 3000 were Indians, under command of Colonel Douglas H. Cooper. With this force he moved to the borders of Missouri, and took position along the line between that State and Arkansas. His advance consisted of a brigade of Missouri Cavalry (two thousand strong, perhaps), lying in and around Newtonia under Colonel Joseph O. Shelby, one of the very best officers I have ever known. The men had all just been recruited in Missouri, and were as fine a body of young fellows as ever fought under any flag.

Hindman had hardly entered Missouri when, on the 10th of September, he was recalled to Little Rock by General Holmes, in order to help organize the troops in that neighborhood for his expedition. He left Rains in command, with orders not to provoke an engagement. Matters remained quiet till the 30th of September, when General Frederick Salomon with a part of Blunt's reënforcements approached Newtonia. Cooper with 4000 or 5000 Indians and mixed troops had previously joined Shelby. Together they attacked Salomon and drove him back in confusion. Schofield marched at once to the assistance of Salomon, and on the 4th of October reached Newtonia. Cooper and Shelby fell back toward Rains. Thereupon Schofield continued to advance, driving the Confederates before him out of Missouri and into the mountains of Arkansas. Thence Cooper continued to retreat toward the Indian Territory, while Rains made his way to Huntsville. Schofield sent Blunt in pursuit of Cooper, who was overtaken at Old Fort Wayne near Maysville on the 22d of October and completely routed and driven into the Indian Territory.

Hindman had meanwhile returned to Fort Smith on the 15th of October. Learning there of the disasters that had befallen his army, he hastened to the front, relieved Rains, assumed command himself, and was about to take a strong position near Fayetteville, whither reënforcements were hastening to him, when Schofield on the 27th of October again advanced. Hindman thereupon retreated somewhat precipitately to the banks of the Arkansas, whence he wrote to Holmes that with another division he could "move into Missouri, take Springfield, and winter on the Osage at least."

Schofield, whose effective strength had been increased by reënforcements to

MAJOR-GENERAL JAMES G. BLUNT.
FROM A PHOTOGRAPH.

over sixteen thousand men, having accomplished the object of his expedition, now returned toward Springfield with two divisions of the Army of the Frontier, leaving Blunt with another division in the vicinity of Fayetteville to guard the mountain passes. Believing that hostilities were ended for the winter, and being ill, he turned over the command of the Army of the Frontier to Blunt on the 20th of November, and went to St. Louis.

Blunt was a typical Kansas man of that period. Born in Maine, he had practiced medicine in Ohio, and gone thence to Kansas when that territory was the battle-field between slavery and freedom. Deeply inspired by the fierce passions which that savage conflict generated, he was one of the first to enlist

FAYETTEVILLE, ARKANSAS. FROM A PHOTOGRAPH.

for the defense of the Union and the abolition of slavery. He was rapidly promoted, and on the 8th of April, 1862, was made brigadier-general and assigned to the command of the Department of Kansas. He was then 36 years old.

While Hindman was actively reorganizing his army on the Arkansas, about fifty miles south of Fayetteville (where Blunt was), and getting ready to move again into Missouri, Holmes, who was doing all that he could to reënforce him, was ordered by reason of the exigencies of the war on the eastern side of the Mississippi to abandon the Missouri expedition.

The disastrous defeat of Van Dorn at Corinth in October, 1862, opened the way to Grant to move overland against Vicksburg, which stronghold and Port Hudson were the only places that the Confederates then held on the Mississippi. Leaving Grand Junction on the 4th of November Grant advanced toward Holly Springs, Van Dorn falling back before him. McClernand was at the same time concentrating at Memphis a large force which was to move by the river and coöperate in the attack upon Vicksburg. Alarmed by these great preparations the Confederate Government, which had sent Pemberton, who had been in command of the Department of South Carolina and Georgia, to supersede Van Dorn, instructed Holmes, under date of November 11th, to send ten thousand men to Vicksburg if possible. Holmes, on receiving this order, straightway ordered Hindman to abandon the invasion of Missouri and return to Little Rock with his army. Hindman protested; and to entreaties from Van Dorn, Pemberton, and Joseph E. Johnston (who on the 24th of November had been assigned to the command), and to the reiterated orders of the President and Secretary of War requiring him to reënforce Vicksburg, Holmes only replied that he could do nothing as "two-thirds of his force was in north-western Arkansas to meet a heavy advance from Springfield." He nevertheless again ordered Hindman to bring his army to Little Rock without further delay.

Hindman, however, had made up his mind to attack Blunt before obeying Holmes's order. He had already sent Marmaduke toward Cane Hill with a division of cavalry; and skirmishing was taking place almost daily between him and Blunt, who had some 7000 or 8000 men. At last Blunt attacked in force on the 28th of November, and drove Marmaduke back to the vicinity of Van Buren. Blunt then took position at Cane Hill.

Hindman resolved to attack him there with his whole available force. Leaving Van Buren on the 3d of December with 9000 infantry, 2000 cavalry, and 22 pieces of artillery, about 11,500 men in all, he drove in Blunt's pickets on the evening of the 6th, and was getting ready to attack him the next evening, when he learned that General F. J. Herron was coming to reënforce Blunt with about 4000 infantry, 2000 cavalry, and 30 guns, and was already entering Fayetteville.

Blunt had learned on the 24th of December that Hindman was moving his infantry from the south side of the Arkansas to the north side of that river. He immediately ordered Herron, who was encamped with two divisions of the Army of the Frontier near Springfield, to come instantly to Cane Hill. That excellent officer broke camp on the morning of the 3d, and, marching 110 miles in 3 days, reached Elkhorn on the evening of the 6th of December.

There seemed nothing to prevent Hindman from first destroying Herron and then turning upon Blunt and defeating him; for Herron and Blunt were twelve miles apart and the Confederates lay between them. Indeed that was what Hindman determined to do. Masking his movement from Blunt by so

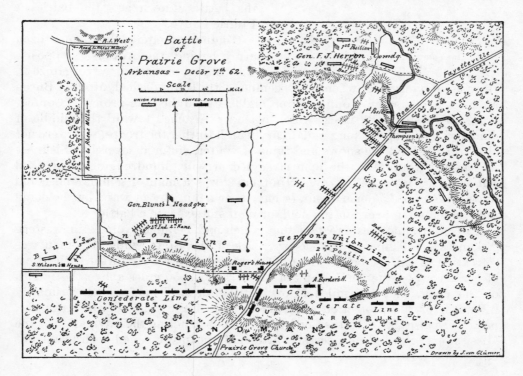

disposing a brigade of cavalry as to deceive him into believing that it was he whom he was about to attack, Hindman moved at 3 o'clock on the morning of December 7th against Herron. His cavalry under Marmaduke soon encountered Herron's on the march to Blunt, and drove them back upon the main body. Herron brought up his entire force, and Marmaduke gave way in turn. Hindman thereupon brought up his infantry, but, instead of attacking, as he ought to have done, took a strong position and awaited Herron's attack. This fatal mistake gave the victory to Blunt. Herron did attack at noon. The moment that Blunt heard Herron's guns he rushed to his assistance, and Hindman had then to confront the united army, which was not only stronger than his own in numbers, but very much stronger in organization, arms, artillery, and leadership. Darkness ended the battle. During the night Hindman withdrew his army and retreated toward Van Buren. Blunt did not pursue. Hindman's loss in killed, wounded, and missing was 1317; Blunt's was 1251, of which 918 belonged to Herron's two divisions, which bore the brunt of the battle, known as "the battle of Prairie Grove."

BRIGADIER-GENERAL T. J. CHURCHILL, C. S. A.
FROM A PHOTOGRAPH.

Hindman sheltered his demoralized army behind the Arkansas, opposite Van Buren, and tried to reorganize it. It was still lying there when, on December 28th, Blunt dashed into Van Buren at the head of a small mounted force, and hastened the long-projected Confederate retreat to Little Rock, which place was reached toward the middle of January. During the long and dreary march thither the troops, who were not clad to withstand the snows and rains of winter, suffered severely. Sickness increased alarmingly; the men straggled at will; hundreds deserted; and Hindman's army faded away. Hindman "was a man of genius and could have commanded a department, or have been a minister of war; but he could not command an army in the field, or plan and execute a battle."

A disaster almost as great as that which had befallen Holmes in western Arkansas befell him in the eastern part of the State while Hindman was retreating to Little Rock. The Confederates had strongly fortified the Post of Arkansas, on the north bank of the Arkansas, 50 miles above the mouth of the river, and 117 miles below Little Rock. The fort was primarily intended for the protection of that city and of the valley of the Arkansas, but it was also useful to the Confederates in obstructing the navigation of the Mississippi. Several unsuccessful attempts to capture it had been made, but now it was about to fall.

When Grant was ready to move overland against Vicksburg he ordered Sherman, in the absence of McClernand, ⸀ to take all the troops at Memphis and Steele's division at Helena, and to move with Porter's fleet by the river and coöperate in the attack. Grant had advanced a part of his own immediate army as far as Holly Springs, where he established a great depot of supplies, and was about to move forward when Van Dorn, by a splendid dash upon Holly Springs, ⚓ on the 20th of December, and Forrest, by a brilliant raid into east Tennessee, so broke Grant's communications and destroyed his supplies that he was forced to abandon his

⸀ On the 21st of October, 1862, Secretary Stanton by a confidential order authorized Major-General John A. McClernand, then in Washington, to proceed to the States of Indiana, Illinois, and Iowa for the purpose of raising and organizing troops for an expedition, to be commanded by him, having for its object the capture of Vicksburg, the freeing of the Mississippi, and the opening of navigation to New Orleans. On the 9th of November General Banks was ordered to relieve General Butler, at New Orleans, and proceed to open the Mississippi from below. General McClernand was authorized to show his confidential orders to the governors of the States named, but they were not communicated to General Grant, who, on October 16th, was formally assigned to the command of the Department of the Tennessee, a command he had been exercising ever since Halleck went to Washington in July. ☆ Being advised, however, of the President's strong desire for a movement against Vicksburg, General Grant made his preparations for a combined attack on that stronghold by a force descending the river on transports from Memphis and a heavier force under his own command moving by land along the general line of the Jackson railroad. Some correspondence took place by telegraph between General Grant and General Halleck, as General-in-Chief, regarding a commander for the river column, to which McClernand's levies were assigned as they reported at Cairo, and General Grant was authorized to designate the commander, unless otherwise ordered. General Grant had already indicated to Halleck his purpose of assigning Sherman; General Halleck replied, December 9th, that Sherman would be his choice, but that the President might insist on naming the commander. Finally, just as the expedition was ready to start from Memphis, General Grant, at Oxford, Mississippi, received General Halleck's telegram of December 18th, directing him to give the command to McClernand. General McClernand, who had also been in correspondence with the Government on this subject and had now received corresponding orders direct, was at that moment on

his way to report for duty. General Grant's telegram to him at Cairo did not find him promptly, and General Grant's telegram to Sherman, intended to cause him to wait for McClernand, did not reach Memphis until after Sherman with the advance of his troops had started. The capture of Holly Springs on the 20th of December broke up General Grant's coöperating movement by land. Sherman, knowing nothing of the enforced change of Grant's plans, attacked alone the reënforced garrison of Vicksburg, at Chickasaw's Bluffs, and was repulsed with heavy loss. [See p. 462.] The following day, January 4th, General McClernand arrived and took command of the expedition, to which he gave the name of the "Army of the Mississippi," dividing it into two corps, commanded by Major-General Sherman and Brigadier-General George W. Morgan. Without waiting for further instructions, McClernand at once moved up the Arkansas River and captured the works known as Arkansas Post, with about five thousand prisoners. Grant at first disapproved of the movement as having been made without orders. McClernand, however, considered himself an independent commander. All question as to McClernand's position disappeared in the reorganization of the forces under General Grant, December 18th, 1862, into four army corps: the Thirteenth to be commanded by McClernand, the Fifteenth by Sherman, the Sixteenth by Hurlbut, the Seventeenth by McPherson.

EDITORS.

⚓ The post at Holly Springs was commanded by Colonel R. C. Murphy, 8th Wisconsin Volunteers, and the force there consisted of the 8th Wisconsin and a portion of the 62d Illinois Infantry, and six companies of the 2d Illinois Cavalry. The surprise was made at daylight, and was complete, but many of the soldiers resisted capture. The cavalrymen distinguished themselves by bold attacks on isolated parties of the enemy, and lost nine killed and thirty-nine wounded in these affrays. The value of the stores destroyed was estimated by Grant at $400,000, and by Van Dorn at $1,500,000. Fifteen hundred prisoners were taken by Van Dorn.— EDITORS.

☆ The origin of the expedition down the Mississippi, December 12th to January 4th, under Sherman's command, is given in General Grant's "Personal Memoirs" (C. L. Webster & Co.), as follows:

"During the delay at Oxford in repairing railroads, I learned that an expedition down the Mississippi now was inevitable, and, desiring to have a competent commander in charge, I

ordered Sherman, on the 8th of December, back to Memphis to take charge. . . . As stated, my action in sending Sherman back was expedited by a desire to get him in command of the forces separated from my direct supervision. I feared that delay might bring McClernand, who was his senior and who had authority from the President and Secretary of War, to exercise that particular command,— and independently."

EDITORS.

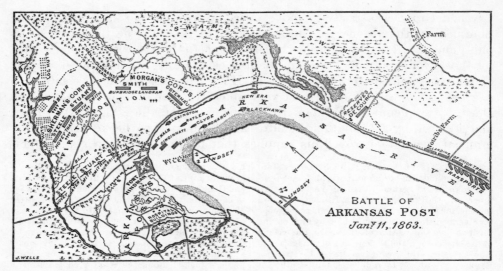

BATTLE OF
ARKANSAS POST
Jan.ʸ 11, 1863.

movement;↓ and on the 23d of December he ordered Sherman to delay his expedition. But Sherman was already on the way to Vicksburg, whence, after making an ineffectual attempt to capture the place [see p. 462], he reëmbarked his army and retired to Milliken's Bend.

McClernand arrived at Milliken's Bend on the 3d of January, 1863, and the next day assumed command of the expedition. Having nothing better to do, he determined to capture the Post of Arkansas, and to occupy the State. Accordingly, on the 4th of January, he embarked his army, 32,000 strong, on transports, and set sail for the Arkansas, accompanied by Porter's fleet — 3 iron-clads and 6 gun-boats. Reaching the vicinity of the Post on the 9th he disembarked his men the next day. The garrison consisted of about five thousand men under command of Brigadier-General Thos. J. Churchill. The iron-clads began the attack on the 10th. It was renewed the next day by

↓ On the 11th of December General N. B. Forrest moved with his brigade from Columbia, Tennessee, toward the Tennessee river, at Clifton, crossing on the 15th, under instructions from Bragg, who was at Murfreesboro', to operate against Grant's communications in west Tennessee. On the 16th Forrest captured Lexington, securing a number of prisoners, including Colonel Robert G. Ingersoll and Major L. H. Kerr, 11th Illinois Cavalry. Two detachments were now sent to cut the Mobile and Ohio Railroad at points north and south of Jackson, and on the 19th Forrest, with the remainder of his men, about four hundred, advanced on the town. A force, consisting of the 43d and 61st Illinois Infantry and portions of the 11th Illinois, 5th Ohio, and 2d West Tennessee Cavalry, under Colonel Adolph Engelmann of the 43d Illinois, disputed the advance of Forrest, and kept up a running fight until within reach of the fortifications and reënforcements had arrived from the south. General Forrest now withdrew and moved with united forces on Humboldt and Trenton, capturing both posts and destroying the stockades and garrison stores. From Trenton, Forrest moved north to Union City, near the Kentucky line, capturing that point and destroying railway bridges and trestling northward. From Union City the raiders passed along the North-western Railway to McKenzie's Station, at the junction of the North-western and the Memphis and Ohio Railroads. On the 28th Forrest started from McKenzie southward toward Lexington. Meanwhile the Union troops along Forrest's line of march that had escaped capture, strengthened by reënforcements from below Jackson, had resumed their stations at Trenton and Humboldt, and were preparing to cut off Forrest's retreat. On the 31st the main body of the raiders was intercepted at Parker's Cross Roads, on the road to Lexington, by a brigade under Colonel C. L. Dunham, subsequently joined by Colonel J. W. Fuller's brigade, and after a desperate engagement Forrest retired toward the Tennessee. Forrest's estimate of his force in this battle is 1800 men. On January 2d, the whole command recrossed the Tennessee at Clifton.— EDITORS.

both army and navy, and after a terrific bombardment of nearly four hours Churchill surrendered. The Confederate loss was 60 killed, 75 or 80 wounded, and 4791 prisoners; the Union loss was 1061 killed and wounded. The next day McClernand received peremptory orders from Grant to return forthwith to Milliken's Bend with his entire command.

By the disasters in the northwestern part of the State and the capture of the Post of Arkansas, and through the demoralization consequent upon those events, the fine army which Hindman had turned over to Holmes on the 12th of August, 1862, had been reduced within less than five months to about 10,000 effectives, most of which were in camp near Little Rock.

The ill consequences of Holmes's incompetence to command a department and of Hindman's unfitness to command an army, now began to be seriously felt by the Confederacy. For

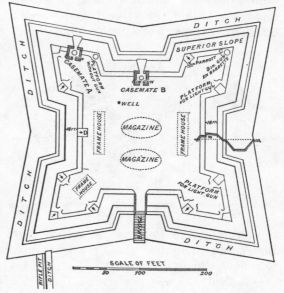

PLAN OF FORT HINDMAN, ARKANSAS POST.

not only was Holmes wholly unable to do anything for the relief of Vicksburg, but his weakness relieved the Federal general-in-chief of all apprehension of another invasion of Missouri, and of all fear for the safety of Helena. Halleck consequently ordered 19,000 of the force at Helena, including those with which Steele had joined Sherman in December, to be sent to Grant, leaving a garrison of only about 5000 men for the defense of the place. All this was done before the 19th of January, 1863. Curtis was also ordered to send all the men that could be spared from Missouri to the Mississippi to coöperate in the capture of Vicksburg.

Schofield, who had resumed command of the Army of the Frontier, immediately after the battle of Prairie Grove, began in

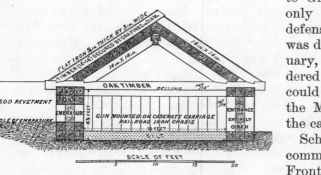

SECTION OF A CASEMATE OF FORT HINDMAN.

consequence of this order to withdraw the greater part of his army, which was then 18,000 strong, from north-western Arkansas and put it on the march through Missouri to north-eastern Arkansas, where it was to be joined by Davidson with six thousand cavalry from St. Louis.

Schofield proposed that ten thousand of these men should be sent to Grant instead.   This led to the culmination of long-existing differences between Curtis and Schofield, the former of whom represented the Radical or Abolition faction of the Union men of Missouri, while the latter represented the Conservative faction, at whose head was Governor Gamble.   Curtis desired to retain the 45,000 "effectives" that were in the State in order to dragoon the Southern sympathizers into submission.   Schofield thought that a part of these men could be better employed elsewhere.   Curtis was sustained by the Government, and on the 1st of April Schofield was, at his own request, relieved from duty in Missouri.   Curtis's conduct, however, soon raised such a storm in Missouri that the President on the 10th of March ordered General E. V. Sumner, from the Army of the Potomac, to relieve him.   Sumner died on the way to St. Louis, and thereupon the President, on the 13th of May, ordered Schofield to relieve Curtis.

CASEMATE ON THE EASTERN CURTAIN OF FORT HINDMAN, SHOW-
ING THE EFFECT OF SHOT FROM THE UNION GUNS.

Schofield at once postponed further operations against Arkansas until after the all-important struggle for Vicksburg had been decided, and sent nearly twelve thousand of his men thither and to Tennessee, making more than thirty thousand men that were sent out of Missouri to reënforce Grant at Vicksburg, a force which gave him the victory there and opened all the Western waters to the Union fleets and armies.

Even President Davis at last saw that General Holmes was unfit for his great command, and on the 7th of February, 1863, ordered Lieutenant-General Edmund Kirby Smith to relieve him, and sent General Price to report to Smith.   The latter assumed command of the Department of the Trans-Mississippi at Alexandria, in Louisiana, on the 7th of March, 1863.   Taylor was left in command of Louisiana, and Magruder of Texas.   Holmes was put in command of the District of Arkansas.   The change resulted in very little, if any, advantage to the Confederacy, for Smith was even feebler than Holmes, and though attempting to do a great deal more did almost nothing.

General Price reached Little Rock on the 25th of March and was assigned to the command of Hindman's division.   The state of affairs in Arkansas at that time is quite accurately depicted in a letter which the Confederate Secretary of War addressed to General Smith on the 18th of March.   He says:

"From a variety of sources, many of which I cannot doubt, the most deplorable accounts reach this department of the disorder, confusion, and demoralization everywhere prevalent both with the armies and people of that State.   The commanding general [Holmes] seems, while esteemed for his virtues, to have lost the confidence and attachment of all; and the next in command, General Hindman, who is admitted to have shown energy and ability, has rendered him-

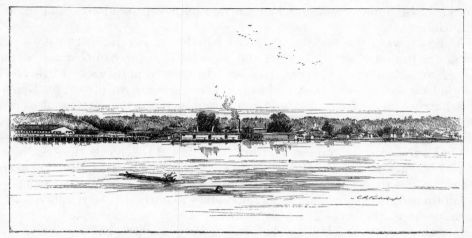

HELENA, ARKANSAS. FROM A PHOTOGRAPH MADE IN 1888.

self by alleged acts of violence and tyranny perfectly odious. The consequences as depicted are fearful. The army is stated to have dwindled by desertion, sickness, and death from 40,000 or 50,000 men to some 15,000 or 18,000, who are disaffected and helpless, and are threatened with positive starvation from deficiency of mere necessaries. The people are represented as in a state of consternation, multitudes suffering for means of subsistence, and yet exposed from gangs of lawless marauders and deserters to being plundered of the little they have."

Such was the outlook in Arkansas when Price assumed command of a division at Little Rock on the 1st of April. Holmes's entire force in Arkansas and the Indian Territory at that time (exclusive of Walker's division which was soon sent to Taylor in Louisiana) aggregated less than 12,500 officers and men. Seven thousand of these constituted Price's division, which was stationed near Little Rock. With them Price

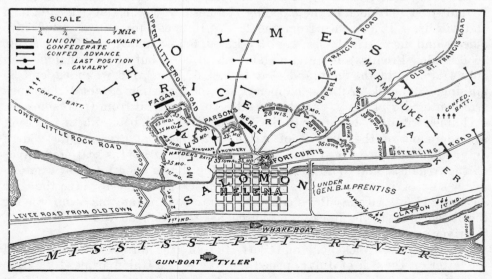

MAP OF THE BATTLE OF HELENA, ARKANSAS.

would have done something had he not been repressed by both Smith and Holmes.

At last toward the middle of June Kirby Smith determined to do something for the relief of Vicksburg, and as the President had frequently suggested an attack upon Helena he ordered Holmes to move from Little Rock for that place. He could hardly have done anything more unwise, for Helena was garrisoned by 5000 men, and was strongly fortified. It was also protected by gun-boats, and could not have been held 24 hours even if it had been taken.

The Confederates bivouacked within five miles of Helena on the evening of the 3d of July, and Holmes then learned for the first time the difficulties which he was to encounter. Between him and the city rose a succession of precipitous hills over which it was impossible to move artillery, and difficult to manœuvre infantry. The hills nearest the city were occupied by strong redoubts,— Graveyard Hill in the center, Fort Righter on the north, and Fort Hindman on the south,— and these redoubts were all connected by a line of bastions. In the low ground between these hills and Helena was a strong work,— Fort Curtis,— and in the river lay the gun-boat *Tyler*, Lieutenant Commanding James M. Prichett, whose great guns were to do no little execution. The Union forces were under the command of General B. M. Prentiss. [See organization, p. 460.]

Holmes, nothing daunted, for he was both brave and fearless, ordered the attack to be made at daybreak of the 4th of July. Price with 3095 men was to take Graveyard Hill; Fagan with 1770 men to attack Fort Hindman; and Marmaduke and L. M. Walker were sent with 2781 men against Fort Righter. The attack was made as ordered; Price carried Graveyard Hill in gallant style and held it, but Fagan and Marmaduke were both repulsed, and the fire of the forts, rifle-pits, and gun-boat was then all concentrated against Price. By half-past 10 o'clock in the morning Holmes saw that his attack had failed and withdrew Price's men from the field. Holmes's force aggregated 7646 officers and men. His losses were 173 killed, 687 wounded, and 776 missing, 1636 in all. Prentiss's force aggregated about 5000, but he says that he had only 4129 men in the fight, and that he lost 57 killed, 146 wounded, and 36 missing, 239 in all. All this happened on the day that Grant's victorious army entered Vicksburg, and that Lee began his retreat from Gettysburg.

Holmes withdrew his army to the White River, and, being ill, turned over the command of the District of Arkansas to General Price on the 23d of July. Price at once urged General Smith to concentrate his scattered forces on the Arkansas and to do something, but Smith was then too busy organizing a sort of independent Trans-Mississippi Confederacy to have time for anything else. All that Price could do was to concentrate his own force for the defense of Little Rock, the approaches to which on the north side of the river he now began to fortify.

The capture of Vicksburg and Port Hudson (the former on the 4th and the latter on the 8th of July) opened the way to the Union armies for active operations in Arkansas. Major-General Frederick Steele was accordingly

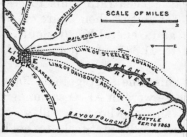

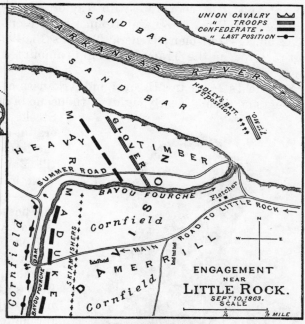

MAP OF THE CAPTURE OF LITTLE ROCK.

sent with a force to Helena, and instructed to form a junction with Brigadier-General Davidson, who was moving south from Missouri, by Crowley's Ridge, and to " break up Price and occupy Little Rock."

Steele organized his expedition at Helena on the 5th of August, and moved thence with two divisions of infantry, a brigade of cavalry, and 39 guns to the White River, where he effected a junction with Davidson, who had 6000 cavalry, taught as dragoons, and three batteries. On the 18th of August Steele moved from Devall's Bluff upon Little Rock with 13,000 officers and men and 57 pieces of artillery. He was reënforced a few days later by True's brigade, which raised his aggregate to nearly 14,500 "present." Of this number 10,500 were " present for duty." On the morning of the 10th of September he had come within eight miles of Little Rock.

Price had " present for duty " 7749 men of all arms. About 6500 of these occupied the trenches on the north side of the Arkansas, and about 1250 were disposed on the south side with orders to prevent the enemy from crossing the river. This was not easy to do, as the river was fordable at many points, and Davidson did in fact effect a crossing below Little Rock, about 10 o'clock, without much difficulty.

As soon as Price learned that his fortified position on the north side of the river had been turned by Davidson he withdrew his troops across the Arkansas, and evacuated Little Rock about 5 o'clock in the afternoon. Two brigades of Steele's cavalry, under Colonel Lewis Merrall, started in pursuit, followed Marmaduke for a day, and returned to Little Rock on the 12th. General Price's total casualties in the series of operations around Little Rock amounted to 64 killed, wounded, and missing; General Steele's to 137.

Price continued his retreat undisturbed to Arkadelphia. There Holmes resumed command on the 25th of September. On the 7th of October Smith ordered him to fall back to Camden, whence he could either safely retreat to Shreveport or coöperate with Taylor, who was concentrating his forces on the Red River. General Holmes's "present for duty" then aggregated 8532 officers and men; General Taylor's 13,649; and General Kirby Smith's entire force in the Trans-Mississippi amounted to 41,887, of whom 32,971 were "present for duty."

Schofield's force in Missouri and Arkansas at this time aggregated 47,000 officers and men. Nearly eighteen thousand of these were in Arkansas under Steele. Halleck, who was still general-in-chief, ordered Steele to hold the line of the Arkansas, and to wait till Banks was ready to coöperate with him from Port Hudson in an attack upon Shreveport, and in taking possession of the Red River and its valley.

MAJOR-GENERAL FREDERICK STEELE.
FROM A PHOTOGRAPH.

Holmes, not being pressed by Steele, settled his infantry quietly at Camden, while his cavalry indulged in a sort of spasmodic activity, the main object of which was to procure forage for their horses.

A division of infantry—consisting of Churchill's Arkansas brigade and Parsons's Missouri brigade, the two having some five thousand effectives—was near Spring Hill. On their left flank was Cabell's brigade of Arkansas cavalry; and on their right, toward Camden, was Marmaduke with a division of Missouri cavalry—Shelby's and Greene's brigades. Cabell had about 1200 men for duty; Marmaduke about 2000. East of the Washita were Dockery's brigade of cavalry and some other mounted men.

Lieutenant-General E. Kirby Smith was kept very busy at Shreveport organizing bureaus and sub-bureaus; fortifying his capital; issuing orders and countermanding them; and planning campaigns that were never to be fought.

Throughout all his great department hostilities were virtually suspended during the autumn, throughout the winter, and far into the spring. His soldiers lay idle in their camps, and the people gave themselves up to cotton-trading and money-getting. Neither soldiers nor civilians did anything to sustain, or even to encourage, the armies which were fighting in Virginia and Tennessee against overwhelming odds.

It was to no purpose that Dick Taylor and General Price begged Kirby Smith to concentrate the troops that were scattered through Louisiana, Arkansas and Texas, and to move them northward and into Missouri, where they would at least create a diversion in favor of Lee and of Johnston, even if they did not regain Arkansas and Missouri. Smith listened, but did nothing. Yes!—he asked the President to relieve General Holmes from service in the Trans-Mississippi, and toward the middle of March this was done.

General Price was then put in temporary command of what was left of the District of Arkansas—that small portion of the State which lies south of a line drawn east and west through Camden.

General Price's lines extended from Monticello in the east to the Indian Territory in the west, where General Samuel B. Maxey (who, from March, 1875, till March, 1887, represented Texas in the United States Senate) had a mixed command of Texans and Indians, some two thousand strong.

THE OPPOSING FORCES IN ARKANSAS.

December 7th, 1862–September 14th, 1863.

The composition, losses, and strength of each army as here stated give the gist of all the data obtainable in the Official Records. K stands for killed; w for wounded; m w for mortally wounded; m for captured or missing; c for captured.

PRAIRIE GROVE, DECEMBER 7TH, 1862.

UNION: ARMY OF THE FRONTIER.—Brig.-Gen. James G. Blunt.

FIRST DIVISION, Brig.-Gen. James G. Blunt.
First Brigade, Brig.-Gen. Frederick Salomon: 6th Kan. Cav., Col. William R. Judson; 9th Kan. Cav., Col. Edward Lynde; 3d Wis. Cav. (6 co's), Maj. Elias A. Calkins; 9th Wis. Inf. (train guard), Col. Charles E. Salomon. Brigade loss: m, 1. *Second Brigade,* Col. William Weer: 3d Indian Home Guard, Col. William A. Phillips; 10th Kan., Maj. Henry H. Williams; 13th Kan., Col. Thomas M. Bowen; 1st Kan. Battery, Lieut. Marcus D. Tenney. Brigade loss: k, 16; w, 117; m, 5 = 138. *Third Brigade,* Col. William F. Cloud: 1st Indian Home Guard, Lieut.-Col. Stephen H. Wattles; 2d Kan. Cav., Lieut.-Col. Owen A. Bassett; 11th Kan., Col. Thomas Ewing, Jr.; 2d Ind. Battery, Capt. John W. Rabb; 2d Kan. Battery, Capt. Henry Hopkins. Brigade loss: k, 8; w, 63 = 71.
SECOND DIVISION, Col. Daniel Huston, Jr.
Escort: 1st Mo. Cav. (2 co's), Maj. Charles Banzhaf.
First Brigade, Col. John G. Clark: 26th Ind., Col. John G. Clark; 7th Mo. Cav., Maj. Eliphalet Bredett (k), Capt. Wesley R. Love; A, 2d Ill. Art'y, Lieut. Herman Borris. Brigade loss: k, 30; w, 181; m, 132 = 343. *Second Brigade,* Col. William McE. Dye: 37th Ill., Lieut.-Col. John C. Black (w), Maj. Henry M. Frisbie; 20th Iowa, Lieut.-Col. Joseph B. Leake; 2d Battalion, 6th Mo. Cav.,

Maj. Samuel Montgomery; F, 1st Mo. Art'y, Capt. David Murphy. Brigade loss: k, 17; w, 99; m, 38 = 154.
THIRD DIVISION, Brig.-Gen. Francis J. Herron (in command of Second and Third Divisions combined).
Escort, etc.: 1st Mo. Cav. (battalion), Maj. James M. Hubbard (c), Capt. Amos L. Burrows. Loss: w, 5; m, 13 = 18.
First Brigade, Lieut.-Col. Henry Bertram: 10th Ill. Cav.,⌡ Lieut.-Col. James Stuart; 1st Iowa Cav.,⌡ Col. James O. Gower; 1st Battalion, 2d Wis. Cav.,⌡ Maj. William H. Miller; 20th Wis., Maj. Henry A. Starr; L, 1st Mo. Art'y, Capt. Frank Backof. Brigade loss: k, 51; w, 159; m, 13 = 223. *Second Brigade,* Col. William W. Orme: 94th Ill., Lieut.-Col. John McNulta; 19th Iowa, Lieut.-Col. Samuel McFarland (k), Maj. Daniel Kent; 8th Mo. Cav.,⌡ Col. Washington F. Geiger; E, 1st Mo. Art'y, Lieut. Joseph Foust. Brigade loss: k, 49; w, 185; m, 14 = 248. *Unattached:* 1st Ark. Cav., Col. M. La Rue Harrison; 14th Mo. S. M. Cav., Col. John M. Richardson. Unattached loss: k, 4; w, 4; m, 47 = 55.
Total Union loss: Killed, 174; wounded, 813; captured or missing, 263 = 1251. General Blunt says ("Official Records," Vol. XXII., Pt. I., p. 76): "The entire force . . . engaged did not exceed 7000, about 3000 cavalry not having been brought into action."

CONFEDERATE: FIRST CORPS, TRANS-MISSISSIPPI ARMY.—Maj.-Gen. Thomas C. Hindman.

FOURTH (CAVALRY) DIVISION, Brig.-Gen. John S. Marmaduke.
Carroll's Brigade, Col. J. C. Monroe: Ark. Reg't, Maj. John B. Thompson; Ark. Reg't, Maj. —— Johnston. Brigade loss: k, 3; w, 12 = 15. *Shelby's Brigade,* Col. Joseph O. Shelby: 1st Mo., Lieut.-Col. B. F. Gordon; 2d Mo., Col. Beal G. Jeans; 3d Mo., Col. G. W. Thompson; Scouts, Maj. B. Elliott; Quantrill's Co., Lieut. —— Gregg; Mo. Battery, Capt. H. M. Bledsoe; Mo. Battery, Capt. Westley Roberts. *MacDonald's Brigade,* Col. Emmett MacDonald: Lane's Tex. Reg't, Lieut.-Col. R. P. Crump; Mo. Reg't, Lieut.-Col. M. L.

Young; Ark. Battery, Capt. Henry C. West. Brigade loss: k, 5; w, 22; m, 8 = 35.
There are no official reports of the other divisions engaged, and their composition is not given. Generals Frost and Shoup were the division commanders, and the commanders of brigades were Roane, Fagan, Parsons, McRae, and Shaver. Major-General Thomas C. Hindman says ("Official Records," Vol. XXII., Pt. I., p. 140) that he had "for the fight less than 10,000 men of all arms." He also (*ibid,* p. 142) reports his loss as 164 killed, 817 wounded, and 336 missing = 1317.

⌡ Temporarily organized as a cavalry brigade under Col. Dudley Wickersham.

ARKANSAS POST (FORT HINDMAN), JANUARY 11TH, 1863.

UNION: ARMY OF THE MISSISSIPPI. ☫ — Major-General John A. McClernand.

THIRTEENTH ARMY CORPS, Brig.-Gen. George W. Morgan.

Escort: A, 3d Ill. Cav., Capt. Richard H. Ballinger.
FIRST DIVISION, Brig.-Gen. Andrew J. Smith.

Escort: C, 4th Ind. Cav., Capt. Joseph P. Lesslie.

First Brigade, Brig.-Gen. Stephen G. Burbridge: 16th Ind., Lieut.-Col. John M. Orr (w), Maj. James H. Redfield, Col. Thomas J. Lucas; 60th Ind., Col. Richard Owen; 67th Ind., Col. Frank Emerson (w); 83d Ohio, Lieut.-Col. William H. Baldwin; 96th Ohio, Col. Joseph W. Vance; 23d Wis., Col. Joshua J. Guppey. Brigade loss: k, 37; w, 305; m, 7 = 349. *Second Brigade,* Col. William J. Landram: 77th Ill., Col. David P. Grier; 97th Ill., Col. Friend S. Rutherford; 108th Ill., Col. John Warner; 131st Ill. (not in action), Lieut.-Col. R. A. Peter; 19th Ky., Lieut.-Col. John Cowan; 48th Ohio, Lieut.-Col. Job R. Parker (w), Capt. S. G. W. Peterson (temporarily). Brigade loss: k, 8; w, 77 = 85. *Artillery,* Mercantile (Ill.) Battery, Capt. Charles G. Cooley: 17th Ohio Battery, Capt. Ambrose A. Blount. Artillery loss: w, 1. *Cavalry:* Squadron 6th Mo., Col. Clark Wright.

SECOND DIVISION, Brigadier-General Peter J. Osterhaus.

First Brigade, Col. Lionel A. Sheldon: 118th Ill., Col. John G. Fonda; 69th Ind., Col. Thomas W. Bennett; 120th Ohio, Col. Daniel French. Brigade loss: k, 3; w, 14; m, 11 = 28. *Second Brigade,* Col. Daniel W. Lindsey: 49th Ind., Col. James Keigwin; 3d Ky., Capt. Andrew H. Clark; 114th Ohio, Lieut.-Col. Horatio B. Maynard. *Third Brigade,* Col. John F. DeCourcy: 54th Ind., Col. Fielding Mansfield; 22d Ky., Maj. William J. Worthington; 16th Ohio, Capt. Eli W. Botsford; 42d Ohio, Lieut.-Col. Don A. Pardee. *Artillery:* 7th Mich., Capt. Charles H. Lanphere; 1st Wis., Capt. Jacob T. Foster. *Ky. Engineers,* Capt. W. F. Patterson.

FIFTEENTH ARMY CORPS, Maj.-Gen. William T. Sherman.

FIRST DIVISION, Brig.-Gen. Frederick Steele.

Escort: Kane County (Ill.) Cav., Capt. William. C. Wilder.

First Brigade, Brig.-Gen. Frank P. Blair, Jr.: 13th Ill., Lieut.-Col. A. B. Gorgas; 29th Mo., Col. John S. Cavender; 30th Mo., Lieut.-Col. Otto Schadt; 31st Mo., Lieut.-Col. Samuel P. Simpson; 32d Mo., Col. Francis H. Manter; 58th Ohio, Capt. Bastian Benkler; 4th Ohio Battery, Capt. Louis Hoffmann. Brigade loss: w, 9. *Second Brigade,* Brig.-Gen. Charles E. Hovey (w): 25th Iowa, Col. George A. Stone; 31st Iowa, Col. William Smyth; 3d Mo., Col. Isaac F. Shepard; 12th Mo. (not in action), Col. Hugo Wangelin; 17th Mo., Col. F. Hassendeubel; 76th Ohio, Col. Charles R. Woods; 1st Mo. Horse Battery (not in action), Capt. C. Landgraeber. Brigade loss: k, 38; w, 182; m, 2 = 222. *Third Brigade,* Brig.-Gen. John M. Thayer: 4th Iowa, Col. J. A. Williamson; 9th Iowa, Lieut.-Col. W. H. Coyl; 26th Iowa, Col. Milo Smith; 30th Iowa, Lieut.-Col. W. M. G. Torrence; 34th Iowa, Col. George W. Clark; 1st Iowa Battery, Capt. Henry H. Griffiths. Brigade loss: k, 24; w, 156 = 180. *Cavalry:* 3d Ill., Col. Lafayette McCrillis.

SECOND DIVISION, Brig.-Gen. David Stuart.

First Brigade, Col. Giles A. Smith: 113th Ill., Col. George B. Hoge; 116th Ill., Lieut.-Col. James P. Boyd; 6th Mo., Lieut.-Col. James H. Blood; 8th Mo., Lieut.-Col. David C. Coleman (w); Maj. Dennis T. Kirby; 13th U. S. (1st Battalion), Maj. Dudley Chase. Brigade loss: k, 18; w, 84 = 102. *Second Brigade,* Col. T. Kilby Smith: 55th Ill., Lieut.-Col. Oscar Malmborg; 127th Ill., Col. J. Van Arman; 83d Ind., Col. Benjamin J. Spooner; 54th Ohio, Capt. S. B. Yoeman (w); 57th Ohio, Col. William Mungen. Brigade loss: k, 6; w, 70; m, 9 = 85. *Artillery:* A, 1st Ill., Capt. Peter P. Wood; B, 1st Ill., Capt. Samuel E. Barrett; H, 1st Ill., Lieut. Levi W. Hart; 8th Ohio, Lieut. J. F. Putnam. *Cavalry:* A and B, Thielemann's (Ill.) Battalion, Capt. Berthold Marschner; C, 10th Mo., Lieut. Daniel W. Ballou.

The total loss of the Union Army was 134 killed, 898 wounded, and 29 missing = 1061. The strength of McClernand's expeditionary force was about "32,000 infantry, 1000 cavalry, and 40 or more pieces of artillery." (See "Official Records," Vol. XVII., Pt. II., p. 553.)

THE CONFEDERATE FORCES.—Brigadier-General Thomas J. Churchill.

First Brigade, Col. Robert R. Garland: 6th Tex., Lieut.-Col. T. S. Anderson; 24th Tex. Cav. (dismounted), Col. F. C. Wilkes; 25th Tex. Cav. (dismounted), Col. C. C. Gillespie; Ark. Battery, Capt. William Hart; La. Cav., Capt. W. B. Denson. Brigade loss: k, 25; w, 64; m, 68 = 157. *Second Brigade,* Col. James Deshler: 10th Tex., Col. Roger Q. Mills; 15th Tex. Cav. (dismounted), Maj. V. P. Sanders; 17th Tex. Cav. (dismounted), Col. James R. Taylor; 18th Tex. Cav. (dismounted), Lieut.-Col. John T. Coit. Brigade loss not separately reported. *Third Brigade* (composition probably incomplete), Col. John W. Dunnington: 19th Ark., Lieut.-Col. A. S. Hutchinson. *Miscellaneous:* 24th Ark. (detachment), Col. E. E. Portlock, Jr.; Tex. Cav., Capt. Alfred Johnson; La. Cav., Capt. L. M. Nutt; Tex. Cav., Capt. Samuel J. Richardson.

General Churchill says ("Official Records," Vol. XVII., Pt. I., p. 782): "My loss will not exceed 60 killed and 75 or 80 wounded." He also states (*ibid*, p. 780) that the whole force under his command numbered about 3000 effective men. General McClernand (*ibid*, p. 708) reports 5000 prisoners captured, and General Sherman (*ibid*, p. 757) says that 4791 prisoners of war were embarked on transports.

HELENA, JULY 4TH, 1863.

UNION: DISTRICT OF EASTERN ARKANSAS.—Maj.-Gen. B. M. Prentiss.

THIRTEENTH DIVISION (THIRTEENTH ARMY CORPS), Brig.-Gen. Frederick Salomon.

First Brigade, Col. William E. McLean: 43d Ind., Lieut.-Col. John C. Major; 35th Mo., Lieut.-Col. Horace Fitch; 28th Wis., Lieut.-Col. Edmund B. Gray. Brigade loss: k, 9; w, 28; m, 5 = 42. *Second Brigade,* Col. Samuel A. Rice: 29th Iowa, Col. Thomas H. Benton, Jr.; 33d Iowa, Lieut.-Col. Cyrus H. Mackey; 36th Iowa, Col. Charles W. Kittredge; 33d Mo., Lieut.-Col. William H. Heath. Brigade loss: k, 43; w, 99; m, 30 = 172. *Cavalry Brigade,* Col. Powell Clayton: 1st Ind., Lieut.-Col. Thomas N. Pace; 5th Kan., Lieut.-Col. Wilton A. Jenkins. Brigade loss: k, 5; w, 18; m, 1 = 24. *Artillery,* 3d Iowa, Lieut. Melvil C. Wright; K, 1st Mo., Lieut. John O'Connell. Artillery loss, w, 1. *Unattached:* 2d Ark. (colored) ——.

Total Union loss: killed, 57; wounded, 146; captured or missing, 36 = 239. Effective strength: 4129.

☫ So styled, provisionally, by General McClernand, the Thirteenth Army Corps being designated as the First, and the Fifteenth Army Corps as the Second Corps of said army.

CONFEDERATE: DISTRICT OF ARKANSAS.—Lieut.-Gen. Theophilus H. Holmes.

PRICE'S DIVISION, Maj.-Gen. Sterling Price.

McRae's Brigade, Brig.-Gen. Dandridge McRae: 32d Ark., Col. L. C. Gause; 36th Ark., Col. J. E. Glenn; 39th Ark., Col. R. A. Hart (w); Ark. Battery, Capt. John G. Marshall. Brigade loss: k, 46; w, 168; m, 133 = 347. *Parsons's Brigade*, Brig.-Gen. M. Monroe Parsons: 7th Mo., Col. L. M. Lewis; 8th Mo., Col. S. P. Burns; 9th Mo., Col. J. D. White; 10th Mo., Col. A. C. Pickett; 1st Battalion Sharp-shooters, Maj. L. A. Pindall; Mo. Battery, Capt. C. B. Tilden. Brigade loss: k, 62; w, 304; m, 365 = 731. *Fagan's Brigade*, Brig.-Gen. J. F. Fagan: 6th Ark., Col. A. T. Hawthorn; 34th Ark., Col. W, H. Brooks; 35th Ark., Col. J. P. King; 37th Ark., Col. S S. Bell (c), Maj. T. H. Blacknall; Denson's Cav. (3 co's), Capt. W. B. Denson; Ark. Battery (section), Lieut. John

C. Arnett; Ark. Battery, Capt. W. D. Blocker. Brigade loss: k, 47; w, 115; m, 273 = 435.

WALKER'S DIVISION, Brig.-Gen. L. M. Walker.

5th Ark. Cav., Col. Robert C. Newton; Ark. Cav., Col. Archibald S. Dobbin. Loss: k, 4; w, 8 = 12.

MARMADUKE'S DIVISION, Brig.-Gen. J. S. Marmaduke.

Staff loss: k, 1.

Greene's Brigade, Col. Colton Greene: 3d Mo. Cav., —————; 8th Mo. Cav., —————; Young's Battalion, —————. Brigade loss: k, 5; w, 7 = 12. *Shelby's Brigade*, Col. Joseph O. Shelby (w): 5th Mo. Cav., —————; 6th Mo. Cav., —————; Jeans's Regiment, —————; Mo. Battery (Bledsoe's), —————. Brigade loss: k, 8; w, 45; m, 1 = 54.

Total Confederate loss: killed, 173; wounded, 687; captured or missing, 776 = 1636. Effective strength, 7646.

LITTLE ROCK EXPEDITION, AUGUST 1ST–SEPTEMBER 14TH, 1863.

THE UNION ARMY.— Maj.-Gen. Frederick Steele.

Escort: D, 3d Ill. Cav., Lieutenant James K. McLean; Kane County (Ill.) Cav., Lieutenant Eben C. Litherland.

FIRST (CAVALRY) DIVISION, Brig.-Gen. John W. Davidson.

First Brigade, Col. Washington F. Geiger, Col. Lewis Merrill: 2d Mo., Maj. Garrison Harker; 7th Mo., Lieut.-Col. John L. Chandler; 8th Mo., Lieut.-Col. J. W. Lisenby, Col. Washington F. Geiger. *Second Brigade*, Col. John M. Glover: 10th Ill., Col. Dudley Wickersham, Lieut.-Col. James Stuart; 1st Iowa, Lieut.-Col. Daniel Anderson, Maj. Joseph W. Caldwell; 3d Mo., Lieut.-Col. T. G. Black. *Reserve Brigade*, Col. John F. Ritter: 13th Ill., Maj. Lothar Lippert; 3d Iowa, Maj. George Duffield; 32d Iowa, Lieut.-Col. Edward H. Mix, Maj. Gustavus A. Eberhart; 1st Mo., Capt. J. W. Fuller. *Artillery*, Capt. Julius L. Hadley: K, 2d Mo., Lieut. T. S. Clarkson; M, 2d Mo., Capt. Gustav Stange; 25th Ohio, Capt. Julius L. Hadley.

SECOND DIVISION, Col. William E. McLean, Col. Adolph Engelmann.

First Brigade, Col. William H. Graves: 18th Ill., Col. Daniel H. Brush; 43d Ill., Maj. Charles Stephani; 54th Ill., Col. Greenville M. Mitchell; 61st Ill., Lieut.-Col. Simon P. Ohr; 106th Ill., Lieut.-Col. Henry Yates; 12th Mich., Lieut.-Col. Dwight May. *Second Brigade*, Col. Oliver Wood: 126th Ill., Lieut.-Col. Ezra M. Beardsley; 40th Iowa, Lieut.-Col. Samuel F. Cooper; 3d Minn., Col.

Christopher C. Andrews; 22d Ohio, Lieut.-Col. Homer Thrall; 27th Wis., Col. Conrad Krez.

THIRD DIVISION, Brig.-Gen. Samuel A. Rice.

First Brigade, Col. Charles W. Kittredge: 43d Ind., Lieut.-Col. John C. Major; 36th Iowa, Lieut.-Col. Francis M. Drake; 77th Ohio, Col. William B. Mason. *Second Brigade*, Col. Thomas H. Benton, Jr.: 29th Iowa, Lieut.-Col. Robert F. Patterson; 33d Iowa, Lieut.-Col. Cyrus H. Mackey; 28th Wis., Maj. Calvert C. White. CAVALRY BRIGADE, Col. Powell Clayton: 1st Ind., Lieut.-Col. Thomas N. Pace; 5th Kans., Lieut.-Col. Wilton A. Jenkins. ARTILLERY, Capt. Mortimer M. Haden: 3d Iowa, Lieut. Melvil C. Wright; K, 1st Mo., Capt. Stillman O. Fish; 5th Ohio, Lieut. John D. Burner; 11th Ohio, Capt. Frank C. Sands. UNATTACHED BRIGADE, Col. James M. True; 49th Ill., Col. Phineas Pease; 62d Ill., Lieut.-Col. Stephen M. Meeker; 50th Ind., Lieut.-Col. Samuel T. Wells; 27th Iowa, Col. James I. Gilbert; Ill. Battery, Capt. Thomas F. Vaughn.

At the beginning of the campaign the Union forces aggregated about 12,000 for duty. (See "Official Records," Vol. XXII., Pt. I., p. 475.) From Devall's Bluff, Sept. 1, General Steele reported that his force, for duty, was considerably short of 12,000 (*ibid*, p. 474). According to the return for Sept. 10th (*ibid*, Part II., p. 523), the "present for duty" amounted to 10,477.

The total loss was 18 killed, 118 wounded, and 1 missing = 137.

CONFEDERATE: DISTRICT OF ARKANSAS.—Maj.-Gen. Sterling Price.

WALKER'S DIVISION, Brig.-Gen. Lucius Marsh Walker, Col. Archibald S. Dobbin, Col. Robert C. Newton.

Arkansas Cavalry Brigade, Col. Archibald S. Dobbin, Col. Robert C. Newton: Dobbin's regiment, Maj. Samuel Corley (k); Newton's regiment, Col. Robert C. Newton, Maj. John P. Bull. *Texas Cavalry Brigade* (composition not stated), Col. George W. Carter. *Artillery:* Ark. Battery, Capt. C. B. Etter; Tex. Battery, Capt. J. H. Pratt. *Miscellaneous Commands:* Spy Company, Capt. Alf. Johnson; La. Cav. Company, Capt. W. B. Denson; Tex. Squadron, Maj. C. L. Morgan.

MARMADUKE'S DIVISION, Brig.-Gen. John S. Marmaduke.

Marmaduke's Brigade, Col. William L. Jeffers: Jeffers's regiment, Lieut.-Col. S. J. Ward; Kitchen's regiment, Col. S. G. Kitchen; Burbridge's regiment, Lieut.-Col. W. J. Preston; Greene's regiment, Maj. L. A. Campbell; Young's Battalion, Lieut.-Col. M. L. Young; Bell's Battery, Lieut. C. O. Bell (m w). *Shelby's Brigade*, Lieut.-

Col. B. Frank Gordon, Col. G. W. Thompson: Elliott's Battalion, Maj. Benjamin Elliott; Gordon's regiment, Capt. George Gordon; Thompson's regiment, Lieut.-Col. J. C. Hooper; Gilkey's regiment, Col. C. A. Gilkey (m w); Jeans's regiment, Capt. R. H. Adams; Bledsoe's Battery, Capt. Joseph Bledsoe. *Unattached Artillery:* Mo. Battery, Capt. S. T. Ruffner; Mo. Battery, Capt. R. A. Collins.

PRICE'S DIVISION, Brig.-Gen. D. M. Frost.

[Consisted of Fagan's, Parsons's, McRae's, and Clark's brigades; Tappan's brigade unattached. The composition of these brigades is not given in detail.]

Strength of Confederate forces: General Price says ("Official Records," Vol. XXII., Part I., p. 521) that he "had barely 8000 men of all arms."

Losses: An incomplete statement of casualties ("Official Records," as above, p. 523) shows 12 killed, 34 wounded, and 18 captured or missing = 64.

CHICKASAW BAYOU AND THE VICKSBURG BLUFFS. (THE CANNON INDICATE THE POSITION OF GENERAL MORGAN L. SMITH'S UNION DIVISION.) FROM A WAR-TIME SKETCH.

THE ASSAULT ON CHICKASAW BLUFFS.

BY GEORGE W. MORGAN, BRIGADIER-GENERAL, U. S. V.

PRESIDENT LINCOLN early determined to obtain control of the Mississippi, in its entire length. In pursuance of his plan, Island Number Ten in the north and Forts Jackson and St. Philip in the south had been captured, and New Orleans occupied by our troops in the spring of 1862; and in the fall of that year General McClernand was assigned to the command of a river expedition against Vicksburg.

The day following the receipt of this order by Grant at Oxford, Mississippi, Sherman, who was then at Memphis, in telegraphic communication with Grant, commenced the embarkation of a column upon three grand flotillas, each bearing a division, to be joined by a fourth (Steele's) at Helena.

In his "Memoirs," ∤ General Sherman says:

"The preparations at Memphis were necessarily hasty in the extreme, but it was the essence of the whole plan, viz., to reach Vicksburg, as it were, by surprise, while General Grant held in check Pemberton's army about Grenada, leaving me to contend only with the smaller garrison of Vicksburg and its well-known strong batteries and defenses."

In his written directions to his division commanders, December 23d, 1862, General Sherman said: "Already the gun-boats have secured the Yazoo, for twenty miles, to a fort on the Yazoo, on Haynes's Bluff."

This movement of the gun-boats not only rendered a surprise impossible, but gave notice to the enemy of the coming attack. On the 24th, General

∤ "Memoirs of General William T. Sherman. By himself." Vol. I., p. 285.
(New York: D. Appleton & Co.)

John C. Pemberton, who was in command of the Confederate army at Grenada, received "definite and reliable information" of the operations of the gun-boats, and at noon on the 26th he reached Vicksburg in person, before Sherman had arrived at the mouth of the Yazoo. The strong brigades of Barton, Gregg, and Vaughn were promptly transferred from Grenada to Vicksburg, and formed the enemy's sole defense between Vicksburg and McNutt Lake, a distance of six miles.

General Pemberton describes the battle-ground as follows in his official report:

"Swamps, lakes, and bayous, running parallel with the river, intervene between the bank and the hills, and leave but four practicable approaches to the high ground from Snyder's Mills to the Mississippi River, but all outside of the fortifications of Vicksburg."

In its entire length Chickasaw Bayou is tortuous and in its course is known by different names. As we advanced along the road leading from the Yazoo to the bluffs, the bayou was on our left for some distance; on our right was a forest intersected by sloughs, more or less filled with water, and perpendicular to the bayou and parallel to the bluffs. Opposite the point where the bayou turns abruptly to the left, and on the right side of the road, the forest was felled and formed a tangled abatis to the point where the bayou divides into two branches, over one of which was a narrow corduroy bridge.

The ground on which the battle was fought was a triangle, the apex of which was at the point of divergence of the two branches of the bayou, the high and rugged bluff in front being the base. Standing at the apex and facing the base of the triangle, its left side was formed by the left branch of the bayou, which flowed obliquely to (and I believe through) a break in the bluffs; while the right was formed by a broken line of rifle-pits that ran obliquely from the base toward the apex, and by the other branch of the bayou, which first runs obliquely to the right, then parallel to the bluffs, and forms McNutt Lake.

Our troops had not only to advance from the narrow apex of a triangle, whose short base of about four hundred yards and sharp sides bristled with the enemy's artillery and small-arms, but had to wade the bayou and tug through the mucky and tangled swamp, under a withering fire of grape, canister, shells, and minie-balls, before reaching dry ground. Such was the point chosen for the assault by General Sherman. What more could be desired by an enemy about to be assailed in his trenches!

In a letter to the author of this article, in regard to the assault at Chickasaw, General Stephen D. Lee, who commanded the enemy's defenses at that point, says:

"Had Sherman moved a little faster after landing, or made his attack at the mound [Sherman's bluff, or sand-bar], or at any point between the bayou and Vicksburg, he could have gone into the city. As it was, he virtually attacked at the apex of a triangle while I held the base and parts of the two sides."

Sherman did make an attack at the mound, or sand-bar, but only sent one regiment, the 6th Missouri, to the assault; and in making it that gallant regiment lost fifty-seven men.

Sherman's army was composed of four splendid divisions, commanded by Brigadier-Generals A. J. Smith, Morgan L. Smith, George W. Morgan, and Frederick Steele. The entire force was about 30,000 strong. [See map, next page.]

On the night of the 28th of December Sherman ordered Steele to abandon his position, leave a small force to observe the road leading to Snyder's Mills, form in rear of Morgan, and give him such support as he might ask for. Blair's brigade had been ordered by General Sherman to report to Morgan, and was sent by him across the bayou and over the road which De Courcy and Thayer afterward advanced to the assault, to occupy the ground between the bayou and Thompson's Lake. This was promptly done.

The city of Vicksburg formed the extreme left of the enemy's position, and its immediate rear was the weakest point in the entire line of defense.

On the 28th and 29th the city was occupied and defended solely by the 27th Louisiana regiment, under Colonel Marks, and by the batteries commanding the Mississippi; and on the 29th there was but a single regiment, under General Vaughn, between the city and "the mound," "sand-bar," or "bluff," as it was differently called, four miles in rear of Vicksburg.

In the immediate rear of the city there were redans and redoubts connected by rifle-pits; but on the 28th and 29th these were empty, every soldier and every gun having been withdrawn and sent to the defense of "the swamp," or "county road."

In the original formation, Vaughn's brigade rested on a heavy abatis at the race-course. On his right was the brigade of Barton, and in their rear the brigade of Gregg was held as a reserve. On the right of Barton was S. D. Lee, who had had the command of the entire line from Vicksburg to Snyder's Mills prior to the arrival of the brigades of Vaughn, Barton, and Gregg from Grenada. Early on the 28th one of Vaughn's regiments was sent to reënforce Lee, and another to reënforce Barton; and thus Vaughn was left with only one regiment to protect the immediate rear of the city, with the whole of A. J. Smith's division opposed to him. This division was ordered to make a feint, and, in doing so, lost two men. Had a real attack been ordered by General Sherman, Vicksburg would have fallen, for Morgan L. Smith's division would have occupied Barton and Gregg at the "mound," "sand-bar," or "dry lake," while the divisions of Morgan and Steele would have held Lee at Chickasaw.

In his "Memoirs" (I., 290), General Sherman says:

" On reconnoitering the front in person, I became satisfied that General A. J. Smith could not cross the intervening obstacles under the heavy fire of the forts immediately in his front."

That front was the immediate rear of the city. There was skirmishing on the 27th and 28th, and the enemy was driven back to his trenches.

My division consisted of the brigades of Sheldon, Lindsey, and De Courcy.

General Blair's brigade, as already stated, had been detached from Steele's division, and ordered to report to me. December 28th, I directed Blair, then on the north side of the bayou, to reconnoiter his front, and with De Courcy, who was on the opposite side of the bayou from Blair, I reconnoi-

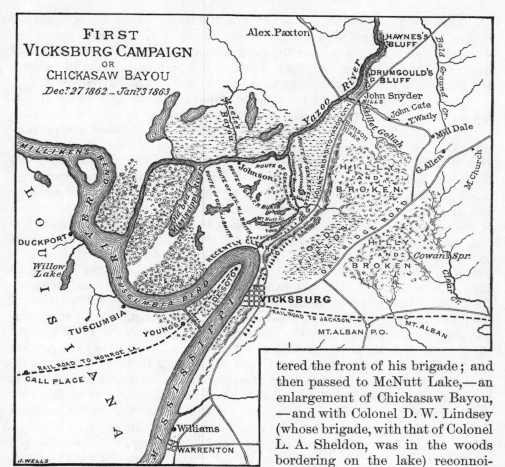

FIRST
VICKSBURG CAMPAIGN
OR
CHICKASAW BAYOU
Dec.ʳ 27 1862 _ Jan.ʸ 3 1863

J. WELLS

tered the front of his brigade; and then passed to McNutt Lake,—an enlargement of Chickasaw Bayou,—and with Colonel D. W. Lindsey (whose brigade, with that of Colonel L. A. Sheldon, was in the woods bordering on the lake) reconnoitered his front. The enemy had relied on the depth and width of the lake as a sufficient defense, and at that place had neither troops nor works of any kind between the lake and the bluffs. I determined to bridge the lake during the night, and at dawn on the 29th to send Lindsey and Sheldon with their brigades to seize and hold the swamp road and bluff in their front, while the brigades of Blair and De Courcy should advance to the assault in parallel columns from my left. Could this plan have been executed, the day might have been ours. Fate willed it otherwise.

Captain W. F. Patterson, an intelligent and efficient officer, had a small body of engineer-mechanics, and I directed him, with the aid of a detail, to bring the pontoons, eight in number, from the steamers, and bridge the lake before daylight at a point indicated. The night was intensely dark, and Patterson by mistake bridged, instead of the lake, a wide and deep slough, parallel to the bluff and filled with water. It was nearly dawn when I learned of the mistake, whereupon I ordered Patterson to take up the bridge and throw it across the lake at the point selected.

I again reconnoitered the ground beyond the lake. There was no apparent change in the situation, and I still felt strong hopes of success. But in the extreme haste to get away from Memphis, General Sherman had not provided trestles on which to lay the plank between the pontoons, hence the bridge had to be built by laying the pontoons side by side. The bayou was 80 feet wide, and the eight pontoons thus placed would only form a bridge of 48 feet in length; for the rest it was necessary to make trestles or construct a raft.

The withdrawal of Steele from Sherman's left enabled the enemy to concentrate his right on the threatened point at Chickasaw. As soon as he discovered that a bridge was being thrown over McNutt Lake, Barton occupied the woods bordering the lake on the bluff side. Patterson had succeeded in placing and flooring six pontoons when the enemy opened a fire of artillery and small-arms on the pontoniers and drove them from their work. Two of the boats were damaged and a number of the men killed or wounded.

A short time previous to this, while standing near Foster's 1st Wisconsin battery, I saw approaching from the enemy's right, about a mile away, a caisson, with gunners on the ammunition boxes, and a few horsemen in front. I asked Foster if he could blow up that caisson. He replied, "I can try, sir." He waited until the caisson came within fair range, and fired. The report of the gun and the explosion of the caisson seemed to be instantaneous; caisson and gunners were blown into the air; every man and horse was killed, and a shout went up from around Foster and his battery. On the next day, when our flag of truce to the enemy had returned, I learned that one of the victims of the explosion was Captain Paul Hamilton, assistant adjutant-general on the staff of General S. D. Lee. He was but twenty-one years of age, was distinguished for his gallantry, and had gone through several battles without a scar. As he deserved, his death is mourned over to this day.

The fire of Barton was promptly returned by Lindsey, but it was certain the bridge could not be completed while the enemy covered it with his guns.

I now regarded an attack from my left, by way of the narrow road or causeway leading across the bayou, as impracticable, and reported the fact to General Sherman by my acting assistant adjutant-general, Lieutenant E. D. Saunders, with the request that he would come to my front. Upon his arrival I reported to him the condition of things on my right, and requested him to accompany me down the causeway leading to the corduroy bridge over the bayou. He did so. I called his attention to our very narrow and difficult front; to the bayou in its tortuous course on our left; to the mucky marsh beyond the bayou and bridge, all within easy range of the enemy's guns.

For a time General Sherman made no reply. At length, pointing toward the bluffs, he said: "That is the route to take!" And without another word having been exchanged he rode away to his headquarters behind the forest. ⚓

⚓ As to this interview, General Sherman and myself are at variance. He states that he gave me an order to lead the assault in person, and that I replied I would be on the top of those hills in ten minutes after the signal for the assault was given. I am positive that no such order was given; nor was there such an understanding. A well-mounted horseman, unobstructed by an enemy, could not have reached the top of those hills in double that length of time. The circumstances of the occasion must decide between us.
G. W. M.

I was in the actual command of two divisions, that of Steele and my own. In his report Steele says:

"I received orders from the general commanding to halt the brigade [Thayer's] and subsequently to render General Morgan any assistance he might ask for. General Morgan finally told me that he was going to storm the heights without waiting for the completion of the bridge. He requested me to support the storming party with what force I had. . . . I gave no orders on the field that day, except at the suggestion of General Morgan, save that I followed the movement, encouraging the men while they were advancing, and endeavoring to check them when they fell back." ↓

In addition to the assaulting force of nine regiments, I held two of Blair's regiments in support of my artillery, to be used as circumstances might require; and the brigades of Lindsey and Sheldon, and four regiments of Thayer's brigade of Steele's division were on my right. I was the senior officer in the immediate presence of the enemy, and occupied a position on the causeway, near Foster's battery, ready to take such action as the chances of battle might call for.

Not long after the brief reconnoissance with General Sherman, Major John H. Hammond, his assistant adjutant-general, came to the front, and said that he had just come from General Sherman, and would give me his exact words: "Tell Morgan to give the signal for the assault; that we will lose 5000 men before we take Vicksburg, and may as well lose them here as anywhere

LIEUTENANT-GENERAL S. D. LEE, C. S. A.
FROM A PHOTOGRAPH.

else." I told him to say to General Sherman that I would order the assault; that we might lose 5000 men, but that his entire army could not carry the enemy's position in my front; that the larger the force sent to the assault, the greater would be the number slaughtered.

I sent orders to Blair and De Courcy to form their brigades, and a request to Steele to send me another brigade for the assault. Just then Colonel De Courcy, who was an officer of skill and experience, approached and said: "General, do I understand that you are about to order an assault?" To which I replied, "Yes; form your brigade!" With an air of respectful protest he said: "My poor brigade! Your order will be obeyed, General."

Blair was between the bayou and Thompson's Lake. The bayou was on his right; but at a short distance in advance it abruptly turned to the left, in his front. The brigade of De Courcy was massed from the abatis, across the road or causeway, and fronting the corduroy bridge; and I directed Thayer to support De Courcy, and indicated the point to assault. Thayer's brigade

was now composed of five regiments—one being absent on detached duty—
and a battery of artillery which did good service, though it did not cross the
bayou. It was my intention to make the assault with the brigades of Blair,
Thayer, and De Courcy, while Lindsey and Sheldon, by threatening to bridge
McNutt Lake, would prevent the enemy (under Barton) from reënforcing
Lee. By some misunderstanding—a fortunate one, I think, as it turned
out—four of Thayer's regiments diverged to the right, leaving only one
regiment, the 4th Iowa, with him in the assault.

The signal volley was fired, and with a wild shout the troops of De Courcy,
Thayer, and Blair advanced to the assault. As soon as the corduroy bridge
was reached by De Courcy and Thayer, and the bayou to the left by Blair,
the assaulting forces came under a withering and destructive fire. A passage
was forced over the abatis and through the mucky bayou and tangled marsh
to dry ground. All formations were broken; the assaulting forces were
jammed together, and, with a yell of desperate determination, they rushed to
the assault and were mowed down by a storm of shells, grape and canister,
and minie-balls which swept our front like a hurricane of fire. Never did
troops bear themselves with greater intrepidity. They were terribly repulsed,
but not beaten. There was neither rout nor panic, but our troops fell back
slowly and angrily to our own line, halted, re-formed, and, if ordered, would
again have rushed to the assault.

As in all cases of repulse or defeat, contention and crimination have arisen
as to the cause of the disaster. Sherman, in his report, ♭ and Grant, in his
"Memoirs," ⸲ give a satisfactory cause—the true one in my opinion—the
impregnable position of the enemy. Sherman says, in his "Memoirs," Vol.
I., p. 292:

"Had he [General Morgan] used with skill and boldness one of his brigades, in addition to
that of Blair, he could have made a lodgment on the bluff, which would have opened a door
for our whole force to follow."

The fact is that, beside the four regiments of Blair's brigade, the attacking
forces included four regiments led by De Courcy and one by Thayer.

General Sherman also says, in his "Memoirs," that

"one brigade (De Courcy's), of Morgan's troops, crossed the bayou, but took to cover behind
the bank, and could not be moved forward."

In fact, all the troops behaved gallantly, and the assault was as valiant as
it was hopeless. Each of De Courcy's regiments brought back its colors, or
what remained of them. The flag of the 16th Ohio was torn into shreds by
the explosion of a shell in its very center, but the shreds were brought back
adhering to the staff.

The losses speak for themselves. De Courcy had 48 killed, 321 wounded,
and 355 missing; Blair, 99 killed, 331 wounded, 173 missing; Thayer (in the
4th Iowa), 7 killed, 105 wounded: total, for the 9 regiments engaged, 154
killed, 757 wounded, 528 missing,—in all, 1439. In Sherman's whole command the loss was 208 killed, 1005 wounded, 563 missing,—aggregate, 1776.

♭ "Official Records," Vol. XVII., Part I., p. 610.
⸲ "Personal Memoirs of U. S. Grant" (C. L. Webster & Co.), Vol. I., p. 437.

The Confederates report 63 killed, 134 wounded, 10 missing,— aggregate, 207.

Shortly after De Courcy had returned to his command, General Blair came. He said that De Courcy's brigade had behaved badly. At the time I did not know the relative loss of the two brigades, but I did know that each of them, as well as Thayer's, had made a superb assault, and that the enemy's position was impregnable.

Blair did not refer to the matter in his report; but Thayer says in his:

"I found myself within the enemy's works, with one regiment. I then went back to the intrenchments, where I had seen, as we went over, a regiment of our troops lying in the ditch, entirely protected from the rebel fire. I ordered and begged them, but without effect, to come forward and support my regiment, which was now warmly engaged. *I do not know what regiment it was.*" (The italics are mine.— G. W. M.)

MAJOR-GENERAL DABNEY H. MAURY, C. S. A. FROM A PHOTOGRAPH.

But on August 30th, 1887, twenty-four years and eight months after the date of his report, in a letter to me, Thayer says:

"De Courcy and his brigade on that day made no assault whatever, unless against the outside rifle-pits, and were not repulsed. They got into the enemy's rifle-pits, and there remained."

That Thayer and the 4th Iowa behaved gallantly is certain; that had his other regiments been with him they would have borne themselves with equal intrepidity is not less so; but that the statements of himself and Blair do injustice to De Courcy is shown by the fact that the loss of De Courcy's brigade was greater than that sustained by the brigades of Blair and Thayer together.

After it was determined that the assault was not to be renewed, I repaired to General Sherman's headquarters and found him alone, pacing backward and forward with restless strides. In brief terms I described the assault and the repulse, and suggested that a flag be sent to the enemy asking for an armistice of sufficient length to bring in our wounded and bury our dead. This was on the afternoon of the 29th of December.

In reply to my suggestion General Sherman said he did not like to ask for a truce, as it would be regarded as an admission of defeat. To this I replied that we had been terribly cut up, but were not dishonored; that the bearing of our troops was superb, and we held every foot of our own ground; but that our dead and wounded covered the field and could only be reached by a flag. He determined not to ask for a truce. However, at about dusk I was told that General Sherman had said that he had authorized me to send a flag to the enemy, and I immediately addressed a note "to the general commanding the Confederate forces on Chickasaw Bluff," asking for a truce. In the meantime it had become so dark that the flag could not be seen, and the escort was fired upon and driven back. The next morning, December 30th, I sent another flag, with a note explaining the misadventure of the previous evening, when a truce was promptly granted and all of our wounded that had not been carried into the Confederate lines as prisoners, and our dead, were at once brought within our lines.

It has been charged that the enemy on the field of Chickasaw stripped our dead of their clothing. The charge is unjust and should not go into history. I saw our dead as they were brought in; all were in their uniforms; nor did I ever hear of such a charge till long years after the war.

In his report of the battle General Sherman says : ☆

" General Morgan's first report to me was that the troops were not discouraged at all, though the losses in the brigades of Blair and De Courcy were heavy, and he would renew the assault in half an hour; but the assault was not again attempted."

But in his " Memoirs " General Sherman says : ⌡

" At first I intended to renew the assault, but soon became satisfied that the enemy's attention having been drawn to the only two practicable points, it would prove too costly, and accordingly resolved to look elsewhere, below Haynes's Bluff or Blake's Plantation."

While the blood was yet fresh upon the field, McClernand arrived, assumed command, and divided the army into two army corps, one commanded by Major-General W. T. Sherman, and the other by Brigadier-General George W. Morgan.

General Pemberton's report of the defense, on the 29th, is as follows :

" On the 29th, about 9 o'clock, the enemy was discovered in his attempt to throw a pontoon-bridge across the lake. In this he was foiled by a few well-directed shots from a section each of Wofford's and Ward's batteries, that of the latter commanded by Lieutenant Tarleton.

" About 10 o'clock a furious cannonade was opened on General Lee's lines. This ceased about 11 o'clock, when a whole brigade — about six thousand strong, understood to have been Brigadier-General [F. P.] Blair's, though not led by him in person — emerged from the woods in good order and moved gallantly forward under a heavy fire of our artillery. They advanced to within 150 yards of the pits when they broke and retreated, but soon rallied, and dividing their forces sent a portion to their right, which was gallantly driven back by the 28th Louisiana and 42d Georgia regiments with heavy loss. Their attack in front was repulsed with still greater disasters. By a handsome movement on the enemy's flank the 26th and part of the 17th Louisiana threw the enemy into inextricable confusion, and were so fortunate as to capture 4 stand of regimental colors, 21 commissioned officers, 311 non-commissioned officers and privates, and 500 stand of arms. The 3d, 30th, and 80th Tennessee regiments occupied the rifle-pits in front and behaved with distinguished coolness and courage.

" During this assault upon the right the enemy in force was endeavoring to carry our center, commanded by General Barton, by storm. Five resolute efforts were made to carry our breastworks and were as often repulsed with heavy loss. Three times he succeeded in mounting the parapet, and once made a lodgment and attempted to mine. The 52d Georgia, Colonel [C. D.] Phillips, reënforced Colonel Morrison's and Colonel Abda Johnson's regiments early in the day. These troops and the line of skirmishers, formed of companies from the 40th and 42d Georgia, behaved with distinguished courage and steadiness throughout. At this point the enemy did not give up his attack until nightfall."

☆ " Official Records," Vol. XVII., Part I., p. 608.
⌡ " Memoirs of W. T. Sherman " (D. Appleton & Co.), Vol. I., p. 292.

THE OPPOSING FORCES AT CHICKASAW BLUFFS (OR FIRST VICKSBURG), MISS.

December 27th, 1862 – January 3d, 1863.

The composition, losses, and strength of each army as here stated give the gist of all the data obtainable in the Official Records. K stands for killed; w for wounded; m w for mortally wounded; m for captured or missing; c for captured.

THE UNION ARMY.

RIGHT WING, THIRTEENTH ARMY CORPS.— Major-General William T. Sherman.

FIRST DIVISION, Brig.-Gen. Andrew J. Smith (also in command of the Second Division December 29th).
Escort : C, 4th Ind. Cav., Capt. Joseph P. Lesslie.
First Brigade, Brig.-Gen. Stephen G. Burbridge: 16th Ind., Col. Thomas J. Lucas; 60th Ind., Col. Richard Owen ; 67th Ind., Col. Frank Emerson ; 83d Ohio, Lieut.-Col. William H. Baldwin ; 96th Ohio, Col. Joseph W. Vance ; 23d Wis., Col. Joshua J. Guppey. Brigade loss : k, 1 ; w, 1 = 2. *Second Brigade,* Col. William J. Landram : 77th Ill., Col. David P. Grier ; 97th Ill., Col. Friend S. Rutherford ; 108th Ill., Col. John Warner; 131st Ill., Col. George W. Neeley ; 89th Ind., Col. Charles D. Murray ; 19th Ky., Lieut.-Col. John Cowan ; 48th Ohio, Lieut.-Col. Job R. Parker.
SECOND DIVISION, Brig.-Gen. Morgan L. Smith (w), Brig.-Gen. David Stuart. Staff loss : w, 1.
First Brigade, Col. Giles A. Smith : 113th Ill., Col. George B. Hoge ; 116th Ill., Col. Nathan W. Tupper; 6th Mo., Lieut.-Col. James H. Blood ; 8th Mo., Lieut.-Col. David C. Coleman ; 13th U. S. (1st Battalion), Maj. Dudley Chase. Brigade loss : k, 15 ; w, 63 = 78. *Fourth Brigade,* Brig.-Gen. David Stuart, Col. T. Kilby Smith : 55th Ill., Lieut.-Col. Oscar Malmborg ; 127th Ill., Col. John Van Arman ; 83d Ind., Col. Benjamin J. Spooner ; 54th Ohio, Col. T. Kilby Smith ; 57th Ohio, Col. William Mungen. Brigade loss : k, 12 ; w, 39 ; m, 6 = 57.
THIRD DIVISION, Brig.-Gen. George W. Morgan.
First Brigade, Col. Lionel A. Sheldon : 118th Ill., Col. John G. Fonda ; 69th Ind., Col. Thomas W. Bennett; 120th Ohio, Col. Daniel French. Brigade loss : w, 27 ; m, 2 = 29. *Second Brigade,* Col. Daniel W. Lindsey : 49th Ind., Col. James Keigwin ; 3d Ky., Lieut.-Col. Joel W. Ridgell ; 114th Ohio, Lieut.-Col. Horatio B. Maynard. Brigade loss : k, 17 ; w, 68 ; m, 21 = 106. *Third Brigade,* Col. John F. De Courcy : 54th Ind., Col. Fielding Mansfield ; 22d Ky., Lieut.-Col. George W. Monroe (w), Maj. William J. Worthington ; 16th Ohio, Lieut.-Col. Philip Kershner (w and c) ; 42d Ohio, Lieut.-Col. Don A. Pardee. Brigade loss : k, 48 ; w, 321 ; m, 355 = 724. *Artil-*

lery: 7th Mich., Capt. Charles H. Lanphere ; 1st Wis., Capt. Jacob T. Foster. Artillery loss : k, 1 ; w, 13 = 14.
Ky. Engineers, Capt. William F. Patterson.
FOURTH DIVISION, Brig.-Gen. Frederick Steele.
First Brigade, Brig.-Gen. Frank P. Blair, Jr. : 13th Ill., Col. John B. Wyman (k), Lieut.-Col. Adam B. Gorgas ; 29th Mo., Col. John S. Cavender ; 30th Mo., Lieut.-Col. Otto Schadt ; 31st Mo., Col. Thomas C. Fletcher (w and c), Lieut.-Col. Samuel P. Simpson (w) ; 32d Mo., Col. Francis H. Manter ; 58th Ohio, Lieut.-Col. Peter Dister (k) ; 4th Ohio Battery, Capt. Louis Hoffmann ; C, 10th Mo. Cav., Lieut. Daniel W. Ballou. Brigade loss : k, 99 ; w, 331 ; m, 173 = 603. *Second Brigade,* Brig.-Gen. Charles E. Hovey : 25th Iowa, Col. George A. Stone ; 31st Iowa, Col. William Smyth ; 3d Mo., Col. Isaac F. Shepard ; 12th Mo., Col. Hugo Wangelin ; 17th Mo., Col. Francis Hassendeubel ; 76th Ohio, Col. Charles R. Woods ; 1st Mo. Horse Art'y, Capt. Clemens Landgraeber. Brigade loss : k, 6 ; w, 21 ; m, 2 = 29. *Third Brigade,* Brig.-Gen. John M. Thayer : 4th Iowa, Col. James A. Williamson ; 9th Iowa, Lieut.-Col. William H. Coyl ; 26th Iowa, Col. Milo Smith ; 28th Iowa, Col. William E. Miller ; 30th Iowa, Col. Charles H. Abbott ; 34th Iowa, Col. George W. Clark ; 1st Iowa Battery, Capt. Henry H. Griffiths. Brigade loss : k, 7 ; w, 115 ; m, 2 = 124. *Artillery :* A, 1st Ill., Capt. Peter P. Wood ; B, 1st Ill., Capt. Samuel E. Barrett ; H, 1st Ill., Lieut. Levi W. Hart ; Chicago (Ill.) Mercantile, Capt. Charles G. Cooley ; 8th Ohio, Lieut. James F. Putnam ; 17th Ohio, Capt. Ambrose A. Blount. *Cavalry :* 6th Mo., Col. Clark Wright ; 3d Ill., Col. Lafayette McCrillis ; Thielemann's (Ill.) Battalion. The total loss of the Union army was 208 killed, 1005 wounded, and 563 captured or missing = 1776. The effective strength of the expeditionary force is estimated at about 33,000 men. General Sherman says ("Official Records," Vol. XVII., Part I., p. 610) that "the only real fighting was during the assault by Morgan's and Steele's divisions, and at the time of crossing the 6th Missouri, during the afternoon of December 29th, by the Second Division."

THE CONFEDERATE FORCES.

Lieutenant-General John C. Pemberton.

DEFENSES OF VICKSBURG, Major-General Martin L. Smith, Major-General Carter L. Stevenson.
Barton's Brigade, Brig.-Gen. Seth M. Barton : 40th Ga., Col. Abda Johnson (w) ; 42d Ga., Col. R. J. Henderson ; 43d Ga., Lieut.-Col. Hiram P. Bell (w) ; 52d Ga., Col. C. D. Phillips. Brigade loss : k, ' 15 ; w, 39 54. *Vaughn's Brigade,* Brig.-Gen. John C. Vaughn : 79th Tenn., Col. John H. Crawford ; 80th Tenn., Col. John A. Rowan ; 81st Tenn., ——. Brigade loss : k, 8 ; w, 10 = 18. *Gregg's Brigade,* Brig.-Gen. John Gregg : 1st Tenn., —— ; 3d Tenn., Col. C. J. Clack ; 10th Tenn., —— ; 30th Tenn., Col. James J. Turner ; 41st Tenn., —— ; 50th Tenn., —— ; 51st Tenn., ——. Brigade loss : k, 1 ; w, 3 = 4. *Tracy's Brigade,* Brig.-Gen. E. D. Tracy : 20th Ala., —— ; 23d Ala., Col. F. K. Beck ; 30th Ala., —— ; 31st Ala., ——.
PROVISIONAL DIVISION, Brig.-Gen. Stephen D. Lee, Major-Gen. Dabney H. Maury.
Brigade Commanders (Provisional) : Colonels William T. Withers and Allen Thomas. *Troops :* 37th Ala., —— ;

40th Ala., Col. A. A. Coleman ; 1st La., Col. S. R. Harrison ; 17th La., Col. Robert Richardson ; 22d La., Col. Edward Higgins ; 26th La., Col. Winchester Hall ; 28th La., Lieut.-Col. J. O. Landry ; 31st La., Col. C. H. Morrison ; 3d Miss., —— ; 3d Battalion Miss. State Troops, —— ; 4th Miss., Col. Pierre S. Layton ; 30th Miss., —— ; 35th Miss., —— ; 46th Miss., Lieut.-Col. W. K. Easterling ; Miss. Battery, Capt. Robert Bowman ; Miss. Battery, Capt. J. L. Wofford ; Miss. Battery (section), Lieut. Frank Johnston ; Miss. Battery, Capt. N. J. Drew, Lieut. W. J. Duncan ; 2d Tex., Lieut.-Col. W. C. Timmins (w) ; Hill's Co. Cav. ; Johnson's (Miss.) Co. Cav. ; Miss. Light Artillery, Maj. S. M. Ward.
The total Confederate loss is reported by General Pemberton as 63 killed, 134 wounded, and 10 missing = 207.
The effective strength, including the reënforcements prior to the withdrawal of the Union forces, was about 25,000. (See "Official Records," Vol. XVII., Pt. II., pp. 824, 825.)

JEFFERSON DAVIS AND THE MISSISSIPPI CAMPAIGN.↓

BY JOSEPH E. JOHNSTON, GENERAL, C. S. A.

IN Mr. Davis's account of the military operations in Mississippi in 1863,⚓ their disastrous result is attributed to my misconduct. My object in the following statement is to exhibit the true causes of those disasters.

The combination of Federal military and naval forces which produced that result was made practicable by the military errors of the Confederate Government in 1862, and was made successful by its repetition of the gravest of those errors in 1863.↓

In the first half of July, 1862, General Halleck was ordered to Washington as general-in-chief. Before leaving Corinth he transferred General Buell, with his troops, to middle Tennessee, and left General Grant in command of those holding in subjection north-eastern Mississippi and southern West Tennessee. For this object they were distributed in Corinth, Memphis, Jackson, and intermediate places. They numbered about forty-two thousand present for duty by Mr. Davis's estimate. Their wide dispersion put them at the mercy of any superior or equal force, such as the Confederacy could have brought against them readily; but this opportunity, such a one as has rarely occurred in war, was put aside by the Confederate Government, and the army which, properly used, would have secured to the South the possession of Tennessee and Mississippi was employed in a wild expedition into Kentucky, which could have had only the results of a raid.

Mr. Davis extols the strategy of that operation, which, he says, "manœuvred the foe out of a large and to us important territory." This advantage, if it could be called so, was of the briefest. For this "foe" drove us out of Kentucky in a few weeks, and recovered permanently the "large and to us important territory." After General Bragg was compelled to leave Kentucky, the Federal army, which until then had been commanded by General Buell, was established at Nashville, under General Rosecrans. And General Bragg, by a very circuitous route through south-eastern Kentucky and north-eastern Tennessee, brought his troops to the neighborhood of Murfreesboro'. Mr. Davis says ["Rise and Fall," p. 384] that "the strength of the Federal army, as we have ascertained, was 65,000 men." Army returns show that it was a little less than 47,000, and Bragg's, 44,000. [See also this volume, p. 30.]

↓ Reprinted by permission from the "North American Review" for Dec., 1886, Vol. 143, p. 585.

⚓ "The Rise and Fall of the Confederate States," by Jefferson Davis.

↓ The Confederate army that fought at Shiloh was reorganized by General Beauregard at Corinth, and occupied that position until the 29th of May, 1862, when that officer led it to Tupelo in consequence of the near approach of General Halleck's vastly superior forces. There, about the middle of June, General Beauregard was compelled by ill health to transfer his command to General Bragg. The discipline and instruction of those troops had been greatly improved at Corinth and Tupelo; so that they were in excellent condition for marches and for battles before the middle of July. They numbered 45,000. There were 22,000 other Confederate troops in Mississippi, in two bodies, one commanded by Major-General Van Dorn, the other by Major-General Price. Those two officers were independent of each other — and, strange to say, of General Bragg also.— J. E. J.

General Grant was then in northern Mississippi, with an army formed by uniting the detachments that had been occupying Corinth and various points in southern West Tennessee. He was preparing for the invasion of Mississippi, with the special object of gaining possession of Vicksburg by the combined action of his army and Admiral Porter's squadron, which was in readiness. To oppose him, Lieutenant-General Pemberton, who commanded the Department of Mississippi and East Louisiana, had an active army of 23,000 effective infantry and artillery, and above 6000 cavalry, most of it irregular. There were also intrenched camps at Vicksburg and Port Hudson, each held by about six thousand men, protecting batteries of old smoothbore guns, which, it was hoped, would prevent the Federal war vessels from occupying the intermediate part of the Mississippi. Lieutenant-General Holmes was then encamped near Little Rock with an army of above fifty thousand men, as General Cooper, adjutant-general, reported to the President in my presence. There were no Federal forces in Arkansas at the time, except one or two garrisons.

In all the time to which the preceding relates I had been out of service from the effects of two severe wounds received in the battle of Seven Pines [May 31st, 1862]. On the 12th of November, 1862, I reported myself fit for duty. The Secretary of War replied that I would be assigned to service in Tennessee and Mississippi in a few days. Thinking myself authorized to make suggestions in relation to the warfare in which I was to be engaged, I proposed to the Secretary, in his office, that, as the Federal forces about to invade Mississippi were united in that State, ours available for its defense should be so likewise; therefore General Holmes should be ordered to unite his forces with General Pemberton's without delay. As a reply, he read me a letter of late date from himself to General Holmes, instructing that officer to make the movement just suggested, and then a note from the President directing him to countermand his order to General Holmes. A few days after this, General Randolph resigned the office of Secretary of War—unfortunately for the Confederacy. On the 24th of November Mr. Seddon, who had succeeded General Randolph as Secretary of War, assigned me to the command of the departments of General Bragg and Lieutenant-Generals E. Kirby Smith and Pemberton, each to command his department under me. In acknowledging this order, I again suggested the transfer of the army in Arkansas to Mississippi. The suggestion was not adopted or noticed.

The Government placed my headquarters at Chattanooga, but authorized me to move them as occasion might require. On the 4th of December, I received there a telegram from the adjutant-general, informing me that Lieutenant-General Pemberton was falling back before a very superior force; that "Lieutenant-General Holmes has been peremptorily ordered to reënforce him, but that, as his troops may be too late, the President urges on you the importance of sending a sufficient force from General Bragg's command to the aid of Lieutenant-General Pemberton." I replied that Lieutenant-General Holmes's troops could join the army in Mississippi much sooner than General Bragg's, and that the latter officer could not give adequate aid to the army in

Mississippi without exposing himself to inevitable defeat. And further, that there was no object in our retaining troops in Arkansas, where they could find no enemy. For these reasons I declined to weaken General Bragg without further orders to do so.

About the 9th of December the President passed through Chattanooga on his way to Murfreesboro', to decide, at General Bragg's headquarters, whether the army of Tennessee or that of Arkansas should furnish the reënforcements

necessary to enable the Confederacy to hold the Mississippi and its valley. He returned in two or three days and directed me to order General Bragg to send ten thousand of his men under Major-General C. L. Stevenson to report to General Pemberton. The order was given as the President's. He then set out to Mississippi, desiring me to accompany him. In Jackson, which he reached the morning of the 19th of December, he found the Legislature in session. It had been convened by Governor Pettus to bring out the remaining military resources of the State, to aid in its defense.

On the 21st and 22d Mr. Davis inspected the water-batteries and land defenses of Vicksburg, which were then very extensive, but slight—the usual defect of Confederate engineer-

LIEUTENANT-GENERAL J. C. PEMBERTON, C. S. A.
FROM A PHOTOGRAPH.

ing. He also conferred with the commander, Major-General Martin L. Smith, and me, in reference to the forces required to hold that place and Port Hudson, and at the same time to oppose General Grant in the field. We agreed (General Smith and I) that at least twenty thousand more troops were necessary, and I again urged him to transfer the troops in Arkansas to Mississippi. In a friendly note to General Holmes, which I was permitted to read, Mr. Davis pointed out to him that he would benefit the service by sending twenty thousand men into Mississippi, but gave him no order; consequently no troops came.

Thus an army outnumbering that which General Grant was then commanding was left idle, while preparations were in progress, near it, for the conquest of a portion of the Confederacy so important as the valley of the Mississippi.

From Vicksburg the President visited General Pemberton's army in the extensive position it was intrenching near Grenada,—so extensive that it is fortunate for us, probably, that General Grant was prevented from trying its strength. In conversing with the President concerning the operations impending, General Pemberton and I advocated opposite modes of warfare.

On the 25th the President returned to Jackson, and on the 27th information was received from General W. W. Loring, commanding near Grenada, that General Grant's army, which had been advancing, was retiring in consequence of the destruction of the depot of supplies at Holly Springs by the gallant Van Dorn's daring and skillfully executed enterprise, surpassed by none of its character achieved during the war. This depot was to have supplied the Federal army in its march toward Vicksburg. Its destruction frustrated that design. General Van Dorn accomplished it on the 20th of December with a brigade of cavalry, attacking, defeating, and capturing a superior force. The supplies were destroyed by burning the store-houses—to which the consent of the owners was freely given. The destruction of the stores compelled General Grant to fall back and gave the Confederate Government abundant time for thorough preparations to meet his next advance. The most effective, indeed a decisive one, would have required but 12 or 15 days—the uniting Lieutenant-General Holmes's troops with Lieutenant-General Pemberton's, in Mississippi, which would have formed an effective force of little less than 75,000 men.

Before Mr. Davis returned to Richmond I represented to him that my command was a nominal one merely, and useless; because the great distance between the armies of Tennessee and Mississippi, and the fact that they had different objects and adversaries, made it impossible to combine their action; so there was no employment for me unless I should take command of one of the armies in an emergency, which, as each had its own general, was not intended or desirable. He replied that the great distance of these departments from the seat of government made it necessary that there should be an officer near them with authority to transfer troops from one to the other in emergencies. I suggested that each was too weak for its object; and that neither, therefore, could be drawn upon to strengthen the other; and that the distance between them was so great as to make such temporary transfers impracticable. These objections were disregarded, however.

The detaching of almost a fourth of General Bragg's army to Mississippi, while of no present value to that department, was disastrous to that of Tennessee, for it caused the battle of Murfreesboro'. General Rosecrans was, of course, soon informed of the great reduction of his antagonist's strength, and marched from Nashville to attack him. The battle, that of Murfreesboro' or Stone's River, occurred on the 31st of December, 1862, and the 2d of January, 1863, and was one of the most obstinately contested and bloody of the war, in proportion to the numbers engaged. [See articles to follow.] The result of this action compelled the Confederate army to fall back and place itself behind Duck River, at Manchester, Tullahoma, and Shelbyville.

Early in December Grant projected an enterprise against Vicksburg under Sherman's command. He directed that officer to embark at Memphis with about 30,000 men, descend the river with them to the neighborhood of the place, and with the coöperation of Admiral Porter's squadron proceed to reduce it. Sherman entered the Yazoo with his forces on the 26th of December, employed several days in reconnoitering, and on the 29th made a vigorous assault upon the defensive line near Chickasaw Bayou, manned by Brigadier-General S. D. Lee's brigade, which repelled the attack.♭ General Pemberton reported that the Confederate loss was 150, and that of the Federals 1100.♮

The combined land and naval forces then left the Yazoo, and, entering the Arkansas, ascended it to Arkansas Post, which they captured, with its garrison of five thousand Confederate troops. In the meantime General Pemberton brought what had been his active forces into Vicksburg.

On the 20th of January all the troops destined for the operations against Vicksburg were ordered by General Grant to Milliken's Bend and Young's Point, where he joined them on the 29th. These troops were employed until April in cutting a canal through the point of land opposite Vicksburg, to enable the Federal vessels to pass it without exposure to the batteries; but the attempt was unsuccessful.

MAJOR-GENERAL MARTIN L. SMITH, C. S. A.
FROM A PHOTOGRAPH.

In the meantime Brigadier-General Bowen was detached with three brigades to Grand Gulf, to construct batteries there; and Major-General Loring, with a similar detachment, was sent to select and fortify a position to prevent the enemy from approaching Vicksburg by the Yazoo Pass and River. He constructed a field-work for this object at the head of the Yazoo. A flotilla of 9 United States gun-boats and 20 transports, carrying 4500 troops, appeared before it on the 11th of March, and constructed a land-battery, which, with the gun-boats, cannonaded the fort several days; but the steady fire of the little work [Fort Pemberton] compelled the assailants to draw off and return to the Mississippi.

On the 22d of January, while inspecting the works for the defense of Mobile, then in course of construction, I received orders by telegraph from the President to go to General Bragg's headquarters "with the least delay." A letter from the President delivered to me in Chattanooga told for what service. It was to ascertain if General Bragg had so far lost the confidence of the army as to make it expedient to remove him from command. After making the necessary investigation thoroughly, I came to the conclusion that there was no ground for the general's removal, so reported, and resumed the inspection at Mobile. While so employed, I received a telegram from the Secretary of War, in which he ordered me to direct General Bragg to report at the War

♭ Besides Lee's brigade, which met the main attack, three brigades of the Confederates were engaged, commanded respectively by Brigadier-Generals John Gregg, J. C. Vaughn, and S. M. Barton [see p. 462].— EDITORS.

♮ According to the "Official Records" (Vol. XVII., Pt. I, pp. 625 and 668), the Union loss was 208 killed, 1005 wounded, 563 missing,— total, 1776; that of the Confederates, 63 killed, 134 wounded, 10 missing,— total, 207.— EDITORS.

Department for conference; and to assume, myself, direct charge of the army in middle Tennessee. On my return to Tullahoma under this order, I learned that the general was devoting himself to Mrs. Bragg, who was supposed to be at the point of death. So the communication of the order to him was postponed, and the postponement and the cause reported to the Secretary. Mrs. Bragg's condition improved, however; but before it became such as to permit General Bragg to return to military duty, I had become unfit for it, and was compelled to retain him in the command of the Army of Tennessee and put myself under the care of a surgeon. This sickness continued for weeks, and was *reported repeatedly.*

The United States naval officers had already ascertained that their iron-clads could pass the Confederate batteries without great danger. Moreover, as General Pemberton had reported, the wooden vessels *Hartford* and *Albatross* had passed Port Hudson while most of our guns were engaged with the other vessels of Admiral Farragut's squadron. This reduced the value of our water-batteries greatly. Yet, in the first half of April, General Pemberton became convinced that General Grant had abandoned the design against Vicksburg and was preparing to reëmbark his forces, perhaps to join General Rosecrans; and on April 11th he expressed the belief that most of those troops were being withdrawn to Memphis, and stated that he himself was assembling troops at Jackson to follow this movement. This was approved. On the 17th, however, he reported that the Federal army had resumed its offensive operations. He also reported that General Grant was occupying New Carthage, and that there were nine Federal gun-boats between Vicksburg and Port Hudson.

Colonel B. H. Grierson [Federal] set out from La Grange on the 17th of April on his noted raid through Mississippi, terminating at Baton Rouge, May 2d. The mischief reported was the burning of some bridges, engines, and cars near Newton, the destruction of ammunition and cars at Hazelhurst, and the burning of the railroad depot and cars at Brookhaven. Several brigades of infantry were detached to protect such property; but fruitlessly, of course.

Admiral Porter's squadron, and three transports towing barges, passed Vicksburg on the night of April 16th, and ran down to Hard Times, where the army was; and six more transports and barges followed on the night of the 22d. On the two occasions, one transport was sunk, another burned, and six barges rendered unserviceable by the fire of the batteries.

General Grant's plan seems to have been to take possession of Grand Gulf, and thence operate against Vicksburg; for Admiral Porter's squadron commenced firing upon the Confederate works early in the morning of the 29th, and the Thirteenth Corps was ready to seize them as soon as their guns should be silenced; but as their fire had slackened but little at 6 o'clock, Grant changed his plan and sent his troops and transports to the landing-place, six miles from Bruinsburg, on the east bank of the river. The four divisions of the Thirteenth Corps were ferried to that point during the day of the 30th.

General Bowen, at Grand Gulf, observed this, and led parts of his three brigades (five thousand men) to the road from Bruinsburg to Port Gibson, four miles in advance of the latter. By admirable conduct and great advantages of ground, this handful delayed the advance of the Thirteenth Corps six or eight hours. Lieutenant-General Pemberton informed me of this engagement by telegraph during the fighting, adding: " I should have large reënforcements." I replied immediately: "If General Grant's army lands on this side of the river, the safety of Mississippi depends on beating it. For that object you should unite your whole force." And I telegraphed again next day: " If Grant's army crosses, unite all your forces to beat it. Success will give you back what was abandoned to win it." In transmitting General Pemberton's call for reënforcements to the Secretary of War, I said: " They cannot be sent from here without giving up Tennessee."

On the 3d Bowen's troops abandoned Grand Gulf and returned to Vicksburg. On the same day the Seventeenth Corps joined the Thirteenth at Willow Springs, where the two waited for the Fifteenth, which came up on the 8th. The army then marched toward Raymond, the Seventeenth Corps leaving first, and the Fifteenth second.

In the evening of May 9th I received, by telegraph, orders to proceed at once to Mississippi and take chief command of the forces there, and to arrange to take with me, for temporary service, or to have follow without delay, three thousand good troops. I replied instantly: "Your dispatch of this morning received. I shall go immediately, although unfit for service," and took the first train, which was on the morning of the 10th. At Lake Station, on the 13th, I found a telegram from General Pemberton, dated the 12th, informing me that the enemy was apparently moving in heavy force on Edwards's depot, which, as he said, "will be the battle-field if I can carry forward sufficient force, leaving troops enough to secure the safety of this place [Vicksburg]." This was the first intelligence of the Federal army received from General Pemberton since the first of the month.

I arrived in Jackson at nightfall, exhausted by an uninterrupted journey of four days, undertaken from a sick-room; in consequence of which Major Mims, chief quartermaster of the department, the first officer who reported to me, found me in bed. He informed me, among other military occurrences, that two brigades had marched into the town an hour or two before. Brigadier-General Gregg, their senior officer, reported to me soon after that he had been ordered from Port Hudson to Raymond by General Pemberton, but had been driven from that place the day before by the Federal Seventeenth Corps; and, in obedience to the general's instructions for such an event, had fallen back to Jackson, accompanied by Brigadier-General W. H. T. Walker, whom he had met on the way, marching to join him with his brigade. The latter had just come from General Beauregard's department [South Carolina, Georgia, and Florida]. There were about six thousand men in the two brigades.

He said further that Colonel Wirt Adams, of the cavalry, had informed him that General Pemberton's forces were at Edwards's depot, 20 miles from Vicksburg, and his headquarters at Bovina, 8 miles from that place; that the Seventeenth Corps (McPherson's) had moved that day from Raymond to Clinton, 9 or 10 miles from Jackson, on the road to Vicksburg. He added that General Maxey's brigade from Port Hudson was expected in Jackson next day. I had passed General Gist's during that day, on its way from Charleston. The arrival of these troops, and, as I hoped, 3000 from Tennessee, would increase the force in Jackson to near 15,000 men. The most important measure to be executed then was the junction of these reënforcements with the army. For that object, an order in writing was sent without delay to General Pemberton by Captain Yerger, who volunteered to bear it, to move to Clinton at once and attack a Federal corps there, the troops in Jackson to coöperate; to beat that detachment and establish communication, that he might be reënforced. It was delivered at Bovina early next morning, and General Pemberton replied promptly that he " moved at once with his whole available force"; but in the ride of ten or twelve miles to his camp at Edwards's depot he determined to disobey my order, and on his arrival assembled a council of war, which he informed of that intention, and consulted upon the measure to be substituted for the movement to Clinton. It was decided to move southward to a point on the road by which General Grant's forces had advanced, which would have made it impossible for the troops then in Jackson and other expected reënforcements to join Pemberton's army.

Mr. Davis says of this [" Rise and Fall," II., pp. 404–5]:

" When he [Johnston] reached Jackson, learning that the enemy was between that place and the position occupied by General Pemberton's forces, about thirty miles distant, he halted there and opened correspondence with General Pemberton, from which confusion and consequent disasters resulted, which might have been avoided had he, with or without his reënforcements, proceeded to General Pemberton's headquarters in the field."

Mr. Davis knew that I had been sick five or six weeks when ordered to Mississippi, and therefore he had no right to suppose that I was able to make a night ride of thirty miles, after a journey of four days. He knew, too, that my course, which he now condemns, was the only one offering us a hope of success; for he indorsed on a letter of mine, giving a brief account of these events to the Secretary of War: " Do not perceive why a junction was not attempted, which would have made our force nearly equal in number to the estimated strength of the enemy; and might have resulted in a total defeat under circumstances which rendered retreat or reënforcement to him scarcely practicable." It would be doing injustice to Mr. Davis's intelligence to think that he really believes that I am chargeable with the consequences of the disobedience of my indispensable order, or that he is ignorant that our only hope of success lay in the execution of that order, and that to disobey it was to ruin us.

After the decision of the council of war, General Pemberton remained at Edwards's depot at least 24 hours; and instead of marching in the morning of the 14th, his movement was commenced so late on the 15th that he bivouacked at night but three or four miles from the ground he had left. Here, soon after nightfall, the camp-fires of a division were pointed out to him, but he took no measures in consequence. Soon after sunrise on the 16th he received an order from me, the second one, to march toward Clinton that our forces might be united. He made preparations to obey it, and, in acknowledging it, described the route he intended to follow; but he remained passive five or six hours, before a single Federal division, until near noon, when General Grant, having brought up six other divisions, attacked him. Notwithstanding the enemy's great superiority of numbers, General Pemberton maintained a spirited contest of several hours, but was finally driven from the field. This was the battle of Baker's Creek, or Champion's Hill. The Confederate troops retreated toward Vicksburg, but bivouacked at night near the Big Black, one division in some earth-works in front of the bridge, the other a mile or two in rear of it. Loring, whose division was in the rear, in quit-

ting the field, instead of crossing Baker's Creek, turned southward, and by a skillfully conducted march eluded the enemy, and in three days joined the troops from the east, assembling near Jackson. On the near approach of the pursuing army next morning, the troops in front of the bridge abandoned the intrenchments and retreated rapidly to Vicksburg, accompanied by the division that had been posted west of the river. Information of this was brought to me in the evening of that day, and I immediately wrote to General Pemberton that, if invested in Vicksburg, he must ultimately surrender; and that, instead of losing both troops and place, he must save the troops by evacuating Vicksburg and marching to

VICKSBURG COURT HOUSE, A LANDMARK DURING THE SIEGE. FROM A PHOTOGRAPH TAKEN IN 1880.

the north-east. The question of obeying this order was submitted by him to a council of war, which decided that "it was impossible to withdraw the troops from that position with such *morale* and material as to be of further service to the Confederacy." This allegation was refuted by the courage, fortitude, and discipline displayed by that army in the long siege.

The investment of the place was completed on the 19th; on the 20th Gist's brigade from Charleston, on the 21st Ector's and McNair's from Tennessee, and on the 23d Maxey's from Port Hudson joined Gregg's and Walker's near Canton. This force was further increased on the 3d of June by the arrival of Breckinridge's division and Jackson's (two thousand) cavalry from the Army of Tennessee, and Evans's brigade from Charleston. These troops, except the cavalry, having come by railroad, were not equipped for the service before them: that of rescuing the garrison of Vicksburg. They required artillery, draught horses and mules, wagons, ammunition, and provisions, all in large numbers and quantity; the more because it was necessary to include the Vicksburg troops in our estimates.

According to Lieutenant-General Pemberton's report of March 31st, 1863 (the only one I can find), he had then present for duty 2360 officers and 28,221 enlisted men. These were the troops that occupied Vicksburg and the camp at Edwards's depot when General Pemberton received my order dated May 13th. There were, besides, above two thousand cavalry in the northern and south-western parts of the State.

I have General Grant's reports of May 31st and June 30th, 1863. The first shows a force of 2991 officers and 47,500 enlisted men present for duty; the second, 4412 officers and 70,866 en-listed men present for duty. The so-called siege of Vicksburg was little more than a blockade. But one vigorous assault was made, which was on the third day.

Mr. Davis represents that General Pemberton's operations were cramped by a want of cavalry, for which I was responsible. He had cavalry enough; but it was used near the extremities of the State against raiding parties, instead of being employed against the formida-ble invasion near the center. Mr. Davis accepts that officer's idea that a large body of cavalry could have broken Gen-eral Grant's communication with the Mis-sissippi, and so defeated his enterprise. But Grant had no communication with the Mississippi. His troops supplied them-selves from the country around them.

COLONEL S. H. LOCKETT, C. S. A., CHIEF ENGINEER OF THE VICKSBURG DEFENSES. FROM A PHOTOGRAPH.

He accuses me of producing "confusion and consequent disasters" by giving a written order to Lieutenant-General Pemberton, which he terms opening correspondence. But as that order, dated May 13th, was disobeyed, it cer-tainly produced neither confusion nor disaster. But "consequent disaster" was undoubtedly due to the disobedience of that order, which caused the bat-tle of Champion's Hill. When that order was written, obedience to it, which would have united all our forces, might have enabled us to contend with General Grant on equal terms, and perhaps to win the campaign. Strange as it may now seem, Mr. Davis thought so at the time, as the indorsement already quoted proves distinctly.

A proper use of the available resources of the Confederacy would have averted the disasters referred to by Mr. Davis. If, instead of being sent on the wild expedition into Kentucky, General Bragg had been instructed to avail himself of the dispersed condition of the Federal troops in northern Mississippi and west Tennessee, he might have totally defeated the forces with which General Grant invaded Mississippi three months later. Those troops were distributed in Corinth, Jackson, Memphis, and intermediate points, while his own were united, so that he could have fought them in detail, with as much certainty of success as can be hoped for in war. And such success would have prevented the military and naval combination which gave the enemy control of the Mississippi and divided the Confederacy, and would have given the Confederacy the ascendency on that frontier. It is evident, and was so then, that the three bodies of Confederate troops in Mississippi in July, 1862, should have been united under General Bragg. The army of above 65,000 men so formed could not have been seriously resisted by the Federal forces, not only greatly inferior to it in numbers, but so distributed that the various parts could have been attacked separately, and certainly defeated, probably destroyed.

Even after this failure the Confederates were stronger to repel invasion than the Federals to invade. By uniting their forces in Arkansas with those in Mississippi, an army of above 70,000 men would have been formed, to meet General Grant's of 43,000. In all human probability such a force would have totally defeated the invading army, and not only preserved Mississippi but enabled us to recover Tennessee.

But if there were some necessity known only to the President to keep the Confederate troops then in Arkansas on that side of the Mississippi, he could have put General Pemberton on at least equal terms with his antagonist, by giving him the troops in April actually sent to him late in May. This would have formed an army of above fifty thousand men. General Grant landed two corps, less than 30,000 men, on the 30th of April and 1st and 2d of May; and it was not until the 8th of May that the arrival of Sherman's corps increased his force to about 43,000 men. The Confederate reënforcements could have been sent as well early in April as late in May; and then, without bad generalship on our part, the chances of success would have been in our favor, decidedly.

THE DEFENSE OF VICKSBURG.

BY S. H. LOCKETT, C. S. A., CHIEF ENGINEER OF THE DEFENSES.

THE occupation of Vicksburg was the immediate result of the fall of New Orleans on the 25th of April, 1862.[The first military operations were the laying out and construction of some batteries for heavy guns, by Captain (afterward Colonel) D. B. Harris of the Confederate States Engineers, ⚓ the work being mostly done by a force of hired negroes. These batteries were located chiefly below the city; their positions were well chosen; they had fine command of the river against a fleet coming from below.

On the 12th of May, 1862, Brigadier-General Martin Luther Smith arrived and took command, under orders from Major-General Mansfield Lovell, the Department commander. From that day to the end General Smith was never absent from his post, was always equal to every emergency, and never once, while in control, failed to do the right thing at the right time.

On the 20th of June, 1862, I was ordered from the Army of Tennessee, then under General Bragg, to report to General Smith as his Chief Engineer.

[The first troops to go to Vicksburg were from Camp Moore, a rendezvous of the forces which had recently evacuated New Orleans. They were Allen's 4th Louisiana and Thomas's 28th Louisiana. These regiments were soon followed by Marks's 27th Louisiana, De Clouet's 26th Louisiana, Richardson's 17th Louisiana, Morrison's 30th Louisiana, all infantry; and Beltzhoover's Louisiana regiment of artillery, and Ogden's Louisiana battalion of artillery. After these came Mellon's regiment and Balfour's battalion of Mississippi troops. The staff-officers were Major Devereux, Assistant Adjutant-General; Major Girault, Inspector-General; Lieutenant-Colonel Jay, Chief of Artillery; Captain McDon-

ald, Chief of Ordnance, and Lieutenants Harrod and Frost, Aides-de-camp. These troops and officers constituted the garrison of Vicksburg from the beginning to the end of operations. The troops had but recently had a fearful baptism of fire in the fierce bombardment by Admiral Farragut of Forts Jackson and St. Philip, and the batteries of the Chalmette. They were already veterans, and many of them were skilled artillerists. — S. H. L.

⚓ General Beauregard claims to have sent Captain Harris to Vicksburg and to have given the orders under which that officer began the construction of the fortifications. (O. R., XV., 810.) — EDITORS.

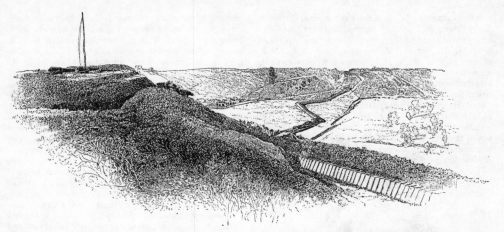

CONFEDERATE LINES IN THE REAR OF VICKSBURG. FROM A WAR-TIME PHOTOGRAPH.

I was with him in that capacity until the 1st of November, when I was made, by General Pemberton, Chief Engineer of the Department of Mississippi and East Louisiana, of which General Pemberton had just taken command. This change extended my field of operations from Holly Springs to Port Hudson, but I never relinquished immediate charge of the defenses of Vicksburg. Hence I may safely claim to have been identified with the defense almost from the beginning to the end of operations.

The series of irregular hills, bluffs, and narrow, tortuous ridges, apparently without system or order, that constitute the strong defensive position of Vicksburg, raised some two hundred feet above the level of the river, owe their character, with all their strangely complex arrangement and configuration, to the natural erosive action of water on the fine, homogeneous, calcareous silt peculiar to the lias or bluff formation.

At the time of my arrival no enemy was near, but the work of preparation was going on vigorously. The garrison was engaged in strengthening the batteries already constructed, in making bomb-proof magazines, and in mounting new guns recently arrived. Several new batteries were laid out by myself on the most commanding points above the city; these were afterward known as the "Upper Batteries." The work of making an accurate map of Vicksburg and vicinity was also begun. But we had not many days for these preliminaries. On the 26th of June the advance of Farragut's fleet arrived in sight. The next morning found it in position for bombarding. A flotilla of mortar-boats was moored close to the farther shore of the river just beyond the range of our lower batteries. A second flotilla had crept along the bank next to us with their masts so covered with the boughs of trees that we did not discover them until they were quite near. They were completely protected from our guns by the bank.

At a signal-gun from one of the iron-clads the guns were opened. I measured one of the holes made by the mortar-shells in hard, compact clay, and found it seventeen feet deep. It was a diffi-

cult matter to make bomb-proofs against such destructive engines. A few shots were fired from our batteries in answer to the challenge of the mortar-boats, but these shots were harmless, and were soon discontinued. The Federal bombardment was likewise nearly harmless. But few soldiers and citizens were killed. Vertical fire is never very destructive of life. Yet the howling and bursting shells had a very demoralizing effect on those not accustomed to them. One of my engineer officers, a Frenchman, a gallant officer who had distinguished himself in several severe engagements, was almost unmanned whenever one passed anywhere near him. When joked about it, he was not ashamed to confess: "I no like ze bomb; I cannot fight him back!"

June 28th was a memorable day. At early dawn the mortar-fleet renewed its heavy bombardment. At the same time the vessels and gun-boats moved up toward the city and opened fire with all their heavy ordnance. Under cover of this tremendous shelling the *Brooklyn* and *Hartford* and several of the iron-clads boldly pushed up stream, and went past our batteries under full headway, pouring into the city broadside after broadside with astonishing rapidity. The Confederate batteries responded with equal energy.

The results of this first encounter with the hitherto redoubtable fleet was highly gratifying to the defenders of Vicksburg. It is true the fleet got past the batteries; but the *Brooklyn* and *Octorora* were temporarily disabled. All the vessels suffered more or less, and many Federal sailors were killed and wounded, as we learned from people who lived across the river. On the Confederate side no gun was disabled, no battery injured, and only thirteen were killed or wounded. Our batteries mounted 29 guns, of which 2 were 10-inch Columbiads, the rest being old style 42 and 32 pounders. The *Brooklyn* alone carried 24 11-inch Dahlgren guns. We expected a land attack at the same time, and were prepared for it by the presence of as many as ten thousand troops, under Breckinridge, Bowen, and Preston, who had just arrived and were in near-supporting distance. They were not called upon, however, and no troops were under fire except the brigade of General M. L. Smith. After this, for two weeks, things moved along at Vicksburg with something akin to monotony. The mortar-fleets kept up a steady bombardment, but even the citizens of the town became so accustomed to it that they went about their daily occupations. The women and children left their caves to watch the shells, and would only betake themselves to their shelters when the fire seemed to be concentrated in their particular neighborhoods. Finally the upper fleet, under Flag-Officer C. H. Davis, came down the

MAJOR-GENERAL C. L. STEVENSON, C. S. A.
FROM A PHOTOGRAPH.

river, joined the vessels that had run our batteries, put a flotilla of mortar-boats in position, and took part in the grand but nearly harmless sport of pitching big shells into Vicksburg. During this period General Thomas Williams commenced the famous canal across the narrow neck of land in front of Vicksburg. But the water fell faster than the ditch was dug, the river refused to make a cut-off, and this effort also proved a failure.

On the 15th of July the monotony of the situation was greatly relieved by one of the most stirring episodes of the war. The little Confederate ram, *Arkansas*, under her gallant commander, I. N. Brown, came out of Yazoo River, where she had been built in imitation of the famous *Merrimac*, and ran the gauntlet of the whole upper fleet. [See article by Captain I. N. Brown, to follow.]

For several days after this the regulation bombardment was kept up. Suddenly, however, on the 25th of July, the lower fleet, big ships, gun-boats, and mortar-boats, weighed anchor and dropped down the river to a distance of several miles below their former position. On the 27th both lower and upper fleets took leave of us, and the 28th of July found Vicksburg once more freed from the presence of a hostile force.

Working parties were at once put upon the river-

batteries to repair damages and increase their strength wherever recent experience had shown it to be necessary. It was also determined to construct a line of defense in rear of Vicksburg, to prepare against an army operating upon land. As chief engineer, it became my duty to plan, locate, and lay out that line of defense. A month was spent in reconnoitering, surveying, and studying the complicated and irregular site to be fortified. No greater topographical puzzle was ever presented to an engineer. The difficulty of the situation was greatly enhanced by the fact that a large part of the hills and hollows had never been cleared of their virgin forest of magnificent magnolia-trees and dense undergrowth of cane. At first it seemed impossible to find anything like a general line of commanding ground surrounding the city; but careful study gradually worked out the problem.

The most prominent points I purposed to occupy with a system of redoubts, redans, lunettes, and small field-works, connecting them by rifle-pits so as to give a continuous line of defense. The work of construction was begun about the 1st of September with a force of negro laborers hired or impressed from the plantations of the adjacent counties. Haynes's Bluff on the Yazoo River and Warrenton, about six miles below Vicksburg, were fortified as flank protections to the main position.

On the 14th of October, 1862, Lieutenant-General John C. Pemberton took command of the Department of Mississippi and East Louisiana, establishing his headquarters at Jackson. About the same time General Grant was placed in supreme command of the Federal forces in north Mississippi. Then followed a succession of movements against Vicksburg, having for their object the turning of that point. They were all uniformly unsuccessful, and were so remote from the city, with one exception, that the garrison of Vicksburg was not involved in the operations which defeated them. I will simply mention them in the order in which they occurred. First was General Grant's advance from Memphis and Grand Junction, via Holly Springs, toward Grenada. This was defeated by the raids of Van Dorn and Forrest upon Grant's communications [December 20th and December 15th to January 3d]. He was forced to retire or starve. Next came General Sherman's attempt to get in rear of Vicksburg by the Chickasaw Bayou road, which ran from the Yazoo River bottom to the Walnut hills, six miles above the city. His column of thirty thousand men was defeated and driven back with dreadful slaughter by General S. D. Lee with one brigade of the Vicksburg garrison [December 20th to January 3d].

After this General Grant himself appeared in front of Vicksburg, occupied the river with an immense fleet and the Louisiana shore with a large army. He renewed the old style of bombardment and the work on the canal, but high water made him abandon that work and his position.

Then came the expedition, via Lake Providence and Bayou Maçon, which was defeated by natural difficulties. Next, the expedition by Yazoo Pass and Hushpuccanaugh Bayou, which was stopped by Fort Pemberton,—a cotton-bale fort made by

PASSAGE, ON THE NIGHT OF APRIL 16, 1863, OF GUN-BOATS AND STEAMERS AT VICKSBURG.
FROM A SKETCH MADE BY COLONEL S. H. LOCKETT, C. S. A.

Captain P. Robinson, of the Confederate States Engineers, on the overflowed bottom-lands of the Tallahatchie and Yallabusha rivers, near their junction [February 24th to April 8th]. Here General Loring, with 3 guns and about 1500 men, turned back a large fleet and land force, and won the sobriquet of "Old Blizzards" by standing on the cotton-bale parapet and shouting "Give them blizzards, boys! Give them blizzards!" Last of these flanking expeditions was one of General Sherman and Admiral Porter, via Steele's Bayou, to reach the Sunflower and Yazoo rivers, above Haynes's Bluff [March 14th–27th]. This came near being as disastrous as that by the Chickasaw Bayou, owing to obstructions made by the Confederates and to a sudden fall in the waters.

Though these expeditions all failed, the desperate nature of most of them convinced us that General Grant was in deep earnest, and not easily discouraged. He made one more effort, which succeeded perhaps beyond his own most sanguine expectations. This had been anticipated by General Pemberton, and, to a certain extent, provided for by sending General John S. Bowen to occupy and fortify Grand Gulf. I accompanied General Bowen and located the works at Grand Gulf, leaving them in charge of Lieutenant Donnellan, of the Confederate States Engineers.

On the night of the 16th of April, 1863, a large part of the upper fleet (then commanded by Admiral David D. Porter), consisting of six gun-boats and several transports, ran the batteries at Vicksburg. Gun-boats had frequently passed the batteries during the operations of the preceding ten

months, but up to that time no one had dreamed that the ordinary river steamboats could do so. They were protected by cotton-bales and by large barges loaded with coal and forage, lashed alongside. One of the transports was fired by our shells, and burned to the water's edge in front of the city. Two other boats were partly disabled, and several of the barges were sunk. Yet eight boats succeeded in getting past both Vicksburg and Warrenton in more or less serviceable condition. The movement of the boats was soon discovered by the Confederate pickets, who nightly patrolled the river in small boats. They immediately crossed the river and fired several houses in the village of DeSoto, so as to illuminate the river. To appreciate the boldness of this action one must try to put himself in the place of these pickets, who ran great risks of being captured in landing on the opposite shore, which was occupied by the Federal forces. In addition, as soon as their work was accomplished, they were exposed to the enemy's sharp-shooters, on the now brightly lighted river, and were in the direct line of fire of the batteries of their friends. Yet they neither failed nor faltered.

Two nights later, four more boats, towing barges of large capacity, passed down the river, and joined the others at New Carthage, a village in Louisiana about half-way between Vicksburg and Grand Gulf. Here there was a fleet of formidable gun-boats, and transports and barges enough to ferry a large force across the river. This gave a serious and threatening aspect to the movement. At the same time a force under General Sherman was again menacing Haynes's Bluff; Grierson's raid

DOUBLE CAVE IN THE RIGBY HILL.

batteries of Grand Gulf, and passed that point with his fleet. This was on the 29th of April. On the next day he crossed the river at Bruinsburg and obtained a lodgment on the eastern shore. Then followed in rapid succession the defeat of Bowen at Port Gibson on May 1st, the defeat of General Gregg at Raymond on the 12th, and the capture of Jackson on the 14th. Meantime General Pemberton had left Jackson and gone to Vicksburg. The writer followed him, after having laid out a line of defenses around Jackson, leaving them to be constructed by Captain Thyssens. General Pemberton first thought that Grant would turn north from Port Gibson and try to force a pas-

"SKY PARLOR HILL," A CONFEDERATE SIGNAL-STATION DURING THE SIEGE, AND (PICTURES ABOVE AND BELOW) CAVES OF THE KIND IN WHICH RESIDENTS OF VICKSBURG SOUGHT REFUGE DURING THE BOMBARDMENT BY THE FLEET. FROM PHOTOGRAPHS.

CAVE NEAR THE MACHINE-SHOP.

was playing havoc with railroads and depots of supplies in the interior of Mississippi; rumors of movements of Federal troops in north Mississippi were rife; and Port Hudson in Louisiana was threatened. General Pemberton, just previous to this time, had sent some troops from his department to General Bragg, at Tullahoma, and had others *en route* to the same destination. As soon as he became convinced that Vicksburg was seriously threatened by General Grant's last move, he strongly pleaded for the return of his troops, and made rapid dispositions of those still left, to meet the various forces operating against him. Lack of reliable information, however, made his efforts unavailing.↓ Before he could determine which was the real attack, and which were mere diversions, General Grant had perfected his arrangements, attacked and temporarily silenced the sage across Big Black River at one of the ferries. He accordingly sent about a brigade each to Hankinson's, Hall's, and Baldwin's ferries, and ordered field-works to be thrown up at these crossings.

After taking measures to establish works for the defense of the important points on our main line of communications at the railroad bridge and

↓ General Pemberton claims that the transfer of his cavalry to Bragg, in Tennessee, by General Johnston's orders, deprived him of the means of ascertaining the Federal movements in time to meet them effectively. This afterward became a subject of controversy between Generals Johnston and Pemberton.— EDITORS.

Edwards's depot, I returned to Vicksburg with Captain Wintter's company of sappers and miners and put them to work on the rear line of defenses, with orders to make necessary repairs and put everything in good condition.

At last General Pemberton became convinced that General Grant's intention was to march up the east bank of Big Black River, to strike the railroad at or near Edwards's depot, and thus cut his communications with Jackson. To prevent this, and at the same time to defeat Grant, if possible, he concentrated all of his forces at Edwards's depot, excepting General Forney's division which was left in Vicksburg, and General Smith's which was posted at and near the railroad bridge. On the 12th of May, under the orders of General Pemberton, I went to Edwards's depot to put the Confederate forces in position upon the ground selected for them to occupy, covering all the approaches from the south and east. The army here assembled consisted of three divisions: Bowen's on the right, Loring's in the center, and C. L. Stevenson's on the left, numbering about 18,000 men. Some slight field-works had been thrown up at favorable points. The position was naturally a strong one, on high ground, with the cultivated valley of Baker's Creek in its front. Here General Pemberton wished to wait to be attacked by Grant. There can be no doubt that if he had been allowed to do so a desperate and bloody battle would have been fought on that ground, the issue of which might have been different from that of the two unfortunate engagements which did actually occur. The army remained at Edwards's depot from the 13th to the 15th. During this time General Pemberton received numerous dispatches from President Davis, and from General J. E. Johnston, who had recently arrived at Jackson. I saw, or heard read, most of these dispatches. They were very conflicting in their tenor, and neither those of Mr. Davis nor those of General Johnston exactly comported with General Pemberton's views. He then made the capital mistake of trying to harmonize instructions from his superiors diametrically opposed to each other, and at the same time to bring them into accord with his own judgment, which was adverse to the plans of both. Mr. Davis's idea was to hold Vicksburg at all hazard, and not to endanger it by getting too far from it. Johnston's plan was to cut loose from Vicksburg altogether, manœuvre so as to avoid a general engagement with Grant until the Confederate forces could be concentrated, and then beat him. Pemberton wished to take a strong position on the line of the Big Black and wait for an attack, believing that it would be successfully resisted, and that then the tables could be turned upon Grant in a very bad position, without any base of supplies, and without a well-protected line of retreat. As I have said, none of these plans was carried out, but a sort of compromise or compound of all these attempts, resulting in the unfortunate battle of Baker's Creek, or Champion's Hill, and the disgraceful stampede of Big Black bridge.

Pemberton moved out from Edwards's depot in obedience to a dispatch from General Johnston, ordering him to attack in the rear a force which he supposed General Johnston was going to engage in front. Instead of this, he encountered Grant's victorious army returning, exultant and eager for more prizes, from the capture of Jackson. Pemberton's army, which was making a retrograde movement at the time, was put into line of battle by being faced to the right with infantry, artillery, baggage, and ordnance wagons just as they were. In a few minutes after this disposition was made, his extreme left, previously the head of his column, was actively engaged with largely superior numbers. Under all the circumstances the Confeder-

BRIGADIER-GENERAL EDWARD HIGGINS, C. S. A.
FROM A PHOTOGRAPH.

ates made a gallant fight, but they were driven from the field with heavy loss in killed, wounded, and captured, and a considerable loss of arms and ammunition. Stevenson's division bore the brunt of this battle and suffered the heaviest losses. Bowen's division sustained its reputation by making one of its grand old charges, in which it bored a hole through the Federal army, and finding itself unsupported turned around and bored its way back again. Loring's division did not coöperate with the other two, through some misunderstanding or misconception, and was scarcely engaged at all during the fight. Tilghman's brigade of this division covered the road by which the Confederates retreated late in the afternoon. While in the discharge of this duty General Tilghman was killed.

Our beaten forces, except Loring's division, retreated across Baker's Creek and took position at nightfall at Big Black bridge; part of the forces, Bowen's division and Vaughn's brigade, being put in position in the *tête-de-pont* on the east bank of the river, and part on the bluffs on the west. Loring's division was moved by its commander, by the right flank, around the Federal army, and finally, after a loss of most of its cannon and wagons, joined General Johnston at Jackson.

The affair of Big Black bridge was one which an ex-Confederate participant naturally dislikes to record. The Federals engaged us early in the morning from a copse of woods on our left. I was standing on the railroad bridge at the time, and soon saw signs of unsteadiness in our men, and reporting the fact to General Pemberton, received orders to prepare to destroy the bridges. Fence-rails and loose cotton saturated with turpentine were piled on the railroad bridge, and a barrel of spirits of turpentine placed on the steamer *Dot*, which was swung across the river and used as a bridge. About 9 o'clock our troops on the left (Vaughn's brigade) broke from their breastworks and came pell-mell toward the bridges. Bowen's men, seeing themselves unsupported, followed the example, and soon the whole force was crossing the river by the bridges and by swimming, hotly pursued by the Federals. I was on the *Dot* at the time.

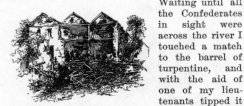

Waiting until all the Confederates in sight were across the river I touched a match to the barrel of turpentine, and with the aid of one of my lieutenants tipped it over. In a moment the boat was in a blaze. The railroad bridge

EFFECT OF THE GUN-BOAT SHELLS ON VICKSBURG HOUSES. FROM A SKETCH MADE THE DAY OF THE SURRENDER.

was likewise fired, and all immediate danger of pursuit prevented.

After the stampede at the bridge orders were issued for the army to fall back to Vicksburg, Major-General Stevenson being placed in command of the retreating forces. General Pemberton rode on himself to Bovina, a small railroad station about two and a half miles from the river. I was the only staff-officer with him. He was very much depressed by the events of the last two days, and for some time after mounting his horse rode in silence. He finally said: "Just thirty years ago I began my military career by receiving my appointment to a cadetship at the U. S. Military Academy, and to-day — the same date — that career is ended in disaster and disgrace." I strove to encourage him, urging that things were not so bad as they seemed to be; that we still had two excellent divisions (Smith's and Forney's) which had not been engaged and were, therefore, fresh and not demoralized; that they could occupy our lines at Vicksburg, covering especially the approaches from the position now occupied by the Federal forces, which they would naturally follow;

that the rest of the troops could be put, at first, in the less exposed parts of the line, or in reserve, until they had steadied themselves; that Vicksburg was strong and could not be carried by assault; and that Mr. Davis had telegraphed to him "to hold Vicksburg at all hazard," adding that "if besieged he would be relieved." To all of which General Pemberton replied that my youth and hopes were the parents of my judgment; he himself did not believe our troops would stand the first shock of an attack. We finally reached Bovina, where the general halted, and at my earnest instance wrote an order directing me to return to Vicksburg in all possible haste, to put the place in a good state of defense. This order directed all officers, of whatsoever rank, to obey all requisitions of the chief engineer for men, materials, and labor, and to render all possible aid in carrying out his plans. Generals Forney and Smith responded heartily, and before nightfall work was under way all along the lines of defense. The main works on the rear line, already described, had, for the most part, exterior ditches from six to ten feet deep, with rampart, parapet, banquette for infantry, and embrasures and platforms for artillery. Not having been occupied they were now much washed and weakened by the winter's rains. The rifle-pits connecting the main works had suffered in the same way, while on many parts of the line these pits had never been finished.

Fatigue parties were set to work making these repairs and connections; at the same time all field-artillery, Parrott guns, and siege pieces on the river front were moved to the rear line, platforms and embrasures were prepared for them, and ammunition was placed in convenient and protected places. The field-artillery brought in by our retreating army was likewise put in position as it arrived, and the morning of the 18th found us with 102 guns ready for service on the rear line. Some portions of our front were protected by abatis of fallen trees and entanglements of telegraph wire. The river-batteries were still strong and intact, having lost none of their sea-coast guns.

The troops were placed in position as I had recommended. General C. L. Stevenson's division extended from the Warrenton road on our extreme right to the railroad; General John H. Forney's division occupied the center, from the railroad to the Graveyard road; General M. L. Smith's division filling up the space between the Graveyard road and the river on our left. General John S. Bowen's Missourians and Waul's Texas Legion were held in reserve. ♮

♮ The defenses were divided into three districts as follows: *First:* General Stevenson's line, Captain P. Robinson, chief engineer, with Captain J. J. Conway, Captain James Couper, Lieutenant A. W. Gloster, Lieutenant R. R. Southard, and Sergeant W. B. H. Saunders as assistants. *Second:* The rest of the rear line: Captain D. Wintter, chief engineer, with Captain James Hogane, Lieutenant E. McMahon, Lieutenant F. Gillooly, Lieutenant S. McD. Vernon, and Lieutenant Blessing as assistants. *Third:* The river front commanded by Colonel Edward Higgins, First Lieutenant William O. Flynn, engineer. The working force under the direct control of the chief engineer was as follows: 26 sappers and miners of Captain Wintter's company; 8

detailed mechanics and firemen, 4 overseers for negroes, 72 hired negroes (20 were sick), 3 four-mule teams, and 25 yoke of oxen.

About five hundred picks and shovels is perhaps a near estimate of the number of intrenching tools. They were distributed to the different brigades according to the amount of work required, and being much scattered along our long lines were considered so precious by both men and officers that when not in actual use they were hidden for fear that they would be stolen by other troops, or ordered to some other part of the line by the chief engineer. They were entirely inadequate for the work, and the men soon improvised wooden shovels, using their bayonets as picks.— H. L. S.

Early on May 18th the Federal forces appeared on the Jackson and Graveyard roads, which were covered by a part of General M. L. Smith's division posted as skirmishers and pickets outside of our main lines. The Federals were held in check, so that during the night General Smith had no difficulty in withdrawing his forces within the main line of defense. The next day, when the Federals discovered that the Confederates were gone from their position of the evening before, they came forward rapidly and took that position, with shout and cheer, and soon after rushed upon the main line of defense, apparently with perfect confidence that there would be another "walk over" such as they had had two days before at Big Black bridge. But this time they struck a rock in General Shoup's brigade which met them with so heavy and well-directed a fire that they were compelled to fall back. A second time they came forward in greater numbers and with more boldness and determination, but with even more fatal results. They were repulsed with great loss, leaving five stand of colors close to our lines and the ground being strewn with their dead and wounded. These assaults extended from Shoup's position toward our right so as to include a part of Forney's division. Thus they were met by troops which had not been in any of the recent disastrous engagements, and were not in the least demoralized. These men stood to their arms like true soldiers, and helped to restore the *morale* of our army.

FIRST MONUMENT THAT STOOD ON THE SPOT OF THE INTERVIEW BETWEEN GENERALS GRANT AND PEMBERTON. FROM A PHOTOGRAPH.

The 20th and 21st of May were occupied by the Federal forces in completing their line, at an average distance of about eight hundred yards from our works. The Confederates utilized the time in putting up traverses against enfilade fires, and in making covered approaches from the camps in rear to the line of works. Many a man and officer had already been picked off by the quick-sighted Federal sharp-shooters, while passing along our lines or between them and the cooking-camps. It took several days for our men to learn the caution necessary to protect themselves.

On the 22d of May the gun-boats moved up within range and opened fire upon the river front. At the same time several dense columns of troops assaulted our lines in the rear. These assaults covered the right of General Smith's position, where General Shoup's brigade was posted, the whole of General Forney's front, and that of Stephen D. Lee's brigade of Stevenson's division. The assaults were made with great determination and admirable courage by the Federal soldiers. Once, twice,

three times they came forward and recoiled from the deadly fire poured upon them by the Confederates, who were now thoroughly restored to their old-time confidence and aroused to an enthusiastic determination to hold their lines. Every assault was repulsed with terrible loss to the attacking parties. At two points on the line — on General Forney's and General S. D. Lee's front — the Federals obtained a lodgment and planted their colors on our parapet; but the brave fellows paid for their success by being either killed or captured and having their colors fall into our hands. On General Lee's line they even succeeded in capturing one of our detached works and drove out the men who held it. But it was retaken in a few minutes by a charge of Waul's Legion, led by Colonel Pettus of Alabama. The losses on both sides were severe; several thousand men, estimated by us

MONUMENT NOW ON THE SPOT OF THE INTERVIEW BETWEEN GENERALS GRANT AND PEMBERTON. FROM A PHOTOGRAPH.

at 3500, were left dead and wounded between the lines.

On the 25th the Federal dead and some of their wounded in the fight of the 22d were still in our front and close to our lines. The dead had become offensive and the living were suffering fearful agonies. General Pemberton, therefore, under a flag of truce, sent a note to General Grant, proposing a cessation of hostilities for two and a half hours, so that the dead and dying men might receive proper attention. This was acceded to by General Grant, and from six o'clock until nearly dark both parties were engaged in performing funeral rites and deeds of mercy to the dead and wounded Federal soldiers. On this occasion I met General Sherman for the first time. Naturally, the officers of both armies took advantage of the truce to use their eyes to the best possible advantage. I was on the Jackson road redan, which had been terribly

LOGAN'S DIVISION ENTERING VICKSBURG BY THE JACKSON ROAD, JULY 4, 1863.
FROM A SKETCH MADE AT THE TIME.

pounded and was the object of constant attention from a battery of heavy guns in its immediate front. The Federals were running toward it in a zigzag approach [see p. 540], and were already in uncomfortable proximity to it. While standing on the parapet of this work a Federal orderly came up to me and said that General Sherman wished to speak to me. Following the orderly, I reached a group of officers standing some two hundred yards in front of our line. One of these came forward, introduced himself as General Sherman, and said: "I saw that you were an officer by your insignia of rank, and have asked you to meet me, to put into your hands some letters intrusted to me by Northern friends of some of your officers and men. I thought this would be a good opportunity to deliver this mail before it got too old." To this I replied: "Yes, General, it would have been very old, indeed, if you had kept it until you brought it into Vicksburg yourself." "So you think, then," said the general, "I am a very slow mail route." "Well, rather," was the reply, "when you have to travel by regular approaches, parallels, and zigzags." "Yes," he said, "that is a slow way of getting into a place, but it is a very sure way, and I was determined to deliver those letters sooner or later."

The general then invited me to take a seat with him on an old log near by, and thus the rest of the time of the truce was spent in pleasant conversation. In the course of it the general remarked: "You have an admirable position for defense here, and you have taken excellent advantage of the ground." "Yes, General," I replied, "but it is equally as well adapted to offensive operations,

and your engineers have not been slow to discover it." To this General Sherman assented. Intentionally or not, his civility certainly prevented me from seeing many other points in our front that I as chief engineer was very anxious to examine.

The truce ended, the sharp-shooters immediately began their work and kept it up until darkness prevented accuracy of aim. Then the pickets of the two armies were posted in front of their respective lines, so near to each other that they whiled away the long hours of the night-watch with social chat. Within our lines the pick and shovel were the weapons of defense until the next morning.

On the night of the 26th, while we were trying to place an obstruction across the swamp between our right and the river, our working party and its support had a sharp engagement with a detachment of Federals who came to see what we were doing. We captured one hundred of our inquisitive friends, and retired without putting in the obstruction. At other parts of the line the work of making traverses, changing guns to more available points, making covered ways along the line and to the rear, and repairing damages, went on as vigorously as our means would allow.

The events of the 27th of May were varied by an attack on our river batteries by the fleet. The *Cincinnati* was badly crippled, and before reaching her former moorings she sank in water not deep enough to cover her deck. She was still within range of our guns, so that the efforts made by the Federals to dismantle her and remove her armament were effectually prevented.

By this time the Federal commander was evidently convinced that Vicksburg had to be taken by regular siege operations. By the 4th of June the Federals had advanced their parallels to within 150 yards of our line. From them they commenced several double saps against our most salient works — the Jackson road redan, the Graveyard road redan, the Third Louisiana redan, on the left of the Jackson road, and the lunette on the right of the Baldwin's Ferry road. In each of these the engineer in charge was ordered to place thundering barrels and loaded shells with short-time fuses, as preparations for meeting assaults. The stockade redan and the stockade on its left, which had been constructed across a low place in our line, had by this time been nearly knocked to pieces by the enemy's artillery. A new line was therefore made to take its place when it should be no longer tenable. So, too, retrenchments, or inner lines, were ordered at all points where breaches seemed imminent or the enemy more than ordinarily near. These retrenchments served us excellently before the siege was terminated.

By the 8th of June, in spite of all efforts to prevent them, the enemy's sap-rollers had approached within sixty feet of two of our works. A private soldier suggested a novel expedient by which we succeeded in destroying the rollers. He took a piece of port-fire, stuffed it with cotton saturated with turpentine, and fired it from an old-fashioned large-bore musket into the roller, and thus set it on fire. Thus the enemy's sappers were exposed and forced to leave their sap and begin a new one some distance back. After this they kept their sap-rollers wet, forcing us to other expedients. ☆ Our next effort was counter-mining. From the ditches of all the threatened works counter-mines were started on the night of the 13th of June. The Third Louisiana redan was located on a very narrow ridge and had no ditch. The counter-mines for it were therefore started from within by first sinking a vertical shaft, with the intention of working out by an inclined gallery under the enemy's sap. Before this work was completed the Federal sappers succeeded in getting under the salient of the redan, and on the 25th they exploded a small mine, but the charge was too small to do much damage. Nevertheless, it tore off the vortex of the redan, and made what the Federals thought was a practicable breach. Into it they poured in strong force as soon as the explosion had expended itself. But they were met by a deadly volley from our men posted behind the retrenchment prepared for this emergency, and after heavy loss were compelled to retire. Six of our counter-miners were buried by this explosion.

On the same day we exploded two of our counter-mines and completely destroyed the enemy's sap-rollers, filled up their saps, and forced them to abandon a parallel very close to our line. Two days later we exploded another mine prematurely, without injury to the enemy, as they had not approached as near our works as we supposed. It was very difficult to determine distances under

ground, where we could hear the enemy's sappers picking, picking, picking, so very distinctly that it hardly seemed possible for them to be more than a few feet distant, when in reality they were many yards away.

On the 29th of June the enemy had succeeded in getting close up to the parapet of the Third Louisiana redan. We rolled some of their unexploded 13-inch shells down upon them and annoyed them so much as to force them to stop operations. At night they protected themselves against this method of attack by erecting a screen in front of their sap. This screen was made of heavy timbers, which even the shells could not move. I finally determined to try the effect of a barrel of powder. One containing 125 pounds was obtained, a time-fuse set to fifteen seconds was placed in the bung-hole, was touched off by myself with a live coal, and the barrel was rolled over the parapet by two of our sappers. The barrel went true to its destination and exploded with terrific force. Timbers, gabions, and facines were hurled into the air in all directions and the sappers once more were compelled to retire. They renewed their operations, however, at night, and in a few days succeeded in establishing their mine under the redan, which they exploded at 1:30 o'clock P. M. on the 1st of July. The charge was enormous — one and a quarter tons, as I subsequently learned from the Federal engineer. The crater made was about twenty feet deep and fifty feet in diameter. The redan was virtually destroyed, and the explosive effect extended back far enough to make a breach of nearly twenty feet width in the retrenchment across the gorge of the work. We expected an assault, but previous experience had made the enemy cautious. Instead, they opened upon the work a most terrific fire from everything that could be brought to bear upon it. Only a few minutes before the explosion I had been down in our counter-mine and had left seven men there, only one of whom was ever seen again; he, a negro, was blown over into the Federal lines but not seriously hurt [see p. 527]. The next thing for us to do was to stop the breach in our retrenchment. This we first tried to accomplish by heaving dirt into the breach with shovels from the two sides, but the earth was swept away by the storm of missiles faster than it could be placed in position. We then tried sand-bags, but they, too, were torn to shreds and scattered. Finally I sent for some tent flies and wagon covers, and with these great rolls of earth were prepared under cover and pushed into place, until at last we had something between us and the deadly hail of shot and shell and minie-balls. Playing into that narrow breach for nearly six hours were 2 9-inch Dahlgren guns, a battery of large Parrotts, 1 or more batteries of field-guns, a Coehorn mortar, and the deadliest fire of musketry ever witnessed by any of us there present. We stopped the breach, but lost in killed and wounded nearly one hundred men by the explosion and the subsequent fusillade. This was really the last

☆ I think this may be the origin of General Grant's notion that we had explosive bullets. I certainly never heard of anything of the sort, and most surely would

have made some use of them if we had had them in circumventing the Federal engineers.—S. H. L. [See statement of General Grant, p. 522.]

stirring incident of the siege. On the 2d of July we exploded one of our mines somewhat prematurely, and we had ready for explosion 11 others, containing from 100 to 125 pounds of powder, and extending at a depth of 6 to 9 feet for a distance of from 18 to 20 feet in front of our works. The fuses were set and everything was primed and ready for the approach of the Federal sappers, but on the 3d of July the flag of truce stopped all operations on both sides, and the efficiency of our preparations was not put to the test.

The Federal engineers had similar preparations made for our destruction at several points. Their men had gradually closed up to our lines so that at some portions, for a hundred yards or more, the thickness of our parapet was all that separated us. Fighting by hand-grenades was all that was possible at such close quarters. As the Federals had the hand-grenades and we had none, we obtained our supply by using such of theirs as failed to explode, or by catching them as they came over the parapet and hurling them back.

The causes that led to the capitulation ↓ are well known. We had been from the beginning short of ammunition, and continued so throughout in spite of the daring exploits of Lamar Fontaine, Captain Saunders, and Courier Walker, who floated down the river on logs and brought us, respectively, 18,000, 20,000, and 200,000 caps. We were short of provisions, so that our men had been on quarter rations for days before the close of the siege; had eaten mule meat, and rats, and young shoots of cane, with the relish of epicures dining on the finest delicacies of the table. We were so short-handed that no man within the lines had ever been off duty more than a small part of each day; and in response to inquiries of the lieutenant-general commanding, every general officer and colonel had reported his men as physically exhausted and unfit for any duty but simply standing in the trenches and firing. Our lines were badly battered, many of our guns were dismounted, and the Federal forces were within less than a minute of our defenses, so that a single dash could have precipitated them upon us in overwhelming numbers. All of these facts were brought out in the council of war on the night of the 2d of July. After that General Pemberton said he had lost all hopes of being relieved by General Johnston; he had considered every possible plan of relieving ourselves, and to his mind there were but two alternatives — either to surrender while we still had ammunition enough left to give us the right to demand terms, or to sell our lives as dearly as possible in what he knew must be a hopeless effort to cut our way through the Federal lines. He then asked each officer present to give his vote on the question, *surrender or not?* Beginning with

the junior officer present, all voted to surrender but two, — Brigadier-General S. D. Lee and Brigadier-General Baldwin, — and these had no reasons to offer. After all had voted General Pemberton said: "Well, gentlemen, I have heard your votes and I agree with your almost unanimous decision, though my own preference would be to put myself at the head of my troops and make a desperate effort to cut our way through the enemy. That is my only hope of saving myself from shame and disgrace. Far better would it be for me to die at the head of my army, even in a vain effort to force the enemy's lines, than to surrender it and live and meet the obloquy which I know will be heaped upon me. But my duty is to sacrifice myself to save the army which has so nobly done its duty to defend Vicksburg. I therefore concur with you and shall offer to surrender this army on the 4th of July." Some objection was made to the day, but General Pemberton said: "I am a Northern man; I know my people; I know their peculiar weaknesses and their national vanity; I know we can get better terms from them on the 4th of July than any other day of the year. ↓ We must sacrifice our pride to these considerations." And thus the surrender was brought about.

During the negotiations we noticed that General Grant and Admiral Porter were communicating with each other by signals from a tall tower on land and a mast-head on Porter's ship. Our signal-service men had long before worked out the Federal code on the principle of Poe's "Gold Bug," and translated the messages as soon as sent. We knew that General Grant was anxious to take us all as prisoners to the Northern prison-pens. We also knew that Porter said that he did not have sufficient transportation to carry us, and that in his judgment it would be far better to parole us and use the fleet in sending the Federal troops to Port Hudson and other points where they were needed. This helped to make General Pemberton more bold and persistent in his demands, and finally enabled him to obtain virtually the terms of his original proposition.

A few minutes after the Federal soldiers marched in, the soldiers of the two armies were fraternizing and swapping yarns over the incidents of the long siege. One Federal soldier seeing me on my little white pony, which I had ridden every day to and from and along the lines, sang out as he passed: "See here, Mister, — you man on the little white horse! Danged if you ain't the hardest feller to hit I ever saw; I've shot at you more 'n a hundred times!"

General Grant says there was no cheering by the Federal troops. My recollection is that on our right a hearty cheer was given by one Federal division "for the gallant defenders of Vicksburg!"

↓ Being constantly at headquarters I was cognizant of every step in the proceedings. I went with General M. L. Smith to General Grant's headquarters with one of the messages, and was present at the final council of war. — S. H. L.

↓ General Pemberton's report repeats this statement; but General Grant has pointed out [see p. 315] that but for the unexpected delays in the negotiations, begun at 10 A. M. on the 3d of July, the surrender would have taken place on that day instead of on the 4th. — EDITORS.

VICKSBURG FROM THE NORTH — AFTER THE SURRENDER. FROM A SKETCH MADE AT THE TIME.

THE VICKSBURG CAMPAIGN. ⹋

BY ULYSSES S. GRANT, GENERAL, U. S. A.

IT is generally regarded as an axiom in war that all great armies moving in an enemy's country should start from a base of supplies, which should be fortified and guarded, and to which the army is to fall back in case of disaster. The first movement looking to Vicksburg and the force defending it as an objective was begun early in November, 1862, and conformed to this axiom. [See map, p. 442.] It followed the line of the Mississippi Central Railroad, with Columbus, Kentucky, as a base, and soon after it started, a coöperating column was moved down the Mississippi River on transports, with Memphis as its base. Both these movements failing, the entire Army of the Tennessee was transferred to the neighborhood of Vicksburg, and landed on the opposite or western bank of the river at Milliken's Bend. The Mississippi flows through a low alluvial bottom many miles in width, and is very tortuous in its course, running to all points of the compass, sometimes within a few miles. This valley is bounded on the east side by a range of high land rising in some places more than two hundred feet above the bottom. At points the river runs up to the bluffs, washing their base. Vicksburg is built on the first high land on the eastern bank below Memphis, and four hundred miles from that place by the windings of the river.

The winter of 1862–63 was unprecedented for continuous high water in the Mississippi, and months were spent in ineffectual efforts to reach high land above Vicksburg from which we could operate against that stronghold, and in making artificial waterways through which a fleet might pass, avoiding the batteries to the south of the town, in case the other efforts should fail.

In early April, 1863, the waters of the Mississippi having receded sufficiently to make it possible to march an army across the peninsula opposite

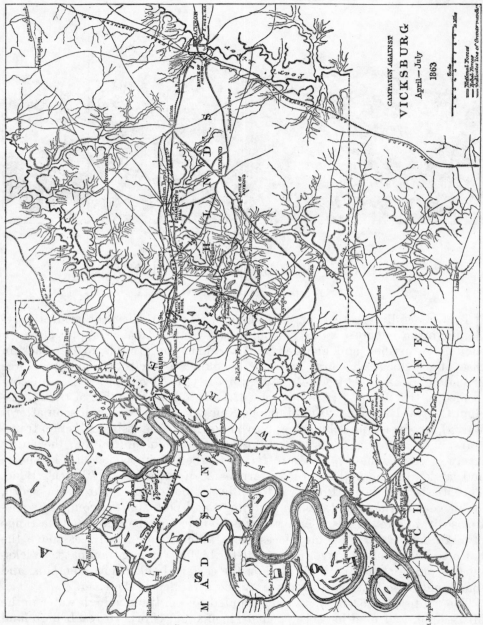

FROM GENERAL BADEAU'S "MILITARY HISTORY OF ULYSSES S. GRANT": D. APPLETON & CO., N. Y.

Vicksburg, I determined to adopt this course, and moved my advance to a point below the town. It was necessary, however, to have transports below, both for the purpose of ferrying troops over the river and to carry supplies. These had necessarily to run the batteries. Under the direction of Admiral Porter this was successfully done. On the 29th, Grand Gulf, the first bluff

FUNERAL ON THE LEVEE AT THE DUCKPORT CANAL, APRIL, 1863. FROM A WAR-TIME SKETCH.

south of Vicksburg on the east side of the river, and about fifty miles below, was unsuccessfully attacked by the navy. The night of the same day the batteries of that place were run by the navy and transports, again under the direction of Admiral Porter, and on the following day the river was crossed by the troops, and a landing effected at Bruinsburg, some nine miles below.

I was now in the enemy's country, with a vast river and the stronghold of Vicksburg between me and my base of supplies. I had with me the Thirteenth Corps, General McClernand commanding, and two brigades of Logan's division of the Seventeenth Corps, General McPherson commanding; in all not more than twenty thousand men to commence the campaign with. These were soon reënforced by the remaining brigade of Logan's division and by Crocker's division of the Seventeenth Corps. On the 7th of May I was further reënforced by Sherman with two divisions of his, the Fifteenth Corps. My total force was then about thirty-three thousand men. The enemy occupied Grand Gulf, Vicksburg, Haynes's Bluff, and Jackson, with a force of nearly sixty thousand men. My first problem was to capture Grand Gulf to use as a base, and then if possible beat the enemy in detail outside the fortifications of Vicksburg. Jackson is fifty miles east of Vicksburg, and was connected with it by a railroad. Haynes's Bluff is eleven miles north, and on the Yazoo River, which empties into the Mississippi some miles above the town.

Bruinsburg is two miles from high ground. The bottom at that point is higher than most of the low land in the valley of the Mississippi, and a good road leads to the bluff. It was natural to expect the garrison from Grand Gulf to come out to meet us, and prevent, if they could, our reaching this

REAR-ADMIRAL PORTER'S FLOTILLA PASSING THE VICKSBURG BATTERIES, NIGHT OF APRIL 16, 1863, THE FLAG-SHIP
"BENTON" LEADING, FOLLOWED BY THE "LOUISVILLE," "LAFAYETTE," "GENERAL PRICE," "MOUND CITY,"
"PITTSBURG," "CARONDELET," AND "TUSCUMBIA"; AND THE TRANSPORTS "HENRY CLAY,"
"FOREST QUEEN," AND "SILVER WAVE." FROM A WAR-TIME SKETCH.

solid base.   Bayou Pierre enters the Mississippi just above Bruinsburg; and
as it is a navigable stream, and was high at the time, in order to intercept us
they had to go by Port Gibson, the nearest point where there was a bridge to
cross upon.   This more than doubled the distance from Grand Gulf to the
high land back of Bruinsburg.   No time was to be lost in securing this foothold.   Our transportation was not sufficient to move all the army across the
river at one trip or even two.   But the landing of the Thirteenth Corps and
one division of the Seventeenth was effected during the day, April 30th, and
early evening.   McClernand was advanced as soon as ammunition and two
days' rations (to last five) could be issued to his men.   The bluffs were reached
an hour before sunset, and McClernand was pushed on, hoping to reach Port
Gibson and save the bridge spanning the Bayou Pierre before the enemy
could get there; for crossing a stream in the presence of an enemy is always
difficult.   Port Gibson, too, is the starting-point of roads to Grand Gulf,
Vicksburg, and Jackson.

McClernand's advance met the enemy about five miles south of Port
Gibson at Thompson's plantation.   There was some firing during the night,
but nothing rising to the dignity of a battle until daylight.   The enemy had
taken a strong natural position with most of the Grand Gulf garrison, numbering about seven or eight thousand men, under General Bowen.   His hope
was to hold me in check until reënforcements under Loring could reach him
from Vicksburg; but Loring did not come in time to render much assistance

south of Port Gibson. Two brigades of McPherson's corps followed McClernand as fast as rations and ammunition could be issued, and were ready
to take position upon the battle-field whenever the Thirteenth Corps could be
got out of the way.

The country in this part of Mississippi stands on edge, as it were, the roads
running along the ridges except when they occasionally pass from one ridge to
another. Where there are no clearings, the sides of the hills are covered
with a very heavy growth of timber, and with undergrowth, and the ravines
are filled with vines and canebrakes, almost impenetrable. This makes it
easy for an inferior force to delay, if not defeat, a far superior one.

Near the point selected by Bowen to defend, the road to Port Gibson divides,
taking two ridges, which do not diverge more than a mile or two at the widest
point. These roads unite just outside the town. This made it necessary for
McClernand to divide his force. It was not only divided, but it was separated
by a deep ravine of the character above described. One flank could not re-
enforce the other except by marching back to the junction of the roads.
McClernand put the divisions of Hovey, Carr, and A. J. Smith upon the right-
hand branch, and Osterhaus on the left. I was on the field by 10 A. M.,
and inspected both flanks in person. On the right the enemy, if not being
pressed back, was at least not repulsing our advance. On the left, however,
Osterhaus was not faring so well. He had been repulsed, with some loss.
As soon as the road could be cleared of McClernand's troops I ordered up
McPherson, who was close upon the rear of the Thirteenth Corps with two
brigades of Logan's division. This was about noon. I ordered him to send
one brigade (General John E. Smith's was selected) to support Osterhaus, and

REAR-ADMIRAL PORTER'S FLOTILLA ARRIVING BELOW VICKSBURG ON THE NIGHT OF APRIL 16, 1863—IN THE
FOREGROUND GENERAL W. T. SHERMAN GOING IN A YAWL TO THE FLAG-SHIP "BENTON."

to move to the left and flank the enemy out of his position. This movement carried the brigade over a deep ravine to a third ridge, and when Smith's troops were seen well through the ravine Osterhaus was directed to renew his front attack. It was successful and unattended by heavy loss. The enemy was sent in full retreat on their right, and their left followed before sunset.

While the movement to our left was going on, McClernand, who was with his right flank, sent me frequent requests for reënforcements, although the force with him was not being pressed. I had been upon the ground, and knew it did not admit of his engaging all the men he had. We followed up our victory until night overtook us, about two miles from Port Gibson; then the troops went into bivouac for the night.

MAJOR-GENERAL WILLIAM W. LORING, C. S. A.
FROM A PHOTOGRAPH.

We started next morning [May 2d] for Port Gibson as soon as it was light enough to see the road. We were soon in the town, and I was delighted to find that the enemy had not stopped to contest our crossing further at the bridge, which he had burned. The troops were set to work at once to construct a bridge across the South Fork of the Bayou Pierre. At this time the water was high, and the current rapid. What might be called a raft-bridge was soon constructed from material obtained from wooden buildings, stables, fences, etc., which sufficed for carrying the whole army over safely. Colonel James H. Wilson, a member of my staff, planned and superintended the construction of this bridge, going into the water and working as hard as any one engaged. Officers and men generally joined in this work. When it was finished the army crossed, and marched eight miles beyond to the North Fork that day. One brigade of Logan's division was sent down the stream to occupy the attention of a rebel battery which had been left behind, with infantry supports, to prevent our repairing the burnt railroad bridge. Two of his brigades were sent up the bayou to find a crossing, and to reach the North Fork to repair the bridge there. The enemy soon left when he found we were building a bridge elsewhere. Before leaving Port Gibson we were reënforced by Crocker's division, McPherson's corps, which had crossed the Mississippi at Bruinsburg and come up without stopping, except to get two days' rations. McPherson still had one division west of the Mississippi River guarding the road from Milliken's Bend to the river below until Sherman's command should relieve it.

When the movement from Bruinsburg commenced we were without a wagon-train. The train, still west of the Mississippi, was carried around, with proper escort, by a circuitous route from Milliken's Bend to Hard Times, seventy or more miles below, and did not get up for some days after the battle of Port Gibson. My own horses, headquarters' transportation, servants, mess-chest, and everything except what I had on, were with this train. General A. J. Smith happened to have an extra horse at Bruinsburg, which I borrowed, with a saddle-tree without upholstering further than stirrups. I had no other for nearly a week.

It was necessary to have transportation for ammunition. Provisions could be taken from the country; but all the ammunition that can be carried on the person is soon exhausted when there is much fighting. I directed therefore, immediately on landing, that all the vehicles and draught animals, whether horses, mules, or oxen, in the vicinity should be collected and loaded to their capacity with ammunition. Quite a train was collected during the 30th, and a motley train it was. In it could be found fine car-riages, loaded nearly to the tops with boxes of cartridges that had been pitched in promiscuously, drawn by mules with plow-harness, straw-collars, rope lines, etc.; long-coupled wagons, with racks for car-rying cotton bales, drawn by oxen, and everything that could be found in the way of transportation on a plantation, either for use or pleas-ure. The making out of provision returns was stopped for the time. No formalities were to retard our progress until a position was se-cured, when time could be spared to observe them.‡

MAJOR-GENERAL J. S. BOWEN, C. S. A.
FROM A PHOTOGRAPH.

During the night of the 2d of May the bridge over the North Fork was repaired, and the troops commenced crossing at 5 the next morning. Be-fore the leading brigade was over, it was fired upon by the enemy from a commanding position; but they were soon driven off. It was evident that the enemy was covering a retreat from Grand Gulf to Vicksburg. Every

‡ "It was at Port Gibson I first heard through a Southern paper of the complete success of Colonel Benjamin H. Grierson, who was making a raid through central Mississippi [from La Grange, Ten-nessee, to Baton Rouge, Louisiana]. He had started from La Grange, April 17th, with three regiments of about 1700 men. On the 21st he had detached Colonel Hatch with one regiment to destroy the railroad between Columbus and Macon and then return to La Grange. Hatch had a sharp fight with the enemy at Columbus and retreated along the railroad, destroying it at Okolona and Tupelo, and arriving in La Grange April 26th. Grierson continued his movement with about 1000 men, breaking the Vicksburg and Meridian railroad and the New Orleans and Jackson railroad, arriving at Baton Rouge May 2d. This raid was of great im-portance, for Grierson had attracted the attention of the enemy from the main movement against Vicks-burg."—From "Personal Memoirs of U. S. Grant."

commanding position from this (Grindstone) crossing to Hankinson's Ferry, over the Big Black, was occupied by the retreating foe to delay our progress. McPherson, however, reached Hankinson's Ferry before night, seized the ferry-boat, and sent a detachment of his command across and several

MAJOR-GENERAL ANDREW J. SMITH. FROM A PHOTOGRAPH.

miles north on the road to Vicksburg. When the junction of the road going to Vicksburg with the road from Grand Gulf to Raymond and Jackson was reached, Logan, with his division, was turned to the left toward Grand Gulf. I went with him a short distance from this junction. McPherson had encountered the largest force yet met since the battle of Port Gibson, and had a skirmish nearly approaching a battle; but the road Logan had taken enabled him to come up on the enemy's right flank, and they soon gave way. McPherson was ordered to hold Hankinson's Ferry, and the road back to Willow Springs, with one division; General McClernand who was now in the rear was to join in this, as well as to guard the line back down the bayou. I did not want to take the chances of having an enemy lurking in our rear.

On the way from the junction to Grand Gulf, where the road comes into the one from Vicksburg to the same place, six or seven miles out, I learned that the last of the enemy had retreated past that place on their way to Vicksburg. I left Logan to make the proper disposition of his troops for the night, while I rode into the town with an escort of about twenty cavalry. Admiral Porter had already arrived with his fleet. The enemy had abandoned his heavy guns and evacuated the place.

When I reached Grand Gulf, May 3d, I had not been with my baggage since the 27th of April, and, consequently, had had no change of underclothing, no meal except such as I could pick up sometimes at other headquarters, and no tent to cover me. The first thing I did was to get a bath, borrow some fresh underclothing from one of the naval officers, and get a good meal on the flag-ship. Then I wrote letters to the general-in-chief informing him of our present position, dispatches to be telegraphed from Cairo, orders to General Sullivan, commanding above Vicksburg, and gave orders to all my corps commanders. About 12 o'clock at night I was through my work, and started for Hankinson's Ferry, arriving there before daylight. While at Grand Gulf I heard from Banks, who was on the Red River,[†] and he said that he could not be at Port Hudson before the 10th of May, and then with only fifteen thousand men. Up to this time my intention had been to secure Grand Gulf as a base of supplies, detach McClernand's corps to Banks, and coöperate with him in the reduction of Port Hudson.

The news from Banks forced upon me a different plan of campaign from the one intended. To wait for his coöperation would have detained me at least a month. The reënforcements would not have reached 10,000 men, after deducting casualties and necessary river-guards, at all high points close to the river, for over 300 miles. The enemy would have strengthened his position and been reënforced by more men than Banks could have brought. I therefore determined to move independently of Banks, cut loose from my base, destroy the rebel force in rear of Vicksburg, and invest or capture the city.

Grand Gulf was accordingly given up as a base, and the authorities at Washington were notified. I knew well that Halleck's caution would lead him to disapprove this course; but it was the only one that gave any chance of success. The time it would take to communicate with Washington and get a reply would be so great that I could not be interfered with until it was demonstrated whether my plan was practicable. Even Sherman, who afterward ignored bases of supplies other than what were afforded by the country while marching through four States of the Confederacy, with an army more than twice as large as mine at this time, wrote me from Hankinson's Ferry, advising me of the impossibility of supplying our army over a single road. He urged me to "stop all troops till your army is partially supplied with wagons, and then act as quick as possible; for this road will be jammed, as sure as life." To this I replied: "I do not calculate upon the possibility of supplying the army with full rations from Grand Gulf. I know it will be impossible without constructing additional roads. What I do expect is to get up what rations of hard bread, coffee, and salt we can, and make the country furnish the balance." We started from Bruinsburg with an average of about two days' rations, and received no more from our own supplies for some days; abundance was found in the meantime. A delay would give the enemy time to reënforce and fortify.

McClernand's and McPherson's commands were kept substantially as they were on the night of the 2d, awaiting supplies to give them three days' rations in haversacks. Beef, mutton, poultry, and forage were found in abundance. Quite a quantity of bacon and molasses was also secured from the country, but bread and coffee could not be secured in quantity sufficient for all the men. Every plantation, however, had a run of stone, propelled by mule-power, to grind corn for the owners and their slaves. All these were kept running while we were stopping day and night, and when we were marching, during the night, at all plantations covered by the troops. But the product was taken by the troops nearest by; so that the majority of the command

---

[†] Banks reached Alexandria on the 7th of May, and was acting in concert with Farragut's and Porter's fleet to control the waters of Red River.— EDITORS.

was destined to go without bread until a new base was established on the Yazoo, above Vicksburg.

While the troops were awaiting the arrival of rations, I ordered reconnoissances made by McClernand and McPherson, with a view of leading the enemy to believe that we intended to cross the Big Black and attack the city at once.

On the 6th Sherman arrived at Grand Gulf, and crossed his command that night and the next day. Three days' rations had been brought up from

Grand Gulf for the advanced troops, and were issued. Orders were given for a forward movement the next day. Sherman was directed to order up Blair, who had been left behind to guard the road from Milliken's Bend to Hard Times with two brigades.

The quartermaster at Young's Point was ordered to send 200 wagons with General Blair, and the commissary was to load them with hard bread, coffee, sugar, salt, and 100,000 pounds of salt meat.

On the 3d Hurlbut, who had been left at Memphis, was ordered to send four regiments from his command to Milliken's Bend to relieve Blair's division, and on

MAJOR-GENERAL RICHARD J. OGLESBY: FROM A PHOTOGRAPH.

the 5th he was ordered to send Lauman's division in addition, the latter to join the army in the field. The four regiments were to be taken from troops near the river, so that there would be no delay.

During the night of the 6th McPherson drew in his troops north of the Big Black and was off at an early hour on the road to Jackson, via Rocky. Springs, Utica, and Raymond. That night he and McClernand were both at Rocky Springs, ten miles from Hankinson's Ferry. McPherson remained there during the 8th, while McClernand moved to Big Sandy and Sherman marched from Grand Gulf to Hankinson's Ferry. The 8th McPherson moved to a point within a few miles of Utica; McClernand and Sherman remained where they were. On the 10th McPherson moved to Utica; Sherman to Big Sandy,—McClernand was still at Big Sandy. The 11th McClernand was at Five Mile Creek; Sherman at Auburn; McPherson five miles advanced from Utica. May 12th McClernand was at Fourteen Mile Creek; Sherman at Fourteen Mile Creek; McPherson at Raymond, after a battle. ⑂

⑂ "After McPherson crossed the Big Black at Hankinson's Ferry, Vicksburg could have been approached and besieged by the south side. It is not probable, however, that Pemberton would have permitted a close besiegement. The broken nature of the ground would have enabled him to hold a strong defensible line from the river south of the city to the Big Black, retaining possession of the

Up to this point our movements had been made without serious opposition. My line was now nearly parallel with the Jackson and Vicksburg Railroad, and about seven miles south of it. The right was at Raymond, eighteen miles from Jackson, McPherson commanding; Sherman in the center on Fourteen Mile Creek, his advance thrown across; McClernand to the left, also on Fourteen Mile Creek, advance across, and his pickets within two miles of Edwards's Station, where the enemy had concentrated a considerable force, and where they undoubtedly expected us to attack. McClernand's left was on the Big Black. In all our moves, up to this time, the left had hugged the Big Black closely, and all the ferries had been guarded to prevent the enemy throwing a force on our rear.

McPherson encountered the enemy, 5000 strong, with 2 batteries, under General Gregg, about 2 miles out of Raymond. This was about 2 P. M. Logan was in advance with one of his brigades. He deployed and moved up to engage the enemy. McPherson ordered the road in rear to be cleared of wagons, and the balance of Logan's division, and Crocker's, which was still farther in rear, to come forward with all dispatch. The order was obeyed with alacrity. Logan got his division in position for assault before Crocker could get up, and attacked with vigor, carrying the enemy's position easily, sending Gregg flying from the field, not to appear against our front again until we met at Jackson.

In this battle McPherson lost 66 killed, 339 wounded, and 37 missing,— nearly or quite all from Logan's division. The enemy's loss was 100 killed, 305 wounded, besides 415 taken prisoners.

I regarded Logan and Crocker as being as competent division commanders as could be found in or out of the army, and both equal to a much higher command. Crocker, however, was dying of consumption when he volunteered. His weak condition never put him on the sick-report when there was a battle in prospect, as long as he could keep on his feet. He died not long after the close of the Rebellion.

When the news reached me of McPherson's victory at Raymond about sundown, my position was with Sherman. I decided at once to turn the whole column toward Jackson and capture that place without delay.⸦

railroad back to that point. It was my plan, therefore, to get to the railroad east of Vicksburg, and approach from that direction. Accordingly McPherson's troops that had crossed the Big Black were withdrawn, and the movement east, to Jackson, commenced.

"As has been stated before, the country is very much broken, and the roads generally confined to the tops of the hills. The troops were moved one (sometimes two) corps at a time, to reach designated points out parallel to the railroad, and only from six to ten miles from it. McClernand's corps was kept with its left flank on the Big Black guarding all the crossings. Fourteen Mile Creek, a stream substantially parallel with the railroad, was reached, and crossings effected by McClernand and Sherman with slight loss. McPherson was to the right of Sherman, extending to Raymond. The cavalry was used in this advance in reconnoitering to find the roads; to cover our advances, and to find the most practicable routes from one command to another, so they could support each other in case of an attack. In making this move I estimated Pemberton's movable force at Vicksburg at about eighteen thousand men, with smaller forces at Haynes's Bluff and Jackson. It would not be possible for Pemberton to attack me with all his troops at one place, and I determined to throw my army between his and fight him in detail. This was done with success, but I found afterward that I had entirely under-estimated Pemberton's strength."—From "Personal Memoirs of U. S. Grant." C. L. Webster & Co.

⸦ "Pemberton was now on my left, with, as I supposed, about 18,000 men; in fact, as I learned afterward, with nearly 50,000. A force was also

Accordingly, all previous orders given during the day for movements on the 13th were annulled by new ones. McPherson was ordered at daylight to move on Clinton, ten miles from Jackson. Sherman was notified of my determination to capture Jackson and work from there westward. He was ordered to start at four in the morning and march to Raymond. McClernand was ordered to march with three divisions by Dillon's to Raymond. One was left to guard the crossing of the Big Black. On the 10th I received a letter from Banks, on the Red River, asking reënforcements. Porter had gone to his assistance, with a part of his fleet, on the 3d, and I now wrote to him describing my position and declining to send any troops. I looked upon side movements, as long as the enemy held Port Hudson and Vicksburg, as a waste of time and material. General Joseph E. Johnston arrived at Jackson in the night of the 13th, from Tennessee, and immediately assumed command of all the Confederate troops in Mississippi. I knew he was expecting reënforcements from the south and east. On the 6th I had written to General Halleck, "Information from the other side leaves me to believe the enemy are bringing forces from Tullahoma."

Up to this time my troops had been kept in supporting distances of each other as far as the nature of the country would admit. Reconnoissances were constantly made from each corps to enable them to acquaint themselves with the most practicable routes from one to another in case a union became necessary.

McPherson reached Clinton with the advance early on the 13th, and immediately set to work destroying the railroad. Sherman's advance reached Raymond before the last of McPherson's command had got out of the town. McClernand withdrew from the front of the enemy, at Edwards's Station, with much skill and without loss, and reached his position for the night in good order. On the night of the 13th McPherson was ordered to march at early dawn upon Jackson, only fifteen miles away. Sherman was given the same order; but he was to move by the direct road from Raymond to Jackson, which is south of the road McPherson was on, and does not approach within two miles of it at the point where it crossed the line of intrenchments which at that time defended the city. McClernand was ordered to move one division of his command to Clinton, one division a few miles beyond Mississippi Springs,— following Sherman's line,— and a third to Raymond. He was also directed to send his siege-guns, four in number, with the troops going by Mississippi Springs. McClernand's position was an advantageous one, in any event. With one division at Clinton, he was in position to reënforce McPherson at Jackson rapidly if it became necessary. The division beyond Mississippi Springs was equally available to reënforce Sherman. The one at

collected on my right at Jackson, the point where all the railroads communicating with Vicksburg connect. All the enemy's supplies of men and stores would come by that point. As I hoped in the end to besiege Vicksburg I must first destroy all possibility of aid. I therefore determined to move swiftly toward Jackson, destroy or drive any force in that direction, and then turn upon Pem-

berton. But by moving against Jackson I uncovered my own communication. So I finally decided to have none — to cut loose altogether from my base and move my whole force eastward. I then had no fears for my communications, and if I moved quickly enough could turn upon Pemberton before he could attack me in the rear."— From "Personal Memoirs of U. S. Grant." C. L. Webster & Co.

Raymond could take either road. He still had two other divisions farther back now that Blair had come up, available within a day at Jackson. If this last command should not be wanted at Jackson, they were already one day's march from there on their way to Vicksburg, and on three different roads leading to the latter city. But the most important consideration in my mind was to have a force confronting Pemberton if he should come out to attack my rear. This I expected him to do; as shown farther on, he was directed by Johnston to make this very move.

I notified General Halleck that I should attack the State capital on the 14th. A courier carried the dispatch to Grand Gulf, through an unprotected country.

Sherman and McPherson communicated with each other during the night, and arranged to reach Jackson at the same hour. It rained in torrents during the night of the 13th and the fore part of the day of the 14th. The roads were intolerable, and in some places on Sherman's line, where the land was low, they were covered more than a foot deep with water. But the troops never murmured. By 9 o'clock Crocker, of McPherson's corps, who was now in advance, came upon the enemy's pickets and speedily drove them in upon the main body. They were outside of the intrenchments, in a strong position, and proved to be the troops that had been driven out of Raymond. Johnston had been reënforced during the night by Georgia and South Carolina regiments, so that his force amounted to eleven thousand men, and he was expecting still more.

Sherman also came upon the rebel pickets some distance out from the town, but speedily drove them in. He was now on the south and south-west of Jackson, confronting the Confederates behind their breastworks; while McPherson's right was nearly two miles north, occupying a line running north and south across the Vicksburg Railroad. Artillery was brought up and reconnoissances made preparatory to an assault. McPherson brought up Logan's division, while he deployed Crocker's for the assault. Sherman made similar dispositions on the right. By 11 A.M. both were ready to attack. Crocker moved his division forward, preceded by a strong skirmish line. These troops at once encountered the enemy's advance and drove it back on the main body, when they returned to their proper regiment, and the whole division charged, routing the enemy completely and driving him into this main line. This stand by the enemy was made more than two miles outside of his main fortifications. McPherson followed up with his command until within range of the guns of the enemy from their intrenchments, when he halted to bring his command into line, and reconnoiter to determine the next move. It was now about noon.

While this was going on, Sherman was confronting a rebel battery which enfiladed the road on which he was marching—the Mississippi Springs road—and commanded a bridge spanning the stream over which he had to pass. By detaching right and left the stream was forced, and the enemy flanked and speedily driven within the main line. This brought our whole line in front of the enemy's line of works, which was continuous on the

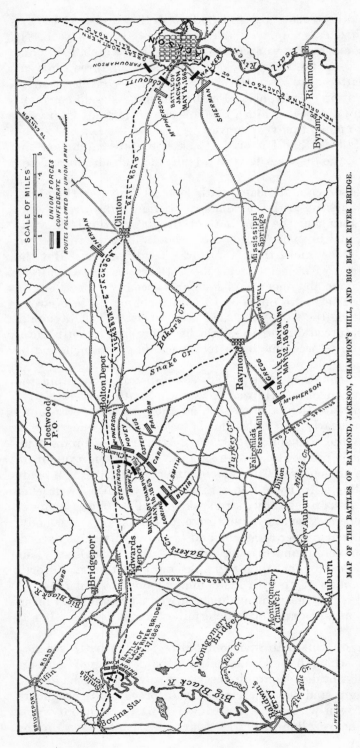

MAP OF THE BATTLES OF RAYMOND, JACKSON, CHAMPION'S HILL, AND BIG BLACK RIVER BRIDGE.

north, west, and south sides, from the Pearl River north of the city to the same river south. I was with Sherman. He was confronted by a sufficient force to hold us back. Appearances did not justify an assault where we were. I had directed Sherman to send a force to the right, and to reconnoiter as far as to the Pearl River. This force — Tuttle's division — not returning, I rode to the right with my staff, and soon found that the enemy had left that part of the line. Tuttle's movement or McPherson's pressure had, no doubt, led Johnston to order a retreat, leaving only the men at the guns to retard us while he was getting away. Tuttle had seen this, and, passing through the lines without resistance, came up in rear of the artillerists confronting Sherman, and captured them, with ten pieces of artillery. I rode immediately to the State House, where I was soon followed by Sherman. About the same time McPherson discovered that the enemy was leaving his front, and advanced Crocker, who was so close upon the enemy that they could not move their guns or destroy them. He captured seven guns, and, moving on, hoisted the National flag over the Confederate capital of Mississippi. Stevenson's brigade was sent to cut off the Confederate retreat, but was too late or not expeditious enough.

Our loss in this engagement was: McPherson, 36 killed, 229 wounded, 3 missing; Sherman, 6 killed, 22 wounded, and 4 missing. The enemy lost 845 killed, wounded, and captured. Seventeen guns fell into our hands, and the enemy destroyed by fire their storehouses, containing a large amount of commissary stores. On this day Blair reached New Auburn and joined McClernand's Fourth Division. He had with him two hundred wagons loaded with rations, the only commissary supplies received during the entire campaign. I slept that night in the room that Johnston had occupied the night before.

About 4 in the afternoon I sent for the corps commanders, and directed the disposition to be made of their troops. Sherman was to remain in Jackson until he destroyed that place as a railroad center and manufacturing city of military supplies. He did the work most effectually. Sherman and I went together into a manufactory which had not ceased work on account of the battle, nor for the entrance of Yankee troops. Our presence did not seem to attract the attention of either the manager, or of the operatives (most of whom were girls). We looked on awhile to see the tent-cloth which they were making roll out of the looms, with C. S. A. woven in each bolt. There was an immense amount of cotton in bales stacked outside. Finally I told Sherman I thought they had done work enough. The operatives were told they might leave and take with them what cloth they could carry. In a few minutes cotton and factory were in a blaze. The proprietor visited Washington, while I was President, to get his pay for this property, claiming that it was private. He asked me to give him a statement of the fact that his property had been destroyed by National troops, so that he might use it with Congress where he was pressing, or proposed to press, his claim. I declined.

On the night of the 13th Johnston sent the following dispatch to Pemberton at Edwards's Station:

"I have lately arrived, and learn that Major-General Sherman is between us with four divisions at Clinton. It is important to establish communication, that you may be reënforced. If practicable, come up in his rear at once. To beat such a detachment would be of immense value. All the troops you can quickly assemble should be brought. Time is all-important."

This dispatch was sent in triplicate by different messengers. One of the messengers happened to be a loyal man, who had been expelled from Memphis some months before, by Hurlbut, for uttering disloyal and threatening sentiments. There was a good deal of parade about this expulsion, ostensibly as a warning to those who entertained the sentiments he expressed; but Hurlbut and the expelled man understood each other. He delivered his copy of Johnston's dispatch to McPherson, who forwarded it to me.

Receiving this dispatch on the 14th, I ordered McPherson to move promptly in the morning back to Bolton, the nearest point where Johnston could reach the road. Bolton is about twenty miles west of Jackson. I also informed McClernand of the capture of Jackson, and sent him the following orders:

"It is evidently the design of the enemy to get north of us and cross the Big Black, and beat us into Vicksburg. We must not allow them to do this. Turn all your forces toward Bolton Station, and make all dispatch in getting there. Move troops by the most direct road from wherever they may be on the receipt of this order."

And to Blair I wrote:

"Their design is evidently to cross the Big Black and pass down the peninsula between the Big Black and Yazoo rivers. We must beat them. Turn your troops immediately to Bolton; take all the trains with you. Smith's division, and any other troops now with you, will go to the same place. If practicable, take parallel roads, so as to divide your troops and train."

Johnston stopped on the Canton road, only six miles north of Jackson, the night of the 14th. He sent from there to Pemberton dispatches announcing the loss of Jackson, and the following dispatch [given here in part.—EDITORS]:

"Can he [Grant] supply himself from the Mississippi? Can you not cut him off from it, and above all, should he be compelled to fall back for want of supplies, beat him? As soon as the reënforcements are all up, they must be united to the rest of the army. I am anxious to see a force assembled that may be able to inflict a heavy blow upon the enemy."

The concentration of my troops was easy, considering the character of the country. McPherson moved along the road parallel with and near the railroad. Of McClernand's command one division (Hovey's) was on the road McPherson had to take, but with a start of four miles; one (Osterhaus's) was at Raymond, on a converging road that intersected the other near Champion's Hill; one (Carr's) had to pass over the same road with Osterhaus's, but, being back at Mississippi Springs, would not be detained thereby; the fourth (Smith's, with Blair's division) was near Auburn, with a different road to pass over. McClernand faced about and moved promptly. His cavalry from Raymond seized Bolton by half-past 9 in the morning, driving out the enemy's pickets and capturing several men.

The night of the 15th Hovey was at Bolton; Carr and Osterhaus were about three miles south, but abreast, facing west; Smith was north of Raymond, with Blair in his rear.

McPherson's command, with Logan in front, had marched at 7 o'clock, and by 4 reached Hovey and went into camp. Crocker bivouacked just in Hovey's rear on the Clinton road. Sherman, with two divisions, was in Jackson, completing the destruction of roads, bridges, and military factories. I rode in person out to Clinton. On my arrival I ordered McClernand to move early in the morning on Edwards's Station, cautioning him to watch for the enemy, and not to bring on an engagement unless he felt very certain of success.

I naturally expected that Pemberton would endeavor to obey the orders of his superior, which I have shown were to attack us at Clinton. This, indeed, I knew he could not do, but I felt sure he would make the attempt to reach that point. It turned out, however, that he had decided his superior's plans were impracticable, and consequently determined to move south from Edwards's Station, and get between me and my base. I, however, had no base, having abandoned it more than a week before. On the 15th Pemberton had actually marched south from Edwards's Station; but the rains had swollen Baker's Creek, which he had to cross, so much that he could not ford it, and the bridges were washed away. This brought him back to the Jackson road, on which there was a good bridge over Baker's Creek. Some of his troops were marching until midnight to get there. Receiving here early on the 16th a repetition of his order to join Johnston at Clinton, he concluded to obey, and sent a dispatch to his chief, informing him of the route by which he might be expected.

About 5 o'clock in the morning (16th) two men who had been employed on the Jackson and Vicksburg Railroad were brought to me. They reported that they had passed through Pemberton's army in the night, and that it was still marching east. They reported him to have 80 regiments of infantry and 10 batteries; in all about 25,000 men.

I had expected to leave Sherman at Jackson another day in order to complete his work. But, getting the above information, I sent him orders to move with all dispatch to Bolton, and to put one division, with an ammunition train, on the road at once, with directions to its commander to march with all possible speed until he came up to our rear. Within an hour after receiving this order, Steele's division was on the road. At the same time I dispatched to Blair, who was near Auburn, to move with all speed to Edwards's Station. McClernand was directed to embrace Blair in his command for the present. Blair's division was a part of the Fifteenth Army Corps (Sherman's); but as it was on its way to join its corps, it naturally struck our left first, now that we had faced about and were moving west. The Fifteenth Corps, when it got up, would be on our extreme right. McPherson was directed to get his trains out of the way of the troops, and to follow Hovey's division as closely as possible. McClernand had two roads, about three miles apart, converging at Edwards's Station, over which to march his troops. Hovey's division of his corps had the advance on a third road (the Clinton) still farther north. McClernand was directed to move Blair's and A. J. Smith's divisions by the southernmost of these roads, and Osterhaus and Carr by the middle road. Orders were to move cautiously, with skirmishers in the front to feel for the enemy. Smith's division, on the most southern road, was the first to encounter the enemy's pickets, who were speedily driven in. Osterhaus, on the middle road, hearing the firing, pushed his skirmishers forward, found the enemy's pickets, and forced them back to the main line. About the same time Hovey encountered the enemy on the northern or direct wagon road from Jackson to Vicksburg. McPherson was hastening up to join Hovey, but was embarrassed by Hovey's trains occupying the roads. I was still back at Clinton. McPherson sent me word of the situation and expressed the wish that I was up. By 7:30 I was on the road and proceeded rapidly to the front, ordering all trains that were in front of troops off the road. When I arrived Hovey's skirmishing amounted almost to a battle.

McClernand was in person on the middle road, and had a shorter distance to march to reach the enemy's position than McPherson. I sent him word by a staff-officer to push forward and attack. These orders were repeated several times without apparently expediting McClernand's advance.

Champion's Hill, where Pemberton had chosen his position to receive us, whether taken by accident or design, was well selected. It is one of the highest points in that section, and commanded all the ground in range. On the east side of the ridge, which is quite precipitous, is a ravine, running first north, then westerly, terminating at Baker's Creek. It was grown up thickly with large trees and undergrowth, making it difficult to penetrate with troops, even when not defended. The ridge occupied by the enemy terminated abruptly where the ravine turns westerly. The left of the enemy occupied the north end of this ridge. The Bolton and Edwards's Station road turns almost due south at this point, and ascends the ridge, which it follows for about a mile, then, turning west, descends by a gentle declivity to Baker's Creek, nearly a mile away. On the west side the slope of the ridge is gradual, and is cultivated from near the summit to the creek. There was, when we were there, a narrow belt of timber near the summit, west of the road.

From Raymond there is a direct road to Edwards's Station, some three miles west of Champion's Hill. There is one also to Bolton. From this latter road there is still another, leaving it about three and a half miles before reaching Bolton, and leading direct to the same station. It was along these two roads that three divisions of McClernand's corps, and Blair, of Sherman's, temporarily under McClernand, were moving. Hovey, of McClernand's command, was with McPherson, farther north on the road from Bolton, direct to Edwards's Station. The middle road comes into the northern road at the point where the latter turns to the west, and descends to Baker's Creek; the southern road is still several miles south and does not intersect the others until it reaches Edwards's Station. Pemberton's lines covered all these roads and faced east. Hovey's line, when it first drove in the enemy's pickets, was formed parallel to that of the enemy, and confronted his left.

By eleven o'clock the skirmishing had grown into a hard-contested battle. Hovey alone, before other troops could be got to assist him, had captured a battery of the enemy. But he was not able to hold his position, and had to abandon the artillery. McPherson brought up his troops as fast as possible — Logan in front — and posted them on the right of Hovey and across the flank of the enemy. Logan reënforced Hovey with one brigade from his division; with his other two he moved farther west to make room for Crocker, who was coming up as rapidly as the roads would admit. Hovey was still being heavily pressed, and was calling on me for more reënforcements. I ordered Crocker, who was now coming up, to send one brigade from his division. McPherson ordered two batteries to be stationed where they nearly enfiladed the enemy's line, and they did good execution.

From Logan's position now a direct forward movement would carry him over open fields in rear of the enemy and in a line parallel with them. He did make exactly this move, attacking, however, the enemy through the belt of woods covering the west slope of the hill for a short distance. Up to this time I had kept my position near Hovey, where we were the most heavily pressed; but about noon I moved with a part of my staff by our right, around, until I came up with Logan himself. I found him near the road leading down to Baker's Creek. He was actually in command of the only road over which the enemy could retreat; Hovey, reënforced by two brigades from McPherson's command, confronted the enemy's left; Crocker, with two brigades, covered their left flank; McClernand, two hours before, had been within two and a half miles of their center with two divisions, and two divisions — Blair's and A. J. Smith's — were confronting the rebel right; Ransom, with a brigade of McArthur's division, of the Seventeenth Corps (McPherson's), had crossed the river at Grand Gulf a few days before and was coming up on their right flank. Neither Logan nor I knew that we had cut off the retreat of the enemy. Just at this juncture a messenger came from Hovey, asking for more reënforcements. There were none to spare. I then gave an order to move McPherson's command by the left flank around to Hovey. This uncovered the Confederate line of retreat, which was soon taken advantage of by the enemy. ☆

During all this time Hovey, reënforced as he was by a brigade from Logan and another from Crocker, and by Crocker gallantly coming up with two other brigades on his right, had made several assaults, the last one about the time the road was opened to the rear. The enemy fled precipitately. This was between 3 and 4 o'clock. I rode forward, or rather back, to where the middle road intersects the north road, and found the skirmishers of Carr's division just coming in. Osterhaus was farther south, and soon after came up with skirmishers advanced in like manner. Hovey's division, and McPherson's two divisions with him, had marched and fought from early dawn, and were not in the best condition to follow the retreating foe. I sent orders to Osterhaus to pursue the enemy, and to Carr, whom I saw personally, I explained the situation, and directed him to pursue vigorously as far as the Big Black, and to cross it if he could, Osterhaus to follow him. The pursuit was continued until after dark.

The battle of Champion's Hill lasted about four hours of hard fighting, preceded by two or three hours of skirmishes, some of which rose almost to the dignity of battle. Every man of Hovey's division and of McPherson's two divisions was engaged during the battle. No other part of my command was engaged at all, except that (as described before). Osterhaus's and A. J. Smith's had encountered the rebel advanced pickets as early as 7:30. Their

---

☆ Dr. William M. Beach of London, Ohio, sends to the editors this anecdote of General Grant:

"At the time of the Vicksburg campaign I was the Assistant Surgeon of the 78th Ohio Regiment; but I had been detailed by J. H. Boucher, Medical Director of the 17th Army Corps, as the Division Hospital Director of Logan's division. I had a regular service of men and wagons; and at the battle of Champion's Hill — when my division had been assigned to its position — I chose an abandoned farm-house and its surroundings as a proper place to establish our hospital, and immediately proceeded in its preparation. My position was in the rear of our left wing, and not far in the rear of Hovey's right wing. About the time I was fairly ready to receive the wounded the line had advanced across an open field, and had swung to the right and front nearly a quarter of a mile. The steady roar of battle had rolled from Hovey's front by this time to that of Logan's, who was steadily advancing, and where the sound of the conflict was now simply *terrific*. Grant and his staff, coming from the left, dismounted at the front gate, within twenty feet of where I was standing. He had scarcely dismounted, when, — more clearly and distinctly hearing the fury of the contest on our right, — leisurely taking his cigar from his mouth, he turned slowly to one of his staff and said, ' *Go down to Logan and tell him he is making history to-day*.' " EDITORS.

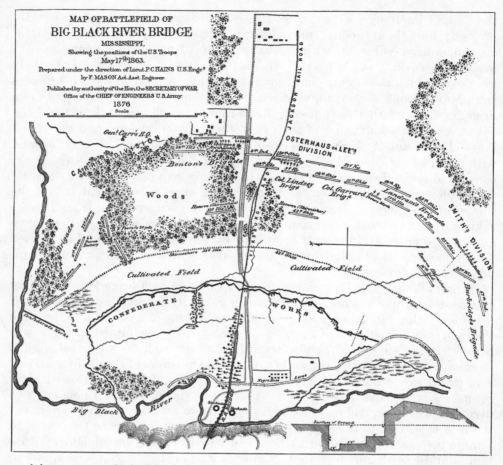

MAP OF BATTLEFIELD OF
BIG BLACK RIVER BRIDGE
MISSISSIPPI,
Showing the positions of the U.S. Troops
May 17th 1863.
Prepared under the direction of Lieut. P.C.HAINS U.S.Engr.
by F. MASON Act.Asst. Engineer.
Published by authority of the Hon.the SECRETARY OF WAR
Office of the CHIEF OF ENGINEERS U.S.Army.
1876
Scale

positions were admirable for advancing upon the enemy's line. McClernand, with two divisions, was within a few miles of the battle-field long before noon, and in easy hearing. I sent him repeated orders by staff-officers fully competent to explain to him the situation. These traversed the road separating us, without escort, and directed him to push forward, but he did not come.⌡ Instead of this he sent orders to Hovey, who belonged to his corps, to join on to his right flank. Hovey was bearing the brunt of the battle at the time. To obey the order he would have had to pull out from the front of the enemy and march back as far as McClernand had to advance to get into battle, and substantially over the same ground. Of course, I did not permit Hovey to obey the order of his intermediate superior.

We had in this battle about fifteen thousand men actually engaged. This excludes those that did not get up — all of McClernand's command except Hovey. Our loss was 410 killed, 1844 wounded, and 187 missing.

⌡ "It is true, in front of McClernand there was a small force of the enemy, and posted in a good position behind a ravine, obstructing his advance; but if he had moved to the right by the road my staff-officers had followed, the enemy must either have fallen back or been cut off."— From "Personal Memoirs of U. S. Grant." C. L. Webster & Co.

Hovey alone lost twelve hundred killed, wounded, and missing,—one-third of his division.

Had McClernand come up with reasonable promptness, or had I known the ground as I did afterward, I cannot see how Pemberton could have escaped with any organized force. As it was he lost over 3000 killed and wounded, and about 3000 captured in battle and in pursuit. Loring's division, which was the right of Pemberton's line, was cut off from the retreating army, and never got back into Vicksburg. Pemberton himself fell back that night to the Big Black River. His troops did not stop before midnight, and many of them left before the general retreat commenced, and no doubt a good part of them returned to their homes. Logan alone captured 1300 prisoners and 11 guns. Hovey captured 300, under fire, and about 700 in all, exclusive of 500 sick and wounded, whom he paroled, thus making 1200.

McPherson joined in the advance as soon as his men could fill their cartridge-boxes, leaving one brigade to guard our wounded. The pursuit was continued as long as it was light enough to see the road. The night of the 16th of May found McPherson's command bivouacked from two to six miles west of the battle-field, along the line of the road to Vicksburg. Carr and Osterhaus were at Edwards's Station, and Blair was about three miles southeast. Hovey remained on the field where his troops had fought so bravely and bled so freely. Much war material abandoned by the enemy was picked up on the battle-field, among it thirty pieces of artillery. I pushed through the advancing column· with my staff, and kept in advance until after night. Finding ourselves alone we stopped and took possession of a vacant house. As no troops came up we moved back a mile or more, until we met the head of the column just going into bivouac on the road. We had no tents, so we occupied the porch of a house which had been taken for a rebel hospital, and which was filled with wounded and dying who had been brought from the battle-field we had just left.

While a battle is raging one can see his enemy mowed down by the thousand and the ten thousand, with great composure. But after the battle these scenes are distressing, and one is naturally disposed to do as much to alleviate the suffering of an enemy as of a friend.

We were now assured of our position between Johnston and Pemberton, without the possibility of a junction of their forces. Pemberton might indeed have made a night march to the Big Black, crossed the bridge there, and, by moving north on the west side, have eluded us, and finally returned to Johnston. But this would have given us Vicksburg. It would have been his proper move, however, and the one Johnston would have made had he been in Pemberton's place. In fact, it would have been in conformity with Johnston's orders to Pemberton.

Sherman left Jackson with the last of his troops about noon on the 16th, and reached Bolton, twenty miles west, before halting. His rear-guard did not get in until 2 A. M. the 17th, but renewed their march by daylight. He paroled his prisoners at Jackson, and was forced to leave his own wounded,— in care of surgeons and attendants however. At Bolton he was informed of

GENERAL BLAIR'S DIVISION CROSSING BIG BLACK RIVER.   FROM A WATER-COLOR.

our victory.   He was directed to commence the march early next day, and to diverge from the road he was on, to Bridgeport, on the Big Black River, some eleven miles above where we expected to find the enemy.   Blair was ordered to join him there with the pontoon train as early as possible.

This movement brought Sherman's corps together, and at a point where I hoped a crossing of the Big Black might be effected, and Sherman's corps used to flank the enemy out of his position in our front, and thus open a crossing for the remainder of the army.   I informed him that I would endeavor to hold the enemy in my front while he crossed the river.

The advanced division, Carr's (McClernand's corps), resumed the pursuit at 3:30 A. M. on the 17th, followed closely by Osterhaus; McPherson bringing up the rear with his corps.   As I expected, the enemy was found in position on the Big Black.   The point was only six miles from that where my advance had rested for the night, and was reached at an early hour.   Here the river makes a turn to the west, and has washed close up to the high land.   The east side is a low bottom, sometimes overflowed at very high water, but was cleared and in cultivation.   A bayou runs irregularly across this low land, the bottom of which, however, is above the surface of the Big Black at ordinary stages.   When the river is full, water runs through it, converting the point of land into an island.   The bayou was grown up with timber, which the enemy had felled into the ditch.   All this time there was a foot or two of water in it.   The rebels had constructed a parapet along the inner bank of this bayou, by using cotton bales from the plantation close by and throwing dirt over them.   The whole was thoroughly commanded from the height west of the river. At the upper end of the bayou there was a strip of uncleared land, which afforded a cover for a portion of our men. Carr's division was deployed on our right, Lawler's brigade forming his extreme right, and reaching through these woods to the river above. Osterhaus's division was deployed to the left of Carr, and covered the enemy's entire front. McPherson was in column on the road, the head close by, ready to come in whenever he could be of assistance.

While the troops were standing as here described, an officer from Banks's staff ⚓ came up and presented me with a letter from General Halleck, dated the 11th of May. It had been sent by the way of New Orleans to Banks to forward to me. It ordered me to return to Grand Gulf, and to coöperate from there with Banks, against Port Hudson, and then to return with our combined forces to besiege Vicksburg. I told the officer that the order came too late, and that Halleck would not give it then if he knew our position. The bearer of the dispatch insisted that I ought to obey the order, and was giving arguments to support his position, when I heard great cheering to the right of our line, and, looking in that direction, saw Lawler, in his shirt-sleeves, leading a charge upon the enemy. I immediately mounted my horse and rode in the direction of the charge, and saw no more of the officer who delivered the dispatch, I think not even to this day.

The assault was successful. But little resistance was made. The enemy fled from the west bank of the river, burning the bridge behind them, leaving the men and guns on the east side to fall into our hands. Many tried to escape by swimming the river. Some succeeded and some were drowned in the attempt. Eighteen guns were captured, and 1751 prisoners. Our loss was 39 killed, 237 wounded, and 3 missing. The enemy probably lost but few men except those captured and drowned. But for the successful and complete destruction of the bridge, I have but little doubt that we should have followed the enemy so closely as to prevent his occupying his defenses around Vicksburg.

As the bridge was destroyed and the river was high, new bridges had to be built. It was but little after 9 o'clock A. M. when the capture took place. As soon as work could be commenced, orders were given for the construction of three bridges. One was taken charge of by Lieutenant Peter C. Hains, of the Engineer Corps, one by General McPherson himself, and one by General Ransom, a most gallant and intelligent volunteer officer. My recollection is that Hains built a raft-bridge; McPherson a pontoon, using cotton bales in large numbers for pontoons; and that Ransom felled trees on opposite banks of the river, cutting only on one side of the tree, so that they would fall with their tops interlacing in the river, without the trees being entirely severed from their stumps. A bridge was then made with these trees to support the roadway. Lumber was taken from buildings, cotton-gins, and wherever found, for this purpose. By 8 o'clock on the morning of the 18th all three bridges were complete and the troops were crossing.

Sherman reached Bridgeport about noon of the 17th, and found Blair with

⚓ Brigadier-General William Dwight, afterward of Banks's staff. According to Banks, Dwight reported that Grant said "he would give me 5000 men, but that I should not wait for them."— EDITORS.

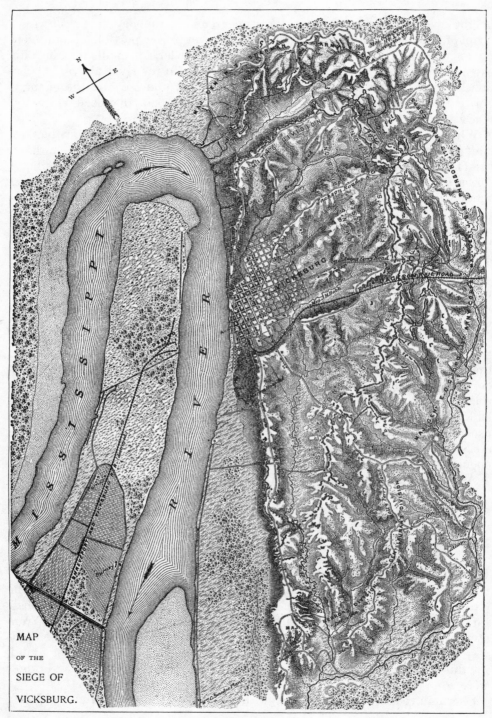

MAP

OF THE

SIEGE OF

VICKSBURG.

FROM GENERAL BADEAU'S "MILITARY HISTORY OF ULYSSES S. GRANT."   D. APPLETON & CO., N. Y.

the pontoon train already there. A few of the enemy were intrenched on the west bank, but they made little resistance, and soon surrendered. Two divisions were crossed that night, and the third the following morning.

On the 18th I moved along the Vicksburg road in advance of the troops, and as soon as possible joined Sherman. My first anxiety was to secure a base of supplies on the Yazoo River above Vicksburg. Sherman's line of march led him to the very point on Walnut Hills occupied by the enemy the December before, when he was repulsed. Sherman was equally anxious with myself. Our impatience led us to move in advance of the column, and well up with the advanced skirmishers. There were some detached works along the crest of the hill. These were still occupied by the enemy, or else the garrison from Haynes's Bluff had not all got past on their way to Vicksburg. At all events, the bullets of the enemy whistled by thick and fast for a short time. In a few minutes Sherman had the pleasure of looking down from the spot coveted so much by him the December before,—on the ground where his command lay so helpless for offensive action [Chickasaw Bayou]. He turned to me, saying that up to this minute he had felt no positive assurance of success. This, however, he said, was the end of one of the greatest campaigns in history, and I ought to make a report of it at once. Vicksburg was not yet captured, and there was no telling what might happen before it was taken; but whether captured or not, this was a complete and successful campaign. I do not claim to quote Sherman's language, but the substance only. My reason for mentioning this incident will appear farther on.

McPherson, after crossing the Big Black, came into the Jackson and Vicksburg road which Sherman was on, but to his rear. He arrived at night near the lines of the enemy, and went into camp. McClernand moved by the direct road near the railroad to Mount Albans, and then turned to the left, and put his troops on the road from Baldwin's Ferry to Vicksburg. This brought him south of McPherson. I now had my three corps up to the works built for the defense of Vicksburg on three roads,—one to the north, one to the east, and one to the south-east of the city. By the morning of May 19th the investment was as complete as my limited number of troops would allow. Sherman was on the right and covered the high ground from where it over-looked the Yazoo as far south-east as his troops would extend. McPherson joined on to his left, and occupied ground on both sides of the Jackson road. McClernand took up the ground to his left, and extended as far toward War-renton as he could, keeping a continuous line.

On the 19th there was constant skirmishing with the enemy while we were getting into better position. The enemy had been much demoralized by his defeats at Champion's Hill and the Big Black, and I believed would not make much effort to hold Vicksburg. Accordingly at 2 o'clock I ordered an assault. It resulted in securing more advanced positions for all our troops, where they were fully covered from the fire of the enemy.

The 20th and 21st were spent in strengthening our position, and·in making roads in rear of the army, from Yazoo River, or Chickasaw Bayou. Most of the army had now been for three weeks with only five days' rations issued by the commissary. They had an abundance of food, however, but began to feel the want of bread. I remember, that in passing around to the left of the line on the 21st, a soldier, recognizing me, said in rather a low voice, but yet so that I heard him, "*Hard-tack*." In a moment the cry was taken up all along the line, "*Hard-tack! Hard-tack!*" I told the men nearest to me that we had been engaged ever since the arrival of the troops in building a road over which to supply them with everything they needed. The cry was instantly changed to cheers. By the night of the 21st all the troops had full rations issued to them. The bread and coffee were highly appreciated.

I now determined on a second assault. Johnston was in my rear, only fifty miles away, with an army not much inferior in numbers to the one I had with me, and I knew he was being reënforced. There was danger of his coming to the assistance of Pemberton, and, after all, he might defeat my anticipations of capturing the garrison, if, indeed, he might not prevent the capture of the city. The immediate capture of Vicksburg would save sending me the re-enforcements, which were so much wanted elsewhere, and would set free the army under me to drive Johnston from the State. But the first consideration of all was: the troops believed they could carry the works in their front, and would not have worked so patiently in the trenches if they had not been allowed to try.

The attack was ordered to commence on all parts of the line at 10 o'clock A. M. on the 22d with a furious cannonading from every battery in position. All the corps commanders set their time by mine, so that all might open the engagement at the same minute. The attack was gallant, and portions of each of the three corps succeeded in getting up to the very parapets of the enemy, and in planting their battle-flags upon them; but at no place were we able to enter. General McClernand reported that he had gained the enemy's intrenchments at several points, and wanted reënforcements. I occupied a position from which I believed I could see as well as he what took place in his front, and I did not see the success he reported. But his request for re-enforcements being repeated, I could not ignore it, and sent him Quinby's division of the Seventeenth Corps. Sherman and McPherson were both ordered to renew their assaults as a diversion in favor of McClernand. This last attack only served to increase our casualties, without giving any benefit whatever. As soon as it was dark, our troops that had reached the enemy's line and had been obliged to remain there for security all day, were withdrawn, and thus ended the last assault on Vicksburg.

I now determined upon a regular siege,— to "out-camp the enemy," as it were, and to incur no more losses. The experience of the 22d convinced officers and men that this was best, and they went to work on the defenses and approaches with a will. With the navy holding the river the investment of Vicksburg was complete. As long as we could hold our position, the enemy was limited in supplies of food, men, and munitions of war, to what they had on hand. These could not last always.

The crossing of troops at Bruinsburg commenced April 30th. On the 18th of May the army was in rear of Vicksburg. On the 19th, just twenty days after the crossing, the city was completely invested and an assault had been made: five distinct battles—besides continuous skirmishing—had been fought and won by the Union forces; the capital of the State had fallen, and its arsenals, military manufactories, and everything useful for military purposes had been destroyed; an average of about 180 miles had been marched by the troops engaged; but 5 days' rations had been issued, and no forage; over 6000 prisoners had been captured, and as many more of the enemy had been killed or wounded; 27 heavy cannon and 61 field-pieces had fallen into our hands; 250 miles of the river, from Vicksburg to Port Hudson, had become ours. The Union force that had crossed the Mississippi River up to this time was less than 43,000 men. One division of these—Blair's—only arrived in time to take part in the battle of Champion's Hill, but was not engaged there; and one brigade—Ransom's—of McPherson's corps reached the field after the battle. The enemy had at Vicksburg, Grand Gulf, Jackson, and on the roads between these places, over sixty thousand men. They were in their own country, where no rear-guards were necessary. The country is admirable for defense, but difficult to conduct an offensive campaign in. All their troops had to be met. We were fortunate, to say the least, in meeting them in detail: at Port Gibson, 7000 or 8000; at Raymond, 5000; at Jackson, from 8000 to 11,000; at Champion's Hill, 25,000; at the Big Black, 4000. A part of those met at Jackson were all that were left of those encountered at Raymond. They were beaten in detail by a force smaller than their own, upon their own ground. Our loss up to this time was:

	Killed.	Wounded.	Missing.
Port Gibson	131	719	25
South Fork, Bayou Pierre		1	
Skirmishes, May 3d	1	9	
Fourteen Mile Creek	6	24	
Raymond	66	339	37
Jackson	42	251	7
Champion's Hill	410	1844	187
Big Black	39	237	3
Bridgeport		1	
Total .... [In all, 4379]	695	3425	259

Of the wounded many were but slightly so, and continued on duty. Not half of them were disabled for any length of time. ✚

After the unsuccessful assault on the 22d, the work of the regular siege began. Sherman occupied the right, starting from the river above Vicksburg; McPherson the center (McArthur's division now with him); and McClernand the left, holding the road south to Warrenton. Lauman's division arrived at this time and was placed on the extreme left of the line.

In the interval between the assaults of the 19th and 22d, roads had been completed from the Yazoo River and Chickasaw Bayou, around the rear of the army, to enable us to bring up supplies of food and ammunition; ground

✚ The revised statements (unpublished "Official Records," Vol. XXIV., part I., p. 167) show that the aggregate Union losses, including the above, from May 1st to July 4th, were: killed, 1514; wounded, 7395; captured or missing, 453,—total, 9362.—EDITORS.

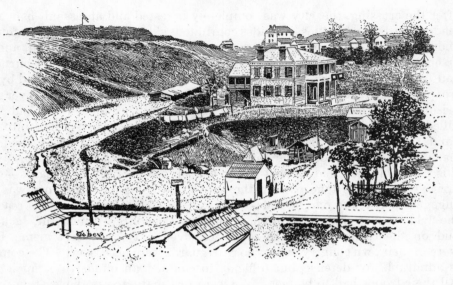

HEADQUARTERS OF THE UNION SIGNAL CORPS, VICKSBURG. FROM A WAR-TIME PHOTOGRAPH.

had been selected and cleared, on which the troops were to be encamped, and tents and cooking utensils were brought up. The troops had been without these from the time of crossing the Mississippi up to this time. All was now ready for the pick and spade. With the two brigades brought up by McArthur, which reached us in rear of Vicksburg, and Lauman's division brought from Memphis, and which had just arrived, we had now about forty thousand men for the siege. Prentiss and Hurlbut were ordered to send forward every man that could be spared. Cavalry especially was wanted to watch the fords along the Big Black, and to observe Johnston. I knew that Johnston was receiving reënforcements from Bragg, who was confronting Rosecrans in Tennessee. Vicksburg was so important to the enemy that I believed he would make the most strenuous efforts to raise the siege, even at the risk of losing ground elsewhere.

My line was more than fifteen miles long, extending from Haynes's Bluff to Vicksburg, thence south to Warrenton. The line of the enemy was about seven. In addition to this, having an enemy at Canton and Jackson, in our rear, who was being constantly reënforced, we required a second line of defense facing the other way. I had not troops enough under my command to man these. But General Halleck appreciated the situation, and, without being asked, forwarded reënforcements with all possible dispatch.

The ground about Vicksburg is admirable for defense. On the north it is about two hundred feet above the Mississippi River at the highest point, and very much cut up by the washing rains; the ravines were grown up with cane and underbrush, while the sides and tops were covered with a dense forest. Farther south the ground flattens out somewhat, and was in cultivation. But here, too, it was cut by ravines and small streams. The enemy's line of defense followed the crest of a ridge, from the river north of the city, eastward, then southerly around to the Jackson road, full three miles back of the city; thence in a south-westerly direction to the river. Deep ravines of the description given lay in front of these defenses.

As there is a succession of gullies, cut out by rains, along the side of the ridge, the line was necessarily very irregular. To follow each of these spurs with intrenchments, so as to command the slopes on either side, would have lengthened their line very much. Generally, therefore, or in many places, their line would run from near the head of one gully nearly straight to the head of another, and an outer work, triangular in shape, generally open in the rear, was thrown up on the point; with a few men in this outer work they commanded the approaches to the main line completely.

The work to be done to make our position as strong against the enemy as his was against us, was very great. The problem was also complicated by our wanting our line as near that of the enemy as possible. We had but four engineer officers with us. Captain F. E. Prime, of the Engineer Corps, was the chief, and the work at the beginning was mainly directed by him. His health soon gave out, when he was succeeded by Captain Cyrus B. Comstock, also of the Engineer Corps. To provide assistants on such a long line, I directed that all officers who had been graduated at West Point, where they had necessarily to study military engineering, should, in addition to their other duties, assist in the work.

The chief quartermaster and the chief commissary were graduates. The chief commissary, now the commissary-general of the army [General Robert Macfeely], begged off, however, saying that there was nothing in engineering that he was good for, unless he would do for a sap-roller. As soldiers require rations while working in the ditches as well as when marching and fighting, and we would be sure to lose him if he was used as a sap-roller, I let him off. The general is a large man,—weighs two hundred and twenty pounds, and is not tall.

We had no siege-guns except six 32-pounders, and there were none in the West to draw from. Admiral Porter, however, supplied us with a battery of navy-guns, of large caliber, and with these, and the field-artillery used in the campaign, the siege began. The first thing to do was to get the artillery in batteries, where they would occupy commanding positions; then establish the camps, under cover from the fire of the enemy, but as near up as possible; and then construct rifle-pits and covered ways, to connect the entire command by the shortest route. The enemy did not harass us much while we were constructing our batteries. Probably their artillery ammunition was short; and their infantry was kept down by our sharp-shooters, who were always on the alert and ready to fire at a head whenever it showed itself above the rebel works.

In no place were our lines more than six hundred yards from the enemy. It was necessary, therefore, to cover our men by something more than the ordinary parapet. To give additional protection sand-bags, bullet-proof, were placed along the tops of the parapets, far enough apart to make loop-holes for musketry. On top of these, logs were put. By these means the men were enabled to walk about erect when off duty, without fear of annoyance from sharp-shooters. The enemy used in their defense explosive musket-balls, thinking, no doubt, that, bursting over the men in the trenches, they would do some execution; but I do not remember a single case where a man was injured by a piece of one of the shells. When they were hit, and the ball exploded, the wound was terrible. In these cases a solid ball would have hit as well. Their use is barbarous, because they produce increased suffering without any corresponding advantage to those using them. [See p. 491.]

The enemy could not resort to the method we did to protect their men, because we had an inexhaustible supply of ammunition to draw upon, and used it freely. Splinters from the timber would have made havoc among the men behind.

WOODEN COEHORN ON GRANT'S LINES. FROM A SKETCH MADE AT THE TIME.

There were no mortars with the besiegers, except what the navy had in front of the city; but wooden ones were made by taking logs of the toughest wood that could be found, boring them out for six or twelve pounder shells, and binding them with strong iron bands. These answered as coehorns, and shells were successfully thrown from them into the trenches of the enemy.

The labor of building the batteries and intrenching was largely done by the pioneers, assisted by negroes who came within our lines and who were paid for their work, but details from the troops had often to be made. The work was pushed forward as rapidly as possible, and when an advanced position was secured and covered from the fire of the enemy, the batteries were advanced. By the 30th of June there were 220 guns in position, mostly light field-pieces, besides a battery of heavy guns belonging to, manned, and commanded by the navy. We were now as strong for defense against the garrison of Vicksburg as they were against us. But I knew that Johnston was in our rear, and was receiving constant reënforcements from the east. He had at this time a larger force than I had prior to the battle of Champion's Hill.

As soon as the news of the arrival of the Union army behind Vicksburg reached the North, floods of visitors began to pour in. Some came to gratify curiosity; some to see sons or brothers who had passed through the terrible ordeal; members of the Christian and Sanitary Commissions came to minister to the wants of the sick and the wounded. Often those coming to see a son or brother would bring a dozen or two of poultry. They did not know how little the gift would be appreciated; many soldiers had lived so much on chickens, ducks, and turkeys, without bread, during the march, that the sight of poultry, if they could get bacon, almost took away their appetite. But the intention was good.

Among the earliest arrivals was the Governor of Illinois [Yates], with most of the State officers. I naturally wanted to show them what there was of most interest. In Sherman's front the ground was the most broken and most

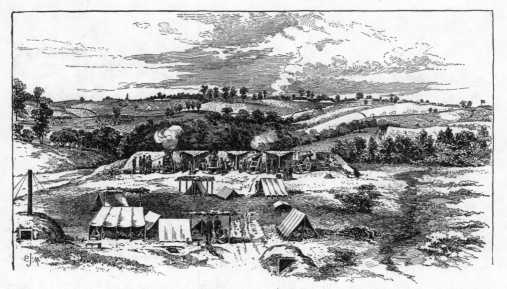

POSITION OF HOVEY'S DIVISION OF McCLERNAND'S CORPS.   FROM A LITHOGRAPH.

In the foreground is the siege-battery; below is the wooded ravine; from left to right are seen the camps of the 34th Indiana, 29th Wisconsin, 11th Indiana, 46th Indiana, and 25th Indiana; half-way to the summit are the rifle-pits of Hovey's division, confronting Confederate works and forts on the farthest ridge, which was a part of the Confederate line held by General C. L. Stevenson.

wooded, and more was to be seen without exposure. I therefore took them to Sherman's headquarters and presented them. Before starting out to look at the lines—possibly while Sherman's horse was being saddled—there were many questions asked about the late campaign, about which the North had been so imperfectly informed. There was a little knot about Sherman and around me, and I heard Sherman repeating in the most animated manner what he had said to me, when we first looked down from Walnut Hills upon the land below, on the 18th of May, adding: "Grant is entitled to every bit of the credit for the campaign; I opposed it. I wrote him a letter about it." But for this speech it is not likely that Sherman's opposition would have ever been heard of. His untiring energy and great efficiency during the campaign entitled him to a full share of all the credit due for its success. He could not have done more if the plan had been his own.

On the 26th of May I sent Blair's division up the Yazoo to drive out a force of the enemy supposed to be between the Big Black and the Yazoo. The country was rich, and full of supplies of both fruit and forage. Blair was instructed to take all of it. The cattle were to be driven in for the use of our army, and the food and forage to be consumed by our troops or destroyed by fire; all bridges were to be destroyed, and the roads rendered as nearly impassable as possible. Blair went forty-five miles, and was gone almost a week. His work was effectually done. I requested Porter at this time to send the Marine brigade — a floating nondescript force which had been assigned to his command, and which proved very useful — up to Haynes's Bluff to hold it until reënforcements could be sent.

POSITION OF QUINBY'S DIVISION OF McCLERNAND'S CORPS. FROM A LITHOGRAPH.

On the ridge in the background are Confederate forts connected by breastworks, and on the right is pictured the blowing up, June 25th, of the Confederate works on the Jackson road, in front of General Logan's division. The Union rifle-pits are at the farther edge of the ravine, in which the troops were protected. On the left is Battery Archer, 2 siege-guns; center, 12th Wisconsin Battery; right, 6th Wisconsin Battery. The trees in front of the explosion mark the scene of the conference between Grant and Pemberton.

On the 26th I also received a letter from Banks, asking me to reënforce him with ten thousand men at Port Hudson. ⟆ Of course I could not comply with his request, nor did I think he needed them. He was in no danger of an attack by the garrison in his front, and there was no army organizing in his rear to raise the siege. On the 3d of June a brigade from Hurlbut's command arrived, General Nathan Kimball commanding. ⟆ It was sent to Mechanicsburg, some miles north-east of Haynes's Bluff, and about midway between the Big Black and the Yazoo. A brigade of Blair's division and twelve hundred cavalry had already, on Blair's return from up the Yazoo, been sent to the same place—with instructions to watch the crossings of the Big Black River, to destroy the roads in his (Blair's) front, and to gather or destroy all supplies.

On the 7th of June our little force of colored and white troops across the Mississippi, at Milliken's Bend, were attacked by about three thousand men from Richard Taylor's Trans-Mississippi command. With the aid of the gun-boats these were speedily repelled. I sent Mower's brigade over with instructions to drive the enemy beyond the Tensas bayou; and we had no further

⟆ On May 25th General Grant wrote to General Banks that it seemed to him advisable to collect as large a force at Vicksburg as possible, and says, "I would be pleased, General, to have you come, with such force as you are able to spare." In the same letter General Grant makes this statement:

"When I commenced writing this, it was my intention to propose sending you, if you will furnish transportation, 8000 or 10,000 men to coöperate with you on Port Hudson; but, whilst writing, a courier came in from my cavalry, stating that a force of the enemy are now about thirty miles north-east of here. . . . At present, therefore, I do not deem it prudent to send off any men I have, or even safe, . . ."

On May 23d, 1863, General Halleck wrote to General Banks:

"I assure you that the Government is exceedingly disappointed that you and General Grant are not acting in conjunction. It thought to secure that object by authorizing you to assume the entire command as soon as you and General Grant could unite."

In Halleck's instructions, dated November 9th, 1862, General Banks was authorized "to assume control of any military forces from the Upper Mississippi which may come within your command. . . . You will exercise superior authority as far as you may ascend the river. . . ."—EDITORS.

⟆ General Kimball was wounded at Fredericksburg, and on recovering was assigned to the command of a division in the West.—EDITORS.

POSITION OF LOGAN'S DIVISION OF McPHERSON'S CORPS.   FROM A LITHOGRAPH.

In the middle-ground is seen the main line of works, which on the right ascends the hill to the White House at the end of the curtain of trees. On the ridge to the left of the White House is the Union sap leading to the exploding mine under the Confederate fort near the Jackson road.   Between the Union and Confederate lines, a little to the left of the center, are the trees that mark the conference between Grant and Pemberton.

trouble in that quarter during the siege.   This was the first important engagement of the war in which colored troops were under fire. ☆ These were very raw, having all been enlisted since the beginning of the siege, but they behaved well.

On the 8th of June a full division arrived from Hurlbut's command, under General Sooy Smith. It was sent immediately to Haynes's Bluff, and General C. C. Washburn was assigned to the general command at that point.

On the 11th a strong division arrived from the Department of the Missouri under General Herron, which was placed on our left. This cut off the last possible chance of communication between Pemberton and Johnston, as it enabled Lauman to close up on McClernand's left, while Herron intrenched from Lauman to the water's edge. At this point the water recedes a few hundred yards from the high land. Through this opening, no doubt, the Confederate commanders had been able to get messengers under cover of night.

On the 14th General Parke arrived with two divisions of Burnside's corps,⌡ and was immediately dispatched to Haynes's Bluff. These latter troops — Herron's and Parke's — were the reënforcements already spoken of, sent by Halleck in anticipation of their being needed. They arrived none too soon.

I now had about seventy-one thousand men. More than half were disposed of across the peninsula, between the Yazoo, at Haynes's Bluff, and the

☆ Colored troops had been under fire on the 27th of May at Port Hudson.— EDITORS.

⌡ These troops came from the Department of the Ohio (Burnside), June 14th to 17th, having been transferred from the Army of the Potomac in the previous March.   After Vicksburg they returned to Burnside's command and took part in the East Tennessee campaign.— EDITORS.

Big Black, with the division of Osterhaus watching the crossings of the latter river farther south and west, from the crossing of the Jackson road to Baldwin's Ferry, and below.

There were eight roads leading into Vicksburg, along which and the immediate sides of which our work was specially pushed and batteries advanced; but no commanding point within range of the enemy was neglected.

On the 17th I received a letter from General Sherman and on the 18th one from McPherson, saying that their respective commands had complained to them of a fulsome congratulatory order published by General McClernand to the Thirteenth Corps, which did great injustice to the other troops engaged in the campaign.

This order had been sent north and published, and now papers containing it had reached our camps. The order had not been heard of by me, and certainly not by troops outside of McClernand's command, until brought in this way. I at once wrote McClernand, directing him to send me a copy of this order. He did so, and I at once relieved him from the command of the Thirteenth Army Corps, and ordered him back to Springfield, Illinois. The publication of his order in the press was in violation of War Department orders and also of mine.

On the 22d of June positive information was received that Johnston had crossed the Big Black River for the purpose of attacking our rear, to raise the siege and release Pemberton. The correspondence between Johnston and Pemberton shows that all expectation of holding Vicksburg had by this time passed from Johnston's mind. I immediately ordered Sherman to the command of all the forces from Haynes's Bluff to the Big Black River. This amounted now to quite half the troops about Vicksburg. Besides these, Herron's and A. J. Smith's divisions were ordered to hold themselves in readiness to reënforce Sherman. Haynes's Bluff had been strongly fortified on the land side, and on all commanding points from there to the Big Black, at the railroad crossing, batteries had been constructed. The work of connecting by rifle-pits, where this was not already done, was an easy task for the troops that were to defend them.

We were now looking west, besieging Pemberton, while we were also looking east to defend ourselves against an expected siege by Johnston. But as against the garrison of Vicksburg we were as substantially protected as they were against us. When we were looking east and north we were strongly fortified, and on the defensive. Johnston evidently took in the situation and wisely, I think, abstained from making an assault on us, because it would simply have inflicted loss on both sides without accomplishing any result.

We were strong enough to have taken the offensive against him; but I did not feel disposed to take any risk of loosing our hold upon Pemberton's army, while I would have rejoiced at the opportunity of defending ourselves against an attack by Johnston.

From the 23d of May the work of fortifying and pushing forward our position nearer to the enemy had been steadily progressing. At three points on the Jackson road in front of Ransom's brigade a sap was run up to the

THE FIGHT IN THE CRATER AFTER THE EXPLOSION OF THE UNION MINE UNDER THE CONFEDERATE FORT
ON THE JACKSON ROAD, JUNE 25, 1863.   FROM A LITHOGRAPH.

To the right and left are seen part of the approaches from the main Union line at the White
House, as shown in the plan on p. 540.

enemy's parapet, and by the 25th of June we had it undermined and the
mine charged.   The enemy had countermined, but did not succeed in reaching our mine.   At this particular point the hill on which the rebel work stands
rises abruptly.   Our sap ran close up to the outside of the enemy's parapet.
In fact, this parapet was also our protection.   The soldiers of the two sides
occasionally conversed pleasantly across this barrier; sometimes they exchanged the hard bread of the Union soldiers for the tobacco of the Confederates; at other times the enemy threw over hand-grenades, and often our
men, catching them in their hands, returned them.

Our mine had been started some distance back down the hill, consequently
when it had extended as far as the parapet it was many feet below it.   This
caused the failure of the enemy in his search to find and destroy it.   On
the 25th of June, at 3 o'clock, all being ready, the mine was exploded.   A
heavy artillery fire all along the line had been ordered to open with the
explosion.   The effect was to blow the top of the hill off and make a crater
where it stood.   The breach was not sufficient to enable us to pass a column
of attack through.   In fact, the enemy, having failed to reach our mine, had
thrown up a line farther back, where most of the men guarding that point
were placed.   There were a few men, however, left at the advance line, and
others working in the counter-mine, which was still being pushed to find ours.
All that were there were thrown into the air, some of them coming down on
our side, still alive.   I remember one colored man, who had been under ground
at work, when the explosion took place, who was thrown to our side.   He was

not much hurt, but was terribly frightened. Some one asked him how high he had gone up. "Dunno, Massa, but t'ink 'bout t'ree mile," was the reply. General Logan commanded at this point, and took this colored man to his quarters, where he did service to the end of the siege.

As soon as the explosion took place the crater was seized upon by two regiments of our troops who were near by, under cover, where they had been placed for the express purpose. The enemy made a desperate effort to expel them, but failed, and soon retired behind the new line. From here, however, they threw hand-grenades, which did some execution. The compliment was returned by our men, but not with so much effect. The enemy could lay their grenades on the parapet, which alone divided the contestants, and then roll them down upon us; while from our side they had to be thrown over the parapet, which was at considerable elevation. During the night we made efforts to secure our position in the crater against the missiles of the enemy, so as to run trenches along the outer base of their parapet, right and left; but the enemy continued throwing their grenades, and brought boxes of field ammunition (shells) the fuses of which they would light with port-fires, and throw them by hand into our ranks. We found it impossible to continue this work. Another mine was consequently started, which was exploded on the 1st of July, destroying an entire rebel redan, killing and wounding a considerable number of its occupants, and leaving an immense chasm where it stood. No attempt to charge was made this time, the experience of the 25th admonishing us. Our loss in the first affair was about thirty killed and wounded. The enemy must have lost more in the two explosions than we did in the first. We lost none in the second.

From this time forward the work of mining and of pushing our position nearer to the enemy was prosecuted with vigor, and I determined to explode no more mines until we were ready to explode a number at different points and assault immediately after. We were up now at three different points, one in front of each corps, to where only the parapet of the enemy divided us.

At this time an intercepted dispatch from Johnston to Pemberton informed me that Johnston intended to make a determined attack upon us, in order to relieve the garrison of Vicksburg. I knew the garrison would make no forcible effort to relieve itself. The picket lines were so close to each other — where there was space enough between the lines to post pickets — that the men could converse. On the 21st of June I was informed, through this means, that Pemberton was preparing to escape, by crossing to the Louisiana side under cover of night; that he had employed workmen in making boats for that purpose; that the men had been canvassed to ascertain if they would make an assault on the "Yankees" to cut their way out; that they had refused, and almost mutinied, because their commander would not surrender and relieve their sufferings, and had only been pacified by the assurance that boats enough would be finished in a week to carry them all over. The rebel pickets also said that houses in the city had been pulled down to get material to build these boats with. Afterward this story was

IN THE SAPS BETWEEN THE WHITE HOUSE AND
THE VICKSBURG CRATER, JULY 2, 1863. FROM
A SKETCH MADE AT THE TIME.

verified.   On entering the city we found a large number of very rudely constructed boats.

All necessary steps were at once taken to render such an attempt abortive.
Our pickets were doubled; Admiral Porter was notified so that the river
might be more closely watched; material was collected on the west bank of
the river to be set on fire and light up the river if the attempt was made;
and batteries were established along the levee crossing the peninsula on
the Louisiana side.   Had the attempt been made, the garrison of Vicksburg would have been drowned or made prisoners on the Louisiana side.
General Richard Taylor was expected on the west bank to coöperate in this
movement, I believe, but he did not come, nor could he have done so with a
force sufficient to be of service.   The Mississippi was now in our possession
from its source to its mouth, except in the immediate front of Vicksburg
and Port Hudson.   We had nearly exhausted the country, along a line drawn
from Lake Providence to opposite Bruinsburg.   The roads west were not of
a character to draw supplies over for any considerable force.

By the 1st of July our approaches had reached the enemy's ditch at a number of places.   At ten points we could move under cover to within from five
to 100 yards of the enemy.   Orders were given to make all preparations for
assault on the 6th of July.   The debouches were ordered widened, to afford
easy egress, while the approaches were also to be widened to admit the troops
to pass through four abreast.   Plank and sand-bags, the latter filled with cotton packed in tightly, were ordered prepared, to enable the troops to cross
the ditches.

On the night of the 1st of July Johnston was between Brownsville and the
Big Black, and wrote Pemberton from there that about the 7th of the month
an attempt would be made to create a diversion to enable him to cut his way
out.   Pemberton was a prisoner before this message reached him.

On July 1st Pemberton, seeing no hope of outside relief, addressed the following letter to each of his four division commanders :

" Unless the siege of Vicksburg is raised, or supplies are thrown in, it will become necessary very shortly to evacuate the place. I see no prospect of the former, and there are many great, if not insuperable, obstacles in the way of the latter. You are, therefore, requested to inform me with as little delay as possible as to the condition of your troops, and their ability to make the marches and undergo the fatigues necessary to accomplish a successful evacuation."

Two of his generals suggested surrender, and the other two practically did the same ; they expressed the opinion that an attempt to evacuate would fail. Pemberton had previously got a message to Johnston suggesting that he should try to negotiate with me for a release of the garrison with their arms. Johnston replied that it would be a confession of weakness for him to do so ; but he authorized Pemberton to use his name in making such an arrangement.

On the 3d, about 10 o'clock A. M., white flags appeared on a portion of the rebel works. Hostilities along that part of the line ceased at once. Soon two persons were seen coming toward our lines bearing a white flag. They proved to be General Bowen, a division commander, and Colonel Montgomery, aide-de-camp to Pemberton, bearing the following letter to me :

" I have the honor to propose an armistice for ——— hours, with the view to arranging terms for the capitulation of Vicksburg. To this end, if agreeable to you, I will appoint three commissioners, to meet a like number to be named by yourself, at such place and hour to-day as you may find convenient. I make this proposition to save the further effusion of blood, which must otherwise be shed to a frightful extent, feeling myself fully able to maintain my position for a yet indefinite period. This communication will be handed you, under a flag of truce, by Major-General John S. Bowen."

It was a glorious sight to officers and soldiers on the line where these white flags were visible, and the news soon spread to all parts of the command. The troops felt that their long and weary marches, hard fighting, ceaseless watching by night and day in a hot climate, exposure to all sorts of weather, to diseases, and, worst of all, to the gibes of many Northern papers that came to them, saying all their suffering was in vain, Vicksburg would never be taken, were at last at an end, and the Union sure to be saved.

Bowen was received by General A. J. Smith, and asked to see me. I had been a neighbor of Bowen's in Missouri, and knew him well and favorably before the war ; but his request was refused. He then suggested that I should meet Pemberton. To this I sent a verbal message saying that if Pemberton desired it I would meet him in front of McPherson's corps, at 3 o'clock that afternoon. I also sent the following written reply to Pemberton's letter :

" Your note of this date is just received, proposing an armistice for several hours, for the purpose of arranging terms of capitulation through commissioners to be appointed, etc. The useless effusion of blood you propose stopping by this course can be ended at any time you may choose, by the unconditional surrender of the city and garrison. Men who have shown so much endurance and courage as those now in Vicksburg will always challenge the respect of an adversary, and I can assure you will be treated with all the respect due to prisoners of war. I do not favor the proposition of appointing commissioners to arrange the terms of capitulation, because I have no terms other than those indicated above."

At 3 o'clock Pemberton appeared at the point suggested in my verbal message, accompanied by the same officers who had borne his letter of the morning. Generals Ord, McPherson, Logan, A. J. Smith, and several officers of my staff accompanied me. Our place of meeting was on a hill-side within a few hundred feet of the rebel lines. Near by stood a stunted oak-tree, which was made historical by the event. It was but a short time before the last vestige of its body, root, and limb had disappeared, the fragments being taken as trophies. Since then the same tree has furnished as many cords of wood, in the shape of trophies, as "The True Cross."

Pemberton and I had served in the same division during a part of the Mexican war. I knew him very well, therefore, and greeted him as an old acquaintance. He soon asked what terms I proposed to give his army if it surrendered. My answer was the same as proposed in my reply to his letter. Pemberton then said, rather snappishly, "The conference might as well end," and turned abruptly as if to leave. I said, "Very well." General Bowen, I saw, was very anxious that the surrender should be consummated. His manners and remarks while Pemberton and I were talking showed this. He now proposed that he and one of our generals should have a conference. I had no objection to this, as nothing could be made binding upon me that they might propose. Smith and Bowen accordingly had a conference, during which Pemberton and I, moving some distance away toward the enemy's lines, were in conversation. After a while Bowen suggested that the Confederate army should be allowed to march out, with the honors of war, carrying their small-arms and field-artillery. This was promptly and unceremoniously rejected. The interview here ended, I agreeing, however, to send a letter giving final terms by 10 o'clock that night. I had sent word to Admiral Porter soon after the correspondence with Pemberton had commenced, so that hostilities might be stopped on

FIRST CONFERENCE BETWEEN GRANT AND PEMBERTON, JULY 3, 1863.
FROM A SKETCH MADE AT THE TIME.

Grant and Pemberton met near the tree and went aside to the earth-work, where they sat in conference. To their right is a group of four, including General John S. Bowen, C. S. A., General A. J. Smith, General James B. McPherson, and Colonel L. M. Montgomery. Under the tree are Chief-of-Staff John A. Rawlins, Assistant Secretary of War Charles A. Dana, and Theodore R. Davis, special artist, who made the above and many other sketches of the Vicksburg siege, in this work.— EDITORS.

GENERAL GRANT.   MASTER FRED. D. GRANT.   CHARLES A. DANA,
                                                 ASSISTANT SECRETARY OF WAR.

UNION HEADQUARTERS, JULY 3. GENERAL GRANT RECEIVING GENERAL PEMBERTON'S MESSAGE.
FROM A SKETCH MADE AT THE TIME.

In his "Personal Memoirs" (C. L. Webster & Co.) General Grant says: "On leaving Bruinsburg for the front I left my son Frederick, who had joined me a few weeks before, on board one of the gun-boats asleep, and hoped to get away without him until after Grand Gulf should fall into our hands; but on waking up he learned that I had gone, and being guided by the sound of the battle raging at Thompson's Hill—called the battle of Port Gibson—found his way to where I was. He had no horse to ride at the time, and I had no facilities for even preparing a meal. He therefore foraged around the best he could until we reached Grand Gulf. Mr. C. A. Dana, then an officer of the War Department, accompanied me on the Vicksburg campaign and through a portion of the siege. He was in the same situation as Fred so far as transportation and mess arrangements were concerned. The first time I call to mind seeing either of them, after the battle, they were mounted on two enormous horses, grown white from age, equipped with dilapidated saddles and bridles. Our trains arrived a few days later, after which we were all perfectly equipped. My son accompanied me throughout the campaign and siege, and caused no anxiety either to me or to his mother, who was at home. He looked out for himself and was in every battle of the campaign. His age, then not quite thirteen, enabled him to take in all he saw, and to retain a recollection of it that would not be possible in more mature years."

the part of both army and navy. It was agreed on my parting with Pemberton that they should not be renewed until our correspondence should cease.

When I returned to my headquarters I sent for all the corps and division commanders with the army immediately confronting Vicksburg. (Half the army was from eight to twelve miles off, waiting for Johnston.) I informed them of the contents of Pemberton's letters, of my reply, and the substance of the interview, and was ready to hear any suggestion; but would hold the power of deciding entirely in my own hands. This was the nearest to a "council of war" I ever held. Against the general and almost unanimous judgment of the council I sent the following letter:

"In conformity with agreement of this afternoon I will submit the following proposition for the surrender of the city of Vicksburg, public stores, etc. On your accepting the terms proposed I will march in one division as a guard, and take possession at 8 A. M. to-morrow. As soon as rolls can be made out and paroles be signed by officers and men, you will be allowed to march out of our lines, the officers taking with them their side-arms and clothing; and the field, staff, and cavalry officers one horse each. The rank and file will be allowed all their clothing, but no other property. If these conditions are accepted, any amount of rations you may deem necessary can be taken from the stores you now have, and also the necessary cooking-utensils for preparing them. Thirty wagons also, counting two-horse or mule teams as one, will be allowed to transport such articles as cannot be carried along. The same conditions will be allowed to all sick and wounded officers and soldiers as fast as they become able to travel. The paroles for these latter must be signed, however, whilst officers present are authorized to sign the roll of prisoners."

By the terms of the cartel then in force, prisoners captured by either army were required to be forwarded, as soon as possible, to either Aiken's Landing below Dutch Gap, on the James River, or to Vicksburg, there to be exchanged, or paroled until they could be exchanged. There was a Confederate Commissioner at Vicksburg, authorized to make the exchange. I did not propose to take him prisoner, but to leave him free to perform the functions of his office. Had I insisted upon an unconditional surrender, there would have been over thirty-odd thousand men to transport to Cairo, very much to the inconvenience of the army on the Mississippi; thence the prisoners would have had to be transported by rail to Washington or Baltimore; thence again by steamer to Aiken's—all at very great expense. At Aiken's they would have to be paroled, because the Confederates did not have Union prisoners to give in exchange. Then again Pemberton's army was largely composed of men whose homes were in the south-west; I knew many of them were tired of the war and would get home just as soon as they could. A large number of them had voluntarily come into our lines during the siege and requested to be sent north where they could get employment until the war was over and they could go to their homes.

Late at night I received the following reply to my last letter:

" I have the honor to acknowledge the receipt of your communication of this date, proposing terms of capitulation for this garrison and post. In the main, your terms are accepted; but, in justice both to the honor and spirit of my troops manifested in the defense of Vicksburg, I have to submit the following amendments, which, if acceded to by you, will perfect the agreement between us. At 10 o'clock A. M. to-morrow I propose to evacuate the works in and around Vicksburg, and to surrender the city and garrison under my command, by marching out with my colors and arms, stacking them in front of my present lines, after which you will take possession. Officers to retain their side-arms and personal property, and the rights and property of citizens to be respected."

This was received after midnight; my reply was as follows:

" I have the honor to acknowledge the receipt of your communication of 3d July. The amendment proposed by you cannot be acceded to in full. It will be necessary to furnish every officer and man with a parole signed by himself, which, with the completion of the roll of prisoners, will necessarily take some time. Again, I can make no stipulations with regard to the treatment of citizens and their private property. While I do not propose to cause them any undue annoyance or loss, I cannot consent to leave myself under any restraint by stipulations. The property which officers will be allowed to take with them will be as stated in my proposition of last evening; that is, officers will be allowed their private baggage and side-arms, and mounted officers one horse each. If you mean by your proposition for each brigade to march to the front of the lines now occupied by it, and stack arms at 10 o'clock A. M., and then return to the inside and there remain as prisoners until properly paroled, I will make no objection to it. Should no notification be received of your acceptance of my terms by 9 o'clock A. M.,

I shall regard them as having been rejected, and shall act accordingly. Should these terms be accepted, white flags should be displayed along your lines to prevent such of my troops as may not have been notified from firing upon your men."

Pemberton promptly accepted these terms.

During the siege there had been a good deal of friendly sparring between the soldiers of the two armies, on picket and where the lines were close together. All rebels were known as "Johnnies"; all Union troops as "Yanks." Often "Johnny" would call, "Well, Yank, when are you coming into town?" The reply was sometimes: "We propose to celebrate the 4th of July there." Sometimes it would be: "We always treat our prisoners with kindness and do not want to hurt them"; or, "We are holding you as prisoners of war while you are feeding yourselves." The garrison, from the commanding general down, undoubtedly expected an assault on the 4th. They knew from the temper of their men it would be successful when made, and that would be a greater humiliation than to surrender. Besides it would be attended with severe loss to them.

The Vicksburg paper, which we received regularly through the courtesy of the rebel pickets, said prior to the 4th, in speaking of the "Yankee" boast that they would take dinner in Vicksburg that day, that the best receipt for cooking rabbit was, "First ketch your rabbit." The paper at this time, and for some time previous, was printed on the plain side of wall paper. The last was issued on the 4th and announced that we had "caught our rabbit."

I have no doubt that Pemberton commenced his correspondence on the 3d for the twofold purpose; first, to avoid an assault, which he knew would be successful, and second, to prevent the capture taking place on the great national holiday,—the anniversary of the Declaration of American Independence. Holding out for better terms, as he did, he defeated his aim in the latter particular.

At the 4th, at the appointed hour, the garrison of Vicksburg marched out of their works, and formed line in front, stacked arms, and marched back in good order. Our whole army present witnessed this scene without cheering.

Logan's division, which had approached nearest the rebel works, was the first to march in, and the flag of one of the regiments of his division was soon floating over the court-house. Our soldiers were no sooner inside the lines than the two armies began to fraternize. Our men had had full rations from the time the siege commenced to the close. The enemy had been suffering, particularly toward the last. I myself saw our men taking bread from their haversacks and giving it to the enemy they had so recently been engaged in *starving out.* It was accepted with avidity and with thanks.

Pemberton says in his report: "If it should be asked why the 4th of July was selected as the day for surrender, the answer is obvious. I believed that upon that day I should obtain better terms. Well aware of the vanity of our foe, I knew they would attach vast importance to the entrance, on the 4th of July, into the stronghold of the great river, and that, to gratify their national vanity, they would yield then what could not be extorted from them at any other time." This does not support my view of his reasons for selecting the day he did for surrendering. But it must be recollected that his first letter asking terms was received about 10 o'clock, A. M., July 3d. It then could hardly be expected that it would take 24 hours to effect a surrender. He knew that Johnston was in our rear for the purpose of raising the siege, and he naturally would want to hold out as long as he could. He knew his men would not resist an assault, and one was expected on the 4th. In our interview he told me he had rations enough to hold out some time—my recollection is two weeks. It was this statement that induced me to insert in the terms that he was to draw rations for his men from his own supplies.

On the 3d, as soon as negotiations were commenced, I notified Sherman, and directed him to be ready to take the offensive against Johnston, drive him out of the State, and destroy his army if he could. Steele and Ord were directed at the same time to be in readiness to join Sherman as soon as the surrender took place. Of this Sherman was notified.

I rode into Vicksburg with the troops, and went to the river to exchange congratulations with the navy upon our joint victory. At that time I found that many of the citizens had been living under-ground. The ridges upon which Vicksburg is built, and those back to the Big Black, are composed of a deep yellow clay, of great tenacity. Where roads and streets are cut through, perpendicular banks are left, and stand as well as if composed of stone. The magazines of the enemy were made by running passage-ways into this clay at places where there were deep cuts. Many citizens secured places of safety for their families by carving out rooms in these embankments. A door-way in these cases would be cut in a high bank, starting from the level of the road or street, and after running in a few feet a room of the size required was carved out of the clay, the dirt being removed by the door-way. In some instances I saw where two rooms were cut out, for a single family, with a door-way in the clay wall separating them. Some of these were carpeted and furnished with considerable elaboration. In these the occupants were fully secure from the shells of the navy, which were dropped into the city, night and day, without intermission. [See "Naval Operations," p. 551.]

I returned to my old headquarters outside in the afternoon, and did not move them into the town until the 6th. On the afternoon of the 4th I sent Captain William M. Dunn, of my staff, to Cairo, the nearest point where the telegraph could be reached, with a dispatch to the general-in-chief. It was as follows:

" The enemy surrendered this morning. The only terms allowed is their parole as prisoners of war. This I regard as a great advantage to us at this moment. It saves, probably, several days in the capture, and leaves troops and transports ready for immediate service. Sherman, with a large force, moves immediately on Johnston, to drive him from the State. I will send troops to the relief of Banks, and return the Ninth Army Corps to Burnside."

At the same time I wrote to General Banks informing him of the fall, and sending him a copy of the terms, also saying I would send him all the troops he wanted to insure the capture of the only foothold the enemy now had on the Mississippi River. General Banks had a number of copies of this letter printed, or at least a synopsis of it, and very soon a copy fell into the hands of General Gardner, who was then in command of Port Hudson. Gardner at once sent a letter to the commander of the National forces, saying that he had been informed of the surrender of Vicksburg and telling how the information reached him. He added that if this was true it was useless for him to hold out longer. General Banks gave him assurances that Vicksburg had been surrendered, and General Gardner surrendered unconditionally on the 9th of July.) Port Hudson, with nearly 6000 prisoners, 51 guns, and 5000 small-arms and other stores, fell into the hands of the Union forces. From that day on, the river remained under National control.

Pemberton and his army were kept in Vicksburg until the whole could be paroled. The paroles were in duplicate, by organization (one copy for each, National and Confederate), signed by the commanding officers of the companies or regiments. Duplicates were also made for each soldier, and signed by each individually, one to be retained by the soldier signing, and one to be retained by us. Several hundred refused to sign their paroles, preferring to be sent north as prisoners to being sent back to fight again. Others again kept out of the way, hoping to escape either alternative.

Pemberton appealed to me in person to compel these men to sign their paroles, but I declined. It also leaked out that many of the men who had signed their paroles intended to desert and go to their homes as soon as they got out of our lines. Pemberton, hearing this, again appealed to me to assist him. He wanted arms for a battalion, to act as guards in keeping his men together while being marched to a camp of instruction, where he expected to keep them until exchanged. This request was also declined. It was precisely what I expected and hoped that they would do. I told him, however, I would see that they marched beyond our lines in good order. By the 11th, just one week after the surrender, the paroles were completed, and the Confederate garrison marched out. Many deserted; fewer of them were ever returned to the ranks to fight again than would have been the case had the surrender been unconditional and the prisoners been sent to the James River to be paroled.

As soon as our troops took possession of the city, guards were established along the whole line of parapet, from the river above to the river below. The prisoners were allowed to occupy their old camps behind the intrenchments. No restraint was put upon them, except by their own commanders. They were rationed about as our own men, and from our supplies. The men of the two armies fraternized as if they had been fighting for the same cause. When they passed out of the works they had so long and so gallantly defended, between lines of their late antagonists, not a cheer went up, not a remark was made that would give pain. I believe there was a feeling of sadness among the Union soldiers at seeing the dejection of their late antagonists.

The day before the departure the following order was issued:

"Paroled prisoners will be sent out of here to-morrow. They will be authorized to cross at the railroad-bridge and move from there to Edwards's Ferry,⸲ and on by way of Raymond. Instruct the commands to be orderly and quiet as these prisoners pass, to make no offensive remarks, and not to harbor any who fall out of ranks after they have passed."

) See article on Port Hudson, to follow.— EDITORS.   ⸲ Meant Edwards's Station.— U. S. G.

On the 8th a dispatch was sent from Washington by Halleck, saying:

" I fear your paroling the prisoners at Vicksburg without actual delivery to a proper agent, as required by the seventh article of the cartel, may be construed into an absolute release, and that the men will immediately be placed in the ranks of the enemy. Such has been the case elsewhere. If these prisoners have not been allowed to depart, you will detain them until further orders."

Halleck did not know that they had already been delivered into the hands of Major Watts, Confederate Commissioner for the Exchange of Prisoners.

At Vicksburg 31,600 prisoners were surrendered, together with 172 cannon, about 60,000 muskets, and a large amount of ammunition. The small-arms of the enemy were far superior to the bulk of ours. Up to this time our troops at the west had been limited to the old United States flint-lock muskets changed into percussion, or the Belgian musket imported early in the war — almost as dangerous to the person firing it as to the one aimed at — and a few new and improved arms. These were of many different calibers, a fact that caused much trouble in distributing ammunition during an engagement. The enemy had generally new arms, which had run the blockade, and were of uniform caliber. After the surrender I authorized all colonels, whose regiments were armed with inferior muskets, to place them in the stack of captured arms, and replace them with the latter. A large number of arms, turned in to the ordnance department as captured, were these arms that had really been used by the Union army in the capture of Vicksburg.

In this narrative I have not made the mention I should like of officers, dead and alive, whose services entitle them to special mention. Neither have I made that mention of the navy which its services deserve. Suffice it to say, the close of the siege found us with an army unsurpassed, in proportion to its numbers, taken as a whole, officers and men. A military education was acquired which no other school could have given. Men who thought a company was quite enough for them to command properly, at the beginning, would have made good regimental or brigade commanders; most of the brigade commanders were equal to the command of a division, and one, Ransom, would have been equal to the command of a corps at least. Logan and Crocker ended the campaign fitted to command independent armies.

General F. P. Blair joined me at Milliken's Bend, a full-fledged general, without having served in a lower grade. He commanded a division in the campaign. I had known Blair in Missouri, where I had voted against him in 1858 when he ran for Congress. I knew him as a frank, positive, and generous man, true to his friends even to a fault, but always a leader. I dreaded his coming. I knew from experience that it was more difficult to command two generals desiring to be leaders, than it was to command one army, officered intelligently, and with subordination. It affords me the greatest pleasure to record now my agreeable disappointment in respect to his character. There was no man braver than he, nor was there any who obeyed all orders of his superior in rank with more unquestioning alacrity. He was one man as a soldier, another as a politician.

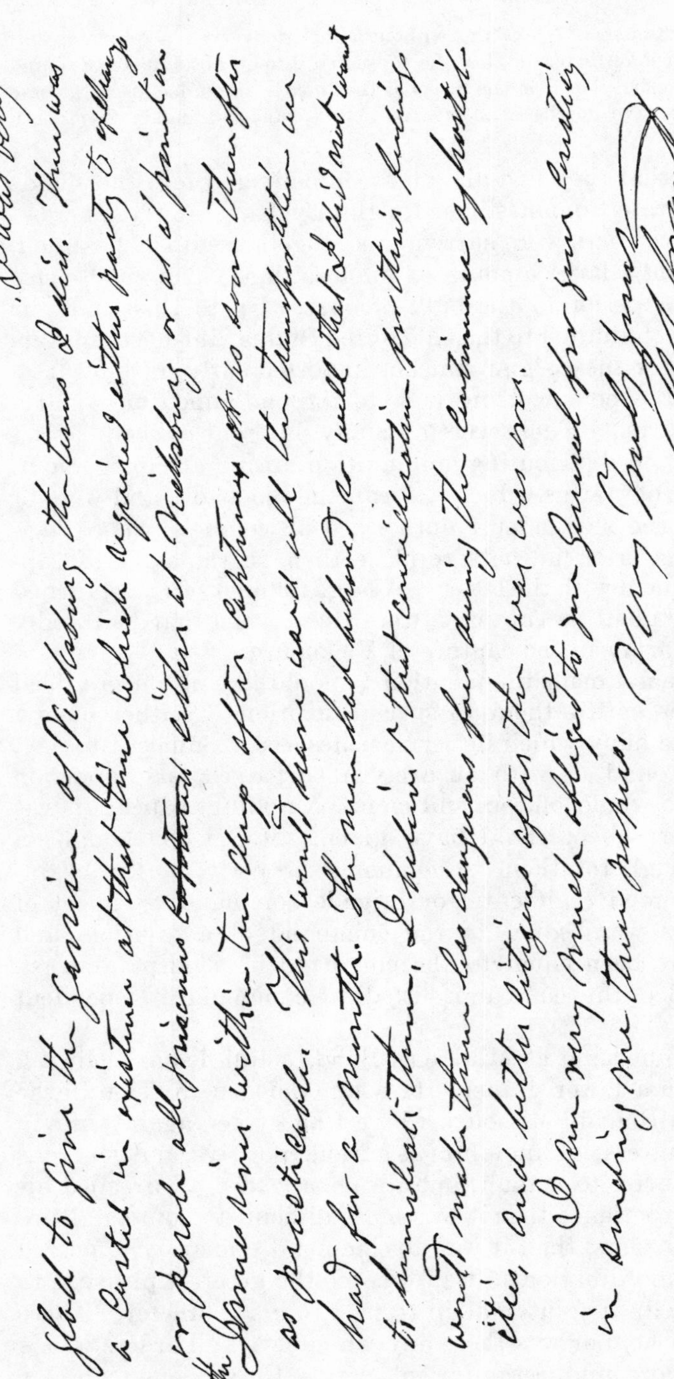

The navy, under Porter, was all it could be, during the entire campaign. Without its assistance the campaign could not have been successfully made with twice the number of men engaged. It could not have been made at all, in the way it was, with any number of men, without such assistance. The most perfect harmony reigned between the two arms of the service. There never was a request made, that I am aware of, either of the flag-officer or any of his subordinates, that was not promptly complied with.

The campaign of Vicksburg was suggested and developed by circumstances. The elections of 1862 had gone against the prosecution of the war: voluntary enlistments had nearly ceased, and the draft had been resorted to; this was resisted, and a defeat, or backward movement, would have made its execution impossible. A forward movement to a decisive victory was necessary. Accordingly I resolved to

Dear Sir:

glad to give the garrison of Vicksburg the terms I did. There was a cartel in existence at that time which required either party to exchange or parole all prisoners captured either at Vicksburg or at Port ____ the James river within ten days after capturing or so soon thereafter as practicable. This would have used all the transportation we had for a month. The men had behaved so well that I did not want to humiliate them. I believe that consideration for this feeling would make them less dangerous foes during the continuance of hostilities, and better citizens after the war was over.

I am very much obliged to you General for your courtesy in sending me these pictures.

Very truly yours,
U. S. Grant

FROM A LETTER TO GEN. MARCUS J. WRIGHT, C. S. A., DATED NEW YORK, NOV. 30, 1884.

get below Vicksburg, unite with Banks against Port Hudson, and make New Orleans a base; and, with that base and Grand Gulf as a starting-point, move our combined forces against Vicksburg. Upon reaching Grand Gulf, after running its batteries and fighting a battle, I received a letter from Banks informing me that he could not be at Port Hudson under ten days, and then with only fifteen thousand men. The time was worth more than the reënforcements; I therefore determined to push into the interior of the enemy's country.

With a large river behind us, held above and below by the enemy, rapid movements were essential to success. Jackson was captured the day after a new commander had arrived, and only a few days before large reënforcements were expected. A rapid movement west was made; the garrison of Vicksburg was met in two engagements and badly defeated, and driven back into its stronghold and there successfully besieged.

THE WHITE HOUSE, OR SHIRLEY, AT THE ENTRANCE TO M^cPHERSON'S SAPS AGAINST THE "THIRD LOUISIANA REDAN," VICKSBURG. FROM A WAR-TIME SKETCH.

THE VICKSBURG MINE.

BY ANDREW HICKENLOOPER, BREVET BRIGADIER-GENERAL, U. S. V., CHIEF ENGINEER OF THE SEVENTEENTH ARMY CORPS.

AFTER the failure of the general assault on May 22d, orders were issued to commence regular siege operations. General J. B. McPherson occupied the center with the Seventeenth Army Corps, covering the main Jackson road, on which the Confederates had constructed the most formidable redoubt on the entire line, and intrusted its defense to the 3d Louisiana, a veteran regiment. Because of its strength, commanding position, and heavy armament, this redoubt became the main objective point of the engineer-ing operations of the Seventeenth Army Corps. It was approachable only over a broad, flat ridge, forming a comparatively level plateau, extending eastwardly from the fort for a distance of almost five hundred yards before descending into one of the numerous ravines or depressions which extended in almost every conceivable direction over the ground lying between the contending armies. The Third Division, commanded by General Logan, occupied the position immediately in front of the fort, and upon these troops—more especially those of the brigade commanded by General M. D. Leggett, working under the direction of the chief engineer of the corps — was imposed the greater part of the labor.

The "pioneers" of the corps were at once sent to the cane-brakes, swamps, and lowlands in the rear to construct sap-rollers, gabions, and fascines, and details of 150 men for day and the same number for night duty were made for work on the main sap, which was commenced on the Jackson road at a point about 150 feet south-east of a large frame plantation house, known as the White House, which for some unexplained reason had been left standing by the enemy. Up to this point troops could be marched in comparative safety under cover of the intervening hills, supplemented by the construction of parapets at exposed points. The line of the first section was selected during the night of the 23d under cover of an attack made upon the enemy's pickets. Upon this line the workmen were placed at intervals of about five feet, each equipped with a gabion, pick, and shovel, with instructions to cover themselves securely and dig a connection through to the adjoining burrow before daylight. The day relief was engaged in deepening and widening the sap thus commenced, and on the following night the second section was laid out and occupied in the same manner.

On the 25th of May the Confederate commander sent in a flag of truce, for the purpose of tendering permission to bury the Federal dead who had fallen in front of their works during the heroic assault of the 22d, which was gladly accepted. This incident afforded the chief engineer a much-needed opportunity of closely inspecting the ground to be passed over, of fixing the salient points in his mind, and of determining upon the general direction of the various sections of the sap. The highest point between the fort and the White House was selected as a spot upon which to locate a battery and "place at arms" (afterward known as Battery Hickenlooper), the guns of which rendered valuable service in covering the extensions of the sap beyond that point. Two 8-inch naval guns located in battery south-east of this point also rendered effective service in silencing the guns of the Confederate fort; thus leaving the Union soldiers exposed only to the ever-vigilant sharp-shooters of the enemy. Not even a hand could be safely raised above the parapets; and heavy rope shields, or aprons, were hung in front of the embrasures for the protection of the gunners while they were sighting their pieces. A favorite amusement of the soldiers was to place a cap on the end of a ramrod and to raise it just above the head-logs, betting on the number of bullets which would pass through it within a given time.

The sap-roller, used to protect the workmen from an enfilading fire during the opening of each section of the sap, was a wicker casing five feet in diameter by ten feet in length compactly filled with cotton. The roller was several times found to be on fire, and on the night of June 9th it was totally consumed; but through what agency was, at the time, a great mystery. After the capitulation it was ascertained that cotton saturated with turpentine and placed in the hollow of a minie-ball had been fired from a musket into the packing of the roller. [See p. 491.]

It was difficult for the sharp-shooters to reach the Confederates by direct firing, and the artillerymen found it impossible to gauge their shells so as to cause the explosion immediately behind the Confederate parapets. To overcome this latter difficulty, when the sap reached the vicinity of the fort we caused "Coehorn mortars" to be made from short sections of gum-tree logs bored out and hooped with iron bands. These novel engines of warfare, being accurately charged with just sufficient powder to lift six or twelve pound shells over the parapet and drop them down immediately behind, proved exceedingly effective.

The general plan of conducting the work with flying-sap by night and deepening and widening by day was pushed forward with the utmost energy until June 22d, when the head of the sap reached the outer ditch surrounding the fort. A few days previous an order had been issued for all men in the corps having a practical knowledge of coal-mining to report to the chief engineer. Out of those reporting thirty-six of the strongest and most experienced were selected and divided into two shifts for day and night duty, and each shift was divided into

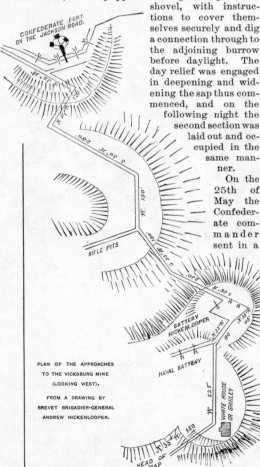

CONFEDERATE FORT ON THE JACKSON ROAD.

RIFLE PITS

BATTERY HICKENLOOPER

NAVAL BATTERY

WHITE HOUSE OR SHIRLEY

HEAD OF SAP

PLAN OF THE APPROACHES TO THE VICKSBURG MINE (LOOKING WEST).

FROM A DRAWING BY BREVET BRIGADIER-GENERAL ANDREW HICKENLOOPER.

LOGAN. McPHERSON.   VICKSBURG.

EXPLOSION OF THE MINE UNDER THE CONFEDERATE FORT ON THE JACKSON ROAD.
FROM A SKETCH MADE AT THE TIME.

The foreground shows the Union sap near the White House, where stand Generals McPherson, Logan, and Leggett with three other officers. In the distance is seen "Coonskin's" Tower, ⌡ a lookout and perch for sharp-shooters, adjoining Battery Hickenlooper, near which were massed the troops that charged into the crater.

three reliefs. On the night of the 22d these men, properly equipped with drills, short-handled picks, shovels, etc., under the immediate command of Lieutenant Russell of the 7th Missouri and Sergeant Morris of the 32d Ohio, commenced the mining operations by driving a gallery, four feet in width by five feet in height, in at right angles to the face of the parapet of the fort. Each relief worked an hour at a time, two picking, two shoveling, and two handing back the grain-sacks filled with earth, which were deposited in the ditch until they could be carried back. The main gallery was carried in 45 feet, and then a smaller gallery extended in on the same line 15 feet, while from the end of the main gallery two others were run out on either side at angles of 45 degrees for a distance of 15 feet. The soil through which this gallery was driven was a reddish clay of remarkable tenacity, easily cut and requiring but little bracing. So rapidly was this work executed that on the morning of the 25th the miners commenced depositing the powder, 800 pounds at the extreme end of the main gallery and 700 pounds at the end of each of the lateral galleries, making a total of 2200 pounds. From each of these deposits there were laid two strands of safety fuse,— obtained, as was the powder, from the navy,— this duplication being made to cover the possible contingency of one failing to burn with the desired regularity and speed. These six strands were cut

⌡ Coonskin's Tower, according to Brevet Brigadier-General William E. Strong, was built under the direction of Second-Lieutenant Henry C. Foster, of Company B, 23d Indiana Volunteers. A newspaper slip sent to the editors by General Hickenlooper contains the following account of "Coonskin" (Lieutenant Foster), which W. P. Davis, who was Lieutenant-Colonel of the 23d Indiana, says is substantially correct:

"He was an unerring shot, and wore a cap made of raccoon fur. From this he was called 'Coonskin' the Seventeenth Corps through, and wherever he was, woe to the Confederate head that appeared above a parapet. 'Coonskin' went out once in the night-time, crept up toward the Confederate defenses and built himself a burrow in the ground, with a peep-hole in it. There he would frequently take provisions with him, and stay several days at a time, watching for Confederates. At length he built 'Coonskin's Tower.' The Jackson and Vicksburg railway had been torn up for miles in the rear of Vicksburg, and railway iron and cross-ties lay all about. Taking advantage of the night hours, Coonskin built himself a tower of the loose railroad ties. Learned in backwoods lore, he knew how to construct the genuine pioneer log-cabin. Working several nights, he at length built the tower so high that by climbing toward its top he could actually look over the Confederate parapets. He could see the men inside the works. Then, taking aim through the chinks of the logs, he would pick off the enemy. The tower was a terror to the Confederates. They could not use their artillery against it, that having been already quite silenced by the Union batteries. All they could do was to fire musket-balls at it, which whistled around its corners or buried themselves in its logs."

EDITORS.

to exactly the same length, and having been carefully laid, the earth, which had been previously removed in grain-sacks, was carried back and deposited in the most compact manner possible, and well braced by heavy timbers, beyond the junction point of the three galleries. From this point out to the entrance it was more loosely packed in. The Confederate garrison, surmising the object in view, were active in efforts to thwart the purpose of the Union forces by throwing hand-grenades and rolling shells with lighted fuses over their parapet down into the trench in front of the fort. They also countermined in hopes of tapping the gallery. So near were they to the attainment of this object that during the last day the miners could distinctly hear the conversation and orders given in the counter-mine.

The powder was brought up in barrels and kept in the main sap at a safe distance from the enemy's hand-grenades and shells, and there opened and placed in grain-sacks, each one of which contained about 25 pounds. These were taken upon the backs of the miners, who made the run over the exposed ground during the intervals between the explosion of the enemy's shells; and so well timed were these movements that, although it required nearly one hundred trips with the dangerous loads, all were landed in the mine without a single accident.

The commanding general having been advised on the day previous that the work would be completed before 3 P. M. of the 25th, general orders were issued directing each corps commander to order up the reserves and fully man the trenches, and immediately following the explosion to open with both artillery and musketry along the entire twelve miles of investing line; under cover of which the assaulting columns, composed of volunteers from the 31st and 45th Illinois, preceded by ten picked men from the pioneer corps under charge of the chief engineer, were to move forward and take possession of the fort. For an hour or two previous to the time of the explosion the scene from "Battery Hickenlooper," where General Grant and his subordinate commanders had taken their positions, was one of the most remarkable ever witnessed. As far as the eye could reach to the right and left could be seen the long winding columns of blue moving to their assigned positions behind the besiegers' works. Gradually as the hour of 3 approached the booming of artillery and incessant rattle of musketry, which had been going on day and night for thirty days, suddenly subsided, and a deathlike and op-

pressive stillness pervaded the whole command. Every eye was riveted upon that huge redoubt standing high above the adjoining works. At the appointed moment it appeared as though the whole fort and connecting outworks commenced an upward movement, gradually breaking into fragments and growing less bulky in appearance, until it looked like an immense fountain of finely pulverized earth, mingled with flashes of fire and clouds of smoke, through which could occasionally be caught a glimpse of some dark objects,—men, gun-carriages, shelters, etc. Fire along the entire line instantly opened with great fury, and amidst the din and roar of 150 cannon and the rattle of 50,000 muskets the charging column moved forward to the assault. [See p. 527.] But little difficulty was experienced in entering the crater, but the moment the assaulting forces attempted to mount the artificial parapet, which had been formed by the falling débris about midway across the fort, completely commanded by the Confederate artillery and infantry in the rear, they were met by a withering fire so severe that to show a head above the crest was certain death. Two lines were formed on the slope of this parapet, the front line raising their muskets over their heads and firing at random over the crest while the rear rank were engaged in reloading. But soon the Confederates began throwing short-fused shells over the parapet, which, rolling down into the crater crowded with the soldiers of the assaulting column, caused the most fearful destruction of life ever witnessed under like circumstances. The groans of the dying and shrieks of the wounded became fearful, but bravely they stood to their work until the engineers constructed a casemate out of the heavy timbers found in the crater, and upon which the earth was thrown until it was of sufficient depth to resist the destructive effects of the exploding shells. As soon as this work was completed, and a parapet was thrown up across the crater on a line with the face of the casemate, the troops were withdrawn to the new line beyond the range of exploding shells. The crater being secured, again the miners were set at work running a new gallery under the left wing of the fort. This mine was exploded on the 1st of July, leaving the fort a total wreck.

In the meantime the main sap had been widened sufficiently to admit of the convenient movement of troops in "column of fours" during the contemplated assault, the necessity for which was happily avoided by the surrender on the following day.

VICKSBURG, FROM THE RIVER. FROM A PHOTOGRAPH.

ARRIVAL OF GENERAL GRANT AT GENERAL PEMBERTON'S VICKSBURG HOUSE, JULY 4, 1863. FROM A SKETCH MADE AT THE TIME.

THE TERMS OF SURRENDER.

I. BY JOHN C. PEMBERTON, LIEUTENANT-GENERAL, C. S. A.

PHILADELPHIA, June 12, 1875.

DEAR SIR·—I give you with pleasure my version of the interview between General Grant and myself on the afternoon of July 3, 1863, in front of the Confederate lines at Vicksburg.

If you will refer to the first volume of Badeau's life of U. S. Grant, you will find a marked discrepancy between that author's account of it and mine. I do not fear, however, to trust to the honest memory of any officer then present to confirm the statement I shall make.

Passing over all preceding events, I come at once to the circumstance that brought about the personal interview referred to.

Feeling assured that it was useless to hope longer for assistance from General Johnston, either to raise the siege of Vicksburg or to rescue the garrison, ⚓ I summoned division and brigade commanders, with one or two others, to meet in my quarters on the night of the 2d of July. All the correspondence that had taken place during the siege between General Johnston and myself

For this letter, addressed to Lieutenant-Colonel John P. Nicholson, the American editor of the Comte de Paris's "History of the Civil War," we are indebted to General Marcus J. Wright, Agent of the War Department for the Collection of Confederate Records. See General Grant's reply, addressed to General Pemberton, p. 545; also his paper, "The Vicksburg Campaign," p. 493.—EDITORS.

⚓ Among General Pemberton's papers was found a copy of the following letter, accompanied by a note stating that the original had "miscarried and was never received, but General Johnston was kind enough to furnish me a copy":

was laid before these officers. After much consideration it was advised that I address a note to General Grant, proposing the appointment of commissioners to arrange terms of capitulation.

The following, having been read to the council and approved, was sent to General Grant under a flag of truce by the hands of Major-General J. S. Bowen, on the morning of the 3d:

"VICKSBURG, July 3d, 1863. MAJOR-GENERAL GRANT, Commanding United States Forces near Vicksburg, Mississippi. GENERAL: I have the honor to propose to you an armistice of —— hours, with a view to arrange terms of capitulation of Vicksburg. To this end, if agreeable to you, I will appoint three commissioners to meet a like number, to be named by yourself, at such place and hour to-day as you may find convenient. I make this proposition to save further effusion of blood, which must otherwise be shed to a frightful extent, feeling myself fully able to maintain my position for a yet indefinite period. This communication will be handed you under flag of truce by Major-General John S. Bowen. I am, General, very respectfully, your obedient servant, JOHN C. PEMBERTON, Lieutenant-General Commanding."

"June 27, 1863. GENERAL PEMBERTON: Your dispatch of the 22d received. General E. K. Smith's troops have been mismanaged, and have fallen back to Delhi. I have sent a special messenger, urging him to assume direct command. The determined spirit you manifest and his expected co-operation encourage me to hope that something may yet be done to save Vicksburg and to postpone both of the modes suggested of merely extricating the garrison. Negotiations with Grant for the relief of the garrison, should they become necessary, must be made by you. It would be a confession of weakness on my part, which I ought not to make, to propose them. When it becomes necessary to make terms, they may be considered as made under my authority.— J. E. JOHNSTON, General."

In due time the following reply was handed to me:

"HEADQUARTERS, DEPARTMENT OF THE TENNESSEE, NEAR VICKSBURG, July 3d, 1863. LIEUTENANT-GENERAL JOHN C. PEMBERTON, Commanding Confederate Forces, etc. GENERAL: Your note of this date is just received, proposing an armistice for several hours for the purpose of arranging terms of capitulation through commissioners to be appointed, etc. The useless effusion of blood you propose stopping by this course can be ended at any time you may choose, by an unconditional surrender of the city and garrison. Men who have shown so much endurance and courage as shown now in Vicksburg, will always challenge the respect of an adversary, and I can assure you will be treated with all the respect due to prisoners of war. I do not favor the proposition of appointing commissioners to arrange the terms of capitulation, because I have no terms other than those indicated above. I am, General, very respectfully, your obedient servant, U. S. GRANT, Major-General."

I at once expressed to General Bowen my determination not to surrender unconditionally. He then stated that General Grant would like to have an interview with me if I was so disposed, and would meet me at a designated point between the two lines at 3 P. M. that day. I was not aware that the suggestion had originated with General Bowen, but acceded to the proposed meeting at the joint request of my four division commanders.

On reaching the place appointed, accompanied by Major-General Bowen and Colonel Montgomery, then temporarily serving on my personal staff, I found General Grant and a number of his generals and other officers already arrived and dismounted. To the general himself, with whom my acquaintance dated as far back as the Mexican war,—as well as to several of the group who surrounded him,—I was formally introduced by General Bowen.

After a few remarks and inquiries on either side, a pause ensued, which was prolonged on my part in expectation that General Grant would introduce the subject, the discussion of which I supposed to be the object of our meeting. Finding that he did not do so, I said to him that I understood that he had expressed a wish to have a personal interview with me. He replied that he had not. I was much surprised, and, turning to General Bowen, remarked, "Then there is a misunderstanding; I certainly understood differently." The matter, however, was satisfactorily explained to me in a few words, the mistake, no doubt, having been my own. Again addressing General Grant, I said: "In your letter this morning you state that you have no other terms than an unconditional surrender." He answered promptly, "I have no other." To this I rejoined: "Then, sir, it is unnecessary that you and I should hold any further conversation; we will go to fighting again at once"; and I added: "I can assure you, sir, you will bury many more of your men before you will enter Vicksburg." General Grant did not, as Badeau represents, reply, "Very well," nor did he "turn off." He did not change his position, nor did he utter a word. The movement to withdraw, so far as there was any movement, was on my part, and was accompanied by the remark that if he

(General Grant) supposed that I was suffering for provisions he was mistaken, that I had enough to last me for an indefinite period, and that Port Hudson was better supplied than Vicksburg. General Bowen made no suggestion whatever in regard to a consultation between any parties during this interview, as he is represented to have done by Badeau; but General Grant *did* at this time propose that he and I should step aside, and on my assenting, he added that if I had no objection, he would take with him Generals McPherson and A. J. Smith. I replied, certainly, and that General Bowen and Colonel Montgomery would accompany me. General Grant then suggested that these gentlemen withdraw and see whether, on consultation, they could not arrive at some satisfactory arrangement. It will be readily understood that I offered no objection to this course, as it was, in fact, a withdrawal by General Grant from the position he had so unqualifiedly assumed, to wit, unconditional surrender—and it really submitted, as I had desired it should, the discussion of the question of terms to a commission, although that commission was now necessarily an *impromptu* one.

Pending the interchange of views by the officers named, General Grant and I remained apart from them, conversing only upon topics that had no relation to the important subject that brought us together. The terms which this commission agreed to propose were in the main those that were afterward proffered by General Grant, and eventually accepted by me. During this discussion I stated to him that as he declined to appoint commissioners when invited to do so by me, it was now his part to propose the terms. He agreed to this, and said I should hear from him by 10 P. M. When about to part I notified General Grant that I held myself in no manner pledged to any agreement, but should consult my division and brigade commanders. He replied that I must understand him in the like manner, and that he, too, should consult his corps commanders. With this our interview ended.

Mr. Badeau's statement is a misrepresentation of the facts as they occurred, and, whether intentional or otherwise, conveys false impressions to his readers. If he was present at the interview he knows, if he was absent, he could readily have ascertained, that after General Grant's verbal declaration that he had no other terms than unconditional surrender, all suggestions and all overtures looking to terms arose directly from General Grant himself, and neither directly nor indirectly from me or my subordinates. There was no display by General Grant as to the result of this interview, nor did he feel indifferent. On the night of the 3d of July a dispatch was intercepted by my signal-officer from Admiral Porter to General Grant. The former inquired as to the chances of a surrender on the 4th. General Grant replied through the same medium, mentioning in a general way the terms offered, stating that the arrangement was *against his feelings*, but that his officers advised it on the ground that it would free his river transportation for other important uses, etc., etc. If this message was sent it should be found in the reports of the signal-officers. Will you have it looked up? No doubt both these gentlemen remember the circumstances. I am, Colonel, very truly yours,

J. C. PEMBERTON.

II. BY ULYSSES S. GRANT, GENERAL, U. S. A.

THE following letter, dated New York, November 30th, 1884, and printed for the first time in "The Century" magazine for August, 1887, was addressed to General Marcus J. Wright, Agent of the War Department for the Collection of Confederate Records, by whose permission it is here given, from the original manuscript.—EDITORS.

DEAR GENERAL: Herewith I send you General Pemberton's account of the surrender of Vicksburg. As the written matter [printed above] is "Copy," and supposing you have what it has been copied from, I do not return it, though I will if you inform me that you want it.

A gentleman from Philadelphia sent me the same matter I return herewith, last summer. I probably left the paper at Long Branch, but do not know certainly. All there is of importance in the matter of the surrender of Vicksburg is contained in the correspondence between General Pemberton and myself. The fact is, General Pemberton, being a Northern man commanding a Southern army, was not at the same liberty to surrender an army that a man of Southern birth would be. In adversity or defeat he became an object of suspicion, and felt it. Bowen was a Southern man all over, and knew the garrison of Vicksburg had to surrender or be captured, and knew it was best to stop further effusion of blood by surrendering. He did all he could to bring about that result.

Pemberton is mistaken in several points. It was Bowen that proposed that he and A. J. Smith should talk over the matter of the surrender and submit their views. Neither Pemberton nor I objected, but we were not willing to commit ourselves to accepting such terms as they might propose. In a short time those officers returned. Bowen acted as spokesman; what he said was substantially this: The Confederate army was to be permitted to march out with the honors of war, carrying with them their arms, colors, and field-batteries. The National troops were then to march in and occupy the city, and retain the siege-guns, small-arms not in the hands of the men, all public property remaining. Of course I rejected the terms at once. I did agree, however, before we separated, to write Pemberton what terms I would give. The correspondence is public and speaks for itself. I held no council of war; hostilities having ceased, officers and men soon became acquainted with the reason why. Curiosity led officers of rank—most all the general officers—to visit my headquarters with the hope of getting some news. I talked with them very freely about the meeting between General Pemberton and myself, our correspondence, etc., but in no sense was it a council of war. I was very glad to give the garrison of Vicksburg the terms I did. There was a cartel in existence at that time which required either party to exchange or parole all prisoners either at Vicksburg or at a point on the James River within ten days after captures or as soon thereafter as practicable. This would have used all the transportation we had for a month. *The men had behaved so well that I did not want to humiliate them. I believed that consideration for their feelings would make them less dangerous foes during the continuance of hostilities, and better citizens after the war was over.*

I am very much obliged to you, General, for your courtesy in sending me these papers. Very truly yours,

U. S. GRANT.

III. CORRESPONDENCE BETWEEN GENERAL PEMBERTON AND GENERALS GRANT AND BLAIR.

General Pemberton to General Grant :‡

WARRENTON, FAUQUIER, VIRGINIA, January 30, 1874. His Excellency, U. S. GRANT, PRESIDENT OF THE UNITED STATES. SIR: A statement of some historic significance and of considerable interest to me personally, has lately come to my notice in a way that induces me to address you as the single individual competent to confirm or refute it. I am aware that I have no claim to your special consideration; should you, however, deem it not improper to respond to my inquiry, I shall feel myself indebted to your kindness. The statement I refer to was from a general officer of the Army of the Tennessee, and was in the words following:

"It was generally understood in our army that General Johnston's courier, conveying dispatches to you previous to the battle of Baker's Creek or Champion Hills, betrayed his dispatches to General Grant, and also your answers to General Johnston's orders. I do not know positively from General Grant these facts, but the matter was spoken of by the officers of our army in such a way as to leave no doubt in my mind."

Permit me to add that this information has tended to confirm my own suspicion, excited at the time by the (otherwise) inexplicable delay in the receipt of General Johnston's dispatch of the 14th of May, which, as you, sir, are probably aware, was not handed to me until after 5 P. M. on the 16th, when my army was in full retreat. My inquiry is confined simply to two points: first, the truth (or reverse) of the facts discussed by the officers of the Army of the Tennessee; second, the correctness (or the reverse) of my surmises as to the dispatch of the 14th, above referred to. I am, sir, most respectfully your obedient servant,

J. C. PEMBERTON.

General Grant to General Pemberton :

EXECUTIVE MANSION, WASHINGTON, January 31, 1874. GENERAL J. C. PEMBERTON, Warrenton, Virginia. General: Your letter of yesterday was duly received this morning, and the President authorizes me to say that the statement of the officer to which you refer was correct, and he thinks you are also correct as to your surmises in regard to the delay in receipt of your dispatch. He says the dispatches were brought in our lines and given to General McPherson, and by him immediately brought to headquarters. I have the honor to remain, sir, your obedient servant,

LEVI P. LUCKEY, Secretary.

‡ On the 19th of January, 1874, General Pemberton addressed a letter, substantially to the same effect, to General Frank P. Blair, whose reply follows General Grant's.—EDITORS.

General Blair to General Pemberton:

St. Louis, January 24, 1874. General J. C. Pemberton, Fauquier County, Virginia. Dear General: I take pleasure, in answer to your letter of the 19th of January, in saying that it was generally understood in our army that General J. Johnston's courier, conveying dispatches to you previous to the battle of Baker's Creek or Champion Hills, betrayed his dispatches to General Grant, and also your answers to General Johnston's orders, so that, in fact, General Grant had the most precise information as to your movements and those of General Johnston. I do not know positively from General Grant these facts, but the matter was spoken of by the officers of our army in such a way as to leave no doubt in my mind. Very respectfully, your obedient servant,   Frank P. Blair.

CONFEDERATE RIVER-BATTERY ON THE RIDGE SOUTH OF VICKSBURG.   FROM A SKETCH MADE AFTER THE SURRENDER.

THE OPPOSING FORCES IN THE VICKSBURG CAMPAIGN.
May 1st–July 4th, 1863.

The composition, losses, and strength of each army as here stated give the gist of all the data obtainable in the Official Records. K stands for killed; w for wounded; m w for mortally wounded; m for captured or missing; c for captured.

UNION FORCES: ARMY OF THE TENNESSEE, Maj.-Gen. Ulysses S. Grant.

Escort: A, 4th Ill. Cav., Capt. Embury D. Osband.   *Engineers:* 1st Batt. Eng. Regt. of the West, Maj. W. Tweeddale.

NINTH ARMY CORPS (joined June 14–17), Maj.-Gen. John G. Parke.

FIRST DIVISION, Brig.-Gen. Thomas Welsh.

First Brigade, Col. Henry Bowman: 36th Mass., Lieut.-Col. John B. Norton; 17th Mich., Lieut.-Col. Constant Luce; 27th Mich., Col. Dorus M. Fox; 45th Pa., Col. John I. Curtin. *Third Brigade,* Col. Daniel Leasure: 2d Mich., Col. William Humphrey; 8th Mich., Col. Frank Graves; 20th Mich., Lieut.-Col. W. Huntington Smith; 79th N. Y., Col. David Morrison; 100th Pa., Lieut.-Col. Mathew M. Dawson. *Artillery:* D, Pa., Capt. G.W. Durell.

SECOND DIVISION, Brig.-Gen. Robert B. Potter.

First Brigade, Col. Simon G. Griffin: 6th N. H., Lieut.-Col. Henry H. Pearson; 9th N. H., Col. Herbert B. Titus; 7th R. I., Col. Zenas R. Bliss. *Second Brigade,* Brig.-Gen. Edward Ferrero: 35th Mass., Col. Sumner Carruth; 11th N. H., Lieut.-Col. Moses N. Collins; 51st N. Y., Col. Charles W. Le Gendre; 51st Pa., Col. John F. Hartranft. *Third Brigade,* Col. Benjamin C. Christ: 29th Mass., Lieut.-Col. Joseph H. Barnes; 46th N. Y., Col. Joseph Gerhardt; 50th Pa., Lieut.-Col. Thomas S. Brenholtz. *Artillery:* L, 2d N. Y., Capt. Jacob Roemer.

ARTILLERY RESERVE, E, 2d U. S., Lieut. Samuel N. Benjamin.

THIRTEENTH ARMY CORPS, Maj.-Gen. John A. McClernand, Maj.-Gen. Edward O. C. Ord.

Escort: L, 3d Ill. Cav., Capt. David R. Sparks.

Pioneers: Indpt. Co., Ky. Inf., Capt. Wm. F. Patterson.

NINTH DIVISION, Brig.-Gen. Peter J. Osterhaus (w).

Brig.-Gen. Albert L. Lee, Brig.-Gen. Peter J. Osterhaus. Staff loss: Big Black Bridge, w, 1.

First Brigade, Brig.-Gen. Theophilus T. Garrard, Brig.-Gen. Albert L. Lee (w), Col. James Keigwin: 118th Ill., Col. John G. Fonda; 49th Ind., Col. James Keigwin, Maj. Arthur J. Hawhe, Lieut.-Col. Joseph H. Thornton; 69th Ind., Col. Thomas W. Bennett, Lieut.-Col. Oran Perry; 7th Ky., Maj. H. W. Adams, Lieut.-Col. John Lucas, Col. Reuben May; 120th Ohio, Col. Marcus M. Spiegel. Brigade loss: Port Gibson, k, 18; w, 102; m, 3 = 123. Champion's Hill, k, 11; w, 44; m, 13 = 68. Big Black Bridge, w, 1. Vicksburg, assault May 19th, k, 1; w, 28 = 29; assault May 22d, k, 15; w, 87 = 102. *Second Brigade,* Col. Lionel A. Sheldon, Col. Daniel W. Lindsey: 54th Ind., Col. Fielding Mansfield; 22d Ky., Lieut.-Col. George W. Monroe; 16th Ohio, Capt. Eli W. Botsford, Maj. Milton Mills; 42d Ohio, Lieut.-Col. Don A. Pardee, Maj. William H. Williams, Col. Lionel A. Sheldon; 114th Ohio, Col. John Cradlebaugh (w), Lieut.-Col. John H. Kelly. Brigade loss: Port Gibson, k, 15; w, 66 = 81. Champion's Hill, k, 6; w, 42; m, 13 = 61. Big Black Bridge, k, 10; w, 14; m, 1 = 25. Vicksburg, assault May 19th, k, 1; w, 34 = 35; assault May 22d, k, 14; w, 63; m, 1 = 78. *Cavalry:* 2d Ill. (5 co's), Lieut.-Col. Daniel B. Bush, Jr.; 3d Ill. (3 co's), Capt. John L. Campbell; 6th Mo. (7 co's), Col. Clark Wright. Cavalry loss: Champion's Hill, k, 2; w, 2 = 4. *Artillery,* Capt. Jacob T. Foster: 7th Mich., Capt. Charles H. Lanphere; 1st Wis., Lieut. Charles B. Kimball, Lieut. Oscar F. Nutting. Artillery loss: Port Gibson, k, 3; w, 7 = 10. Big Black Bridge, w, 4.

TENTH DIVISION, Brig.-Gen. Andrew J. Smith.

Escort: C, 4th Ind. Cav., Capt. Andrew P. Gallagher.

First Brigade, Brig.-Gen. Stephen G. Burbridge: 16th Ind., Col. Thomas J. Lucas, Maj. James H. Redfield; 60th Ind., Col. Richard Owen; 67th Ind., Lieut.-Col. Theodore E. Buehler; 83d Ohio, Col. Frederick W. Moore; 96th Ohio, Col. Joseph W. Vance; 23d Wis., Lieut. Joshua J. Guppey, Lieut.-Col. William F. Vilas. Brigade loss: Port Gibson, w, 8. Champion's Hill, w, 16. Big Black Bridge, w, 1; m, 1 = 2. Vicksburg, assault May 19th, k, 2; w, 15 = 17; assault May 22d, k, 14; w, 82; m, 2 = 98. *Second Brigade,* Col. William J. Landram: 77th Ill., Col. David P. Grier; 97th Ill., Col. Friend S. Rutherford, Lieut.-Col. Lewis D. Martin; 130th Ill., Col. Nathaniel Niles; 19th Ky., Lieut.-Col. John Cowan, Maj. Josiah J. Mann; 48th Ohio, Lieut.-Col. Job R. Parker, Col. Peter J. Sullivan. Brigade loss: Port Gibson, k, 2; w, 21; m, 8 = 31. Champion's Hill, w, 6. Vicksburg, assault May 19th, k, 3; w, 15 = 18; assault May 22d, k, 44; w, 210; m, 30 = 284. *Artillery:* Mercantile (Ill.) Battery, Capt. Patrick H. White; 17th Ohio, Capt. Ambrose A. Blount, Capt. Charles S. Rice. Artillery loss: Champion's Hill, w, 3. Vicksburg, assault May 22d, w, 3. TWELFTH DIVISION, Brig.-Gen. Alvin P. Hovey.

Escort: C, 1st Ind. Cav., Lieut. James L. Carey.

First Brigade, Brig.-Gen. George F. McGinnis: 11th Ind., Col. Daniel Macauley (w), Lieut.-Col. William W. Darnall; 24th Ind., Col. William T. Spicely (w); 34th Ind., Col. Robert A. Cameron, Lieut.-Col. William Swaim (m w), Maj. Robert B. Jones, Col. Robert A. Cameron; 46th Ind., Col. Thomas H. Bringhurst; 29th Wis., Col. Charles R. Gill, Lieut.-Col. William A. Greene. Brigade loss: Port Gibson, k, 30; w, 187; m, 1 = 218. Champion's Hill, k, 103; w, 507; m, 26 = 636. *Second Brigade,* Col. James R. Slack: 87th Ill., Col. John E. Whiting; 47th Ind., Lieut.-Col. John A. McLaughlin; 24th Iowa, Col. Eber C. Byam, Lieut.-Col. John Q. Wilds; 28th Iowa, Col. John Connell; 56th Ohio, Col. William H. Raynor. Brigade loss: Port Gibson, k, 16; w, 62; m, 11 = 89. Champion's Hill, k, 108; w, 365; m, 93 = 566. *Artillery:* A, 1st Mo., Capt. George W. Schofield; 2d Ohio, Lieut. Augustus Beach; 16th Ohio, Capt. James A. Mitchell (m w), Lieut. George Murdock, Lieut. Russell P. Twist. Artillery loss: Port Gibson, w, 3.
FOURTEENTH DIVISION, Brig.-Gen. Eugene A. Carr.

Escort: G, 3d Ill. Cav., Capt. Enos McPhial (k), Capt. Samuel S. Marrett.

First Brigade, Brig.-Gen. William P. Benton, Col. Henry D. Washburn, Col. David Shunk: 33d Ill., Col. Charles E. Lippincott; 99th Ill., Col. George W. K. Bailey, Lieut.-Col. Lemuel Parke; 8th Ind., Col. David Shunk, Maj. Thomas J. Brady; 18th Ind., Col. Henry D. Washburn, Capt. Jonathan H. Williams; 1st U. S. (siege guns), Maj. Maurice Maloney. Brigade loss: Port Gibson, k, 28; w, 134 = 162. Champion's Hill, k, 1; w, 2 = 3. Big Black Bridge, k, 1; w, 22; m, 1 = 24. Vicksburg, assault May 22d, k, 61; w, 273; m, 7 = 341. *Second Brigade,* Col. Charles L. Harris, Col. William M. Stone, Brig.-Gen. Michael K. Lawler: 21st Iowa, Col. Samuel Merrill (w), Lieut.-Col. Cornelius W. Dunlap (k), Maj. Salue G. Van Anda; 22d Iowa, Col. William M. Stone (w), Lieut.-Col. Harvey Graham (w and c), Maj. Joseph B. Atherton, Capt. Charles N. Lee; 23d Iowa, Col. William H. Kinsman (k), Col. Samuel L. Glasgow; 11th Wis., Lieut.-Col. Charles A. Wood, Col. Charles L. Harris, Maj. Arthur Platt. Brigade loss: Port Gibson, k, 13; w, 88 = 101. Big Black Bridge, k, 27; w, 194 = 221. Vicksburg, assault May 22d, k, 54; w, 285; m, 29 = 368. *Artillery:* A, 2d Ill., Lieut. Frank B. Fenton, Capt. Peter Davidson; 1st Ind., Capt. Martin Klauss. Artillery loss: Port Gibson, k, 2. Big Black Bridge, k, 1. Vicksburg, assault May 22d, w, 1.
FIFTEENTH ARMY CORPS, Maj.-Gen. William T. Sherman.

FIRST DIVISION, Maj.-Gen. Frederick Steele.

First Brigade, Col. Francis H. Manter, Col. Bernard G. Farrar: 13th Ill., Col. Adam B. Gorgas; 27th Mo., Col. Thomas Curly; 29th Mo., Col. James Peckham; 30th Mo., Lieut.-Col. Otto Schadt; 31st Mo., Col. Thomas C. Fletcher, Maj. Frederick Jaensch, Lieut.-Col. Samuel P. Simpson; 32d Mo., Maj. Abraham J. Seay. Brigade loss: Vicksburg, assault May 19th, k, 1; w, 9 = 10; assault

May 22d, k, 2; w, 5 = 7. *Second Brigade,* Col. Charles R. Woods: 25th Iowa, Col. George A. Stone; 31st Iowa, Col. William Smyth, Maj. Theodore Stimming; 3d Mo., Lieut.-Col. Theodore Meumann; 12th Mo., Col. Hugo Wangelin; 17th Mo., Col. Francis Hassendeubel (m w), Lieut.-Col. John F. Cramer; 76th Ohio, Lieut.-Col. William B. Woods. Brigade loss: Vicksburg, assault May 19th, k, 1; w, 3 = 4; assault May 22d, k, 37; w, 145; m, 8 = 190. *Third Brigade,* Brig.-Gen. John M. Thayer: 4th Iowa, Col. James A. Williamson, Lieut.-Col. George Burton; 9th Iowa, Maj. Don A. Carpenter, Capt. Frederick S. Washburn, Col. David Carskaddon; 26th Iowa, Col. Milo Smith; 30th Iowa, Col. Charles H. Abbott (k), Col. William M. G. Torrence. Brigade loss: Vicksburg, assault May 19th, k, 7; w, 43 = 50; assault May 22d, k, 35; w, 119; m, 1 = 155. *Artillery:* 1st Iowa, Capt. Henry H. Griffiths; F, 2d Mo., Capt. Clemens Landgraeber; 4th Ohio, Capt. Louis Hoffmann. Artillery loss: Vicksburg, assault May 22d, w, 1. *Cavalry:* Kane County (Ill.) Company, Lieut. Thomas J. Beebe; D, 3d Ill., Lieut. Jonathan Kershner.
SECOND DIVISION, Maj.-Gen. Frank P. Blair, Jr.

First Brigade, Col. Giles A. Smith: 113th Ill., Col. George B. Hoge, Lieut.-Col. John W. Paddock; 116th Ill., Col. Nathan W. Tupper; 6th Mo., Lieut.-Col. Ira Boutell, Col. James H. Blood; 8th Mo., Lieut.-Col. David C. Coleman; 13th U. S. (1st Battalion), Capt. Edward C. Washington (m w), Capt. Charles Ewing, Capt. Charles C. Smith. Brigade loss: Vicksburg, assault May 19th, k, 37; w, 164; m, 1 = 202; assault May 22d, k, 20; w, 81; m, 1 = 102. *Second Brigade,* Col. Thomas Kilby Smith, Brig.-Gen. J. A. J. Lightburn: 55th Ill., Col. Oscar Malmborg; 127th Ill., Col. Hamilton N. Eldridge; 83d Ind., Col. Benjamin J. Spooner; 54th Ohio, Lieut.-Col. Cyrus W. Fisher; 57th Ohio, Col. Americus V. Rice, Lieut.-Col. Samuel R. Mott. Brigade loss: Vicksburg, assault May 19th, k, 29; w, 125; m, 1 = 155; assault May 22d, k, 11; w, 45 = 56. *Third Brigade,* Brig.-Gen. Hugh Ewing: 30th Ohio, Lieut.-Col. George H. Hildt, Col. Theodore Jones; 37th Ohio, Lieut.-Col. Louis von Blessingh, Maj. Charles Hipp, Col. Edward Siber; 47th Ohio, Col. Augustus C. Parry; 4th W. Va., Col. James H. Dayton. Brigade loss: Vicksburg, assault May 19th, k, 54; w, 194; m, 6 = 254; assault May 22d, k, 25; w, 116; m, 3 = 144. *Artillery:* A, 1st Ill., Capt. Peter P. Wood; B, 1st Ill., Capt. Samuel E. Barrett, Lieut. Israel P. Rumsey; H, 1st Ill., Capt. Levi W. Hart; 8th Ohio, Capt. James F. Putnam. Artillery loss: Vicksburg, assault May 19th, w, 2; assault May 22d, k, 2. *Cavalry:* A and B, Thielemann's (Ill.) Battalion, Capt. Milo Thielemann; C, 10th Mo., Capt. D. W. Ballou, Lieut. Ben. Joel.
THIRD DIVISION, Brig.-Gen. James M. Tuttle.

First Brigade, Brig.-Gen. Ralph P. Buckland, Col. William L. McMillen: 114th Ill., Col. James W. Judy; 93d Ind., Col. De Witt C. Thomas; 72d Ohio, Lieut.-Col. Le Roy Crockett (w), Maj. Charles G. Eaton; 95th Ohio, Col. William L. McMillen, Lieut.-Col. Jefferson Brumback. Brigade loss: Jackson, k, 4; w, 9 = 13. Vicksburg, assault May 19th, k, 4; w, 30 = 34; assault May 22d, w, 9. *Second Brigade,* Brig.-Gen. Joseph A. Mower: 47th Ill., Col. John N. Cromwell (k), Lieut.-Col. Samuel R. Baker; 5th Minn., Col. Lucius F. Hubbard; 11th Mo., Col. Andrew J. Weber (m w), Lieut.-Col. William L. Barnum; 8th Wis., Col. George W. Robbins. Brigade loss: Jackson, k, 1; w, 9; m, 3 = 13. Vicksburg, assault May 22d, k, 17; w, 136; m, 29 = 182. *Third Brigade,* Brig.-Gen. Charles L. Matthies, Col. Joseph J. Woods: 8th Iowa, Col. James L. Geddes; 12th Iowa, Col. Joseph J. Woods, Lieut.-Col. Samuel R. Edgington; 35th Iowa, Col. Sylvester G. Hill. Brigade loss: Jackson, k, 1; w, 1; m, 1 = 3. Vicksburg, assault May 19th, k, 1; w, 1 = 2; assault May 22d, w, 5. *Artillery,* Capt. Nelson T. Spoor: E, 1st Ill., Capt. Allen C. Waterhouse; 2d Iowa, Lieut. Joseph R. Reed. Artillery loss: Jackson, w, 3. Vicksburg, assault May 22d, k, 1; w, 4 = 5. *Cavalry:* 4th Iowa, Lieut.-Col. Simeon D. Swan.
SIXTEENTH ARMY CORPS (detachment), Maj.-Gen. Cadwallader C. Washburn.
FIRST DIVISION (joined June 12th), Brig.-Gen. Wm. Sooy Smith.

Escort: B, 7th Ill. Cav., Capt. Henry C. Forbes.

First Brigade, Col. John M. Loomis: 26th Ill., Maj. John B. Harris; 90th Ill., Col. Timothy O'Meara; 12th Ind., Col. Reuben Williams; 100th Ind., Lieut.-Col. Albert Heath. *Second Brigade,* Col. Stephen G. Hicks: 40th Ill., Maj. Hiram W. Hall; 103d Ill., Col. Willard A. Dickerman; 15th Mich., Col. John M. Oliver; 46th Ohio, Col. Charles C. Walcutt. *Third Brigade,* Col. Joseph R. Cockerill: 97th Ind., Col. Robert F. Catterson; 99th Ind., Col. Alexander Fowler; 53d Ohio, Col. Wells S. Jones; 70th Ohio, Maj. Wm. B. Brown. *Fourth Brigade,* Col. Wm. W. Sanford: 48th Ill., Lieut.-Col. Lucien Greathouse; 6th Iowa, Col. John M. Corse. *Artillery,* Capt. Wm. Cogswell: F, 1st Ill., Capt. John T. Cheney; I, 1st Ill., Lieut. Wm. N. Lansing; Cogswell, Ill., Lieut. Henry G. Eddy; 6th Ind., Capt. Michael Mueller.

FOURTH DIVISION (joined May 13th to 20th, and temporarily attached to Fifteenth Corps), Brig.-Gen. Jacob G. Lauman.

First Brigade, Col. Isaac C. Pugh: 41st Ill., Lieut.-Col. John H. Nale; 53d Ill., Lieut.-Col. Seth C. Earl; 3d Iowa, Col. Aaron Brown; 33d Wis., Col. Jonathan B. Moore. *Second Brigade,* Col. Cyrus Hall: 14th Ill., Lieut.-Col. Wm. Cain, Capt. Augustus H. Cornman; 15th Ill., Col. Geo. C. Rogers; 46th Ill., Col. Benj. Dornblaser; 76th Ill., Col. Samuel T. Busey; 53d Ind. (transferred to Third Brigade June 22d), Col. Walter Q. Gresham. *Third Brigade,* Col. Geo. E. Bryant, Col. Amory K. Johnson: 28th Ill., Maj. Hinman Rhodes; 32d Ill., Col. John Logan, Lieut.-Col. Wm. Hunter; 12th Wis., Lieut.-Col. DeWitt C. Poole, Col. Geo. E. Bryant. *Cavalry:* F and I, 15th Ill., Maj. James G. Wilson. *Artillery,* Capt. Geo. C. Gumbart: E, 2d Ill., Lieut. Geo. L. Nispel; K, 2d Ill., Capt. Benj. F. Rodgers; 5th Ohio, Lieut. Anthony B. Burton; 7th Ohio, Capt. Silas A. Burnap; 15th Ohio, Capt. Edward Spear, Jr.

PROVISIONAL DIVISION (joined June 3d), Brig.-Gen. Nathan Kimball.

Engelmann's Brigade, Col. Adolph Engelmann: 43d Ill., Lieut.-Col. Adolph Dengler; 61st Ill., Maj. Simon P. Ohr; 106th Ill., Maj. John M. Hunt; 12th Mich., Col. Wm. H. Graves. *Richmond's Brigade,* Col. Jonathan Richmond: 18th Ill., Col. Daniel H. Brush; 54th Ill., Col. Greenville M. Mitchell; 126th Ill., Maj. Wm. W. Wilshire; 22d Ohio, Col. Oliver Wood. *Montgomery's Brigade,* Col. Milton Montgomery: 40th Iowa, Col. John A. Garrett; 3d Minn., Col. Chauncey W. Griggs; 25th Wis., Lieut.-Col. Samuel J. Nasmith; 27th Wis., Col. Conrad Krez.

SEVENTEENTH ARMY CORPS, Maj.-Gen. James B. McPherson.

Escort: 4th Co. Ohio Cav., Capt. John S. Foster. Loss: Port Gibson, w, 1.

THIRD DIVISION, Maj.-Gen. John A. Logan.

Escort: A, 2d Ill. Cav., Lieut. William B. Cummins.

First Brigade, Brig.-Gen. John E. Smith, Brig.-Gen. Mortimer D. Leggett: 20th Ill., Lieut.-Col. Evan Richards (k), Maj. Daniel Bradley; 31st Ill., Col. Edwin S. McCook (w), Lieut.-Col. John D. Rees (m w), Maj. Robert N. Pearson; 45th Ill., Col. Jasper A. Maltby; 124th Ill., Col. Thomas J. Sloan; 23d Ind., Lieut.-Col. William P. Davis. Brigade loss: Port Gibson, k, 5; w, 27 = 32. Raymond, k, 35; w, 175; m, 25 = 235. Champion's Hill, k, 22; w, 104; m, 9 = 135. Vicksburg, assault May 22d, k, 7; w, 72; m, 2 = 81. *Second Brigade,* Brig.-Gen. Elias S. Dennis, Brig.-Gen. Mortimer D. Leggett, Col. Manning F. Force: 30th Ill., Lieut.-Col. Warren Shedd; 20th Ohio, Col. Manning F. Force, Capt. Francis M. Shaklee; 68th Ohio, Lieut.-Col. John S. Snook (k), Col. Robert K. Scott; 78th Ohio, Lieut.-Col. Greenberry F. Wiles. Brigade loss: Port Gibson, w, 3. Raymond, k, 10; w, 75 = 85. Champion's Hill, k, 21; w, 189 = 210. Vicksburg, assault May 22d, w, 6. *Third Brigade,* Brig.-Gen. John D. Stevenson: 8th Ill., Col. John P. Post, Lieut.-Col. Robert H. Sturgess; 17th Ill., Lieut.-Col. Francis M. Smith, Maj. Frank F. Peats; 81st Ill., Col. James J. Dollins (k), Col. Franklin Campbell; 7th Mo., Maj. Edwin Wakefield, Lieut.-Col. William S. Oliver (w), Capt. Robert Buchanan, Capt. William B. Collins; 32d Ohio, Col. Benjamin F. Potts. Brigade loss: Port Gibson, k, 1; w, 8; m, 2 = 11. Raymond, k, 18; w, 85; m, 12 = 115.

Champion's Hill, k, 7; w, 36; m, 18 = 61. Vicksburg, assault May 22d, k, 34; w, 238 = 272. *Artillery,* Maj. Charles J. Stolbrand: D, 1st Ill., Capt. Henry A. Rogers (k), Lieut. George J. Wood, Capt. Frederick Sparrestrom; G, 2d Ill., Capt. Frederick Sparrestrom, Lieut. John W. Lowell; L, 2d Ill., Capt. William H. Bolton; 8th Mich., Capt. Samuel De Golyer (m w), Lieut. Theodore W. Lockwood; 3d Ohio, Capt. William S. Williams. Artillery loss: Port Gibson, w, 2. Raymond, w, 1. Champion's Hill, k, 1.

SIXTH DIVISION, Brig.-Gen. John McArthur.

Escort: G, 1st Ill. Cav., Lieut. Stephen S. Tripp.

First Brigade, Brig.-Gen. Hugh T. Reed: 1st Kan., Col. William Y. Roberts; 16th Wis., Col. Benjamin Allen. *Second Brigade,* Brig.-Gen. Thomas E. G. Ransom: 11th Ill., Lieut.-Col. Garrett Nevins (k), Lieut.-Col. James H. Coates; 72d Ill., Col. Frederick A. Starring; 95th Ill., Col. Thomas W. Humphrey, Lieut.-Col. Leander Blanden; 14th Wis., Col. Lyman M. Ward; 17th Wis., Lieut.-Col. Thomas McMahon, Col. Adam K. Malloy. Brigade loss: Vicksburg, assault May 19th, k, 14; w, 110 = 124; assault May 22d, k, 57; w, 275; m, 32 = 364. *Third Brigade,* Col. William Hall, Col. Alexander Chambers: 11th Iowa, Lieut.-Col. John C. Abercrombie, Col. William Hall; 13th Iowa, Col. John Shane; 15th Iowa, Col. William W. Belknap; 16th Iowa, Lieut.-Col. Addison H. Sanders. Brigade loss: Vicksburg, assault May 22d, k, 1; w, 2 = 3. *Artillery,* Maj. Thomas D. Maurice: F, 2d Ill., Capt. John W. Powell; 1st Minn., Lieut. Henry Hunter, Capt. William Z. Clayton; C, 1st Mo., Capt. Charles Mann; 10th Ohio, Capt. Hamilton B. White, Lieut. William L. Newcomb.

SEVENTH DIVISION, Brig.-Gen. Marcellus M. Crocker, Brig.-Gen. Isaac F. Quinby, Brig.-Gen. John E. Smith.

Escort: F, 4th Mo. Cav., Lieut. Alexander Mueller. Loss: Raymond, k, 1; w, 1 = 2.

First Brigade, Col. John B. Sanborn: 48th Ind., Col. Norman Eddy; 59th Ind., Col. Jesse I. Alexander; 4th Minn., Lieut.-Col. John E. Tourtellotte; 18th Wis., Col. Gabriel Bouck. Brigade loss: Jackson, k, 4; w, 33 = 37. Champion's Hill, k, 5; w, 51 = 56. Vicksburg, assault May 22d, k, 36; w, 176; m, 2 = 214. *Second Brigade,* Col. Samuel A. Holmes, Col. Green B. Raum: 56th Ill., Col. Green B. Raum, Capt. Pinckney J. Welsh; 17th Iowa, Col. David B. Hillis, Col. Clark R. Wever, Maj. John F. Walden; 10th Mo., Lieut.-Col. Leonidas Horney (k), Maj. Francis C. Deimling; E, 24th Mo., Lieut. Daniel Driscoll; 80th Ohio, Col. Matthias H. Bartilson, Maj. Pren. Metham. Brigade loss: Jackson, k, 30; w, 182; m, 3 = 215. Champion's Hill, k, 12; w, 87; m, 4 = 103. Vicksburg, assault May 22d, k, 1; w, 11 = 12. *Third Brigade,* Col. George B. Boomer (k), Col. Holden Putnam, Brig.-Gen. Charles L. Matthies: 93d Ill., Col. Holden Putnam, Lieut.-Col. Nicholas C. Buswell, Col. Holden Putnam; 5th Iowa, Lieut.-Col. Ezekiel S. Sampson, Col. Jabez Banbury; 10th Iowa, Col. William E. Small; 26th Mo., Capt. Benjamin D. Dean. Brigade loss: Jackson, k, 1; w, 10 = 11. Champion's Hill, k, 111; w, 388; m, 11 = 510. Vicksburg, assault May 19th, k, 2; w, 3 = 5; assault May 22d, k, 14; w. 100 = 114. *Artillery,* Capt. Frank C. Sands, Capt. Henry Dillon: M, 1st Mo., Lieut. Junius W. MacMurray; 11th Ohio, Lieut. Fletcher E. Armstrong; 6th Wis., Capt. Henry Dillon, Lieut. Samuel F. Clark; 12th Wis., Capt. William Zickerick. Artillery loss: Jackson, w, 2. Champion's Hill, w, 2.

HERRON'S DIVISION (joined June 11), Maj.-Gen. Francis J. Herron.

First Brigade, Brig.-Gen. Wm. Vandever: 37th Ill., Col. John C. Black; 26th Ind., Col. John G. Clark; 20th Iowa, Col. Wm. McE. Dye; 34th Iowa, Col. George W. Clark; 38th Iowa, Col. D. Henry Hughes; E, 1st Mo. Art'y, Capt. Nelson Cole; F, 1st Mo. Art'y, Capt. Joseph Foust. *Second Brigade,* Brig.-Gen. Wm. W. Orme: 94th Ill., Col. John McNulta; 19th Iowa, Lieut.-Col. Daniel Kent; 20th Wis., Col. Henry Bertram; B, 1st Mo. Art'y, Capt. Martin Welfley.

UNATTACHED CAVALRY, Col. Cyrus Bussey: 5th Ill., Maj. Thomas A. Apperson; 3d Iowa, Maj. Oliver H. P. Scott; 2d Wis., Col. Thomas Stephens.

DISTRICT NORTH-EAST LOUISIANA.— Brig.-Gen. Elias S. Dennis.

DETACHED BRIGADE, Col. George W. Neeley: 63d Ill., Col. Joseph B. McCown; 108th Ill., Lieut.-Col. Charles Turner; 120th Ill., Col. George W. McKeaig; 131st Ill., Col. George W. Neeley, Maj. Joseph L. Purvis; 10th Ill. Cav. (4 co's), Maj. Elvis P. Shaw.

AFRICAN BRIGADE, Col. Isaac J. Shepard.

Post of Milliken's Bend, Col. Hiram Scofield: 8th La., Col. Hiram Scofield; 9th La., Col. Herman Lieb, Maj. Erastus N. Owen, Lieut.-Col. Charles J. Paine; 11th La., Col. Edwin W. Chamberlain, Lieut.-Col. Cyrus Sears; 13th La., Lieut. H. Knoll; 1st Miss., Lieut.-Col. A. Watson Webber; 3d Miss., Col. Richard H. Ballinger.

Post of Goodrich's Landing, Col. Wm. F. Wood: 1st Ark., Lieut.-Col. James W. Campbell; 10th La., Lieut.-Col. Frederick M. Crandall.

Grant's losses during the campaign were:

ENGAGEMENTS.	Kill'd.	Wounded.	Capt-ured or Missi'g.	Total.
Port Gibson	131	719	25	875
Raymond	66	339	37	442
Jackson	42	251	7	300
Champion's Hill	410	1,844	187	2,441
Big Black Bridge	39	237	3	279
Assault of May 19	157	777	8	942
Assault of May 22	502	2,550	147	3,199
Siege Operations	104	419	7	530
Miscellane's Skirmishes.	63	259	32	354
Aggregate	1,514	7,395	453	9,362

The effective force ranged from 43,000 at the beginning to 75,000 at the close of the campaign.

CONFEDERATE FORCES: Lieut.-General John C. Pemberton.

FIRST DIVISION, ☆ Maj.-Gen. W. W. Loring.

First Brigade, Brig.-Gen. Lloyd Tilghman (k), Col. A. E. Reynolds: 1st Confederate Battalion, Maj. G. H. Forney; 6th Miss., Col. Robert Lowry; 15th Miss., Col. M. Farrell; 20th Miss., Col. D. R. Russell; 23d Miss., Col. J. M. Wells; 26th Miss., Col. A. E. Reynolds, Maj. T. F. Parker; Miss. Battery, Capt. J. J. Cowan; Miss. Battery, Capt. Jacob Culbertson. Brigade loss: Champion's Hill, k, 5; w, 10; m, 42 = 57. *Second Brigade*, Brig.-Gen. Winfield S. Featherston: 3d Miss., Col. T. A. Mellon; 22d Miss., Lieut.-Col. H. J. Reid; 31st Miss., Col. J. A. Orr; 33d Miss., Col. D. W. Hurst; 1st Miss. Battalion Sharpshooters, Maj. W. A. Rayburn. Brigade loss: Champion's Hill, w, 2; m, 1 = 3. *Third Brigade*, Brig.-Gen. Abram Buford: 27th Ala., Col. James Jackson; 35th Ala., Col. Edward Goodwin; 54th Ala., Col. Alpheus Baker (w); 55th Ala., Col. John Snodgrass; 9th Ark., Col. Isaac L. Dunlop; 3d Ky. (4 co's), Maj. J. H. Bowman; 7th Ky., Col. Edward Crossland; 12th La., Col.T. M. Scott; Pointe Coupée (La.) Artillery, Capt. Alcide Bouanchaud. Brigade loss: Champion's Hill, k, 11; w, 49 = 60.

STEVENSON'S DIVISION, Maj.-Gen. Carter L. Stevenson.

Staff loss: Champion's Hill, k, 1.

First Brigade, Brig.-Gen. Seth M. Barton: 40th Ga., Col. Abda Johnson, Lieut.-Col. Robert M. Young; 41st Ga., Col. William E. Curtiss; 42d Ga., Col. R. J. Henderson; 43d Ga., Col. Skidmore Harris (k), Capt. M. M. Grantham; 52d Ga., Col. C. D. Phillips (m), Maj. John J. Moore; Miss. Battery (Hudson's), Lieut. Milton H. Trantham; La. Battery (Pointe Coupée Artillery), Section Co. A, Lieut. John Yoist; La. Battery (Pointe Coupée Artillery), Co. C, Capt. Alexander Chust. Brigade loss: Champion's Hill, k, 58; w, 106; m, 737 = 901. Vicksburg (siege), k, 6; w, 20; m, 5 = 31. *Second Brigade*, Brig.-Gen. E. D. Tracy (k), Col. Isham W. Garrott, Brig.-Gen. Stephen D. Lee; 20th Ala., Col. Isham W. Garrott (k), Col. Edward W. Pettus; 23d Ala., Col. F. K. Beck; 30th Ala., Col. Charles M. Shelley, Capt. John C. Francis; 31st Ala., Col. D. B. Hundley (w), Lieut.-Col. T. M. Arrington, Maj. G. W. Mathieson; 46th Ala., Col. Michael L. Woods (c), Capt. George E. Brewer; Ala. Battery, Capt. James F. Waddell. Brigade loss: Port Gibson, k, 18; w, 112 ; m, 142 = 272. Champion's Hill, k, 53; w, 152; m, 609 = 814. Vicksburg (siege), k, 79; w, 177; m, 7 = 263. *Third Brigade*, Brig.-Gen. Alfred Cumming: 34th Ga., Col. James A. W. Johnson; 36th Ga., Col. Jesse A. Glenn, Maj. Charles E. Broyles; 39th Ga., Col. J. T. McConnell (w), Lieut.-Col. J. F. B. Jackson; 56th Ga., Col. E. P. Watkins (w), Lieut.-Col. J. T. Slaughter; 57th Ga., Lieut.-Col. C. S. Guyton, Col. William Barkuloo; Ga. Battery (Cherokee Artillery), Capt. M. Van Der Corput. Brigade loss: Champion's Hill, k, 121; w, 269; m, 605 = 995. Vicksburg (siege), k, 22; w, 74 = 96. *Fourth Brigade*, Col. A. W. Reynolds: 3d Tenn. (Prov.

Army), Col. N. J. Lillard; 31st Tenn., Col. William M. Bradford; 43d Tenn., Col. James W. Gillespie; 59th Tenn., Col. William L. Eakin; 3d Md. Battery, Capt. F. O. Claiborne (k), Capt. John B. Rowan. Brigade loss: Champion's Hill, m, 152. Big Black Bridge, m, 12. Vicksburg (siege), k, 14; w, 25; m, 14 = 53. *Texas Legion*, Col. T. N. Waul: 1st Battalion (infantry), Maj. Eugene S. Bolling; 2d Battalion (infantry), Lieut.-Col. James Wrigley; Cav. Battalion, Lieut. Thomas J. Cleveland; Art'y Co., Capt. J. Q. Wall. Legion loss: Vicksburg (siege), k, 47; w, 190; m, 8 = 245. *Attached Troops:* C, 1st Tenn. Cav. (Carter's), Capt. R. S. Vandyke; Va. Battery (Botetourt Art'y), Capt. J. W. Johnston, Lieut. James P. Wright.

FORNEY'S DIVISION, Maj.-Gen. John H. Forney.

Hébert's Brigade, Brig.-Gen. Louis Hébert: 3d La., Lieut.-Col. S. D. Russell, Maj. David Pierson (w); 21st La., Col. Charles H. Herrick (m w), Lieut.-Col. J. T. Plattsmier; 36th Miss., Col. W. W. Witherspoon; 37th Miss., Col. O. S. Holland; 38th Miss., Capt. D. B. Seal; 43d Miss., Col. Richard Harrison; 7th Miss. Battalion, Capt. A. M. Dozier; C, 2d Ala. Art'y Battalion, Lieut. John R. Sclater; Ark. (Appeal) Battery, Capt. W. N. Hogg (k), Lieut. R. N. Cotten. Brigade loss: Vicksburg (siege), k, 219; w, 455; m, 21 = 695. *Moore's Brigade*, Brig.-Gen. John C. Moore: 37th Ala., Col. J. F. Dowdell; 40th Ala., Col. John H. Higley; 42d Ala., Col. John W. Portis, Lieut.-Col. Thomas C. Lanier; 1st Miss. Light Art'y (Batteries A, C, D, E, G, and I), Col. William T. Withers; 35th Miss., Col. William S. Barry, Lieut.-Col. C. R. Jordan; 40th Miss., Col. W. B. Colbert; 2d Tex., Col. Ashbel Smith; Ala. Battery, Capt. H. H. Sengstak; La. Battery (Pointe Coupée Art'y), Capt. William A. Davidson. Brigade loss: Vicksburg (siege), k, 121; w, 304 = 425.

SMITH'S DIVISION, Maj.-Gen. Martin L. Smith.

First Brigade, Brig.-Gen. W. E. Baldwin: 17th La., Col. Robert Richardson; 31st La., Col. S. H. Griffin (k), Lieut.-Col. James W. Draughon; 4th Miss., Lieut.-Col. T. W. Adaire (w), Capt. Thomas P. Nelson; 46th Miss., Col. C. W. Sears; Tenn. Battery, Capt. Thomas F. Tobin. Brigade loss: Port Gibson, k, 12; w, 48; m, 27 = 87. *Vaughn's Brigade*, Brig.-Gen. J. C. Vaughn: 60th Tenn., Capt. J. W. Bachman; 61st Tenn., Lieut.-Col. James G. Rose; 62d Tenn., Col. John A. Rowan. *Third Brigade*, Brig.-Gen. Francis A. Shoup: 26th La., Col. Winchester Hall (w), Lieut.-Col. William C. Crow; 27th La., Col. L. D. Marks (m w), Lieut.-Col. L. L. McLaurin (k), Capt. Joseph T. Hatch; 28th La., Col. Allen Thomas; Ark. Battery (McNally's). Brigade loss: Vicksburg (siege), k, 107; w, 199 = 306. *Mississippi State Troops* (under Vaughn's command), Brig.-Gen. John V. Harris: 5th Reg't, Col. H. C. Robinson; 3d Battalion, Lieut.-Col. Thomas A. Burgin. *Attached Troops:* 14th

☆ The major portion of this division was separated from Pemberton after the battle of Champion's Hill, and joined the forces with General Joseph E. Johnston (Pemberton's superior officer) at Jackson, Mississippi.— EDITORS.

Miss. Art'y Battalion, Maj. M. S. Ward ; Miss. Partisan Rangers, Capt. J. S. Smyth.

BOWEN'S DIVISION, Maj.-Gen. John S. Bowen.

First (Missouri) *Brigade*, Col. Francis M. Cockrell : 1st and 4th Mo., Col. A. C. Riley ; 2d Mo., Lieut.-Col. P. S. Senteny (k), Maj. Thomas M. Carter ; 3d Mo., Lieut.-Col. F. L. Hubbell (m w), Col. W. R. Gause, Maj. J. K. McDowell ; 5th Mo., Lieut.-Col. R. S. Bevier, Col. James McCown ; 6th Mo., Col. Eugene Erwin (k), Maj. Stephen Cooper ; Mo. Battery (Guibor's), Lieut. William Corkery, Lieut. Cornelius Hefferman ; Mo. Battery, Capt. John C. Landis, Lieut. John M. Langan ; Mo. Battery, (Wade's), Lieut. Richard C. Walsh. Brigade loss : Port Gibson, k, 13 ; w, 97 ; m, 96 = 206. Champion's Hill, k, 65 ; w, 293 ; m, 242 = 600. Big Black Bridge, k, 2. Vicksburg (siege), k, 113 ; w, 446 = 559. *Second Brigade*, Brig.-Gen. Martin E. Green (k), Col. T. P. Dockery : 15th Ark., Capt. Caleb Davis ; 19th Ark., Col. T. P. Dockery, Capt. James K. Norwood ; 20th Ark., Col. D. W. Jones ; 21st Ark., Col. J. E. Cravens, Capt. A Tyler ; 1st Ark. Cav. Battalion (dismounted), Capt. John J. Clark ; 12th Ark. Battalion Sharp-shooters, Capt. Griff. Bayne (w), Lieut. John S. Bell ; 1st Mo. Cav. (dismounted), Col. Elijah Gates, Major William C. Parker ; 3d Mo. Cav. (dismounted), Captain Felix Lotspeich ; 3d Mo. Battery, Captain William E. Dawson ; Mo. Battery (Lowe's), Lieutenant Thomas B. Catron ; Stirman's Battalion, Colonel Ras. Stirman. Brigade loss : Port Gibson, k, 17 ; w, 83 ; m, 122 = 222. Champion's Hill, k, 65 ; w, 137 ; m, 65 = 268. Big Black Bridge, k, 1 ; w, 9 ; m, 1012 = 1022.

RIVER-BATTERIES, Col. Edward Higgins : 1st La. Artillery, Lieut.-Col. D. Beltzhoover ; 8th La. Artillery Battalion, Maj. F. N. Ogden ; 23d La., Capt. Samuel Jones ; 1st Tenn. Artillery, Col. A. Jackson, Jr. ; Tenn. Battery, Capt. J. B. Caruthers ; Tenn. Battery, Capt. T. N. Johnston ; Tenn. Battery, Capt. J. P. Lynch ; Miss. Battery (Vaiden), Capt. S. C. Bains.

MISCELLANEOUS TROOPS : 54th Ala. (detachment), Lieut. Joel P. Abney ; City Guards, Capt. E. B. Martin ; Miss. Cavalry, Col. Wirt Adams.

JOHNSTON'S FORCES (engaged only at Raymond and Jackson), General Joseph E. Johnston (in chief command of the departments of Generals Bragg, E. Kirby Smith, and Pemberton).

Gregg's Brigade, Brig.-Gen. John Gregg : 1st Tenn. Battalion, Maj. S. H. Colms ; 3d Tenn., Col. C. H. Walker ; 10th and 30th Tenn., Col. R. W. MacGavock (k), Lieut.-Col. James J. Turner ; 41st Tenn., Col. R. Farquharson ; 50th Tenn., Lieut.-Col. T. W. Beaumont (w) ; 7th Tex., Col. H. B. Granbury ; Mo. Battery, Capt. H. M. Bledsoe. Brigade loss : Raymond, k, 73 ; w, 251 ; m, 190 = 514. *Gist's Brigade*, Col. Peyton H. Colquitt : 46th Ga. (5 co's), Capt. T. B. Hancock ; 14th Miss., Lieut.-Col. W. L. Doss ; 24th S. C., Lieut.-Col. Ellison Capers ; Miss. Bat'y, Capt. J. A. Hoskins. Brigade loss : Jackson, k, 17 ; w, 64 ; m, 118 = 198. *Walker's Brigade*, Brig.-Gen. W. H. T. Walker : 1st Bat'n Ga. Sharp-shooters, Maj. A Shaaff ; Ga. Bat'y, Capt. R. Martin. *Unattached*, 3d Ky. (mounted), Col. A. P. Thompson ; 8th Ky. (mounted), Col. H. B. Lyon.

After Grant's withdrawal from Jackson to Vicksburg the reënforcements received by Johnston consisted of the brigades of Rust and Maxey from Port Hudson ; Ector's and McNair's brigades and the divisions of Breckinridge and W. H. Jackson from Tennessee ; Evans's brigade from Charleston ; and the division of Loring, from the force under Pemberton. [See p. 487.] On June 4th Johnston's effectives numbered, according to his own report, 24,000. [See also pp. 478, 479, 480.] — EDITORS.

Incomplete reports of Confederate losses from May 1st to July 3d, inclusive, aggregate 1260 killed, 3572 wounded, and 4227 captured or missing = 9059. Complete returns would doubtless swell the number to over 10,000. According to the parole lists on file in the War Department the number surrendered on July 4th was 29,491. Of course this included all the non-combatants. Pemberton's greatest available force, including the troops confronting Grant at Raymond and Jackson, probably numbered over 40,000. General Grant estimated it at nearly 60,000. General Pemberton says in his official report that when he moved within the defenses of Vicksburg his effective aggregate did not exceed 28,000.

WRECK OF THE "STAR OF THE WEST," IN THE TALLAHATCHIE RIVER, OPPOSITE THE SITE OF FORT PEMBERTON. FROM A PHOTOGRAPH TAKEN IN 1887.

It was the steamer *Star of the West* that was used in the unsuccessful effort to reënforce Fort Sumter in January, 1861. She was at New Orleans when Louisiana seceded, and was seized by the State authorities. S. B. Morgan, of Greenwood, Mississippi, wrote to the editors, January 12th, 1888, that the *Star of the West* was sunk in the Tallahatchie on March 13th, 1863, under the parapet of Fort Pemberton, to prevent Union gun-boats, that had entered by way of Yazoo Pass, from passing from the Tallahatchie into the Yazoo River. [See map, p. 442.]

NAVAL OPERATIONS IN THE VICKSBURG CAMPAIGN.

BY PROFESSOR JAMES RUSSELL SOLEY, U. S. N.

B Y the 1st of July, 1862, the Mississippi had been traversed by the fleet of Davis from Cairo down, and by that of Farragut from the Passes up, and the only point where the Confederates retained a strong foothold was at Vicksburg. The objects of the river operations were to establish communication from the Ohio to the Gulf, and to cut off the important supplies drawn by the Confederacy from Arkansas, Louisiana, and Texas. The commanders of the Mississippi squadron during this period were, first, Charles Henry Davis, and later, David D. Porter, the transfer of the command taking place October 15th, 1862. The operations of the navy at this time were unique in maritime warfare in the energy and originality with which complex conditions were met.

After the defeat of Montgomery's flotilla at Memphis, on the 6th of June, by the combined forces of Flag-Officer Davis and Colonel Ellet [see Vol. I., pp. 449–459], the Mississippi squadron remained at Memphis for three weeks. Immediately after the battle Davis had formed the project of sending a force up the Arkansas and White rivers to cut off the Confederate gun-boats which were supposed to have taken refuge there, among them the *Van Dorn*, the only vessel remaining of Montgomery's flotilla. Davis did not know that the *Van Dorn* had made her way into the Yazoo. There were, however, two Confederate gun-boats in White River, the *Maurepas* and *Pontchartrain*, which had previously been in the flotilla of Hollins at Island Number Ten— the former under Lieutenant Joseph Fry and the latter under Lieutenant John W. Dunnington.

On the 10th Davis received a telegram from General Halleck urging him to open communication by way of Jacksonport with General Curtis, then moving through Arkansas toward the Mississippi. Davis accordingly altered his plan, and directed that the expedition should confine its operations to the White River. The force detached for the purpose was composed of the iron-clads *Mound City* and *St. Louis*, and the wooden gun-boats *Conestoga* and *Tyler*, under Commander A. H. Kilty, of the *Mound City*, and the 46th Indiana, Colonel Graham N. Fitch. Ascending the White River, the expedition arrived on the evening of the 16th in the neighborhood of St. Charles, ninety miles from the mouth. [See map, p. 442.]

Anticipating this movement, Hindman had taken steps to obstruct the channel at this point, where the first bluffs touch the river. One hundred men, under Captain A. M. Williams, C. S. Engineers, were the only force which could be spared for the defense of the place, and their only arms were thirty-five Enfield rifles which Hindman had impounded at Memphis. Lieutenant Dunnington had placed two rifled 32-pounders in battery on the bluffs, and had manned them with part of the crew of the *Pontchartrain*. Finally, Fry had stationed the *Maurepas* in the river below.

The approach of Kilty's gun-boats was first discovered on the afternoon of June 16th.   Expecting an immediate attack, Fry placed the *Maurepas* across the stream and prepared to defend her.   Finding that the gun-boats remained below, Fry now landed his guns and scuttled his ship, sinking her across the channel.   Two transports also were sunk, and the imperfect obstruction thus created was completed about daylight.   During the night a small rifled Parrott gun was placed in position four hundred yards below Dunnington's battery, under Midshipman F. M. Roby.   Two rifled Parrott 8-pounders were also moved up soon after daylight, and placed near Roby's gun, and the three guns were manned by the crew of the *Maurepas*, and fought personally by Fry, the senior officer present.   Below this second battery Captain Williams was stationed with his thirty-five men, those without arms having been sent to the rear.   He was presently reënforced by the 12-pounder howitzer from the *Maurepas*, manned by some of her crew.   The total force under Fry's command comprised the men with Williams, and 79 seamen from the two gun-boats,— in all, 114 persons, to resist the attack of Fitch's Indiana regiment, and four gun-boats, two of them iron-clads.   Rarely has it happened to such a feeble force to accomplish so much by a determined resistance.

Early on the morning of June 17th the troops landed about two miles below the bluffs.   At half-past 8 the gun-boats advanced to the attack, the *Mound City* ahead, followed closely by the *St. Louis*, the *Lexington* and the *Conestoga* bringing up the rear.   They moved slowly, endeavoring to discover the enemy's position, but in total ignorance of the whereabouts of his guns, which were covered by the trees and bushes on the bluffs.   About 9 o'clock Williams's men were engaged by Fitch's skirmishers.   The firing disclosed the enemy's advanced position, and the gun-boats opened a heavy fire of grape and shell upon it, compelling Williams to fall back.   Fry's battery of four light guns, manned by the crew of the *Maurepas*, now became engaged with the gun-boats.   At 10 Dunnington opened with his rifled 32-pounders. Kilty had now to some extent made out the location of the Confederate guns, and, moving up, replied with a rapid fire, aimed carefully in what was supposed to be the direction of the batteries, the vessel taking a position at point-blank range from both of them.   At the same time Fitch sent word to him that the troops were ready to storm the batteries, unless he desired to silence them with the gun-boats.   Kilty, unfortunately for himself and his crew, gallantly decided on the latter course.

The *Mound City* had been in position less than half an hour, about 600 yards from the batteries, when one of the 32-pounder rifle shot, directed by the skillful and experienced eye of Lieutenant Dunnington, penetrated the port casemate of the *Mound City* just forward of the armor, or, as Colonel Fitch rather comically described it in his report, " the larboard forequarter of the gun-boat," and, after killing 8 men at the gun, struck the steam-drum, and went through it directly fore and aft.   At the time, the *Mound City* was turning her wheel over slowly, and, being in slack water, the wheel kept on turning until the steam was exhausted, and the boat slowly forged ahead, running her nose directly under the battery.   Lieutenant Blodgett immediately ran up in the *Conestoga*, with great gallantry, and making fast to the *Mound City*, towed her away from the bank and out of action. Fitch, seeing the catastrophe, and apprehensive lest another fortunate shot from the enemy should deprive him of his support afloat, gave the signal to cease firing, and assaulted the works simultaneously in front and in flank. They were quickly carried; Dunnington and Williams made good their retreat, but Fry, who was badly wounded, was taken prisoner with about thirty of his men. General Hindman reported the Confederate loss as 6 killed, 1 wounded, and 8 missing.

The scene on board the *Mound City*, upon the explosion of the steam-drum, was beyond description. The gun-deck was at once filled with scalding steam, and many of the crew were instantly killed,— literally cooked alive. Others, in an agony of pain, jumped into the water, where they were shot at by sharp-shooters from the bluff, under orders from Dunnington and Williams. The boats from the other vessels put off at once to the rescue, and were riddled with shot while picking up their comrades. Out of 175 officers and men on board the *Mound City*, only 23 answered to their names at the roll-call that evening, and these were men and boys that were in the shell-room and magazine when the explosion took place. The only officers unhurt were Dominy, the first master, and McElroy, the gunner. Eighty-two men perished in the casemate, 43 were killed in the water or drowned, and 25 were severely wounded. The latter, among whom was the gallant Kilty, were sent at once to Memphis in the *Conestoga*. The *Mound City* remained at St. Charles, under First Master John H. Duble, of the *Conestoga*, with a crew of one hundred of Fitch's men, her injuries being temporarily repaired.

The expedition continued up White River as far as Crooked Point Cut-off, 63 miles above St. Charles, where the gun-boats were compelled to turn back by the falling of the water. Halleck and Grant meantime had decided to increase Fitch's command by the addition of two regiments, which sailed for White River on the 26th of June, under convoy of the *Conestoga*. Commander John A. Winslow, of *Kearsarge-Alabama* fame, who was at this time in command of the forces afloat in White River, was ordered to give additional convoy as far up as the state of the water would permit. The bulk of the naval force was then withdrawn, the *Lexington* remaining to support Fitch in his subsequent operations up the river. Curtis reached Helena on the 13th of July without communicating with the gun-boats. [See p. 445.]

During the months of May and June, 1862, Farragut's fleet had been slowly working up from New Orleans, receiving the surrender of the principal cities on the way, and having an occasional encounter with the Confederate batteries along the river. None of the latter were at this time of any great importance, although those at Grand Gulf inflicted some damage on two of the gun-boats which attacked them on June 9th. No serious obstruction, however, to the passage of the river from Cairo to the sea now existed, except at Vicksburg.

The advance division of Farragut's squadron under Commander Lee in the *Oneida* had summoned Vicksburg to surrender on the 18th of May, but had met with a refusal. Farragut, arriving soon after, held a consultation with

COLONEL CHARLES RIVERS ELLET.
FROM AN AMBROTYPE.

General Williams, who commanded a small detachment of Butler's army, and the two came to the conclusion that they had not enough men to make an attempt on Vicksburg with any hope of success, and Farragut went back to New Orleans.

Soon after, Farragut received pressing instructions from the Navy Department to attack Vicksburg, and in consequence returned up the river with his squadron, the mortar-boats under Porter, and 3000 troops under Williams. On the night of the 26th of June Porter placed his mortar-boats in position, nine on the eastern and eight on the western bank, the latter, as at New Orleans, being dressed with bushes to prevent an accurate determination of their position. The next day they opened upon Vicksburg. On the 28th Farragut passed the batteries with all the vessels of his fleet, except the *Brooklyn*, *Katahdin*, and *Kennebec*, which dropped back, owing to a too rigid adherence to their original orders. No impression of any consequence was made on the forts, nor were the ships materially injured, notwithstanding the great advantage which the forts possessed in their plunging fire. The *Hartford* was principally damaged by the battery above the town, which was able to rake a passing ship in a position from which the latter could not reply. Farragut, in his report of July 2d, sums up the situation with the phrase:

"The forts can be passed, and we have done it, and can do it again as often as may be required of us. It will not, however, be an easy matter for us to do more than silence the batteries for a time, as long as the enemy has a large force behind the hills to prevent our landing and holding the place."

While Farragut with the Western Gulf Squadron, so called, was passing the batteries at Vicksburg, the Mississippi flotilla was still at Memphis, except the rams now commanded by Lieutenant-Colonel Alfred W. Ellet, which had left Memphis about the 20th, and arrived above Vicksburg on the afternoon of the 24th. Here Ellet opened communication with Farragut across the neck of land opposite Vicksburg. Farragut replied, suggesting the coöperation of Davis's iron-clads. Davis received this message at Memphis on the 28th, and the next day started down the river. During the interval, Ellet's audacity was rewarded by another extraordinary success. Taking the *Monarch* and the *Lancaster*, the latter under Charles Rivers Ellet, a mere boy nineteen years of age, he steamed fifty miles up the Yazoo River. Ellet was in perfect ignorance of what he might find there, whether batteries, gun-boats, or torpedoes. His rams carried no armament. As a matter of fact there were at the time in the river two of Hollins's former fleet, the *Polk* and the *Livingston*, and the last of Montgomery's vessels, the *Van Dorn*. These were tied up abreast of a battery at Liverpool Landing, and above them was a barrier made from a raft. The *Arkansas* was at Yazoo City above the barrier, completing her preparations. The officer in charge at Liverpool Landing, Commander Robert F. Pinkney, on the approach of the rams set fire to his three gun-boats, and the purpose of Ellet's visit being thus easily accomplished, he withdrew again to the Mississippi. ☆

Davis arrived above Vicksburg on the 1st of July, and joined Farragut with four gun-boats and six mortar-boats. The fleets remained here at anchor for several days, while the army was attempting to make a cut-off across the neck of the land opposite Vicksburg, and thus create a new channel out of range of the batteries on the bluffs. During this time Porter continued his daily bombardment. Beyond this nothing was attempted, there being no force of troops to make it worth while.

While matters were in this condition, it was resolved between the two flag-officers that a detachment of gun-boats should make a reconnoissance in force up the Yazoo River. The shoalness and narrowness of the stream led them to take vessels of the upper squadron in preference to those of the lower, and the following were selected: the *Carondelet*, Commander Henry Walke; *Tyler*, Lieutenant William Gwin, and *Queen of the West*. The *Arkansas*, an armored ram with a heavy battery, was known to be up the river, and Farragut in his report mentions her as one of the objects of investigation.

The engagement that followed has been the subject of much discussion [see p. 572]. The *Queen of the West*, which had no weapons except her ram and the muskets of the sharp-shooters, and possibly a borrowed howitzer, immediately proceeded down the river. The *Tyler*, a very vulnerable wooden gun-boat, also retreated, placing herself under the protection of the *Carondelet*. The latter therefore became the principal antagonist of the Confederate ram. It now became a question for Walke of the *Carondelet* to decide whether he would advance to meet the *Arkansas* bows on, trusting to the skillful management of the helm to avoid a ram-thrust, or would retreat, engaging her with his stern guns. He chose the latter course. ⌡

☆ Lieutenant-Colonel Alfred W. Ellet soon after received a brigadier-general's commission, with instructions to organize and equip the Mississippi Marine Brigade for future work in patrolling the river. He also received commissions for such of his men as he chose to recommend. Charles Rivers Ellet, though but nineteen years of age, received a colonel's commission, and succeeded to the command of the ram fleet which his father, Charles Ellet, Jr., had created.— EDITORS.

⌡ In a note to the editors Admiral Walke states:

"When the *Tyler* was passing the *Carondelet*, I hailed the commander of the *Tyler*, and ordered him to go down to our fleet and report the arrival of the *Arkansas;* but the *Tyler* ran under the protection of the *Carondelet*. The latter, while advancing, fired several rounds of her bow-guns and all her starboard broadside guns at the *Arkansas*, which, returning the fire, raked the *Carondelet* from stem to stern, striking her forward three times. One shot glanced on the forward plating, one went through it and broke up, one from forward passed through the officers' rooms on the starboard side, and through the captain's cabin. Being a stern-wheel boat, the *Carondelet* required room and time to turn around. To avoid being sunk immediately, she turned and retreated. I was not such a simpleton as to 'take the bull by the horns,' to be fatally rammed, and sacrifice my command through fear of the criticisms of any man, or the vaunting opinion of much less-experienced officers. If I had continued fighting, bows on, in that narrow river, a collision, which the enemy desired, would have been inevitable, and would have sunk the *Carondelet* in a few minutes."

THE CONFEDERATE RAM "ARKANSAS" RUNNING THROUGH THE UNION FLEET AT VICKSBURG, JULY 15, 1862.

The *Arkansas* was decidedly the superior vessel. Apart from the fact that she was larger, and had at the beginning of the contest somewhat greater speed, she had a more efficient battery, and a far more complete and impenetrable armor protection. Indeed the Eads gun-boats, of which the *Carondelet* was one, were by no means fully armored, their two and one-half inch plating on the casemate covering only the forward end and that part of the sides abreast of the machinery. The stern was not armored at all. The side armor had no heavy backing, and such as it was could only ward off a shot directly abeam. It was by no means a complete protection to the boilers, as was shown in the catastrophe at St. Charles. The *Arkansas* on the other hand had three inches of railroad iron surrounding her casemate, with a heavy backing of timber and cotton bales. She had, besides, her ram, which experience had shown was a weapon much to be dreaded. However, the position adopted by Walke was the one which, by exposing his weakest point, gave the enemy the benefit of his superiority. The *Carondelet*, instead of presenting her armored bow, armed with three rifled guns, 30, 50, and 70 pounders, presented her unarmored stern, armed with two smooth-bore 32-pounders. That she escaped total destruction in the running fight of an hour or so that ensued with the two 8-inch guns in the *Arkansas's* bow is little short of a miracle. Walke made a very good fight of it, and both he and Gwin of the *Tyler*, who pluckily supported the *Carondelet*, inflicted much injury on their antagonist, riddling her smoke-stack so as nearly to destroy her speed, wounding her captain twice, damaging her wheel, and killing her Yazoo pilot. When near the mouth of the river, the *Carondelet's* steering gear was disabled and she ran in close to the bank, where the water was too shoal for the *Arkansas* to follow her. The latter, therefore, passed her, the two vessels exchanging broadsides, and the *Arkansas* continued on her course to Vicksburg.

Her approach caught the two flag-officers fairly napping. Notwithstanding their knowledge of her presence in the Yazoo, and the heavy firing that had been heard for more than an hour, there was, out of the combined fleet of twenty vessels or thereabouts, but one that had steam up, the captured ram *General Bragg*, and she did nothing. The *Arkansas* dashed boldly through the mass of clustered vessels, receiving the broadside of each ship as she passed, and delivering her fire rapidly in return. Her audacity was rewarded by success, for though she was badly battered, she was neither stopped nor disabled. On the other hand, her shot, penetrating the boiler of the ram *Lancaster*, used up that vessel and caused considerable loss of life among her crew. The *Benton*, Davis's flagship, got under way after Brown had passed, and followed him "at her usual snail's pace," to borrow Davis's phrase, without overtaking him. In a few minutes the *Arkansas* was under the guns of Vicksburg.

A week before, on the 7th of July, Farragut had written to the department that he hoped "soon to have the pleasure of recording the combined attack by army and navy, for which we all so ardently long." In the course of the week that had elapsed these hopes had been pretty well extinguished. The canal had turned out a failure, and the prospect that a considerable force of troops would arrive had been growing every day more remote. Before the *Arkansas* made her appearance, therefore, Farragut had already been meditating a return down the river, and the falling of the water and the prevalence of sickness in his crews admonished him to hasten. He also wished to damage the *Arkansas* in the rush by, so as to recover in some measure the prestige lost through her successful passage of the fleet. Preparations were therefore made for the descent on that very afternoon.

Already on the 10th Porter had left his station below Vicksburg with twelve of his mortar-boats, which were to be sent round to the James River. Most of the gun-boats of the mortar-flotilla went with him to tow the schooners down. The force that remained was composed of six mortar-schooners, under Commander W. B. Renshaw, with the ferry-boat *Westfield*. On the afternoon of the 15th these were moved up into position on the west bank of the river (with the exception of one, the *Sidney C. Jones*, which had run on shore and was blown up), and by half-past 3 they were engaged with the batteries. Davis, in the river above, also stationed three of his vessels, the *Benton*, *Louisville*, and *Cincinnati*, in position to attack the upper batteries, and to aid in covering Farragut's passage. Toward 7 in the evening the fleet got under way, consisting of the four sloops, the *Hartford*, *Richmond*, *Oneida*, and *Iroquois*, four gun-boats, and the ram *Sumter*, which Davis had lent for the special purpose of attacking the *Arkansas*. The fleet made a gallant dash past the batteries, meeting with little loss, but the attack on the *Arkansas* was a failure, for she had shifted her position and could not be readily distinguished by the flashes of the guns.   A single 11-inch shot, however, reached the ram and inflicted very serious injury, especially to the engine.

Early on the morning of the 22d, Farragut's reunited squadron being now at anchor below Vicksburg, another attempt was made on the *Arkansas*. While the upper and the lower fleets were drawing the fire of the batteries in their neighborhood, the *Essex*, under Commodore William D. Porter, started down the river, followed by the *Queen of the West*, Lieutenant-Colonel A. W. Ellet.   The crew of the *Arkansas* was small, but they were skillfully handled. The assailants tried to ram her in succession, but as each came on the beak of the Confederate was turned toward them, and they only succeeded in giving a glancing blow, and, sheering off, ran on the bank.   Extricating themselves with difficulty, they withdrew as rapidly as they could from their perilous position, the *Essex* going below and the *Queen*, temporarily disabled, resuming her station with the upper squadron.   One shot from the *Essex* did serious damage on board the *Arkansas*.

The *Essex* and *Sumter* were now permanently detained below Vicksburg. Shortly after the last engagement Farragut sailed down the river with Williams and his troops.   Davis had expected Farragut's departure, but he had relied on the occupation by the land forces of the point opposite Vicksburg, by which he communicated with his vessels below.   As these had now departed, nothing could be gained by staying longer in the neighborhood. Davis accordingly withdrew to Helena, and for the next four months Vicksburg was left unmolested.

Williams remained at Baton Rouge, with the *Essex, Kineo, Katahdin*, and *Sumter*, while Farragut continued to New Orleans with the rest of his fleet.   At daylight on the 5th of August, Baton Rouge was unsuccessfully attacked by the Confederates under General John C. Breckinridge, and on the 6th the *Arkansas* was destroyed. [See pp. 579 and 583.]   The remaining events of the summer of 1862 were of little importance.   Early in August a reconnoissance showed that the White River had fallen three feet and was impracticable for gun-boats.   Later in the month a more important expedition was sent down the river.   It was composed of the *Benton, Mound City*, and *Bragg*, together with four of Ellet's rams, the *Switzerland, Monarch, Samson*, and *Lioness*, all under Lieutenant-Commander Phelps, with a detachment of troops under Colonel Charles R. Woods.   At Milliken's Bend, thirty miles above Vicksburg, the Confederate transport steamer *Fairplay* was captured, loaded with a heavy cargo of arms and ammunition.   The gun-boats then penetrated far up the Yazoo River, and two of the rams even ascended the Sunflower for twenty miles.   When the expedition returned to Helena, it had destroyed or captured a vast quantity of military supplies.   It taught the Confederates a lesson, however, and it was a long time before the Federal fleet could again enter the Yazoo with impunity.

The experience of the gun-boats in the White River showed the necessity of obtaining light-draught vessels for service in the uncertain channels of the tributaries of the Mississippi, and each additional operation in these rivers confirmed the impression. As early as the 27th of June Davis had urgently recommended this step, and his recommendations, sustained by the earnest appeals of other officers, resulted in the creation of the "tin-clads," or "light-draughts," which during the next year performed invaluable service.

On the 15th of October Davis was relieved of this command, having been appointed Chief of the Bureau of Navigation at the Navy Department. He was succeeded by Porter. Two important and much-needed changes in organization took place about this time, the first being the formal transfer of the squadron on the 1st of October from the War Department, under which it had first come into existence, to the Navy Department, which henceforth exercised exclusive direction of it. The second was the order of the Secretary of War of November 8th, directing Ellet to report "for orders and duty" to Porter. These two changes made the vessels in the Mississippi for the first time a homogeneous naval force, and swept away all the complications of command which had hitherto vexed and harassed its commander-in-chief.

Porter, as acting rear-admiral, assumed command of the Mississippi squadron at the naval depot at Cairo, which was now the headquarters. He received from Davis intact the squadron as it had come from Foote — the *Benton*, the seven Eads iron-clads, and the three Rodgers gun-boats. He had also Ellet's nine rams and several very valuable captured vessels, including the *Eastport*, and Montgomery's rams captured at Memphis — the *Bragg*, *Pillow*, *Price*, and *Little Rebel*. The only vessels that had been withdrawn were the *Essex* and *Sumter*, now in the river below Vicksburg. Porter was also getting at this very time an accession to his force in the new tin-clads,— the *Brilliant*, *Rattler*, *Romeo*, *Juliet*, *Marmora*, *Signal*, and others,— and an equally important accession of iron-clads, the *Lafayette* and *Choctaw*, altered steamboats of great power, and the newly (and rather badly) constructed boats, *Chillicothe*, *Indianola*, and *Tuscumbia*.

On the 21st of November Porter issued orders from Cairo to Captain Henry Walke, then in command of the gun-boats patrolling the river below Helena, to enter the Yazoo and destroy the batteries as far up as possible. Accordingly, on the 11th of December the *Marmora* and *Signal* entered the river for twenty miles. They found that in the interval since Phelps's raid in August, the Confederates had been by no means idle. The channel was full of scows and floats, indicating torpedoes, one of which exploded near the *Signal*, while another was discharged by musket-balls from the *Marmora*. Next day, as the river was rising, the light-draughts went in again, supported by two iron-clads, the *Cairo*, Lieutenant-Commander T. O. Selfridge, and the *Pittsburgh*, Lieutenant Hoel. The *Queen of the West* also went in. About a dozen miles up, the *Cairo* was struck by two torpedoes, one exploding under her bow, the other under her quarter. She sank in twelve minutes, disappearing completely save the tops of her smoke-stacks. The discipline of the crew was perfect, the men remaining at quarters until they were ordered away, and no lives were lost. Several torpedoes were removed before the expedition returned to the mouth of the river.

The object of both these expeditions was to prepare for the attack on

Chickasaw Bluffs.   On December 23d, Porter, who had now come down from Cairo, went up the Yazoo with the *Benton*, *Tyler*, and *Lexington*, three tin-clads, and two rams.   By three days' incessant labor, under musketry fire from the banks, the fleet worked up to a point within range of the enemy's heavy batteries at Haynes's Bluff, whose fire the *Benton* sustained for two hours.   The ship was not much damaged, but her commander, Gwin, one of the best officers in the squadron, was mortally wounded.

After the failure of the army at that point (December 29th) came the expedition against Arkansas Post.   The vessels detailed by Porter for this movement were the iron-clads *De Kalb*, Lieutenant-Commander John G. Walker, *Louisville*, Lieutenant-Commander Elias K. Owen, and *Cincinnati*, Lieutenant George M. Bache; the ram *Monarch*, Colonel C. R. Ellet; the gun-boats *Black Hawk*, Lieutenant-Commander K. R. Breese, and *Tyler*, Lieutenant-Commander James W. Shirk; and the tin-clads, *Rattler*, Lieutenant-Commander Watson Smith, and *Glide*, Lieutenant S. E. Woodworth.   McClernand's force, comprising Sherman's and Morgan's corps, accompanied the fleet in transports.   As a feint the vessels ascended the White River, crossing over to the Arkansas by the cut-off.   On the 9th of January the army landed three miles below the fort.

Fort Hindman was a square bastioned work, standing at a bend of the river, sufficiently high to command the surrounding country.   It was commanded by Lieutenant Dunnington, who had done such good service at St. Charles, and defended by troops under General Churchill.   On the side facing the river were three casemates, two of them at the angles containing each a 9-inch gun, and the intermediate one an 8-inch.   On the opposite side the approaches were defended by a line of trenches a mile in length, beginning at the fort and terminating in an impassable swamp.   [See map and cuts, pp. 452, 453.]   In the main work and in the trenches were mounted fourteen lighter pieces, several of them rifled.   Two or three outlying works were built on the levee below the fort, but these were exposed to an enfilading fire from the gun-boats, and at the first attack by the latter were promptly abandoned.

On the afternoon and night of the 10th, the army marched up past the abandoned outworks, and took position about one thousand yards from the fort.   On the afternoon of the same day the three iron-clads advanced to within 300 or 400 yards of the fort and opened with their heavy guns. When they had become hotly engaged, Porter moved up the *Black Hawk* and the *Lexington*, together with the light-draughts, which threw in a destructive fire of shrapnel and rifle-shells.   When the guns on the river-side had been partly silenced, Lieutenant-Commander Smith in the *Rattler* was ordered to pass the fort and enfilade it, which he did in a very gallant and handsome manner.   The *Rattler* suffered somewhat, being raked by a heavy shell, and having her cabin knocked to pieces.   After passing the fort she was entangled in the snags above and obliged to return.   As night came on and the troops were not yet in position, the vessels were withdrawn, and tied up to the bank below.

The next day at 1 o'clock the army was reported ready, and the fleet moved up to a second attack. The same disposition was made of the vessels. All of the casemate-guns were silenced, No. 3, which was in the casemate assigned to the *Cincinnati*, being reduced to a complete wreck. At the same time the troops gradually advanced, and were just preparing for a final assault, when white flags were run up all along the works. Lieutenant Dunnington surrendered to Porter, and General Churchill to McClernand.

On the 30th of January Grant assumed command of the army before Vicksburg. The enemy's right flank rested on the Yazoo Valley, a vast tract of partly overflowed country, oval in shape, two hundred miles long, and intersected by innumerable streams and bayous. This oval valley was bounded by the Mississippi on the west, and on the north, east, and south by what was in reality one long stream, known in its successive parts as the Coldwater, Tallahatchie, and Yazoo rivers. The bounding streams made the valley almost an island, the only break in their continuity being at the northern end of the valley, at Yazoo Pass, a bayou which had formerly connected the Coldwater with the Mississippi, but which had been closed by the erection of a levee several years before. The greater part of the valley was impassable for troops, and the streams were deemed impassable for vessels. The district was a rich storehouse of Confederate supplies, which were carried in small vessels through obscure passages and channels to Yazoo City, and thence to Vicksburg. At Yazoo City also, protected from assault by torpedoes and by the forts at Haynes's Bluff, was a large navy-yard, where several gun-boats were in course of erection.

Porter's plan was to cut the levee at Yazoo Pass, thus restoring the entrance and raising the water in the rivers, and by this means to get in the rear of Yazoo City before the enemy could prepare his defenses. Involving, as it did, a circuit of some two hundred miles through the tributary streams in the enemy's country, it was an audacious and original conception, but still a sagacious piece of naval strategy.

General Grant adopted the plan, and on the 2d of February the work of cutting the levee was begun by Colonel James Harrison Wilson of the Engineers. On the evening of the 3d a mine was exploded in the remaining portion of the embankment, and the waters of the Mississippi rushed through in a torrent, cutting a passage forty yards wide, and sweeping everything before them. The difference in the levels was eight or nine feet, and some days elapsed before the new entrance was practicable for vessels. The first reconnoissance developed the fact that the Confederates had already been vigilant enough to block the way to the Coldwater by felling trees on the banks of the Pass. The removal of these occasioned a further delay of two weeks, when time was of great importance.

The naval expedition, which was commanded by Lieutenant-Commander Watson Smith, was composed of two iron-clads, the *Chillicothe*, Lieutenant-Commander James P. Foster, and the *DeKalb*, Lieutenant-Commander John G. Walker, and the tin-clads *Rattler*, *Forest Rose*, *Romeo*, *Marmora*, *Signal*, and *Petrel*. To these were added two vessels of the ram fleet, the *Fulton* and

Lioness. The only troops at first ordered to accompany the vessels were four thousand men comprising the division under Brigadier-General L. F. Ross, which, being delayed by the want of boats, only left Helena on the 23d, arriving a week later at the Cold-water. Meantime, as the feasibility of the project became more apparent, Grant enlarged his plan, and McPherson's corps,

THE "BLACKHAWK," ADMIRAL PORTER'S
FLAG-SHIP, VICKSBURG, 1863.

about 30,000 men, was ordered up, but, owing to delays, only a small part of this force under Brigadier-General I. F. Quinby took part in the movement.

On the 28th of February Smith's flotilla reached the Coldwater. Notwithstanding the work which had been done by the army pioneers in removing obstructions, the progress of the flotilla had been excessively slow,—hardly more than three miles a day. The tortuous windings of the stream, which imposed the utmost caution on the vessels navigating them in a swift current, and the overhanging branches of the dense growth of trees lining the banks, which damaged the smoke-stacks and light upper works, made the passage slow and difficult, and caused a number of mishaps. There appears to be little doubt, however, that if the gun-boats had been pushed they might have got on considerably faster, perhaps with a saving of three or four days. In the Coldwater they made better time, though still moving slowly, and they only reached the Tallahatchie on the 6th of March. After four days more of rather dilatory navigation, they arrived at the junction of the Tallahatchie and the Yazoo. The transports were close behind them.

The Confederates had put to the fullest use the time given them by Smith's dilatory advance. A hastily constructed work of earth and cotton bales, called Fort Pemberton, was thrown up at the junction of the Tallahatchie and Yazoo, and though barely completed when the gun-boats arrived, it was armed and garrisoned, and in condition to receive them. The old *Star of the West*, of Fort Sumter fame, was sunk in the river as an obstruction. [See p. 550.] The *Chillicothe* and *DeKalb* attacked the fort on three different days, but their guns alone were not enough to reduce it, and the troops under Ross could find no firm ground for a landing. The *Chillicothe* was badly racked by the enemy's fire, showing plainly her defective construction. Smith, who had started on the expedition in failing health, was now sent back in the *Rattler* (he died shortly after), and the command of the vessels fell to Foster of the *Chillicothe*. Finding that nothing more could be accomplished, Foster decided to return. On the way back he met General Quinby's troops descending the Tallahatchie, and at that officer's request steamed down again to Fort Pemberton. On the 5th of April the expedition withdrew, and on the 10th arrived in the Mississippi, about two months after it had started.

About the middle of March, before the Yazoo Pass expedition returned, Porter decided to try another route, through a series of narrow streams and bayous which made a circuitous connection between the Mississippi and the Sunflower, a tributary of the Yazoo River. Steele's Bayou was a sluggish stream which entered the Mississippi a few miles above the mouth of the Yazoo. Black Bayou, which was little better than a narrow ditch, connected Steele's Bayou with Deer Creek, a tortuous river with a difficult and shallow channel. A second lateral bayou, called Rolling Fork, connected Deer Creek with the Sunflower. From Rolling Fork the way was easy, but the difficulties of reaching that point were such that no commander with less than Porter's indefatigable energy and audacious readiness to take risks that promised a bare chance of success, would have ventured on the expedition.

The flotilla, consisting of the remaining five Eads gun-boats, the *Carondelet*, *Cincinnati*, *Louisville*, *Mound City*, and *Pittsburgh*, started on the 14th of March, Porter commanding in person, while a coöperating detachment of troops under Sherman marched through the swamps. After overcoming obstacles that would have been insurmountable to almost any other commander, it arrived early at Rolling Fork. Here Porter was attacked by a small force, which was evidently only the advance-guard of a large army on its way up from Vicksburg.   Sherman could not come to his assistance, being himself entangled in the swamp.   At the same time Porter learned that detached parties of the enemy were felling trees in his rear, which would shortly render the bayous impassable, and place his five iron-clads in a position from which they could not be extricated.   Under these circumstances, he wisely abandoned all thought of farther advance, and after dropping down Deer Creek until he fell in with the army, he succeeded, notwithstanding the additional obstructions which had been placed in the rivers, in retracing his course; and on the 24th of March, after almost incredible difficulties, his iron-clads arrived safe in the Mississippi.

While the two expeditions were at work in the Yazoo Valley, a series of detached operations had been going on below Vicksburg.   The portion of the river that was virtually held by the enemy, from Vicksburg to Port Hudson, included the outlet of the Red River, by which provisions and stores from Louisiana and Texas, arms and ammunition from the Rio Grande, and detachments of men, were forwarded through the trans-Mississippi country. On the 2d of February Porter sent the *Queen of the West*, under Colonel Charles R. Ellet, to the Red River.   Her passage of the Vicksburg batteries alone and by daylight—for her start had been delayed for necessary repairs—was made in the true Ellet fashion.   She was struck thrice before she got abreast of the town.   At this point she turned and delivered a ram-thrust at the enemy's steamer *Vicksburg*, which lay at one of the wharves, and damaged her badly; a second attempt to ram was prevented by a conflagration in the cotton bales which Ellet had placed around his deck.   These were quickly pitched overboard, the ram dashed past the lower batteries, and though struck a dozen times by the enemy's shot, in an hour or two she was ready for active operations and started down the river.

For once the Confederates were fairly taken by surprise, and before they knew of his approach, Ellet had run down one hundred miles to the Red River and pounced upon three heavily laden store-ships.   These were burned, and the *Queen*, ascending again until near Vicksburg, coaled from a barge which Porter had set adrift the night before, and which had passed the batteries without mishap.   A tender was also found in the *De Soto*, a little ferry-boat captured by the army.   With her the *Queen* started on February 10th on a second raid, burning and destroying as occasion offered.   Without meeting any serious opposition, this novel expedition proceeded down the Mississippi, up the Red River, down the Atchafalaya, and back again, then farther up the Red River.   The Confederate ram *Webb*, which was regarded as its most dangerous antagonist, was nowhere to be seen.   But the catastrophe was coming.   On the 14th, some fifty miles from the river-mouth, Ellet captured a transport, the *Era No. 5*.   Leaving her at this point, the *Queen* hastened up again, followed by the *De Soto*, but in rounding a bend of the river she ran aground under a 4-gun battery, whose fire made havoc with her, finally cutting her steam-pipe.   Part of the crew made for the *De Soto* in a boat, and the remainder, Ellet among them, jumped overboard on cotton bales, and drifted down the stream.   Upon reaching the *Era*, the *De Soto*, which had lost her rudder, was burned, the floating contingent was picked up, and the prize, now manned by the crews of the abandoned vessels, made her way to the Mississippi.

Shortly before this Porter had sent down the iron-clad *Indianola*, under Lieutenant-Commander George Brown, to support Ellet in his isolated position. She had passed Vicksburg and Warrenton at night without a scratch,

THE "MISSISSIPPI."

and descending the river met the *Era* coming up. Both vessels continued on their way, the *Era* to Vicksburg, and the *Indianola* to the mouth of Red River, where she lay for three days. She then moved up toward Vicksburg, the two coal barges

which she had brought with her being lashed alongside. While she was working slowly up, the Confederates, who had meantime repaired the *Queen*, fitted out an expedition composed of their prize, together with the *Webb* and two cotton-clad steamers. These followed the *Indianola* and overtook her a short distance below Warrenton. Engaging

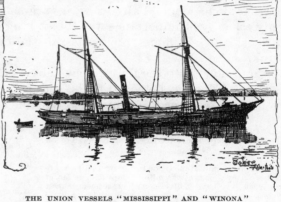

THE UNION VESSELS "MISSISSIPPI" AND "WINONA"
AT BATON ROUGE.

her at night, which gave them peculiar advantages, they succeeded in ramming her seven times, disabling her steering gear, and opening at last one great hole in her side. The Union vessel, reduced to a sinking condition, was then run ashore and surrendered.

A day or two later, Porter, whose buoyancy of spirit never deserted him, set adrift from his anchorage a dummy-monitor, constructed out of a coal-barge surmounted by barrels. The incident was in the nature of a stupendous joke, but it had very practical results. The dummy passed the Vicksburg batteries under a terrific fire. When the *Queen of the West*, acting as a picket to the grounded *Indianola*, saw this new antagonist coming she only stopped to give the alarm, and fled down the river. The supposed monitor stuck fast a mile or two above the *Indianola*, but the Confederate officer in charge of the work on board the latter did not wait for an attack, but set fire to the recent prize, which was in great part destroyed.

Less than three weeks after, on the 14th of March, Farragut ran the batteries at Port Hudson. ☆ Most of his fleet, including the *Richmond*, *Monongahela*, *Genesee*, and *Kineo*, failed to get through, and the *Mississippi* was burnt;⎮ but the *Hartford* and *Albatross* made the passage, and, coming up to Vicksburg, communicated with the vessels above. At Farragut's request, General Ellet sent two of his rams, the *Lancaster* and *Switzerland*, to join the *Hartford*. The *Lancaster* was sunk in passing the batteries, but the *Switzerland* managed to get through. From this time the Union forces retained control of the mouth of the Red River and the adjacent waters of the Mississippi.

The navy was now called upon to coöperate with General Grant's plan of attacking Vicksburg by the left and rear. Porter rapidly made his preparations to descend the river, and on the night of April 16th started with seven of his iron-clads, the *Benton*, *Lafayette*, and *Tuscumbia*, and the Eads gun-boats *Carondelet*, *Louisville*, *Mound City*, and *Pittsburgh*. The ram *General Price* and three transports laden with stores accompanied the fleet. The passage was one of the most brilliant and successful of the many dashes of this kind that were made on the river. Some of the vessels lost the coal-barges which they carried alongside, and all met with various mischances and damages, but the only casualty of importance was the sinking of one of the transports. About a week later six more transports ran the batteries. Of these also one was sunk.

From now on to the fall of Vicksburg, for over two months, Porter was in command of three detached fleets, acting from three distinct bases of operation — one the squadron which had remained above Vicksburg, and which was

---

☆ In a letter to the editors Rear-Admiral T. A. Jenkins says, in reference to Farragut's plan of an attack on Port Hudson:

"The great importance, not to say necessity, of coöperation by a part of the military forces, in so far, at the least, as to cause a diversion upon the enemy's rear, was decided upon, whereupon the commanding general (Banks) was conferred with with great frequency, until at last in the early part of March, 1863, it was arranged that a considerable force (8000 or 10,000) of all arms should rendezvous at Baton Rouge, preparatory to moving to the rear of the Port Hudson works, a little time before the vessels should move from Poplar Island, which lay just out of range of the Port Hudson heavy guns. After a review of the military forces at Baton Rouge, and after Admiral Farragut had attended to the minutest details of inspection of the vessels,— the removal of the sick, the necessary changes of officers and men, and last, but most difficult at that time, the employment of a sufficient number of competent river pilots,— the vessels got under way in their usual order of steaming, led by the *Hartford*, and stood up to Poplar Island, where the *Essex* and the bomb-vessels were lying. During a brief stay here, the commanders of the vessels were called on board and their instructions were repeated to them. Every contingency, even the most minute, every casualty that could or might happen, was discussed, and proposed remedies pointed out. On the night of the 14th of March, at dark, everything was prepared for a quiet, and it was hoped unperceived, movement of the vessels up the river. Near the last moment before the actual firing commenced, Admiral Farragut's attention was called to an approaching river steamer with flaring lights and steam-whistles blowing. He was

calm, but the lights and noise of the little steamer ruffled him a good deal. He saw at once that the enemy's attention had been specially called to him and his little squadron. The commander of the steamer came within speaking distance, reporting that General Banks's army was within 'five miles of the rear of the Port Hudson works.' That was all. The *Hartford* moved up against a current of three to five knots, while her greatest speed was not exceeding seven knots. The noise and flaring lights of the messenger steamer had evidently put the enemy on both sides of the river on the alert, for a shot from one of the enemy's lower batteries soon whistled harmlessly overhead, and, as if by magic, at the next moment the piles of pine-knots placed on the right bank of the river blazed up, illuminating for a time the entire breadth of the river, making the dark hulls of the vessels as they passed between the immense piles of burning pine a target for the Port Hudson gunners. The smoke of the guns in battery and on shipboard soon obscured these lights, and the darkness of Erebus and the noises of Pandemonium followed and continued, until the *Hartford*, with her little cockle-shell consort (the *Albatross*) anchored out of range of the enemy's guns, abreast of a huge pine-knot fire, to which the rebels before leaving added a small wooden building."

⎮ The *Mississippi* passed the lower batteries, but, running at high speed, struck on the spit opposite Port Hudson. Failing after half an hour to get her off, and being under fire of three batteries, Captain Melancton Smith had the sick and wounded taken off with the crew, and then set fire to the ship. At 3 A. M. she floated off, drifting through the fleet, and half an hour later blew up.— EDITORS.

now to operate along the Yazoo River, the second that which had passed the batteries and was occupied with the river from Vicksburg 25 miles or more to Grand Gulf, and the third the vessels in Red River. Porter moved from one to the other as occasion required. His first duty lay at Grand Gulf, which was really the southern extremity of the Vicksburg forts. The batteries were well armed, and one hundred or more feet above the river. On the 29th of April the seven iron-clads of the lower fleet engaged them for four hours, silencing them, but not destroying the guns. As the elevation of the batteries made it impossible for the fleet to capture them, the army was landed lower down the river, which resulted in the evacuation of Grand Gulf on the 3d of May. ⚓

As Grant advanced into the interior, Porter turned his attention to the Red River. For the last fortnight Farragut had been blockading the river with

⚓ Rear-Admiral Henry Walke writes as follows to the editors regarding this engagement, in which he commanded the *Lafayette*:

"To one approaching Grand Gulf on the river from the northward, six miles above, Bald Head presents a very formidable appearance. Rising abruptly 180 feet, surrounded by hills higher still, and with the wide gulf beneath, it is not unlike a little Gibraltar, as it is called. Here the river turns due west, and the principal fortification was on the Point of Rocks, a precipitous bluff about fifty feet high, at the foot of Bald Head. Three-quarters of a mile east of it is the mouth of Big Black River, which was defended with two 8-inch Columbiads. Here the gulf is about a mile and a half wide, and two hundred yards north or in front of the Point of Rocks there is a shoal which becomes an island at low water. The lower fort of heavy guns was three-quarters of a mile west of Bald Head and four hundred yards from the river, and sixty feet above the river at its ordinary level. The battery on the Point of Rocks mounted two 100-pounder rifles, one 64-pounder shell gun, and one 30-pounder rifle. A sunken road connected this fort with the batteries below. Seven or eight guns of smaller and various caliber were mounted on high points between them. The lower fort mounted one 100-pounder rifle, two 8-inch shell guns, and two 32-pounders.

"The fleet, under Rear-Admiral Porter, got into line at 7:30 A. M. of the 29th, steaming down to the Grand Gulf batteries, the *Pittsburgh*, Lieutenant W. R. Hoel, leading; then the *Louisville*, Lieutenant-Commander E. K. Owen; *Carondelet*, Lieutenant J. M. Murphy; *Mound City*, Lieutenant-Commander Byron Wilson (attacking the lower batteries); *Lafayette*, Captain Henry Walke; *Benton* (flag-ship), Lieutenant J. A. Greer, and *Tuscumbia*, Lieutenant-Commander J. W. Shirk; steaming slowly with a current of five or six knots, 150 yards apart and 100 yards from the shore, except the *Lafayette*, which rounded to above the fort on the Point of Rocks, ran into the shoal water, and took a flanking position 600 yards north-east from it. The battle was commenced by the leading gun-boat, *Pittsburgh*, at 7:55 A. M.; the other gun-boats followed in succession four minutes after. All the gun-boats fired into the upper fort with their bow and broadside guns as they passed up or down. The *Pittsburgh* rounded to opposite the battery of light guns half-way between the upper and lower batteries; the *Louisville* next below, the *Carondelet* next, opposite the lower battery, and the *Mound City* just below the lower battery. The flag-steamer *Benton* and the *Tuscumbia* gallantly opened fire close under the Point of Rocks at 8:15 with their bow and broadside guns, rounded to, heading up the river, the enemy firing on them with musketry. At 9 a shell entered the *Benton's* starboard quarter, setting her on fire; it was soon extinguished. At 9:05 a shell from No. 5 gun carried

away the enemy's flag-staff; at 10 the admiral made signal for the *Lafayette* to assist the boats below; at 10:10 the *Benton* was caught in the eddy; in turning around she dropped fifteen hundred yards and then ran into shore to turn around with her head up stream; continuing the engagement, she steamed up to the batteries on the bluffs again. At 12:25 the *Benton* went up the river to communicate with General Grant, who was on a tug above with three of McClernand's divisions on transports.

"In the engagement the *Benton* fired 347 shot and shell, and was struck 47 times, nearly every shot penetrating her iron plating. The *Tuscumbia*, following the *Benton*, engaged the upper batteries until noon. She was obliged to drop out of action about noon, and landed about four miles below Grand Gulf, having been struck by shot, shell, grape, and shrapnel eighty-one times, two shells having exploded inside her turret. As the *Lafayette* approached the upper battery at 8:15 A. M., ahead of the *Benton* and *Tuscumbia*, she fired 11-inch and 9-inch shell into it, but in turning to take her position on the other side of the port, she was whirled around so quickly between the swift current and the counter-current, that her gunners could not get good aim with broadside guns, but as soon as she turned her 100-pounder rifles on the battery in a flanking position in the eddy, every shell seemed to strike the mark; but even there it was difficult to hold her steady for good aim. After firing 35 rounds, about 9 A. M. her 11-inch bow guns were turned upon the fort and fired with such precision that we expected to silence it, as their fire was dying away. This was the position our whole squadron should have taken, but it was not known that that part of the gulf was navigable. The heaviest guns of the enemy could point to the northward and westward, but not to the eastward, where the *Lafayette* was exempt from that terrible battering which the *Benton* and *Tuscumbia* received, while they were revolving at the mercy of the currents, in constant danger of running ashore.

"At 9:20 A. M. the admiral made a preconcerted signal for the *Lafayette* to go to the assistance of the gun-boats at the lower batteries, thinking no doubt that his two heaviest vessels could silence the upper fort. This move was not after the lower batteries were silenced (as has been stated), but about two hours before. The *Lafayette* proceeded immediately with all speed and rounded to about 10 A. M. opposite the lower battery. She joined battle with the gun-boats there, firing her 11-inch shell from her bow guns into it and to bring her head up stream and her starboard side guns to bear on it quickly. The pilot ran her low into the bank of the river under the fort. She continued firing with the starboard broadside guns within five hundred yards of the lower fort, and with the other gun-boats continued firing on the lower batteries, enfilading the upper fort until 11:30,

UPPER BATTERIES.   "LOUISVILLE."   "PITTSBURGH." " MOUND CITY."   MIDDLE AND LOWER BATTERIES.
TRENTON."   " TUSCUMBIA."   "CARONDELET."   " LAFAYETTE."

BATTLE OF GRAND GULF (SECOND POSITION).

the *Hartford* and *Albatross*, a service of great importance in view of the active operations on foot along the river, and at the end of that time he was joined by a detached force of gun-boats which had been operating in the Teche, and which had reached Red River through the Atchafalaya. Banks was then moving against Alexandria, and a light squadron was formed to go up and coöperate with him. At this juncture Porter arrived with three iron-clads, and with these and a part of Farragut's detached squadron he steamed up to Alexandria, where Banks arrived on May 7th. After clearing out the Red River and its tributary the Black, and destroying much property, the expedition returned, Banks going to Port Hudson and Porter returning to his old station above Vicksburg.

The Yazoo River now became for a short time the central point of Porter's operations. Nothing had been done there since December except a demonstration during the attack of April 29–30 on Grand Gulf, which, though conducted with spirit and gallantry, was really only a feint to prevent the enemy from reënforcing his works below Vicksburg. In the fortnight that had elapsed, however, Grant's environment of the town on the east had cut off Haynes's Bluff and the whole Yazoo Valley above it. Porter immediately sent up the *De Kalb*, *Choctaw*, and four light-draughts under Lieutenant-Com-

when the lower batteries were silenced, and all the gun-boats, except the *Pittsburgh*, steamed close to and passed the Point of Rocks (which had not been silenced), raking it with their bow guns. The *Benton* had just then gone up the river.

"The remainder of the squadron continued firing on the upper fort. The *Lafayette* took her former position, flanking the fort. The *Louisville*, *Mound City*, and *Carondelet* steamed around in a circle, firing as they bore in front of the fort. The *Pittsburgh* remained in her original position, raking it with her bow guns from the west. The enemy, thus involved, fought desperately to the last; their guns, ceasing one by one at long intervals, were at last silent; whereupon the admiral made signal for his squadron to follow his motions. But the fort, as if to give us notice that it was not silenced, fired the last gun after we had started to go up the river."

mander K. R. Breese to open communication. Pushing on to Haynes's Bluff the *De Kalb*, Lieutenant-Commander John G. Walker, in advance, it was found that evacuation had already begun, and the small force left in the works hastily abandoned them. The fortifications were of great strength and covered a large area. On the 20th Walker with the *De Kalb* and *Choctaw* and three of the light-draughts, steamed up to Yazoo City. The work of destruction, begun by the retreating enemy, was completed by the gun-boats. The navy-yard, a large and well-equipped establishment, and the only one now remaining to the Confederates, with its mills and machine-shops and its stores of lumber, was burned, as were also three formidable vessels then in course of construction. A second expedition under Walker, a few days later, struck out into the tributary streams, the Sunflower, Rolling Fork, and the smaller bayous, burning the transports that had taken refuge there. Several steamers were sunk by the enemy on Walker's approach, and three were captured and burnt by his vessels. Navigation in the Yazoo Valley was broken up, and the destruction of military supplies and provisions was enormous.

During Grant's assault on the 22d of May, the fleet below Vicksburg kept up a heavy fire on the hill and water batteries, and during the siege the mortar-boats were incessantly at work, shelling the city and the batteries. From time to time the gun-boats joined in the bombardment, notably on May 27th and June 20th. On the first of these occasions, the *Cincinnati*, Lieutenant George M. Bache, engaged alone the battery on Fort Hill, the principal work above Vicksburg, while the other iron-clads, under Commander Woodworth, were similarly occupied below. The fire from the upper battery was too much for the *Cincinnati*, which sank not far from the shore, losing a considerable number of her crew. On the second occasion three heavy guns mounted on scows were placed in position on the point opposite Vicksburg, where they did good execution under Lieutenant-Commander F. M. Ramsay, enfilading the rifle-pits in front of Sherman's position and rendering them untenable. The lower squadron also took part in this bombardment. In addition to the work of the squadron afloat, when the army called for siege-guns thirteen heavy cannon were landed from the gun-boats and placed in position in the rear of Vicksburg, where they were constantly and efficiently worked by naval crews, first under Selfridge, and later under Walker. At the same time the squadron was engaged in the duty of patrolling the rivers, keeping open lines of communication, convoying transports, and coöperating with troops in beating off the enemy at detached points.

On the 25th of May Banks, who had returned with his army from Alexandria, had invested Port Hudson, which had been subjected for several nights previous to a bombardment from the *Essex* and the mortar flotilla, under Commander Caldwell. During the month of June a naval battery of 9-inch guns, under Lieutenant-Commander Edward Terry of the *Richmond*, rendered efficient service in the siege operations. On the 9th of July Port Hudson surrendered and the Mississippi was now clear of obstructions to its mouth.

Besides the main operations at Vicksburg and Port Hudson, the navy had been occupied from time to time in detached bodies at other points. A cut-off, at the mouth of the Arkansas, ingeniously made by Selfridge in April, had contributed materially to the facility of operations at that place. In May Lieutenant-Commander Wilson in the *Mound City* effectually destroyed a water-battery at Warrenton. In June an attack was made on Milliken's Bend by Confederate troops from Arkansas under Taylor, and the garrison was driven from their works to the levee. At this critical moment Ramsay, in the *Choctaw*, turned his guns on the successful assailants, and though unable to see the enemy on account of the intervening bank, he hailed the troops on shore to ascertain their position; and so well placed were the hundred or more shell and shrapnel that he fired that the Confederates were soon in full retreat.

LIEUTENANT-COMMANDER JAMES M. PRICHETT.
FROM A PHOTOGRAPH.

Finally, on the 4th of July, the day of the fall of Vicksburg, General Holmes made his attack on Helena [see pp. 455–6] with a force of about 8000 men, then garrisoned by 4000 under B. M. Prentiss. The enemy had placed batteries in opposition above and below the town, and, making a spirited attack in front, succeeded in carrying a portion of the outlying works. The garrison fought stubbornly, but were heavily outnumbered. The wooden gun-boat *Tyler*, under Lieutenant-Commander James M. Prichett, had been covering the approach by the old town road, but seeing the strategic points of the enemy's position, Prichett with masterly skill placed his vessel where her bow and stern guns could reach the batteries above and below, while her broadside enfiladed the ravines down which the enemy was pouring in masses. The gun-boat's rapid discharge of shrapnel and shell told heavily upon the Confederates, who, after sustaining it for a time, fled in disorder, Prentiss's men pursuing them with the bayonet. The destructive fire of the *Tyler* caused an unusually severe loss.

The fall of Vicksburg was followed by successful gun-boat raids, one in July under Selfridge in the Red, Black, and Tensas rivers, the other in August under Bache in White River. General Herron and Lieutenant-Commander Walker also proceeded up the Yazoo and retook Yazoo City, but with the loss of the *De Kalb*, destroyed by torpedoes near Yazoo City. [See p. 580.] The vessel sank in fifteen minutes, but all hands were saved. Porter accepted the misfortune with that true understanding of the business of war which had been the secret of so much of his success — that without taking risks you cannot achieve results.

GULF OPERATIONS IN 1862 AND 1863. [

BY PROFESSOR JAMES RUSSELL SOLEY, U. S. N.

THE regular monotony of the blockade of Mobile by the West Gulf squadron was interrupted only by the two successful passages of the *Oreto* or *Florida*, under Commander J. N. Maffitt, C. S. N., past the blockading squadron, inward on the 4th of September, 1862, and outward on the 16th of January, 1863. The first passage was made in broad daylight, under the disguise of an English gun-vessel, at a time when the *Oreto* was short-handed, the captain and crew ill, and the battery incapable of resistance. As a bold dash, it was hardly paralleled during the war. The second passage was made at night, without disguise, after the squadron had received full warning, and had been reënforced specially to capture the cruiser.

On the Texas coast the blockade was only of moderate efficiency, and in the summer of 1862 Farragut determined to convert it at the principal points into an occupation. With this object, he sent out three expeditions. The first, under Acting-Lieutenant J. W. Kittredge, successfully attacked Corpus Christi August 16th–18th, but having no troops to hold the place withdrew to the bay. The second expedition, composed of the *Kensington* and *Rachel Seaman*, under Acting-Master Frederick Crocker, was sent in September to Sabine Pass, a point of great importance in blockade-running operations on account of the neighboring railroad, and at that time under purely formal blockade. Crocker ascended the river, captured the fort at Sabine City, destroyed the railroad bridge, and broke up a Confederate camp. Raids in the passes resulted in the capture of the steamer *Dan* and the schooner *Velocity*, which were left with the *Rachel Seaman* to maintain the blockade.

The third and most important expedition, under Commander W. B. Renshaw, composed of the ferry-boats *Westfield* and *Clifton*, the latter under Lieutenant-Commander R. L. Law; the *Harriet Lane*, Commander J. M. Wainwright, and the *Owasco*, Lieutenant-Commander John Guest, took possession of Galveston in October without a conflict. Colonel Burrell, with only 260 men, was sent to hold the town. The flotilla, which carried a heavy armament, was disposed about the harbor and bay, and held the town for two months, but without proper precautions against attack.

At daybreak on the 1st of January, 1863, General Magruder, commanding the Confederate forces in Texas, made a vigorous attack on the city. The bridge by which alone troops could march to the town, and which might easily have been destroyed, was left unguarded. The Confederates, early in the night, planted batteries unobserved just outside the town, and abreast of the *Harriet Lane*, which lay in a narrow channel near the shore. A little farther to the eastward, abreast of the town, were the gun-boat *Sachem* and the yacht *Corypheus*. A mile farther down the bay were the *Clifton* and *Owasco*, and two miles away the *Westfield*, Renshaw's vessel. The enemy had two cotton-clad

steamers, the *Bayou City* and *Neptune*, the first carrying a rifled 32-pounder, and the second two howitzers. Each had from 150 to 200 sharp-shooters.

Of the vessels the *Harriet Lane* bore the brunt of the attack, the *Owasco* being the only one of her consorts that lent any assistance. The *Bayou City's* rifle burst at the third fire, and the *Neptune* stove in her bow in an attempt to ram, and sank on the flats. The *Bayou City* then ran alongside the *Harriet Lane* and opened a withering musketry fire from behind the cotton-bales, in which Commander Wainwright was killed and his first-lieutenant, Lea, mortally wounded. The Confederates then carried the *Lane* by boarding, the officer in command surrendering without serious attempt at resistance. Hostilities were now suspended awaiting an answer from Renshaw to the demand for a surrender of all the vessels. The *Clifton* carried this message to the *Westfield*, and took back Renshaw's refusal, after which she executed her orders, which were to take the vessels out of the harbor. Meantime the enemy had moved up their lines. Burrell surrendered the town, and the *Westfield*, getting aground, was set on fire at Renshaw's order, and blew up prematurely, killing Renshaw and several of his men. Law, of the *Clifton*, now the senior officer, immediately steamed away, and the blockade was raised. (See also pp. 586–7.)

On the 8th the blockade was resumed by Commodore Bell, with the *Brooklyn*, *Hatteras*, and several gun-boats. On the 11th the *Hatteras* was sent after the *Alabama*, supposed to be a blockade-runner. The *Alabama*, after drawing the *Hatteras* away from her consorts, sank her in a fifteen-minute fight.

On the 21st of January the blockading force at Sabine Pass, composed of the sailing-ship *Morning Light*, and the schooner *Velocity*, was attacked by two cotton-clad steamers, and, being unable to manœuvre, surrendered. The blockade was resumed the next day by the *New London* and *Cayuga*.

After the fall of Port Hudson, General Banks took up the question of Texas. His first plan was to land at Sabine Pass and strike the railroad. The expedition was composed of troops under Franklin, and the *Clifton*, *Sachem*, *Granite City*, and *Arizona* under Lieutenant Crocker. On the 8th of September the gun-boats moved up the pass to attack the enemy's fort. The *Clifton* ran ashore, and soon after got a shot in her boiler. The *Sachem's* boiler also was penetrated, and both vessels surrendered after heavy loss. The remainder retreated.

Banks now decided to attack Texas near the Rio Grande, and his troops, escorted by the *Monongahela* and other vessels under Commander J. H. Strong, landed at Brazos November 2d. Brownsville, Corpus Christi, Aransas, and Fort Esperanza at Pass Cavallo, were captured, but owing to the lack of troops to hold the various points, no further operations were attempted.

] See Vol. II., p. 13.

THE CONFEDERATE GUN-BOAT "ARKANSAS."

BY HER COMMANDER, ISAAC N. BROWN, CAPTAIN, C. S. N.

AFTER the Appomattox capitulation, the observance of which, nobly maintained by General Grant, crowns him as the humane man of the age, I took to the plow, as a better implement of reconstruction than the pen; and if I take up the latter now, it is that justice may be done to the men and the memory of the men of the *Arkansas*.

On the 28th of May, 1862, I received at Vicksburg a telegraphic order from the Navy Department at Richmond to "proceed to Greenwood, Miss., and assume command of the Confederate gun-boat *Arkansas*, and finish and equip that vessel without regard to expenditure of men or money." I knew that such a vessel had been under construction at Memphis, but I had not heard till then of her escape from the general wreck of our Mississippi River defenses. Greenwood is at the head of the Yazoo River, 160 miles by river from Yazoo City. It being the season of overflow, I found my new command four miles from dry land. Her condition was not encouraging. The vessel was a mere hull, without armor; the engines were apart; guns without carriages were lying about the deck; a portion of the railroad iron intended as armor was at the bottom of the river, and the other and far greater part was to be sought for in the interior of the country. Taking a day to fish up the sunken iron, I had the *Arkansas* towed to Yazoo City, where the hills reach the river. Here, though we were within fifty miles of the Union fleets, there was the possibility of equipment. Within a very short time after reaching Yazoo City we had two hundred men, chiefly from the nearest detachment of the army, at work on the deck's shield and hull, while fourteen blacksmith forges were drawn from the neighboring plantations and placed on the bank to hasten the iron-work. Extemporized drilling-machines on the steamer *Capitol* worked day and night fitting the railway iron for the bolts which were to fasten it as armor. This iron was brought from many points to the nearest railroad station and thence twenty-five miles by wagons. The trees were yet growing from which the gun-carriages had to be made — the most difficult work of all, as such vehicles had never been built in Mississippi. I made a contract with two gentlemen of Jackson to pay each his own price for the full number of ten. The executive officer, Mr. Stevens, gave the matter his particular attention, and in time, along with the general equipment, we obtained five good carriages from each contractor. This finishing, armoring, arming, and equipment of the *Arkansas* within five weeks' working-time under the hot summer sun, from which we were unsheltered, and under the depressing thought that there was a deep channel, of, but six hours' steaming between us and the Federal fleet, whose guns were within hearing, was perhaps not inferior under all the circumstances to the renowned effort of Oliver Hazard Perry in cutting a fine ship from

the forest in ninety days. We were not a day too soon, for the now rapid fall of the river rendered it necessary for us to assume the offensive without waiting for the apparatus to bend the railway iron to the curve of our quarter and stern, and to the angles of the pilot-house. Though there was little thought of showing the former, the weakest part, to the enemy, we tacked boiler-plate iron over it for appearance' sake, and very imperfectly covered the pilot-house shield with a double thickness of one-inch bar iron. Our engines' twin screws, one under each quarter, worked up to eight miles an hour in still water, which promised about half that speed when turned against the current of the main river. We had at first some trust in these, not having discovered the way they soon showed of stopping on the center at wrong times and places; and as they never both stopped of themselves at the same time, the effect was, when one did so, to turn the vessel round, despite the rudder. Once, in the presence of the enemy, we made a circle, while trying to make the automatic stopper keep time with its sister-screw.

The *Arkansas* now appeared as if a small sea-going vessel had been cut down to the water's edge at both ends, leaving a box for guns amidships. The straight sides of the box, a foot in thickness, had over them one layer of railway iron; the ends closed by timber one foot square, planked across by six-inch strips of oak, were then covered by one course of railway iron laid up and down at an angle of thirty-five degrees. These ends deflected overhead all missiles striking at short range, but would have been of little security under a plunging fire. This shield, flat on top, covered with plank and half-inch iron, was pierced for 10 guns — 3 in each broadside and 2 forward and aft. The large smoke-stack came through the top of the shield, and the pilot-house was raised about one foot above the shield level. Through the latter led a small tin tube by which to convey orders to the pilot.‡ The battery was respectable for that period of the war: 2 8-inch 64-pounders at the bows; 2 rifled 32s (old smooth-bores banded and rifled) astern; and 2 100-pounder Columbiads and a 6-inch naval gun in each broadside,—10 guns in all, which, under officers formerly of the United States service, could be relied on for good work, if we could find the men to load and fire. We obtained over 100 good men from the naval vessels lately on the Mississippi, and about 60 Missourians from the command of General Jeff Thompson. These had never served at great guns, but on trial they exhibited in their new service the cool courage natural to them on land. They were worthily commanded, under the orders of our first lieutenant, by Captain Harris. Our officers were Lieutenants Stevens, Grimball, Gift, Barbot, Wharton, and Read, all of the old service, and Chief Engineer City, Acting Masters Milliken and Nicholls, of the Volunteer Navy, and

‡ In this action 68 shot-holes were made in the stack, and 4 minie-balls passed through the tin tube.—I. N. B.

BUILDING THE "ARKANSAS."

Midshipmen Scales, ⚓ R. H. Bacot, Tyler, and H. Cenas. The only trouble they ever gave me was to keep them from running the *Arkansas* into the Union fleet before we were ready for battle. On the 12th of July we sent our mechanics ashore, took our Missourians on board, and dropped below Satartia Bar, within five hours of the Mississippi. I now gave the executive officer a day to organize and exercise his men.

The idea exists that we made "a run," or "a raid," or in some way an "attack by surprise" upon the Union fleet. I have reason to think that we were expected some hours before we came. ↓

On Monday A. M., July 14th, 1862, we started from Satartia. Fifteen miles below, at the mouth of Sunflower River, we found that the steam from our imperfect engines and boiler had penetrated our forward magazine and wet our powder so as to render it unfit for use. We were just opposite the site of an old saw-mill, where the opening in the forest, dense everywhere else, admitted the sun's rays. The day was clear and very hot; we

made fast to the bank, head down-stream, landed our wet powder (expecting the enemy to heave in sight every moment), spread tarpaulins over the old saw-dust and our powder over these. By constant shaking and turning we got it back to the point of ignition before the sun sank below the trees, when, gathering it up, we crowded all that we could of it into the after magazine and resumed our way, guns cast loose and men at quarters, expecting every moment to meet the enemy. I had some idea of their strength, General Van Dorn, commanding our forces at Vicksburg, having written to me two days before that there were then, I think he said, thirty-seven men-of-war in sight and more up the river. Near dark we narrowly escaped the destruction of our smoke-stack from an immense overhanging tree. From this disaster we were saved by young Grimball, who sprang from the shield to another standing tree, with rope's-end in hand, and made it fast. We anchored near Haynes's Bluff at midnight and rested till 3 A. M., when we got up anchor for the fleet, hoping

⚓ Dabney M. Scales was from the Naval Academy at Annapolis; he distinguished himself afterward in the *Shenandoah*, and is now a prominent lawyer of Memphis.— I. N. B.

↓ A Federal letter relating to the *Arkansas*, and evidently press correspondence, was captured by Confederates at Greenville, Miss. It began by saying, "Last night at 10 o'clock [it seems to have been written on the day of the combat] two deserters from Grandpré's sharp-shooters at the Yazoo, who had stolen a skiff, came alongside the admiral's ship, the *Hartford*, and reported that the *Arkansas* had cut the raft and would be down at daylight to attack the fleet. Upon this a council of

war was immediately [that night] called on board the *Hartford*," etc., etc. The same letter, bearing every internal evidence of truth and sincerity, went on to say, "At daylight [following the night council] the little tug which [Admiral] Davis had sent up the Yazoo as a look-out came down like a streak of lightning, screaming, 'The *Arkansas* is coming! The *Arkansas* is coming!'" and then follows the account of excitement and preparation. Now all this may have been only in the imagination of the correspondent, but there *was* a detachment of our sharp-shooters under Captain Grandpré at the raft, and we *did* cut and pass through it as stated. [See also p. 556.]— I. N. B.

THE CONFEDERATE RAM "ARKANSAS," ALONGSIDE THE UNION GUN-BOAT "CARONDELET."

to be with it at sunrise, but before it was light we ran ashore and lost an hour in getting again afloat. At sunrise we gained Old River—a lake caused by a "cut-off" from the Mississippi; the Yazoo enters this at the north curve, and, mingling its deep waters with the wider expanse of the lake, after a union of ten miles, breaks through a narrow strip of land, to lose itself finally in the Mississippi twelve miles above Vicksburg. We were soon to find the fleet midway between these points, but hid from both by the curved and wooded eastern shore. As the sun rose clear and fiery out of the lake on our left, we saw a few miles ahead, under full steam, three Federal vessels in line approaching. These, as we afterward discovered, were the iron-clad *Carondelet*, Captain Henry Walke,♭ the wooden gun-boat *Tyler*, Lieutenant William Gwin, and a ram, the *Queen of the West*, Lieutenant James M. Hunter. Directing our pilot to stand for the iron-clad, the center vessel of the three, I gave the order not to fire our bow guns, lest by doing so we should diminish our speed, relying for the moment upon our broadside guns to keep the ram and the *Tyler* from gaining our quarter, which they seemed eager to do. I had determined, despite our want of speed, to try the ram or iron prow upon the foe, who were gallantly approaching; but when less than half a mile separated us, the *Carondelet* fired a wildly aimed bow gun, backed round, and went from the *Arkansas* at a speed which at once perceptibly increased the space between us. The *Tyler* and ram followed

this movement of the iron-clad, and the stern guns of the *Carondelet* and the *Tyler* were briskly served on us. Grimball and Gift, with their splendid sixty-fours, were now busy at their work, while Barbot and Wharton watched for a chance shot abeam. Read chafed in silence at his rifles. The whole crew was under the immediate direction of the first lieutenant, Henry Stevens, a religious soldier, of the Stonewall Jackson type, who felt equally safe at all times and places. I was on the shield directly over our bow guns, and could see their shot on the way to the *Carondelet*, and with my glasses I thought that I could see the white wood under her armor. This was satisfactory, for I knew that no vessel afloat could long stand rapid raking by 8-inch shot at such short range. We soon began to gain on the chase, yet from time to time I had to steer first to starboard, then to port, to keep the inquisitive consorts of the *Carondelet* from inspecting my boiler-plate armor. This gave the nearer antagonist an advantage, but before he could improve it he would be again brought ahead. While our shot seemed always to hit his stern and disappear, his missiles, striking our inclined shield, were deflected over my head and lost in air. I received a severe contusion on the head, but this gave me no concern after I had failed to find any brains mixed with the handful of clotted blood which I drew from the wound and examined. A moment later a shot from the *Tyler* struck at my feet, penetrated the pilot-house, and, cutting off a section of the wheel, mortally hurt

♭ The commander of the *Carondelet* and I had been friends in the old navy and messmates on a voyage around the world.—I. N. B.

Chief Pilot Hodges and disabled our Yazoo River pilot, Shacklett, who was at the moment much needed, our Mississippi pilots knowing nothing of Old River. James Brady, a Missourian of nerve and equal to the duty, took the wheel, and I ordered him to "keep the iron-clad ahead." All was going well, with a near prospect of carrying out my first intention of using the ram, this time at a great ad-

CAPTAIN I. N. BROWN, C. S. N. FROM A PHOTOGRAPH.

vantage, for the stern of the *Carondelet* was now the objective point, and she seemed to be going slow and unsteady. Unfortunately the *Tyler* also slowed, so as to keep near his friend, and this brought us within easy range of his small-arms. I saw with some concern, as I was the only visible target outside our shield, that they were firing by volleys. I ought to have told Stevens to hold off Grimball and Gift from the iron-clad till they could finish the *Tyler*, but neither in nor out of battle does one always do the right thing. I was near the hatchway at the moment when a minie-ball, striking over my left temple, tumbled me down among the guns. I awoke as if from sleep, to find kind hands helping me to a place among the killed and wounded. I soon regained my place on the shield. I found the *Carondelet* still ahead, but much nearer, and both vessels entering the willows, which grew out on the bar at the inner curve of the lake. To have run into the mud, we drawing 13 feet (the *Carondelet* only 6), would have ended the matter with the *Arkansas*. The *Carondelet's* position could only be accounted for by supposing her steering apparatus destroyed.⁋ The deep water was on our starboard bow, where at some distance I saw the *Tyler* and the ram, as if awaiting our further entanglement. I gave the order "hard a-port and depress port guns." So near were we to the chase that this action of the helm brought us alongside, and our port broadside caused her to heel to port and then roll back so deeply as to take the water over her deck forward

of the shield. Our crew, thinking her sinking, gave three hearty cheers. In swinging off we exposed our stern to the *Carondelet's* broadside, and Read at the same time got a chance with his rifles. The *Carondelet* did not return this fire of our broadside and stern guns. Had she fired into our stern when we were so near, it would have destroyed or at least have disabled us.

Though I stood within easy pistol-shot, in uniform, uncovered, and evidently the commander of the *Arkansas*, no more notice was taken of me by the *Carondelet* than had been taken of my ship when, to escape running into the mud, I had exposed the *Arkansas* to being raked. Their ports were closed, no flag was flying, not a man or officer was in view, not a sound or shot was heard. She was apparently "disabled."

We neither saw nor felt the *Carondelet* again, but turned toward the spiteful *Tyler* and the wary ram. As these were no longer a match for the *Arkansas*, they very properly took advantage of a speed double our own to gain the shelter of their fleet, the *Tyler* making good practice at us while in range with her pivot gun, and getting some attention in the same way from our bows. Under the ordinary circumstances of war we had just got through with a fair hour's work; but knowing what was ahead of us, we had to regard it in the same light as our Missouri militia did, as "a pretty smart skirmish."

On gaining the Mississippi, we saw no vessels but the two we had driven before us. While following these in the direction of Vicksburg I had the opportunity of inspecting engine and fire rooms, where I found engineers and firemen had been suffering under a temperature of 120° to 130°. The executive officer, while attending to every other duty during the recent firing, had organized a relief party from the men at the guns, who went down into the fire-room every fifteen minutes, the others coming up or being, in many instances, hauled up, exhausted in that time; in this way, by great care, steam was kept to service gauge, but in the conflict below the fire department broke down. The connection between furnaces and smoke-stack (technically called the breechings) were in this second conflict shot away, destroying the draught and letting the flames come out into the shield, raising the temperature there to 120°, while it had already risen to 130° in the fire-room. It has been asked why the *Arkansas* was not used as a ram. The want of speed and of confidence in the engines answers the question. We went into action in Old River with 120 pounds of steam, and though every effort was made to keep it up, we came out with but 20 pounds, hardly enough to turn the engines.

Aided by the current of the Mississippi, we soon approached the Federal fleet—a forest of masts and smoke-stacks—ships, rams, iron-clads, and other gun-boats on the left side, and ordinary river steamers and bomb-vessels along the right. To any one having a real ram at command the genius of havoc could not have offered a finer view, the panoramic effect of which was intensified by the city of men spread out with innumerable tents opposite

⁋ Such was the fact.— EDITORS.

on the right bank. We were not yet in sight of Vicksburg, but in every direction, except astern, our eyes rested on enemies. I had long known the most of these as valued friends, and if I now had any doubts of the success of the *Arkansas* they were inspired by this general knowledge rather than from any awe of a particular name. It seemed at a glance as if a whole navy had come to keep me away from the heroic city,—six or seven rams,

LIEUTENANT JOHN GRIMBALL, C. S. A.
FROM A PHOTOGRAPH.

four or five iron-clads, without including one accounted for an hour ago, and the fleet of Farragut generally, behind or inside of this fleet. The rams seemed to have been held *in reserve*, to come out between the intervals. Seeing this, as we neared the head of the line I said to our pilot, "Brady, shave that line of men-of-war as close as you can, so that the rams will not have room to gather head-way in coming out to strike us." In this way we ran so near to the wooden ships that each may have expected the blow which, if I could avoid it, I did not intend to deliver to any, and probably the rams running out at slow speed across the line of our advance received in the smoke and fury of the fight more damage from the guns of their own men-of-war than from those of the *Arkansas*.

As we neared the head of the line our bow guns, trained on the *Hartford*, began this second fight of the morning (we were yet to have a third one before the day closed), and within a few minutes, as the enemy was brought in range, every gun of the *Arkansas* was at its work. It was calm, and the smoke settling over the combatants, our men at times directed their guns at the flashes of those of their opponents. As we advanced, the line of fire seemed to grow into a circle constantly closing. The shock of missiles striking our sides was literally continuous, and as we were now surrounded,

without room for anything but pushing ahead, and shrapnel shot were coming on our shield deck, twelve pounds at a time, I went below to see how our Missouri backwoodsmen were handling their 100-pounder Columbiads. At this moment I had the most lively realization of having steamed into a real volcano, the *Arkansas* from its center firing rapidly to every point of the circumference, without the fear of hitting a friend or missing an enemy. I got below in time to see Read and Scales with their rifled guns blow off the feeble attack of a ram on our stern. Another ram was across our way ahead. As I gave the order, "Go through him, Brady!" his steam went into the air, and his crew into the river. A shot from one of our bow guns had gone through his boiler and saved the collision. We passed by and through the brave fellows struggling in the water under a shower of missiles intended for us. It was a little hot this morning all around; the enemy's shot frequently found weak places in our armor, and their shrapnel and minie-balls also came through our port-holes. Still, under a temperature of 120°, our people kept to their work, and as each one, acting under the steady eye of Stevens, seemed to think the result depended on himself, I sought a cooler atmosphere on the shield, to find, close ahead and across our way, a large iron-clad displaying the square flag of an admiral. Though we had but little head-way, his beam was exposed, and I ordered the pilot to strike him amidships. He avoided this by steaming ahead, and, passing under his stern, nearly touching, we gave him our starboard broadside, which probably went through him from rudder to prow. This was our last shot, and we received none in return.

We were now at the end of what had seemed the interminable line, and also past the outer rim of the volcano. I now called the officers up to take a look at what we had just come through and to get the fresh air; and as the little group of heroes closed around me with their friendly words of congratulation, a heavy rifle-shot passed close over our heads: it was the parting salutation, and if aimed two feet lower would have been to us the most injurious of the battle. We were not yet in sight of Vicksburg, but if any of the fleet followed us farther on our way I did not perceive it.

The *Arkansas* continued toward Vicksburg without further trouble. When within sight of the city, we saw another fleet preparing to receive us or recede from us, below: one vessel of the fleet aground and in flames. With our firemen exhausted, our smoke-stack cut to pieces, and a section of our plating torn from the side, we were not in condition just then to begin a third battle; moreover humanity required the landing of our wounded— terribly torn by cannon-shot—and of our dead. We were received at Vicksburg with enthusiastic cheers. Immediate measures were taken to repair damages and to recruit our crew, diminished to one-half their original number by casualties, and by the expiration of service of those who had volunteered only for the trip to Vicksburg.

We had left the Yazoo River with a short supply of fuel, and after our first landing opposite the city-hall we soon dropped down to the coal depot, where we began coaling and repairing, under the fire of the lower fleet, to which, under the circumstances, we could make no reply. Most of the enemy's shot fell short, but Renshaw, in the *Westfield*, made very fine practice with his 100-pounder rifle gun, occasionally throwing the spray from his shot over our working party, but with the benefit of sprinkling down the coal dust. Getting in our coal, we moved out of range of such sharp practice, where, under less excitement, we hastened such temporary repairs as would enable us to continue the offensive. We had intended trying the lower fleet that evening, but before our repairs could be completed and our crew reënforced by suitable selections from the army, the hours of night were approaching, under the shadows of which (however favorable for running batteries) no brave man cares from choice to fight.

About sunset of the same day, a number of our antagonists of the morning, including the flag-ship *Hartford* and the equally formidable *Richmond*, were seen under full steam coming down the river. Before they came within range of the *Arkansas*, we had the gratification of witnessing the beautiful reply of our upper shore-batteries to their gallant attack. Unfit as we were for the offensive, I told Stevens to get under way and run out into the midst of the coming fleet. Before this order could be executed one vessel of the fleet sent a 160-pound wrought-iron bolt through our armor and engine-room, disabling the engine and killing, among others, Pilot Gilmore, and knocking overboard the heroic Brady, who had steered the *Arkansas* through our morning's work. This single shot caused also a very serious leak, destroyed all the contents of the dispensary (fortunately our surgeon, Dr. Washington, was just then away from his medicines), and, passing through the opposite bulwarks, lodged between the wood-work and the armor. Stevens promptly detailed a party to aid the carpenter in stopping the leak, while our bow and port-broadside guns were rapidly served on the passing vessels. So close were these to our guns that we could hear our shot crashing through their sides, and the groans of their wounded; and, incredible as it now seems, these sounds were heard with a fierce delight by the *Arkansas's* people. Why no attempt was made to ram our vessel, I do not know. Our position invited it, and our rapid firing made that position conspicuous; but as by this time it was growing dark, and the *Arkansas* close inshore, they may have mistaken us for a water-battery. We had greatly the advantage in pointing our guns, the enemy passing in line ahead, and being distinctly visible as each one for the time shut out our view of the horizon. And now this busy day, the 15th of July, 1862, was closed with the sad duty of sending ashore a second party of killed and wounded, and the rest which our exhaustion rendered necessary was taken for the night under a dropping fire of the enemy's 13-inch shells.

During the following week we were exposed day and night to these falling bombs, which did not hit the *Arkansas*, but frequently exploded under water

near by. One shell, which fell nearly under our bows, threw up a number of fish. As these floated by with the current, one of our men said: "Just look at that, will you? Why, the upper fleet is killing fish for the lower fleet's dinner!" In time we became accustomed to this shelling, but not to the idea that it was without danger; and I know of no more effective way of curing a man of the weakness of thinking that he is without the feeling of fear than for him, on a dark night, to watch two or three of these double-fused descending shells, all near each other, and seeming as though they would strike him between the eyes.

In three days we were again in condition to move and to menace at our will either fleet, thus compelling the enemy's entire force, in the terrible July heat, to keep up steam day and night. An officer of the fleet writing at this time, said: "Another council of war was held on board the admiral's [flag-ship] last night, in which it was resolved that the *Arkansas* must be destroyed at all hazards, a thing, I suspect, much easier said than done; but I wish that she was destroyed, for she gives us no rest by day nor sleep by night." We constantly threatened the offensive, and our raising steam, which they could perceive by our smoke-stack, was the signal for either fleet to fire up. As the temperature at that season was from 90° to 100° in the shade, it was clear that unless the *Arkansas* could be "destroyed" the siege, if for sanitary reasons alone, must soon be raised.

The result of our first real attempt to resume the offensive was that before we could get within range of the mortar fleet, our engine completely broke down, and it was with difficulty that we regained our usual position in front of the city.

The timely coming of the iron-clad *Essex*, fresh from the docks, and with a new crew, enabled the Union commander to attack us without risk to his regular or original blockading force. They could not have taken us at a more unprepared moment. Some of our officers and all but twenty-eight of our crew were in hospitals ashore, and we lay helplessly at anchor, with a disabled engine. I made known to the general commanding at Vicksburg the condition of our vessel, and with great earnestness personally urged him to give me, without delay, enough men to fight my guns, telling him that I expected an attack every hour. I was promised that the men (needed at the moment) should be sent to me the next day. The following morning at sunrise the *Essex*, Commodore William D. Porter, with the *Queen of the West*, no doubt the best ram of the Ellet flock (though as far as my experience went they were all ordinary sheep and equally harmless), ran down under full steam, regardless of the fire of our upper shore-batteries, and made the expected attack. We were at anchor and with only enough men to fight two of our guns; but by the zeal of our officers, who mixed in with these men as part of the guns' crews, we were able to train at the right moment and fire all the guns which could be brought to bear upon our cautiously coming assailants. With a view perhaps to avoid our bow guns, the *Essex* made the mistake, so far as her success was concerned,

COMMODORE W. D. PORTER. FROM A PHOTOGRAPH.

of running into us across the current instead of coming head-on with its force. At the moment of collision, when our guns were muzzle to muzzle, the *Arkansas's* broadside was exchanged for the bow guns of the assailant; a shot from one of the latter struck the *Arkansas's* plating a foot forward of the forward broadside port, breaking off the ends of the railroad bars and driving them in among our people; the solid shot followed, crossed diagonally our gun-deck, and split on the breech of our starboard after-broadside gun. This shot killed eight and wounded six of our men, but left us still half our crew. What damage the *Essex* received I did not ascertain, but that vessel drifted clear of the *Arkansas* without again firing, and after receiving the fire of our stern rifles steamed in the face and under the fire of the Vicksburg batteries to the fleet below. Had Porter at the moment of the collision thrown fifty men on our upper deck, he might have made fast to us with a hawser, and with little additional loss might have taken the *Arkansas* and her twenty men and officers. We were given time by the approaching ram to reload our guns, and this second assailant, coming also across instead of with the current, "butted" us so gently that we hardly felt the shock. The force of his blow was tempered to us no doubt by the effect of our three broadside guns,

which were fired into him when he was less than fifty feet distant. Apparently blinded by such a blow in the face, he drifted astern and ran ashore under the muzzles of Read's rifles, the bolts from which were probably lost in the immense quantity of hay in bales which seemed stowed over and around him. Getting clear of the bank, the ram wore round without again attempting to strike the *Arkansas,* and steamed at great speed up the river, receiving in passing a second broadside from our port battery, and in the excitement of getting away neglecting the caution of his advance, he brought himself within range of our deadly bow guns, from which Grimball and Gift sent solid shot that seemed to pass through him from stem to stern. As he ran out of range he was taken in tow and was run up into the Davis fleet.

Thus closed the fourth and final battle of the *Arkansas,* leaving the daring Confederate vessel, though reduced in crew to twenty men all told for duty, still defiant in the presence of a hostile force perhaps exceeding in real strength that which fought under Nelson at Trafalgar. The conduct of our men and officers was on this occasion, as on every former trial, worthy of the American name. Moving quickly in a squad, from gun to gun, reloading, and running out each one separately, and then dividing into parties sufficient to train and fire, they were as determined and cheerful as they could have been with a full crew on board. The closeness of this contest with the *Essex* may be inferred from the circumstance that several of our surviving men had their faces blackened and were painfully hurt by the unburnt powder which came through our port-holes from the assailant's guns.

It was perhaps as much a matter of coal as of cannon, of health as of hostility, that the Union commanders had now to decide upon. If the *Arkansas* could not be destroyed, the siege must be raised, for fifty ships, more or less, could not keep perpetual steam to confine one little 10-gun vessel within her conceded control of six miles of the Mississippi River. It was, indeed, a dilemma, and doubtless the less difficult horn of it was chosen. Soon after our contribution to the *Essex's* laurels, and between sunset and sunrise, the lower fleet started for the recuperative atmosphere of salt-water, and about the same time the upper fleet — rams, bombs, and iron-clads — steamed for the North. Thus was dissipated for the season the greatest naval force hitherto assembled at one time in the New World.

Vicksburg was now without the suspicion of an immediate enemy. I had taken, with my brave associates, for the last sixty days, my share of labor and watchfulness, and I now left them for four days, only, as I supposed, to sustain without me the lassitude of inaction. Important repairs were yet necessary to the engines, and much of the iron plating had to be refastened to her shattered sides. This being fairly under way, I called, Thursday P. M., upon General Van Dorn, commanding the forces, and told him that, having obtained telegraphic permission from the Navy Department to turn over the command of the vessel temporarily to the officer next in rank, First Lieutenant Stevens, I would go to Grenada, Miss., and that I would return on the following Tuesday A. M., by which time the *Arkansas*, I hoped, would be ready once more to resume the offensive. Almost immediately on reaching Grenada I was taken violently ill, and while in bed, unable, as I supposed, to rise, I received a dispatch from Lieutenant Stevens saying that Van Dorn required him to steam at once down to Baton Rouge to aid in a land attack of our forces upon the Union garrison holding that place. I replied to this with a positive order to remain at Vicksburg until I could join him; and without delay caused myself to be taken to the railroad station, where I threw myself on the mail-bags of the first passing train, unable to sit up, and did not change my position until reaching Jackson, 130 miles distant. On applying there for a special train to take me to Vicksburg, I learned that the *Arkansas* had been gone from that place four hours.☆ Van Dorn had been persistent beyond all reason in his demand, and Stevens, undecided, had referred the question to a senior officer of the Confederate navy, who was at Jackson, Miss., with horses and carriages, furnished by Government in place of a flag-ship, thus commanding in chief for the Confederacy on the Mississippi, sixty miles from its nearest waters. This officer, whose war record was

yet in abeyance, had attained scientific celebrity by dabbling in the waters of the Dead Sea, at a time when I was engaged in the siege of Vera Cruz and in the general operations of the Mexican war. Ignorant or regardless of the condition of the *Arkansas*, fresh from Richmond on his mission of bother, not communicating with or informing me on the subject, he ordered Stevens to obey Van Dorn without any regard to my orders to the contrary.

Under the double orders of two commanders-in-chief to be at Baton Rouge at a certain date and hour, Stevens could not use that tender care which his engines required, and before they completed their desperate run of three hundred miles against time, the starboard one suddenly broke down, throwing the vessel inextricably ashore. This misfortune, for which there was no present remedy, happened when the vessel was within sight of Baton Rouge. Very soon after, the *Essex* was seen approaching under full steam. Stevens, as humane as he was true and brave, finding that he could not bring a single gun to bear upon the coming foe, sent all his people over the bows ashore, remaining alone to set fire to his vessel; this he did so effectually that he had to jump from the stern into the river and save himself by swimming; and with colors flying, the gallant *Arkansas*, whose decks had never been pressed by the foot of an enemy, was blown into the air.

☆ I was entirely cured by this intelligence, and immediately hurried to Pontchatoula, the nearest approach by rail to Baton Rouge, and thence arrived nearly in time to see the explosion of the *Arkansas*.—I. N. B.

DESTRUCTION OF THE CONFEDERATE RAM "ARKANSAS."

NOTE TO THE FOREGOING ARTICLE.— The condition of the *Carondelet* in the fight with the *Arkansas* is exhibited by the following extracts from the log of the vessel, here printed from the original manuscript:

"*July* 15*th.* Commences and until 4 A. M. clear and warm. At 3 : 30 called all hands and hove up our anchor.— EDW'D E. BRENNAND.

"From 4 to 8: At 4 got under way and proceeded up the river, gun-boat *Taylor* [*Tyler*] and ram *Queen of the West* following us; at 4 : 30 entered Yazoo River; at 5 *Taylor* and *Queen of the West* passed us; at 6 discovered a boat coming down the river; immediately went to quarters and cleared the boat for action. Rebel ram opened fire upon the *Queen of the West* and gun-boat *Taylor*, and they immediately rounded to. We found the advancing rebel boat to be a powerful gunboat and ram. We rounded to and headed down-stream, at the same time firing upon her with all our batteries as we brought them in range. Captain Walke hailed the *Taylor* as she passed, and ordered Lieutenant-Commander Gwin to go ahead and inform the commodore of the *Arkansas's* approach. The ram made for us, and for an hour we continued a running fight (she gaining on us); distance, 500 to 50 yards. Our wheelropes were shot away, steam-escape pipe cut, exhaust pipe cut, cold-water supply pipe riddled with pieces of shot, and steam-gauge shot away; the boat becoming unmanageable.

"Our tiller ropes and box being shot away, the *Carondelet* was unmanageable, and ran upon a small stump after the *Arkansas* passed by us. As she passed by us we called the boarders up on deck, and we gave her our starboard broadside and bow guns, firing them as the enemy came in range. At this time the *Arkansas's* flag was down, and not hoisted again while in sight. Our backing-bell and speaking-trumpet being shot away, the pilot could not communicate readily with the engineer. By this time the ram had passed by us, and was following the *Taylor*. After remaining at the bank for a short time to repair damages we made our way down the river, and found that the rebel boat had succeeded in passing by the whole of the flotilla and rams. We received five shots in the captain's cabin and three in the ward-room, three of the shots passing clear through the wheel-house, one lodging in the steerage mess-room, one going through wheel-house carrying away deck-pump, passing through bulkhead aft of steam drum, glancing up, passing over steam drum, striking carlines, carrying away four of them, and falling into fireroom. One going through wheel-house, carrying away steam-escape pipes, going through two coppers on the galley, through smoke-pipe, through ventilators, through bulkhead forward of fire-room, through loose timbers placed upon the bulkhead, and entering four pieces of ¼-inch iron. One coming in captain's cabin on starboard corner, carrying away twelve carlines, striking chambers of side pipe, glancing upward and cutting exhaust pipe, and striking upper deck over engine-room and falling to the main deck. One coming in ward-room just amidships, cutting away eight carlines, passing through the chief engineer's, surgeon's, and gunner's rooms, carrying away bulkheads, and striking the deck and fetching up against the after stanchion on port side. Another shot came through starboard quarter, passing through 2d and 1st masters' room and through the captain's cabin out of the after-port. Another shot came through the iron on starboard side, breaking in casemate, and the shot breaking in pieces; two shots carrying away iron, and coming through the iron into the wood on the inside. Both cutters shot away; two boats' davits carried away; all boats' falls on starboard side shot away; three awning stanchions shot away. One shell burst on starboard side of upper deck, cutting awning in pieces and setting starboard hammocknetting on fire. We expended during the engagement one 32-pound gun, weight 43 hundred-weight, struck on the lower part of the muzzle, splitting the gun in two places; six boarding pikes, one musket, three revolvers, and four cutlasses, belts, and accouterments were lost and shot to pieces during the engagement. Robert Letty, Charles A. Wiggins, Charles Schraw, and Oliver Greggs were killed. There were also 15 wounded and 16 missing. Expended ninety rifle and solid shots. . . . EDW'D E. BRENNAND, 1st Master."

The reader is also referred to Admiral Walke's statement on p. 555.— EDITORS.

CONFEDERATE TORPEDOES IN THE YAZOO.

BY ISAAC N. BROWN, CAPTAIN, C. S. N.

IT was rather by inference than by any direct orders that after the sacrifice of the *Arkansas* I was left to guard the Yazoo River. At this juncture Messrs. McDonald (or McDonough) and Ewing, acting masters in the Confederate navy, offered to aid me with torpedoes. So poor in resources were we, that in order to make a beginning I borrowed a five-gallon glass demijohn, and procuring from the army the powder to fill it and an artillery friction tube to explode it, I set these two enterprising men to work with a coil of small iron wire which they stretched from bank to bank, the demijohn filled with inflammable material being suspended from the middle, some feet below the surface of the water, and so connected with the friction tube inside as to ignite when a vessel should come in contact with the wire. Soon after it was put in position the iron-clad *Cairo* came up the river [December 12th, 1862], and, keeping the middle of the stream, hit the demijohn, and within twelve minutes went to the bottom in thirty feet of water. In this way a belligerent vessel was "neutralized" by an enemy's torpedo. The moral strength thus added to our defenses may be inferred from an anecdote reported to me soon after. One of our Confederate people went on board a Union gun-boat off the mouth of the Yazoo, under flag of truce, and met there an old messmate and friend, and said banteringly to him, "Tom, why don't you go up and clean out the Yazoo?" "I would as soon think of going to —— at once," was the answer, "for Brown has got the river chock-full of torpedoes."

I also made a contract with Dr. Fretwell and Mr. Norman, then at Yazoo City, for fifty or more of these destructives on Dr. Fretwell's plan — automatic action on being brought in contact with a vessel or boat. But the difficulty of procuring materials prevented the completion of the contract for the whole number in time.

On the morning of the Union advance upon Yazoo City [July 13th, 1863], I had myself placed two of these "Fretwells" half a mile below our landbattery of one rifle 6-inch gun — handled by the same men — the same gun, in fact, that had aided in the defense of Fort Pemberton. The *De Kalb* had there felt this gun, and it came twice within its range on this day,— retiring both times without unreasonable delay,— but when our sailor crew found themselves uncovered by our land force, and a whole division of Union men within riflerange, they withdrew under orders, and the *De Kalb*, seeing our gun silent, advanced for the third time, getting as far as the torpedoes, and there suddenly disappearing beneath the waters of the Yazoo. [See also pp. 559 and 570.]

UNION VESSELS IN THE VICKSBURG OPERATIONS.

THE MISSISSIPPI FLOTILLA.—Rear-Admiral David D. Porter, commanding; Commander A. M. Pennock, Fleet Captain, Naval Station, Cairo.

GUN-BOATS.— *Benton*, Lieut.-Com. S. L. Phelps, Lieut.-Com. W. Gwin (Yazoo River, December, 1862), Lieut.-Com. J. A. Greer (Vicksburg, Grand Gulf), 16 guns; *Essex*, Com. W. D. Porter, Com. C. H. B. Caldwell (Port Hudson), Com. R. Townsend, 5 guns, 1 howitzer; July, 1862, 7 guns, 1 howitzer; June 10th, 1863, 8 guns, 2 howitzers; August 1st, 1863, 8 guns, 4 howitzers.

EADS IRON-CLADS.—*St. Louis (Baron De Kalb)*, Lieut. W. McGunnegle (St. Charles), Lieut.-Com. J. G. Walker (Yazoo River, Arkansas Post, Yazoo Pass, Haynes's Bluff, Yazoo City), 13 guns (reduced to 7, May, 1863); *Cairo*, Lieut.-Com. T. O. Selfridge, 13 guns, 1 howitzer; *Carondelet*, Com. Henry Walke (action with *Arkansas*, July 15th, 1862), Lieut. J. M. Murphy (Steele's Bayou, Vicksburg, and Grand Gulf), 13 guns, 1 howitzer; May 15th, 1863, 11 guns; *Cincinnati*, Lieut.-Com. B. Wilson (Vicksburg, July, 1862), Lieut. George M. Bache (Arkansas Post, Steele's Bayou, Vicksburg, May 27th), 13 guns, 1 howitzer; *Louisville*, Com. B. M. Dove (Vicksburg, July, 1862), Lieut.-Com. E. K. Owen (Arkansas Post, Steele's Bayou, Vicksburg, and Grand Gulf), 13 guns, 1 howitzer; *Mound City*, Com. A. H. Kilty (St. Charles), Lieut.-Com. W. Gwin (Yazoo River Raid, Aug., '62), Lieut. B. Wilson (Steele's Bayou, Vicksburg, and Grand Gulf, Warrenton), 13 guns, 1 howitzer; May 28, '63, 15 guns; July 26, '63, 13 guns; *Pittsburgh*, Act. V. Lieut. W. R. Hoel, 13 guns; Sept., '62, 12 guns, 1 howitzer; May 18, '63, 13 guns; Dec., '63, 14 guns.

LATER IRON-CLADS.— *Choctaw* (turret), Lieut.-Com. F. M. Ramsay (Haynes's Bluff, Yazoo River, Yazoo City, Milliken's Bend), April 9th, 1863, 4 guns; May, 1863, 4 guns, 2 howitzers; June 8th, 1863, 6 guns, 2 howitzers; *Lafayette*, Capt. H. Walke (Vicksburg and Grand Gulf), 6 guns, 4 howitzers; *Chillicothe*, Lieut.-Com. J. P. Foster (Yazoo Pass), 2 guns; *Indianola*, Lieut.-Com. George Brown, 4 guns; *Tuscumbia*, Lieut.-Com. J. W. Shirk (Vicksburg and Grand Gulf), 5 guns.

RODGERS GUN-BOATS.—*Conestoga*, Lieut. G. W. Blodgett (St. Charles), Lieut.-Com. T. O. Selfridge, 4 guns, 1 howitzer; *Lexington*, Lieut. James W. Shirk (St. Charles, Yazoo River, Dec., '62, Arkansas Post); Lieut.-Com. S. L. Phelps (Cumberland River, Jan.,'63); Lieut.-Com. Le Roy Fitch (Tennessee and Cumberland rivers); Lieut. G. M. Bache (White River), 6 guns; Sept.,'62, 7 guns, 1 howitzer; *Tyler*, Lieut. William Gwin (action with *Arkansas*, July 15, '62); Lieut.-Com. J. M. Prichett (Yazoo River, Dec., '62, Helena), 7 guns; Sept., '62, 9 guns, 1 howitzer.

ELLET RAMS.—Lieut.-Col. A. W. Ellet, Col. C. R. Ellet. (Originally employed without armament; subsequently howitzers or other light guns were mounted from time to time. Frequent changes were also made in commanding officers. Those engaged in important actions are mentioned below. The vessels were the *Fulton*, *Horner*, *Lancaster*, Lieut.-Col. J. A. Ellet (passage of Vicksburg, March 25th, 1863); *Lioness*, Master T. O'Reilly (Yazoo River, December, 1862); *Mingo*, *Monarch*, Sergt. E. W. Davis (Yazoo River raid, August, 1862), Col. C. R. Ellet (Ark. Post); *Queen of the West*, Lieut. J. M. Hunter (action of July 15th, 1862), Lieut.-Col. A. W. Ellet (July 22d, 1862), Capt. E. W. Sutherland (Yazoo River, December, 1862), Col. C. R. Ellet (Red River cruise); *Sampson*, *Switzerland*, Lieut.-Col. A. W. Ellet (Yazoo River raid, August, 1862), Col. C. R. Ellet (passage of Vicksburg, March 25th, 1863).

PRIZES. — *Alfred Robb*, Act. V. Lieut. J. Goudy, Act. Ens. W. C. Hanford, 4 howitzers; *Eastport*, Lieut.-Com. S. L. Phelps, 8 guns, 2 howitzers; *Fair Play*, Lieut.-Com. Le Roy Fitch; Act. Master Geo. J. Groves, September, 1862, 4 howitzers; May, 1863, 1 gun, 6 howitzers; *General Bragg*, Lt. Joshua Bishop, September, 1862, 2 guns, 1 howitzer; *General Pillow*, Act. Ens. J. Moyer, September, 1862, 2 howitzers; *General Price*, Com. S. E. Woodworth (Vicksburg, April–July, 1863), 4 guns; *Little*

Rebel, Act. V. Lieut. T. B. Gregory, September, 1862, 3 howitzers; March, 1863, 4 howitzers; *Sumter*, Lieut. Henry Erben (Vicksburg, July 15th, 1862), 4 guns, 1 howitzer.

TIN-CLADS.—*Brilliant*, Act. V. Lieut. C. G. Perkins, September, 1862, 4 howitzers; February, 1863, 6 howitzers; *Cricket*, Act. V. Lieut. A. R. Langthorne, 6 howitzers; *Forest Rose*, Act. V. Lieut. George W. Brown, December, 1862, 2 guns, 4 howitzers; August 19th, 1863, 4 guns, 4 howitzers; *Glide*, Act. Lt. S. E. Woodworth (Ark. Post); *Juliet*, Act. V. Lieut. Ed. Shaw, 6 howitzers; *Linden*, Act. V. Lieut. T. E. Smith, Act. Master T. M. Farrell, 6 howitzers; *Marmora*, Act. V. Lieut. Robert Getty, September, 1862, 4 howitzers; December, 1862, 8 howitzers; *Petrel*, Act. Master T. McElroy, Act. V. Lieut. John Pearce; *Rattler*, Lieut.-Com. Watson Smith (Ark. Post, Yazoo Pass), Act. Master W. E. H. Fentress, 8 howitzers; *Romeo*, Act. Ens. R. B. Smith (Yazoo River, December, 1862), Act. Master T. Baldwin, 6 howitzers; *Signal*, Act. V. Lieut. John Scott, Act. V. Lieut. C. Dominy, September, 1862, 4 howitzers; May, 1863, 6 howitzers; November, 1863, 2 guns, 6 howitzers.

VARIOUS VESSELS.—*Alexandria*, Act. Master D., P. Rosenmiller, 2 howitzers; *Argosy*, Act. Ens. J. C. Morong, 7 howitzers; *Black Hawk*, Lieut.-Com. K. R. Breese (Ark. Post and Vicksburg), 9 guns, 2 howitzers; *Champion*, Act. Master Alfred Phelps, 2 guns, 2 howitzers; *Covington*, Act. V. Lieut. J. S. Hurd, Act. V. Lieut. Geo. P. Lord, 4 guns, 4 howitzers; *Curlew*, Act. Ens. H. B. O'Neill, 8 howitzers; *Exchange*, Act. V. Lieut. J. S. Hurd, 2 guns, 5 howitzers; *Fort Hindman*, Act. V. Lieut. John Pearce, 6 guns; *Hastings*, Act. V. Lieut. A. R. Langthorne, 4 guns, 4 howitzers; *Kenwood*, Act. Master John Swaney, May, 1863, 2 guns, 4 howitzers; *Key West*, Act. V. Lieut. E. M. King, May, 1863, 6 howitzers; June 16th, 1863, 8 howitzers; *Moose*, Lieut.-Com. LeRoy Fitch, 6 howitzers; *Naumkeag*, Act. Master John Rogers, 2 guns, 4 howitzers; *New Era*, Act. Master F. W. Flanner, Act. Master J. C. Bunner, 6 howitzers; *Pawpaw*, Act. Master A. F. Thompson, 2 guns, 6 howitzers; *Peosta*, Act. V. Lieut. T. E. Smith, 6 guns, 8 howitzers; *Prairie Bird*, Act. V. Lieut. E. E. Brennand, 8 howitzers; *Queen City*, Act. V. Lieut. J. Goudy, Act. V. Lieut. G. W. Brown, April, 1863, 4 guns, 4 howitzers; *Reindeer*, Act. V. Lieut. H. A. Glassford, 6 howitzers; *St. Clair*, Act. V. Lieut. J. S. Hurd, Act. V. Lieut. T. B. Gregory, September, 1862, 4 howitzers; February 1863, 6 howitzers; *Silver Cloud*, Act. V. Lieut. A. F. O'Neil, 6 howitzers; *Silver Lake*, Act. Master J. C. Coyle, 6 howitzers; *Springfield*, Act. Master J. Watson, 6 howitzers; *Tawah*, Act. V. Lieut. J. Goudy, 2 guns, 6 howitzers; *Victory*, Act. Master F. Read, 6 howitzers.

MORTAR-BOATS, Gunner Eugene Mack; Ensign Miller.

AUXILIARY.—*Abraham*, Act. Ens. W. Wagner (inspection boat); *Clara Dolsen*, Lieut.-Com. T. Pattison (receiving ship at Cairo), 1 gun; *General Lyon*, Pilot R. E. Birch (dispatch boat), 2 howitzers; *Grampus*, Act. Master E. Sells (receiving ship); *Great Western*, (ordnance boat), Act. V. Lieut. W. F. Hamilton; *Judge Torrence*, (ordnance boat), Act. V. Lieut. J. F. Richardson; *New National*, Act. Master A. M. Grant (receiving ship), 1 howitzer; *Red Rover*, Act. Master W. R. Wells (hospital steamer), 1 gun; *Sovereign* (storeship, no battery), Act. Master T. Baldwin; *William H. Brown* (dispatch steamer), Act. V. Lieut. J. A. French.

WEST GULF SQUADRON: Passage of Port Hudson, March 14th-15th, 1863.— Rear-Admiral D. G. Farragut commanding; Capt. Thornton A. Jenkins, Fleet Captain. *Hartford* (flag-ship), Capt. James S. Palmer; *Mississippi*, Capt. Melancton Smith; *Monongahela*, Capt. J. P. McKinstry; *Richmond*, Com. James Alden; *Genesee*, Com. W. H. Macomb; *Albatross*, Lieut.-Com. John E. Hart: *Kineo*, Lieut.-Com. John Watters. Coöperating vessels of West Gulf Squadron, in Red River, May, 1863: *Albatross*, Lieut.-Com. John E. Hart; *Estrella*, Lieut.-Com. A. P. Cooke; *Arizona*, Act. V. Lieut. Daniel P. Upton.

MILITARY OPERATIONS IN LOUISIANA IN 1862.

BY RICHARD B. IRWIN, LIEUTENANT-COLONEL, ASSISTANT ADJUTANT-GENERAL, U. S. V.

ON the 1st of May General Butler took possession of New Orleans, and immediately afterward of all its outlying defenses. ⚓ His instructions from General McClellan, as General-in-Chief, dated February 23d, the main object of which had now been so successfully accomplished, looked to the occupation of Baton Rouge as the next step, "and the opening of communication with the northern column, bearing in mind the occupation of Jackson, Mississippi." Mobile was to follow. The whole force assigned to General Butler, for all purposes, was 18,000, but his actual force can at no time have exceeded 15,000; it was now probably about 13,000.↓

Two weeks before this the "northern column," under Pope, had been called from Fort Pillow to Corinth; consequently there was no longer a northern column to coöperate with; and Jackson, Mississippi, meant Beauregard's rear.

Promptly on the 2d of May Farragut moved the fleet up the river, and on the 8th General Butler sent Brigadier-General Thomas Williams, with 1400 men of the 4th Wisconsin and 6th Michigan regiments, and two sections of Everett's 6th Massachusetts battery. On the 12th the troops landed at Baton Rouge and took possession of the town. The advance of the fleet anchored below Vicksburg on the 18th, when Commander Lee and General Williams jointly demanded from "the authorities" the surrender of the town, which was refused.

The whole available force of the department, as things were then, could not have held Vicksburg. Farragut's guns were heavily handicapped by the extreme elevation required to reach the batteries on the bluff, 200 feet above the river, while Williams could not land till the batteries

were silenced. After a thorough reconnoissance on the 25th it was decided to drop down the river, leaving six vessels to keep up a blockade and an occasional bombardment. The Confederates now rushed the work on their batteries on the river-front, and in a short time the whole ten were completed and about 25 heavy guns mounted. ♭

On the 29th of May the troops were back at Baton Rouge, where they landed and went into camp for the first time in three weeks; indeed, the men had been almost continuously on the crowded transports, in a great state of discomfort, since the 17th of April. General Butler sent up reënforcements, and with them orders "to proceed to Vicksburg with the flag-officer, and then take the town or have it burned at all hazards."

Accordingly, on the 20th of June, General Williams again set out for Vicksburg, under convoy, this time with four regiments and ten guns: the 4th Wisconsin, 30th Massachusetts, 9th Connecticut, 7th Vermont, Nims's 2d Massachusetts battery, and two sections of Everett's; leaving the 21st Indiana, 6th Michigan, the remaining section of Everett's battery, and Magee's troop of cavalry to hold Baton Rouge against a possible attack from Camp Moore, near Tangipahoa. At Ellis's Bluffs, and again at Grand Gulf, troops were landed to drive off the field-batteries that had been firing upon the gun-boats. On the 25th the troops were back at Vicksburg where the bulk of the fleet and sixteen of Commodore Porter's mortar-boats, or "bombers," as they were rather familiarly called, were now lying at anchor.

After the failure of the attack by Farragut and Porter's fleets on the 28th of June, Farragut sent an urgent appeal for aid to Halleck, at Corinth,

---

↓ For an account of the Naval Operations, see p. 551.

⚓ General Butler at once declared martial law (by a proclamation dated May 1st), abridging the liberty of the press and placing the telegraph under military espionage. On the 6th a military commission was established to try capital and other serious offenses. On the 13th an order was issued forbidding fasting and prayer under the proclamation of Jefferson Davis; on the 15th an order (No. 28) prescribing that women guilty of insulting Union soldiers should be treated as "women of the town"; and on the 16th an order forbidding the city and the banks from receiving Confederate money, and fixing the 27th of May as a date when all circulation of Confederate notes and bills should cease in the Department of the Gulf. William B. Mumford, who hauled down the flag which by Farragut's order had been raised over the Mint, was convicted of treason, and by General Butler's order was hanged on the 7th of June from a gallows placed under the flag-staff of the Mint. Mumford, who was a North Carolinian, though long a resident of New Orleans, addressed a vast crowd from the gallows. He spoke with perfect self-possession, and said that his offense had been committed under excitement.— EDITORS.

↓ General Butler raised, on his own motion, two good regiments of infantry, the 1st Louisiana, Colonel Richard

E. Holcomb, and 2d Louisiana, Colonel Charles J. Paine, well commanded and well officered; three excellent troops of Louisiana cavalry under fine leaders, Captains H. F. Williamson, Richard Barrett, and J. F. Godfrey; and three colored regiments with white field and staff officers, designated as the 1st, 2d, and 3d "Louisiana Native Guards" (a name "captured" by General Butler), Colonels Spencer H. Stafford, Nathan W. Daniels, and John A. Nelson. I believe these were the first negro troops mustered into the service of the United States.— R. B. I.

♭ On the way down the river a Confederate battery at Grand Gulf fired about sixty shots at short range at the transports, killing one private and wounding one officer (Captain Chauncey J. Bassett) of the 6th Michigan regiment. The gun-boat Kineo, Lieutenant-Commander Ransom, shelled the town, and General Williams sent four companies of the 4th Wisconsin, under Major Frederick A. Boardman, to disperse the neighboring Confederate camp. A skirmish in the dark followed, in which Lieutenant George DeKay, Aide-de-Camp to General Williams, was mortally wounded, while in front of the advance-guard.

De Kay was a most estimable young man, much loved by all that knew him, and was the first officer killed in the department.— R. B. I.

saying : "My orders, General, are to clear the river. This I find impossible without your assistance. Can you aid me in this matter to carry out the peremptory order of the President?" Unfortunately, Halleck's army was broken up; he was sending reënforcements to Curtis and Buell, and was being asked to send 25,000 men to McClellan. The Confederates, however, were able to send 10,000 men to the support of the defenders. Finally the *Arkansas* came out of the Yazoo and put an end to the operations, and the two fleets turned

their backs on each other and on Vicksburg, and on the 26th of July, abandoning the canal, the troops landed once more at Baton Rouge.

Overwork, malaria, and scurvy, the result of privation, had done their work on Williams's men; of the 3200 men that went up the river barely 800 came back fit for duty.⸶

Van Dorn at once prepared to assume the offensive. As the last of the fleet steamed away from Vicksburg, Breckinridge set out for Camp Moore with five thousand picked men. There he was to pick up the troops under Brigadier-General Daniel Ruggles, raising the whole force to six thousand, and promptly attack Baton Rouge, in coöperation with the *Arkansas*. The plan was admirably conceived and put in motion with great promptness. As Van Dorn estimated Williams's force at 3500 (it was in fact less), with four or five of the same gun-boats that the *Arkansas* had already treated so cavalierly, he had a right to look for success.

⸶ The work on the canal had proved especially exhausting, though the troops had the help of about 1200 to 1500 negroes. By the 11th of July, the cut, originally intended to be 4 feet deep and 5 feet wide, had been excavated through the clay (with much felling of trees and grubbing of roots) to a depth of 13 feet, and a width of 18 feet; the length of the canal was about a mile and half. The grade was now about 18 inches below the river level,

Breckinridge organized his force in two divisions, the first commanded by Brigadier-General Charles Clark, consisting of the brigades of Brigadier-General B. H. Helm and Colonel T. B. Smith, 20th Tennessee; the second division under Brigadier-General Daniel Ruggles, comprising the brigades of Colonel A. P. Thompson, 3d Kentucky, and Colonel H. W. Allen, 4th Louisiana. To these forces were attached three batteries of artillery, two mounted companies and 250 Partisan Rangers.

Shortly after daylight on the 5th of August, a dense fog prevailing, Breckinridge moved to the attack, Ruggles deployed on the left of the road from Greenwell Springs to Baton Rouge, Clark on its right. Williams stood to receive the attack, his troops deployed in a single line, with reserves, covering the rear of the town. No attempt at intrenching had been made, and from the nature of the country, for the most part an elevated plateau surmounting the bluff, the line was open to attack from any direction except the river. From left to right the troops were posted thus: 4th Wisconsin beyond Bayou Grosse; 9th Connecticut next; 14th Maine at the crossing of the Bayou Sara and Greenwell Springs roads on the left of the latter; 21st Indiana on its

PRIVATE HOUSES (IN NEW ORLEANS) IN WHICH CONFEDERATE OFFICERS WERE CONFINED.

right; 6th Michigan across the Perkins and Clay Cut roads near their fork; 7th Vermont and 30th Massachusetts in reserve supporting the center and right; the batteries from left to right, Manning, Everett, Nims, with Brown in reserve.

Ruggles was soon engaged; Clark took up the attack; and falling on fiercely they at first carried everything before them. Some of the tents that were in advance of the line of battle were occupied, and Brown's two guns were captured by the

and in a few hours the water was to have been let in. Suddenly the banks began to cave, and before anything could be done to remedy this, the river, falling rapidly, was once more below the bottom of the cut. Williams at once set about collecting more hands and tools, with the purpose of carrying the cut below the lowest stage of water, forty feet if necessary ; this he calculated would take three months.— R. B. I.

4th Louisiana, but immediately retaken by the 6th Michigan, together with the colors of their opponents. Then as the attack spent its vigor and developed its direction, Williams re-formed the 21st Indiana and 6th Michigan, rather roughly handled at first, on the new line. The 9th Connecticut moved by the flank to the support of their left; the 30th Massachusetts covered the interval on the left of the 6th Michigan, and the 4th Wisconsin went to the assistance of the 14th Maine, which had been stoutly holding its own against the onset of Clark. Finally the Union troops advanced to the attack, the Confederates in their turn were driven back in some disorder, and at 10 o'clock the battle was over, with the attack thrown off and the battle-field in the hands of the defenders.

The Union loss was 84 killed, 266 wounded, 33 missing, in all 383. Among the killed were Colonel George T. Roberts, 7th Vermont, and the gallant commander, Brigadier-General Thomas Williams, who fell pierced by a rifle-ball in the chest, just after giving the final order to attack. An extremely rigid disciplinarian, a thoroughly trained and most accomplished officer, and a man of the highest courage and honor, General Williams's death was long and deeply regretted in the department.

The Confederate loss was 84 killed, 315 wounded, 57 missing,— total, 456. Brigadier-General Charles Clark, commanding the First Division, was severely wounded and made prisoner, and also among the wounded were three brigade commanders, Colonels Thomas H. Hunt, A. P. Thompson, and H. W. Allen, the last two severely.

The iron-clad *Essex*, Commander William D. Porter, with the *Cayuga* and *Sumter* above the town, and the gun-boats *Kineo*, Lieutenant-Commander George M. Ransom, and *Katahdin*, Lieutenant F. A. Roe, contributed materially to the defense.

The numbers engaged cannot have been far from equal — about 2500 on either side.

When Williams fell, Colonel Thomas W. Cahill, of Connecticut, succeeded to the command. On the 6th he was relieved by Colonel Halbert E. Paine, 4th Wisconsin, who had been sent up from New Orleans by Butler on receiving the first news of the battle. Being still menaced by Breckinridge, the troops took up a new and shorter line, extending from Bayou Grosse by the tannery and penitentiary to the neighborhood of the capitol; at 3 o'clock every morning they stood to arms, and by the 13th Colonel Paine, with characteristic care and energy, had strongly intrenched the arsenal grounds, with 24 guns in position, and with the coöperation of the navy concerted every measure for an effective defense against numbers. By General Butler's orders the library and a statue of Washington, in the capitol, were packed and shipped to New Orleans. On the 20th, by Butler's orders, Baton Rouge was quietly evacuated, and the troops, with all their material, proceeded to Camp Parapet, at Carrollton, just above New Orleans, where they set to work to extend and

strengthen the old Confederate lines and put everything in good condition for defense.

Breckinridge had fallen back to Port Hudson, where, by Van Dorn's orders, the strong works were begun that were long to prove a formidable obstacle to the Union operations on the Mississippi. On the 19th of August Breckinridge was ordered by Bragg to leave the command in the hands of Ruggles and return to Mississippi.

The "Official Records" covering this period afford several strong hints of a Confederate plan for the recapture of New Orleans. Major-General Richard Taylor appears to have had that object committed to his special care when he was assigned (August 20th) to command in western Louisiana, and it seems likely that the troops of Van Dorn's department, as well as those at Mobile, were expected to take part.

Toward the end of September, Lieutenant Godfrey Weitzel, of the Engineers, having been made a brigadier-general on Butler's recommendation, was placed in command of a brigade of 4 regiments of infantry, 2 batteries and 4 troops of cavalry, and General Butler committed to his hands the preparations for dislodging Taylor's force and occupying the district of the La Fourche, important to the security of New Orleans because comprising or controlling all the fertile region between the Mississippi and the Atchafalaya. With the funds of the army, four light-draught gun-boats, the *Estrella*, *Calhoun*, *Kinsman*, and *Diana*, were quickly built, equipped, turned over to the navy, and sent to Berwick Bay, under Commander T. McKean Buchanan. When all was ready Weitzel took transports, under convoy, landed below Donaldsonville, entered the town, and on the 27th of October moved on Thibodeaux, the heart of the district. At Georgia Landing, two miles above Labadieville, he encountered the Confederates under Brigadier-General Alfred Mouton, consisting of the 18th and 33d Louisiana, Crescent and Terre Bonne regiments, Ralston's and Semmes's batteries, and 2d Louisiana Cavalry,— in all reported by Mouton as 1392 strong; they had taken up a defensive position on both sides of the bayou. After a short but spirited engagement, Mouton's force was routed and pursued about four miles. Mouton then called in his other troops, burned the bridges, and evacuated the district, Buchanan's gun-boats having been prevented by a gale from arriving in time to cut off the retreat. Mouton's report accounts for 5 killed, 8 wounded, and 186 missing,— in all, 199. Among the killed was Colonel G. P. McPheeters of the Crescent regiment.

Weitzel followed through Thibodeaux, and went into camp beyond the town. He claims to have taken 208 prisoners and 1 gun; his loss was 18 killed, 74 wounded, and 5 missing,— total, 97.

So ended operations in Louisiana for this year. Taylor continued to occupy the Teche country, and Weitzel the La Fourche, until the spring of 1863. On the 9th of November, 1862, General N. P. Banks was assigned to the command of the Department of the Gulf to relieve General Butler.

BURNING OF THE STATE-HOUSE, BATON ROUGE, ON SUNDAY, DECEMBER 28, 1862. FROM A SKETCH MADE AT THE TIME.

THE OPPOSING FORCES AT BATON ROUGE, LA.
August 5th, 1862.

The composition, losses, and strength of each army as here stated give the gist of all the data obtainable in the "Official Records." K stands for killed; w for wounded; m w for mortally wounded; m for captured or missing; c for captured.

THE UNION FORCES: Brig.-Gen. Thomas Williams (k), Col. Thomas W. Cahill.

Troops : 9th Conn., Col. Thomas W. Cahill, Lieut.-Col. Richard Fitz-Gibbons; 21st Ind., Lieut.-Col. John A. Keith (w), Capt. James Grimsley; 14th Me., Col. Frank S. Nickerson (commanding the left wing), Lieut.-Col. Thomas W. Porter; 30th Mass., Col. Nathan A. M. Dudley (commanding the right wing), Maj. Horace O. Whittemore; 6th Mich., Capt. Charles E. Clarke; 7th Ver., Col. George T. Roberts (m w), Capt. Henry M. Porter, Lieut.-Col. Volney S. Fullam; 4th Wis., Lieut.- Col. Sidney A. Bean; 2d Co. Mass. Cav., Captain James M. Magee; Ind. Battery (3 guns), Lieut. James H. Brown; 2d Mass. Battery, Lieut. George G. Trull; 4th Mass. Battery, Capt. Charles H. Manning; 6th Mass. Battery, Lieut. William W. Carruth.

The total Union loss was 84 killed, 266 wounded, 33 captured or missing = 383. The "force engaged numbered less than 2500." (See "Official Records," Vol. XV., p. 54.)

THE CONFEDERATE FORCES: Major-Gen. John C. Breckinridge.

FIRST DIVISION, Brig.-Gen. Charles Clark (w and c), Col. T. B. Smith. Staff loss: w, 2; m, 1 = 3.

Second Brigade, Brig.-Gen. Benjamin H. Helm (w), Col. Thomas H. Hunt (w), Capt. John A. Buckner: 4th Ky., Capt. John H. Millett; 5th Ky., Col. Thomas H. Hunt, Lieut.-Col. John W. Caldwell, Maj. J. C. Wickliffe; 31st Miss., Maj. H. E. Topp; 31st Ala., Col. Jeptha Edwards; 4th Ala. Battalion, Lieut.-Col. John Snodgrass; Miss. Battery (Pettus's Flying Art'y), Lieut. J. R. Sweaney. Brigade loss: k, 29; w, 111; m, 3 = 143. *Fourth Brigade,* Col. T. B. Smith: 19th, 20th, 28th, and 45th Tenn. (Battalion), Lieut.-Col. B. F. Moore; 15th Miss. (in reserve), Maj. J. R. Binford; 22d Miss., Capt. F. Hughes (m w); Ky. Battery, Capt. Robert Cobb. Brigade loss: k, 15; w, 41; m, 3 = 59.

SECOND DIVISION, Brig.-Gen. Daniel Ruggles.

First Brigade, Col. A. P. Thompson (w), Col. J. W. Robertson: 35th Ala., Col. J. W. Robertson, Lieut.-Col. Edward Goodwin; 3d Ky., Capt. J. W. Bowman; 6th Ky., Lieut.-Col. M. H. Cofer; 7th Ky., Col. Edward Crossland; Sharp-shooters, Lieut. G. C. Hubbard. Brigade loss: k, 12; w, 70; m, 3 = 85. *Second Brigade,* Col. H. W. Allen (w), Col. Gustavus A. Breaux: 4th La., (Co. I, 39th Miss., attached), Lieut.-Col. S. E. Hunter; 30th La. (battalion), Col. Gustavus A. Breaux; La. Battalion (Stewart's Legion), Lieut.-Col. Samuel Boyd (w), Capt. Thomas Bynum; Confederate Light Battery, Capt. O. J. Semmes. Brigade loss: k, 28; w, 91; m, 47 = 166.

UNATTACHED, La. Partisan Rangers, Col. Francis Pond, Jr., and Maj. J. De Baun.

The total Confederate loss was 84 killed, 315 wounded, and 57 captured or missing = 456. General Breckinridge says ("Official Records," Vol. XV., p. 77): "I did not carry into action more than 2600 men. This estimate does not include some 200 Partisan Rangers . . . who, from the nature of the ground, took no part in the action."

THE CAPTURE OF PORT HUDSON.

BY RICHARD B. IRWIN, LIEUTENANT-COLONEL, ASSISTANT ADJUTANT-GENERAL, U. S. V.

GENERAL BANKS arrived in New Orleans on the 14th of December, 1862, with the advance of a fleet of transports from New York and Hampton Roads, bringing reënforcements for the Department of the Gulf. ⌡ On the 15th he took command of the department, Butler then formally taking leave of the troops. His orders were to move up the Mississippi, in order to open the river, in coöperation with McClernand's column from Cairo. Banks was to take command of the combined forces as soon as they should meet.

On the 16th General Grover, with 12 regiments and a battery, without disembarking at New Orleans, accompanied by two batteries and two troops of cavalry from the old force, and convoyed by a detachment of Farragut's fleet under Captain James Alden, of the *Richmond*, was sent to occupy Baton Rouge. The next morning the town was evacuated by the small Confederate detachment which had been posted there, and General Grover quietly took possession. The town was held without opposition until the war ended.

An attempt followed to occupy Galveston, apparently under importunity from Brigadier-General Andrew J. Hamilton, and in furtherance of the policy that had led the Government to send him with the expedition as military governor of Texas. This resulted on the 1st of January in a military and naval disaster in which three companies of the 42d Massachusetts regiment, under Colonel Isaac S. Burrell, were taken prisoners by the Confederates under Magruder. ⌘

Weitzel, who was occupying the La Fourche, was strengthened so as to enable him to make the district safe in view of the projected operations on the Mississippi; a strong work was constructed at Donaldsonville commanding the head of the bayou; and intrenchments were thrown up at Brashear City to prevent, with the aid of the navy, any approach of the enemy from the direction of Berwick Bay. On the 14th of January, having crossed the bay, Weitzel ascended the Teche, accompanied by the gun-boats *Calhoun*, *Estrella*, and *Kinsman*, under Lieutenant-Commander Buchanan, forced the Confederates to destroy the gun-boat *Cotton*, and took 50 prisoners, with a loss of 6 killed and 27 wounded. Among the dead was Buchanan, who was succeeded by Lieutenant-Commander A. P. Cooke.

⌡ These reënforcements finally included 39 regiments of infantry (of which 22 were 9-months' men), six batteries of artillery, and one battalion of cavalry.

⌘ On the 21st of December three companies of the 42d Massachusetts, under Colonel Isaac S. Burrell, were dispatched from New Orleans, without disembarking. Holcomb's 2d Vermont battery was sent with them, but, waiting for its horses to arrive, did not go ashore. Burrell landed at Kuhn's wharf on the 24th, took nominal possession of the town, but really occupied only the wharf itself, protected by barricades and the 32

guns of the fleet under Commander W. B. Renshaw. Major-General J. B. Magruder, who had been barely a month in command of the district of Texas, had directed his attention as soon as he arrived to the defenseless condition of the coast, menaced as it was by the blockading fleet; thus it happened that Burrell's three companies found themselves confronted by two brigades (Scurry's and Sibley's, under Colonel Reily), an artillery regiment, 14 heavy guns, and 14 field-pieces. Magruder had also caused two improvised gun-boats to be equipped under an old California steamboat man, Captain Leon Smith; these were the *Bayou*

MAGRUDER'S MEN BOARDING THE "HARRIET LANE" AT GALVESTON.   SEE PREVIOUS PAGE.

After providing for the garrisons and the secure defense of New Orleans, Banks organized his available forces in four divisions, commanded by Major-General C. C. Augur and Brigadier-Generals Thomas W. Sherman, William H. Emory, and Cuvier Grover. Each division was composed of three brigades with three field-batteries, and there were also two battalions and six troops of cavalry, numbering about 700 effectives, and a regiment of heavy artillery, the 1st Indiana (21st Infantry) to man the siege train. The veteran regiments that had served in the department from the beginning were distributed so as to leaven the mass and to furnish brigade commanders of some experience; of the eight colonels commanding brigades, all but two belonged

City, Captain Henry Lubbock, and *Neptune*, Captain Sangster. Early in the morning of the 1st of January Magruder, having perfected his plans, under cover of a heavy artillery fire, assaulted the position of the 42d Massachusetts with two storming parties of 300 and 500 men respectively, led by Colonels Green, Bagby, and Cook, with the remainder of the troops under Brigadier-General W. R. Scurry in support. A sharp fight followed, but the defenders had the concentrated fire of the fleet to protect them; the scaling-ladders proved too short to reach the wharf, and as day began to break the assailants were about to draw off, when suddenly the Confederate gun-boats appeared on the scene, and in a few moments turned the defeat into a signal victory. The *Neptune* was disabled and sunk by the *Harriet Lane*; the *Harriet Lane*

herself was boarded and captured by the *Bayou City*; the *Westfield* ran aground and was blown up by her gallant commander, and soon the white flag, first displayed on the *Harriet Lane*, was flying from all the fleet. Thereupon Burrell surrendered. The Confederates ceased firing on him as soon as they perceived his signal; but the navy, observing that the firing on shore went on for some time, notwithstanding the naval truce, thought it had been violated; accordingly the *Clifton, Owasco*, and *Sachem* put to sea, preceded by the army transport steamers, the *Saxon*, which had brought the three unlucky companies of the 42d, and the *Mary A. Boardman*, with Holcomb's 2d Vermont battery still aboard. The Confederates lost 26 killed and 117 wounded; the Union troops 5 killed and 15 wounded.— R. B. I. [See also p. 571.]

to these regiments. The whole force available for active operations was about 25,000. Two-thirds were, however, new levies, and of these, again, half were nine-months' men; some were armed with guns that refused to go off, others did not know the simplest evolutions, while in one instance (afterward handsomely redeemed) the colonel was actually unable to disembark his men except by the novel command, "Break ranks, boys, and get ashore the best way you can!"

The cavalry was poor, except the six old companies, and was quite insufficient in numbers. Of land and water transportation, both indispensable to any possible operation, there was barely enough for the movement of a single division. In Washington, Banks had been led to expect that he would find in the depots, or in the country, all material required for moving his army; yet the supplies in the depots barely sufficed for the old force of the department, while the country could furnish very little at best, and nothing at all until it should be occupied. Banks had finally to send his chief quartermaster back to Washington before these deficiencies could be supplied.

Again, Banks had not been informed until he reached New Orleans that the Confederates held in force any fortified place below Vicksburg, yet Port Hudson, 135 miles above New Orleans, was found strongly intrenched, with

21 heavy guns in position, and a garrison of 12,000 men—increased to 16,000 before Banks could have brought an equal number to the attack.

Banks could not communicate with the commander of the northern column, and knew practically nothing of its movements.

Under these conditions, all concert between the coöperating forces was rendered impossible from the start, and it became inevitable that the expectations of the Government that Banks would go against Vicksburg immediately on landing in Louisiana should be doomed to disappointment.

The Confederate occupation of Port Hudson had completely changed the nature of the problem confided to General Banks for solution, for he had now to choose among three courses, each involving an im-

SHARP-SHOOTERS OF THE 75TH N. Y. VOLUNTEERS PICKING OFF THE GUNNERS OF THE CONFEDERATE GUN-BOAT "COTTON," IN THE ACTION AT BAYOU TECHE, LA., JANUARY 14, 1863. FROM A SKETCH MADE AT THE TIME.

RETURN OF A FORAGING PARTY OF THE 24TH CONNECTICUT VOLUNTEERS TO BATON ROUGE.
FROM A SKETCH MADE AT THE TIME.

possibility: to carry by assault a strong line of works, three miles long, impregnable on either flank and defended by 16,000 good troops; to lay siege to the place, with the certainty that it would be relieved from Mississippi and the prospect of losing his siege train in the venture; to leave Port Hudson in his rear and go against Vicksburg, thus sacrificing his communications, putting New Orleans in peril, and courting irreparable and almost inevitable disaster as the price of the remote chance of achieving a great success. No word came from Grant or McClernand.

Meanwhile Banks was trying to find a way of turning Port Hudson on the west by means of the Atchafalaya, the mouth of Red River, and the net-work of bayous, interlacing and intersecting one another, that connect the Atchafalaya with the Mississippi, in time of flood overflowing and fertilizing, at other seasons serving as highways for the whole region between the two rivers. [See map, p. 442.] The Mississippi was unusually high, the narrow and tortuous bayous were swollen and rapid; the levees, nearly everywhere neglected since the outbreak of the war, had in some places been cut by the Confederates; a large area of the country was under water; while great rafts of drift-logs added to the difficulty of navigation occasioned by the scarcity of suitable steamers and skilled pilots. Every attempt to penetrate the bayous having failed, Banks was just turning his attention to the preparations for gaining the same end by a movement from Berwick Bay by the Atchafalaya or Teche, when the news came that two of Ellet's rams, the *Queen of the West* and *Indianola,* after successfully running the batteries of Vicksburg, had been captured by the Confederates. These gun-boats must therefore be reckoned with in any movement on or beyond the Atchafalaya, while their presence above Port Hudson as a hostile force, in place of the reënforcement expected from Admiral Porter, greatly increased the anxiety Admiral Farragut had for some time felt to pass the batteries of Port Hudson with part of his fleet, control the long reach above, and cut off the Confederate supplies from the Red River country. General Banks fell in with the admiral's plans, and, concentrating 17,000 men at Baton Rouge, moved to the rear of Port Hudson on the 14th of March, with the divisions of Augur, Emory, and Grover, for the purpose of coöperating with the fleet by dividing the attention of the garrison and gaining a flank fire of artillery on the lower batteries on the bluff. The field-returns showed 12,000 men in line after providing for detachments and for holding Baton Rouge. Admiral Farragut had intended to pass the batteries on the 15th, in the gray of the morning, but at the last moment saw reason to change this plan and moved to the attack before midnight. In a naval affair like this the coöperation of the army could not have been very effective at best; the change of hour left us little more than spectators and auditors of the battle between the ships and the forts. The *Hartford* and *Albatross* passed up comparatively uninjured, but in the smoke and darkness the rest of the fleet could not go by, and the *Mississippi,* stranding, was set on fire and blown up — the grandest display of fireworks I ever witnessed, and the costliest. [See p. 566.]

This gave the navy command of the mouth of Red River, and, accordingly, Banks at once reverted to the execution of his former plan,— a turning movement by the Atchafalaya. That involved disposing of Taylor's force of about 4000 or 5000 men encamped and intrenched on the Teche below Franklin. Our force was so much stronger than Taylor's as to suggest the idea of capturing him in his position, by getting in his rear, simultaneously with a front attack; and this was particularly to be desired, as otherwise he might retire indefinitely into the vast open country behind him and return at his leisure at some inopportune moment. So perfectly was the movement masked that Taylor was actually preparing to attack the force in his front (Weitzel) when the main army began crossing Berwick Bay.

Weitzel crossed on the 9th; Emory followed; they then bivouacked on the west bank to wait for Grover's movement. So few were the facilities that it took Grover two days to embark. Six hours more were lost by a dense fog, and four by the stranding of the *Arizona.* When the proposed landing-place at Madame Porter's plantation was reached after dark, the road was found to be under water and impassable, but a practicable way was discovered six miles farther up the lake, at McWilliams's plantation. There the landing began early on the 13th, and with great difficulty, owing to the shallowness of the water, was completed by 4 o'clock in the afternoon. Favored by the woods and undergrowth, which concealed their numbers, Vincent's 2d Louisiana and Reily's 4th Texas Cavalry, with a section of Cornay's battery, delayed the advance until Dwight's brigade, supported by two regiments of Birge's and

MARCH OF THE NINETEENTH ARMY CORPS BY THE BAYOU SARA ROAD TOWARD PORT HUDSON,
SATURDAY, MARCH 14, 1863.   FROM A SKETCH MADE AT THE TIME.

by Closson's battery, went out and drove them away. At 6 the division took
up the line of march to the Teche and bivouacked at nightfall on Madame
Porter's plantation, five miles distant.

Meanwhile Banks had moved Emory and Weitzel slowly up the Teche,
seeking to hold Taylor's forces in position until Grover could gain their
rear. Taylor fell back behind the intrenched lines below Centreville known
as Fort Bisland, and there a brisk engagement took place on the 13th,
Banks only seeking to gain a good position on both sides of the bayou,
and to occupy the enemy's attention, while he listened in vain for Grover's
guns, which were to have been the signal for a direct and determined attack
in front.

At night, knowing that Grover's movement must certainly have been
seen and reported during his passage up Grand Lake and surmising some
miscarriage, Banks gave orders to carry the works by assault at daylight.
However, early in the night, Taylor ordered his whole force to fall back on
Franklin; the sounds of the movement were heard, and toward daylight
reconnoitering parties discovered the evacuation. Banks's whole force at
once moved in pursuit.

Early in the morning Taylor met Grover advancing against his line of
retreat, which here follows the great bow of the Teche, known as Irish Bend,
struck Birge's brigade in flank, forced Grover to develop, and with the

assistance of the *Diana*‡ held him just long enough to make good the retreat.

Taylor had made a gallant fight and had extricated himself cleverly. His reports show his whole force to have been 5000. Grover had about the same. We lost at Bisland 40 killed and 184 wounded,—total, 224; at Irish Bend, 49 killed, 274 wounded, 30 missing,—total, 353. The losses of the Confederates are not reported, but they destroyed their two gun-boats and all their transport steamers except one, which we captured, and their troops began to disperse soon after passing Franklin. We captured many prisoners on the march. Their gun-boats came down the Atchafalaya too late to dispute Grover's landing, were defeated by our flotilla, under Lieutenant-Commander A. P. Cooke, and the *Queen of the West* was destroyed. On the 20th Butte-à-la-Rose, with sixty men and two heavy guns, surrendered to Cooke, and the same day Banks occupied Opelousas.

Here he received his first communication from General Grant, dated before Vicksburg, March 23d, and sent through Admiral Farragut. This opened a correspondence, the practical effect of which was to cause General Banks to conform his movements to the expectation that General Grant would send an army corps to Bayou Sara to join in reducing Port Hudson.

Banks moved on to Alexandria, on the Red River, to push Taylor farther out of the way. Taylor retired toward Shreveport. On the 14th of May the

‡ A Union gun-boat captured by the Confederates and afterward set on fire and destroyed by them, as mentioned above.—EDITORS.

THE BAGGAGE TRAIN OF GENERAL AUGUR'S DIVISION CROSSING BAYOU MONTECINO ON THE MARCH TO PORT HUDSON. FROM A SKETCH MADE AT THE TIME.

whole command marched on Simsport, crossed the Atchafalaya, and moved to Bayou Sara, where the advance of the army crossed the Mississippi on the night of the 23d and moved immediately to the rear of Port Hudson.

There communication was made with Augur's two brigades, which had established themselves in position on the 21st, after a brisk engagement, known as the battle of Plains Store, ‖ just in time, apparently, to prevent the evacuation, which had been ordered by General Johnston and afterward countermanded by President Davis. With Augur we found T. W. Sherman and two brigades from New Orleans.

When the investment was completed on the 26th, we had about 14,000 men of all arms in front of the works, and behind them the Confederates had about 7000, under Major-General Frank Gardner. Part of the garrison (three brigades, as it proved) was known to have gone to succor Vicksburg, and all reports, apparently confirmed by the comparative feebleness of the attack on Augur at Plains Store, indicated a reduction even greater than had actually taken place. Nothing was known, of course, of the phenomenal success of Grant's operations, nor could it have been surmised, while his precarious position in the event of a defeat or even a serious check was obvious enough; the magnitude of the Confederate forces in Mississippi and the energy habitual to their commanders everywhere, added an additional reason against delay. Finally the troops themselves, elated by their success in the Teche campaign, were in the best of spirits for an immediate attack. For these reasons General Banks, with the full concurrence of all his commanders, save one, ordered a general assault to be made on the morning of the 27th of May.

Early in the morning Weitzel, who commanded the right wing on this day, moved to the attack in two lines, Dwight at first leading, and steadily drove the Confederates in his front into their works. Thus unmasked, the Confederate artillery opened with grape and canister, but our batteries, following the infantry as closely as possible, soon took commanding positions within 200 and 300 yards of the works that enabled them to keep down the enemy's fire. The whole fight took place in a dense forest of magnolias, mostly amid a thick undergrowth, and among ravines choked with felled or fallen timber, so that it was difficult not only to move but even to see; in short, in the phrase of the day, the affair was "a gigantic bush-whack." Soon after Weitzel's movement began Grover, on his left, moved to the attack at two points, but only succeeded in gaining and holding commanding positions within about two hundred yards of the works. This accomplished, and no sound of battle coming from his left, Grover determined to wait where he was for the attack that had been expected in that quarter, or for further orders, and Weitzel conformed his action to Grover's: properly in both cases, although it was afterward made apparent that had Weitzel continued to press his attack a few minutes longer he would probably have broken through the Confederate defense and taken their whole line in reverse. To make a diversion, Dwight caused the two colored regiments on the extreme

‖ Augur lost 15 killed, 71 wounded, 14 missing,— total, 100; the Confederates, 89.

OPENING OF THE NAVAL ATTACK ON PORT HUDSON, MARCH 13, 1863.

right to form for the attack; they had hardly done so when the extreme left of the Confederate line opened on them, in an exposed position, with artillery and musketry and forced them to abandon the attempt with great loss. In Augur's front the Confederate works were in full view, but the intervening plain was obstructed by tangled abatis of huge trees felled with their great branches spread as if to receive us with open arms, and these obstructions were commanded by the fire of nearly a mile of the works. His movement had therefore been meant for a demonstration, mainly in aid of Sherman, to be converted into a real attack if circumstances should favor; but as the morning wore away and no sound came from Sherman, General Banks rode to the left and gave fresh orders for that assault; then, returning to the center about two o'clock, he ordered Augur to attack simultaneously. At the word Chapin's brigade moved forward with great gallantry, but was soon caught and cruelly punished in the impassable abatis. Sherman gallantly led his division on horseback, surrounded by his full staff, likewise mounted, but though the ground in his front was less difficult than that which Augur had to traverse, it was very exposed, and the formation was, moreover, broken by three parallel lines of fence. No progress was possible, and when night fell the result was that we had gained commanding positions, yet at a fearful cost.

The next day a regular siege was begun. Grover was assigned to the command of the right wing, embracing his own and Paine's divisions and Weitzel's brigade; while Dwight was given command of Sherman's division, raised to three brigades by transferring regiments. From left to right, from this time, the lines were held in the order of Dwight, Augur, Paine, Grover, and Weitzel.

On the 14th of June, time still pressing, the lines being everywhere well advanced, the enemy's artillery effectually controlled by ours, every available man having been brought up, and yet our force growing daily less by casualties and sickness, Taylor menacing our communications on the west bank of the Mississippi, and the issue of Grant's operations before Vicksburg in suspense, Banks ordered a second assault to be delivered simultaneously at daybreak on the left and center, preceded by a general cannonade of an hour's duration. Dwight's attack on the left was misdirected by its guides and soon came to naught. Paine attacked with great vigor at what proved to be the strongest point of the whole work, the priest-cap near the Jackson road. He himself almost instantly fell severely wounded at the head of his division, and this attack also ended in a disastrous repulse, our men being unable to cross the crest just in front of the work, forming a natural glacis so swept by the enemy's fire that in examining the position afterward I found this grass-crowned knoll shaved bald, every blade cut down to the roots as by a hoe.

Our loss in the two assaults was nearly 4000, including many of our best and bravest officers. The heat, especially in the trenches, became almost insupportable, the stenches quite so, the brooks dried up, the creek lost itself in the pestilential swamp, the springs gave out, and the river fell, exposing to the tropical sun a wide margin of festering ooze. The illness and mortality were enormous. The labor of the siege, extending over a front of seven miles, pressed so severely upon our numbers, far too weak for such an undertaking, that the men were almost incessantly on duty; and as the numbers for duty diminished, of course the work fell the more heavily upon those that remained. From first to last we had nearly 20,000 men of all arms engaged before Port Hudson, yet the effective strength of infantry and artillery at no time exceeded 13,000, and at the last hardly reached 9000, while even of these every other man might well have gone on the sick-report if pride and duty had not held him to his post.

Meanwhile Taylor with his forces, reorganized and reënforced until they again numbered four or five thousand, had crossed the Atchafalaya at Morgan's Ferry and Berwick Bay, surprised and captured the garrisons at Brashear City and Bayou Bœuf almost without resistance, menaced Donaldsonville, carried havoc and panic through the La Fourche, and finally planted batteries on the Mississippi to cut off our communication with New Orleans. At Donaldsonville, however, an assault by about 1500 Texans was repulsed by about 200 men, including convalescents, under Major J. D. Bullen, 28th Maine,\ and at La Fourche Crossing Taylor's forces suffered another check at the hands of a detachment under Lieutenant-Colonel Albert Stickney, 47th Massachusetts. Otherwise Taylor, whose operations were conducted with marked skill and vigor, had everything his own way. In New Orleans great was the excitement when it was known that the Confederate forces were on the west bank within a few miles of the city; but fortunately the illness that had deprived Emory's division of its commander in the field had given New

---

\ Aided by the gun-boats *Princess Royal*, Commander M. B. Woolsey, and *Winona*, Lieutenant-Commander A. W. Weaver.

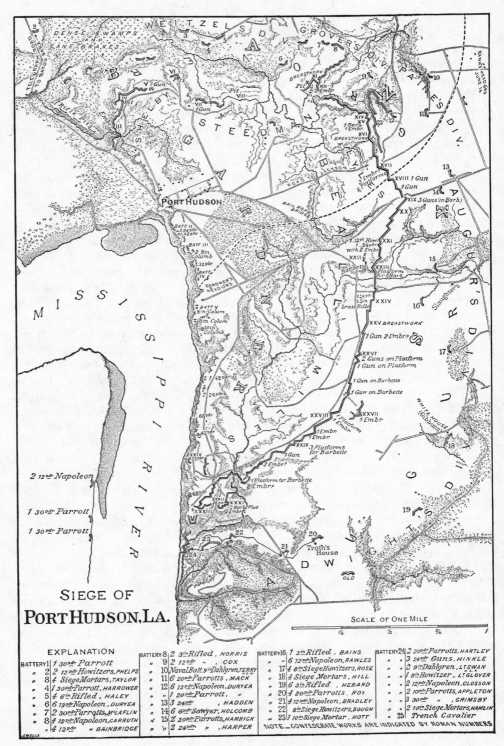

Orleans a commander of a courage and firmness that now, as always, rose with the approach of danger, with whom difficulties diminished as they drew near, and whose character had earned the respect of the inhabitants. Still by the 4th of July things were at such a pass that General Emory plainly told General Banks he must choose between Port Hudson and New Orleans. However, Banks was convinced that Port Hudson must be in his hands within three days.

His confidence was justified. At last on the 7th of July, when the sap-head was within 16 feet of the priest-cap, and a storming party of 1000 volunteers had been organized, led by the intrepid Birge, and all preparations had been made for springing two heavily charged mines, word came from Grant that Vicksburg had surrendered. Instantly an aide was sent to the "general-of-the-trenches" bearing duplicates in "flimsy" of a note from the adjutant-general announcing the good news. One of these he was directed to toss into the Confederate lines. Some one acknowledged the receipt by calling back, "That's another damned Yankee lie!" Once more the cheers of our men rang out as the word passed, and again the forest echoed with the strains of the "Star-spangled Banner" from the long-silent bands. Firing died away, the men began to mingle in spite of everything, and about 2 o'clock next morning came the long, gray envelope that meant *surrender*.

Formalities alone remained; these were long, but the articles were signed on the afternoon of the 8th; a moment later a long train of wagons loaded with rations for the famished garrison moved down the Clinton road, and on the morning of the 9th a picked force of eight regiments, under Brigadier-General George L. Andrews, marched in with bands playing and colors flying; the Confederates stacked arms and hauled down their flag, and the National ensign floated in its stead. By General Banks's order, General Gardner's sword was returned to him in the presence of his men in recognition of the heroic defense—a worthy act, well merited.

But, stout as the defense had been, the besiegers had on their part displayed some of the highest qualities of the soldier; among these valor in attack, patient endurance of privation, suffering, and incredible toil, and perseverance under discouragement. And to defenders and besiegers it is alike unjust to say, even though it has been said by the highest authority, that Port Hudson surrendered only because Vicksburg had fallen. The simple truth is that Port Hudson surrendered because its hour had come. The garrison was literally starving. With less than 3000 famished men in line, powerful mines beneath the salients, and a last assault about to be delivered at 10 paces, what else was left to do?

With the post there fell into our hands 6340 prisoners, 20 heavy guns, 31 field-pieces, about 7500 muskets, and two river steamers.☆ Many of the guns were ruined, some had been struck over and over again, and the depots and magazines were empty. The garrison also lost about 500 prisoners or

☆ *Starlight* and *Red Chief*, found aground in Thompson's Creek, floated and brought into the river by the ingenuity and skill of Major Joseph Bailey, 4th Wisconsin, whose success here led to its repetition on the Red River the next year, when Admiral Porter's fleet was rescued.—R. B. I.

deserters before the surrender, and about 700 killed and wounded. Our loss was 707 killed, 3336 wounded, 319 missing,— total, 4362.

The army was greatly assisted by Admiral Farragut's fleet above and below Port Hudson, and directly by two fine batteries forming part of the siege-works, manned by seamen under Lieutenant-Commander Edward Terry.

While the ceremonies of capitulation were going on, Weitzel led Augur's division aboard the transports and hastened to Donaldsonville to drive Taylor out of the La Fourche. Grover followed. On the 13th, at Koch's plantation, Green and Major suddenly fell upon Weitzel's advance, composed of Dudley's brigade and Dwight's under Colonel Joseph S. Morgan, and handled them roughly. We lost 50 killed, 223 wounded, 186 missing,— total, 465,— as well as 2 guns, while Green's loss was 3 killed and 30 wounded. As the gun-boats could not be got round to Berwick Bay in time to cut off Taylor, he crossed Berwick Bay on the 21st with all his spoils that he could carry away and took post on the lower Teche, until in September the Nineteenth Corps, reorganized and placed under the command of Franklin, once more advanced into the Teche country and drove him back toward Opelousas.

After the fall of Vicksburg and Port Hudson, Grant sent Herron's division, and the Thirteenth Corps under Ord, to report to Banks. Banks went to Vicksburg to consult with Grant, and Grant came to New Orleans; together they agreed with Admiral Farragut in urging an immediate attack on Mobile. This was the only true policy; success would have been easy and must have influenced powerfully the later campaigns that centered about Chattanooga and Atlanta; but for reasons avowedly political rather than military, the Government ordered, instead, an attempt to "plant the flag at some point in Texas." The unaccountable failure at Sabine Pass followed,⌋ then the occupation of the Texan coast by the Thirteenth Corps. So the favorable moment passed and 1863 wore away.

⌋ In September a detachment of the Nineteenth Corps, under Franklin, convoyed by the navy, was sent by sea to effect a landing at Sabine Pass, and thence operate against Houston and Galveston; but the gun-boats meeting with a disaster in an encounter with the Confederate batteries, the expedition returned to New Orleans without having accomplished anything.— R. B. I.

THE OPPOSING FORCES AT PORT HUDSON, LA.
May 23d–July 8th, 1863.

The composition, losses, and strength of each army as here stated give the gist of all the data obtainable in the Official Records. K stands for killed; w for wounded; m w for mortally wounded; m for captured or missing; c for captured.

THE UNION ARMY.
NINETEENTH ARMY CORPS.— Major-General Nathaniel P. Banks.

FIRST DIVISION, Maj.-Gen. Christopher C. Augur.
First Brigade, Col. Edward P. Chapin (k), Col. Charles J. Paine: 2d La., Col. Charles J. Paine, Lieut.-Col. Charles Everett; 21st Me., Col. Elijah D. Johnson; 48th Mass., Col. Eben F. Stone; 49th Mass., Lieut.-Col. Burton D. Deming (k), Maj. Charles T. Plunkett; 116th N. Y., Capt. John Higgins. Brigade loss: k, 94; w, 412; m, 20 = 526. *Second Brigade,* Brig.-Gen. Godfrey Weitzel (also commanding the right wing, a provisional division, etc.), Col. Stephen Thomas: 12th Conn., Lieut.-Col. Frank H. Peck (w); 75th N. Y., Col. Robert B. Merritt;

114th N. Y., Col. Elisha B. Smith (m w), Lieut.-Col. Samuel R. Per Lee; 160th N. Y., Lieut.-Col. John B. Van Petten; 8th Vt., Col. Stephen Thomas, Lieut.-Col. Charles Dillingham. Brigade loss: k, 67; w, 406; m, 16 = 489. *Third Brigade,* Col. Nathan A. M. Dudley: 30th Mass., Lieut.-Col. William W. Bullock; 50th Mass., Col. Carlos P. Messer; 161st N. Y., Col. Gabriel T. Harrower; 174th N. Y., Maj. George Keating. Brigade loss: k, 5; w, 47; m, 3 = 55. *Artillery:* 1st Ind. Heavy, Col. John A. Keith; 1st Me., Lieut. John E. Morton; 6th Mass., Lieut. John F. Phelps; 12th Mass. (section), Lieut. Edwin M. Chamberlin; 18th N. Y., Capt. Albert G. Mack; A, 1st U. S., Capt. Edmund C. Bainbridge; G, 5th U. S., Lieut. Jacob B. Rawles. Artillery loss: k, 10; w, 49; m, 10 = 69. *Unattached :* 1st La. Eng's, Corps d'Afrique, Col. Justin Hodge; 1st La. Native Guards, Lieut.-Col. Chauncey J. Bassett; 3d La. Native Guards, Col. John A. Nelson, Capt. Charles W. Blake; 1st La. Cav., Maj. Harai Robinson; 2d R. I. Cav., Lieut.-Col. Augustus W. Corliss. Unattached loss: k, 57; w, 171; m, 43 = 271.

SECOND DIVISION, Brig.-Gen. Thomas W. Sherman (w), Brig.-Gen. George L. Andrews, Brig.-Gen. Frank S. Nickerson, Brig.-Gen. William Dwight. Staff loss: w, 2.

First Brigade, Brig.-Gen. Neal Dow (w and c), Col. David S. Cowles (k), Col. Thomas S. Clark: 26th Conn., Lieut.-Col. Joseph Selden; 6th Mich., Col. Thomas S. Clark, Lieut.-Col. Edward Bacon; 15th N. H., Col. John W. Kingman; 128th N. Y., Col. David S. Cowles, Capt. Francis S. Keese, Lieut.-Col. James Smith; 162d N. Y., Col. Lewis Benedict, Lieut.-Col. Justin W. Blanchard. Brigade loss: k, 81; w, 498; m, 12 = 591. *Third Brigade*, Brig.-Gen. Frank S. Nickerson: 14th Me., Col. Thomas W. Porter; 24th Me., Col. George M. Atwood; 28th Me., Col. Ephraim W. Woodman; 165th N. Y., Lieut.-Col. Abel Smith, Jr. (m w), Maj. Gouverneur Carr (w), Capt. Felix Agnus; 175th N. Y., Col. Michael K. Bryan (k), Maj. John Gray; 177th N. Y., Col. Ira W. Ainsworth. Brigade loss: k, 34; w, 199; m, 5 = 238. *Artillery:* 21st N. Y., Capt. James Barnes; 1st Vt., Capt. George T. Hebard. Artillery loss: k, 1; w, 6 = 7.

THIRD DIVISION, Brig.-Gen. Halbert E. Paine (w), Col. Hawkes Fearing, Jr. Staff loss: w, 1.

First Brigade, Col. Timothy Ingraham, Col. Samuel P. Ferris: 28th Conn., Col. Samuel P. Ferris, Lieut.-Col. Wheelock T. Batcheller, Maj. William B. Wescome; 4th Mass., Col. Henry Walker; 16th N. H., Col. James Pike; 110th N. Y., Col. Clinton H. Sage. Brigade loss: k, 20; w, 127; m, 20 = 167. *Second Brigade*, Col. Hawkes Fearing, Jr., Maj. John H. Allcot, Col. Lewis M. Peck: 8th N. H., Lieut.-Col. Oliver W. Lull (k), Capt. William M. Barrett; 133d N. Y., Col. Leonard D. H. Currie (w), Capt. James K. Fuller; Maj. John H. Allcot; 173d N. Y., Maj. A. Power Gallway (m w), Capt. George W. Rogers; 4th Wis., Col. Sidney A. Bean (m w), Capt. Webster P. Moore. Brigade loss: k, 115; w, 483; m, 86 = 684. *Third Brigade*, Col. Oliver P. Gooding: 31st Mass. (7 co's), Lieut.-Col. W. S. B. Hopkins; 38th Mass., Lieut.-Col. William L. Rodman (k), Maj. James P. Richardson; 53d Mass., Col. John W. Kimball; 156th N. Y., Col. Jacob Sharpe. Brigade loss: k, 48; w, 265; m, 8 = 321. *Artillery*, Capt.

Richard C. Duryea: 4th Mass., Lieut. Frederick W. Reinhard; F, 1st U. S., Capt. Richard C. Duryea; 2d Vt., Capt. Pythagoras E. Holcomb. Artillery loss: k, 1; w, 4; m, 2 = 7.

FOURTH DIVISION, Brig.-Gen. Cuvier Grover.

First Brigade, Col. Richard E. Holcomb (k), Col. Joseph S. Morgan: 1st La., Lieut.-Col. William O. Fiske; 22d Me., Col. Simon G. Jerrard; 90th N. Y., Col. Joseph S. Morgan; Maj. Nelson Shaurman; 91st N. Y., Col. Jacob Van Zandt; 131st N. Y., Lieut.-Col. Nicholas W. Day. Brigade loss: k, 84; w, 359; m, 27 = 470. *Second Brigade*, Col. William K. Kimball: 24th Conn., Col. Samuel M. Mansfield; 12th Me., Lieut.-Col. Edward Ilsley; 52d Mass., Col. Halbert S. Greenleaf. Brigade loss: k, 32; w, 125; m, 3 = 160. *Third Brigade*, Col. Henry W. Birge: 13th Conn., Capt. Apollos Comstock; 25th Conn., Lieut.-Col. Mason C. Wild; 26th Me., Col. Nathaniel H. Hubbard; 159th N. Y., Lieut.-Col. Charles A. Burt. Brigade loss: k, 34; w, 128; m, 10 = 172. *Artillery*, Capt. Henry W. Closson: 2d Mass., Capt. Ormand F. Nims; L, 1st U. S., Capt. Henry W. Closson; C, 2d U. S., Lieut. Theodore Bradley. Artillery loss: w, 5; m, 3 = 8.

CAVALRY, Col. Benjamin H. Grierson.

6th Ill., Col. Reuben Loomis; 7th Ill., Col. Edward Prince, 1st La., Maj. Harai Robinson; 3d Mass., Col. Thomas E. Chickering; 14th N. Y., ——. Cavalry loss: k, 10; w, 37; m, 47 = 94.

CORPS D'AFRIQUE: 6th Inf., ——; 7th Inf., ——; 8th Inf., ——; 9th Inf., ——; 10th Inf., ——. Corps d'Afrique loss: k, 15; w, 12; m, 4 = 31.

Total Union loss: killed, 708; wounded, 3336; captured or missing, 319 = 4363.

General Banks, in his official report, says that on May 27th, when he first assaulted the enemy's works, his effective force had been reduced to less than 13,000, and that at the time of the surrender "the besieging force was reduced to less than 10,000 men." But the returns of Banks's command for May 31st ("Official Records," Vol. XXVI., Pt. I., pp. 526–528) show not less than 30,000 officers and men of all arms "present for duty" at Port Hudson, besides the Corps d'Afrique, which is not reported on any of the returns for that month. According to the return for June 30th ("Official Records," Vol. XXVI., Pt. I., p. 611), the "present for duty" (including the Corps d'Afrique) aggregated 23,962, but Colonel Irwin, who (as assistant adjutant-general) made all these figures, informs us that those for May 31st and June 30th were totals of former months carried forward, whereas the actual strength was as given by him on page 595.—EDITORS.

THE CONFEDERATE ARMY.

Major-General Frank Gardner.

Line Commanders : Brig.-Gen. W. N. R. Beall, Col. W. R. Miles, and Col. I. G. W. Steedman.

Garrison Troops: 1st Ala., Col. I. G. W. Steedman, Lieut.-Col. M. B. Locke, Maj. Samuel L. Knox; 49th Ala., Maj. T. A. Street; Maury (Tenn.) Artillery (attached to 12th La. Heavy Art'y Battalion); 1st Ark. Battalion, Lieut.-Col. B. Jones; 10th Ark., Lieut.-Col. M. B. Locke, Lieut.-Col. E. L. Vaughan, Maj. C. M. Cargile; 11th and 17th Ark. (detachment); 12th Ark., Col. T. J. Reid, Jr.; 14th Ark., Lieut.-Col. Pleasant Fowler; 15th Ark., Col. Ben. W. Johnson; 16th Ark., Col. David Provence; 18th Ark., Lieut.-Col. W. N. Parish; 23d Ark., Col. O. P. Lyles; 4th La. (detachment), Capt. Charles T. Whitman; 9th La. Battalion (infantry), Capt. R. B. Chinn; 9th La. Battalion (Partisan Rangers), Lieut.-Col. J. H. Wingfield, Maj. James De Baun; 12th La. Heavy Art'y Battalion, Lieut.-Col. P. F. De Gournay; 30th La. (detachment), Capt. T. K. Porter; La. Legion, Col. W. R. Miles, Lieut.-Col. Frederick B. Brand; La. Battery Capt. R. M. Boone (w), Capt. S. M. Thomas; La. Battery (Watson), Lieut. E. A. Toledano; 1st Miss., Lieut.-Col. A. S. Hamilton, Maj. Thomas H. Johnston; 39th Miss., Col. W. B. Shelby; Claiborne (Miss.) Light Infantry, Capt. A. J. Lewis; 1st Miss. Light Artillery (Abbay's,

Bradford's, and Herod's batteries); Miss. Battery (English's), Lieut. P. J. Noland; Miss. Battery (Seven Stars Art'y), Lieut. F. G. W. Coleman; B and G, 1st Tenn. Heavy Art'y (attached to 12th La. Heavy Art'y Battalion), Lieut. Oswald Tilghman and Capt. James A. Fisher; Tenn. Battalion (composed of details from 41st, 42d, 48th, 49th, 53d, and 55th Tenn. regiments), Capt. S. A. Whiteside.

Cavalry and Mounted Infantry (operating outside of the post), Col. John L. Logan: 11th and 17th Ark. (consolidated), ——; 9th Tenn. Battalion, ——; Cochran's Battalion, ——; Garland's Battalion, ——; Hughes's Battalion, ——; Stockdale's Battalion, ——; Robert's Battery (section), ——.

According to an incomplete report ("Official Records," Vol. XXVI., Pt. I., p. 144), the loss of the garrison of Port Hudson during the siege was 176 killed, and 447 wounded = 623. General Banks reports ("Official Records," Vol. XXVI., Pt. I., p. 55), "that with the post there fell into our hands over 5500 prisoners." There appears to be no statement of the strength of the garrison at any time during the investment. The effective strength of Logan's command, June 25th, was 1296. See "Official Records," Vol. XXVI., Pt. II., p. 82.

BRAGG'S ADVANCE AND RETREAT.[1]

BY DAVID URQUHART, COLONEL, C. S. A.; MEMBER OF GENERAL BRAGG'S STAFF.

GENERAL BRAGG'S Kentucky campaign has drawn on him more criticism than any other part of his career as a military commander. During that memorable march I rode at his side from day to day, and it was his habit to confide to me his hopes and fears.

About the end of June, 1862, General Bragg was visited by many prominent citizens of Kentucky, who had abandoned their homes, and who assured him that Kentuckians were thoroughly loyal to the South, and that as soon as they were given an opportunity it would be proven. Fired with this idea, he planned his offensive campaign. On the 21st of July, 1862, the movement of the Army of Mississippi from Tupelo was ordered. The infantry moved by rail, the artillery and cavalry across the country. Headquarters were established at Chattanooga on the 29th. On the 30th Major-General Kirby Smith visited General Bragg at that point, and it was arranged that Smith should move at once against the Federal forces under General George W. Morgan in Cumberland Gap. In this interview General Bragg was very certain that he would begin his forward move in ten or fifteen days at latest, and if Kirby Smith was successful in his operation against Morgan he would be on his offensive against Buell. Kirby Smith took the field on the 13th of August, 1862. On the 28th, after some inevitable delays, Bragg crossed the Tennessee, his right wing, under Polk, 13,537 strong; the left wing, under Hardee, 13,763 strong,— total effective, 27,320 rank and file.

General Bragg by this time was deeply impressed with the magnitude of his undertaking. He had lost faith somewhat in the stories that had been told him of Kentucky's desire to join the South, but he proposed to give the people a chance of so doing by the presence of Southern troops. At the same time he was resolved to do nothing to imperil the safety of his army, whose loss, he felt, would be a crushing blow to the Confederacy. He reached Carthage on the 9th of September. On the 12th he was at Glasgow, Kentucky, where he issued a proclamation to Kentuckians. About that time also the corps of Polk and Hardee were ordered to unite. Buell was now moving on Bowling Green from the south. On the 16th our army surrounded and invested Munfordville, and General Wilder, with its garrison of four thousand men, was forced to capitulate. General Kirby Smith, having found Morgan's position impregnable, detached a part of his forces to invest it, and, advancing on Lexington, defeated the Federal forces encountered at Richmond, Ky. He was relying on an early junction with General Bragg.

On the 17th of September Generals Polk and Hardee were called to a council at Munfordville. With the map and the cavalry dispatches outspread before him, General Bragg placed General Buell and his army in our rear, with Munfordville on the direct line of his march to Louisville, the

[1] See also articles by General Wheeler and General Buell, pp. 1 and 32.

GENERAL BRAXTON BRAGG, C. S. A. FROM A WAR-TIME PHOTOGRAPH.

assumed objective point of his movement, General Bragg then explaining his plan, which was discussed and approved by his lieutenants. Our advance was then resumed, leaving General Buell to pursue his march unmolested. This action was subsequently severely criticised by military men, and at the time it was greatly deplored by many officers of his command. At 1 o'clock on the morning of the 18th of September, indeed, Bragg was on the point of rescinding the order to continue the march, and of directing instead an immediate offensive movement against Buell. The importance of recovering Nashville induced the proposed change of operation. But, upon further consideration, he reverted to his previous plans, saying to me with emphasis, "This campaign must be won by marching, not by fighting." He used similar language at subsequent stages of the campaign before the battle of Perryville. At the moment he evinced no regret at having allowed Buell to pass on our left flank.

The success of the column under Kirby Smith in its combat at Richmond, Ky., elated him. He was worried by the delays that retarded his junction with that officer, and was greatly relieved when all the Confederate forces in Kentucky were united at Lexington.

Here a brilliant entertainment was given to the two generals by our old comrade, General William Preston, in his delightful Kentucky home. But it was here, also, that General Bragg fully realized that the reported desire of Kentucky to cast her lot with the South had passed away, if indeed such a disposition had ever existed; for not only was Kentucky unprepared to enter the Confederacy, but her people looked with dread at the prospect of their State being made a battle-field. Under these circumstances he remarked to me again and again, "The people here have too many fat cattle and are too well off to fight." He was now aware that he had embarked in a campaign that was to produce no favorable result, and that he had erred in departing from his original plan of taking the offensive in the outset against Buell by an operation on that general's communications. He was determined, however, not to expose his army to disaster, nor to take any chances. The information we were receiving indicated that Buell was being heavily reënforced.

It was now the eve of the battle of Perryville, and Kirby Smith, at Salvisa, twenty miles to the north-east, was calling for reënforcements, as he was confident that the feint was against Perryville, and that the main attack would surely fall on him. Thus urged, General Bragg, against his own judgment, yielded, and detached two of his best divisions (Withers's and Cheatham's) to Smith's aid. The former division could not be recalled in time, and the latter arrived the morning of the battle. Having placed General Polk in command of the troops, Bragg had gone to Frankfort, the capital of the State of Kentucky, to witness the inauguration of the secessionist governor, Hawes. The inaugural was being read when the booming of cannon, shortly followed by dispatches from our cavalry outposts, announced the near presence of the enemy. As the hall was chiefly filled by the military, who hurried away to their respective commands, the governor was obliged to cut short his inaugural address.

The field of Perryville was an open and beautiful rolling country, and the battle presented a grand panorama. There was desperate fighting on both sides. I saw a Federal battery, with the Union flag planted near its guns, repulse six successive Confederate charges before retiring, saving all but one gun, and eliciting praise for their bravery from their desperate foes.

About dark, Polk, convinced that some Confederate troops were firing into each other, cantered up to the colonel of the regiment that was firing, and asked him angrily what he meant by shooting his own friends. The colonel, in a tone of surprise, said: "I don't think there can be any mistake about it. I am sure they are the enemy." "Enemy! Why, I have just left them myself. Cease firing, sir. What is your name?" rejoined the Confederate general. "I am Colonel —— of the —— Indiana. And pray, sir, who are you?" Thus made aware that he was with a Federal regiment and that his only escape was to brazen it out, his dark blouse and the increasing obscurity happily befriending him, the Confederate general shook his fist in the Federal colonel's face and promptly said: "I will show you who I am, sir. Cease firing at once!" Then, cantering down the line again, he shouted authoritatively to the men, " Cease firing ! " Then, reaching the cover of a small copse, he spurred his horse and was soon back with his own corps, which he immediately ordered to open fire.

The battle of Perryville, a hard-fought fight against many odds, was merely a favorable incident which decided nothing. Our army, however, was elated and did not dream of a retreat, as we had held the field and bivouacked on it. But the commanding general, full of care, summoned his lieutenant-generals to a council in which both advised retreat.

The next day General Smith's army was called to Harrodsburg, where a junction of the two forces was effected, and where a position was selected to receive Buell's attack ;—this, however, not being made, Bragg was enabled to take measures for an immediate retrograde. Forrest was at once dispatched by forced marches to take position at Murfreesboro', and prepare it for occupancy by the retreating Confederates.

The conduct of the retreat was intrusted to Polk. Our army fell back first to Camp Dick Robinson, whence the retreat began in earnest, a brigade of cavalry leading. All the supplies which it was impossible to carry from this depot were burned; the rest were hauled away in wagons, including provisions, merchandise of all kinds, and captured muskets, while captured cannon were drawn by oxen. Refugees, with their families, slaves, and a great deal of household stuff; omnibuses, stages, and almost every other description of vehicle were to be seen in this heterogeneous caravan. Thousands of beef cattle, sheep, and hogs were driven along under the charge of Texans as reckless as the affrighted cattle they were driving.

General Smith's army and Polk's and Hardee's corps followed the trains. The Federal army promptly took up the pursuit and made an effort by a flank movement to intercept our long unwieldly trains. General Wheeler with his cavalry brought up the rear—fighting by day and obstructing the roads at night. Before the pursuit was abandoned at Rock Castle, that officer was engaged over twenty-six times. His vigilance was so well known by the infantry that they never feared a surprise. Hard marching, stony roads, and deep fords lay before us until we had crossed Cumberland Gap. But at last almost all that had been taken out of Kentucky was safely conveyed to Morristown, Tenn.

About the 31st of October, 1862, General Bragg, having made a short visit to Richmond, there obtained the sanction of the Confederate Government for a movement into middle Tennessee. Returning to Knoxville, General Bragg made preparations with the utmost rapidity for the advance to Murfreesboro', where General Breckinridge was already posted, and General Forrest was operating with a strong, active cavalry force. Our headquarters were advanced to Tullahoma on the 14th of November, and on the 26th to Murfreesboro'. Notwithstanding long marches and fighting, the condition of the troops was very good ; and had they been well clad, the Confederate army would have presented a fine appearance.

On November 24th, 1862, the commands of Lieutenant-General Pemberton at Vicksburg, and that of General Bragg in Tennessee, were placed under

General Joseph E. Johnston, and his official headquarters were established at Chattanooga. Immediately thereafter General Johnston visited Murfreesboro', where he passed some days devoted to a thorough inspection of the army. Our forces numbered somewhat over 40,000 men. General Johnston's visit was followed during the second week in December by that of President Davis and his aide, General Custis Lee. The President asked Bragg if he did not think he could spare a division of his army to reënforce Pember-

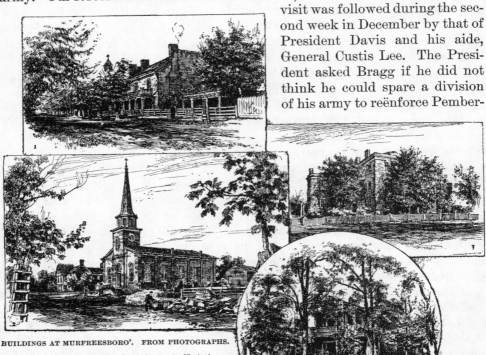

BUILDINGS AT MURFREESBORO'. FROM PHOTOGRAPHS.

1. General Rosecrans's Headquarters. 2. Christian Church, used as a post chapel by the Union army. 3. Soule Female College, used as a hospital. 4. Headquarters of General Bragg; afterward of Generals Thomas and Garfield. 5. Union University, used as a hospital.

ton. Bragg assented and dispatched a division of 8000 men under Stevenson. This step was contrary to the decided opinion previously expressed to Mr. Davis by General Johnston. [See p. 473.]

So well satisfied was General Bragg at having extricated his army from its perilous position in Kentucky, that he was not affected by the attacks upon him by the press for the failure of the campaign. He was cheerful, and would frequently join the staff about the camp-fire, and relate with zest incidents of his services under General Taylor in Mexico.⚓ On the 26th General

⚓ He told how on one occasion, when he was asleep, the men of his battery had placed under his cot a shell, which exploded, tearing everything to pieces, but without harming him. He told us also that at the battle of Buena Vista General Taylor did not use the words so frequently quoted, "A

Wheeler, commanding the cavalry outposts,↓ sent dispatches in quick succession to headquarters reporting a general advance of Rosecrans's army. Soon all was bustle and activity. General Hardee's corps at Triune was ordered to Murfreesboro'. Camps were at once broken up and everything was made ready for active service. On the 27th of December our army was moving.

On Sunday, December 28th, Polk and Hardee met at General Bragg's headquarters to learn the situation and his plans. Rosecrans was advancing from Nashville with his whole army. Wheeler with his cavalry was so disposed at the moment as to protect the flanks, and, when pressed, to fall back toward the main army. Hardee's corps, consisting of the divisions of Breckinridge and Cleburne, with Jackson's brigade as a reserve, constituted our right wing, with its right resting on the Lebanon Pike and its left on the Nashville road. Polk's corps, composed of Withers's and Cheatham's divisions, was to take post with its right touching Hardee on the Nashville road, and its left resting on the Salem Pike ; McCown's division was to form the reserve and to occupy our center. Such was the position of the Confederate army on the 29th of December.

On Tuesday, December 30th, Rosecrans was in our front, a mile and a half away. At 12 o'clock artillery on both sides was engaged. At 3 o'clock the Federal infantry advanced and attacked our lines, but were repulsed by the Louisiana and Alabama brigade, under Colonel Gibson, commanding

little more grape, Captain Bragg," but had ridden up to him and exclaimed, "Captain, give them hell!" He also often related anecdotes of Buell, Thomas, and Sherman. Thomas had been in his old battery and he never could praise him too much. While at Murfreesboro' flags of truce were the order of the day, and almost always some kind message from old army friends was sent thereby to General Hardee, usually accompanied by a bottle of brandy.— D. U.

↓ Wheeler had shortly before relieved our dashing cavalryman, John H. Morgan, who, since the return from Kentucky, had commanded a brigade picketing our front. As early as the 1st of December Morgan had been ordered by Bragg to operate on Rosecrans's lines of communication in rear of Nashville, and to prevent him from foraging north of the Cumberland. Learning that the Union force at Hartsville, at the crossing of the Cumberland, was isolated [see map, p. 635], Morgan resolved to capture it, and while two brigades of Cheatham's division, with Wheeler's cavalry, made a demonstration before Nashville, he set out on the 6th from Baird's Mills, with four regiments and one battalion of cavalry under Colonel Basil W. Duke, and two regiments of infantry and Cobb's battery from Hanson's brigade, under Colonel T. H. Hunt. The Union force at Hartsville consisted of Colonel A. B. Moore's brigade of Dumont's division and numbered about two thousand men. At Castalian Springs, nine miles distant, there were two brigades numbering 5000, and at Gallatin, other forces, all belonging to Thomas's command. Morgan crossed the Cumberland on

the night of the 6th, and disposed his forces so as to cut off the retreat from Hartsville on the roads to Lebanon, Gallatin, and Castalian Springs, and, closing in, attacked the troops who were drawn up to receive him. Morgan won a complete victory after a stubborn fight of an hour and a half, and promptly retired with his prisoners and some wagons, animals, and stores. While he was retiring, the advance of a brigade of reënforcements under Colonel John M. Harlan, coming up from Castalian Springs, reached Hartsville and attacked the Confederate rear-guard.

The Union loss was : k, 58 ; w, 204 ; m, 1834,— total, 2096. The Confederate loss was 139 in all. Colonel Moore was taken prisoner and his assistant adjutant-general, Captain W. G. Gholson, was killed.— EDITORS.

I have been present in my life at many marriages, religious and civil, but only once did I witness one purely military, and never one with which I was so much impressed as that of John H. Morgan. A few days before the battle of Stone's River his marriage ceremony was performed at the house of the bride. General Bragg and his staff, with a few of Morgan's comrades, were gathered as witnesses in the front parlor. General Polk, Bishop of Louisiana, performed the ceremony and gave the blessing. That evening Morgan and his command left Murfreesboro' on a raid toward Kentucky. Social recreation at Murfreesboro' at this time was at its zenith ; Christmas was approaching. The young officers of our army were all bent on fun and gayety. Invitations were out for a ball on the day after Christmas.— D. U.

in the absence of General Daniel Adams. But night soon interposed, quiet prevailed, and the two armies bivouacked opposite to each other. General Bragg was on the field the entire day, but returned to his headquarters that evening at Murfreesboro'. He called his corps commanders together and informed them that his advices convinced him that Rosecrans, under cover of the day's attack, had been massing his troops for a move on our left flank. It was then agreed that Hardee should at once move to the extreme left Cleburne's division of his corps and the reserve (McCown), and that, next morn-

ing, Hardee should take command in that quarter and begin the fight.

At daylight on the 31st (Wednesday), Hardee, with Cleburne's and Mc-Cown's divisions, attacked McCook's corps of the Federal army. For a

THE NASHVILLE PIKE OUT OF MUR-FREESBORO', LOOKING NORTH-WEST TOWARD THE RISE OF GROUND WHICH WAS THE SITE OF FORT-RESS ROSECRANS, CONSTRUCTED AFTER THE WITHDRAWAL OF BRAGG. FROM A PHOTOGRAPH TAKEN IN 1884.

while the enemy were dis-organized, many of the men being still engaged in cooking their break-fasts, but they very soon got under arms and in

VIEW OF MURFREESBORO' FROM THE VICINITY OF FORTRESS ROSECRANS. FROM A PHOTOGRAPH TAKEN IN 1884.

position, and resisted the attack with desperation. At this juncture Polk advanced with Withers's and Cheatham's divisions, and after hard fighting McCook's corps was driven back between three and four miles. Our attack had pivoted the Federals on their center, bending back their line, as one half-shuts a knife-blade. At 12 o'clock we had a large part of the field, with many prisoners, cannon, guns, ammunition, wagons, and the dead and wounded of both armies.

Between 2 and 3 o'clock, however, Rosecrans massed artillery on the favorable rising ground to which his line had been forced back. On this ground cedar-trees were so thick that his movements had not been perceived. Our line again advanced. Stewart's, Chalmers's, Donelson's, and Maney's brigades, supported by Slocomb's, Cobb's, and Byrne's batteries, were hurled against the Federal line, but could not carry it. Reënforced by Gibson's and Jackson's brigades, another charge was ordered, but the position was not carried and many were killed and wounded on our side.

A bitter cold night was now on us. We were masters of the field. The sheen of a bright moon revealed the sad carnage of the day, and the horrors of war became vividly distinct. That night General Bragg again made his headquarters at Murfreesboro', whence he gave orders for the care of the wounded. All the churches and public buildings were turned into hospitals. He announced to Richmond by telegraph: "God has granted us a happy New Year."

We had indeed routed the Federal right wing, but the bloody work was not over. During January 1st Rosecrans's army was intrenching itself, but General Bragg was of the opinion that their quiet meant a retreat.

During the morning of the 2d (Friday) quiet prevailed, except some shelling on our right. At about noon General Bragg determined to dislodge the force on his right. Orders were given to that end, and our best troops were carefully selected. Hanson's,

BRIGADIER-GENERAL JAMES E. RAINS, C. S. A., KILLED AT STONE'S RIVER. FROM A PHOTOGRAPH.

Preston's, Gibson's, and Hunt's brigades, with Cobb's and Wright's batteries, were placed under Major-General Breckinridge. A gun fired by one of our batteries at 4 o'clock was the signal for the attack. After a fierce fight we carried the hill. The orders were to take its crest, and there remain intrenched. General Breckinridge endeavored to execute this order, but the commanders of the brigades engaged could not restrain the ardor of their men, who pushed on beyond support. The Federal batteries that had been massed on the other side of the stream now opened on them and drove the Confederates back with terrible slaughter, fully 2000 of our men being killed and wounded in this attack. At 10 o'clock P. M. the news of this disastrous charge, led by the *élite* of the Confederate army, cast a gloom over all.

Saturday, January 3d, the two armies faced each other, with little fighting on either side.

The miscarriage of the 2d determined General Bragg to begin to fall back on Tullahoma; but all day of the 3d our forces maintained their line of battle taken up early that morning. That night the evacuation of Murfreesboro' was effected.

General Rosecrans entered Murfreesboro' on Sunday, the 4th of January, 1863. Meantime his adversary was in full retreat on Tullahoma, thirty-six miles distant.   By this time General Bragg's corps commanders, as well as their subordinates down to the regimental rank and file, scarcely concealed their want of confidence in him as the commander of the army.   On the 11th of January he invited from his corps, division, and brigade commanders an expression of their opinion on that point, and their replies, while affirming their admiration for his personal courage, devotion to duty, and ability as

BRIGADIER-GENERAL R. W. HANSON, C. S. A., KILLED AT STONE'S RIVER.   FROM A PHOTOGRAPH.

an organizer, frankly confessed that his army had lost confidence to such an extent in his capacity for chief command as wholly to impair his further usefulness.   On the 4th of February General Polk went so far indeed as to write direct to President Davis with regard to the dissatisfaction felt, and the necessity for the immediate substitution of another commander. ♭

To vindicate himself, General Bragg at once made an official report of the battle of the 31st of December, especially in relation to the miscarriage of the effort to break the enemy's center.⸦

The feeling outside as well as inside of his army, however, waxed so strong against Bragg that President Davis ordered General Johnston, then near Vicksburg, to go to Tennessee, with authority, if he thought it wise, to relieve Bragg from command.   Johnston's arrival was hailed with joy, for our army specially wanted him as their commander.   But after spending more than a week looking into its condition, he decided that he would not relieve Bragg, and thereupon returned toward Vicksburg with his staff.   This result quieted the bad feeling somewhat, but did not restore harmony between the corps

♭ Colonel Brent once showed me an order from General Bragg to place General Polk under arrest. Knowing what feeling against General Bragg such a step would produce, I was deeply pained and hastened to the latter's tent, where I besought, as a personal favor to myself, that the order should not be executed at present.   After a short conversation General Bragg authorized me to direct Colonel Brent to withhold the arrest.   The next morning, however, General Bragg, sent for me, and expressed his appreciation of what I had said, and said that he realized the feeling it would excite against himself, but that he felt that the urgent exactions of discipline made General Polk's arrest absolutely requisite.   The arrest was therefore made, but it was not sustained by the Richmond authorities.   It is hardly necessary to say that the incident deepened General Bragg's unpopularity with his army, while the feeling between his two corps commanders and himself grew from "bad to worse."   On the eve of the

battle of Chickamauga his relations with General Longstreet were no better than with the other two.— D. U.

⸦ In his report General Bragg says, in part:

"To meet our successful advance and retrieve his losses in the front of his left, the enemy early transferred a portion of his reserve from his left to that flank, and by 2 o'clock had succeeded in concentrating such a force on Lieutenant-General Hardee's front as to check his further progress.   Our two lines had, by this time, become almost blended, so weak were they by losses, exhaustion, and extension to cover the enemy's whole front.   As early as 10 A. M. Major-General Breckinridge was called on for one brigade, and soon after for a second, to reënforce or act as a reserve to General Hardee.   His reply to the first call represented the enemy crossing Stone's River in heavy force in his immediate front; and on receiving the second order he informed me they had already crossed in heavy force and were advancing on him in two lines. He was immediately ordered not to wait attack but to advance and meet them.   About this same time a report reached me that a heavy force of the enemy's infantry was advancing on the Lebanon Road about five miles in

commanders and their commanding general. Seldom did either of them visit headquarters except officially. On the other hand, Bragg was on good terms with the division and brigade commanders, namely, Wheeler, Cleburne, and Withers, Patton Anderson, J. C. Brown, J. K. Jackson, Bate, and Walthall.

The certainty he felt that General Rosecrans would retire from his front had led him to suffer the 1st to pass without advancing his right to cover the rising ground, thus giving ample leisure to Rosecrans to intrench and to restore order to his army after the fight of the 31st, when all the advantages of battle had remained with us. But on Friday, the 2d of January, he was convinced that Rosecrans was not going to retreat and that fighting must soon be resumed. After riding over the ground early on the morning of the 2d, at 11 o'clock he had adopted the following plan: To seize and carry by a vigorous assault that rising ground now occupied by the Federal forces, allowing only one hour to intervene between the time of the attack and dark, so that night should stop the fighting and give us opportunity to fortify at once. It was for that reason the hour of 4 P. M. was selected for the operation. The failure of Friday to secure the heights on our right necessitated an entire change of our lines, and Saturday his determination was to fall back to Tullahoma and await General Rosecrans's advance. No such move, however, having been made, our army went into winter quarters, undisturbed.

While the army was at Murfreesboro', no firing of guns being allowed, the country remained full of rabbits, some of which during the battle, alarmed by the din, rushed swiftly past one of our regiments, which at the time was advancing under a heavy fire of musketry. One of our soldiers was heard by a staff-officer to yell out, "Go it, cotton-tail; I'd run too if I hadn't a reputation."

At Tupelo an order had been issued forbidding the men firing their muskets when in camp. One of the volunteers shooting at a chicken killed a man; he was tried and shot, not, as unjustly stated, for disobedience of orders, but for killing the man. During one of General Bragg's rides near Tullahoma, he happened to meet a countryman dressed in his "butternut" garb, one of those rough, independent citizens of the mountain district of Tennessee, who, after intelligently giving all the information asked of him about the roads we were looking for, was also asked by the general if he did not "belong to Bragg's army." "Bragg's army?" was the reply. "He's got none; he shot half of them in Kentucky, and the other got killed up at Murfreesboro'." The general laughed and rode on.

Breckinridge's front. Brigadier-General Pegram, who had been sent to that road to cover the flank of the infantry with the cavalry brigade (save two regiments, detached with Wheeler and Wharton), was ordered forward immediately to develop such movement. The orders for the two brigades from Breckinridge were countermanded, whilst dispositions were made at his request to reënforce him. Before they could be carried out the movements ordered disclosed the facts that no force had crossed Stone's River; that the only enemy in our immediate front there were a small body of sharp-shooters, and that there was no advance on the Lebanon Road.

"These unfortunate misapprehensions on that part of the field (which, with proper precaution, could not have existed) withheld from active operations three fine brigades until the enemy had succeeded in checking our progress, had reëstablished his lines, and had collected many of his broken battalions."

The orders referred to by General Bragg as having been sent to General Breckinridge were in part written by me, and the receipts for their delivery were given to and retained by me for some time. General Bragg cordially said to me afterward that my preservation of those receipts had saved his reputation.— D. U.

THE OPPOSING FORCES AT STONE'S RIVER, TENN.

The composition, losses, and strength of each army as here stated give the gist of all the data obtainable in the Official Records. K stands for killed; w for wounded; m w for mortally wounded; m for captured or missing; c for captured.

THE UNION ARMY.

ARMY OF THE CUMBERLAND (Fourteenth Army Corps), Maj.-Gen. William S. Rosecrans.

Provost-Guard: 10th Ohio, Lieut.-Col. Joseph W. Burke. *Escort:* Anderson Troop Pa. Cav., Lieut. Thomas S. Maple. Staff and escort loss: k, 4; w, 5 = 9.

RIGHT WING, Maj.-Gen. Alexander McD. McCook.
FIRST (LATE NINTH) DIVISION, Brig.-Gen. Jefferson C. Davis.

Escort: Cavalry Co. B, 36th Ill., Capt. Samuel B. Sherer; G, 2d Ky. Cav., Capt. Miller R. McCulloch (k), Lieut. Harvey S. Park. Escort loss: k, 1; w, 4; m, 6 = 11.

First (late Thirtieth) Brigade, Col. P. Sidney Post: 59th Ill., Capt. Hendrick E. Paine; 74th Ill., Col. Jason Marsh; 75th Ill., Lieut.-Col. John E. Bennett; 22d Ind., Col. Michael Gooding. Brigade loss: k, 25; w, 144; m, 155 = 324. *Second (late Thirty-first) Brigade,* Col. William P. Carlin: 21st Ill., Col. J. W. S. Alexander (w), Lieut.-Col. Warren E. McMackin; 38th Ill., Lieut.-Col. Daniel H. Gilmer; 101st Ohio, Col. Leander Stem (m w and c), Lieut.-Col. Moses F. Wooster (m w and c), Maj. Isaac M. Kirby, Capt. Bedan B. McDonald; 15th Wis., Col. Hans C. Heg. Brigade loss: k, 129; w, 498; m, 194 = 821. *Third (late Thirty-second) Brigade,* Col. William E. Woodruff: 25th Ill., Col. Thomas D. Williams (k), Capt. Wesford Taggart; 35th Ill., Lieut.-Col. William P. Chandler; 81st Ind., Lieut.-Col. John Timberlake. Brigade loss: k, 32; w, 179; m, 47 = 258. *Artillery:* 2d Minn. (2d Brigade), Capt. William A. Hotchkiss; 5th Wis. (1st Brigade), Capt. Oscar F. Pinney (m w), Lieut. Charles B. Humphrey; 8th Wis. (3d Brigade), Capt. Stephen J. Carpenter (k), Sergt. Obadiah German, Lieut. Henry E. Stiles. Artillery loss embraced in brigades to which attached.

SECOND DIVISION, Brig.-Gen. Richard W. Johnson.

First (late Sixth) Brigade, Brig.-Gen. August Willich (c), Col. William Wallace, Col. William H. Gibson: 89th Ill., Lieut.-Col. Charles T. Hotchkiss; 32d Ind., Lieut.-Col. Frank Erdelmeyer; 39th Ind., Lieut.-Col. Fielder A. Jones; 15th Ohio, Col. William Wallace, Capt. A. R. Z. Dawson, Col. William Wallace; 49th Ohio, Col. William H. Gibson, Lieut.-Col. Levi Drake (k), Capt. Samuel F. Gray. Brigade loss: k, 90; w, 373; m, 701 = 1164. *Second (late Fifth) Brigade,* Brig.-Gen. Edward N. Kirk (w), Col. Joseph B. Dodge: 34th Ill., Lieut.-Col. Hiram W. Bristol, Maj. Alexander P. Dysart; 79th Ill., Col. Sheridan P. Read (k), Maj. Allen Buckner; 29th Ind., Lieut.-Col. David M. Dunn (c), Maj. Joseph P. Collins; 30th Ind. Col. Joseph B. Dodge, Lieut.-Col. Orrin D. Hurd; 77th Pa., Lieut.-Col. Peter B. Housum (k), Capt. Thomas E. Rose. Brigade loss: k, 99; w, 384; m, 376 = 859. *Third (late Fourth) Brigade,* Col. Philemon P. Baldwin: 6th Ind., Lieut.-Col. Hagerman Tripp; 5th Ky., Lieut.-Col. William W. Berry (w); 1st Ohio, Maj. Joab A. Stafford; 93d Ohio, Col. Charles Anderson (w). Brigade loss: k, 59; w, 244; m, 209 = 512. *Artillery:* 5th Ind. (3d Brigade), Capt. Peter Simonson; A, 1st Ohio (1st Brigade), Lieut. Edmund B. Belding; E, 1st Ohio (2d Brigade), Capt. Warren P. Edgarton (c). Artillery loss embraced in the brigades to which attached. *Cavalry:* G, H, I, and K, 3d Ind., Maj. Robert Klein. Loss: k, 4; w, 6; m, 15 = 25.

THIRD (LATE ELEVENTH) DIVISION, Brig.-Gen. Philip H. Sheridan.

Escort: L, 2d Ky. Cav., Lieut. Joseph T. Forman.

First (late Thirty-seventh) Brigade, Brig.-Gen. Joshua W. Sill (k), Col. Nicholas Greusel: 36th Ill., Col. Nicholas Greusel, Maj. Silas Miller (w and c), Capt. Porter C. Olson; 88th Ill., Col. Francis T. Sherman; 21st Mich. Lieut.-Col. William B. McCreery; 24th Wis., Maj. Elisha C. Hibbard. Brigade loss: k, 104; w, 365; m,

200 = 669. *Second (late Thirty-fifth) Brigade,* Col. Frederick Schaefer (k), Lieut.-Col. Bernard Laiboldt: 44th Ill., Capt. Wallace W. Barrett (w); 73d Ill., Maj. William A. Presson (w); 2d Mo. Lieut.-Col. Bernard Laiboldt, Maj. Francis Ehrler; 15th Mo., Lieut.-Col. John Weber. Brigade loss: k, 71; w, 281; m, 46 = 398. *Third Brigade,* Col. George W. Roberts (k), Col. Luther P. Bradley: 22d Ill., Lieut.-Col. Francis Swanwick (w and c), Capt. Samuel Johnson; 27th Ill., Col. Fazilo A. Harrington (k), Maj. William A. Schmitt; 42d Ill., Lieut.-Col. Nathan H. Walworth; 51st Ill., Col. Luther P. Bradley, Capt. Henry F. Wescott. Brigade loss: k, 62; w, 343; m, 161 = 566. *Artillery:* Capt. Henry Hescock: C, 1st Ill. (3d Brigade), Capt. Charles Houghtaling; 4th Ind. (1st Brigade), Capt. Asahel K. Bush; G, 1st Mo. (2d Brigade), Capt. Henry Hescock. Artillery loss embraced in brigades to which attached.

CENTER, Maj.-Gen. George H. Thomas. Staff and escort loss: k, 1; w, 1 = 2.

Provost-Guard: 9th Mich., Col. John G. Parkhurst.
FIRST (LATE THIRD) DIVISION, Maj.-Gen. Lovell H. Rousseau. Staff and escort loss: w, 2.

First (late Ninth) Brigade, Col. Benjamin F. Scribner: 38th Ind., Lieut.-Col. Daniel F. Griffin; 2d Ohio, Lieut.-Col. John Kell (k), Maj. Anson G. McCook; 33d Ohio, Capt. Ephraim J. Ellis; 94th Ohio, Col. Joseph W. Frizell (w), Lieut.-Col. Stephen A. Bassford; 10th Wis., Col. Alfred R. Chapin. Brigade loss: k, 33; w, 189; m, 57 = 279. *Second (late Seventeenth) Brigade,* Col. John Beatty: 42d Ind., Lieut.-Col. James M. Shanklin (c); 88th Ind., Col. George Humphrey (w), Lieut.-Col. Cyrus E. Briant; 15th Ky., Col. James B. Forman (k), Lieut.-Col. Joseph R. Snider; 3d Ohio, Lieut.-Col. Orris A. Lawson. Brigade loss: k, 53; w, 240; m, 96 = 389. *Third (late Twenty-eighth) Brigade,* Col. John C. Starkweather: 24th Ill., Col. Geza Mihalotzy; 79th Pa., Col. Henry A. Hambright; 1st Wis., Lieut.-Col. George B. Bingham; 21st Wis., Lieut.-Col. Harrison C. Hobart. Brigade loss: k, 2; w, 31; m, 113 = 146. *Fourth Brigade,* Lieut.-Col. Oliver L. Shepherd: 1st Battalion, 15th U. S., Maj. John H. King (w), Capt. Jesse Fulmer; 1st Battalion, 16th U. S., and B, 2d Battalion, Maj. Adam J. Slemmer (w), Capt. R. E. A. Crofton; 1st Battalion, and A and D, 3d Battalion, 18th U. S., Maj. James N. Caldwell; 2d Battalion, and B, C, E, and F, 3d Battalion, 18th U. S., Maj. Frederick Townsend; 1st Battalion, 19th U. S., Maj. Stephen D. Carpenter (k), Capt. James B. Mulligan. Brigade loss: k, 94; w, 497; m, 50 = 641. *Artillery,* Capt. Cyrus O. Loomis: A, Ky. (3d Brigade), Capt. David C. Stone; A, 1st Mich. (2d Brigade), Lieut. George W. Van Pelt; H, 5th U. S. (4th Brigade), Lieut. Francis L. Guenther. Artillery loss embraced in brigades to which attached. *Cavalry:* 2d Ky. (6 co's), Maj. Thomas P. Nicholas. Loss: w, 3.

SECOND (late EIGHTH) DIVISION, Brig.-Gen. James S. Negley.

First (late Twenty-fifth) Brigade, ∤ Brig.-Gen. James G. Spears: 1st Tenn., Col. Robert K. Byrd; 2d Tenn. Lieut.-Col. James M. Melton; 6th Tenn., Col. Joseph A. Cooper. Brigade loss: k, 5; w, 28 = 33. *Second (late Twenty-ninth) Brigade,* Col. Timothy R. Stanley: 19th Ill., Col. Joseph R. Scott (w), Lieut.-Col. Alexander W. Raffen; 11th Mich., Col. William L. Stoughton; 18th Ohio, Lieut.-Col. Josiah Given; 69th Ohio, Col. William B. Cassilly (w), Maj. Eli J. Hickcox, Capt. David Putman, Capt. Joseph H. Brigham, Lieut.-Col. George F. Elliott. Brigade loss: k, 76; w, 336; m, 101 = 513. *Third*

∤ The 14th Mich., 85th Ill., and two sections 10th Wis. Battery temporarily attached Jan. 2d and 3d.

(late Seventh) Brigade. Col. John F. Miller: 37th Ind., Col. James S. Hull (w,) Lieut.-Col. William D. Ward; 21st Ohio, Lieut.-Col. James M. Neibling; 74th Ohio, Col. Granville Moody (w); 78th Pa., Col. William Sirwell. Brigade loss: k, 80; w, 471; m, 97 = 648. *Artillery:* B, Ky., Lieut. Alban A. Ellsworth; G, 1st Ohio, Lieut. Alexander Marshall; M, 1st Ohio (2d Brigade), Capt. Frederick Schultz. Artillery loss embraced in brigades to which attached.

THIRD (LATE FIRST) DIVISION.

First Brigade, ⚓ Col. Moses B. Walker: 82d Ind., Col. Morton C. Hunter; 17th Ohio, Col. John M. Connell; 31st Ohio, Lieut.-Col. Frederick W. Lister; 38th Ohio, Col. Edward H. Phelps. Brigade loss: w, 22. *Artillery:* D, 1st Mich., Capt. Josiah W. Church.

LEFT WING.—Maj.-Gen. Thomas L. Crittenden. Staff loss: w, 1.

FIRST (LATE SIXTH) DIVISION, Brig.-Gen. Thomas J. Wood (w), Brig.-Gen. Milo S. Hascall. Staff loss: w, 1.

First (late Fifteenth) Brigade, Brig.-Gen. Milo S. Hascall, Col. George P. Buell: 100th Ill., Col. Frederick A. Bartleson; 58th Ind., Col. George P. Buell, Lieut.-Col. James T. Embree; 3d Ky., Col. Samuel McKee (k), Maj. Daniel R. Collier; 26th Ohio, Capt. William H. Squires. Brigade loss: k, 50; w, 316; m, 34 = 400. *Second (late Twenty-first) Brigade,* Col. George D. Wagner: 15th Ind., Lieut.-Col. Gustavus A. Wood; 40th Ind., Col. John W. Blake, Lieut.-Col. Elias Neff (w), Maj. Henry Leaming; 57th Ind., Col. Cyrus C. Hines (w), Lieut.-Col. George W. Lennard (w), Capt. John S. McGraw; 97th Ohio, Col. John Q. Lane. Brigade loss: k, 57; w, 291; m, 32 = 380. *Third (late Twentieth) Brigade,* Col. Charles G. Harker: 51st Ind., Col. Abel D. Streight; 73d Ind., Col. Gilbert Hathaway; 13th Mich., Col. Michael Shoemaker; 64th Ohio, Lieut.-Col. Alexander McIlvain; 65th Ohio, Lieut.-Col. Alexander Cassil (w), Maj. Horatio N. Whitbeck (w). Brigade loss: k, 108; w, 330; m, 101 = 539. *Artillery,* Maj. Seymour Race: 8th Ind. (First Brigade), Lieut. George Estep; 10th Ind. (Second Brigade), Capt. Jerome B. Cox; 6th Ohio (Third Brigade), Capt. Cullen Bradley. Artillery loss embraced in brigades to which attached.

SECOND (LATE FOURTH) DIVISION, Brig.-Gen. John M. Palmer. Staff loss: w, 1.

First (late Twenty-second) Brigade, Brig.-Gen. Charles Cruft: 31st Ind., Col. John Osborn; 1st Ky., Col. David A. Enyart; 2d Ky., Col. Thomas D. Sedgewick; 90th Ohio, Col. Isaac N. Ross. Brigade loss: k, 44; w, 227; m, 126 = 397. *Second (late Nineteenth) Brigade,* Col. William B. Hazen: 110th Ill., Col. Thomas S. Casey; 9th Ind., Col. William H. Blake; 6th Ky., Col. Walter C. Whitaker; 41st Ohio, Lieut.-Col. Aquila Wiley. Brigade loss: k, 45; w, 335; m, 29 = 409. *Third (late Tenth) Brigade,* Col. William Grose: 84th Ill., Col. Louis H. Waters; 36th Ind., Maj. Isaac Kinley (w), Capt. Pyrrhus Woodward; 23d Ky., Maj. Thomas H. Hamrick; 6th Ohio, Col. Nicholas L. Anderson (w); 24th Ohio, Col. Frederick C. Jones (k), Maj. Henry Terry (k), Capt. Enoch Weller

(k), Capt. A. T. M. Cockerill. Brigade loss: k, 107; w, 478; m, 74 = 659. *Artillery,* Capt. William E. Standart: B, 1st Ohio, Capt. William E. Standart; F, 1st Ohio, Capt. Daniel T. Cockerill (w), Lieut. Norval Osburn; H and M, 4th U. S., Lieut. Charles C. Parsons. Artillery loss: k, 9; w, 40; m, 11 = 60. *Third (late Fifth) Division,* Brig.-Gen. Horatio P. Van Cleve (w), Col. Samuel Beatty. Staff loss: w, 1. *First (late Eleventh) Brigade,* Col. Samuel Beatty, Col. Benjamin C. Grider: 79th Ind., Col. Frederick Knefler; 9th Ky., Col. Benjamin C. Grider, Lieut.-Col. George H. Cram; 11th Ky., Maj. Erasmus L. Mottley; 19th Ohio, Maj. Charles F. Manderson. Brigade loss: k, 67; w, 371; m, 83 = 521. *Second (late Fourteenth) Brigade,* Col. James P. Fyffe: 44th Ind., Col. William C. Williams (w), Lieut.-Col. Simeon C. Aldrich; 86th Ind., Lieut.-Col. George F. Dick; 13th Ohio, Col. Joseph G. Hawkins (k), Maj. Dwight Jarvis, Jr.; 59th Ohio, Lieut.-Col. William Howard. Brigade loss: k, 78; w, 239; m, 240 = 557. *Third (late Twenty-third) Brigade,* Col. Samuel W. Price: 35th Ind., Col. Bernard F. Mullen; 8th Ky., Lieut.-Col. Reuben May, Maj. Green B. Broaddus; 21st Ky., Lieut.-Col. James C. Evans; 51st Ohio, Lieut.-Col. Richard W. McClain; 99th Ohio, Col. Peter T. Swaine (w), Lieut.-Col. John E. Cummins. Brigade loss: k, 79; w, 361; m, 143 = 583. *Artillery,* Capt. George R. Swallow: 7th Ind., Capt. George R. Swallow; B, Pa., Lieut. Alanson J. Stevens; 3d Wis., Lieut. Cortland Livingston. Artillery loss: k, 6; w, 19 = 25.

CAVALRY, Brig.-Gen. David S. Stanley.

CAVALRY DIVISION, Col. John Kennett.

First Division, Col. Robert H. G. Minty: M, 2d Ind., Capt. J. A. S. Mitchell; 3d Ky., Col. Eli H. Murray; 4th Mich., Lieut.-Col. William H. Dickinson; 7th Pa., Maj. John E. Wynkoop. Brigade loss: k, 5; w, 24; m, 77 = 106. *Second Brigade,* Col. Lewis Zahm: 1st Ohio, Col. Minor Milliken (k), Maj. James Laughlin; 3d Ohio, Lieut.-Col. Douglas A. Murray; 4th Ohio, Maj. John L. Pugh. Brigade loss: k, 18; w, 44; m, 59 = 121. *Artillery:* D, 1st Ohio (section), Lieut. Nathaniel M. Newell. Loss: k, 1.

RESERVE CAVALRY: ‡ 15th Pa., Maj. Adolph G. Rosengarten (k), Maj. Frank B. Ward (m w), Capt. Alfred Vezin; 1st Middle (5th) Tenn., Col. William B. Stokes; 2d Tenn., Col. Daniel M. Ray. Reserve cavalry loss: k, 12; w, 25; m, 67 = 104.

UNATTACHED: 3d Tenn., Col. William C. Pickens; 4th U. S., Capt. Elmer Otis. Loss: k, 3; w, 10; m, 12 = 25.

MISCELLANEOUS.—PIONEER BRIGADE, Capt. James St. C. Morton: 1st Battalion, Capt. Lyman Bridges (w); 2d Battalion, Capt. Calvin Hood; 3d Battalion, Capt. Robert Clements; Stokes's Ill. Battery, Capt. James H. Stokes. Brigade loss: k, 15; w, 33 = 48.

ENGINEERS AND MECHANICS: 1st Mich., Col. William P. Innes. Loss: k, 2; w, 9; m, 5 = 16.

Total loss of Union army (in the campaign): killed, 1730; wounded, 7802; captured or missing, 3717 = 13,249. Effective force December 31st, 1862, 43,400. (See "Official Records," Vol. XX., Pt. I., p. 201.)

⚓ This brigade and Church's battery were the only troops of this division engaged in the battle.
‡ Under the immediate command of General Stanley, chief of cavalry.

THE CONFEDERATE ARMY.

ARMY OF TENNESSEE.— General Braxton Bragg.

POLK'S CORPS, Lieut.-Gen. Leonidas Polk.

FIRST DIVISION, Maj.-Gen. B. F. Cheatham.

First Brigade, Brig.-Gen. Daniel S. Donelson: 8th Tenn., Col. W. L. Moore (k), Lieut.-Col. J. H. Anderson; 16th Tenn., Col. John H. Savage; 38th Tenn., Col. John C. Carter; 51st Tenn., Col. John Chester; 84th Tenn., Col. S. S. Stanton; Tenn. Battery, Capt. W. W. Carnes. Brigade loss: k, 108; w, 575; m, 17 = 700. *Second Brigade,* Brig.-Gen. Alexander P. Stewart: 4th and 5th Tenn., Col. Oscar F. Strahl; 19th Tenn., Col. Francis M. Walker; 24th Tenn., Col. H. L. W. Bratton (m w), Maj. S. E. Shannon; 31st and 33d Tenn., Col. E. E. Tansil; Miss. Battery, Capt. T. J. Stanford. Bri-

gade loss: k, 63; w, 334; m, 2 = 399. *Third Brigade,* Brig.-Gen. George Maney: 1st and 27th Tenn., Col. H. R. Feild; 4th Tenn. (Prov. army), Col. J. A. McMurry; 6th and 9th Tenn., Col. C. S. Hurt; Tenn. Sharp-shooters, Capt. Frank Maney; Miss. Battery (Smith's), Lieut. William B. Turner. Brigade loss: k, 22; w, 163; m, 8 = 193. *Fourth Brigade,* Col. A. J. Vaughan, Jr.: 12th Tenn., Maj. J. N. Wyatt; 13th Tenn., Lieut.-Col. W. E. Morgan (m w), Capt. R. F. Lanier; 29th Tenn., Maj. J. B. Johnson; 47th Tenn., Capt. W. M. Watkins; 154th Tenn., Lieut.-Col. M. Magevney, Jr.; 9th Tex., Col. W. H. Young; Tenn. Sharp-shooters (Allin's), Lieut. J. R. J. Creighton (w), Lieut. T. F. Pattison; Tenn. Battery

Capt. W. L. Scott. Brigade loss: k, 105; w, 564; m, 38=707.

SECOND DIVISION, Maj.-Gen. Jones M. Withers.

First Brigade, Col. J. Q. Loomis (w), Col. J. G. Coltart: 19th Ala., ——; 22d Ala., ——; 25th Ala., ——; 26th Ala., ——; 39th Ala., ——; 17th Ala. Battalion Sharp-shooters, Capt. B. C. Yancey; 1st La. (Regulars), Lieut.-Col. F. H. Farrar, Jr. (m w); Fla. Battery, Capt. Felix H. Robertson. Brigade loss: k, 53; w, 533; m, 5=591. *Second Brigade,* Brig.-Gen. James R. Chalmers (w), Col. T. W. White: 7th Miss., ——; 9th Miss., Col. T. W. White; 10th Miss., ——; 41st Miss., ——; 9th Miss. Battalion Sharp-shooters, Capt. O. F. West; Blythe's Miss., ——; Ala. Battery (Garrity's), ——. Brigade loss: k, 67; w, 445; m, 36 = 548. *Third Brigade,* Brig.-Gen. J. Patton Anderson: 45th Ala., Col. James G. Gilchrist; 24th Miss., Lieut.-Col. R. P. McKelvaine; 27th Miss., Col. Thomas M. Jones, Lieut.-Col. James L. Autry (k), Capt. E. R. Neilson (w); 29th Miss., Col. W. F. Brantly (w), Lieut.-Col. J. B. Morgan; 30th Miss., Lieut.-Col. J. I. Scales; 39th N. C., Capt. A. W. Bell; Mo. Battery, Capt. O. W. Barret. Brigade loss: k, 130; w, 620; m, 13=763. *Fourth Brigade,* Col. A. M. Manigault: 24th Ala., ——; 28th Ala., ——; 34th Ala., ——; 10th and 19th S. C., Col. A. J. Lythgoe (k); Ala. Battery, Capt. D. D. Waters. Brigade loss: k, 73; w, 428; m, 16 = 517.

HARDEE'S CORPS, Lieut.-Gen. William J. Hardee.

FIRST DIVISION, Maj.-Gen. John C. Breckinridge.

First Brigade, Brig.-Gen. Daniel W. Adams (w), Col. Randall L. Gibson: 32d Ala., Lieut.-Col. Henry Maury (w), Col. Alexander McKinstry; 13th and 20th La., Col. Randall L. Gibson, Maj. Charles Guillet; 16th and 25th La., Col. S. W. Fisk (k), Maj. F. C. Zacharie; 14th La. Battalion, Maj. J. E. Austin; 5th Battery Washington (La.) Art'y, Lieut. W. C. D. Vaught. Brigade loss: k, 112; w, 445; m, 146 = 703. *Second Brigade,* Col. J. B. Palmer, Brig.-Gen. Gideon J. Pillow: 18th Tenn., Lieut.-Col. W. R. Butler, Col. J. B. Palmer (w); 26th Tenn., Col. John M. Lillard; 28th Tenn., Col. P. D. Cunningham (k); 45th Tenn., Col. A. Searcy; Ga. Battery (Moses's), Lieut. R. W. Anderson. Brigade loss: k, 49; w, 324; m, 52 = 425. *Third Brigade,* Brig.-Gen. William Preston: 1st and 3d Fla., Col. William Miller (w); 4th Fla., Col. William L. L. Bowen; 60th N. C., Col. J. A. McDowell; 20th Tenn., Col. T. B. Smith (w), Lieut.-Col. F. M. Lavender, Maj. F. Claybrooke; Tenn. Battery, Capt. E. E. Wright (k), Lieut. J. W. Phillips. Brigade loss: k, 58; w, 384; m, 97=539. *Fourth Brigade,* Brig.-Gen. R. W. Hanson (k), Col. R. P. Trabue: 41st Ala., Col. H. Talbird, Lieut.-Col. M. L. Stansel (w); 2d Ky., Maj. James W. Hewitt (w), Capt. James W. Moss; 4th Ky., Col. R. P. Trabue, Capt. T. W. Thompson; 6th Ky Col. Joseph H. Lewis; 9th Ky., Col. T. H. Hunt; Ky. Battery, Capt. Robert Cobb. Brigade loss: k, 47; w, 273; m, 81=401. *Jackson's Brigade* (temporarily attached), Brig.-Gen. John K. Jackson: 5th Ga., Col. W. T. Black (k), Maj. C. P. Daniel; 2d Ga. Battalion Sharp-shooters, Maj. J. J. Cox; 5th Miss., Lieut.-Col. W. L. Sykes (w); 8th Miss., Col. J. C. Wilkinson (w and c), Lieut.-Col. A. McNeill; Ga. Battery (Pritchard's), ——; Ala. Battery (Lumsden's), Lieut. H. H. Cribbs. Brigade loss: k, 41; w, 262 = 303. *Unattached:* Ky. Battery, Capt. E. P. Byrne.

SECOND DIVISION, Maj.-Gen. P. R. Cleburne. Staff loss: w, 2.

First Brigade, Brig.-Gen. L. E. Polk: 1st Ark., Col. John W. Colquitt; 13th Ark., ——; 15th Ark., ——; 5th Confederate, Col. J. A. Smith; 2d Tenn., Col. W. D. Robison; 5th Tenn., Col. B. J. Hill; Ark. Battery (Helena Art'y), Lieut. T. J. Key. Brigade loss: k, 30; w, 298; m, 19 = 347. *Second Brigade,* Brig.-Gen. St. John

R. Liddell : 2d Ark., Col. D. C. Govan ; 5th Ark., Lieut.-Col. John E. Murray ; 6th and 7th Ark., Col. S. G. Smith (w), Lieut.-Col. F. J. Cameron (w), Maj. W. F. Douglass ; 8th Ark., Col. John H. Kelly (w), Lieut.-Col. G. F. Baucum ; Miss. Battery (Swett's), Lieut. H. Shannon. Brigade loss : k, 86 ; w, 503 ; m, 18 = 607. *Third Brigade,* Brig.-Gen. Bushrod R. Johnson : 17th Tenn., Col. A. S. Marks (w), Lieut.-Col. W. W. Floyd ; 23d Tenn., Lieut.-Col. R. H. Keeble ; 25 Tenn., Col. J. M. Hughs (w), Lieut.-Col. Samuel Davis ; 37th Tenn., Col. Moses White (w), Maj. J. T. McReynolds (k), Capt. C. G. Jarnagin ; 44th Tenn., Col. John S. Fulton ; Miss. Battery (Jefferson Art'y), Capt. Put. Darden. Brigade loss : k, 61 ; w, 488 ; m, 57 = 606. *Fourth Brigade,* Brig.-Gen. S. A. M. Wood : 16th Ala., Col. W. B. Wood (w) ; 33d Ala., Col. Samuel Adams ; 3d Confederate, Maj. J. F. Cameron ; 45th Miss., Lieut.-Col. R. Charlton ; 15th Miss. Battalion Sharp-shooters, Capt. A. T. Hawkins ; Ala. Battery, Capt. Henry C. Semple. Brigade loss : k, 52 ; w, 339 ; m, 113 = 504.

McCOWN'S DIVISION (of Kirby Smith's corps, serving with Hardee), Maj.-Gen. J. P. McCown.

First Brigade (serving as infantry), Brig.-Gen. M. D. Ector: 10th Tex. Cav., Col. M. F. Locke; 11th Tex. Cav., Col. J. C. Burks (m w), Lieut.-Col. J. M. Bounds; 14th Tex. Cav., Col. J. L. Camp; 15th Tex. Cav., Col. J. A. Andrews; Tex. Battery, Capt. J. P. Douglas. Brigade loss: k, 28; w, 276; m, 48 = 352. *Second Brigade,* Brig.-Gen. James E. Rains (k), Col. R. B. Vance: 3d Ga. Battalion, Lieut.-Col. M. A. Stovall; 9th Ga. Battalion, Maj. Joseph T. Smith; 29th N. C., Col. R. B. Vance; 11th Tenn., Col. G. W. Gordon (w), Lieut.-Col. William Thedford; Ala. Battery (Eufaula Light Art'y), Lieut. W. A. McDuffie. Brigade loss: k, 20; w, 161; m, 18 = 199. *Third Brigade,* Brig.-Gen. Evander McNair, Col. R. W. Harper; 1st Ark. Mt'd Rifles (dismounted), Col. R. W. Harper, Maj. L. M. Ramsaur (w); 2d Ark. Mt'd Rifles (dismounted), Lieut.-Col. J. A. Williamson; 4th Ark., Col. H. G. Bunn; 30th Ark., Maj. J. J. Franklin (w and c), Capt. W. A. Cotter; 4th Ark. Battalion, Maj. J. A. Ross; Ark. Battery, Capt. J. T. Humphreys. Brigade loss: k, 42; w, 330; m, 52 = 424.

CAVALRY, Brig.-Gen. Joseph Wheeler.

Wheeler's Brigade, Brig.-Gen. Joseph Wheeler: 1st Ala., Col. W. W. Allen (w); 3d Ala., Maj. F. Y. Gaines, Capt. T. H. Maudlin; 51st Ala., Col. John T. Morgan; 8th Confederate, Col. W. B. Wade; 1st Tenn., Col. James E. Carter; Tenn. Battalion, Maj. DeWitt C. Douglass; Tenn. Battalion, Maj. D. W. Holman; Ark. Battery, Capt. J. H. Wiggins. Brigade loss: k, 22; w, 61; m, 84=167. *Buford's Brigade,* Brig.-Gen. Abraham Buford: 3d Ky., Col. J. R. Butler; 5th Ky., Col. D. H. Smith; 6th Ky., Col. J. W. Grigsby. Brigade loss: k, 1; w, 11; m, 6 = 18. *Pegram's Brigade,* Brig.-Gen. John Pegram: 1st Ga., ——; 1st La., ——. Brigade loss, not reported. *Wharton's Brigade,* Brig.-Gen. John A. Wharton: 14th Ala. Battalion, Lieut.-Col. James C. Malone; 1st Confederate, Col. John T. Cox; 3d Confederate, Lieut.-Col. William M. Estes; 2d Ga., Lieut.-Col. J. E. Dunlop, Maj. F. M. Ison; 3d Ga. (detachment), Maj. R. Thompson; 2d Tenn., Col. H. M. Ashby; 4th Tenn., Col. Baxter Smith; Tenn. Battalion, Maj. John R. Davis; 8th Tex., Col. Thomas Harrison: Murray's Tenn., Maj. W. S. Bledsoe; Escort Co., Capt. Paul F. Anderson; McCown's Escort Co., Capt. L. T. Hardy; Tenn. Battery, Capt. B. F. White, Jr. Brigade loss: k, 20; w, 131; m, 113 = 264.

The total Confederate loss (minus Pegram's cavalry brigade, not reported) was 1294 killed, 7945 wounded, and 1027 captured or missing = 10,266. The number present for duty on December 31st, 1862, was 37,712. (See " Official Records," Vol. XX., Pt. I., p. 674.)

THE BATTLE OF STONE'S RIVER.

BY G. C. KNIFFIN, LIEUT.-COLONEL, U. S. V., OF GENERAL CRITTENDEN'S STAFF.

ON the 26th of December, 1862, General W. S. Rosecrans, who on the 20th of October had succeeded General Buell in the command of the Army of the Cumberland, set out from Nashville with that army with the purpose of attacking the Confederate forces under General Braxton Bragg, then concentrated in the neighborhood of Murfreesboro', on Stone's River, Tenn.

The three corps into which the army was organized moved by the following routes: General Crittenden by the Murfreesboro' turnpike, arriving within two miles of Murfreesboro' on the night of the 29th; General Thomas's corps by the Franklin and Wilkinson turnpikes, thence by cross-roads to the Murfreesboro' pike, arriving a few hours later; and General McCook's corps, marching by the Nolensville pike to Triune, and bivouacking at Overall's Creek on the same night. The forward movement had not been accomplished without some sharp fighting. The advance of Crittenden had a spirited action at La Vergne, and again at the Stewart's Creek bridge. McCook fought at Nolensville, and the cavalry, under General Stanley, found the march a continuous skirmish; but the Confederate advance pickets had fallen back upon the main line, where they rejoined their divisions.

The armies were about equally matched. Bragg's effective strength on December 10th was 39,304 infantry, 10,070 cavalry, and 1758 artillery,—total, 51,132; while on December 15th General Rosecrans's returns showed a present for duty of 51,822 infantry and artillery, and 4849 cavalry,—total, 56,671. In each army these figures were diminished by the usual details for hospital and transportation service, train guards, and other purposes, so that Rosecrans reported his force actually engaged, December 31st, at 43,400, while Bragg placed his own force at 37,712. ⌡

Rosecrans's left wing, under Crittenden, bivouacked on the night of the 29th within seven hundred yards of the Confederate lines in front of Murfreesboro'. Crittenden's orders had been to go into Murfreesboro', and he was inclined to obey them. Riding forward, he found the two advance divisions arranged in line of battle, and, against the remonstrance of General Wood, ordered a forward movement. Palmer united with Wood, however, in a protest on the ground that an advance at night over unknown ground, in the face of a force of unknown strength, was too hazardous to be undertaken.

General Crittenden finally suspended the execution of the order one hour, and soon after it was countermanded by General Rosecrans, who

---

⌡ One reason for the unreliability of official returns for historical purposes is that the absence of tri-monthly and monthly returns of numerous organizations frequently require the use of the returns "last on file," which may be three months old, thus leaving out of the account, as rendered by the brigade, division, or corps adjutant, the numerous casualties that have tended to diminish the actual strength of those organizations since last reported.—G. C. K.

came up to Crittenden's headquarters at the toll-house on the Nashville turnpike.

Crittenden's line of battle was the base of a triangle of which Stone's River on his left and the line of a dense cedar thicket on his right formed the other sides. General Wood's division occupied the left, with his flank resting on the river, General Palmer's the right, while General Van Cleve was in reserve near a ford of Stone's River. Of Thomas's two divisions, Negley formed on the right of Palmer, with his right on the Wilkinson pike, while Rousseau was in reserve. ⚓

The soldiers lay down on the wet ground without fires, under a drenching rain. The slumbers of the commanding general were disturbed at half-past 3 on the morning of the 30th by a call from General McCook, who had just come up and who was instructed to rest the left of his corps upon Negley's right. Of his divisions, Sheridan therefore, preceded by Stanley's cavalry, moved on the Wilkinson turnpike, closely followed by R. W. Johnson and Davis. Skirmishing into position, the line was formed by resting the left of Sheridan's division on the Wilkinson pike, Davis taking position on his right and Johnson in reserve.

The general course of the Nashville and Murfreesboro' turnpike, and of the railroad where they crossed the line of battle, is south-east. On the left of the turnpike, and opposite the toll-gate house, was a grove of trees of about four acres in extent, crowning a slight elevation known as the " Round

⚓ An important cavalry raid by General Wheeler around the Union army had engaged two of Thomas's brigades, Starkweather's and Walker's. During the night of the 29th General Wheeler, who had moved from the left to the right of Murfreesboro', advancing by the Lebanon and Jefferson pikes, gained the rear of Rosecrans's army and attacked Starkweather's brigade of Rousseau's division, at Jefferson, at daylight on the 30th. The head of his brigade train, consisting of sixty-four wagons, had just arrived in camp, and was driving into park, when Wheeler dashed down upon it with three thousand cavalry. But he had encountered an antagonist as vigilant as himself. Wheeler's men, dismounted, advanced gallantly to the charge, when they were as gallantly met. After two hours' contest twenty wagons in the rear of the train were taken and destroyed, but the assault upon the brigade was handsomely repulsed. The Confederates fell back, followed by Starkweather for more than a mile, when he returned to camp. The Union loss in killed, wounded, and missing was 122.

From Jefferson Wheeler proceeded toward La Vergne, picking up stragglers and a small forage train, arriving at La Vergne about noon of the same day, where he captured the immense supply trains of McCook's corps, moving slowly forward under insufficient guard.

Seven hundred prisoners and nearly a million dollars' worth of property was the penalty paid by the Government for not heeding the requests of the commanding general for more cavalry. The work of paroling prisoners, burning wagons, exchanging arms and horses, and driving off mules commenced at once and occupied the remainder of the day and night. Early on the morning of the 31st Colonel M. B. Walker's Union brigade (of Fry's division, Thomas's corps), on its night march from Nolensville to Stewartsboro', arrived within two and a half miles of La Vergne, and advanced at once to the scene of devastation. The turnpike, as far as the eye could reach, was filled with burning wagons. The country was overspread with disarmed men, broken-down horses and mules. The streets were covered with empty valises and trunks, knapsacks, broken guns, and all the indescribable débris of a captured and rifled army train. A few shells, judiciously administered, sufficed to set Wheeler's stragglers scampering after the main body, now far on its way toward Rock Spring. Walker recaptured eight hundred men and all the train animals, and saved some of the stores. A train there, and another at Nolensville, shared the fate of that at La Vergne, and three hundred paroled prisoners were left to carry the tidings back to Nashville. At 2 o'clock on the morning of the 31st Wheeler came up bright and smiling upon the left flank of the Confederate army in front of Murfreesboro', having made the entire circuit of Rosecrans's army in forty-eight hours, leaving miles of road strewn with burning wagons and army supplies, remounting a portion of his cavalry, and bringing back to camp a sufficient number of minie-rifles and accouterments to arm a brigade.—G. C. K.

Forest," in which Wagner's brigade was posted. The line of battle trending irregularly southward, facing east and accommodating itself to the character of the ground, was much nearer the Confederate line in front of McCook than on the left, where the flanks of the contending armies were separated by Stone's River. At 4 o'clock General McCook reported the alignment of the right wing, together with the fact that two divisions of Polk's corps and two of Hardee's were in his front, extending far to his right out the Salem pike. General Rose- crans objected to the direction of McCook's line, and said it should face strongly south, and that Johnson's division, in column of regi- ments at half distance, should be held in reserve in rear of Davis's right at close musket- range; but he left the arrangement of his right

wing with the corps command- er, who had been over the ground.↓ The right wing, generally occupy- ing a wooded ridge with open ground in front, was further protected from surprise by an outlook over a narrow cultivated

1. MONUMENT TO THE DEAD OF THE REGULAR BRIGADE, STONE'S RIVER CEMETERY.
2. CANNON INSCRIBED WITH THE NUMBER BURIED IN STONE'S RIVER CEMETERY.
3. STONE'S RIVER CEMETERY (SEE MAP, P. 616) — THE NASHVILLE RAILROAD IN THE FOREGROUND. FROM PHOTOGRAPHS MADE IN 1884.

↓ During the afternoon, General McCook being informed that his line was greatly overlapped by the enemy, Johnson's division was moved up on Davis's right. Kirk's brigade on the left was formed on the right of Post, but was advanced slightly to obtain position in the front edge of a woodland, commanding the ground in front. Willich's line was refused to the right and rear of Kirk's, and Baldwin was in reserve. The left wing maintained substantially the same position it had assumed the previous night. The pioneer brigade, under Captain Morton, was posted on Stone's River, in rear of Wood, to prepare fords. Rousseau came up with Scribner's, Beatty's and the Regular brigade, and took position in rear of Negley. — G. C. K.

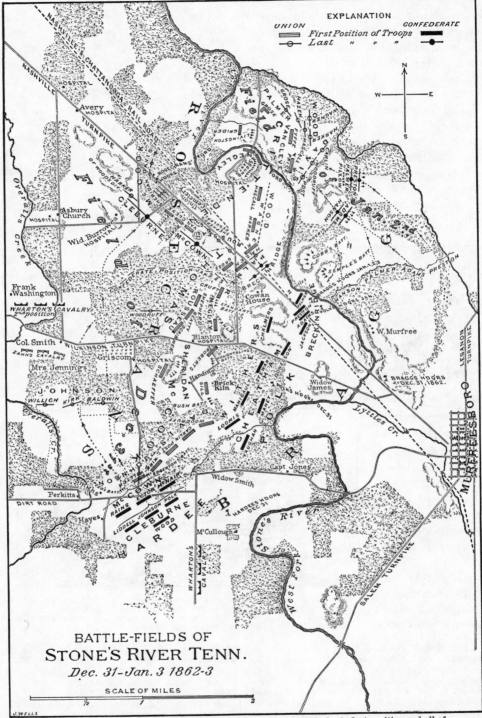

BATTLE-FIELDS OF
STONE'S RIVER TENN.
Dec. 31–Jan. 3 1862-3

SCALE OF MILES

½   1   2

J. WELLS

The Round Forest mentioned in the text included the right of Harker's first position and all of
Hazen's position, field of December 31st.

valley, widening from left to right from 200 to 500 yards, beyond which, in a dense cedar thicket, the enemy's lines were dimly visible. Confidence in the strength and staying qualities of his troops, and reluctance to yield a favorable position without a struggle, together with the fact that the retirement of his line must be executed in the night, induced General McCook to make the fatal mistake of leaving his position unchanged.

The plan of battle was as follows: General McCook was to occupy the most advantageous position, refusing his right as much as was practicable and necessary to secure it; to receive the attack of the enemy, or, if that did not come, to attack sufficiently to hold all the forces in his front. General Thomas and General Palmer were to

VIEW ON THE NASHVILLE PIKE AT THE UNION CEMETERY, LOOKING SOUTH-EAST TOWARD MURFREESBORO'. FROM A PHOTOGRAPH TAKEN IN 1884.

open with skirmishing and engage the enemy's center and left as far as the river. Crittenden was to cross Van Cleve's division at the lower ford (covered and supported by Mor-

MONUMENT TO THE DEAD OF HAZEN'S BRIGADE, ON THE POSITION HELD BY HIS BRIGADE IN THE ANGLE BETWEEN THE PIKE AND THE RAILROAD. FROM A PHOTOGRAPH TAKEN IN 1884.

ton's Pioneers, 1700 strong) and to advance on Breckinridge. Wood's division was to cross by brigades at the upper ford, and, moving on Van Cleve's right, was to carry everything before it to Murfreesboro'. This move was intended to dislodge Breckinridge, and to gain the high ground east of Stone's River, so that Wood's batteries could enfilade the heavy body of troops massed in front of Negley and Palmer. The center and left, using Negley's right as a pivot, were to swing round through Murfreesboro' and take the force confronting McCook in rear, driving it into the country toward Salem. The successful execution of General Rosecrans's design depended not more upon the spirit and gallantry of the assaulting column than upon the courage and obstinacy with which the position held by the right wing should be maintained. Having explained this fact to General McCook, the commanding general asked him if, with a full knowledge of the ground, he could, if attacked, hold his position three hours,—again alluding to his dissatisfaction with the direction which his line had assumed, but, as before, leaving that to the corps commander,—to which McCook replied, " I think I can."

Swift witnesses had borne to the ears of General Bragg the movements of General Rosecrans. He had in his army about the same proportion of raw troops to veterans as General Rosecrans, and the armies were equally well armed. By a singular coincidence Bragg had formed a plan identical with that of his antagonist. If both could have been carried out simultaneously the spectacle would have been presented of two large armies turning upon an axis from left to right. Lieutenant-General Hardee was put in command of the Confederate left wing, consisting of McCown's and Cleburne's divisions, and received orders to attack at daylight. Hardee's attack was to be taken up by Polk with the divisions of Cheatham and Withers, in succession to the right flank, the move to be made by a constant wheel to the right, on Polk's right flank as a pivot. The

BRIGADIER-GENERAL EDWARD N. KIRK, KILLED AT
STONE'S RIVER. FROM A PHOTOGRAPH.

object of General Bragg was by an early and impetuous attack to force the Union army back upon Stone's River, and, if practicable, by the aid of the cavalry, cut it off from its base of operations and supplies by the Nashville pike.

As has been shown, the Union and Confederate lines were much nearer together on the Union right than on the left. In point of fact the distance to be marched by Van Cleve to strike Breckinridge on Bragg's right, crossing Stone's River by the lower ford, was a mile and a half. To carry out the order of General Bragg to charge upon Rosecrans's right, the Confederate left wing, doubled, with McCown in the first line and Cleburne in support, had only to follow at double-quick the advance of the skirmish line a few hundred paces, to find themselves in close conflict with McCook.

The Confederate movement began at daybreak. General Hardee moved his two divisions with the precision that characterized that able commander. McCown, deflecting to the west, as he advanced to the attack, left an opening between his right and Withers's left, into which Cleburne's division fell, and together the two divisions charged upon R. W. Johnson and Davis, while yet the men of those divisions were preparing breakfast. There was no surprise. The first movement in their front was observed by the Union skirmish line, but that first movement was a rush as of a tornado. The skirmishers fell back steadily, fighting, upon the main line, but the main line was overborne by the fury of the assault. Far to the right, overlapping R. W. Johnson, the Confederate line came sweeping on like the resistless tide, driving artillerists from their guns and infantry from their encampments. Slowly the extreme right fell back, at first contesting every inch of ground. In Kirk's brigade 500 men were killed or wounded in a few minutes. Willich lost nearly as many. Goodspeed's battery, on Willich's right, lost three guns. The swing of Bragg's left flank toward the right brought McCown's brigades upon the right of Davis's division. Leaving the detachments in R. W. Johnson's division to the attention of two of his brigades and Wheeler's cavalry, McCown turned McNair to the right, where Cleburne was already heavily engaged. Driving Davis's skirmishers before him, Cleburne advanced with difficulty in line of battle, bearing to the right over rough ground cut up with numerous fences and thickets, and came upon the main line at a distance of three-fourths of a mile from his place of bivouac. It was not yet daylight when he began his march, and he struck the Union line at 6 o'clock. General Davis now changed

the front of Colonel Post's brigade nearly perpendicular to the rear. Pinney's battery was moved to the right, and the 59th Illinois assigned to its support. One-fourth of a mile to the right of Post, Baldwin's brigade, with Simonson's battery on its right, took position behind a fence on the margin of a wood. Carlin's, Woodruff's, and Sill's brigades were on the main battle line. Against this force, about seven thousand strong without works of any kind, Hardee hurled the seven brigades commanded by Manigault, Loomis, Polk, Bushrod Johnson, Wood, Liddell, and McNair — 10,000 men. The engagement which followed (being the second distinct stage of the battle on the right) was one of the fiercest of the day. Baldwin was the first to give way. After half an

BRIGADIER-GENERAL JOSHUA W. SILL, KILLED AT STONE'S RIVER. FROM A STEEL ENGRAVING.

hour's spirited resistance, finding the left of McCown's division, in pursuit of the remnants of Willich's and Kirk's brigades, advancing far beyond his right, Baldwin withdrew to the edge of the woods in rear of the front line, and tried to make a stand, but was driven back. The salient angle formed by the junction of Post's brigade with Carlin's, which at this time formed the right of the extreme Union line of battle, was in the meantime fiercely assailed. In front of Post, the Confederates under McCown, in command of McNair's brigade of his own division, and Liddell of Cleburne's division, received a decided repulse; and Cleburne was for a time equally unsuccessful in pushing back the main Union line.

Three successive assaults were made upon this position. In the second, Vaughan's and Maney's brigades of Cheatham's division relieved Loomis's and Manigault's. In the third attack Post's brigade was enveloped by Hardee's left, which, sweeping toward his rear, made withdrawal a necessity. Sill had been killed in the first assault. Schaefer's Union brigade was brought forward to the support of the front line. The dying order from General Sill to charge was gallantly obeyed, and Loomis was driven back to his first position. Manigault advanced at about 8 o'clock and attacked directly in

GENERAL ROSECRANS'S HEADQUARTERS AT STONE'S RIVER. FROM A PHOTOGRAPH TAKEN IN 1884.

his front, but, meeting with the same reception, was compelled to retire. A second attack resulted like the first. Maney's brigade now came up and advanced in line with Manigault's

BRIDGE OVER OVERALL'S CREEK. FROM A PHOTOGRAPH TAKEN IN 1884.

supported by Vaughan's. Turner's Confederate battery took position near the brick-kiln [see map, p. 616], and opened fire, under cover of which Manigault made an unsuccessful dash upon Houghtaling's Union battery. Colonel Roberts was killed, and Colonel Bradley, of the 51st Illinois, succeeded to the command of the brigade. Having completed the formation of his line, Hardee gave the order for a general advance, and that portion of the right wing, which up to this time had resisted every assault made upon it, retreated in perfect order toward the left and rear, with empty cartridge-boxes but with courage undaunted. Schaefer's brigade, being entirely out of ammunition, obeyed Sheridan's order to fix bayonets and await the charge. Roberts's brigade, having a few cartridges left, fell back, resisting the enemy. With the country to the right and rear overrun by McCown's infantry and

Wheeler's cavalry in pursuit of R. W. Johnson's routed division, one-half of which were either killed, wounded, or captured, and with a strong, determined enemy pressing them upon front and flank, Davis and Sheridan now found themselves menaced by another powerful auxiliary to defeat. Their ammunition was nearly exhausted, and there was none nearer than the Nashville-Murfreesboro' pike in the rear of Crittenden. On the other hand, McCown, in his report, refers to the necessity of replenishing his ammunition at this juncture, Liddell's brigade having exhausted forty rounds per man.

Carlin's brigade retired and re-formed on the Murfreesboro' pike. Woodruff held out some time longer, but finally followed Carlin toward the left, taking all the artillery with him, with the exception of one gun from Pinney's battery. Captain Pinney, dangerously wounded, was left upon the field. The withdrawal of the artillery was a matter of greater difficulty. Nearly all the horses having been killed, the attempt was made to withdraw the pieces by the use of prolonges. Lieutenant Taliaferro, commanding a section of Hescock's battery, was killed, and his sergeant brought off his two guns by hand. The ground, however, was too rough, and the road to safety too long, and in consequence the six guns of Houghtaling's battery were abandoned. Dragging the remaining pieces of artillery with them, Sheridan's division at 11 o'clock emerged from the cedars on Palmer's right, passing Rousseau on his way to the front. Cheatham's Confederates advanced in line of battle over the ground vacated by the Union right wing, and came up with Stewart's brigade hotly engaged with Negley, while Cleburne and McCown, sweeping toward the Nashville pike, driving hundreds of fugitives before them, encountered a new line improvised by Rosecrans to meet the emergency.

Thus far the plan of battle formed by Bragg had been carried out in strict conformity with its requirements. It now remained for Withers and Cheatham to drive the Union center back on the Union left. The retirement of Sheridan's division precipitated the entire command of Cheatham and a portion of Withers's upon Negley's two brigades and two brigades of Rousseau, on the left of the Wilkinson pike, taking them in front, left flank, and rear. The roar of artillery and the sharp rattle of musketry had aroused these brigades early, and they had stood in line, for hours, in momentary expectation of an attack upon their front. This, it is possible, would have been repulsed; but when it came in such a questionable shape, preceded by a cloud of retreating troops, but one course appeared to present itself to the commander, and that was to fall back. Nevertheless, he faced Colonel T. R. Stanley's brigade to the right, and ordered Colonel John F. Miller to hold his position to the last extremity. Miller arranged his brigade in convex order, with Schultz's battery on his right and Ellsworth's battery on his left. Simultaneously with Cheatham's advance upon his right, Stewart's and Anderson's brigades attacked Miller in front. Miller's lines were barely formed when a heavy musketry and artillery fire opened upon his men, who met the charge with a well-directed fire. On his right was Stanley, and the rapid discharge of Schultz's and Ellsworth's guns told with terrible precision upon the ranks of the advancing Confederates who soon halted, but did not abate their

GENERAL SAMUEL BEATTY'S BRIGADE (VAN CLEVE'S DIVISION) ADVANCING TO SUSTAIN THE UNION RIGHT
NEAR THE NASHVILLE PIKE (SEE MAP, P. 616). FROM A LITHOGRAPH.

fire. The 29th and 30th Mississippi, of Anderson's brigade, made a dash upon
Schultz's battery, but were hurled back behind the friendly cover of a stone
wall, where Stewart passed them in his charge upon Miller. A bayonet
charge was met by the 21st Ohio, and repulsed with great gallantry. The
fighting at this point was terrific. All along the front the dead and wounded
lay in heaps, and over their bodies came the assaulting host, seemingly
strong and brave as when the first charge was made in the morning. But
the inevitable result of a successful flank movement, by which the ammunition trains had been captured, came to Negley's strong fighting brigades as
it had come to those of Sheridan and Davis. Ammunition was nearly
exhausted, and it could only be replenished in rear of Crittenden, whose
lines still stood intact. Negley ordered Stanley to retire, which he did in
perfect order; and Miller's brigade, after holding its position until the
ammunition on the persons of the killed and wounded was all used, slowly
fell back to re-form in Palmer's rear.

Rosecrans, having arranged his plan of battle, had risen early to superintend its execution. Crittenden, whose headquarters were a few paces
distant, mounted at 6 A. M., and with his staff rode to an eminence, where
Rosecrans, surrounded by his staff-officers, was listening to the opening guns
on the right. The plan of Bragg was instantly divined, but no apprehension of danger was felt. Suddenly the woods on the right in the rear of
Negley appeared to be alive with men wandering aimlessly in the direction
of the rear. The roar of artillery grew more distinct, mingled with the con-

tinuous volleys of musketry. The rear of a line of battle always presents the pitiable spectacle of a horde of skulkers, men who, when tried in the fierce flame of battle, find, often to their own disgust, that they are lacking in the element of courage. But the spectacle of whole regiments of soldiers flying in panic to the rear was a sight never seen by the Army of the Cumberland except on that occasion. Captain Otis, from his position on the extreme right, dispatched a messenger, who arrived breathless, to inform General Rosecrans that the right wing was in rapid retreat. The astounding intelligence was confirmed a moment later by a staff-officer from McCook, calling for reënforcements. "Tell General McCook," said Rosecrans, "to contest every inch of ground. If he holds them we will swing into Murfreesboro' and cut them off." Then Rousseau with his reserves was sent into the fight, and Van Cleve, who, in the execution of the initial movement on the left, had crossed Stone's River at 6 A. M. at the lower ford, and was marching in close column up the hill beyond the river (preparatory to forming a line of battle for a movement to the right, where Wood was to join him in an assault upon Breckinridge), was arrested by an order to return and take position on the turnpike facing toward the woods on the right. A few moments later this gallant division came dashing across the fields, with water dripping from their clothing, to take a hand in the fray. Harker's brigade was withdrawn from the left and sent in on Rousseau's right, and Morton's Pioneers, relieved at the ford by Price's brigade, were posted on Harker's right. The remaining brigades of Van Cleve's division (Beatty's and Fyffe's) formed on the extreme right, and thus an improvised line half a mile in extent presented a new and unexpected front to the approaching enemy. It was a trying position to these men to stand in line while the panic-stricken soldiers of McCook's beaten regiments, flying in terror through the woods, rushed past them. The Union lines could not fire, for their comrades were between them and the enemy. Rosecrans seemed ubiquitous. All these dispositions had been made under his personal supervision. While riding rapidly to the front, Colonel Garesché, his chief-of-staff, was killed at his side by a cannon-ball. Finding Sheridan coming out of the cedars into which Rousseau had just entered, Rosecrans directed Sheridan to the ammunition train, with orders to fill his cartridge-boxes and march to the support of Hazen's brigade, now hotly engaged on the edge of the Round Forest. The left was now exposed to attack by Breckinridge, and riding rapidly to the ford, Rosecrans inquired who commanded the brigade. "I do, sir," said Colonel Price. "Will you hold this ford?" "I will try, sir." "Will you hold this ford?" "I will die right here." "Will you hold this ford?" for the third time thundered the general. "Yes, sir," said the colonel. "That will do"; and away galloped Rosecrans to Palmer, who was contending against long odds for the possession of the Round Forest.

At half-past 10 o'clock Rousseau's reserve division, shorn of one brigade, under command of Major-General Lovell H. Rousseau, was ordered into action on the right of General Negley. The two brigades commanded by Colonels John Beatty and B. F. Scribner, known as the 17th and 9th of the

SCENE OF THE FIGHTING OF PALMER'S AND ROUSSEAU'S DIVISIONS. FROM A LITHOGRAPH.

In the distance between the railroad on the left and the pike in the center was the first position of Hazen, of Palmer's division. On the right are the cedars in which Negley's division and the regulars of Rousseau's division were so roughly handled. In the foreground are seen the batteries of Loomis and Guenther.

old Army of the Ohio, were the same that only three months before had hurled back the strong fighting brigades of Hardee on the bloody slopes of Chaplin Hills or Perryville. The regular brigade, composed of five battalions of the 15th, 16th, 18th, and 19th United States Infantry, commanded by Colonel Oliver L. Shepherd, under perfect discipline, was placed on the extreme right. The line was formed in a dense cedar brake, through which Cleburne's and McCown's victorious columns were advancing, sweeping everything before them. On the left the roar of battle in Negley's front showed that all was not lost, and to his right Colonel John Beatty's brigade was formed. Scribner was held in reserve. The shock of battle fell heaviest upon the regulars; over one-third of the command fell either killed or wounded. Major Slemmer, of Fort Pickens fame, was wounded early. Steadily, as if on drill, the trained battalions fired by file, mowing down the advancing Confederate lines. Guenther's battery could not long check the fury of the charge that bore down upon the flanks and was fast enveloping the entire command.

Lieutenant-Colonel Kell, the commander of the 2d Ohio, was killed; Colonel Forman, the boy Colonel of the 15th Kentucky, and Major Carpenter, of the 19th Infantry, fell mortally wounded. There was no resource but to retreat upon support. At this moment Negley's division, with empty cartridge-boxes, fell back, and Rousseau, finding his flanks exposed, after a heroic fight of over two hours, fell back slowly and stubbornly to the open field, where his flanks could be more secure. Captain Morton, with the Pioneers and the Chicago Board of Trade battery, pushed into the cedars, and disappeared from view on their way to the front simultaneously with Harker. The general course of the tide of the stragglers toward the rear struck the Nashville turnpike at the point where Van Cleve stood impatiently awaiting the order to advance. All along the line men were falling, struck by the bullets of the enemy, who soon appeared at the edge of the woods on

Morton's flank. At the order to charge, given by General Rosecrans in person, Van Cleve's division sprang forward, reserving their fire for close quarters. It was the crisis in the battle. If this line should be broken all would be lost. Steadily the line moved forward, sending a shower of bullets to the front.

The brigades of Stanley and Miller having fallen back, as previously described, and the entire strength of Cheatham and three brigades of Withers and Cleburne having come upon Rousseau, the latter had fallen back into the open field, where he found Van Cleve. Loomis's and Guenther's batteries, double-shotted with canister, were posted on a ridge, and as the Confederate line advanced, opened upon it with terrific force. Men fell all along the line, but it moved straight ahead. The field was covered with dead and wounded men. The deep bass of the artillery was mingled with the higher notes of the minie-rifles, while in the brief pauses could be distinguished the quickly spoken orders of commanding officers and the groans of the wounded. It was the full orchestra of battle. But there is a limit to human endurance. The Confederate brigades, now melted to three-fourths their original numbers, wavered and fell back; again and again they re-formed in the woods and advanced to the charge, only to meet with a bloody repulse. All along the line from Harker's right to Wood's left, the space gradually narrowed between the contending hosts. The weak had gone to the rear; there was no room now for any but brave men, and no time given for new dispositions; every man who had a stomach for fighting was engaged on the front line. From a right angle the Confederate left had been pressed back by Van Cleve and Harker and the Pioneers to an angle of 45 degrees. This advance brought Van Cleve within view of Rousseau, who at once requested him to form on his right.

General Harker, entering the woods on the left of Van Cleve, passed to his right, and now closed up on his flank. The enemy had fallen back, stubbornly fighting, and made a stand on the left of Cheatham. Brave old Van Cleve, his white hair streaming in the wind, the blood flowing from a wound in his foot, rode gallantly along the line to where Harker was stiffly holding his position, with his right "in the air." Bidding him hold fast to every inch of ground, he rode on to Swallow's battery, which was working with great rapidity. He then passed to the left, where General Samuel Beatty's brigade were firing with their minie-rifles at a line of men which seemed to be always on the point of advancing.

The advance of Bragg's left wing had brought it into a position at right angles with the original line. The entire strength of the center, and most of the left, was concentrated upon the angle formed by Rousseau and the right of Palmer's division. Chalmers's Confederate brigade, which up to 10 o'clock had lain concealed in the rifle-pits on the right of Withers's line, arose at the order, and, under a terrific fire, dashed forward across the open field upon Palmer's front. Finding that the time had come for a decisive blow, General Bragg now directed General Breckinridge to send two brigades to the left to reënforce Polk. General Pegram, who, with his cavalry, was posted on the Lebanon pike in advance of Breckinridge's right, had observed Van Cleve's movement, and notified General Breckinridge that a heavy column of infantry and artillery had crossed Stone's River and was advancing along the river bank upon the position occupied by Hanson's brigade. Interpreting this as the initial movement in a plan which was intended to strike his division, Breckinridge declined to obey Bragg's order, which in his report he terms a "suggestion." At ten minutes after ten he replied, "The enemy is undoubtedly advancing upon me." Soon after he wrote Bragg, "The Lebanon road is unprotected, and I have no troops to fill out my line to it." At half-past eleven, upon Bragg ordering him to move forward and attack the Union left, Breckinridge replied, "I am obeying your order, but my left is now engaged with the enemy, and if I advance my whole line farther forward, and still retain communication with my left, it will take me clear away from the Lebanon road, and expose my right and that road to a heavy force of the enemy advancing from Black's." The withdrawal of Van Cleve appears to have passed unnoticed by Breckinridge, and was undiscovered until too late to accomplish any good by complying with Bragg's order. Thus, by simply thrusting forward the left flank of his army and at once withdrawing it, General Rosecrans had held four Confederate brigades inactive at a time when their presence in support of Chalmers might have administered the *coup de grace* to the center of the Union line.

The movement of Crittenden's left and center divisions upon Bragg's right wing having been arrested, Wood's division was in position to cross at the upper ford. Wagner's brigade was at the river bank. Hascall was in reserve some distance to the rear of the opening between Wagner's right and Hazen's left. The withdrawal of Negley from Palmer's right precipitated the attack of Donelson's and Chalmers's brigades against the right and Adams and Jackson against the left. Chalmers's attack was made with great fury. His men had been confined, without fires, in their rifle-pits for forty-eight hours, and when finally the order came at 10 o'clock to "up and at 'em," they came forward like a pack of hounds in full cry. Cruft recoiled from the attack in the open field between the Round Forest and the wood in which Negley was engaged, and, falling back, met the charge at the time that Negley moved to the rear. Now Cruft's right was in the air and exposed to attack by Donelson following Negley. Cruft repulsed Chalmers in his front, but Donelson's brigade, pouring to his rear, threatened to envelop him. Grose, from his position in reserve, faced to the right, and soon after to the rear, and bore back the charging columns, enabling Cruft to withdraw.

When Chalmers's assault first fell upon Palmer's right, Hazen faced his two right regiments, the 6th Kentucky and 9th Indiana, to the rear, where the impetus of Chalmers's assault upon Cruft had borne him, at the same time retiring the two left regiments, the 41st Ohio and 110th Illinois, some fifty yards to the left of the pike and engaged to the front, the 40th Indiana having fallen back. A burnt brick house [Cowan's] in the immediate front of the Round Forest afforded cover for the enemy, and in the steady, persistent effort to force back the front of Hazen's line the action became terrific. All of Hascall's brigade, and two regiments of Wagner's, being engaged on the right of the 6th Kentucky, and Wagner's remaining regiments being in position at the ford some distance to the left, the assault on the left was borne by Hazen, whose brigade was thought by Polk to be the extreme left of the Union line. Upon this point, as on a pivot, the entire army oscillated from front to rear for hours. Hazen's horse fell shot square in the forehead. Word came that the ammunition of the 41st Ohio was nearly exhausted. "Fix bayonets and hold your ground!" was the order. To the 110th Illinois, who had no bayonets, and whose cartridges were expended, the order was given to club their muskets, but to hold the ground. The 9th Indiana now dashed across the line of fire, from a battery in front, to the left, to relieve the 41st Ohio. Cannon-balls tore through their ranks, but they were rapidly closed up, and the men took their place in the front line, the 41st retiring with thinned ranks, but in excellent order, to refill their empty cartridge-boxes. An ominous silence succeeded, soon followed by the charge of Donelson's fresh Confederate brigade and the remains of Chalmers's. The time had been occupied in the readjustment of Palmer's line. The 24th Ohio, commanded by Colonel Fred. Jones, and the 36th Indiana, shorn of half its strength in the previous assault, were sent to Hazen's support. Parsons's battery was posted on the left. The 3d Kentucky, led by McKee, dashed forward and took position on the right of the 9th Indiana across the turnpike. The terrible slaughter in this regiment attests its courage.

While Hazen and Wagner were thus gallantly defending the left of the line from 9 o'clock in the morning until 2 in the afternoon, the fight raged not less furiously on their immediate right. Here a line was formed, composed of two brigades of Palmer's division and Hascall of Wood's, filled out by the remains of Sheridan's and Negley's divisions, who, after they had replenished their ammunition, formed behind the railroad embankment at right angles with Hazen's brigade, which alone retained its position upon the original line. Farther to the right was Rousseau, with Van Cleve, Harker, and Morton on his right. At this supreme moment the chances of victory were evenly balanced. The undaunted soldiers of the left and center had swept past the crowd of fugitives from the right wing, and now in strong array they stood like a rock-bound coast beating back the tide which threatened to engulf the rear.

Along this line rode Rosecrans; Thomas, calm, inflexible, from whose gaze skulkers shrank abashed; Crittenden, cheerful and full of hope, complimenting his men as he rode along the lines; Rousseau, whose impetuosity no disaster could quell; Palmer, with a stock of cool courage and presence of mind equal to any emergency; Wood, suffering from a wound in his heel, staid in the saddle, but had lost that jocularity which usually characterized him. "Good-bye, General, we'll all meet at the hatter's, as one coon said to another when the dogs were after them," he had said to Crittenden early in the action. "Are we doing it about right now, General?" asked Morton, as he glanced along the blazing line of muskets to where the Chicago battery [Stokes's] was hard at work. "All right, fire low," said Rosecrans as he dashed by. Colonel Grose, always in his place, had command of the Ammen brigade, of Shiloh memory, which, with Hazen's and Cruft's brigades, had driven the right of Beauregard's victorious army off that field. After the formation of this line at noon it never receded; the right swung around until, at 2 o'clock, considerable of the lost ground had been retaken. The artillery, more than fifty guns, was massed in the open ground behind the angle in the line (twenty-eight Union guns had been captured), where they poured iron missiles continuously upon the Confederate line. They could not fire amiss. The fire from Cox's battery was directed upon Hanson's brigade across the river, whence Cobb, with his Napoleons, returned the compliment with zeal and precision. Schaefer's brigade, having received a new stock of cartridges, formed on Palmer's right, where later its commander received his death wound, the last of Sheridan's brigade commanders to fall during the day. At 4 o'clock it became evident to the Confederate commander that his only hope of success lay in a charge upon the Union left, which, by its overpowering weight, should carry everything before it. The movement of Cleburne to the left in support of McCown had deprived him of reserves; but Breckinridge had two brigades unemployed on the right, and these were peremptorily ordered across the river to the support of General Polk.

The charge of Adams and Jackson, and the subsequent attack of Preston's and Palmer's brigades, have been described. The error made by General Polk in making an attack with the two brigades that first arrived upon the field, instead of waiting the arrival of General Breckinridge with the remaining brigades, was so palpable as to render an excuse for failure necessary. This was easily found in the tardy execution of Bragg's order by Breckinridge, and resulted in sharp criticism of the latter. The Union 3d Kentucky, now nearly annihilated, was relieved by the 58th Indiana, Colonel George P. Buell. The 6th Ohio, Colonel Nicholas L. Anderson at its head, took position on the right of the 26th Ohio, with its right advanced so that its line of fire would sweep the front of the regiments on its left. The 97th Ohio and 100th Illinois came up and still further strengthened the position. They had not long to wait for the Confederate attack. These dispositions had hardly been made when a long line of infantry emerged from behind the hill. Adams's and Jackson's brigades were on the right, and Donelson's and Chalmers's, badly cut up but stout of heart, were on the left. On they came in splendid style, full six thousand strong. Estep's case-shot tore through their ranks, but the gaps closed up. Parsons sent volley after volley of grape-shot against them, and the 6th and the 26th Ohio, taking up the refrain, added the sharp rattle of minie-rifles to the unearthly din. Still the line pressed forward, firing as they came, until met by a simultaneous and destructive volley of musketry. They staggered, but quickly re-formed and, reënforced by Preston and the Confederate Palmer, advanced again to the charge. The battle had hushed on the extreme right, and the gallantry of this advance is indescribable. The right was even with the left of the Union line, and the left stretched far past the point of woods from which Negley had retired. It was such a charge as this that at Shiloh broke the strong lines of W. H. L. Wallace and Hurlbut, and enveloped Prentiss. The Confederates had no sooner moved into the open field from the cover of the river bank than they were received with a blast from the artillery. Men plucked the cotton from the boles at their feet and stuffed it in their ears. Huge gaps were torn in the Confederate line at every discharge. The Confederate line staggered forward half the distance across the fields, when the Union infantry lines added minie-balls to the fury of the storm. Then the Confederates wavered and fell back, and the first day's fight was over.

New Year's was a day of fair weather. During the night Rosecrans retired his left to a more advantageous position, the extreme left resting on Stone's River at the lower ford, where Van Cleve had crossed on the previous morning, the line of battle extending to Stokes's battery, posted on a knoll on Rosecrans's right. Walker's and Starkweather's brigades having come up, the former bivouacked in close column in reserve in rear of McCook's left, and the latter, posted on Sheridan's left, next morning relieved Van Cleve's division, now commanded by Colonel Samuel Beatty, which crossed the river and took position on the margin of a woodland that covered a gentle slope extending from the river to an open field in its front.

Across this field the Lebanon road, running nearly at right angles with Beatty's line, was nearly in sight. In his front and right, an elevation still held by Hanson's brigade of Breckinridge's division was crowned by Cobb's battery of artillery. On the left and rear, Grose's brigade of Palmer's division occupied a knoll in support of Livingston's battery on the following day.

The Confederate line, formed by Polk and Breckinridge on the right and Hardee on the left, extended from the point on Stone's River where

POSITION OF STARKWEATHER'S AND SCRIBNER'S BRIGADES ON JANUARY 1, 2, AND 3. FROM A LITHOGRAPH.

Chalmers's brigade had bivouacked since the 25th, in a direction almost at right angles with its original line.

At dawn on the 1st of January the right flank of General Polk was advanced to occupy the ground vacated by the Union army on the west bank of the river. Neither commander deemed it advisable to attack, but each was watchful of every movement of the other. The picket lines on either side were thrust forward within sight of the main lines of the opposing force, on the alert to notify their commanders of any movement in their front. Weaker in numbers, but more compact, and decidedly stronger in morale, each awaited the order to advance and close in a final struggle.

General Bragg confidently expected to find the Union troops gone from his front on the morning of the 2d. His cavalry had reported the turnpike full of troops and wagons moving toward Nashville, but the force east of Stone's River soon attracted his attention. Reconnoissance by staff-officers revealed Beatty's line, enfilading Polk in his new position. It was evident that Polk must be withdrawn or Beatty dislodged. Bragg chose the latter alternative, and Breckinridge, against his earnest protest, was directed to concentrate his division and assault Beatty. Ten Napoleon guns were added to his command, and the cavalry was ordered to cover his right. The line was formed by placing Hanson's brigade of Kentuckians, who had thus far borne no part in the engagement, on the extreme left, supported by Adams's brigade, now commanded by Colonel Gibson. The Confederate Palmer's brigade, commanded by General Pillow, took the right of the line, with Preston in reserve. The artillery was ordered to follow the attack and go into position on the summit of the slope when Beatty should be driven from it. The total strength of the assaulting column was estimated by Bragg at six thousand men. His cavalry took no part in the action.

In the assault that followed a brief cannonade, Hanson's left was thrown forward close to the river bank, with orders to fire once, then charge with the bayonet. On the right of Beatty was Colonel S. W. Price's brigade, and the charge made by Hanson's 6th Kentucky was met by Price's 8th Kentucky regiment, followed by Hanson and Pillow in successive strokes from right to left of Beatty's line. Overborne by numerical strength, the Union brigades of Price and Fyffe were forced back upon Grider, in reserve, the right of whose brigade was rapidly being turned by Hanson, threatening to cut the division off from the river. Beatty ordered retreat, and assailants and assailed moved in a mass toward the river. The space between the river bank and the ridge occupied by Grose now presented a scene of the wildest confusion. The pursuit led the Confederate column to the right of Grose, and Lieutenant Livingston opened upon it with his artillery, but he was quickly ordered across the river. Crittenden, turning to his chief-of-artillery, said, "Mendenhall, you must cover my men with your guns." Never was there a more effective response to such a request; the batteries of Swallow, Parsons, Estep, Stokes, Stevens, Standart, Bradley, and Livingston dashed forward, wheeled into position, and opened fire. In all, fifty-eight pieces of artillery played upon the enemy. Not less than one hundred shots per minute were fired. As the mass of men

POSITION OF MENDENHALL'S FIFTY-EIGHT GUNS (AS SEEN FROM THE EAST BANK ABOVE THE FORD) WHICH REPELLED THE CHARGE OF BRECKINRIDGE, JANUARY 2, 1863. FROM A PHOTOGRAPH TAKEN IN 1884.

swarmed down the slope they were mowed down by the score. Confederates were pinioned to the earth by falling branches. For a few minutes the brave fellows held their ground, hoping to advance, but the west bank bristled with bayonets.

Hanson was mortally wounded, and his brigade lost over 400 men; the loss in the division was 1410. There was no thought now of attacking Grose, but one general impulse to get out of the jaws of death. The Union infantry was soon ordered to charge. Colonel John F. Miller with his brigade and two regiments of Stanley's was the first to cross the river, on the extreme left. He was quickly followed on the right by Davis and Morton and by Hazen in the center. Beatty quickly re-formed his division and recrossed the river and joined in the pursuit. The artillery ceased firing, and the Union line with loud cheers dashed forward, firing volley after volley upon the fugitives, who rallied behind Robertson's battery and Anderson's brigade in the narrow skirt of timber from which they had emerged to the assault. The Union line advanced and took possession of the ground from which Beatty had been driven an hour before, and both armies bivouacked upon the battlefield. General Spears, with a brigade guarding a much-needed supply train, came up and took position on the right, relieving Rousseau on the following morning.

General Bragg had been promptly notified by General Joseph Wheeler of the arrival of this reënforcement to his antagonist, and says in his report:

ADVANCE OF COLONEL M. B. WALKER'S UNION BRIGADE, AT STONE'S RIVER, ON THE EVENING OF
JANUARY 2, 1863.   FROM A LITHOGRAPH.

Walker's position is in the cedars near the right of Rousseau's line (see map, page 616).   In the right of the picture
is seen the 4th Michigan Battery.   The front line was composed of the 31st and 17th
Ohio, and the second line of the 82d Indiana and 38th Ohio.

" Common prudence and the safety of my army, upon which even the safety of our cause depended, left no doubt on my mind as to the necessity of my withdrawal from so unequal a contest."

Bragg acknowledged a loss of over 10,000 men, over 9000 of whom were
killed or wounded,— nearly 25 per cent. of the total force engaged.   The
loss in the Union army was, in killed, 1533; wounded, 7245 = 8778; and in
prisoners, McCook, 2092; Thomas, 576; Crittenden, 821,— total, 3489.   Appre-
hending the possible success of a flank movement against his left, General
Bragg had caused all the tents and baggage to be loaded on wagons and
sent to the rear.   On the night of the 3d he began his retreat and continued
it south of Elk River, whence he was ordered back to Tullahoma by General
Johnston.

THE UNION LEFT AT STONE'S RIVER.

BY THOMAS L. CRITTENDEN, MAJOR-GENERAL, U. S. V.

THE battle of Stone's River, Tennessee, on the
31st of December, 1862, and the 2d of January, 1863, was one of the most fiercely contested
and bloody conflicts of the war.   The two armies
that met in this conflict were made up of soldiers
who, for the most part, had been disciplined by
capable instructors and hardened by service in
the field, both having made many long marches,
and neither having been strangers to the perils of
the battle-field.   Moreover, these armies were ably
commanded by graduates of the Military Academy
at West Point — a military school, I think, not surpassed, if equaled, anywhere else.   The duration
of the battle, and the long list of the killed and
wounded, show the stuff of which the two armies
were composed.   I do not think that two better

armies, as numerous and so nearly matched in
strength, ever met in battle.

I had the good fortune to command the left wing
of our army, and, thanks to the skill and bravery of
the officers and men of my command, the enemy
were not able to drive them from our first line of
battle.   On the 31st of December my extreme left
was strongly posted, but my right was in an open
field back from the stream.   Still it was a fairly
strong position by reason of the railroad and the
railroad cut and the woods.   Thomas's position in
the center was not so strong as mine ; of McCook's,
on our right, I knew nothing; that it was less strong
than ours, I presume from the fact that in spite of
the most stubborn resistance McCook was driven
back two miles or more, the whole right of the

army hinging on its center, while the left held its ground. Thomas, with Rousseau's division, including a brigade of regulars (Lieutenant-Colonel O. L. Shepherd's), undertook to support McCook, but they were all driven along. Every time the right was driven in I thought (and I now think) that nothing but a most extraordinary blunder on the part of a soldier of the experience of Bragg hindered him from breaking Rosecrans's army in two and leaving me standing with my troops looking at Murfreesboro'. It is a pretty well-established maxim in military tactics that you should always press your advantage. Bragg had the advantage; all that he had to do (it seems to me) was to pursue it, and leave me alone with my success. Instead of that, he attempted to drive the left; but he could not drive us; and meanwhile our right was reorganized. I did not know on the 31st when they would come right upon our rear. I was facing Murfreesboro'. My right division under Palmer changed its place somewhat, to conform to our movements on the right, but that line was maintained by stubborn fighting. Thomas was then not far back, and that helped me more. (McCook was too far away for any protection to my flank.) Rousseau's men were driven out of the woods, a regular dense thicket, and Shepherd's regulars suffered fearfully in there. They moved in by the head of column. There was no fighting of consequence on the 1st of January.

The last attack made by the enemy was upon my extreme left, on the 2d of January, and it was disastrous to them. Van Cleve's division, under Colonel Samuel Beatty, had crossed the river on the 1st, and Grose and Hazen had followed with their brigades on the 2d. The fight opened on Colonel Beatty's line and lasted about twenty minutes. Before this battle I had been inclined to underrate the importance of artillery in our war, but I never knew that arm to render such important service as at this point. The sound judgment, bravery, and skill of Major John Mendenhall, who was my chief-of-artillery, enabled me to open 58 guns almost simultaneously on Breckinridge's men and to turn a dashing charge into a sudden retreat and rout, in which the enemy lost 1700 or 1800 men in a few moments. I witnessed the effect of this cannonade upon the Confederate advance. Mendenhall's guns were about 100 yards back from the river. Van Cleve's division of my command was retiring down the opposite slope, before overwhelming numbers of the enemy, when the guns, the fire of which had been held till our men should no longer be exposed to it, opened upon the swarming enemy. The very forest seemed to fall before our fire, and not a Confederate reached the river. ⌡

⌡ General Breckinridge says in his report:

"It now appeared that the ground we had won was commanded by the enemy's batteries, within easy range, on better ground, upon the other side of the river. I do not know how many guns he had. He had enough to sweep the whole position from the front, the left, and the right, and to render it wholly untenable by our force present of artillery and infantry."   EDITORS.

⚓ The fact being that the enemy were repulsed and flying in confusion before the terrific guns of my chief-

Mendenhall did not receive adequate recognition in the report of General Rosecrans. ⚓

As to our general's plan of battle, I don't remember that I was ever advised of it. The battle was fought according to the plan of General Bragg. Indeed, our uniform experience was — at Perryville, at Stone's River, at Chickamauga — that whenever we went to attack Bragg we were attacked by him, and so our plan had to be extemporized. I knew Bragg. His reputation was that of a martinet. He was a severe disciplinarian, a good soldier, and a hard fighter.

During the fight I had the experience of eating a horse-steak, the only one I ever tasted; it was simply because although we had supplies there we couldn't get at them. I had to go to sleep without my wagon, and as I said something about being hungry, one of the men said: "General, I will get you a first-rate beefsteak." Next morning I found that the steak had been cut from a horse that had been killed. I didn't know this at the time I ate it.

On the night of the 31st a wagon-train arrived from Nashville escorted by a thousand men, and these men, I learned, were sent back. I won't say whom they were under, but I know I felt and thought it was unwise that a thousand men who hadn't been in the fight at all should be sent away. All the wagons in the world wouldn't have made me send back a thousand fresh men. They could have staid there and eaten horse for a while until they had won the fight.

I regard Rosecrans as of the first order of military mind. He was both brave and generous, impulsively so; in fact, in his impulsiveness lay a military defect, which was to issue too many orders while his men were fighting. When I met him on the field on the 31st I saw the stains of blood on his breast, and exclaimed: "Are you wounded, General?" "Oh, no," said he, "that is the blood of poor Garesché, who has just been killed." ⌡

After the fight on the night of the 31st a number of general officers were assembled by Rosecrans's order, including McCook, Thomas, Stanley, and myself. There was some talk of falling back. I do not remember who started the subject, but I do remember that I expressed the opinion that my men would be very much discouraged to have to abandon the field after their good fight of the day, during which they had uniformly held their position. I spoke of the proposition as resembling the suggestion of General Wool to General Taylor at Buena Vista, when Taylor responded: "My wounded are behind me, and I will never pass them alive." Rosecrans called McCook to accompany him on a ride,

of-artillery, Major John Mendenhall, and were only pursued by Negley and Morton, as they were also pursued by portions of my command under Cruft, Hazen, Grose, and a part of General Jefferson C. Davis's command.— T. L. C.

⌡ Lieutenant-Colonel Julius P. Garesché, assistant adjutant-general, U S. A., and since November 13th chief-of-staff of the Army of the Cumberland, was killed on the afternoon of the 31st of December, by a shell which carried off his head after narrowly missing General Rosecrans.— EDITORS.

BRIGADIER-GENERAL JOHN H. MORGAN, C. S. A.
FROM A PHOTOGRAPH.

directing us to remain until their return. McCook has since told me that the purpose of this ride was to find a position beyond Overall's Creek to which the army might retire. Upon approaching the creek Rosecrans, perceiving mounted men moving up and down with torches, said to McCook: "They have got entirely in our rear and are forming a line of battle by torchlight." They returned then to where we were, and Rosecrans told us to

go to our commands and prepare to fight or die. The explanation of the torches is that the men were making fires, and the torches were firing-brands being carried from one point to another by cavalrymen. I had received an order from General Rosecrans not to allow the men to make fires; but upon looking out of my quarters I discovered that the fires were already made from one end of my line to the other. I sent Rosecrans word that as the men were cold and were not being disturbed by the enemy, and as it would take all night to put out the fires, we had better leave them. The men would have suffered very much if they had staid there all night without fire.

The battle was fought for the possession of middle Tennessee. We went down to drive the Confederates out of Murfreesboro', and we drove them out. They went off a few miles and camped again. And we, although we were the victors, virtually went into hospital for six months before we could march after them again. Whether we would take Murfreesboro' or go back to Nashville was doubtful until the last moment. As in most of our battles, very meager fruits resulted to either side from such partial victories as were for the most part won. Yet it was a triumph. It showed that in the long run the big purse and the big battalions—both on our side—must win; and it proved that there were no better soldiers than ours.

The results of the battle were not what we had hoped, and yet there was a general feeling of elation. One day, after we had gone into Murfreesboro', I accompanied General Rosecrans in a ride about our camp. We had come across some regiment or brigade that was being drilled, and they raised a shout, and as he rode along he took off his cap and said: "All right, boys, all right; Bragg's a good dog, but Hold Fast's a better." This well expressed my feeling as to the kind of victory we had won.

MORGAN'S OHIO RAID.

IN the summer of 1863, the Confederate army at Tullahoma having been weakened by detachments for the defense of Vicksburg, Bragg found himself exposed to the risk of an attack by Rosecrans from Murfreesboro' simultaneously with a movement by Burnside from the Ohio to drive Buckner out of Knoxville. Bragg therefore determined to fall back to Chattanooga. To cover the retreat he ordered Brigadier-General John H. Morgan with a picked force from his division of mounted infantry [to ride into Kentucky, breaking up the railroad, attacking Rosecrans's detachments, and threatening Louisville. To gain more time, Morgan wanted to extend the raid by a wide sweep beyond the Ohio, but Bragg would not consent.

Morgan set out from Burkesville, on the 2d of July, with 2460 men and 4 guns, ostensibly to execute Bragg's orders, but really bent on carrying out his own plan. Although ten thousand Federal troops under Generals Hartsuff and Judah were watching the Cumberland at various points, Morgan skillfully effected the difficult crossing, overcame Judah's opposition, and rode north, followed by all the Federal detachments within reach.

On the 4th he attacked the 25th Michigan, Col. Orlando H. Moore, in a strong position guarding the bridge over Green River, and drew off with heavy loss. On the 5th he defeated and captured the garrison of Lebanon, and then marched, by Springfield and Bardstown, to Brandenburg, on the Ohio, where he arrived on the morning of the

[Brig.-Gen. B. W. Duke commanded the First Brigade, and Colonel Adam R. Johnson the Second.— EDITORS.

9th, and at once began crossing on two captured steamboats. The passage was disputed by a gun-boat, and by some home-guards with a field-piece on the Indiana shore, but by midnight the whole command was in Indiana. Twenty-four hours later General E. H. Hobson followed, leading the advance of Judah's forces in pursuit. But Indiana and Ohio were now in arms, and at every step their militia had to be eluded or overcome; to do either caused delay.

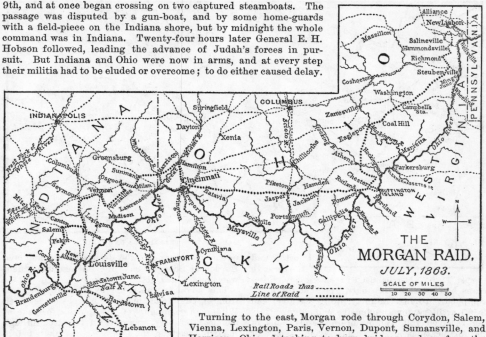

THE
MORGAN RAID,
JULY, 1863.
SCALE OF MILES
10 20 30 40 50

MAP OF MORGAN'S OHIO RAID.

Turning to the east, Morgan rode through Corydon, Salem, Vienna, Lexington, Paris, Vernon, Dupont, Sumansville, and Harrison, Ohio, detaching to burn bridges and confuse the pursuit, impressing fresh horses, his men pillaging freely. Under cover of a feint on Hamilton, Ohio, he marched by night unmolested through the suburbs of Cincinnati, and at last, after dark on the evening of July 18th, reached the bank of the Ohio, near Buffington Bar and Blennerhassett's Island, where from the first he had planned to escape. Morning found his pursuers closing in from all directions. Morgan, with about half his men, eluded the net. ⚓ All the rest were killed or captured. ↓ After nearly reaching the West Virginia shore Morgan himself returned, and with the remnant made for Pennsylvania, hotly pursued, and finally surrendered on the 26th of July, near Beaver Creek, with 364 officers and men. ♭

Later on he commanded in south-western Virginia. After another disastrous raid into Kentucky, he was killed at Greenville, Tennessee, on the 4th of September, 1864.— EDITORS.

⚓ Of these many were drowned, but about three hundred escaped across the river.

↓ About 120 were killed and wounded, and 700 captured.

♭ Morgan was confined in the State Penitentiary at Columbus, Ohio, until November 26th, when he made his escape by tunneling.

MANŒUVRING BRAGG OUT OF TENNESSEE.

BY GILBERT C. KNIFFIN, LIEUTENANT-COLONEL, U. S. V.

THE brief campaign which resulted in forcing the Confederate army to evacuate their works at Tullahoma and Shelbyville, Tenn., and retire behind the Tennessee River, began on the 23d of June, was prosecuted in the midst of drenching rains, and terminated July 4th, 1863. Both armies had occupied the time since the battle of Stone's River in recruiting their strength and in fortifying their respective positions. Murfreesboro' was Rosecrans's secondary base of supplies, while Tullahoma was Bragg's barrier against Rosecrans's farther advance toward Chattanooga, the stra-

tegic importance of which, as controlling Confederate railroad communication between the East and West, had rendered it the objective point of all the campaigns of the armies of the Ohio and the Cumberland.

As the contending armies stood facing each other on the 20th of June, 1863, General Bragg estimated the effective strength of his army at 30,449 infantry, 13,962 cavalry, and 2254 artillery. Polk and Hardee commanded his two corps of infantry, and Wheeler and Forrest the cavalry. Deducting the garrisons of Nashville and points

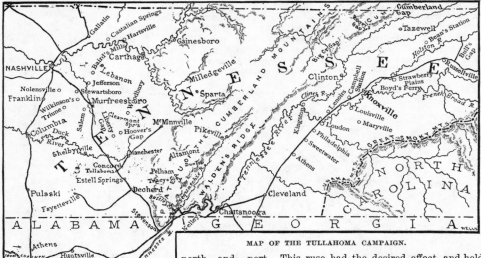

MAP OF THE TULLAHOMA CAMPAIGN.

north, and the Reserve Corps, 12,575, to be used in emergency, Rosecrans had at the same date "present for duty, equipped," 40,746 infantry, 6806 cavalry, and 3065 artillery, for an offensive campaign. Having received full and accurate descriptions of the fortifications at Tullahoma, where a part of Polk's corps was intrenched behind formidable breastworks, protected by an abatis of fallen trees six hundred yards in width, and at Shelbyville, where Hardee had fortified his position with equal engineering skill, General Rosecrans determined to force the Confederate army out of its works, and if possible engage it in the open field. A glance at the map will show Shelbyville directly south of Murfreesboro', and Tullahoma, on the line of the Nashville and Chattanooga railroad, eighteen miles south-east. The high state of cultivation of the country west of Shelbyville, and the connection of the towns by broad turnpike roads, would naturally suggest the route of march for the Union army; moreover, the region to the east of the railroad consisted of sterile uplands through which winding country roads offered continuous obstacles to the rapid advance of an army. Precisely for this reason Rosecrans chose the latter route for one of his corps, while the other two corps were directed against the center of the line at Tullahoma. Sending his supply trains out on the Shelbyville road, the cavalry under Stanley was ordered to Eagleville, twenty miles west, and a little south of Murfreesboro', with orders to advance on Shelbyville on the 24th of June in bold array, and at night to fill the country to their rear with camp-fires extending from Hardee's left to the Shelbyville road and beyond, indicating the presence of a heavy infantry force in his support. This ruse had the desired effect, and held Hardee at Shelbyville, while the real movement was against his right.

This advance was made by Hoover's Gap⌋ in front of Tullahoma, and to this end Colonel J. G. Wilder, in command of his splendid brigade of mounted infantry, was ordered to "trot through the gap," pushing the Confederate pickets before him, while Thomas was directed to follow as closely in his rear as possible. Wilder obeyed his orders literally, paying no attention to the frequent stands made by the retiring pickets, but driving them back upon their reserves, who in turn fell back upon Stewart's division, posted on the Garrison Fork of Elk River, which is about four miles south of Tullahoma. General Stewart sent Bushrod Johnson's brigade forward, and a brisk fight ensued. The head of Thomas's column was six miles in the rear, but Wilder's plucky regiments used their Spencer rifles to such good purpose as to hold their ground until Reynolds's division secured possession of the bridge, when Stewart, finding that the movement was really an advance in force, that the Gap he was posted to guard was lost, and that a heavy infantry column was crossing the bridge, fell back upon the main line.

Thomas was followed closely by McCook with the Twentieth Corps, Granger with the Reserve Corps holding the ground in front of Murfreesboro'. Meantime, Crittenden with the Twenty-first Corps, who had seventeen miles to march, over a road that seemingly had no bottom, was toiling through the mud between Woodbury and Manchester on his way to his position before Bragg's right flank and rear. Colonel John F. Miller with his brigade of Negley's division attacked Liberty Gap, and fell in a fierce fight there, badly wounded; but the

⌋ A range of hills dividing the waters of Duck River from the head-waters of Stone's River, about eleven miles from Murfreesboro' and running nearly east and west, is pierced by several gaps. Hoover's Gap, nearly north from Wartrace, Liberty, and Guy's Gaps, and

the Railroad Gap were all guarded by heavy pickets. Cleburne's division was stationed at Wartrace, and Stewart's division held possession of Hoover's Gap and the bridge over the Garrison fork of Duck River five or six miles north of Tullahoma.— EDITORS.

Gap was held by the brigade until relieved by the Twentieth Corps, which then passed Thomas and took the lead on the Manchester road, both corps camping within two miles of Tullahoma. In front of Stanley, Guy's Gap, held by a battery supported by cavalry, was charged, driving the Confederates toward Shelbyville, near which town they made a stand; but Colonel Minty attacked them on the left with the 4th Regular Cavalry of his brigade, sabering the gunners and pursuing the remainder through the town.

Bragg had ordered Hardee to the support of Polk's threatened left flank, leaving Shelbyville with its elaborately planned fortifications to fall before a cavalry charge after a brief struggle by the rear-guard.

The unforeseen inclemency of the weather retarded Crittenden's advance to such an extent that, notwithstanding the continued exertions of both officers and men, he was four days in marching seventeen miles. Horses and mules, floundering in the mud, were unhitched, and artillery and ammunition wagons dragged through deep morasses by the infantry. In some places mules perished in the mud, unable to extricate themselves. But

for the heavy rains Crittenden would have joined McCook and Thomas two days earlier, and the campaign might have had a different ending. When he came up, line of battle was formed fronting the works at Tullahoma, to mask a flank movement through the woods to Elk River Bridge, four miles in rear of Bragg's position. Between the lines the treacherous soil was filled with quicksand, which only needed the soaking of the week's rain to render it impassable. To advance against the Confederate works over this ground, through a dense abatis of tangled tree-tops, in the face of a storm of grape-shot and minie-balls, would have been to doom one-half the army to destruction. Finding, when too late, that the advance against Hardee was only a feint to cover the real movement upon his left and rear, and alive to the paramount importance of protecting Chattanooga, General Bragg again faced his army southward, and crossed the Tennessee River at Bridgeport, the mouth of Battle Creek, and at Kelley's Ferry. The advance of the column against Elk River Bridge arrived in time to witness the crossing of the rear of Bragg's army, and on the afternoon of the 3d of July Sheridan's division occupied Tullahoma. ☽

☽ The Union loss aggregated 84 killed, 473 wounded, and 13 captured or missing = 570. The Confederate loss is only partially reported. In Liddell's, Bushrod John-

son's, and Bate's brigades the casualties amounted to 50 killed, 228 wounded, and 23 missing = 291. The loss in other commands is not indicated.— EDITORS.

THE OLD JOHN ROSS HOUSE AT ROSSVILLE — MISSIONARY RIDGE ON THE RIGHT. (SEE MAP, P. 648.)
FROM A WAR-TIME PHOTOGRAPH.

CONFEDERATE LINE OF BATTLE IN THE
CHICKAMAUGA WOODS.

CHICKAMAUGA—THE GREAT BATTLE OF THE WEST.↓

BY DANIEL H. HILL, LIEUTENANT-GENERAL, C. S. A.

ON the 13th of July, 1863, while in charge of the defenses of Richmond and Petersburg and the Department of North Carolina, I received an unexpected order to go West. I was seated in a yard of a house in the suburbs of Richmond (the house belonging to Mr. Poe, a relative of the poet), when President Davis, dressed in a plain suit of gray and attended by a small escort in brilliant uniform, galloped up and said: "Rosecrans is about to advance upon Bragg; I have found it necessary to detail Hardee to defend Mississippi and Alabama. His corps is without a commander. I wish you to command it." "I cannot do that," I replied, "as General Stewart ranks me." "I can cure that," answered Mr. Davis, "by making you a lieutenant-general. Your papers will be ready to-morrow. When can you start?" "In twenty-four hours," was the reply. Mr. Davis gave his views on the subject, some directions in regard to matters at Chattanooga, and then left in seemingly good spirits. ⚓

↓ At the beginning of the Civil War I was asked the question, "Who of the Federal officers are most to be feared?" I replied: "Sherman, Rosecrans, and McClellan. Sherman has genius and daring, and is full of resources. Rosecrans has fine practical sense, and is of a tough, tenacious fiber. McClellan is a man of talents, and his delight has always been in the study of military history and the art and science of war." Grant was not once thought of. The light of subsequent events thrown upon the careers of these three great soldiers has not changed my estimate of them; but I acquiesce in the verdict which has given greater renown to some of their comrades. It was my lot to form a more intimate acquaintance with the three illustrious officers who I fore-saw would play an important part in the war. I fought against McClellan from Yorktown to Sharpsburg (Antietam), I encountered Rosecrans at Chickamauga, and I surrendered to Sherman at Greensboro', N. C.— each of the three commanding an army.— D. H. H.

⚓ His cheerfulness was a mystery to me. Within a fortnight the Pennsylvania campaign had proved abortive. Vicksburg and Port Hudson had fallen, and Federal gun-boats were now plying up and down the Mississippi, cutting our communications between the east and west. The Confederacy was cut in two, and the South could readily be beaten in detail by the concentration of Federal forces, first on one side of the Mississippi and then on the other. The end of our glorious dream could not

The condition of our railroads even in 1863 was wretched, so bad that my staff and myself concluded to leave our horses in Virginia and resupply ourselves in Atlanta. On the 19th of July I reported to General Bragg at Chattanooga. I had not seen him since I had been the junior lieutenant in his battery of artillery at Corpus Christi, Texas, in 1845. The other two lieutenants were George H. Thomas and John F. Reynolds. We four had been in the same mess there. Reynolds had been killed at Gettysburg twelve days before my new assignment. Thomas, the strongest and most pronounced Southerner of the four, was now Rosecrans's lieutenant. It was a strange casting of lots that three messmates of Corpus Christi should meet under such changed circumstances at Chickamauga.

My interview with General Bragg at Chattanooga was not satisfactory. He was silent and reserved and seemed gloomy and despondent. He had grown prematurely old since I saw him last, and showed much nervousness. His relations with his next in command (General Polk) and with some others of his subordinates were known not to be pleasant. His many retreats, too, had alienated the rank and file from him, or at least had taken away that enthusiasm which soldiers feel for the successful general, and which makes them obey his orders without question, and thus wins for him other successes. The one thing that a soldier never fails to understand is victory, and the commander who leads him to victory will be adored by him whether that victory has been won by skill or by blundering, by the masterly handling of a few troops against great odds, or by the awkward use of overwhelming numbers. Long before Stonewall Jackson had risen to the height of his great fame, he had won the implicit confidence of his troops in all his movements. "Where are you going?" one inquired of the "foot cavalry" as they were making the usual stealthy march to the enemy's rear. "We don't know, but old Jack does," was the laughing answer. This trust was the fruit of past victories, and it led to other and greater achievements.

I was assigned to Hardee's old corps, consisting of Cleburne's and Stewart's divisions, and made my headquarters at Tyner's Station, a few miles east of Chattanooga on the Knoxville railroad. The Federals soon made their appearance at Bridgeport, Alabama, and I made arrangements to guard the crossings of the Tennessee north of Chattanooga.‡ On Fast Day,

be far off. But I was as cheerful at that interview as was Mr. Davis himself. The bitterness of death had passed with me before our great reverses on the 4th of July. The Federals had been stunned by the defeat at Chancellorsville, and probably would not have made a forward movement for months. A corps could have been sent to General Joe Johnston, Grant could have been crushed, and Vicksburg, "the heart of the Confederacy," could have been saved. The drums that beat for the advance into Pennsylvania seemed to many of us to be beating the funeral march of the dead Confederacy. Our thirty days of mourning were over before the defeat of Lee and Pemberton. Duty, however, was to be done faithfully and unflinchingly to the last. The calmness of our Confeder-

ate President may not have been the calmness of despair, but it may have risen from the belief, then very prevalent, that England and France would recognize the Confederacy at its last extremity, when the Northern and Southern belligerents were both exhausted. Should the North triumph, France could not hope to retain her hold upon Mexico. Besides, the English aristocracy, as is well known, were in full sympathy with the South.—D. H. H.

‡ A regiment was placed at Sivley's Ford, another at Blythe's Ferry, farther north, and S. A. M. Wood's brigade was quartered at Harrison, in supporting distance of either point. The railroad upon which Rosecrans depended for his supplies ran south of Chattanooga, and had he crossed the

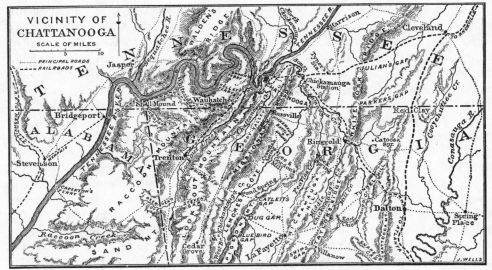

MAP OF THE CHICKAMAUGA CAMPAIGN.

August 21st, while religious services were being held in town, the enemy appeared on the opposite side of the river and began throwing shells into the houses. ♭ Rev. B. M. Palmer, D. D., of New Orleans, was in the act of prayer when a shell came hissing near the church. He went on calmly with his petition to the Great Being "who rules in the armies of heaven and among the inhabitants of earth," but at its close, the preacher, opening his eyes, noticed a perceptible diminution of his congregation. Some women and children were killed and wounded by the shelling. Our pickets and scouts had given no notice of the approach of the enemy. On Sunday, August 30th, we learned through a citizen that McCook's corps had crossed at Caperton's Ferry, some thirty-five miles below Chattanooga, the movement having begun on the 29th. Thomas's corps was also crossing at or near the same point.

The want of information at General Bragg's headquarters was in striking contrast with the minute knowledge General Lee always had of every operation in his front, and I was most painfully impressed with the feeling that it was to be a hap-hazard campaign on our part. ↖ Rosecrans had effected the crossing of the river (Thomas's corps) and had occupied Will's Valley, between Sand and Lookout mountains, without opposition, and had established his

river above the town he would have been separated many miles from his base and his depot. But he probably contemplated throwing a column across the Tennessee to the north of the town to cut off Buckner at Knoxville from a junction with Bragg, and inclose him between that column and the forces of Burnside which were pressing toward Knoxville.—D. H. H.

Buckner's division was promptly withdrawn south of the Hiawassee.—EDITORS.

♭ Colonel J. T. Wilder, who led the reconnoissance, says: "The enemy opened fire upon the com-

mand from their batteries, which was replied to by Captain Lilly's 18th Indiana battery."—EDITORS.

↖ My sympathies had all been with Bragg. I knew of the carping criticisms of his subordinates and the cold looks of his soldiers, and knew that these were the natural results of reverses, whether the blame lay with the commander or otherwise. I had felt, too, that this lack of confidence or lack of enthusiasm, whichever it might be, was ominous of evil for the impending battle. But ignorance of the enemy's movements seemed a still worse portent of calamity.—D. H. H.

headquarters at Trenton. Lookout Mountain now interposed to screen all the enemy's movements from our observation. ☆

On the 7th of September Rosecrans sent McCook to cross Lookout Mountain at Winston's Gap, forty-six miles south of Chattanooga, and to occupy Alpine, east of the mountains. Thomas was ordered to cross the mountain at Stevens's and Cooper's gaps, some twenty-five miles from Chattanooga, and to occupy McLemore's Cove on the east, a narrow valley between Lookout and Pigeon mountains. Pigeon Mountain is parallel to the former, not so high and rugged, and does not extend so far north, ending eight miles south of Chattanooga. Crittenden was left in Will's Valley to watch Chattanooga.

General Bragg had had some inclosed works constructed at Chattanooga, and the place could have been held by a division against greatly superior forces. By holding Chattanooga in that way, Crittenden's corps would have been neutralized, and a union between Rosecrans and Burnside would have been impossible. Moreover, the town was the objective point of the campaign, and to lose it was virtually to lose all east Tennessee south of Knoxville. If Bragg knew at the time of the prospective help coming to him from the Army of Northern Virginia, it was of still more importance to hold the town, that he might be the more readily in communication with Longstreet on his arrival. Under similar circumstances General Lee detached Early's division to hold the heights of Fredericksburg, and neutralized Sedgwick's corps, while he marched to attack Hooker at Chancellorsville. Bragg, however, may have felt too weak to spare even one division from his command. Whatever may have been his motive, he completely abandoned the town by the 8th, and Crittenden took possession of it next day. My corps, ǀ consisting of Breckinridge's and Cleburne's divisions, had led in the withdrawal, and was halted at Lafayette, twenty-two miles from, and almost south of, Chattanooga, and east of Pigeon Mountain, which separates it from McLemore's Cove, into which the columns of Thomas began to pour on the 9th. I placed Breckinridge in charge of the Reserve Artillery and the wagon-train at Lafayette, while Cleburne was sent to hold the three gaps in Pigeon Mountain, Catlett's on the north, Dug in the center, and Blue Bird on the south. Cleburne pitched his tent by the road leading to the center gap. Notwithstanding the occupation of Chattanooga, Rosecrans did not attempt to concentrate his forces there, but persisted in pushing two of his corps to our left and rear.

As the failure of Bragg to beat Rosecrans in detail has been the subject of much criticism, it may be well to look into the causes of the failure. So far as the commanding general was concerned, the trouble with him was: first, lack of knowledge of the situation; second, lack of personal supervision of the execution of his orders. No general ever won a permanent fame who was

---

☆ General Bragg had said petulantly a few days before the crossing into Will's Valley: "It is said to be easy to defend a mountainous country, but mountains hide your foe from you, while they are full of gaps through which he can pounce upon you at any time. A mountain is like the wall of a house full of rat-holes. The rat lies hidden at his hole ready to pop out when no one is watching. Who can tell what lies hidden behind that wall?" said he, pointing to the Cumberland range across the river.—D. H. H.

ǀ Breckinridge's division of my corps had come up from Mississippi and was substituted for Stewart's, sent to Knoxville to join Buckner.

D. H. H.

wanting in these grand elements of success, knowledge of his own and his enemy's condition, and personal superintendence of operations on the field.⚓

The failure to attack Negley's division in the cove on September 10th↓ was owing to Bragg's ignorance of the condition of the roads, the obstructions at Dug Gap, and the position of the enemy. He attributed the failure to make the attack on the same force on the 11th to the major-general [Hindman] who had it in charge,—whether justly or unjustly, I do not know.♮ All day of the 11th my signal corps and scouts at Blue Bird Gap reported the march of a heavy column to our left and up the cove. These reports were forwarded to the commanding general, but were not credited by him.

On the morning of the 13th I was notified that Polk was to attack Critten-den at Lee and Gordon's Mills, and the Reserve Artillery and baggage trains were specially intrusted to my corps. Breckinridge guarded the roads leading south from Lafayette, and Cleburne guarded the gaps in Pigeon Mountain. The attack was not made at Lee and Gordon's Mills, and this was the second of the lost opportunities. Bragg in his official report, speaking of this fail-ure, quotes his first order to Polk to attack, dated 6 P. M. September 12th, Lafayette, Ga.:

"GENERAL: I inclose you a dispatch from General Pegram. This presents you a fine oppor-tunity of striking Crittenden in detail, and I hope you will avail yourself of it at daylight to-morrow. This division crushed, and the others are yours. We can then turn again on the force in the cove. Wheeler's cavalry will move on Wilder so as to cover your right. I shall be delighted to hear of your success."

This order was twice repeated at short intervals, the last dispatch being:

"The enemy is approaching from the south — and it is highly important that your attack in the morning should be quick and decided. Let no time be lost."

The rest of the story is thus told by General Bragg:

"At 11 P. M. a dispatch was received from the general [Polk] stating that he had taken up a strong position for defense, and requesting that he should be heavily reënforced. He was

---

⚓ Invidious critics have attributed many of Stonewall Jackson's successes to lucky blunders, or at best to happy inspirations at the moment of striking. Never was there a greater mistake. He studied carefully (shall I add prayerfully?) all his own and his adversary's movements. He knew the situation perfectly, the geography and the topography of the country, the character of the officers opposed to him, the number and ma-terial of his troops. He never joined battle with-out a thorough personal reconnoissance of the field. That duty he trusted to no engineer officer. When the time came for him to act, he was in the front to see that his orders were carried out, or were modified to suit the ever-shifting scenes of battle.— D. H. H.

↓ Thomas's corps, after crossing at Bridgeport, Shell Mound, and Caperton's Ferry, arrived, Sep-tember 4th, near Trenton, in Will's Valley (east of Sand Mountain). On the 6th Negley's division, with Baird's supporting, reached Johnson's Crook, and on the 10th crossed Missionary Ridge into McLemore's Cove. On the 11th Negley and Baird retired to Stevens's Gap after feeling the enemy in front of Dug Gap, in Pigeon Mountain. Mean-time Davis's and Johnson's divisions of McCook's corps crossing the Tennessee at Caperton's Ferry passed over Sand Mountain and seized Winston's Gap, while Sheridan's division, moving via Tren-ton, was close at hand. On the 10th McCook's three divisions were at Alpine. Crittenden's corps by September 4th was across the Tennessee (at Bridgeport, Shell Mound, and Battle Creek). On the 9th Wood's division occupied Chattanooga, and Palmer and Van Cleve marched to Rossville. On the 10th Crittenden, leaving Wagner's bri-gade to occupy Chattanooga, pursued the enemy toward Dalton and Ringgold. Wood reached Lee and Gordon's Mills on the 11th, and Crittenden was now ordered to close up his whole force on Wood.— EDITORS.

♮ The Comte de Paris states that Bragg sent word to Hindman, at 11 A. M. September 11th, to retire if he deemed it not prudent to attack.— EDITORS.

promptly ordered not to defer his attack,—his force being already numerically superior to the enemy,—and was reminded that his success depended upon the promptness and rapidity of his movements. He was further informed that Buckner's corps would be moved within supporting distance the next morning. Early on the 13th I proceeded to the front, ahead of Buckner's command, to find that no advance had been made upon the enemy and that his forces [the enemy's] had formed a junction and recrossed the Chickamauga. Again disappointed, immediate measures were taken to place our trains and limited supplies in safe positions, when all our forces were concentrated along the Chickamauga threatening the enemy in front."

ALEXANDER'S BRIDGE FROM THE CONFEDERATE SIDE OF THE CHICKAMAUGA LOOKING UP STREAM. FROM A PHOTOGRAPH TAKEN IN 1884.

During the active operations of a campaign the post of the commander-in-chief should be in the center of his marching columns, that he may be able to give prompt and efficient aid to whichever wing may be threatened. But whenever a great battle is to be fought, the commander must be on the field to see that his orders are executed and to take advantage of the ever-changing phases of the conflict. Jackson leading a cavalry fight by night near Front Royal in the pursuit of Banks, Jackson at the head of the column following McClellan in the retreat from Richmond to Malvern Hill, presents a contrast to Bragg sending, from a distance of ten miles, four consecutive orders for an attack at daylight, which he was never to witness.

Surely in the annals of warfare there is no parallel to the coolness and nonchalance with which General Crittenden marched and counter-marched for a week with a delightful unconsciousness that he was in the presence of a force of superior strength. On the 11th we find him with two divisions (Van Cleve's and Palmer's) at Ringgold, twenty miles from Chattanooga, and with his third (Thomas J. Wood's), ten miles from Ringgold, at Lee and Gordon's Mills, where it remained alone and unsupported, until late in the day of the 12th. Crittenden was at the mills with his whole corps on the 13th and morning of the 14th, moving back to Missionary Ridge during the 14th all his divisions except Wood's, which remained all that day. Crittenden seemed to think that so long as the bridge there was held, there was no danger of the rebels passing to his rear on the road toward Chattanooga, though there were other bridges and several good fords over the Chickamauga at other points. It was to the isolation of Wood that Bragg refers in his order dated Lafayette, 6 P. M., on the 12th. Captain Polk (in the Southern Historical Society papers) says:

"General Bragg, in his official report of the battle of Chickamauga, charges General Polk with the failure to crush Crittenden's forces in their isolated position at Ringgold. It will be noted, however, that General Polk was ordered to take position at a particular spot,—Rock Spring,—thence, if not attacked, to advance by daylight of the 13th of September, and assume the offensive against the opposing forces, which were expected from the way of Ringgold. But Crittenden was at Gordon's Mills behind the Chickamauga on the evening of the 12th. The order was simply impracticable."

The concentration at Rock Spring, seven miles south-west from Ringgold and four and a half miles south-east from Lee and Gordon's Mills, was apparently to interpose between Crittenden's columns, and to strike in detail whichever should present itself. But General Crittenden, unaware, apparently, of his danger, crossed the Chickamauga at the mills, and united with Wood about nightfall on the 12th. General Polk discovered that there was a large force in front of him on the night of the 12th, and not a single division, and hence he thought only of a defensive attitude. It is probable that, from his long experience of Bragg's ignorance of the situation, he was skeptical in regard to the accuracy of the general's information on the present occasion. Bragg certainly did not know of the union of Crittenden's forces in the afternoon and night of the 12th. But, even with that knowledge, he would have acted wisely in falling upon the combined forces on the 13th and 14th. [See letter from Captain Polk, p. 662.]

The truth is, General Bragg was bewildered by "the popping out of the rats from so many holes." The wide dispersion of the Federal forces, and their confrontal of him at so many points, perplexed him, instead of being a source of congratulation that such grand opportunities were offered for crushing them one by one. He seems to have had no well-organized system of independent scouts, such as Lee had, and such as proved of inestimable service to the Germans in the Franco-Prussian war. For information in regard to the enemy, apparently he trusted alone to his very efficient cavalry. But the Federal cavalry moved with infantry supports, which could not be brushed aside by our cavalry. So General Bragg only learned that he was encircled by foes, without knowing who they were, what was their strength, and what were their plans. His enemy had a great advantage over him in this respect. The negroes knew the country well, and by dividing the numbers given by them by three, trustworthy information could be obtained. The waning fortunes of the Confederacy were developing a vast amount of "latent uniónism" in the breasts of the original secessionists — those fiery zealots who in '61 proclaimed that "one Southerner could whip three Yankees." The negroes and the fire-eaters with "changed hearts" were now most excellent spies.

The 13th of September was a day of great anxiety to me at Lafayette, in charge of the Reserve Artillery and the wagons trains, with only two weak divisions, less than nine thousand strong, to protect them. During the 11th and 12th my signal corps on Pigeon Mountain had been constantly reporting the march of a heavy column to our left and rear. These reports were communicated by me to the commanding general, and were discredited by him. At 8 A. M. on the 13th Lieutenant Baylor came to my camp with a note from General Wharton, of the cavalry, vouching for the lieutenant's entire trustworthiness. Lieutenant Baylor told me that McCook had encamped the night before at Alpine, twenty miles from Lafayette, toward which his march was directed. Our cavalry pickets had been driven in on the Alpine road the afternoon before, and had been replaced by infantry. Soon after the report by Lieutenant Baylor, a brisk fire opened upon the Alpine road, two miles from Lafayette. I said to my staff, as we galloped toward the firing, " It is to be South Mountain over again." This referred to the defense, on the 14th of September, 1862, of the passes of that mountain by my gallant division, reduced by fighting and marching to five thousand men. We learned, on reaching the Alpine road, that General Daniel Adams's skirmishers had been attacked by two regiments of cavalry, which were repulsed. General Adams said to me, " The boldness of the cavalry advance convinces me that an infantry column is not far off." Lucius Polk's brigade was brought down from Pigeon Mountain, and every disposition was made to celebrate appropriately the next day — the anniversary of South Mountain. But that was not to be. General McCook (Federal) had been ordered to Summerville, eleven miles south of Lafayette on the main road to Rome, Ga. But he had become cautious after hearing that Bragg was not making the hot and hasty retreat that Rosecrans had supposed. He therefore ordered his wagon-train back to the top of Lookout Mountain, and remained all day of the 13th at Alpine. His cavalry had taken some prisoners from General Adams, and he thus learned certainly that Bragg had been reënforced. At midnight on the 13th McCook received the order to hurry back to join Thomas [in McLemore's Cove]. Then began the race of life and death, the crossing back over Lookout Mountain, the rapid exhausting march north through Lookout Valley, and the junction at last at Stevens's Gap on the 17th. The contemporary accounts represent McCook's march as one of fatigue and suffering.

General Bragg returned to Lafayette on the afternoon of the 13th, and I communicated to him verbally that night the report of Lieutenant Baylor. He replied excitedly, " Lieutenant Baylor lies. There is not an infantry soldier of the enemy south of us." The next morning he called his four corps commanders, Polk, Buckner, W. H. T. Walker, and myself, together, and told us that McCook was at Alpine, Crittenden at Lee and Gordon's Mills, and Thomas in McLemore's Cove. McCook was at that very time making that famous march, estimated by Rosecrans at fifty-seven miles, to join Thomas at Stevens's Gap. But the Confederate commander did not know of this withdrawal, and possibly the fear of an attack in his rear by McCook kept him from falling upon Thomas and Crittenden in his front. The nightmare upon Bragg for the next three days was due, doubtless, to his uncertainty about the movements of his enemy, and to the certainty that there was not that

LEE AND GORDON'S MILLS ON THE CHICKAMAUGA. FROM A WAR-TIME PHOTOGRAPH.

mutual confidence between him and some of his subordinates that there ought to be between a chief and his officers to insure victory. Bragg's want of definite and precise information had led him more than once to issue "impossible" orders, and therefore those intrusted with their execution got in the way of disregarding them. Another more serious trouble with him was the disposition to find a scapegoat for every failure and disaster. This made his officers cautious about striking a blow when an opportunity presented itself, unless they were protected by a positive order. ⸆

In reference to the long intervals between battles in the West, I once said to General Patton Anderson, "When two armies confront each other in the East, they get to work very soon; but here you look at one another for days and weeks at a time." He replied with a laugh, "Oh, we out here have to crow and peck straws awhile before we use our spurs." The crowing and pecking straws were now about over. On the 13th Rosecrans awoke from his delusion that Bragg was making a disorderly retreat, and issued his orders for the concentration of his army in McLemore's Cove. Granger's corps came up from Bridgeport, occupied Rossville on the 14th, and remained there until the battle of the 20th. Rossville is at the gap in Missionary Ridge through which runs the road from Chattanooga to Lafayette and Rome, Ga. General Rosecrans had felt it to be of vital importance to hold this gap at all hazards, in case of a disaster to his arms. On the 16th Rosecrans had his forces well in hand, extending from Lee and Gordon's Mills to

⸆ General Lee sought for no vicarious victim to atone for his *one* disaster. "I alone am to blame; the order for attack was mine," said he, after the repulse of the assault upon Cemetery Ridge at Gettysburg. Lee and Bragg were cast in different molds.—D. H. H.

Stevens's Gap, in a line running from east to south-west some eleven miles long. On the same day Bragg, with headquarters still at Lafayette, held the gaps in Pigeon Mountain, and the fords to Lee and Gordon's Mills. Each commander was in position, on the 17th, to turn the left flank of his adversary,—Bragg by crossing the Chickamauga at points north of Lee and Gordon's Mills; but by this he risked fighting with his back to the river,—a hazardous situation in case of defeat. He risked too, to some extent, his trains, which had yet to be moved toward Ringgold and Dalton. His gain, in case of a decided victory, would be the cutting off of Rosecrans from Chattanooga, and possibly the recapture of that place. Rosecrans could have flanked Bragg by crossing at the Mills and at the fords between that place and Catlett's. This would have cut off Bragg from Rome certainly, and from Dalton in case of his advance upon Chattanooga, or else would have compelled him to come out and fight upon ground selected by his antagonist. The risk to Rosecrans was an insecure line of retreat in case of defeat, and possibly the loss of Chattanooga. But he had Granger's corps to hold the fortifications of Chattanooga, and he held also the gaps in Lookout Mountain. Bragg showed superior boldness by taking the initiative. Rosecrans determined to act upon the defensive. He says that he knew on the 17th that Bragg would try to seize the Dry Valley and Rossville roads—the first on the west and the second on the east of Missionary Ridge. He thus divined the plan of his enemy twelve hours before Bragg's order was issued. Therefore Rosecrans, on the afternoon of the 17th, ordered McCook to take the place of Thomas at Pond Spring, Thomas to relieve the two divisions of Crittenden at Crawfish Springs, and Crittenden to take these divisions and extend them to the left of Wood at Lee and Gordon's, so as to protect the road to Chattanooga. McCook's corps reached its position at dark, Crittenden's near midnight. Thomas marched all night uninterruptedly, and the head of his columns reached the Widow Glenn's (Rosecrans's headquarters) at daylight on the 19th.

On the 18th Bragg issued, from Leet's tan-yard, his order for battle:

" 1. [Bushrod] Johnson's column (Hood's), on crossing at or near Reed's Bridge, will turn to the left by the most practicable route, and sweep up the Chickamauga toward Lee and Gordon's Mills.

" 2. Walker, crossing at Alexander's Bridge, will unite in this move and push vigorously on the enemy's flank and rear in the same direction.

" 3. Buckner, crossing at Tedford's Ford, will join in the movement to the left, and press the enemy up the stream from Polk's front at Lee and Gordon's.

" 4. Polk will press his forces to the front of Lee and Gordon's Mills, and if met by too much resistance to cross will bear to the right and cross at Dalton's Ford or at Tedford's, as may be necessary, and join the attack wherever the enemy may be.

" 5. Hill will cover our left flank from an advance of the enemy from the cove, and, by pressing the cavalry in his front, ascertain if the enemy is reënforcing at Lee and Gordon's Mills, in which event he will attack them in flank.

" 6. Wheeler's cavalry will hold the gaps in Pigeon Mountain, and cover our rear and left, and bring up stragglers.

" 7. All teams, etc., not with troops should go toward Ringgold and Dalton beyond Taylor's Ridge. All cooking should be done at the trains; rations when cooked will be forwarded to the troops.

" 8. The above movement will be executed with the utmost promptness, vigor, and persistence."

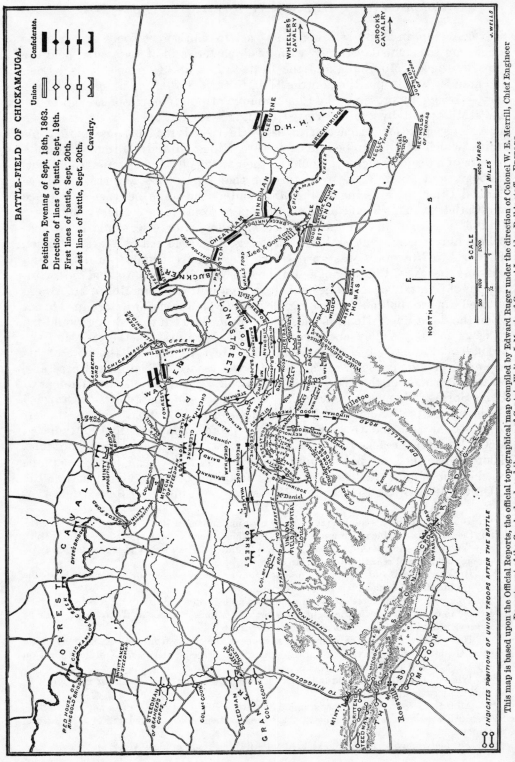

BATTLE-FIELD OF CHICKAMAUGA.

Positions, Evening of Sept. 18th, 1863.
Direction of lines of battle, Sept. 19th.
First lines of battle, Sept. 20th.
Last lines of battle, Sept. 20th.

Confederate.

Union.

Cavalry.

SCALE

500   1000   2000   4000 YARDS
½   1   2 MILES

NORTH

S

E   W

J. WELLS.

INDICATES POSITIONS OF UNION TROOPS AFTER THE BATTLE

This map is based upon the Official Reports, the official topographical map compiled by Edward Ruger under the direction of Colonel W. E. Merrill, Chief Engineer Department of the Cumberland, and the maps of Captain Walter J. Morris of General Leonidas Polk's staff.— EDITORS.

Had this order been issued on any of the four preceding days, it would have found Rosecrans wholly unprepared for it, with but a single infantry division (Wood's) guarding the crossings of the Chickamauga, and that at one point only, Lee and Gordon's — the fords north of it being watched by cavalry. Even if the order had been given twenty-four hours earlier, it must have been fatal to Rosecrans in the then huddled and confused grouping of his forces.

All that was effected on the 18th was the sending over of Walker's small corps of a little more than 5000 men near Alexander's Bridge, and Bushrod Johnson's division of 3600 men at Reed's Bridge, farther north. These troops drove off Wilder's mounted infantry from the crossings immediately south of them, so as to leave undisputed passage for Bragg's infantry, except in the neighborhood of Lee and Gordon's. On the night of the 18th Bragg's troops were substantially as follows: Hill's corps on the extreme left, with center at Glass's Mill; Polk's at Lee and Gordon's; Buckner's at Byram's Ford; Hood's at Tedford's Ford. ☆ During the night Cheatham's division of Polk's corps was detached, moved down the Chickamauga, and crossed at Hunt's Ford about 7 A. M. on the 19th. On that morning the Federal line of battle ran, in the main, parallel to the Chattanooga road from Lee and Gordon's to beyond Kelly's farm, and consisted of the divisions of Wood, Van Cleve, and Palmer of Crittenden's corps, and Baird's and Brannan's of Thomas's corps, in the order named from right to left. Negley and Reynolds, commanders under Thomas, had not come up at the opening of the battle of the 19th. The leading division (R. W. Johnson's) of McCook's corps reached Crawfish Springs at an early hour that day, and the divisions of Davis and Sheridan soon followed. It is about five miles from Crawfish Springs to Kelly's farm.

Soon after getting into position at Kelly's after his night march, General Thomas was told by Colonel Daniel McCook, commanding a brigade of the Reserve Corps, that there were no rebel troops west of the Chickamauga, except one brigade that had crossed at Reed's Bridge the afternoon before, and which could easily be captured, as he (McCook) had burned the bridge behind the rebels. Thomas ordered Brannan to take two brigades and make a reconnoissance on the road to Reed's Bridge, and place a third brigade on the road to Alexander's Bridge. This order took the initiative away from Bragg, and put it in the hands of Thomas with his two divisions in line to crush the small Confederate force west of the river, and then with *his* supports, as they came, beat, in detail, the *Confederate* supports, delayed, as they must be, by the crossings and the distances to march. Croxton's brigade, of Brannan's division, met Forrest's cavalry on the Reed's Bridge road, and drove it back on the infantry — two small brigades under Ector and Wilson. These advanced with the " rebel yell," pushed Croxton back, and ran over his battery, but were in turn beaten back by Brannan's and Baird's forces. Baird now began the readjustment of his lines, and during the confusion of the movement Liddell's (Confederate) division, two thousand strong, struck the brigades of Scribner and King, and drove them in disorder, capturing Loomis's battery, commanded by Lieutenant Van Pelt. Bush's Indiana battery was

☆ Hood's division, about 5000, was the only part of Longstreet's corps in the action of the 19th.—D. H. H.

CRAWFISH SPRINGS. FROM A PHOTOGRAPH
TAKEN IN 1884.

captured at the same time. The defeat had become a panic, and Baird's and Brannan's men were going pell-mell to the rear, when the victorious Liddell found himself in the presence of a long line of Federal troops overlapping both flanks of his little force. These were the troops of Brannan's reorganized division on his right, and of the freshly arrived division of R. W. Johnson from McCook. Liddell extricated himself skillfully, losing heavily, however, and being compelled to abandon his captured guns. It was by Rosecrans's own order, at 10:15 A. M., that R. W. Johnson had been hurried forward five miles from Crawfish Springs, just in time to save the Federal left from a grave disaster. At 11 A. M. Bragg ordered Cheatham to the relief of Liddell, but he reached the ground after Johnson—too late to drive Brannan as well as Baird off the field. Cheatham's veteran division of seven thousand men advanced gallantly, driving the enemy before it, when it was in its turn hurled back by an attacking column which Thomas had organized after the defeat of Liddell and the arrival of two fresh divisions, viz., Palmer's of Crittenden's corps and Reynolds of his own corps.

Unfortunately for the Confederates, there was no general advance, as there might have been along the whole line—an advance that must have given a more decisive victory on the 19th than was gained on the 20th. It was desultory fighting from right to left, without concert, and at inopportune times. It was the sparring of the amateur boxer, and not the crushing blows of the trained pugilist. From daylight on the 19th until after midday, there was a gap of two miles between Crittenden and Thomas, into which the Confederates could have poured, turning to right or left, and attacking in flank whichever commander was least prepared for the assault. As Cheatham was falling back, A. P. Stewart's division of Buckner's corps, 3400 strong, attacked Palmer's division of Crittenden's corps, which was flanking Cheatham, drove it back, and marching forward met Van Cleve's division of the same corps hastening to the assistance of Thomas, and hurled it back also. Hood, with his own division and Bushrod Johnson's, moved at 2:30 P. M., and gained for a time a most brilliant success, crushing the right center of the Federal army, capturing artillery, and seizing the Chattanooga road. The three Confederate divisions, after their first triumphs, had to encounter the four fresh divisions of Wood, Davis, Sheridan, and Negley, and were in turn driven back to the east of the road.

Stewart had recaptured the battery lost by Cheatham's division, twelve pieces of Federal artillery, over two hundred prisoners, and several hundred rifles. Hood and Bushrod Johnson had met with a similar success at first, but, of course, three divisions could not stand the combined attack of six.

On our extreme left a good deal of demonstrating had been done by the Federals on the 17th and 18th; infantry had been crossed over at Owen's Ford, and threats made at Glass's Mill. On the 19th I ordered an attack at the latter place. Slocomb's battery had a bloody artillery duel with one on the west of the river, and, under cover of the artillery fire, Helm's brigade of Breckinridge's division was crossed over, and attacked Negley's infantry and drove it off. Riding over the ground with Breckinridge, I counted eleven dead horses at the Federal battery, and a number of dead infantrymen that had not been removed. The clouds of dust rolling down the valley revealed the precipitate retirement of the foe, not on account of our pressure upon him, but on account of the urgency of the order to hurry to their left. This was the time to have relieved the strain upon our right by attacking the Federal right at Lee and Gordon's. My veteran corps, under its heroic division commanders, Breckinridge and Cleburne, would have flanked the enemy out of his fortifications at this point, and would by their brilliant onset have confounded Rosecrans in his purpose of massing upon his left; but Bragg had other plans. |

At 3 P. M. I received an order to report to the commander-in-chief at Tedford's Ford, to set Cleburne's division in motion to the same point, and to relieve Hindman at Gordon's with Breckinridge's division. Cleburne had six miles to march over a road much obstructed with wagons, artillery, and details of soldiers. He got into position on the extreme right after sundown. Thomas had, in the meanwhile, moved Brannan from his left to his right, and was retiring Baird and R. W. Johnson to a better position, when

---

| The great commander is he who makes his antagonist keep step with him. Thomas, like the grand soldier he was, by attacking first, made Bragg keep step with him. He who begins the attack assumes that he is superior to his enemy, either in numbers or in courage, and therefore carries with him to the assault all the moral advantage of his assumed superiority.—D. H. H.

Cleburne, with Cheatham upon his left, moved upon them " in the gloaming " in magnificent style, capturing three pieces of artillery, a number of caissons, two stand of colors, and three hundred prisoners. The contest was obstinate, for a time, on our left, where log breastworks were encountered; and here that fine soldier, Brigadier-General Preston Smith, of Cheatham's division, lost his life. Discovering that our right extended beyond the enemy, I threw two batteries in advance of our fighting line and almost abreast of that of the enemy. These caused a hasty abandonment of the breastworks and a falling back of some half a mile. This ended the contest for the day.

General Rosecrans made a very natural mistake about our overwhelming numbers. But it *was* a big mistake. The South, from patriotic pride, still kept up its old military organizations, for how could it merge together divisions and brigades around which clustered such glorious memories? But the waste of war had reduced them to mere skeleton divisions and brigades. My corps at Chickamauga was but little more than one-third of the size of my division at Yorktown, and so it was through the whole Southern army. Captain W. M. Polk, from data furnished him by General Marcus J. Wright, has given an estimate of the numbers in the respective corps and divisions of the two armies; he concludes that the Federals had 45,855 and the Confederates 33,897 in the battle of the 19th.

I witnessed some of the heaviest fighting on the afternoon of the 19th, and never saw so little straggling from the field. I saw but one deserter from Hood's ranks, and not one from Cleburne's. The divisions of Hindman, Breckinridge, and Preston had not been put into the fight, and two brigades of McLaws's (Kershaw's and Humphreys's) were expected next day. Rosecrans had put in all but two of his brigades. The outlook seemed hopeful for the Confederates. Longstreet arrived at 11 P. M. on the 19th.☨

Soon after, General Bragg called together some of his officers and ventured upon that hazardous experiment, a change of organization in face of the enemy. He divided his army into two wings; he gave to Polk the right wing, consisting of the corps of Hill and Walker, and the division of Cheatham,— comprising in all 18,794 infantry and artillery, with 3500 cavalry under Forrest; to Longstreet he gave the left wing, consisting of the corps of Buckner and Hood, and the division of Hindman,— 22,849 infantry and artillery, with 4000 cavalry under Wheeler. That night Bragg announced his purpose of adhering to his plan of the 19th for the 20th, viz., successive attacks from right to left, and he gave his wing commanders orders to begin at daylight. I left Cleburne, after his fight, at 11 P. M., and rode with Captains Coleman and Reid five miles to Tedford's Ford, where the orders for the

☨ While lying on the Rapidan in August, after that disastrous day at Gettysburg, Longstreet had suggested to General Lee the reënforcing of Bragg. The general went to Richmond, and after a time got the consent of the Confederate authorities to send Longstreet, without artillery or cavalry, with the much reduced divisions of McLaws and Hood. Lee followed Longstreet to his horse to see him off, and as he was mounting said, " General, you must beat those people." (Lee always called the Federals "those people.") Longstreet said, " General, if you will give your orders that the enemy, when beaten, shall be destroyed, I will promise to give you victory, if I live; but I would not give the life of a single soldier of mine for a barren victory." Lee replied, "The order has been given and will be repeated."— D. H. H. [See p. 676 for strength of Longstreet's force.]

day announced that Bragg's headquarters would be, that I might get instructions for the next day.   On the way I learned from some soldiers that Breckinridge was coming up from Lee and Gordon's.   I sent Captain Reid to him to conduct him to Cleburne's right.   General Polk, however, as wing commander, gave General Breckinridge permission to rest his weary men, and took him to his own headquarters.   It was after 2 o'clock when General Breckinridge moved off under the guidance of Captain Reid, and his division did not get into position until after sunrise.   Captain Coleman and myself reached the ford after midnight, only to learn that Bragg was not there.   Some time after the unsuccessful search, my other staff-officers came up, and my chief-of-staff gave me a message from General Polk that my corps had been put under his command, and that he wished to see me at Alexander's Bridge.   He said not a word to any of them about an attack at daylight, nor did he to General Breckinridge, who occupied the same room with him that night.   I have by me written statements from General Breckinridge and the whole of my staff to that effect.   General Polk had issued an order for an attack at daylight, and had sent a courier with a copy, but he had failed to find me.   I saw the order for the first time nineteen years afterward in Captain Polk's letter to the Southern Historical Society.   At 3 A. M. on the 20th I went to Alexander's Bridge, but not finding the courier who was to be posted there to conduct me to General Polk, I sent Lieutenant Morrison, aide-de-camp, to hunt him up and tell him I could be found on the line of battle, which I reached just after daylight, before Breckinridge had got into position.   Neither of my division commanders had heard anything of the early attack, and cooked rations were being distributed to our men, many of whom had not eaten anything for twenty-four hours.   At 7:25 an order was shown me from General Polk, directed to my major-generals, to begin the attack.   I sent a note to him that I was adjusting my line, and· that my men were getting their rations.   Polk soon after came up, and assented to the delay.   Still nothing was said of the daylight attack.   Bragg rode up at 8 A. M. and inquired of me why I had not begun the attack at daylight.   I told him that I was hearing then for the first time that such an order had been issued and had not known whether we were to be the assailants or the assailed.   He said angrily, " I found Polk after sunrise sitting down reading a newspaper at Alexander's Bridge, two miles from the line of battle, where he ought to have been fighting."

However, the essential preparations for battle had not been made up to this hour and, in fact, could not be made without the presence of the commander-in-chief.   The position of the enemy had not been reconnoitered, our line of battle had not been adjusted, and part of it was at right angles with the rest; there was no cavalry on our flanks, and no order had fixed the strength or position of the reserves.   My corps had been aligned north and south, to be parallel to the position of the enemy.   Cheatham's division was at right angles to my line, and when adjusted was found to be exactly behind Stewart's, and had therefore to be taken out after the battle was begun, and placed in reserve.   Kershaw's brigade of Longstreet's corps was also out of place, and was put in reserve.

GENERAL THOMAS'S BIVOUAC AFTER THE FIRST DAY'S BATTLE.

Rosecrans in person made a careful alignment of his whole line in the morning, arranging it so as to cover the Rossville (Chattanooga) and the Dry Valley roads. It began four hundred yards east of the Rossville road, on a crest which was occupied from left to right by Baird's division (Thomas's corps), R. W. Johnson's division (McCook's), Palmer's division (Crittenden's), and Reynolds's division (Thomas's). These four divisions became isolated during the day, and the interest of the battle centers largely in them. They lay behind substantial breastworks of logs,↓ in a line running due south and bending back toward the road at each wing. "Next on the right of Reynolds," says a Federal newspaper account, "was Brannan's division of Thomas's corps, then Negley's of the same corps, its right making a crotchet to the rear. The line across the Chattanooga road toward Missionary Ridge was completed by Sheridan's and Davis's divisions of McCook's corps: Wood's and Van Cleve's divisions of Crittenden's corps were in reserve at a proper distance." The line from Reynolds extended in a south-westerly direction. Minty's cavalry covered the left and rear at Missionary Mills; Mitchell's and

---

↓ The ringing of axes in our front could be heard all night.—D. H. H.

These breastworks were described as follows by William F. G. Shanks, war correspondent of the "New York Herald":

"General Thomas had wisely taken the precaution to make rude works about breast-high along his whole front, using rails and logs for the purpose. The logs and rails ran at right angles to each other, the logs keeping parallel to the proposed line of battle and lying upon the rails until the proper height was reached. The spaces between these logs were filled with rails, which served to add to their security and strength. The spade had not been used."   EDITORS.

Wilder's cavalry covered the extreme right. Rosecrans's headquarters were at Widow Glenn's house.

The Confederate line ran at the outset from north to south, Hill's corps on the right, next Stewart's division, Hood in reserve, then Bushrod Johnson's, then Hindman's on the extreme left, Preston's in reserve. After the fighting had actually begun, Walker's and Cheatham's divisions and Kershaw's brigade were taken out and put in reserve. Wheeler's cavalry covered our left, and Forrest had been sent, at my request, to our right. The Confederates were confronted with eight Federal divisions protected generally by breastworks. The battle can be described in a few words. The Confederate attack on the right was mainly unsuccessful because of the breastworks, but was so gallant and persistent that Thomas called loudly for reënforcements, which were promptly sent, weakening the Federal right, until finally a gap was left. This gap Longstreet entered. Discovering, with the true instinct of a soldier, that he could do more by turning to the right, he disregarded the order to wheel to the left and wheeled the other way, striking the corps of Crittenden and McCook in flank, driving them with their commanders and the commanding general off the field.‖ Thomas, however, still held his ground, and, though ordered to retreat, strongly refused to do so until nightfall, thus saving the Federals from a great disaster. Longstreet, then, was the organizer of victory on the Confederate side, and Thomas the savior of the army on the other side.

Longstreet did not advance until noon, nor did he attack the breastworks on the Federal left (Thomas's position) at all, though Federal writers at the time supposed that he did. Those assaults were made first by the divisions of Breckinridge and Cleburne of Hill's corps, and then by the brigades of Gist, Walthall, Govan, and others sent to their assistance. Stewart began his brilliant advance at 11 A. M., and before that time Thomas began his appeals for help.

Breckinridge moved at 9:30 A. M., and Cleburne fifteen minutes later, according to the order for attack. Forrest dismounted Armstrong's division of cavalry to keep abreast of Breckinridge, and held Pegram's division in reserve. Breckinridge's two right brigades, under Adams and Stovall, met but little opposition, but the left of Helm's brigade encountered the left of the breastworks, and was badly cut up. The heroic Helm was killed, and his command repulsed. His brigade, now under the command of that able officer, Colonel J. H. Lewis, was withdrawn. The simultaneous advance of Cleburne's troops would have greatly relieved Helm, as he was exposed to a flank as well as a direct fire. General Breckinridge suggested, and I cordially approved the suggestion, that he should wheel his two brigades to the left, and get in rear of the breastworks. These brigades had reached the Chattanooga road, and their skirmishers had pressed past Cloud's house, where

‖ General Bushrod Johnson was the first to enter the gap with his division and, with the coolness and judgment for which he was always distinguished, took in the situation at a glance and began the flank movement to the right. General Longstreet adopted the plan of his lieutenant, and made his other troops conform to Bushrod Johnson's movement.—D. H. H.

there was a Federal field-hospital. The wheeling movement enabled Stovall to gain a point beyond the retired flank of the breastworks, and Breckinridge says in his report, "Adams had advanced still farther, being actually in rear of his intrenchments. A good supporting line to my division at this moment would probably have produced decisive results." Federal reënforcements had, however, come up. Adams was badly wounded and fell into the enemy's hands, and the two brigades were hurled back. Beatty's brigade of Negley's division had been the first to come to Baird's assistance. General Thomas says:

THE SINK-HOLE NEAR WIDOW GLENN'S HOUSE. FROM A RECENT PHOTOGRAPH.

This sink-hole contained the only water to be had in the central part of the battle-field. Colonel Wilder's brigade of mounted infantry at one time gained the pool after a hard contest and quenched their thirst. In the water were lying dead men and horses that had been wounded and had died while drinking.

"Beatty, meeting with greatly superior numbers, was compelled to fall back until relieved by the fire of several regiments of Palmer's reserve, which I had ordered to the support of the left, being placed in position by General Baird, and which, with the coöperation of Van Derveer's brigade ⸸ of Brannan's division, and a portion of Stanley's brigade of Negley's division, drove the enemy entirely from Baird's left and rear."

Here was quite a sensation made by Breckinridge's two thousand men. American troops cannot stand flank and rear attacks. While Breckinridge was thus alarming Thomas for his left, Cleburne was having a bloody fight with the forces behind the breastworks. From want of alignment before the battle, Deshler's brigade had to be taken out that it might not overlap Stewart. L. E. Polk's brigade soon encountered the enemy behind his logs, and after an obstinate contest was driven back. Wood's (Confederate) brigade on the left had almost reached Poe's house (the burning house) on the Chattanooga road, when he was subjected to a heavy enfilading and direct fire, and driven back with great loss. Cleburne withdrew his division four hundred yards behind the crest of a hill. The gallant young brigadier Deshler was killed while executing the movement, and his brigade then fell into the able hands of Colonel R. Q. Mills. The fierce fight on our right lasted until 10:30 A. M. It was an unequal contest of two small divisions against four full ones behind fortifications. Surely, there were never nobler leaders than Breckinridge and Cleburne, and surely never were nobler troops led on a more desperate "forlorn-hope"—against odds in

⸸ General Adams was captured by Van Derveer's men.—D. H. H.

numbers and superiority in position and equipment. But their unsurpassed and unsurpassable valor was not thrown away. Before a single Confederate soldier had come to their relief, Rosecrans ordered up other troops to the aid of Thomas, in addition to those already mentioned. At 10:10 A. M. he ordered McCook to be ready at 10:30; Sheridan's division to support Thomas.

General McCook says that he executed the order and marched the men at double-quick. This weakening of his right by Rosecrans to support his left was destined soon to be his ruin. So determined had been the assaults of Breckinridge and Cleburne, that, though repulsed and badly punished, they were not pursued by the enemy, who did not venture outside of his works.

At 11 A. M. Stewart's division advanced under an immediate order from Bragg. His three brigades under Brown, Clayton, and Bate advanced with Wood of Cleburne's division, and, as General Stewart says, " pressed on past the corn-field in front of the burnt house, two or three hundred yards beyond the Chattanooga road, driving the enemy within his line of intrenchments. . . . Here they encountered a fresh artillery fire on front and flank, heavily supported by infantry, and had to retire."

This was the celebrated attack upon Reynolds and Brannan which led directly to the Federal disaster. In the meantime our right was preparing to renew the attack. I proposed to the wing commander, Polk, to make a second advance, provided fresh troops were sent forward, requesting that the gap in Breckinridge's left, made by the withdrawal of Helm, should be filled by another brigade. General J. K. Jackson's was sent for that purpose, but unfortunately took its position too far in rear to engage the attention of the enemy in front, and every advance on our right during the remainder of the day was met with flank and cross fire from that quarter. Gist's brigade and Liddell's division of Walker's corps reported to me. Gist immediately attacked with great vigor the log-works which had repulsed Helm so disastrously, and he in turn was driven back. Liddell might have made as great an impression by moving on the Chattanooga road as Breckinridge had done, but his strong brigade (Walthall's) was detached, and he advanced with Govan's alone, seized the road for the second time that day, and was moving behind the breastworks, when, a column of the enemy appearing on his flank and rear, he was compelled to retreat.

This was simultaneous with the advance of Stewart. The heavy pressure on Thomas caused Rosecrans to support him by sending the divisions of Negley and Van Cleve and Brannan's reserve brigade. In the course of these changes, an order to Wood, which Rosecrans claims was misinterpreted, led to a gap being left into which Longstreet stepped with the eight brigades (Bushrod Johnson's original brigade and McNair's, Gregg's, Kershaw's, Law's, Humphreys's, Benning's, and Robertson's) which he had arranged in three lines to constitute his grand column of attack. Davis's two brigades, one of Van Cleve's, and Sheridan's entire division were caught in front and flank and driven from the field. Disregarding the order of the day, Longstreet now gave the order to wheel to the right instead of the left, and thus take in reverse the strong position of the enemy. Five of McCook's brigades were speedily driven off the field. He estimates their loss at forty per cent. Certainly that flank march was a bloody one. I have never seen the Federal dead lie so thickly on the ground, save in front of the sunken wall at Fredericksburg.

But that indomitable Virginia soldier, George H. Thomas, ☆ was there and was destined to save the Union army from total rout and ruin, by confronting with invincible pluck the forces of his friend and captain in the Mexican war. Thomas had ridden to his right to hurry up reënforcements, when he discovered a line advancing, which he thought at first was the expected succor from Sheridan, but he soon heard that it was a rebel column marching upon him. He chose a strong position on a spur of Missionary Ridge, running east

and west, placed upon it Brannan's division with portions of two brigades of Negley's; Wood's division (Crittenden's) was placed on Brannan's left. These troops, with such as could be rallied from the two broken corps, were all he had to confront the forces of Longstreet, until Steedman's division of Granger's corps came to his relief about 3 P. M. Well and nobly did Thomas and his gallant troops hold their own against foes flushed with past victory and confident of future success. His new line was nearly at right angles with the line of log-works on the west side of the Rossville road, his right being an almost impregnable wall-like hill, his

GENERAL W. H. LYTLE, COMMANDING THE
FIRST BRIGADE, SHERIDAN'S DIVISION,
KILLED SEPTEMBER 20, 1863.

left nearly an inclosed fortification. Our only hope of success was to get in his rear by moving far to our right, which overlapped the Federal left.

Bushrod Johnson's three brigades in Longstreet's center were the first to fill the gap left by Wood's withdrawal from the Federal right; but the other five brigades under Hindman and Kershaw moved promptly into line as soon as space could be found for them, wheeled to the right, and engaged in the murderous flank attack. On they rushed, shouting, yelling, running over batteries, capturing trains, taking prisoners, seizing the headquarters of the Federal commander, at the Widow Glenn's, until they found themselves facing the new Federal line on Snodgrass Hill. Hindman had advanced a little later than the center, and had met great and immediate success. The brigades of Deas and Manigault charged the breastworks at double-quick, rushed over them, drove Laiboldt's Federal brigade of Sheridan's division off the field down the Rossville road; then General Patton Anderson's brigade of Hindman, having come into line, attacked and beat back the forces of Davis, Sheridan, and Wilder ⏉ in their front, killed the hero and poet General Lytle,

---

☆ Bragg had great respect and affection for the first lieutenant of his battery. The tones of tenderness with which he spoke of "Old Tom" are still remembered by me.—D. H. H.

⏉ James Burns, 39th Indiana Mounted Infantry, writes to the editors from Harper, Kansas:

"Wilder's brigade, with Colonel T. J. Harrison's 39th Indiana Mounted Infantry regiment, which was ordered to report to Colonel Wilder about 9 o'clock A. M. of the 20th of September, was stationed on a hill about one-third of a mile in the rear of the line of battle,— the 39th on the left of the brigade. A few minutes after 11 o'clock A. M. the brigade was ordered to advance

took 1100 prisoners, 27 pieces of artillery, commissary and ordnance trains, etc. Finding no more resistance on his front and left, Hindman wheeled to the right to assist the forces of the center. The divisions of Stewart, Hood, Bushrod Johnson, and Hindman came together in front of the new stronghold of the Federals. [See map, p. 648.]

It was now 2:30 p. m. Longstreet, with his staff, was lunching on sweet-potatoes. A message came just then that the commanding general wished to see him. He found Bragg in rear of his lines, told him of the steady and satisfactory progress of the battle, that sixty pieces of artillery had been reported captured (though probably the number was over-estimated), that many prisoners and stores had been taken, and that all was going well. He then asked for additional troops to hold the ground gained, while he pursued the two broken corps down the Dry Valley road and cut off the retreat of Thomas. Bragg replied that there was no more fight in the troops of Polk's wing, that he could give Longstreet no reënforcements, and that his headquarters would be at Reed's Bridge. He seems not to have known that Cheatham's division and part of Liddell's had not been in action that day.↥

Some of the severest fighting had yet to be done after 3 p. m. It probably never happened before for a great battle to be fought to its bloody conclusion with the commanders of each side away from the field of conflict. But the Federals were in the hands of the indomitable Thomas, and the Confederates were under their two heroic wing commanders Longstreet and Polk. In the lull of the strife I went with a staff-officer to examine the ground on our left. One of Helm's wounded men had been overlooked, and was lying alone in the woods, his head partly supported by a tree. He was shockingly injured.↓

across the valley where the ammunition train was stationed, and up the hill to the support of Captain Lilly's battery, and to hold the hill at all hazards until the train was got out of the way. My company, 'A,' 39th Indiana, was in advance, and on reaching the brow of the hill Major Evans gave the commands, '39th Indiana on left into line'; 'Fire at will.' At a distance of less than fifty yards six solid lines of gray were coming with their hats down, their bayonets at a charge, and the old familiar rebel yell. Our first volley did not check their advance, but as volley after volley from our Spencer rifles followed, with scarce a second's intermission, and regiment after regiment came on left into line on our right, and poured the same steady, deadly fire into their fast-thinning ranks, they broke and fled.

"Colonel Wilder and Colonel Harrison rode along our lines, directing that if they charged us again, no shot must be fired until the word of command was given. In a few moments those lines of gray once more emerged from the sheltering timber on the opposite side of the field, and steadily, as if on parade, they advanced to the charge till the line had reached to the point at which they broke before, when the command 'Fire' was given, and again they broke and fled in wild confusion. Three times more did those brave men advance at a charge, and each time were they hurled back. A lieutenant of the 17th Indiana went down with a few men under cover of the fire of the brigade, and brought in the flag of an Alabama regiment. We then received orders to move off, remount and guard the ammunition train to Chattanooga, which we did successfully."

↥ General Longstreet wrote to me in July, 1884:
"It is my opinion that Bragg thought at 3 p. m. that the battle was lost, though he did not say so positively.

I asked him at that time to reënforce me with a few troops that had not been so severely engaged as mine, and to allow me to go down the Dry Valley road, so as to interpose behind Thomas and cut off his retreat to Chattanooga, at the same time pursuing the troops that I had beaten back from my front. His reply, as well as I can remember, was that he had no troops except my own that had any fight left in them, and that I should remain in the position in which I then was. After telling me this, he left me, saying, 'General, if anything happens, communicate with me at Reed's Bridge.' In reading Bragg's report, I was struck with his remark that the morning after the battle 'he found the ever-vigilant General Liddell feeling his way to find the enemy.' Inasmuch as every one in his army was supposed to know on the night of the battle that we had won a complete victory, it seemed to me quite ludicrous that an officer should be commended for his vigilance the next morning in looking for the enemy in his immediate presence. I know that I was then laying a plan by which we might overhaul the enemy at Chattanooga or between that point and Nashville. It did not occur to me on the night of the 20th to send Bragg word of our complete success. I thought that the loud huzzas that spread over the field just at dark were a sufficient assurance and notice to any one within five miles of us. . . . Rosecrans speaks particularly of his apprehension that I would move down the Dry Valley road."   D. H. H.

↓ He belonged to Von Zinken's regiment, of New Orleans, composed of French, Germans, and Irish. I said to him: "My poor fellow, you are badly hurt. What regiment do you belong to?" He replied: "The Fifth Confederit, and a dommed

Hindman and Bushrod Johnson organized a column of attack upon the front and rear of the stronghold of Thomas. It consisted of the brigades of Deas, Manigault, Gregg, Patton, Anderson, and McNair. Three of the brigades, Johnson says, had each but five hundred men, and the other two were not strong. Deas was on the north side of the gorge through which the Crawfish road crosses, Manigault across the gorge and south, on the crest parallel to the Snodgrass Hill, where Thomas was. The other three brigades extended

along the crest with their faces north, while the first two faced east. Kershaw, with his own and Humphreys's brigade, was on the right of Anderson and was to coöperate in the movement. It began at 3:30 P. M. A terrific contest ensued. The bayonet was used, and men were killed and wounded with clubbed muskets. A little after 4, the enemy was reënforced, and advanced, but was repulsed by Anderson and Kershaw.

General Bushrod Johnson claims that his men were surely, if slowly, gaining ground at all points, which must have made untenable the stronghold of Thomas. Relief was,

GENERAL J. M. BRANNAN.
FROM A PHOTOGRAPH TAKEN IN MAY, 1865.

however, to come to our men, so hotly engaged on the left, by the advance of the right. At 3 P. M. Forrest reported to me that a strong column was approaching from Rossville, which he was delaying all he could. From prisoners we soon learned that it was Granger's corps. We were apprehensive that a flank attack, by fresh troops, upon our exhausted and shattered ranks might prove fatal. Major-General Walker strongly advised falling back to the position of Cleburne, but to this I would not consent, believing that it would invite attack, as we were in full view. ♭ Cheatham's fine division was sent to my assistance by the wing commander. But Granger, who had gallantly marched without orders to the relief of Thomas, moved on "to the sound of the firing, attacked with vigor and broke

good regiment it is." The answer, though almost ludicrous, touched me as illustrating the *esprit de corps* of the soldier — his pride in and his affection for his command. Colonel Von Zinken told me afterward that one of his desperately wounded Irishmen cried out to his comrades, "Charge them, boys; they have cha-ase (cheese) in their haversacks." Poor Pat, he has fought courageously in every land in quarrels not his own.— D. H. H.

♭ Major-General Walker claims that he proposed to me to make an advance movement with his whole corps, and complains that his command was disintegrated by sending it in by brigades.

General Walker did propose, as he says, to fall back and align upon Cleburne, when we saw Granger's corps approaching on our right, and I did refuse to permit this, believing that a withdrawal in full view of Granger would invite an attack upon our flank, and this might be fatal to troops more or less demoralized by the bloody repulse which they had sustained. The proposal to advance with his whole corps was never heard by me, and was, at best, impossible, as two of his five brigades had been detached, the one by Polk and the other by myself, to fill gaps in the line.— D. H. H.

our line."⸲ Rosecrans thus describes the timely help afforded by Granger to the sorely beset Thomas:

"Arrived in sight, Granger discovered at once the peril and the point of danger — the gap — and quick as thought he directed his advance brigade upon the enemy. General Steedman, taking a regimental color, led the column. Swift was the charge and terrible the conflict, but the enemy was broken. A thousand of our brave men killed and wounded paid for its possession."

Longstreet was determined to send Preston with his division of three brigades under Gracie, Trigg, and Kelly, aided by Robertson's brigade of Hood's division, to carry the heights — the main point of defense. His troops were of the best material and had been in reserve all day; but brave, fresh, and strong as they were, it was with them alternate advance and retreat, until success was assured by a renewal of the fight on the right. At 3:30 P. M. General Polk sent an order to me to assume command of the attacking forces on the right and renew the assault. Owing to a delay in the adjustment of our lines, the advance did not begin until 4 o'clock. The men sprang to their arms with the utmost alacrity, though they had not heard of Longstreet's success, and they showed by their cheerfulness that there was plenty of "fight in them." Cleburne ran forward his batteries, some by hand, to within three hundred yards of the enemy's breastworks, pushed forward his infantry, and carried them. General J. K. Jackson, of Cheatham's division, had a bloody struggle with the fortifications in his front, but had entered them when Cheatham with two more of his brigades, Maney's and Wright's, came up. Breckinridge and Walker met with but little opposition until the Chattanooga road was passed, when their right was unable to overcome the forces covering the enemy's retreat. As we passed into the woods west of the road, it was reported to me that a line was advancing at right angles to ours. I rode to the left to ascertain whether they were foes or friends, and soon recognized General Buckner. The cheers that went up when the two wings met were such as I had never heard before, and shall never hear again.

Preston gained the heights a half hour later, capturing 1000 prisoners and 4500 stand of arms. But neither right nor left is entitled to the laurels of a complete triumph. It was the combined attack which, by weakening the enthusiasm of the brave warriors who had stood on the defense so long and so obstinately, won the day.

Thomas had received orders after Granger's arrival to retreat to Rossville, but, stout soldier as he was, he resolved to hold his ground until nightfall. An hour more of daylight would have insured his capture. Thomas had under him all the Federal army, except the six brigades which had been driven off by the left wing.☆

⸲ According to the official returns the entire loss during the afternoon in Steedman's two brigades [including 613 captured or missing] was 1787. A Federal writer says that of the eight staff-officers of Brig.-Gen. Whitaker "three were killed, three wounded, and one killed or captured."—D. H. H.

☆ In regard to the relative strength of the two armies [see also p. 676], Colonel Archer Anderson says:

"From an examination of the original returns in the War Department, I reckon, in round numbers, the Federal infantry and artillery on the field at 59,000, and the Confederate infantry and artillery at 55,000. The Federal cavalry, about 10,000 strong, was outnumbered by the Confederates by 1000 men. Thus speak

Whatever blunders each of us in authority committed before the battles of the 19th and 20th, and during their progress, the great blunder of all was that of not pursuing the enemy on the 21st. The day was spent in burying the dead and gathering up captured stores. Forrest, with his usual promptness, was early in the saddle, and saw that the retreat was a rout. Disorganized masses of men were hurrying to the rear; batteries of artillery were inextricably mixed with trains of wagons; disorder and confusion pervaded the broken ranks struggling to get on. Forrest sent back word to Bragg that "every hour was worth a thousand men." But the commander-in-chief did not know of the victory until the morning of the 21st, and then he did not order a pursuit. Rosecrans spent the day and the night of the 21st in hurrying his trains out of town. A breathing-space was allowed him; the panic among his troops subsided, and Chattanooga — the objective point of the campaign — was held. There was no more splendid fighting in '61, when the flower of the Southern youth was in the field, than was displayed in those bloody days of September, '63. But it seems to me that the *élan* of the Southern soldier was never seen after Chickamauga — that brilliant dash which had distinguished him was gone forever. He was too intelligent not to know that the cutting in two of Georgia meant death to all his hopes. He knew that Longstreet's absence was imperiling Lee's safety, and that what had to be done must be done quickly. The delay in striking was exasperating to him; the failure to strike after the success was crushing to all his longings for an independent South. He fought stoutly to the last, but, after Chickamauga, with the sullenness of despair and without the enthusiasm of hope. That "barren victory" sealed the fate of the Southern Confederacy.

the returns. Perhaps a deduction of 5000 men from the reported strength of each army would more nearly represent the actual strength of the combatants. But in any case it is, I think, certain that Rosecrans was stronger in infantry and artillery than Bragg by at least 4000 men."

The Federal estimate of their loss, in captured or missing, is below the mark by 1000, if the Confederate claim of the capture of 6500 prisoners is correct. The Confederates also claim to have taken 51 pieces of artillery, 15,000 stand of arms, and a large amount of ordnance stores, camp-equipage, etc.— D. H. H.

GENERAL POLK AT CHICKAMAUGA.

BY HIS SON, CAPTAIN W. M. POLK, OF HIS STAFF.

THE reason given by General Polk for the delay in attack on the morning of September 20th, 1863, was that General Hill's corps was not ready for the assault. General Polk sent General Hill an order at midnight to attack at daylight, but General Hill could not be found (either on his line of battle or at Tedford's Ford, where his headquarters were reported to be). Upon learning this fact General Polk issued an order, dated 5 : 30 A. M., direct to Hill's division commanders to attack as soon as they could get into position. This second order was delivered in the presence of General Hill by Captain Wheless soon after sunrise, about 6 : 15. To this General Hill replied that his men were getting rations and that he would not be ready to move for an hour or more. General Polk reported this reply to General Bragg, in a note dated 7 A. M.,

and stated that the attack would be made as soon as General Hill was ready. This, of course, conflicts with the time given by General Hill for the reception of the second order, viz., 7 : 25 A. M. These facts are derived from the official statements of General Polk, Captain Wheless, and of John H. Fisher, on file in the War Records office.

As to the whereabouts of General Polk, on the morning of the 20th: General Polk left his camp at Alexander's Bridge, 1200 yards in rear of his line, between daylight and sunrise, and, as is shown by the statement of General Cheatham ("Official Records"), was on the line of battle at sunrise, where he remained and where he first met General Bragg (Captain Wheless, "Official Records"). These facts I state from my personal knowledge.

General Bragg's statement that General Polk

was away from his line of battle at this time was not derived from his own knowledge, but from a statement of one of his staff-officers, as is shown in the following extract from an unpublished private letter from General Bragg, dated Mobile, February 8th, 1873:

"The staff-officer sent to General Polk (Major Lee, A. I. G.) to urge his compliance with the orders of the previous night, reported to me that he found him at a farm-house, three miles from the line of his troops, about one hour after sunrise, sitting on the gallery reading a newspaper, and waiting as he (the general) said, for his breakfast."

The facts of the records above quoted are sufficient answer to this absurd statement. But I can add further that I saw Major Lee when he delivered General Bragg's message to General Polk, at his (Polk's) camp in the woods, at Alexander's Bridge, 1200 yards from his line, before sunrise. General Polk was then preparing to mount his horse.

I will also add of my own knowledge that General Polk had ridden from one end of his line to the other, and had met General Hill and each of the division commanders before General Bragg came upon his line of battle. They met on the line about 7:45 A. M.

As to the failure to attack on the 13th, the object of Polk's movement was to intercept Crittenden before he should cross to the west side of the Chickamauga and unite with other portions of Rosecrans's army. Polk was told that he would find Crittenden east of the creek about Pea Vine Church on the Graysville road, and was directed to attack him there at daylight of the 13th. He moved as ordered and found no enemy, Crittenden having crossed to the west of the creek the evening before. General Bragg in his report neglects to take this fact into account, and thus leaves the impression that Crittenden's escape was due to Polk's tardiness in moving rather than to his own tardiness in ordering the movement. It should have been ordered for the morning of the 12th.

THE CRISIS AT CHICKAMAUGA. [

BY GATES P. THRUSTON, BREVET BRIGADIER-GENERAL, U. S. V.

THE furious initial attack on the Federal left, on the morning of the 20th, although repulsed, unfortunately led to changes in Rosecrans's army materially affecting the results of the general conflict. Thomas, discovering his position turned and his front assaulted, hurried messengers to Rosecrans for assistance. Two aides, in rapid succession, called for reënforcements. All was still on the Federal right. The fight was raging with grand fury on the left.

Rosecrans felt that his apprehensions of the morning were to be realized. The Confederates were doubtless massing on his left. They had reached the much-coveted Chattanooga road. McCook was at once notified that Thomas was heavily pressed, that the left must be held at all hazards, and that he must be ready to reënforce Thomas at a moment's warning. Five minutes later came the order to hurry Sheridan's two brigades to the left. Negley's troops, replaced by Wood, had started. Van Cleve, with two brigades, was also sent to aid Thomas. McCook was now left with one of Sheridan's brigades and two of Jefferson C. Davis's, all depleted by Saturday's losses. They were unable to form a connected front, but joined Wood on their left. Captain Kellogg, of Thomas's staff, hurrying along the line with orders, unfortunately reported to Rosecrans that he had noticed "Brannan was out of line, and Reynolds's right exposed."

Turning to an aide (Major Frank Bond), Rosecrans directed him to order Wood "to close up on Reynolds as fast as possible and support him." In fact, Reynolds was not needing help, and Brannan was in position on his right, but slightly in rear. Wood, whose left connected with Brannan's right, passed to the rear of Brannan to reach Reynolds's position; thus a wide gap was left in the Union line. McCook had already called up Wilder to strengthen his front, and sent for the main cavalry to protect the right. The right had unexpectedly become, as it were, the rear of the army.

Unhappily for the National army, Bragg was not now massing his forces on our left. He had just been defeated and repulsed there. Bragg's main plan had failed; but in the quiet forest, within almost a stone's-throw of our right, and in the still overclouding mist, were Longstreet and Buckner, with the left wing of the Confederate army massed in battle array, impatiently awaiting the signal for attack.

Longstreet's troops were placed in column of brigades at half distance,—a masterpiece of tactics. Hood, a soldier full of energy and dash, was to lead the column, his own division being massed five brigades deep, with the brigades of Kershaw and Humphreys as additional supports.

The order to advance came at last. The deep Confederate lines suddenly appeared. The woods in our front seemed alive. On they came like an angry flood. They struck McCook's three remaining brigades, the remnants of the Federal right. Under the daring personal exertions of McCook and Davis, they made a gallant but vain resistance. The massed lines of the enemy swarmed around their flanks. Pouring through the opening made by Wood's withdrawal, they struck his last brigade as it was leaving the line. It was slammed back like a door, and shattered. Brannan, on Wood's left, was struck in front and flank. His right was flung back; his left stood fast. Sheridan, hastening to the left with two brigades, was called back, and rushed to the rescue. His little force stayed the storm for a time. Wave after wave of Con-

} Condensed from the "Southern Bivouac" for December, 1886.— EDITORS.

federates came on; resistance only increased the multitude. Brannan's artillery, attacked in flank, rushed to the rear for clearer ground, and, with the Confederates at their heels, suddenly plunged into Van Cleve marching to the aid of Thomas. Disorder ensued; effective resistance was lost. The Reserve Artillery of the center, well posted in rear, unable to manœuvre in the undergrowth, hedged around by infantry a half hour before, was now without immediate support. The sudden rush of Longstreet's compact column through the forest had foiled all plans. The astonished artillerists were swept from their guns. General Negley, with one of his brigades isolated in rear, shared the general fate of the right.

When Longstreet struck the right, Rosecrans was near McCook and Crittenden. Seeing our line swept back, he hurried to Sheridan's force for aid. With staff and escort he recklessly strove to stem the tide. They attempted to pass to the left through a storm of canister and musketry, but were driven back.

All became confusion. No order could be heard above the tempest of battle. With a wild yell the Confederates swept on far to their left. They seemed everywhere victorious. Rosecrans was borne back in the retreat. Fugitives, wounded, caissons, escort, ambulances, thronged the narrow pathways. He concluded that our whole line had given way, that the day was lost, that the next stand must be made at Chattanooga. McCook and Crittenden, caught in the same tide of retreat, seeing only rout everywhere, shared the opinion of Rosecrans, and reported to him for instructions and coöperation.

Briefly, this is the story of the disaster on our right at Chickamauga: We were overwhelmed by numbers; we were beaten in detail. Thirty minutes earlier Longstreet would have met well-organized resistance. Thirty minutes later our marching divisions could have formed beyond his column of attack.

But Longstreet had now swept away all organized opposition in his front. Four divisions only of the Union army remained in their original position—Johnson, of McCook's corps; Palmer, of Crittenden's, and Baird and Reynolds, of Thomas's. Three had been cut off and swept away. Longstreet's force separated them. He says he urged Bragg to send Wheeler's cavalry in pursuit. Strange to report, no pursuit was ordered.

An incident of the battle perhaps contributed to the delay. When Sheridan and others were sent to the left, the writer hastened down toward Crawfish Springs, instructed by McCook to order the cavalry to the left to fill the gaps made by the withdrawal of infantry. I was but fairly on the run when Longstreet struck our right: The storm of battle was sweeping over the ground I had just left. Hastily giving the orders and returning, I found the 39th Indiana regiment coming from a cross-road,—a full, fresh regiment, armed with Spencer's repeating-rifles, the only mounted force in our army corps. Calling upon Colonel T. J. Harrison, its commander, to hurry to the left, we led the regiment at a gallop to the Widow Glenn's.

The sound of battle had lulled. No Union force was in sight. A Confederate line near by was advancing against the position. Harrison, dismounting his men, dashed at the enemy in a most effective charge. Wilder, coming up on our right, also attacked. Wilder had two regiments armed with the same repeating-rifles. They did splendid work. Longstreet told Wilder after the war that the steady and continued racket of these guns led him to think an army corps had attacked his left flank. Bragg, cautious by nature, hesitated. By the time he was ready to turn Longstreet's force against Thomas, valuable time had elapsed.

Brannan, partly knocked out of line, had gathered his division on a hill at right angles to his former position, and a half mile in rear of Reynolds. General Wood came up with Harker's brigade and part of George P. Buell's, and posted them near Brannan's left. Some of Van Cleve's troops joined them, and fragments of Negley's.

General Thomas, ignorant of these movements and of the disaster to the right of the Union army, had again been attacked by Breckinridge and Forrest. They were again in Baird's rear with increased force. Thomas's reserve brigades, Willich, Grose, and Van Derveer, hurried to meet the attack. After a fierce struggle the Confederates were beaten back. Thomas, expecting the promised assistance of Sheridan, had sent Captain Kellogg to guide him to the left. Kellogg, hurrying back, reported that he had been fired on by a line of Confederates advancing in the woods in rear of Reynolds, who held the center of our general line.

The men in gray were coming on the right instead of Sheridan! Wood and Harker hoped the force advancing in the woods on their new front was a friendly one. The National flag was waved; a storm of bullets was the response. It was Stewart and Bate coming with their Tennesseeans. They had finally forced their way across the ragged edge of the Federal right, and were following Hood. Fortunately Thomas had just repulsed Breckinridge's attack on his left, and Stanley, Beatty, and Van Derveer had double-quicked across the "horseshoe" to our new right. They did not come a moment too soon. The improvised line of Federals thus hastily formed on "Battery Hill" now successfully withstood the assault of the enemy. The Union line held the crest. Longstreet was stayed at last. Gathering new forces, he soon sent a flanking column around our right. We could not extend our line to meet this attack. They had reached the summit, and were coming around still farther on through a protected ravine. For a time the fate of the Union army hung in the balance. All seemed lost, when unexpected help came from Gordon Granger and the right was saved.

When Longstreet first struck our right I was hurrying toward Crawfish Springs, as stated above, to order the cavalry to the left. I brought back with me Harrison's regiment, which, with Wilder's brigade, gallantly charged the Confederates in flank. Harrison captured some two hundred prisoners and turned again upon the enemy. Finding no Federal infantry in sight, I passed to the northward, taking with me Harrison's disarmed prisoners, partly under charge of my small escort, to prevent their recapture. We had a lively double-quick race, pushing our prisoners at the point of sword and carbine to get them to a place of safety. Only the predominance of the gray uniforms prevented the Confederates, three hundred yards away, from riddling our little party in the chase. We soon reached our retreating forces. Placing the prisoners in safe custody, I turned and rode over the Ridge toward the front, no enemy appearing.

Riding on, I struck the Dry Valley road, running along the east slope of the Ridge. Near by, on the left, I found Sheridan and Davis, with the remnants of their five brigades. General Phil was furious. Like the great Washington on several occasions, he was *swearing* mad, and no wonder. The devoted Lytle and the truest and bravest had fallen in vain resistance around him. His splendid fighting qualities and his fine soldiers had not had half a chance. He had lost faith. Hearing the sound of battle on our left, I offered to ascertain the situation with Thomas on the left, and report as soon as possible. I hurried off at a racing gallop, directly through the open woodland, with my few faithful soldiers of the 2d Kentucky cavalry (of the Headquarters escort), toward the increasing sound of musketry. As we neared the firing we came suddenly upon a line of gray much too close to be agreeable. Fortunately it was intent on other game in its front, and we escaped with only a few whizzing compliments. We were too far to the right. We had struck the wrong side, and were behind the Confederates. Circling to the left we were soon among the soldiers in blue in rear of the Union lines.

Galloping through the wounded as best we could, I checked my horse before the form of an officer borne in the arms of his comrades to find that it was an old home friend, Colonel Durbin Ward, a moment before severely wounded.

I soon reached General Thomas. He was intently watching the conflict near the crest, a few steps in rear of the battle-line. General Wood and other officers were near. I reported briefly the situation on the right. Thanking me, he requested me to try to bring up Sheridan's and Davis's troops to aid his right. In his official report he states that I came with General Garfield. We probably reached him about the same time, but General Garfield had come out from Rossville, by

the Lafayette road, and I had crossed almost directly from the extreme right. We gave him the first tidings from the troops cut off. Hurrying back on my mission, full of hope that the day was not lost, we soon reached the identical spot on the Dry Valley road where we had left Sheridan and Davis. Strange to say, no Confederate cavalry or infantry appeared, and there seemed still no pursuit. Forrest, Wheeler, Wharton, Roddey,— half the cavalry of the Confederacy,— were with Bragg, yet no cavalry apparently came through the gap of a mile or more to pursue or follow our retreating forces on the right. At our recent fight at Murfreesboro', Wheeler's whole force had been smashing around in our rear. It had been about as uncomfortable for nervous recruits there as on the battle-front.

Unfortunately Sheridan's and Davis's force had drifted down the road toward Rossville. Hastening after them, we found they had already entered the narrow road or defile at McFarland's Gap. I tried to halt the rear of the column, but without success. The miseries of a mounted officer trying to pass marching infantry on a narrow roadway can be well imagined. Time was precious. I rode furiously through the thicket, alongside, and appealed to officers. "See Jeff, Colonel?" they said. "See Phil?" Some old trudger in the ranks called out, "We'll talk to you, my son, when we get to the Ohio River!"

A long half-hour was lost in scrambling along this wretched defile before I reached the head of the column. There I found Generals Sheridan, Davis, and Negley. We were about half-way between the field and Rossville. We held a hasty conference. Davis ordered a "right-about" at once, and marched briskly to the front; Lieutenant-Colonel William M. Ward followed with the 10th Ohio. Sheridan was still without faith. He may have thought there was danger at Rossville, or that his troops had not regained their fighting spirit. He insisted on going to Rossville. Darkness would catch him before he could reach the field from that direction. Negley was vacillating: he finally went to Rossville.

We soon reached the battle-field with Davis's and Ward's troops, but the night was then near. They did not get into action, but it was a cheerful sight to see at least some of the troops cut off in the morning in line again on the right of General Thomas, ready for an emergency.

REËNFORCING THOMAS AT CHICKAMAUGA.

BY J. S. FULLERTON, BREVET BRIGADIER-GENERAL, U. S. V.; AT CHICKAMAUGA CHIEF-OF-STAFF TO GENERAL GORDON GRANGER.

ON the 19th day of September, 1863, the Reserve Corps of the Army of the Cumberland, General Gordon Granger in command, was distributed over a long stretch of country, its rear at Murfreesboro' and its van on the battle-field of Chickamauga. These troops had been posted to cover the rear and left flank of the army. During September 19th, the first day of the battle, they were engaged in some skirmishing and stood at arms expecting an attack. On the evening of the 19th every indication pointed to a renewal of the battle early the next day. The night was cold for that time of the year. Tell-tale fires were prohibited. The men slept on their arms. All was quiet save in the field-hospitals in the rear. A bright moon lighted up the fields and woods.

THE SNODGRASS FARM-HOUSE. FROM A RECENT PHOTOGRAPH.

General Thomas's headquarters on the second day were in the field this side of the house. The hills called
the "Horse-shoe," made famous by the defense of Brannan and Steedman, lie on the
opposite side of the house. See map, p. 648.—EDITORS.

Along the greater part of a front of eight miles
the ground was strewn with the intermingled dead
of friend and foe. The morning of Sunday, the
20th, opened with a cloudless sky, but a fog had
come up from the warm water of the Chickamauga
and hung over the battle-field until 9 o'clock. A
silence of desertion was in the front. This quiet
continued till nearly 10 o'clock; then, as the
peaceful tones of the church-bells, rolling over the
land from the east, reached the meridian of
Chickamauga, they were made dissonant by the
murderous roar of the artillery of Bishop Polk,
who was opening the battle on Thomas's front.
Granger, who had been ordered at all hazards
to hold fast where he was, listened and grew impatient. Shortly before 10 o'clock, calling my
attention to a great column of dust moving from
our front toward the point from which came the
sound of battle, he said, "They are concentrating
over there. That is where we ought to be." The
corps flag marked his headquarters in an open
field near the Ringgold road. He walked up and
down in front of his flag, nervously pulling his
beard. Once stopping, he said, "Why the ——
does Rosecrans keep me here? There is nothing
in front of us now. There is the battle"—pointing in the direction of Thomas. Every moment
the sounds of battle grew louder, while the many
columns of dust rolling together here mingled with
the smoke that hung over the scene.

At 11 o'clock, with Granger, I climbed a high hay-
rick near by. We sat there for ten minutes listening and watching. Then Granger jumped up, thrust
his glass into its case, and exclaimed with an oath:

"I am going to Thomas, orders or no orders!"

"And if you go," I replied, "it may bring disaster to the army and you to a court-martial."

"There's nothing in our front now but ragtag,
bobtail cavalry," he replied. "Don't you see
Bragg is piling his whole army on Thomas? I am
going to his assistance."

We quickly climbed down the rick, and, going
to Steedman, Granger ordered him to move his
command "over there," pointing toward the place
from which came the sounds of battle. Colonel
Daniel McCook was directed to hold fast at McAfee
Church, where his brigade covered the Ringgold
road. Before half-past 11 o'clock Steedman's
command was in motion. Granger, with his staff
and escort, rode in advance. Steedman, after
accompanying them a short distance, rode back to
the head of his column.

Thomas was nearly four miles away. The day
had now grown very warm, yet the troops marched
rapidly over the narrow road, which was covered
ankle-deep with dust that rose in suffocating
clouds. Completely enveloped in it, the moving
column swept along like a desert sandstorm. Two
miles from the point of starting, and three-
quarters of a mile to the left of the road, the
enemy's skirmishers and a section of artillery
opened fire on us from an open wood. This force
had worked round Thomas's left, and was then
partly in his rear. Granger halted to feel them.
Soon becoming convinced that it was only a large
party of observation, he again started his column
and pushed rapidly forward. I was then sent to
bring up Colonel McCook's brigade, and put it in

position to watch the movements of the enemy, to keep open the Lafayette road, and to cover the open fields between that point and the position held by Thomas. This brigade remained there the rest of the day. Our skirmishers had not gone far when they came upon Thomas's field-hospital, at Cloud's house, then swarming with the enemy. They came from the same body of Forrest's cavalry that had fired on us from the wood. They were quickly driven out, and our men were warmly welcomed with cheers from dying and wounded men.

A little farther on we were met by a staff-officer sent by General Thomas to discover whether we were friends or enemies; he did not know whence friends could be coming, and the enemy appeared to be approaching from all directions. All of this shattered Army of the Cumberland left on the field was with Thomas; but not more than one-fourth of the men of the army who went into battle at the opening were there. Thomas's loss in killed and wounded during the two days had been dreadful. As his men dropped out his line was contracted to half its length. Now its flanks were bent back, conforming to ridges shaped like a horse-shoe.

On the part of Thomas and his men there was no thought but that of fighting. He was a soldier who had never retreated, who had never been defeated. He stood immovable, the "Rock of Chickamauga." Never had soldiers greater love for a commander. He imbued them with his spirit, and their confidence in him was sublime.

To the right of Thomas's line was a gorge, then a high ridge, nearly at right angles thereto, running east and west. Confederates under Kershaw (McLaws's division of Hood's corps) were passing through the gorge, together with Bushrod Johnson's division, which Longstreet was strengthening with Hindman's division; divisions were forming on this ridge for an assault; to their left the guns of a battery were being unlimbered for an enfilading fire. There was not a man to send against the force on the ridge, none to oppose this impending assault. The enemy saw the approaching colors of the Reserve Corps and hesitated.

At 1 o'clock Granger shook hands with Thomas. Something was said about forming to fight to the right and rear.

"Those men must be driven back," said Granger, pointing to the gorge and ridge. "Can you do it?" asked Thomas.

"Yes. My men are fresh, and they are just the fellows for that work. They are raw troops, and they don't know any better than to charge up there."

Granger quickly sent Aleshire's battery of 3-inch rifle guns which he brought up to Thomas's left to assist in repelling another assault about to be made on the Kelly farm front. Whitaker's and Mitchell's brigades under Steedman were wheeled into position and projected against the enemy in the gorge and on the ridge. With ringing cheers they advanced in two lines by double-quick — over open fields, through weeds waist-high, through a little valley, then up the ridge. The enemy opened on them first with artillery, then with a murderous musketry fire. When well up the ridge the men, almost exhausted, were halted

for breath. They lay on the ground two or three minutes, then came the command, "Forward!" Brave, bluff old Steedman, with a regimental flag in his hand, led the way. On went the lines, firing as they ran and bravely receiving a deadly and continuous fire from the enemy on the summit. The Confederates began to break and in another minute were flying down the southern slope of the ridge. In twenty minutes from the beginning of the charge the ridge had been carried.

Granger's hat had been torn by a fragment of shell; Steedman had been wounded; Whitaker had been wounded, and four of his five staff-officers killed or mortally wounded. Of Steedman's two brigades, numbering 3500, twenty per cent. had been killed and wounded in that twenty minutes; and the end was not yet.

The enemy massed a force to retake the ridge. They came before our men had rested; twice they assaulted and were driven back. During one assault, as the first line came within range of our muskets, it halted, apparently hesitating, when we saw a colonel seize a flag, wave it over his head, and rush forward. The whole line instantly caught his enthusiasm, and with a wild cheer followed, only to be hurled back again. Our men ran down the ridge in pursuit. In the midst of a group of Confederate dead and wounded they found the brave colonel dead, the flag he carried spread over him where he fell.

Soon after 5 o'clock Thomas rode to the left of his line, leaving Granger the ranking officer at the center. The ammunition of both Thomas's and Granger's commands was now about exhausted. When Granger had come up he had given ammunition to Brannan and Wood, and that had exhausted his supply. The cartridge-boxes of both our own and the enemy's dead within reach had been emptied by our men. When it was not yet 6 o'clock, and Thomas was still on the left of his line, Brannan rushed up to Granger, saying, "The enemy are forming for another assault; we have not another round of ammunition — what shall we do?" "Fix bayonets and go for them," was the reply. Along the whole line ran the order, "Fix bayonets." On came the enemy — our men were lying down. "Forward," was sounded. In one instant they were on their feet. Forward they went to meet the charge. The enemy fled. So impetuous was this counter-charge that one regiment, with empty muskets and empty cartridge-boxes, broke through the enemy's line, which, closing in their rear, carried them off as in the undertow.

One more feeble assault was made by the enemy; then the day closed, and the battle of Chickamauga was over. Of the 3700 men of the Reserve Corps who went into the battle that afternoon, 1175 were killed and wounded; 613 were missing, many of whom were of the regiment that broke through the lines. Our total loss was 1788, nearly 50 per cent.

Gordon Granger was rough in manner, but he had a tender heart. He was inclined to insubordination, especially when he knew his superior to be wrong. Otherwise he was a splendid soldier. Rosecrans named him well when he wrote of him, "Granger, great in battle."

HOUSE OF MR. J. M. LEE, CRAWFISH SPRINGS, ROSECRANS'S HEADQUARTERS BEFORE THE BATTLE, AND SITE OF THE UNION FIELD-HOSPITAL FOR THE RIGHT WING. FROM A PHOTOGRAPH TAKEN IN 1884.

NOTES ON THE CHICKAMAUGA CAMPAIGN.

BY EMERSON OPDYCKE, BREVET MAJOR-GENERAL, U. S. V.

CHATTANOOGA was the indispensable key to all the objects committed to the Army of the Cumberland, and General Halleck planned two widely separated movements toward their accomplishment. General Burnside, starting from the Ohio River with one column, was to cross the mountains of eastern Kentucky. To overcome the great advantage of the enemy's position and works, and secure at one blow a decisive victory, General Rosecrans conceived a series of brilliant movements from Murfreesboro' where his four corps were concentrated. On the 23d of June he began the formidable operations which sent the enemy out of middle Tennessee and left our army at the western base of the Cumberland mountains.

General Rosecrans halted there till the 16th of August, and between him and Halleck the question of delay was renewed with spirit. Rosecrans justly urged that, before crossing the Tennessee River, his right and rear ought to be protected by the part of our army made idle by the surrender of Vicksburg, because the enemy's superiority in cavalry forced him constantly to weaken his line of battle, to protect the long line over which supplies were brought to him. This sound view, however, did not prevail, and if General Bragg had perceived the advantage to him of Halleck's error, I am sure that the peremptory order by which Rosecrans was sent across the Tennessee River and into the mountains between Bridgeport and Chattanooga would have proved disastrous.

If Bragg had stubbornly defended his several

positions, he certainly could have retained Chattanooga and assumed the offensive, for reënforcements soon made his army larger than ours. It would have been rash for Rosecrans to move his force on the theory that the enemy would not defend at least some of the formidable positions that now separated the two armies. He had to assume that his adversary's conduct would be stubbornly defensive.

On the 16th of August he put his army in motion, crossed the Cumberland mountains, and caused his main columns to appear at several points on the river, the extremes fifty miles apart. These movements so deceived Bragg that he was comparatively harmless where we really wished to cross ; and by the 4th of September the army, followed by its artillery, wagons, and beeves, safely reached the south bank of the Tennessee River. Then, throwing as much energy into his movements as though he had approved them, Rosecrans promptly marched upon Chattanooga.

With but slight opposition his columns wound through the defiles of Raccoon Mountain and came to the western base of the Lookout range. On its highest point the enemy's signal-flags were seen announcing to Bragg in Chattanooga the presence of our army. There are only three routes by which armies can cross the range, respectively 2 miles, 26 miles, and 42 miles south of Chattanooga. Unless Bragg should defend these passes, he could remain in the town only to surrender, because the two more distant routes would give us ready access to his line of supplies and enable us to close all avenues of retreat.

Time had now become of pressing importance to him, because heavy reënforcements were advancing to his aid: two divisions from Mississippi, one from Knoxville, and a renowned corps under Longstreet from the army of General Lee. He was in a few days to feel the mistake of allowing us so easily to come to the last barrier of Chattanooga. Fortunately for our army, the Confederate general, while easily defending the pass nearest the town, gave no attention to the other two. Thomas was directed to the 26 and McCook to the 42 mile pass, while Crittenden made demonstrations near Chattanooga. These admirable movements endangered Bragg's communications and forced him to choose between immediate retreat and ultimate surrender. He retreated; and on the 9th of September Crittenden entered Chattanooga. These operations drew Buckner from Knoxville to the aid of Bragg, and Burnside marched into Knoxville.

It is surprising that the events of the last sixty days did not suggest to General Halleck concentrations that must have ended the war in 1863. By the 4th of July Meade had seriously defeated and permanently weakened Lee at Gettysburg, and Grant, by giving us Vicksburg and 30,000 prisoners, had ended all important operations near the Mississippi River. In the main, this left Grant's army of 75,000 men free to be sent in whatever directions lay the best chance of decisive work. Is it not, therefore, clear, that Rosecrans should have been heavily reënforced and made able to crush Bragg at Chickamauga? He then could have marched irresistibly through east Tennessee, to the aid of Meade against Lee, whose army could not have existed a single day if it had held its ground, before such a concentration of forces. The order thus to reënforce the Army of the Cumberland could have been as easily made and executed before as after Chickamauga. I am convinced that it would have saved us the slaughter and the expense of 1864. But Halleck only ordered Burnside to reënforce Rosecrans. Burnside, though without an opposing force of importance, failed utterly to obey the orders of Halleck, as well as the plain suggestions of the situation.

Up to the 9th of September — the day Rosecrans entered Chattanooga — his plans and movements, aside from the delay in beginning operations, had been brilliant and faultless. He had not achieved the highest success — the destruction of his adversary, but he had forced from the enemy strategic advantages from which immense results were afterward gained by his successors. But the moment he entered Chattanooga he should have concentrated his army there long enough to accumulate supplies, ascertain the position and intentions of his adversary, and whether or not Burnside would reënforce him. He was now 337 miles from the Ohio River, 150 from Nashville, and his prudence, not his impetuosity, should have increased. Halleck, himself deceived, misled Rosecrans, who judged that his present work was to pursue an alarmed adversary, and, accordingly,

on the 10th of September, ordered Crittenden's corps to seek the enemy in the direction of Ringgold,—thus still farther separating his army.

General Wood's division, to which I belonged, happened to be the rear of Crittenden's column, and in the evening a simple negro informed Wood of the position of Bragg's army. Instead of an alarmed retreat, the enemy's movement had been a leisurely march of thirty miles south to Lafayette. The divergent movements which had placed Thomas near to and west of Lafayette, McCook sixteen miles farther south, and was now placing Crittenden farther north than McCook was south of the Confederate army, made it convenient for Bragg to overwhelm in succession our separated corps before any two of them could be united. Wood hurried the momentous information to Rosecrans at Chattanooga; and, notwithstanding the incredulity with which it was received, Harker's brigade of Wood's division was ordered to countermarch at daybreak to the Lafayette road, and to make a reconnoissance in the direction indicated by the negro. Soon meeting an opposing force that was feeling its way toward Chattanooga, Harker slowly forced it back across the Chickamauga River, at Lee and Gordon's Mills, only eighteen miles from Lafayette. Crittenden was now ordered to the mills, Thomas to Lafayette, and McCook to Summerville, twenty-five miles south of Lafayette; for Rosecrans did not yet believe that the enemy's entire army was there, preparing to assume the offensive. Most happily, Bragg, although correctly informed of the isolation of our corps, took no decisive advantage of our helplessness.

McCook found that the enemy's cavalry, when driven, always retreated in the direction of Lafayette; and in advancing toward that place Thomas met a resistance that convinced him that he was in the presence of the Confederate army, while Crittenden's reconnoissance south from the mills sustained the opinion of Thomas.

On the 12th, however, Rosecrans also became at last convinced that the enemy had faced about at Lafayette, and orders were issued to attack them at that place.

By the 15th he learned that the enemy was receiving heavy reënforcements. Doctor Hale, chief-of-scouts for General Thomas, found large numbers of prisoners whom Grant had paroled at Vicksburg. They spoke freely of the fact that they had been ordered on duty, although not yet exchanged, and all were confident that the concentration then going on would result in our annihilation. Stunned by the disasters to their cause at Gettysburg and Vicksburg, the Confederate chiefs were secretly hurrying reënforcements to Bragg, hoping to neutralize the effects of those disasters by overwhelming Rosecrans. These well-planned movements were not, until too late, even suspected by Halleck, who sent us the report that Bragg was reënforcing Lee!

As already indicated, if Rosecrans had opened his campaign when the other two great armies were carrying forward the Gettysburg and Vicksburg campaigns, his operations could not now have been disturbed by these reënforcements.

If he should be defeated when so far from his base, and with such obstacles to the rear, the destruction of his army would be probable; while if he should have the good fortune to defeat his adversary, it would not be possible, without surplus supplies at Chattanooga, to pursue far enough to gather the fruits of a victory. With so much to lose and so little to gain, it is clear that the battle of Chickamauga ought not to have been fought.

It has been said that this battle was necessary to secure us Chattanooga. But the error of that assertion may be seen in the fact that Rosecrans, before the battle, still had time to assume impregnable positions around that town. Three days were enough for this, and it was seven days before Bragg seriously interfered with the freedom of our movements. Moreover, Chattanooga, won at the cost of Chickamauga, became a peril instead of a gain. But, deciding not to fall back, Rosecrans slowly concentrated his corps on the north bank of the Chickamauga River, at Lee and Gordon's Mills, twelve miles south of Chattanooga. Bragg decided to move down the valley up which he had retired because, first, of all the routes open to him that one was least obstructed; and, secondly, because it would continue his army near the railway of his supplies, which was also bringing him Longstreet. Rosecrans did not get his corps united and well in position, before the enemy, on the 19th, began the battle of Chickamauga.

The country in which the next two days' operations took place lies between the river and Missionary Ridge, and was covered by woods of varying density, broken here and there by cleared fields. The Chickamauga River, winding slowly through the forest of the region, flows into the Tennessee eight miles above Chattanooga. Bragg's aim was to turn our left and gain the road into Chattanooga, now indispensable to the existence of our army. Thomas commanded our left; and as Bragg sent division after division against that wing, Rosecrans sent successive divisions to Thomas. The fighting was close and stubborn; batteries were taken and retaken till the day closed, without material advantage to either side. It was clear, however, that we were outnumbered; for, while we had put nearly every regiment into the action, the enemy, meeting us with equal numbers in line of battle, still had heavy reserves.

In the night both commanders prepared for the decisive conflict which all felt must come on the 20th. Still covering the Chattanooga road, Rosecrans placed his army in a somewhat better position, both flanks well refused. From left to right his divisions were: Baird's, R. W. Johnson's, Palmer's, Reynolds's, Brannan's, Negley's, Davis's, Sheridan's; Wood's and Van Cleve's were in reserve; and three brigades of Granger's corps were near Rossville, four miles away. Thomas commanded six divisions at the left, McCook two at the right, and Crittenden the two in reserve. Thomas covered his front with a slight barricade of rails and old logs found in the woods, and so greatly aided his men.

Early in the morning Thomas discovered, and reported to Rosecrans, that another division was needed to maintain our extreme left against the enemy's longer line. Rosecrans, therefore, brought Wood from reserve to relieve Negley, and ordered Negley at once to report his division to Thomas; and Thomas was informed that Negley would immediately join him at the line. But Negley, disappearing from the line, drifted away from the field to Rossville. Two of his brigades reached the left, but so far apart, and so ill-timed, as to be of little value. It is important to remember Negley's conduct, because from it came the misapprehensions that were soon to result in disaster to our right wing.

The Confederate plan was to turn and envelop our left, and then to advance upon our divisions in succession, and involve the whole in one common ruin. Their right wing was commanded by Polk, and their left by Longstreet.

Polk was ordered to begin the battle at daybreak, but the first shots were not heard before 8:30; and, in an hour, the action at the left became furious. Polk's right division began to envelop our left and to appear upon our rear; but Thomas hurried some reserves against it and drove it away in disorder. Having been able, in the absence of Negley's division, to find the way to our left and rear, the enemy would naturally reappear there with decisive numbers. Thomas, therefore, knowing nothing of Negley's conduct, and wishing to add only a division to his left, sent again and again for the promised reënforcements. The attack soon extended heavily to Johnson, Palmer, and Reynolds; and, by 10:30, lightly to Brannan. Naturally supposing that Negley had already reached Thomas, Rosecrans inferred, from the requests of Thomas and from other indications, that Bragg was moving his left wing to the extreme right of the Confederate line of battle. The conflict had been raging against Thomas for two hours, while Wood, Davis, and Sheridan were untouched; and, not suspecting that Longstreet (a reconnoissance of ten minutes would have developed it) was already formed for attack and about to advance in full force against our right wing, Rosecrans, in the short space of fifteen minutes,—10:30 to 10:45,—ordered to his left Van Cleve, from the reserve, and Sheridan, from the extreme right; and, by the blunder of an aide in wording an order, sent Wood out of line to "close up on Reynolds and support him as soon as possible," while McCook was to move Davis by the left flank into the position vacated by Wood. These disconnected and fatal movements of Van Cleve, Wood, Sheridan, and Davis were in progress when Longstreet attacked them with six divisions of the Confederate left wing. Disaster was the immediate and inevitable result.

Sheridan's routed division moved back to Rossville. Heroism could not save Davis; his division was overwhelmed, and scattered in fragments that were afterward collected behind Missionary Ridge. Wood's movement uncovered Brannan's right, and, in temporary confusion, that division hurried away to a new position. This exposed Reynolds's right, made it necessary for him to change front to the rear at right angles on his left; but *there* he held firmly to Palmer's right. The rush of disordered troops and artillery, disintegrating Van Cleve's division, destroyed its further usefulness in this battle.

Rosecrans, seeing this appalling demolition of his right wing, and finding that the enemy had interposed between him and Thomas, hastened around to Rossville. Finding there men of Negley's division, which he had supposed to be with Thomas, Rosecrans thought the day lost, and deemed it his duty to hasten to Chattanooga, there to prepare for the reception and disposition of what *seemed to him* his disordered and defeated army. Rosecrans and Garfield, his chief-of-staff, separated at Rossville — Rosecrans riding to Chattanooga and Garfield to Thomas at the front. Rosecrans says that he sent Garfield to the front; while Garfield has many times said that he himself insisted upon going — that the sound of the battle proved that Thomas was still holding the enemy in check. McCook and Crittenden soon joined Rosecrans at Chattanooga; but Thomas remained on the field. Brannan brought his division to a good position, but so far to the right of Reynolds that the space of a division lay open between them. While Wood was moving toward this gap, Longstreet, advancing to complete the work, came within musket-range.

The moment was critical, because if Wood should be unable to occupy and hold the gap, Longstreet would pass through, permanently cut off Brannan, again turn, and then overwhelm Reynolds, and attack the rear of Palmer, Johnson, and Baird, who were still confronted by Polk. Wood coolly changed front under fire, so as to face south instead of east, and caused one of his brigades to charge with fixed bayonets. The audacity of the charge probably made the enemy believe that there was force enough near to sustain it, for they soon bolted, and then fled out of range just before our bayonets reached their ranks. The needed moments were snatched from the enemy, and Wood brought his division into the gap between Reynolds and Brannan.

Except some fragments from the broken divisions, our line was now composed of Baird's, Johnson's, Palmer's, Reynolds's, Wood's, and Brannan's divisions, naming them from left to right. In front stood the whole army of the enemy, eager to fall upon us with the energy that comes from great success and greater hopes. But close behind our line rode a general whose judgment never erred, whose calm, invincible will never bent; and around him thirty thousand soldiers resolved to exhaust the last round of ammunition, and then to hold their ground with their bayonets. Soldiers thus inspired and commanded, are more easily killed than defeated.

For five long hours the shocks and carnage were as close and deadly as men could make them. Thomas often came within speaking distance of his men, and wherever the energy of the attack most endangered our line, he strengthened it with cannon and regiments drawn from points in less peril; and when the soldiers asked for more ammunition Thomas said: "Use your bayonets." At about 3:30 in the afternoon I saw General Thomas looking in the direction of Chattanooga,

watching with anxious interest a column of dust rising in the air. Our suspense was relieved when Granger and Steedman emerged from the dust, and Garfield dashed up to Thomas.

To prevent a turning movement on the road from Ringgold, through Rossville to Chattanooga, Granger, with three brigades, had been stationed on the Ringgold road; and, by a sound, soldierly judgment, leaving one brigade to do the work assigned to the three, brought two brigades to the field. Thomas himself was then only a little way down the rear slope of the low ridge on which Wood's division was fighting, with every man in the line, and with no reserves. We were hard pressed, and many muskets became so hot that loading was difficult; but Thomas sent up two cannon with the words: "The position must be held." The reply was: "Tell General Thomas that we will hold the position or go to heaven from it."

At about 4 o'clock Longstreet drew back and asked for reënforcements, but was answered that the right wing was already so shattered that it could not aid him. He then brought forward his reserves and re-formed his lines; and, extending beyond our right, advanced in a final attack.

Thomas ordered Granger's reënforcements to the right of Brannan, where the enemy had already begun to appear. The conflict there, and on the divisions of Brannan and Wood, was soon at its fiercest. Our short-range ammunition from the cannon cut great gaps through the enemy's columns, and the steady volleys of musketry, aided by our bayonets, did their remorseless work for about thirty minutes; and then the Confederate left wing, shattered, bleeding, defeated, withdrew from sight. The battle was ended — Thomas had saved the army.

The sun had not yet gone down, and there was time enough to renew the action, but Bragg, if we may trust his official report, had lost two-fifths of his infantry; his army was incapable of making another effort. What now would have been the consequences if General Rosecrans had come upon the field with ammunition and the few thousand soldiers collected near Rossville?

On the 21st Bragg was too prudent to attack, and on the 22d our army was placed in positions around Chattanooga.

Of our men under fire, we had lost more than one-third, and a number of batteries in the woods fell to the enemy by the disaster on the morning of the 20th. About 30,000 men — both sides — were killed and wounded in this battle.

On the 23d and 24th the Confederates came slowly into position on Missionary Ridge and Lookout Mountain, connecting the two by a line of earth-works across Chattanooga Valley; and, by sending a force into Lookout Valley, they commanded our 26-mile wagon route to Bridgeport for supplies. This forced us to an almost impassable mountain route of sixty miles to the same point. Knowing that it would be impossible long to subsist an army by this route, Bragg waited the process of starvation with some probability of success.

THE OPPOSING FORCES AT CHICKAMAUGA, GA.

September 19th–20th, 1863.

For much of the information contained in this list and in similar lists to follow, the editors are indebted (in advance of the publication of the "Official Records") to Brigadier-General Richard C. Drum, Adjutant-General of the Army. K stands for killed; w for wounded; m w for mortally wounded; m for captured or missing; c for captured.

THE UNION ARMY.

ARMY OF THE CUMBERLAND — Major-General William S. Rosecrans.

General Headquarters: 1st Battalion Ohio Sharpshooters, Capt. Gershom M. Barber; 10th Ohio Infantry, Lieut.-Col. William M. Ward; 15th Pa. Cav., Col. William J. Palmer. Loss: w, 2; m, 4 = 6.

FOURTEENTH ARMY CORPS, Maj.-Gen. George H. Thomas. Staff loss: m, 1.

Escort: L, 1st Ohio Cav., Capt. John D. Barker.

FIRST DIVISION, Brig.-Gen. Absalom Baird.

First Brigade, Col. Benjamin F. Scribner: 38th Ind., Lieut.-Col. Daniel F. Griffin; 2d Ohio, Lieut.-Col. Obadiah C. Maxwell (w), Maj. William T. Beatty (w and c), Capt. James Warnock; 33d Ohio, Col. Oscar F. Moore; 94th Ohio, Maj. Rue P. Hutchins; 10th Wis., Lieut.-Col. John H. Ely (m w and c), Capt. Jacob W. Roby. Brigade loss: k, 55; w, 254; m, 423 = 732. *Second Brigade,* Brig.-Gen. John C. Starkweather: 24th Ill., Col. Geza Mihalotzy (w), Capt. August Mauff; 79th Pa., Col. Henry A. Hambright; 1st Wis., Lieut.-Col. George B. Bingham; 21st Wis., Lieut.-Col. Harrison C. Hobart (w), Capt. Charles H. Walker. Brigade loss: k, 65; w, 285; m, 256 = 606. *Third Brigade,* Brig.-Gen. John H. King: 1st Battalion 15th U. S., Capt. Albert B. Dod; 1st Battalion 16th U. S., Maj. Sidney Coolidge (k), Capt. Robert E. A. Crofton; 1st Battalion 18th U. S., Capt. George W. Smith; 2d Battalion 18th U. S., Capt. Henry Haymond; 1st Battalion 19th U. S., Maj. Samuel K. Dawson (w), Capt. Edmund L. Smith. Brigade loss: k, 61; w, 255; m, 523 = 839. *Artillery:* 4th Ind. (Second Brigade), Lieut. David Flansburg (w and c), Lieut. Henry J. Willits; A, 1st Mich. (First Brigade), Lieut. George W. Van Pelt (k), Lieut. Almerick W. Wilber; H, 5th U. S. (Third Brigade), Lieut. Howard M. Burnham (k), Lieut. Joshua A. Fessenden (w). Artillery loss included in that of brigades.

SECOND DIVISION, Maj.-Gen. James S. Negley.

First Brigade, Brig.-Gen. John Beatty: 104th Ill., Lieut.-Col. Douglas Hapeman; 42d Ind., Lieut.-Col. William T. B. McIntire; 88th Ind., Col. George Humphrey; 15th Ky., Col. Marion C. Taylor. Brigade loss: k, 17; w, 189; m, 104 = 310. *Second Brigade,* Col. Timothy R. Stanley (w), Col. William L. Stoughton: 19th Ill., Lieut.-Col. Alexander W. Raffen; 11th Mich., Col. William L. Stoughton, Lieut.-Col. Melvin Mudge (w); 18th Ohio, Lieut.-Col. Charles H. Grosvenor. Brigade loss: k, 20; w, 146; m, 49 = 215. *Third Brigade,* Col. William Sirwell: 37th Ind., Lieut.-Col. William D. Ward; 21st Ohio, Lieut.-Col. Dwella M. Stoughton (m w), Maj. Arnold McMahan (w), Capt. Charles H. Vantine; 74th Ohio, Capt. Joseph Fisher; 78th Pa., Lieut.-Col. Archibald Blakeley. Brigade loss: k, 29; w, 95; m, 142 = 266. *Artillery:* Bridges's Ill. Battery (First Brigade), Capt. Lyman Bridges; G, 1st Ohio (Third Brigade), Capt. Alexander Marshall; M, 1st Ohio (Second Brigade), Capt. Frederick Schultz. Artillery loss included in brigades to which attached.

THIRD DIVISION, Brig.-Gen. John M. Brannan. Staff loss: w, 1.

First Brigade, Col. John M. Connell: 82d Ind., Col. Morton C. Hunter; 17th Ohio, Lieut.-Col. Durbin Ward (w); 31st Ohio, Lieut.-Col. Frederick W. Lister. Brigade loss: k, 49; w, 323; m, 70 = 442. *Second Brigade,* Col. John T. Croxton (w), Col. William H. Hays: 10th Ind., Col. William B. Carroll (m w), Lieut.-Col. Marsh B. Taylor; 74th Ind., Col. Charles W. Chapman, Lieut.-Col. Myron Baker; 4th Ky., Lieut.-Col. P. Burgess Hunt (w), Maj. Robert M. Kelly; 10th Ky., Col. William H. Hays, Maj. Gabriel C. Wharton; 14th Ohio, Lieut.-Col. Henry D. Kingsbury. Brigade loss: k, 131; w, 728; m, 79 = 938. *Third Brigade,* Col. Ferdinand Van Derveer: 87th

Ind., Col. Newell Gleason; 2d Minn., Col. James George; 9th Ohio, Col Gustave Kammerling; 35th Ohio, Lieut.-Col. Henry V. N. Boynton. Brigade loss: k, 144; w, 594; m, 102 = 840. *Artillery:* D, 1st Mich. (First Brigade), Capt. Josiah W. Church; C, 1st Ohio (Second Brigade), Lieut. Marco B. Gary; I, 4th U. S. (Third Brigade), Lieut. Frank G. Smith. Artillery loss included in brigades to which attached.

FOURTH DIVISION, Maj.-Gen. Joseph J. Reynolds. Staff loss: w, 1; m, 1 = 2.

*First Brigade,[|] Col. John T. Wilder: 92d Ill., Col. Smith D. Atkins; 98th Ill., Col. John J. Funkhouser (w), Lieut.-Col. Edward Kitchell; 128th Ill., Col. James Monroe; 17th Ind., Maj. William T. Jones; 72d Ind., Col. Abram O. Miller. Brigade loss: k, 13; w, 94; m, 18 = 125. *Second Brigade,* Col. Edward A. King (k), Col. Milton S. Robinson: 68th Ind., Capt. Harvey J. Espy (w); 75th Ind., Col. Milton S. Robinson, Lieut.-Col. William O'Brien; [|]01st Ind., Lieut.-Col. Thomas Doan; 105th Ohio, Maj. George T. Perkins (w). Brigade loss: k, 50; w, 363; m, 71 = 484. *Third Brigade,* Brig.-Gen. John B. Turchin: 18th Ky., Lieut.-Col. H. Kavanaugh Milward (w), Capt. John B. Heltemes; 11th Ohio, Col. Philander P. Lane; 36th Ohio, Col. William G. Jones (k), Lieut.-Col. Hiram F. Duvall; 92d Ohio, Col. Benjamin D. Fearing (w), Lieut.-Col. Douglas Putman, Jr. (w). Brigade loss: k, 30; w, 227; m, 86 = 343. *Artillery:* 18th Ind. (First Brigade), Capt. Eli Lilly; 19th Ind. (Second Brigade), Capt. Samuel J. Harris (w), Lieut. Robert G. Lackey; 21st Ind. (Third Brigade), Capt. William W. Andrew. Artillery loss included in brigades to which attached.

TWENTIETH ARMY CORPS, Maj.-Gen. Alexander McD. McCook.

Provost-Guard: H, 81st Ind., Capt. Will'm J. Richards.

Escort: I, 2d Ky. Cav., Lieut. George W. L. Batman.

FIRST DIVISION, Brig.-Gen. Jefferson C. Davis.

Second Brigade, Brig.-Gen. William P. Carlin: 21st Ill., Col. John W. S. Alexander (k), Capt. Chester K. Knight; 38th Ill., Lieut.-Col. Daniel H. Gilmer (k), Capt. Willis G. Whitehurst; 81st Ind., Capt. Nevil B. Boone, Maj. James E. Calloway; 101st Ohio, Lieut.-Col. John Messer (w), Maj. Bedan B. McDanald (w), Capt. Leonard D. Smith; 2d Minn. Batt'y, ✠ Lieut. Albert Woodbury (m w), Lieut. Richard L. Dawley. Brigade loss: k, 54; w, 299; m, 298 = 651. *Third Brigade,* Col. Hans C. Heg (k), Col. John A. Martin: 25th Ill., Maj. Samuel D. Wall (w), Capt. Wesford Taggart; 35th Ill., Lieut.-Col. William P. Chandler; 8th Kans., Col. John A. Martin, Lieut.-Col. James L. Abernethy; 15th Wis., Lieut.-Col. Ole C. Johnson (c); 8th Wis. Batt'y, Lieut. John D. McLean. Brigade loss: k, 70; w, 519; m, 107 = 696.

SECOND DIVISION, Brig.-Gen. Richard W. Johnson. Staff loss: k, 1; m, 2 = 3.

First Brigade, Brig.-Gen. August Willich: 89th Ill., Lieut.-Col. Duncan J. Hall (k), Maj. William D. Williams; 32d Ind., Lieut.-Col. Frank Erdelmeyer; 39th Ind.,[|] Col. Thomas J. Harrison; 15th Ohio, Lieut.-Col. Frank Askew; 49th Ohio, Maj. Samuel F. Gray (w). Capt. Luther M. Strong; A, 1st Ohio Art'y, Capt. Wilbur F. Goodspeed. Brigade loss: k, 63; w, 355; m, 117 = 535. *Second Brigade,* Col. Joseph B. Dodge: 79th Ill., Col. Allen Buckner; 29th Ind., Lieut.-Col. David M. Dunn; 30th Ind., Lieut.-Col. Orrin D. Hurd; 77th Pa., Col. Thomas E. Rose (c), Capt. Joseph J. Lawson; 20th Ohio Battery, Capt. Edward Grosskopff. Brigade loss: k, 27; w, 200; m, 309 = 536. *Third Brigade,* Col. Philemon P. Baldwin (k), Col. William W. Berry: 6th Ind., Lieut.-Col.

[|] Detached and serving as mounted infantry.

✠ Captain William A. Hotchkiss, chief of division artillery.

Hagerman Tripp (w), Maj. Calvin D. Campbell; 5th Ky., Col. William W. Berry, Capt. John M. Huston; 1st Ohio, Lieut.-Col. Bassett Langdon; 93d Ohio,Col. Hiram Strong (m w), Lieut.-Col. Wm. H. Martin; 5th Ind. Bat'y, Capt. Peter Simonson. Brigade loss: k, 57; w, 385; m, 126 = 568. THIRD DIVISION, Maj.-Gen. Philip H. Sheridan.

First Brigade, Brig.-Gen. William H. Lytle (k), Col. Silas Miller: 36th Ill., Col. Silas Miller, Lieut.-Col. Porter C. Olson; 88th Ill., Lieut.-Col. Alexander S. Chadbourne; 21st Mich., Col. William B. McCreery (w and c), Maj. Seymour Chase; 24th Wis., Lieut.-Col. Theodore S. West (w and c), Maj. Carl von Baumbach; 11th Ind. Battery, Capt. Arnold Sutermeister. Brigade loss: k, 55; w; 321; m, 84 = 460. *Second Brigade*, Col. Bernard Laiboldt: 44th Ill., Col. Wallace W. Barrett (w); 73d Ill., Col. James F. Jaquess; 2d Mo., Lieut.-Col. Arnold Beck; 15th Mo., Col. Joseph Conrad; G (Capt. H. Hescock, chief of division artillery), 1st Mo. Art'y, Lieut. Gustavus Schueler. Brigade loss: k, 38; w, 243; m, 108 = 389. *Third Brigade*, Col. Luther P. Bradley (w), Col. Nathan H. Walworth: 22d Ill., Lieut.-Col. Francis Swanwick; 27th Ill., Col. Jonathan R. Miles; 42d Ill., Col. Nathan H. Walworth. Lieut.-Col. John A. Hottenstine; 51st Ill., Lieut.-Col. Samuel B. Raymond; C, 1st Ill. Art'y, Capt. Mark H. Prescott. Brigade loss: k, 58; w, 374; m, 64 = 496.

TWENTY-FIRST ARMY CORPS, Maj.-Gen. Thomas L. Crittenden.

Escort: K, 15th Ill. Cav., Capt. S. B. Sherer. Loss: w, 3. FIRST DIVISION, Brig.-Gen. Thos. J. Wood. Staff loss: w, 1.

First Brigade, Col. George P. Buell: 100th Ill., Maj. Frederick A. Bartleson (w and c), Maj. Charles M. Hammond; 58th Ind., Lieut.-Col. James T. Embree; 13th Mich., Col. Joshua B. Culver (w), Maj. Willard G. Eaton; 26th Ohio, Lieut.-Col. William H. Young. Brigade loss: k, 79; w, 443; m, 129 = 651. *Third Brigade*, Col. Charles G. Harker: 3d Ky., Col. Henry C. Dunlap; 64th Ohio, Col. Alexander McIlvain; 65th Ohio, Lieut.-Col. Horatio N. Whitbeck (w), Maj. Samuel C. Brown (m w), Capt. Thomas Powell; 125th Ohio, Col. Emerson Opdycke. Brigade loss: k, 51; w, 283; m, 58 = 392. *Artillery:* 8th Ind. (First Brigade), Capt. George Estep (w); 6th Ohio (Third Brigade), Capt. Cullen Bradley. Artillery loss: k, 2; w, 17; m, 7 = 26. SECOND DIVISION, Maj.-Gen. John M. Palmer. Staff loss: k, 1; w, 2; m, 3 = 6.

First Brigade, Brig.-Gen. Charles Cruft: 31st Ind., Col. John T. Smith; 1st Ky. (5 co's), Lieut.-Col. Alva R. Hadlock; 2d Ky., Col. Thomas D. Sedgewick; 90th Ohio, Col. Charles H. Rippey. Brigade loss: k, 24; w, 213; m, 53 = 290. *Second Brigade*, Brig.-Gen. William B. Hazen: 9th Ind., Col. Isaac C. B. Suman; 6th Ky., Col. George T. Shackelford (w), Lieut.-Col. Richard Rockingham (k), Maj. Richard T. Whitaker; 41st Ohio, Col. Aquila Wiley; 124th Ohio, Col. Oliver H. Payne (w), Maj. James B. Hampson. Brigade loss: k, 46; w, 378; m, 76 = 500. *Third Brigade*, Col. William Grose: 84th Ill., Col. Louis H. Waters; 36th Ind., Lieut.-Col. Oliver H. P. Carey (w), Maj. Gilbert Trusler; 23d Ky., Lieut.-Col. James C. Foy; 6th Ohio, Col. Nicholas L. Anderson (w), Maj. Samuel C. Erwin; 24th Ohio, Col. David J. Higgins. Brigade loss: k, 53; w, 399; m, 65 = 517. *Artillery*, Capt. William E. Standart: B, 1st Ohio (First Brigade), Lieut. Norman A. Baldwin; F, 1st Ohio (Second Brigade), Lieut. Giles J. Cockerill; H, 4th U. S. (Third Brigade), Lieut. Harry C. Cushing; M, 4th U. S. (Third Brigade), Lieut. Francis D. L. Russell. Artillery loss: k, 10; w, 39; m, 6 = 55. THIRD DIVISION, Brig.-Gen.H.P.VanCleve. Staff loss: m,1.

First Brigade, Brig.-Gen. Samuel Beatty: 79th Ind., Col. Frederick Knefler; 9th Ky., Col. George H. Cram; 17th Ky., Col. Alexander M. Stout; 19th Ohio, Lieut.-Col. Henry G. Stratton. Brigade loss: k, 16; w, 254; m, 61 = 331. *Second Brigade*, Col. George F. Dick: 44th Ind.,

Lieut.-Col. Simeon C. Aldrich; 86th Ind., Maj. Jacob C. Dick; 13th Ohio, Lieut.-Col. Elhannon M. Mast (k), Capt. Horatio G. Cosgrove; 59th Ohio, Lieut.-Col. Granville A. Frambes. Brigade loss: k, 16; w, 180; m, 83 = 279. *Third Brigade*, Col. Sidney M. Barnes: 35th Ind., Maj. John P. Dufficy; 8th Ky., Lieut.-Col. James D. Mayhew (c), Maj. John S. Clark; 51st Ohio, Col. Richard W. McClain (c), Lieut.-Col. Charles H. Wood; 99th Ohio, Col. Peter T. Swaine. Brigade loss: k, 20; w, 135; m, 144 = 299. *Artillery:* 17th Ind., Capt. George R. Swallow; 26th Pa., Capt. Alanson J. Stevens (k), Lieut. Samuel M. McDowell; 3d Wis., Lieut. Cortland Livingston. Artillery loss: k, 4; w, 35; m, 13 = 52.

RESERVE CORPS, Maj.-Gen. Gordon Granger. Staff loss: k, 1.

FIRST DIVISION, Brig.-Gen. James B. Steedman.

First Brigade, Brig.-Gen. Walter C. Whitaker: 96th Ill., Col. Thomas E. Champion; 115th Ill., Col. Jesse H. Moore; 84th Ind., Col. Nelson Trusler; 22d Mich., Col. Heber Le Favour. (c), Lieut.-Col. William Sanborn (w), Capt. Alonzo M. Keeler (c); 40th Ohio, Lieut.-Col. William Jones; 89th Ohio, Col. Caleb H. Carlton (c), Capt. Isaac C. Nelson; 18th Ohio Battery, Capt. Charles C. Aleshire. Brigade loss: k, 154; w, 654; m, 518 = 1326. *Second Brigade*, Col. John G. Mitchell: 78th Ill., Lieut.-Col. Carter Van Vleck (w), Lieut. Geo. Green; 98th Ohio, Capt. Moses J.Urquhart (w), Capt. Armstrong J.Thomas; 113th Ohio, Lieut.-Col. Darius B. Warner; 121st Ohio, Lieut.-Col. Henry B. Banning; M, 1st Ill. Art'y, Lieut. Thos. Burton. Brigade loss: k, 58; w, 308; m, 95 = 461. SECOND DIVISION.

Second Brigade, Col. Daniel McCook: 85th Ill.,Col.Caleb J. Dilworth; 86th Ill., Lieut.-Col. D. W. Magee; 125th Ill., Col. Oscar F. Harmon; 52d Ohio, Maj. J. T. Holmes; 69th Ohio, Lieut.-Col. J. H. Brigham; I, 2d Ill. Art'y, Capt. C. M. Barnett. Brigade loss: k, 2; w, 14; m, 18 = 34. CAVALRY CORPS, Brig.-Gen. Robert B. Mitchell. FIRST DIVISION, Col. Edward M. McCook.

First Brigade, Col. Archibald P. Campbell: 2d Mich., Maj. Leonidas S. Scranton; 9th Pa., Lieut.-Col. Roswell M. Russell; 1st Tenn., Lieut.-Col. James P. Brownlow. Brigade loss: k, 2; w, 6; m, 7 = 15. *Second Brigade*, Col. Daniel M. Ray: 2d Ind., Maj. Joseph B. Presdee; 4th Ind., Lieut.-Col. John T. Deweese; 2d Tenn., Lieut.-Col. William R. Cook; 1st Wis., Col. Oscar H. La Grange; D, 1st Ohio Art'y (section), Lieut. Nathaniel M. Newell. Brigade loss: k, 2; w, 10; m, 11 = 23. *Third Brigade*, Col. Louis D. Watkins: 4th Ky., Col. Wickliffe Cooper; 5th Ky., Lieut.-Col. William T. Hoblitzell; 6th Ky., Maj. Louis A. Gratz. Brigade loss: k, 2; w, 8; m, 236 = 246. SECOND DIVISION, Brig.-Gen. George Crook.

First Brigade, Col. Robert H. G. Minty: 3d Ind. (detachment), Lieut.-Col. Robert Klein; 4th Mich., Maj. Horace Gray; 7th Pa., Lieut.-Col. James J. Seibert; 4th U. S., Capt. James B. McIntyre. Brigade loss: k, 7; w, 33; m, 8 = 48. *Second Brigade*, Col. Eli Long: 2d Ky., Col. Thomas P. Nicholas; 1st Ohio, Lieut.-Col. Valentine Cupp (m w), Maj. Thomas J. Patten; 3d Ohio, Lieut.-Col. Charles B. Seidel; 4th Ohio, Lieut.-Col. Oliver P. Robie. Brigade loss: k, 19; w, 79; m, 38 = 136. *Artillery:* Chicago Board of Trade Battery, Capt. James H. Stokes.

Total Union loss: killed 1656, wounded 9749, captured or missing 4774 = 16,179.

Effective strength (partly from official reports and partly estimated):

Fourteenth Army Corps (estimated)	20,000
Twentieth Army Corps (estimated)	11,000
Twenty-first Army Corps (report)	12,052
Reserve Corps (report)	3,913
Cavalry Corps (estimated)	10,000
Total	56,965

THE CONFEDERATE ARMY.

ARMY OF TENNESSEE — General Braxton Bragg.

RIGHT WING, Lieut.-Gen. Leonidas Polk.
CHEATHAM'S DIVISION [Polk's, Corps], Maj.-Gen. B. F. Cheatham.
Escort: G, 2d Ga. Cav., Capt. T. M. Merritt.

Jackson's Brigade, Brig.-Gen. John K. Jackson: 1st Ga. (Confed.) and 2d Ga. Battalion, Maj. J. C. Gordon; 5th Ga., Col. C. P. Daniel; 2d Ga. Battalion Sharpshooters, Maj. R. H. Whiteley; 5th Miss., Lieut.-Col. W.

L. Sykes (k), Maj. J. B. Herring; 8th Miss., Col. J. C. Wilkinson. Brigade loss: k, 55; w, 430; m, 5=490. *Maney's Brigade*, Brig.-Gen. George Maney: 1st and 27th Tenn., Col. H. R. Feild; 4th Tenn. (Prov. Army), Col. J. A. McMurry (k), Lieut.-Col. R. N. Lewis (w), Maj. O. A. Bradshaw (w), Capt. J. Bostick; 6th and 9th Tenn., Col. George C. Porter; 24th Tenn. Battalion Sharp-shooters, Maj. Frank Maney. Brigade loss: k, 54; w, 317; m, 15 = 386. *Smith's Brigade*, Brig.-Gen. Preston Smith (k), Col. A. J. Vaughan, Jr.: 11th Tenn., Col. G. W. Gordon; 12th and 47th Tenn., Col. W. M. Watkins; 13th and 154th Tenn., Col. A. J. Vaughan, Jr., Lieut.-Col. R. W. Pitman; 29th Tenn., Col. Horace Rice; Dawson's Battalion ☆ Sharp-shooters, Maj. J. W. Dawson (w), Maj. William Green. Brigade loss: k, 42; w, 284; m, 36=362. *Wright's Brigade*, Brig.-Gen. Marcus J. Wright: 8th Tenn., Col. John H. Anderson; 16th Tenn., Col. D. M. Donnell; 28th Tenn., Col. S. S. Stanton; 38th Tenn. and Murray's (Tenn.) Battalion, Col. J. C. Carter; 51st and 52d Tenn., Lieut.-Col. John G. Hall. Brigade loss: k, 44; w, 400; m, 43 = 487. *Strahl's Brigade*, Brig.-Gen. O. F. Strahl: 4th and 5th Tenn., Col. J. J. Lamb; 19th Tenn., Col. F. M. Walker; 24th Tenn., Col. J. A. Wilson; 31st Tenn., Col. E. E. Tansil; 33d Tenn., ——. Brigade loss: k, 19; w, 203; m, 28=250. *Artillery*, Maj. Melancthon Smith: Tenn. Battery, Capt. W. W. Carnes; Ga. Battery, Capt. John Scogin; Tenn. Battery (Scott's), Lieut. J. H. Marsh (w), Lieut. A. T. Watson; Miss. Battery (Smith's), Lieut. W. B. Turner; Miss. Bat'y, Capt. T. J. Stanford.

HILL'S CORPS, Lieut.-Gen. Daniel H. Hill.
CLEBURNE'S DIVISION, Maj.-Gen. P. R. Cleburne.
Wood's Brigade, Brig.-Gen. S. A. M. Wood: 16th Ala., Maj. J. H. McGaughy (k), Capt. F. A. Ashford; 33d Ala., Col. Samuel Adams; 45th Ala., Col. E. B. Breedlove; 18th Ala. Battalion, Maj. J. H. Gibson (k), Col. Samuel Adams; 32d and 45th Miss., Col. M. P. Lowrey; Sharp-shooters, Maj. A. T. Hawkins (k), Capt. Daniel Coleman. Brigade loss: k, 96; w, 680=776. *Polk's Brigade*, Brig.-Gen. Lucius E. Polk: 1st Ark., Col. J. W. Colquitt; 3d and 5th Confederate, Col. J. A. Smith; 2d Tenn., Col. W. B. Robertson; 35th Tenn., Col. B. J. Hill; 48th Tenn., Col. G. H. Nixon. Brigade loss: k, 58; w, 541; m, 6 = 605. *Deshler's Brigade*, Brig.-Gen. James Deshler (k), Col. R. Q. Mills: 19th and 24th Ark., Lieut.-Col. A. S. Hutchinson; 6th, 10th, and 15th Tex., Col. R. Q. Mills, Lieut.-Col. T. Scott Anderson; 17th, 18th, 24th, and 25th Tex., Col. F. C. Wilkes (w), Lieut.-Col. John T. Coit, Maj. W. A. Taylor. Brigade loss: k, 52; w, 366=418. *Artillery*, Maj. T. R. Hotchkiss (w), Capt. Henry C. Semple: Ark. Battery (Calvert's), Lieut. Thomas J. Key; Tex. Battery, Capt. J. P. Douglas; Ala. Battery, Capt. Henry C. Semple, Lieut. R. W. Goldthwaite.

BRECKINRIDGE'S DIVISION, Maj.-Gen. J. C. Breckinridge.
Helm's Brigade, Brig.-Gen. Benjamin H. Helm (k), Col. J. H. Lewis: 41st Ala., Col. M. L. Stansel; 2d Ky., Col. J. W. Hewitt (k), Lieut.-Col. J. W. Moss; 4th Ky., Col. Joseph P. Nuckols, Jr. (w), Maj. T. W. Thompson; 6th Ky., Col. J. W. Lewis, Lieut.-Col. M. H. Cofer; 9th Ky., Col. J. W. Caldwell (w), Lieut.-Col. J. C. Wickliffe. Brigade loss: k, 63; w, 408=471. *Adams's Brigade*, Brig.-Gen. Daniel W. Adams (w and c), Col. R. L. Gibson: 32d Ala., Maj. J. C. Kimbell; 13th and 20th La., Col. R. L. Gibson, Col. Leon von Zinken, Capt. E. M. Dubroca; 16th and 25th La., Col. D. Gober; 19th La., Lieut.-Col. R. W. Turner (w), Maj. L. Butler (k), Capt. H. A. Kennedy; 14th La. Battalion, Maj. J. E. Austin. Brigade loss: k, w and m = 429. *Stovall's Brigade*, Brig.-Gen. M. A. Stovall: 1st and 3d Fla., Col. W. S. Dilworth; 4th Fla., Col. W. L. L. Bowen; 47th Ga., Capt. William S. Phillips (w), Capt. Joseph S. Cone; 60th N. C., Lieut.-Col. J. M. Ray (w), Capt. J. T. Weaver. Brigade loss: k, 37; w, 232; m, 46=315. *Artillery*, Maj. R. E. Graves (k): Ky. Battery, Capt. Robert Cobb; Tenn. Battery, Capt. John W. Mebane; La. Battery, Capt. C. H. Slocomb.

RESERVE CORPS, Maj.-Gen. W. H. T. Walker.
WALKER'S DIVISION, Brig.-Gen. S. R. Gist.
Gist's Brigade, Brig.-Gen. S. R. Gist, Col. P. H. Col-

quitt (k), Lieut.-Col. L. Napier: 46th Ga., Col. P. H. Colquitt, Maj. A. M. Speer; 8th Ga. Battalion, Lieut.-Col. L. Napier; 24th S. C., Col. C. H. Stevens (w), Lieut.-Col. Ellison Capers (w). Brigade loss: k, 49; w, 251; m, 36=336. *Ector's Brigade*, Brig.-Gen. M. D. Ector: Stone's Ala. Battalion, ——; Pound's Miss. Battalion, ——; 29th N. C.,——; 9th Texas,——; 10th, 14th, and 32d Tex. Cav. (dismounted), ——. Brigade loss: k,59; w, 239; m,138=436. *Wilson's Brigade*, Col. C. C. Wilson: 25th Ga., Lieut.-Col. A. J. Williams (k); 29th Ga., Lieut. G. R. McRae; 30th Ga., Lieut.-Col. James S. Boynton; 1st Ga. Battalion Sharp-shooters, ——; 4th La. Battalion, ——. Brigade loss: k, 99; w, 426; m, 80=605. *Artillery*: Martin's Battery, ——.

LIDDELL'S DIVISION, Brig.-Gen. St. John R. Liddell.
Liddell's Brigade, Col. Daniel C. Govan: 2d and 15th Ark., Lieut.-Col. R. T. Harvey; 5th and 13th Ark., Col. L. Featherston (k), Lieut.-Col. John E. Murray; 6th and 7th Ark., Col. D. A. Gillespie (w), Lieut.-Col. Peter Snyder; 8th Ark. and 1st La., Lieut.-Col. George F. Baucum (w), Maj. A. Watkins. Brigade loss: k, 73; w, 502; m, 283=858. *Walthall's Brigade*, Brig.-Gen. E. C. Walthall: 24th Miss., Lieut.-Col. R. P. McKelvaine (w), Maj. W. C. Staples (w), Capt. B. F. Toomer, Capt. J. D. Smith (w); 27th Miss., Col. James A. Campbell; 29th Miss., Col. William F. Brantly; 30th Miss., Col. Junius I. Scales (c), Lieut.-Col. Hugh A. Reynolds (k), Maj. J. M. Johnson (w); 34th Miss., Maj. W. G. Pegram (w), Capt. H. J. Bowen, Lieut.-Col. H. A. Reynolds (k). Brigade loss: k, 61; w, 531; m, 196=788. *Artillery*, Capt. Charles Swett: Ala. Battery, Capt. W. H. Fowler (w); Miss. Battery (Warren Light Art'y), Lieut. H. Shannon. Artillery loss included in loss of brigades.

LEFT WING, Lieut.-Gen. James Longstreet.
HINDMAN'S DIVISION [Polk's Corps], Maj.-Gen. T. C. Hindman (w), Brig.-Gen. J. Patton Anderson. Staff loss: w, 1.
Anderson's Brigade, Brig.-Gen. J. Patton Anderson, Col. J. H. Sharp: 7th Miss., Col. W. H. Bishop; 9th Miss., Maj. T. H. Lynam; 10th Miss., Lieut.-Col. James Barr; 41st Miss., Col. W. F. Tucker; 44th Miss., Col. J. H. Sharp, Lieut.-Col. R. G. Kelsey; 9th Miss. Batt. Sharp-shooters, Maj. W. C. Richards; Ala. Battery, Capt. J. Garrity. Brigade loss: k, 80; w, 464; m, 24=568. *Deas's Brigade*, Brig.-Gen. Z. C. Deas: 19th Ala., Col. Samuel K. McSpadden; 22d Ala., Lieut.-Col. John Weedon (k), Capt. H. T. Toulmin; 25th Ala., Col. George D. Johnston; 39th Ala., Col. W. Clark; 50th Ala., Col. J. G. Coltart; 17th Ala. Batt. Sharp-shooters, Capt. Jas. F. Nabers; Robertson's Battery, Lieut. S. H. Dent. Brigade loss: k, 123; w, 578; m, 28=729. *Manigault's Brigade*, Brig.-Gen. A. M. Manigault: 24th Ala., Col. N. N. Davis; 28th Ala., Col. John C. Reid; 34th Ala., Maj. John N. Slaughter; 10th and 19th S. C., Col. James F. Pressley; Ala. Battery (Waters's), Lieut. Charles W. Watkins. Brigade loss: k, 66; w, 426; m, 47=539.

BUCKNER'S CORPS, Maj.-Gen. Simon B. Buckner.
STEWART'S DIVISION, Maj.-Gen. Alexander P. Stewart. Staff loss: w, 1; m, 1=2.
Johnson's Brigade (attached to Johnson's Provisional Division), Brig.-Gen. Bushrod R. Johnson, Col. J. S. Fulton: 17th Tenn., Lieut.-Col. Watt W. Floyd; 23d Tenn., Col. R. H. Keeble; 25th Tenn., Lieut.-Col. R. B. Snowden; 44th Tenn., Lieut.-Col. J. L. McEwen, Jr. (w), Maj. G. M. Crawford; Ga. Battery, Lieut. W. S. Everett. Brigade loss: k, 28; w, 271; m, 74=373. *Brown's Brigade*, Brig.-Gen. John C. Brown (w), Col. Edmund C. Cook: 18th Tenn., Col. J. B. Palmer (w), Lieut.-Col. W. R. Butler (w), Capt. Gideon H. Lowe; 26th Tenn., Col. J. M. Lillard (k), Maj. R. M. Saffell; 32d Tenn., Col. Edmund C. Cook, Capt. C. G. Tucker; 45th Tenn., Col. A. Searcy; 23d Tenn. Batt., Maj. T. W. Newman (w), Capt. W. P. Simpson. Brigade loss: k, 50; w, 426; m, 4=480. *Bate's Brigade*, Brig.-Gen. William B. Bate: 58th Ala.. Col. Bushrod Jones; 37th Ga., Col. A. F. Rudler (w), Lieut.-Col. Joseph T. Smith; 4th Ga. Battalion Sharp-shooters, Maj. T. D. Caswell (w), Capt.

☆ Composed of two companies from the 11th Tenn., two from the 12th and 47th Tenn. (consolidated), and one from the 154th Senior Tenn.

B. M. Turner (w), Lieut. Joel Towers; 15th and 37th Tenn., Col. R. C. Tyler (w), Lieut.-Col. R. D. Frayser (w), Capt. R. M. Tankesley; 20th Tenn., Col. T. B. Smith (w), Maj. W. M. Shy. Brigade loss: k, 63; w, 530; m, 11 = 604. *Clayton's Brigade*, Brig.-Gen. H. D. Clayton (w): 18th Ala., Col. J. T. Holtzclaw (w), Lieut.-Col. R. F. Inge (m w), Maj. P. F. Hunley; 36th Ala., Col. L. T. Woodruff; 38th Ala., Lieut.-Col. A. R. Lankford. Brigade loss: k, 86; w, 518; m, 15 = 619. *Artillery*, Maj. J. W. Eldridge: 1st Ark. Battery, Capt. J. T. Humphreys; Ga. Battery (Dawson's), Lieut. R. W. Anderson; Eufaula Art'y, Capt. McD. Oliver. Artillery loss : k, 4; w, 23 = 27. PRESTON'S DIVISION, Brig.-Gen. William Preston.

Gracie's Brigade, Brig.-Gen. Archibald Gracie, Jr.: 43d Ala., Col. Y. M. Moody; 1st Ala. Battalion, ↓ Lieut.-Col. J. H. Holt (w), Capt. G. W. Huguley; 2d Ala. Battalion, ↓ Lieut.-Col. Bolling Hall, Jr. (w), Capt. W. D. Walden (w); 3d Ala. Battalion, ↓ Maj. Joseph W. A. Sanford; 4th Ala., ↓ Maj. J. D. McLennan; 63d Tenn., Lieut.-Col. A. Fulkerson (w), Maj. John A. Aiken. Brigade loss: k, 90; w, 576; m, 2 = 668. *Trigg's Brigade*, Col. Robert C. Trigg: 1st Fla. Cav. (dismounted), Col. G. T. Maxwell; 6th Fla., Col. J. J. Finley; 7th Fla., Col. R. Bullock; 54th Va., Lieut.-Col. John J. Wade. Brigade loss: k, 46; w, 231; m, 4 = 281. *Kelly's Brigade*, Col. J. H. Kelly: 65th Ga., Col. R. H. Moore; 5th Ky., Col. H. Hawkins; 58th N. C., Col. John B. Palmer (w); 63d Va., Maj. J. M. French. Brigade loss: k, 66; w, 241; m, 3 = 310. *Artillery Battalion*, Maj. A. Leyden: Ga. Battery, Capt. A. M. Wolihin; Ga. Battery, Capt. T. M. Peeples; Va. Battery, Capt. W. C. Jeffress; Ga. Battery (York's). Artillery loss : w, 6.

RESERVE ARTILLERY, Maj. S. C. Williams: Baxter's (Tenn.) Battery; Darden's (Miss.) Battery; Kolb's (Ala.) Battery; McCant's (Fla.) Battery. Artillery loss: k, 2; w, 2 = 4.

JOHNSON'S DIVISION, ♪ Brig.-Gen. Bushrod R. Johnson. *Gregg's Brigade*, Brig.-Gen. John Gregg (w), Col. C. A. Sugg: 3d Tenn., Col. C. H. Walker; 10th Tenn., Col. William Grace; 30th Tenn., —; 41st Tenn., Lieut.-Col. James D. Tillman (w); 50th Tenn., Col. C. A. Sugg, Lieut.-Col. T. W. Beaumont (k), Maj. C. W. Robertson (w), Col. C. H. Walker; 1st Tenn. Battalion, Maj. S. H. Colms (w), Maj. C. W. Robertson; 7th Texas, Col. H. B. Granbury (w), Maj. K. M. Vanzandt; Mo. Battery (Bledsoe's), Lieut. R. L. Wood. Brigade loss: k, 109; w, 474; m, 18 = 601. *McNair's Brigade*, Brig.-Gen. E. McNair (w), Col. D. Coleman: 1st Ark. Mounted Rifles, Col. Robert W. Harper (m w); 2d Ark. Mounted Rifles, Col. James A. Williamson; 25th Ark., Lieut.-Col. Eli Hufstedler (w); 4th and 31st Ark. and 4th Ark. Battalion, Maj. J. A. Ross; 39th N. C., Col. D. Coleman; S. C. Battery, Capt. J. F. Culpeper. Brigade loss : k, 51; w, 336; m, 64 = 451.

LONGSTREET'S CORPS, ¶ Maj.-Gen. John B. Hood (w). Staff loss: w, 1.

McLAWS'S DIVISION, Brig.-Gen. Joseph B. Kershaw, Maj.-Gen. Lafayette McLaws.

Kershaw's Brigade, Brig.-Gen. Joseph B. Kershaw: 2d S. C., Lieut.-Col. F. Gaillard; 3d S. C., Col. James D. Nance; 7th S. C., Lieut.-Col. Elbert Bland (k), Maj. John S. Hard (k), Capt. E. J. Goggans; 8th S. C., Col. John W. Henagan; 15th S. C., Lieut.-Col. Joseph F. Gist; 3d S. C. Battalion, Capt. J. M. Townsend (k). Brigade loss: k, 68; w, 419; m, 1 = 488. *Wofford's Brigade*, ☆ Brig.-Gen. W. T. Wofford: 16th Ga., —; 18th Ga., —; 24th Ga., —; 3d Ga. Battalion Sharp-shooters, —; Cobb's (Ga.) Legion, —; Phillips's (Ga.) Legion, —. *Humphreys's Brigade*, Brig.-Gen. Benjamin G. Humphreys : 13th Miss., —; 17th Miss., —; 18th Miss., —; 21st Miss., —. Brigade loss : k, 20 : w, 132 = 152. *Bryan's Brigade*, ☆ Brig.-Gen. Goode Bryan: 10th Ga., —; 50th Ga., —; 51st Ga., —; 53d Ga., —.

HOOD'S DIVISION, Maj.-Gen. John B. Hood, Brig.-Gen. E. McIver Law.

Jenkins's Brigade, ♪ Brig.-Gen. Micah Jenkins; 1st S. C., —; 2d S. C. Rifles, —; 5th S. C., —; 6th S. C., —; Hampton Legion, —; Palmetto (S. C.) Sharp-shooters, —. *Law's Brigade*, Brig.-Gen. E. McIver Law, Col. James L. Sheffield: 4th Ala., —; 15th Ala., Col. W. C. Oates; 44th Ala., —; 47th Ala., —; 48th Ala., —. Brigade loss : k, 61; w, 329 = 390. *Robertson's Brigade*, ♪ Brig.-Gen. J. B. Robertson, Col. Van. H. Manning: 3d Ark., Col. Van H. Manning; 1st Texas, Capt. R. J. Harding; 4th Texas, Col. John P. Bane (w), Capt. R. H. Bassett (w); 5th Texas, J. C. Rogers (w), Capt. J. S. Cleveland (w), Capt. T. T. Clay. Brigade loss : k, 78; w, 457; m, 35 = 570. *Anderson's Brigade*, ⚓ Brig.-Gen. George T. Anderson: 7th Ga., —; 8th Ga., —; 9th Ga., —; 11th Ga., —; 59th Ga., —. *Benning's Brigade*, Brig.-Gen. Henry L. Benning: 2d Ga., Lieut.-Col. William S. Shepherd (w). Maj. W. W. Charlton; 15th Ga., Col. D. M. Du Bose (w), Maj. P. J. Shannon; 17th Ga., Lieut.-Col. Charles W. Matthews (m w); 20th Ga., Col. J. D. Waddell. Brigade loss : k, 46; w, 436; m, 6 = 488.

CORPS ARTILLERY, ♪ Col. E. Porter Alexander: S. C. Battery (Fickling's); Va. Battery (Jordan's); La. Battery (Moody's); Va. Battery (Parker's); Va. Battery (Taylor's); Va. Battery (Woolfolk's).

RESERVE ARTILLERY, ARMY OF TENNESSEE, Maj. Felix H. Robertson: Barret's (Mo.) Battery; Le Gardeur's (La.) Battery; Havis's (Ala.) Battery; Lumsden's (Ala.) Battery; Massenburg's (Ga.) Battery. Artillery loss: k, 2; w, 6 = 8.

CAVALRY, Maj.-Gen. Joseph Wheeler.

WHARTON'S DIVISION, Brig.-Gen. John A. Wharton.

First Brigade, Col. C. C. Crews: 7th Ga., —; 2d Ga., —; 3d Ga., —; 4th Ga., Col. Isaac W. Avery. *Second Brigade*, Col. Thomas Harrison: 3d Confederate, Col. W. N. Estes; 1st Ky., Lieut.-Col. J. W. Griffith; 4th Tenn., Col. Paul F. Anderson; 8th Texas, —; 11th Texas, —; Ga. Battery (White's).

MARTIN'S DIVISION, Brig.-Gen. William T. Martin.

First Brigade, Col. J. T. Morgan; 1st Ala., —; 3d Ala., Lieut.-Col. T. H. Mauldin; 51st Ala., —; 8th Confederate, —. *Second Brigade*, Col. A. A. Russell: 4th Ala., † —; 1st Confederate, Col. W. B. Wade; Ark. Battery (Wiggins's). *Roddey's Brigade*, Brig.-Gen. P. D. Roddey; 4th Ala., † Lieut.-Col. William A. Johnson; 5th Ala., —; 53d Ala., —; Tenn. Reg't (Forrest's); Ga. Battery (Newell's). Loss of Wheeler's cavalry (estimated), 375 killed, wounded, and missing.

FORREST'S CORPS, Brig.-Gen. N. B. Forrest.

ARMSTRONG'S DIVISION, Brig.-Gen. Frank C. Armstrong. *Armstrong's Brigade*, Col. J. T. Wheeler: 3d Ark., —; 1st Tenn., —; 18th Tenn. Battalion, Maj. Charles McDonald. *Forrest's Brigade*, Col. G. G. Dibrell: 4th Tenn., Col. W. S. McLemore; 8th Tenn., Capt. Hamilton McGinnis; 9th Tenn., Col. J. B. Biffle; 10th Tenn., Col. N. N. Cox; 11th Tenn., Col. D. W. Holman; Shaw's Battalion, Maj. J. Shaw; Tenn. Battery, Capt. A. L. Huggins ; Tenn. Battery, Capt. John W. Morton.

PEGRAM'S DIVISION (composition of division uncertain). Brig.-Gen. John Pegram.

Davidson's Brigade, Brig.-Gen. H. B. Davidson: 1st Ga., —; 6th Ga., Col. John R. Hart; 6th N. C., —; Rucker's Legion, —; Tenn. Battery (Huwald's). *Scott's Brigade*, Col. J. S. Scott: 10th Confederate, Col. C. T. Goode; Detachment of Morgan's command, Lieut.-Col. R. M. Martin; 1st La., —; 2d Tenn., —; 5th Tenn., —; 12th Tenn. Battalion, —; 16th Tenn. Battalion, Capt. J. Q. Arnold (w); La. Battery (section), —. Brigade loss : k, 10; w, 39 = 49.

Total Confederate loss : killed, 2389; wounded, 13,412; captured or missing, 2003 = 17,804.

↓ Hilliard's Legion.

♪ Provisional, embracing Johnson's and, part of the time, Robertson's brigades, as well as Gregg's and McNair's. Sept. 19, attached to Longstreet's corps under Hood.

¶ Organization taken from return of Lee's army for Aug. 31, 1863. Pickett's division was left in Virginia.

☆ Longstreet's report indicates that these brigades did not arrive in time to take part in the battle.

♪ Did not arrive in time to take part in the battle.

⚓ Served part of time in Johnson's Provisional Division.

† Two regiments of the same designation. Lieut.-Col. Johnson commanded that in Roddey's brigade.

As to the strength of the Confederate army at Chickamauga, Major E. C. Dawes contributed to "The Century" magazine, for April, 1888, the following note:

" An examination of the original returns in the War Department, which I have personally made, shows the following result: General Bragg's return, 31st of August, 1863, shows under the heading 'present for duty,' officers and men, 48,998. This return does not include the divisions of General Breckinridge or General Preston, the brigades of Generals Gregg and McNair, or the reënforcement brought by General Longstreet. The strength of each is accurately given in Confederate official returns. The total Confederate force available for battle at Chickamauga was as follows: General Bragg's army, 31st of August, 1863, for duty, 48,998; Longstreet's command (Hood's and McLaws's divisions), by return of Army of Northern Virginia, 31st of August, 1863, for duty, 11,716; Breckinridge's division, by his official report in 'Confederate Reports of Battles,' for duty, 3769; Preston's division, by his official report in 'Confederate Reports of Battles,' for duty, 4509; Brigades of Gregg and McNair, by General Bushrod Johnson's official report (So. Hist. Soc. Papers, Vol. XIII.), for duty, 2559,— total, 71,551."

THE LITTLE STEAMBOAT THAT OPENED THE "CRACKER LINE."

BY WILLIAM G. LE DUC, BREVET BRIGADIER-GENERAL AND ASSISTANT QUARTERMASTER, U. S. V.

IN answer to the urgent demand of Rosecrans for reënforcements, the Eleventh Corps (Howard's) and the Twelfth Corps (Slocum's) were sent from the east to his assistance under command of General Hooker. Marching orders were received on the 22d of September, and the movement was commenced from the east side of the Rappahannock on the 24th; at Alexandria the troops and artillery and officers' horses were put on cars, and on the 27th started for Nashville. On the 2d of October the advance reached Bridgeport, and on the 3d Hooker established headquarters at Stevenson, and Howard the headquarters of the Eleventh Corps at Bridgeport,⎰ then the limit of railroad travel, eight miles east of Stevenson.

The short reach of 26 miles of railroad, or 28 miles of road that ran nearly alongside the railroad, was now all that was necessary for the security of the important position at Chattanooga. But Rosecrans must first secure possession of the route, and then rebuild the long truss-bridge across the Tennessee River, and the trestle, one-quarter of a mile long and 113 feet high, at Whiteside, or Running Water, which would take longer than his stock of provisions and forage would last.

To supply an army of 40,000 or 50,000 men, having several thousand animals, in Chattanooga, by wagons, over country roads 28 miles long, in winter, would be a most difficult, but not an impossible task. Rosecrans determined to build some small, flat-bottomed steamers, that could navigate the river from Bridgeport, and transport supplies to Kelley's Ferry or William's Island (either within easy reach from Chattanooga), which would enable him to supply his army with comfort until the railroad could be repaired. The enemy held Lookout Mountain, commanding both river and railroad above William's Island. This position was then deemed impregnable. The Confederates also had an outpost on Raccoon Mountain, commanding the river completely and also overlooking a road that skirted the river-bank on the north side for a short distance, thus making the long detour over Waldron's Ridge necessary to communication between Stevenson, Bridgeport, and Chattanooga. The river, where it passes through the Raccoon Range, is very rapid and narrow; the place is known as the Suck, and in navigating up stream the aid of windlass and shore-lines is necessary. Kelley's Landing, below the Suck, is the debouchment of a low pass through Raccoon Mountain, from Lookout Valley, and is within eight or ten miles of Chattanooga.

At Bridgeport I found Captain Edwards, Assistant Quartermaster, from Detroit, preparing to build a steamboat to navigate the river, by mounting an engine, boiler, and stern-wheel on a flat-bottomed scow, to be used in carrying and towing up supplies until the completion of the railroad.

I quote from my Diary:

Oct. 5, 1863.— General Hooker was over yesterday . . . and examined the little scow. He appreciated the probable importance of the boat, and ordered me to take it in hand personally and see that work was crowded on it as fast as possible. . . . We also looked over the grade of the Jasper Branch Railroad, which is above high-water mark, and must be used if supplies are sent on the north side of the river. He directed me to send him a report in writing, and a copy for General Rosecrans, of my observations and suggestions, and to go ahead and do what I could without waiting for written orders. I turned my attention to the boat. Captain Edwards has employed a ship-builder from Lake Erie — Turner, an excellent mechanic, who has built lake vessels and steamers, but who is not so familiar with the construction of flat-bottomed, light-draught river steamers. He has a number of ship and other carpenters engaged, with some detailed men from our own troops, making an efficient force. Men who can be serviceable as rough carpenters are abundant; not so with calkers, who will soon be needed, I hope. The frame of the boat is set on blocks, and is

⎰ General Grant says [see p. 689]: " Hooker had brought with him from the east a full supply of land transportation. His animals had not been subjected to hard work on bad roads without forage, but were in good condition."

This should have been the fact, but unfortunately was not. Hooker's command, when ordered west, had land transportation of the most efficient description, more than 6000 mules and horses, seasoned to army work in marches made through Virginia clay and quicksand, from Fredericksburg to Gettysburg and back to the Rappahannock; but against protest they were ordered to be turned into the corrals at Alexandria and Washington. These choice and efficient trains, that could be relied on to do effective work day and night, were thus broken up, and the want of them was soon after most seriously felt on the Tennessee. Hooker's troops were supplied from the corral at Nashville with all sorts of animals, young and old, broken and unbroken. Many died on the road before reaching Bridgeport.— W. G. L.

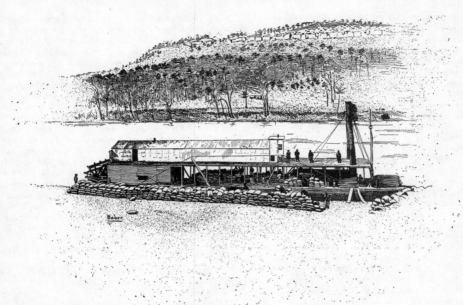

THE "CHATTANOOGA" UNLOADING AT KELLEY'S LANDING, NOVEMBER, 1863. FROM A WAR-TIME PHOTOGRAPH.

only five or six feet above the present water of the river. This mountain stream must be subject to sudden floods, which may make trouble with the boat.

Oct. 16.— . . . I found Turner, the master mechanic, in trouble with the hull of the little boat. The planking was nearly all on, and he was getting ready to calk and pitch her bottom when I went to Stevenson. The water had risen so rapidly that it was within sixteen or eighteen inches of her bottom planks when I returned, and Turner was loading her decks with pig-iron that the rebels had left near the bridge-head. He thought he would thus keep the hull down on the blocking, and after the waters went down would then go on and finish.

"But," I said, "Turner, if the planking gets wet, you cannot calk and pitch until it dries." "That's true ; and it would take two weeks, and may be four, to dry her after she was submerged, and who knows how high it may rise and when it will abate ?" "Then, Turner, what's the use of weighing it down with pig-iron. Rosecrans's army depends on this little boat : he must have supplies before two weeks, or quit Chattanooga. Can't you cross-timber your blocks, and raise the hull faster than the water rises ?" "No ; I've thought of that, and believe it would be useless to try it. Captain Edwards and I concluded the only thing we could do was to weigh it down with pig-iron, and try to hold it, but if the water rises very high it will be swept away, pig-iron and all !" . . . I went rapidly over to Edwards's tent . . . and found him in his bunk, overcome by constant work, anxiety, and despair. . . . In answer to my question if nothing better could be done than weigh the hull down with pig-iron he said, "No ; I've done all I can. I don't know what the

water wants to rise for here. It never rose this way where I was brought up, and they're expecting this boat to be done inside of two weeks, or they will have to fall back !" I turned from his tent, and stood perplexed, staring vacantly toward the pontoon-bridge. I saw a number of extra pontoons tied to the shore — flat-bottomed boats, 10 to 12 feet wide and 30 feet long, the sides 18 inches high. I counted them, and then started double-quick for the boat-yard, hallooing to Turner, "Throw off that iron, quick ! Detail me three carpenters : one to bore with a two-and-a-half or three-inch auger, and two to make plugs to fill the holes. Send some laborers into all the camps to bring every bucket, and find some careful men who are not afraid to go under the boat and knock out blocks as fast as I bring them down a pontoon."

Turner, who had been standing silent and amazed at my excitement and rapid orders, exclaimed, with a sudden burst of conviction, "That's it ! That's it ! That'll do ! Hurrah ! We'll save her yet. Come here with me under the boat, and help knock out a row of blocks." And he jumped into the water up to his arm-pits, leaving me to execute my own orders. The pontoons were dropped down the river, the holes were bored in the end allowing them partly to fill, and they were then pulled under the boat as fast as the blocks were out. The holes were then plugged, and the water was dipped until they began to lift up on the bottom of the hull, and when all were under that were necessary, then rapid work was resumed with the buckets, till by 2 o'clock in the morning she was safely riding on the top of the rising waters. They are now calking and pitching her as rapidly as possible, and fixing beams for wheel and engines; as many men are at work as can get around on her to do anything.

Afternoon, 16*th*.— General Howard rode out with me to examine the bridge work on Jasper road, let out to some citizens living inside our lines. They are dull to comprehend, slow to execute, and need constant direction and supervision. Showed General Howard the unfinished railroad grade to Jasper, and my estimate of the time in which it can be made passable for cars if we can get the iron, and if not, of the time in which we can use it for wagons.

On October 19th, under General Rosecrans's orders to General Hooker, I was charged with the work on this road.

20*th*.— Commenced work on the Jasper branch.

22*d*.— General Grant and Quartermaster-General Meigs arrived on their way to the front with Hooker and staff. I accompanied them as far as Jasper. During the ride I gave Grant what information I had of the country, the streams, roads, the work being done and required to be done on the Jasper branch, also on the steamboat. He saw the impossibility of supplying by the dirt road, and approved the building of the Jasper branch, and extending it if practicable to Kelley's; also appreciated the importance of the little steamboat, which will be ready for launching to-morrow or Saturday. General Meigs . . . approved of the Jasper branch scheme and gave me a message ordering the iron forwarded at once.

23*d*.— Steamboat ready to launch to-morrow. Railroad work progressing.

24*th*.— Steamer launched safely.

26*th*.—Work on boat progressing favorably; as many men are at work on her as can be employed.

Extract from a letter dated Nov. 1st, 1863:

I had urged forward the construction of the little steamer day and night, and started her with only a skeleton of a pilot-house, without waiting for a boiler-deck, which was put on afterward as she was being loaded. Her cabin is now being covered with canvas. On the 29th she made her first trip, with two barges, 34,000 rations, to Rankin's Ferry, and returned. I loaded two more barges during the night, and started at 4 o'clock A. M. on the 30th for Kelley's Ferry, forty-five miles distant by river. The day was very stormy, with unfavorable head-winds. We made slow progress against the wind and the rapid current of this tortuous mountain stream. A hog-chain broke, and we floated down the stream while repairing it with help of block and tackle. I ordered the engineer to give only steam enough to overcome the current and keep crawling up, fearful of breaking some steam-pipe connection, or of starting a leak in the limber half-braced boat. Had another break, and again floated helplessly down while repairing; straightened up once more, and moved on again—barely moved up in some places where the current was unusually strong; and so we kept on, trembling and hoping, under the responsibility of landing safely this important cargo of rations. Night fell upon us—the darkest night possible—with a driving rain, in which, like a blind person, the little boat was feeling her way up an unknown river.

Captain Edwards brought, as captain, a man named Davis, from Detroit, who used to be a mate on a Lake Erie vessel; but, as he was ignorant of river boats or navigation, could not steer, and knew nothing of wheel-house bells or signals, I could not trust him on this important first trip. The only soldier I could find who claimed any knowledge of the business of a river pilot was a man named Williams, who had steered on a steam-ferry running between Cincinnati and Covington. Him I put into the wheel-house, and as I had once owned a fourth interest in a steamboat, and fooled away considerable money and time with her, I had learned enough of the wheel to know which way to turn it, and of the bell-pulls to signal Stop, Back, and Go ahead. I went with Williams into the wheel-house, and put Davis on the bows, to keep a lookout. As the night grew dark, and finally black, Davis declared he could see nothing, and came back wringing his hands and saying we would "surely be wrecked if we did not land and tie up."

"There's a light ahead now, Davis, on the north shore."

"Yes, and another on the south, I think."

"One or both must be rebels' camp-fires."

We tried to keep the middle of the river, which is less than musket-shot across in any part. After a long struggle against wind and tide we got abreast of the first camp-fire, and saw the sentry pacing back and forward before it, and hailed:

"Halloo! there. What troops are those?"

Back came the answer in unmistakable Southern patois: "Ninth Tennessee. Run your old tea-kittle ashore here, and give us some hot whisky."

The answer was not comforting. I knew of no Tennessee regiment in the Union service except one, or part of one, commanded by Colonel Stokes, and where that was I did not know. So we put the boat over to the other shore as fast as possible, and to gain time I called out:

"Who's in command?"

"Old Stokes, you bet."

"Never mind, Williams, keep her in the middle. We're all right.—How far to Kelley's Ferry?"

"Rite over thar whar you see that fire. They're sittin' up for ye, I reckon."

"Steady, Williams. Keep around the bend and steer for the light."

And in due time we tied the steamboat and barges safely to shore, with 40,000 rations and 39,000 pounds of forage, within five miles of General Hooker's men, who had half a breakfast ration left in haversacks; and within eight or ten miles of Chattanooga, where four cakes of hard bread and a quarter pound of pork made a three days' ration. In Chattanooga there were but four boxes of hard bread left in the commissary warehouses on the morning of the 30th [October]. About midnight I started an orderly to report to General Hooker the safe arrival of the rations. The orderly returned about sunrise, and reported that the news went through the camps faster than his horse, and the soldiers were jubilant, and cheering "The Cracker line open. Full rations, boys! Three cheers for the Cracker line," as if we had won another victory; and we had.

CHATTANOOGA.

BY ULYSSES S. GRANT, GENERAL, U. S. A.

AFTER the fall of Vicksburg I urged strongly upon the Government the propriety of a movement against Mobile. General Rosecrans had been at Murfreesboro', Tennessee, with a large and well-equipped army from early in the year 1863, with Bragg confronting him with a force quite equal to his own at first, considering that it was on the defensive. But after the investment of Vicksburg, Bragg's army was largely depleted to strengthen Johnston, in Mississippi, who was being reënforced to raise the siege. I frequently wrote to General Halleck suggesting that Rosecrans should move against Bragg. By so doing he would either detain the latter's troops where they were, or lay Chattanooga open to capture. General Halleck strongly approved the suggestion, and finally wrote me that he had repeatedly ordered Rosecrans to advance, but that the latter had constantly failed to comply with the order, ✠ and at last, after having held a council of war, replied, in effect, that it was a military maxim "not to fight two decisive battles at the same time." If true, the maxim was not applicable in this case. It would be bad to be defeated in two decisive battles fought the same day, but it would not be bad to win them. I, however, was fighting no battle, and the siege of Vicksburg had drawn from Rosecrans's front so many of the enemy that his chances of victory were much greater than they would be if he waited until the siege was over, when these troops could be returned. Rosecrans was ordered to move against the army that was detaching troops to raise the siege. Finally, on the 24th of June, he did move, but ten days afterward Vicksburg surrendered, and the troops sent from Bragg were free to return.↓ It was at this time that I recommended to the general-in-chief the movement against Mobile. I knew the peril the Army of the Cumberland was in, being depleted continually not only by ordinary casualties, but also by having to detach troops to hold its constantly extending line over which to draw supplies, while the enemy in front was as constantly being strengthened. Mobile was important to the enemy, and, in the absence of a threatening force, was guarded by little else than artillery. If threatened by land and from the

✠ In an article in "The Century" magazine for May, 1887, General Rosecrans says:

"Since our forces in rear of Vicksburg would be endangered by General Joseph E. Johnston, if he should have enough troops, we must not drive Bragg out of middle Tennessee until it shall be too late for his command to reënforce Johnston's. Bragg's army is now, apparently, holding this army in check. It is the most important service he can render to his cause. The Confederate authorities know it. They will not order, nor will Bragg venture to send away any substantial detachments. The news that Vicksburg could not hold out over two or three weeks having reached us, we began our movements to dislodge Bragg from his intrenched camp on the 24th of June, 1863. It rained for seventeen consecutive days. The roads were so bad that it required four days for Crittenden's troops to march seventeen miles. Yet, on the 4th of July, we had possession of both the enemy's intrenched camps, and by the 7th, Bragg's army was in full retreat over the Cumberland Mountains into Sequatchie valley, whence he proceeded to Chattanooga, leaving us in full possession of middle Tennessee and of the damaged Nashville and Chattanooga railway, with my headquarters at Winchester, fifty miles from our starting-point, Murfreesboro'. This movement was accomplished in fifteen days, and with a loss of only 586 killed and wounded." EDITORS.

↓ Late in August the divisions of Breckinridge and W. H. T. Walker were transferred from Mississippi to Bragg's army, and the brigades of Gregg and McNair followed early in September. These troops were engaged at Chickamauga.— EDITORS.

water at the same time, the prize would fall easily, or troops would have to be sent to its defense. Those troops would necessarily come from Bragg.

My judgment was overruled, however, and the troops under my command were dissipated over other parts of the country where it was thought they could render the most service. Four thousand were sent to Banks, at New Orleans; five thousand to Schofield, to use against Price, in Arkansas; the Ninth Corps back to Kentucky; and finally, in August, the whole of the Thirteenth Corps to Banks. I also sent Ransom's brigade to Natchez, to occupy that point, and to relieve Banks from guarding any part of the river above what he had guarded before the fall of Port Hudson. Ransom captured a large amount of ammunition and about five thousand beef cattle that were crossing the river going east for the rebel armies. At this time the country was full of deserters from Pemberton's army, and it was reported that many had also left Johnston. These avowed they would never go back to fight against us again. Many whose homes were west of the river went there, and others went North to remain until they could return with security.

Soon it was discovered in Washington that Rosecrans was in trouble and required assistance. The emergency was now too immediate to allow us to give this assistance by making an attack in the rear of Bragg upon Mobile. It was, therefore, necessary to reënforce directly, and troops were sent from every available point. On the 13th of September Halleck telegraphed me to send all available forces to Memphis, and thence east along the Memphis and Charleston railroad to coöperate with Rosecrans. This instruction was repeated two days later, but I did not get even the first until the 23d of the month. As fast as transports could be provided all the troops except a portion of the Seventeenth Corps were forwarded under Sherman, whose services up to this time demonstrated his superior fitness for a separate command. ⟩ I also moved McPherson, with most of the troops still about Vicksburg, eastward, to compel the enemy to keep back a force to meet him. Meanwhile Rosecrans had very skillfully manœuvred Bragg south of the Tennessee River, and through and beyond Chattanooga. If he had stopped and intrenched, and made himself strong there, all would have been right, and the mistake of not moving earlier partially compensated. But he pushed on, with his forces very much scattered, until Bragg's troops from Mississippi began to join him. ⟩ Then Bragg took the initiative. Rosecrans had to fall back in turn, and was able to get his army together at Chickamauga, some miles south-east of Chattanooga, before the main battle was brought on. The

---

⟩ In his "Personal Memoirs" (C. L. Webster & Co.) General Grant says:

"Soon after negotiations were opened with General Pemberton for the surrender of the city, I notified Sherman, whose troops extended from Haynes's Bluff on the left to the crossing of the Vicksburg and Jackson road over the Big Black on the right, and directed him to hold his command in readiness to advance and drive the enemy from the State as soon as Vicksburg surrendered. . . . Johnston heard of the surrender of Vicksburg almost as soon as it occurred, and immediately fell back on Jackson. On the 8th of July Sherman was within ten miles of Jackson, and on the 11th was close up to the defenses of the city and shelling the town. The siege was kept up until the morning of the 17th, when it was found that the enemy had evacuated during the night. The weather was very hot, the roads dusty, and the water bad. Johnston destroyed the roads as he passed, and had so much the start that pursuit was useless; but Sherman sent one division, Steele's, to Brandon, fourteen miles east of Jackson. . . . Sherman was ordered back to Vicksburg, and his troops took much the same position they had occupied before — from the Big Black to Haynes's Bluff." EDITORS.

⟩ Bragg was also reënforced by Longstreet, from the Army of Northern Virginia.—EDITORS.

battle was fought on the 19th and 20th of September, and Rosecrans was badly defeated, with a heavy loss in artillery, and some sixteen thousand men killed, wounded, and captured. The corps under Major-General George H. Thomas stood its ground, while Rosecrans, with Crittenden and McCook, returned to Chattanooga. Thomas returned also, but later, and with his troops in good order. Bragg followed and took possession of Missionary Ridge, overlooking Chattanooga. He also occupied Lookout Mountain, west of the town, which Rosecrans had abandoned, and with it his control of the river and river road as far back as Bridgeport. The National troops were now strongly intrenched in Chattanooga Valley, with the Tennessee River behind them, the enemy occupying commanding heights to the east and west, with a strong line across the valley, from mountain to mountain, and Chattanooga Creek for a large part of the way in front of their line.

On the 29th of September Halleck telegraphed me the above results, and directed all the forces that could be spared from my department to be sent to Rosecrans, suggesting that a good commander like Sherman or McPherson should go with the troops; also that I should go in person to Nashville to superintend the movement. Long before this dispatch was received Sherman was already on his way, and McPherson also was moving east with most of the garrison of Vicksburg. I at once sent a staff-officer to Cairo, to communicate, in my name, directly with the Government, and to forward me any and all important dispatches without the delays that had attended the transmission of previous ones. On the 3d of October a dispatch was received at Cairo ordering me to move with my staff and headquarters to that city, and report from there my arrival. This dispatch reached me on the 10th. I left Vicksburg the same day, reached Columbus *en route* for Cairo on the 16th, and reported my arrival at once. The reply to my telegram from Cairo, announcing my arrival at that point, came on the morning of the 17th, directing me to proceed immediately to the Galt House, Louisville, Kentucky, where I would meet an officer of the War Department with my instructions. I left Cairo within an hour after the receipt of this dispatch, going by rail by the way of Indianapolis, Indiana. Just as the train I was on was starting out of the depot at Indianapolis, a messenger came running up to stop it, saying the Secretary of War was coming into the station and wanted to see me. I had never met Mr. Stanton up to that time, though we had held frequent conversations over the wires, the year before, when I was in Tennessee. Occasionally, at night, he would order the wires between the War Department and my headquarters to be connected, and we would hold a conversation for an hour or two. On this occasion the secretary was accompanied by Governor Brough, of Ohio, whom I had never met, though he and my father had been old acquaintances. Mr. Stanton dismissed the special train that had brought him to Indianapolis and accompanied me to Louisville.

Up to this time no hint had been given me of what was wanted after I left Vicksburg, except the suggestion in one of Halleck's dispatches that I had better go to Nashville and superintend the operation of the troops sent to relieve Rosecrans. Soon after we had started, the secretary handed me two

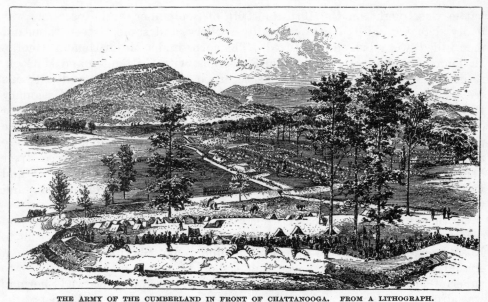

THE ARMY OF THE CUMBERLAND IN FRONT OF CHATTANOOGA.   FROM A LITHOGRAPH.

The picture shows the intrenchments occupied by three divisions of Thomas's corps. In the foreground is seen Fort Grose, manned on the left of the picture by the 24th Ohio and on the right by the 36th Indiana, guns of the First Ohio Battery being in the inclosures. Fort Negley is at the end of the line of works seen in the middle-ground, Lookout Mountain being in the distance.— EDITORS.

orders, saying that I might take my choice of them.   The two were identical in all but one particular.   Both created the Military Division of the Mississippi, giving me the command, composed of the Departments of the Ohio, the Cumberland, and the Tennessee, and all the territory from the Alleghanies to the Mississippi River, north of Banks's command in the south-west.   One order left the department commanders as they were, while the other relieved Rosecrans and assigned Thomas to his place.   I accepted the latter.   We reached Louisville after night, and, if I remember rightly, in a cold, drizzling rain.   The Secretary of War told me afterward that he caught a cold on that occasion from which he never expected to recover.

A day was spent in Louisville, the secretary giving me the military news at the capital, and talking about the disappointment at the results of some of the campaigns.   By the evening of the day after our arrival all matters of discussion seemed exhausted, and I left the hotel to spend the evening away, both Mrs. Grant (who was with me) and myself having relations living in Louisville.   In the course of the evening Mr. Stanton received a dispatch from Mr. C. A. Dana [an officer of the War Department], then in Chattanooga, informing him that unless prevented Rosecrans would retreat, and advising peremptory orders against his doing so.   A retreat at that time would have been a terrible disaster.   It would not only have been the loss of a most important strategic position to us, but it would have been attended with the loss of all the artillery still left with the Army of the Cumberland, and the annihilation of that army itself, either by capture or demoralization.

All supplies for Rosecrans had to be brought from Nashville.   The railroad between this base and the army was in possession of the Government up to Bridgeport, the point at which the road crosses to the south side of the Tennessee River; but Bragg, holding Lookout and Raccoon mountains west of Chattanooga, commanded the railroad, the river, and the shortest and best wagon roads both south and north of the Tennessee, between Chattanooga and Bridgeport. The distance between these two places is but twenty-six miles by rail; but owing to this position of Bragg all supplies for Rosecrans had to be hauled by a circuitous route, north of the river, and over a mountainous country, increasing the distance to over sixty miles. This country afforded but little food for his animals, nearly ten thousand of which had already starved, and none were left to draw a single piece of artillery or even the ambulances to convey the sick. The men had been on half rations of hard bread for a considerable time, with but few other supplies, except beef driven from Nashville across the country. The region along the road became so exhausted of food for the cattle that by the time they reached Chattanooga they were much in the condition of the few animals left alive there, "on the lift." Indeed, the beef was so poor that the soldiers were in the habit of saying, with a faint facetiousness, that they were living on half rations of hard bread and " beef dried on the hoof." Nothing could be transported but food, and the troops were without sufficient shoes or other clothing suitable for the advancing season. What they had was well worn. The fuel within the Federal lines was exhausted, even to the stumps of trees. There were no teams to draw it from the opposite bank, where it was abundant. The only means for supplying fuel, for some time before my arrival, had been to cut trees from the north bank of the river, at a considerable distance up the stream, form rafts of it, and float it down with the current, effecting a landing on the south side, within our lines, by the use of paddles or poles. It would then be carried on the shoulders of the men to their camps. If a retreat had occurred at this time it is not probable that any of the army would have reached the railroad as an organized body, if followed by the enemy.

On the receipt of Mr. Dana's dispatch Mr. Stanton sent for me. Finding that I was out, he became nervous and excited, inquiring of every person he met, including guests of the house, whether they knew where I was, and bidding them find me and send me to him at once. About 11 o'clock I returned to the hotel, and on my way, when near the house, every person met was a messenger from the secretary, apparently partaking of his impatience to see me. I hastened to the room of the secretary and found him pacing the floor rapidly, in a dressing-gown. Saying that the retreat must be prevented, he showed me the dispatch. I immediately wrote an order assuming command of the Military Division of the Mississippi, and telegraphed it to General Rosecrans. I then telegraphed to him the order from Washington assigning Thomas to the command of the Army of the Cumberland; and to Thomas that he must hold Chattanooga at all hazards, informing him at the same time that I would be at the front as soon as possible. A prompt reply was received from Thomas, saying, " We will hold the town till we starve." I appreciated the force of this dispatch later when I witnessed the condition of affairs which prompted it. It looked, indeed, as if but two courses were open: one to starve, the other to surrender or be captured.

On the morning of the 20th of October I started by train with my staff, and proceeded as far as Nashville. At that time it was not prudent to travel beyond that point by night, so I remained in Nashville until the next morning. Here I met for the first time Andrew Johnson, Military Governor of Tennessee. He delivered a speech of welcome. His composure showed that it was by no means his maiden effort. It was long, and I was in torture while he was delivering it, fearing something would be expected from me in response. I was relieved, however, the people assembled having apparently heard enough. At all events they commenced a general hand-shaking, which, although trying where there is so much of it, was a great relief to me in this emergency.

From Nashville I telegraphed to Burnside, who was then at Knoxville, ☆ that important points in his department ought to be fortified, so that they could be held with the least number of men; to Porter at Cairo, that Sherman's advance had passed Eastport, Miss. [see p. 691], and that rations were probably on their way from St. Louis by boat for supplying his army, and requesting him to send a gun-boat to convoy them; and to Thomas, suggesting that large parties should be put at work on the wagon road then in use back to Bridgeport.

On the morning of the 21st we took the train for the front, reaching Stevenson, Alabama, after dark. Rosecrans was there on his way north. He came into my car, and we held a brief interview in which he described very clearly the situation at Chattanooga, and made some excellent suggestions as to what should be done. My only wonder was that he had not carried them out. We then proceeded to Bridgeport, where we stopped for the night. From here we took horses and made our way by Jasper and over Waldron's Ridge to Chattanooga. There had been much rain and the roads were almost impassable from mud knee-deep in places, and from washouts on the mountain-sides. I had been on crutches since the time of my fall in New Orleans,⌡ and had to be carried over places where it was not safe to cross on horseback. The roads were strewn with the débris of broken wagons and the carcasses of thousands of starved mules and horses. At Jasper, some ten or twelve miles from Bridgeport, there was a halt. Howard had his headquarters there. From this point I telegraphed Burnside to make every effort to secure 500 rounds of ammunition for his artillery and small-arms. We stopped for the night at a little hamlet some ten or twelve miles farther on. The next day we reached Chattanooga, a little before dark. I went directly to Thomas's headquarters, and remained there a few days until I could establish my own.

During the evening most of the general officers called in to pay their respects and to talk about the condition of affairs. They pointed out on the maps the line marked with a red or blue pencil which Rosecrans had contemplated falling back upon. If any of them had approved the move, they

<hr/>

☆ General Burnside assumed command of the Department of the Ohio, succeeding General H. G. Wright, on the 25th of March, 1863.—EDITORS.
⌡ In August General Grant went to New Orleans to confer with Banks about coöperating in movements that had been ordered west of the Mississippi. During the visit his horse fell, severely injuring him.—EDITORS.

did not say so to me. I found General W. F. Smith occupying the position of chief engineer of the Army of the Cumberland. I had known Smith as a cadet at West Point, but had no recollection of having met him after my graduation, in 1843, up to this time. He explained the situation of the two armies and the topography of the country so plainly that I could see it without an inspection. I found that he had established a saw-mill on the banks of the river, by utilizing an old engine found in the neighborhood; and by rafting logs from the north side of the river above had got out the lumber and completed pontoons and roadway plank for a second bridge, one flying-bridge being there already. He was also rapidly getting out the materials for constructing the boats for a third bridge. In addition to this he had far under way a steamer for plying between Chattanooga and Bridgeport whenever he might get possession of the river. This boat consisted of a scow made of the plank sawed out at the mill, housed in, with a stern-wheel attached which was propelled by a second engine taken from some shop or factory.

I telegraphed to Washington this night, notifying Halleck of my arrival, and asking to have Sherman assigned to the command of the Army of the Tennessee, headquarters in the field. The request was at once complied with.

The next day, the 24th, I started out to make a personal inspection, taking Thomas and Smith with me, besides most of the members of my personal staff. We crossed to the north side of the river, and, moving to the north of detached spurs of hills, reached the Tennessee, at Brown's Ferry, some three miles below Lookout Mountain, unobserved by the enemy. Here we left our horses back from the river and approached the water on foot. There was a picket station of the enemy, on the opposite side, of about twenty men, in full view, and we were within easy range. They did not fire upon us nor seem to be disturbed by our presence. They must have seen that we were all commissioned officers. But, I suppose, they looked upon the garrison of Chattanooga as prisoners of war, feeding or starving themselves, and thought it would be inhuman to kill any of them except in self-defense. That night I issued orders for opening the route to Bridgeport—a " cracker line," as the soldiers appropriately termed it. [See p. 676.] They had been so long on short rations that my first thought was the establishment of a line over which food might reach them.

Chattanooga is on the south bank of the Tennessee, where that river runs nearly due west. It is at the northern end of a valley five or six miles in width through which runs Chattanooga Creek. To the east of the valley is Missionary Ridge, rising from five to eight hundred feet above the creek, and terminating somewhat abruptly a half-mile or more before reaching the Tennessee. On the west of the valley is Lookout Mountain, 2200 feet above tide-water. Just below the town, the Tennessee makes a turn to the south and runs to the base of Lookout Mountain, leaving no level ground between the mountain and river. The Memphis and Charleston railroad passes this point, where the mountain stands nearly perpendicular. East of Missionary Ridge flows the South Chickamauga River; west of Lookout Mountain is Lookout Creek; and west of that, the Raccoon Mountain. Lookout Mountain

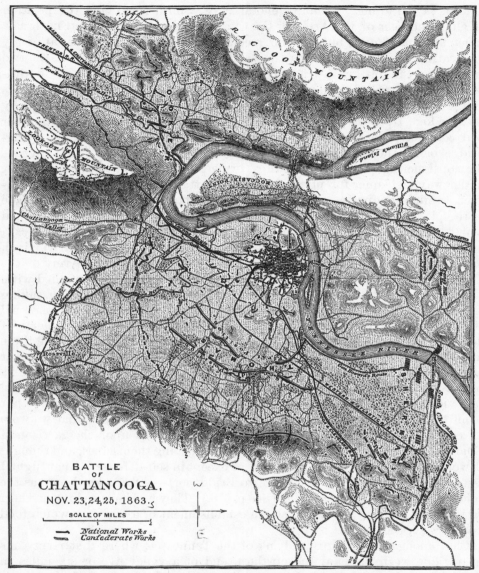

BATTLE
OF
CHATTANOOGA,
NOV. 23, 24, 25, 1863.
SCALE OF MILES

━━ *National Works*
━━ *Confederate Works*

at its northern end rises almost perpendicularly for some distance, then breaks off in a gentle slope of cultivated fields to near the summit, where it ends in a palisade thirty or more feet in height. On the gently sloping ground, between the upper and lower palisades, there is a single farm-house, which is reached by a wagon road from the valley to the east.

The intrenched line of the enemy commenced on the north end of Missionary Ridge and extended along the crest for some distance south, thence across Chattanooga Valley to Lookout Mountain. Lookout Mountain was also fortified and held by the enemy, who also kept troops in Lookout Valley and on Raccoon Mountain, with pickets extending down the river so as to command the road on the north bank and render it useless to us. In addition to this there was an intrenched line in Chattanooga Valley extending from the river east of the town to Lookout Mountain, to make the investment complete. Besides the fortifications on Missionary Ridge there was a line at the base of the hill, with occasional spurs of rifle-pits half-way up the front. The enemy's pickets extended out into the valley toward the town, so far that the pickets of the two armies could converse. At one point they were separated only by the narrow creek which gives its name to the valley and town, and from which both sides drew water. The Union lines were shorter than those of the enemy.

Thus the enemy, with a vastly superior force, was strongly fortified to the east, south, and west, and commanded the river below. Practically the Army of the Cumberland was besieged. The enemy, with his cavalry north of the river, had stopped the passing of a train loaded with ammunition and medical supplies. The Union army was short of both, not having ammunition enough for a day's fighting.

Long before my coming into this new field, General Halleck had ordered parts of the Eleventh and Twelfth corps, commanded respectively by Generals Howard and Slocum, Hooker in command of the whole, from the Army of the Potomac, to reënforce Rosecrans. It would have been folly to have sent them to Chattanooga to help eat up the few rations left there. They were consequently left on the railroad, where supplies could be brought them. Before my arrival Thomas ordered their concentration at Bridgeport.

General W. F. Smith had been so instrumental in preparing for the move which I was now about to make, and so clear in his judgment about the manner of making it, that I deemed it but just to him that he should have command of the troops detailed to execute the design, although he was then acting as a staff-officer, and was not in command of troops.

On the 24th of October, after my return to Chattanooga, the following details were made : General Hooker, who was now at Bridgeport, was ordered to cross to the south side of the Tennessee and march up by Whiteside's and Wauhatchie to Brown's Ferry. General Palmer, with a division of the Fourteenth Corps, Army of the Cumberland, was ordered to move down the river on the north side, by a back road, until opposite Whiteside's, then cross and hold the road in Hooker's rear after he had passed. Four thousand men were at the same time detailed to act under General Smith directly from Chattanooga. Eighteen hundred of them, under General Hazen, were to take sixty pontoon-boats and, under cover of night, float by the pickets of the enemy at the north base of Lookout, down to Brown's Ferry, then land on the south side and capture or drive away the pickets at that point. Smith was to march with the remainder of the detail, also under cover of night, by the north bank of the river, to Brown's Ferry, taking with him all the material for laying the bridge, as soon as the crossing was secured.

On the 26th Hooker crossed the river at Bridgeport and commenced his eastward march. At 3 o'clock on the morning of the 27th Hazen moved into

HAZEN'S MEN LANDING FROM PONTOON-BOATS AT BROWN'S FERRY [SEE MAP, P. 686].
FROM A WAR-TIME SKETCH.

the stream with his sixty pontoons and eighteen hundred brave and well-equipped men. Smith started enough in advance to be near the river when Hazen should arrive. There are a number of detached spurs of hills north of the river at Chattanooga, back of which is a good road parallel to the stream, sheltered from view from the top of Lookout. It was over this road Smith marched. At 5 o'clock Hazen landed at Brown's Ferry, surprised the picket-guard and captured most of it. By 7 o'clock the whole of Smith's force was ferried over and in possession of a height commanding the ferry. This was speedily fortified while a detail was laying the pontoon-bridge. By 10 o'clock the bridge was laid, and our extreme right, now in Lookout Valley, was forti-fied and connected with the rest of the army. The two bridges over the Tennessee River,— a flying one at Chattanooga and the new one at Brown's Ferry,— with the road north of the river, covered from both the fire and the view of the enemy, made the connection complete. Hooker found but slight obstacles in his way, and on the afternoon of the 28th emerged into Lookout Valley at Wauhatchie. Howard marched on to Brown's Ferry, while Geary, who commanded a division in the Twelfth Corps, stopped three miles south. The pickets of the enemy on the river below were cut off and soon came in and surrendered.

The river was now open to us from Lookout Valley to Bridgeport. Between Brown's Ferry and Kelley's Ferry the Tennessee runs through a narrow gorge in the mountains, which contracts the stream so much as to increase the current beyond the capacity of an ordinary steamer to stem. To get up these rapids, steamers must be cordelled, that is, pulled up by ropes from the shore. But there is no difficulty in navigating the stream from Bridgeport to Kelley's

Ferry. The latter point is only eight miles from Chattanooga, and connected with it by a good wagon road, which runs through a low pass in the Raccoon Mountain on the south side of the river to Brown's Ferry, thence on the north side to the river opposite Chattanooga. There were several steamers at Bridgeport, and abundance of forage, clothing, and provisions.

On the way to Chattanooga I had telegraphed back to Nashville for a good supply of vegetables and small rations, which the troops had been so long deprived of. Hooker had brought with him from the east a full supply of land transportation. His animals had not been subjected to hard work on bad roads without forage, but were in good condition. In five days from my arrival at Chattanooga the way was open to Bridgeport, and, with the aid of steamers and Hooker's teams, in a week the troops were receiving full rations. It is hard for any one not an eye-witness to realize the relief this brought. The men were soon reclothed and well fed; an abundance of ammunition was brought up, and a cheerfulness prevailed not before enjoyed in many weeks. Neither officers nor men looked upon themselves any longer as doomed. The weak and languid appearance of the troops, so visible before, disappeared at once. I do not know what the effect was on the other side, but assume it must have been correspondingly depressing. Mr. Davis had visited Bragg but a short time before, and must have perceived our condition to be about as Bragg described it in his subsequent report. "These dispositions," he said, " faithfully sustained, insured the enemy's speedy evacuation of Chattanooga, for want of food and forage. Possessed of the shortest route to his depot and the one by which reënforcements must reach him, we held him at our mercy, and his destruction was only a question of time." But the dispositions were not "faithfully sustained," and I doubt not that thousands of men engaged in trying to "sustain" them now rejoice that they were not.

There was no time during the rebellion when I did not think, and often say, that the South was more to be benefited by defeat than the North. The latter had the people, the institutions, and the territory to make a great and prosperous nation. The former was burdened with an institution abhorrent to all civilized peoples not brought up under it, and one which degraded labor, kept it in ignorance, and enervated the governing class. With the outside world at war with this institution, they could not have extended their territory. The labor of the country was not skilled, nor allowed to become so. The whites could not toil without becoming degraded, and those who did were denominated "poor white trash." The system of labor would have soon exhausted the soil and left the people poor. The non-slaveholders would have left the country, and the small slaveholder must have sold out to his more fortunate neighbors. Soon the slaves would have outnumbered the masters, and, not being in sympathy with them, would have risen in their might and exterminated them. The war was expensive to the South as well as to the North, both in blood and treasure; but it was worth all it cost.

The enemy was surprised by the movement which secured to us a line of supplies. He appreciated its importance, and hastened to try to recover the line from us. His strength on Lookout Mountain was not equal to Hooker's

PANORAMIC VIEW OF THE CHATTANOOGA REGION FROM POINT LOOKOUT, ON LOOKOUT MOUNTAIN. FROM A LITHOGRAPH.

command in the valley below. From Missionary Ridge he had to march twice the distance we had from Chattanooga, in order to reach Lookout Valley. But on the night of the 28th–29th [of October] an attack was made on Geary, at Wauhatchie, by Longstreet's corps. When the battle commenced, Hooker ordered Howard up from Brown's Ferry. He had three miles to march to reach Geary. On his way he was fired upon by rebel troops from a foot-hill to the left of the road, and from which the road was commanded. Howard turned to the left, and charged up the hill, and captured it before the enemy had time to intrench, taking many prisoners. Leaving sufficient men to hold this height, he pushed on to re-enforce Geary. Before he got up, Geary had been engaged for about three hours against a vastly superior force. The night was so dark that the men could not distinguish one another except by the light of the flashes of their muskets. In the darkness and uproar Hooker's teamsters became frightened, and deserted their teams. The mules also became frightened, and, breaking loose from their fastenings, stampeded directly toward the enemy. The latter no doubt took this for a charge, and stampeded in turn. By 4 o'clock in the morning the battle had entirely ceased, and our "cracker line" was never afterward disturbed. ⚓

⚓ Major J. L. Coker, of Darlington, South Carolina, says of General Grant's description of this fighting in Lookout Valley:

"The engagement of Wauhatchie, or Lookout Valley, was of minor importance; but it is well to have errors corrected. General Geary's Federal division was not attacked by Longstreet's corps, but by Jenkins's South Carolina brigade, commanded by Colonel (afterward General) John Bratton. No other troops fired a shot at Geary's men that night. The battle lasted about one hour and a half, and was brought to a close on account of General Howard's advance threatening Bratton's rear, and not by a Confederate stampede caused by a '*mule-charge*' in the dark. When the order to retire was received, the brigade was withdrawn in good order. The writer, acting assistant adjutant-general on Colonel Bratton's staff, was wounded and taken from the field at the close of the battle, and did not observe any disorder. General Howard was opposed by a small force, and made such progress that Jenkins's brigade was in danger of being cut off from the crossing over Lookout Creek. They were ordered out when they seemed to be getting the better of General Geary, who was surprised by the night attack, and no doubt thought himself 'greatly outnumbered,' and reported himself attacked by a corps instead of a brigade."
EDITORS.

In securing possession of Lookout Valley, Smith lost one man killed and four or five wounded. The enemy lost most of his pickets at the ferry by capture. In the night engagement of the 28th–29th Hooker lost 416 killed and wounded. I never knew the loss of the enemy, but our troops buried over 150 of his dead, and captured more than 100.

Having got the Army of the Cumberland in a comfortable position, I now began to look after the remainder of my new command. Burnside was in about as desperate a condition as the Army of the Cumberland had been, only he was not yet besieged. He was a hundred miles from the nearest possible base, Big South Fork of the Cumberland River, and much farther from any railroad we had possession of. The roads back were over mountains, and all supplies along the line had long since been exhausted. His animals, too, had been starved, and their carcasses lined the road from Cumberland Gap, and far back toward Lexington, Kentucky. East Tennessee still furnished supplies of beef, bread, and forage, but it did not supply ammunition, clothing, medical supplies, or small rations, such as coffee, sugar, salt, and rice.

Stopping to organize his new command, Sherman had started from Memphis for Corinth on the 11th of October. His instructions required him to repair the road in his rear in order to bring up supplies. The distance was about 330 miles through a hostile country. His entire command could not have maintained the road if it had been completed. The bridges had all been destroyed by the enemy and much other damage done ; a hostile community lived along the road ; guerrilla bands infested the country, and more or less of the cavalry of the enemy was still in the west. Often Sherman's work was destroyed as soon as completed, though he was only a short distance away.

The Memphis and Charleston road strikes the Tennessee River at Eastport, Mississippi. Knowing the difficulty Sherman would have to supply himself from Memphis, I had previously ordered supplies sent from St. Louis on small steamers, to be convoyed by the navy, to meet him at Eastport. These he got. I now ordered him to discontinue his work of repairing roads, and to move on with his whole force to Stevenson, Alabama, without delay. This order was borne to Sherman by a messenger who paddled down the Tennessee in a canoe, and floated over Muscle Shoals; it was delivered at Iuka on the 27th. In this Sherman was notified that the rebels were moving a force toward Cleveland, east Tennessee, and might be going to Nashville, in which event his troops were in the best position to beat them there. Sherman, with his characteristic promptness, abandoned the work he was engaged upon and pushed on at once. On the 1st of November he crossed the Tennessee at Eastport, and that day was in Florence, Alabama, with the head of column, while his troops were still crossing at Eastport, with Blair bringing up the rear.

Sherman's force made an additional army, with cavalry, artillery, and trains, all to be supplied by the single-track road from Nashville. All indications pointed also to the probable necessity of supplying Burnside's command, in east Tennessee, 25,000 more, by the same road. A

VIEW OF CHATTANOOGA AND MOCCASIN POINT FROM THE SIDE OF LOOKOUT MOUNTAIN. FROM A PHOTOGRAPH.

single track could not do this. I therefore gave an order to Sherman to halt General G. M. Dodge's command of eight thousand men at Athens, and subsequently directed the latter to arrange his troops along the railroad from Decatur, north toward Nashville, and to rebuild that road. The road from Nashville to Decatur passes over a broken country, cut up with innumerable streams, many of them of considerable width, and with valleys far below the road-bed. All the bridges over these had been destroyed and the rails taken up and twisted by the enemy. All the locomotives and cars not carried off had been destroyed as effectually as they knew how to destroy them. All bridges and culverts had been destroyed between Nashville and Decatur, and thence to Stevenson, where the Memphis and Charleston and the Nashville and Chattanooga roads unite. The rebuilding of this road would give us two roads as far as Stevenson over which to supply the army. From Bridgeport, a short distance farther east, the river supplements the road.

General Dodge, besides being a most capable soldier, was an experienced railroad builder. He had no tools to work with except those of the pioneers—axes, picks, and spades. With these he was able to intrench his men and protect them against surprises by small parties of the enemy. As he had no base of supplies until the road could be completed back to Nashville, the first matter to consider, after protecting his men, was the getting in of food and forage from the surrounding country. He had his men and teams bring in all the grain they could find, or all they needed, and all the cattle for beef, and such other food as could be found. Millers were detailed from the ranks to run the mills along the line of the army; when these were not near enough to the troops for protection, they were taken down and moved up to the line of the road. Blacksmith shops, with all the iron and steel found in them, were moved up in like manner. Blacksmiths were detailed and set to work making the tools necessary in railroad and bridge building. Axemen were put to work getting out timber for bridges, and cutting fuel for the locomotives when the road should be completed; car-builders were set to work repairing the locomotives and cars. Thus every branch of railroad-building, making tools to work with, and supplying the workingmen with food, was all going on at once, and without the aid of a mechanic or laborer except what the command itself furnished. But rails and cars the men could not make without material, and there was not enough rolling stock to keep the road we already had worked to its full capacity. There were no rails except those in use. To supply these deficiencies I ordered eight of the ten engineers General McPherson had at Vicksburg to be sent to Nashville, and all the cars he had, except ten. I also ordered the troops in west Tennessee to points on the river and on the Memphis and Charleston road, and ordered the cars, locomotives, and rails from all the railroads, except the Memphis and Charleston, to Nashville. The military manager of railroads, also, was directed to furnish more rolling stock, and, as far as he could, bridge material. General Dodge had the work assigned him finished within forty days after receiving his orders. The number of bridges to rebuild was 182, many of them over deep and wide chasms. The length of road repaired was 182 miles.

The enemy's troops, which it was thought were either moving against Burnside or were going to Nashville, went no farther than Cleveland. Their presence there, however, alarmed the authorities at Washington, and on account of our helpless condition at Chattanooga caused me much uneasiness. Dispatches were constantly coming, urging me to do something for Burnside's relief; calling attention to the importance of holding east Tennessee; saying the President was much concerned for the protection of the loyal people in that section, etc. We had not at Chattanooga animals to pull a single piece of artillery, much less a supply train. Reënforcements could not help Burnside, because he had neither supplies nor ammunition sufficient for them; hardly indeed bread and meat for the men he had. There was no relief possible for him, except by expelling the enemy from Missionary Ridge and about Chattanooga.

On the 4th of November Longstreet left our front with about 15,000 troops, besides Wheeler's cavalry, 5000 more, to go against Burnside. ‡ The situation seemed desperate, and was more exasperating because nothing could be done until Sherman should get up. The authorities at Washington

‡ In the course of the preparation of this paper we asked General Grant, whether the detachment of Longstreet for the attack on Knoxville was not, in his opinion, a great mistake on the part of Bragg. He replied in the affirmative; and when it was further presumed that Bragg doubtless thought his position impregnable, the Victor of Chattanooga answered, with a shrewd look that accented the humor of his words: "Well, it *was* impregnable."—EDITORS.

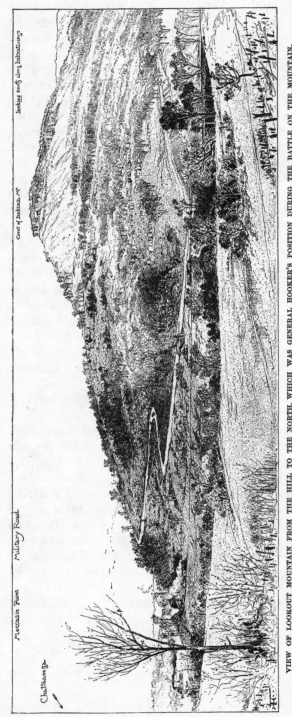

VIEW OF LOOKOUT MOUNTAIN FROM THE HILL TO THE NORTH, WHICH WAS GENERAL HOOKER'S POSITION DURING THE BATTLE ON THE MOUNTAIN, NOVEMBER 24, 1863. FROM A WAR-TIME PHOTOGRAPH.

The military road winding over the north slope of Lookout was built after Hooker captured the mountain.

were now more than ever anxious for the safety of Burnside's army, and plied me with dispatches faster than ever, urging that something should be done for his relief. On the 7th, before Longstreet could possibly have reached Knoxville, I ordered Gen. Thomas peremptorily to attack the enemy's right so as to force the return of the troops that had gone up the valley. I directed him to take mules, officers' horses, or animals wherever he could get them, to move the necessary artillery. But he persisted in the declaration that he could not move a single piece of artillery, and could not see how he could possibly comply with the order. Nothing was left to be done but to answer Washington dispatches as best I could, urge Sherman forward, although he was making every effort to get forward, and encourage Burnside to hold on, assuring him that in a short time he would be relieved. All of Burnside's dispatches showed the greatest confidence in his ability to hold his position as long as his ammunition should hold out. He even suggested the propriety of abandoning the territory he held south and west of Knoxville, so as to draw the enemy farther from his base, and to make it more difficult for him to get back to Chattanooga when the battle should begin. Longstreet had a railroad as far as Loudon; but from there to Knoxville he had to rely on wagon trains. Burnside's suggestion, therefore, was a good one, and it was adopted. On the 14th I telegraphed him:

"Sherman's advance has reached Bridgeport. His whole force will be ready to move from there by Tuesday at furthest. If you can hold Longstreet in check until he gets up, or, by skirmishing and falling back, can avoid serious loss to yourself, and gain time, I will be able to force the enemy back from here, and place a force between Longstreet and Bragg that must inevitably make the former take to the mountain-passes by every available road, to get to his supplies. Sherman would have been here before this but for the high water in Elk River driving him some thirty miles up the river to cross.

Longstreet, for some reason or other, stopped at Loudon until the 13th. That being the terminus of his railroad communications, it is probable he was directed to remain there awaiting orders. ♭ He was in a position threatening Knoxville, and at the same time where he could be brought back speedily to Chattanooga. The day after Longstreet left Loudon, Sherman reached Bridgeport in person, and proceeded on to see me that evening, the 14th, and reached Chattanooga the next day.

My orders for the battle were all prepared in advance of Sherman's arrival, except the dates, which could not be fixed while troops to be engaged were so far away. The possession of Lookout Mountain was of no special advantage to us now. Hooker was instructed to send Howard's corps to the north side of the Tennessee, thence up behind the hills on the north side, and to go into camp opposite Chattanooga; with the remainder of the command Hooker was, at a time to be afterward appointed, to ascend the western slope between the upper and lower palisades, and so get into Chattanooga Valley.

The plan of battle was for Sherman to attack the enemy's right flank, form a line across it, extend our left over South Chickamauga River, so as to threaten or hold the railroad in Bragg's rear, ♮ and thus force him either to weaken his lines elsewhere or lose his connection with his base at Chickamauga Station. Hooker was to perform like service on our right. His problem was to get from Lookout Valley to Chattanooga Valley in the most expeditious way possible; cross the latter valley rapidly to Rossville, south of Bragg's line on Missionary Ridge, form line there across the ridge, facing north, with his right flank extended to Chickamauga Valley east of the ridge, thus threatening the enemy's rear on that flank and compelling him to reënforce this also. Thomas, with the Army of the Cumberland, occupied the center, and was to assault while the enemy was engaged with most of his forces on his two flanks.

To carry out this plan, Sherman was to cross the Tennessee at Brown's Ferry and move east of Chattanooga to a point opposite the north end of

---

♭ In his history, the Comte de Paris says Longstreet was delayed "by the necessity of collecting provisions and organizing his trains."— EDITORS.

♮ A bridge was thrown across the South Chickamauga Creek, at its mouth, and a brigade of cav-
alry was sent across it. That brigade caused the bridge across the Holston River to be burned by the enemy and thus cut off General Longstreet's forces from coming back to General Bragg.— EDITORS.

Missionary Ridge, and to place his command back of the foot-hills out of sight of the enemy on the ridge. There are two streams called Chickamauga emptying into the Tennessee River east of Chattanooga: North Chickamauga, taking its rise in Tennessee, flowing south and emptying into the river some seven or eight miles east; while the South Chickamauga, which takes its rise in Georgia, flows northward, and empties into the Tennessee some three or four miles above the town. There were now 116 pontoons in the North Chickamauga River, their presence there being unknown to the enemy.

At night a division was to be marched up to that point, and at 2 o'clock in the morning moved down with the current, thirty men in each boat. A few were to land east of the mouth of the South Chickamauga, capture the pickets there, and then lay a bridge connecting the two banks of the river. The rest were to land on the south side of the Tennessee, where Missionary Ridge would strike it if prolonged, and a sufficient number of men to man the boats were to push to the north side to ferry over the main body of Sherman's command, while those left on the south side intrenched themselves.☆ Thomas was to move out from his lines facing the ridge, leaving enough of Palmer's corps to guard against an attack down the valley. Lookout Valley being of no present value to us, and being untenable by the enemy if we should secure Missionary Ridge, Hooker's orders were changed. His revised orders brought him to Chattanooga by the established route north of the Tennessee. He was then to move out to the right to Rossville. |

The next day after Sherman's arrival I took him, with Generals Thomas and Smith and other officers, to the north side of the river and showed them the ground over which Sherman had to march, and pointed out generally what he was expected to do. I, as well as the authorities in Washington, was still in a great state of anxiety for Burnside's safety. Burnside himself, I believe, was the only one who did not share in this anxiety. Nothing could be done for him, however, until Sherman's troops were up. As soon, therefore, as the inspection was over, Sherman started for Bridgeport to hasten

☆ This was not, however, the original plan to which Sherman assented, which was to march at once for the north end of the ridge.— EDITORS.

| Hooker's position in Lookout Valley was absolutely essential to us so long as Chattanooga was besieged. It was the key to our line for supplying the army. But it was not essential after the enemy was dispersed from our front, or even after the battle for this purpose was begun. Hooker's orders, therefore, were designed to get his force past Lookout Mountain and Chattanooga Valley, and up to Missionary Ridge. By crossing the north face of Lookout the troops would come into Chattanooga Valley in rear of the line held by the enemy across the valley, and would necessarily force its evacuation. Orders were accordingly given to Hooker to march by this route. But days before the battle began the advantages as well as disadvantages of this plan of action were all considered. The passage over the mountain was a difficult one to make in the face of an enemy. It might consume so much time as to lose us the use

of the troops engaged in it at other points where they were more wanted. After reaching Chattanooga Valley, the creek of the same name, quite a formidable stream to get an army over, had to be crossed.

I was perfectly willing that the enemy should keep Lookout Mountain until we got through with the troops on Missionary Ridge. By marching Hooker to the north side of the river, thence up the stream and recrossing at the town, he could be got in position at any named time; when in this new position he would have Chattanooga Creek behind him; and the attack on Missionary Ridge would unquestionably have caused the evacuation by the enemy of his line across the valley and on Lookout Mountain. Hooker's order was changed accordingly. As explained elsewhere, the original order had to be reverted to because of a flood in the river rendering the bridge at Brown's Ferry unsafe for the passage of troops at the exact juncture when it was wanted to bring all the troops together against Missionary Ridge.—U. S. G.

matters, rowing a boat himself, I believe, from Kelley's Ferry. Sherman had left Bridgeport the night of the 14th, reached Chattanooga the evening of the 15th, made the above-described inspection the morning of the 16th, and started back the same evening to hurry up his command, fully appreciating the importance of time.

His march was conducted with as much expedition as the roads and season would admit of. By the 20th he was himself at Brown's Ferry with head of column, but many of his troops were far behind, and one division, Ewing's, was at Trenton, sent that way to create the impression that Lookout was to be taken from the south. Sherman received his orders at the ferry, and was asked if he could not be ready for the assault the following morning. News had been received that the battle had been commenced at Knoxville. Burnside had been cut off from telegraphic communication. The President, the Secretary of War, and General Halleck were in an agony of suspense. My suspense was also great, but more endurable, because I was where I could soon do something to relieve the situation. It was impossible to get Sherman's troops up for the next day. I then asked him if they could not be got up to make the assault on the morning of the 22d, and ordered Thomas to move on that date. But the elements were against us. It rained all the 20th and 21st. The river rose so rapidly that it was difficult to keep the pontoons in place.

General Orlando B. Willcox, a division commander under Burnside, was at this time occupying a position farther up the valley than Knoxville,—about Maynardsville,—and was still in telegraphic communication with the North. A dispatch was received from him, saying that he was threatened from the east. The following was sent in reply:

" If you can communicate with General Burnside, say to him that our attack on Bragg will commence in the morning. If successful, such a move will be made as, I think, will relieve east Tennessee, if he can hold out. Longstreet passing through our lines to Kentucky need not cause alarm. He would find the country so bare that he would lose his transportation and artillery before reaching Kentucky, and would meet such a force before he got through that he could not return."

Meantime Sherman continued his crossing, without intermission, as fast as his troops could be got up. The crossing had to be effected in full view of the enemy on the top of Lookout Mountain. Once over, the troops soon disappeared behind the detached hills on the north side, and would not come to view again, either to watchmen on Lookout Mountain or Missionary Ridge, until they emerged between the hills to strike the bank of the river. But when Sherman's advance reached a point opposite the town of Chattanooga, Howard, who, it will be remembered, had been concealed behind the hills on the north side, took up his line of march to join the troops on the south side. His crossing was in full view both from Missionary Ridge and the top of Lookout, and the enemy, of course, supposed these troops to be Sherman's. This enabled Sherman to get to his assigned position without discovery.

On the 20th, when so much was occurring to discourage,—rains falling so heavily as to delay the passage of troops over the river at Brown's Ferry, and threatening the entire breaking of the bridge; news coming of a battle raging at Knoxville; of Willcox being threatened by a force from the east,— a letter was received from Bragg which contained these words:

"As there may still be some non-combatants in Chattanooga, I deem it proper to notify you that prudence would dictate their early withdrawal."

Of course I understood that this was a device intended to deceive; but I did not know what the intended deception was. On the 22d, however, a deserter came in who informed me that Bragg was leaving our front, and on that day Buckner's division was sent to reënforce Longstreet, at Knoxville, and another division started to follow, but was recalled. The object of Bragg's letter no doubt was in some way to detain me until Knoxville could be captured, and his troops there be returned to Chattanooga.

During the night of the 21st the rest of the pontoon-boats, completed, one hundred and sixteen in all, were carried up to and placed in North Chickamauga. The material for the roadway over these was deposited out of view of the enemy within a few hundred yards of the bank of the Tennessee where the north end of the bridge was to rest.

Hearing nothing from Burnside, and hearing much of the distress in Washington on his account, I could no longer defer operations for his relief. I determined therefore to do on the 23d, with the Army of the Cumberland, what had been intended to be done on the 24th.

The position occupied by the Army of the Cumberland had been made very strong for defense during the months it had been besieged. The line was about a mile from the town, and extended from Citico Creek, a small stream running near the base of Missionary Ridge and emptying into the Tennessee about two miles below the mouth of the South Chickamauga, on the left, to Chattanooga Creek on the right. All commanding points on the line were well fortified and well equipped with artillery. The important elevations within the line had all been carefully fortified and supplied with a proper armament. Among the elevations so fortified was one to the east of the town, named Fort Wood. It owed its importance chiefly to the fact that it lay between the town and Missionary Ridge, where most of the strength of the enemy was. Fort Wood had in it twenty-two pieces of artillery, most of which would reach the nearer points of the enemy's line. On the morning of the 23d Thomas, according to instructions, moved Granger's corps of two divisions, Sheridan and T. J. Wood commanding, to the foot of Fort Wood, and formed them into line as if going on parade— Sheridan on the right, Wood to the left, extending to or near Citico Creek. Palmer, commanding the Fourteenth Corps, held that part of our line facing south and south-west. He supported Sheridan with one division, Baird's, while his other division, under [R. W.] Johnson, remained in the trenches, under arms, ready to be moved to any point. Howard's corps was moved in rear of the center. The picket lines were within a few hundred yards of each other. At 2 o'clock in the afternoon all were ready to advance. By this time the clouds had lifted so that the enemy could see from his elevated

BRIDGING LOOKOUT CREEK PREPARATORY TO THE ASSAULT BY HOOKER. FROM A WAR-TIME SKETCH.

position all that was going on. The signal for advance was given by a booming of cannon from Fort Wood and other points on the line. The rebel pickets were soon driven back upon the main guards, which occupied minor and detached heights between the main ridge and our lines. These too were carried before halting, and before the enemy had time to reënforce their advance guards. But it was not without loss on both sides. This movement secured to us a line fully a mile in advance of the one we occupied in the morning, and one which the enemy had occupied up to this time. The fortifications were rapidly turned to face the other way. During the following night they were made strong. We lost in this preliminary action about eleven hundred killed and wounded, while the enemy probably lost quite as heavily, including the prisoners that were captured. With the exception of the firing of artillery, kept up from Missionary Ridge and Fort Wood until night closed in, this ended the fighting for the day.

The advantage was greatly on our side now, and if I could only have been assured that Burnside could hold out ten days longer I should have rested more easy. But we were doing the best we could for him and the cause.

By the night of the 23d Sherman's command was in a position to move, though one division (Osterhaus's) had not yet crossed the river at Brown's Ferry. The continuous rise in the Tennessee had rendered it impossible to keep the bridge at that point in condition for troops to cross; but I was determined to move that night, even without this division. Accordingly, orders were sent to Osterhaus to report to Hooker if he could not cross by 8 o'clock on the morning of the 24th. Because of the break in the bridge, Hooker's orders were again changed, but this time only back to those first given to him.

General W. F. Smith had been assigned to duty as chief engineer of the military division. To him was given the general direction of moving troops by the boats from North Chickamauga, laying the bridge after they reached

THE BATTLE OF LOOKOUT MOUNTAIN. FROM A PAINTING LENT BY CAPTAIN W. L. STORK.

This picture shows the Union troops fighting in the woods near the cliffs of Point Lookout.

Early in October, 1863, Jefferson Davis visited Lookout Mountain with General Bragg. As they approached the edge of the cliff, General Bragg, with a wave of the hand, alluded to "the fine view"; whereupon Major Robert W. Wooley, who had little faith in the military outlook, exclaimed to a brother officer, but so that all could hear: "Yes, it's a fine view, but a —— bad prospect."—EDITORS.

their position, and, generally, all the duties pertaining to his office of chief engineer. During the night General Morgan L. Smith's division was marched to the point where the pontoons were, and the brigade of Giles A. Smith was selected for the delicate duty of manning the boats and surprising the enemy's pickets on the south bank of the river. During this night, also, General J. M. Brannan, chief of artillery, moved forty pieces of artillery belonging to the Army of the Cumberland, and placed them on the north side of the river so as to command the ground opposite, to aid in protecting the approach to the point where the south end of the bridge was to rest. He had to use Sherman's artillery horses for this purpose, Thomas having none.

At 2 o'clock in the morning, November 24th, Giles A. Smith pushed out from the North Chickamauga with his 116 boats, each loaded with 30 brave and well-armed men. The boats, with their precious freight, dropped down quietly with the current to avoid attracting the attention of any one who could convey information to the enemy, until arriving near the mouth of South Chickamauga. Here a few boats were landed, the troops debarked, and a rush was made upon the picket-guard known to be at that point. The guard was surprised, and twenty of their number captured. The remainder of the troops effected a landing at the point where the bridge was to start, with equally good results. The work of ferrying over Sherman's command from the north side of the Tennessee was at once commenced, using the pontoons for the purpose. A steamer was also brought up from the town to assist. The rest of M. L. Smith's division came first, then the division of John E. Smith. The troops as they landed were put to work intrenching their position. By daylight the two entire divisions were over, and well covered by the works they had built.

The work of laying the bridge on which to cross the artillery and cavalry was now begun. The ferrying over the infantry was continued with the steamer and the pontoons, taking the pontoons, however, as fast as they were wanted to put in their place in the bridge. By a little past noon the bridge was completed, as well as one over the South Chickamauga, connecting the troops left on that side with their comrades below, and all the infantry and artillery were on the south bank of the Tennessee.

Sherman at once formed his troops for assault on Missionary Ridge. By 1 o'clock he started, with M. L. Smith on his left, keeping nearly the course of Chickamauga River; J. E. Smith next, to the right and a little in the rear; then Ewing, still farther to the right, and also a little to the rear of J. E. Smith's command, in column ready to deploy to the right if an enemy should come from that direction. A good skirmish line preceded each of these columns. Soon the foot of the hill was reached; the skirmishers pushed directly up, followed closely by their supports. By half-past 3 Sherman was in possession of the height, without having sustained much loss. A brigade from each division was now brought up, and artillery was dragged to the top of the hill by hand. The enemy did not seem to have been aware of this movement until the top of the hill was gained. There had been a drizzling rain during the day, and the clouds were so low that Lookout Mountain and the top of Missionary Ridge were obscured from the view of persons in the valley. But now the enemy opened fire upon their assailants, and made several attempts with their skirmishers to drive them away, but without avail. Later in the day a more determined attack was made, but this, too, failed, and Sherman was left to fortify what he had gained.

Sherman's cavalry took up its line of march soon after the bridge was completed, and by half-past three the whole of it was over both bridges, and on its

THE FIGHT EAST OF THE PALISADES ON LOOKOUT MOUNTAIN.   FROM A WAR-TIME SKETCH.

way to strike the enemy's communications at Chickamauga Station.   All of
Sherman's command was now south of the Tennessee.   During the afternoon General Giles A. Smith was severely wounded and carried from the field.

Thomas having done on the 23d what was expected of him on the 24th,
there was nothing for him to do this day, except to strengthen his position.
Howard, however, effected a crossing of Citico Creek and a junction with
Sherman, and was directed to report to him.   With two or three regiments
of his command, he moved in the morning along the banks of the Tennessee
and reached the point where the bridge was being laid.   He went out on the
bridge as far as it was completed from the south end, and saw Sherman
superintending the work from the north side, moving himself south as fast as
an additional boat was put in and the roadway put upon it.   Howard reported
to his new chief across the chasm between them, which was now narrow and
in a few minutes was closed.

While these operations were going on to the east of Chattanooga, Hooker
was engaged on the west.   He had three divisions: Osterhaus's, of the Fifteenth Corps, Army of the Tennessee; Geary's, Twelfth Corps, Army of the
Potomac; and Cruft's, Fourteenth Corps, Army of the Cumberland.   Geary
was on the right at Wauhatchie, Cruft at the center, and Osterhaus near
Brown's Ferry.   These troops were all west of Lookout Creek.   The enemy
had the east bank of the creek strongly picketed and intrenched, and three
brigades of troops in the rear to reënforce them if attacked.   These brigades

occupied the summit of the mountain. General Carter L. Stevenson was in command of the whole. Why any troops except artillery, with a small infantry guard, were kept on the mountain-top, I do not see. A hundred men could have held the summit—which is a palisade for more than thirty feet down—against the assault of any number of men from the position Hooker occupied.

The side of Lookout Mountain confronting Hooker's command was rugged, heavily timbered, and full of chasms, making it difficult to advance with troops, even in the absence of an opposing force. Farther up the ground becomes more even and level, and was in cultivation. On the east side the slope is much more gradual, and a good wagon road, zigzagging up it, connects the town of Chattanooga with the summit.

Early in the morning of the 24th Hooker moved Geary's division, supported by a brigade of Cruft's, up Lookout Creek, to effect a crossing. The remainder of Cruft's division was to seize the bridge over the creek, near the crossing of the railroad. Osterhaus was to move up to the bridge and cross it. The bridge was seized by Grose's brigade after a slight skirmish with the picket guarding it. This attracted the enemy so that Geary's movement farther up was not observed. A heavy mist obscured him from the view of the troops on the top of the mountain. He crossed the creek almost unobserved, and captured the picket of over forty men on guard near by. He then commenced ascending the mountain directly in his front. By this time the enemy was seen coming down from their camp on the mountain slope, and filing into their rifle-pits to contest the crossing of the bridge. By 11 o'clock the bridge was complete. Osterhaus was up, and after some sharp skirmishing the enemy was driven away, with considerable loss in killed and captured.

While the operations at the bridge were progressing, Geary was pushing up the hill over great obstacles, resisted by the enemy directly in his front, and in face of the guns on top of the mountain. The enemy, seeing their left flank and rear menaced, gave way and were followed by Cruft and Osterhaus. Soon these were up abreast of Geary, and the whole command pushed up the hill, driving the enemy in advance. By noon Geary had gained the open ground on the north slope of the mountain with his right close up to the base of the upper palisade, but there were strong fortifications in his front. The rest of the command coming up, a line was formed from the base of the upper palisade to the mouth of Chattanooga Creek.

Thomas and I were on the top of Orchard Knob. Hooker's advance now made our line a continuous one. It was in full view extending from the Tennessee River, where Sherman had crossed, up Chickamauga River to the base of Missionary Ridge, over the top of the north end of the ridge, to Chattanooga Valley, then along parallel to the ridge a mile or more, across the valley to the mouth of Chattanooga Creek, thence up the slope of Lookout Mountain to the foot of the upper palisade. The day was hazy, so that Hooker's operations were not visible to us except at moments when the clouds would rise. But the sound of his artillery and musketry was heard incessantly. The enemy on his front was partially fortified, but was soon driven out of his works. At 2 o'clock the clouds, which had so obscured the top of Lookout all day as to hide whatever was going on from the view of those below, settled down and made it so dark where Hooker was as to stop operations for the time. At 4 o'clock Hooker reported his position as impregnable. By a little after 5, direct communication was established, and a brigade of troops was sent from Chattanooga to reënforce him. These troops had to cross Chattanooga Creek, and met with some opposition, but soon overcame it, and by night the commander, General Carlin, reported to Hooker and was assigned to his left. I now telegraphed to Washington:

" The fight to-day progressed favorably. Sherman carried the end of Missionary Ridge, and his right is now at the tunnel, and his left at Chickamauga Creek. Troops from Lookout Valley carried the point of the mountain, and now hold the eastern slope and a point high up. Hooker reports two thousand prisoners taken, besides which a small number have fallen into our hands, from Missionary Ridge."

The next day the President replied:

" Your dispatches as to fighting on Monday and Tuesday are here. Well done. Many thanks to all. Remember Burnside."

Halleck also telegraphed:

" I congratulate you on the success thus far of your plans. I fear that Burnside is hard pushed, and that any further delay may prove fatal. I know you will do all in your power to relieve him."

The division of Jefferson C. Davis, Army of the Cumberland, had been sent to the North Chickamauga to guard the pontoons as they were deposited in the river, and to prevent all ingress or egress by citizens. On the night of the 24th his division, having crossed with Sherman, occupied our extreme left, from the upper bridge over the plain to the north base of Missionary Ridge. Firing continued to a late hour in the night, but it was not connected with an assault at any point.

At 12 o'clock at night, when all was quiet, I began to give orders for the next day, and sent a dispatch to Willcox to encourage Burnside. Sherman was directed to attack at daylight. Hooker was ordered to move at the same hour, and endeavor to intercept the enemy's retreat, if he still remained; if he had gone, then to move directly to Rossville and operate against the left and rear of the force on Missionary Ridge. Thomas was not to move until Hooker had reached Missionary Ridge. As I was with him on Orchard Knob, he would not move without further orders from me.

The morning of the 25th opened clear and bright, and the whole field was in full view from the top of Orchard Knob. It remained so all day. Bragg's headquarters were in full view, and officers—presumably staff-officers—could be seen coming and going constantly.

The point of ground which Sherman had carried on the 24th was almost disconnected from the main ridge occupied by the enemy. A low pass, over which there is a wagon road crossing the hill, and near which there is a railroad tunnel, intervenes between the two hills. The problem now was to get to the latter. The enemy was fortified on the point, and back farther, where the ground was still higher, was a second fortification commanding the first. Sherman was out as soon as it was light enough to see, and by sunrise his command was in motion. Three brigades held the hill already gained. Morgan L. Smith moved along the east base of Missionary Ridge; Loomis along the west base, supported by two brigades of John E. Smith's division; and Corse with his brigade was between the two, moving directly toward the hill to be captured. The ridge is steep and heavily wooded on the east side, where M. L. Smith's troops were advancing, but cleared and with a more gentle slope on the west side. The troops advanced rapidly and carried the extreme end of the rebel works. Morgan L. Smith advanced to a point which cut the enemy off from the railroad bridge and the means of bringing up supplies by rail from Chickamauga Station, where the main depot was located. The enemy made brave and strenuous efforts to drive our troops from the position we had gained, but without success. The contest lasted for two hours. Corse, a brave and efficient commander, was badly wounded in this assault. Sherman now threatened both Bragg's flank and his stores, and made it necessary for him to weaken other points of his line to strengthen his right. From the position I occupied I could see column after column of Bragg's forces moving against Sherman; every Confederate gun that could be brought to bear upon the Union forces was concentrated upon him. J. E. Smith, with two brigades, charged up the west side of the ridge to the support of Corse's command, over open ground, and in the face of a heavy fire of both artillery and musketry, and reached the very parapet of the enemy. He lay here for a time, but the enemy coming with a heavy force upon his right flank, he was compelled to fall back, followed by the foe. A few hundred yards brought Smith's troops into a wood, where they were speedily re-formed, when they charged and drove the attacking party back to his intrenchments.

Seeing the advance, repulse, and second advance of J. E. Smith from the position I occupied, I directed Thomas to send a division to reënforce him. Baird's division was accordingly sent from the right of Orchard Knob. It had to march a considerable distance, directly under the eyes of the enemy, to reach its position. ☆ Bragg at once commenced massing in the same direction. This was what I wanted. But it had now got to be late in the afternoon, and I had expected before this to see Hooker crossing the ridge in the neighborhood of Rossville, and compelling Bragg to mass in that direction also.

The enemy had evacuated Lookout Mountain during the night, as I expected he would. In crossing the valley he burned the bridges over Chattanooga Creek, and did all he could to obstruct the roads behind him. Hooker was off bright and early, with no obstructions in his front but distance and the destruction above named. He was detained four hours in crossing Chatta-

☆ Concerning this movement General Baird writes as follows: "I was ordered to report to General Sherman to reënforce his command. I marched the distance, about two miles to the rear of his position, and sent an officer to report to him, but I immediately received orders to return and form on the left of the line which was to assault Missionary Ridge. I reached there, and got my troops in position, just as the gun was fired directing the assault."—EDITORS.

BAIRD'S DIVISION FIGHTING FOR THE CREST OF MISSIONARY RIDGE. FROM THE CYCLORAMA.

nooga Creek, and thus was lost the immediate advantages I expected from his forces.   His reaching Bragg's flank and extending across it was to be the signal for Thomas's assault of the ridge.   But Sherman's condition was getting so critical that the assault for his relief could not be delayed any longer.

Sheridan's and Wood's divisions had been lying under arms from early in the morning, ready to move the instant the signal was given.   I now directed Thomas to order the charge at once.⎰   I watched eagerly to see the effect, and became impatient at last that there was no indication of any charge being made.   The center of the line which was to make the charge was near where Thomas and I stood together, but concealed from our view by the intervening forest.   Turning to Thomas to inquire what caused the delay, I was surprised to see General Thomas J. Wood, one of the division commanders who were to make the charge, standing talking to him.   I spoke to General Wood, asking him why he had not charged, as ordered an hour before.   He replied very promptly that this was the first he had heard of it, but that he had been ready all day to move at a moment's notice.   I told him to make the charge at once.   He was off in a moment, and in an incredibly short time loud cheering was heard, and he and Sheridan were driving the enemy's advance before them toward Missionary Ridge.   The Confederates were strongly intrenched

⎰ In this order authority was given for the troops to re-form after taking the first line of rifle-pits preparatory to carrying the ridge.— U. S. G.

on the crest of the ridge in front of us, and had a second line half-way down and another at the base. Our men drove the troops in front of the lower line of rifle-pits so rapidly, and followed them so closely, that rebel and Union troops went over the first line of works almost at the same time. Many rebels were captured and sent to the rear under the fire of their own friends higher up the hill. Those that were not captured retreated, and were pursued. The retreating hordes being between friends and pursuers, caused the enemy to fire high, to avoid killing their own men. In fact, on that occasion the Union soldier nearest the enemy was in the safest position. Without awaiting further orders or stopping to re-form, on our troops went to the second line of works; over that and on for the crest — thus effectually carrying out my orders of the 18th for the battle and of the 24th for this charge. I watched their progress with intense interest. The fire along the rebel line was terrific. Cannon and musket balls filled the air; but the damage done was in small proportion to the ammunition used.⚓ The pursuit continued until the crest was reached, and soon our men were seen climbing over the Confederate barrier at different points in front of both Sheridan's and Wood's divisions. The retreat of the enemy along most of his line was precipitate, and the panic so great that Bragg and his officers lost all control over their men. Many were captured and thousands threw away their arms in their flight.

Sheridan pushed forward until he reached the Chickamauga River at a point above where the enemy had crossed. He met some resistance from troops occupying a second hill in rear of Missionary Ridge, probably to cover the retreat of the main body and of the artillery and trains. It was now getting dark, but Sheridan, without halting on that account, pushed his men forward up this second hill slowly and without attracting the attention of the men placed to defend it, while he detached to the right and left to surround the position. The enemy discovered the movement before these dispositions were complete, and beat a hasty retreat, leaving artillery, wagon trains, and many prisoners in our hands. To Sheridan's prompt movement the Army of the Cumberland and the nation are indebted for the bulk of the capture of prisoners, artillery, and small-arms that day. Except for his prompt pursuit, so much in this way would not have been accomplished.

While the advance up Missionary Ridge was going forward, General Thomas, with his staff, General Gordon Granger, commander of the corps, making the assault, and myself and staff, occupied Orchard Knob, from which the entire field could be observed. The moment the troops were seen going over the last line of rebel defenses I ordered Granger to join his command, and mounting my horse I rode to the front. General Thomas left about the same time. Sheridan, on the extreme right, was already in pur-

---

⚓ Captain Benjamin F. Hegler, of Attica, Indiana, who was second in command of the 15th Indiana in the assault on Missionary Ridge, writes to the editors:

"General Grant says of the assault on Missionary Ridge that 'the fire along the rebel line was terrific. Cannon and musket balls filled the air; but the damage done was in small proportion to the ammunition used.'

The inference might be that the assault, though brilliant, was after all a rather harmless diversion. The 15th Indiana, of Sheridan's division, started up the ridge just to the left of Bragg's headquarters with 337 officers and men, and lost 202 killed and wounded, in just forty-five minutes, the time taken to advance from the line of works at the foot of the ridge and to carry the crest. This report I made officially to General Sheridan near Chickamauga Creek the morning after the battle."

THE CONFEDERATE LINE OPPOSED TO BAIRD'S DIVISION ON MISSIONARY RIDGE. FROM THE CYCLORAMA.

suit of the enemy east of the ridge.   Wood, who commanded the division to
the left of Sheridan, accompanied his men on horseback, but did not join
Sheridan in the pursuit.   To the left, in Baird's front, where Bragg's troops
had massed against Sherman, the resistance was more stubborn, and the
contest lasted longer.   I ordered Granger to follow the enemy with Wood's
division, but he was so much excited, and kept up such a roar of musketry,
in the direction the enemy had taken, that by the time I could stop the firing
the enemy had got well out of the way.   The enemy confronting Sherman,
now seeing everything to their left giving away, fled also.   Sherman, however, was not aware of the extent of our success until after nightfall, when
he received orders to pursue at daylight in the morning.

Hooker, as stated, was detained at Chattanooga Creek by the destruction
of the bridges at that point.   He got his troops over, with the exception of
the artillery, by fording the stream, at a little after 3 o'clock.   Leaving his
artillery to follow when the bridges should be reconstructed, he pushed on
with the remainder of his command.   At Rossville he came upon the flank
of a division of the enemy, which soon commenced a retreat along the ridge.
This threw them on Palmer.   They could make but little resistance in the
position they were caught in, and as many of them as could do so escaped.

Many, however, were captured. Hooker's position during the night of the 25th was near Rossville, extending east of the ridge. Palmer was on his left, on the road to Graysville.

During the night I telegraphed to Willcox that Bragg had been defeated, and that immediate relief would be sent to Burnside if he could hold out; to Halleck I sent an announcement of our victory, and informed him that forces would be sent up the valley to relieve Burnside.

Before the battle of Chattanooga opened I had taken measures for the relief of Burnside the moment the way should be clear. Thomas was directed to have the little steamer that had been built at Chattanooga loaded to its capacity with rations and ammunition. Granger's corps was to move by the south bank of the Tennessee River to the mouth of the Holston, and up that to Knoxville, accompanied by the boat. In addition to the supplies transported by boat, the men were to carry forty rounds of ammunition in their cartridge-boxes, and four days' rations in haversacks.

In the battle of Chattanooga, troops from the Army of the Potomac, from the Army of the Tennessee, and from the Army of the Cumberland participated. In fact, the accidents growing out of the heavy rains and the sudden rise in the Tennessee River so mingled the troops that the organizations were not kept together, under their respective commanders, during the battle. Hooker, on the right, had Geary's division of the Twelfth Corps, Army of the Potomac; Osterhaus's division of the Fifteenth Corps, Army of the Tennessee; and Cruft's division of the Army of the Cumberland. Sherman had three divisions of his own army, Howard's corps from the Army of the Potomac, and Jeff. C. Davis's division of the Army of the Cumberland. There was no jealousy — hardly rivalry. Indeed I doubt whether officers or men took any note at the time of this intermingling of commands. All saw a defiant foe surrounding them, and took it for granted that every move was intended to dislodge him, and it made no difference where the troops came from so that the end was accomplished.

The victory at Chattanooga was won against great odds, considering the advantage the enemy had of position; and was accomplished more easily than was expected by reason of Bragg's making several grave mistakes: first, in sending away his ablest corps commander, with over 20,000 troops; second, in sending away a division of troops on the eve of battle; third, in placing so much of a force on the plain in front of his impregnable position.

It was known that Mr. Davis had visited Bragg on Missionary Ridge a short time before my reaching Chattanooga. It was reported and believed that he had come out to reconcile a serious difference between Bragg and Longstreet, and finding this difficult to do planned the campaign against Knoxville, to be conducted by the latter general. I had known both Bragg and Longstreet before the war, the latter very well. We had been three years at West Point together, and, after my graduation, for a time in the same regiment. Then we served together in the Mexican war. I had known Bragg in Mexico, and met him occasionally subsequently. I could well understand how there might be an irreconcilable difference between them.

Bragg was a remarkably intelligent and well-informed man, professionally and otherwise. He was also thoroughly upright. But he was possessed of an irascible temper, and was naturally disputatious. A man of the highest moral character and the most correct habits, yet in the old army he was in frequent trouble. As a subordinate he was always on the lookout to catch his commanding officer infringing upon his prerogatives; as a post commander he was equally vigilant to detect the slightest neglect, even of the most trivial order.

I heard in the old army an anecdote characteristic of General Bragg. On one occasion, when stationed at a post of several companies, commanded by a field-officer, he was himself commanding one of the companies and at the same time acting post quartermaster and commissary. He was a first lieutenant at the time, but his captain was detached on other duty. As commander of the company he made a requisition upon the quartermaster—himself—for something he wanted. As quartermaster he declined to fill the requisition, and indorsed on the back of it his reason for so doing. As company commander he responded to this, urging that his requisition called for nothing but what he was entitled to, and that it was the duty of the quartermaster to fill it. As quartermaster he still persisted that he was right. In this condition of affairs Bragg referred the whole matter to the commanding officer of the post. The latter, when he saw the nature of the matter referred, exclaimed: "My God, Mr. Bragg, you have quarreled with every officer in the army, and now you are quarreling with yourself."

Longstreet was an entirely different man. He was brave, honest, intelligent, a very capable soldier, subordinate to his superiors, just and kind to his subordinates, but jealous of his own rights, which he had the courage to maintain. He was never on the lookout to detect a slight, but saw one as soon as anybody when intentionally given.

It may be that Longstreet was not sent to Knoxville for the reason stated, but because Mr. Davis had an exalted opinion of his own

DEPARTURE OF THE FIRST HOSPITAL TRAIN FROM CHATTANOOGA, JANUARY, 1864, AND INTERIOR
OF A HOSPITAL CAR. FROM A WAR-TIME SKETCH.

military genius, and thought he saw a chance of "killing two birds with one stone." On several occasions during the war he came to the relief of the Union army by means of his *superior military genius.*

I speak advisedly when I say Mr. Davis prided himself on his military capacity. He says so himself virtually, in his answer to the notice of his nomination to the Confederate Presidency. Some of his generals have said so in their writings since the downfall of the Confederacy. Whatever the cause or whoever is to blame, grave mistakes were made at Chattanooga, which enabled us, with the undaunted courage of the troops engaged, to gain a great victory, under the most trying circumstances presented during the war, much more easily than could otherwise have been attained. If Chattanooga had been captured, east Tennessee would have followed without a struggle. It would have been a victory to have got the army away from Chattanooga safely. It was manifold greater to defeat, and nearly destroy, the besieging army.

In this battle the Union army numbered in round figures about 60,000 men; we lost 752 killed, and 4713 wounded and 350 captured or missing. The rebel loss was much greater in the aggregate, as we captured, and sent North to be rationed there, over 6100 prisoners. Forty pieces of artillery, over seven thousand stand of small-arms, and many caissons, artillery wagons, and baggage wagons fell into our hands. The probabilities are that our loss in killed was the heavier, as we were the attacking party. The enemy reported his loss in killed at 361; but as he reported his missing at 4146, while we held over 6000 of them as prisoners, and there must have been hundreds, if not thousands, who deserted, but little reliance can be placed in this report. There was certainly great dissatisfaction with Bragg, ↓ on the part of the soldiers, for his harsh treatment of them, and a disposition to get away if they could. Then, too, Chattanooga following in the same half-year with Gettysburg in the East, and Vicksburg in the West, there was much the same feeling in the South at this time that there had been in the North the fall and winter before. If the same license had been allowed the people and the press in the South that was allowed in the North, Chattanooga would probably have been the last battle fought for the preservation of the Union.

Bragg's army now being in full retreat, the relief of Burnside's position at Knoxville was a matter for immediate consideration. Sherman marched with a portion of the Army of the Tennessee, and one corps of the Army of the Cumberland, toward Knoxville; but his approach caused Longstreet to abandon the siege long before these troops reached their destination. Knoxville was now relieved; the anxiety of the President was removed, and the loyal portion of the North rejoiced over the double victory: the raising of the siege of Knoxville and the victory at Chattanooga.

SHERMAN'S ATTACK AT THE TUNNEL.

BY S. H. M. BYERS, CAPTAIN, U. S. V.

IT was the eve of the battle of Chattanooga. I had lately returned to the Army of the Tennessee, after a very short furlough, from my home in the West. How well I remember it—ten days of furlough out of four years of war! It was the only time in the whole four years that I slept in a bed. We had helped to capture Vicksburg after a hundred days' siege, and felt entitled to a rest. My regiment, the 5th Iowa, had already marched 2000 miles in two years. But Rosecrans was in straits, Sherman was called for, and we made the forced march of four hundred miles from Memphis to Chattanooga without a murmur.

Our camp was a concealed one in which no fires or lights were permitted—no noises allowed. In the darkness of the previous night, the command had left bright fires burning in a wood, and had secretly marched to this hidden position. Close beside it, the broad and rapid waters of the Tennessee rolled off into the darkness. On the opposite bank, numbers of rebel pickets kept guard, ignorant of our presence. Behind these pickets were the high hills known as Missionary Ridge, thoroughly intrenched and defended by a large rebel army, just fresh from victory. In a little creek close by lay secreted 116 pontoons. What were they there for? The silence, the secrecy, the mystery of the scene, convinced us that there was work ahead—and that we had to do it.

Before sundown two great soldiers had quietly been inspecting the little camp and the banks of the river. They were Grant and Sherman. Other officers, strangers to us, had come and looked at the pontoons in the creek, and a great wagon-load of boat-oars had been quietly placed beside them. We were at supper when the order came to row over the river and assault at midnight. I laid down my knife and fork, and stopped eating. A strange sensation came over me. Certainly I had been in dangerous places before. The regiment had a record for gallantry. The names of five battles were already inscribed upon its banners. Within two years from enlistment, half the men in the regiment had been killed, wounded, or disabled. We already had our third colonel. Numerous of our line officers had been promoted to higher posts. My own red sash had been given me under the guns of Vicksburg. Yes, we had seen fighting, but I had always been a believer in presentiments, and, somehow, something told me that I was doomed—that some calamity was in store for me.

The critical situation and the vast consequences dependent on success or failure were known to us all as we lay in the shadows that evening, waiting the order to move over the dark river and assault the heights of Missionary Ridge.

Midnight came—but we still lay quiet; 2 o'clock, and we heard some gentle splashing in the water near us, and the noise of muffled oars. Every man seized his rifle. "Quiet, boys—fall in quietly," said the captains. Spades were handed to many of us—we did not ask what for, we knew too well. Quietly the pontoon-boats had been slipped out of the little creek to our left, and into the river, and quietly we stepped down the bank, two by two, into the rude craft. "Be prompt as you can, boys, there's room for thirty in a boat," said a tall man who stood on the bank near us, in the darkness. Few of us had ever before heard the voice of our beloved commander. Sherman's kind words, his personal presence, his attention to every detail of the dangerous adventure, waked confidence in every one. He was with us, and sharing the danger.

In a quarter of an hour a thousand of us were out in the middle of the river, afloat in the darkness. Would they fire on us from the opposite shore?—was our constant thought. Those were strange feelings, we soldiers had, out in the middle of the river that night. We were not aware that a boat-load of our comrades in blue had crossed farther up the stream, just at midnight, and had captured the rebel pickets on the bank without firing a shot. We met a boat in the water, full of men—the captured pickets being rowed over to our side of the river. It was a fine ruse that had been played on them. The boys, crossing above, had got in behind them, and then, calling out the "relief," deceived and captured all but one.

In half an hour we were up the opposite bank and creeping along through the thickets—a spade in one hand and a rifle in the other. What might happen any moment, we knew not. Where was the picket that had escaped? Why was not the whole rebel camp alarmed and upon us? Daylight came; but it found us two thousand strong, intrenched with rifle-pits a mile in length. What a sight for Bragg! Hand about, we worked and digged like beavers. An old Quaker came down to expostulate with us for ruining his farm by such digging. The scene was ludicrous, and the boys gave a derisive little cheer for "Broad-brim." The noise drew upon us the shells from a hidden battery, and cost us two wounded men. It very nearly cost our friend his life, as an exploding shell left a hole within a yard of him, twice as broad as his big hat.

Still we dug on at our rifle-pits. Other regiments were ferried across. By noon the pontoon-bridge was down behind us, and soon the whole army corps was over.

All the afternoon we manœuvred and fought for position, chasing the enemy off one high hillspur only to find him better intrenched behind another. These were the outlying hills between Missionary Ridge proper and the banks of the river. The real position was across fields and hollows, and farther up on the mountain. Sullenly and slowly the enemy gave way, preparing in his high position for the battle of the morrow.

That night my regiment stood picket in the wood at the front. All night long we could hear the rebel field-batteries taking position on Missionary Ridge. For a hundred hours we had scarcely slept.

The 25th of November dawned clear and beautiful, and with the sunrise came the bugle-sound for Corse's division at our center to advance on the enemy. All the morning the hills and woods in front of Missionary Ridge resounded with the crash of musketry. The battle raged for over an hour for the possession of a single hill-crest. Once the hail of bullets became so heavy that a temporary halt was made. The enemy had the advantage of position and numbers everywhere. So close were they, and so protected behind rifle-pits, logs, and bowlders, that they could throw stones on the assaulting column and do almost as much harm with them as with bullets. More regiments were sent in to Corse, and the hand-to-hand assault was renewed till Corse himself was borne wounded from the field. Still his men fought on, retreating not a foot. Around to our left, General J. E. Smith's division was gradually getting possession of that part of the enemy's line, and far off across Lookout Valley, Hooker's men, in possession of the heights, were driving in the left flank of the rebel army.

It was 2 o'clock when our division, my own regiment with it, was ordered to fix bayonets and join in the assault on the ridge. We had been concealed from the enemy all the forenoon by the edge of a wood; yet his constant shelling of this wood showed that he knew we were there. As the column came out upon the open ground, and in sight of the rebel batteries, their renewed and concentrated fire knocked the limbs from the trees about our heads. An awful cannonade had opened on us. In front of us was a rail-fence. Its splinters and fragments flew in every direction. "Jump the fence, boys," was the order, and never was a fence scaled more quickly. It was nearly half a mile to the rebel position, and we started on the charge, running across the open fields. I had heard the roaring of heavy battle before, but never such a shrieking of cannon-balls and bursting of shells as met us on that run. We could see the rebels working their guns, while in plain view other batteries galloped up, unlimbered, and let loose upon us. Behind us our own batteries were firing at the enemy over our heads, till the storm and roar became horrible. The line officers screamed at the top of their voices, trying to repeat the orders to the men. "Steady, steady. Bear to the right! Don't fire! Steady, steady," was yelled till every one of us was hoarse, and until the fearful thunder of the cannonade made all commands unheard and useless. In ten minutes the field was crossed, the foot of the ascent was reached, and now the Confederates poured into our faces the reserved fire of their awful musketry. It helped little that we returned it from our own rifles, hidden as the enemy were in rifle-pits, behind logs, and stumps, and trees. Still we charged, and climbed a fence in front of them, and charged again. The order was given to lie down and continue firing. Then some

one cried, "Look to the tunnel!" There, on the right, pouring through a tunnel in the mountain, and out of the railway cut, came the gray-coats by hundreds, flanking us completely. "Stop them!" cried our colonel to those of us at the right. "Push them back!" It was but the work of a few moments to rise to our feet and run to the mouth of the tunnel, firing as we ran. Too late! They were through by hundreds, and a fatal enfilading fire was cutting our line to pieces. No wonder the brigade temporarily faltered and gave way, when a whole army of the enemy seemed concentrated on a single point.

"Come out of that sword," shrieked a big Mississippian at me. "And give me that revolver," cried another. "And get up the hill quicker than hell," cried both of them. It was time; for our own batteries were now pouring a fearful fire on the very spot where we stood. The rocks and the earth flew about us, and everything seemed to smoke. Not only this, our brigade was rallying to charge again, and other brigades were climbing with them to the hill-top. Still more, Thomas was storming the center.

In a moment I reflected that I was a prisoner, and horrible pictures of Libby and Andersonville flashed through my mind—and with them the presentiment of evil I had had the night before the assault. I took a blanket from one of my dead comrades lying near me, and at the point of the bayonet I was hurried on up the mountain, the fire from our own guns constantly increasing. I passed numerous lines of the enemy standing or lying in the rifle-pits with which the whole mountain-side was honeycombed, both in front of Sherman and in front of Thomas. Once I glanced back and to the right. Glorious sight! The troops of Thomas were storming up the slopes of Missionary Ridge. In a hollow, back of the lines, I was mustered with others of my brigade who had been captured. Three of that night's messmates were among them. We were relieved of our watches, our money, our knives, even our pocket-combs, by a chivalrous young officer of the guard.

"Why do your caissons hurry so to the rear?" I inquired of this gallant gentleman as I handed him my pocket-book. "For ammunition, of course," was his prompt reply. "And the cannon," I ventured further, noticing a dozen brass field-pieces being galloped off with; "do they bring ammunition too?" "Fall in," was the quick answer. "Guards, fall in: quick, quick!" In five minutes, prisoners and guards, infantry, artillery, and wagons were on the run pell-mell to the rear. Missionary Ridge had been taken.

Twenty-five miles they marched us down the railroad that night without stopping. Whizzing by us went trains loaded with wounded and dying soldiers. Far behind us we heard our own victorious cannon in pursuit.

For seven months we officers lingered in Libby prison, and then for eight months more in Macon and Columbia. Most of the privates died in Andersonville. When I escaped at Columbia, fifteen months afterward,

only sixteen of the sixty of my regiment who were captured with me on that day were alive. Of the nine of my own company (B) who were taken, only one besides myself was left to tell the tale.— S. H. M. B.

I. BY WILLIAM FARRAR SMITH, BREVET MAJOR-GENERAL, U. S. A.

UMBRELLA ROCK, POINT OF LOOKOUT MOUNTAIN.

ON the 3d of October, 1863, having reported to General Rosecrans at Chattanooga, I was assigned the duty of chief engineer of the Army of the Cumberland, and it devolved on me as a part of my duty, first, to lay out and construct the fortifications so as to enable a comparatively small force to hold the place, and, secondly, to look out for the communications by which the army was supplied. In the performance of that duty I was actively engaged in building boats and material for bridges, and was studying earnestly to find some way of restoring our short line of communications lost by the giving up of Lookout Mountain and Valley. I found a most excellent company of volunteers styled "Michigan Engineers and Mechanics," commanded by Captain Perrin V. Fox. Before my arrival they had set up a saw-mill, and were engaged in making boats and flooring, etc., for military bridges. In pursuance of the paramount necessity of finding some way of shortening our distance to the railroad at Bridgeport, on the 19th of October I started to make a personal examination of the north side of the Tennessee River below Chattanooga. The object was to find some point on the south side, the holding of which would secure to us the river from Bridgeport through the Raccoon Mountain, and the short road in the valley from there to Chattanooga. On returning unsuccessful in my search, to within about five miles of Chattanooga, I saw before me on a bluff, washed by the river, an earth-work in which was posted a field-battery commanding a road through a break in the hills on the opposite side, where had formerly been established a ferry, known as Brown's Ferry. The place struck me as worthy of examination, and learning from the commanding officer of the battery that there was a tacit agreement that the pickets should not fire on each other, I left my horse in the battery and went down to the water's edge. There I spent an hour, studying the character of the hills, the roadway through the gorge, and marking and estimating the distances to the fires of the picket reserves of the enemy. I then rode back to headquarters, to find that during my absence General Rosecrans had been relieved from duty there and General George H. Thomas put in command of the army.

The next morning, October 20th, General Thomas asked me what length of bridge material I had not in use, and directed me to throw another bridge across the river at Chattanooga. I asked him not to give the order till he had heard my report of my examination of the day before and had looked into a plan I had to propose for opening the river to our steamboats, of which there were two then partly disabled, but which had not been repaired by me lest they should eventually serve the purpose of the enemy. After a discussion which I think was finished in two days, and by the 22d of October, he gave his approval to the plan, and I went to work at once, he giving the necessary orders for the coöperating movements from Bridgeport, which were a vital part of the operations. After that there was but one discussion between General Thomas and myself, which was as to the relative time at which Hooker's column was to move from Bridgeport. That took place after the arrival of General Grant at Chattanooga, all others having been concluded before General Grant made his appearance.

When Grant had been but about twelve hours in Chattanooga, and before he had even started on his trip to Brown's Ferry, Mr. Dana had sketched to the Secretary of War the substance of the whole movement.⸗ That General Thomas had, after General Grant's arrival, to put before him the plan which he had determined upon, and that General Grant's approval was necessary, and that it was proper for him to go to Brown's Ferry at once to see the position before he gave his approval to it, cannot be gainsaid, but there is not the slightest reason for doubting that Thomas would have made the same move with the same men and with the same results, had General Grant been in Louisville, from which place he had telegraphed the order putting Thomas in command of the Army of the Cumberland. General Grant does not overstate the importance of this movement to the army. It gave at once to the army food and clothing, with forage for the animals which were yet alive, and last, but not least, ammunition, of which General Grant says the Union army had "not enough for a day's fighting." From being an army in a condition in which it could not retreat, it became an army which, so soon as it was reënforced by the troops with Sherman, assumed the offensive, and under the leadership of General Grant helped to win the battle of Missionary Ridge, inflicting a mortal blow upon the army under Bragg. General Thomas was a man who observed strictly the proprieties and courtesies of military life; and had the plan "for opening the route to Bridgeport," and the orders necessary for its execution, emanated from General Grant, Thomas would hardly have noticed the subject in the following words:

"To Brigadier-General W. F. Smith, chief engineer, should be accorded great praise for the ingenuity which conceived, and the ability which executed, the movement at Brown's Ferry. The preparations were all made in secrecy, as was also the boat expedition which passed under the overhanging cliffs of Lookout, so much so that when the bridge was thrown at Brown's

⸗ Telegrams of Dana to Stanton, October 23d and 24th, 10 A. M.

714

Ferry, on the morning of the 27th, the surprise was as great to the army within Chattanooga as it was to the army besieging it from without." [From the report of the Committee on the Conduct of the War.]

With some hesitation I will give a copy of a letter from General Grant to the Secretary of War, which, though speaking of me in possibly much too high terms, is yet important in this connection from its date. It was written two weeks after the opening of the river, and two weeks before the battle of Missionary Ridge. It could hardly have been written from General Grant's previous knowledge of me, for he says he "had no recollection of having met me, after my [his] graduation, in 1843, up to this time,"— the night of his arrival at Chattanooga,— October 23d, 1863. It could not have been written because I had shown zeal in establishing a saw-mill, making a steamboat or any amount of bridge material, nor yet because I had commanded two brigades in a surprise attack at Brown's Ferry. No other movement than the successful opening of the river had been made from the time of General Grant's arrival to the date of this letter. Was it possible that it rose from any other reason than that General Grant, appreciating fully the great and prompt change in the condition of the army, arising from the opening of the river, had perhaps over-estimated the ability of the one who within his own knowledge had planned the movement? Circumstances afterward occurred to change the relations between General Grant and myself, to which it is not necessary to refer, and his opinion of me may and probably did afterward undergo a change, but at the time at which the letter was written there was some striking reason which produced it:

"HEADQUARTERS, MILITARY DIVISION OF THE MISS.
"CHATTANOOGA, TENNESSEE, November 12th, 1863.
"HON. E. M. STANTON, Secretary of War.
"SIR: I would respectfully recommend that Brigadier-General William F. Smith be placed first on the list for promotion to the rank of major-general. He is possessed of one of the clearest military heads in the army — is very practical and industrious — no man in the service is better qualified than he for our largest commands.
"I have the honor to be, very respectfully, your obedient servant,   "U. S. GRANT,
      (Official)   "Major-General.
"Signed, GEO. K. LEET, Assistant Adjutant-General."

Not only is it due to the truth of history that this evidence of General Grant's military appreciation of the movement on Brown's Ferry should appear, but it also establishes his generosity of character in giving credit where he felt it to be due.

At some future time I may have an opportunity of doing justice to the memory of General George H. Thomas, whose comparatively early death was so great a loss to the country. The civil war developed no higher character than his, viewed in all its aspects, either as soldier or civilian. There are no clouds on it to mar the brightness of his glory.

General Grant's narrative [see p. 679] is in text and inference so unjust to the memory of the late Major-General George H. Thomas that it is proper to make a statement of facts taken in the main from official papers.

In November, 1863, Mr. Charles A. Dana, Assistant Secretary of War, was at Chattanooga. Under date of November 5th, 11 A. M., he telegraphed to Mr. Stanton:

" . . . Grant and Thomas considering plan proposed by W. F. Smith to advance our pickets on the left to Citico Creek, about a mile in front of the position they have occupied from the first, and to *threaten* the seizure of the north-west extremity of Missionary Ridge. This, taken in connection with our present demonstration in Lookout Valley, will compel them to concentrate and come back from Burnside to fight here."

It is perhaps well to explain here that at that time no plan for future operations had been discussed. On the supposition that Sherman's forces would be united with those of Thomas in front of Chattanooga, more space than we occupied was necessary for the proper encampments and probable developments for a battle. This made a move to the front at that time for the acquisition of more ground a proper one under all circumstances. It will be seen that in the plan proposed by me, as chief engineer, only a *threat to seize* the north-west end of Missionary Ridge was intended, and with the idea that such a feint might force the recall of Longstreet. I think I may safely state that I did not propose at that time, in view of the condition of the Army of the Cumberland, to suggest anything that would bring on a general battle unless under the guns of our forts at Chattanooga. The next telegram to Secretary Stanton referring to this move is dated November 7th at 10 A. M., and states:

"Before receiving this information [report of a rebel deserter] Grant had ordered Thomas to execute the movement on Citico Creek which I reported on the 5th as proposed by Smith. Thomas, who rather preferred an attempt on Lookout Mountain, desired to postpone the operation until Sherman should come up, but Grant has decided that for the sake of Burnside the attack must be made at once, and I presume the advance on Citico will take place to-morrow evening, and that on Missionary Ridge immediately afterward. If successful, this operation will divide Bragg's forces in Chattanooga valley from those in the valley of the Chickamauga, and will compel him either to retreat, leaving the railroad communication of Cheatham and Longstreet exposed, or else fight a battle with his diminished forces."

From General Grant's order of November 7th the following extract is made:

" . . . I deem the best movement to *attract* the enemy to be an attack on the north end of Missionary Ridge with all the force you can bring to bear against it, and, when that is *carried, to threaten,* and even attack if possible, the enemy's line of communication between Dalton and Cleveland. . . . The movement should not be made one moment later than to-morrow morning."

It will be seen from this order that the plan proposed by me had been entirely changed, for while I had proposed only to threaten the seizure of the north-west end of Missionary Ridge, General Grant proposed "to attack the enemy" by carrying the ridge, and then "to threaten, and even attack if possible," the lines of communication; *that is, to bring on a general engagement.* When it is remembered that eighteen days after this Sherman with six perfectly appointed divisions failed to carry this same point of Missionary Ridge, at a time when Thomas with four divisions stood threatening Bragg's center, and Hooker with nearly three divisions was driving in Bragg's left flank (Bragg having no more strength than on the 7th), it will not be a matter of surprise that the order staggered Thomas. After the order had been issued I sought a conversation with General Grant for the purpose of inducing a modification, and began by asking General Grant what was the plan proposed by General Thomas for carrying out the order. To this General Grant replied, "*When I have sufficient confidence in a general to leave him in command of an army, I have enough confidence in him to leave his plans to himself.*" This answer seemed to cut off all discussion, and nothing more was said on the subject.

Shortly after that General Thomas sent for me, and under the impression that the order related to my plan, referred to in Mr. Dana's dispatch of November 5th, said, "If I attempt to carry out the order I have received, my army will be terribly beaten. You must go and get the order revoked." Without replying to this I asked General Thomas to go up the river with me, and we set out directly, going to a hill opposite the mouth of the South Chickamauga Creek, where we spent an hour or more. We looked carefully over the ground on which Thomas would have to operate, noted the extreme of Bragg's camp-fires on Missionary Ridge, and then, becoming convinced that Thomas with his force could not outflank Bragg's right without endangering our connection with Chattanooga, on our return I went directly to General Grant, and reported to him that after a careful reconnoissance of the ground I was of the decided opinion that no movement could be made in that direction until the arrival of Sherman's forces. That very evening the order for Thomas to move was countermanded, and no further effort to aid Burnside was attempted till the Army of the Tennessee had joined the army at Chattanooga. On the 8th of November, at 11 A. M., Mr. Dana sent to the Secretary of War the following dispatch:

"Reconnoissance of Citico Creek and head of Missionary Ridge made yesterday by Thomas, Smith, and Brannan from the heights opposite on the north of the Tennessee proved Smith's plan for attack impracticable. The creek and country are wrongly laid down on our maps, and no operation for the seizure of Missionary Ridge can be undertaken with the force which Thomas can now command for the purpose. That force cannot by any effort be made to exceed eighteen thousand men."

General Grant in his official report says:

"Directions were given for a movement against Missionary Ridge, with a view to carrying it, ... of which I informed Burnside on the 7th of November by telegraph. After a thorough reconnoissance of the ground, however, it was deemed *utterly impracticable* to make the move until Sherman could get up, because of the inadequacy of our forces and the condition of the animals then at Chattanooga."

The writer of an article entitled "General Grant," in "The Century" for May, 1885, says of Chattanooga: "Few battles in any war have ever been fought so strictly according to the plan. This battle was fought as nearly according to the plan laid down in advance as any recorded in the schools."

Holding at the time the position of chief engineer of the Army of the Cumberland under General Thomas, and being at the same time chief engineer of the Military Division of the Mississippi under General Grant, it was absolutely necessary that I should know the plan to be able to direct the engineering operations. Let me compare the original plan as "laid down in advance" with a sketch of the battle as fought.

The original plan of the battle of Chattanooga was to turn Bragg's right flank on Missionary Ridge, thereby throwing his army away from its base and natural line of retreat. This, the first thing to be done, was confided to Sherman, *and the plan was not adopted* till after Sherman had carefully examined the situation and asserted that he could do the work assigned to him. Thomas was to hold the center and right of our front, to coöperate with Sherman, and attack when the proper time arrived.

The preliminary movements were simple. Sherman was to effect a lodgment on the left bank of the Tennessee River, just below the mouth of the South Chickamauga Creek. This was to be done by landing a brigade of troops from the boats, which were to be used in the bridge to be thrown at that point across the Tennessee for the crossing of Sherman's army. One division of Sherman's army was to march up the Lookout Valley, on the extreme right of our operations, and threaten a pass in Lookout Mountain, ostensibly to turn Bragg's *left* flank. The march was to be made in daylight, in sight of the enemy, and after dark the division was to retrace its steps, cross the Tennessee at Brown's Ferry, and join the main body of Sherman's force, which was to be massed during the night preceding the intended attack at the point where the bridge was to be laid. Hooker with his small force was to hold Lookout Valley and threaten Lookout Mountain at the point where it strikes the Tennessee. This general plan was filled in with all necessary details, embracing all the initial movements of the whole force under Grant. At the very outset began the changes in this plan. The division which made the threat against Bragg's left flank on returning found the bridge at Brown's Ferry impassable; and as it could not join Sherman, it was turned over to Hooker, who was ordered, with his command thus strengthened, to assault the works on his front on Lookout Mountain. This was a most decided change from the plan "laid down in advance."

On the evening of the first day the results could be summed up as follows: Sherman had crossed the Tennessee River at the point selected, but had not turned Bragg's right flank. Thomas had drawn out the Army of the Cumberland facing Missionary Ridge, had connected with Sherman, but had had no fighting other than skirmishing varied by some artillery practice. Hooker had carried Lookout Mountain after a fight which has been celebrated in song as "the battle above the clouds." This victory of Hooker's compelled Bragg to withdraw his troops from the Chattanooga Valley, and retreat or concentrate for a battle on

Missionary Ridge. On the morning of the second day Hooker was ordered by Thomas to march for and *carry* the Rossville Gap in Missionary Ridge, and as soon as that was done to send an aide or courier to him, in order that he might then make the assault of the " Ridge" with the Army of the Cumberland. Sherman with severe fighting continued his efforts to reach the crest of Missionary Ridge. As the day wore on, and no news came from Hooker, Thomas grew anxious, but could give no order to assault the works on his front till one at least of the enemy's flanks had been turned.

Finally, in the afternoon, General Grant sent orders directly to the division commanders of the Army of the Cumberland to move forward and carry the rifle-pits in their front at the base of Missionary Ridge. This was very easily done, and after capturing the rifle-pits the soldiers, seeing that they could not remain there under the fire from the crest of the ridge, and having no intention of giving up any ground won by them, demanded to be led up the hill to storm the works on the crest, which was successfully done, and Bragg's

headquarters were in their possession just before the sun went down on the second day of the battle. This assault was, of course, the crisis of the whole battle, and the successful carrying of Missionary Ridge was doubtless due in a measure to the position of Sherman and the threatening movement of Hooker.

The battle was then ended and nothing left but a retreat by one and a pursuit by the other opposing general. A condensed statement of the history of the original plan and the battle of Chattanooga as fought is this: The original plan contemplated the turning of Bragg's right flank, which *was not done.* The secondary plan of Thomas looked toward following up the success of Hooker at Lookout Mountain by turning the left flank of Bragg, and then an attack by Thomas along his entire front. The Rossville Gap was not carried in time to be of more than secondary importance in the battle.

The assault on the center before either flank was turned was never seriously contemplated, and was made without plan, without orders, and as above stated.

II. BY HENRY M. CIST, BREVET BRIGADIER-GENERAL, U. S. V.

GENERAL SMITH very clearly shows that the plan for the movement was originated some time prior to General Grant's arrival at Chattanooga, and that the only part of the plan Grant was concerned in was the approval he gave to it, on it being submitted to him by General Thomas and General Smith. The necessary orders for the execution of the plan and the approval of the movement, however, had been given even prior to the date at which General Thomas assumed command of the Army of the Cumberland, which was the 20th of October,1863.

After the battle of Chickamauga and the return of the troops to Chattanooga, the first aim of General Rosecrans was to secure his command behind earth-works and fortifications on the front, sufficiently strong to enable the army successfully to resist any attack that might be made upon it in that quarter. This being accomplished, the next important demand was that of rations and supplies for the troops. In the execution of all of this General Rosecrans was ably seconded by the very efficient services of his chief engineer, General Smith; any plan of the latter, however, could only be carried into execution upon the approval of the commanding general.

The general plan for the fortifications, and also for the relief of the army with supplies, were those of the officer in command of the army. The preliminaries and details of these plans were, of course, intrusted to the chief executive officer of his staff in that branch of his service — his chief engineer. In the execution of his general plan, General Rosecrans, prior to the date of the order relieving him, had selected William's Island as a depot of supplies. He had also contracted for the rebuilding of the railroad bridge across the Tennessee and over Running Water, and had ordered the construction of four steamboats, for the use of

his army on the river. He had also directed that a sufficient number of pontoons should be built, by which he could throw a bridge across the Tennessee below the mouth of Lookout Creek, on which to march and take possession of Lookout Valley.

One of the last subjects of conference between Generals Rosecrans and Thomas after midnight of October 19th, 1863, and after Rosecrans's order relinquishing the command had been written and signed, grew out of the request of General Thomas to Rosecrans, " Now, General, I want you to be kind enough to describe the exact plan for the taking of Lookout Valley as you proposed it." General Rosecrans went over it again, explaining how it was his purpose to cross the river and where ; how he intended to occupy Lookout Valley, and to secure the use of the road on the south side of the river—the plan as afterward matured and carried out.

When General Smith was assigned to duty the plan for the fortifications had been fully considered, and that for the relief of the troops in regard to rations was well under way. Under General Rosecrans's orders General Smith gave his attention to the details of both plans, and brought his skill to bear upon the best method to accomplish the desired results. When General Thomas assumed command of the Army of the Cumberland, General Smith was retained as chief engineer, and Thomas *continued* the preparations for the plan afterward so successfully carried out in the "Brown's Ferry movement," under the supervision of the chief engineer as to the details. As General Smith says, " Thomas would have made the same move with the same men, and with the same results, had General Grant been in Louisville."

General Smith says that General Thomas is entitled to the credit of the successful consummation of these plans. Certainly he is as against the claim of General Grant. But as to Rosecrans, let us see what General Thomas himself says. In his report, dated November 7th, 1863, of "The Battle of Wauhatchie," he says:

"Preliminary steps had already been taken to execute this vitally important movement before the command of the department devolved on me. The bridge which it was necessary to throw across the river at Brown's Ferry to gain possession of the northern end of Lookout Valley and open communication with Bridgeport by road and river was nearly completed."

If all this had been accomplished by General Rosecrans, the plan must have been under his consideration with his approval for some weeks prior to his removal.

On November 4th, 1863, in the report of the part taken by the troops under him of the movement that actually opened up the road to Brown's Ferry and Kelley's Ferry, General Smith says:

"On the 19th of October I was instructed by General Rosecrans to reconnoiter the river in the vicinity of William's Island with a view of making the island a cover for a steamboat landing and store-houses, etc."

I do not wish to appear as detracting from the honor that belongs to General Smith, who executed the plan, to General Thomas, who ordered the execution, to General Grant, who approved the plan, but I think the truth of history calls for a repetition of the statement as made by General Thomas that he took up the work where his predecessor in command left it, and that he carried out the plan of General Rosecrans in the final movement.

III. POSTSCRIPT BY GENERAL W. F. SMITH.

GENERAL ROSECRANS never said anything to me about a bridge into Lookout Valley, or a movement by Hooker's command from Bridgeport, although I was his chief engineer and troops under my command were making boats for bridges. Mr. Dana telegraphed to Mr. Stanton early in October that Rosecrans would throw a bridge from Moccasin Point into Lookout Valley. A bridge from Moccasin Point could not have been thrown, for the nose of Lookout Mountain was strongly held by the enemy, and if the bridge had been thrown it could not have been maintained, as it would have been under close fire of artillery.

Mr. Dana also telegraphed to Mr. Stanton that Rosecrans had ordered Hooker to concentrate his troops with a view to moving his force through the Raccoon Mountain into Lookout Valley. If that could have been done the operations at Brown's Ferry were useless, as it would have been only necessary to throw a bridge after the arrival of Hooker's troops in that Valley. With Bragg's force, the passes in the Raccoon Mountain could have been held so as to make it impossible for Hooker to get through them.

Shortly after my arrival at Chattanooga I told General Rosecrans that he could not supply his army over the mountain roads as soon as the fall rains began. He said I was mistaken, that he was getting double the number of rations that he used. I never said anything more on the subject. Seeing that we were daily falling behind, even after the troops had been put on half rations, I tried to hurry on the defenses, and was all the time trying to work out some plan for shortening the line of supplies. It seemed to me that, by holding the country between Bridgeport and the Raccoon Mountain and the nose of Raccoon Mountain where it struck the Tennessee River, we might use William's Island as a depot of supplies, the transportation from Bridgeport being by water. Determined to go and see if such a plan were practicable, I went to General Rosecrans on the evening of the 18th of October and said, "General, I wish to go down the river to-morrow to see if we cannot hold the river as far as William's Island, and use that for a depot." General Rosecrans said, "Go, by all means, and I will go with you." We started at an early hour the next morning, but after crossing the river General Rosecrans stopped to go through the hospital and I pushed on and made the examination entirely alone. When I reached camp General Rosecrans had been relieved; he left that night, I think, and I did not say a word to him about what I had discovered and what I had to propose. It is impossible that Rosecrans could have developed any plan for opening the river to General Thomas which was satisfactory to Thomas, for any plan would have required a bridge to be thrown below Chattanooga, and General Thomas directed me, when I went to report to him the next day, to throw a bridge at the town. That would have left nothing for another bridge, and it took time to prepare boats and bridge materials.

General Rosecrans could not have informed his generals, with whom he was on confidential terms, of any such plan, for when Thomas explained my plan to them they opposed it strongly, and it took two or three interviews to get General Thomas to adopt the plan. Finally it was carried out exactly as I had suggested it. General Thomas was a very careful man about his statements and was very particular in his use of words. In his order he was careful to give me credit for planning as well as executing, and if he had had any such plan given to him by General Rosecrans he would certainly have not committed the injustice of giving me the credit for the plan.

General Cist's quotation from my report refers only to the William's Island project, which I gave up as soon as I saw the ground, and that may have been an idea of General Rosecrans, but he certainly had never taken any steps to find out if it were practicable, which I found it was not. I never heard of Brown's Ferry till I saw it. I did not report on it to Rosecrans, and I do not believe that Rosecrans had matured any scheme for shortening the line of communications. If he had, why did he not execute it; for at the time he was relieved the Army of the Cumberland could not have remained a week at Chattanooga, under the then existing lines for obtaining supplies.

MILITARY BRIDGE OVER THE TENNESSEE RIVER AT CHATTANOOGA, BUILT IN OCTOBER, 1863. FROM A PHOTOGRAPH.

THE ARMY OF THE CUMBERLAND AT CHATTANOOGA.

BY JOSEPH S. FULLERTON, BREVET BRIG.-GEN., U. S. V., ASSISTANT ADJ.-GEN., 4TH ARMY CORPS.

AFTER it became apparent that Bragg would not assault Rosecrans at Chattanooga, it was thought that he might cross the river above, threaten our lines of communication with the rear, and thus repeat, on the north side, the manœuvre of Rosecrans. Longstreet advised such a movement, but Bragg preferred to adopt the plan of starving us out.

On September 24th a brigade that had held the point of Lookout Mountain was withdrawn. Bragg at once took possession, and sent Longstreet's corps over into Lookout Valley. He also extended his pickets down the south bank of the river, nearly to Bridgeport, our base of supplies. This cut us off from the river and the roads on its north and south banks, and left us but one open road to the rear. Over this, for a time, we might haul supplies; but we were in a state of semi-siege.

The trees within our lines were soon cut down for use in the fortifications, or for fuel. There had been but little rain since early in July. The earth was parched and blistered. Leaves had dried up on the trees, and all the grass had withered and turned gray. The moving of men and animals stirred up blinding clouds of dust which every breeze sent whirling through the camps. With the first week in October came the rains, and it was a question whether the deep and sticky mud was not more objectionable than the dust.

Our whole army was obliged to depend for every ration and every pound of forage on the mules that hauled the army wagons over the sixty miles of horrible road from Bridgeport. Some of the hills along this route were so steep that a heavy wagon was almost a load going up, and, now that the rains were falling, that part of it in the little valleys had become so soft and was so cut up that a lightly loaded wagon would sink up to the axles.

In the third week of the occupation of Chattanooga, no one, from commanding general down, any longer expected or even thought of an attack. Missionary Ridge, summit, side, and base, was furrowed with rifle-pits and studded with batteries. The little valley of Chattanooga was dammed up with earth-works; and Lookout Mountain, now a mighty fortress, lifted to the low hanging clouds its threatening head crowned with siege-guns. The two lines of pickets were not more than three hundred yards apart; but, by common consent, there was no picket firing. On a still night, standing on the picket line, one could hear the old negro song "Dixie," adopted by the Confederates as their national music; while from our line came, in swelling response, "Hail Columbia" and "The Star-spangled Banner." With a glass Bragg's headquarters on Missionary Ridge, even the movement of his officers and orderlies, could be seen; while from the ridge or Lookout Mountain our whole camp was clearly in view. By daylight our troops could be counted, our reveille heard, our roll-call noted, our scanty meals of half rations seen — the last without envy. And we were not only heard and seen, but the enemy's signal-flag on Lookout talked, over our heads, with the signal-flag on Missionary Ridge.

The fall rains were beginning, and hauling was becoming each day more difficult. Ten thousand dead mules walled the sides of the road from Bridgeport to Chattanooga. In Chattanooga the men were on less than half rations. Guards stood at the troughs of artillery horses to keep the soldiers from taking the scant supply of corn allowed these starving animals. Many horses died of starvation, and most of those that survived grew too weak for use in pulling the lightest guns. Men followed the wagons as they came over the river, picking up the grains of corn and bits of crackers that fell to the ground. Yet there was no murmur of discontent.

Ever since Longstreet got into Lookout Valley, Rosecrans had been making preparation to drive him out. A small stern-wheel steamboat was built at Bridgeport; a captured ferry-boat, reconstructed, was made an available transport; and material for boats and pontoons, or either, with stringers and flooring for bridges, was prepared at Chattanooga as rapidly as possible, at an improvised saw-mill. But the plan finally adopted was conceived and worked out by General William F. Smith, Chief Engineer of the Army of the Cumberland. On the 20th of October, after having been fully matured, it was submitted, and was warmly approved by Thomas, who had then succeeded Rosecrans, and who at once gave orders to General Smith, General Hooker, and others to carry it into execution with all possible expedition. General Grant reached Chattanooga the evening of the 23d. General Smith's plan was explained to him, and he heartily approved it and directed its execution.

Everything necessary for the movement being in readiness, it was commenced with the greatest possible haste and secrecy on the night of the 26th. After midnight, fourteen hundred picked men from Hazen's and Turchin's brigades, under command of Brigadier-General Hazen, quietly marched to the river-bank at Chattanooga; the rest of the troops of these two brigades, with three batteries of artillery under Major John Mendenhall, crossed the river and marched over Moccasin Point to a place near Brown's Ferry, where, under cover of the woods, they awaited the arrival of General Hazen's force. The success of this expedition depended on surprising the enemy at Brown's Ferry. It was known that he had there 1000 infantry, 3 pieces of artillery, and a squadron of cavalry, while Longstreet's corps was not far off. At 3 o'clock in the morning, 52 pontoons, filled with Hazen's 1400 men, and under the direction of Colonel T. R. Stanley, 18th Ohio Infantry, noiselessly started down the river on the nine-mile course to Brown's Ferry. There was a full moon, but the light was dimmed by floating clouds and by a fog rising from the water. Oars were used till the first picket fire of the enemy was approached; then the boats were steered close to the right bank and allowed to float with the current. On top of Lookout a signal torch was seen flashing against the sky, but not a gun had yet been fired,—not an alarm given. Brown's Ferry was reached at break of dawn. Suddenly the oars were put into use, and before the enemy could make out the sounds the boats were rowed to the left bank. The pickets on guard greeted them with a volley of musketry, and then fell back on their reserves. The fourteen hundred men quickly and in perfect order occupied the crest of the hill and began to throw up light breastworks. But they had not proceeded far in this work when the enemy appeared and made a fruitless effort to drive them from the hill. In the meantime the boats were bringing over the river the rest of the two brigades that had marched to the north ferry landing. When the transfer had been accomplished, the boats were used in the construction of a pontoon-bridge, which was finished by 3 o'clock in the afternoon, and over which Mendenhall's artillery crossed.

At daylight on the morning of October 28th General Hooker crossed the river at Bridgeport with the Eleventh and Geary's division of the Twelfth Corps, and moved along the direct road to Brown's Ferry by the base of Raccoon Mountain. He brushed away the enemy's pickets and light bodies of skirmishers, and moved cautiously, as he knew Longstreet was in Lookout Valley and might at any moment appear to oppose his advance. At 5 o'clock in the afternoon the head of his column reached a point about one mile from the ferry, up Lookout Valley; and here his command went into camp, excepting Geary's division, which was left three miles in the rear, in a position covering the ferry. A short distance from the ferry, up the little valley of Lookout, was Longstreet, with his troops. When Longstreet discovered Hooker's object, he did not even wait the light of day to repeat his old tactics. The night of the 28th was clear and the air crisp. The moon shone bright from before midnight till morning. Hooker's troops were sleeping soundly after their hard march of nearly twenty-five miles, when Longstreet's men came crowding down the valley. An hour past midnight a terrific onslaught was made on Geary's division. It was assaulted on three sides. Artillery in the valley and on Lookout opened a severe fire. Our men, who slept in line of battle, sprang to their feet at the first shot of a sentinel. The contest lasted for three hours, till Longstreet's line was broken and his men driven from the field. It was Longstreet's intention to crush Geary; then, with his whole force, to attack General Howard's Eleventh Corps, nearly three miles away. In order to hold Howard where he was, and to prevent him from lending assistance to Geary, he had sent a smaller column to move round his camp, and, almost in its rear, to occupy a steep hill nearly two hundred feet high. General Howard ordered Colonel Orland Smith, with his brigade, to carry the hill. In gallant response a magnificent charge was made up the steep side, and the enemy was driven from the barricades on top at the point of the bayonet. Longstreet, routed at every point, retreated up the valley, leaving it at daybreak. Four hundred and twenty of our men, and many more of the enemy, were killed and wounded. Hooker thus gained Lookout Valley; the siege of Chattanooga was raised; the "cracker line" was opened!

The credit of this result is chiefly due to General W. F. Smith, Chief Engineer of the Army of the Cumberland, who conceived the plan of operations, and under whose directions it was mostly carried out. The raising of the siege of Chattanooga, by opening up the river and the road on its south bank, was determined upon by the commanding officers of the Army of the Cumberland soon after the occupation, though the plan of operations was adopted later, but before General Grant came to Chattanooga.

On November 15th General Sherman reached Chattanooga in advance of his troops. General Grant's plan, in brief, now was to turn Bragg's right. He selected his old army—the Army of the Tennessee, under Sherman—to open the battle, to make the grand attack, and to carry Missionary Ridge as far as Tunnel Hill. The Army of the Cumberland was simply to get into position and coöperate.

No battle-field in our war, probably none in history, where large armies were engaged, was so spectacular or so well fitted for a display of soldierly courage and daring as the amphitheater of Chattanooga. Late on the night of November 22d a sentinel who had deserted from the enemy was brought to General Sheridan, and informed him that Bragg's baggage was being reduced and that he was about to fall back. On account of these indications and reports, General Grant decided not to wait longer for General Sherman's troops to come up, but to find out whether Bragg was in fact withdrawing, and, if so, to attack him at once. Therefore, at 11 o'clock on the morning of the 23d, he directed General Thomas to "drive in the enemy's pickets," and feel his lines for the purpose of finding out whether he still held in force. Thus Grant was about to change his plans. He was compelled to depart from his original purpose, and was obliged to call on troops of the Army of the Cumberland to make the first offensive movement.

General Thomas ordered General Granger, commanding the Fourth Corps, to throw one division forward in the direction of Orchard Knob, with a second division in support, to discover if the enemy still remained near his old camp.

Orchard Knob is a rough, steep hill, one hundred feet high, covered with a growth of small timber, rising abruptly from the Chattanooga Valley, and lying about half-way between our outer pits and the breastworks of logs and stones. At its western base, and extending for a mile beyond, both north and south of the hill, were other rifle-pits, hid in part by a heavy belt of timber that extended about a quarter of a mile from the foot of the hill into the plain. Between this belt of timber and our lines were open fields, in which there was not a tree, fence, or other obstruction, save the bed of the East Tennessee Railroad. On the plain were hundreds of little mounds, thrown up by our own and the enemy's pickets, giving it the appearance of an overgrown prairie-dog village.

At noon General Grant, Assistant Secretary of War Dana, General Thomas, Generals Hooker, Granger, Howard, and other distinguished officers stood on the parapet of Fort Wood facing Orchard Knob, waiting to see this initial movement,—the overture to the battle of Chattanooga. At half-past twelve, Wood's division, supported by Sheridan, marched out on the plain in front of the fort. It was an inspiring sight. Flags were flying; the quick, earnest steps of thousands beat equal time. The sharp commands of hundreds of company officers, the sound of the drums, the ringing notes of the bugle, companies wheeling and countermarching and regiments getting into line, the bright sun lighting up ten thousand polished bayonets till they glistened and flashed like a flying shower of electric sparks,—all looked like preparations for a peaceful pageant, rather than for the bloody work of death. Groups of officers on Missionary Ridge looked down through their glasses, and the enemy's pickets, but a few hundred yards away, came out of their pits and stood idly looking on, unconcernedly viewing what they supposed to be preparations for a grand review. But at half-past one o'clock the advance was sounded. Instantly Wood's division, moving with the steadiness of a machine, started forward. Not a straggler or laggard was on the field, and, what was probably hardly ever before seen, drummers were marching with their companies, beating the charge. Now the enemy

realized, for the first time, that it was not a review. His pickets fell back to their reserves. The reserves were quickly driven back to the main line. Firing opened from the enemy's advanced rifle-pits, followed by a tremendous roll of musketry and roar of artillery. Men were seen on the ground, dotting the field over which the line of battle had passed. Ambulances came hurrying back with the first of the wounded. Columns of puffy smoke arose from the Orchard Knob woods. A cheer, faint to those on the parapet of Fort Wood, indicated that the boys in blue were carrying the breastworks on the Knob! A sharp, short struggle, and the hill was ours.

About 4 o'clock in the afternoon of November 23d, when it became certain that Osterhaus, cut off by the breaking of the pontoon-bridge at Brown's Ferry, would be attached to Hooker's command, General Thomas directed Hooker to make a demonstration against Lookout Mountain the next morning, and, if the demonstration showed it could be carried, to proceed to take it. Later in the day, orders to the same effect came to General Hooker from General Grant. The success at Orchard Knob, and the breaking of the bridge, caused this radical change to be made in Grant's plans. Yet he still held to the chief feature, which was to turn Bragg's right.

The morning of November 24th opened with a cold, drizzling rain. Thick clouds of mist were settling on Lookout Mountain. At daybreak Geary's division, and Whitaker's brigade of Cruft's division, marched up to Wauhatchie, the nearest point at which Lookout Creek, swelled by recent rains, could be forded, and at 8 o'clock they crossed. The heavy clouds of mist reaching down the mountain-side hid the movement from the enemy, who was expecting and was well prepared to resist a crossing at the Chattanooga road below. As soon as this movement was discovered, the enemy withdrew his troops from the summit of the mountain, changed front, and formed a new line to meet our advance, his left resting at the palisade, and his right at the heavy works in the valley, where the road crossed the creek. Having crossed at Wauhatchie, Whitaker's brigade, being in the advance, drove back the enemy's pickets, and quickly ascended the mountain till it reached the foot of the palisade. Here, firmly attaching its right, the brigade faced left in front, with its left joined to Geary's division. Geary now moved along the side of the mountain, and through the valley, thus covering the crossing of the rest of Hooker's command. In the meantime Grose's brigade was engaging the enemy at the lower road crossing, and Wood's brigade of Osterhaus's division was building a bridge rather more than half a mile farther up the creek. Geary, moving down the valley, reached this point at 11 o'clock, just after the bridge was finished, and as Osterhaus's division and Grose's brigade were crossing. Hooker's command, now united in the enemy's field, was ready to advance and sweep around the mountain. His line, hanging at the base of the palisades like a great pendulum, reached down the side of the mountain to the valley, where the force

GENERAL HOOKER AND STAFF ON THE HILL NORTH OF LOOKOUT CREEK, FROM WHICH HE DIRECTED
THE BATTLE. FROM A WAR-TIME PHOTOGRAPH.

that had just crossed the creek was attached as its weight. Now, as, at the command of Hooker, it swung forward in its upward movement, the artillery of the Army of the Cumberland, on Moccasin Point, opened fire, throwing a stream of shot and shell into the enemy's rifle-pits at the foot of the mountain, and into the works thickly planted on the "White House" plateau. At the same time the guns planted by Hooker on the west side of the creek opened on the works which covered the enemy's right. Then followed a gallant assault by Osterhaus and Grose. After fighting for nearly two hours, step by step up the steep mountain-side, over and through deep gullies and ravines, over great rocks and fallen trees, the earth-works on the plateau were assaulted and carried, and the enemy was driven out and forced to fall back. He did so slowly and reluctantly, taking advantage of the rough ground to continue the fight. It was now 2 o'clock. A halt all along the line was ordered by General Hooker, as the clouds had grown so thick that further advance was impracticable, and as his ammunition was almost exhausted and more could not well be brought up the mountain. But all the

enemy's works had been taken. Hooker had carried the mountain on the east side, had opened communication with Chattanooga, and he commanded the enemy's line of defensive works in Chattanooga Valley.⚓

At 2 o'clock Hooker reported to General Thomas and informed him that he was out of ammunition. Thomas at once sent Carlin's brigade from the valley, each soldier taking with him all the small ammunition he could carry. At 5 o'clock Carlin was on the mountain, and Hooker's skirmishers were quickly supplied with the means of carrying on their work.

In the morning it had not been known in Chattanooga, in Sherman's army, or in Bragg's camp, that a battle was to be fought. Indeed, it was not definitely known even to General Grant; for Hooker was only ordered to make a demonstration, and, if this showed a good chance for success, then to make an attack. Soon after breakfast, Sherman's men at the other end of the line, intent on the north end of Missionary Ridge, and Thomas's men in the center, fretting to be let loose from their intrenchments, were startled by the sound of

⚓ Colonel D. R. Hundley, of Greenbrier, Alabama, writing to the editors, May 27th, 1887, said: "The impression conveyed in the above is that Osterhaus and Grose were confronted by at least a reasonably large force in their fight up the mountain-side and at the earth-works. The fact is, the only force opposed to them on the side of the mountain were skirmishers from the weak brigade in charge of the earth-works, and the only force to confront them in the earth-works was the same weak brigade, but little over a thousand strong, commanded by General Walthall, of Mississippi. Nearly half of this

weak force was killed or captured, but the rest fought their way gallantly back to the Craven farm, where, for the first time, they received reënforcements. I personally know that no step backward was taken from that hour, and that the conflict raged furiously for some time on that ground before the Federals ceased firing. General Hooker had no occasion to 'order a halt all along the line'—the 'boys in gray' in his front, concealed in the mist and hid behind trees and rocks, had already most effectually halted the gallant 'boys in blue.'"

artillery and musketry firing in Lookout Valley. Surprise possessed the thousands who turned their anxious eyes toward the mountain. The hours slowly wore away ; the roar of battle increased, as it came rolling around the point of the mountain, and the anxiety grew. A battle was being fought just before and above them. They could hear, but could not see how it was going. Finally, the wind, tossing about the clouds and mist, made a rift that for a few minutes opened a view of White House plateau. The enemy was seen to be in flight, and Hooker's men were in pursuit! Then went up a mighty cheer from the thirty thousand in the valley that was heard above the battle by their comrades on the mountain.

As the sun went down the clouds rolled away, and the night came on clear and cool. A grand sight was old Lookout that night. Not two miles apart were the parallel camp-fires of the two armies, extending from the summit of the mountain to its base, looking like streams of burning lava, while in between, the flashes from the skirmishers' muskets glowed like giant fire-flies.

The next morning there was silence in Hooker's front. Before daylight eight adventurous, active volunteers from the 8th Kentucky Infantry scaled the palisades and ran up the Stars and Stripes. The enemy had stolen away in the night.

Although General Grant had twice changed his original plan, first in the movement from the center, then in the reconnoissance and resulting attack on Lookout Mountain, he still adhered to his purpose of turning Bragg's right, and made no change in the instructions given to General Sherman, except as to the time of attack. Every necessary preparation for crossing Sherman's troops had been made secretly, under direction of General W. F. Smith ; 116 pontoons had been placed in North Chickamauga Creek, and in ravines near its mouth, and many wagon-loads of " balks" (stringers) and chess (flooring) had been hid near by. Before dark on the evening of November 23d General Sherman had his troops well massed and hid behind the hills on the north side of the river opposite the end of Missionary Ridge. After dark General Barnett, Chief of Artillery of the Army of the Cumberland, planted fifty-six guns on the low foot-hills on the north bank of the river, to cover Sherman's crossing and to protect the pontoon-bridge when laid. Everything now being in readiness for the movement, at midnight General Giles A. Smith's brigade entered the pontoons, floated out of North Chickamauga Creek, and was rowed to the south bank of the river. Landing quietly, he surprised and captured the enemy's pickets, and secured a firm foothold. The pontoons were sent across the river, and with these and the small steamboat brought up from Chattanooga General Morgan L. Smith's and General John E. Smith's divisions were ferried over the river. As soon as these troops had been landed, work was commenced on the pontoon-bridge, which was skillfully laid under the supervision of General W. F. Smith. The bridge was 1350 feet in length, and was completed by 11 o'clock in the morning, when General Ewing's division and Sherman's artillery

crossed. At 1 o'clock, just as Hooker was rounding the front of Lookout Mountain, the roar of his battle stirring the blood of the veterans of the Army of the Tennessee, General Sherman gave the command, " Forward!" At 3:30 General Sherman took the hill which was supposed to be the north end of the ridge, and soon afterward took another hill a little in advance, both separated by a deep depression from the heavily fortified Tunnel Hill, on which Bragg's right flank rested and which was Sherman's objective point.

None of the men of the Army of the Cumberland, who for nine weeks were buried in the trenches at Chattanooga, can ever forget the glorious night of the 24th of November. As the sun went down, the clouds rolled up the mountain, and the mist was blown out of the valley. Night came on clear, with the stars lighting up the heavens. But there followed a sight to cheer their hearts and thrill their souls. Away off to their right, and reaching skyward, Lookout Mountain was ablaze with the fires of Hooker's men, while off to their left, and reaching far above the valley, the north end of Missionary Ridge was aflame with the lights of Sherman's army. The great iron crescent that had, with threatening aspect, so long hung over them, was disappearing. The only thought that dampened their enthusiasm was that the enemy was being destroyed on the flanks, while they were tied down in the center, without a part in the victories. But late that night General Grant, thinking that General Sherman had carried Tunnel Hill, and acting in that belief, gave orders for the next day's battle. General Sherman was directed to attack the enemy at early dawn, Thomas to coöperate with him, and Hooker, to be ready to advance into Chattanooga Valley, to hold the road that zigzagged from the valley to the summit. Early the next morning, when General Grant learned that the ridge had not been carried as far as Tunnel Hill, and that Lookout Mountain had been evacuated by the enemy, he suspended his orders, except those to Sherman, and directed Hooker to come down from the mountain, to carry the pass at Rossville, and then operate on Bragg's left and rear. Bragg's army was now concentrated on Missionary Ridge, and in the valley at the east foot. Cheatham's and Stevenson's divisions had been withdrawn from Lookout Mountain on the night of the 24th, and, marching all night, were seen at dawn the next morning moving along the summit of Missionary Ridge, on the way to reënforce Bragg's right. For several hours after daylight the flowing of this steady stream of troops continued.

Early in the morning of the 25th General Grant and General Thomas established their headquarters on Orchard Knob, a point from which the best view of the movements of the whole army could be had. At sunrise General Sherman commenced his attack, but after repeated assaults and severe fighting, it appearing to be impossible for General Sherman to take the enemy's works, operations ceased early in the afternoon.

Meanwhile Hooker was detained three hours at Chattanooga Creek, while a bridge that the

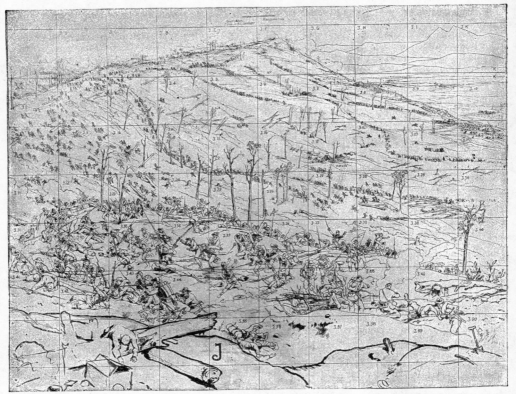

THE CHARGE UP MISSIONARY RIDGE BY BAIRD'S, WOOD'S, SHERIDAN'S, AND JOHNSON'S DIVISIONS.
FROM THE ROUGH SKETCH FOR ONE SECTION OF THE CYCLORAMA OF THE BATTLE OF MISSIONARY RIDGE.

retreating enemy had burned was being rebuilt. As soon as he had taken Rossville, he moved against the south end of Missionary Ridge. The ridge was quickly carried, and, sweeping northward, Hooker soon came upon Stewart's division, posted on the summit, and behind the earth-works which the Army of the Cumberland had thrown up the day after Chickamauga. Cruft's division assaulted and carried the works, thus having the good fortune of retaking the works they themselves had constructed. It was by this time nearly sundown. Hooker reached the south end of the ridge too late in the day to relieve the pressure on Sherman, who was at the north end six miles off. Bragg's right had not been turned. Success had not followed Sherman's movement. The battle as planned had not been won.

Late on this memorable afternoon there was an accident — an accident like the charge at Balaklava; though, unlike this theme for poetry, it called for greater daring, and was attended by complete success, and yielded most important results, for it led to the complete shattering of the enemy's army, and drove him from the field. On Orchard Knob, and opposite the center of Missionary Ridge, were four divisions of the Army of the Cumberland. On the left was Baird's division; then Wood's and Sheridan's divisions occupying

the lines which, two days before, they had taken in their magnificent advance; on the right was R. W. Johnson's division, — all under the personal command of Thomas. It was past 3 o'clock. General Sherman had ceased operations. General Hooker's advance had not yet been felt. The day was dying, and Bragg still held the ridge. If any movement to dislodge him was to be made that day it must be made at once. At half-past three o'clock an attack was ordered by General Grant. He had changed his plan of battle. At once orders were issued that at the firing, in rapid succession, of six guns on Orchard Knob, Thomas's whole line should instantaneously move forward, Sheridan's and Wood's divisions in the center, Sheridan to be supported on the right by Johnson, and Wood on the left by Baird. This demonstration was to be made to relieve the pressure on Sherman. The only order given was to move forward and take the rifle-pits at the foot of the ridge. In Sheridan's division the order was, "As soon as the signal is given, the whole line will advance, and you will take what is before you."

Between Orchard Knob and Missionary Ridge was a valley, partly covered with a small growth of timber. It was wooded in front of the right of Baird's and of the whole of Wood's division. In front of Sheridan's and Johnson's it had been almost entirely cleared. At the foot of the ridge were heavy rifle-pits, which could be seen from Orchard Knob, and extending in front of them, for four and five hundred yards, the ground was covered with felled trees. There was a good plain for both direct and enfilading fire from the rifle-pits, and the approaches were commanded by the enemy's artillery. At this point the ridge is five or six hundred feet high. Its side, scored with gullies and showing but little timber, had a rough and bare appearance. Half-way up was another line of rifle-pits, and the summit was furrowed with additional lines and dotted over with epaulements, in which were placed fifty pieces of artillery. Directly in front of Orchard Knob, and on the summit of the ridge, in a small house, was Bragg's headquarters.

At twenty minutes before four the signal-guns were fired. Suddenly twenty thousand men rushed forward, moving in line of battle by brigades, with a double line of skirmishers in front, and closely followed by the reserves in mass. The big siege-guns in the Chattanooga forts roared above the light artillery and musketry in the valley. The enemy's rifle-pits were ablaze, and the whole ridge in our front had broken out like another Ætna. Not many minutes afterward our men were seen working through the felled trees and other obstructions. Though exposed to such a terrific fire, they neither fell back nor halted. By a bold and desperate push they broke through the works in several places and opened flank and reverse fires. The enemy was thrown into confusion, and took precipitate flight up the ridge. Many prisoners and a large number of small-arms were captured. The order of the commanding general had now been fully and most successfully carried out. But it did not go far enough to satisfy these brave men, who thought the time had come to finish the battle of Chickamauga. There was a halt of but a few minutes, to take breath and to re-form lines; then, with a sudden impulse, and without orders, all started up the ridge. Officers, catching their spirit, first followed, then led. There was no thought of supports or of protecting flanks, though the enemy's line could be seen, stretching on either side. ↓

As soon as this movement was seen from Orchard Knob, Grant quickly turned to Thomas, who stood by his side, and I heard him say angrily: "Thomas, who ordered those men up the ridge?" Thomas replied, in his usual slow, quiet manner: "I don't know; I did not." Then, addressing General Gordon Granger, he said, "Did you order them up, Granger?" "No," said Granger; "they started up without orders. When those fellows get started all hell can't stop them." General Grant said something to the effect that somebody would suffer if it did not turn out well, and then, turning, stoically watched the ridge. He gave no further orders.

As soon as Granger had replied to Thomas, he turned to me, his chief-of-staff, and said: "Ride at once to Wood, and then to Sheridan, and ask them if they ordered their men up the ridge, and tell them, if they can take it, to push ahead." As I was mounting, Granger added: "It is hot over there, and you may not get through. I shall send Captain Avery to Sheridan, and other officers after both of you." As fast as my horse could carry me, I rode first to General Wood, and delivered the message. "I didn't order them up," said Wood; "they started up on their own account, and they are going up, too! Tell Granger, if we are supported, we will take and hold the ridge!" As soon as I reached General Wood, Captain Avery got to General Sheridan, and delivered his message. "I didn't order them up," said Sheridan; "but we are going to take the ridge!" He then asked Avery for his flask and waved it at a group of Confederate officers, standing just in front of Bragg's headquarters, with the salutation, "Here's at you!" At once two guns—the "Lady Breckinridge" and the "Lady Buckner"—in front of Bragg's headquarters were fired at Sheridan and the group of officers about him. One shell struck so near as to throw dirt over Sheridan and Avery. "Ah!" said the general, "that is ungenerous; I shall take those guns for that!" Before Sheridan received the message taken by Captain Avery, he had sent a staff-officer to Granger, to inquire whether "the order given to take the rifle-pits meant the rifle-pits at the base, or those on the top of the ridge." Granger told this officer that "the order given was to take those at the base." Conceiving this to be an order to fall back, the officer, on his way to Sheridan, gave it to General Wagner, commanding the Second Brigade of the division, which was then nearly half-way up the ridge. Wagner ordered his brigade back to the rifle-pits at the base, but it only remained there till Sheridan, seeing the mistake, ordered it forward. It again advanced under a terrific fire.

The men, fighting and climbing up the steep hill, sought the roads, ravines, and less rugged parts. The ground was so broken that it was impossible to keep a regular line of battle. At times their movements were in shape like the flight of migratory birds—sometimes in line, sometimes in mass, mostly in V-shaped groups, with the points toward the enemy. At these points regimental flags were flying, sometimes drooping as the bearers were shot, but never reaching the ground, for other brave hands were there to seize them. Sixty flags were advancing up the hill. Bragg was hurrying large bodies of men from his right to the center. They could be seen hastening along the ridge. Cheatham's division was being withdrawn from Sherman's front. Bragg and Hardee were at the center, urging their men to stand firm and drive back the advancing enemy, now so near the summit—indeed, so near that the guns, which could not be sufficiently depressed to reach them, became useless. Artillerymen were lighting the

↓ The Confederate line from right to left on the ridge was as follows: Hardee's corps on the right, Cleburne's division confronting Sherman; Stevenson and Cheatham came next, the latter joining on Breckinridge's corps, which occupied the slope of the ridge, with outposts in trenches at the foot of the slope. Breckinridge's own division, under General Bate, was in the center, in front of Truman's house, Bragg's headquarters. [See map, p. 686.] Stewart's division, deployed, formed the left of the line.— EDITORS.

fuses of shells, and bowling them by hundreds down the hill. The critical moment arrived when the summit was just within reach. At six different points, and almost simultaneously, Sheridan's and Wood's divisions broke over the crest,—Sheridan's first, near Bragg's headquarters; and in a few minutes Sheridan was beside the guns that had been fired at him, and claiming them as captures of his division. Baird's division took the works on Wood's left almost immediately afterward; and then Johnson came up on Sheridan's right. The enemy's guns were turned upon those who still remained in the works, and soon all were in flight down the eastern slope. Baird got on the ridge just in time to change front and oppose a large body of the enemy moving down from Bragg's right to attack our left. After a sharp engagement, that lasted till dark, he drove the enemy back beyond a high point on the north, which he at once occupied. ꝑ

The sun had not yet gone down, Missionary Ridge was ours, and Bragg's army was broken and in flight! Dead and wounded comrades lay thickly strewn on the ground: but thicker yet were the dead and wounded men in gray. Then followed the wildest confusion, as the victors gave vent to their joy. Some madly shouted; some wept from very excess of joy; some grotesquely danced out their delight,—even our wounded forgot their pain, to join in the general hurrah. But Sheridan did not long stop to receive praise and congratulations. With two brigades he started down the Mission Mills road, and found, strongly posted on a second

hill, the enemy's rear. They made a stout resistance, but by a sudden flank movement he drove them from the heights and captured two guns and many prisoners. The day was succeeded by a clear moonlight night. At 7 o'clock General Granger sent word to General Thomas that by a bold dash at Chickamauga Crossing he might cut off a large number of the enemy now supposed to be leaving Sherman's front, and that he proposed to move in that direction. It was midnight before guides could be found, and then General Sheridan again put his tired and well-worn men in motion. He reached the creek just as the rear-guard of the enemy was crossing, and pressed it so closely that it burned the pontoon-bridge before all its troops were over. Here Sheridan captured several hundred prisoners, a large number of quartermasters' wagons, together with caissons, artillery, ammunition, and many small-arms.

In this battle Sheridan's and Wood's divisions —the two center assaulting divisions — took 31 pieces of artillery, several thousand small-arms, and 3800 prisoners. In that one hour of assault they lost 2337 men in killed and wounded,— over twenty per cent. of their whole force! On the northern end of the ridge General Sherman lost in his two days' fighting 1697 in killed and wounded. Of these, 1268 were in his own three divisions. During the night the last of Bragg's army was withdrawn from Missionary Ridge, and Chattanooga from that time remained in undisputed possession of the Union forces.

ꝑ Governor John A. Martin, of Kansas, colonel of the 8th Kansas Volunteers, of Willich's brigade, Wood's division, in a letter to General Fullerton, dated November 16th, 1886, describes the charge as follows:

"When the advance on Missionary Ridge was ordered, on November 25th, my regiment went out directly from Orchard Knob. General Willich, in communicating to me the orders received, distinctly stated that we were directed to take the line of Confederate works at the foot of the hill. We reached these works without serious difficulty, the losses being very small. Shortly after, we emerged from the woods into the open field, and were charging the Confederate works on the double-quick; the soldiers there threw down their arms, and, holding up their hands, in token of surrender, jumped to our side. I had ridden my horse to this line, and, on reaching it, halted my regiment behind the enemy's intrenchments. Dismounting, I ran forward to the little huts that were built by the Confederates, on the plateau just back of their line, with a view of ascertaining what the situation was. I had seen, as soon as I reached the first line of works, as did every soldier in the command, that it was impossible for the troops to remain there long. The line was within easy range of the musketry on the summit of the ridge, and was raked by the artillery fire on the projecting points of the ridge on either side. Reaching the foot of the ridge east of the plateau, I found the position there fairly well protected,— that is, not so easily reached, either by the musketry or artillery of the enemy,— and I at once ran back to near where my regiment had been halted. Just as I got there General Willich came up, and I said to him, 'We can't live here, and ought to go forward.' He gave me directions to move ahead, and I at once ordered my regiment forward. By that time, or about that time, it seemed to me that there was a simultaneous advance of many of the regiments in different parts of the line, and I got the impression that possibly orders had been communicated for an advance on the ridge, which I had not received; hence I hurried my regiment forward as rapidly as possible. When I reached the foot of the ridge again, with the regiment, my orderly came up with my horse, and I mounted it, as my adjutant did his. The advance to the ridge was as rapid as the nature of the ground would permit; and I think, from the position I occupied, I had a fair opportunity to see what was going on, not only immediately above me, but to

the right and left. I was impressed with the idea, I know, that a sharp rivalry had sprung up between several regiments, including my own, as to which should reach the summit first. Another idea, I remember distinctly, which impressed me, was that the different regiments had assumed the form of a triangle or wedge — the advance point in nearly every case being the regimental battle-flag. I have always believed that my own regiment made the first break in the enemy's lines on the summit of Missionary Ridge; but the difference between the break thus made by the 8th Kansas and the progress made by one or two regiments of Hazen's brigade on our right and the 25th Illinois of our own brigade, was exceedingly brief.

"But that the first break in the enemy's lines was made in front of our division, I have not the slightest doubt. After we passed through the Confederate works, and while the men were rushing with great enthusiasm after the fleeing Confederates, who were running down the hill on the other side, my attention was directed to the right, where, at the point of a knob, I saw other troops were still engaged in a fierce struggle with the Confederates, who were yet in force behind their works; and while thus, for a moment, watching the progress of the fight to the right, a Confederate battery on a point to the left of our position was swung round, and poured a fire directly down our line. Immediately I ordered my bugler to sound the recall, and began forming all the troops I could gather at that point, with a view of moving to the left to clear the enemy's works in that direction. I had assembled probably a hundred men, when suddenly the whole Confederate line, both to the right and left, gave way before the furious attack of our troops, and was soon in full retreat through the woods and down the roads to the rear.

"I have stated hastily some of my impressions of the battle, but the principal point, which, in my judgment, should always be made prominent, is the fact that Missionary Ridge was fought without orders from the commander-in-chief. I remember, too, and this only confirms what I have said, that shortly after the battle was over General Granger rode along our lines, and said, in a joking way, to the troops, 'I am going to have you all court-martialed! You were ordered to take the works at the foot of the hill, and you have taken those on top! You have disobeyed orders, all of you, and you know that you ought to be court-martialed!'"

EDITORS.

GENERAL BRAGG'S COMMENTS ON MISSIONARY RIDGE.

GENERAL BRAGG made a brief report on the Chattanooga campaign on November 30th, 1863, and on the 2d of December was relieved of command. Of the battle of Missionary Ridge, the report says:

"About 11 A. M. the enemy's forces were being moved in heavy masses from Lookout and beyond to our front, while those in front extended to our right. They formed their lines with great deliberation just beyond the range of our guns and in plain view of our position. Though greatly outnumbered, such was the strength of our position that no doubt was entertained of our ability to hold it, and every disposition was made for that purpose. During this time they [the enemy] had made several attempts on our extreme right, and had been handsomely repulsed with very heavy loss by Major-General Cleburne's command, under the immediate directions of Lieutenant-General Hardee. . . . About 8:30 P. M. the immense force in the front of our left and center advanced in three lines, preceded by heavy skirmishers. Our batteries opened with fine effect, and much confusion was produced before they reached musket-range. In a short time the roar of musketry became very heavy, and it was soon apparent the enemy had been repulsed in my immediate front. While riding along the crest congratulating the troops, intelligence reached me that our line was broken on my right, and the enemy had crowned the ridge. Assistance was promptly dispatched to that point under Brigadier-General Bate, who had so successfully maintained the ground in my front, and I proceeded to the rear of the broken line to rally our retiring troops and return them to the crest to drive the enemy back. General Bate found the disaster so great that his small force could not repair it. About this time I learned that our extreme left had also given way, and that my position was almost surrounded. Bate was immediately directed to form a second line in the rear, where, by the efforts of my staff, a nucleus of stragglers had been formed upon which to rally. Lieutenant-General Hardee, leaving Major-General Cleburne in command on the extreme right, moved toward the left when he heard the heavy firing in that direction. He reached the right of Anderson's division just in time to find it had nearly all fallen

back, commencing on its left, where the enemy had first crowned the ridge. By a prompt and judicious movement, he threw a portion of Cheatham's division directly across the ridge facing the enemy, who was now moving a strong force immediately on his left flank. By a decided stand here the enemy was entirely checked, and that portion of our force to the right remained intact. All to the left, however, except a portion of Bate's division, was entirely routed and in rapid flight. . . . A panic which I had never before witnessed seemed to have seized upon officers and men, and each seemed to be struggling for his personal safety, regardless of his duty or his character. In this distressing and alarming state of affairs General Bate was ordered to hold his position covering the road for the retreat of Breckinridge's command, and orders were immediately sent to Generals Hardee and Breckinridge to retire their forces upon the depot at Chickamauga. . . . No satisfactory excuse can possibly be given for the shameful conduct of our troops on the left in allowing their line to be penetrated. The position was one which ought to have been held by a line of skirmishers against any assaulting column, and wherever resistance was made the enemy fled in disorder after suffering heavy loss. Those who reached the ridge did so in a condition of exhaustion from the great physical exertion in climbing which rendered them powerless, and the slightest effort would have destroyed them. Having secured much of our artillery, they soon availed themselves of our panic, and turning our guns upon us enfiladed the lines, both right and left, rendering them entirely untenable. Had all parts of the line been maintained with equal gallantry and persistence, no enemy could ever have dislodged us, and but one possible reason presents itself to my mind in explanation of this bad conduct in veteran troops who never before failed in any duty assigned them, however difficult and hazardous: They had for two days confronted the enemy, marshaling his immense forces in plain view, and exhibiting to their sight such a superiority in numbers as may have intimidated weak-minded and untried soldiers. But our veterans,had so often encountered similar hosts when the strength of position was against us, and with perfect success, that not a doubt crossed my mind."

OPPOSING FORCES IN THE CHATTANOOGA CAMPAIGN.

November 23d–27th, 1863.

For much of the information contained in this list and in similar lists to follow, the editors are indebted (in advance of the publication of the "Official Records") to Brigadier-General Richard C. Drum, Adjutant-General of the Army. K stands for killed; w for wounded; m w for mortally wounded; m for captured or missing; c for captured.

THE UNION ARMY: Maj.-Gen. Ulysses S. Grant.

ARMY OF THE CUMBERLAND.—Maj.-Gen. George H. Thomas.

General Headquarters: 1st Ohio Sharp-shooters, Capt. G. M. Barber; 10th Ohio, Lieut.-Col. W. M. Ward.

FOURTH ARMY CORPS, Maj.-Gen. Gordon Granger.

FIRST DIVISION, Brig.-Gen. Charles Cruft.

Escort: E, 92d Ill., Capt. Matthew Van Buskirk.

Second Brigade, Brig.-Gen. Walter C. Whitaker: 96th Ill., Col. Thomas E. Champion, Maj. George Hicks; 35th Ind., Col. Bernard F. Mullen; 8th Ky., Col. Sidney M. Barnes; 40th Ohio, Col. Jacob E. Taylor; 51st Ohio, Lieut.-Col. Charles H. Wood; 99th Ohio, Lieut.-Col. John E. Cummins. Brigade loss: k, 17; w, 63; m, 2=82. *Third Brigade,* Col. William Grose: 59th Ill., Maj. Clayton Hale; 75th Ill., Col. John E. Bennett; 84th Ill., Col. Louis H. Waters; 9th Ind., Col. Isaac C. B. Suman; 36th Ind., Maj. Gilbert Trusler; 24th Ohio, Capt. George M. Bacon. Brigade loss: k, 4; w, 60=64.

SECOND DIVISION, Maj.-Gen. Philip H. Sheridan.

First Brigade, Col. Francis T. Sherman: 36th Ill., Col. Silas Miller,⌡ Lieut.-Col. Porter C. Olson; 44th Ill., Col. Wallace W. Barrett; 73d Ill., Col. James F. Jaques;

74th Ill., Col. Jason Marsh; 88th Ill., Lieut.-Col. George W. Chandler; 22d Ind., Col. Michael Gooding; 2d Mo., Col. Bernard Laiboldt,⌡ Lieut.-Col. Arnold Beck; 15th Mo., Col. Joseph Conrad (w), Capt. Samuel Rexinger; 24th Wis., Maj. Carl von Baumbach. Brigade loss: k, 30; w, 268; m, 3=301. *Second Brigade,* Brig.-Gen. George D. Wagner: 100th Ill., Maj. Chas. M. Hammond; 15th Ind., Col. Gustavus A. Wood,⌡ Maj. Frank White (w), Capt. Benjamin F. Hegler; 40th Ind., Lieut.-Col. Elias Neff; 57th Ind., Lieut.-Col. George W. Lennard; 58th Ind., Lieut.-Col. Joseph Moore; 26th Ohio, Lieut.-Col. William H. Young; 97th Ohio, Lieut.-Col. Milton Barnes. Brigade loss: k, 70; w, 660=730. *Third Brigade,* Col. Charles G. Harker: 22d Ill., Lieut.-Col. Francis Swanwick; 27th Ill., Col. Jonathan R. Miles; 42d Ill., Col. Nathan H. Walworth,⌡ Capt. Edgar D. Swain; 51st Ill., Maj. Charles W. Davis (w), Capt. Albert M. Tilton; 79th Ill., Col. Allen Buckner; 3d Ky., Col. Henry C. Dunlap; 64th Ohio, Col. Alexander McIlvain; 65th Ohio, Lieut.-Col. William A. Bullitt; 125th Ohio, Col. Emerson Opdycke,⌡ Capt. Edward P. Bates. Brigade loss: k, 28; w, 269=297. *Artillery,* Capt War-

⌡ Temporarily in command of a demi-brigade.

ren P. Edgarton: M, 1st Ill., Capt. George W. Spencer; 10th Ind., Capt. William A. Naylor; G, 1st Mo., Lieut. G. Schueler; I, 1st Ohio, Capt. H. Dilger; G, 4th U. S., Lieut. C. F. Merkle; H, 5th U. S., Capt. F. L. Guenther. THIRD DIVISION, Brig.-Gen. Thomas J. Wood.

First Brigade, Brig.-Gen. August Willich: 25th Ill., Col. Richard H. Nodine; 35th Ill., Lieut.-Col. William P. Chandler; Lieut.-Col. William D. Williams; 32d Ind., Lieut.-Col. Frank Erdelmeyer; 68th Ind., Lieut.-Col. Harvey J. Espy; 8th Kans., Col. John A. Martin; 15th Ohio, Lieut.-Col. Frank Askew; 49th Ohio, Maj. Samuel F. Gray; 15th Wis., Capt. John A. Gordon. Brigade loss: k, 46; w, 291; m, 1 = 338. *Second Brigade,* Brig.-Gen. William B. Hazen: 6th Ind., Maj. Calvin D. Campbell; 5th Ky., Col. William W. Berry (w), Lieut.-Col. John L. Treanor; 6th Ky., Maj. Richard T. Whitaker; 23d Ky., Lieut.-Col. James C. Foy; 1st Ohio, Lieut.-Col. Bassett Langdon (w), Maj. Joab A. Stafford; 6th Ohio, Lieut.-Col. Alex. C. Christopher; 41st Ohio, Col. Aquilla Wiley (w), Lieut.-Col. Robert L. Kimberly; 93d Ohio, Maj. William Birch (k), Capt. Daniel Bowman (w), Capt. Samuel B. Smith; 124th Ohio, Lieut.-Col. James Pickands. Brigade loss: k, 92; w, 430; m, 7 = 529. *Third Brigade,* Brig.-Gen. Samuel Beatty: 79th Ind., Col. Frederick Knefler; 86th Ind., Col. George F. Dick; 9th Ky., Col. George H. Cram; 17th Ky., Col. Alexander M. Stout; 13th Ohio, Col. Dwight Jarvis, Jr.; 19th Ohio, Col. Charles F. Manderson; 59th Ohio, Maj. Robert J. Vanosdol. Brigade loss: k, 14; w, 160; m, 1 = 175. *Artillery,* Capt. Cullen Bradley: Ill., Battery, Capt. Lyman Bridges; 6th Ohio, Lieut. Oliver H. P. Ayres; 20th Ohio, Capt. Edward Grosskopff; B, Pa., Lieut. Samuel M. McDowell.

ELEVENTH CORPS,[¶] Maj.-Gen. O. O. Howard.

General Headquarters, Independent Co., 8th N. Y. Infantry, Capt. Anton Bruhn.

SECOND DIVISION, Brig.-Gen. Adolph von Steinwehr.

First Brigade, Col. Adolphus Buschbeck: 33d N. J., Col. George W. Mindil; 134th N. Y., Col. Allen H. Jackson; 154th N. Y., Col. Patrick H. Jones; 27th Pa., Maj. Peter A. McAloon (m w), Capt. August Reidt; 73d Pa., Lieut.-Col. Joseph B. Taft (k), Capt. Daniel F. Kelly (c), Lieut. Samuel D. Miller. Brigade loss: k, 28; w, 148; m, 108 = 284. *Second Brigade,* Col. Orland Smith: 33d Mass., Lieut.-Col. Godfrey Rider, Jr.; 136th N. Y., Col. James Wood, Jr.; 55th Ohio, Col. C. B. Gambee; 73d Ohio, Maj. S. H. Hurst. Brigade loss: k, 4; w, 21: m, 4 = 29.

THIRD DIVISION, Maj.-Gen. Carl Schurz.

First Brigade, Brig.-Gen. Hector Tyndale: 101st Ill., Col. Charles H. Fox; 45th N. Y., Maj. Charles Koch; 143d N. Y., Col. Horace Boughton; 61st Ohio, Col. Stephen J. McGroarty; 82d Ohio, Lieut.-Col. David Thomson. Brigade loss: k, 1; w, 4 = 5. *Second Brigade,* Col. Wladimir Krzyzanowski: 58th N. Y., Capt. Michael Esembaus; 119th N. Y., Col. John T. Lockman; 141st N. Y., Col. William K. Logie; 26th Wis., Capt. Frederick C. Winkler. Brigade loss: w, 3. *Third Brigade,* Col. Frederick Hecker: 80th Ill., Capt. James Neville; 82d Ill., Lieut.-Col. Edward S. Salomon; 68th N. Y., Maj. Albert von Steinhausen; 75th Pa., Maj. August Ledig. Brigade loss: k, 1; w, 9 = 10. *Artillery,* Maj. Thomas W. Osborn: I, 1st N. Y., Capt. Michael Wiedrich; 13th N. Y., Capt. W. Wheeler; K, 1st Ohio, Lieut. Nicholas Sahm.

TWELFTH ARMY CORPS.

SECOND DIVISION, Brig.-Gen. John W. Geary.

First Brigade, Col. Charles Candy, Col. William R. Creighton (k), Col. Thomas J. Ahl: 5th Ohio, Col. John H. Patrick; 7th Ohio, Col. William R. Creighton, Lieut.-Col. Orrin J. Crane (k), Capt. Ernest J. Kreiger; 29th Ohio, Col. William F. Fitch; 66th Ohio, Lieut.-Col. Eugene Powell, Capt. Thomas McConnell; 28th Pa., Col. Thomas J. Ahl, Capt. John Flynn; 147th Pa., Lieut.-Col. Ario Pardee, Jr. Brigade loss: k, 25; w, 117 = 142. *Second Brigade,* Col. George A. Cobham, Jr.: 29th Pa., Col. William Rickards, Jr.; 109th Pa., Capt. Frederick L. Gimber; 111th Pa., Col. Thomas M. Walker. Brigade loss: k, 4; w, 18 = 22. *Third Brigade,* Col. David Ire-

land: 60th N. Y., Col. Abel Godard; 78th N. Y., Col. Herbert von Hammerstein; 102d N. Y., Col. James C. Lane; 137th N. Y., Capt. Milo B. Eldridge; 149th N. Y., Lieut.-Col. Charles B. Randall. Brigade loss: k, 26; w, 151 = 177. *Artillery,* Maj. J. A. Reynolds: E, Pa., Lieut. J. D. McGill; K, 5th U. S., Capt. E. C. Bainbridge.

FOURTEENTH CORPS, Maj.-Gen. J. M. Palmer.

Escort: L, 1st Ohio Cav., Capt. John D. Barker.

FIRST DIVISION, Brig.-Gen. Richard W. Johnson.

First Brigade, Brig.-Gen. William P. Carlin: 104th Ill., Lieut.-Col. Douglas Hapeman; 38th Ind., Lieut.-Col. Daniel F. Griffin; 42d Ind., Lieut.-Col. William T. B. McIntire; 88th Ind., Col. Cyrus E. Briant; 2d Ohio, Col. Anson G. McCook; 33d Ohio, Capt. James H. M. Montgomery; 94th Ohio, Maj. Rue P. Hutchins; 10th Wis., Capt. Jacob W. Roby. Brigade loss: k, 25; w, 134 = 159. *Second Brigade,* Col. Marshall F. Moore, Col. William L. Stoughton: 19th Ill., Lieut.-Col. Alexander W. Raffen; 11th Mich., Capt. Patrick H. Keegan; 69th Ohio, Maj. James J. Hanna; 1st Battalion, 15th U. S., Capt. Henry Keteltas; 2d Battalion, 15th U. S., Capt. William S. McManus; 1st Battalion, 16th U. S., Maj. Robert E. A. Crofton; 1st Battalion, 18th U. S., Capt. George W. Smith; 2d Battalion, 18th U. S., Capt. Henry Haymond; 1st Battalion, 19th U. S., Capt. Henry S. Welton. Brigade loss: k, 23; w, 149; m, 2 = 174. *Third Brigade,* Brig.-Gen. John C. Starkweather: 24th Ill., Col. Geza Mihalotzy; 37th Ind., Col. James S. Hull; 21st Ohio, Capt. Charles H. Vantine; 74th Ohio, Maj. Joseph Fisher; 78th Pa., Maj. Augustus B. Bonnaffon; 79th Pa., Maj. Michael H. Locher; 1st Wis., Lieut.-Col. George B. Bingham; 21st Wis., Capt. Charles H. Walker. *Artillery:* C, 1st Ill., Capt. Mark H. Prescott; A, 1st Mich., Francis E. Hale.

SECOND DIVISION, Brig.-Gen. J. C. Davis. Staff loss: w, 1.

First Brigade, Brig.-Gen. James D. Morgan: 10th Ill., Col. John Tillson; 16th Ill., Lieut.-Col. James B. Cahill; 60th Ill., Col. William B. Anderson; 21st Ky., Col. Samuel W. Price; 10th Mich., Lieut.-Col. Christopher J. Dickerson. Brigade loss: w, 9. *Second Brigade,* Brig.-Gen. John Beatty: 34th Ill., Lieut.-Col. Oscar Van Tassell; 78th Ill., Lieut.-Col. Carter Van Vleck; 98th Ohio, Maj. James M. Shane; 108th Ohio, Lieut.-Col. Carlo Piepho; 113th Ohio, Maj. L. Starling Sullivant; 121st Ohio, Maj. John Yager. Brigade loss: k, 3; w, 17; m, 1 = 21. *Third Brigade,* Col. Daniel McCook: 85th Ill., Col. Caleb J. Dilworth; 86th Ill., Lieut.-Col. David W. Magee; 110th Ill., Lieut.-Col. E. Hibbard Topping; 125th Ill., Col. Oscar F. Harmon; 52d Ohio, Maj. James T. Holmes. Brigade loss: k, 2; w, 4; m, 5 = 11. *Artillery,* Capt. William A. Hotchkiss: I, 2d Ill., Lieut. Henry B. Plant; 2d Minn., Lieut. Richard L. Dawley; 5th Wis., Capt. George Q. Gardner.

THIRD DIVISION, Brig.-Gen. Absalom Baird.

First Brigade, Brig.-Gen. John B. Turchin: 82d Ind., Col. Morton C. Hunter; 11th Ohio, Lieut.-Col. Ogden Street; 17th Ohio, Maj. Daniel Butterfield (w), Capt. Benjamin H. Showers; 31st Ohio, Lieut.-Col. Frederick W. Lister; 36th Ohio, Lieut.-Col. Hiram F. Duval; 89th Ohio, Capt. John H. Jolly; 92d Ohio, Lieut.-Col. Douglas Putman, Jr. (w), Capt. Edward Grosvenor. Brigade loss: k, 50; w, 231; m, 3 = 284. *Second Brigade,* Col. Ferdinand Van Derveer: 75th Ind., Col. Milton S. Robinson; 87th Ind., Col. Newell Gleason; 101st Ind., Lieut.-Col. Thomas Doan; 2d Minn., Lieut.-Col. Judson W. Bishop; 9th Ohio, Col. Gustave Kammerling; 35th Ohio, Lieut.-Col. Henry V. N. Boynton (w), Maj. Joseph L. Budd; 105th Ohio, Lieut.-Col. William R. Tolles. Brigade loss: k, 19; w, 142; m, 2 = 163. *Third Brigade,* Col. Edward H. Phelps (k), Col. William H. Hays: 10th Ind., Lieut.-Col. Marsh B. Taylor; 74th Ind., Lieut.-Col. Myron Baker; 4th Ky., Maj. Robert M. Kelly; 10th Ky., Col. William H. Hays, Lieut.-Col. Gabriel C. Wharton; 14th Ohio, Lieut.-Col. Henry D. Kingsbury; 38th Ohio, Maj. Charles Greenwood. Brigade loss: k, 18; w, 100; m, 1 = 119. *Artillery,* Capt. George R. Swallow: 7th Ind., Lieut. Otho

[¶] Maj.-Gen. Joseph Hooker, commanding Eleventh and Twelfth Army Corps, had under his immediate command the First Division, Fourth Corps; the Second Division, Twelfth Corps; portions of the Fourteenth Corps, and the First Division, Fifteenth Corps. Co. K, 15th Ill. Cav., Capt. Samuel B. Sherer, served as escort to Gen. Hooker.

H. Morgan; 19th Ind., Lieut. Robert G. Lackey; I, 4th U. S., Lieut. Frank G. Smith.

ENGINEER TROOPS, Brig.-Gen. William F. Smith.

Engineers: 1st Mich. Engineers (detachment), Capt. Perrin V. Fox; 13th Mich., Maj. Willard G. Eaton; 21st Mich., Capt. Loomis K. Bishop; 22d Mich. Inf., Maj. Henry S. Dean; 18th Ohio, Col. Timothy R. Stanley. *Pioneer Brigade,* Col. George P. Buell: 1st Battalion, Capt. Charles J. Stewart; 2d Battalion, Capt. Cornelius Smith; 3d Battalion, Capt. William Clark.

ARTILLERY RESERVE, Brig.-Gen. J. M. Brannan.

FIRST DIVISION, Col. James Barnett.

First Brigade, Maj. Charles S. Cotter: B, 1st Ohio, Lieut. Norman A. Baldwin; C, 1st Ohio, Capt. Marco B. Gary; E, 1st Ohio, Lieut. Albert G. Ransom; F, 1st Ohio, Lieut. Giles J. Cockerill. *Second Brigade:* G, 1st Ohio, Capt. Alexander Marshall; M, 1st Ohio, Capt. Frederick Schultz; 18th Ohio, Lieut. Joseph McCafferty.

SECOND DIVISION.

First Brigade, Capt. Josiah W. Church: D, 1st Mich., Capt. Josiah W. Church; A, 1st Tenn., Lieut. Albert F. Beach; 3d Wis., Lieut. Hiram F. Hubbard; 8th Wis., Lieut. Obadiah German; 10th Wis., Capt. Yates V. Beebe. *Second Brigade,* Capt. Arnold Sutermeister: 4th Ind., Lieut. Henry J. Willits; 8th Ind., Lieut. George Estep; 11th Ind., Capt. Arnold Sutermeister; 21st Ind., Lieut. W. E. Chess; C, 1st Wis. Heavy, Capt. John R. Davies.

CAVALRY. ☆

Second Brigade (Second Division), Col. Eli Long: 98th Ill., Lieut.-Col. Edward Kitchell; 17th Ind., Lieut.-Col. Henry Jordan; 2d Ky., Col. Thomas P. Nicholas; 4th Mich., Maj. Horace Gray; 1st Ohio, Maj. Thomas J. Patten; 3d Ohio, Lieut.-Col. C. B. Seidel; 4th Ohio (battalion), Maj. G. W. Dobb; 10th Ohio, Col. C. C. Smith.

POST OF CHATTANOOGA, Col. John G. Parkhurst: 44th Ind., Lieut.-Col. Simeon C. Aldrich; 15th Ky., Maj. William G. Halpin; 9th Mich., Lieut.-Col. William Wilkinson.

ARMY OF THE TENNESSEE, Maj.-Gen. William T. Sherman. ⎰

FIFTEENTH CORPS, Maj.-Gen. Frank P. Blair, Jr.

FIRST DIVISION, Brig.-Gen. Peter J. Osterhaus.

First Brigade, Brig.-Gen. Charles R. Woods: 13th Ill., Lieut.-Col. Frederick W. Partridge (w), Capt. Geo. P. Brown; 3d Mo., Lieut.-Col. Theodore Meumann; 12th Mo., Col. Hugo Wangelin (w), Lieut.-Col. Jacob Kaercher; 17th Mo., Lieut.-Col. John F. Cramer; 27th Mo., Col. Thomas Curly; 29th Mo., Col. James Peckham (w), Maj. Philip H. Murphy; 31st Mo., Lieut.-Col. Samuel P. Simpson; 32d Mo., Lieut.-Col. Henry C. Warmoth; 76th Ohio, Maj. Willard Warner. Brigade loss: k, 33; w, 203; m, 41 = 277. *Second Brigade,* Col. James A. Williamson: 4th Iowa, Lieut.-Col. George Burton; 9th Iowa, Col. David Carskaddon; 25th Iowa, Col. George A. Stone; 26th Iowa, Col. Milo Smith; 30th Iowa, Lieut.-Col. Aurelius Roberts; 31st Iowa, Lieut.-Col. Jeremiah W. Jenkins. Brigade loss: k, 19; w, 134; m, 2 = 155. *Artillery,* Capt. Henry H. Griffiths: 1st Iowa, Lieut. James M. Williams; F, 2d Mo., Capt. Clemens Landgraeber; 4th Ohio, Capt. George Froehlich.

SECOND DIVISION, Brig.-Gen. Morgan L. Smith.

First Brigade, Brig.-Gen. Giles A. Smith (w), Col. Nathan W. Tupper: 55th Ill., Col. Oscar Malmborg; 116th Ill., Col. Nathan W. Tupper, Lieut.-Col. James P. Boyd; 127th Ill., Lieut.-Col. Frank S. Curtiss; 6th Mo., Lieut.-Col. Ira Boutell; 8th Mo., Lieut.-Col. David C. Coleman; 57th Ohio, Lieut.-Col. Samuel R. Mott; 1st Battalion, 13th U. S., Capt. Charles C. Smith. Brigade loss: w, 14; m, 2 = 16. *Second Brigade,* Brig.-Gen. Joseph A. J. Lightburn: 82d Ind., Col. Benjamin J. Spooner; 30th Ohio, Col. Theodore Jones; 37th Ohio, Lieut.-Col. Louis Von Blessingh; 47th Ohio, Col. Augustus C. Parry; 54th Ohio, Maj. Robert Williams, Jr.; 4th W. Va., Col. James H. Dayton. Brigade loss: k, 10; w, 76 = 86. *Artillery:* A, 1st Ill., Capt. Peter P. Wood; B, 1st Ill., Capt. Israel P. Rumsey; H, 1st Ill., Lieut. Francis DeGress. Artillery loss: w, 1.

FOURTH DIVISION, Brig.-Gen. Hugh Ewing.

First Brigade, Col. John Mason Loomis: 26th Ill., Lieut.-Col. Robert A. Gillmore; 90th Ill., Col. Timothy O'Meara (k), Lieut.-Col. Owen Stuart; 12th Ind., Col. Reuben Williams; 100th Ind., Lieut.-Col. Albert Heath. Brigade loss: k, 37; w, 331; m, 18 = 386. *Second Brigade,* Brig.-Gen. John M. Corse (w), Col. Charles C. Walcutt: 4th Ill., Maj. Hiram W. Hall; 103d Ill., Col. William A. Dickerman; 6th Iowa, Lieut.-Col. Alexander J. Miller; 46th Ohio, Col. Charles C. Walcutt, Capt. Isaac N. Alexander. Brigade loss: k, 34; w, 201; m, 2 = 237. *Third Brigade,* Col. Joseph R. Cockerill: 48th Ill., Lieut.-Col. Lucien Greathouse; 97th Ind., Col. Robert F. Catterson; 99th Ind., Col. Alexander Fowler; 53d Ohio, Col. Wells S. Jones; 70th Ohio, Maj. William B. Brown. Brigade loss: w, 3. *Artillery,* Capt. Henry Richardson: F, 1st Ill., Capt. John T. Cheney; I, 1st Ill., Lieut. Josiah H. Burton; D, 1st Mo., Lieut. Byron M. Callender. Artillery loss: w, 2.

SEVENTEENTH ARMY CORPS.

SECOND DIVISION, Brig.-Gen. John E. Smith.

First Brigade, Col. Jesse I. Alexander: 63d Ill., Col. Joseph B. McCown; 48th Ind., Lieut.-Col. Edward J. Wood; 59th Ind., Capt. Wilford H. Welman; 4th Minn., Lieut.-Col. John E. Tourtellotte; 18th Wis., Col. Gabriel Bouck. Brigade loss: w, 4. *Second Brigade,* Col. Green B. Raum (w), Col. Francis C. Deimling, Col. Clark R. Wever: 56th Ill., Maj. Pinckney J. Welsh (w); 17th Iowa, Col. Clark R. Wever, Maj. John F. Walden; 10th Mo., Col. Francis C. Deimling, Lieut.-Col. Christian Hoppee, Col. Francis C. Deimling; E, 24th Mo., Capt. William W. McCammon; 80th Ohio, Lieut.-Col. Pren Metham. Brigade loss: k, 40; w, 140; m, 24 = 204. *Third Brigade,* Brig.-Gen. Charles L. Matthies (w), Col. Benjamin D. Dean, Col. Jabez Banbury: 93d Ill., Col. Holden Putnam (k), Lieut.-Col. Nicholas C. Buswell; 5th Iowa, Col. Jabez Banbury, Lieut.-Col. Ezekiel S. Sampson; 10th Iowa, Lieut.-Col. Paris P. Henderson; 26th Mo., Col. Benjamin D. Dean. Brigade loss: k, 49; w, 145; m, 121 = 315. *Artillery,* Capt. Henry Dillon: Ill. Battery, Capt. William Cogswell; 6th Wis., Lieut. Samuel F. Clark; 12th Wis., Capt. William Zickerick.

Total Union loss: killed, 752; wounded, 4713; captured or missing, 350 = 5815. Effective strength (est.), 60,000.

THE CONFEDERATE ARMY: General Braxton Bragg.

HARDEE'S CORPS, Lieut.-Gen. William J. Hardee.

CHEATHAM'S DIVISION, Brig.-Gen. John K. Jackson.

Jackson's Brigade, Col. C. J. Wilkinson: 1st Ga. (Confederate), Maj. J. C. Gordon; 2d Battalion Ga. Sharpshooters, Lieut.-Col. R. H. Whiteley; 5th Ga., Col. C. P. Daniel; 47th Ga., Lieut.-Col. A. C. Edwards; 65th Ga., Lieut.-Col. J. W. Pearcy; 5th Miss., Maj. J. B. Herring; 8th Miss., Maj. J. F. Smith. Brigade loss not reported. *Walthall's Brigade,* Brig.-Gen. E. C. Walthall: 24th

Miss., Col. William F. Dowd; 27th Miss., Col. J. A. Campbell; 29th Miss., Col. W. F. Brantley; 30th Miss., Maj. J. M. Johnson; 34th Miss., Capt. H. J. Bowen. Brigade loss: k, 8; w, 111; m, 853 = 972. *Moore's Brigade,* Brig.-Gen. John C. Moore: 37th Ala., Lieut.-Col. A. A. Green; 40th Ala., Col. J. H. Higley; 42d Ala., Lieut.-Col. Thomas C. Lanier. Brigade loss: k, 9; w, 39; m, 206 = 254. *Wright's Brigade,* Brig.-Gen. Marcus J. Wright, Col. John H. Anderson: 8th Tenn., Col. John H. Anderson,

---

☆ Corps headquarters and the First and Second Brigades and 18th Ind. Battery, of the First Division, at and about Alexandria, Tenn.; Third Brigade at Caperton's Ferry, Tennessee River. First and Third Brigades and Chicago Board of Trade Battery, of the Second Division, at Maysville, Ala.

⎰ General Sherman had under his immediate command the Eleventh Corps, and the Second Division, Fourteenth Corps of the Army of the Cumberland; the Second and Fourth Divisions, Fifteenth Corps, and the Second Division, Seventeenth Corps.

Lieut.-Col. Chris. C. McKinney; 16th Tenn., Col. D. M. Donnell; 28th Tenn., Col. S. S. Stanton; 38th Tenn. (at Charleston, Tenn.), Col. John C. Carter; 51st and 52d Tenn., Lieut.-Col. John G. Hall. Brigade loss: k, 1; w, 11 = 12. *Artillery Battalion,* Maj. M. Smith: Ala. Battery, Capt. W. H. Fowler; Fla. Battery, Capt. Robert P. McCants; Ga. Battery, Capt. John Scogin; Miss. Battery, Capt. W. B. Turner. Battalion loss: m, 7.

STEVENSON'S DIVISION, Maj.-Gen. Carter L. Stevenson, Brig.-Gen. John C. Brown (temporarily).

Brown's Brigade, Brig.-Gen. John C. Brown: 3d Tenn., Col. C. H. Walker; 18th and 26th Tenn, Lieut.-Col. W. R. Butler; 32d Tenn., Maj. J. P. McGuire; 45th Tenn. and 23d Tenn. Battalion, Col. A. Searcy. Brigade loss: k, 2; w, 35; m, 13 = 50. *Pettus's Brigade,* Brig.-Gen. E. W. Pettus: 20th Ala., Capt. John W. Davis; 23d Ala., Lieut.-Col. J. B. Bibb; 30th Ala., Col. C. M. Shelley; 31st Ala., Col. D. R. Hundley; 46th Ala., Capt. George E. Brewer. Brigade loss: k, 17; w, 93; m, 17 = 127. *Cumming's Brigade,* Brig.-Gen. Alfred Cumming: 34th Ga., Col. J. A. W. Johnson (w), Lieut.-Col. J. W. Bradley; 36th Ga., Lieut.-Col. Alexander M. Wallace (w), Capt. J. A. Grice; 39th Ga., Col. J. T. McConnell (k); 56th Ga., Lieut.-Col. J. T. Slaughter, Capt. J. L. Morgan. Brigade loss: k, 17; w, 156; m, 30 = 203. *Reynolds's Brigade* (of Buckner's division), Brig.-Gen. Alexander W. Reynolds: 58th N. C., Col. J. B. Palmer; 60th N. C., Maj. James T. Weaver; 54th Va., Lieut.-Col. J. J. Wade; 63d Va., Maj. J. M. French. *Artillery:* Ga. Battery, Capt. Max. Van Den Corput; Md. Battery, Capt. John B. Rowan; Tenn. Battery, Capt. W. W. Carnes; Tenn. Battery, Capt. Edward Baxter.

CLEBURNE'S DIVISION, Maj.-Gen. P. R. Cleburne.

Lowrey's Brigade, Brig.-Gen. Mark P. Lowrey: 16th Ala., Maj. F. A. Ashford; 33d Ala., Col. Samuel Adams; 45th Ala., Lieut.-Col. H. D. Lampley; 32d and 45th Miss., Col. A. B. Hardcastle; 15th Battalion Sharp-shooters, Capt. T. M. Steger. *Polk's Brigade,* Brig.-Gen. Lucius E. Polk: 2d Tenn., Col. W. D. Robison (w); 35th and 48th Tenn., Col. B. J. Hill; 1st Ark., Col. J. W. Colquitt; 3d and 5th Confederate, Lieut.-Col. J. C. Cole (m w), Capt. W. A. Brown, Capt. M. H. Dixon. *Liddell's Brigade,* Col. D. C. Govan: 2d, 15th, and 24th Ark., Lieut.-Col. E. Warfield; 5th and 13th Ark., Col. John E. Murray; 6th and 7th Ark., Lieut.-Col. Peter Snyder; 8th and 19th Ark., Lieut.-Col. A. S. Hutchinson. *Smith's Brigade,* Col. Hiram A. Granbury: 7th Tex., Capt. C. E. Talley; 6th, 10th, and 15th Tex., Capt. John R. Kennard; 17th, 18th, 24th, and 25th Tex. (dismounted cavalry), Maj. W. A. Taylor. *Artillery Battalion,* Capt. J. P. Douglas: Ala. Battery (Semple's), Lieut. R. W. Goldthwaite; Ark. Battery (Calvert's), Lieut. T. J. Key; Miss. Battery (Sweet's), Lieut. H. Shannon. Battalion loss: k, 6; w, 16 = 22. Division loss: k, 62; w, 367; m, 12 = 441.

WALKER'S DIVISION, Brig.-Gen. States R. Gist.

Gist's Brigade: 8th Ga. Battalion, Lieut.-Col. Z. L. Walters; 46th Ga., Lieut.-Col. W. A. Daniel; 16th S. C., Col. James McCullough; 24th S. C., Col. C. H. Stevens. *Wilson's Brigade,* Brig.-Gen. Claudius C. Wilson: 1st Ga. Battalion Sharp-shooters and 25th Ga., Maj. A. Shaaff; 26th Ga. Battalion, Maj. J. W. Nisbet; 29th and 30th Ga., Maj. Thomas W. Mangham; 66th Ga., Col. J. C. Nisbet. *Maney's Brigade,* Brig.-Gen. George E. Maney (w): 4th Confederate, Capt. Joseph Bostick; 1st and 27th Tenn., Col. H. R. Feild; 6th and 9th Tenn., Col. George C. Porter; 41st Tenn., Col. R. Farquharson; 50th Tenn., Col. C. A. Sugg; 24th Tenn. Battalion Sharp-shooters, Maj. Frank Maney. *Artillery Battalion,* Maj. Robert Martin: Ga. Battery, Capt. E. P. Howell; Mo. Battery, Capt. H. M. Bledsoe; Ferguson's Battery, Capt. T. B. Ferguson. Division loss: k, 14; w, 118; m, 190 = 322.

BRECKINRIDGE'S CORPS, Maj.-Gen. John C. Breckinridge.

HINDMAN'S DIVISION, Brig.-Gen. J. Patton Anderson.

Anderson's Brigade, Col. W. F. Tucker: 7th and 9th Miss., Col. W. H. Bishop; 10th and 44th Miss., Col. James Barr; 41st Miss., ———; 9th Battalion Miss. Sharpshooters, Maj. W. C. Richards. *Manigault's Brigade,* Brig.-Gen. Arthur M. Manigault: 24th Ala., Col. N. N. Davis; 28th Ala., Lieut.-Col. W. L. Butler; 34th Ala., Capt. R. G. Welch; 10th and 19th S. C., Col. James F. Pressley. *Deas's Brigade,* Brig.-Gen. Z. C. Deas: 19th Ala., Col. S. K. McSpadden; 22d Ala.; Lieut.-Col. B. R. Hart; 25th Ala., Col. G. D. Johnston; 39th Ala., Lieut.-Col. W. C. Clifton; 50th Ala., Col. J. G. Coltart; 17th Ala. Battalion Sharp-shooters, Capt. J. F. Nabers. *Vaughan's Brigade,* Brig.-Gen. A. J. Vaughan: 11th Tenn., Lieut.-Col. William Thedford; 12th and 47th Tenn., Col. W. M. Watkins; 13th and 154th Tenn., Lieut.-Col. R. W. Pitman; 29th Tenn., Col. Horace Rice. *Artillery Battalion,* Maj. A. R. Courtney: Ala. Battery, Capt. James Garrity; Dent's Battery, Capt. S. H. Dent; Tex. Battery, Capt. J. P. Douglas. Division loss: k, 76; w, 476; m, 1124 = 1676.

BRECKINRIDGE'S DIVISION, Brig.-Gen. William B. Bate.

Bate's Brigade, Col. R. C. Tyler (w), Col. A. F. Rudler (w), Lieut.-Col. James J. Turner: 37th Ga., Col. A. F. Rudler, Lieut.-Col. J. T. Smith; 10th Tenn., Maj. John O'Neill; 15th and 37th Tenn., Lieut.-Col. R. D. Frayser; 20th Tenn., Capt. John F. Guthrie; 30th Tenn., Lieut.-Col. James J. Turner; Caswell's Battalion, Lieut. Joel Towers. *Lewis's Brigade,* Brig.-Gen. Joseph H. Lewis: 2d Ky., Col. James W. Moss; 4th Ky., Lieut.-Col. T. W. Thompson; 5th Ky., Col. H. Hawkins; 6th Ky., Lieut.-Col. W. L. Clarke; 9th Ky., Lieut.-Col. John C. Wickliffe. *Finley's Brigade,* Brig.-Gen. Jesse J. Finley: 1st and 3d Fla., Lieut.-Col. E. Mashburn; 4th Fla., Lieut.-Col. E. Badger; 6th Fla., Lieut.-Col. A. D. McLean; 7th Fla., Lieut.-Col. T. Ingram; 1st Fla. Cav. (dismounted), Col. G. T. Maxwell. *Artillery Battalion,* Capt. Robert Cobb: Ky. Battery (Cobb's), Lieut. F. J. Gracie; La. Battery, Capt. C. H. Slocomb; Tenn. Battery, Capt. J. W. Mebane. Division loss: k, 44; w, 244; m, 591 = 859.

STEWART'S DIVISION, Maj.-Gen. Ambrose P. Stewart.

Stovall's Brigade, Brig.-Gen. Marcellus A. Stovall: 40th Ga., Lieut.-Col. R. M. Young; 41st Ga., Col. W. E. Curtis; 42d Ga., Maj. W. H. Hulsey; 43d Ga., Lieut.-Col. H. C. Kellogg; 52d Ga., Maj. John J. Moore. Brigade loss: k, 5; w, 32; m, 47 = 84. *Strahl's Brigade,* Brig.-Gen. Oscar F. Strahl: 4th Tenn., Lieut.-Col. L. W. Finley; 5th Tenn., Col. J. J. Lamb; 19th Tenn., Col. F. M. Walker; 24th Tenn., Col. John A. Wilson; 31st Tenn., Lieut.-Col. F. E. P. Stafford; 33d Tenn., Lieut.-Col. H. C. McNeill. Brigade loss: k, 16; w, 93; m, 150 = 259. *Clayton's Brigade,* Col. J. T. Holtzclaw: 18th Ala., Maj. Shep. Ruffin; 32d and 58th Ala., Col. Bush. Jones; 36th and 38th Ala., Col. L. T. Woodruff. Brigade loss: k, 21; w, 100; m, 706 = 827. *Adams's Brigade,* Col. R. L. Gibson: 13th and 20th La., Maj. F. L. Campbell; 19th La., Maj. H. A. Kennedy; 16th and 25th La., Col. D. Gober; 14th La. Battalion Sharp-shooters, Maj. J. E. Austin; 4th La. Battalion, Maj. S. L. Bishop. Brigade loss: k, 28; w, 96; m, 233 = 357. *Artillery Battalion,* Eufaula Battery (Oliver's), Lieut. William J. McKenzie; La. Battery, Capt. Charles E. Fenner; Miss. Battery, Capt. T. J. Stanford. Battalion loss: k, 1; w, 6; m, 5 = 12. *Escort company,* loss: w, 1; m, 1 = 2.

RESERVE ARTILLERY.

Robertson's Battalion, Capt. Felix H. Robertson: Ala. Battery (Lumsden's), Lieut. H. H. Cribbs; Ga. Battery (Havis's), Lieut. J. R. Duncan; Ga. Battery, Capt. R. W. Anderson; Mo. Battery, Capt. Oberton W. Barret. Battalion loss: k, 1; w, 4; m, 6 = 11. *Williams's Battalion,* Maj. S. C. Williams: Ala. Battery, Capt. R. Kolb; Jeffress's Battery, Capt. W. C. Jeffress; Miss. Battery (Darden's), Lieut. H. W. Bullen. Battalion loss: w, 2.

CAVALRY: Parts of the 3d, 8th, and 10th Confederate, and 1st, 2d, 4th, and 5th Tenn.

Total Confederate loss: killed, 361; wounded, 2180; captured or missing, 4146 = 6687.

CONFEDERATE ASSAULT ON FORT SANDERS.

THE DEFENSE OF KNOXVILLE.

BY ORLANDO M. POE, BREVET BRIGADIER-GENERAL, U. S. A.

IT was determined by the Federal authorities to make strenuous efforts
during the summer of 1863 to effect permanent lodgments in east
Tennessee, both at Chattanooga and Knoxville, not only for the purpose of
interrupting railway communication by that route, | but to afford relief to a
section where Union sentiments were known to exist to a very considerable
extent. It was accordingly arranged that Rosecrans should move from
Murfreesboro' against Bragg, while a force should be organized in central
Kentucky to move toward Knoxville in coöperation. The latter movement
was intrusted to General Burnside, who occupied Knoxville on the 2d of
September, 1863, with part of the Twenty-third Corps, and on the 9th received
the surrender of the Confederate force under General John W. Frazer at
Cumberland Gap.

The greater portion of General Burnside's force was now expected to move
down the Valley of the Tennessee to a connection (possibly a junction) with
Rosecrans, then at Chattanooga or its vicinity. This involved leaving Knoxville to be held by a small force, and rendered it necessary to fortify the place.
Accordingly, as chief engineer, I was instructed to arrange for a garrison of
600 men, intended only to hold the place against a cavalry " dash."

During the enemy's occupation of Knoxville, a very small beginning had
been made toward the erection of earth-works. An insignificant line had
been thrown up on the hill north-west of the college, and a slight epaulement

| At the beginning of 1863 the Confederates
had two lines of railway communication between
their eastern and western forces: one by the coast-
wise system to Savannah or Augusta, and thence
southward or westward; the other by way of
Lynchburgh, Knoxville, and Chattanooga, where
it branched toward Memphis and Atlanta. [See
also p. 746.]—O. M. P.

on the bluff overlooking the railway station. Neither of these was of use in the construction of our works. The plans for two works were submitted,— one, afterward known as Fort Sanders, on the site of the imperfect work first mentioned; and the other, afterward known as Fort Huntington Smith, on Temperance Hill in East Knoxville. These plans were approved by General Burnside, and work was at once begun by the engineer battalion of the Twenty-third Corps and a small force of negroes, but progressed slowly on account of the difficulty of getting suitable materials. The forts were not entirely completed until after the siege of Knoxville. Meanwhile our lines were extended down the valley toward Chattanooga. By the 18th of September, a battalion of cavalry in the extreme advance reached Cleveland, and the prospect for a junction was good until Chickamauga put an end to further movements in that direction, and Sweetwater became our outpost.

Early in October a force of the enemy under General John S. Williams, coming from the eastward, moved down the railroad to the vicinity of Bull's Gap, and pressed heavily upon our forces in that quarter. With such troops as could readily be concentrated, General Burnside attacked them at Blue Springs on the 10th and drove them well back toward Bristol.

On the 22d of October our outpost at Sweetwater and our reserve at Philadelphia were attacked successfully. Subsequent operations and reconnoissances resulted in the determination to abandon temporarily the Valley of the Tennessee south of Loudon. The troops were all withdrawn and the pontoon-bridge was transferred from Loudon to Knoxville, where General Sanders's cavalry command crossed it to the south side of the river, on the 1st of November. The abandonment of Loudon had in view the occupation of a stronger position on the northern bank of the river from Kingston to Lenoir's, where a pontoon-bridge was to be thrown across the Holston and the line prolonged by the right bank of the Little Tennessee.

On the 13th of November it was ascertained that the enemy had constructed a pontoon-bridge at Huff's Ferry, near Loudon, and were crossing in force to the northern bank of the Tennessee. At the same time General Wheeler, with nearly the whole of his four brigades of cavalry, made a rapid night march and crossed the Little Tennessee with a view to cutting off Sanders's command and occupying the heights opposite Knoxville; or, as stated by Longstreet, "failing in this, to threaten the enemy at Knoxville so as to prevent his concentrating against us before we reached Knoxville." Wheeler was foiled in this attempt, and soon withdrew to the north bank of the river, which he crossed at Louisville. He rejoined Longstreet on the 17th of November, after the latter had fought the battle of Campbell's Station.

Upon learning of Longstreet's movement, General Burnside took personal command of the troops available to oppose him. The operations of our forces during the next few days had for their object to delay the advance of the enemy to enable us to get our trains into Knoxville, and to forward the defensive works at that place, where it had been determined to make a stand.

Longstreet advanced from Loudon in two columns, McLaws's division taking the left road, leading to Campbell's Station, and Hood's division (commanded by Jenkins), the one to the right, following the line of the railroad to Lenoir's. The latter soon came in contact with the Federal skirmishers and drove them slowly back, but failed to reach Lenoir's that day. Every effort was made during the night to ascertain Burnside's movements, but his bold and vigilant rear-guard succeeded in completely concealing them. By daybreak the whole force was on the road, and when the Confederates advanced they found Lenoir's deserted.

The road upon which Burnside was moving, followed by Jenkins, intersects that along which McLaws was advancing, about a mile south-west of Campbell's Station. It was therefore essential to the safety of his train, if not of his entire command, that Burnside should reach the junction before McLaws. Just before daylight on the 16th of November, Hartranft's division took the advance of Burnside's column from Lenoir's and pushed forward as rapidly as the roads permitted, followed by the trains and by the other troops. McLaws, with full knowledge of the importance of seizing the intersection of the roads, was making every endeavor to get possession before the arrival of Burnside. He was opposed by a small force, but his march, like Hartranft's, was impeded by the mud resulting from heavy rains. It thus became a race for the position. Hartranft won by perhaps half an hour, and, turning west on the Kingston road, quickly deployed his division in such manner as to confront McLaws, and at the same time cover the Loudon road along which our trains were moving.

During the movement from Lenoir's, Burnside's rear-guard, composed of Colonel William Humphrey's brigade, had several sharp encounters with Jenkins's advance, in which Humphrey handled his forces so well as to excite the admiration of both friends and foes, always standing long enough, but never too long.

Scarcely had Hartranft's dispositions been made when McLaws appeared and attacked, but Hartranft steadfastly held his ground until the remainder of our troops and all our trains had safely passed. The trains continued on the road to Knoxville, while the troops were formed in line of battle about half a mile beyond the junction, with Ferrero's division on the right, and White's in prolongation to the left, whereupon Hartranft withdrew from his advanced position and took his place in line on the left of White. A small cavalry force scouted the roads on each flank of the line. About noon Longstreet unsuccessfully attacked our right, and afterward our left center. Later, taking advantage of a wooded ridge to conceal the march, he attempted to turn our left flank with three brigades of Jenkins's division, but our scouts soon discovered and reported the movement. Burnside had determined to retire to a new position about two-thirds of a mile to his rear, and this development but slightly hastened his withdrawal from the first line. The difficult and hazardous undertaking was successfully accomplished in the face of the enemy. All who saw it say that the troops moved with the greatest coolness, deliberation, and precision under a heavy and continuous fire.

McLaws's division promptly advanced to attack the new position, while Jenkins continued his turning movement, but the difficulties of the ground delayed him until nightfall and stopped his further progress. McLaws attacked and failed to make an impression, and at the close of the action Burnside remained in possession of his own ground until after dark, and then continued his movement to Knoxville, the head of his column appearing there about daybreak next morning, November 17th. He had gained his object and therefore was fairly entitled to claim a victory.

Burnside placed his whole loss in this important affair of Campbell's Station at about 300. Jenkins reported his as 174. It is probable that the losses on both sides, including McLaws's, were about equal.

During the fight Burnside had instructed me to select lines of defense around Knoxville and have everything prepared to put the troops into position as fast as they should arrive. I was well acquainted with the ground, and but little further examination was necessary to enable me to designate, in writing, the proposed location of each organization.

The topographical features of the vicinity of Knoxville give that place decided strength as a military position. [See maps, pp. 636 and 736.] On the northern or right bank of the Holston, a narrow table-land, or ridge, beginning about two miles east of the town, extends down the river to Lenoir's, some 24 miles. This ridge is generally elevated about 150 feet above the river, but with many higher points. Its width at Knoxville is about 1300 yards, and the valley bounding it on the north-west, parallel with the river, is perhaps 50 feet above that stream at the ordinary stage of water. The East Tennessee, Virginia and Georgia railroad is located along the valley, which was almost entirely clear of timber. At short intervals the ridge is cut through by small streams emptying into the Holston, two of which, called First and Second Creeks, run through the town at a distance apart of about one thousand yards. The main portion of Knoxville, as it existed at the time of the siege, occupied that portion of the table-land included between the two creeks, the river and the valley. East Knoxville was situated next east of First Creek, upon an elevation known as Temperance Hill. East of Temperance Hill, and separated from it by a depression in the ridge, is Mabry's Hill, the highest ground on the north side of the Holston within cannon-range of the town. Beyond this the ground, with a few minor elevations, gradually descends to the level of the valley. Flint Hill is immediately upon the bank of the river, south of Temperance Hill. Third Creek, a little more than a mile westward from Second Creek, forms the south-westerly limit of another natural division of the ridge, including the hill north-west from the college. North-westerly from the river are found successive ridges; the most important was occupied by the Confederates, across the valley a mile from our line. South of the Holston the ground rises in a series of prominent points, or knobs, the highest of which is directly opposite Knoxville on the prolongation of Gay street. These knobs form a range, the crest line of which is parallel with the river at an average distance from it of about half a mile, with a wide valley beyond.

On the Knoxville side of the Holston, our line rested upon the river about a quarter of a mile below the mouth of Second Creek, extended from there at an angle of about 82° with the river for 900 yards to Battery Noble,⚓ then, bending about 50° to the northward, continued a little more than 600 yards to Fort Sanders, where it changed direction about 65° to the eastward, and, overlooking the valley, followed the crest of the bluff, parallel with the general course of the river for some 1600 yards to Battery Wiltsie, opposite the railroad station, including, in this part of the line, Battery Zoellner, between Fort Sanders and Second Creek, Battery Galpin, just east of Second Creek, and Fort Comstock, between Battery Galpin and Battery Wiltsie. From the last named, with a slight change of direction toward the river, the line continued along the crest of the bluff, over Temperance Hill to Mabry's Hill, a distance of 2400 yards, including Battery Billingsley just west of First Creek, Fort Huntington Smith on Temperance Hill, Battery Clifton Lee and Battery Stearman in the depression between Temperance Hill and Mabry's Hill, and Fort Hill on the extreme easterly point of Mabry's Hill. From here it turned sharply to the southward for 1300 yards and reached the river at a ravine about 1000 yards above the mouth of First Creek. A continuous line of infantry cover connected all these positions, and dams were built at the crossing of First and Second Creeks which, by backing the water, formed considerable obstacles, especially in front of Temperance Hill, where the line was parallel with the course of First Creek for 1200 yards, and the pond impassable without bridges.

A short interior line was established from Fort Sanders to Second Creek, near its mouth. This included Fort Byington, built around the college. Another line extended from Temperance Hill to Flint Hill, terminating in Battery Fearns.

On the south side of the river such of the heights (four in number) as were necessary to the defense were occupied by detached works with extensions for infantry cover, insufficient, however, to make the line continuous, or even approximately so. Fort Stanley was built on the hill directly opposite Knoxville, and a line of ordinary rifle-trenches was carried eastward from it across the Sevierville road and to the adjacent height. The hill nearly opposite the mouth of Second Creek was occupied by Fort Dickerson, and the next one to the westward by Fort Higley.

The arrangements for the defense of the position on the north side of the Holston were necessarily made in the most hurried manner. The earth-works known as Fort Sanders and Fort Huntington Smith, intended for a very different condition of affairs, were so far advanced toward completion when Longstreet appeared before Knoxville, that their use without modification was compulsory. Neither of the plans was what it would have been had the works been designed for parts of a continuous line. Especially was this the case with respect to Fort Sanders, the trace of which was such that under the stress of circumstances its north-western bastion became a prominent salient of the main line, and notwithstanding the measures taken to remedy this objec-

---

⚓ The several positions along the line were not named until after the lines were established,—Fort Sanders on the 18th of November, and the others after the siege was raised. All were named after officers who had been killed during the siege or in the operations preceding it.—O. M. P.

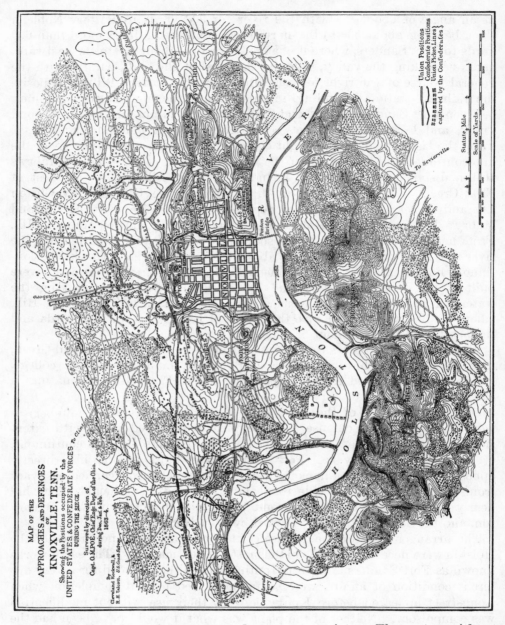

MAP OF THE
APPROACHES AND DEFENCES
OF
KNOXVILLE, TENN.
Showing the Positions occupied by the
UNITED STATES & CONFEDERATE FORCES
DURING THE SIEGE
Surveyed by direction of
Capt. O. M. POE, Chief Engr Dept. of the Ohio.
during Dec., Jan. & Feb.
1863-4.
By
Cleveland Rockwell &
R. H Talcott, U. S Coast Survey

tionable feature, its existence caused us great anxiety. The sector without
fire of the bastion referred to (the one attacked) would have been a sector
without fire for the line, but for the arrangements made on either side of it to
overcome the defect as far as possible. The fire thus obtained in front of this
bastion was not all that could have been desired, but the event proved that
it was sufficient. That Longstreet's renowned infantry failed to carry it by
assault demonstrated that there were no very serious defects unprovided for.

As already stated, the head of Burnside's column appeared at Knoxville at daybreak on the 17th of November. It was met near Third Creek, and the organizations were directed to their respective stations, formed upon the lines, and told to dig, and to do it with all their might. By the middle of the fore-noon all were hard at work. The locations of but few of the organizations were changed during the siege, and these but slightly.

Except the incomplete forts, Sanders and Huntington Smith, nothing in the way of defensive works had been previously contemplated. Lines of rifle-trenches soon appeared, only to grow rapidly into continuous infantry parapets. Batteries for the artillery were ready in the shortest possible time.

During the night of the 16th of November Sanders had crossed his division of cavalry to the north side of the river and moved out on the Loudon road to cover our forces, approaching from Campbell's Station, until they could get into position and make some progress in the construction of defensive works. Slowly falling back as the enemy advanced on the 17th, he finally made a stand with one brigade of about 700 men under his immediate command, upon a hill just north of the Loudon road, a mile from Fort Sanders and about 800 yards west from where that road crossed Third Creek; while the other brigade (two regiments of mounted infantry), commanded by Colonel C. D. Pennebaker, turned at bay where the Clinton road crossed the ridge about a mile north-west from Fort Sanders.

For the remainder of the 17th these commands stubbornly held their ground, in full view of our lines, the principal Confederate attacks being directed upon the position of Sanders, who kept up a fierce and gallant contest with Longstreet's infantry and Alexander's guns, ceasing only with the darkness. About 11 P. M. General Burnside sent for me, and upon reporting to him at his headquarters at Crozier's house, I found him in conversation with Sanders. He asked me how long it would take to make the works defensible, and was informed that it could be done by noon of the next day, the 18th. Turning to Sanders he asked him if he would maintain his position until that time, and received an assuring promise. Sanders accompanied me to my quarters, where we discussed the matter until after midnight, and then lay down upon the same blanket to get some rest, but before daylight he was called by the guard, and left to join his command.

As day dawned the attacks upon Sanders were renewed, with the evident determination to dislodge him in the shortest possible time. As hour after hour passed, and that cavalry continued to stand against the pressure, it excited the wonder of the rest of our army. The contest was very unequal, and occasionally a few of our men would leave their position behind the piles of fence rails which constituted their only cover, with the apparent intention of retreating. At such critical times Sanders would walk up to the rail piles and stand there erect, with fully half his height exposed to a terrific fire at short range, until every retreating man, as if ashamed of himself, would return to his proper place. He held his ground until noon as he had promised, and then, in accordance with an understanding with me, continued to hold it, intending to do so until actually driven away. At about half-past two he fell, mortally

THE NORTH-WESTERN BASTION OF FORT SANDERS, VIEWED FROM THE NORTH. FROM A WAR-TIME PHOTOGRAPH.

wounded, and the screen which he had so stubbornly interposed between the enemy and our hard-working troops was quickly rolled aside.

Every spadeful of earth turned while Sanders was fighting aided in making our position secure, and he had determined to sacrifice himself if necessary for the safety of the rest of the army. Hence he maintained his position so strenuously, and but for his fall it is possible he would have held it until night, as I sincerely believe he meant to do. His fine presence, soldierly bearing, extreme gallantry, and unvarying courtesy attached to him the incongruous elements composing his command, and enabled him to handle it as he did on this occasion, when its behavior was certainly worthy the commendation it received. The fort in front of which he fell was immediately named after him in commemoration of the service rendered.

Early on the 18th eight or ten of the enemy had established themselves in the upper story of the tower of a brick house which stood about 750 yards beyond Sanders's line, and from this advantageous position greatly annoyed his command by their accurate fire. He sent a request to Benjamin, in Fort Sanders, to try the effect upon these sharp-shooters of a few shots from his 20-pounder Parrotts. The distance was 2500 yards, but Benjamin's gunner put a shot directly through the compartment occupied by the sharp-shooters, badly wrecking it (as was ascertained by examination after the siege), and abating the nuisance. During the whole war I saw no prettier single shot.

By the night of the 18th our infantry trenches on the north side of the river had been made nearly continuous, and our heavier works were well advanced. The enemy's skirmishers pushed up in front of ours, and the siege was fairly on. On the 19th he extended to his left, and during the day threw shells into Knoxville from a battery posted on the Tazewell road, about a mile and a half from our main line. On the 20th the enemy's offensive lines began to appear, his right approaching the river near Armstrong's house just west of Third Creek. From there he extended toward the left across the valley and along the ridge beyond on a line nearly concentric with ours. The earth-works on each side seemed to grow like magic, but we were apparently doing more digging than they. Indeed, they never constructed any works of consequence east of the Jacksboro' road.

A large brick house, with two log barns, stood within the enemy's skirmish line in front of Fort Sanders, and served as cover for troublesome sharp-shooters. Why these buildings were not destroyed by us as we fell back I do not know, but it soon became evident that it must be done now, and the 17th Michigan Infantry was detailed for the purpose. At 9 P. M. the regiment, passing to the rear and left of Fort Sanders, advanced to our skirmish line, where they halted a few moments to adjust the line, and again moved forward. The enemy soon discovered the movement and opened fire, whereupon our men charged at a run, and quickly gained possession of the buildings; a baking-pan full of warm biscuits in the house indicating the completeness of the surprise. A party of five volunteers under charge of Major F. W. Swift had been formed to set fire to

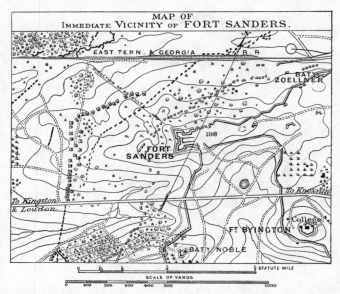

MAP OF
IMMEDIATE VICINITY of FORT SANDERS.

the buildings. These were effectually fired, and our men were half-way on their return to our lines before the light of the burning buildings revealed the party to the enemy, who then opened a cannonade upon them.

The siege and defensive operations progressed in the usual manner until the 22d, when we received information↓ that the enemy was constructing a raft at Boyd's Ferry, on the Holston, about six miles above Knoxville by the course of the river, intending to set it adrift in the hope that it would reach our pontoon-bridge and carry it away, thus breaking our communication with the south side. About dark we began stretching an iron cable boom across the river above the bridge, with a view to catching the raft. The cable was about a thousand feet long, formed by linking together all the iron bars we could get, and was borne by wooden floats. Under my personal supervision the boom was completed by 9 o'clock next morning.

On the evening of the 23d the enemy advanced upon our skirmishers in front of Fort Comstock and drove them back, but not until they had set fire to all the buildings in the immediate vicinity. We regained the position next

↓ John C. Phillips, of Chicago, captain and chief of artillery during the siege, writes to the editors that this information came in the form of a message in a bottle sent down the river by a Union woman living near the point where the raft was being constructed.

morning. Nearly due west from Fort Sanders the enemy had advanced his line to within about 600 yards of the fort, and had thrown up a continuous line of infantry trench, with its right resting on the railroad and extending about 300 yards to the left. Early in the morning of the 24th a detail of 169 men of the 2d Michigan Infantry attacked and carried this work. After they had held it for some time without reënforcements, the enemy made a counter-attack in largely increased force, with lamentable results to us, our men being driven back with a loss of nearly half their number.

BRIGADIER-GENERAL WILLIAM P. SANDERS, KILLED AT KNOXVILLE. FROM A PHOTOGRAPH.

Strange as it may seem, this sortie was made without my knowledge, and although I made considerable effort afterward to ascertain who was responsible for it, I never succeeded. It would be difficult to conceive a more ill-advised movement. It would have been proper if we had intended to bring on a general engagement, in which case the sortie should have been supported with our whole force. If such was not the intention, the sortie should not have been made at all. Carried out in the manner it was, the affair was simply murderous. This is strong language, but every word of it is justified by the unnecessary loss of about eighty-three of our very best men. The notes which I made at the time show that if I could have found any one to stand sponsor for the order, my condemnation of it would have then been quite as decided as now.

About the same time the enemy crossed the Holston below his lines and unsuccessfully attacked our forces on the south side of the river. He established batteries of rifled guns on the heights nearly opposite the mouth of Third Creek (never occupied by us), distant about 2300 yards from Fort Sanders, rendering it necessary to defilade this work against them.

The reports of a destructive raft being renewed, another boom, 1500 feet long, and made of long timbers fastened together at the ends by fifth chains from the wagon trains, was stretched across the river above the first one.

Prior to our occupation of Knoxville, the enemy had begun the erection of an earth-work, called by them Fort Loudon, on the site afterward occupied by Fort Sanders. A second growth of pines, averaging about five inches in diameter, thickly covered the hillside in front, and were cut down by them, leaving stumps perhaps eighteen inches high. The necessity for using every possible means of obstructing the approach over the sector without fire in front of the north-western bastion of Fort Sanders, included in the area covered by these stumps, was evident to every one, and became more pressing as the probability of an assault at this point grew more apparent. At this time Mr. Hoxie, in charge of the railroad property at Knoxville, informed me that he had a lot of old telegraph wire at the depot which he thought might be of service to us as an obstruction. Its use as a net-work entanglement, by carrying it from stump to stump over the sector without fire referred to, was so obvious that no time was lost in putting it in place. The part it played in causing the repulse was much overrated. Owing to its rusty color, nearly that of the pine litter just under it, and the imperfect light of the foggy morning, it doubtless did have some effect in breaking up the coherency of the assaulting column, and may possibly have detained it long enough to permit the defense to deliver a couple of rounds more, a matter of some consequence.

The wet, foggy, and generally disagreeable weather of the preceding days still continued, when, at about 11 o'clock on the night of the 28th, our picket lines in front of Fort Sanders were attacked with such spirit as to indicate an important movement, and after sharp skirmishing for some length of time were finally carried. This was, in fact, the prelude to an assault upon the main work, and had for its immediate effect to put us on the alert and keep us in readiness for the serious business which we knew was close at hand.

The enemy's arrangements for the assault provided that it be made in two columns, from McLaws's division, directed against the north-west angle of Fort Sanders, the one on the left to be composed of Wofford's brigade, in column of regiments, with the 16th Georgia leading; while the other, formed in like order, was to consist of Humphreys's brigade, led by the 13th Mississippi, and closely followed by three regiments of Bryan's brigade. The attack was to be made with fixed bayonets, without cheering or firing a shot, and the men were to be urged to rush forward with a determination to succeed. The sharp-shooters were to keep up a continuous fire into the embrasures of the fort and along the adjacent works, to prevent the use of artillery against the assaulting force and to disturb the fire of all arms. Anderson's brigade, following the main attack, was to carry the works about a hundred yards to the left, and, in case the assault on Fort Sanders should prove successful, was then to wheel to the left, and, followed by Benning's and Jenkins's brigades, sweep down our lines to the eastward. But if the main attack should fail, Anderson was to wheel to the right and endeavor to carry Fort Sanders from the rear. Kershaw's brigade was to advance to the assault of the works on the right of the fort as soon as it had fallen. The unassigned brigades of McLaws's and Jenkins's divisions, together with the brigades of Bushrod Johnson and Gracie, were to be held in readiness to follow up any success. Thus the plan of assault had been well studied, carefully elaborated, and clearly formulated. The preparations for resisting it were the wire entanglements already described, a slight abatis, the strong profile of Fort Sanders, and the arrangements for both a direct and a cross fire in front of the salient not only from the garrison of the fort itself, but also from the troops occupying the adjacent intrenchments.

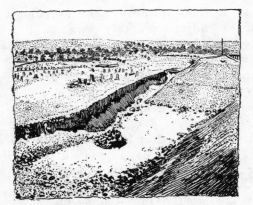

THE NORTH-WESTERN BASTION OF FORT SANDERS,
VIEWED FROM THE SOUTH-WESTERN BASTION.
FROM A PHOTOGRAPH.

Fort Sanders was laid out in strict accordance with the rules for constructing bastioned earth-works, but upon shorter exterior lines than were desirable. It was built upon an irregular quadrilateral of which the western side was 95 yards, the northern 125 yards, the eastern 85 yards, and the southern 125 yards; the north-western bastion being traced in the right angle between the first two sides. The western front was completed, and the two adjoining ones had been carried far enough to give us the advantage of their flanking arrangements. The eastern front had been intentionally left open. Provision had been made by pan-coupés for an artillery fire along the capitals of the two completed bastions, and a 12-pounder gun had been placed in the one attacked. The trace of the interior crest was so located on the slopes of the hill that when a parade of about forty feet in width had been formed, the undisturbed ground behind it served some of the minor purposes of a traverse. The ditch was made twelve feet wide at the bastion faces, and from six to eight feet in depth, depending upon the accidents of the ground, the average being about seven feet. The result of this location of the interior crest and depth of ditch, was an unusually high relief to the work, especially at the north-western bastion. The scarps were practically vertical, and the berme at the foot of the exterior slope was cut away. The counterscarps were continued until they intersected, and all the material between them and the curtain excavated to the general level of the bottom of the ditch, thus obviating all dead angles. A banquette was formed in the counterscarp at the north-western salient, of sufficient extent for the location of about forty men, whose fire could be delivered in the direction of the capital. In addition to the ordinary flank fire, three 12-pounders were so located in notches in the immediate eastward extension of the northern front as to admit of their firing into the left flank of the assaulting column; and a fire, more or less efficient, could be delivered over the same ground from our intrenchments as far eastward as Battery Zoellner. A similar fire into their front and right flank was obtained from our lines to the southward of Fort Sanders as far as Battery Noble.

The garrison of Fort Sanders at the time of the assault, usually estimated at about 500 men, consisted of Benjamin's and Buckley's batteries and one section of Roemer's (four 20-pounder Parrotts, six 12-pounder Napoleons, and two 3-inch rifled guns), and an infantry force made up of some 120 men of the 79th New York, 75 men of the 29th Massachusetts, 60 men of the 2d Michigan, and 80 men of the 20th Michigan. About forty men of the 2d Michigan, under command of Captain Charles H. Hodskin, occupied the banquette in the counterscarp salient as long as the position was tenable, and then ran through the ditch to the southward; they entered the fort around the southeastern angle as they had been instructed to do, and took further part in the defense.

The number actually within the fort at the moment of the supreme struggle and repulse probably did not exceed 440 men. The discrepancy arises from the different ways of reckoning the limits of the fort, due to the open eastern front. The smaller estimate includes only the troops that were within the bastioned trace. Yet some very effective work was done against the assaulting column by the fire coming from the intrenchments beyond the original Fort Sanders, and it has always seemed to me only fair that troops delivering this fire should be counted in estimating the strength of the garrison, in which case the total would be increased to more than three times the number given.

About 6 A. M. on Sunday, November 29th, the enemy opened a heavy artillery fire upon Fort Sanders, to which no reply was made, because our limited supply of ammunition made it necessary to reserve it for use at a more critical moment. The fire continued for about twenty minutes and then slackened, whereupon the columns moved to the assault, and were at once met by all the fire that could be concentrated upon them from our lines. Encountering the wire entanglements, their organization was somewhat disturbed, but the movement was not seriously checked thereby, nor did the slight abatis retard it. Although suffering from the terribly destructive fire to which they were subjected, they soon reached the outer brink of the ditch. There could be no pause at that point, and, leaping into the ditch in such numbers as nearly to fill it, they endeavored to scale the walls. Having no scaling-ladders, a portion of the men, scrambling over the shoulders of their comrades, planted the battle-flags of the 13th and 17th Mississippi and the 16th Georgia upon the parapet, but every man who rallied to them was either killed or captured, and the flags were taken.

Meanwhile those who remained in the ditch found themselves under a deadly flank fire of musketry and canister, supplemented by shells thrown as hand-grenades from inside the fort, without the slightest possibility of returning a blow. Advance and retreat were about equally difficult, and it needed but a very short exposure to convince them that if any were to leave the ditch alive it could only be by the promptest surrender. Those who were able to walk were brought through the ditch to the south-eastern angle and there entered our lines as prisoners. Such of the assaulting forces as had not entered the ditch fell back, at first sullenly and slowly, but flesh and blood could not stand the storm of shot and shell that was poured upon them, and they soon broke in confused retreat.

The assault had been gallantly made, but was repulsed in little more time than is required to describe it. When the result became apparent Longstreet directed the withdrawal of the supporting brigade, but the order did not reach Anderson in time to prevent his troops from pushing on as though the assault had been successful. They swerved, however, somewhat to their left, and attacked a short distance to the eastward of the designated point, only to meet with as decided, though not so bloody, a repulse.

The assaulting columns were rallied under partial cover some five or six hundred yards from Fort Sanders and there reorganized, but no further open attempt to carry our lines was made.

Many reasons have been assigned for the failure of this assault, and there is some difference of opinion in regard to the matter. Some of those opposed to us, of unquestioned ability and fairness, have attributed it to the warning given us by taking our picket line the night before, the insufficient use of their artillery, and the improper direction taken by two of the columns, resulting in their intermingling and consequent confusion. The opinion has been confidently expressed that a subsequent assault would have been successful. All this assumes, first, that we were not already vigilant and waiting for the attack; second, that a heavy and continued artillery fire would have greatly damaged and demoralized us; third, that the confusion arising from the convergence of the advancing columns would not have occurred again; fourth, that the works were "very faulty in plan and very easy to take by a properly managed assault"; and last, but not least, that the troops of the enemy were better than ours. The first of these assumptions is erroneous; the second greatly exaggerated; the

BRIGADIER-GENERAL E. P. ALEXANDER, C. S. A.
FROM A PHOTOGRAPH.

third might have been verified, but again might not; the fourth is correct only within the limits and to the extent already explained; and the last has no evidence to sustain it.

No one is more ready and willing than the writer to admit the excellence of the troops that fought us at Knoxville. They had few equals, and I believe no superiors. But in making this admission I do not abate one particle of my confidence in the valor and persistency of those who opposed them. They possessed those qualities in as high degree as General Longstreet's men or any others, and the succession of events had only served to improve their morale. It may fairly be doubted whether any disaster to our arms was imminent.

Again, the repulse may have been due to the existence of fewer faults in the works than supposed; to the measures adopted by us to remedy the faults which did exist; ♭ to the passive obstacles of wire entanglements, depth of ditch and unusual relief of the parapet; to the enemy's error in deciding it to be unnecessary to provide scaling-ladders for the storming party; and, finally and emphatically, to a sufficient garrison of the coolest, bravest, and most determined men. Each of these reasons seems to me to have contributed its share to the result, and some of them were surely of much graver moment than any of those assigned by the other side.

The successful resistance of the 29th did not lead to any remission of labor on our defenses. Work was continued by the troops with the energy that had characterized their efforts thus far, but the enemy gave little indication of a purpose to do anything further upon their works of attack. On the 1st of December large trains belonging to the enemy were seen moving to the eastward, and again on the 3d and 4th and on the night of the 4th his troops were withdrawn and the siege was raised. We had not yet heard the result of General Grant's operations at Chattanooga.

The signal defeat of Bragg at Missionary Ridge and the happy conclusion of the siege of Knoxville confirmed our hold upon the direct line of communication between the enemy's forces east and west and achieved the permanent relief of the friends of our cause in east Tennessee.

The conduct of the men who stood in the trenches at Knoxville cannot be overpraised. Half starved, with clothing tattered and torn, they endured without a murmur every form of hardship and exposure that falls to the lot of the soldier. The question with them was not whether they could withstand the assaults of the enemy, but simply whether sufficient food could be obtained to enable them to keep their places in the line. That they were not reduced to the last extremity in this regard is due to the supplies sent in by the loyalists of the French Broad settlements, who took advantage of Longstreet's inability to invest the place completely, and under cover of the night-fogs floated down to us such food and forage as they could collect.

♭ "On the morning of December 6th I rode from Marysville into Knoxville, and met General Burnside. . . . We examined his lines of fortifications, which were a wonderful production for the short time allowed in their selection of ground and construction of work. It seemed to me that they were nearly impregnable. We examined the redoubt named 'Sanders,' where on the Sunday previous three brigades of the enemy had assaulted and met a bloody repulse."— Extract from General Sherman's official report of December 19th, 1863.

LONGSTREET AT KNOXVILLE.

BY E. PORTER ALEXANDER, BRIGADIER-GENERAL, C. S. A.

AFTER the return of the Army of Northern Virginia from Gettysburg, it took position south of the Rapidan River, in the vicinity of Orange Court House, to recuperate from the losses and fatigue of the campaign. We settled ourselves in comfortable camps among the wooded hills, enjoyed better rations than we ever got again, gradually collected horses, recruits, conscripts, and returning sick and wounded, and altogether we felt about as well satisfied with the situation and prospect as we had ever done before. The enjoyment of our pleasant camps and still pleas-

anter rest was suddenly broken, on September 9th, by orders for Hood's and McLaws's divisions of Longstreet's corps, about 11,000 strong, with my battalion of artillery, 23 guns, to go under the personal command of General Longstreet to reënforce Bragg in Georgia.

It was clear that our now, however, adversary, the Army of the Potomac, could not resume the offensive for some months, and there would be ample time to send this force out to enable Bragg to crush Rosecrans, and bring it back to Virginia before it would be needed there. It was the only occasion during the war, I believe, when the Confederates availed themselves of the possession of the interior and shorter lines, and transferred a force of any magnitude rapidly from the eastern to the western army to meet an emergency, and then to return.

The orders were received September 9th, and the troops were put in motion immediately for Petersburg, whence we were to have railroad transportation to the vicinity of Chattanooga via Wilmington, N. C., and Augusta and Atlanta, Ga. This line at the time was the only one open from Virginia to Georgia, the East Tennessee line, the only other then existing, being held by the enemy at Knoxville. Consequently it was taxed with the entire business of the Confederacy between those States, and that it managed to do it at all has always seemed to me a feat in railroad management deserving great praise. The roads had had but a small business before the war, and their equipment and motive power were light even for those days. The gauges were not uniform, and often the tracks of connecting roads were joined through the cities only by lines of drays, and there was no interchange of cars. There was no manufactory of locomotives in the South, and but one small rolling-mill, at Atlanta, that could make a rail. Yet, in spite of all these drawbacks and the enormous business suddenly thrown upon them, and frequent raids by the enemy, destroying bridges, tearing up tracks, burning ties, and bending and twisting rails, the railroads always came up again smiling, and stuck to the contest as faithfully as did the army.

My battalion brought up the rear, leaving Petersburg September 17th, and arriving at Ringgold, the railroad terminus near Chickamauga, on the 25th. Our artillery was distributed about our lines, the station of my own battalion being on Lookout Mountain, whence we threw shells over the enemy's territory, and fought daily with a vicious little battery in Moccasin Bend, almost directly under us. This battery had nearly buried itself in the ground under high parapets, and fired up at us like a man shooting at a squirrel in a tree. We propped our trails high up in the air to depress the muzzles, and tried to mash our opponents into the earth with solid shot and percussion-shells; but we never hurt them much, and when we left the mountain they were still as lively as ever.

It was at last decided by General Bragg not to attempt to manœuvre Rosecrans out of Chattanooga, but to detach Longstreet and send him up to try to capture Burnside, who was at Knoxville with a force of about 12,000 effective men. On the night of November 4th we withdrew from Lookout Mountain, and the next day marched to Tyner's Station, whence, with Longstreet's two divisions of infantry, Hood's (under Jenkins) and McLaws's, about 10,000 infantry, ↓ we were to be taken by rail as far as Sweetwater. The infantry

were sent in advance, and the railroad was so taxed to do this that we were detained at Tyner's until the 10th, and meanwhile nearly starved, as rations had been provided for only half that time.

At length, about noon on the 10th, a train of flat cars came for us and the guns and men were loaded, the horses being sent afoot. It was a cold and windy night, and we suffered a great deal on the open cars. There was a very insufficient water and wood supply on the road, and the troops had to bail water and chop up fence rails for the engine. The journey of only sixty miles occupied the whole afternoon and night. On the 13th we moved from Sweetwater with the infantry and a pontoon-train, and our artillery was reënforced by Leyden's battalion of 12 guns, giving us in all 35. Owing to the scarcity of horses we were compelled to use oxen to haul the caissons.

We encamped near Sweetwater for two days, while secret reconnoissances were made of the enemy's position across the Tennessee River at Loudon, and commissary, quartermaster, and ordnance trains were organized and equipped. On the 13th, Friday, we marched to Huff's Ferry, about two miles by land below Loudon, which point had been selected for our crossing. Everything was kept out of sight of the enemy, and soon after dark some pontoons were carried by hand to the river, a half mile below the ferry, and a party of infantry ferried over, to try to surround and capture the Federal picket which was posted on their side. This part of the programme, however, failed, from the vigilance of the Federal sentries. They all escaped, and probably carried the news to Burnside that we were crossing in force, for early next morning a strong reconnoissance was pushed on us by the enemy as the last of our troops were crossing the pontoon which had been constructed during the night. We drove it back, and organizing a strong advance-guard under Lieutenant-Colonel (afterward General) T. M. Logan, of Hampton's Legion, with Parker's battery of my battalion, we pushed forward vigorously in the effort to bring Burnside to bay and defeat him before he could get back and concentrate behind the fortifications about Knoxville. This he had set out to do as soon as he appreciated the situation, sending his trains ahead and covering them with his whole force. For three days there ensued a sort of running skirmish covering the whole distance to Knoxville, about thirty miles. It was not rapid progress, but the days were short, the roads axle-deep in mud, and a strong rear-guard of the enemy skirmished with us for every hill and wood and stream on the road. Twice — at Lenoir's the first afternoon, the 15th, and at Campbell's Station the next — we seemed to have brought him to bay, and behind our advance-guard our whole force was brought up and formed for attack. But the approach of night prevented an action on both occa-

THE NORTH-WESTERN BASTION OF FORT SANDERS, SHOWING THE GROUND OVER WHICH THE
CONFEDERATES CHARGED. FROM A PHOTOGRAPH.

sions, though on the latter we got in a sharp and pretty artillery duel over some nice open ground unusually favorable for it, during which one of our guns, a 20-pounder Parrott, exploded, but fortunately without killing any one. Here we found out that we had opposite to us an old friend, Benjamin's battery of 20-pounder Parrotts, which had been our vis-à-vis at Fredericksburg, where it had pounded us from "Mary Scott's Hill."

The night of the third day, the 17th, Burnside was safe in Knoxville, and we encamped at Hazen's, a short distance off. The next day we began reconnoitering for the best place to assault.

A Federal cavalry brigade, under General W. P. Sanders, held a line of rail breastworks on a hill near the Armstrong house, and interfered seriously with our freedom of motion. Our skirmishers having vainly tried to move them, and artillery ammunition being too scarce for much of a cannonade on a minor point, we got up two of Taylor's Napoleons, so they could not be seen, behind a house which stood about 250 yards from the enemy's line, and asked for two regiments of infantry to charge it as soon as we made an impression. All being ready, the guns were run out from behind the house and opened vigorously with solid shot, being helped also by Moody's 24-pounder howitzers with shrapnel, a short distance to the left. At the close range Taylor made the rails fly at every shot, and the enemy began to desert them

rapidly and run back over the hill. Then the 2d and 3d South Carolina regiments of Kershaw's brigade rose from their cover and dashed at them. Sanders and his officers rallied their men gallantly and brought most of them back to the line, and poured a heavy fire upon the Carolinians. The latter advanced rapidly without returning it until they reached two cedar-trees within thirty yards of the enemy, when they halted, lay down, and opened fire. This was from a misapprehension of their orders, which were not to go farther forward than the enemy's line near the cedar-trees. In three minutes, however, the mistake was appreciated, and, rising with a yell, they dashed upon and carried the rail breastwork, killing and capturing quite a number of the enemy. ⚓

On the 19th, the enemy being now pretty closely confined to the town, we began preparations to assault him. It was first necessary to study his lines and find the most favorable point.

The town had been partly fortified a year before by the Confederates, and the topography being generally favorable to defense, it was not easy to find a weak spot, especially as we were all unfamiliar with the locality, and without even maps of the city.

It soon appeared that there was but one point of the lines which it was possible to assault with any hope of success. That was a fort which had been started by the Confederates under the name

⚓ This action was very sharp for a small affair and was well fought on both sides. When our infantry line halted and lay down, Captain S. Winthrop, of my staff, galloped up to and through them as they rose, and right up to the breastworks. A dozen muskets could be seen blazing at him, and he fell forward on his horse's neck with a bullet through the collar-bone. He had been a captain in Her Majesty's 24th regiment, and came to the Confederacy to get a taste of active service, and on other

occasions than this also fully sustained the reputation of British pluck.

The Federal general, Sanders, was mortally wounded in this skirmish. He was from Mississippi, and I believe was a distant relative of President Davis. We had been intimate at West Point, and had met in San Francisco in 1861, as I was about resigning to cast my fortunes with my native State. We parted with no anticipations of such a meeting.— E. P. A.

of Fort Loudon, and had been finished by the Federals and by them called Fort Sanders. It was upon a hill that fell off to the north-west, so that a large force could be marched under cover and approach within two hundred yards of the fort without being exposed to view or to fire either from the fort or the adjacent lines on either side, which here made an obtuse angle. [See p. 739.]

All of our artillery, thirty-four guns, was posted in the most available positions to fire upon this fort and enfilade the adjacent lines, except four howitzers, which were rigged as mortars to drop shells behind the parapets and to search out spaces sheltered from direct fire. To accomplish this, skids were prepared inclined at an angle of forty-five degrees, one end resting on the ground and the other on a horizontal pole supported about six feet from the ground by forked posts. The axle of the howitzer was run up on these skids, raising the wheels in the air on each side of the skids, and leaving the trail on the ground between them, until the piece had an elevation of about sixty degrees. I had experimented with the arrangement in Virginia, and also at Chattanooga, and found it to work nicely and to give very fair mortar practice. Of course the range was regulated by the charge of powder used. We also rigged up an old flat-boat and made a ferry with some telegraph wire, by which we carried Parker's rifle-guns to the south side of the river and established a battery on a commanding hill, from which we could enfilade the western front of the fort at a range of 2600 yards. All of our guns were protected by earth-works.

These arrangements occupied us closely until Tuesday, the 24th. The attack was ordered to begin at sunrise on the 25th, and was to be made as follows: First, the mortars were to open and get the range by slow and deliberate practice. Next, the direct-fire guns were to do the same. Next, a strong line of sharp-shooters was to capture and occupy the enemy's line of rifle-pits in which their pickets were posted, and from these pits, an average distance of 200 yards, maintain a concentrated fire upon the parapet and embrasures of the fort. Next, all thirty of the guns and mortars were to pour a rapid fire into the fort for about a half hour, to dismount its guns and demoralize its garrison, and under cover of this fire and the sharp-shooters the storming column, previously massed under shelter, was to advance. As it approached, the guns would shift their fire to the right and left, and the mortars would resume their natural functions as howitzers and limber up and follow the storming column.

On the night of the 24th we learned that Bushrod Johnson's and Gracie's brigades, about 2600 men, were on their way to reënforce us, and would arrive the next night. The attack was accordingly postponed to await their arrival. With them came General Leadbetter, chief engineer to Bragg, who had been stationed at Knoxville and was familiar with its fortifications. Under his advice Longstreet again postponed the attack, and the next day went in person with him to look at the enemy's lines above the town, with a view to making the attack there. On their return Thursday night I was ordered to withdraw our guns from the south side of the river, as it was intended to move up above the town and make the assault on Mabry's Hill.

On Friday I accompanied Generals Longstreet, Leadbetter, and others on a careful reconnoissance of this locality with a force of cavalry under General Wheeler, who drove in the enemy's pickets. This reconnoissance convinced every one that an attack in that quarter was impossible. The hill was strongly fortified, the approaches inundated, and there was no cover within a mile for the formation and advance of an assaulting column. It was unanimously decided to go back to the plan of assaulting Fort Sanders, and I was ordered to get the guns back upon the hills across the river early Saturday morning. This was done, but the day turned out rainy and the assault was again postponed until Sunday, the 28th. So General Leadbetter's advent cost us three as valuable days as the sun ever shone upon. Meanwhile a rumor reached us that Bragg had had a severe battle at Chattanooga, and had been defeated and driven back to Dalton.

Late on Saturday afternoon General Longstreet suddenly changed the plan of attack (I believe under advice of General Leadbetter) and ordered that instead of beginning at sunrise, and being preceded by a crushing fire of artillery concentrated on the fort and covered by an enveloping swarm of sharp-shooters, a surprise should be attempted just before dawn by the infantry alone. This was a bitter disappointment to the artillery, after so many days spent in preparation. We believe that in daylight, with our aid, the result would have been different.

About 11 o'clock that night our infantry skirmishers were ordered to move forward and capture the enemy's pickets, which was successfully accomplished with a little firing, and our sharp-shooters established themselves in the enemy's line of rifle-pits within 150 yards of the fort. But it put the enemy on the alert, and during the rest of the night they fired occasional rounds of canister over our ground. The troops were brought up as soon as the rifle-pits were taken and formed in the sheltered ground in the rear. Those assigned to the storming of the fort were Humphreys's Mississippi brigade, and Bryan's and Wofford's Georgia brigades (the latter under Colonel Ruff), all of McLaws's division. Anderson's Georgia brigade, of Jenkins's division, was to support their left flank. The brigades averaged about one thousand men each.

The night was wretched, the temperature freezing, and a fine mist falling. The troops lay upon their arms without fires and suffered greatly.

At the earliest indication of dawn three signal-guns were fired in rapid succession from different batteries. Their shells were visible like meteors in the air and they exploded over the fort. Instantly the recumbent ranks of gray sprang to their feet and formed for a charge, not so famous in history as Pickett's charge at Gettysburg, and not so inspiriting a sight to see, for only the flashes of guns were visible in the dim light, but a charge that illustrated as well as Pickett's or any other ever made those splendid qualities of Longstreet's infantry which made them at once an admiration and a delight to their comrades in the artillery.

For a few minutes about a dozen guns poured a hot fire into the angle of the lines back of the fort, and the success with which they threw their shells about it, even in the dim light, made it all the harder to bear that the plan of attack had been changed and the artillery was not allowed to try its full strength. Then we ceased firing to leave a clear field for the storming column, except a few shots from a battery that could reach the ground in rear of the fort.

Meanwhile the assaulting column formed, advanced to the line of rifle-pits, and then swarmed over them and rushed for the fort. Almost immediately they found themselves in an entanglement of telegraph wires stretched a few inches above the ground and fastened to stumps and stakes. This, however, was quickly broken up, and the men pressed forward rapidly to the ditch around the fort, receiving a severe musketry fire from its parapet and two or three discharges of canister from guns which were able to reach a part of the ground traversed. It was impossible, however, to maintain ranks in this rapid advance, in darkness, over unknown ground with such obstacles, and under so close a fire. It resulted that the three brigades converged in a mass and without order around the north-west bastion. It was here that the ditch was supposed to be easily passable.

On the western face, indeed, it proved to be only about four-and-a-half feet deep, and ordinarily a ditch of that depth would not be a serious obstacle. But that morning the ground was frozen and very slippery, and, in addition, Colonel O. M. Poe, General Burnside's chief engineer, anticipating an assault, had made a very important variation in the ordinary profile of the ditch and parapet. Ordinarily there is left a space of about a foot between the edge of the ditch and the foot of the parapet, which space is called the "berme." [See cut, p. 750.]

It will be readily seen that to a man attempting to scale the parapet the berme is a great assistance, giving a foothold whence it is easy to rush up the exterior slope, which cannot be made steeper than forty-five degrees. Here the berme had been entirely cut away. To the right and left of the western face of the bastion the ditch grew deeper until it reached ten feet in places, and the parapet was raised in places by cotton bales. The advance was, of course, checked by the ditch, and the men generally swarmed along the edge, uncertain what

to do, and firing into the embrasures and at such of the enemy as ventured to show their heads over the parapet. This soon silenced the direct fire upon them from the parapet, except an occasional musket raised overhead to the level of the interior crest and fired without aim. The fort was so nearly silenced that looking on from the guns we thought it had surrendered, though some fire continued to come from the left.

Meanwhile many of the officers, color-bearers, and men jumped into the ditch and attempted to scale the parapet. The slippery slopes and the absence of a berme prevented their success in such numbers as to accomplish any result, and the gallant fellows going up one by one were shot down

FORT STANLEY, KNOXVILLE. FROM A PHOTOGRAPH.

from the inside as fast as they crowned the parapet. Nowhere in the war was individual example more splendidly illustrated than on that fatal slope and in that bloody ditch.

Some of the battle-flags were planted on the exterior crest and maintained there for some time by a succession of color-bearers. ↓ For fully twenty minutes the men stood around the ditch unable to get at their adversaries, but unwilling to retreat. Lieutenant Benjamin, commanding the artillery within the fort, made hand-grenades of his shells and exploded several within the ditch. Longstreet, seeing the flash of their explosions, and thinking them to be our own shells falling short, ordered the cessation of the slight artillery fire which we had continued to throw on the flanks and beyond the fort. [See note, p. 744.] At last, daylight having succeeded dawn, and further effort being plainly hopeless, the men sulkily withdrew. As the main force fell back Anderson's brigade of Jenkins's division, which was to take up the

↓ Colonel S. Z. Ruff, 18th Georgia, commanding Wofford's brigade; Colonel H. P. Thomas, of the 16th Georgia; and Colonel Kennon McElroy, 13th Mississippi, were killed, and Lieutenant-Colonel Fiser, 17th Mississippi, lost an arm upon the parapet. Adjutant T. W. Cumming, of the 16th Georgia, penetrated the

fort through an embrasure and was captured inside, assuring his captors that they would all be his prisoners within a few minutes. Lieutenant Munger, of the 9th Georgia, got into another embrasure and, finding himself alone, emptied a revolver at the gunners and made his escape.— E. P. A.

attack upon the left of the assaulting column only in case of its success, unwilling to see the assault fail without trying it themselves, rushed forward to the ditch. Longstreet endeavored to have them stopped, but was too late. They repeated the scenes of the first attack, and after losing nearly two hundred men they likewise withdrew. The ranks were re-formed, however, close behind the line of the

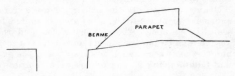

VERTICAL SECTION OF FORT SANDERS.

enemy's rifle-pits, which our sharp-shooters still occupied. It had been a bloody repulse, though occupying but about forty minutes. ♭

Soon after the repulse I heard, with great delight, that Jenkins had asked and obtained permission to make a fresh attempt, for I felt the utmost confidence that a concentrated fire by daylight from our 34 guns and mortars, with 1000 sharp-shooters whom we could shelter within close range, could silence the fort entirely, enabling a storming column to plant ladders, fill the ditch with fascines, and cut footholds in the scarp, so that an overwhelming force might reach the interior. But before arrangements could be made Longstreet received official intelligence of Bragg's disaster and an order to abandon the siege of Knoxville and to move promptly to join Bragg. A renewal of the attack was, therefore, thought inexpedient, and orders were at once given to move all trains to the rear, in preparation for a retreat southward that night.

Under cover of night it was intended that we should abandon the siege and get a good start on our march to join Bragg, but before nightfall we got news from Bragg himself that a large force under Sherman was being moved to intercept us, and that an early junction with him was impossible. Under these circumstances it was finally decided to remain and threaten Knoxville as long as possible, and draw Sherman off from the pursuit of Bragg, and then to retreat northward into east Tennessee. We remained before Knoxville until the night of December 4th.

About noon the next day we encamped at Blain's Cross-roads, having made eighteen miles; that was, I think, about the very worst night march I ever went through. The roads were in fearful

condition, and in the inky darkness and pouring rain neither men nor animals could see. Frequently guns or wagons would be mired so that the column behind would be blocked in the mud until extra teams and men at the wheels could set the column going for a few minutes. Strict orders had been given that the men should not use fence rails for fuel, but that night they were ignored, and miles of fence were fired merely to light up the road.

I recall some incidents illustrating how poorly our army was provided with even prime necessaries, although we were in our own country. We were so badly off for horse-shoes that on the advance to Knoxville we stripped the shoes from all the dead horses, and we killed for the purpose all the wounded and broken-down animals, both our own and those left behind by the enemy. During the siege the river brought down to us a number of dead horses and mules, thrown in within the town. We watched for them, took them out, and got the shoes and nails from their feet. Our men were nearly as badly off as the animals — perhaps worse, as they did not have hoofs. I have myself seen bloody stains on frozen ground, left by the barefooted where our infantry had passed. We of the artillery took the shoes off the drivers and gave them to the cannoneers who had to march.

Early in the advance Longstreet gave permission to the men to "swap" shoes with the prisoners whenever any were taken, but each man was strictly required to have something to "swap," and not leave the prisoner barefoot. It was quite an amusing sight (to us) to see a ragged rebel with his feet tied up in a sort of raw beef-hide moccasin, which the men learned to make, come up to a squad of prisoners, inspect their feet, and select the one he would "swap" with. Generally, however, the prisoners took it all very good-humoredly, guyed one another, and swapped jokes also with the swappers. It looked a little rough, but, as one of the victims said, "When a man is captured, his shoes are captured too."

On Sunday the 6th we marched fifteen miles farther, to Rutledge; on the 8th seventeen more, to Mooresburg; and on the 9th nine more, in the direction of Rogersville. Here we remained until the 14th, when we marched back, hoping to be able to surprise and capture a small force of the enemy that had followed us to Bean's Station and had become separated from its support. ⟨

We spent the winter between Russellville and Greenville, living off the country, having occasional

---

♭ Our losses had been 129 killed, 458 wounded, and 226 captured,— total, 813. The enemy's loss inside the fort was, I believe, only about 20.— E. P. A.

⟨ Gracie's brigade had quite a sharp engagement here, General Gracie being severely wounded, and Kershaw's and Bushrod Johnson's brigades and two of my batteries were slightly engaged; but darkness came on before we could get a sufficient force into position and line, and under cover of it the enemy retreated. It had been intended to cut off his retreat with a force of cavalry, but the plan miscarried in some way— as plans are always liable to do. Our loss was 290, more than half of

it in Gracie's brigade. This virtually ended the fighting of the campaign, in which our entire losses were 198 killed, 850 wounded, 248 missing,— total, 1296. Burnside's losses were 92 killed, 393 wounded, and 207 missing,— total, 692.— E. P. A.

The Union force at Bean's Station consisted of 4000 cavalry, under General Shackelford, who led the advance of a column commanded by General Parke. Parke, with the infantry, was approaching, and sent a division against Martin's cavalry, preventing the flank movement here referred to as having miscarried.— EDITORS.

expeditions, and alarms enough to destroy most of the comfort of winter-quarters. ☆

In the latter part of March we moved back to Bristol, and in April General Lee sent for us to rejoin him by rail. Reaching Gordonsville on the

☆ We had some of our foraging wagons captured and men killed by the "bushwhackers." The latter were supposed to be guerrilla troops in the Federal service

22d of April, we were once more with the Army of Northern Virginia, just twelve days before it entered the Wilderness and began the death-grapple that was only to end, after eleven months of daily fighting, at Appomattox.

recruited among the people of that section whose sympathies were anti-Confederate. They seldom fought, but they cut off small parties and took no prisoners.—E. P. A.

KNOXVILLE IN 1870. FROM A WATER-COLOR SKETCH.

THE OPPOSING FORCES AT KNOXVILLE, TENN.
November 17th–December 4th, 1863.

For much of the information contained in this list and in similar lists to follow, the editors are indebted (in advance of the publication of the " Official Records") to Brigadier-General Richard C. Drum, Adjutant-General of the Army. K stands for killed ; w for wounded ; m w for mortally wounded ; m for captured or missing ; c for captured.

THE UNION ARMY.

ARMY OF THE OHIO — Major-General Ambrose E. Burnside.

NINTH ARMY CORPS, Brig.-Gen. Robert B. Potter. *Escort:* 6th Ind. Cav. (4 co's), Col. James Biddle. Loss: k, 1 ; w, 1 ; m, 1 = 3.
FIRST DIVISION, Brig.-Gen. Edward Ferrero.
First Brigade, Col. David Morrison : 36th Mass., Maj. William F. Draper ; 8th Mich., Lieut.-Col. Ralph Ely ; 79th N. Y., Capt. William S. Montgomery ; 45th Pa., Lieut.-Col. Francis M. Hills. Brigade loss : k, 4 ; w, 19 ; m, 6 = 29. *Second Brigade,* Col. Benjamin C. Christ : 29th Mass., Col. Ebenezer W. Peirce ; 27th Mich., Maj. William B. Wright ; 46th N. Y., Capt. Alphons Serieri ; 50th Pa., Maj. Edward Overton, Jr. Brigade loss : k, 15 ; w, 25 ; m, 24 = 64. *Third Brigade,* Col. William Humphrey : 2d Mich., Maj. Cornelius Byington (m w), Capt. John C. Ruehl ; 17th Mich., Lieut.-Col. Lorin L. Comstock (k), Capt. Frederick W. Swift ; 20th Mich., Maj. Byron M. Cutcheon ; 100th Pa., Lieut.-Col. Matthew M. Dawson. Brigade loss : k, 18 ; w, 102 ; m, 46 = 166. *Artillery :* 34th N. Y., Capt. Jacob Roemer ; D, 1st R. I., Capt. William W. Buckley. Artillery loss : w, 2.
SECOND DIVISION, Col. John F. Hartranft.
First Brigade, Col. Joshua K. Sigfried : 2d Md., Col. Thomas B. Allard ; 21st Mass., Lieut.-Col. George P. Hawkes ; 48th Pa., Maj. Joseph A. Gilmour. Brigade loss : k, 5 ; w, 27 ; m, 32 = 64. *Second Brigade,* Lieut.-Col. Edwin Schall : 35th Mass., Maj. Nathaniel Wales ; 11th N. H., Capt. Leander W. Cogswell ; 51st Pa., Maj. William J. Bolton. Brigade loss : k, 4 ; w, 7 ; m, 3 = 14.

UNATTACHED : E, 2d U. S. Art'y, Lieut. Samuel N. Benjamin.
TWENTY-THIRD ARMY CORPS, Brig.-Gen. Mahlon D. Manson.
General Headquarters : McLaughlin's Ohio Squadron Cav., Maj. Richard Rice ; Eng. Battalion, Capt. O. S. McClure.
SECOND DIVISION, Brig.-Gen. Julius White. Staff loss : m, 2.
Second Brigade, Col. Marshall W. Chapin : 107th Ill., Lieut.-Col. Francis H. Lowry ; 13th Ky., Col. William E. Hobson ; 23d Mich., Maj. William W. Wheeler ; 111th Ohio, Maj. Isaac R. Sherwood ; Ill. Battery, Capt. Edward C. Henshaw. Brigade loss : w, 13 ; m, 4 = 17.
THIRD DIVISION, Brig.-Gen. Milo S. Hascall.
First Brigade, Col. James W. Reilly : 44th Ohio, Maj. Alpheus S. Moore ; 100th Ohio, Col. Patrick S. Slevin ; 104th Ohio, Lieut.-Col. Oscar W. Sterl ; D, 1st Ohio Art'y, Lieut. William H. Pease. Brigade loss : k, 2 ; w, 15 ; m, 7 = 24. *Second Brigade,* Col. Daniel Cameron : 65th Ill., Lieut.-Col. William S. Stewart ; 24th Ky., Col. John S. Hunt ; 103d Ohio, Capt. John T. Philpot ; Ind. Battery, Capt. Hubbard T. Thomas. Brigade loss : k, 9 ; w, 97 ; m, 2 = 108.
RESERVE ARTILLERY, Capt. Andrew J. Konkle : 24th Ind., Capt. Joseph A. Sims ; 19th Ohio, Capt. Joseph C. Shields.
Provisional Brigade, Col. William A. Hoskins : 12th

Ky., Maj. Joseph M. Owens; 8th Tenn., Col. Felix A. Reeve. *Tennessee Brigade*, Col. John S. Casement.
CAVALRY CORPS, Brig.-Gen. James M. Shackelford.
FIRST DIVISION, Brig.-Gen. William P. Sanders (m w), Col. Frank Wolford. Staff loss : m w, 1.
First Brigade, Col. Frank Wolford, Lieut.-Col. Silas Adams : 1st Ky., Lieut.-Col. Silas Adams ; 11th Ky., ——— ; 12th Ky., ——— ; Law's Howitzer Battery,———. Brigade loss : k, 5 ; w, 9 ; m, 10 = 24. *Second Brigade*, Lieut.-Col. Emery S. Bond : 112th Ill. (mounted infantry), Maj. Tristram T. Dow ; 8th Mich., ——— ; 45th Ohio (mounted infantry), ——— ; 15th Ind. Battery, ———. Brigade loss : k, 25 ; w, 63 ; m, 64 = 152. *Third Brigade*,

Col. Charles D. Pennebaker : 11th Ky., Col. S. Palace Love ; 27th Ky., Lieut.-Col. John H. Ward. Brigade loss : k, 4 ; w, 12 ; m, 1 = 17.
SECOND DIVISION.
First Brigade, Col. Israel Garrard : 2d Ohio, Lieut.-Col. George A. Purington ; 7th Ohio, ——— ; 2d Tenn. (infantry), ———. Brigade loss : m, 5. Total Union loss : killed 92, wounded 394, captured or missing, 207 = 693.
In his official report General Burnside says : " Our force at this time [commencement of the siege] in Knoxville was about 12,000 effective men, exclusive of the new recruits of loyal Tennesseeans."

THE CONFEDERATE ARMY.

Lieut.-Gen. James Longstreet.   Staff loss : w, 1.

McLAWS'S DIVISION, Maj.-Gen. Lafayette McLaws.
Kershaws's Brigade, Brig.-Gen. Joseph B. Kershaw : 2d S. C., Col. John D. Kennedy (w), Lieut.-Col. F. Gaillard ; 3d S. C., Col. James D. Nance ; 7th S. C., Capt. E. J. Goggans ; 8th S. C., Col. J. W. Henagan, Capt. D. McIntyre ; 15th S. C., Maj. William M. Gist (k), Capt. J. B. Davis ; 3d S. C. Battalion, Lieut.-Col. W. G. Rice. Brigade loss : k, 19 ; w, 116 ; m, 3 = 138. *Wofford's Brigade*, Col. S. Z. Ruff (k), Lieut.-Col. N. L. Hutchins, Jr. : 16th Ga., Lieut.-Col. Henry P. Thomas (k) ; 18th Ga., Capt. John A. Crawford ; 24th Ga., Capt. N. J. Dortch ; Cobb's (Ga.) Legion, Maj. William D. Conyers ; Phillips (Ga.) Legion, Maj. Joseph Hamilton (w) ; 3d Ga. Battalion Sharp-shooters, Lieut.-Col. N. L. Hutchins, Jr. Brigade loss : k, 48 ; w, 121 ; m, 81 = 250. *Humphreys's Brigade*, Brig.-Gen. Benjamin G. Humphreys : 13th Miss., Col. Kennon McElroy (k), Maj. G. L. Donald ; 17th Miss., Lieut.-Col. John C. Fiser (w) ; 18th Miss., Col. Thomas M. Griffin ; 21st Miss., Col. W. L. Brandon. Brigade loss : k, 21 ; w, 105 ; m, 56 = 182. *Bryan's Brigade*, Brig.-Gen. Goode Bryan : 10th Ga., Lieut.-Col. Willis C. Holt ; 50th Ga., Col. P. McGlashan ; 51st Ga., Col. E. Ball ; 53d Ga., Col. James P. Simms (w). Brigade loss : k, 27 ; w, 121 ; m, 64 = 212.
HOOD'S DIVISION, Brig.-Gen. Micah Jenkins.
Jenkins's Brigade, Col. John Bratton : 1st S. C., Col. F. W. Kilpatrick ; 2d S. C. Rifles, Col. Thomas Thomson ; 5th S. C., Col. A. Coward ; 6th S. C. ——— ; Hampton (S. C.) Legion, Col. M. W. Gary ; Palmetto (S. C.) Sharp-shooters, Col. Joseph Walker. Brigade loss : k, 22 ; w, 109 ; m, 5 = 136. *Robertson's Brigade*, Brig.-Gen. Jerome B. Robertson : 3d Ark., Col. Van H. Manning ; 1st Tex., Col. A. T. Rainey ; 4th Tex., Col. J. C. G. Key ; 5th Tex., Col. R. M. Powell. Brigade loss : k, 9 ; w, 18 ; m, 6 = 33. *Law's Brigade*, Brig.-Gen. E. McIver Law : 4th Ala., Col. P. D. Bowles ; 15th Ala., Col. W. C. Oates ; 44th Ala., Col. W. F. Perry ; 47th Ala., Col. M. J. Bulger ; 48th Ala., Col. James L. Sheffield. Brigade loss : k, 15 ; w, 69 ; m, 8 = 92. *Anderson's Brigade*, Brig.-Gen. G. T. Anderson : 7th Ga., Col. W. W. White ; 8th Ga., Col. John R. Towers ; 9th Ga., Col. Benjamin Beck ; 11th Ga., Col. F. H. Little ; 59th Ga., Col. Jack Brown. Brigade loss : k, 36 ; w, 186 ; m, 25 = 247. *Benning's Brigade*, Brig.-Gen. Henry L. Benning : 2d Ga., Col. E. M. Butt ; 15th Ga., Col. D. M. Du Bose ; 17th Ga., Col. Wesley C. Hodges ; 20th Ga., Col. J. D. Waddell. Brigade loss : k, 1 ; w, 5 = 6.

☆ Joined November 26th-28th.

ARTILLERY, Col. E. P. Alexander.
Leyden's Battalion, Maj. A. Leyden : Ga. Battery, Capt. Tyler M. Peeples ; Ga. Battery, Capt. A. M. Wolihin ; Ga. Battery, Capt. B. W. York. *Alexander's Battalion*, Maj. Frank Huger : La. Battery, Capt. G. V. Moody ; Va. Battery, Capt. W. W. Fickling ; Va. Battery, Capt. Tyler C. Jordan ; Va. Battery, Capt. William W. Parker ; Va. Battery, Capt. Osmond B. Taylor ; Va. Battery, Capt. Pichigru Woolfolk, Jr. Artillery loss : k, 2 ; w, 2 = 4.
BUCKNER'S DIVISION, ☆ Brig.-Gen. Bushrod R. Johnson.
Gracie's Brigade, Brig.-Gen. Archibald Gracie, Jr. : 41st Ala., Lieut.-Col. T. G. Trimmier ; 43d Ala., Col. Y. M. Moody ; 59th Ala., Lieut.-Col. J. D. McLennan ; 60th Ala., Col. J. W. A. Sanford. Brigade loss : k, 1 ; w, 1 = 2. *Johnson's Brigade*, Col. John S. Fulton : 17th and 23d Tenn., Lieut.-Col. W. W. Floyd ; 25th and 44th Tenn., Lieut.-Col. J. L. McEwen, Jr. ; 63d Tenn., Maj. J. A. Aiken. Brigade loss : k, 2 ; w, 19 = 21.
CAVALRY CORPS, Maj.-Gen. Joseph Wheeler, Maj.-Gen. William T. Martin.
Division commanders : Maj.-Gen. William T. Martin, Brig.-Gen's F. C. Armstrong and John T. Morgan. *Brigade commanders :* Colonels Thomas Harrison, A. A. Russell, C. C. Crews, and George G. Dibrell. *Troops :* Parts of 4th, 8th, 9th, and 11th Tenn., 1st, 2d, 3d, 4th, and 6th Ga., 1st, 3d, 4th, 7th, and 51st Ala., 3d Ark., 8th and 11th Tex., and 1st and 8th Confederate regiments, and Wiggins's Battery. Cavalry loss (estimated) : k, w and m, 200.
RANSOM'S CAVALRY. ╎
Jones's Brigade, Brig.-Gen. William E. Jones : 8th Va., Col. James M. Corns ; 21st Va., ——— ; 27th Va. Battalion, ——— ; 34th Va. Battalion, Col. V. A. Witcher ; 36th Va. Battalion, ——— ; 27th Va. Battalion, ———. *Giltner's Brigade*, Col. H. L. Giltner : 16th Ga. Battalion, Maj. E. Y. Clark ; 4th Ky., Maj. N. Parker ; 10th Ky., Lieut.-Col. Edwin Trimble ; 1st Tenn., Col. James E. Carter ; 64th Va., Col. Campbell Slemp ; Va. Battery, Capt. William N. Lowry.
The total Confederate loss (minus the cavalry, not reported) was 182 killed, 768 wounded, and 192 captured or missing = 1142. The loss in the cavalry is estimated at 250.
The effective strength of the forces under Longstreet's command probably numbered 20,000.

╎ Joined November 27th-28th.

END OF VOLUME III.